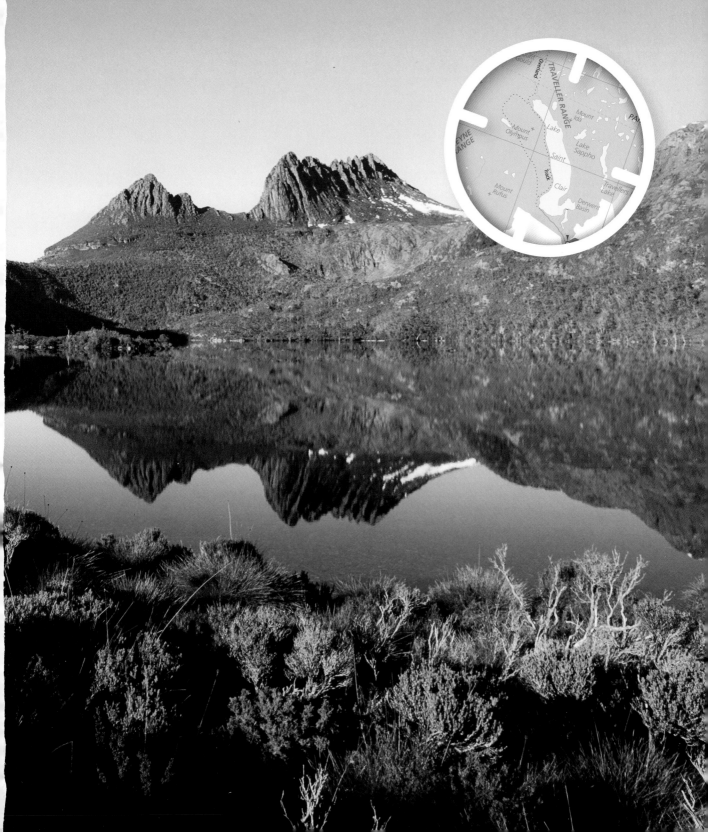

EXPLORE
AUSTRALIA
2011

EXPLORE
AUSTRALIA
2011

CONTENTS

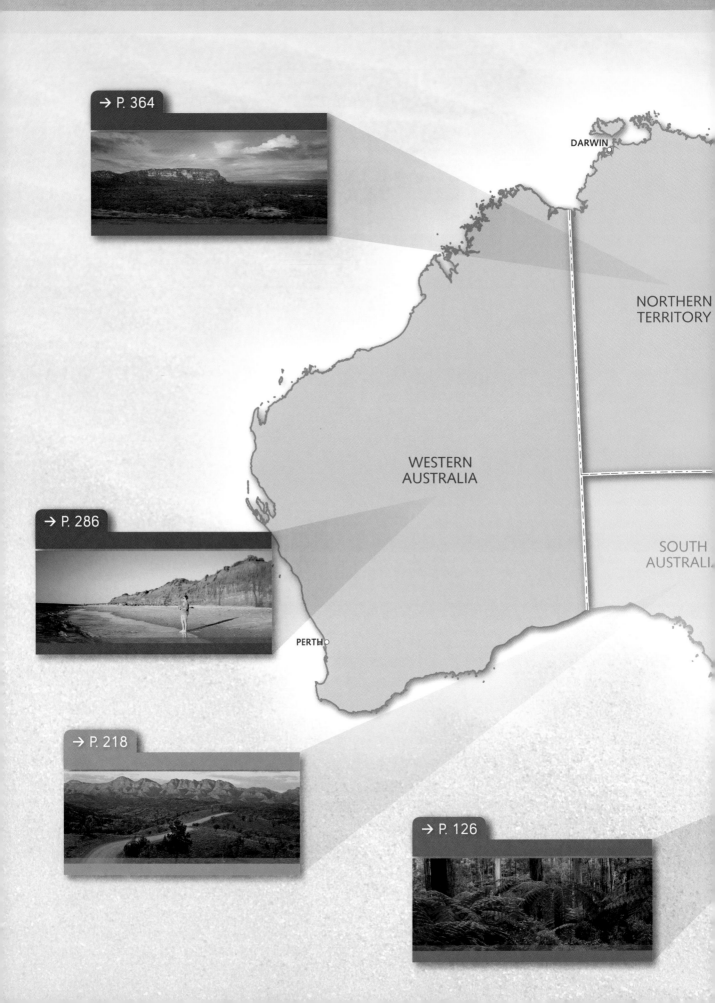

DARWIN

NORTHERN
TERRITORY

WESTERN
AUSTRALIA

SOUTH
AUSTRALIA

PERTH

QUEENSLAND

NEW
SOUTH
WALES

VICTORIA

TASMANIA

ACT

BRISBANE

SYDNEY

CANBERRA

MELBOURNE

HOBART

DELAIDE

→ P. 396

→ P. viii

→ P. 112

→ P. 484

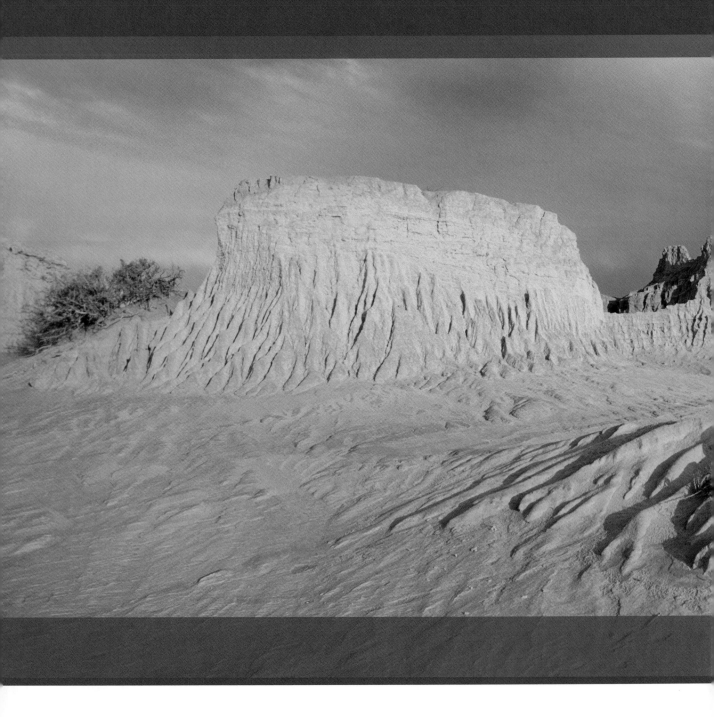

NEW SOUTH WALES is...

Bodysurfing at **BONDI** / Viewing the Three Sisters rock formation in the **BLUE**

MOUNTAINS / Skiing at Thredbo in **KOSCIUSZKO NATIONAL PARK** / Tasting

wines at cellar doors in the **HUNTER VALLEY** / A country music experience

in **TAMWORTH** / Seeing weather-eroded sand formations and skeletons of

NEW SOUTH WALES

[THE WALLS OF CHINA, MUNGO NATIONAL PARK]

megafauna in MUNGO NATIONAL PARK / Walking along Byron Bay's beaches to

CAPE BYRON LIGHTHOUSE, Australia's most easterly point / A whale-watching

boat tour in MERIMBULA / Strolling through the historic town of BERRIMA,

visiting antique shops along the way / Fossicking for opals at LIGHTNING RIDGE

NEW SOUTH WALES

NEW SOUTH WALES is a land of contrasts. Lush rainforests, pristine beaches, snowfields and the rugged beauty of the outback all vie for visitors' attention.

Beaches are a clear drawcard, with those at Bondi and Byron Bay among the most popular. Surfing, swimming and whale-watching can be enjoyed almost anywhere along the coast, but Hyams Beach in Jervis Bay National Park is home to the whitest sand in the world.

The discovery of Mungo Man and Woman, the miraculously preserved remains of two ancient Aboriginal people found in a dune over three decades ago, prove that civilisation existed here 40 000 years ago. Numerous Aboriginal nations have called the state home, and still do. Well-preserved fish traps in Brewarrina are thought by some to be the oldest man-made structures in the world.

After the American War of Independence spelt the end for British penal settlements in North America, the recently annexed New South Wales was an obvious solution to the problem of overcrowded prisons. Conditions were harsh; the first inmates of Maitland Gaol, who

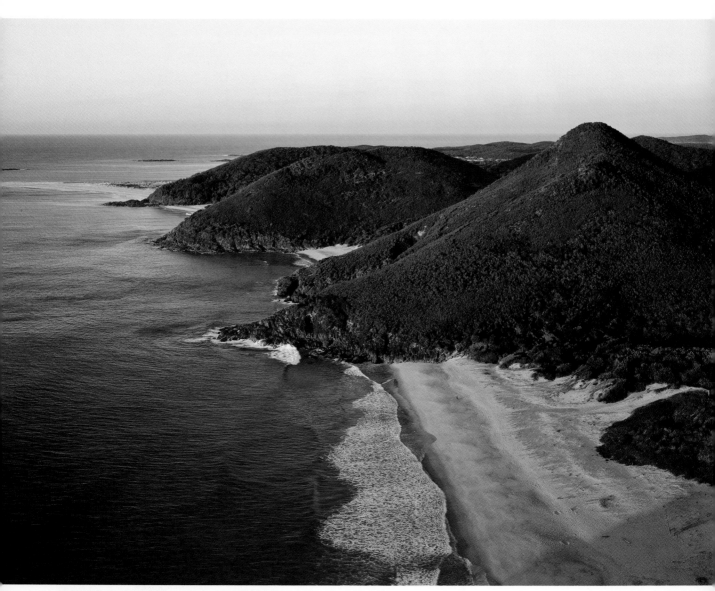

[ZENITH BEACH AT SUNRISE, TOMAREE NATIONAL PARK]

included many children, were forced to march the 6 kilometres from the wharf at Morpeth to the prison in shackles and chains.

Harsh conditions were not limited to the prisons. In 1845, due to the pitiless terrain explorer Charles Sturt lost his second-in-command and was stranded for six months in the outback near Milparinka. Today remote Silverton stands as a reminder of outback isolation, with its buildings and stark surrounds featuring in Australian films such as *Mad Max II* and *The Adventures of Priscilla, Queen of the Desert*.

In stunning contrast, Sydney's bright lights and sophistication sit beside the sparkling waters of the largest natural harbour in the world. The iconic Harbour Bridge and Opera House, along with the successes of the 2000 Olympics and the popular Gay and Lesbian Mardi Gras, have ensured Sydney and New South Wales a place on the world stage.

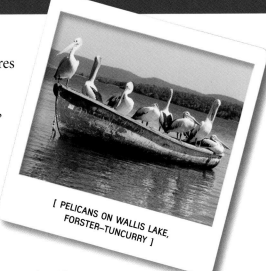

[PELICANS ON WALLIS LAKE, FORSTER–TUNCURRY]

fact file

Population 7 165 400
Total land area 800 628 square kilometres
People per square kilometre 8.5
Sheep per square kilometre 48
Length of coastline 2007 kilometres
Number of islands 109
Longest river Darling River (1390 kilometres)
Largest lake Lake Eucumbene (dam), (145 square kilometres)
Highest mountain Mount Kosciuszko (2228 metres)
Highest waterfall Wollomombi Falls (220 metres), Oxley Wild Rivers National Park
Highest town Cabramurra (1488 metres)
Hottest place Bourke (average 35.6°C in summer)
Coldest place Charlotte Pass (average 2.6°C in winter)
Wettest place Dorrigo (average 2004 millimetres per year)
Most remote town Tibooburra
Strangest place name Come-by-Chance
Most famous person Nicole Kidman
Quirkiest festival Stroud International Brick and Rolling Pin Throwing Competition
Number of 'big things' 49
Most scenic road Lawrence Hargrave Drive, Royal National Park
Favourite food Sydney rock oysters
Local beer Tooheys
Interesting fact The Stockton Sand Dunes, 32 kilometres long, 2 kilometres wide and up to 30 metres high, form the largest moving coastal sand mass in the Southern Hemisphere

gift ideas

Cookies (Byron Bay Cookie Company, Byron Bay) Drool-worthy cookies in flavours like triple choc fudge or white choc chunk and macadamia nut. See Byron Bay p. 53, 557 O3

Australian country music CD (Big Golden Guitar Tourist Centre, Tamworth) Bring back a music sample by one of Australia's talented country music legends. See Tamworth p. 96, 556 H9

Mead (Dutton's Meadery, Manilla) Manilla is home to one of only two meaderies in Australia, producing this ancient alcoholic beverage from fermented local honey and water. Purchase some bottles and see the private museum. Barraba St, Manilla. See Manilla p. 79, 556 H8

Replica of Sydney Opera House (Opera House Shop, Sydney) Take home a tiny replica of this icon in gleaming pewter or sparkling Waterford crystal. See Sydney Opera House p. 11, 8 C2

Sydney Harbour Bridge coathanger (Pylon Lookout Shop, Sydney) A quirky – and useful – variation on the old 'Coathanger' itself. See Sydney Harbour Bridge p. 13, 8 C1

Beach gear (Bondi Beach) Sun hats, beach towels and unique swimwear that sport the name of this iconic beach in bold letters are available from various stores. See Bondi Beach p. 17, 6 D6, C5

Arts and crafts (Paddington Markets) Local artisans sell fabulous artworks, jewellery, clothing and collectibles. See Markets p. 14, 6 C5

Gumnut products (Nutcote, Neutral Bay) The home of May Gibbs sells beautiful books, postcards, CDs, DVDs, tea towels and more, featuring the enchanting lives of Snugglepot, Cuddlepie and the Banksia Men. See Nutcote p. 18, 6 C3

Wool products (The Big Merino, Goulburn) Stylish woollen clothing, slippers lined with lambs wool and beauty products made from lanolin. See Goulburn p. 65, 565 E3

Wine (Hunter Valley) Try the shiraz and chardonnay from one of Australia's most renowned wine-producing districts. See Hunter Valley & Coast p. 26, 543 D1

SYDNEY is...

Bodysurfing at BONDI / Wandering through the lanes and alleyways of THE ROCKS / Views from SYDNEY TOWER / A trip on the MANLY FERRY / Fish and chips at WATSONS BAY / Soaking up the atmosphere of KINGS CROSS / A picnic at TARONGA ZOO / Harbour views from MRS MACQUARIES CHAIR / A performance at the SYDNEY OPERA HOUSE / Climbing the SYDNEY HARBOUR BRIDGE / A stroll through BALMAIN / Bargain hunting at PADDY'S MARKETS / Following the Games Trail at OLYMPIC PARK / Visiting ELIZABETH FARM in Parramatta

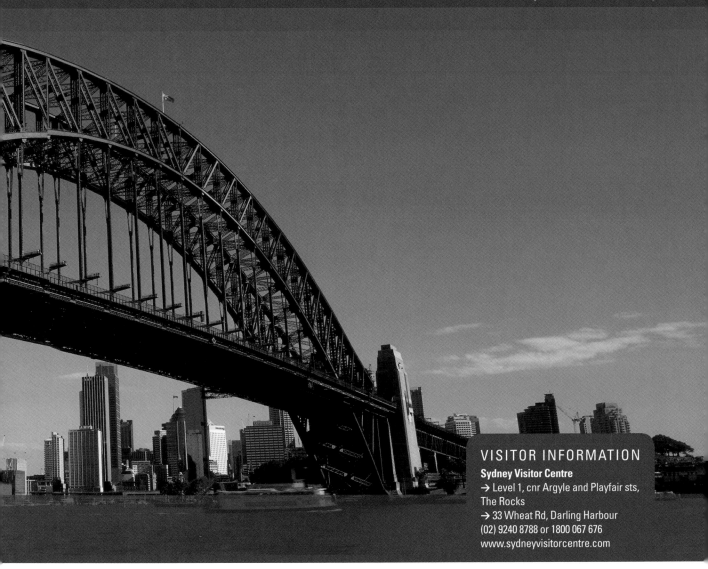

VISITOR INFORMATION
Sydney Visitor Centre
→ Level 1, cnr Argyle and Playfair sts, The Rocks
→ 33 Wheat Rd, Darling Harbour
(02) 9240 8788 or 1800 067 676
www.sydneyvisitorcentre.com

Australia's largest city stretches from the shores of the Tasman Sea to the foot of the Blue Mountains. Along with outstanding natural assets – stunning beaches, extensive parklands and the vast expanse of the harbour – Sydney boasts an impressive list of urban attractions, including world-class shopping and a host of superb restaurants and nightclubs.

Sydney began life in 1788 as a penal colony, a fact long considered a taint on the city's character. Today, echoes of those bygone days remain in areas such as The Rocks, Macquarie Street and the western suburb of Parramatta.

Since those early days, the one-time prison settlement has become one of the world's great cities. Home to two of Australia's most famous icons, the Sydney Harbour Bridge and the Sydney Opera House, Sydney attracts more than two million international visitors a year. For a true Sydney experience, try watching a Rugby League Grand Final at ANZ Stadium with a crowd of 80 000 cheering fans. Or if good food and fine wine are more your style, sample the waterfront dining at Circular Quay or Darling Harbour, and multicultural flavours in inner-city Darlinghurst.

With a population of 4 340 000, Sydney offers a multitude of activities. Surf the breakers at Bondi Beach or jump on a Manly ferry and see the harbour sights. Whatever you do, Sydney is a great place to explore.

City Centre

Taking in the area between Martin Place, Bathurst Street, Elizabeth Street and George Street, this is primarily a retail district, with Pitt Street Mall, the main shopping precinct, situated between King and Market streets, and the exclusive shops of Castlereagh Street to the east.

Martin Place 8 B4

A sweeping vista of buildings in the High Victorian and Art Deco styles line Martin Place all the way to Macquarie Street. Chief among these notable buildings is the old **GPO** on the corner of Martin Place and George Street, which was designed by colonial architect James Barnet and has been gloriously transformed into the **Westin Sydney**, a five-star hotel with stunning interiors. The lower ground floor contains an up-market food hall along with a carefully preserved part of the old **Tank Stream**, which until recently was thought to be irretrievably lost below the streets of Sydney. Once a major source of water for the Eora people, it was also a deciding factor in the choice of Sydney Cove as a settlement site.

Pitt Street Mall 8 B4

If you head south along Pitt Street from Martin Place you will come to a busy pedestrian precinct. This is Pitt Street Mall, the heart of the CBD's retail area, which is connected to a network of overhead walkways, small arcades and underground tunnels that lead to places as far away as David Jones and the QVB (the Queen Victoria Building). The mall houses beautiful department stores, stylish boutiques and vast emporiums selling music and books. Here too is the lovely **Strand**, the last of the old arcades in what was once a city of arcades. The Strand has three levels of beautiful and unusual shops to explore.

Sydney Tower 8 B4

A visit to Sydney Tower is a must for any visitor. Accessed by way of the Centrepoint shopping complex in Pitt Street Mall, your ticket grants you access to the 250-metre observation tower, which commands superb views of Sydney, all the way from the Blue Mountains to the Pacific Ocean. Included in your ticket price is OzTrek, a virtual tour of Australia and the outback. For those who like to live dangerously, there's the new Skywalk, an outdoor walk over the roof of the Sydney Tower. *100 Market St; tickets www.myfun.com.au; open 9am–10.30pm daily.*

State Theatre 8 B4

An extravagant mix of Art Deco, Italianate and Gothic architecture, the State Theatre is the final word in opulence. Built in 1929 as a 'Palace of Dreams' with marble columns, mosaic floors and plush furnishings, it boasts a beautiful chandelier, the Koh-I-Noor, and several paintings by well-known Australian artists. Classified by the National Trust, it is still a working theatre and has seen performances by artists such as Bette Midler and Rudolf Nureyev. Self-guide tours of the building are available, but it's best to ring first to check times. *49 Market St; (02) 9373 6862.*

Queen Victoria Building 8 B4

It's astonishing to realise now that the QVB was once in danger of becoming a multistorey carpark, but this was indeed the case. Built in 1898 to replace the old Sydney markets, it was later used for a number of purposes, at various times housing a concert hall and the city library before being restored in 1984 to its former splendour. Now one of Sydney's most cherished landmarks, it is considered by some to be the most beautiful shopping centre in the world, with three levels of stylish shops and cafes. The QVB features elaborate stained-glass windows, intricate tiled floors, arches, pillars, balustrades and a mighty central dome. The building's best-kept secret is the old ballroom on the third floor, now used as the supremely elegant Tea Room. *455 George St.*

Sydney Town Hall 8 B4

Immediately to the south of the QVB stands the Sydney Town Hall, a wildly extravagant piece of Victoriana, now the seat of city government. Erected in 1869, it was built on the site of a convict burial ground – as recently evidenced by the accidental discovery of an old brick tomb. While you're here, slip inside for a look at the Grand Organ, which was installed in the Concert Hall in 1890. Free lunchtime concerts are held occasionally. *483 George St; (02) 9265 9189.*

climate

Sydney is blessed with a warm, sunny climate, often described as Mediterranean, making it possible to enjoy outdoor activities all year-round. The driest time of year occurs in spring, with autumn being the wettest season. Summers are hot and humid, with temperatures often in the mid-30s, while winters are cool and mostly dry, with temperatures usually around 15–17°C.

J	F	M	A	M	J	J	A	S	O	N	D	
25	25	24	22	19	16	16	17	19	22	23	25	MAX °C
18	18	17	14	11	9	8	8	11	13	15	17	MIN °C
102	116	130	125	122	128	97	81	69	77	83	77	RAIN MM
8	8	9	8	8	8	7	7	7	8	8	8	RAIN DAYS

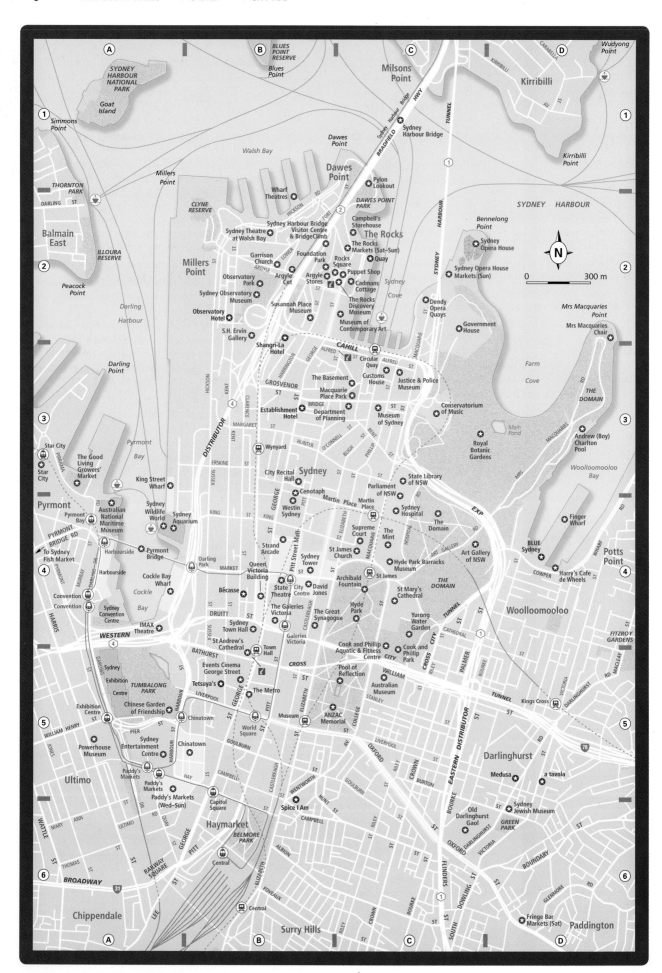

Hyde Park & Macquarie Street

One of the most historically significant areas of Sydney, this district contains one of the oldest parks in the city, Australia's first museum, a Gothic cathedral and the beautiful old buildings of Macquarie Street, once the heart of Sydney's fashionable society.

Hyde Park 8 C4, C5

Originally laid out as the city's first racecourse, Hyde Park is now a place of sunny lawns and wide avenues shaded by spreading trees. At the quiet end of the park, near Liverpool Street, you will find the beautiful Art Deco **ANZAC Memorial** and the **Pool of Reflection**. In the offices below the memorial there's an excellent ongoing exhibition, 'Spirit of ANZAC'. At the busy end of the park stands the gorgeously kitsch **Archibald Fountain**, which commemorates the association of France and Australia during World War I.

Australian Museum 8 C5

On the corner of William and College streets, you will find the excellent Australian Museum. Established in 1827, the present complex is an intriguing mix of Victorian museum and 21st-century educational centre. It houses several unique natural history collections as well as a superb display of Indigenous Australian culture, with lots of hands-on activities and weekly sessions of Aboriginal music and dance. *6 College St; open 9.30am–5pm daily.*

Cook and Phillip Park 8 C5

For a change of pace, do as the locals do and go for a swim at the **Cook and Phillip Park Aquatic & Fitness Centre**, which is located across from the Australian Museum at the southern end of the park. The complex offers a full range of swimming and

recreational activities, including a wave pool, but it's worth visiting just to see the mural that graces the western wall of the Olympic pool. Inspired by the life of Australian swimming champion Annette Kellerman, it consists of eight painted panels depicting scenes from a long and colourful career. Also worth a look is the **Yurong Water Garden** near the northern end of the park.

St Mary's Cathedral 8 C4

The cathedral is located on the east side of Hyde Park North, and was designed by William Wardell in a soaring Gothic Revival style that recalls the cathedrals of medieval Europe. Work on the cathedral began in 1868 and was finished in 1928, leaving the twin towers in the southern facade without their spires. The completed spires were added to the cathedral in 2000 by helicopter – much to the delight of watching Sydneysiders. A particular highlight is the crypt beneath the nave, which features a stunning terrazzo mosaic floor. *College St, facing Hyde Park.*

St James Church 8 C4

This fine sandstone church, with its elegant tower and copper-sheathed spire, is the oldest ecclesiastical building in the city. The commemorative tablets on the walls read like a page from a history of early Australia. Don't miss the little children's chapel either, which is located in the crypt. The chapel is decorated with an enchanting mural inspired by the Christmas carol 'I Saw Three Ships Come Sailing In', which depicts the land and seascapes of Sydney Harbour. *173 King St, opposite Hyde Park.*

Macquarie Street 8 C4

Named after one of Sydney's most dynamic and far-seeing governors, Macquarie Street was a thriving centre of upper-class society during the 19th century, evidence of which can still be seen in the magnificent buildings that line the eastern side of the street. In keeping with its old-world character, Macquarie Street is also home to a number of statues. Up near Hyde Park, for example, you will find **Queen Victoria** and her royal consort,

 getting around

Sydney has an extensive network of rail, bus and ferry services. When negotiating the inner city, buses are probably best, with regular services on George and Elizabeth streets, between Park Street and Circular Quay, including the free 555 CBD Shuttle. The Red Explorer bus covers city attractions, and the Blue Explorer bus focuses on the eastern beach and harbourside suburbs. Trains are another option, with services every two or three minutes on the City Circle line, which runs in a loop between Central Station and Circular Quay.

The monorail, an elevated ride through the streets of Sydney, is an experience in itself. It runs in a circle that includes the north, west and south sides of Darling Harbour, and Liverpool, Pitt and Market streets.

The light rail service runs from Central Station to the inner-west suburb of Lilyfield. As Sydney's only tram service, it is particularly useful for accessing places such as Star City and the Sydney Fish Market.

Ferries are also a great way to travel, with services to many locations on the inner and outer harbour (*see Getting around on ferries, p. 10*). Inquire about Travel 10, MyMulti Day Pass and weekly tickets, as these can considerably reduce the cost of your trip.

If you're driving, an up-to-the-minute road map is essential. There are ten tollways in Sydney, including the Harbour Bridge and the Cross-City Tunnel. Tolls can sometimes be paid on the spot, but the Cross-City Tunnel, Sydney

Harbour Bridge, Sydney Harbour Tunnel, Lane Cove Tunnel, Falcon Street Gateway and M7 will only accept payment by E-tag, an electronic device that can be obtained through the Roads and Traffic Authority (RTA).

Public transport Train, bus and ferry information line 13 1500.

Airport rail service Airport Link (02) 8337 8417.

Tollways Roads and Traffic Authority (RTA) 13 2213.

Motoring organisation NRMA 13 1122.

Car rental Avis 13 6333; Bayswater Car Rental (02) 9360 3622; Budget 13 2727; Hertz 13 3039; Thrifty 1300 367 227.

Specialty trips Monorail and Metro Light Rail (02) 8584 5288.

Harbour cruises Sydney Harbour Ferries 13 1500; Captain Cook Cruises (02) 9206 1111.

Taxis ABC Taxis 13 2522; Legion Cabs 13 1451; Manly Warringah Cabs 13 1668; Premier Cabs 13 1017.

Water taxis Water Taxis Combined 1300 666 484; Yellow Water Taxis 1300 138 840.

Tourist bus Red Explorer, Blue Explorer 13 1500.

Bicycle hire Centennial Park Cycles (02) 9398 5027; Bonza Bike Tours (02) 9247 8800.

getting around on ferries

Ferries are a great way to get about and see the harbour. Sydney Ferries and private operators run daily services from Circular Quay to more than 30 locations around the harbour and Parramatta River. Timetables, network maps and information about link tickets (combining a ferry fare with admission to various tourist attractions) can be obtained from the Sydney Ferries Information Centre at Circular Quay. Matilda Catamarans and Captain Cook Cruises are the main private ferry operators. They run ferry cruises and some express services to various points around Sydney Harbour, including some not serviced by Sydney Ferries.

Sydney Ferries from Circular Quay

Manly Ferry Departs Wharf 3.

Manly JetCat Express service to Manly, departs Wharf 2.

Taronga Zoo Ferry Departs Wharf 2.

Watsons Bay Ferry Darling Point (Mon–Fri only), Double Bay, Rose Bay and Watsons Bay, departs Wharf 4.

Mosman Ferry Mosman and Cremorne, departs Wharf 4 (Mon–Sat) and Wharf 2 (Sun).

North Sydney Ferry Kirribilli, North Sydney, Neutral Bay and Kurraba Point, departs Wharf 4.

Woolwich Ferry North Shore, Balmain, Cockatoo Island and Drummoyne, departs Wharf 5 (Mon–Sat) and Wharf 4 (Sun).

Parramatta RiverCat Express service to Parramatta, departs Wharf 5.

Rydalmere RiverCat North Sydney, Balmain, Darling Harbour and the Parramatta River to Rydalmere, departs Wharf 5.

Birkenhead Point Ferry North Sydney, Balmain and Birkenhead Point, departs Wharf 5 (Mon–Fri).

Darling Harbour Ferry North Sydney, Balmain and Darling Harbour, departs Wharf 5.

Private services from Darling Harbour and Circular Quay

Manly Flyer Catamaran service to Manly from Circular Quay and Darling Harbour. Tickets may be purchased on board.

Matilda Catamaran City Loop Service Darling Harbour to Circular Quay via Luna Park. Tickets may be purchased on board.

Matilda Catamaran Cruise + Attraction Combines Matilda Harbour Express ferry ticket with entry to one of the following harbourside attractions: Taronga Zoo, Shark Island or Fort Denison. Bookings on (02) 9264 7377.

Captain Cook Cruises Hop-on and hop-off cruise departs Darling Harbour, stopping at Luna Park, Circular Quay, Taronga Zoo, Shark Island, Fort Denison and Watsons Bay. Bookings on 1800 804 843.

Aboriginal Cruise An island visit, a welcome dance, and the Aboriginal names and history of the harbour. Bookings on (02) 9206 1111.

Prince Albert. While you're in this part of Macquarie Street, take the lift to the 14th floor of the **Supreme Court** building and visit the **Buena Vista** cafe. You can enjoy one of the best harbour views in Sydney, all for the price of a latte.

Gardens & Domain

One of the loveliest parts of the city, this area consists of extensive parkland, much of which was once part of the property surrounding the first Government House. It is thanks to the wisdom of governors Phillip and Macquarie that so much of this land was preserved, saving it from 200 years of ferocious development.

Hyde Park Barracks Museum 8 C4

Every elegant line and delicate arch of Hyde Park Barracks, one of the loveliest of Sydney's older buildings, bears the stamp of its convict architect, Francis Greenway. Built in 1819, the barracks have provided accommodation for a wide range of individuals including convicts. Various ongoing exhibitions reveal the many layers of this building's rich social history, with poignant displays of artefacts gleaned from recent excavations. *Cnr College and Macquarie sts; open 9.30am–5pm daily.*

The Mint 8 C4

Once the South Wing of the old Rum Hospital, the site of the colony's first mint is now the headquarters of the Historic Houses Trust. Besides a pleasant reading room there's a good cafe on the upper floor with balcony seating and fine views of Macquarie Street and Hyde Park. The mint artefacts are now housed in the Powerhouse Museum (*see p. 14*). *Open 9am–5pm Mon–Fri; general admission free.*

Sydney Hospital 8 C4

Now housing both the Sydney Hospital and the Sydney Eye Hospital, this imposing complex of sandstone buildings occupies the original site of the centre wing of the old Rum Hospital. Tours of the hospital's historic buildings are available (bookings essential). The little cobbled walkways that lead to the rear of the complex bring you to the oldest building, the Nightingale Wing, which houses the **Lucy Osborne-Nightingale Foundation Museum**. Among other items, you can see the sewing basket used by Florence Nightingale in the Crimea. *Museum open 10am–3pm Tues; tours (02) 9382 7111.*

Before you move on, don't forget to pay a visit to '**Il Porcellino**', a favourite photo opportunity with tourists and a 'collector' of money for the hospital. It is considered lucky to rub the statue's nose, then toss a coin in the fountain and make a wish.

Parliament of New South Wales 8 C4

Between the Sydney Hospital and the State Library stands the northern wing of the old Rum Hospital, now the seat of the Parliament of New South Wales. Tours of Parliament House begin at 9.30am and every 90 minutes thereafter except on sitting days, when both houses are in session. On sitting days tours commence at 1.30pm, and are followed by attendance at Question Time. Bookings for these days are essential. *(02) 9230 3444; open daily; general admission free.*

State Library of New South Wales 8 C3

Facing the Royal Botanic Gardens, on the corner of Macquarie Street and Shakespeare Place, the state library houses a remarkable collection of Australian books, records, personal papers, drawings, paintings and photographs, most of which are regularly displayed in the library's five public galleries. The magnificent Mitchell Library Reading Room is a highlight, as is the exquisite mosaic on the floor of the lobby, which depicts Abel Tasman's map of Australia. Just outside the library, check out the statues of **Matthew Flinders** and his beloved cat **Trim**. Stolen at least four times, Trim now perches on a sandstone ledge, well beyond the reach of souvenir hunters. *Open 9am–8pm Mon–Thurs, 9am–5pm Fri, 10am–5pm Sat–Sun.*

Royal Botanic Gardens 8 C3

A landscaped oasis on the edge of the harbour, the gardens are a wonderful place in which to stroll or relax with a picnic. Aside from its sweeping parklands, there are several formal gardens, including the Aboriginal garden, Cadi Jam Ora, and a stunning rose garden. Stock up on bush tucker, take in the botanical drawings at the Red Box Gallery, see a film by moonlight (summer only), or even adopt a tree. Ask at the Gardens Shop for details. *Mrs Macquaries Rd.*

Government House 8 C2

Government House is located in the north-west corner of the Botanic Gardens, close to Macquarie's old stables, now the **Conservatorium of Music** *(see Grand old buildings, p. 16)*. Built in 1845, Government House is an elaborate example of the Gothic Revival style, with extensive gardens and harbour views. Free guided tours of the state apartments are available, and there are 'Behind the Scenes' tours of the servants' halls, cellars, kitchens and dairies run by the Historic Houses Trust requiring an admission fee. Contact Trust headquarters at the Mint *(see The Mint, facing page)* for details.

The Domain 8 C4

Separated from the Botanic Gardens by the Cahill Expressway, the Domain falls into two distinct parts. South of the expressway, it's a wide green park where soapbox orators and an attendant crowd of hecklers once gathered each Sunday to debate the issues of the day. Now a place where office workers come to soak up the sun and play some lunchtime soccer, this area comes into its own in January when it hosts popular jazz, opera and symphony concerts. North of the Cahill, the rest of the Domain runs along the promontory to **Mrs Macquaries Chair**, a bench that was carved out of the sandstone bluff specifically so that Elizabeth Macquarie could sit in comfort as she watched for ships arriving from England with longed-for letters from home.

Art Gallery of New South Wales 8 C4

The gallery is situated to the south of the Cahill Expressway, opposite the South Domain. Built in an imposing Classical Revival style with ultra-modern additions, it houses an impressive collection of both Australian and international artworks, including a large permanent collection of Aboriginal art and a superb Asian collection. *Art Gallery Rd, The Domain; open 10am–5pm Thurs–Tues, 10am–9pm Wed; general admission free.*

Andrew (Boy) Charlton Pool 8 D3

A sensational place for a quick dip, a swimming lesson or a leisurely bite at the harbourside cafe. Boy Charlton was just 14 when he won a major swimming championship and became a national idol. His status was confirmed when he beat the Swedish world record holder Arne Borg three times in early 1924, and he went on to compete in three Olympic Games (1924, 1928 and 1932).

Around Circular Quay

Bounded by the 19th-century streetscape of Bridge Street and including the promenades of East and West Circular Quay, this area contains one of Sydney's most famous icons. It also houses two must-see museums and boasts one of the few corners of the CBD that has remained unaltered for almost 200 years.

[SYDNEY OPERA HOUSE AT NIGHT]

Circular Quay 8 C3

Since the moment that Sydney was declared a settlement, Circular Quay has been where it all happens. With many journeys beginning and ending here, it's a major junction for bus, rail and ferry transport *(see Getting around, p. 9)*, and a natural meeting place. There's entertainment on the quay itself in the form of buskers and street performers, while the many excellent cafes and bars offer stunning views of the harbour.

Sydney Opera House 8 C2

One of the great buildings of the 20th century, the Sydney Opera House stands at the far end of East Circular Quay, breathtaking in its beauty against the backdrop of Sydney Harbour. Thought by many to echo the sails seen in the harbour, it was in fact the natural fall of a segmented orange that inspired Jørn Utzon's design, although Utzon never saw the completed building. After resigning in anger over changes made to the interior design, he left, swearing never to return. The recent renovations to the interior were carried out under his direction prior to his death in November 2008. With nearly 1000 rooms that include theatres and concert halls, rehearsal studios and dressing-rooms, a guided tour is recommended (bookings essential). *Tours (02) 9250 7250.*

top events

Sydney Festival   A celebration of the city, this includes cultural events at Sydney's most stunning indoor and outdoor venues. January.

Gay and Lesbian Mardi Gras   A two-week cultural festival culminating in a spectacular street parade. February–March.

Royal Easter Show   The country comes to the city in the Great Australian Muster. Easter.

Archibald Prize   The Archibald national portrait prize and exhibition is one of Sydney's most controversial events. March–May.

Sydney Comedy Festival   Three weeks of local and international comedy acts at various venues around Sydney. April–May.

Sydney Film Festival   A showcase for the newest offerings in cinema. June.

City to Surf   A 14-kilometre fun run, from Hyde Park to Bondi. August.

Crave Sydney   A month-long festival of food and outdoor art, including the Sydney International Food Festival, Darling Harbour Fiesta and Art & About. October.

Rugby League Grand Final   The leaders of the football competition compete for the title in the final match of the season. October.

Sydney to Hobart Yacht Race   Classic blue-water sailing event. 26 December.

museums

Brett Whiteley Studio   Paintings and sculptures in the former studio and home of this great Australian artist. 2 Raper St, Surry Hills; open 10am–4pm Sat–Sun.

Mary MacKillop Place Museum   A tribute to this remarkable woman who brought education to the children of the bush. 7 Mount St, North Sydney; open 10am–4pm daily.

Royal Australian Navy Heritage Centre   Over 100 years of navy history in the harbourside setting of Garden Island. Take Watsons Bay ferry from Circular Quay to Garden Island; last ferry departs Garden Island 4.06pm Mon–Fri, 4.16pm Sat–Sun. Open daily; admission free.

Sydney Jewish Museum   A history of the Jewish people in Australia, along with a poignant tribute to the victims of the Holocaust. Cnr Darlinghurst Rd and Burton St, Darlinghurst; closed Sat and Jewish holidays.

Justice and Police Museum   Located in the old Water Police Station, with exhibitions on crime and punishment in Sydney, including the city's most notorious cases. Cnr Albert and Phillip sts, Circular Quay; open 10am–5pm Sat–Sun, daily Jan.

Victoria Barracks Museum   Military pride in a colonial setting, with a stirring flag-raising ceremony, followed by a guided tour of the barracks and the museum. Oxford St, Paddington; open 10am–1pm Thurs, 10am–4pm Sun; admission free.

Sydney Tramway Museum   Historic trams from Sydney, Nagasaki, Berlin and San Francisco. Entry fee includes unlimited rides on the trams. Cnr Pitt St and Princes Hwy, Loftus; open 10am–3pm Wed, 10am–5pm Sun, daily during school holidays.

The Rocks Discovery Museum   A fascinating glimpse into the chequered past of The Rocks, featuring both interactive technology and archaeological artefacts. 2–8 Kendall La, The Rocks; open 10am–5pm daily; admission free.

Australian Centre for Photography   Exhibitions of work by the world's best art, fashion and documentary photographers. 257 Oxford St, Paddington; open 12–7pm Tues–Fri, 10am–6pm Sat–Sun; admission free.

See also Australian Museum, p. 9, Hyde Park Barracks Museum, p. 10, Museum of Sydney, this page, Museum of Contemporary Art, this page, Susannah Place Museum, p. 13, Australian National Maritime Museum, p. 14, Powerhouse Museum, p. 14, La Perouse Museum, p. 18

Museum of Sydney 8 C3

A gem of a museum built of sandstone, steel and glass, the Museum of Sydney is situated on the site of the first Government House, the original foundations of which can still be seen. Through a series of intriguing displays, exhibitions and films, the many layers that have gone into the making of Sydney are revealed. *Cnr Phillip and Bridge sts; open 9.30am–5pm daily.*

Macquarie Place Park 8 C3

On the corner of Loftus and Bridge streets stands a remnant of the old Government House garden, now known as Macquarie Place Park and hardly changed from the days when Macquarie designated it the city centre. The elegant sandstone obelisk near the south-east corner of the park marks the place from which all distances in the colony were once measured. The nearby anchor and small gun belonged to Arthur Phillip's flagship *Sirius*. More of this ship has since been recovered, and can be viewed at the Australian National Maritime Museum *(see p. 14).*

The Rocks

Once the haunt of pickpockets, prostitutes and sailors, The Rocks contains some of the city's most important historic sites, and is one of Sydney's most treasured attractions. Divided into two parts by the approaches to the Harbour Bridge, the area on the eastern side of the Argyle Cut is centred on the lanes north of George Street, while the area to the west takes in one of Sydney's most beautiful parks and the gracious 19th-century houses of Lower Fort Street.

Sydney Visitor Centre 8 B2

A visit to The Rocks should begin with a visit to the excellent Sydney Visitor Centre, where you'll find all the detailed information you'll need regarding accommodation, dining, shopping and sightseeing in the area. Of special interest are the many guided tours available, including several walking tours, a ghost tour and a tour of the area's historic pubs. *Cnr Argyle and Playfair sts; open 9.30am–5.30pm daily.*

George Street — north 8 B2, C2

Much of The Rocks' previous character as a notorious seaport rookery can still be glimpsed in the winding streets and tiny lanes that run behind George Street. There are quiet courtyard cafes and some unusual shops to be found here, including the enchanting **Puppet Shop**, with hundreds of exquisitely handcrafted marionettes hanging from the ceilings of four rooms. Located in the sandstone cellars of 77 George Street, it's a must-see, and not just for children.

Museum of Contemporary Art 8 C2

The museum occupies the old Maritime Services building – a brooding Art Deco structure that dominates the western side of Circular Quay. But once inside, the large, open white rooms offer an ideal setting to showcase works by Australian and international contemporary artists. Visitors can expect an ever-changing display of innovative sculptures, paintings, photographs and video installations. Make sure to visit the giftshop. *Open 10am–5pm daily; general admission free.*

Cadmans Cottage 8 C2

This charming little cottage has the distinction of being Sydney's oldest surviving residence. Built in 1816, for many years it was the home of John Cadman, an ex-convict and boatman to Governor Macquarie. Today it is the Sydney Harbour National Park Information Centre and the starting point for tours of the harbour islands *(see Harbour islands, p. 20). 110 George St; (02) 9247 5033; open 10am–4.30pm Tues–Sun.*

Playfair Street 8 B2

The heart and soul of The Rocks, Playfair Street is the place to be, particularly on the weekends. There's corn-on-the-cob, wandering street performers, endless live entertainment, and a fantastic vibe from the crowd that is constantly on the move. Find a seat in **Rocks Square** and soak it all up. Not far away is **Argyle Stores**, a converted warehouse that now houses a collection of open-plan shops specialising in beautiful and unusual clothes. The main entrance to the stores is on Argyle Street, by way of Mary Reibey's old bond stores. As you pass through the arched gateway, spare a thought for this remarkable woman who arrived in Australia in 1792 at the age of 14 and is today remembered as one of the most successful businesswomen in the colony of New South Wales. Her portrait appears on the 20-dollar note.

Foundation Park 8 B2

Hidden behind a row of souvenir shops in Playfair Street, the quirky and charming Foundation Park occupies the almost vertical site of three former dwellings that were built into the face of the sandstone escarpment. A front door was situated at the top of the cliff, and a back door halfway down. All that remains now are a few scattered foundations among the grassy terraces of the park and a steep stairway or two leading nowhere, but here and there you can find a chair, a fireplace, a clock or a table, recalling those long-vanished homes.

Susannah Place Museum 8 B2

From the top of Foundation Park, this wonderful museum is just up the Argyle Stairs and around the corner in Gloucester Street. Occupying four terrace houses, it affords a glimpse of what it was like for working-class people living in The Rocks at varying stages in its history. The museum is extremely people-friendly, with visitors encouraged to linger among the exhibits and try the piano in the parlour of No. 64. Take a moment to look around the little shop before you go; re-created in turn-of-the-century style, it sells toys, sweets, soft drinks and other goods from that era. *58–64 Gloucester St; open 2–6pm Mon–Fri, 10am–5pm Sat–Sun and school holidays.*

Sydney Harbour Bridge 8 C1

With almost every view in The Rocks dominated by its soaring arch, it's hard to ignore the presence of Sydney's magnificent harbour bridge. With its longest span at 503 metres, it was completed and opened to traffic in 1932. One of the best views of Sydney can be had from the **Pylon Lookout**, which contains an excellent exhibition detailing the bridge's history. The **Sydney Harbour Bridge Visitor Centre** also contains an exhibition and cinemas showing how the bridge was built. The same entrance leads to **BridgeClimb Sydney**, offering unique and unforgettable tours to the very top of the span *(see Walks & tours, p. 15)*. *3 Cumberland St; open 10am–5pm daily.*

Argyle Cut 8 B2

Work on the cutting connecting the eastern and western sides of The Rocks commenced in 1843, with chained convicts doing most of the hard labour. Initially much narrower than it is now, it was once the haunt of 'pushes' (larrikin youths who specialised in gang warfare and rolling the lone passer-by). In the heyday of the pushes, even the police went through the Argyle Cut in pairs.

Observatory Park 8 B2

High above The Rocks stands what is perhaps the loveliest park in Sydney. It has an old-world ambience and stunning views of the western harbour. For stargazers, there's the **Sydney Observatory Museum**, which hosts exhibitions on astronomy as well as talks, films and viewings of the night sky (bookings essential). *Bookings (02) 9921 3485; open 10am–10pm daily; day admission free.*

Not far from the observatory, hidden by a curve of the Cahill Expressway, stands the old Fort Street School for Girls, now the headquarters for the National Trust. This is where you will find the **S. H. Ervin Gallery**, which is renowned for its innovative and unusual art exhibitions.

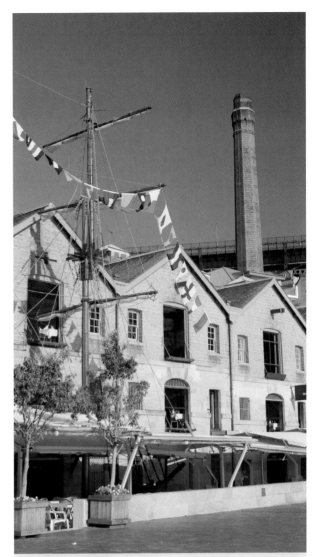

[THE HISTORIC ROCKS PRECINCT]

shopping

Pitt Street Mall, City Sydney's major shopping area.

Castlereagh Street, City Sheer indulgence with some of the world's leading designer labels.

The Galeries Victoria, City A dazzling array of top-quality fashion and lifestyle brands.

The Rocks The place to go for top-quality Australian art, jewellery and clothing.

Oxford Street, Darlinghurst Up-to-the-minute street fashion and funky alternative clothing.

Oxford Street, Paddington Cutting-edge designers and a mecca for antique hunters.

Double Bay Sydney's most exclusive shopping suburb.

Birkenhead Point, Drummoyne Designer shopping at bargain prices in a historic venue.

Military Road, Mosman Classy shopping in a village atmosphere.

Darling Harbour

Located to the immediate west of the CBD and easily accessed by ferry, light rail and monorail, Darling Harbour is the focus of much of the city's culture and entertainment. In the inner-west area, families will delight in Australia's largest and most popular museum, the Powerhouse. There's also the glitz of Star City casino, and food lovers should head to the Sydney Fish Market, the largest market of its kind in the Southern Hemisphere.

Darling Harbour East 8 A4

Once very much a working harbour, Darling Harbour has a maritime past reflected in the structures that surround its landscaped promenades and parks. One good example is the National Trust–classified **Pyrmont Bridge**, which spans the harbour from east to west. North-east of the bridge are **King Street Wharf** and **Cockle Bay Wharf**, renowned for exclusive

markets

Paddy's Markets   Sydney's most famous markets, with superb fresh produce and bargains in clothing, souvenirs, toys and gifts. Haymarket; Wed–Sun. 8 A5

The Rocks Markets   Classic street market with a dedicated designers section, some superb Indigenous art, stylish homewares and exquisite jewellery for sale. Sat–Sun, Fri evening Nov–Mar, farmers market Fri–Sat. 8 C2

Sydney Opera House Markets   Australian souvenirs, arts and crafts in a glorious harbour setting. Sun. 8 C2

Paddington Markets   Fabulous mix of fashion, artworks, jewellery and collectibles in one of Sydney's trendiest suburbs. Sat. 6 C5

Sydney Flower Market   Freshly cut flowers at wholesale prices, and breakfast at the market cafes. Flemington; Mon–Sat. 545 K9

EQ Village Markets   Gourmet food, produce and coffee in the village-like atmosphere of the Showring. Moore Park; Wed & Sat, Kidz Zoo Wed, Sat–Sun. 6 C5

Balmain Market   Jewellery and leather goods, arts and craft in the grounds of an old sandstone church. St Andrews Church; Sat. 6 B3

Bondi Markets   Clothes, jewellery, a range of new and second-hand collectibles, and a lively beachside atmosphere. Sun. 6 E5

The Good Living Growers' Market   The gourmet's choice, with superb breads, cheeses, fruit and vegetables, close to Darling Harbour. 1st Sat each month. 8 A3

Glebe Markets   Decorative homewares, arts and crafts, new and second-hand clothing, with a background of live music. Sat. 6 B4

Paddy's Swap and Sell Market   Sydney's biggest garage sale where second-hand goods are bought and sold and occasionally even swapped. Flemington; Sat. 545 K9

Eveleigh Farmers Market   Fresh seasonal produce, flowers and wines at the CarriageWorks arts centre. Eveleigh; Sat. 6 B5

Fringe Bar Markets   The Unicorn Hotel opens up its space for trendy new fashions and vintage clothing. Paddington; Sat. 8 D6

Manly West Organic Market   Stock up on exclusively organic produce at this market at Manly West Public School. Sat. 6 E1

See also Sydney Fish Market, facing page

shopping and dining. South-east of Pyrmont Bridge, the ultra-modern **Imax Theatre** boasts the largest cinema screen in the world and offers films in both 2D and 3D format.

Sydney Aquarium 8 A4

The Sydney Aquarium rates high among the world's aquariums for sheer spectacle-value. Highlights include the fabulous underwater tunnels that enable you to walk with the stingrays and stroll with the sharks, a Great Barrier Reef exhibition that's pure magic, two of only six dugongs in captivity in the world, and the Seal Sanctuary, where you can watch the seals flirt and frolic all around you. *Aquarium Pier; open 9am–10pm daily.*

Sydney Wildlife World 8 A4

Situated right next door to the Aquarium, Sydney Wildlife World takes you deep into the heart of the Australian bush, from the rainforests of the tropical north to the deserts of the Red Centre. Over 250 different Australian species live within their own natural habitats and ecosystems. *Aquarium Pier; 9am–5.30pm daily.*

Chinese Garden of Friendship 8 A5

Tucked away to the south is this garden, where airy pavilions and tiny arched bridges stand reflected in tranquil lakes, surrounded by weeping willows and graceful bamboo. There's an elegant teahouse that serves traditional Chinese teas, as well as a tiny pavilion where for a small fee you can dress up in costumes from the Peking Opera. *Open 9.30am–5pm daily.*

Australian National Maritime Museum 8 A4

Located to the north of Pyrmont Bridge, several imaginative and awe-inspiring exhibitions highlight Australia's multifaceted relationship with the sea, from the days of convict transports and immigrant ships, to the beach culture of today. Special exhibitions include tours of the museum's fleet. *2 Murray St, Darling Harbour; open 9.30am–5pm daily; general admission free.*

South of the harbour 8 A5, B5

Just past the **Sydney Entertainment Centre**, host to the world's biggest music stars, you'll find **Paddy's Markets** *(see Markets, this page)*. Opposite the Thomas Street entrance to the market is Dixon Street, the main thoroughfare of **Chinatown**. There are colourful shops offering everything from inexpensive souvenirs to beautiful and costly Chinese items, as well as superb Asian cuisine to suit every taste.

Powerhouse Museum 8 A5

South-west of Darling Harbour, the museum is best accessed by monorail. One of Sydney's most fascinating museums, it houses an extraordinary collection of oddments and treasures. Highlights include the Hall of Transport, with its fleet of aeroplanes suspended from the ceiling, and the tiny 1930s-style cinema with its program of old newsreels and documentaries. Free guided tours are available as well as a broad range of daily activities. *500 Harris St, Ultimo; open 10am–5pm daily.*

Star City 8 A3

Star City, Sydney's only official casino, can be found to the north-west of Darling Harbour. It is worth a visit just to see its extraordinary interiors, with glittering lights and dazzling aquatic displays. Star City is also home to two of Sydney's finest theatres and several restaurants that offer fine dining with panoramic views of Darling Harbour. *80 Pyrmont St, Pyrmont; open 24 hours.*

[CHINESE GARDEN OF FRIENDSHIP, DARLING HARBOUR]

Sydney Fish Market 6 B4

The Sydney Fish Market is still within walking distance of Darling Harbour, but is probably best accessed by light rail. Fast-paced and vibrant, with a good bakery, an excellent deli and some of the best and freshest seafood you're ever likely to find, the market is a great place to visit. There are guided tours that enable you to watch a Dutch auction (where the price actually *drops* every minute), but only for the early risers. *Bank St, Pyrmont; tours (02) 9004 1143; open 7am–4pm daily.*

Inner West

The inner west starts at the beginning of Parramatta Road near Sydney University and takes in the historic suburbs of Glebe and Balmain. Glebe has retained many of its grand Victorian homes, Federation houses and modest workers' cottages, and has a reputation as an alternative suburb. With its arty flair, in complete contrast to its previous population of dockland workers, Balmain sits on a peninsula in Port Jackson, adjacent to the suburbs of Rozelle to the south-west, Birchgrove to the north-west and Balmain East.

Glebe 6 B4

Once a predominantly working-class suburb, Glebe has become more refined over the years. With Sydney University close by, you can find excellent bookshops, lively cafes and some great weekend markets here *(see Markets, facing page)*. Its leafy streets lined with old weatherboard houses, Victorian terraces and the occasional mansion, Glebe is a fabulous area to explore on foot. At the far end of Glebe Point Road is **Glebe Park**, which features landscaped walks with views of Blackwattle Bay and Anzac Bridge.

Balmain 6 B4

Tucked away on its own little peninsula, Balmain is another suburb of quaint houses, stepped lanes and harbour views. The main shopping centre is in Darling Street, a lively area with cafes, boutiques and top-quality shops. Quickly and easily reached by ferry, this is another suburb that is best seen on foot.

walks & tours

The Rocks Walking Tours The history of The Rocks and its many colourful characters are brought to life during this 90-minute tour. Bookings on (02) 9247 6678.

Harbour Circle Walk For a comprehensive overview of Sydney's harbour, starting and ending at Observatory Hill, this walk covers 26 kilometres and could take you the whole day. Download a map from planning.nsw.gov.au

BridgeClimb Sydney Various tours of the Sydney Harbour Bridge that involve climbing to the top of the span clad in protective clothing and secured with a harness. Bookings on (02) 8274 7777.

Sculpture by the Sea During November, this free outdoor exhibition on the Bondi to Tamarama coastal walk draws large crowds viewing over 100 modern art pieces with the sea as their backdrop.

Sydney Ferry Harbour Walks Discover some of Sydney's more out-of-the-way places on foot. Pick up a brochure at the Sydney Ferries Information Centre at Circular Quay, take a ferry to any of the listed destinations, and start walking.

The Rocks Pub Tour Tales of scandal and intrigue unfold on this pub crawl with a difference, as you knock back a schooner or two at The Rocks' most famous hotels. Bookings on 1300 458 437.

Oz Jet Boating Tours Tour the harbour in a high-performance V8 jet boat. Bookings on (02) 9808 3700.

Destiny Tours Stories of sex, scandal and the supernatural. Explore Sydney's darker side on this night-time minibus tour. Bookings on (02) 9487 2895.

Harley-Davidson Tours See Sydney from the back of an East Coast Harley-Davidson. Bookings on 1300 882 065.

Gourmet Safaris Choose from a range of foodie tours that uncover Sydney's multicultural world of gourmet food. Experienced chefs will take you to local shops and invite you to try traditional Greek, Italian, Lebanese, Portuguese, Turkish or Vietnamese cuisine. Bookings on (02) 9960 5675.

City Sightseeing Sydney and Bondi Tours Cover the city and the eastern suburbs in a double-decker, open-topped bus, hopping on and off as often as you like. (02) 9567 8400.

Chocolate Espresso Tours Tour the city's CBD and shopping districts, with a focus on either coffee or chocolate. Bookings on 0417 167 766.

Inner East

The inner-eastern suburbs begin just beyond the Domain and include Kings Cross, the old maritime suburb of Woolloomooloo, Paddington and Darlinghurst, once the haunt of some of the city's most notorious gangsters and now home to some very trendy cafes and restaurants.

Woolloomooloo 8 D4

While there are buses that service this area, the best way to get to Woolloomooloo is to take the stairs near the Art Gallery in Mrs Macquaries Road. These will bring you down close to Woolloomooloo's most recent and controversial development, the **Finger Wharf**. A remnant of the days when the 'Loo had a reputation for toughness and lawlessness, the Finger Wharf is

grand old buildings

Customs House   Elegant sandstone building designed by colonial architect James Barnet in the Classical Revival style. Alfred St, Circular Quay.

Department of Planning   This building is particularly noteworthy for the statues of famous explorers and legislators that grace the exterior. 22–33 Bridge St.

Conservatorium of Music   Much altered, but the castellated facade still recalls Macquarie's fancy Government House Stables. Macquarie St.

Cadmans Cottage   Sydney's oldest surviving residence, now a NPWS office. 110 George St, The Rocks.

Campbell's Storehouse   Built from bricks made by convicts, its serried roof has long been a Sydney landmark. Hickson Rd, The Rocks.

The Garrison Church   View the red-cedar pulpit and the beautiful stained-glass window. Lower Fort St, Millers Point.

The Great Synagogue   Exotic and remarkable in its originality, with a gorgeous mix of Byzantine and Gothic architecture, and sumptuous interiors. Elizabeth St.

St Andrew's Cathedral   With twin towers that recall York Minster, it is best seen in November through a cloud of purple jacaranda. Cnr Bathurst and George sts.

Old Darlinghurst Gaol   An impressive early Victorian sandstone prison with an imposing entrance, it now houses the National Art School.

The University of Sydney   Landscaped grounds and historic sandstone buildings. Parramatta Rd, Broadway.

See also Queen Victoria Building, p. 7, Sydney Town Hall, p. 7, Hyde Park Barracks Museum, p. 10, Government House, p. 11

now one of Sydney's most exclusive addresses. For a traditional Sydney culinary experience, try **Harry's Cafe de Wheels**, a pie-wagon and long-time Sydney icon on the eastern side of the bay.

Kings Cross 8 D5

If driving to Kings Cross, head towards the Coca-Cola sign – a landmark since the days of the Vietnam War. The Cross is one of the most fascinating parts of Sydney. At night, when the strip clubs of Darlinghurst Road swing into action, the vibe is raw and edgy. But by daylight it retains the charm of its bohemian past, with gracious tree-lined streets and pretty sidewalk cafes. Look for the **El Alamein Fountain**, the most photographed fountain in Sydney. For something completely different, you could indulge in a dip and massage at the **Body Inc Bathhouse and Spa** at Level 1, 224 Victoria Street.

Elizabeth Bay House 6 C4

Designed by John Verge as a home for Alexander Macleay (whose family history is displayed on the walls of St James Church in Queens Square), the house is particularly famous for the stunning proportions of its elegant oval saloon with a sky-lit dome, and beautiful curving staircase. After spending many years as a shabby boarding house and artists' squat, it is now a Historic Houses Trust museum, and its rooms have been restored to their former 19th-century graciousness. *7 Onslow Ave, Elizabeth Bay; open 9.30am–4pm Fri–Sun.*

Paddington 6 C5

Considered an eyesore until quite recently, Paddington is now one of Sydney's most beautiful suburbs. Its backstreets are lined with rows of iron-lace-trimmed terraces decked with flowers, and its main thoroughfare, Oxford Street, is home to dozens of boutiques, galleries and cafes. Always busy, it is at its most vibrant on weekends, when the **Paddington Markets** are in full swing *(see Markets, p. 14)*. Paddington is easily accessed by bus – you can disembark on Oxford Street and walk around.

East

Sydney's east is dominated by the city's green lungs, Centennial Park. Stretching south of Paddington, the park is a magnet for joggers, sun-worshippers, picnickers, tai-chi exponents, horseriders and lovers of the great outdoors.

Centennial Park 6 C5

South of Paddington lies Centennial Park, a massive complex of parklands, playing fields, bridle paths and riding tracks. It's a great place to get away from it all and relax with a picnic. Once a huge catchment of creeks, swamps, springs, sand dunes and ponds fed by groundwater, it was traditionally home to the Gadi people. The distinctive Federation Pavilion commemorates the site of the inauguration of Australian Federation on 1 January 1901.

Inner South

The Moore Park precinct in the city's inner south takes in the Entertainment Quarter, one of Sydney's premier leisure playgrounds. It was the home of the Royal Agricultural Society and the Sydney Royal Easter Show until January 1998, when they were relocated to Sydney Olympic Park.

Entertainment Quarter 6 C5

One of Sydney's newer entertainment centres, the Entertainment Quarter occupies the site of the old showgrounds and is located next to the **Sydney Cricket Ground** at Moore Park. While film studios and sound sets occupy much of the site, the Showring is now a vast village green, adjacent to a vibrant pedestrian precinct lined with top-quality fashion and homewares outlets. The Entertainment Quarter also boasts two cinema complexes and more than a dozen cafes, restaurants and bars. Always lively, the village atmosphere is most noticeable when the weekly markets set up their stalls in the Showring *(see Markets, p. 14)*.

Equestrian Centre 6 C5

There are five riding schools at the **Centennial Parklands Equestrian Centre**, offering park rides for those who have experience and riding lessons for those who do not. The Equestrian Centre is located on the corner of Lang and Cook roads in Moore Park. If riding a bike is more your style, try one of the bicycle-hire shops in Clovelly Road, on the south side of the park *(see Getting around, p. 9)*.

Eastern Beachside

Vaucluse is one of Sydney's most exclusive suburbs, and old and new money abounds in the lavish homes gracing the harbour foreshore. The suburb's nearby cousin, Watsons Bay, on the southern head of the harbour entrance, is recognised as Australia's oldest fishing village. It was Governor Phillip's first landing point after discovering the harbour in 1788.

Vaucluse House 6 E4

In the heart of Vaucluse, not far from the harbour, this early 19th-century house was once owned by the flamboyant William Charles Wentworth. Now a Historic Houses Trust museum, it is a beautifully preserved example of an early Victorian well-to-do household. The gardens are open to the public daily; guided tours of the house are available on request. *Open 9.30am–4pm Fri–Sun.*

Watsons Bay 7 E3

All roads in the eastern suburbs lead to Watsons Bay. This is where you will find the spectacular ocean cliffs known as **The Gap** and **Doyles**, a famous seafood restaurant with superb views of the city. Nearby is **Camp Cove**, a popular family beach and the starting point of a 1.5-kilometre walking track, which takes you past Sydney's first nude-bathing beach, **Lady Bay**, to the windswept promontory of **South Head**. South Head boasts magnificent views across the harbour to Manly and a poignant memorial to the crew and passengers of the *Dunbar* who were all lost in 1853 when the ill-fated ship ran aground and sank just outside the heads.

Bondi Beach 6 E5

On a hot summer's day, Bondi is about as iconic as it gets – a sweep of pale sand covered with a rainbow of towels and umbrellas, encircling the blue-and-white breaks of the bay. Interestingly, Bondi Beach was privately owned until 1856, when the government purchased it for the 'pleasure of the people'. The suburb was a bohemian and immigrant enclave from the 1950s onwards, and even today with soaring real estate prices, it retains a diverse mix of professionals, artists, students and surfers. The beach stretches 800 metres between a set of headlands, from the **Icebergs** sea baths in the south to a rockpool at the northern end. In the south is where you'll find sizeable, if a little inconsistent, surf, while the more sheltered north is suitable for families.

Bondi to Coogee walk 6 D6, C5

Though all these suburbs are easily accessed by bus, the best way to view them is by taking the walking track that starts at the southern end of **Bondi Beach**, known for its excellent weekend market *(see Markets, p. 14)* and chic sidewalk cafes. From Bondi, the walking track winds south along the cliffs through the tiny boutique beach of **Tamarama**. In November, this section of the track becomes crowded with people viewing the Sculpture by the Sea exhibition *(see Walks & tours, p. 15)*. **Bronte**, a lovely beach with a natural-rock swimming pool known as the Bogey Hole, completes the track. For those who want to explore further, the walk extends through **Waverley Cemetery** (where you can find the grave of Henry Lawson), past **Clovelly** (a popular swimming place), to **Coogee**. Along with the shops and cafes of Arden Street, you can visit the **Coogee Bay Hotel**, a lively pub with a sunny waterfront beer garden, which lies directly opposite the beach.

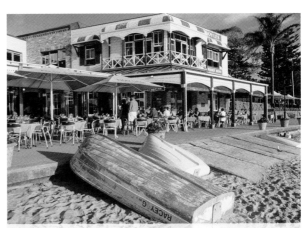

[DOYLES RESTAURANT, WATSONS BAY]

South-eastern Beachside

The city of Botany Bay, on the northern shores of Botany Bay, is Australia's largest municipality. Botany Bay National Park straddles the bay's headlands, and at its entrance is the suburb of La Perouse, home to an intriguing combination of natural and cultural heritage.

La Perouse 545 M10

La Perouse is situated on the northern head of Botany Bay. Originally the home of the Muru-ora-dial people, it was named after the Comte de La Perouse, a French navigator who arrived in Botany Bay around the same time as the First Fleet, as part of a competing French contingent. With some beautiful beaches and interesting walks, it also contains an excellent museum *(see p. 18)*.

where to eat

a tavola Authentic Italian in an intimate dining room setting in the heart of Sydney's trendy inner east. 348 Victoria St, Darlinghurst; (02) 9331 7871; open Fri for lunch and Mon–Sat for dinner. 8 D5

Bécasse Discover imaginative contemporary French flair at this popular inner-city restaurant. 204 Clarence St; (02) 9283 3440; open Mon–Fri for lunch and Mon–Sat for dinner. 8 B4

Berowra Waters Inn Spectacular regional location and cuisine make this star definitely worth the journey. Via Public Wharf; (02) 9456 1027; open Fri–Sun for lunch and Fri–Sat for dinner. 454 L5

Burlington Bar and Dining Dining excellence without the hefty price tag. Experience what locals are raving about. 6 Burlington St, Crows Nest; (02) 9439 7888; open Mon–Fri for lunch and Mon–Sat for dinner. 6 C2

Quay Right at the top of everyone's list for first-class dining. The location – directly opposite the Opera House – isn't bad either. Upper Level, Overseas Passenger Terminal, Circular Quay West; (02) 9251 5600; open Tues–Fri for lunch and daily for dinner. 8 C2

Spice I Am It might not look like much, but Spice I Am has the best Thai food in Sydney and at affordable prices. 90 Wentworth Ave, Surry Hills; (02) 9280 0928; open Tues–Sun for lunch and dinner. 8 B5

Tetsuya's Experience a genius of Japanese-French fusion and individuality with the incredible degustation at Tetsuya's. 529 Kent St; (02) 9267 2900; open Sat for lunch and Tues–Sat for dinner. 8 B5

[BEACHGOERS, COOGEE]

entertainment

Cinema   Located in George Street, between Bathurst and Liverpool streets, the 17-screen Event Cinemas George Street complex is the major cinema centre in the CBD. Arthouse cinemas include the Chauvel at Paddington Town Hall; the Dendy at Newtown and Circular Quay; and the Cinema Paris at the Entertainment Quarter. For a unique cinema experience, try the Hayden Orpheum Picture Palace in Cremorne, famous for its Art Deco interior and Wurlitzer pipe organ. See the newspapers for details of films being shown.

Live music   Sydney has always had a strong live music scene with some excellent venues throughout the city. Apart from the larger, more formal places for live bands that include the Enmore Theatre, the Metro in George Street and the Forum at the Entertainment Quarter, the city's pubs are the main focus for live music. Try the Annandale Hotel, a popular venue for local indie bands; or the legendary Bridge Hotel in Rozelle, which specialises in blues and pub rock. For jazz lovers, there's the Vanguard in Newtown and the famous Basement at Circular Quay. Check newspaper lift-outs such as 'Metro' for what's on, or get hold of one of the free magazines such as *3D World* or *Drum Media* for details.

Classical music and performing arts   The ultimate venue for theatre, dance and classical music, the Sydney Opera House plays host to companies such as the Sydney Symphony Orchestra, the Sydney Theatre Company, Opera Australia and the Australian Ballet. It's worth checking out some of the smaller venues, such as the City Recital Hall in Angel Place or the Conservatorium of Music. Other venues for excellent live theatre include the Belvoir St Theatre in Surry Hills, and the Wharf Theatres and the Sydney Theatre, both at Walsh Bay. If you are interested in dance, you can catch the Sydney Dance Company and the Bangarra Aboriginal dance group between tours at the Sydney Theatre or at the Sydney Opera House. For details, check the *Sydney Morning Herald*'s Friday lift-out, 'Metro', or *Time Out Sydney* magazine.

Bare Island 545 M10

From the earliest days of European settlement, La Perouse was considered to be crucial to the defence of the colony. Governor Macquarie built the sandstone tower that stands at the highest point of the promontory, and the fortifications at Bare Island were added in 1885. Guided tours are the only way to view these buildings (which movie fans will recognise from *Mission: Impossible 2*). *Accessed via a footbridge from Anzac Pde; guided tours Sun 1.30pm, 2.30pm and 3.30pm.*

La Perouse Museum 545 M10

This highly recommended museum occupies the old Cable Station, and presents the rich and varied history of La Perouse – it was once the site of an Aboriginal mission station and a Depression-era shanty town. The real focus of the museum is the life and times of La Perouse himself, with galleries devoted to the history of Pacific exploration, the voyage to Botany Bay and the eventual wreck and loss of the entire expedition. Not far from the museum is a monument to La Perouse near the grave of Father Receveur, the chaplain on the expedition. *Anzac Pde, La Perouse; open 10am–4pm Wed–Sun.*

Inner North

Sydney's inner north includes some of the city's most sought-after suburbs, including Neutral Bay, Mosman and the harbour beach suburb of Balmoral. The main shopping districts of Neutral Bay and Mosman sit along Military Road, the only connection to the Spit Bridge spanning Mosman and Seaforth on Middle Harbour.

Nutcote 6 C3

Nutcote is a must-see for anyone who remembers the characters of Snugglepot, Cuddlepie and the Banksia Men. Once home to May Gibbs, one of Australia's best-known authors and illustrators of children's books, Nutcote is situated in the exclusive harbourside suburb of Neutral Bay. It has been restored and furnished as it would have been in the 1930s, when May Gibbs lived there. It is now a centre for children's literature, the arts and the environment. *5 Wallaringa Ave; open 11am–3pm Wed–Sun.*

Taronga Zoo 6 D3

Located at the end of Bradleys Head Road in Mosman, Taronga Zoo is best accessed by ferry from Circular Quay. A world-class institution, it has an impressive reputation in the fields of conservation, and the care and management of rare and endangered species. It houses over 2000 animals, most of which enjoy stunning views of the harbour and city. Visitors can enjoy animal feeding, keeper talks and displays. The zoo boasts plenty of places for picnics and barbecues. It is also the venue for the ever-popular *Twilight at Taronga* open-air concerts, which take place in February and March. *Open 9am–5pm daily.*

Balmoral 6 D2

Some say Balmoral, with its curving promenade, shady trees and elegant bridge connecting a rocky outcrop to the mainland, is reminiscent of Edwardian Sydney. Extremely popular in summer, Balmoral has a lovely beach with a fenced-in pool, pleasant foreshore and some excellent restaurants.

North-east

Manly 7 F2

A ferry company once promoted Manly as 'Seven miles from Sydney, and a thousand miles from care'. Today it still retains much of the holiday atmosphere of a seaside village. The Manly ferry, which travels to and from Circular Quay, is an experience in itself, and the most pleasant way of getting there. With two beaches, an aquarium *(see next entry)*, the Old Quarantine Station *(see entry on this page)* and the carnival atmosphere of Manly Corso, a visit to Manly is a must.

Oceanworld Manly 7 F2

Situated to the west of the ferry terminal, Oceanworld is an exciting bottom-of-the-sea experience. With colourful displays of marine life that include a touch pool and an underwater tunnel, it also reveals some of the scarier aspects of the continent's wildlife. There are shark-feedings daily, exhibitions that involve some of Australia's deadliest snakes and spiders, plus the chance to dive with sharks. *West Esplanade, Manly; open 10am–5.30pm daily.*

Q Station 7 F2

On the west side of North Head, up the road from Manly, the Old Quarantine Station has been transformed into the Q Station, a unique resort with accommodation, a restaurant, interactive tours and a theatre experience within Sydney National Park. Built to house incoming passengers and crew suspected of carrying contagious diseases from the 1830s to 1984, there's an extensive collection of 65 heritage buildings as well as some fascinating 19th-century rock carvings that were made by the crew and passengers interned here. Access is via car or water shuttle from The Rocks and Manly, and tour bookings are essential. *North Head Scenic Dr, Manly; (02) 9976 6220; open Wed–Sun.*

West

Sydney Olympic Park, Homebush Bay 545 K8

The site of the 2000 Olympic Games, the park now hosts Sydney's yearly Royal Easter Show and is home to several other attractions and events. It can be accessed by Parramatta Road, by rail or

sport

Sydneysiders have always been passionate about their sport. As a city that has recently hosted the Olympic Games, Sydney is now home to some of the best sporting facilities in the world.

Football, cricket and racing dominate the sporting scene. Although Sydney does have an **AFL** (Australian Football League) team – the Sydney Swans – Rugby League and Rugby Union hold more sway here, with the season for both codes beginning in March. Key games throughout the **Rugby League** season are played at the Sydney Football Stadium at Moore Park, with the Grand Final taking place in September at ANZ Stadium, in Olympic Park. A particular highlight is the **State of Origin** competition, which showcases the cream of Rugby League talent in a series of three matches between Queensland and New South Wales. These take place in the middle of the season, and the New South Wales matches are played at ANZ Stadium.

The Waratahs are the New South Wales side in the Super 12s, the **Rugby Union** competition in which local and overseas teams go head to head. These games are played at Sydney Football Stadium, while the **Bledisloe Cup** games (between Australia's Wallabies and the New Zealand All Blacks) are played at ANZ Stadium and attract up to 80 000 spectators.

In summer, **cricket** takes centre stage. The highlight is the New Year's Day Test, followed by the One-Day Internationals, all of which are played at the Sydney Cricket Ground (SCG). Sydney's official **soccer** (football) team is Sydney FC, which competes in the Hyundai A-League at Sydney Football Stadium.

Other sporting highlights include the **Spring and Autumn Racing Carnivals**, with the world's richest horserace for two-year-olds, the Golden Slipper, being held just before Easter.

where to stay

BLUE Sydney Stunning Sydney waterfront accommodation nestled at one of Sydney's premier landmarks: Woolloomooloo Wharf. The Wharf at Woolloomooloo, 6 Cowper Wharf Rd; (02) 9331 9000. 8 D4

Establishment Hotel Experience fabulous luxury in the heart of the city at this celebrity-studded jewel. 5 Bridge La; (02) 9240 3100. 8 B3

Medusa Eclectic bohemian colour and life burst from this unique boutique hotel cradled in one of Sydney's funkiest districts. 267 Darlinghurst Rd, Darlinghurst; (02) 9331 1000. 8 D5

Observatory Hotel Timeless elegance and luxury saturate this old-world treasure tucked away at The Rocks. 89–113 Kent St; (02) 9256 2222. 8 B2

Shangri-La Hotel Guests' concept of contemporary comfort is catapulted sky high at this statuesque beauty towering over Sydney Harbour. 176 Cumberland St; (02) 9250 6000. 8 B3

other suburbs

Surry Hills   Where old Sydney meets new urban chic, with 19th-century streetscapes, trendy cafes, bars and clusters of fashion warehouses close to Central Station. 8 B6

Newtown   A suburb with a funky, alternative feel, Newtown seems to sleep late and party late. It is best visited in the afternoon and early evening, when the shops and cafes of King Street come alive. 6 A5

Leichhardt   Sydney's little Italy, with some of the city's best Italian restaurants, superb shopping in Norton Street and the unique shopping and dining precinct of Italian Forum. 6 A4

Cabramatta   The heart of the Vietnamese community, with a vibrant shopping strip specialising in good-quality fabrics, fresh Asian produce and fabulous pho (rice noodle soup). 545 J9

Avalon   Pretty beachside village with a stunning backdrop of bush-clad hills, and a laid-back shopping precinct crammed with delis, cafes and some very up-market clothing and homewares stores. 545 N6

Penrith   Close to the Nepean River, this is a paradise for watersports enthusiasts, with the Cables Waterski Park and the Whitewater Stadium located here. There is a pleasant shopping precinct with some good eateries, and an excellent regional gallery. 544 H6

Camden   One of Sydney's most far-flung suburbs, with a pleasant rural atmosphere, pretty, old-world streetscapes and good cafes. 544 G11

Cronulla   With some interesting shops and cafes in the main street and a superb beach close by, this is a good starting point for trips to Royal National Park and the important historical site of Kurnell (Captain Cook's landing site and the birthplace of modern Australia). 545 L11

harbour islands

Sydney Harbour is dotted with islands, but only five of them are open to the public. Four come under the authority of the National Parks & Wildlife Service, which charges a $7 landing fee per person. Visits must be prebooked and prepaid, so the information and tour booking office located in Cadmans Cottage, George St, The Rocks, is the starting point for any tour or visit to the islands (except Cockatoo Island).

Fort Denison   Crime, punishment and the defence of Sydney Harbour are all part of Fort Denison's past. Now it plays a vital role in assessing and predicting the tides, and is the site of the One O'clock Gun. Access is by guided tour only, and there is a restaurant on the island. 6 C3

Shark Island   Sandy beaches, shaded grassy areas and superb views of the harbour make this the perfect place for a picnic. Matilda Catamarans runs a daily ferry service from Darling Harbour and Circular Quay to Shark Island, with the fare including the landing fee. 6 D4

Clark Island   Named for Ralph Clark, an officer of the First Fleet who once planted a vegetable garden here, Clark Island is now a place of unspoiled bushland and pleasant grassy areas, and is popular with picnicking families. Access by private vessel or water taxi. 6 D4

Rodd Island   Another favourite picnic place, Rodd Island has a colonial-style hall, which dates back to 1889, and 1920s summer houses that shelter long tables, making the island suitable for picnicking in all seasons. Access by private vessel or water taxi. 6 A4

Cockatoo Island   A former prison and shipyard, Cockatoo Island has abandoned workshops and wharves, a camping ground and cafe, and hosts art and concert events. Tours are available. It's free to visit and accessible by regular ferries from Circular Quay Wharf 5 or 4. 6 A3

by RiverCat from Circular Quay. Take a lift to the Observation Deck on the 17th floor of the Novotel Hotel to see fantastic views of the entire park. There are various activities available, as well as **Bicentennial Park**, with its extensive wetlands and bird sanctuaries, and the fabulous **Aquatic Centre**.

Outer West

Elizabeth Farm, Rosehill 21 D3

Elizabeth Macarthur was one of the more fascinating and unusual characters in early Australian history. With her husband, John, she gave the Australian wool industry a kick-start, running their large merino farm while John was away in England. The lovely sandstone building surrounded by gardens is now a museum run by the Historic Houses Trust. Visitors are encouraged to wander the rooms, touch the furniture, try the featherbeds and generally behave as if they are guests of the family. *Alice St; open 9.30am–4pm Fri–Sun.*

Hambledon Cottage, Harris Park 21 C3

Not far from Elizabeth Farm is the charming Hambledon Cottage, built for a Miss Penelope Lucas, governess of the Macarthur children. Small but elegant, it has been restored and furnished in a style that reflects the early reign of Queen Victoria. It is surrounded by trees said to have been planted by John Macarthur himself. *Hassall St; open 11am–4.30pm Thurs–Sun.*

Parramatta 21 B2

The quickest way to get to Parramatta is probably by train, but the most pleasant and relaxing way to travel is by RiverCat. The area was discovered not long after the arrival of the First Fleet, and Arthur Phillip immediately recognised its farming potential. The colony's first private farm was established here in November 1788, making this outer suburb almost as old as Sydney itself. With places of historical interest around every corner and the lively commercial atmosphere of a busy regional centre, Parramatta is a fascinating spot to visit.

Once you arrive in Parramatta, your first stop should be the **Parramatta Heritage Centre**. Located alongside the Parramatta River, the centre presents a number of exhibitions highlighting the experiences of those who helped to shape this part of Sydney. *346A Church St; open 9am–5pm daily.*

The nearby **Riverside Walk** takes on a whole new meaning when you follow the 800-metre painted path. A combination of paintings, interpretive plaques and native gardens help to reveal the history of this area and its inhabitants, all from the perspective of the Aboriginal people. The walk culminates in a moving soundscape of music and spoken words – it is an experience that should not be missed.

Nearby in the sweeping grounds of Parramatta Regional Park, **Old Government House** stands as one of the oldest public buildings in Australia. Built between 1799 and 1818, chiefly by Governors Hunter and Macquarie, it is very much Macquarie's house. It has been restored to reflect the life and times of the Macquarie family, and includes a fine collection of their own furniture. Guided tours are available and a ghost tour runs on the third Friday of each month; bookings essential. *(02) 9635 8149; open 10am–4.30pm Tues–Fri, 10.30am–4pm Sat–Sun.*

parramatta

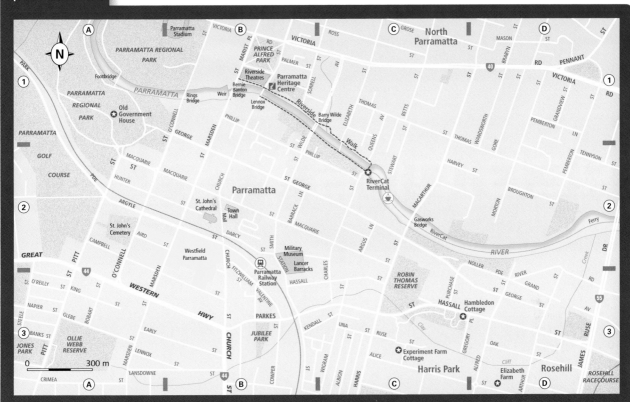

A visit to Parramatta would not be complete without visiting the **Experiment Farm Cottage**. Built in 1798 and named because it was built on the site of Australia's first private farm, the cottage is now run by the National Trust. It features lovely gardens as well as an excellent collection of 1830s furniture. If you are fortunate, your visit may coincide with one of the National Trust exhibitions that are held there from time to time. *Ruse St; open 10.30am–3.30pm Tues–Fri, 11am–3.30pm Sat–Sun.*

Far Outer West

Featherdale Wildlife Park, Doonside 545 l7

This is the place to get up close and personal with Australian wildlife. Over 2000 animals live in a beautiful bushland setting, and there are opportunities to cuddle koalas and handfeed kangaroos. It is also a perfect venue for picnics and barbecues. *217 Kildare Rd; open 9am–5pm daily.*

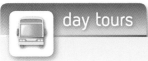

day tours

Blue Mountains Only 100 kilometres from Sydney, the brooding sandstone cliffs and deep, tree-lined gorges of the Blue Mountains provide a superb natural retreat. Aboriginal cave art, cool-climate gardens, charming mountain villages, walking trails and adventure activities are among the many attractions. For more details see p. 23

Southern Highlands Nestled into the folds and hills of the Great Dividing Range, the Southern Highlands offer pretty rural scenery, historic townships with superb European-style gardens, a variety of festivals, and wonderful guesthouses and restaurants. For more details see p. 24

Central Coast & Hawkesbury Stretching north from Sydney Harbour to Broken Bay, the northern beaches are one of Sydney's loveliest natural assets. Pittwater Road takes you from Manly through the beach suburbs of Dee Why, Long Reef, Collaroy and Narrabeen. Barrenjoey Road leads to more exclusive beaches, culminating in posh Whale Beach and Palm Beach. The Upper Hawkesbury, north-west of Sydney, encompasses a scenic river landscape dotted with charming Georgian villages. It is Australia's most historic rural area. For more details see p. 25

Ku-ring-gai Chase North of Sydney, Ku-ring-gai Chase National Park encloses a magnificent stretch of bushland, set around the glittering waters of the Hawkesbury River and Broken Bay. Fishing, river cruises and bushwalking are popular activities here. For more details see p. 25

South along the coast Abutting Sydney's southern suburbs, Royal National Park encloses a landscape of sandstone outcrops, wild heathland, rainforest, plunging cliffs and secluded beaches – perfect for walks, fishing, wildlife-watching and camping. Beyond the park you'll find the city of Wollongong and a magnificent stretch of surf coast dotted with pleasant resort towns. For more details see p. 24

Hunter Valley Located about 160 kilometres north-west of Sydney, the Lower Hunter area is Australia's oldest winegrowing district, with over 60 wineries radiating from the town of Cessnock. Take a tour of the wineries, starting with a visit to the wine centre in town, or book into one of the many excellent restaurants. For more details see p. 26

REGIONS
new south wales

[NEDS BEACH, LORD HOWE ISLAND]

[SKIING AT THREDBO, SNOWY MOUNTAINS]

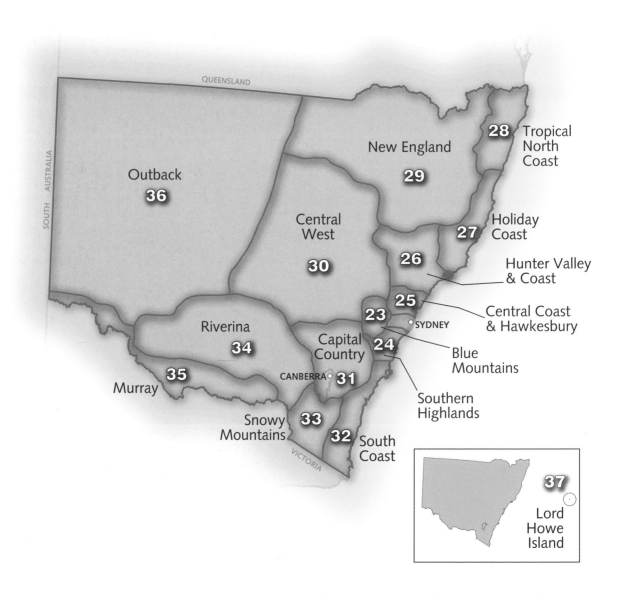

QUEENSLAND

SOUTH AUSTRALIA

Outback
36

New England
29

28 Tropical North Coast

Central West
30

Holiday Coast
27

26

Hunter Valley & Coast

25

Central Coast & Hawkesbury

23

SYDNEY

Riverina
34

Capital Country

24

Blue Mountains

35

CANBERRA **31**

Southern Highlands

Murray

33

32

Snowy Mountains

South Coast

VICTORIA

37

Lord Howe Island

BLUE MOUNTAINS

The misty, bush-clad cliffs and valleys of the Blue Mountains provide a beautiful nature retreat for nearby Sydney residents.

[JENOLAN CAVES HOUSE]

Zig Zag Railway When it was built in 1869, the Zig Zag Railway was a revolutionary engineering achievement, opening up Blue Mountains towns such as Lithgow, which had previously been isolated from the coast. Today it operates as a tourist railway, passing through beautiful mountain scenery, with trips departing from Clarence (10 kilometres east of Lithgow) daily at 11am, 1pm and 3pm. Kids will love the special Friends of Thomas days, when Thomas the Tank Engine himself heads the train.

Jenolan Caves Formed 400 million years ago, the Jenolan Caves make up one of the most extensive and complex underground limestone cave systems in the world. Of the 300 or so 'rooms', nine are open to the public – by tour only.

Heritage Centre The Blue Mountains Heritage Centre east of Blackheath has a wealth of knowledge on the geology, history, flora and fauna of the mountains, and also on the network of walking trails leading into their heart. Nearby Govetts Leap Lookout, high above the Grose Valley, is the starting point for a handful of trails.

Wentworth Falls One of the most beautiful towns in the Blue Mountains, Wentworth Falls offers bushwalks with phenomenal views. A corridor of trees leads to picturesque Wentworth Falls Lake, a popular picnic spot, and the massive waterfall after which the town was named.

Three Sisters and Echo Point The lookout at Echo Point is the best vantage point to view the famous Three Sisters. Echo Point and the Three Sisters were once joined, but over time great blocks of rock broke off and fell away into the Jamison Valley. Visitors can ride on the Scenic Railway, the steepest railway in the world, or enjoy views from the Scenic Skyway.

TOP EVENTS

APR	Ironfest (Lithgow)
JUNE	Winter Magic Festival (Katoomba)
JUNE–AUG	Yulefest (throughout region)
SEPT	Daffodil Festival (Oberon)
OCT	Leura Gardens Festival (Leura)
NOV	Rhododendron Festival (Blackheath)

CLIMATE

KATOOMBA

J	F	M	A	M	J	J	A	S	O	N	D	
23	22	20	17	13	10	9	11	14	18	20	22	MAX °C
13	13	11	9	6	4	3	3	5	8	10	12	MIN °C
160	174	170	123	104	117	85	82	73	90	103	124	RAIN MM
13	13	13	11	10	10	9	9	9	11	11	12	RAIN DAYS

GARDENS

Volcanic soil and cool-climate conditions have made the Blue Mountains one of the best-known gardening regions in Australia. Visit Everglades near Leura, a 6-hectare classically designed garden that melds with the surrounding bush. Mount Wilson is a tiny village of grand, historic estates, nearly all with large gardens of formal lawns, cool-climate plantings and tall European trees; many properties are open to the public. Mount Tomah Botanic Garden is the cool-climate annexe of Sydney's Royal Botanic Gardens. Here specialist displays bring together thousands of rare species from around the world, with a focus on those from the Southern Hemisphere. One feature is the grove of young Wollemi pines – this species was only discovered in 1994 in Wollemi National Park.

→ For more detail see maps 544–5, 546–7 & 554–5. For descriptions of ⊕ towns see Towns from A–Z (p. 38).

SOUTHERN HIGHLANDS

This region offers European-style rural scenery, combined with a stretch of typically Australian coastline — both are great settings for holiday-makers.

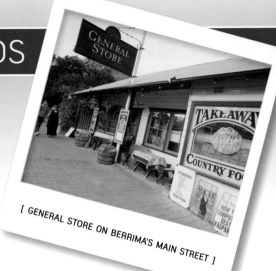

[GENERAL STORE ON BERRIMA'S MAIN STREET]

Wollongong   'Australia's most liveable regional city' is set along 17 surf beaches and surrounded by fantastic mountain scenery. Visit the city's boat harbour, fish co-op and restaurants on Flagstaff Point; drive north through the old coalmines for coastal views; and see Nan Tien Temple, the largest Buddhist temple in the Southern Hemisphere.

Minnamurra Falls   Minnamurra Falls, in Budderoo National Park, is one of several waterfalls formed by the massive sandstone escarpment that defines the edge of the Southern Highlands. Nearby is the Minnamurra Rainforest Centre, which incorporates a raised walkway leading into pockets of dense temperate and subtropical rainforest.

Morton National Park   The northern reaches of Morton National Park were once known as the Bundanoon Gullies; in autumn, mists roll out and engulf the town, giving it the feeling of Brigadoon. Explore the sandstone cliffs, wooded valleys and waterfalls of the park on one of the various walking tracks from the town.

Kangaroo Valley   This valley, known for its lovely combination of rural and native scenery, can be explored on the scenic route leading from the highlands to the coast (from Moss Vale to Nowra). The route takes in the 80-metre-high Fitzroy Falls, crosses Australia's oldest suspension bridge, and passes through the historic township of Kangaroo Valley.

TOP EVENTS

JAN	Illawarra Folk Festival (Bulli)
MAR	Jazz and Blues Festival (Kiama)
APR	Bundanoon is Brigadoon Highland Gathering (Bundanoon)
SEPT	Festival in the Forest (Shellharbour)
SEPT–OCT	Tulip Time Festival (Bowral)
NOV	Festival of Fisher's Ghost (Campbelltown)

CLIMATE

BOWRAL

J	F	M	A	M	J	J	A	S	O	N	D	
25	25	22	19	15	12	12	13	16	19	21	24	MAX °C
13	13	11	8	5	3	2	3	5	7	9	11	MIN °C
87	91	97	86	77	82	46	66	59	75	92	71	RAIN MM
14	13	14	11	13	11	10	10	11	12	13	12	RAIN DAYS

TOWNS OF THE HIGHLANDS

Bowral, with its historic streetscapes, restaurants and cafes, guesthouses and superb gardens, is the centre of the highlands. Historic Berrima, once the commercial heart of the district, now serves as a timepiece of colonial Australia. Nearby Mittagong boasts lovely gardens as well as good cafes and interesting shopfront architecture. Sutton Forest and Moss Vale are pretty towns with an air of the English countryside, while Bundanoon, further south, is known for its excellent guesthouses, health resort and views across Morton National Park. Away from the main tourist route are Robertson and Burrawang, peaceful settlements steeped in history. Don't miss Burrawang's general store (c. 1875), still with a sign advertising the *Sydney Morning Herald* for a penny. The rolling hills of this district were the backdrop for the Australian film *Babe* (1995). To the south is Berry, set in the dairy country of the Shoalhaven River district and boasting charming heritage buildings, galleries, antique shops and guesthouses.

→ For more detail see maps 542, 544–5, 552, 553 & 565. For descriptions of ⊤ towns see Towns from A–Z (p. 38).

CENTRAL COAST & HAWKESBURY

Discover rugged wilderness, Australia's most historic farming district, and the glittering waters of one of the country's most popular national parks.

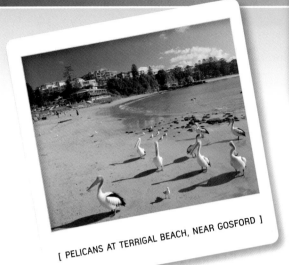

[PELICANS AT TERRIGAL BEACH, NEAR GOSFORD]

Wollemi National Park   This 500 000-hectare wilderness includes areas still unmapped. In 1994 the discovery of a new tree species – the Wollemi pine – in a rainforest gully was compared to finding a living dinosaur. See Newnes' historic ruins, walk to the Glow Worm Tunnel, or visit the secluded beaches along the Colo River.

Pelican feeding at The Entrance   Every day at 3.30pm sharp, dozens of entertaining pelicans wander in to the pelican pavilion on The Entrance's foreshore for a feed, and every year tens of thousands of people turn up to watch them. What has become one of the Central Coast's most popular tourist attractions started out by accident over 20 years ago, when someone working at a local fish 'n' chip shop threw out some scraps …

Lower Hawkesbury   The mouth of the Hawkesbury River opens up into a dazzling network of calm, bush-lined waterways, which provides the perfect setting for a houseboat holiday or a day of boating and fishing. Hop aboard Australia's last river postal run: the Riverboat Postman departs from Brooklyn at 9.30am on weekdays.

Macquarie towns   In 1810 Governor Macquarie established a number of towns on fertile river plains north-west of Sydney. The area now preserves some of Australia's oldest buildings and sites. In Windsor is a cemetery containing the graves of some of the pioneers who arrived in the First Fleet, and to the north in Ebenezer is Australia's oldest church, built in 1809.

Ku-ring-gai Chase National Park   This scenic 15 000-hectare bush, river and sandstone landscape forms a border on the edge of Sydney's northern suburbs. Hidden coves, sheltered beaches and panoramic lookouts combine with a rich Aboriginal heritage. See the Guringgai rock engravings on the Basin Trail at West Head.

TOP EVENTS

MAY	Bridge to Bridge Powerboat Classic (Windsor)
JULY	Terrigal Food and Wine Festival (Terrigal)
SEP	CoastFest (Gosford)
SEPT–NOV	Fruits of the Hawkesbury Festival (Windsor and Richmond)
DEC	Tuggerah Lakes Mardi Gras Festival (The Entrance)

CLIMATE

GOSFORD

J	F	M	A	M	J	J	A	S	O	N	D	
27	27	26	24	20	18	17	19	21	24	25	27	MAX °C
17	17	15	12	8	6	5	5	8	11	13	15	MIN °C
139	148	150	136	119	128	79	76	69	83	92	102	RAIN MM
11	11	11	11	9	10	8	8	8	9	10	10	RAIN DAYS

FISHING

Fishing is one of the area's great attractions. There are plenty of boat ramps and boat-hire outlets, and no shortage of local bait-and-tackle suppliers. The trouble-free waters of the Hawkesbury are good for bream, luderick, mulloway and flathead, with bass in the upper reaches. Bream and whiting are a possibility for anglers in the calm stretches of Brisbane Water and Tuggerah Lake. On the coast, beach fishing yields bream, tailor and mulloway. There are rock platforms, particularly around Terrigal, where anglers try for some of the big ocean fish, including tuna and kingfish.

→ For more detail see maps 542, 543, 544–5 & 555. For descriptions of ❂ towns see Towns from A–Z (p. 38).

HUNTER VALLEY & COAST

Taste wines at cellar doors in the Hunter Valley, one of Australia's premier wine-tourism destinations.

[PEPPER TREE WINES CELLAR DOOR, HUNTER VALLEY]

Barrington Tops National Park   The World Heritage–listed Barrington Tops are situated on one of the highest points of the Great Dividing Range (1600 metres). This landscape of rugged basalt cliffs, rainforests, gorges and waterfalls, with a touch of snow in winter, is a mecca for walkers, campers and climbers.

Port Stephens   Port Stephens, reached via the township of Nelson Bay, is a haven of calm blue waters and sandy beaches, offering excellent boating, fishing and swimming. It is also something of a wildlife haven: over 100 bottlenose dolphins are permanent residents here; migrating whales can be seen in season on a boat cruise; and koalas can be spotted at Tilligerry Habitat.

Stockton Sand Dunes   This huge dune area, the largest moving coastal sand mass in the Southern Hemisphere, extends for 32 kilometres, rises to a height of 30 metres and is, understandably, a popular place for sand boarding. Deep within its midst, you'd be forgiven for thinking you were in the Sahara, not coastal New South Wales. Access is from Anna Bay or Williamtown by four-wheel drive or safari (book at the Port Stephens visitor centre).

Lower Hunter   The Lower Hunter is Australia's oldest and best-known wine-producing district. Around 3000 hectares of vines and over 60 wineries sprawl across the foothills of the Broken Back Range. A day tour should start at the Wine and Visitors Centre in Cessnock. Excellent food and accommodation are available throughout the region.

Newcastle   Australia's second oldest city was founded as a penal colony in 1804. Newcastle rises up the surrounding hills from a spectacular surf coastline, its buildings a pleasant chaos of architectural styles from different periods. The city boasts a range of attractions including cosmopolitan restaurants, a premier regional art gallery and many historic sites.

TOP EVENTS

MAR	Hamilton Music, Food and Wine Festival (Hamilton)
MAR–APR	Harvest Festival (throughout region)
SEPT	Jazz Festival (Morpeth)
OCT	Jazz in the Vines (Cessnock)
OCT	Opera in the Vineyards (Cessnock)
DEC	King Street Fair (Newcastle)

WINES

Over 130 wineries – with over 100 cellar doors – can be found in the Hunter Valley. The region built its reputation on outstanding semillon, shiraz, chardonnay and verdelho, but exciting new wines are emerging, including merlot, chambourcin and pinot noir. The wine industry here is huge, taking up over 4000 hectares and making around $200 million worth of wine each year. The red earth found on the hillsides produces some of the country's great reds, including Tyrell's Shiraz, Lake's Folly Cabernet and McWilliams Rosehill Shiraz. The alluvial soils of the river flats produce excellent semillons, many coming from Tyrell's and McWilliams Lovedale. To complete a day of tasting, enjoy a night in one of the valley's gourmet restaurants or boutique hotels.

CLIMATE

CESSNOCK

	J	F	M	A	M	J	J	A	S	O	N	D	
	30	29	27	25	21	18	18	20	23	25	27	30	MAX °C
	18	18	15	12	9	6	5	5	8	11	14	16	MIN °C
	91	100	90	58	57	50	33	38	41	58	69	69	RAIN MM
	10	10	11	9	9	9	7	8	8	9	11	9	RAIN DAYS

→ For more detail see maps 548, 549 & 555. For descriptions of ⊤ towns see Towns from A–Z (p. 38).

HOLIDAY COAST

This is classic Australian holiday territory: miles of perfect beaches, friendly seaside towns, areas of pristine wilderness and a near-perfect subtropical climate.

[DIAMOND HEAD, CROWDY BAY NATIONAL PARK]

Dorrigo National Park This World Heritage–listed park preserves rugged escarpment country and the continent's most accessible area of temperate rainforest. There are excellent walking tracks, lookouts and picnic areas, and opportunities to see lyrebirds and brush turkeys. The popular Skywalk is an elevated walkway high above the rainforest canopy.

Bellingen Bat Island This 3-hectare island, in the centre of Bellingen, is home to a colony of around 40 000 grey-headed flying foxes (fruit bats). At dusk you can witness the bats setting off in search of food, filling the sky to spectacular effect in the process. The best time to see them is between September and March; access is via Bellingen Caravan Park in Dowle Street. Don't forget your hat.

Coffs Harbour During the holiday season the population of Coffs quadruples. Attractions include the Big Banana, marking one of the area's largest industries; the Pet Porpoise Pool, which features trained sea mammals; and Muttonbird Island, the breeding ground of thousands of wedge-tailed shearwaters, which you can access via a short walk along the sea wall.

Timbertown This re-created 1880s sawmilling village near Wauchope is a step back in time to the days of horsedrawn wagons, bullock teams and blacksmiths. Features include a wood-turning workshop, a craft gallery and a leather goods outlet; the activities range from rides on a restored steam train to sleeper-cutting demonstrations. Australian bush songs, roast meats and damper can be enjoyed in the authentic 1880s hotel.

Myall Lakes The 'Murmuring Myalls' are 10 000 hectares of connected lakes protected from the South Pacific by a long line of windswept dunes. Hire a houseboat and explore the calm waters, or enjoy fishing, windsurfing or canoeing. There are 40 kilometres of spectacular beaches and lookouts along the adjoining coast.

Map labels

Dorrigo
DORRIGO NP
COFFS HARBOUR
BONGIL BONGIL NATIONAL PARK
Bellingen
Urunga
Nambucca Heads
Macksville
YARRAHAPPINI NP
South West Rocks
HAT HEAD NATIONAL PARK
KUMBATINE NATIONAL PARK
Kempsey
Crescent Head
Wauchope
PORT MACQUARIE
TAPIN TOPS NATIONAL PARK
Laurieton
CROWDY BAY NATIONAL PARK
Wingham
Gloucester
TASMAN SEA
TAREE
FORSTER–TUNCURRY
Wallis Lake
Myall Lake
Elizabeth Beach
Stroud
MYALL LAKES NATIONAL PARK
Bulahdelah
Boolambayte Lake
0   20 km
N

TOP EVENTS

JAN	Golden Lure Tournament (Port Macquarie)
EASTER	Gaol Break Swim (South West Rocks, near Kempsey)
MAY	Shakespeare Festival (Gloucester)
JULY	International Brick and Rolling Pin Throwing Competition (Stroud)
OCT	Global Carnival (Bellingen)
OCT–NOV	Country Music Festival (Kempsey)

CLIMATE

PORT MACQUARIE

	J	F	M	A	M	J	J	A	S	O	N	D	
	26	26	25	23	21	19	18	19	20	22	23	25	MAX °C
	18	18	17	14	11	9	7	8	10	13	15	17	MIN °C
	153	177	176	170	147	132	98	83	83	94	102	127	RAIN MM
	12	13	14	13	11	10	9	9	9	11	11	11	RAIN DAYS

BEACHES

Just like the towns here, the beaches of this region cover both ends of the scale; you can choose a stretch of sand with a lively social scene, a secluded inlet, or one of the many options in between. Elizabeth Beach (near Forster) is calm, seasonally patrolled and popular with families. Solitude seekers and nature lovers should explore the bays and coves protected by Crowdy Bay National Park. Further north, top spots include Crescent Head (popular with surfers, particularly longboard riders), South West Rocks, the beaches of Hat Head National Park and those around Coffs Harbour.

→ For more detail see maps 550, 551, 555 & 557. For descriptions of T towns see Towns from A–Z (p. 38).

TROPICAL NORTH COAST

Exquisite beaches, wide rivers and World Heritage rainforest feature in this area, which is also famous for attracting alternative-lifestylers.

[JACARANDA TREES, GRAFTON]

Mount Warning National Park
The summit of Mount Warning is the first place in Australia to be lit by the morning sun, being the highest point along Australia's eastern fringe. A bushwalking track leads up from the carpark through pockets of subtropical and warm–temperate rainforest. The park is World Heritage–listed and the mountain itself is the plug of one of the world's oldest volcanoes, which stretches as far as Cape Byron.

Grafton This picturesque rural town, with a number of 19th-century buildings, is best known for its beautiful civic landscaping, particularly for the mature jacaranda trees with their vivid purple springtime blossom. Located on the Clarence River, Grafton is also a busy centre for watersports, including whitewater rafting and canoeing.

Holiday coast The combination of excellent weather and pristine beaches makes this region popular with visitors year-round. Visit family-friendly Tweed Heads on the Queensland border, or the fishing towns of Iluka and Yamba, great for their fresh seafood. Iluka is also worth a visit for the World Heritage–listed Iluka Nature Reserve, which contains the largest area of coastal rainforest in New South Wales and is great for birdwatching and walking.

Byron Bay Byron Bay's excellent beaches, laid-back feel and great weather have long made it a hideaway for surfers, backpackers and alternative-lifestylers. The town centre has a vast array of restaurants, cafes, New Age shops, galleries, day spas, yoga centres and natural therapy parlours. Byron also hosts many great events, such as the blues festival over Easter. You can stand at Australia's most easterly point at the tip of Cape Byron and, during the cooler months, watch for migrating humpback whales offshore.

TOP EVENTS

EASTER	East Coast Blues and Roots Festival (Byron Bay)
JUNE	Wintersun Carnival (Tweed Heads)
AUG	Tweed Valley Banana Festival and Harvest Week (Murwillumbah)
SEPT	Chincogan Fiesta (Mullumbimby)
OCT	Rainforest Week (Tweed Heads)
OCT–NOV	Jacaranda Festival (Grafton)
NOV	Fairymount Festival (Kyogle)

RAINFOREST

The region's tropical heat and humidity create perfect conditions for the lush rainforest that is the largest remaining area of rainforest in New South Wales. With rainforest comes abundant wildlife, especially native reptiles and mammals, and tours can be arranged through the National Parks & Wildlife Service. Kyogle is known as the 'gateway to the rainforests' as it is almost completely surrounded by them; nearby Border Ranges National Park is a forest full of gorges, creeks and waterfalls. The stunning swimming hole of Wanganui Gorge, west of Mullumbimby, is surrounded by rainforest and strangler figs, and Rotary Rainforest Reserve is 6 hectares of rainforest in the centre of Lismore.

CLIMATE

BYRON BAY

	J	F	M	A	M	J	J	A	S	O	N	D	
	28	28	27	25	22	20	19	20	22	23	25	26	MAX °C
	21	21	20	17	15	12	12	13	14	16	18	20	MIN °C
	161	192	215	185	188	158	100	92	66	102	118	143	RAIN MM
	15	16	17	15	15	12	10	9	9	11	12	13	RAIN DAYS

→ For more detail see map 551. For descriptions of ⊕ towns see Towns from A–Z (p. 38).

NEW ENGLAND

As its name suggests, this region features chilly winters, golden autumns and heritage buildings; it is also famous for gem fossicking.

[NEW ENGLAND NATIONAL PARK]

Lightning Ridge This opal-mining town is one of the few places in the world, and the only place in Australia, where black opal can be found. Local Aboriginal legend says that the opals were created when a huge wheel of fire fell to earth. Visitors can tour the opal mines and museums, and those who feel lucky can fossick for their own gems.

Tenterfield Saddler Tenterfield is perhaps best known from Peter Allen's 1970s song 'Tenterfield Saddler', which he wrote about his grandfather, George Woolnough. You can visit the famous saddlery, which is still open for business in Tenterfield's High Street and classified by the National Trust of Australia. Since the shop's inception in 1870, its customers have included none other than the illustrious Banjo Paterson.

Armidale Armidale is a sophisticated town with over 30 National Trust–listed buildings, two cathedrals, and the first Australian university established outside a capital city, all set in gracious tree-lined streets. Visit the New England Regional Art Museum, featuring the multimillion-dollar Hinton and Coventry collections, Australia's most significant provincial art holdings.

Tamworth Tamworth is Australia's country music capital, hosting the huge Tamworth Country Music Festival each January. Beneath the 12-metre Golden Guitar you will find the Gallery of Stars Wax Museum, with replicas of favourite country artists, and the Country Music Roll of Renown – Australia's highest country music honour. The Hands of Fame Park contains the handprints of over 200 country music stars.

Oxley Wild Rivers National Park The centrepiece of this World Heritage–listed rainforest park is the stunning Wollomombi Falls – at 220 metres, they are one of the highest falls in Australia. The ruggedly beautiful Dangars Falls drop 120 metres into a spectacular gorge. Activities in the park include camping, canoeing, walking and horseriding.

TOP EVENTS

JAN	Tamworth Country Music Festival
MAR	Bavarian Beer Fest (Tenterfield)
APR–MAY	Australian Celtic Festival (Glen Innes)
OCT	Gourmet in the Glen (Glen Innes)
NOV	Land of the Beardies Bush Festival (Glen Innes)
DEC	Great Inland Fishing Festival (Inverell)

CLIMATE

ARMIDALE

J	F	M	A	M	J	J	A	S	O	N	D	
27	26	24	21	16	13	12	14	18	21	24	27	MAX °C
13	13	11	8	4	2	0	1	4	7	10	12	MIN °C
105	87	65	46	44	57	49	48	52	68	80	89	RAIN MM
10	10	10	8	8	10	9	9	8	9	9	10	RAIN DAYS

FOSSICKING

The New England district is a fossicker's paradise. Quartz, jasper, serpentine and crystal are common finds, while sapphires, diamonds and gold present more of a challenge. Fossickers Way is a well-signposted route that introduces visitors to the district, beginning at Nundle and travelling north as far as Glen Innes. It passes through a number of towns including Inverell, the world's largest producer of sapphires. In the far west of the district, Lightning Ridge is known as a source of the famed black opal.

→ For more detail see maps 556–7. For descriptions of 🅣 towns see Towns from A–Z (p. 38).

CENTRAL WEST

The open spaces and clear skies are ideal spots for the two observatories here, while natural features include the Warrumbungles rock formations.

[PARKES CSIRO RADIO TELESCOPE]

Western Plains Zoo Five kilometres from Dubbo, this excellent open-range zoo covers 300 hectares and is home to animals representing five continents. The zoo is renowned throughout the world for its breeding programs, particularly of endangered species. Visitors can use their own cars, hire bikes or walk along the trails to all areas.

Warrumbungle National Park The Warrumbungles are extraordinary rock formations created by ancient volcanic activity. Best known is The Breadknife, which juts savagely out of the surrounding bushland. The 21 000-hectare national park marks the area where the flora and fauna of the Western Plains merge with that of the Great Dividing Range.

Siding Springs Observatory Located west of Coonabarabran on the road to Warrumbungle National Park, Siding Springs Observatory is home to Australia's largest optical telescope; in all there are 12 telescopes dotted around the site. Unfortunately there is no night viewing available; however, the observatory is open to the public during the day, and its Exploratory Centre has hands-on activities and a great astronomy exhibition.

Wellington Caves One of the largest stalagmites in the world (with a circumference of 32 metres) can be viewed in the limestone caves west of Wellington. The caves also contain rare cave coral and for thousands of years have acted as natural animal traps. Fossils of a diprotodon and a giant kangaroo have been found here.

Bathurst This is Australia's oldest inland settlement. Founded in 1815, Bathurst is noted for its colonial and Victorian architecture, including Miss Traill's House (1845), open to the public. Also of interest are Ben Chifley's cottage, the excellent regional art gallery and Mount Panorama, venue for the V8 Supercars 1000 (Bathurst 1000).

Map labels

Coonamble
Nyngan
WARRUMBUNGLE NATIONAL PARK
Coonabarabran
Gilgandra
RANGE
Dunedoo
DUBBO
Gulgong
Wellington
Mudgee
GOOBANG NATIONAL PARK
Lake Burrendong
DIVIDING
Rylstone
Lake Cargelligo
PARKES
Lake Windamere
Kandos
WOLLEMI NATIONAL PARK
Forbes
Eugowra
ORANGE
Lake Cowal
Canowindra
BATHURST
GREAT
Blayney
CONIMBLA NATIONAL PARK
Cowra
Grenfell
Lake Wyangala

0   50 km
N

TOP EVENTS

EASTER	Western Plains Country Music Festival (Dubbo)
SEPT	Red Ochre Festival (Dubbo)
SEPT	Mudgee Wine Festival (Mudgee)
SEPT–OCT	Sakura Matsuri (cherry blossom festival, Cowra)
OCT	Festival of the Stars (Coonabarabran)
OCT	V8 Supercars 1000 (Bathurst)

CLIMATE

DUBBO

J	F	M	A	M	J	J	A	S	O	N	D	
33	32	29	25	20	16	15	17	21	25	29	32	MAX °C
18	18	15	11	7	4	3	4	6	10	13	16	MIN °C
61	54	48	45	48	49	45	45	44	49	51	50	RAIN MM
6	5	5	5	6	8	8	8	7	7	6	6	RAIN DAYS

MUDGEE REGION WINES

German settler Adam Roth planted vines at Mudgee in the 1850s. Thirteen wineries were established by 1890, but just three survived the Depression later in the decade. The red-wine boom of the 1960s saw many new vines planted, and today the Mudgee region, stretching from Dunedoo in the north down through Gulgong, Mudgee, Rylstone and Kandos, has over 40 vineyards, most of which offer tastings. Warm summers favour the production of full-bodied shiraz and chardonnay. Try Huntington's shiraz; the organic, preservative-free wines of Botobolar; Craigmoor's chardonnay; or the cabernet sauvignon from Thistle Hill.

→ For more detail see maps 554–5, 556, 559 & 561. For descriptions of Ⓣ towns see Towns from A–Z (p. 38).

CAPITAL COUNTRY

Best known for its colonial history, this region also has boutique cool-climate wineries and beautiful areas of natural bushland.

[GOULBURN COURTHOUSE]

Murrumbateman wineries
The first vines in this hilly terrain were planted in 1971. Many of the original winemakers had no experience in winemaking and came from government or science jobs in the ACT. Their wine was slow to take off, but the industry has seen a reversal of fortunes now. The region produces a great range of styles, including riesling and shiraz viognier. Cellar doors include Clonakilla, Helm and Jeir Creek. Stop for lunch at Poachers' Pantry in Hall and pick up some gourmet produce to enjoy with your wine purchases.

Goulburn   Established in 1833, this town displays elaborate 19th-century architecture, a legacy of early wool-growing wealth. On the town's outskirts, the Big Merino sells wool products, has an educational display on the history of wool, and provides a lookout with sweeping views of Goulburn and surrounds.

Namadgi National Park   Namadgi takes in much of the Brindabella Range, covering almost half of the ACT. It boasts significant Aboriginal rock art and a beautiful environment of mountains, valleys and bush, regenerating after the 2003 bushfires. Camping and bushwalking are popular. The excellent Namadgi Visitor Centre is just south of Tharwa.

Braidwood   Braidwood's elegant Georgian buildings recall early agricultural settlement, while ornate Victorian structures mark the town's goldmining boom. It was once the haunt of bushrangers such as Ben Hall, and today is the haunt of people making movies about bushrangers (and other subjects). Films made here include *Ned Kelly* in 1969, and *On Our Selection* in 1994.

TOP EVENTS

FEB	Australian Blues Music Festival (Goulburn)
MAR	Celebration of Heritage and Roses (Goulburn)
MAY	Heritage Festival (Braidwood)
OCT	Lilac City Festival (Goulburn)
NOV	Festival of Wine, Roses and all that Jazz (throughout Murrumbateman district)
NOV–DEC	National Cherry Festival (Young)

CLIMATE

GOULBURN

	J	F	M	A	M	J	J	A	S	O	N	D	
	27	26	24	20	16	12	12	13	16	19	22	26	MAX °C
	13	14	11	8	5	2	1	2	5	7	9	12	MIN °C
	61	59	57	53	49	47	45	58	51	56	66	55	RAIN MM
	10	9	9	9	11	11	12	12	11	11	12	9	RAIN DAYS

HISTORY

The first inhabitants of the area were the Ngunnawal, whose ancestors may have arrived anywhere from 75 000 to 12 000 years ago according to archaeological evidence from Lake George. Europeans sighted the district in the late 1790s and the Goulburn plains were named in 1818. Settlers arrived between the 1820s and the 1850s, first attracted by the rich grazing land and later by the discovery of gold. Today a number of towns, including Yass, Young, Gunning, Bungendore and Braidwood, features heritage buildings and charming streetscapes. The district as a whole provides an evocative glimpse of 19th-century life in rural Australia.

→ For more detail see maps 554, 562, 563, 564, 565 & 566–7. For descriptions of ⓣ towns see Towns from A–Z (p. 38).

SOUTH COAST

This region of sandy beaches, fishing villages and native forests is popular with holiday-makers in summer, yet never loses its laid-back feel.

[BOURNDA LAGOON, BOURNDA NATIONAL PARK]

Jervis Bay   Part of this area is in Jervis Bay Territory (the third and least-known mainland territory of Australia) and includes the national capital's seaport. The bay, partially flanked by Jervis Bay National Park, is known for its dramatic underwater landscapes and its dolphins; diving and dolphin cruises are available.

Central Tilba   Classified by the National Trust as an 'unusual mountain village', picturesque Central Tilba is a showcase for late-19th-century town architecture, set in a magnificent rural landscape. New buildings are required to meet National Trust specifications, maintaining the original charm of the streetscapes. Central Tilba was founded in 1895 as a goldmining town, but now caters for tourists with cafes, galleries and art and craft shops.

Mogo   Mogo is an old goldmining town that has been restored and turned into a tourist destination, with several craft shops and a zoo that specialises in raising endangered species. Visitors can pan for gold and take a mine tour at Goldfields Park, visit the reconstructed 19th-century goldmining village of Old Mogo Town or enjoy the sclerophyll forest of the Mogo Bushwalk.

Montague Island Nature Reserve   This isolated island, accessed only by guided tour, is a major shearwater breeding site and home to 8000 pairs of little penguins and 600 Australian fur seals. Cruise from nearby Narooma to tour the island and learn about its history as a fertile hunting ground for the Walbanga and Djiringanj tribes, or you can see migrating humpback and killer whales off the island's coast from September to November on a whale-watching cruise. Recently, stays in the lighthouse keeper's quarters were introduced.

Mimosa Rocks National Park   The park, named after a wrecked paddlesteamer, crosses a landscape of beaches, sea caves, cliffs, forests and wetlands. Rocks tumble across the beaches and form impressive sculptural stacks. There are several secluded campsites, and swimming, walking, diving, fishing and birdwatching are among the activities on offer.

Map labels

NOWRA
JERVIS BAY NP
Huskisson
Jervis Bay
MORTON NATIONAL PARK
JBT BOODEREE NP
Ulladulla
Bawley Point
MONGA NP
Batemans Bay
Mogo
DEUA NP
Moruya
TASMAN SEA
Mount Dromedary
Narooma
Montague Island
Central Tilba
Wallaga Lake
Bermagui
WADBILLIGA NP
MIMOSA ROCKS NATIONAL PARK
Bega
Tathra
BOURNDA NP
Bombala
Merimbula
SOUTH EAST FOREST NATIONAL PARK
Eden
Twofold Bay
BEN BOYD NATIONAL PARK
VICTORIA

0   20 km   N

TOP EVENTS

JAN	Blue Water Fishing Classic (Bermagui)
EASTER	Tilba Festival (Central Tilba)
OCT	Great Southern Blues and Rockabilly Festival (Narooma)
OCT–NOV	Eden Whale Festival (Eden)
NOV	Riverside Festival (Bombala)
NOV	Country Music Festival (Merimbula)

CLIMATE

MERIMBULA

J	F	M	A	M	J	J	A	S	O	N	D	
24	25	23	21	19	16	16	17	18	20	21	23	MAX °C
15	15	14	11	8	6	4	5	7	9	12	14	MIN °C
77	79	91	83	65	69	41	42	56	69	88	78	RAIN MM
10	10	10	9	9	9	7	9	11	11	13	11	RAIN DAYS

ABORIGINAL CULTURE

Before European colonisation, the Yuin occupied the area from Jervis Bay to Twofold Bay, sustained by the produce of coast and rivers. Today the area remains steeped in Yuin history. At Wallaga Lake the Umbarra Cultural Centre offers tours, including one to the summit of Mount Dromedary (Gulaga) where, according to legend, the great creation spirit, Daramulun, ascended to the sky. Booderee National Park, in Jervis Bay Territory, is once again Yuin land after a successful 1995 land claim. Jointly managed by the Wreck Bay Aboriginal Community and Parks Australia, Booderee has middens and other significant sites, and an art and craft centre. The Murramarang Aboriginal Area, near Bawley Point, offers a self-guide interpretive walk.

→ For more detail see maps 553, 554–5, 565 & 567. For descriptions of ⊕ towns see Towns from A–Z (p. 38).

SNOWY MOUNTAINS

[SNOW GUMS, KOSCIUSZKO NATIONAL PARK]

This region features Kosciuszko National Park, which offers skiing in winter and bushwalking, mountain-bike riding and watersports in summer.

Yarrangobilly Caves   Among myriad natural wonders in Kosciuszko National Park, Yarrangobilly Caves stand out as a world-class attraction. Of the 70 caves formed some 2 million years ago, six are open to the public, with highlights including underground pools, frozen waterfalls and a bizarre web of limestone formations. Visitors can marvel at the radiant white, orange and grey limestone flows, stalactites and stalagmites, or take a dip in the naturally formed thermal pool offering year-round swimming.

Alpine Way   Stretching 111 kilometres from Jindabyne to Khancoban, this spectacular route winds around the Thredbo slopes, passes through Dead Horse Gap, and crosses the valley of the Murray headwaters. It is best driven during spring and summer, although the winter scenery is superb.

Snowy River power   This once mighty river was dammed and diverted for the Snowy Mountains Scheme. Some 100 000 men from 30 countries worked for 25 years on the largest engineering project of its kind in Australia. Drop in at the Snowy Mountains Authority Information Centre in Cooma, or visit the power stations near Khancoban.

Thredbo   This charming alpine village with its European-style lodges and hotels makes for an unusual sight in the Australian landscape. Packed and brimming with life during winter, it is also popular in summer with wildflower enthusiasts, anglers, mountain-bike riders and bushwalkers wanting to tackle Mount Kosciuszko. A chairlift drops people at the beginning of a 6-kilometre walk to the summit.

Lake Jindabyne   Created as part of the Snowy Mountains Scheme, this huge lake, along with nearby Lake Eucumbene, has a reputation as one of the best inland fishing destinations in the state, particularly for trout. Sailing, windsurfing and waterskiing are popular in summer.

TOP EVENTS

JAN	Blues Festival (Thredbo)
FEB	Rodeo (Cooma)
MAY	Jazz Festival (Thredbo)
NOV	Cooma Street Fair (Cooma)
NOV	Snowy Mountains Trout Festival (throughout region)

CLIMATE

THREDBO

	J	F	M	A	M	J	J	A	S	O	N	D	
	21	21	18	14	10	6	5	6	10	13	16	19	MAX °C
	7	7	4	2	0	−3	−4	−2	−1	1	4	5	MIN °C
	108	87	112	114	165	166	192	192	212	206	155	117	RAIN MM
	11	10	11	13	15	16	17	17	18	16	15	12	RAIN DAYS

SKI RESORTS

The Snowy Mountains resorts are well equipped in terms of lessons, lifts, ski hire, transport, food, accommodation and entertainment. Perisher, Smiggin Holes, Guthega and Mount Blue Cow (near Guthega) are collectively known as Perisher Blue, the largest ski resort in Australia, with 50 lifts and a variety of slopes. A good range of accommodation is available at Perisher and Smiggin Holes, but overnight parking is limited (many visitors leave their cars at Bullocks Flat and take the Skitube). Accommodation is limited at Guthega and not available at Blue Cow. Thredbo, the main village, has excellent skiing and tourist facilities. Charlotte Pass provides access to some of the region's most spectacular runs for experienced skiers. In the north of the park, Mount Selwyn is a good place for families and beginners, and is one of the main centres for cross-country skiing.

→ For more detail see maps 565 & 566. For descriptions of ⊤ towns see Towns from A–Z (p. 38).

RIVERINA

A landscape of far horizons and clear skies makes touring these fertile plains a pleasure; regional towns feature heritage buildings and good restaurants.

[RESTORED HISTORIC BUILDING, COOTAMUNDRA]

Griffith The main township of the Riverina, Griffith developed in the early days of irrigation and was designed by Walter Burley Griffin, architect of Canberra. It is surrounded by farms and vineyards, but nearby, in Cocoparra National Park, there is also an opportunity to glimpse the landscape as it once was.

Riverina wineries The Riverina is responsible for 60 per cent of the grapes grown in New South Wales. There are 14 wineries in the district, mostly around Griffith, including the De Bortoli and McWilliams estates. This region is best known for its rich botrytised semillon (semillon improved by flavour-enhancing fungus).

Hay Hay lies at the centre of a huge stretch of semi-arid grazing country known as the Hay Plains. Established in 1859, the town boasts an interesting collection of late-19th-century buildings. The POW Internment Camp Interpretive Centre tells the fascinating and sometimes inspirational stories of Hay's role as a prison camp in World War II.

Wagga Wagga On the banks of the Murrumbidgee, Wagga Wagga is the state's largest inland city and a major centre for commerce, agriculture and education. Visit the Museum of the Riverina (incorporating the Sporting Hall of Fame), the Botanic Gardens and the Regional Art Gallery, home of the National Art Glass Collection. River walks and cruises are also on offer.

Dog on the Tuckerbox Originally mentioned in the poem *Bill the Bullocky* by Bowyang Yorke, this monument to pioneer teamsters and their dogs, situated on the highway 8 kilometres north of Gundagai, is recognised throughout the nation as an Australian icon. The faithful bronze dog was unveiled in 1932 by former prime minister Joseph Lyons and celebrated in the song 'Where the Dog Sits on the Tuckerbox' by Jack O'Hagan (who also penned the famous 'Along the Road to Gundagai').

Map labels

Murrumbidgee
COCOPARRA NATIONAL PARK
West Wyalong
Balranald
GRIFFITH
Hanwood
Temora
Hay
Leeton
River
Narrandera
Cootamundra
OOLAMBEYAN NATIONAL PARK
N 0 40 km
WAGGA WAGGA
Gundagai
Tumut
Adelong
Lake Urana
Batlow
Blowering Reservoir
Tumbarumba
VIC

TOP EVENTS

FEB	Tumbafest (food and wine, Tumbarumba)
MAR	John O'Brien Bush Festival (Narrandera)
AUG	Wattle Time Festival (Cootamundra)
OCT	Apple Blossom Festival (Batlow)
NOV	Dog on the Tuckerbox Festival and Snake Gully Cup (Gundagai)
NOV	Festival of Gardens (Griffith)

CLIMATE

TEMORA

J	F	M	A	M	J	J	A	S	O	N	D	
31	31	28	23	18	14	13	15	18	22	26	30	MAX °C
16	16	13	9	6	3	2	3	5	8	11	14	MIN °C
48	37	41	43	45	43	47	45	42	54	45	41	RAIN MM
5	5	5	6	9	10	13	12	9	9	7	6	RAIN DAYS

REGIONAL PRODUCE

The Riverina produces vast quantities of rice, citrus and stone fruit, grapes, poultry and vegetables. To learn about the rice industry, visit the Sunrice Country Visitors Centre in Leeton. For fruit products, tour the Catania Fruit Salad Farm at Hanwood (near Griffith). For the gourmet, Mick's Bakehouse in Leeton makes excellent breads and award-winning pies. Drop in to Charles Sturt University Winery and Cheese Factory in Wagga Wagga for local products.

→ For more detail see maps 554, 558–9 & 565. For descriptions of ⊕ towns see Towns from A–Z (p. 38).

MURRAY

Australia's most important river supports this region's agriculture, but is also a holiday destination with activities including golf and watersports.

[RED GUM TREES ALONG THE MURRAY RIVER]

Perry Sandhills The vast orange dunes of Perry Sandhills near Wentworth cover 10 hectares and were formed after an ice age around 40 000 years ago. They hold the remains of megafauna such as kangaroos, wombats, emus and lions. Today the dunes are often used as a backdrop in film and television production.

Corowa Corowa is the quintessential Australian river town, with wide streets and turn-of-the-century architecture. Federation got a jump-start here in 1893 at the Corowa Federation Conference, now commemorated in the Federation Museum. In 1889 Tom Roberts completed his iconic painting *Shearing the Rams* at a sheep station nearby.

Cobram Barooga Golf Club There are many renowned golf courses along the banks of the Murray River, and the Cobram Barooga Golf Club has two of the best. The two 18-hole, championship-standard golf courses, good for pros and novices alike, are consistently rated in Australia's top resort courses. With many holes surrounded by beautiful red gums and pines, and the odd kangaroo looking on, this is a great spot to have a swing.

Lake Mulwala The construction of the Yarrawonga Weir in 1939 created this 6000-hectare artificial lake, around which the town of Mulwala has grown. The lake is now a premier destination for watersports, offering yachting, sailboarding, swimming, canoeing and fishing, and the largest waterskiing school in the world.

Albury Once a meeting place for the local Aboriginal tribes, today Albury is a large regional centre familiar to motorists who travel the busy Hume Highway. Attractions include interesting heritage buildings, a large regional art gallery and good restaurants. Nearby Lake Hume, one of Australia's biggest artificial lakes, is another popular spot for watersports. Wineries around Albury can be explored on a camel trek.

Map labels: SA, Lake Victoria, Wentworth, MILDURA (Vic.), MALLEE CLIFFS NATIONAL PARK, Robinvale (Vic.), N, 0 30 km, VICTORIA, Murray River, Barham, Deniliquin, Jerilderie, Finley, Tocumwal, Barooga, Culcairn, Holbrook, WOOMARGAMA NATIONAL PARK, Cobram (Vic.), Mulwala, Corowa, Lake Hume, Lake Mulwala, ALBURY, WODONGA (Vic.)

TOP EVENTS

JAN	Sun Festival (Deniliquin)
JAN	Federation Festival (Corowa)
FEB	Border Flywheelers Vintage Engine Rally (Barham)
MAR–APR	Albury Gold Cup Racing Carnival (Albury)
SEPT–OCT	Play on the Plains Festival and Ute Muster (Deniliquin)
SEPT–OCT	Food and Wine Festival (Albury)

ALONG THE RIVER

The Murray River provides endless opportunities for swimming, boating, watersports and fishing. Perch, catfish and yabbies are plentiful, and Murray cod is the catch that almost every angler seeks. The parklands of Albury feature pleasant riverside walks and picnic facilities, and at Corowa Yabby Farm visitors can catch and cook their own yabbies. Lake Mulwala was formed by damming the Murray and is now a haven for watersports. The Rocks of Tocumwal, on the banks of the river, change colour according to the weather and, as Aboriginal legend has it, the mysterious Blowhole nearby was the home of a giant Murray cod that liked to eat young children. The Barham Lakes consist of four artificial lakes stocked with yabbies and fish, with walking trails through the surrounding bushland.

CLIMATE

ALBURY

	J	F	M	A	M	J	J	A	S	O	N	D	
	31	31	27	23	18	14	13	15	18	21	25	29	MAX °C
	15	15	12	9	6	4	3	4	6	8	11	13	MIN °C
	55	36	43	49	64	71	87	89	72	72	53	51	RAIN MM
	6	6	6	7	11	14	16	15	13	11	9	7	RAIN DAYS

→ For more detail see maps 558–9. For descriptions of ⊤ towns see Towns from A–Z (p. 38).

OUTBACK

A series of national parks preserve this sparsely populated region's stunning landscapes, natural heritage and rich Indigenous history.

[OUTBACK FARMHOUSE]

Sturt National Park Occupying 310 000 hectares of Corner Country – the point where three states meet – this park offers a varied landscape of hills, rocks and plains, congregations of native birds and animals, and wonderful wildflowers after rain. Camping is available; check in at the park office in Tibooburra and take advantage of their tours.

White Cliffs The area around White Cliffs has been rendered a moonscape, thanks to 5000 abandoned opal digs. Owing to soaring temperatures in summer much of the town has been built underground, where the temperature remains a steady 27°C. Opals are still mined here, and nearby is spectacular Mutawintji National Park with its sandstone cliffs, river red gums, gorges, rockpools, desert plains and some of the state's best Aboriginal rock art.

Broken Hill Broken Hill was established in the 1880s to service the mining of massive deposits of silver, lead and zinc in the Barrier Ranges. With its historic buildings, 30 or so art galleries and decent eating options, it is an oasis of civilisation in a sparse landscape. Nearby Silverton is a quintessential outback town, made famous in films such as *Mad Max II* (1981).

Bourke 'If you know Bourke you know Australia,' said Henry Lawson. This Darling River town has become synonymous with the outback and is rich in heritage sites. The Back O'Bourke Exhibition Centre is a fascinating and important modern facility set among river red gums. It tells the story of the river and the outback from the Dreamtime until now.

Mungo National Park The focal point of the 240 000–hectare Willandra Lakes World Heritage Area, Mungo National Park's weather-eroded, sculptural sand formations have become one of outback Australia's signature sights. Around the area's dry lakes astounding remains have been uncovered, including ancient Aboriginal artefacts and Mungo Man, a full male skeleton estimated to be around 40 000 years old. The undoubted highlight is the huge Walls of China crescent-shaped dune, which you can visit on a 70-kilometre self-guide drive through the park.

TOP EVENTS

OCT	Festival of the Miner's Ghost (Cobar)
OCT	Red Desert Live! (Broken Hill)

CLIMATE

BROKEN HILL

J	F	M	A	M	J	J	A	S	O	N	D	
33	32	29	24	19	16	15	17	21	25	29	31	MAX °C
18	18	16	12	9	6	5	6	9	12	15	17	MIN °C
23	25	20	18	23	21	19	19	21	25	20	22	RAIN MM
3	3	3	3	5	5	6	5	4	5	4	3	RAIN DAYS

RUGGED REPUTATION

Charles Sturt was marooned north-west of Milparinka for six months while waiting for rain to replenish his party's drinking water in 1845. Although some towns have been successfully established in this harsh but beautiful environment, unpredictable conditions suggest that it will never be tamed. The land of Broken Hill has brought forth valuable minerals, which can be viewed at White's Mineral Art and Mining Museum. White Cliffs receives the most solar radiation in New South Wales and so was the natural choice for Australia's first solar-power station. Sturt National Park is home to the red sands and reptiles of the Strzelecki Desert; here day temperatures are often over 40°C and nights can be below freezing.

→ For more detail see maps 558–9 & 560–1. For descriptions of ☉ towns see Towns from A–Z (p. 38).

LORD HOWE ISLAND

This World Heritage—listed site has great natural beauty and some of the rarest flora and fauna on earth.

[MOUNT LIDGBIRD AND MOUNT GOWER]

Dining at Arajilla Widely regarded as 'the' place to dine on Lord Howe Island, Arajilla exudes casual elegance and lashings of style from its coveted forest location. Seafood is the focus of the contemporary menu, with the restaurant host personally reeling in the catch of the day brought fresh to your plate. The wine list features an impressive array of Australian and New Zealand labels, making it easy to linger over your meal under the beautiful canopy of trees.

The Lagoon A coral reef encloses the crystal waters of this 6-kilometre long lagoon on the western side of the island. Spend the day relaxing and swimming at Old Settlement Beach or snorkel at Escotts Hole, about 1 kilometre out. Glass-bottomed boat and snorkelling tours are available.

Mount Gower This 875-metre mountain is the island's highest point. Take a nine-hour guided walk to the summit through areas of stunted rainforest – a fairytale world of gnarled trees, orchids and moss-covered basalt outcrops. Mists permitting, the panoramic view from the summit is spectacular.

Neds Beach Lush forests of kentia and banyan trees, two of the island's most prolific and distinctive species, fringe this beautiful surf beach. Handfeed the tropical fish, swim, surf, snorkel or take a 45-minute walk up Malabar Hill on the northern headland for superb island views.

Golf at Mount Lidgbird Situated at the base of imposing Mount Lidgbird, Lord Howe Island's golf course is one of Australia's most scenic – its nine holes incorporate lush vegetation and open fairways with superb coastal views. Visitors are welcome to tee off at any time on this World Heritage turf, and you can even participate in the annual Lord Howe Open Golf Tournament held in November.

Balls Pyramid This extraordinary cathedral-shaped rock rises 551 metres out of the sea 25 kilometres south-east of the main island. Once nearly 6 kilometres wide, the rock's width has been eroded to only 400 metres. It is a major breeding ground for seabirds and can be seen by air charter or boat cruise. Deep-sea fishing in the vicinity is excellent.

Map labels

Roach Island
LORD HOWE ISLAND PERMANENT PARK PRESERVE NATURE RESERVE
Fishy Point
Malabar Hill
North Head
Neds Beach
Old Settlement Beach
Searles Point
Clear Place Point
The Lagoon
LORD HOWE ISLAND
SOUTH PACIFIC OCEAN
Blinky Beach
Blinkenthorpe Bay
Mutton Bird Island
Mutton Bird Point
Boat Harbour Point
East Point
Mount Lidgbird
Red Point
LORD HOWE ISLAND PERMANENT PARK PRESERVE NATURE RESERVE
Mount Gower
South Head
King Point
Gower Island
Lord Howe Island
25 km
Balls Pyramid
Observatory Rock
Wheatsheaf Islet
Balls Pyramid
0   1 km
N

TOP EVENTS

FEB	Discovery Day
OCT–NOV	Gosford to Lord Howe Island Yacht Race
NOV	Lord Howe Island Golf Open

CLIMATE

LORD HOWE ISLAND

	J	F	M	A	M	J	J	A	S	O	N	D	
	25	26	25	23	21	19	19	19	20	21	22	24	MAX °C
	20	20	20	18	16	14	13	13	14	15	17	19	MIN °C
	108	114	122	149	160	177	178	141	135	127	116	117	RAIN MM
	11	13	15	18	21	22	23	21	17	14	12	12	RAIN DAYS

A WORLD OF ITS OWN

The Lord Howe Group of Islands comprises a series of seven-million-year-old volcanic formations. Because of its isolation and the absence of humans until recent times, Lord Howe has a unique natural history. Fifty-seven of the islands' 180 flowering plants and 54 fern species are not found anywhere else. At settlement (1834) there were 15 species of land birds, 14 of which were unique. Five species survive today. Hundreds of thousands of seabirds roost on the islands. These include sooty terns, brown noddies, several shearwater species, the world's largest colony of red-tailed tropic birds and the world's only breeding colony of providence petrels.

[SNOW GUM WOODLANDS AT SUNRISE, MORTON NATIONAL PARK]

LEGEND

ⓘ VISITOR INFORMATION

RADIO STATIONS

IN TOWN

WHAT'S ON

WHERE TO EAT

WHERE TO STAY

NEARBY

Adaminaby

Pop. 235

Map ref. 554 E12 | 565 B6 | 566 E7 | 581 D2

ⓘ Snowy Region Visitor Centre, Kosciuszko Rd, Jindabyne; (02) 6450 5600 or 1800 004 439; www.snowymountains.com.au

97.7 Snow FM, 1602 AM ABC Local

Over 100 buildings were moved in the 1950s to Adaminaby's current town site. The remaining town and surrounding valley were flooded to create Lake Eucumbene as part of the Snowy Mountains Hydro-Electric Scheme. The lake is regularly restocked with trout and Adaminaby is now a haven for anglers. Due to its proximity to Selwyn Snowfields, Adaminaby is also a popular base in winter for skiers.

 The Big Trout The world's largest fibreglass rainbow trout was erected after a local angler, attempting to drink a gallon of Guinness while fishing, was pulled into the water by a large trout and almost drowned. Legend has it the man then managed to finish the Guinness, but the 10 m high trout stands as a tribute to 'the one that got away'. Lions Club Park at town entrance.

Leigh Stewart Gallery: displays historical information including pictures and films; Main St. *Historic buildings:* several buildings, including 2 churches that were moved from Adaminaby's original site; details from visitor centre.

San Michele Resort: secluded contemporary accommodation; 1512 Caddigat Rd; (02) 6454 2229. *Snowy Mountains Alpine Cabins:* self-contained mountain cabins; 6078 Snowy Mountains Hwy; (02) 6454 1120.

Kosciuszko National Park On the road to Tumut is the historic goldmining site of Kiandra. North of the road, via Long Plain Rd, is historic Coolamine Homestead. All of New South Wales' ski fields exist inside Kosciuszko National Park; the focal point is Mt Kosciuszko, Australia's highest mountain. The summit can be reached easily via the Kosciuszko Express Chairlift (operating all year), which drops you at the beginning of a 13 km return walk. Among a myriad of natural wonders in the park, the Yarrangobilly Caves are a highlight. The string of 70 limestone caves, some 2 million years old, comprise marine sediments dating back 440 million years. Six caves are open to the public, featuring underground pools, frozen waterfalls, a bizarre web of limestone formations and a naturally formed thermal pool offering year-round swimming. For guided and self-guide tours, call (02) 6454 9597; more details from visitor centre.

Lake Eucumbene It is said that anyone can catch a trout in Lake Eucumbene, the largest of the Snowy Mountains artificial lakes. Its abundance of rainbow trout, brown trout and Atlantic salmon make it a popular spot for anglers. In recent years droughts have lowered the water level in the dam, revealing ruins of the old town. The Snowy Mountains Trout Festival draws hundreds of anglers every November. Fishing boats can be hired at Old Adaminaby and for fly-fishing tours, contact the visitor centre. Access via Old Adaminaby. 9 km sw.

Old Adaminaby Racetrack: featured in the film *Phar Lap* (1984); on the road to Rosedale, Cooma side of town. *Power stations:* tours and interactive displays; details from visitor centre.

See also SNOWY MOUNTAINS, p. 33

Adelong

Pop. 827
Map ref. 554 D10 | 565 A4 | 566 B2 | 585 P2

ⓘ Tumut Region Visitor Centre, 5 Adelong Rd, Tumut; (02) 6947 7025; www.tumut.nsw.gov.au

📻 96.3 FM Sounds of the Mountain, 99.5 FM ABC Radio National

Adelong was established and thrived as a goldmining town in the late 19th century. Wilham Williams discovered gold and prospectors flocked to Adelong to seek their fortunes. Legend has it that Williams bought a mining claim for £40 000, only to sell it later the same day for £75 000. By World War I, over a million ounces of gold had been extracted from the mines, leaving little behind. The people began to disappear immediately. What is left is a charming rural village with a turn-of-the-century feel.

Historic buildings Many of the beautifully preserved buildings in Adelong have been classified by the National Trust. Take a stroll through Adelong's streets to discover banks, hotels and churches of the gold-rush era.

🍴 *Coat of Arms Kaffeehaus Restaurant:* authentic European; Beaufort Guest House, 77 Tumut St; (02) 6946 2273.

🛏 *Beaufort House:* heritage-listed B&B; 77 Tumut St; (02) 6946 2273.

Adelong Falls Reserve Richie's Gold Battery was one of the foremost gold-processing and quartz-crushing facilities in the country. See the ruins of its reefer machine, including water wheels and a red-brick chimney. Three clearly signposted walks explore the falls, and other ruins in the reserve. 1 km N.

See also RIVERINA, p. 34

Albury

Pop. 43 784
Map ref. 554 A12 | 559 O12 | 585 K6 | 587 I2

ⓘ Gateway Visitor Information, Gateway Island, Hume Highway, Wodonga; 1300 796 222; www.destinationalburywodonga.com.au

📻 105.7 FM The River, 990 AM ABC Radio National

The twin towns of Albury–Wodonga are 7 kilometres apart on opposite sides of the Murray River, which is also the New South Wales–Victoria border. Originally inhabited by Aboriginal people, the Albury area was 'discovered' in 1824 by explorers Hume and Hovell, who carved their comments into the trunks of two trees. Hume's tree was destroyed by fire, but Hovell's still stands today in Hovell Tree Park.

Albury Library Museum Exhibits include a display on one of Australia's largest postwar migrant centres, which existed at nearby Bonegilla. Free wireless is also available. Cnr Kiewa and Swift sts; (02) 6023 8333.

Botanical Gardens: array of native and exotic plants and signposted rainforest and heritage walks; cnr Wodonga Pl and Dean St. *The Parklands:* comprises Hovell Tree, Noreuil and Australia parks. Enjoy riverside walks, swimming, kiosk and picnic areas; Wodonga Pl. *Monument Hill:* spectacular views of town and alps; Dean St. *Albury Regional Art Centre:* extensive Russell Drysdale collection; Dean St; (02) 6023 8187. *Wonga Wetlands:* rehabilitated wetland along the Murray River, home to the black cormorant; Riverina Hwy.

🌴 *Rotary Community Market:* Townsend St; Sun. *Opera in the Alps:* Jan. *Kinross Country Muster:* Feb. *Albury Gold Cup*

Racing Carnival: Mar/Apr. *Food and Wine Festival:* Sept/Oct. *Mungabareena Ngan-Girra (Festival of the Bogong Moth):* Nov.

🍴 *sourcedining:* contemporary Australian; 664 Dean St; (02) 6041 1288. *Green Zebra:* classic cafe fare; 484 Dean St; (02) 6023 1100.

🛏 *Chifley Albury:* 140 studio rooms; cnr Dean and Elizabeth sts; (02) 6021 5366. *Quest Albury:* 104 serviced apartments; 550 Kiewa St; (02) 6058 0900 or 1800 334 033. *Table Top Mountain:* self-contained bushland cottages; Bells Rd, Gregory; (02) 6026 0529.

 Ettamogah A tiny but famous town in Australia, which is home to the original Ettamogah Pub, inspired by cartoonist Ken Maynard. 12 km NE. The OZE Wildlife Resort is worth a visit and Cooper's Ettamogah Winery is 3 km further along.

Lake Hume: watersports, camping and spectacular dam wall; 14 km E. *Hume Weir Trout Farm:* handfeeding and fishing for rainbow trout; Lake Hume; 14 km E. *Jindera Pioneer Museum:* originally a German settlement featuring a general store, a slab hut and a wattle and daub cottage; 14 km NW. *Albury–Wodonga Trail System:* walking trails in the footsteps of Hume and Hovell; maps available from visitor centre. *Hume and Hovell Walking Track:* 23-day, 440 km trek from Albury to Yass. For a kit, including maps, contact Department of Lands, Sydney (02) 6937 2700.

See also MURRAY, p. 35

Alstonville

Pop. 5001
Map ref. 551 G5 | 557 O3 | 653 N12

ⓘ Ballina Visitor Information Centre, cnr Las Balsas Plaza and River St, Ballina; (02) 6686 3484 or 1800 777 666; www.discoverballina.com

📻 101.9 Paradise FM, 738 AM ABC Local

Alstonville is between Lismore and Ballina, surrounded by macadamia and avocado plantations. It's known for its immaculate gardens and purple tibouchina trees that blossom in March, as well as quirky antique and gift shops.

Lumley Park: walk-through reserve of native plants, flying fox colony and open-air pioneer transport museum; Bruxner Hwy. *Budgen Avenue:* several shops and galleries with local art and craft. *Elizabeth Ann Brown Park:* rainforest park with picnic facilities; Main St.

🍴 *E.S.P Espresso Bar:* excellent coffee and food; Shop 1A/76 Main St; (02) 6628 3433.

🛏 *Hume's Hovell B&B:* B&B; Dalwood Rd; (02) 6629 5371. *Tallaringa Views:* self-contained cottages; 1344 Eltham Rd; (02) 6628 5005. *Deux Belettes:* French-style guesthouse; Victoria Park Rd, Dalwood; (02) 6629 5377.

Victoria Park Nature Reserve This remarkable rainforest reserve contains 68 species of trees in only 17.5 ha, 8 ha of which remain largely untouched. The area is also home to red-legged pademelons, potoroos, water rats and possums. There is a boardwalk, clearly marked walking trails and a spectacular lookout taking in the surrounding countryside. 8 km S.

Summerland House with No Steps: nursery, avocado and macadamia orchard, garden, crafts, fruit-processing plant, kids water park and Devonshire tea. Completely run by people with disabilities; (02) 6628 0610; 3 km S.

See also TROPICAL NORTH COAST, p. 28

Armidale

Pop. 19 483
Map ref. 550 B1 | 557 J8

 82 Marsh St; (02) 6772 4655 or 1800 627 736; www.armidaletourism.com.au

92.1 2ARM FM, 720 AM ABC Radio National

Armidale is the largest town of the New England district. It is home to New England University, the first university in Australia established outside a capital city. The transplanted birch, poplar and ash trees that line the streets make Armidale seem like an English village. It is one of those rare towns in Australia that enjoy four distinct seasons, with autumn turning the leaves stunning shades of crimson and gold. National parks in the area offer breathtaking forests, gorges and waterfalls.

New England Regional Art Museum The museum (closed Mon) has over 40 000 visitors each year and 8 gallery spaces, an audiovisual theatre, artist studio and cafe. The Howard Hinton and Chandler Coventry collections are among the most important and extensive regional collections, and include works by legendary Australian artists such as Arthur Streeton, Tom Roberts, Margaret Preston and John Coburn. There is also a separate Museum of Printing (open Thurs–Sun) featuring the F. T. Wimble & Co collection. Kentucky St; (02) 6772 5255.

Armidale Heritage Tour: includes Railway Museum, St Peter's Anglican Cathedral (built with 'Armidale blues' bricks) and University of New England; departs daily from visitor centre. *Aboriginal Cultural Centre and Keeping Place:* includes museum, education centre and craft displays; Kentucky St. *Armidale Folk Museum:* National Trust–classified building with comprehensive collection of pioneer artefacts from the region including toys and buggies; open 1–4pm daily; Cnr Faulkner and Rusden sts; (02) 6770 3536. *Self-guide heritage walk and heritage drive:* 3 km walk and 25 km drive provide history and points of interest in and around the town; maps from visitor centre.

Armidale Markets: Beardy St; last Sun each month (3rd Sun in Dec). *Autumn Festival:* Mar.

Archie's on the Park: modern Australian in historic homestead; Moore Park Inn, New England Hwy; (02) 6772 2358. *Caffiends on Marsh:* great coffee and food; Shop 1, 110 Marsh St; (02) 6771 3178. *Split Dining:* modern Australian; 1/117 Beardy St; (02) 6772 8313.

Annie's B&B: cosy, charming, self-contained; 37 Ellowera Rd; (02) 6772 5335. *Claremont Crossing:* self-contained farmhouse; 353 Claremont Rd; (02) 6775 1012. *Petersons Armidale Winery & Guesthouse:* luxury country manor; Dangarsleigh Rd; (02) 6772 0422.

Oxley Wild Rivers National Park World Heritage–listed with the largest area of dry rainforest in NSW, this park includes Dangars Falls (21 km SE), a 120 m waterfall in a spectacular gorge setting, and Wollomombi Falls (40 km E), which at 220 m is one of the highest falls in the state.

University of New England: features Booloominbah Homestead, Antiquities Museum, Zoology Museum and kangaroo and deer park; 5 km NW. *Saumarez Homestead:* National Trust–owned house offering tours (closed mid-June to end Sept); 5 km S. *Dumaresq Dam:* walking trails, boating, swimming and trout fishing (Oct–June); 15 km NE. *Hillgrove:* former mining town with Rural Life and History Museum featuring goldmining equipment (open Fri–Mon) and self-guide walk through old town site; brochure at visitor centre; 31 km E.

See also NEW ENGLAND, p. 29

Ballina

Pop. 14 675
Map ref. 551 G5 | 557 O4 | 653 N12

 Cnr Las Balsas Plaza and River St; (02) 6686 3484 or 1800 777 666; www.discoverballina.com

101.9 Paradise FM, 738 AM ABC Local

Ballina sits on an island at the mouth of the Richmond River in northern New South Wales surrounded by the Pacific Ocean and nearby fields of sugarcane. The sandy beaches, clear water and warm weather make the area popular. Ballina's name comes from the Aboriginal word 'bullenah', which is said to mean 'place where oysters are plentiful'. This is still the case, with fresh seafood readily available in many seaside restaurants.

Shelly Beach A superb spot for the whole family. Dolphins can be seen frolicking in the waves all year-round and humpback whales migrate through these waters June–July and Sept–Oct. The beach itself has rockpools, a wading pool for toddlers and a beachside cafe. Off Shelly Beach Rd.

Naval and Maritime Museum: features a restored Las Balsas Expedition raft that sailed from South America in 1973; Regatta Ave; (02) 6681 1002. *Kerry Saxby Walkway:* from behind the visitor centre to the river mouth with great river and ocean views. *The Big Prawn:* art and craft and fresh seafood; Pacific Hwy. *Richmond Princess and Bennelong:* river cruises; bookings at visitor centre. *Shaws Bay:* swimming and picnic area; off Compton Dr. *Ballina Water Slide:* River St.

Ballina Markets: Canal Drive; 3rd Sun each month. *Ballina Cup:* horserace; Sept.

Ballina Manor Boutique Hotel: modern Australian in Edwardian manor; 25 Norton St; (02) 6681 5888. *Pelican 181:* waterfront seafood, eat in or takeaway; 12–24 Fawcett St; (02) 6686 9181. *Sandbar and Restaurant:* modern European, tapas; 23 Compton Dr; (02) 6686 6602.

Ballina Beach Resort: incredible beachfront location; Compton Dr; (02) 6686 8888. *Ballina Manor Boutique Hotel:* award-winning, heritage-listed manor; 25 Norton St; (02) 6681 5888.

Lennox Head A beachside town with a good market on the 2nd and 5th Sun each month on the shores of Lake Ainsworth (also a popular spot for windsurfing). The lake has been nicknamed the Coca-Cola lake due to coloration from surrounding tea trees. Pat Morton Lookout affords excellent views along the coast, with whale-watching June–July and Sept–Oct. Below is The Point, a world-renowned surf beach. The outskirts of town offer scenic rainforest walks. 10 km N.

Thursday Plantation: tea-tree plantation with product sales and maze; (02) 6620 5150; 3 km W. *Macadamia Castle:* features macadamia products, industry displays, minigolf and children's wildlife park; (02) 6687 8432; 15 km N. *Whale-watching:* bookings at visitor centre.

See also TROPICAL NORTH COAST, p. 28

Balranald

Pop. 1217
Map ref. 558 H7 | 589 M9

 Heritage Park, Market St; (03) 5020 1599; www.balranald.nsw.gov.au

93.1 FM ABC Radio National, 102.1 FM ABC Local

Balranald is the oldest town on the lower part of the Murrumbidgee River. Situated on saltbush and mallee plains, the area now embraces the viticulture, horticulture and tourism industries. A string of dry lake beds stretches to the north of Balranald, the most famous of which are preserved in Mungo National Park. Recently, the oldest human footprints in Australia were found in the park, estimated to be up to 23 000 years old.

 Heritage Park Investigate the old gaol, the Murray pine schoolhouse, local history displays and a historical museum. There are also picnic and barbecue facilities. Market St.

Art gallery: exhibitions by local artists, housed in 1880s Masonic Lodge; Mayall St. *Balranald Weir:* barbecues, picnics, fishing. *Memorial Drive:* great views. *Frog Sculptures:* 14 throughout town. *Self-guide town walk:* historically significant buildings in the town; maps available from visitor centre.

 Balranald Cup: horserace; Feb/Mar.

Riverview on the Edward: B&B situated on a working sheep and cattle farm; Balpool Rd, Moulamein; (03) 5887 5241.

 Mungo National Park This park is the focal point of the Willandra Lakes World Heritage Area, a 240 000 ha region dotted with 17 dry lakes. These lakes display astounding evidence of ancient Aboriginal life and of creatures that existed during the last Ice Age. The highlight is the 33 km crescent-shaped dune on the eastern edge of Lake Mungo, called the Walls of China. The park contains some remarkable animal remains, as well as ancient fireplaces, artefacts and tools. The Mungo Visitor Centre delves into the heritage of the Willandra Lakes, and has a replica of the diprotodon, a massive wombat-like marsupial; Arumpo Rd; (03) 5021 8900 or 1300 361 967. A 70 km self-guide drive tour, suitable for conventional vehicles, takes in the Walls of China, old tanks and wells and an old homestead site. Accommodation in the park includes the old Mungo Shearers' Quarters and a campground. 100 km N.

Moulamein The oldest town in the Riverina, Moulamein has fascinating historic structures to explore including its restored courthouse (1845) and Old Wharf (1850s). There are picnic areas by the Edward River and Lake Moulamein. 99 km SE.

Yanga Lake: fishing and watersports; 7 km SE. *Homebush Hotel:* built in 1878 as a Cobb & Co station, the hotel now provides meals and accommodation; (03) 5020 6803; 25 km N. *Kyalite:* home to Australia's largest commercial pistachio nut farm and popular with campers and anglers; 36 km S. *Redbank Weir:* barbecues and picnics; Homebush–Oxley Rd; 58 km N.

See also RIVERINA, p. 34

Barham

Pop. 1131
Map ref. 559 I10 | 584 A2 | 591 O4

i Golden Rivers Tourism, 15 Murray St; (03) 5453 3100.

107.7/102.5 Mix FM, 594 AM ABC Local

Barham and its twin town, Koondrook, sit beside the Murray River and the New South Wales–Victoria border. Barham is known as the southern gateway to Golden Rivers country and is surrounded by river flats and red hills. The Murray River makes Barham a great place for anglers with Murray cod, golden perch, catfish and yabbies in abundance. Barham Bridge is one of the oldest bridges on the Murray and was lifted manually until 1997.

 Barham Lakes Complex The complex is popular with locals and visitors alike. It has 4 artificial lakes stocked with fish and

yabbies, grasslands with hundreds of native plants, a walking track and barbecue facilities. Murray St.

Border Flywheelers Vintage Engine Rally: Feb. *The Country Music Stampede:* Feb and Aug. *Jazz Festival:* June. *Barham Produce and Food Festival:* Aug. *Golden Rivers Red Gum Forest to Furniture Showcase:* Oct.

Barham Caravan and Tourist Park: fantastic family park on Murray River; 1 Noorong St; (03) 5453 2553.

 Koondrook State Forest Koondrook State Forest is 31 000 ha of native bushland that is perfect for birdwatchers and nature enthusiasts. The forest has over 100 bird species, kangaroos, emus and wild pigs. Forest drives winding through the park are well signposted. 12 km NE.

Koondrook: old sawmilling town and river port with historic buildings and tramway; 5 km SW. *Murrabit:* largest country markets in the region; 1st Sat each month; Murrabit Rd; 24 km NW.

See also MURRAY, p. 35

Barraba

Pop. 1163
Map ref. 556 H7

i 112 Queen St; (02) 6782 1255.

99.1 FM ABC Local, 648 AM ABC Local

The tree-lined streets of Barraba lie in the valley of the Manilla River. Surrounded by the Nandewar Ranges, Horton Valley and undulating tablelands, Barraba is a quiet and idyllic town. The area was once busy with mining and, although some mines still operate, the main industries today centre around sheep and wool.

 Heritage walk The walk takes in a heritage-listed organ and historic buildings such as the courthouse, church, clock tower and the visitor centre itself. The Commercial Hotel on Queen St was once a Cobb & Co changing station.

Clay Pan and Fuller Gallery: exhibits art, craft and pottery; Queen St. *The Playhouse:* accommodation including a theatre and exhibition space; Queen St; (02) 6782 1109.

 Market: 1st Sat each month; Queen St. *Australia's Smallest Country Music Festival:* Jan. *Barraba Agricultural Show and Rodeo:* Feb/Mar. *Australia's Smallest Jazz and Blues Festival:* Easter. *Frost Over Barraba:* art show; July. *BarrArbor Festival:* celebration of culture; Nov. *Horton Valley Rodeo:* Dec.

Barraba Motel: traditional, charming motel accommodation; 17 Edward St; (02) 6782 1555. *Playhouse Hotel:* comfortable accommodation adjacent to theatre; 121–123 Queen St; (02) 6782 1109.

 Mt Kaputar National Park This park is excellent for hiking, rising as high as 1200 m, and is the site of the now extinct Nandewar Volcano. The diverse vegetation ranges from semi-arid woodland to wet sclerophyll forest and alpine growth. Wildlife is abundant, especially bats, birds and quolls. Access to the park from Barraba is by foot only, although permission for 4WD access can be granted by the visitor centre. 48 km W.

Adams Lookout: panoramic views of the town and countryside; 5 km NE. *Millie Park Vineyard:* organic wine cellar-door tastings and sales; 5 km N. *Glen Riddle Recreation Reserve:* on Manilla River north of Split Rock Dam, for boating, fishing

BATEMANS BAY

Pop. 10 843

Map ref. 554 H12 | 565 F6 | 567 L6

ⓘ **Cnr Princes Hwy and Beach Rd; (02) 4472 6900 or 1800 802 528; www.eurobodalla.com.au**

📻 103.5 FM ABC South East, 104.3 Power FM

Batemans Bay is a popular town for holiday-makers at the mouth of the Clyde River. It has something for everyone with rolling surf beaches, quiet coves and rockpools, and wonderful views upriver to the hinterland mountains and out to sea to the islands on the horizon. Batemans Bay is the home of the famous Clyde River oyster and other excellent fresh seafood.

🏠 **Birdland Animal Park:** native wildlife and rainforest trail; Beach Rd. **River cruises:** daily cruises on the *Merinda* to historic Nelligen depart from the wharf behind The Boatshed; contact visitor centre for times. **Houseboat hire and fishing charters:** bookings at visitor centre. **Corn Trail:** a picturesque but challenging 12.5 km walking and horseriding track through Buckenboura State Forest, following a pioneer route from the top of Clyde Mountain down the valley to the coast; maps available from visitor centre. **Joy-flights over the Clyde River:** scenic flights or skydiving over the coast and Clyde River from Moruya Airport; inquiries 1800 802 528 or at visitor centre. **Scenic lookouts:** panoramic views of coast and hinterland from Big Bit Lookout or Folders Hill Lookout (north of town), Holmes Lookout (west) and Round Hill Lookout (south).

🎪 **Batemans Bay Market:** Museum Place, 1st, 2nd and 4th Sat each month; high school, 3rd Sun each month.

🍴 **Briars Restaurant:** modern Australian; Princes Hwy; (02) 4472 9200. **On the Pier:** waterfront seafood; 2 Old Punt Rd; (02) 4472 6405. **Starfish Deli Restaurant:** relaxed dining; The Promenade, 2 Clyde St; (02) 4472 4880.

🛏 **Chalet Swisse Spa at Surf Beach Retreat:** bushland and rainforest setting; 676 The Ridge Rd; (02) 4471 3671. **Mariners on the Waterfront:** resort-style accommodation; Orient St; (02) 4472 6222. **The Bower at Broulee:** romantic self-contained eco cabins; George Bass Dr, Broulee; (02) 4471 8666.

🧭 **Mogo** Alive with a quaint village atmosphere, Old Mogo Town re-creates a 19th-century goldmining town. Take a guided tour to experience gold-rush life, bushranger legends, goldmine workings and workshops. Wildlife enthusiasts will enjoy Mogo Zoo – it specialises in raising endangered species such as tigers, white lions, snow leopards and red pandas. Mogo offers fabulous village-style shopping and cafes, including antique and collectibles stores, art galleries and specialty shops. Mogo State Forest is popular with birdwatchers and bushwalkers, and is home to lorikeets, kookaburras, rosellas and cockatoos. 8 km s.

Eurobodalla Native Botanic Gardens: native plants, walking tracks, nursery and picnic area; open Wed–Sun; 5 km s. **Murramarang National Park:** undisturbed coastline and abundant kangaroos, particularly at Pebble Beach; good swimming, excellent surf beaches and plenty of picnic spots; rock and beach fishing are popular; 10 km NE. **Murramarang Aboriginal Area:** signposted walk through 12 000-year-old Aboriginal sites, including the largest complex of shell middens and stone tools on the south coast; just north of Murramarang National Park. **Nelligen:** an important Clyde River port in pioneer days, when goods were shipped from here down to Sydney or sent into the hinterland; nowadays holiday-makers use the historic town as a base for waterskiing, fishing and houseboat vacations; 10 km NW. **Malua Bay:** excellent surfing; 14 km SE. **Durras Lake:** fishing, kayaking and swimming; 16 km NE. **Tomakin:** coastal holiday village by the Tomaga River with long stretches of pristine family-friendly beaches and forested hinterland. 15 km s.

See also SOUTH COAST, p. 32

[BODY SURFERS CATCHING A WAVE AT MALUA BAY]

and picnicking; 15 km SE. *Ironbark Creek:* gold and mineral fossicking, with ruins of old village; 18 km E. *Horton River Falls:* 83 m waterfall, swimming and bushwalking; 38 km W. *Birdwatching trails:* the 165 species in the area include the rare regent honeyeater. Guides are available from the visitor centre.

See also NEW ENGLAND, p. 29

Bathurst

Pop. 30 748
Map ref. 554 H5

ⓘ Kendall Ave; (02) 6332 1444 or 1800 681 000; www.visitbathurst.com.au

📻 96.7 FM ABC Radio National, 99.3 B-Rock FM

Bathurst, on the western side of the Great Dividing Range, is Australia's oldest inland city. Originally occupied by the Wiradjuri people, it was the site of enormous conflict in 1824 between its original inhabitants and the European settlers. Since then, Bathurst has become known as the birthplace of Ben Chifley, Australian prime minister 1945–49, and for its magnificent Georgian and Victorian architecture. Today it is best known for its motor racing circuit, Mount Panorama.

🏠 **Miss Traill's House** Ida Traill (1889–1976) was a fourth-generation descendant of pioneers William Lee and Thomas Kite who came to Bathurst in 1818. Her house, a colonial Georgian bungalow filled with artefacts and bequeathed to the National Trust, was built in 1845, making it one of the oldest houses in Bathurst. The 19th-century cottage garden is particularly charming in spring. Russell St; (02) 6332 4232.

Bathurst District Historical Museum: features notable local Aboriginal artefacts in the east wing of the Neoclassical Bathurst Courthouse; Russell St; (02) 6330 8455. *Australian Fossil and Mineral Museum:* exhibits close to 2000 fossil and mineral specimens, including rare and unique displays, housed in the 1876 public school building; Howick St; (02) 6331 5511. *Bathurst Regional Art Gallery:* focuses on Australian art after 1955, with frequently changing exibitions; Keppel St; (02) 6333 6555. *Machattie Park:* Victorian-era park in the heart of the city, with a begonia house full of blooms Feb–Apr; Keppel, William and George sts. *Self-guide historical walking tour and self-drive tour:* takes in Bathurst Gaol, the courthouse and historic homes, including Ben Chifley's house; map from visitor centre.

🎪 **Gold Crown Festival:** harness racing; Mar. *Autumn Colours:* variety of events celebrating autumn; Mar–May. *V8 Supercars 1000:* Oct.

🍴 **Cobblestone Lane:** Italian brasserie; 2/173–179 George St; (02) 6331 2202. *Lamplighters Restaurant:* bistro-style fare; 56 Keppel St; (02) 6331 5800. *The Crowded House Cafe:* modern Australian; 1 Ribbon Gang La; (02) 6334 2300.

🛏 **Bishop's Court Estate Boutique Hotel:** Victorian hilltop guesthouse; 226 Seymour St; (02) 6332 4447. *Encore Apartments:* contemporary self-contained apartments; 187 Piper St; (02) 6333 6000.

⊗ **Mt Panorama** The inaugural Bathurst 1000 was held here in 1960 and has since become an Australian institution. The 6.2 km scenic circuit is open year-round, and while the lap record is 129.7 seconds (over 170 km/h), visitors are limited to 60 km/h. The National Motor Racing Museum at the circuit displays race cars, trophies, memorabilia and special exhibits; (02) 6332 1872. Also at Mt Panorama are the Bathurst Goldfields, a reconstruction of a historic goldmining area, and McPhillamy Park, which features the Sir Joseph Banks Nature Reserve with great views over Bathurst, especially at sunrise and sunset. 2 km S.

Abercrombie House: impressive 1870s baronial-style Gothic mansion; Ophir Rd; 6 km W. *Bathurst Sheep and Cattle Drome:* visitors can milk a cow and see shearing and sheepdog demonstrations; Limekilns Rd; 6 km NE. *Bathurst Observatory:* program varies throughout the year. The visitor centre features mineral, fossil and space displays. The complex is closed in inclement weather; 12 km NE. *Wallaby Rocks:* wall of rock rising from the Turon River and a popular spot for kangaroos and wallabies. Also an ideal swimming and picnic spot; 40 km N. *Sofala:* historic gold town and the setting for scenes from the films *The Cars That Ate Paris* (1974) and *Sirens* (1994); 42 km N. *Hill End Historic Site:* former goldfield with many original buildings. The area has inspired painters Russell Drysdale, Donald Friend, John Olsen and Brett Whiteley. There is a National Parks & Wildlife Service visitor centre in old Hill End Hospital, which has a historical display and information on panning and fossicking, with equipment for hire; (02) 6337 8206. Old gold towns nearby include Peel, Wattle Flat, Rockley, O'Connell and Trunkey; 86 km NW.

See also CENTRAL WEST, p. 30

Batlow

Pop. 997
Map ref. 554 D11 | 565 A5 | 566 C4 | 585 P3

ⓘ Tumut Region Visitor Centre, 5 Adelong Rd, Tumut; (02) 6947 7025; www.tumut.nsw.gov.au

📻 96.3 FM Sounds of the Mountain, 675 AM ABC Local Radio

In the 19th-century gold rush prospectors converged on nearby Reedy Creek, which sparked a sudden demand for fresh produce. The resulting orchards and farms became the town of Batlow. Set in the low-lying mountains of the state's south-west slopes, Batlow is a picturesque town still surrounded by orchards of delicious apples, pears, berries, cherries and stone fruit.

🏠 **Batlow Woodworks:** discover a range of art, pottery, woodworks and crafts, serving morning and afternoon tea; Pioneer St; (02) 6949 1265. *Weemala Lookout:* breathtaking views of town and Snowy Mountains; H. V. Smith Dr.

🎪 **Apple Blossom Festival:** Oct.

🍴 **Mountain View Cafe:** popular cafe; Pioneer St; (02) 6949 1110.

🛏 **Batlow House:** self-contained Federation cottage; 5 Pioneer St; 0437 378 768.

⊗ **Hume and Hovell Lookout:** great views over Blowering Valley and Blowering Reservoir, with picnic area at the site where explorers rested in 1824; 6 km E. *Tumut Rd:* fresh fruit along the road. Springfield Orchard, 6 km N, grows 16 apple varieties and has picnic and barbecue facilities. *Kosciuszko National Park:* this alpine park to the east includes nearby Bowering Reservoir and Buddong Falls; *for more details see Adaminaby.* **Hume and Hovell Walking Track:** access to short sections of the 440 km track via Tumut Rd. Maps available from visitor centre.

See also RIVERINA, p. 34

 RADIO STATIONS IN TOWN WHAT'S ON WHERE TO EAT WHERE TO STAY NEARBY

Bega

Pop. 4536
Map ref. 565 E9 | 567 J12 | 581 H6

 Lagoon St; (02) 6491 7645; www.sapphirecoast.com.au

 102.5 Power FM, 810 AM ABC Local

It is possible to ski and surf on the same day around Bega, set in a fertile valley with the mountains of the Kosciuszko snow resorts to the west and breathtaking coastline to the east. Bega is best known for its dairy industry, particularly cheese-making.

Bega Family Museum: houses town memorabilia including silverware, ball gowns, farm machinery and photographs; open Mon–Sat Sept–May, Tues and Fri June–Aug; Cnr Bega and Auckland sts; (02) 6492 1453.

Bega Valley Art Awards: Oct.

Bega Downs Restaurant: modern Australian; Bega Downs Motor Inn, cnr Princes Hwy and High St; (02) 6492 2944. **Pepperberry Restaurant:** friendly cafe; Shop 1, Ayres Walkway; (02) 6492 0361.

Rock Lily Cottages: self-contained cottages; 864 Warrigal Range Rd, Brogo via Bega; (02) 6492 7364.

Biamanga National Park Now a popular spot for swimming, bushwalking and picnics, Biamanga National Park has long been a sacred site to the Yuin people. Mumbulla Mountain was an initiation site for young men and Mumbulla Creek was used to wash off ceremonial ochre. Visitors can now enjoy the rockpools, natural water slides, boardwalks, viewing platforms and picnic sites of this culturally significant area. 19 km NE.

Bega Cheese Heritage Centre: restored cheese factory with cheese-tasting and displays of cheese-making equipment; (02) 6491 7762; 3 km N. **Lookouts:** excellent views at Bega Valley Lookout (3 km N) and Dr George Lookout (8 km NE). **Candelo:** charming and peaceful village with market on 1st Sun each month; 24 km SW. **Brogo Dam:** haven for native birdlife such as sea eagles and azure kingfishers. Also popular for bass fishing, swimming, picnicking, boating and canoeing (canoe hire on-site; (02) 6492 7328); 30 km NW.

See also SOUTH COAST, p. 32

Bellingen

Pop. 2878
Map ref. 550 G1 | 551 D12 | 557 M8

 Hyde St; (02) 6655 1522; www.bellingermagic.com

107.3 2BBB FM, 738 AM ABC Local

Bellingen is an attractive tree-lined town on the banks of the Bellinger River, surrounded by rich pasturelands. Traditionally serving dairy farmers and timber cutters, Bellingen is now a haven for urban folk fleeing the big cities, attracted to the relaxed and alternative lifestyle on offer. City touches can be found in shops and cafes, but the town retains its laid-back feel. The area is the setting for Peter Carey's novel *Oscar and Lucinda*.

Bellingen Bat Island This 3 ha island is home to a colony of up to 40 000 grey-headed flying foxes (fruit bats). At dusk the flying foxes set off in search of food, filling the sky. The best time to visit is Sept–Mar. Access is via Dowle St (north of the river).

Horse-drawn carriage tours: guided tours of town and river picnics (operate during holidays and by appt); 0423 671 581. **Bellingen Museum:** features extensive photo collection of early pioneer life and early transportation; Hyde St; (02) 6655 1259. **Hammond and Wheatley Emporium:** the first concrete block construction in Australia, the emporium has been magnificently restored – including a grand staircase leading to a mezzanine floor – and is now home to boutiques, homewares retailers and jewellery galleries; Hyde St. **Local art and craft:** galleries thoughout the town including The Yellow Shed, Cnr Hyde and Prince sts, and The Old Butter Factory, Doepel St.

Bellingen Markets: Bellingen Park, Church St; 3rd Sat each month. **Jazz Festival:** Aug. **Global Carnival:** world music; Oct.

 Elite Espresso Gallery: great coffee and food; 62 Hyde St; (02) 6655 0509. **Lodge 241 Gallery Cafe:** historic riverside cafe; 117–212 Hyde St; (02) 6655 2470. **No 2 Oak Street:** modern Australian; 2 Oak St; (02) 6655 9000.

Casa Belle: Tuscan-style guesthouse; 90 Gleniffer Rd; (02) 6655 9311. **Kumbaingiri Retreat:** luxurious self-contained retreat; 184 Kalang Rd; 0434 074 075. **Promised Land Cottages:** self-contained cottages; 934 Promised Land Rd, Promised Land; (02) 6655 9578.

Raleigh Vineyard and Winery: tastings available; (02) 6655 4388; 11 km E. **Walking, cycling, horseriding and canoeing:** along the Bellinger River and in forest areas; information and maps from visitor centre. **Scenic drive:** north-east through wooded valleys and farmlands, across Never Never Creek to Promised Land; map available from visitor centre.

See also HOLIDAY COAST, p. 27

Bermagui

Pop. 1298
Map ref. 565 E8 | 567 K11

 Bunga St; (02) 6493 3054 or 1800 645 808; www.sapphirecoast.com.au

102.5 Power FM, 105.9 FM 2EC, 810 AM ABC Local

Bermagui is a charming and sleepy coastal village. The continental shelf is at its closest to the mainland off Bermagui and this results in excellent fishing for marlin, tuna and shark. Zane Grey was a famous visitor in the 1930s and the town featured in two of his books. Bermagui is also the centre of a mystery involving a geologist, Lamont Young, who was sent to investigate goldfields in 1880. When he decided to head north to investigate further, he and his assistant were offered passage on a small boat with three men. All five disappeared en route. When their boat was discovered, it was found to have five bags of clothing, Young's books and papers, and a bullet in the starboard side. Despite extensive searches and media attention, no trace of the men was ever found.

Fish Co-op: freshly caught fish and prawns; Fishermans Wharf, harbourside. **Blue Pool:** large and attractive saltwater rockpool offering an unusual swimming experience; off Scenic Dr. **Horseshoe Bay Beach:** safe swimming spot. **Good surfing beaches:** Beares, Mooreheads, Cuttagee and Haywards beaches; maps from visitor centre. **Gamefishing, deep-sea fishing and reef-fishing:** bookings at visitor centre.

Craft Market: Dickinson Park; last Sun each month. **Blue Water Fishing Classic:** Jan. **Seaside Fair:** Mar. **Tag and Release Gamefishing Tournament:** Mar. **Four Winds Festival:** even-numbered years, Easter. **Victorian Southern Gamefish Challenge:** Easter.

Bermagui Mudworks & Cafe: cafe with Balinese feel; 23 Alexander Dr; (02) 6493 4661. **Saltwater:** seafood cafe; 59 Lamont St; (02) 6493 4328.

Bermagui Beach House: contemporary beach house; address provided on inquiry; 0402 337 396. ***Bimbimbi House:*** modern self-contained beach house; 62 Nutleys Creek Rd; (02) 6493 4456. ***Wu Wei House:*** luxurious, Japanese-inspired holiday home; address provided on inquiry; 0410 081 599.

 Gulaga National Park The Wallaga Lakes area has an 8 km coastal walk through wetland flora and fauna reserves and remnants of the Montreal Goldfield north to Wallaga Lake. It passes Camel Rock, an unusual rock formation in the general shape of a camel. The park is hilly with steep gullies, so it is best explored by boat (available for hire from Regatta Pt and Beauty Pt). Guided tours are available through Montreal Goldfield (bookings at visitor centre). There are good walking trails, including one to the summit of Mt Dromedary. The park is excellent for boating, fishing, swimming, picnicking and bushwalking. The Yuin people run Aboriginal cultural tours from the Umballa Cultural Centre, sharing Dreamtime stories that have never been recorded on paper. Activities include ochre painting, bark-hut building and boomerang throwing. Bookings and information (02) 4473 7232; 6 km N.

Mimosa Rocks National Park: 17 km s; *see Tathra.* ***Mystery Bay:*** the site of the discovery of Lamont Young's abandoned boat and a memorial; 17 km N. ***Cobargo:*** historic working village with art galleries, wood and leather crafts, antiques, pottery and tearooms. A country market on 4th Sat each month at RSL hall grounds; 20 km W.

See also SOUTH COAST, p. 32

Berridale

Pop. 844
Map ref. 565 C8 | 566 F10 | 581 D4

 Snowy Region Visitor Centre, Kosciuszko Rd, Jindabyne; (02) 6450 5600 or 1800 004 439; www.snowymountains.com.au

 97.7 Snow FM, 810 AM ABC Local

This charming small town calls itself the 'Crossroads of the Snowy' and is a popular stopover point in winter between Cooma and the snowfields. In the 1860s and 1870s it was known as Gegedzerick, but later changed its name to Berridale, the name of a local property. The main street is lined with poplars that provide a striking show in autumn. The trees were planted about 100 years ago by children from Berridale School.

Ray Killen Gallery: landscape photographs from around Australia; Jindabyne Rd. ***Historic buildings:*** St Mary's (1860), Mary St; Berridale School (1883), Oliver St; Berridale Inn (1863), Exchange Sq; Berridale Store (1863), Exchange Sq. ***Boulders:*** unique granite boulders near to the main road were formed from crystallised magma 400 million years ago.

Snowy River Winery: charming restaurant, wine tastings; Jindabyne Rd; (02) 6456 4015.

Snowy Mountains Coach and Motor Inn: resort-style accommodation; Jindabyne Rd; (02) 6456 3283. ***The Range:*** lodge-style accommodation; Kosciuszko Rd; (02) 6456 3368.

Dalgety: small town featuring historic Buckley's Crossing Hotel, marking the spot where cattle crossed the Snowy River; 18 km s. ***Eucumbene Trout Farm:*** sales, horseriding and tours; (02) 6456 8866; 19 km N. ***Snowy River Ag Barn***

and Fibre Centre: museum, craft and fibre shop, animals and restaurant; 21 km s.

See also SNOWY MOUNTAINS, p. 33

Berrima

Pop. 867
Map ref. 553 B5 | 555 I8 | 565 G2

 Berrima Courthouse, cnr Wilshire and Argyle sts; (02) 4877 1505; www.berrimavillage.com.au

102.9 FM 2ST, 675 AM ABC Local

A superbly preserved 1830s village, Berrima is nestled in a valley next to the Wingecarribee River. The National Heritage Council declared the village a historic precinct in the 1960s. Many buildings have been restored as antique shops, restaurants and galleries.

Berrima Courthouse The courthouse was the scene in 1841 of Australia's first trial by jury, in which Lucretia Dunkley and Martin Beech were accused of having an affair and tried for murdering Lucretia's much older husband, Henry, with an axe. They were both found guilty and hanged. The building, said to be the finest in town, now houses displays on the trial and early Berrima. Cnr Wilshire and Argyle sts; (02) 4877 1505.

Berrima District Historical Museum: displays focus on colonial settlement and the struggles of pioneer days; Market Pl; (02) 4877 1130. ***Harpers Mansion:*** Georgian house built in 1834, now owned by the National Trust; Wilkinson St. ***Australian Alpaca Centre:*** sales of knitwear and toys; Market Pl. ***The Surveyor General:*** built in 1835, Australia's oldest continually licensed hotel; Old Hume Hwy. ***Berrima Gaol:*** Bushranger Paddy Curran was the first man hanged there in 1842 and Lucretia Dunkley was the first and only woman executed there; Argyle St.

Market: 2nd Sun each month; school grounds; Oxley St.

 Eschalot: modern Australian; 24 Old Hume Hwy; (02) 4877 1977. ***Josh's Cafe:*** popular eatery with Middle Eastern influences; 2/9 Old Hume Hwy; (02) 4877 2200.

Jellore Cottage and Settlers Hut: luxury self-contained cottages; 16 and 16A Jellore St; 0404 951 884. ***Surveyor General Inn:*** colonial-style pub; Old Hume Hwy; (02) 4877 1226.

Wineries: numerous in the area with cellar-door tastings including Southern Highland Wines in Sutton Forest ((02) 4868 2300); 10 km s; and Mundrakoona Estate in Mittagong ((02) 4872 1311); 10 km NE; maps from visitor centre.

See also SOUTHERN HIGHLANDS, p. 24

Berry

Pop. 1485
Map ref. 553 D8 | 555 J9 | 565 G3

 Shoalhaven Visitors Centre, cnr Princes Hwy and Pleasant Way, Nowra; (02) 4421 0778 or 1300 662 808; www.berry.org.au

94.9 Power FM, 603 AM Radio National

The local chamber of commerce named Berry 'The Town of Trees' because of the extensive stands of English oaks, elms and beech trees planted by settlers in the 1800s. Berry is a popular weekend destination for Sydneysiders searching for bargains in the antique and craft shops and looking to enjoy the laid-back atmosphere. With the Cambewarra Ranges as its backdrop, Berry is the first truly rural town south of Sydney.

 RADIO STATIONS   IN TOWN   WHAT'S ON   WHERE TO EAT   WHERE TO STAY   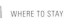 NEARBY

Berry Historical Museum: records and photographs of early settlement; open 11am–2pm Sat, 11am–3pm Sun, daily during school holidays; Queen St; (02) 4464 3097. *Precinct Galleries:* local contemporary art, craft and design; Alexandra St. *Great Warrior Aboriginal Art Gallery:* contemporary and traditional Aboriginal art, weapons, artefacts and didgeridoos; Queen St. *Antique and craft shops:* contact visitor centre for details.

Country Fair Markets: showground, cnr Alexandra and Victoria sts, 1st Sun each month (except Feb); Great Southern Hotel, Queen St, 3rd Sun each month. *Musicale festival:* June. *Garden Festival:* Oct.

Hungry Duck: modern Asian/Australian; 85 Queen St; (02) 4464 2323. *The Posthouse:* modern Australian; 137 Queen St; (02) 4464 2444.

Sojourn at Far Meadow: contemporary self-contained cabins; 47 Bryces Rd; (02) 4448 5497. *Crystal Creek Meadows:* eco-friendly retreat; 1655 Kangaroo Valley Rd, Kangaroo Valley; (02) 4465 1406.

Coolangatta: convict-built cottages, winery (open for tastings) and accommodation on site of first European settlement in area; 11 km se. *Other wineries in area:* open for tastings and sales; map from visitor centre. *Mild to Wild Tours:* adventure tours including sea-kayaking with dolphins, rock climbing, moonlight canoeing and mountain-biking; bookings (02) 4464 2211.

See also SOUTHERN HIGHLANDS, p. 24

Bingara

Pop. 1205
Map ref. 556 H5

ⓘ Roxy Theatre Building, Maitland St; (02) 6724 0066 or 1300 659 919; www.bingara.com.au

102.9 Gem FM, 648 AM ABC Local

Located in the centre of an area known as Fossickers Way, Bingara is an old gold- and diamond-mining town in the Gwydir River Valley. Gold was discovered here in 1852. Prospectors have been attracted to the town ever since, drawn by the chance of discovering their own fortunes in gold, tourmaline, sapphires and garnets, and by the peaceful cypress-covered mountain surrounds.

Orange Tree Memorial Orange trees along Finch St and Gwydir Oval stand as a memorial to those who have fallen in war. It is a town tradition that during the Orange Festival, Bingara's children pick the fruit and present it to hospital patients and the elderly.

All Nations Goldmine: a stamper battery is the only visible remnant; Hill St. *Bingara Historical Museum:* slab building (1860) displays gems and minerals and 19th-century furniture and photographs; Maitland St. *Visitor Information Centre:* set in the beautifully restored 1930s Art Deco Roxy Theatre complex; Maitland St. *Gwydir River Rides:* trail rides; Keera St. *Gwydir River:* walking track along the bank, and reportedly the best Murray cod fishing in NSW. *Self-guide historical/scenic town walk and drive:* contact visitor centre for maps.

Bingara Cup Race Meeting: Feb. *Bingara Fishing Competition:* Easter. *Campdraft:* Apr. *Orange Festival:* Aug.

Bingara Fossickers Way Motel: friendly, comfortable accommodation; 2 Finch St; (02) 6724 1373.

Three Creeks Goldmine: working mine open to the public for gold panning, crystal fossicking and bushwalking; 24 km s.

Myall Creek Memorial: monument to 28 Aboriginal men, women and children killed in the massacre of 1838; Delungra–Bingara Rd; 27 km ne. *Rocky Creek glacial area:* unusual conglomerate rock formations; 37 km sw. *Sawn Rocks:* pipe-shaped volcanic rock formations; 70 km sw. *Birdwatching and fossicking:* maps available from visitor centre.

See also NEW ENGLAND, p. 29

Blackheath

Pop. 4178
Map ref. 544 C4 | 546 F6 | 555 I6

ⓘ Heritage Centre, Govetts Leap Rd; (02) 4787 8877; www.visitbluemountains.com.au

89.1 BLU FM, 675 AM ABC Local

This pretty resort town, the highest in the Blue Mountains, has breathtaking views. Known for its guesthouses, gardens and bushwalks, Blackheath is in an ideal location at the edge of Blue Mountains National Park. It is also known as 'Rhododendron Town' for the myriad varieties that bloom every November.

National Parks & Wildlife Heritage Centre More than just an information resource, the centre features an interactive display on the geology, wildlife, Aboriginal and European history of the area and offers historical tours and guided walks. It is the starting point for the Fairfax Heritage Walk, a gentle bushwalk with wheelchair access and facilities for the visually impaired. The 4 km return trail goes to Govetts Leap Lookout for views across several waterfalls and the Grose Valley. Govetts Leap Rd.

Govett statue: commemorates the bushranger known as Govett, said to have ridden his horse over a cliff rather than be captured by police; centre of town.

Markets: Growers Market, Community Hall, Great Western Hwy, 2nd Sun each month; Community Market, School Grounds, 1st Sun each month. *Blue Mountains Food and Wine Fair:* Apr. *Rhododendron Festival:* Nov.

Ashcrofts: modern Australian; 18 Govetts Leap Rd; (02) 4787 8297. *Vulcan's:* modern Australian; 33 Govetts Leap Rd; (02) 4787 6899.

Lavender Cottage and Manor: self-contained cottages; 117 Evans Lookout Rd; (02) 4782 2385. *Secrets Hideaway:* self-contained cottages; 173 Evans Lookout Rd; (02) 4787 8453. *Woolshed Cabins:* modern, spacious, self-contained cabins; Kanimbla Dr; (02) 4787 8199.

Mount Victoria National Trust–classified Mount Victoria is the westernmost township of the Blue Mountains. There are buildings from the 1870s, including the Imperial Hotel, St Peter's Church of England and The Manor House. Also in town are craft shops, a museum at the train station and the Mount Vic Flicks historic cinema (open Thurs–Sun and school holidays). Mount Victoria has wonderful views of the mountains and many picnic spots and walking trails. 6 km nw.

Blue Mountains National Park In the area east of Blackheath are various waterfalls and lookout points, including the much photographed Hanging Rock (around 9 km n via Ridgewell Rd). The Blue Mountains have been home to Aboriginal people for at least 22 000 years – the Gundungurra people in the north, the Dharug people in the south and the Wiradjuri people in the west. It is an area rich not only with Dreamtime stories but also with over 700 heritage sites that descendants of the original inhabitants continue to protect today. *For other parts of the park see Katoomba and Glenbrook.*

Bacchante Gardens: rhododendrons and azaleas; 1.5 km N.
Mermaid Cave: picturesque rock cave where parts of *Mad Max III* (1985) were filmed; Megalong Rd; 4 km S. **Shipley Gallery:** art exhibitions (open weekends); Shipley Rd; 4.6 km S. **Pulpit Rock Reserve and Lookout:** sweeping views of Mt Banks and Grose Valley; 6 km E. **Hargraves Lookout:** overlooking Megalong Valley; Panorama Point Rd; 7.4 km SW via Shipley Gallery. **Mt Blackheath Lookout:** views of Kanimbla Valley; Mount Blackheath Rd; 8.2 km N via Shipley Gallery. **Megalong Australian Heritage Centre:** horseriding, adventure tours and tourist farm; (02) 4787 8188; 9 km S. **Werriberri Trail Rides:** various trail rides on horseback; bookings (02) 4787 9171.

See also BLUE MOUNTAINS, p. 23

Blayney

Pop. 2748
Map ref. 554 G5

 97 Adelaide St; (02) 6368 3534; www.blayney.nsw.gov.au

105.9 Star FM, 576 AM ABC Radio National

Blayney is a farming town in the central tablelands. National Trust–classified buildings and avenues of deciduous trees add a touch of charm to the town, particularly in autumn.

Heritage Park: small wetland area, barbecue facilities and tennis courts; Adelaide St. **Local craft shops:** contact visitor centre for details. **Self-guide heritage walk:** includes churches and the courthouse; brochure from visitor centre.

Mams Coffee Shoppe: rustic cafe; 129B Adelaide St; (02) 6368 3262.

Blayney Goldfields Motor Inn: comfortable accommodation option; 48 Martha St; (02) 6368 2000.

Carcoar The National Trust–classified town of Carcoar, surrounded by oak trees on the banks of the Belubula River, has a wealth of historic buildings. In early settlement days, convicts and bushrangers caused a lot of trouble in the town. Johnny Gilbert and John O'Meally committed Australia's first daylight bank robbery in 1863 at the Commercial Bank (still standing) on Belubula St. The hold-up was unsuccessful and the robbers fled when a teller fired a shot into the ceiling. 14 km SW.

Millthorpe: National Trust–classified village with quaint shopfronts, art and craft shops, historic churches and a museum with blacksmith's shop and old-style kitchen. Also visit the Golden Memories museum for displays of life in the 19th century; 11 km NW. **Wind farm:** with 15 turbines and an interpretive centre, the largest farm of its kind in Australia; 11 km SW. **Carcoar Dam:** watersports and camping with picnic and barbecue facilities; 12 km SW. **Newbridge:** historic buildings and craft shops; 20 km E. **Abercrombie Caves:** cave system in a 220 ha reserve that features the largest natural limestone arch in the Southern Hemisphere. Carols in the Caves is held here in Dec. Various tours are available; contact visitor centre for details. 50 km SE.

See also CENTRAL WEST, p. 30

Bombala

Pop. 1204
Map ref. 565 C9 | 581 F7

 Platypus Country Tourist Information Centre, Railway Park, Monaro Hwy; (02) 6458 4622; www.platypuscountry.org.au

87.6 Bombala FM, 103.7 Monaro FM, 810 AM Radio Local

Situated halfway between the Snowy Mountains and the Sapphire Coast, this charming small town has remained largely untouched by time. It is the centre for the surrounding wool, beef, lamb, vegetable and timber industries. The Bombala River is well known as a platypus habitat and for trout fishing. Bombala was considered as a site for Australia's capital city but missed out due to lack of water.

Railway Park There is much to see at Railway Park, including the historic engine shed (open by appt) and the museum of local artefacts and farm implements. The most unusual, though, is Lavender House, home to the oldest lavender association in the country. Lavender House has education facilities, displays on distillation and an array of lavender products such as lavender jams, soaps and oils. Monaro Hwy.

Endeavour Reserve: features a 2 km return walking track to a lookout with views over town; Caveat St. **Bicentennial Park:** wetlands and a pleasant river walk; Mahratta St. **Self-guide historical walk:** 1 hr walk includes courthouse (1882) and School of Art (1871); leaflet available from visitor centre.

Market: Imperial Hotel, Cnr Forbes and Maybe sts; 1st Sat each month. **Wool and Wood Festival:** Jan. **Celebrate Lavender:** Jan. **Celebration of Motorcycles:** Nov. **Riverside Festival:** celebration of diversity of regional crafts and products; Nov. **Historic Engine Shed Engine Rally:** even-numbered years, Nov.

Cosmo Cafe: country-style cafe; 133 Maybe St; (02) 6458 3510. **The Heritage Guest House:** eatery in heritage house; 121 Maybe St; (02) 6458 4464.

The Heritage Guest House: historic guesthouse; 121 Maybe St; (02) 6458 4464.

Platypus Sanctuary Bombala has one of the densest populations of platypus in NSW. They can be seen here in their natural environment from the Platypus Reserve Viewing Platform. The best times for viewing are at dawn and dusk, when platypus are at their most active, but they can be seen at any time of day. Off Monaro Hwy on the road to Delegate; 3 km S.

Cathcart: charming township with historical town walk and Cathcart Collectables, a fascinating collection of Monaro history; brochure from visitor centre; 14 km NE. **Myanba Gorge:** boardwalk and bushwalks through old-growth eucalypt forest with spectacular views of waterfalls, granite boulders and Towamba Valley. Enjoy a picnic or barbecue at the gorge. South East Forest National Park; 20 km SE. **Delegate:** scenic town with Early Settlers Hut, believed to be the first dwelling on the Monaro plains, and Platypus Walk and River Walk (leaflets from visitor centre); 36 km SW. **Scenic drive:** gold fossicking en route to Bendoc Mines in Victoria; 57 km SW. **Fly-fishing and trout fishing:** maps from visitor centre. **Mountain-biking:** there are many trails in nearby state forest areas; maps from visitor centre.

See also SOUTH COAST, p. 32

Bourke

Pop. 2145
Map ref. 561 M5

 Old Railway Station, Anson St; (02) 6872 1222; www.backobourke.com.au

101.1 FM ABC Radio National, 104.9 Rebel FM

The saying 'back o' Bourke' has come to mean the middle of nowhere, which is why Bourke is known as the gateway to the real outback. Bourke is a prosperous country town in the centre of thriving wool, cotton and citrus areas on the Darling River. It wasn't always so. Charles Sturt described it as 'unlikely to become the haunt of civilised man'. In 1835 Sir Thomas Mitchell came to the area and, thinking that the local Aboriginal people were a great threat, built himself a sturdy fort out of logs. Fort Bourke, as it became known, encouraged permanent settlement. Bourke quickly became a bustling major town, with Henry Lawson describing it as 'the metropolis of great scrubs'.

Back O' Bourke Exhibition Centre This fascinating modern facility is set among river red gums on the Darling River. It tells the story of the river and the outback from the Dreamtime to 100 years into the future. Visitors walk through colourful displays that re-create the past: paddleboats, early settlers and pastoralists, Afghan cameleers, Cobb & Co coaches, the history of unionism and Aboriginal heritage. The centre also looks at the sustainability of agriculture and the social structures of the outback. Kidman Way; (02) 6872 1321.

Old Railway Station: displays of Aboriginal artefacts and local history; Anson St. *Fred Hollows' Grave and Memorial:* the eye surgeon and famous humanitarian is buried in the cemetery; Cobar Rd. *Historic wharf replica:* reminder of days when Bourke was a busy paddlesteamer port. Take a paddlesteamer ride on the river; Sturt St. *Mateship Country Tours:* include historic buildings of Bourke (such as the Carriers Arms Inn, frequented by Henry Lawson) and surrounding citrus and grape farms; bookings at visitor centre.

Gecko Cafe: pasta, sandwiches; 27 Oxley St; (02) 6872 1701. *Morralls Bakery and Cafe:* sandwiches, pies; 37 Mitchell St; (02) 6872 2086.

Bourke Riverside Motel: heritage-listed accommodation; 3 Mitchell St; (02) 6872 2539. *Kidman's Camp:* riverside tourist park; Kidman Way, North Bourke; (02) 6872 1612.

Gundabooka National Park The park is a woodland haven for wildlife. There are over 130 species of bird, including the endangered pink cockatoo, pied honeyeater and painted honeyeater. Kangaroos, euros and endangered bats also make their homes here. Mt Gundabooka offers great walking tracks and a spectacular lookout. The Ngemba people have a history of ceremonial gatherings in the area and their art can be seen in some caves (to book tours, contact National Parks & Wildlife Service (02) 6872 2744). The park also provides excellent camping and barbecue facilities. 74 km s.

Fort Bourke Stockade replica: memorial to Sir Thomas Mitchell, who built the original fort; 20 km sw. *Mt Oxley:* home to wedge-tailed eagles and with views of plains from the summit. A key is needed for access to the mountain (collect from visitor centre); 40 km se. *Comeroo Camel Station:* working sheep and cattle station with artesian spa and outback experiences including a camel-drawn wagon; accommodation available; (02) 6874 7735; 150 km nw.

See also Outback, p. 36

Bowral

Pop. 11 496
Map ref. 553 C5 | 555 I8 | 565 G2

ⓘ **Southern Highlands Visitor Information Centre, 62–70 Main St, Mittagong; (02) 4871 2888 or 1300 657 559; www.southern-highlands.com.au**

102.9 2ST FM, 1431 AM ABC Radio National

Bowral is best known as the home town of 'the boy from Bowral', cricketing legend Sir Donald Bradman. There are Bradman tours,

a sporting ground and a museum. Now an up-market tourist town and the commercial centre of the Southern Highlands, Bowral's close proximity to Sydney made it a popular retreat for the wealthy in earlier times. This is still evident today in the magnificent mansions and gardens around town.

Bradman Museum A comprehensive history of cricket is on display, including an oak bat from the 1750s. The Don Bradman memorabilia collection includes the bat he used to score 304 at Headingley in 1934. A cinema plays Bradman footage and newsreels. The Bradman Walk through town takes in significant sites including the Don's two family homes. A leaflet is available from the museum. Bradman Oval; St Jude St; (02) 4862 1247.

The Milk Factory Gallery: art and design exhibition centre and cafe; Station St. *Bong Bong Street:* specialty shopping including books and antiques. *Historic buildings:* mostly in Wingecarribee and Bendooley sts; leaflet available from visitor centre.

Produce Market: Bowral Public School, Bendooley St; 2nd Sat each month. *Autumn Gardens in the Southern Highlands:* throughout region; Apr. *Tulip Time Festival:* Sept–Oct. *Bong Bong Races:* Nov.

Centennial Vineyards Restaurant: local produce, vineyard views; Woodside, Centennial Rd; (02) 4861 8701. *Hordern's Restaurant:* modern Australian; Milton Park Country House Hotel, Horderns Rd; (02) 4861 1522. *Onesta Cucina:* modern Italian; Shop 2, The Penders, cnr Station and Wingecarribee sts; (02) 4861 6620.

Milton Park Country House: historic resort-style accommodation; Horderns Rd; (02) 4861 8100. *Strathburn Cottage:* award-winning historic bed and breakfast: 85 Bowral St; (02) 4862 3391.

Mittagong This small and appealing town has historic cemeteries and buildings. Lake Alexandra in Queen St is artificial and great for birdwatching and walking. There is a market at the Uniting Church hall on the 3rd Sat each month. 8 km ne.

Mt Gibraltar: bushwalking trails and lookout over Bowral and Mittagong; 2 km n. *Box Vale Mine walking track:* begins at the northern end of Welby, passes through old railway tunnel; 12 km n. *Nattai National Park:* protects landforms, geological features, catchments and biodiversity in the Sydney Basin. Only low-impact activities are encouraged and there is a 3 km exclusion zone around Lake Burragorang; via Hilltop; 19 km n.

See also Southern Highlands, p. 24

Braidwood

Pop. 1108
Map ref. 554 H11 | 565 E5 | 567 K4

ⓘ **National Theatre, Wallace St; (02) 4842 1144; www.visitbraidwood.com.au**

94.5 Braidwood FM, 103.5 FM ABC Local

Braidwood is an old gold-rush area that has been declared a historic town by the National Trust. Gold was plentiful here in the 1800s, the largest gold discovery being 170 kilograms in 1869. With the discovery of gold came bushrangers, such as the Clarke Gang and Ben Hall, and Braidwood became one of the most infamous and dangerous towns in the region. The 19th-century buildings have been carefully maintained and restored, and are still in use. The town appears to be from a bygone era, which has come in handy for film producers, who have found Braidwood a perfect setting for movies such as *Ned Kelly* (1969), *The Year My Voice Broke* (1986) and *On Our Selection* (1994).

Braidwood Museum Built of local granite and originally the Royal Mail Hotel, the museum houses over 2100 artefacts and 900 photographs. On display are exhibits of Aboriginal history, goldmining, the armour worn by Mick Jagger in *Ned Kelly*, a machinery shed and a library of local records, newspapers and family histories. An unusual collection is from the Namchong family, who came here from China during the gold rush and became traders in town from the 1870s to the 1990s. Open Fri–Mon, daily during school holidays; Wallace St; (02) 4842 2310.

Galleries and craft and antique shops: details from visitor centre. *Tallaganda Heritage Trail and scenic drive:* tours of historic buildings such as the Royal Mail Hotel and St Andrew's Church; leaflet from visitor centre.

Picnic Race Meeting: Feb. *Braidwood Heritage Festival:* May. *Music at the Creek:* Nov. *The Quilt Event:* Nov.

Braidwood Bakery: pies, sandwiches; 99 Wallace St; (02) 4842 2541. *Braidwood Deli:* sandwiches, pies; Shop 1, 91 Wallace St; (02) 4842 1201.

Araluen Old Courthouse: fascinating historical B&B; The Old Courthouse, Araluen Rd; (02) 4846 4053. *Mona:* romantic retreat; 140 Little River Rd; (02) 4842 1288.

Monga National Park This park features a boardwalk through rainforest areas dating back to the ancient Gondwana period. Penance Grove, a small pocket of rainforest, is filled with ancient plumwood trees and tree ferns. Maps at visitor centre. Access via Kings Hwy; 20 km SE.

The Big Hole and Marble Arch The Big Hole is thought to have formed when overlying sandstone collapsed into a subterranean limestone cavern creating an impressive chasm 96 m deep and 50 m wide. Wildlife in the area includes native birds, echidnas, wallabies, wombats and tiger quolls. Marble Arch is a narrow canyon 3–4 m wide and 25 m deep. It is over 1 km in length and bands of marble are visible along the walls. There are caves along the way, but special permission is required to enter some of them. Some are very dark and require a torch, so it is best to check with the NSW National Parks & Wildlife Service if you intend to explore. Inquiries (02) 4887 7270; near Gundillion; 45 km S.

Scenic drives: rugged countryside; brochure from visitor centre. *Fishing:* good trout fishing, especially in the Mongarlowe and Shoalhaven rivers; details from visitor centre.

See also CAPITAL COUNTRY, p. 31

Brewarrina
Pop. 1123
Map ref. 561 O5

i Bathurst St; (02) 6830 5152; www.breshire.com

106.5 2CUZ FM, 657 AM ABC Local

This charming outback town on the banks of the Barwon River is affectionately known as Bre. It was developed in the 1860s as a river crossing for stock, but later thrived because of its position on a Cobb & Co route. Brewarrina was once a meeting place for Aboriginal tribes, with sacred sites including burial and ceremonial grounds, pointing to a culture that revolved around the river. By far the most impressive relics are the ancient stone fish traps of the Barwon River estimated to be 40 000 years old – among the oldest constructions in the world.

Aboriginal fish traps The traditional Aboriginal story states that the traps were built during a drought. Gurrungga, the water hole at Brewarrina, dried up and this opportunity was used to build the traps in the dry bed. The Ngemba people, who were facing famine, were never hungry again. Anthropologists claim the traps are impressive evidence of early engineering, river hydrology and knowledge of fish biology. Around 500 m long, these traps relied on the currents to sweep the fish inside, where they would be confined when the water level dropped. Thousands of years ago, the traps formed the centrepiece of a seasonal festival, regularly attended by up to 50 000 people from Aboriginal groups along the east coast. At night they held corroborees and shared stories around campfires in a language common to the region. The traps preserve the memory of these ancient times. Guided tours are available from visitor centre.

Aboriginal Cultural Museum: displays on aspects of Aboriginal life, from tales of the Dreamtime to the present; open Mon–Fri; Bathurst St. *Barwon Bridge:* one of two surviving examples of the first series of lift span bridges in the state (1889); Bridge Rd. *Wildlife park:* native fauna in bush setting; Doyle St. *Self-guide drive:* 19th-century buildings; brochure from visitor centre.

Barwon River Rodeo: Easter. *Brewarrina Annual Races:* May.

Bokhara Hutz: self-contained accommodation; Bokhara Plains; (02) 6874 4921.

Narran Lake Nature Reserve: wetlands and a breeding ground for native and migratory birds; access permits from visitor centre; 50 km NE. *Culgoa National Park:* wildlife unique to the western flood plains including falcons, striped-faced dunnat and pied bats. Information from visitor centre; 100 km N. *Fishing:* plentiful Murray cod in the Barwon River. *Start of Darling River Run:* self-drive tour; brochure from visitor centre.

See also OUTBACK, p. 36

Broken Hill
see inset box on next page

Bulahdelah
Pop. 1092
Map ref. 549 H4 | 550 C10 | 555 N3

i Cnr Pacific Hwy and Crawford St; (02) 4997 4981; www.greatlakes.org.au

101.5 FM Great Lakes, 1233 AM ABC Local

Bulahdelah is a pretty town at the foot of Bulahdelah Mountain (known to locals as Alum Mountain because of the alunite that was mined here). Surrounded by rainforests and the beautiful Myall Lakes, it is a popular destination for bushwalkers and watersports enthusiasts.

Bulahdelah Mountain Park A park of contrasts, with meandering walking trails taking in tall forest, rare orchids in spring and the remains of mining machinery. There are picnic and barbecue facilities and a lookout over Bulahdelah and the Myall Lakes. Meade St.

Bulahdelah Court House: museum featuring Bulahdelah's logging past, with cells out the back; open Sat mornings or by appt; Cnr Crawford and Anne sts; bookings on (02) 6597 4838.

Market: beside visitor centre, Crawford St; 1st Sat each month. *Bulahdelah Music Festival:* Jan. *The Bass Bash:* fishing festival; Feb. *Junior Rodeo:* July. *Bulahdelah Show:* campdraft and rodeo; Sept.

 RADIO STATIONS   IN TOWN   WHAT'S ON   WHERE TO EAT   WHERE TO STAY   NEARBY

BROKEN HILL

Pop. 18 856

Map ref. 560 B10 | 603 P1 | 605 O8

ⓘ **Cnr Blende and Bromide sts; (08) 8080 3560; www.visitbrokenhill.com.au**

📻 106.9 Hill FM, 999 AM ABC Local

In the vast, arid lands of far-western New South Wales, Broken Hill was first an intermittent home for the Willyama people; its lack of water made it impossible to settle permanently. When Charles Sturt encountered the area while searching for an inland sea, he described it as some of the most barren and desolate land he had ever seen. Enthusiasm was soon generated, however, with the discovery of silver and Broken Hill was born. A syndicate of seven men quickly bought much of the land and in 1885 they discovered the world's largest silver-lead-zinc lodes. Later that same year they decided to form a company and float shares. That company was Broken Hill Proprietary (BHP), now BHP Billiton, the largest mining company in the world. Referred to as the 'Silver City', Broken Hill is also the centre of the 16-million-hectare West Darling pastoral industry, which has 1.75 million merino sheep surrounded by a 600-kilometre dog-proof fence. As you would expect of a hot, arid mining town, Broken Hill has many pubs. Note that Broken Hill operates on Central Standard Time, half an hour behind the rest of New South Wales.

🏚 **Line of Lode Miners Memorial and Visitor Centre:** perched on top of the mullock heap at the centre of town, and delving into Broken Hill's mining heritage; Federation Way. **Railway, Mineral and Train Museum:** displays on old mining and rail services. Also incorporates the Hospital Museum and Migrant Museum; open 10am–3pm; Bromide St. **Geocentre:** displays of minerals, mining specimens and a silver tree; Cnr Crystal and Bromide sts; (08) 8087 6538. **Photographic Recollections:** more than 600 photos telling Broken Hill's history; Eyre St. **White's Mineral Art and Mining Museum:** walk-in mine and mining models; Allendale St. **Joe Keenan's Lookout:** view of town and mining dumps; Marks St. **Thankakali Aboriginal Arts and Crafts:** see works created on the premises, talk to artists and purchase pieces; cnr Buck and Beryl sts. **Muslim Mosque:** built by Afghan community in 1891; open 2–4pm Sun or by appt; Buck St. **Zinc Twin Lakes:** popular picnic spot at lakes used as a water source for mines; off Wentworth Rd, South Broken Hill. **Art galleries:** over 30 in town including Pro Hart Gallery, Wyman St; Jack Absalom Gallery, Chapple St; and Broken Hill Regional Art Gallery, Argent St, the oldest regional gallery in the state. **Heroes, Larrikins and Visionaries of Broken Hill Walk and Silver Trail self-guide historical town drive:** leaflets from visitor centre.

🌴 **St Patrick's Race Day:** horseraces; Mar/Apr. **Outback 4x4 Challenge:** 4WD rally; May. **Red Desert Live!:** music festival; Oct.

🍴 **Bells Milk Bar:** diner serving delicious milkshakes; 160 Patton St; (08) 8087 5380. **Broken Hill Musicians Club:** cafe, community club; 276 Crystal St; (08) 8088 1777.

🛏 **Royal Exchange Hotel:** Art Deco building; 320 Argent St; (08) 8087 2308 or 1800 670 160. **The Imperial Fine Accommodation:** luxury heritage-listed retreat; 88 Oxide St; (08) 8087 7444.

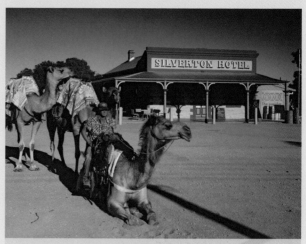

[CAMELS OUTSIDE THE SILVERTON HOTEL]

⊗ **Silverton** This National Trust–classified town was established when silver chloride was found 27 km NW of Broken Hill in 1883. It now has less than 100 inhabitants and is surrounded by stark, arid plains, making it popular with filmmakers wanting an outback setting. *Mad Max II* (1981), *Razorback* (1983), *Young Einstein* (1988), *The Adventures of Priscilla, Queen of the Desert* (1994) and *Dirty Deeds* (2001) have all been filmed here, and the Silverton Hotel displays photographs of the film sets on its walls. Take the Silverton Heritage Walking Trail (leaflet from visitor centre) and visit Silverton Gaol Museum. Silverton Camel Farm offers 15 min rides around the outskirts of town and 3-day safaris. Mundi Mundi Plain Lookout, a further 10 km N, affords views of the desolate yet awe-inspiring landscape. Daydream Mine, 13 km NE, operated in the 1880s and is now open for 1 hr guided tours, 10am–3.30pm daily.

Mutawintji National Park Bushwalks lead through a rugged terrain of colourful gorges, rockpools and creek beds, while Aboriginal rock engravings and paintings tell stories of creation. The land was returned to its traditional owners in 1998, and a historic site in the centre containing a vast gallery of rock art is accessed by tour only. Mutawintji Heritage Tours leave Homestead Creek Campground at 11am Wed and Sat Apr–Oct; contact Broken Hill Area Office for details (08) 8080 3200; 130 km NE.

Royal Flying Doctor Service base and visitor centre: headquarters, radio room and aircraft hangar open to visitors; at airport; 10 km S. **Living Desert:** magnificent sandstone sculptures set on a hillside (particularly striking at sunrise and sunset) and walking trails through the mulga-dotted landscape; leaflet available from visitor centre; Nine Mile Rd; 11 km N. **Dingo Fence:** longest fence in the world at 5300 km from Jimbour in Queensland to the Great Australian Bight. Originally constructed in the 1880s to halt rabbit invasion, now maintained to keep dingoes out of sheep grazing areas; 150 km NW. **Tours:** for 4WD, camel safaris, outback excursions and scenic flights; bookings at visitor centre.

See also OUTBACK, p. 36

Detours Cafe: homemade hamburgers; 82 Stroud St; (02) 4997 4755. *Myalla Cafe:* traditional cafe fare; 84 Stroud St; (02) 4997 4900.

Bombah Point Eco Cottages: luxurious self-contained cottages; 969 Bombah Point Rd; (02) 4997 4401. *Peacehaven Country Cottages:* self-contained cottages; 353 Upper Myall Rd; (02) 4997 8247.

Myall Lakes National Park Unspoiled coastal lakes and 40 km of beaches make this national park one of the most visited in the state. It is ideal for all types of watersports – canoe and houseboat hire is available, and Broughton Island, 2 km offshore, is a popular spot for diving. Enjoy the bushwalks and campsites set in the rainforest, heathlands and eucalypt forest. 12 km E.

Bulahdelah State Forest: with scenic picnic area and walking trails along old mining trolley lines, and one of the tallest trees in NSW – the 84 m flooded gum (*Eucalyptus grandis*); off The Lakes Way; 14 km N. *Wootton:* charming small town with a 6 hr rainforest walk along an old timber railway; 15 km N. *Sugar Creek Toymakers:* fine wooden toys and hand-painted dolls; (02) 4997 6142; 31 km E. *Seal Rocks:* fishing village with seals sometimes resting on the offshore rocks. Grey nurse sharks breed in underwater caves and whales pass by June–Aug. Sugarloaf Point Lighthouse (1875) has a lookout tower, and there are pleasant beaches and camping areas; 40 km E. *Wallingat National Park:* walking trails and picnic facilities. Stop at Whoota Whoota Lookout for sweeping views of forest, coast and lakes; 43 km NE.

See also HOLIDAY COAST, p. 27

Bundanoon

Pop. 2035
Map ref. 553 A6 | 555 I9 | 565 G3

Southern Highlands Visitor Information Centre, 62–70 Main St, Mittagong; (02) 4871 2888 or 1300 657 559; www.southern-highlands.com.au

97.3 FM ABC Local, 107.1 Highlands FM

Bundanoon is a quiet village with a European feel thanks to its green, tree-lined avenues. The first European to investigate the district was ex-convict John Wilson, who was sent by Governor Hunter to collect information on the area that would discourage Sydney convicts from trying to escape in this direction. Today the sleepy town is a popular yet unspoiled tourist destination with many delightful guesthouses and a health resort.

Craft shops and art galleries: several featuring local work; contact visitor centre for details. *Drive and walk to several lookouts:* map from visitor centre.

Market: Memorial Hall, Railway Ave; 1st Sun each month. *Bundanoon is Brigadoon:* highland gathering; Apr. *Village Garden Ramble:* Oct.

Ye Olde Bicycle Shoppe: popular cafe and bike hire; 9 Church St; (02) 4883 6043.

Tree Tops Country Guesthouse: Edwardian-style guesthouse; 101 Railway Ave; (02) 4883 6372.

Morton National Park, Bundanoon section This section of the park has stunning views, lookouts and walking trails. The park consists mainly of rainforest and eucalypts and is home to myriad native fauna including wallabies, potoroos and bush rats. See glow worms at night in the remarkable Glow Worm Glen.

1 km S. *For other sections of the park see Nowra, Robertson and Ulladulla.*

Exeter: quaint village with an English feel; 7 km N.

See also SOUTHERN HIGHLANDS, p. 24

Byron Bay
see inset box on next page

Camden
Pop. 3179
Map ref. 544 G11 | 553 E1 | 555 J7 | 565 H1

John Oxley Cottage, Camden Valley Way; (02) 4658 1370; www.visitcamden.com.au

C91.3 FM Campbelltown, 684 AM ABC Local

Camden, in a picturesque setting on the Nepean River just south-west of Sydney, was once a hunting ground of the Gundungurra people, who called it 'Benkennie', meaning 'dry land'. Governor Macquarie sent men to kill or imprison the Aboriginal people in 1816, and although records are poor, the brutal mission had some success. European settlement began after eight cattle wandered off four months after the First Fleet landed. They were not seen again until 1795 when it was discovered their number had grown to more than 40. The site on which they were found was named Cowpasture Plains, but was later changed to Camden. Camden was home to John and Elizabeth Macarthur, pioneers of the Australian wool industry, and also the first in Australia to grow tobacco, use mechanical irrigation, produce wine of respectable quality and quantity and make brandy. The Macarthurs sent thousands of vines to the Barossa Valley and are thereby credited with helping to start South Australia's wine industry.

Self-guide walk and scenic drive: includes historic buildings such as the Macarthur Camden Estate, St John the Evangelist Church and Kirkham Stables; brochure from visitor centre.

Produce Market: Cnr Exeter and Mitchell sts; 2nd and 4th Sat each month. *Craft and Fine Food Market:* Camden Showground; 3rd Sat each month (except Jan). *Food, Wine and Music Festival:* Sept. *Camden House Open Weekend:* Nov.

Enzo Italian Restaurant: modern Italian; 39 John St; (02) 4655 9260. *Impassion:* modern Australian; Level 1, 100 Argyle St; (02) 4655 8163.

Camden Valley Inn: stylish, comfortable accommodation; Remembrance Dr (Old Hume Hwy); (02) 4655 8413.

Camden Museum of Aviation This privately owned museum has the largest specialist aircraft collection in Australia. Where possible, the aircraft have been painstakingly restored (to a standard allowing them to taxi along a runway but not necessarily fly), with accurate wartime markings and camouflage colours carefully researched through service records and photographs. Open Sun and public holidays; (02) 4648 2419; 3 km NE.

Struggletown Fine Arts Complex: gallery featuring stained glass, pottery, traditional art and a restaurant; 3 km N. *Belgenny Farm:* includes Belgenny Cottage (1820) and the oldest surviving collection of farm buildings in Australia; (02) 4655 9651; 6 km SE. *Camden Aerodrome:* ballooning, gliding and scenic flights with vintage aircraft on display; (02) 4655 8064; 3 km NW. *Cobbity:* historic rural village with market 1st Sat each month; 11 km NW. *The Oaks:* small town in open countryside featuring the slab-built St Matthew's Church and Wollondilly Heritage Centre, a social history museum; 16 km W. *Burragorang Lookout:* views over Lake Burragorang; 24 km w. *Yerranderie:* this fascinating old silver-mining town can be reached by normal vehicle only in dry conditions, otherwise only by 4WD or plane; 40 km w. *Wineries:* several in the area; contact visitor centre for map; Gledswood (10 km N) features a working colonial farm.

See also SOUTHERN HIGHLANDS, p. 24

Campbelltown

Pop. 147 460

Map ref. 544 H11 | 553 F1 | 555 J7 | 565 H1

 15 Old Menangle Rd; (02) 4645 4921; www.visitmacarthur.com.au

C91.3 FM Campbelltown, 603 AM ABC Radio National

Campbelltown was founded in 1820 by Governor Macquarie and named after his wife, Elizabeth Campbell. While the town is being engulfed by the urban sprawl of Sydney, it manages to combine the best of two worlds, enjoying the convenience of city living with the rustic charm of 19th-century buildings. It is also the location of the legend of Fisher's ghost. In 1826 an ex-convict, Frederick Fisher, disappeared. Another ex-convict, George Worrell, claimed that Fisher had left town, leaving him in charge of Fisher's farm. A farmer claimed to have seen the ghost of Fisher pointing at the creek bank where his body was subsequently found. Worrell was tried and hanged for Fisher's murder.

Campbelltown Arts Centre Visitors can see, explore and participate in art-creation at this interactive centre. Exhibitions are diverse and include local, regional, national and international shows of art and craft. Behind the gallery is a sculpture garden established in 2001 as a Centenary of Federation project. New permanent sculptures are added to the garden on a regular basis. Adjacent to the gallery is the Koshigaya-tei Japanese Teahouse and Garden, a bicentennial gift to the people of Campbelltown from its sister city, Koshigaya. The garden is a peaceful area with a waterfall, koi pond and timber bridge, perfect for picnics and tranquil contemplation. Art Gallery Rd; (02) 4645 4100.

Campbelltown Visitor Information Centre: formerly St Patrick's, the first Catholic school in Australia, displays include early world maps, desks, inkwells, canes and curriculums (1840); Old Menangle Rd. *Stables Museum:* display of historic farm equipment and household goods on 1st, 3rd and 5th Sun each month; Lithgow St. *Self-guide heritage walks:* take in numerous historic buildings including St Peter's Church (1823), Emily Cottage (1840) and Fisher's Ghost restaurant, formerly Kendall's Millhouse (1844); leaflet from visitor centre.

Ingleburn Festival: Mar. *Autumn Harvest Food and Wine Fair:* Mar/Apr. *Festival of Fisher's Ghost:* Nov.

The Barn Restaurant: modern Australian; 12 Queen St; (02) 4625 4521.

Campbelltown Colonial Motor Inn: heritage-listed sandstone motel; 20 Queen St; (02) 4625 2345. *Rydges Hotel and Resort:* contemporary hotel; Old Menangle Rd; (02) 4645 0500.

Mt Annan Botanic Garden Australia's largest botanic garden is a striking 400 ha garden with 20 km of walking trails. Attractions include two ornamental lakes with picnic areas, a nursery, an arboretum, themed gardens, the rare and endangered plants garden and the banksia garden. The botanic garden is a haven to over 160 bird species and mammals such as the wallaroo and swamp wallaby. The human sundial allows visitors to tell the time by standing in its centre and raising their arms. Guided tours are available; (02) 4648 2477; 3 km w.

Sugarloaf Horse Centre: heritage-listed site with amazing views and trail-rides for all skill levels; (02) 4625 9565; 2.2 km sw. *Macarthur Centre for Sustainable Living:* showcasing sustainable homes, gardens and lifestyles. To promote sustainable living, the centre is entirely self-sufficient. Regular workshops are also held throughout the year; (02) 4647 9828; 3 km w. *Steam and Machinery Museum:* history of Australia's working past, including interactive displays; Menangle Rd; 5 km sw. *Menangle:* small town featuring a historic homestead (1834) and The Store (1904), an old-style country store with everything from antiques to ice-creams, and the Menangle Railway Bridge (1863), the colony's first iron bridge; 9 km sw. *Eschol Park House:* grand colonial home (1820) set in landscaped gardens; 15 km N. *Appin:* historic coalmining town with a monument to Hume and Hovell (who began their 1824 expedition to Port Phillip from this district). Also weekend markets in 10 locations (leaflet available from visitor centre) and a celebration of Scottish links through the Highland Gathering and Pioneer Festival each Nov; 16 km s.

See also SOUTHERN HIGHLANDS, p. 24

Canowindra

Pop. 1501

Map ref. 554 F5

 Age of Fishes Museum, Gaskill St; (02) 6344 1008; www.ageoffishes.org.au

104.3 FM ABC Radio National, 105.1 2GZ FM

Canowindra, meaning 'home' in the Wiradjuri language, is in the Lachlan Valley with sandstone mountains to the west and the old volcano, Mount Candobolas, to the north-east. Ben Hall and his gang struck in the town twice in 1863. During the first visit they robbed two homesteads and then forced residents and local police into Robinson's Inn (now the Royal Hotel), where they held an impromptu and compulsory two-day party. Two weeks later they returned and held a similar three-day party, reportedly at their own expense. Today Canowindra is still a genuine old-style country town with a National Trust–classified main street (Gaskill St) that follows the crooked path of an old bullock track. It is now known for balloons, fossils and boutique cellar doors. Canowindra calls itself the 'balloon capital of Australia' because there are more hot-air balloon flights here than anywhere else in the country. In 1956, 3500 fish fossils over 360 million years old were found in the area. Another major dig took place in 1993.

Age of Fishes Museum Long before dinosaurs walked the earth bizarre fish populated local rivers, including fish with armoured shells, fish with lungs and fish with jaws like crocodiles. The museum displays many of the fossils from the Devonian era found during the 1956 and 1993 digs along with information about the digs. There are also live aquarium displays and re-creations of life in the Devonian period. Gaskill St.

Historical museum: local history displays and agricultural equipment; weekends or by appt; Gaskill St. *Hot-air balloon rides:* over picturesque Lachlan Valley; Mar–Nov (weather permitting); details at visitor centre. *Historical tourist drive and riverbank self-guide walks:* include historic buildings of Gaskill St; brochure available from visitor centre.

Springfest: wine and art; Oct.

Taste Canowindra: lunches and cakes; 42 Ferguson St; (02) 6344 2332. *Tom's Waterhole Winery:* ploughman's lunches; 'Felton', Longs Corner Rd; (02) 6344 1819.

Everview Retreat: luxury self-contained cottages; 72 Cultowa La; (02) 6344 3116. *Falls Vineyard Retreat:* luxury homestead guesthouse; Belubula Way; (02) 6344 1293.

BYRON BAY

Pop. 4978

Map ref. 551 H4 | 557 O3 | 653 N12

ℹ️ 80 Jonson St; (02) 6680 8558; www.visitbyronbay.com

📻 92.2 FM North Coast Radio, 720 AM ABC Local

Byron Bay's excellent beaches, laid-back feel and great weather have made it a long-time destination for surfers, backpackers and alternative-lifestylers. A forward-thinking council moved early to ban all drive-in takeaway food outlets and all buildings more than three storeys high. Now people from all walks of life, including celebrities, flock to Byron Bay for whale-watching, surfing, swimming and relaxing. The town centre has an array of restaurants and cafes, shops selling discount surfboards, New Age products and interesting clothing, and galleries with everything from handmade jewellery to timber furniture. Day spas, yoga centres and natural therapy parlours offer expert pampering.

🏠 **Tours and activities:** everything from diving and sea-kayaking to surf lessons, skydiving and gliding; contact visitor centre for details. **Beach Hotel:** well-established venue for live music and dining, with a beer garden that has ocean views; cnr Jonson and Bay sts. **Beaches:** safe swimming at the patrolled Main Beach, and surfing at Clarkes Beach and the Pass; look out for 'sandologist' Steve Machell and his fabulous sand sculptures on Main or Clarkes beaches; there's more surfing at Wategos, child-friendly swimming at secluded Little Wategos, dogs are welcome at Belongil and Brunswick Heads, or go horseriding or beach-fishing at Seven Mile Beach stretching towards Lennox Head. **Health and wellbeing:** relax and unwind with a massage at Byron's numerous spas, including the tropical day spa at Buddha Gardens Balinese Spa, (02) 6680 7844; and Relax Haven at Belongil Beachhouse, (02) 6685 7868, with massage therapy and float tanks. **Byron Bay Arts & Industry Park:** arts precinct 3 km from town with artists', jewellers' and sculptors' studios, galleries, cafes and restaurants; Artist Trail guide from visitor centre.

🌴 **Market:** Butler St Reserve; 1st Sun each month. **Farmers Market:** Thurs mornings; Butler St Reserve. **East Coast Blues and Roots Festival:** Easter. **Splendour in the Grass:** music festival; July/Aug. **Byron Bay Writers Festival:** July/Aug. **Taste of Byron Food Fest:** Sept. **Buzz–Byron Bay Film Fest:** Oct.

🍴 **Byron Beach Cafe:** modern Australian; Clarkes Beach, Lawson St; (02) 6685 8400. **Dish Restaurant & Marvell Bar:** modern European; cnr Jonson and Marvel sts; (02) 6685 7320. **Fishmongers Cafe:** gourmet fish and chips; Bay La; (02) 6680 8080. **Pacific Dining Room:** modern Australian; Bay St; (02) 6680 7055. **Red Ginger:** eat dumplings in the store's front window; 2/111 Jonson St; (02) 6680 9779. **The Balcony Bar & Restaurant:** bohemian charm, world menu; cnr Lawson and Jonson sts; (02) 6680 9666. **Twisted Sista Cafe:** light meals and desserts; 1/4 Lawson St; (02) 6685 6810.

🛏️ **Amber Gardens Guesthouse:** small, reasonably priced guesthouse; 66 Plantation Dr, Ewingsdale; (02) 6684 8215. **Byron Retreat:** contemporary self-contained accommodation; Ewingsdale (address given on inquiry); 1300 660 422. **Rae's on Watego's:** iconic Byron Bay resort; 8 Marine Pde, Wategos Beach; (02) 6685 5366. **The Garden Burées:** Balinese-inspired bungalows and chalets; 17 Gordon St; (02) 6685 5390.

🌀 **Cape Byron** This headland forms part of the world's oldest caldera – the rim of an enormous extinct volcano (the centre is Mt Warning). It is the easternmost point on the mainland and provides breathtaking views up and down the coast. Dolphins can be seen year-round and humpback whales migrate up the coast June–July and back down Sept–Oct. Cape Byron Lighthouse, the 22 m structure completed in 1901, houses a visitor centre with displays of the area's cultural and natural history. 3 km SE.

Julian Rocks Aquatic Reserve: protects 450 underwater species and is great for diving; 3 km S. **Broken Head Nature Reserve:** rainforest, secluded beaches and dolphin-watching; 9 km S. **Bangalow:** scenic village with antique shops, arts and crafts, walking tracks and a popular market on 4th Sun each month; 10 km SW.

See also TROPICAL NORTH COAST, p. 28

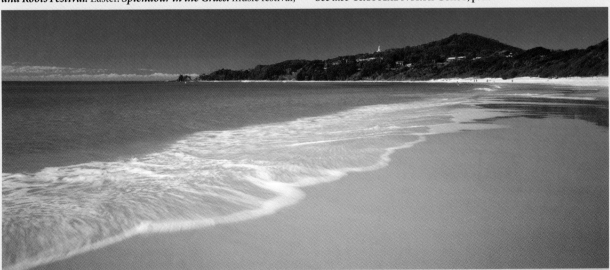

[BYRON BAY'S MAIN BEACH]

 RADIO STATIONS   IN TOWN   WHAT'S ON   WHERE TO EAT   WHERE TO STAY   NEARBY

CESSNOCK

Pop. 18 318

Map ref. 543 E2 | 549 A8 | 555 L4

i 455 Wine Country Dr, Pokolbin; (02) 4990 0900;
www.winecountry.com.au

96.5 CHR-FM Community Radio, 1044 AM ABC Local

Cessnock was once a coalmining town, but that was before the Hunter Valley, of which Cessnock is at the southern end, began producing some of Australia's best wines. A visit to Cessnock almost guarantees relaxation as it focuses on fresh produce and wine in the spectacular scenery of rainforests and green valleys.

Galleries and antique and craft shops: brochures from visitor centre.

Harvest Festival: throughout region; Mar–Apr. *Hunter Semillon and Seafood Festival:* Apr. *Jazz in the Vines:* Oct. *Opera in the Vineyards:* Oct.

Swill N Grill: international; The Australia Hotel, 136 Wollombi Rd; (02) 4990 1256. *The Kurrajong Restaurant:* pub bistro; Cessnock Hotel, 234 Wollombi Rd; (02) 4990 1002. *Esca Bimbadgen:* modern Australian; Bimbadgen Estate, 790 McDonalds Rd, Pokolbin; (02) 4998 7585.

Cessnock Heritage Inn: comfortable, affordable B&B; 167 Vincent St; (02) 4991 2744. *Greta Main Pay Office B&B:* guesthouse in historic surrounds; 988 Wollombi Rd, Greta Main; (02) 4998 1703. *Peppers Guest House:* 48 deluxe rooms; Ekerts Rd, Pokolbin; (02) 4993 8999.

Hunter Valley Wine Region Over 120 wineries, most open for cellar-door tastings. Older establishments include Tyrrell's (Broke Rd, Pokolbin; (02) 9889 4450), while newcomers include Tulloch Wines (Cnr McDonalds and DeBeyers rds, Pokolbin; (02) 4998 7580). Bimbadgen Estate is a lovely place to stop for lunch (790 McDonalds Rd, Pokolbin; (02) 4998 7585). Further details from visitor centre.

Watagan National Park: this park features several lookout points over mountains and valleys, including the lookout at Gap Creek Falls that reveals rainforest gullies of magnificent red

[OAK BARRELS AT ALLANDALE WINERY, LOWER HUNTER VALLEY]

cedar and Illawarra flame trees. There are many scenic rainforest walks along the creek, which is ideal for swimming. Some walks lead to picnic and barbecue facilities at Heaton, Hunter and McLean's lookouts and the serene Boarding House Dam picnic area; 33 km SE. *Hunter Valley Zoo:* hands-on zoo where most animals (native and introduced) can be patted and fed; 7 km NW. *Lovedale:* home of the Long Lunch (food, wine and music), held at various vineyards in May; 10 km N. *Bimbadeen Lookout:* spectacular views over Hunter Valley; 10 km E. *Hunter Valley Cheese Factory:* factory tours, tastings and sales; McGuigan Cellars Complex, McDonalds Rd; 13 km NW. *Richmond Vale Railway Museum:* rail and mining museum with steam-train rides and John Brown's Richmond Main Colliery, once the largest shaft mine in the Southern Hemisphere; 17 km NE. *Wollombi:* picturesque village with a wealth of historic sandstone buildings. Tour the Aboriginal cave paintings (inquire at general store). Visit Undercliff Winery and Studio (for etchings); 29 km SW. *Galleries and craft shops:* arts and crafts by local artists; maps from visitor centre.

See also HUNTER VALLEY & COAST, p. 26

Gondwana Dreaming Historical Fossil Digs Tours of 1–6 days can be arranged to go on real archaeological digs led by palaeontologists to learn about and possibly find fossils. The tours promote hands-on learning and focus on the area as a whole, including local flora and fauna. This program funds ongoing scientific research. Bookings on (02) 6285 1872.

Wineries and vineyards: cellar-door tastings and tours; maps from visitor centre.

See also CENTRAL WEST, p. 30

Casino

Pop. 9398

Map ref. 551 E5 | 557 N3 | 653 M12

i 86 Centre St; (02) 6662 3566;
www.richmondvalley.nsw.gov.au

107.9 COW FM, 738 AM ABC Local

Beside the Richmond River in the north-east of the state, Casino is a town of grand old buildings and magnificent parklands.

Casino is named after the beautiful Italian town of Monte Cassino and is known as the beef capital of Australia. More than 12 000 cattle are sold each year at the Casino Livestock Selling Centre.

 Jabiru Geneebeinga Wetlands These parklands have picnic facilities and are home to native bird species and wildlife including the jabiru (black-necked stork), egret and black swan. The park is circled by a mini-railway that operates each Sun. West St.

Casino Folk Museum: locally significant documents and photographs; open Mon, Wed afternoons and Sun mornings; Walker St. *Self-guide heritage and scenic walks and drives:* include Bicentennial Mural, St Mark's Church of England and Cecil Hotel; maps available from visitor centre.

Flower and Art Show: Mar. *Beef Week Festival:* May. *Gold Cup:* horseracing; May. *Primex:* primary industry exhibition; June.

Clydesdale Motel and Steak Barn: steakhouse; Bruxner Hwy; (02) 6662 5982.

Clydesdale Motel and Steak Barn: unpretentious country accommodation; Bruxner Hwy; (02) 6662 5982.

 Fossicking: gold, labradorite and quartz (both smoky and clear types); maps from visitor centre. *Freshwater fishing:* Cookes Weir and Richmond River are popular fishing spots; maps from visitor centre.

See also TROPICAL NORTH COAST, p. 28

Cobar

Pop. 4127
Map ref. 561 L9

ⓘ Great Cobar Heritage Centre, Barrier Hwy; (02) 6836 2448; www.cobar.nsw.gov.au

📻 103.7 Zoo FM, 810 AM ABC Local

Cobar got its name from the Aboriginal word 'kubbur', meaning 'burnt earth'. The story goes that three European settlers were camping at Kubbur watering hole near where Cobar is today when they noticed the unusual colour of the water. They took samples and showed them to the publicans at the Gilgunnia Pub who identified them as copper ore. From this discovery, the Cobar mining industry was born. The mines made Cobar so prosperous that at one point the town had a population of 10 000 and its own stock exchange. Mines still operate, including the CSA Copper Mine which is the deepest in Australia. Today Cobar is a surprisingly green and picturesque outback town.

🏠 **Great Cobar Outback Heritage Centre** This centre has displays on the local mining of copper, gold and silver-lead-zinc, an authentic re-creation of a local woolshed and displays on Aboriginal culture. Learn about the chronic water shortages in the early days of European settlement and the bush skills the settlers needed to survive the harsh environment. The Centenary of Federation Walking Track begins here and is a 2 hr scenic walk past mines and a slag dump. Barrier Hwy; (02) 6836 2448.

Commonwealth Meteorological Station: visitors can view the radar tracking process and the launching of weather balloons at 9.15am and 3.15pm daily (Eastern Standard Time). Louth Rd; inquiries (02) 6836 2149. *Golden Walk:* tour the operating Peak Gold Mine or view from observation deck; Kidman Way; (02) 6830 2265. *Self-guide heritage walks and heritage bus tours:* historic buildings including the courthouse and the Great Western Hotel (with the longest iron-lace verandah in NSW), and mining and agricultural sites around town; brochure from visitor centre.

🌴 *Festival of the Miner's Ghost:* Oct.

🍴 *Copper City Restaurant:* modern Australian; 40 Lewis St; (02) 6836 1022. *Empire Hotel:* steaks, pub food; 6 Barton St; (02) 6836 2725.

🌐 **Mt Grenfell Historic Site** The 5 km Ngiyambaa Walkabout leads visitors on a scenic tour with breathtaking views of the Cobar area. There are hundreds of Aboriginal stencils and paintings of great cultural significance in spectacular reds, yellows and ochres on rock overhangs along the trail. Picnic and barbecue facilities are available. Off Barrier Hwy; 67 km NW.

The Old Reservoir and Devil's Rock: Devil's Rock was a site for ceremonial rites for the Ngemba people. Good swimming and watersports at the reservoir; 3 km N. *Mount Drysdale:* deserted mining town where visitors can investigate old mine shafts and remains of the town. Features historic Aboriginal sites including rock wells; permission required (02) 6836 3462; 34 km N.

See also OUTBACK, p. 36

Coffs Harbour

see inset box on next page

Cooma

Pop. 6587
Map ref. 565 C7 | 566 G9 | 581 E3

ⓘ 119 Sharp St; (02) 6450 1742 or 1800 636 525; www.visitcooma.com.au

📻 92.1 FM 2XL, 97.7 Snow FM, 810 AM ABC Local

The regional centre of the Snowy Mountains, Cooma was once dubbed Australia's most cosmopolitan city, thanks to the thousands of migrants who flocked to the region to work on the Snowy Mountains Hydro-Electric Scheme. It is a charming and bustling centre with visitors coming for the snow in winter and the greenery and crisp mountain air in summer. Motorists are advised to stop here to check tyres and stock up on petrol and provisions before heading into the alpine country.

🏠 **Centennial Park** Originally a swamp, Centennial Park was established in 1890. During WW II slit trenches were dug here in case of air attacks. The Avenue of Flags was constructed in 1959 to commemorate the 10th anniversary of the Snowy Mountains Hydro-Electric Scheme with one flag for each of the 27 nationalities of the workers. The Time Walk depicts the district's history in 40 ceramic mosaics laid below the flags. There is also a sculpture of Banjo Paterson's famous 'Man from Snowy River'. Sharp St.

Snowy Mountains Hydro-Information and Education Centre: interactive displays, photographs, models and films on the scheme. A memorial next door commemorates the 121 people killed while working on it. Monaro Hwy; inquiries 1800 623 776. *NSW Corrective Services Museum:* features unique displays of over 200 years of history, from convicts through to the modern prison system in the old Cooma Gaol; Vale Street; (02) 6452 5974. *Southern Cloud Park:* features Southern Cloud Memorial, a display of remains of the aircraft *Southern Cloud*, which crashed in the region in 1931 and was found in 1958. *Bike path:* picturesque path following Cooma Creek between Lambie St and Rotary Oval. *Historic railcar:* trips from Cooma to Bunyan on weekends; bookings at visitor centre. *Lambie Town self-guide walk:* designed in 1985, with over 5 km of easy walking. The tour incorporates three National Trust heritage areas including Lambie St, lined with huge oaks, pines and elms, and St Paul's Church, constructed with local alpine ash and granite and with striking stained-glass windows; brochure available from visitor centre.

🌴 *Market:* Centennial Park; 3rd Sun each month. *Rodeo:* Feb. *Back to Earth Festival:* Apr. *Cooma Festival:* Oct. *Cooma Street Fair:* celebrating Cooma's multicultural society; Nov. *Cooma Races and Sundowner Cup:* Dec.

🍴 *The Lott Food Store:* excellent cafe and bakery; 178–180 Sharp St; (02) 6452 1414.

🏠 *Feathers B&B:* romantic retreat; 12 Cosgrove St, Bredbo; (02) 6454 4151.

Tuross Falls Part of Wadbilliga National Park, the stunning Tuross Falls are a drop of 35 m. A picturesque 2 km walk from the camping area at Cascades leads visitors to the lookout platform, with views of the falls and the Tuross River Gorge. 30 km E.

Kosciuszko Memorial: donated in 1988 by the Polish government to commemorate Tadeuz Kosciuszko, after whom Australia's highest mountain is named; 2.5 km N. *Mt Gladstone Lookout:* impressive views, mountain-bike trails and Austrian teahouse; 6.5 km W. *Transylvania Winery:* cellar-door tastings of cool-climate organic wines; Monaro Hwy; 14 km N. *Whitewater rafting:* Snowy River tours from half-day to 2-day overnight trips; pick-up from Cooma, Jindabyne or Thredbo; bookings on 1800 677 179.

See also SNOWY MOUNTAINS, p. 33

Coonabarabran

Pop. 2605
Map ref. 556 E9

🛈 Newell Hwy; (02) 6849 2144 or 1800 242 881; www.warrumbungleregion.com.au

📻 92.9 FM Tamworth's Hit Music Station, 549 AM ABC Local

Coonabarabran is located on the Castlereagh River and is nestled in the foothills of the stunning Warrumbungle Mountain Range. It is known as the 'Astronomy Capital of Australia' as it has some of the clearest skies in the country, and is the gateway to the striking scenery of the Warrumbungles.

Information centre The Australian Museum worked with Warrumbungle Shire Council to produce the unique Diprotodon Display. The diprotodon is the largest marsupial that ever lived and the skeleton on show was found in a creek bed 40 km east of town in 1979. Newell Hwy.

Crystal Kingdom: unique collection of minerals, including zeolite crystals and fossils, from the Warrumbungle Range; Newell Hwy; (02) 6842 1927. *Newcastle Hats:* hat factory outlet store; Ulan St. *The Art Gallery of C:* regularly changing exhibitions by local artist, Claudia Stern; Cassilis St; (02) 6842 1462.

Market: Dalgamo St; last Sun each month. *Bunny Bazaar:* includes markets; Easter. *Festival of the Stars:* includes Coona Cup Racing Carnival; Oct.

Blue Wren Cafe: cafe and pottery shop; Pilliga Pottery, Dandry Rd; (02) 6842 2239. *Tulips Restaurant:* international cuisine; Country Comfort Coonabarabran, cnr Newell and Oxley hwys; (02) 6842 1188 or 1300 650 464.

Acacia Motor Lodge: contemporary, spacious accommodation; Newell Hwy; (02) 6842 1922. *Amber Court:* 21 ground-floor units; Newell Hwy; (02) 6842 1188. *El Paso Motel:* convenient ground-floor suites; Newell Hwy; (02) 6842 1722. *Pilliga Pottery Old Schoolhouse:* unique, spacious retreat; Pilliga Pottery, Dandry Rd; (02) 6842 2239.

 Warrumbungle National Park Forested ridges, rocky spires and deep gorges coupled with excellent camping and visitor facilities have made this one of the state's most popular parks. Highlights include the Breadknife, a 90 m high rock wall, and the Grand High Tops walking trail with fabulous views of ancient volcanic remains. The park is outstanding for rock climbing, but climbing is prohibited on the Breadknife and permits are required for other areas (contact visitor centre). The Crooked Mountain Open Air Concert takes place here in Nov. Guided

nature walks are conducted during school holidays or by appt. 35 km W.

Warrumbungle Observatory: night-sky viewing of the stars through computerised telescopes; National Park Road; 0488 425 112; 10 km W. *Siding Springs Observatory:* Australia's largest optical telescope, with a hands-on exhibition, science shop and cafe; National Park Rd; (02) 6842 6211; 27 km W. *Pilliga Pottery:* terracotta pottery, showrooms and tearooms in an attractive bushland setting; off Newell Hwy; (02) 6842 2239; 34 km NW. *Barkala Bird Tours:* guided birdwatching tours; off Newell Highway; (02) 6842 2239, 34 km NW. *Sandstone caves:* formed by natural erosion of sandstone, these impressive caves are not signposted, so visitors are advised to seek directions from the visitor centre; 35 km N. *Pilliga Forest:* 450 000 ha of white cypress and ironbark trees, with plains of dense heath and scrub. It is an excellent habitat for koalas, which can be spotted from signposted viewing areas. Also scenic forest drives and walking trails; maps available from the visitor centre; 44 km NW. *Local wineries:* open for tastings and cellar-door sales; contact visitor centre for details.

See also CENTRAL WEST, p. 30

Coonamble

Pop. 2550
Map ref. 556 C8

🛈 26 Castlereagh St; (02) 6822 4532; www.coonamble.org

📻 91.9 MTM FM, 648 AM ABC Local

Coonamble owes its existence to the discovery of artesian water in the area in the 1890s. On the Great Inland Way, the route via Coonamble provides an alternative to the more commonly taken coastal route between Queensland and the southern states. This town lost many of its buildings in the great fire of 1929. Castlereagh Street had to be rebuilt, so most constructions are relatively modern. Coonamble is also the birthplace of Sir Edward Hallstrom, the pioneer of refrigeration.

Historical Museum Housed in the old police station, the museum outlines the rich Aboriginal and pastoral history of Coonamble through photographs, household items and stables. Behind the museum is an authentic Cobb & Co coach and stables. Open by appt (02) 6822 4532; Aberford St.

Warrana Creek Weir: swimming, boating and fishing; southern outskirts of town. *Self-guide town walk:* takes in historic sites; brochure from visitor centre.

Rodeo and Campdraft: largest combined event in Southern Hemisphere; June. *Gold Cup Race Meeting:* Oct.

Sons of the Soil Hotel: bistro-style meals; 54 Castlereagh St; (02) 6822 1009.

Castlereagh Lodge Motel: comfortable, affordable accommodation; 81 Aberford St; (02) 6822 1999. *Coonamble Motel:* comfortable riverside accommodation; 86 Castlereagh St; (02) 6822 1400.

Quambone Locally known as the gateway to Macquarie Marshes, Quambone also has Australia's smallest library and the Marthaguy Picnic Races in Sept. 55 km W.

Gulargambone: a small town with a restored steam train in Memorial Park; 45 km S. *Macquarie Marshes:* 80 km W; *see Nyngan.*

See also CENTRAL WEST, p. 30

COFFS HARBOUR

Pop. 47 710
Map ref. 550 H1 | 551 E12 | 557 N8

[COFFS HARBOUR'S HISTORIC JETTY]

ℹ️ Cnr Pacific Hwy and McLean St; (02) 6648 4990 or 1300 369 070; www.coffscoast.com.au

📻 107.9 2AIR FM, 819 AM ABC Local

Coffs Harbour, a subtropical holiday town on Coffs Coast, is known for its banana plantations (and the iconic Big Banana) and for its great fishing. The combination of great weather, stunning hinterland forests, sandy beaches and a growing cosmopolitan centre make Coffs Harbour a popular spot for tourists seeking fun and relaxation.

🏠 **Muttonbird Island Nature Reserve** Visitors can get an up-close look at the life cycle of one of Australia's most interesting migratory birds. The wedge-tailed shearwaters (muttonbirds) fly thousands of kilometres from South-East Asia each August, with large numbers settling at Muttonbird Island to breed. A walking trail winds through the burrows of the birds, which can be seen Aug–Apr. Muttonbird Island is also a vantage point for whale-watching June–Nov and is a great place for fishing and picnics. Access is via a 500 m walk along the sea wall from the harbour.

Bunker Cartoon Gallery: largest private collection of cartoons in the Southern Hemisphere, housed in a WW II bunker; City Hill; (02) 6651 7343. *Legends Surf Museum:* displays of classic photography, videos and equipment; Sapphire. *Coffs Harbour City Gallery:* varied program of contemporary art exhibitions; Cnr Coff and Duke sts. *Coffs Harbour Historical Museum:* pioneer artefacts and photographs, and the original lantern of the lighthouse built on Split Solitary Island in 1880; Harbour Dr. *Coffs Harbour International Marina:* departure point for fishing charters, scuba diving and whale-watching trips (June–Nov); Marina Dr. *North Coast Regional Botanical Gardens Complex:* rainforest, mangrove boardwalks, herbarium and diverse birdlife; Hardacre St. *Pet Porpoise Pool:* performing dolphins and seals with research and nursery facilities; Orlando St. *Self-guide walks:* include Jetty Walk and Coffs Creek Walk; maps from visitor centre.

🌴 *Growers market:* Harbour Dr; Thurs Nov–Mar. *Market:* jetty, Harbour Dr; Sun. *Uptown Market:* Vernon St; Sun.

Pittwater and Coffs Harbour Offshore Series: yachting; Jan. *Sawtell Chilli Festival:* July. *International Buskers and Comedy Festival:* Sept–Oct. *Food and Wine Festival:* Oct.

🍴 *Butterfly House Maze & Tearooms:* cafe, tourist attraction; 5 Strouds Rd; (02) 6653 4766. *Caffe Fiasco:* northern Italian; 22 Orlando St; (02) 6651 2006. *Ocean Front Brasserie:* spectacular views and seafood platters; Coffs Harbour Deep Sea Fishing Club, 1 Jordan Espl; (02) 6651 2819. *Shearwater Restaurant:* seafood; 321 Harbour Dr; (02) 6651 6053.

🛏️ *Breakfree Aanuka Beach:* absolute beachfront accommodation; 11 Firman Dr, Diggers Beach; (02) 6652 7555. *Sante Fe Luxury B&B:* casually elegant accommodation; 235 The Mountain Way; (02) 6653 7700.

🧭 **Big Banana** Large banana-shaped landmark with displays on the banana industry, a skywalk, giant water slide and an Aboriginal Dreamtime cave experience; 4 km N.

Bindarri National Park Not for the unseasoned bushwalker, Bindarri National Park is a largely untouched forest without facilities, but amazing views reward those who make the effort. The headwaters of the Urumbilum River form breathtaking waterfalls in a remote and rugged setting. Pockets of old-growth forest are scattered across the plateau and rich rainforest protects the steeper slopes. While there are no campgrounds, backpack camping is allowed and there are bushwalking trails to follow. 20 km W.

Clog Barn: Dutch village with clogmaking; Pacific Hwy; 2 km N. *Bruxner Park Flora Reserve:* dense tropical jungle area of vines, ferns and orchids with bushwalking trails, picnic area and Sealy Lookout; Korora; 9 km NW. *Butterfly House:* enclosed subtropical garden with live native and exotic butterflies; Bonville; 9 km S. *Adventure tours:* include whitewater rafting, canoeing, reef-fishing, diving, horseriding through rainforest, surf rafting, skydiving, helicopter flights, go-karting and surf schools; see visitor centre for brochures and bookings.

See also HOLIDAY COAST, p. 27

Cootamundra

Pop. 5565
Map ref. 554 D8 | 565 A2

 Railway station, Hovell St; (02) 6942 4212; www.cootamundra.nsw.gov.au

107.7 Star FM, 675 AM ABC Local

This prosperous rural service centre and major junction on the railway line between Sydney and Melbourne prides itself on being the birthplace of cricketing legend Sir Donald Bradman. Much reference is made to him and to cricket around the town. Cootamundra also lends its name to the famous Cootamundra wattle (*Acacia baileyana*), which blooms in the area each July and August, and Cootamundra Gold, the locally produced canola oil.

Pioneer Park This natural bushland reserve on the northern outskirts of town has a scenic 1.3 km walking trail to the top of Mt Slippery. At the summit there are panoramic views. The park also has excellent picnic sites. Backbrawlin St.

Bradman's birthplace: restored cottage where 'the greatest batsman the world has ever known' was born. Contains memorabilia from cricket and his life in the Cootamundra district; Adams St. *Arts Centre:* community arts space with exhibitions, workshops, art sales and a theatre; Wallendoon St. *Memorabilia Cottage:* displays local history memorabilia and bric-a-brac; Adams St. *Captains Walk:* bronze sculptures of Australia's past cricket captains; Jubilee Park, Wallendoon St. *Heritage Centre:* local memorabilia including an Olympic cauldron and war relics; railway station, Hovell St. *Self-guide 'Two Foot Tour':* includes Sir Donald Bradman's birthplace and the town's historic buildings; brochure from visitor centre. *Local crafts:* at visitor centre and at Art and Craft Centre, Hovell St.

Markets: Fisher Park, 2nd Sun each month; Wallendbeen, 1st Sun each month. *Wattle Time Festival:* Aug. *Rose Show:* Nov.

Country Cuisine: cafe with homemade sweet treats; 265 Parker St; (02) 6942 1788. *Helen's Coffee Lounge:* cafe-style fare or hearty mains; 248 Parker St; (02) 6942 7400.

Heritage Motel: executive motel accommodation; 94 Hurley St; 1300 221 000. *The White Ibis:* elegant boutique B&B; 21 Wallendoon St; (02) 6942 1850.

Murrumburrah This small rural community has the Harden–Murrumburrah Historical Museum, which is open weekends and features pioneer artefacts, an old chemist shop exhibit and early Australian kitchenwares. Also in town are local craft shops and some outstanding picnic spots. 35 km NE. Stocks Native Nursery in Harden, 2 km E on Simmonds Rd, features 1.5 ha of native bush garden with a scenic walking trail and billabong. The Picnic Races are held here in Nov.

Green Tree Indigenous Food Gardens: Australian bush garden divided into different zones providing education on how indigenous people survived on bush tucker; tours available; (02) 6943 2628; 8 km N. *Migurra Reserve:* bushland walking trail with birdwatching and 5 species of wattles; 15 km SW. *The Milestones:* cast-concrete sculptures representing the importance of wheat to the area; 19 km NE. *Bethungra:* dam ideal for canoeing and sailing. The rail spiral is an unusual engineering feat; 23 km SW. *Kamilaroi Cottage Violets:* violet farm with tours by appt; bookings (02) 6943 2207; 25 km N. *Illabo:* charming town with impressive clock museum; 33 km SW. *Cellar doors:* in the Harden area; winery brochure from visitor centre.

See also RIVERINA, p. 34

Corowa

Pop. 5628
Map ref. 559 M12 | 585 I5 | 586 F1

 88 Sanger St; (02) 6033 3221 or 1800 814 054; www.visitcorowashire.com.au

105.7 FM The River, 675 AM ABC Local

Corowa has been known for its goldmining, winemaking, timber milling and as the 'birthplace of Federation'. Traders in the 19th century had to pay taxes both in New South Wales and Victoria when taking goods over the border, which caused much agitation. It was argued that free trade would benefit everyone and the Border Federation League was formed in Corowa, which led to the 1893 Corowa Federation Conference. In 1895 the proposals put forth at the conference were acted upon and on 1 January 1901 the Commonwealth of Australia was born.

Federation Museum This museum focuses on the reasons behind Federation and Corowa's involvement in it. Also on display are local Aboriginal artefacts, Tommy McRae sketches, horse-drawn vehicles and saddlery, and antique agricultural implements. Open Sat and Sun afternoons; Queen St.

Murray Bank Yabby Farm: catch and cook yabbies, go canoeing and enjoy a picnic or barbecue; Federation Ave; (02) 6033 2922. *Self-guide historical town walk:* includes Sanger St, Corowa's historic main street with its century-old verandahed buildings. Guide available for groups; brochure from visitor centre.

Market: Bangerang Park; 1st Sun each month (except Feb). *Federation Festival:* Jan. *Billycart Championships:* Easter.

Easdown House Restaurant: modern Australian; 1 Sanger St; (02) 6033 4077.

Rivergum Holiday Retreat: family resort-style accommodation; 386 Honour Ave; (02) 6033 1990. *Savernake Farmstay Cottage:* self-catering cottage; Mulwala–Savernake Rd; (02) 6035 9415.

All Saints Estate Situated in the respected Rutherglen district, All Saints is a winery like no other. Behind the hedge fence and imposing set of gates lies an enormous medieval castle built by the original owner, George Smith, based on the Castle of Mey in Scotland. Now owned and operated by Peter Brown (of the famous Brown Brothers), All Saints offers a large cellar-door operation, a renowned restaurant, The Keg Factory, Indigo Cheese and beautiful gardens. Inquiries (02) 6035 2222; 5 km SW.

Corowa Jump Shak: skydiving and gliding weekends, weather permitting; off Redlands Rd; (02) 6033 2435. *Savernake Station:* offers eco-heritage tours of their 400 ha woodland including 120 bird species, woodshed and shearers quarters (1912) and cooks museum (1930) and store; inquiries (02) 6035 9415; 50 km NW.

See also MURRAY, p. 35

Cowra

Pop. 8426
Map ref. 554 F6

 Olympic Park, Mid Western Hwy; (02) 6342 4333; www.cowratourism.com.au

99.5 Star FM, 549 AM ABC Local

Cowra is nestled in the Lachlan Valley, where you can enjoy local food and wine. The peaceful air of this town on the Lachlan River belies its dramatic history. The Cowra Breakout is an infamous World War II incident in Australia when 1000 Japanese POWs staged a mass breakout that was the biggest in British and

Australian war history. While it remains what Cowra is most famous for, the town has moved forward.

 Australia's World Peace Bell Each country has only one peace bell and it is normally located in the nation's capital, but Cowra was awarded Australia's Peace Bell owing to local efforts for peace. The bell is a replica of the United Nations World Peace Bell in New York City and was made by melting down coins donated from 103 member countries of the United Nations. It is rung each year during the Festival of International Understanding. Darling St.

Japanese Garden This garden, opened in 1979, is complete with a cultural centre (with a collection of Japanese artwork and artefacts), a traditional teahouse, a bonsai house and a pottery. The garden itself represents the landscape of Japan, with mountain, river and sea re-created. From here gracious Sakura Ave, lined with cherry trees that blossom in spring, leads to the site of the POW camp and to the Australian and Japanese cemeteries. The camp includes the original foundations and replica guardtower, with photo displays and signage; audio tours available. Off Binni Creek Rd; (02) 6341 2233.

Olympic Park: information centre with a fascinating interpretive POW display and theatre. Also here is Cowra Rose Garden with over 1000 rose bushes in over 100 varieties; Mid Western Hwy. *Cowra–Italy Friendship Monument:* in recognition of Italians who died in WW II (Italian POWs interned at Cowra formed a strong friendship with the town); Kendal St. *Lachlan Valley Railway Museum:* displays and train rides; Campbell St. *Cowra Mill Winery:* winery in former flour mill (1861) with cellar-door tastings and restaurant; Vaux St; (02) 6341 4141. *Aboriginal murals:* by local artist Kym Freeman on pylons of bridge over the Lachlan River. *Cowra Heritage Walk:* Federation, colonial and Victorian buildings including the town's first hotel and oldest home; map from visitor centre.

Farmers market: showgrounds; 3rd Sat each month. *Festival of International Understanding:* Mar. *Picnic Races:* July. Cowra Wine Show: July. *Sakura Matsuri:* cherry blossom festival; Sept/Oct. *Cowra Cork and Fork:* Nov.

Neila: modern Australian; 5 Kendal St; (02) 6341 2188.

Country Gardens Motor Inn: spacious, comfortable accommodation; 75 Grenfell Rd; (02) 6341 1100. *Old Milburn Schoolhouse B&B:* award-winning B&B with great food; Nangaree Reg Hailstone Way; (02) 6345 1276. *Tinnies at Back Creek Vineyard:* self-contained cottage; Chiverton Rd; (02) 6342 9251.

Cowra museums: war, rail and rural museums all in one complex; Sydney Rd; 5 km E. *Darby Falls Observatory:* one of the largest telescopes accessible to the public. Check opening times; (02) 6345 1900 or 0417 461 162; Observatory Rd; 25 km SE. *Conimbla National Park:* known for its wildflowers, rock ledges, waterfalls, bushwalks and picnics; 27 km W. *Lake Wyangala and Grabine Lakeside State Park:* ideal for watersports and fishing; 40 km SE. *Self-guide drives:* through countryside including a wine-lovers' drive; brochure from visitor centre. *Local wineries:* open for cellar-door tastings; brochure from visitor centre.

See also CENTRAL WEST, p. 30

Crookwell

i 106 Goulburn St; (02) 4832 1988; www.upperlachlantourism.com

106.1 2GN FM, 846 AM ABC Radio National

This picturesque tree-lined township is a service centre to the local agricultural and pastoral district, and enjoys a cool climate and lush gardens. Australia's first grid-connected wind farm was opened here in 1998 and is capable of supplying electricity to 3500 homes. The Country Women's Association was formed here in 1922 and has since spread nationwide.

Crookwell Wind Farm: viewing platform and information board; Goulburn Rd.

Market: Uniting Church, Goulburn St; 1st Sat each month. *Crookwell Country Festival:* traditional country festival with music, markets, sports and a parade; Mar. *Open Gardens weekends:* spring and autumn (dates from visitor centre).

Paul's Cafe: sandwiches, burgers, fish and chips; 102 Goulburn St; (02) 4832 1745.

Gundowringa Homestead: charming country manor; Goulburn Rd; (02) 4848 1212.

Wombeyan Caves There are 5 caves open to the public including Figtree Cave, widely regarded as the best self-guide cave in NSW. Junction Cave has a colourful underground river; Wollondilly Cave has 5 main chambers with outstanding formations; Mulwarree Cave is intimate, with delicate formations; and Kooringa Cave is huge and majestic. Wombeyan Gorge is made of marble, providing an unusual swimming experience. There are several campgrounds and walking trails in the area. 60 km E.

Redground Lookout: excellent views of surrounding area; 8 km NW. *Willow Vale Mill:* restored flour mill with restaurant and accommodation; Laggan; (02) 4837 3319; 9 km NE. *Lake Wyangala and Grabine Lakeside State Park:* upper reaches ideal for waterskiing, picnicking, fishing, bushwalking and camping; 65 km NW. *Bike riding:* the area surrounding Crookwell is popular for bike riding; trail maps from visitor centre. *Historic villages:* associated with goldmining, coppermining and bushrangers, these villages include Tuena, Peelwood, Laggan, Bigga, Binda (all north) and Roslyn (south), the birthplace of poet Dame Mary Gilmore; maps from visitor centre. *Historical and scenic drives:* explore sites and countryside frequented by bushrangers such as Ben Hall; brochure from visitor centre.

See also CAPITAL COUNTRY, p. 31

Culcairn

i Greater Hume Shire Visitor Information Centre, 15 Wallace St, Holbrook; (02) 6036 2422; www.greaterhume.nsw.gov.au/tourism.html

93.1 Star FM, 675 AM ABC Local

Culcairn is located at the heart of 'Morgan country' where Dan 'Mad Dog' Morgan terrorised the district between 1862 and 1865. This peaceful town owes its tree-lined streets and lush green parks to an underground water supply discovered in 1926.

Stationmaster's Residence: beautifully restored museum (1883) reflects the importance of the railway; just across railway line. *Billabong Creek:* good fishing, one of the longest creeks in the Southern Hemisphere. *National Trust–classified buildings:* includes historic Culcairn Hotel (1891), still operating; Railway Pde and Olympic Way.

Henty This historic pastoral town has the Headlie Taylor Header Memorial, a tribute to the mechanical header harvester that revolutionised the grain industry. The nearby Sergeant Smith Memorial Stone marks the spot where Morgan fatally wounded a police officer, and the adjacent Doodle Cooma Swamp is 2000 ha of breeding area for waterbirds. 24 km N.

John McLean's grave: McLean was shot by Mad Dog Morgan; 3 km E. *Premier Yabby Farm:* tours through yabby-related displays and open ponds; also fishing, picnicking and barbecue facilities; (02) 6029 8351; 6 km SW. *Round Hill Station:* where Morgan committed his first hold-up in the area; Holbrook Rd; 15 km E. *Walla Walla:* old schoolhouse (1875) and the largest Lutheran church in NSW (1924); 18 km SW. *Morgan's Lookout:* granite outcrop on otherwise flat land, allegedly used by Morgan to look for approaching victims and police; 18 km NW.

See also MURRAY, p. 35

Deniliquin
Pop. 7433
Map ref. 559 J10 | 584 D2

i Peppin Heritage Centre, George St; (03) 5898 3120 or 1800 650 712; www.denitourism.com.au

99.3 FM ABC Radio National, 102.5 Classic Rock FM

Deniliquin, at the centre of Australia's largest irrigation system, lies on the Edward River, part of the Murray River and formed by a fault in the earth. Situated next to the world's largest red-gum forest, birdlife and wildlife remain abudant, despite the drought currently crippling the town's rice-growing industry. 'Deni' proclaims itself the 'ute capital of the world', holding the official record for most utes mustered in one place in 2007.

Peppin Heritage Centre This museum is dedicated to George Hall Peppin and his sons' development of the merino sheep industry. Dissatisfied with the quality and yield of the wool from merino sheep, they developed a new breed, the peppin, that was better adapted to the harsh Australian conditions. Peppin sheep now predominate among flocks in New Zealand, South Africa and South America. The museum is housed in the National Trust–classified Old George Street Public School (1879), which still has an intact classroom on display. There is also a lock-up gaol from Wanganella and a 1920s thatched ram shed. George St.

Island Sanctuary: features kangaroos and birdlife, and the burial site of 'Old Jack', a member of the Melville gang who visited Deniliquin in 1851; off Cressy St footbridge. *Ute on a Pole:* confirms Deniliquin's status as 'ute capital of the world'; near National Bridge. *Waring Gardens:* originally a chain of lagoons, the park was established in the 1880s; Cressy St. *Pioneer Steam Museum:* private collection of steam engines and pumps; Hay Rd. *Long Paddock River Walk:* old stock route, includes interpretive panels; from Heritage Centre to Island Sanctuary. *Self-guide walks:* historical and nature walks taking in National Trust–classified buildings and town gardens; brochure from visitor centre.

Market: Waring Gardens; 4th Sat each month. *Sun Festival:* includes gala parade and international food and entertainment; Jan. *RSL Fishing Classic*: Jan. *Play on the Plains Festival and Ute Muster:* celebration of music and cars; Sept/Oct.

Deniliquin Bakery: coffee and snacks; 69 Davidson St; (03) 5881 2278. *The Federal Hotel:* pub bistro; 46 Napier St; (03) 5881 1260.

Centrepoint Motel: affordable 4-star accommodation; 399 Cressy St; (03) 5881 3544.

Pioneer Tourist Park A modern caravan park including charming features of the past (open to the public), with an antique steam and pump display and a blacksmith shop. 2 km N.

Irrigation works: at Lawsons Syphon (7 km E) and Stevens Weir (25 km W). *Clancy's Winery:* cellar-door tastings and sales; 18 km N. *Conargo Pub:* authentic bush pub with photo gallery depicting history of merino wool in the area; 25 km NE. *Bird Observatory Tower:* excellent vantage point for birdwatching; Mathoura; 34 km S.

See also MURRAY, p. 35

Dorrigo
Pop. 970
Map ref. 550 G1 | 551 C12 | 557 M8

i Hickory St; (02) 6657 2486; www.bellingermagic.com

105.5 Star FM, 738 AM ABC Local

Dorrigo is known as 'Australia's national park capital'. It is entirely surrounded by national parks including Dorrigo and Cathedral Rock. The Dorrigo Plateau provides crisp, clean air and wonderful views in all directions. The town is small enough to be friendly, but popular enough to provide excellent facilities.

Historical museum: memorabilia, documents and photographs detailing the history of Dorrigo and surrounding national parks; Cudgery St. *Local crafts:* at Pinnata Gallery; Hickory St. *Wood-fired bakery:* produces popular products with local produce; Hickory St. *Waterfall Way Winery:* unique fruit wines and fortified wines; tastings available; Hickory St.

Market: showground, Armidale Rd; 1st Sat each month. *Arts and Crafts Exhibition:* Easter. *Bluegrass Festival:* Oct.

Lick the Spoon: cafe and provedore; 51–53 Hickory St; (02) 6657 1373. *Tallawalla Teahouse:* cafe in stunning surrounds; 113 Old Coramba Rd; (02) 6657 2315.

Fernbrook Lodge B&B: charming country guesthouse; 4705 Waterfall Way; (02) 6657 2573. *Gracemere Grange:* laid-back country guesthouse; 325 Dome Rd; (02) 6657 2630. *Moss Grove B&B:* English-style traditional B&B; 589 Old Coast Rd; (02) 6657 5388.

Dorrigo National Park This park takes in World Heritage–listed rainforest and offers plenty for visitors to see and do. Attractions include spectacular waterfalls and a variety of birds such as bowerbirds and lyrebirds. The Rainforest Centre has picnic facilities, a cafe, a video theatre and exhibitions. There is also the Skywalk, a boardwalk offering views over the canopy of the rainforest, and the Walk with the Birds boardwalk. 3 km E.

Cathedral Rock National Park Giant boulders, sculpted rock, distinctive granite hills and wedge-tailed eagles make Cathedral Rock spectacular viewing and popular among photographers. Walks include a 3 hr circuit walk to the summit of Cathedral Rock for amazing 360-degree views of the tableland. 56 km SW.

Trout fishing: in streams on the Dorrigo Plateau (between Dorrigo and Urunga); contact visitor centre for locations. *Dangar Falls:* viewing platform over beautiful 30 m waterfall; 2 km N. *Griffiths Lookout:* sweeping views of the mountains;

6 km s. ***Guy Fawkes River National Park:*** rugged and scenic surrounds with limited facilities, but worth the effort for experienced bushwalkers. Ebor Falls has cliff-top viewing platforms above and there is also good canoeing and fishing; 40 km w. ***L. P. Dutton Trout Hatchery:*** educational visitor centre and trout feeding; 63 km sw. ***Point Lookout:*** in New England National Park for spectacular panoramic views of Bellinger Valley and across to the ocean; 74 km sw.

See also Holiday Coast, p. 27

Dubbo

Pop. 34 318
Map ref. 554 F1 | 556 C12

 Cnr Newell Hwy and Macquarie St; (02) 6801 4450 or 1800 674 443; www.dubbotourism.com.au

92.7 Zoo FM, 549 AM ABC Local

One of Australia's fastest growing inland cities, Dubbo is most famous for its world-class open-range zoo. The city, on the banks of the Macquarie River, is thriving and prosperous with more than half a million visitors each year. Dubbo prides itself on city standards with a country smile.

Western Plains Cultural Centre The centre includes the Dubbo Regional Gallery – the Armati Bequest, Dubbo Regional Museum and the Community Arts Centre. It exhibits local and national visual arts, heritage and social history. In 2007, the gallery received a generous gift from the Armati Family including Michael Riley's celebrated 'Cloud' series of photographs. To acknowledge this, the gallery was renamed the Armati Bequest. It specialises in the theme of Animals in Art, collecting works in a broad range of media and styles by artists from all areas. The museum, housed in the original Dubbo High School building, features a permanent space devoted to the story of Dubbo entitled 'People Places Possessions' and a temporary exhibition space. Closed Tues; Wingewarra Street; (02) 6801 4444.

Old Dubbo Gaol Closed as a penal institution in 1966, Old Dubbo Gaol now offers a glimpse at convict life. See the original gallows (where 8 men were hanged for murder) and solitary confinement cells, or walk along the watchtower. An amazing animatronic robot tells historical tales. There are also holograms and theatrical enactments. Macquarie St; (02) 6801 4460.

Shoyoen Sister City Garden: Japanese garden and teahouse designed and built with the support of Dubbo's sister city, Minokamo; Coronation Dr East. ***Jedda Boomerangs:*** Aboriginal art and culture displays; also makes and sells boomerangs. Decorate your own, or take throwing lessons (bookings essential); closed Sat; Minore Rd; (02) 6882 3110. ***The Clay Pan Gallery:*** exhibits include paintings, pottery, silver jewellery, woodturning, ceramics and local craft; closed Tues; Depot Rd. ***Traintasia:*** detailed operating model railway display with spectator interaction; Yarrandale Road; (02) 6884 9944.

Markets: Macquarie Lions Park, 1st and 3rd Sat each month; Dubbo Showground, Wingewarra St, 2nd Sun each month. ***Western Plains Country Music Championships:*** Easter. ***Jazz Festival:*** Aug. ***Red Ochre Festival:*** Sept.

Rose Garden Thai Restaurant: takeaway available; 208 Brisbane St; (02) 6882 8322. ***Two Doors Tapas & Wine Bar:*** Spanish; 215B Macquarie St; (02) 6885 2333.

No 95 Dubbo: stylish, good-value motel; 95 Cobra St; (02) 6882 7888. ***Taronga Western Plains Zoo:*** lodge accommodation or camping at the zoo; Zoofari Lodge (02) 6881 1488, Roar and Snore (02) 6881 1405.

Taronga Western Plains Zoo Australia's first open-range zoo, with over 1000 animals from 5 continents, is set on more than 300 ha of bushland. The zoo is renowned for its breeding programs (especially with endangered species), conservation programs and education facilities and exhibits. There are talks by the keepers and early morning walks, as well as accommodation at Zoofari Lodge. The Tracker Riley Cycleway paves the 5 km from Dubbo to the zoo and bicycles and maps are available from the visitor centre. Inquiries (02) 9969 2777; 5 km s.

Dubbo Observatory: explore the skies via Schmidt Cassegrain telescopes. Open nightly; Camp Road; (02) 6885 3022; 5.5 km s. ***Dundullimal Homestead:*** an 1840s restored squatter's slab-style homestead with working saddler, blacksmith and farm animals; Obley Rd; 7 km SE. ***Terramungamine Rock Grooves:*** the 150 rock grooves were created by the Tubbagah people; Burraway Rd via Brocklehurst; 10 km N. ***Narromine:*** agricultural centre well known for gliding and an outstanding aviation museum. The Air Pageant and Evolution of Flight Festival is held here each Sept/Oct; 40 km E. ***Heritage drives and river cruises:*** brochures from visitor centre. ***Wineries:*** several in region offering cellar-door tastings; brochure from visitor centre.

See also Central West, p. 30

Eden

Pop. 3010
Map ref. 565 E10 | 581 H3

 Eden Gateway Centre, Princes Hwy; (02) 6496 1953; www.sapphirecoast.com.au

102.5 Power FM, 810 AM ABC Local

Situated on the Sapphire Coast, the aptly named Eden is an idyllic and peaceful town on Twofold Bay. The location is excellent, with national park to the north and south, water to the east and woodland to the west. The beautiful bay is rimmed with mountains. Originally settled by whalers, it is now a fishing port and a popular, but relatively undeveloped, tourist town.

Aslings Beach: surf beach with rockpools and excellent platforms for whale-watching Oct–Nov; Aslings Beach Rd. ***Snug Cove:*** working fishing port with plenty of restaurants and cafes. ***Eden Killer Whale Museum:*** fascinating displays on the history of the local whaling industry including the skeleton of 'Old Tom' the killer whale; Imlay St; (02) 6496 2094.

Market: Calle Calle St; 1st Sat each month. ***Eden Seafood and Arts Festival:*** Easter. ***Eden Whale Festival:*** Oct/Nov.

Eden Fishermen's Club: steak and seafood; 217 Imlay St; (02) 6496 1577. ***Essentially Eden:*** modern Australian; The Great Southern Inn, 158 Imlay St; (02) 6496 1515.

Crown & Anchor: traditional B&B in 1840s inn; 239 Imlay St; (02) 6496 1017. ***Quarantine Bay Beach Cottages:*** self-contained cottages; Princes Hwy; (02) 6496 1483.

Ben Boyd National Park This park's scenery includes rugged stretches of coastline, unique rock formations, heaths and banksia forest. The area is excellent for fishing, swimming, wreck diving, bushwalking and camping. Boyd's Tower at Red Point,

32 km SE, was originally built for whale-spotting. Cape Green Lighthouse, 45 km SE, is the first cast-concrete lighthouse in Australia and the second tallest in NSW; tours by appt; bookings (02) 6495 5000. The Pinnacles, 8 km N, are an unusual earth formation with red gravel atop white sand cliffs.

Jiggamy Farm: Aboriginal cultural and bush tucker experience; 9 km N. *Boydtown:* former rival settlement on the shores of Twofold Bay with convict-built Seahorse Inn (still licensed), safe beach and good fishing; 9 km S. *Davidson Whaling Station Historic Site:* provides unique insight into the lives of 19th-century whalers; Kiah Inlet; 30 km SE. *South East Fibre Exports Visitors Centre:* logging and milling displays; Jews Head; bookings essential (02) 6496 0222; 34 km SE. *Nadgee Nature Reserve:* walking track, access via Wonboyn Lake; 35 km SE. *Wonboyn Lake:* scenic area with good fishing and 4WD tracks; 40 km S.

See also SOUTH COAST, p. 32

Eugowra
Pop. 532
Map ref. 554 E5

 i Cnr Byng and Peisley sts; (02) 6393 8226 or 1800 069 466; www.orange.nsw.gov.au

105.9 Star FM, 549 AM ABC Local

Situated on the rich basin of the Lachlan River, Eugowra is a tiny country town known for its crafts. Nearby on the Orange–Forbes road, the famous Gold Escort Robbery took place in 1862.

Eugowra Museum and Bushranger Centre: displays on pioneer life, a pistol used in the Gold Escort Robbery, gemstones, early farm equipment, wagons and Aboriginal artefacts; open Wed–Sun; (02) 6859 2214. *Local craft shops:* leaflet from visitor centre. *Self-guide bushranging tour:* maps from visitor centre.

Escort Rock Cafe: hearty country meals; 61 Nanima St; (02) 6859 2727. *The Lady Bushranger:* quaint cafe; Shop 2, 51 Nanima St; (02) 6859 2900.

Nangar National Park The horseshoe-shaped red cliffs of the Nangar–Murga Range stand out against the central west's plains. Nangar National Park's flowering shrubs and timbered hills provide an important wildlife refuge among mostly cleared land. Rocky slopes and pretty creeks make it a scenic site for bushwalks and popular for rock climbing. The park does not have facilities, so visitors are advised to take water and provisions with them and to give friends or family their itinerary. 10 km E.

Escort Rock: where bushranger Frank Gardiner and gang (including Ben Hall) hid before ambushing the Forbes gold escort. A plaque on the road gives details; 3 km E. *Nanami Lane Lavender Farm:* products and plants for sale and workshops on growing lavender; 19 km SE.

See also CENTRAL WEST, p. 30

Evans Head
Pop. 2629
Map ref. 551 G6 | 557 O4

 i Ballina Visitor Information Centre, cnr Las Balsas Plaza and River St, Ballina; (02) 6686 3484 or 1800 777 666; www.tropicalnsw.com.au

92.9 FM North Coast Radio, 738 AM ABC Local

Evans Head is located at the mouth of the Evans River. It was the first prawning port in Australia and is still predominantly a fishing village, but with 6 kilometres of safe surfing beaches, sandy river flats and coastal scenery, it is also a tourist town. There is excellent rock, beach and ocean fishing.

Goanna Headland: site of great mythical importance to the Bundjalung people and favourite spot of serious surfers. **Razorback Lookout:** views up and down the coast. On a clear day, Cape Byron Lighthouse can be seen to the north; Ocean Dr.

Market: Cnr Oak and Park sts; 4th Sat each month. *Fishing Classic:* July. *Evans Head Flower Show:* Sept. *Evans Head Longboard Invitational:* Sept.

 New Italy A monument and remains are all that are left of this settlement that was the result of the ill-fated Marquis de Rays expedition in 1880. The Marquis tricked 340 Italians into purchasing nonexistent property in a Pacific paradise. Disaster struck several times for the emigrants, as they travelled first to Papua New Guinea and then to New Caledonia. Eventually Sir Henry Parkes arranged for their passage to Australia, where the 217 survivors built this village. Also in the New Italy Complex, Guuragai Aboriginal Arts and Crafts offers quality works and information on Aboriginal culture. 23 km SW.

Bundjalung National Park: Aboriginal relics, fishing, swimming and bushwalking; 2 km S. *Broadwater National Park:* bushwalking, birdwatching, fishing and swimming; 5 km N. *Woodburn:* friendly town on the Richmond River with great spots for picnicking, swimming, fishing and boating; flower show in Aug; 11 km NW.

See also TROPICAL NORTH COAST, p. 28

Finley
Pop. 2053
Map ref. 559 L11 | 584 F3

 i Tocumwal Visitor Centre, 41 Deniliquin St, Tocumwal; (03) 5874 2131 or 1800 677 271.

102.5 FM Classic Rock, 675 AM ABC Local

This town, on the Newell Highway and close to the Victorian border, is a tidy and peaceful spot. It is the centre of the Berriquin Irrigation Area. The main street spans Mulwala Canal, the largest irrigation channel in Australia.

Mary Lawson Wayside Rest Features a log cabin that is an authentic replica of a pioneer home. It houses the Finley and District Historical Museum with displays of antique pumping equipment and machinery. Newell Hwy.

Finley Lake: popular boating, sailboarding and picnic area; Newell Hwy. *Finley Livestock Exchange:* experience a cattle sale; Fri mornings.

Rodeo: Jan.

Berrigan: charming historic town known for its connections to horseracing; 22 km E. *Sojourn Station Art Studio:* spacious rural property providing accommodation for visiting artists; 25 km SE via Berrigan. *Grassleigh Woodturning and Crafts:* displays of woodturning in action and wood products; 37 km NE via Berrigan.

See also MURRAY, p. 35

Forbes
Pop. 6954
Map ref. 554 D4

 i Railway station, Union St; (02) 6852 4155; www.forbes.nsw.gov.au

97.9 Valley FM, 104.3 FM Radio National

When John Oxley passed through in 1817, he was so unimpressed by the area's clay soil, poor timber and swamps that he claimed 'it is impossible to imagine a worse country'. Today Forbes is a pleasant spot bisected by Lake Forbes, a large lagoon in the middle of town. It was the discovery of gold that caused the town to be built and the legends of old bushrangers that keep it buzzing today.

 Albion Hotel The first hotel in Forbes, the Albion Hotel was so popular during the gold rush that it allegedly sold more alcohol in the 1860s than any hotel in Australia – not bad for an outback town. The hotel is a former Cobb & Co depot and now houses displays on the history of the gold strikes and the must-see Bushranger Hall of Fame. Lachlan St.

Historical Museum: features relics associated with bushranger Ben Hall, a vintage colonial kitchen and antique farm machinery; open 2–4pm; Cross St; (02) 6851 6600. *Cemetery:* graves of Ben Hall, Kate Foster (Ned Kelly's sister), Rebecca Shields (Captain Cook's niece) and French author Paul Wenz; Bogan Gate Rd. *King George V Park:* memorial where 'German Harry' discovered gold in 1861, and a pleasant spot for picnics and barbecues; Lawler St. *Dowling Street Park:* memorial marks the spot where John Oxley first passed through in 1817; Dowling St. *Lake Forbes:* picnic spots, barbecue facilities, fishing, and a walking and cycling track; off Gordon Duff Dr. *Historical town walk:* includes the post office (1862) and the town hall (1861) where Dame Nellie Melba performed in 1909; map from visitor centre. *Local arts and crafts:* brochure from visitor centre.

 Jazz Festival: Jan.

Signatures Restaurant: modern Australian; Forbes Services Golf Club, 41–43 Templar St; (02) 6851 2022. *Wattle Cafe:* light lunches; 85 Rankin St; (02) 6852 4310.

Lake Forbes Motel: affordable accommodation, picturesque views; 8 Junction St; (02) 6852 2922.

Gum Swamp Sanctuary: birdlife and other fauna, best seen at sunrise or sunset; 4 km s. *Banderra Estate Vineyard:* French winemaker with cellar-door tastings; off Orange Rd; 5 km E. *Chateau Champsaur:* oldest winery in the area (1886), with cellar-door tastings; (02) 6852 3908; 5 km SE. *Ben Hall's Place:* marks the site where the bushranger was shot dead by policemen; 8 km w. *Jemalong Weir:* with parklands by the Lachan River, good spot for fishing and picnicking; 24 km s.

See also CENTRAL WEST, p. 30

 Forster–Tuncurry

Pop. 18 374

Map ref. 550 E9 | 555 O2

i Little St, Forster; (02) 6554 8799 or 1800 802 692; www.greatlakes.org.au

95.5 FM ABC Local, 107.3 Max FM

Located in the Great Lakes district, Forster is connected to its twin town, Tuncurry, by a concrete bridge across Wallis Lake, forming one large resort town. The area has an excellent reputation for its fishing and seafood, particularly its oysters.

Forster Arts and Crafts Centre: the largest working craft centre in NSW; Breese Pde. *Tobwabba Art Studio:* specialises in urban coastal Aboriginal art; cnr Breckenridge and Little sts, Forster. *Pebbly Beach Bicentennial Walk:* gentle and scenic 2 km walk to Bennetts Head, beginning at baths off North St, Forster. *Wallis Lake Fishermen's Co-op:* fresh and cooked oysters and ocean fish; Wharf St, Tuncurry. *Dolphin-spotting and lake*

cruises: bookings at visitor centre. Dolphins can also be seen from Tuncurry Breakwall and Bennetts Head.

 Forster Market: Town Park; 2nd Sun each month. *Tuncurry Market:* John Wright Park; 4th Sat each month.

Ripples: modern Australian; Shop 6, 24–30 Memorial Dr, Forster; (02) 6555 3949.

Tokelau Guest House: Federation guesthouse; 2 Manning St, Tuncurry; (02) 6557 5157.

Booti Booti National Park An ideal spot for water activities, Booti Booti National Park has beautiful beaches including Elizabeth, Boomerang and Blueys beaches, all fabulous for surfing, swimming and fishing. Elizabeth Beach is patrolled by lifesavers in season. The lookout tower on Cape Hawke offers 360-degree views over Booti Booti and Wallingat national parks, the foothills of the Barrington Tops, Seal Rocks and Crowdy Bay. The park offers a variety of walking trails. 17 km s.

Cape Hawke: steep 400 m track to summit for views of Wallis Lake, Seal Rocks and inland to Great Dividing Range; 8 km s. *The Green Cathedral:* open-air church with pews and altar, sheltered by cabbage palm canopy; Tiona, on the shores of Wallis Lake; 13 km s. *Smiths Lake:* sheltered lake for safe swimming; 30 km s. *Tours of Great Lakes area:* kayak, 4WD, nature and eco-tours, including bushwalks; brochure from visitor centre.

See also HOLIDAY COAST, p. 27

Gilgandra

Pop. 2679

Map ref. 556 C10

i Coo-ee Heritage Centre, Coo-ee March Memorial Park, Newell Hwy; (02) 6817 8700; www.gilgandra.nsw.gov.au

101.3 Star FM, 549 AM ABC Local

A historic town at the junction of three highways, 'Gil' is the centre for the surrounding wool and farming country. The 1915 Coo-ee March in which 35 men, given no support from the army, marched the 500 kilometres to Sydney to enlist for World War I left from here. Along the way they recruited over 200 men, announcing their arrival with a call of 'coo-ee!' The march sparked seven other such marches from country towns.

 Coo-ee Heritage Centre Memorabilia from the 1915 Coo-ee March, and items relating to the Breelong Massacre, which took place after an Aboriginal man was insulted for marrying a white woman, and on which Thomas Keneally's *The Chant of Jimmy Blacksmith* was based. Coo-ee Memorial Park, Newell Hwy.

Rural Museum: vast collection of agricultural artefacts including antique farm machinery and early model tractors on display; Newell Hwy. *Hitchen House Museum:* the home of the Hitchen brothers, who initiated the Coo-ee March. The museum has memorabilia from WW I, WW II and Vietnam; Miller St. *Orana Cactus World:* almost 1000 different cacti on display collected over 40 years; open most weekends and by appt; Newell Hwy; bookings (02) 6847 0566. *Gilgandra Observatory:* Newtonian reflector and refractor telescopes and a sundial; open 7–10pm (8.30–10pm during daylight saving) Mon–Sat; Cnr Wamboin and Willie sts; (02) 6847 2646. *Tourist drives:* around town; brochure from visitor centre.

Rodeo: Oct. *Coo-ee Festival:* Oct.

Cafe Country Style: home-style meals; 44 Miller St; (02) 6487 1571. *Holland's Family Diner:* classic cafe; 11 Castlereagh St; (02) 6847 1199.

Anna's Place B&B: friendly, comfortable accommodation; 13 Morris St; (02) 6847 2790.

Warren Its location on the Macquarie River makes Warren a popular spot with anglers. For a stroll along the riverbank take the River Red Gum Walk, for birdwatching go to Tiger Bay Wildlife Reserve, and for a day of picnicking and swimming visit Warren Weir. The racecourse is known as the 'Randwick of the west' and hosts some fantastic race days. 85 km w.

Gilgandra Flora Reserve: 8.5 ha of bushland, perfect for picnics and barbecues. Most plants flower in spring, making the park particularly spectacular Sept–Nov; 14 km NE. *Emu Farm:* raised for oil, leather and meat, guided tours; Tooraweenah; 40 km NW.

See also CENTRAL WEST, p. 30

Glen Innes

Pop. 5944

Map ref. 557 K5

(i) 152 Church St; (02) 6730 2400; www.gleninnestourism.com

106.7 Gem FM, 819 AM ABC Local

This beautiful town, set among rolling hills on the northern tablelands of New South Wales at an elevation of 1075 metres, is known for its fine parks, which are especially striking in autumn. It was the scene of many bushranging exploits in the 19th century, including some by the infamous Captain Thunderbolt. In the 1830s, two particularly hairy convict stockmen, Chandler and Duval, advised and guided settlers to new land where they settled stations. Because of Chandler and Duval, people came to know Glen Innes as the 'land of the beardies', a nickname that has stuck to this day. The town is undeniably proud of its Celtic beginnings (the first settlers were predominantly Scots), as illustrated by its attractions and festivals.

Centennial Parklands The site of Celtic monument 'Australian Standing Stones', which was built with 38 giant granite monoliths in recognition of the contribution made in Australia by people of Celtic origin. A full explanation of the stones can be read at Crofters Cottage, which also sells Celtic food and gifts. St Martin's Lookout provides superb views. Meade St.

Land of the Beardies History House: folk museum in the town's first hospital building; it has a reconstructed slab hut, period room settings and pioneer relics; Cnr Ferguson St and West Ave; (02) 6732 1035. *Self-guide walks:* past historic public buildings, especially on Grey St; brochure from visitor centre.

Market: Grey St; 2nd Sun each month. *Minerama Gem Festival:* world-class gems on display and guided fossicking trips to unique locations; Mar. *Australian Celtic Festival:* Apr/May. *Gourmet in the Glen:* Oct. *Land of the Beardies Festival:* Nov.

Ramona's Restaurant: modern Australian; 160 Church St; (02) 6732 2922. *The Hereford Steakhouse:* award-winning steakhouse; Rest Point Motel, New England Hwy; (02) 6732 2255.

Kings Plains Castle: beautiful Scottish castle; King Plains Rd; (02) 6733 6808. *Tudor House Boutique B&B:* excellent boutique accommodation; 139–141 Church St; (02) 6732 3884 or 1800 139 149.

Gibraltar Range National Park and Washpool National Park These adjoining parks were World Heritage–listed in 1986 because of their ancient and isolated remnants of rainforest and their great variety of plant and animal species. Gibraltar Range is known for its scenic creeks and cascades and its unusual granite formations, The Needles and Anvil Rock. Gibraltar Range also contains over 100 km of excellent walking trails. 70 km NE. Washpool has the largest remaining stand of coachwood trees in the world and a unique array of eucalypt woods and rainforest. It has some of the least disturbed forest in NSW. 75 km NE.

Stonehenge: unusual balancing rock formations; 18 km S. *Emmaville:* the Australian beginnings of St John Ambulance occurred here. Includes a mining museum; 39 km NW. *Deepwater:* good fishing for trout, perch and cod with regular fishing safaris; bookings at visitor centre; 40 km N. *Mann River Nature Reserve:* popular camping spot due to fantastic swimming holes; 40 km NW. *Torrington:* gem fossicking, bushwalks and unusual rock formations; 66 km NW. *Convict-carved tunnel:* road tunnel halfway between Glen Innes and Grafton; Old Grafton Rd; 72 km W. *Horse treks:* accommodation at historic pubs; bookings at visitor centre.

See also NEW ENGLAND, p. 29

Glenbrook

Pop. 5138

Map ref. 544 G6 | 547 L10 | 555 J6

(i) Blue Mountains Visitor Information Centre, Great Western Hwy; 1300 653 408; www.visitbluemountains.com.au

89.1 BLU FM, 576 AM ABC Radio National

Glenbrook is a picturesque village on the edge of the Blue Mountains. It was originally known as Watertank because it was used for the storage of water for local steam trains. Today it is a charming town with a large lagoon, close to the impressive Red Hands Cave that lies in Blue Mountains National Park.

Lapstone Zig Zag Walking Track The track follows the 3 km path of the original Lapstone Zig Zag Railway. The track includes convict-built Lennox Bridge (the oldest surviving bridge on the mainland), the abandoned Lucasville Station and numerous lookouts with views of Penrith and the Cumberland Plain. Nearby there is a monument to John Whitton, a pioneer in railway development. Starts in Knapsack St.

Glenbrook Lagoon: filled with ducks, and a perfect picnic spot with walking trails.

Market: Infants School, Ross St; 3rd Sat each month. *Spring Festival:* Nov.

Mash Cafe Restaurant: modern Australian, vegetarian and gluten-free options; 19 Ross St; (02) 4739 5908.

Lorikeet Cottage: self-contained cottage; 7 Powell St, Blaxland; 0418 602 690.

Faulconbridge This scenic town features the Corridor of Oaks, a line of trees, each one planted by an Australian prime minister. There is also the grave of Sir Henry Parkes, 'the father of Federation', and the stone cottage where Norman Lindsay lived, now a gallery and museum dedicated to his life and work. Lindsay was the author of Australian classics such as *The Magic Pudding* and was the subject of the film *Sirens* (1994). 16 km NW.

Wascoe Siding Miniature Railway: 300 m of steam and motor railway plus picnic and barbecue facilities. Trains operate 1st Sun each month; off Great Western Hwy; 2.5 km W. *Blue Mountains National Park:* Red Hands Cave is accessed by a 6 km return walk. The cave features hand stencils (mostly red, although some are white or orange) that were created between 500 and 1600 years ago. The artists created the stencils by placing their hands against the cave wall and blowing a mixture of ochre and water from their mouths. Euroka Clearing, 4 km s, is a popular camping spot home to many kangaroos. *For other parts of the park see Katoomba and Blackheath.* **Springwood:** galleries and craft and antique shops. Also home to the Ivy Markets; 2nd Sat each month (except Jan); civic centre, Macquarie Rd; 12 km NW. **Linden:** impressive Kings Cave with Caleys Repulse Cairn nearby commemorating early surveyor George Caley; 20 km w.

See also BLUE MOUNTAINS, p. 23

Gloucester

Pop. 2446
Map ref. 550 C8 | 555 M1 | 557 K12

 27 Denison St; (02) 6558 1408; www.gloucester.org.au

97.7 Breeze FM, 100.9 FM ABC Local

At the foot of the impressive monolithic hills of the Bucketts Range, Gloucester calls itself the base camp to the Barrington Tops. This green and peaceful town is known for its top-quality produce including Barrington beef and perch.

Minimbah Aboriginal Native Gardens: bush-tucker gardens; Gloucester District Park. **Folk Museum:** pioneer household relics, toys, and gemstones and rocks; open 10am–2pm Thurs and Sat, 11am–3pm Sun; Church St; (02) 6558 9989. *Town heritage walk:* includes Lostrochs Cordial Factory and Gloucester Powerhouse; brochure from visitor centre. **Walking trails:** through nearby parks, brochure from visitor centre.

Shakespeare Festival: May. **Mountain Man Triathlon:** kayaking, mountain-biking and running; Sept.

Perenti: chic cafe with local produce; 69 Church St; (02) 6558 9219.

Altamira Retreat: nestled in scenic countryside; 1507 Bakers Creek Rd; (02) 6550 6558. **Arrowee House B&B:** traditional B&B; 152 Thunderbolts Way; (02) 6558 2050.

Barrington Tops National Park This World Heritage–listed rainforest is enormous and has a great variety of landscapes, flora and fauna. There are some good walking trails, beautiful forest drives and breathtaking views from Mt Allyn, 1100 m above sea level. The Barrington Tops Forest Dr from Gloucester to Scone has rainforest walks and picnic spots en route; brochure from visitor centre. 60 km w.

Copeland State Conservation Area Easily accessible dry rainforest, well known for its gold production in the 1870s and large stands of red cedar. Walking trails that utilise the old wagon and logging tracks are open to the public; 17km w. **The Bucketts Walk:** 90 min return with great views of town; Bucketts Rd; 2 km w. **Lookouts:** amazing views of the national park, town and surrounding hills at Kia-ora Lookout (4 km N), Mograni Lookout (5 km E) and Berrico Trig Station (14 km w). **Goldtown:** former site of the Mountain Maid Goldmine (1876), now mostly covered with rainforest. Also a historical museum, gold panning and underground mine tours; 16 km w.

See also HOLIDAY COAST, p. 27

Gosford

Pop. 166 626
Map ref. 543 D8 | 545 O3 | 555 L5

 200 Mann St; (02) 4343 2353 or 1300 130 708; www.visitcentralcoast.com.au

92.5 FM ABC Local, 101.3 Sea FM

Part of the idyllic Central Coast region, Gosford is surrounded by national parks, steep hills and valleys, rainforest, lakes and ocean beaches. Understandably, Gosford continues to increase in popularity and has grown into a bustling city known for its high standard of tourism and its orchards and seafood.

Art galleries and craft and antique shops: many in town; contact visitor centre for details.

Gosford Country Show: May. *Springtime Flora Festival:* Sept. *CoastFest:* arts festival; Oct. *Gosford to Lord Howe Island Yacht Race:* Oct/Nov.

BodyFuel: fresh, healthy cafe meals; 1/9 William Court; (02) 4323 6669. *Upper Deck:* seafood, great views; 61 Masons Pde; (02) 4324 6705. *Flair:* modern Australian; 1/488 The Entrance Rd, Erina Heights; (02) 4365 2777.

Wombats B&B: traditional B&B; 144 Brisbane Water Dr; (02) 4325 5633. *Claddagh House B&B:* romantic retreat; 421 Avoca Dr, Green Point; (02) 4369 5251.

Ku-ring-gai Chase National Park Here the Hawkesbury River meets the sea with winding creeks, attractive beaches, hidden coves and clear water. Highlights are Resolute Track, with Aboriginal rock engravings and hand stencils; Bobbin Head, with a visitor centre and marina; and West Head Lookout, with panoramic views over the water. 33 km sw.

Gosford City Arts Centre: local art and craft and Japanese garden; 3 km E. *Henry Kendall Cottage:* museum in the poet's sandstone home. Also picnic and barbecue facilities in the grounds; 3 km sw. *Australian Rainforest Sanctuary:* walking trails through peaceful rainforest. The Firefly Festival is held here Nov–Dec; 14 km NW. *Firescreek Fruit Wines:* Holgate; (02) 4365 0768; 10 km NE. *Australian Reptile Park:* snakes, spiders and Galapagos tortoises. See shows throughout the day. Somersby Falls nearby provide an ideal picnic spot; Somersby; 15 km NW. *Australian Walkabout Wildlife Park:* native forest with 2 km of walking trails. Animals extinct in the area have been re-introduced with success thanks to the fence that keeps out feral animals; Calga; 20 km NW. *Brooklyn:* access to lower Hawkesbury for houseboating, fishing and river cruises. Historic Riverboat Postman ferry leaves Brooklyn weekdays for cruises and postal deliveries; 32 km s.

See also CENTRAL COAST & HAWKESBURY, p. 25

Goulburn

Pop. 20 131
Map ref. 554 H9 | 565 E3

 201 Sloane St; (02) 4823 4492 or 1800 353 646; www.igoulburn.com

93.5 Eagle FM, 103.3 FM Community Radio, 1098 AM ABC Radio National

Goulburn is at the junction of the Wollondilly and Mulwaree rivers, at the centre of a wealthy farming district. It was one of Australia's first inland settlements and the last proclaimed city in the British Empire. It is now known for its merino wool industry.

 RADIO STATIONS   IN TOWN   WHAT'S ON   WHERE TO EAT   WHERE TO STAY   NEARBY

The Big Merino Even though it was only built in 1985, the Big Merino is an instantly recognisable landmark associated with Goulburn and its thriving merino wool industry. The 15 m high and 18 m long sculptured sheep has 3 floors, with a souvenir shop, an educational display on the history of wool in the area and a lookout. Cnr Hume and Sowerby sts; (02) 4882 8013.

Old Goulburn Brewery: tours of Australia's oldest brewery designed by colonial architect Francis Greenway. Brewing to original recipe; Bungonia Rd; (02) 4821 6071. *Goulburn and District Arts and Crafts Centre:* gallery and giftshop showcasing arts and crafts including jewellery, pottery and textiles; Blackshaw Rd; (02) 4822 7889. *Goulburn Historic Waterworks:* displays antique waterworks engines, beside attractive parkland with picnic and barbecue facilities on Marsden Weir; off Fitzroy St. *Rocky Hill War Memorial and Museum:* erected in 1925 as a tribute to the Goulburn men and women who served during WW I, it offers outstanding views across the city. Museum open weekends and holidays; Memorial Dr. *Self-guide tour:* historic buildings include Goulburn Courthouse and St Saviour's Cathedral; brochure from visitor centre.

Australian Blues Music Festival: Feb. *Celebration of Heritage and Roses:* Mar. *Lilac City Festival:* Oct.

Bungonia State Conservation Area Popular for adventurers with perfect terrain for canyoning, caving and canoeing. Walking trails offer fantastic river and canyon views. One walk passes through the spectacular Bungonia Gorge. 35 km E.

Pelican Sheep Station: farm tours, shearing and sheepdog demonstrations by appt; bookings (02) 4821 4668. Accommodation is available; 10 km s. *Lake George:* 25 km long lake that regularly fills and empties. It has excellent picnic sites; 40 km sw. *Wombeyan Caves:* Daily guided and self-guide cave tours through ancient and spectacular limestone cave system; inquiries (02) 4843 5976; 70 km N.

See also CAPITAL COUNTRY, p. 31

Grafton
Pop. 17 499
Map ref. 551 D9 | 557 N6

ⓘ Clarence River Visitor Information Centre, Pacific Hwy, South Grafton; (02) 6642 4677; www.clarencetourism.com

📻 104.7 FM Clarence Coast, 738 AM ABC Local

With over 6500 trees in 24 parks, Grafton is known for its riverbank parks and jacaranda trees. Its city centre adds to the charm with wide streets, elegant Victorian buildings and the Clarence River passing through. Water lovers are spoiled for choice with everything from whitewater adventures, waterskiing and fishing.

Susan Island This rainforest recreation reserve in the Clarence River is home to a large fruit bat colony. Dusk is the time to visit to watch the bats flying off in search of food (wearing a hat is advisable if visiting at this time). During the day the island is a good spot for rainforest walks, barbecues and picnics. Access is via hired boat, skippered cruise or Clarence Islander ferry.

Grafton Regional Gallery: rated as one of the most outstanding regional galleries in Australia, the Grafton Regional Gallery inside Prentice House has permanent exhibitions such as the Jacaranda Art Society and Contemporary Australian Drawing collections; closed Mon; Fitzroy St; (02) 6642 3177. *National Trust–classified buildings:* include Schaeffer House, home of the Clarence River Historical Society, Christ Church Cathedral and the notorious Grafton Gaol; heritage trail brochure from visitor centre. *Local art and craft shops:* brochure from visitor centre.

Markets: Lawrence Rd, last Sat each month; Prince St, Grafton Showgrounds, 3rd Sat each month; Armidale Rd, South Grafton, every Sat morning. *Autumn Artsfest:* Apr. *Grafton Cup:* horserace; July. *Grafton to Inverell Cycling Classic:* Sept. *Bridge to Bridge Ski Race:* Oct. *Jacaranda Festival:* Oct–Nov.

✕ *Georgie's:* modern Australian and art gallery; Grafton Regional Gallery, 158 Fitzroy St; (02) 6642 6996. *Moos Restaurant:* steakhouse; Pacific Hwy; (02) 6642 2833. *Victoria's Restaurant:* international; Quality Inn Grafton, 51 Fitzroy St; (02) 6640 9100.

🛏 *Blooms Cottage:* self-contained cottage; 6 Queen St; 0407 297 764. *Ivy Cottage:* B&B; 130 Centenary Dr; (02) 6642 3202.

Museum of Interesting Things Australian actor Russell Crowe chose Nymboida's coaching station for the home of his amazing collection of film memorabilia (mostly from Crowe's films like *Gladiator* and *L.A. Confidential*), vintage cars, motorcycles, a giant Cobb & Co coach and other 'interesting things'. Open 11am–3pm Mon–Fri, 10am–5pm Sat, 10am–3pm Sun; 3970 Armidale Rd, Nymboida; (02) 6649 4126. 47 km sw.

Nymboida: Waters pumped by the hydro-electric power station from the Nymboida River into Goolang Creek provide a high-standard canoe course that hosts competitions throughout the year. Canoe hire and lessons are on offer and facilities range from the learners' pond for beginners to grade III rapids for the experienced, thrill-seeking canoeist. The beautiful rainforest surrounds are excellent for bushwalking, abseiling, trail rides and platypus viewing. 47 km sw.

Ulmarra Village: National Trust–classified turn-of-the-century river port with exceptional galleries, craft shops and studios where you can watch artists at work; 12 km NE. *Yuraygir National Park:* highlights include Wooli for unspoiled surf beaches and Minnie Water for walking trails, secluded beaches, camping and abundant wildlife (especially the very friendly wallabies). Minnie Lagoon is a popular swimming, picnicking and boating spot; 50 km SE. *Fishing:* river fishing for saltwater or freshwater fish, depending on time of year and rainfall; details at visitor centre.

See also TROPICAL NORTH COAST, p. 28

Grenfell
Pop. 1991
Map ref. 554 D6

ⓘ CWA Craft Shop and Visitors Centre, 68 Main St; (02) 6343 1612; www.grenfell.org.au

📻 99.5 Star FM, 549 AM ABC Local

Nestled at the foot of the Weddin Mountains, Grenfell is best known as the birthplace of writer Henry Lawson. The wealth appropriated during the days of the gold rush is evident in the opulent original buildings on Main Street. Originally named Emu Creek, the town was renamed after Gold Commissioner John Granville Grenfell, who was gunned down by bushrangers.

 Henry Lawson Obelisk: memorial on the site of the house where the poet is believed to have been born; next to Lawson Park on the road to Young. *Grenfell Museum:* local relics (and their stories) from world wars, the gold rush, Henry Lawson and bushrangers; open weekends 2–4pm; Camp St. *O'Brien's Reef Lookout:* views of the town on a gold-discovery site with walkway and picnic facilities; access from O'Brien St. *Weddin Bird Trails:*

NEW SOUTH WALES

unique Grenfell birdlife; maps from visitors centre. *Historic buildings:* walk and drive tours; brochures from visitor centre.

Guinea Pig Races: Easter and June. *Henry Lawson Festival of Arts:* June. *Amateur Country Music Festival:* Sept. *Open Day:* Oct.

Happy Inn Chinese Restaurant: traditional Chinese; Main St; (02) 6343 1366.

Weddin Mountains National Park The park is a rugged crescent of cliffs and gullies providing superb bushwalking, camping and picnicking spots. Two of the highlights of the bushwalks are Ben Hall's Cave, where the bushranger hid from the police, and Seaton's Farm, a historic homestead set on beautiful parkland. The bush is also rich with fauna including wedge-tailed eagles, honeyeaters and wallabies. 18 km sw.

Company Dam Nature Reserve: excellent bushwalking area; 1 km nw. *Site of Ben Hall's farmhouse and stockyards:* memorial; Sandy Creek Rd, off Mid Western Hwy; 25 km w.

See also CENTRAL WEST, p. 30

Griffith

Pop. 16 185
Map ref. 559 M7

Cnr Banna and Jondaryan avenues; (02) 6962 4145 or 1800 681 141; www.griffith.com.au

99.7 Star FM, 549 AM ABC Local

Griffith is surrounded by low hills and fragrant citrus orchards in the heart of the Murrumbidgee Irrigation Area. It was designed by Walter Burley Griffin and named after Sir Arthur Griffith, the first Minister for Public Works in New South Wales. It is one of the largest vegetable-production regions and produces more than 60 per cent of the state's wine.

Hermits Cave and Sir Dudley de Chair's Lookout Hermits Cave is located down a path below the lookout. The cave is named because it was once home to Valerio Ricetti, an Italian miner from Broken Hill. After being jilted, he left his home and job and became a hermit in this cave. After many years of solitude he fell and broke his leg, and when he was hospitalised he was recognised by people who had known him in Broken Hill. In later years he became ill and local citizens collected money to send him back home to Italy, where he died three months later. Scenic Dr.

Pioneer Park Museum: the 11 ha of bushland features 40 replica and restored buildings, early 20th-century memorabilia and re-created Bagtown Village; Remembrance Dr. *Italian Museum:* exhibiting the lives of the early Italian migrants to Griffith including collections of memorabilia and stories from local families; Remembrance Dr. *Griffith Regional Art Gallery:* exhibition program of international and Australian artists that changes monthly; Banna Ave. *Griffith Cottage Gallery:* local paintings, pottery and handicrafts with exhibitions at various times throughout the year; Bridge Rd. *Two Foot Tour and self-drive tour:* feature the city's historic buildings and surrounding pastures; brochure from visitor centre.

Market: Griffith Showground; each Sun morning. *La Festa:* food and wine festival celebrating cultural diversity; Easter. *UnWined in the Riverina:* food and wine festival; June. *Festival of Gardens:* Oct.

The Clock Restaurant & Wine Lounge: modern Australian; 239–242 Banna Ave; (02) 6962 7111. *La Scala:* traditional Italian; 455B Banna Ave; (02) 6962 4322.

Ingleden Park Cottages: self-contained cottages; Coghlan Rd; (02) 6963 6527. *Kidman Wayside Inn:* comfortable motel; 58–72 Jondaryan Ave; (02) 6964 5666. *Wilga Park Cottage:* self-contained cottage; 6 Condon Rd, via Bilpul; (02) 6968 1661.

Cocoparra National Park Original Riverina forest full of wattles, orchids and ironbarks, the park is spectacular in spring, when the wildflowers bloom. The site is ideal for bushwalking, camping, birdwatching and picnicking, and the rugged terrain and vivid colours also make it popular with photographers. 25 km NE.

Altina Wildlife Park: range of exotic and native wildlife, on the banks of the Murrumbidgee River, horserides and cart rides; inquiries 0412 060 342; 35 km s. *Catania Fruit Salad Farm:* horticultural farm with tours at 1.30pm daily; Cox Rd, Hanwood; (02) 6963 0219; 8 km s. *Lake Wyangan:* good spot for variety of watersports and picnicking; 10 km NW. *Many wineries:* include De Bortoli and McWilliams, open for cellar-door tastings; map from visitor centre.

See also RIVERINA, p. 34

Gulgong

Pop. 1904
Map ref. 554 H2

109 Herbert St; (02) 6374 1202; www.gulgong.net

93.1 Real FM, 107.1 FM ABC Local

Gulgong was named by the Wiradjuri people (the name means 'deep waterhole'.) The town did not excite European interest until gold was discovered in 1866. By 1872 there were 20 000 people living in the area. By the end of the decade 15 000 kilograms of gold had been unearthed, the prospectors had gone and almost all of the local Aboriginal people had been slaughtered. Today, the town stands visually almost unchanged from these times. The narrow, winding streets follow the paths of the original bullock tracks past iron-lace verandahs, horse troughs and hitching rails.

Henry Lawson Centre Housed in the Salvation Army Hall, which was built in 1922, the year Lawson died, the centre has the largest collection of Lawson memorabilia outside Sydney's Mitchell Library. It includes original manuscripts, artefacts, photographs, paintings and an extensive collection of rare first editions. 'A Walk Through Lawson's Life' is an exhibition that uses Lawson's words to illustrate the poverty, family disintegration, deafness and alcoholism that shaped his life, as well as the causes he was passionate about such as republicanism, unionism and votes for women. Mayne St; (02) 6374 2049.

Pioneers Museum: illustrates every era of Gulgong's history. Exhibits include a replica of a classroom from the 1880s, period clothing and rare antique crockery; Cnr Herbert and Bayly sts. *Red Hill:* site of the town's original gold strike, featuring restored stamper mill, poppet head and memorial to Henry Lawson; off White St. *Mayne Street Symbols:* inscribed in the pavement by a local artist, to depict the 'language of the road' used by diggers to advise their mates who may have followed them from other goldfields. *Town trail:* self-guide walking tour of historic buildings such as Prince of Wales Opera House and Ten Dollar Town Motel; brochure from visitor centre.

Folk Festival: Jan. *Henry Lawson Festival:* June.

Butcher Shop Cafe: relaxed atmosphere, delicious food; 113 Mayne St; (02) 6374 2622. *Phoebe's Licensed Restaurant:* modern Australian; cnr Mayne and Medley sts; (02) 6374 1204.

Green Gables B&B: quaint B&B; 8 Tallawang Rd; (02) 6374 2855.

Goulburn River National Park The park follows approximately 90 km of the Goulburn River with sandy riverbanks making easy walking trails and beautiful camping sites. Rare and threatened plants abound here, as do wombats, eastern grey kangaroos, emus and birds. Highlights include the Drip, 50 m curtains of water dripping through the rocks alongside the Goulburn River, sandstone cliffs honeycombed with caves, and over 300 significant Aboriginal sites. 30 km NE.

Ulan: Ulan Coal Mine has viewing areas overlooking a large open-cut mine. Also here is Hands on the Rock, a prime example of Aboriginal rock art; 22 km NE. *Talbragar Fossil Fish Beds:* one of the few Jurassic-period fossil deposits in Australia; 35 km NE. *Wineries:* cellar-door tastings; brochure from visitor centre.

See also CENTRAL WEST, p. 30

Gundagai
Pop. 1999
Map ref. 554 D9 | 565 A3 | 566 C1 | 585 P1

i 249 Sheridan St; (02) 6944 0250; www.gundagai.local-e.nsw.gov.au

94.3 FM Sounds of the Mountain, 549 AM ABC Local

Gundagai is a tiny town on the Murrumbidgee River at the foot of Mount Parnassus. The town and the nearby Dog on the Tuckerbox statue have been celebrated through song and verse for many years. Banjo Paterson, C. J. Dennis and Henry Lawson all included the town in their works. It was also the scene in 1852 of Australia's worst flood disaster when 89 of the 250 townsfolk died. The count could have been worse but for a local Aboriginal man, Yarri, who paddled his bark canoe throughout the night to rescue stranded victims. Gundagai was moved to higher ground soon after, and there are monuments celebrating Yarri's efforts. Near the visitor centre are statues of Dad, Dave, Mum and Mabel (characters from the writings of Steele Rudd).

 Marble Masterpiece In an amazing display of patience and determination, local sculptor Frank Rusconi, who is also responsible for the Dog on the Tuckerbox statue, worked to create a cathedral in miniature. He built it in his spare time over 28 years, hand-turning and polishing the 20 948 individual pieces required to build it. Visitor centre, Sheridan St.

Gabriel Gallery: outstanding collection of photographs, letters and possessions illustrating Gundagai's unique history; Sheridan St. *Gundagai Museum:* relics include Phar Lap's saddle, Frank Rusconi's tools, and artefacts from the horse and buggy era; Homer St. *Lookouts:* excellent views of the town and surrounding green valleys from the Mt Parnassus Lookout in Hanley St and the Rotary Lookout in Luke St; South Gundagai. *Historical town walk:* includes the National Trust–classified Prince Alfred Bridge and St John's Anglican Church; leaflet from visitor centre.

Turing Wave Festival: celebrating Irish heritage; Sept. *Spring Flower Show:* Oct. *Dog on the Tuckerbox Festival:* Nov. *Snake Gully Cup Carnival:* horserace; Nov. *Rodeo:* Dec.

The Poets' Recall Motel & Licensed Restaurant: country restaurant; Cnr Pinch and West sts; (02) 6944 1777.

Bengarralong B&B: riverside homestead; Tarrabandra Rd; (02) 6944 1175. *Gundagai Historic Cottages:* heritage self-contained exclusive-use accommodation; 51 Punch St; (02) 6944 2385. *Gundagai Tourist Park:* camping, basic cabins, caravan sites; 1 Nangus Rd; (02) 6944 4440 or 1300 722 906.

 The Dog on the Tuckerbox Originally mentioned in the poem *Bill the Bullocky* by Bowyang Yorke, this monument to pioneer teamsters and their dogs is recognised throughout the nation as an Australian icon. It was celebrated in the song 'Where the Dog Sits on the Tuckerbox' by Jack O'Hagan (the songwriter responsible for 'Along the Road to Gundagai'). The dog was unveiled in 1932 by Prime Minister Joseph Lyons. 8.5 km N.

See also RIVERINA, p. 34

Gunnedah
Pop. 7541
Map ref. 556 G9

i Anzac Park, South St; (02) 6740 2230 or 1800 562 527; www.infogunnedah.com.au

97.5 FM Triple G, 1044 AM ABC Local

At the heart of the Namoi Valley, Gunnedah is instantly recognisable by the grain silos that tower over the town. The area is abundant with native wildlife, especially koalas. Gunnedah claims to be the koala capital of the world, with one of the largest koala populations in the country; they are often seen wandering around town. A large centre, Gunnedah still manages to keep a laid-back atmosphere and has been home to famous Australians such as Dorothea Mackellar and Breaker Morant.

Anzac Park The Water Tower Museum here, housed in the town's main water tower, has a mural and display of early explorers, memorabilia from several wars and schools, and an Aboriginal history display (open 2–5pm Sat and most Mon). Dorothea Mackellar, the renowned Australian poet responsible for *My Country*, has a memorial statue in the park. Memorabilia of her life and of the annual national school poetry competition in her name can be viewed at the park's visitor centre. South St.

Rural Museum: early agricultural machinery and the largest privately owned firearm collection in the country; Mullaley Rd. *Red Chief Memorial:* to Aboriginal warrior Cumbo Gunnerah, of the Gunn-e-dar people of the Kamilaroi tribe; State Office building, Abbott St. *Old Bank Gallery:* local art and craft; Conadilly St. *Bicentennial Creative Arts Centre:* art and pottery display and the watercolour series 'My Country' by Jean Isherwood; open 10am–4pm Fri–Sun; Chandos St. *Plains of Plenty:* local craft and produce; South St. *Eighth Division Memorial Avenue:* with 45 flowering gums, each with a plaque in memory of men who served in the Eighth Division in WW II; Memorial Ave. *Breaker Morant Drive:* a plaque tells the story of Henry Morant, known as 'the breaker' because of his skill with horses. A 500 m path shows sites where he jumped horses; Kitchener Park. *Poets Drive:* celebration of Australian Poetry, the Poets Drive is a self-guide drive tour inspired by Gunnedah's iconic landmarks and local heroes. *Bindea walking track and town walk:* memorials, koala and kangaroo sites, lookouts and porcupine reserve; brochure from visitor centre.

Market: Wolseley Park, Conadilly St; 3rd Sat each month. *National Tomato Competition:* search for Australia's biggest tomato, and related celebrations; Jan. *Week of Speed:* races include go-karts, cars, bikes and athletics; Mar. *Gunnedah Bird Expo and Sale:* Apr. *Ag Quip:* agricultural field days; Aug. *North-West Swap Meet:* vintage cars; Sept.

Two Rivers Brasserie: hearty bistro meals; 313 Conadilly St; (02) 6742 0400. *The Verdict Coffee:* modern cafe; 147 Conadilly St; (02) 6742 0310.

Alyn Motel: comfortable contemporary accommodation; 351 Conadilly St; (02) 6742 5028.

Lake Keepit This lake is great for watersports, fishing and boating, and there is even a children's pool. If you want to stay a while longer, there is the Keepit Country Campout. The Campout provides all the facilities needed to camp without roughing it too much, including tents, a kitchen and showers and toilets, and there is a campfire amphitheatre for evening entertainment. For the daytime, there is all the equipment needed for canoeing, kayaking, rock climbing, gliding and bushwalking. 34 km NE.

Porcupine Lookout: views over town and surrounding agricultural area; 3 km SE. *Waterways Wildlife Park:* abundant with native animals such as kangaroos, koalas, wombats and emus; Mullaley Rd; 7 km W. *150° East Time Meridian:* the basis of Eastern Standard Time, crossing the Oxley Hwy; 28 km W.

See also NEW ENGLAND, p. 29

Guyra

Pop. 1755
Map ref. 557 J7

Rafters of Guyra Restaurant and Visitor Information Centre, New England Highway; (02) 6779 1876.

100.3 FM, 720 AM ABC Radio National

Guyra is the highest town on the New England tablelands at an altitude of 1320 metres on the watershed of the Great Dividing Range. Snow is not unusual in winter and at other times the town is crisp and green.

Mother of Ducks Lagoon The reserve is a rare high-country wetland and home to hundreds of waterbirds. The migratory Japanese snipe is known to stop here and it is a nesting site for swans. There is a viewing platform with an identification board covering dozens of different birds. McKie Pde.

Blush Tomatoes: largest greenhouse growing tomatoes in the Southern Hemisphere. It has boosted Guyra's population and economy enormously over the last 3 years; Elm St. *Historical Society Museum:* themed room displaying town memorabilia and the story of the Guyra ghost; open by appt; Bradley St; bookings (02) 6779 2132. *Railway Station:* large display of antique machinery, rail train rides; Bradley St.

Lamb and Potato Festival: includes Hydrangea Festival; Jan.

Rafters Seafood: hearty fare; New England Hwy; (02) 6779 1876.

George's Creek Cottages: self-contained cottages on working sheep and cattle farm; 'Cabarfeidh', Wandsworth via Guyra; (02) 6779 4235. *Top of the Range Retreat:* luxury self-contained cottages; 93 Ollera St; (02) 6779 2336.

Thunderbolt's Cave: picturesque and secluded cave, rumoured to be where the bushranger Captain Thunderbolt hid from police; 10 km S. *Handcraft Hall – The Pink Stop:* hand-knitted garments, paintings, pottery and Devonshire teas; 10 km N. *Chandler's Peak:* spectacular views of the tablelands from an altitude of 1471 m; 20 km E.

See also NEW ENGLAND, p. 29

Hay

Pop. 2632
Map ref. 559 J7

407 Moppett St; (02) 6993 4045; www.visithay.com.au

92.1 Hay FM, 100.9 FM ABC Radio National

Located in the heart of the Riverina, the most striking thing about Hay is the incredibly flat plains in which it sits. The saltbush flats afford amazing views across the land, especially at sunrise and sunset, and the terrain makes bicycles a popular and easy mode of transport for residents. American travel writer Bill Bryson described Hay as 'a modest splat' and 'extremely likeable'.

POW Internment Camp Interpretive Centre Housed in Hay's magnificent restored railway station, the centre documents the WW II internment in Hay of over 3000 prisoners of war. The first internees were known as the 'Dunera boys', Jewish intellectuals who had fled Germany and Austria. The camp established a garrison band and a newspaper and printed camp money. The Dunera boys even ran their own 'university', teaching subjects such as atomic research and classical Greek. The Dunera boys held a reunion in Hay in 1990 and there is a memorial on Showground Rd. Murray St; inquiries (02) 6993 4045.

Shear Outback Centre – The Australian Shearers Hall of Fame: interactive experiences and shearing deomonstrations with sheep dogs, historic Murray Downs Woolshed and exhibitions; Sturt Hwy; inquiries (02) 6993 4000. *Witcombe Fountain:* ornate drinking fountain presented to the people of Hay by mayor John Witcombe in 1883; Lachlan St. *Coach house:* features an 1886 Cobb & Co coach, which travelled the Deniliquin–Hay–Wilcannia route until 1901; Lachlan St. *Hay Gaol Museum:* contains memorabilia and photographs of the town, and the building's history from 1878 as a gaol, maternity hospital, hospital for the insane and POW compound; Church St; inquiries (02) 6993 4045. *War Memorial High School Museum:* built in recognition of those who served in WW I, with war memorabilia and an honour roll. The building still operates as a school, so call for opening times (02) 6993 1408; Pine St. *Bishop's Lodge:* restored 1888 iron house, now a museum and gallery with a unique and remarkable collection of heritage roses. Holds a market 3rd Sun in Oct. Open 2–4.30pm Mon–Sat; Cnr Roset St and Sturt Hwy. *Ruberto's Winery:* cellar-door tastings; Sturt Hwy. *Hay Wetlands:* especially spectacular in spring, the land is a breeding ground for over 60 inland bird species with a breeding island and tree plantation; north-western edge of town; brochure from visitor centre. *Hay Park:* pleasant picnic spot with a nature walk along the banks of the river; off Brunker St. *Murrumbidgee River:* excellent sandy river beaches and calm water, perfect for waterskiing, canoeing, swimming and picnics. Enjoy excellent freshwater fishing for Murray cod, yellow-belly perch and redfin. A licence is required; available from outlets in town, including visitor centre. *Heritage walk and scenic drive:* walk includes city structures built for the harsh outback such as the beautifully restored courthouse (1892) on Moppett St and the shire office (1877) on Lachlan St. The drive takes in the parklands, river and surrounding saltbush plains; brochure from visitor centre.

Sheep Show: June. *Rodeo:* Oct. *Hay Races:* Nov.

Cumquats Cuisine: popular cafe; 161 Lachlan St; (02) 6993 4399. *Jolly Jumbuck Bistro:* relaxed bistro; 148 Lachlan St; (02) 6993 1137.

BIG 4 Hay Plains Holiday Park: basic cabins, camping sites; 4 Nailor St; (02) 6993 1875 or 1800 251 974. *Saltbush*

Motor Inn: contemporary motel; 193 Lachlan St; (02) 6993 4555. *The Bank:* heritage-listed, centrally located; 86 Lachlan St; (02) 6993 1730.

 Booligal In an area known as the 'devil's claypan', this hot and dusty sheep- and cattle-town is mentioned in Banjo Paterson's poem *Hay and Hell and Booligal*. The poem says that a visit to Booligal is a fate worse than hell with topics of complaint including heat, flies, dust, rabbits, mosquitoes and snakes. On the plus side, the atmosphere is relaxed and friendly. It is off the beaten tourist track and there is a memorial to John Oxley, the first European in the area, in the shape of a giant theodolite (surveyor's tool). 78 km N. Halfway to Booligal, look out for the lonely ruins of One Tree Hotel.

Hay Weir: on the Murrumbidgee River, excellent for picnics, barbecues and Murray cod fishing; 12 km w. *Sunset viewing area:* the vast plains provide amazingly broad and spectacular sunsets; Booligal Rd; 16 km N. *Maude Weir:* surprisingly green and lush oasis, ideal for picnics and barbecues; 53 km w. *Goonawarra Nature Reserve:* no facilities for visitors, but the flood plains with river red gum forests and black box woodlands are still worth a visit – waterfowl in the billabongs, plenty of Murray cod in the Lachlan River and kangaroos and emus on the plains; 59 km N. *Oxley:* tiny town with river red gums and prolific wildlife (best seen at dusk); 87 km NW.

See also RIVERINA, p. 34

Holbrook

Pop. 1339
Map ref. 554 B11 | 559 P11 | 585 M4

ⓘ Greater Hume Shire Visitor Information Centre, 15 Wallace St; (02) 6036 2422; www.holbrook.nsw.au

📻 93.1 Star FM, 990 AM ABC Radio National

Holbrook is a well-known stock-breeding centre rich with history. Originally called The Germans because of its first European settlers, the name was later changed to Germanton. During World War I, with the allies fighting the Germans, even this name became unacceptable and a new name had to be found. British Commander Norman Holbrook was a war hero and had been awarded the Victoria Cross and the French Legion of Honour, so it was decided the town would be named after him.

 Otway Submarine The 30 m vessel, once under the command of Norman Holbrook, was decommissioned in 1995. The town was given the fin of the submarine by the Royal Australian Navy and was busily trying to raise funds to purchase the full piece of history, when a gift of $100 000 from Commander Holbrook's widow made the purchase possible. Mrs Holbrook was the guest of honour at the unveiling in 1996. The Submarine Museum next door features submariner memorabilia, including a control room with working periscope, and Commander Holbrook Room. Hume Hwy.

Bronze statue: Commander Holbrook and his submarine, a scale model of the one in which Holbrook won the VC in WW I; Holbrook Park, Hume Hwy. *Woolpack Inn Museum:* 22 rooms furnished in turn-of-the-century style, horse-drawn vehicles and farm equipment surrounded by lovely gardens; Albury St. *Ten Mile Creek Gardens:* attractive gardens, excellent for picnics. Also features a miniature railway, operating on the 2nd and 4th Sun each month, and every Sat during holidays; behind museum. *National Museum of Australian Pottery:* extensive range of 19th- and early-20th-century domestic pottery, and photographs;

closed Wed, and Aug; Albury St. *Ian Geddes Walk:* through tranquil bushland, following Ten Mile Creek. Begins behind Grimwood's Craft Shop; Hume Hwy.

 Planes, Trains and Submarines Festival: Mar.

ⓧ *Holbrook Airfield:* ultralight flights over town and surrounds available; 3 km N. *Hume and Hovell Walking Track:* access to short sections of the 440 km track from Albury to Yass via Woomargama; 15 km s. For a kit, including maps, contact Department of Lands, Sydney (02) 9228 6666.

See also MURRAY, p. 35

Huskisson

Pop. 3391
Map ref. 553 D11 | 555 J10 | 565 G4 | 567 O2

ⓘ Shoalhaven Visitors Centre, cnr Princes Hwy and Pleasant Way, Nowra; (02) 4421 0778 or 1300 662 808; www.shoalhaven. nsw.gov.au

📻 94.9 Power FM, 603 AM Radio National

Huskisson is a sleepy holiday resort and fishing port on Jervis (pronounced 'Jarvis') Bay. It was named after British politician William Huskisson, secretary for the colonies and leader of the House of Commons, who was killed by a train in 1830 while talking to the Duke of Wellington at a railway opening. The idyllic bay is renowned for its white sand and clear water, and there are usually several pods of dolphins living in the bay, making the area ideal for cruises and diving.

🏛 **Lady Denman Heritage Complex** The centre features displays on the history of wooden shipbuilding at Huskisson. There is also Laddie Timbery's Aboriginal Art and Craft Centre, with bush tucker demonstrations and talks on request, and the Museum of Jervis Bay Science and the Sea with fine maritime and surveying collections. Woollamia Rd; inquiries (02) 4441 5675.

🎪 *Market:* Huskisson Sporting Ground; 2nd Sun each month. *White Sands Carnival:* stalls, music and entertainment; Easter.

🍴 *Huskisson Bakery and Cafe:* sandwiches, homemade pies; 11 Currambene St; (02) 4441 5015. *Locavore:* cafe with organic and Fair Trade products; 2/66 Owen St; (02) 4441 5464. *Seagrass Brasserie:* seafood; 13 Currambene St; (02) 4441 6124.*The Gunyah Restaurant:* modern Australian, stunning treetop views; Paperbark Camp, 571 Woollamia Rd, Woollamia; (02) 4441 7299.

🛏 *Sandholme Guesthouse:* romantic boutique coastal retreat; 2 Jervis St; (02) 4441 8855. *Paperbark Camp:* luxury safari-style tree houses; 571 Woollamia Rd, Woollamia; (02) 4441 6066 or 1300 668 167.

ⓧ **Booderee National Park** This park is jointly managed by the Wreck Bay Aboriginal Community and Environment Australia. Highlights include Aboriginal sites, the Cape George Lighthouse, Booderee Botanic Gardens and magnificent beaches. Barry's Bush Tucker Tours offers guided walks drawing on Aboriginal food and culture. Bookings on (02) 4442 1168; 11 km s.

Jervis Bay National Park: walking tracks, mangrove boardwalk and amazing beaches (Hyams Beach claims the whitest sand in the world); north and south of town. *Jervis Bay Marine Park:* the clear waters, reefs and deep-water cliffs with caves offer superb diving. Bookings are taken at the visitor centre for dolphin-watching cruises.

See also SOUTH COAST, p. 32

Iluka

Pop. 1739
Map ref. 551 F7

 Lower Clarence Visitor Centre, Ferry Park, Pacific Hwy, Maclean; (02) 6645 4121; www.clarencetourism.com

104.7 FM Clarence Coast's FM, 738 AM ABC Local

Located at the mouth of the Clarence River on the north coast, Iluka is a relatively uncommercial fishing and holiday village. Its attractiveness is evident in the long stretches of sandy white beaches and rare and accessible rainforest. Iluka Nature Reserve has the largest remnant of littoral rainforest (trees obtaining water via filtration through coastal sand and nutrients from airborne particles) in New South Wales.

River cruises: day cruises and evening barbecue cruises (Wed only); Wed, Fri and Sun; from the Boatshed. *Passenger ferry:* travelling daily to Yamba; from the Boatshed. *Iluka Fish Co-op:* fresh catches on sale from 9am; adjacent to the Boatshed. *Walking track:* picturesque coastline walk; access via Iluka Bluff to the north and Long St to the south.

Makuti Cafe: waterfront cafe; 2A Charles St; (02) 6646 5212.

Iluka Nature Reserve This area, nestled on the narrow peninsula where the Clarence River meets the ocean, was World Heritage–listed in 1986. It happens to be the largest remaining coastal rainforest in NSW. It is rich with birdlife and is a beautiful spot for activities such as fishing, swimming, surfing, canoeing, walking and camping. 1 km N.

Iluka Bluff Beach: safe swimming beach with good surf and a whale-watching lookout; brochure from visitors centre; 1 km N. *Bundjalung National Park:* protects ancient rainforest and the Esk River, the largest untouched coastal river system on the north coast. Woody Head has rare rainforest with campground, fishing and swimming; 4 km N. *Woombah Coffee Plantation:* world's southernmost coffee plantation; tours by appt; bookings (02) 6646 4121; 12 km NW.

See also TROPICAL NORTH COAST, p. 28

Inverell

Pop. 9748
Map ref. 557 I5

 Campbell St; (02) 6728 8161 or 1800 067 626; www.inverell-online.com.au

95.1 Gem FM, 738 AM ABC Local

This town on the Macintyre River at the centre of the New England tablelands is known as the 'Sapphire City'. It is also rich in other mineral deposits, including zircons, industrial diamonds and tin. The country here has lush farm and grazing land and excellent weather conditions with cool nights and warm sunny days. A Scottish immigrant gave Inverell its name, which means 'meeting place of the swans' in Gaelic.

Pioneer Village This collection of homes and buildings dating from 1840 was moved from its original site to form a 'village of yesteryear'. Attractions include Grove homestead, Paddy's Pub and Mt Drummond Woolshed. Gooda Cottage has an impressive collection of gems and minerals. Tea and damper are served by prior arrangement. Tingha Rd; (02) 6722 1717.

Visitor Centre and Mining Museum: local and imported gems, a static display on the local mining industry, photographs and a video of local mines, and a working scale model of a sapphire plant; Water Towers Complex, Campbell St. *Inverell Art Centre:* paintings, pottery and craft; Evans St. *Gem Centre:* visitors can see local stones being processed; Byron St. *Transport Museum:* over 200 vehicles on display with an impressive collection of rarities; Taylor Ave. *Town Stroll:* includes sites such as the National Trust–classified courthouse and the CBC Bank building with stables at the rear; brochure from visitor centre. *Arts, crafts and wood-turning:* work by local artists; brochure from visitor centre.

Market: Campbell Park: 1st (except Jan) and 3rd Sun each month. *Outback Festival:* Sept. *Grafton to Inverell Cycling Classic:* Sept. *Sapphire City Festival:* Oct. *Antique Machinery Rally:* Oct. *Great Inland Fishing Festival:* Dec. *Inverell Jockey Club Boxing Day Meeting:* Dec.

The Royal Club Hotel: international cuisine; 260 Byron St; (02) 6722 2811.

Blair Athol Estate: luxury country guesthouse; Warialda Rd; (02) 6722 4288. *Fossickers Rest Tourist Park:* lovely holiday park; Lake Inverell Dr; (02) 6722 2261.

Kwiambal National Park The Macintyre River flows through gorges and plunge pools to Macintyre Falls and then leads into the Severn River. The park is rich with protected woodlands of white cypress pine, box and ironbark. Bat nurseries can be viewed with a torch in the remarkable Ashford Caves, which until the 1960s were mined for guano (bat droppings) to be used as fertiliser on local farms. The park makes a serene site for swimming, bushwalking and camping. Encounters with kangaroos, emus and koalas are common. 90 km N.

McIlveen Lookout: excellent views of town and surrounding pastures and nature reserve; 2 km W. *Lake Inverell Reserve:* 100 ha of unique aquatic sanctuary for birds and wildlife. Also an excellent site for picnics, bushwalking, birdwatching and fishing; 3 km E. *Draught Horse Centre:* 6 breeds of horse and displays of harnesses and memorabilia, horses are paraded twice daily; Fishers Rd; 4 km E. *Goonoowigall Bushland Reserve:* rough granite country rich with birdlife and marsupials, it offers superb birdwatching, remains of a Chinese settlement, bushwalking trails and picnic areas; 5 km S. *Morris' Honey Farm:* visitors can see working bees, taste honey and learn how it is produced. Ride the miniature train and explore the animal park and bottle museum; inquiries (02) 6723 6281; 8 km SW. *Copeton Dam State Recreation Area:* perfect for boating, waterskiing, swimming, fishing, bushwalking and rock climbing. It also has adventure playgrounds, water slides, and picnic and barbecue facilities. Kangaroos graze on the golf course at dusk; inquiries (02) 6723 6269; 17 km S. *DeJon Sapphire Centre:* working sapphire mine with sales; Glen Innes Rd; (02) 6723 2222; 19 km E. *Gwydir Ranch 4WD Park:* rugged and colourful gorge country ideal for canoeing, camping, fishing, bushwalking and swimming. Also popular with photographers and artists; 28 km W. *Green Valley Farm:* working sheep property with zoo, accommodation, extensive gardens, playground and picnic and barbecue facilities. The highlight is Smith's Mining and Natural History Museum, with a rare collection of gems and minerals, local Aboriginal artefacts, antiques and period clothing; inquiries (02) 6723 3370; 36 km SE. *Pindari Dam:* fishing, swimming, camping and picnic and barbecue facilities; 58 km N. *Gwydir River:* one of the best whitewater rafting locations in the country during the summer months; brochure from visitor centre. *Warm-weather wineries:*

cellar-door tastings; brochure from visitor centre. *Fossicking sites:* great spots for searching for tin, sapphires, quartz or even diamonds; maps at visitor centre.

See also NEW ENGLAND, p. 29

Jamberoo

Pop. 935
Map ref. 553 E7 | 555 J9 | 565 H3

 Jamberoo Newsagency Visitor Centre, Shop 2, 18 Allowrie St; (02) 4236 0100; www.kiama.com.au

98 FM, 603 AM ABC Radio National

One of the most picturesque areas of the New South Wales coast, Jamberoo was once tropical forest. The town is surrounded by nature reserves and national parks, but is now situated on the lush green dairy pastures that have made Jamberoo prosperous as a dairy farming region. The surrounding forests are popular with bushwalkers and birdwatchers.

Jamberoo Hotel: charming 1857 building with meals and Sun afternoon entertainment; Allowrie St.

Market: Kevin Walsh Oval; last Sun each month.

Ben Ricketts Environmental Preserve: basic self-contained cabins; 774 Jamberoo Mountain Rd; (02) 4236 0208. *Cedar Mists Cottage:* rustic rainforest cottage; 130 Misty La; (02) 4237 6199. *The Birdhouse:* contemporary self-contained cottage; location provided with booking; 0432 445 229.

Budderoo National Park This park offers views from a plateau across sandstone country, heathlands and rainforest. There are excellent walking trails, including one that is accessible by wheelchair, and there are 3 lookouts with views of Carrington Falls. The Minnamurra Rainforest Centre is the highlight with an elevated boardwalk through rainforest and a steep paved walkway to Minnamurra Falls. 4 km w.

Jamberoo Action Park: family fun park with water slides, speedboats, racing cars and bobsleds; (02) 4236 0114; 3 km N. *Jerrara Dam:* a picturesque reserve on the banks of a 9 ha dam that was once the town's main water supply. Picnic area surrounded by remnant rainforest and freshwater wetland; 4 km SE. *Saddleback Lookout:* 180-degree views of the coast and the starting point for Hoddles Trail, a 1 hr walk with beautiful views to Barren Grounds escarpment; 7 km S. *Barren Grounds Nature Reserve:* this 1750 ha heathland plateau on the Illawarra Escarpment protects over 450 species of plant and 150 species of bird, including the rare ground parrot and eastern bristlebird. It has fabulous bushwalking and birdwatching; guided tours available (bookings (02) 4423 2170); park details from Fitzroy Falls Visitor Centre (02) 4887 7270; 10 km SW.

See also SOUTHERN HIGHLANDS, p. 24

Jerilderie

Pop. 769
Map ref. 559 L10 | 584 G1

 The Willows Museum, 11 Powell St; (03) 5886 1666.

94.1 FM ABC Radio National, Classic Rock 102.5 FM

Jerilderie is an important merino stud area, but is better known for its links with the Kelly Gang. In 1879 the gang captured the police, held the townspeople hostage for two days, cut the telegraph wires and robbed the bank. It was here that Kelly handed over the famous Jerilderie Letter, justifying his actions and voicing his disrespect for police, whom he called 'a parcel of big ugly fat-necked wombat-headed, big-bellied, magpie-legged, narrow-hipped, splay-footed sons of Irish bailiffs or English

landlords'. The town of Jerilderie is now the gateway to the Kidman Way, an 800-kilometre outback highway.

Telegraph Office and The Willows Museum The well-preserved Telegraph Office is where the Kelly Gang cut the telegraph wires in 1879. The Willows Museum next door houses photographs, including some of the Kelly Gang, documents of local historical significance and the cell door from the old police station. Samples of local craft are also on display and Devonshire teas are available. Powell St.

St Luke Park: features Steel Wings, one of the largest windmills in the Southern Hemisphere. The park runs along the bank of Lake Jerilderie, which is popular for all watersports, especially waterskiing. *Mini Heritage Steam Rail:* runs along charming Billabong Creek, which also features the 1.8 km Horgans Walk. Entry behind The Willows Museum; runs 2nd and 5th Sun each month. *Ned Kelly Heritage Trail:* retraces the gangs' visit; brochure from visitor centre.

Coleambally Officially opened in 1968, Coleambally is NSW's newest town and is at the centre of the Coleambally Irrigation Area. It features the Wineglass Water Tower and a dragline excavator used in the irrigation scheme. The excavator is still in working order and can be viewed in the Lions Park at the town's entrance. Tours of the rice mill and of the farms are possible. The area is a haven for birdlife and kangaroos. 62 km N.

See also MURRAY, p. 35

Jindabyne

Pop. 1902
Map ref. 565 B8 | 566 E10 | 581 C4

 Snowy Region Visitor Centre, Kosciuszko Rd; (02) 6450 5600; www.snowymountains.com.au

97.1 FM Radio National, 97.7 Snow FM

Jindabyne, adjacent to the south-eastern section of Kosciuszko National Park (*see Adaminaby and Thredbo*) and just below the snowline, was relocated from its original site on the banks of the Snowy River to make way for the Snowy Mountains Hydro-Electric Scheme. The original town was flooded, but a few of the buildings were moved to their current site beside Lake Jindabyne. The area is popular with skiers in the winter and with anglers, bushwalkers and whitewater rafters in the summer.

Walkway and cycleway: around Lake Jindabyne's foreshore, from Banjo Paterson Park on Kosciuszko Rd to Snowline Caravan Park. *Winter shuttle bus service:* several operators depart from various spots in town to Bullocks Flat and Thredbo; contact visitor centre for more information.

Speed and Marathon Championships: Lake Jindabyne; Jan. *Flowing Festival:* music and dragon-boat races: Feb. *Lake Light Sculpture:* Apr. *Snowy Mountains Trout Festival:* fishing competition throughout region; Nov. *Boxing Day Rodeo:* Dec.

Mario's Mineshaft Restaurant and Bar: modern Italian; Lakeview Plaza Motel, 2 Snowy River Ave; (02) 6456 2727.

Jindy Inn: simple accommodation, gorgeous lake views; 18 Clyde St; (02) 6456 1957. *Wanderers Retreat:* B&B or self-contained units; 54 Gippsland St; (02) 6456 2091.

Perisher The largest ski resort in Australia with an impressive 1250 ha of skiing area, Perisher caters for all levels of skier and snowboarder. State-of-the-art equipment includes many high-quality snow guns and Australia's first 8-seater chairlifts. The resort consists of slopes, accommodation, restaurants, bars and all the facilities and equipment hire needed to enjoy winter sports at Perisher and the nearby skiing areas of Smiggin Holes, Mt Blue Cow and Guthega. 30 km w.

Lake Jindabyne: well stocked with rainbow trout and ideal for boating, waterskiing and other watersports. When the water level is low, remains of the submerged town can be seen; western edge of town. *Kunama Gallery:* over 200 paintings by local artists and work by acclaimed water colourist Alan Grosvenor. Also panoramic views of Lake Jindabyne; (02) 6456 1100; 7 km NE. *Snowy Valley Lookout:* stunning views of Lake Jindabyne; 8 km N. *Gaden Trout Hatchery:* daily tours and barbecues along Thredbo River; (02) 6451 3400; 10 km NW. *Wildbrumby Schnapps Distillery:* boutique schnapps made from seasonal fruits, with cafe and cellar door; Wollondibby Rd; (02) 6457 1447; 11 km W. *Crackenback Cottage:* local craft, maze, restaurant and guesthouse; (02) 6456 2198; 12 km SW. *Sawpit Creek:* the Kosciuszko Education Centre can be found here. The start of the Palliabo (walking) Track is at the Sawpit Creek picnic area; 14 km NW. *Bullocks Flat:* terminal for Skitube, a European-style alpine train to Perisher ski resort; operates daily during ski season; 20 km SW. *Wallace Craigie Lookout:* views of Snowy River Valley; 40 km SW. *Charlotte Pass:* highest ski resort in Australia with challenging slopes for experienced skiers. Magnificent 24 km walking track past Blue Lake in summer; 45 km W. *Scenic walks:* varying lengths; brochures from visitor centre. *Alpine Way:* 111 km road through mountains to Khancoban provides superb scenic touring in summer; chains frequently required in winter.

See also SNOWY MOUNTAINS, p. 33

Katoomba
see inset box on next page

Kempsey
Pop. 8139
Map ref. 550 G4 | 557 M10

 Cultural Centre, Pacific Hwy, South Kempsey; (02) 6563 1555 or 1800 642 480; www.macleayvalleycoast.com.au

 105.1 ROX FM, 684 AM ABC Local

Kempsey is an attractive town in the Macleay River Valley on the mid-north coast, with white sandy beaches and an unspoiled hinterland. It claims two quintessential Aussies as its own: singer Slim Dusty was born here in 1927 (while he died in 2003, he remains one of the country's best-loved country singers) and the Akubra hat has been made here since 1974.

Wigay Aboriginal Cultural Park: Aboriginal cultural experience, including introduction to bush tucker, learning about the use of plants and throwing a boomerang; Sea St. *Cultural Centre:* incorporates the Macleay River Historical Society Museum and visitor centre, a settlers cottage, displays on Akubra hats and Slim Dusty, and a working model of a timber mill; Pacific Hwy, South Kempsey. *Historical walks:* carefully restored historic buildings include the courthouse, post office and West Kempsey Hotel; brochure from visitor centre.

Markets: showground, 1st Sat each month; South West Rocks, 2nd Sat each month. *Gaol Break Swim:* 2.7 km race along Trial Bay beach to South West Rocks; Easter. *Kempsey Cup:* horserace; May. *Akubra Classic Motorcycle Championships:* June. *Truck and Ute Show:* Oct. *Kempsey Country Music Festival:* Oct/Nov.

Netherby Cafe: tranquil cafe; 5 Little Rudder St; (02) 6563 1777.

Netherby House B&B: tranquil retreat; 5 Little Rudder St, East Kempsey; (02) 6563 1777. *Grass Trees Escape:* self-contained cottages; Fern Tree Close, Arakoon; (02) 9907 1440.

Limeburners Creek Nature Reserve Showcases a beautiful coastline of heathlands, banksia and blackbutt forests. The rare rainforest of Big Hill is home to the threatened ground parrot. The beach is popular for swimming, surfing and fishing and there are camping areas with varying levels of facilities. 33 km SE.

South West Rocks Attractions include a pristine white beach, a maritime history display at the restored Boatmans Cottage and the opportunity to handfeed fish at the Everglades Aquarium. The area is excellent for watersports, diving, camping and boating. The nearby Trial Bay Gaol (1886) was a public works prison until 1903 and reopened to hold 'enemy aliens' in WW I. Smoky Cape has a lighthouse offering tours and accommodation and clear views up and down the coast. Fish Rock Cave, just off the cape, is well known for its excellent diving. 37 km NE.

Frederickton: 'Fredo' has beautiful views of river flats, and its award-winning pie shop boasts 148 varieties; 8 km NE. *Kundabung:* tiny village with Australasian bullriding titles in Oct; 14 km S. *Gladstone:* fishing, antiques and crafts; 15 km NE. *Crescent Head:* this seaside holiday town has good surfing. There is an Aboriginal bora ring (ceremonial ground) just to the north. The Sky Show with kites, flying displays and fireworks is held each June and the Crescent Head Malibu Longboard Classic is in May (the largest longboard competition in Australia); 20 km SE. *Barnett's Rainbow Beach Oyster Barn:* direct purchases and viewing of oyster processing; 31 km NE. *Hat Head National Park:* magnificent dunes and unspoiled beaches, popular for birdwatching, snorkelling, swimming and walking. Korogoro Point is a fabulous spot for whale-watching May–July and Sept–Oct; 32 km E. *Bellbrook:* classified by the National Trust as a significant example of a turn-of-the-century hamlet; 50 km NW. *Walks and self-guide drives:* nature-reserve walks and historical and scenic drives; details from visitor centre.

See also HOLIDAY COAST, p. 27

Kiama
Pop. 12 290
Map ref. 553 F7 | 555 J9 | 565 H3

 Blowhole Point Rd; (02) 4232 3322 or 1300 654 262; www.kiama.com.au

98 FM, 1431 AM ABC Radio National

This popular holiday town, hosting one million visitors each year, is best known as the home of the Kiama Blowhole. The rocky coastline, sandy beaches and appealing harbour provide an attractive contrast to the green rolling hills of the lush dairy pastures of the hinterland.

Kiama Blowhole The spectacular blowhole sprays to heights of 60 m and is floodlit at night. Beside the blowhole is a constructed rockpool and a cafe. Pilots Cottage Historical Museum has displays on the blowhole, early settlement, the dairy industry and shipping. Blowhole Pt; (02) 4232 1001.

Family History Centre: world-wide collection of records for compiling and tracing family history; Railway Pde; (02) 4233 1122. *Heritage walk:* includes terraced houses in Collins St and Pilots Cottage; leaflet from visitor centre. *Specialty and craft shops:* several in town showcasing local work; leaflet from visitor centre. *Beaches:* perfect for surfing, swimming and fishing.

Craft market: Black Beach; 3rd Sun each month. *Produce market:* Black Beach; 4th Sat each month. *Rotary Antique Fair:* Jan. *Jazz and Blues Festival:* Mar. *Big Fish Classic:* game-fishing competition; Apr.

55 on Collins: modern Australian; 55 Collins St; (02) 4232 2811. *Cargo's Wharf Restaurant:* seafood; Kiama Wharf; (02) 4233 2771.

Seashells Kiama: self-contained family accommodation; 72 Bong Bong St; (02) 4232 2504. *Spring Creek Retreat:* resort-style accommodation; 41 Jerrara Rd; (02) 4232 2700. *Bellachara Boutique Hotel:* chic boutique hotel; 1 Fern St, Gerringong; (02) 4234 1359.

 Gerringong A coastal town with a renowned heritage museum featuring remarkable scale models of the Illawarra coast. Gerringong's name comes from the Wodi Wodi language and is said to mean 'place of peril'. It is unclear where the peril lies, however, with safe beaches ideal for surfing, swimming and fishing. Heavy rainfall means the hinterland is lush and green. 10 km s.

Little Blowhole: smaller but more active than the Kiama Blowhole; off Tingira Cres; 2 km s. *Bombo Headland:* blue-metal quarrying in the 1880s left an eerie 'moonscape' of basalt walls and columns, which have been used in commercials and video clips; 2.5 km N. *Cathedral Rocks:* scenic rocky outcrop best viewed at dawn; Jones Beach; 3 km N. *Kingsford Smith Memorial and Lookout:* site of Charles Kingsford Smith's 1933 take-off in the *Southern Cross*, with panoramic views; 14 km s. *Seven Mile Beach National Park:* surrounded by sand dunes, this low forest is inhabited by birds and small marsupials. It makes a pretty spot for picnics and barbecues, beach fishing and swimming; 17 km s. *Scenic drives:* in all directions to visit beaches, rock formations, cemeteries and craft shops; brochure from visitor centre.

See also SOUTHERN HIGHLANDS, p. 24

Kyogle

Pop. 2730
Map ref. 551 E4 | 557 N3 | 653 M12

i Summerland Way; (02) 6632 2700; www.tropicalnsw.com.au

104.3 FM 2LM, 738 AM ABC Local

Located at the upper reaches of the Richmond River and the base of the charmingly named Fairy Mountain, Kyogle is known as the 'gateway to the rainforests'. It is almost completely surrounded by the largest remaining areas of rainforest in New South Wales.

Captain Cook Memorial Lookout: at the top of Mt Fairy, the lookout provides stunning views of the town and surrounding countryside; Fairy St. *Botanical Gardens:* combination of formal gardens and revegetated creek environments on the banks of Fawcetts Creek; Summerland Way.

Campdraft: July. *Fairymount Festival – Hell on Hooves:* bullriding; July. *Gateway to the Rainforest Motorcycle Rally:* Sept. *Fairymount Festival – Remembering Yesterday, Dreaming Tomorrow:* Nov.

Ripples on the Creek: popular restaurant/cafe; Lions Road Tourist Drive, Gradys Creek; (02) 6636 6132.

 Border Ranges National Park World Heritage–listed, this 30 000 ha park has walking tracks, camping, swimming, rock climbing and fantastic views of Mt Warning and the Tweed Valley. Sheepstation Creek is an attractive picnic spot. The Tweed Range Scenic Drive (64 km) is a breathtaking journey of rainforest, deep gorges and waterfalls. Brochure from visitor centre. 27 km N.

Wiangaree: rural community with rodeo in Mar; 15 km N. *Roseberry Forest Park:* picturesque picnic spot; 23 km N. *Moore Park Nature Reserve:* tiny reserve with the most important example of black bean rainforest in NSW; 26 km NW. *Toonumbar Dam:* built from earth and rocks, this offers scenic bushwalking with picnic and barbecue facilities. Nearby Bells Bay is known for its bass fishing and has a campsite; 31 km W. *Toonumbar National Park:* contains 2 World Heritage–listed rainforests and the volcanic remnants of Edinburgh Castle, Dome Mountain and Mt Lindesay; 35 km W. *Richmond Range National Park:* protected rainforest perfect for camping, birdwatching, picnics and barbecues, with good bushwalking on a 2 km or 6 km track; 40 km W. *Scenic forest drive:* via Mt Lindesay (45 km NW), offers magnificent views of both the rainforest and the countryside; brochure from visitor centre.

See also TROPICAL NORTH COAST, p. 28

Lake Cargelligo

Pop. 1149
Map ref. 554 A4 | 559 N4

i 1 Foster St; (02) 6898 1501; www.heartofnsw.com.au

99.7 Star FM, 549 AM ABC Local

Lake Cargelligo is a surprisingly attractive small town in the heart of the wide, brown Riverina plains. Built beside the lake of the same name, the town's activities revolve around the water with fishing and regular lake festivals.

Lake Cargelligo The lake dominates the town and is popular for fishing (silver perch, golden perch and redfin), boating, sailing, waterskiing and swimming. It is also appealing to birdwatchers, being home to many bird species including the rare black cockatoo. There is a historic walkway and bicycle track.

Wagon Rides and Working Horse Demonstrations: can be arranged by appt on (02) 6898 1384. *Information centre:* houses a large gem collection and carved stone butterflies; Foster St. *Kejole Koori Studio:* Aboriginal art, jewellery and didgeridoos; Grace St.

Blue Waters Art Exhibition and Competition: June. *Lake Show:* Sept. *Lake Cargelligo Fisharama:* Oct.

 Willandra National Park Once one-eighth of a huge merino sheep station, the 20 000 ha park features a restored homestead (offering accommodation), stables, a shearing complex and men's quarters. The buildings house a display of pastoral and natural history of the area. Plains, wetlands and Willandra Creek make up the rest of the park, with a walking track that is best at dawn or dusk to see the myriad waterbirds, kangaroos and emus. The creek is popular for canoeing and fishing. 163 km W.

Murrin Bridge Vineyard: Australia's first Aboriginal wine producer; 13 km N. *Cockies Shed Lavender Farm and Crafty Corner:* Tullibegeal; 13 km E. *Lake Brewster:* 1500 ha birdwatcher's paradise with fishing and picnic area. No guns, dogs or boats; 41 km W. *Nombinnie Nature Reserve:* birdwatching, bushwalking and abundant spring wildflowers Sept–Dec; 45 km N. *Hillston:* main street lined with palms, thanks to its situation on top of a large artesian basin. Hillston Lake is popular for watersports and picnics, and a swinging bridge provides access to a nature reserve and walking trail; 93 km SW.

See also CENTRAL WEST, p. 30

KATOOMBA

Pop. 7923
Map ref. 544 D5 | 546 F9 | 555 I6

ⓘ Echo Point Rd; 1300 653 408;
www.visitbluemountains.com.au

📻 89.1 BLU FM, 97.3 FM ABC Local

Originally named Crushers but renamed a year later, Katoomba stands at an elevation of 1017 metres and is the region's principal tourist destination. Blue Mountains National Park lies to the north and south of town. The explanation for why these mountains look blue lies in the eucalyptus trees covering them; they disperse eucalyptus oil into the atmosphere, highlighting the sun's rays of blue light.

🏠 *The Edge Cinema:* daily screenings of *The Edge* (images of Blue Mountains) on a 6-storey screen; Great Western Hwy (access through Civic Pl); programs (02) 4782 8900. *The Carrington Hotel:* Katoomba's first hotel; Katoomba St.

🌴 *Market:* 1st Sat each month; St Canice's Primary School. *Blue Mountains Festival of Folk, Roots and Blues:* Mar. *Six Foot Track Festival:* Mar. *Winter Magic Festival:* June. *Yulefest:* throughout region; June–Aug. *Spring Gardens Festival:* throughout region; Sept–Nov.

✕ *Darley's Restaurant:* modern Australian; Lilianfels Blue Mountains Resort & Spa, Lilianfels Ave; (02) 4780 1200. *Echoes:* modern Australian, great location; 3 Lilianfels Ave; (02) 4782 1966. *The Gallery Restaurant:* French; Katoomba Fine Art, 98 Lurline St; (02) 4782 1220. *Hominy Bakery:* best bread in the Blue Mountains; 185 Katoomba St; (02) 4782 9816. *The Conservation Hut Cafe:* modern Australian; Fletcher St, Wentworth Falls; (02) 4757 3827. *Seven:* Italian; 7 Station St, Wentworth Falls; (02) 4757 4997. *Silks Brasserie:* modern Australian; 128 The Mall, Leura; (02) 4784 2534. *Solitary:* French-influenced menu, great views; 90 Cliff Dr, Leura; (02) 4782 1164.

🛏 *Echoes Boutique Hotel:* boutique hotel; 3 Lilianfels Ave; (02) 4782 1966. *Lilianfels Blue Mountains Resort & Spa:* luxury resort and spa; Lilianfels Ave; (02) 4780 1200. *Chalet Fontanelle:* heritage-listed self-contained suites; 178–186 Falls Rd, Wentworth Falls; (02) 4757 1449. *The Falls:* luxury self-contained accommodation; The Avenue (off Falls Rd), Wentworth Falls; (02) 4757 8801.

⌚ **Leura** Considered the most urbane and sophisticated village in the Blue Mountains, Leura has a beautiful tree-lined main street with impressive gardens, specialty shops, galleries and restaurants. Everglades Gardens (Everglades Ave) is a celebrated 1930s garden with a gallery devoted to its creator, Paul Sorensen. Leuralla (Olympian Pde) is a historic Art Deco mansion with a major collection of toys, dolls, trains and railway memorabilia. There are spectacular mountain views from Sublime Pt and Cliff Dr. Markets are on the 1st Sun each month at the public school on the Great Western Hwy. The Leura Gardens Festival is held in Oct. Lyrebird Dell, near Leura, is an Aboriginal campsite estimated to be 12 000 years old. Relics can be found throughout the area, including rock engravings, axe-grinding grooves and cave paintings. All Aboriginal sites, discovered or undiscovered, are protected and are not to be disturbed by visitors. 3 km E.

[THREE SISTERS, ECHO POINT]

Blue Mountains National Park Echo Pt is the best place to view the Three Sisters, which are floodlit at night. Aboriginal Dreamtime legend tells of three beautiful sisters, Meehni, Wimlah and Gunnedoo, who lived in the Jamison Valley with the Katoomba people. The girls fell in love with three brothers from the Nepean people, but tribal law forbade their marriages. The brothers would not accept this and attempted to capture the sisters, causing a major battle. A witchdoctor from the Katoomba people feared that the girls were in danger, so he turned them to stone to protect them, intending to return them to their true forms when the battle was over. This was not to be, however, as the witchdoctor was killed in battle and the three sisters, at 922 m, 918 m and 906 m high, remain trapped as a magnificent rock formation. Nearby Orphan Rock is thought to be the witchdoctor. Also at Echo Pt is the Giant Stairway: 800 steps leading to the valley floor. Near Wentworth Falls, 7 km E, is an eco-designed cafe with great views, and the Valley of the Waters picnic area. *For other parts of the park see Blackheath and Glenbrook.*

Blue Mountains Scenic World Located near Katoomba Falls, the Three Sisters and Echo Pt, Scenic World takes in some of the best scenery in the national park. Take a ride on the Scenic Railway, which was originally built to transport coal and miners and is the world's steepest railway, or on the Scenic Skyway, a 7 km ride in a cable car high up over the Jamison Valley. There is also Sceniscender, which descends into the heart of the valley, and plenty of other attractions to explore on foot. South of town.

Explorers Tree: blackbutt tree reportedly carved with initials of Blaxland, Wentworth and Lawson (there is some question about whether this was done by the explorers or by early tourism operators); west of town, off hwy. *Hazelbrook:* small village with Selwood Science and Puzzles featuring a puzzle room, science kits, bookshop and local artwork. Hazelbrook hosts Regatta Day in Feb on Wentworth Falls Lake; 17 km E.

See also BLUE MOUNTAINS, p. 23

Laurieton

Pop. 2088
Map ref. 550 F7 | 555 O1 | 557 M12

 i Greater Port Macquarie Tourism, cnr Gordon and Gore sts, Port Macquarie; (02) 6581 8000 or 1300 303 155; www.portmacquarieinfo.com.au

100.7 2MC FM, 684 AM ABC Local

Laurieton is on an attractive tidal inlet at the base of North Brother Mountain. The mountain, which was named by Captain Cook in 1770, provides Laurieton with shelter from the wind, so the weather is mild all year-round. There are spectacular views and bushwalks on the mountain and the inlet is popular for estuary fishing.

Historical museum: documents history of the town in old post office; open by appt; Laurie St; bookings (02) 6559 9096. *Armstrong Oysters:* oyster farm on the river open to the public for fresh oysters; Short St.

Riverwalk Market: Cnr Tunis and Short sts; 3rd Sun each month. *Camden Haven Music Festival:* internationally acclaimed music artists from all genres; Apr. *Watermark Literary Muster:* biennial event attracting scholars, authors and writers from around the world; odd-numbered years, Oct.

Rock Lobster Cafe: cafe favourites and gelato; Shop 3, 80 Bold St; (02) 6559 8322.

Gypsy Falls Retreat: secluded self-contained cottages; Tipperary Rd, Lorne; (02) 6556 9702.

Crowdy Bay National Park The park is known for its prolific birdlife and magnificent ocean beach. Diamond Head is an interesting sculpted rock formation and the hut beneath is where Kylie Tennant wrote *The Man and the Headland*. A headland walking track offers stunning views and the area is also popular for fishing, birdwatching and the abundant wildlife. Campsites are at Diamond Head, Indian Head and Kylies Beach. 5 km s.

Dunbogan: this seaside village borders the river and ocean. A fisherman's co-op offers the best fish and chips in the region. River cruises and patrolled swimming beach; 2 km SE. *Kattang Nature Reserve:* in spring the Flower Bowl Circuit leads through stunning wildflowers. Enjoy good coastal views all year-round from sharp cliffs jutting into the ocean; 5 km E. *Dooragan National Park:* according to local Aboriginal legend, Dooragan (North Brother Mountain) was the youngest of three brothers who avenged his brothers' deaths at the hands of a witch by killing the witch and then killing himself. Blackbutt and subtropical forest is home to gliders, bats and koalas. Viewing platforms on North Brother Mountain provide some of the best views anywhere on the NSW coast; 6 km W. *North Haven:* riverside dining, boutique gift shops and patrolled swimming beach; 6 km NE. *Queens Lake Picnic Area:* a beautiful reserve with St Peter the Fisherman Church nearby. Kayak access to the river; 6 km W. *Kendall:* poets walk, art and craft galleries. Also market 1st Sun each month on Logans Crossing Rd; 10 km W. *Big Fella Gum Tree:* 67 m flooded gum tree in Middle Brother State Forest; 18 km SW. *Lorne Valley Macadamia Farm:* tours at 11am and 2pm, products for sale and cafe; open Sat–Thurs; 23 km W.

See also HOLIDAY COAST, p. 27

Leeton

Pop. 6829
Map ref. 559 N7

 i 10 Yanco Ave; (02) 6953 6481; www.leetontourism.com.au

99.7 Star FM, 549 AM ABC Local

Leeton was designed by Walter Burley Griffin, the American architect who designed Canberra. Like Canberra, the town is built in a circular fashion with streets radiating from the centre. The Murrumbidgee Irrigation Area brought fertility to the dry plains of the Riverina and now Leeton has 102 hectares of public parks and reserves and a thriving primary industry.

Visitor centre: beautifully restored building with photographic displays, local artwork and a heritage garden; Yanco Ave. *Sunrice Centre:* product displays and tastings, with 'Paddy to Plate' video presentation at 9.30am and 2.45pm on weekdays; Calrose St. *Mick's Bakehouse:* home of award-winning pies; Pine Ave. *Art Deco streetscape:* includes Roxy Theatre and historic Hydro Motor Inn; Chelmsford Pl.

Bidgee Classic Fishing Competition: Mar. *Sunrice Festival:* even-numbered years, Easter. *Picnic Races:* May. *Australian Birdfair:* Nov. *Light up Leeton:* Dec.

Pages on Pine Restaurant: modern Australian; 119B Pine Ave; (02) 6953 7300.

Historic Hydro Guest House: landmark heritage-listed guesthouse; Chelmsford Pl; (02) 6953 1555. *Leeton Heritage Motor Inn:* traditional motel with rustic twist; 439 Yanco Ave; (02) 6953 4100.

Yanco This town is the site where Sir Samuel McCaughey developed the irrigation scheme that led to the establishment of the Murrumbidgee Irrigation Area. Attractions in town include McCaughey Park, the Powerhouse Museum and a miniature train that runs on market days. Village Markets are held at Yanco Hall on the last Sun each month. 8 km s.

Fivebough Wetlands: 400 ha home to over 150 species of waterbird with interpretive centre, walking trails and viewing hides; 2 km N. *Brobenah Airfield:* gliding and hot-air ballooning; 9 km N. *McCaughey's Mansion:* 1899 mansion with stained-glass windows and attractive gardens, now an agricultural high school, but drive-through inspections welcome. Yanco Agricultural Institute nearby is open to the public and provides farmer-training facilities, research and advisory services; 11 km s. *Murrumbidgee State Forest:* scenic drives; brochure from visitor centre; 12 km s. *Whitton Historical Museum:* housed in old courthouse and gaol with photographs, documents and early farming equipment; 23 km W. *Gogeldrie Weir:* pleasant spot for fishing, picnics and camping; 23 km SW. *Wineries:* cellar-door tastings and tours at Toorak and Lillypilly Estate; brochure at visitor centre.

See also RIVERINA, p. 34

Lightning Ridge

Pop. 2598
Map ref. 556 B3 | 652 E12

 i Lions Park, Morilla St; (02) 6829 1670; www.lightningridge.net.au

91.3 NOW FM, 549 AM ABC Local

This famous opal-mining town is the only place in Australia where true black opals are found. Miners on the opal fields in most cases need to provide their own electricity and catch or cart their own water as these services are not available, making residents pretty creative and resilient. The otherwise desolate area receives 80 000 visitors each year and has modern facilities in an otherwise minimalist town. Famous finds in the region include Big Ben and the Flame Queen, which was sold for £80 because the miner who found it had not eaten properly in three weeks. Local Aboriginal legend explains the opals by saying that a huge wheel of fire fell to earth, spraying the land with brilliant stones. Lightning Ridge is notoriously hot in summer but boasts ideal weather in winter, and has lots of native marsupials and birdlife.

Bottle House Museum: collection of bottles, minerals and mining relics; originally a miner's camp; Opal St. *Big Opal:* opal-cutting demonstrations and daily underground working-mine tours; Three Mile Rd. *John Murray Art:* exclusive outlet for original paintings, limited-edition prints, postcards and posters; Opal St. *Goondee Aboriginal Keeping Place:* Aboriginal artefacts and educational tours of the premises; open by appt; Pandora St. *Chambers of the Black Hand:* unique underground sculptures and carvings in sandstone walls of an old mine; also underground shop; Three Mile Rd. *Displays of art and craft:* including beautiful displays of black opal in the many opal showrooms; several locations; leaflet from visitor centre. *Ridgelightning:* local lightning photography gallery and shop; Gem St. *Car Door Explorer Tours:* follow painted car doors to find attractions; brochure from visitor centre.

Local craft market: Morilla St; every Fri and most Sun. *Great Goat Race:* Easter. *Rodeo:* Easter. *Opal Open Pistol Shoot:* June. *Opal and Gem Festival:* July.

Chats on Opal: homemade cakes, gourmet sandwiches; Shop 1, 5 Opal St; (02) 6829 4228. *Morilla's Cafe:* light meals, cakes; 2 Morilla St; (02) 6829 0066. *Nobbies Restaurant:* bistro; cnr Onyx and Morilla sts; (02) 6829 0304.

Sonja's B&B: friendly, unpretentious accommodation; 60 Butterfly Ave; (02) 6829 2010.

Walk-In Mine: working mine with easy access and tours on demand. Also a cactus nursery nearby; off Bald Hill Rd; 2 km N. *Hot artesian bore baths:* open baths with average temperature 42°C; 2 km NE. *Kangaroo Hill Tourist Complex:* displays of antiques, bottles, shells, rocks and minerals, and mining memorabilia with a fossicking area outside; 3 km S. *Opal fields:* Grawin (65 km w) and Sheepyards (76 km w); brochure from visitor centre. *Designated fossicking areas:* maps from visitor centre.

See also NEW ENGLAND, p. 29

Lismore

Pop. 30 088
Map ref. 551 F5 | 557 O3 | 653 N12

 Cnr Ballina and Molesworth sts; (02) 6626 0100 or 1300 369 795; www.visitlismore.com.au

92.9 FM North Coast Radio, 738 AM ABC Local

This regional centre of the Northern Rivers district is on the banks of the Wilsons River. European settlement came in 1840 when John Brown broke an axle near a small chain of ponds and stopped to have a look around. He liked what he saw and decided to settle. Called Browns Water Hole until 1853, it was changed to Lismore after a town in Ireland. The town is now known for its ecotourism.

Rotary Rainforest Reserve There are 6 ha of original tropical rainforest in the middle of the city, but this is only a small remnant of the original 'Big Scrub' that stood here before European settlement. Over 3 km of paths, including a boardwalk, lead visitors past hoop pines and giant figs, with rare species of labelled rainforest plants. Rotary Dr.

Visitor centre: indoor rainforest walk, historical displays, and local art and craft. The surrounding Heritage Park has pleasant picnic areas and a mini steam train offering rides (10am–2pm Thurs and public holidays, 10am–4pm Sat, Sun and school holidays). Cnr Ballina and Molesworth sts. *Richmond River Historical Museum:* geological specimens, Aboriginal artefacts and pioneer clothing, implements, furniture and handiwork; Molesworth St. *Lismore Regional Art Gallery:* permanent collection of paintings, pottery and ceramics with changing exhibitions by local and touring artists; Molesworth St. *Robinson's Lookout:* views south across the river to South Lismore and north to the mountains; Robinson Ave. *Claude Riley Memorial Lookout:* views over Lismore city; New Ballina Rd. *Wilsons Park:* contains original rainforest with labelled trees; Wyrallah St, East Lismore. *Riverside Walk:* along the banks of the Wilsons River from the town centre to Spinks Park, where there are picnic and barbecue facilities. *Koala Care Centre:* looks after injured and orphaned koalas. Guided tours 10am and 2pm Mon–Fri, and 10am Sat; Rifle Range Rd. *Cafe and Culture Trail:* self-guide walk through sites of historical significance and cafes in the town centre. *Heritage walk:* historic buildings and churches; brochure from visitor centre.

Car Boot Markets: Shopping Sq, Uralba St; 1st and 3rd Sun each month. *Rainbow Region Organic Markets:* Lismore Showground, Tues morning until 11am; Alexander Pde. *Lismore Gemfest:* May. *Lantern Parade:* June. *Cup Day:* horserace; Sept.

Fire in the Belly: modern Italian; 109 Dawson St; (02) 6621 4899. *Paupiettes:* French; 56 Ballina St; (02) 6621 6135. *The Left Bank:* seafood; 133 Molesworth St; (02) 6622 2338.

Elindale House B&B: rustic B&B; 34 Second Ave; (02) 6622 2533. *Melville House:* Art Deco B&B; 267 Ballina St; (02) 6621 5778. *The Lismore Wilson Motel:* heritage-listed motel; 119 Ballina Rd; (02) 6622 3383.

Boatharbour Reserve: 17 ha of rainforest, wildlife sanctuary, picnic area and walking tracks; maps from visitor centre; 6 km E. *Tucki Tucki Koala Reserve:* woodland planted by local residents to protect the diminishing koala population, with walking track and Aboriginal bora ring nearby; 15 km S. *Rocky Creek Dam:* between Nightcap National Park and Whian Whian State Forest, includes spectacular views of the lake, boardwalks, walking trails, platypus-viewing platform, barbecues and a playground; 18 km N.

See also TROPICAL NORTH COAST, p. 28

Lithgow

Pop. 11 298
Map ref. 544 B2 | 546 D2 | 555 I5

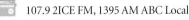 Great Western Hwy; 1300 760 276; www.tourism.lithgow.com

107.9 2ICE FM, 1395 AM ABC Local

Lithgow promotes itself as being 'surrounded by nature'. Easy access to several of the state's finest national parks and the city's charm make it worth visiting this isolated but staggeringly beautiful region. It was isolated from the coastal cities until the revolutionary Zig Zag Railway, built with gently sloping ramps to cut through the mountains, opened it up in 1869.

Eskbank House Museum Built in 1842, this sandstone Georgian mansion houses an extensive collection of Lithgow pottery, memorabilia and photographs. The front 4 rooms are authentically furnished with Regency and Victorian furniture. In the gardens are a stone stable, coach house and picnic area. Open Wed–Sun or by appt; (02) 6351 3557; Bennett St.

Blast Furnace Park: ruins of Australia's first blast furnace complex (1886) with a pleasant walk around adjacent Lake Pillans Wetland; off Inch St. **State Mine Railway Heritage Park:** mining and railway equipment and historic mining buildings; State Mine Gully Rd. **Small Arms Museum:** established in 1912, some argue that this is the birthplace of modern manufacturing in Australia. Displays range from firearms to sewing machines. Open 9.30am–2.30pm Tues and Thurs, 10am–4pm Sat, Sun, public and school holidays; Methven St.

Ironfest: cultural festival celebrating metal; Apr. **Rally of Lithgow:** May. **Celebrate Lithgow:** Nov.

Secret Creek Cafe and Restaurant: modern/native Australian; 35 Crane Rd; (02) 6352 1133. **Lochiel House:** modern Australian; 1259 Bells Line of Road, Kurrajong Heights; (02) 4567 7754.

The Bowen Inn Motel: contemporary motel; 5 Col Drewe Dr; (02) 6352 5111 **Rustic Spirit:** award-winning cottages; 23 Glenara Rd, Kurrajong Heights; (02) 4567 7170.

Wollemi National Park This is the largest wilderness area in NSW and is a breathtaking display of canyons, cliffs and undisturbed forest. Highlights include historic ruins at Newnes, the beaches of the Colo Gorge and the glow worms in a disused rail tunnel. The park also includes Glen Davis, home to more species of birds than anywhere else in the Southern Hemisphere. Mt Wilson, surrounded by the park, is a 19th-century village with large homes and superb gardens, many open to the public. Via the town is the Cathedral of Ferns; begins 16 km E.

Blue Mountains SpaRadise: Japanese bathhouse; Bowenfels; 1 km N. **Hassans Walls Lookout:** spectacular views of the Blue Mountains and Hartley Valley; via Hassans Walls Rd; 5 km S. **Lake Lyell:** stunning lake in mountain setting, popular for activities such as power-boating, waterskiing, trout fishing and picnics. Also canoe and boat hire available on-site; 9 km W. **Zig Zag Railway:** built in 1869, and later restored, it offers train trips of 1 hr 40 min return, departing 11am, 1pm and 3pm daily; via Bells Line of Road, Clarence; 10 km E. **Lake Wallace:** sailing and trout fishing; 11 km NW. **Jannei Goat Dairy:** produces cheeses, yoghurt and milk and is open to visitors, with free cheese tastings; 11 km NW. **Hartley:** became obsolete after the construction of the Great Western Railway in 1887. Explore 17 historical buildings administered by the National Parks & Wildlife Service; 14 km SE. **Portland:** charming town with a power station offering tours and interactive exhibits, a museum with much Australian memorabilia and several pleasant picnic areas; 17 km NW. **Mt Piper Power Station:** hands-on exhibits in the information centre and daily tours at 11am; 21 km NW. **Gardens of Stone National Park:** fascinating pagoda rock formations, sandstone escarpments and beehive-shaped domes caused by erosion. This is a great spot for rock climbing and picnics; 30 km N. **Mount Tomah Botanic Garden:** 5000 species of cool-climate plants at over 1000 m above sea level. Also award-winning restaurant; 35 km E.

See also BLUE MOUNTAINS, p. 23

Macksville	Pop. 2658
	Map ref. 550 G2 | 557 M9

ⓘ Cnr Pacific Hwy and Riverside Dr, Nambucca Heads; (02) 6568 6954 or 1800 646 587; www.nambuccatourism.com

 105.9 FM Radio Nambucca, 738 AM ABC Local

Macksville is a fishing and oyster-farming town on the banks of the Nambucca River. There is an abundance of water-based activities, with picnic areas and riverside parks from which dolphins can often be observed. The town bustles with activities and festivals including the country's second oldest footrace, the Macksville Gift, each November.

Mary Boulton Pioneer Cottage: replica of a pioneer home and farm buildings with horse-drawn vehicles. Open by appt 2–4pm Wed–Sat; River St; (02) 6568 1280. **Hotels:** Star Hotel, River St, and Nambucca Hotel, Cooper St, both heritage buildings from late 1800s with many original features; both offer meals and accommodation. **Nambucca MacNuts Factory:** macadamia products at wholesale prices; Yarrawonga St.

Market: Scout Hall, Partridge St; 4th Sat each month. **Patchwork and Quilt Display:** Easter. **Rusty Iron Rally:** heritage machinery show; Sept. **Macksville Gift:** Nov.

Dangerous Dan's Butchery: excellent butchery; 13 Princess St; (02) 6568 1036. **Short Order Cafe:** light meals, cakes; Shop 1, 10 Princess St; (02) 6568 4550.

Jacaranda Country Lodge: charming B&B; 292 Wilson Rd; (02) 6568 2737.

Bowraville This unspoiled town has much to see with a National Trust–classified main street, the Bowra Folk Museum, Frank Partridge VC Military Museum, Bowra Art Gallery and many craft galleries. There are markets on 3rd Sun each month, regular races at the racecourse and the Bowraville Hinterland Festival each Oct. 16 km NW.

Mt Yarahappini Lookout: the highest point in Nambucca Valley with fabulous 360-degree views, in Yarriabini National Park; 10 km S. **Scotts Head:** coastal town with good beaches for surfing, swimming, fishing and dolphin-watching; 18 km SE. **Pub with No Beer:** built in 1896, this is the hotel that was made famous in Slim Dusty's song 'The Pub with No Beer', so named because it would often run out of beer before the next quota arrived. It is still largely in its original form and offers meals; 26 km SW. **Bakers Creek Station:** old cattle station, now an impressive resort offering horseriding, fishing, rainforest walking, canoeing and picnicking as well as accommodation; (02) 6564 2165; 30 km W. **Local craft:** featured in several shops and galleries in the area; leaflet from visitor centre.

See also HOLIDAY COAST, p. 27

Maitland	Pop. 61 431
	Map ref. 543 F1 | 549 C7 | 550 A11 | 555 L3

ⓘ Ministers Park, cnr New England Hwy and High St; (02) 4931 2800; www.maitlandhuntervalley.com.au

 106.9 NX FM, 549 AM ABC Local

Maitland is in the heart of the world-class Hunter Valley wine region, on the Hunter River. Built on flood plains, it has suffered 15 major floods since settlement. The city has a significant Polish contingent as a result of immigration after World War II.

Maitland Gaol The gaol was built in 1844 and served as a maximum security prison for 154 years. The first inmates were convicts, including some children, and were forced to march 6 km from the wharf at Morpeth in shackles and chains. It has been home to some of Australia's most notorious and dangerous criminals and is now said to be the most haunted gaol in the country. Audio tours are available or there are guided tours with ex-inmates and ex-officers. For the extremely brave, there are also overnight stays. John St, East Maitland; bookings (02) 4936 6482.

Grossman House: National Trust–classified Georgian-style house, now a museum with pioneer silverware, porcelain and handmade clothing; Church St. *Maitland Regional Gallery:* city's art collection specialising in local works; High St. *Self-guide heritage walks:* showcasing Maitland, Morpeth, Lorn and East Maitland; brochures from visitor centre.

Market: showground; 1st Sun each month (except Jan). *Hunter Valley Steamfest:* celebration of steam trains; Apr. *Garden Ramble:* Sept. *Bitter & Twisted International Boutique Beer Festival:* Nov.

The Angels Inn Restaurant: modern Australian; Molly Morgan Motor Inn, New England Hwy; (02) 4933 5422. *The Old George & Dragon Restaurant:* modern European; 48 Melbourne St; (02) 4933 7272. *Organic Feast:* excellent provedore; 10–12 William St, East Maitland; (02) 4934 7351.

The Old George & Dragon Guesthouse: English-style romantic retreat; 50 Melbourne St; (02) 4934 6080. *Pindari House:* luxury guesthouse; 78 Winders La, Lochinvar; (02) 4930 7480.

Morpeth This riverside village has been classified by the National Trust. The town can be explored on foot and features magnificent old sandstone buildings such as St James Church (1830s), and antique and craft shops. There is the Weird and Wonderful Novelty Teapot Exhibition in Aug. A self-guide heritage walk brochure is available from the visitor centre. 5 km NE.

Walka: a scenic drive from Maitland, this former pumping station, now an excellent recreation area, is popular for picnics and bushwalks; 3 km N. *Tocal Homestead:* historic Georgian homestead; open by appt; bookings (02) 4939 8888; 14 km N. *Paterson:* signposted scenic drive leads to this charming hamlet on the Paterson River; 16 km N.

See also HUNTER VALLEY & COAST, p. 26

Manilla
Pop. 2081
Map ref. 556 H8

ℹ 197 Manilla St; (02) 6785 1207; www.manillamuseum.org.au

📻 92.9 FM, 648 AM ABC Local

This rural town is located at the junction of the Manilla and Namoi rivers and surrounded by attractive rural countryside. Its location between Lake Keepit and Split Rock Dam has made it a popular setting for myriad outdoor activities, especially aerosports. Nearby Mount Borah hosted the world's paragliding championships in 2007. Manilla is also known for its production of mead (an alcoholic drink made from fermented honey and water). It is home to one of only two meaderies in the country.

Dutton's Meadery: tastings and sales of honey and mead; Barraba St. *Manilla Heritage Museum:* incorporates Royce Cottage Collection and exhibits pioneer items such as clothing and furniture, and a bakery. Also has displays on platypus, which are often found in the area. *Manilla St:* antique and coffee shops.

National and international paragliding competitions: Nov–Apr.

Oakhampton Homestead: homely farmstay accommodation; Oakhampton Rd; (02) 6785 6517.

Warrabah National Park At this peaceful riverside retreat you'll find enormous granite boulders sitting above still valley pools and rapids suitable for experienced canoeists. Activities include swimming and fishing in the Namoi and Manilla rivers and rock climbing on the cliffs. 40 km NE.

Manilla Paragliding: offers tandem flights; a 2-day introduction, and a 9-day 'live in' licensing course with equipment supplied; Mt Borah; (02) 6785 6545; 12 km N. *Split Rock Dam:* watersports, boating, camping and fishing for species such as Murray cod and golden perch; turn-off 15 km N. *Manilla Ski Gardens:* area at the northern end of Lake Keepit with waterskiing, fishing and swimming; 20 km SW. *For more details on Lake Keepit see Gunnedah.*

See also NEW ENGLAND, p. 29

Menindee
Pop. 331
Map ref. 560 D11

ℹ Yartla St; (08) 8091 4274.

📻 95.7 FM ABC Radio National, 97.3 FM ABC Western Plains

Menindee is like an oasis in the middle of a desert. Although located in the state's arid inland plains, its immediate surrounds comprise fertile land, thanks to the 20 lakes in the area fed by the Darling River and a dam constructed in the 1960s. The orchards and vegetable farms provide a stark contrast to the vast freshwater lakes full of dead trees, and surrounding saltbush and red soil, on the way into this tiny settlement.

Maiden's Menindee Hotel: Burke and Wills lodged here in 1860. Meals and accommodation are available; Yartla St. *Ah Chung's Bakehouse Gallery:* William Ah Chung established one of the first market gardens in town. His bakery (c. 1880) now houses a gallery featuring local artists. Open for groups by appt from visitor centre; Menindee St. *Heritage trail:* through town; maps from visitor centre.

National and international paragliding competitions: Nov–Apr.

Bindara Station: working heritage homestead farm; Bindara Station, via Broken Hill; (08) 8091 7412.

Kinchega National Park When full, the lakes support waterbirds such as egrets, cormorants, black swans and spoonbills, and numerous other wildlife. There are giant river red gums growing along the banks of the Darling River, and campsites along the river in the north. Attractions include the wreck of paddlesteamer *Providence*, the old homestead and woolshed from Kinchega Station, and accommodation in the restored shearers' quarters. There is also a cemetery near the homestead. Activities include swimming, fishing and canoeing. 1 km W.

Menindee Lakes: in dry times only the upper lakes have water, making them the most reliable for fishing, swimming, birdwatching and watersports, and the best place for camping; details from visitor centre. *Menindee Lake Lookout:* good views of the lake; 10 km N. *Copi Hollow:* great spot for waterskiers, swimmers and powerboat enthusiasts, with campsites on the waterfront; 18 km N.

See also OUTBACK, p. 36

Merimbula
Pop. 3851
Map ref. 565 E10 | 581 H7

ℹ Beach St; (02) 6495 1129; www.merimbulatourism.com.au

📻 105.5 2EC FM, 810 AM ABC South East

Merimbula is a modern seaside town known for its surfing, fishing and oyster farming. Middens found in the area indicate that oysters were gathered here by Aboriginal people well before the arrival of Europeans. The town began as a private village belonging to the Twofold Bay Pastoral Association, who opened it as a port in 1855.

Merimbula Aquarium Twenty-seven tanks here present a wide range of sea life and an oceanarium showcases large ocean fish including sharks. Fish feeding time is 11.30am Mon, Wed and Fri (Mon–Fri in school holidays). Excellent seafood restaurant on-site. Merimbula Wharf, Lake St.

Old School Museum: town history displayed in excellent collection of photos, documents and memorabilia; Main St. *Scenic flights:* view the Sapphire Coast from the air. Bookings through Merimbula Air Services; (02) 6495 1074. *Trike Tours:* enjoy the beauty of the coast on three wheels; (02) 6495 2300.

Seaside Markets: Ford Oval; 3rd Sun each month. *Jazz Festival:* June. *Country Music Festival:* Nov.

Poppy's Courtyard Cafe: peaceful cafe; 15 The Plaza; (02) 6495 1110. *Zanzibar Cafe:* modern Australian; Cnr Main and Market sts; (02) 6495 3636.

Robyns Nest: absolute waterfront accommodation; 188 Merimbula Dr; (02) 6495 4956.

Pambula This historic sister village of Merimbula has excellent fishing on the Pambula River and a market 2nd Sun each month. Pambula Beach has a scenic walking track and lookout, with kangaroos and wallabies gathering on the foreshore at dawn and dusk; 7 km sw.

Magic Mountain Family Recreation Park: rollercoaster, water slides, minigolf and picnic area; Sapphire Coast Dr; 5 km N. *Tura Beach:* resort town with excellent beach for surfing; 5 km NE. *Yellow Pinch Wildlife Park:* peaceful bushland setting with array of native animals, birds and reptiles; 5 km E. *Oakland Farm Trail Rides:* scenic trail rides to the Pambula River; Princes Hwy, South Pambula; 0428 957 257; 10 km sw. *Whale-watching (Oct–Nov), boat cruises and boat hire:* bookings at visitor centre.

See also SOUTH COAST, p. 32

Merriwa

Pop. 944
Map ref. 555 J1 | 556 G12

ℹ Vennacher St; (02) 6548 2607.

📻 101.9 FM ABC Local, 102.7 Power FM

This small town in the western Hunter region beside the Merriwa River is known for its majestic early colonial buildings. It is the centre of a vast farming district of cattle, sheep, horses, wheat and olive trees. People converge on the town each year for the Festival of the Fleeces, which includes shearing competitions, yard dog trials and a woolshed dance.

Historical Museum: in stone cottage (1857) with documented history of the region and the belongings of European pioneers; Bettington St. *Bottle Museum:* over 5000 bottles of all shapes and sizes; open Mon–Fri; visitor centre. *Self-guide historical walk:* early school buildings, Holy Trinity Anglican Church (1875) and the Fitzroy Hotel (1892); brochure from visitor centre.

Polocrosse Carnival: June. *Festival of the Fleeces:* June. *Merriwa Motorcycle River Rally:* Oct.

Merriwa Cakes and Pastries: bakery; 147 Bettington St; (02) 6548 2851.

Hidden Valley Escapes: B&B, farmstay; 3615 Willow Tree Rd; (02) 6548 8588 or 1800

Coolah Tops National Park The plateaus at high altitude in this park provide wonderful lookouts over the Liverpool plains and some spectacular waterfalls. Vegetation consists of giant grass trees and tall open forests of snow gums, providing a home for wallabies, gliders, eagles and rare owls. There are superb campsites, walking trails and picnic spots. 107 km NW.

Cassilis: tiny village with historic sandstone buildings including St Columba's Anglican Church (1899) and the courthouse/police station (1858). The main streets have been declared an urban conservation area; 25 km NW. *Flags Rd:* old convict-built road leading to Gungal; 25 km sw. *Gem-fossicking area:* open to the public; 27 km sw. *Goulburn River National Park:* mostly sandstone walking tracks along the Goulburn River, honeycombed with caves; good rafting and access for boats; 35 km s.

See also HUNTER VALLEY & COAST, p. 26

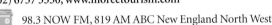

Moree

Pop. 8085
Map ref. 556 G4

ℹ Lyle Houlihan Park, cnr Newell and Gwydir hwys; (02) 6757 3350; www.moreetourism.com

📻 98.3 NOW FM, 819 AM ABC New England North West

Moree sits at the junction of the Mehi and Gwydir rivers and is the centre of the thriving local farming district. Thanks to its rich black-soil plains, one local claimed, 'You could put a matchstick in the ground overnight and get a walking-stick in the morning'. The town is also known for its artesian spas, with therapeutic qualities said to cure arthritis and rheumatism.

Spa complex These spas were discovered accidentally when settlers were searching for reliable irrigation water. A bore was sunk into the Great Artesian Basin and the water that emerged was 41°C. The complex also has an outdoor heated pool and an array of leisure activities that attract 300 000 visitors each year. Cnr Anne and Gosport sts.

Moree Plains Regional Gallery: contemporary Aboriginal art and artefacts and changing exhibitions; Frome St. *The Big Plane:* DC3 transport plane with tours available at Amaroo Tavern; Amaroo Dr. *Dhiiyaan Indigenous Centre:* located in the town's library, this was the first Aboriginal genealogy centre where Indigenous people could access historical family information and photographs; Cnr Balo and Albert sts. *Barry Roberts Historical Walk:* self-guide tour includes the courthouse and the Moree Lands Office, which was restored after a fire in 1982; brochure from visitor centre.

Market: Jellicoe Park; 1st Sun each month (not Jan). *Opera in the Paddock:* odd-numbered years; Mar. *Picnic Races:* May. *Moree on a Plate:* food and wine festival; May. *Australian Cotton Trade Show:* May. *Harmony on the Plains Multicultural Festival:* Aug. *Golden Grain Festival:* Nov.

Dragon & Phoenix Palace: Chinese; 361 Frome St; (02) 6752 4444.

Artesian Spa Motor Inn: comfortable accommodation; 2 Webb Ave, Newell Hwy; (02) 6752 2466. *Moree Spa Motor Inn:* traditional motel accommodation; Cnr Alice and Gosport sts; (02) 6752 3455.

Trewalla Pecan Farm: largest orchard in the Southern Hemisphere yielding 95 per cent of Australia's pecans; tour bookings at visitor centre; 35 km E. *Cotton Gins:* inspections during harvest; Apr–July; details at visitor centre. *Birdwatching:* several excellent sites in the area; brochure from visitor centre.

See also NEW ENGLAND, p. 29

Moruya

Pop. 2433
Map ref. 565 F7 | 567 L7

🛈 Vulcan St; (02) 4474 1345 or 1800 802 528; www.eurobodalla.com.au

📻 104.3 Power FM, 105.1 FM ABC Radio National

This town on the Moruya River was once a gateway to local goldfields, but is now a riverside township. It is known for dairying and oyster farming, and also for its granite, which can be seen in some of the older buildings in town and was also used to build the pylons of the Sydney Harbour Bridge.

🏠 *Eurobodalla Historic Museum:* depicts gold discovery at Mogo and the district history of shipping, dairying and goldmining; town centre. *South Head:* beautiful views across the river mouth.

🌴 *Market:* Main St; Sat. *Jazz Festival:* Oct. *Rodeo:* New Year's Day.

🍴 *The River Moruya:* modern European, fantastic views; 16B Church St; (02) 4474 5505.

🛏 *Blue Hills B&B:* romantic getaway; 59 Hawdon St; (02) 4474 0028. *Mogendoura Farm Holidays:* self-catering cottages; 189 Hawdons Rd; (02) 4474 2057 *The Knoll:* self-contained accommodation; 182 South Head Rd; 0408 629 752.

⊘ *Deua National Park* A wilderness of rugged mountain ranges, plateaus, gentle and wild rivers and a magnificent limestone belt, the area is popular for canyoning and caving. The rivers are a base for most water activities, including swimming, fishing and canoeing. There are scenic walking and 4WD tracks and 4 main campsites to choose from. 20 km W.

Broulee: great surfing and swimming; 12 km NE. *Bodalla:* All Saints Church, built from local granite, is of historical significance; 24 km S. *Comans Mine:* visit the historic tramway and stamper battery used to crush ore and separate the gold; 40 km SW. *Nerrigundah:* former goldmining town with a monument to Miles O'Grady, who was killed here in a battle with the Clarke bushranging gang; 44 km SW.

See also SOUTH COAST, p. 32

Moss Vale

Pop. 6725
Map ref. 553 B6 | 555 I9

🛈 Southern Highlands Visitor Centre, 62–70 Main St, Mittagong; (02) 4871 2888 or 1300 657 559; www.southern-highlands.com.au

📻 102.9 FM 2ST, 1431 AM ABC Radio National

Moss Vale is the industrial and agricultural centre of Wingecarribee Shire and the Southern Highlands. Once it was home to the Dharawal people, but by the 1870s they had all been driven off or killed. The town stands on part of the 1000 acres (approximately 400 hectares) of land granted to explorer Charles Throsby by Governor Macquarie in 1819. For most of the last century Moss Vale was a railway town and is dominated by the architecture of the Victorian railway station.

🏠 *Leighton Gardens:* picturesque area popular for picnics; Main St. *Historical walk:* includes Aurora College (formerly Dominican Convent) and Kalourgan, believed to have been a residence of Mary MacKillop; brochure from visitor centre.

🌴 *Southern Highlands Country Fair:* showgrounds; 4th Sun each month. *Autumn Gardens in the Southern Highlands:* throughout region; Apr. *Tulip Time Festival:* throughout region; Sept–Oct.

🍴 *Katers:* modern Australian; Peppers Manor House, 52 Kater Rd, Sutton Forest; (02) 4860 3111.

🛏 *Church Hill Grange:* self-contained apartment; 18 Church St; (02) 4869 3744. *Heronswood House:* traditional B&B; 165 Argyle St; (02) 4869 1477.

 Sutton Forest Set among green hills, this tiny town has a shop called A Little Piece of Scotland for all things Scottish, and The Everything Store, c. 1859. Hillview House, just north, was the official residence of NSW governors 1882–1958. 6 km SW.

Throsby Park Historic Site: owned for 150 years by the Throsby family. Buildings that depict early settlement life include original stables, former barn, flour mill, Gundagai Cottage and Christ Church. Access is by tour only; bookings (02) 4887 7270; 1.5 km E. *Cecil Hoskins Nature Reserve:* tranquil wetland with over 90 bird species, one-third of which are waterfowl; 3 km NE.

See also SOUTHERN HIGHLANDS, p. 24

Mudgee

Pop. 8248
Map ref. 554 H2

🛈 84 Market St; (02) 6372 1020; www.visitmudgeeregion.com.au

📻 93.1 Real FM, 549 AM ABC Central West

Mudgee derives its name from the Wiradjuri word 'moothi', meaning 'nest in the hills'. The name is apt as the town is situated among green and blue hills in the Cudgegong River Valley. Mudgee is graced with wide streets and historic Victorian buildings and is the centre of the Mudgee Wine Region, one of the largest winegrowing regions in Australia. Local produce features heavily in town and includes fresh silver perch, yabbies, venison, lamb, asparagus, summer berries, peaches and hazelnuts.

 Colonial Inn Museum: local history in photographs, documents, machinery, dolls and agricultural implements; check opening times (02) 6372 3365; Market St. *Honey Hive:* honey, jam and mustard tastings, and bees under glass; Church St. *Heart of Mudgee:* a gourmand's delight where you can enjoy the local produce, tastings, local art and craft; Court St. *Lawson Park:* home to possums, water rats and tortoises. Includes a playground, barbecues and duck pond; Short St. *Mandurah at the Railway:* local art and craft cooperative at the historic railway station; Cnr Inglis and Church sts. *Mudgee Brewing Company:* enjoy some pale ale at this home-grown brewery; Church St. *Roth's Wine Bar:* oldest wine bar in NSW with displays of wine history in the region and a wide selection of local wines; Market St. *Mudgee Observatory:* astronomical wonders of the NSW sky. Day and night sessions available; Old Grattai Rd. *Melrose Park Deer Farm:* deer roam in parkland setting; venison tastings and sales; Melrose Rd. *Town trail:* self-guide walk taking in National

Trust buildings including St John's Church of England (1860) and the Regent Theatre; brochure available from visitor centre.

🌴 **Markets:** St John's Anglican Church, 1st Sat each month; Lawson Park, 2nd Sat each month; St Mary's Catholic Church, 3rd Sat each month; Railway Station, 4th Sat each month. **Small Farm Field Days:** July. **Mudgee Wine and Food Fair:** Aug. **Mudgee Wine Festival:** Sept. **Mudgee Cup:** Dec.

🍴 **Deeb's Kitchen:** Lebanese; Cnr Buckeroo La and Cassilis Rd; (02) 6373 3133. **Eltons Brasserie:** modern Australian; 81 Market St; (02) 6372 0772.

🏨 **Lauralla Guest House:** Victorian guesthouse; 25 Lewis St; (02) 6372 4480. **Wildwood Guesthouse:** secluded B&B; Henry Lawson Dr; (02) 6373 3701. **Wombadah and Tierney House:** luxury B&B; 46 Tierney La; (02) 6373 3176.

⊚ **Munghorn Gap Nature Reserve** Over 160 bird species have been identified here, including the rare regent honeyeater. For bushwalkers, the Castle Rock walking trail is an 8 km journey with stunning views from sandstone outcrops. Camping, barbecue and picnic facilities are available; 34 km NE.

Mount Vincent Mead: one of the few places in the country producing mead (an alcoholic drink made from fermented honey and water). Tastings and sales available; 4 km SW. **Site of Old Bark School:** attended by Henry Lawson and made famous in several of his poems. Eurunderee Provisional School is nearby with historical displays of school life; 6 km N. **Fragrant Farm:** garden and craft shop with doll museum; 8 km SW. **Pick Your Own Farm:** variety of fruit and vegetables; open Oct–May; 12 km S. **Windermere Dam:** watersports, trout fishing and camping facilities; 24 km SE. **Hargraves:** old goldmining town where Kerr's Hundredweight was discovered in 1851, yielding 1272 oz of gold. Ask at general store for gold-panning tours; 39 km SW. **Wineries:** over 100 in the area (many offering cellar-door tastings) including Poet's Corner, Huntington Estate and Botobolar; self-guide drives brochure from visitor centre.

See also CENTRAL WEST, p. 30

Mullumbimby

Pop. 3130
Map ref. 551 G4 | 557 O3 | 653 N12

ℹ️ Byron Visitor Centre, 80 Jonson St, Byron Bay; (02) 6680 8558; www.tropicalnsw.com.au

📻 103.5 Radio 97 FM, 720 AM ABC North Coast

When Mullumbimby's economy, based on local agriculture, started to flag in the late 1960s, the town was saved by becoming an alternative-lifestyle centre. Drawn by lush subtropical countryside and excellent weather conditions, people settled at the foot of Mount Chincogan. The town still has a delightful laid-back feel today with all the facilities of a mature tourist town.

🏛 **Brunswick Valley Historical Museum** The museum covers local history in detail, including timber-getters, dairy farmers, pioneers and local government. It is in a pleasant park on the banks of Saltwater Creek. Outdoor displays include horse-drawn agricultural equipment and a pioneer slab cottage. Opening times vary so check with museum; Stuart St; (02) 6685 1385.

Mullumbimby Art Gallery: changing exhibitions of paintings, sculptures and prints; Cnr Burringbar and Stuart sts. **Cedar House:** National Trust–classified building housing an antiques gallery; Dalley St. **Brunswick Valley Heritage Park:** over 200 rainforest plants, including palms, and a 2 km park and river walk; Tyagarah St.

🌴 **Market:** Stuart St; 3rd Sat each month. **Chincogan Fiesta:** community celebration with stalls, parade and mountain footrace; Sept.

🍴 **Milk and Honey:** Mediterranean/Italian; Shop 5, 59A Station St; (02) 6684 1422. **Poinciana:** funky 'global' cafe; 55 Station St; (02) 6684 4036.

🏨 **Mooyabil Farm Holidays:** affordable self-contained accommodation; 448 Left Bank Rd; (02) 6684 1128. **Figgy Byron Bay:** luxury boutique accommodation; 1 Fig Tree La, Myocum; (02) 6684 7977.

⊚ **Brunswick Heads** This town on the Brunswick River estuary is a charming mix of quiet holiday retreat and large commercial fishing town. Despite having some truly beautiful beaches, Brunswick Heads has managed to remain remarkably serene and unassuming. Enjoy the excellent seafood in town. Highlights during the year include a wood-chopping festival in Jan and the Kite and Bike Festival in Mar. 7 km W.

Crystal Castle: spectacular natural crystal display, jewellery and gifts; 7 km SW. **Tyagarah Airstrip:** skydiving and paragliding; Pacific Hwy; 13 km SW. **Wanganui Gorge:** scenic 4 km bushwalk through the gorge with rainforest trees, enormous strangler figs and a pretty swimming hole; 20 km W. **Crystal Creek Miniatures:** enjoy the amazing world of minature animals; 40 km NW.

See also TROPICAL NORTH COAST, p. 28

Mulwala

Pop. 1629
Map ref. 559 M12 | 584 H5 | 586 D1

ℹ️ Irvine Pde, Yarrawonga; (03) 5744 1989 or 1800 062 260; www.yarrawongamulwala.com.au

📻 96.9 Sun FM, 675 ABC AM Riverina

Mulwala and Yarrawonga (in Victoria) are twin towns sitting astride the Murray River. Mulwala prides itself on being an 'inland aquatic paradise', with plenty of water-based activities for visitors to enjoy. It is surrounded by forests and vineyards.

🏠 **Lake Mulwala** This artificial lake was formed by the 1939 damming of the Murray River at Yarrawonga Weir and is now home to myriad birdlife. The eastern end has river red gums up to 600 years old. The lake is popular for yachting, sailboarding, canoeing, swimming and fishing (especially for Murray cod). The Mulwala Water Ski Club is the largest in the world with 6000 members; it offers lessons and equipment hire for skiing, wakeboarding, and banana and tube rides. Day and evening cruises can be booked at the visitor centre.

Linley Park Animal Farm: working farm with horse and pony rides, and opportunity to handfeed native and exotic animals. Open weekends and school holidays; Corowa Rd. **Pioneer Museum:** historic farming exhibits, photographs and local artefacts; open Wed–Sun; Melbourne St. **Tunzafun Amusement Park:** minigolf, mini-train and dodgem cars; Melbourne St.

🌴 **E.C. Griffiths Cup:** powerboat racing; Apr.

🍴 **La Porchetta:** Italian; Mulwala Waterski Club, Melbourne St; (03) 5744 1507. **Yarrawonga & Border Golf Club:** lively country bistro; Gulai Rd; (03) 5744 1911.

🏨 **Club Mulwala:** motel-style rooms; 271 Melbourne St; (03) 5744 2331. **Lake Mulwala Holiday Park:** includes 18-hole golf course; Melbourne St; (03) 5744 1050. **Lake Mulwala Hotel Motel:** centrally located affordable accommodation; 88 Melbourne St; (03) 5744 2499. **Mulwala Paradise Palms**

NEW SOUTH WALES

Motel: modern, comfortable motel; 121 Melbourne St; (03) 5743 2555. *Yarrawonga & Border Golf Club:* apartments, suites and cabins; Gulai Rd; (03) 5744 1911.

 Savenake Station Woolshed: 1930s-style woolshed in working order producing merino wool; open by appt; bookings (02) 6035 9415; 28 km N. *Everglade and swamp tours:* to waterbird rookeries and native animal habitats; bookings at visitor centre. *Local wineries:* several in area offering cellar-door tastings; brochure from visitor centre.

See also MURRAY, p. 35

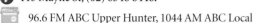
Pop. 804
Map ref. 556 H11

ℹ 113 Mayne St; (02) 6546 6446.

📻 96.6 FM ABC Upper Hunter, 1044 AM ABC Local

Murrurundi (pronounced 'Murrurund-eye') is a rural town set in the lush Pages River Valley at the foot of the Liverpool Ranges. It is a well-preserved, quiet town and any changes have been gradual, thanks to the lack of heavy industry in the region. The main street has been declared an urban conservation area.

Paradise Park This horseshoe-shaped park lies at the base of a steep hill. Behind the park take a walk through the 'Edge of the Needle', a small gap in the rocks that opens to a path leading to the top of the hill and fantastic views. Paradise Rd.

St Joseph's Catholic Church: 1000-piece Italian marble altar; Polding St. *Self-guide heritage walk:* National Trust–classified sites; brochure from visitor centre.

Murrurundi Markets: last Sun of the month; outside visitor centre. *Australia Day Carnival:* markets, parade and activities; Jan. *King of the Ranges Stockman's Challenge:* May. *Bushmans Rodeo and Campdraft Carnival:* Oct. *Murrurundi Stampede:* Dec.

Cafe Telegraph: cafe with wine cellar; 155 Mayne St; (02) 6546 6733.

Combadello Cottage: luxury self-contained cottage; Pages River Rd; 0400 461 363.

Wallabadah Rock The second largest monolith in the Southern Hemisphere, the rock is a large plug (959 m high) of an extinct volcano. There are spectacular flowering orchids in Oct. The rock is on private property, with a good view from the road. Access is possible with the owner's permission (02) 6546 6881. 26 km NE.

Chilcotts Creek: diprotodon remains were found here (now in Australian Museum, Sydney); 15 km N. *Burning Mountain:* deep coal seam that has been smouldering for at least 5000 years; 20 km s.

See also NEW ENGLAND, p. 29

Pop. 7954
Map ref. 551 G2 | 557 O2 | 645 F12 | 653 N11

ℹ World Heritage Rainforest Centre, cnr Tweed Valley Way and Alma St; (02) 6672 1340 or 1800 674 414; www.tweedtourism.com.au

📻 101.3 Tweed Coast Country, 720 AM ABC Local

Murwillumbah is located on the banks of the Tweed River near the Queensland border. It is a centre for sugarcane, banana and cattle farms. In 1907 Murwillumbah was almost completely wiped out by fire. The town was rebuilt and many of those buildings can still be seen on the main street today.

Tweed River Regional Art Gallery This gallery displays a variety of paintings, portraits, glasswork, pottery, ceramics and photography. The two main themes are Australian portraits (nationwide subjects in all mediums), and depictions of the local area by regional artists. It is also home to the Doug Moran National Portrait Prize, the richest portrait prize in the world. Past winners are on display along with changing exhibitions. Mistral Rd; (02) 6670 2790.

Escape Gallery: sculpture, glass and fine arts showcasing local and regional artists, exhibitions changing constantly; Brisbane St. *World Heritage Rainforest Centre:* visitor centre with displays on local vegetation and wildlife, local Aboriginal and European history, and World Heritage regions; Cnr Pacific Hwy and Alma St. *Tweed River Regional Museum:* war memorabilia, genealogy documents, and domestic items and clothing through the ages; open Wed, Fri and 4th Sun each month, or by appt on (02) 6672 1865; Cnr Queensland Rd and Bent St.

Market: Knox Park, 1st and 3rd Sat each month; showground, 4th Sun each month. *Tweed Valley Banana Festival and Harvest Week:* Aug. *Speed on Tweed:* classic car rally; Sept.

Escape Gallery & Coffee Lounge: cafe and fine art gallery; 1 Brisbane St; (02) 6672 2433. *The Modern Grocer:* provedore; Shop 3, 1 Wollumbin St; (02) 6672 5007.

Ripples on Tweed: absolute waterfront B&B; 21 Tweed Valley Way; (02) 6672 2515. *Ecoasis:* eco-friendly accommodation; 55 Tateywan St, Uki; (02) 6679 5959.

Mt Warning National Park World Heritage–listed Mt Warning is the rhyolite plug of a massive ancient volcano left behind after surrounding basalt eroded away. The local Bundjalung nation calls the mountain Wollumbin. It is a traditional place of cultural law, initiation and spiritual education, so visitors are requested not to climb the mountain. For those who ignore this advice, it is steep in places and the return trip takes 4–5 hours, so take plenty of water and make sure there is enough time to return before sunset. The National Parks & Wildlife Service conducts regular tours in the park; contact visitor centre for bookings. 17 km sw.

Lisnagar: historic homestead in lush surrounds; northern edge of town just past showgrounds; open Sun. *Stokers Siding:* historic village at the foot of the Burringbar Ranges, includes pottery gallery with resident potter; 8 km s. *Madura Tea Estates:* tea plantation with tastings and tours by appt; bookings (02) 6677 7215; 12 km NE. *Banana Cabana:* garden and shop with over 20 bush-tucker species and exotic fruits; Chillingham; 12 km NW. *Mooball:* small town with a cow theme that has painted almost anything that stands still in the style of a black and white cow, including buildings, cars and electricity poles; 19 km SE.

See also TROPICAL NORTH COAST, p. 28

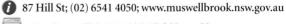
Pop. 10 225
Map ref. 555 K2

ℹ 87 Hill St; (02) 6541 4050; www.muswellbrook.nsw.gov.au

📻 98.1 Power FM, 1044 AM ABC Upper Hunter

Muswellbrook (the 'w' is silent) is in the Upper Hunter Valley and prides itself on being 'blue heeler country'. Here cattle

 RADIO STATIONS IN TOWN WHAT'S ON WHERE TO EAT WHERE TO STAY NEARBY

farmers developed the blue heeler dog by crossing dingoes with Northumberland Blue Merles to produce a working dog that thrives in Australia's harsh conditions. The blue heeler is now in demand all over the world. There are several open-cut coal mines in the local area and the Upper Hunter Valley has many fine wineries.

Muswellbrook Art Gallery: in the restored town hall and School of the Arts building, its centrepiece is the Max Watters collection, which displays pieces from renowned Australian artists in paintings, drawings, ceramics and sculptures; Bridge St. *Upper Hunter Wine Centre:* displays on the local wine industry and information on Upper Hunter wineries; Loxton House, Bridge St. *Historical town walk:* 4.5 km walk featuring St Alban's Church, the police station and the town hall; map from visitor centre.

Muswellbrook Cup: Apr. *Spring Festival:* Aug–Nov.

Hunter Belle Cheese: cheese factory with cheese tastings; Purple Olive, 75 Aberdeen St, New England Hwy; (02) 6541 5066. *Pukara Estate:* olive grove with tastings; 1440 Denman Rd; (02) 6547 1055. *SSS BBQ Barn:* steakhouse; Cnr Hill Street and New England Highway; (02) 6541 4044.

Red Cedar Motel: simple, comfortable motel; 12 Maitland St (New England Hwy); (02) 6543 2852.

Aberdeen This small town is famous for its prize-winning beef cattle. There are markets at St Joseph's High School on the 3rd Sun each month and the famous Aberdeen Highland Games are held each July. The Scottish festivities including Scottish food and music, Highland dancing, caber tossing, a jousting tournament, a warriors competition and a kilted dash. 12 km N.

Bayswater Power Station: massive electricity source with coal-fired boilers and cooling towers; 16 km S. *Sandy Hollow:* picturesque village surrounded by horse studs and vineyards, with Bush Ride in Apr; 36 km SW. *Local wineries:* those open for cellar-door tastings include Arrowfield Wines (28 km S) and Rosemount Estate (35 km SW); brochure from visitor centre.

See also HUNTER VALLEY & COAST, p. 26

Nambucca Heads

Pop. 5874
Map ref. 550 H2 | 557 M9

i Cnr Pacific Hwy and Riverside Dr; (02) 6568 6954 or 1800 646 587; www.nambuccatourism.com

105.9 2NVR FM, 684 AM ABC Mid North Coast

Located at the mouth of the Nambucca River, this is a beautiful coastal holiday town. The stunning long white beaches offer perfect conditions for fishing, swimming, boating and surfing.

V-Wall Breakwater Also known as the Graffiti Gallery, this rock wall gives visitors the opportunity to paint their own postcards on a rock. Mementos from all over the world are on display, including cartoons, paintings and poetry. Wellington Dr.

Headland Historical Museum: photographic history of the town and its residents, historic documents, antique farming implements and household tools; Headland Reserve. *Model Train Display:* miniature display models, including the Ghan and the Indian Pacific; Pelican Cres. *Stringer Art Gallery:* showcases local art and craft; Ridge St. *Valley Community Art:* cooperative of local artists and crafters with work for sale; Bowra St. *Mosaic sculpture:* the history of the town portrayed in a mosaic wrapped around a corner of the police station; Bowra St. *Gordon Park Rainforest:* unique walking trails through rainforest in the middle of urban development; between town centre and Inner

Harbour. *Foreshore Walk:* 5 km pathway from Pacific Hwy to V-Wall with storyboards on shipbuilding yards and mills.

Market: Nambucca Plaza; 2nd Sun each month. *Country Music Jamboree:* Easter. *Breakfast by the River:* Apr. *VW Spectacular:* odd-numbered years, July–Aug. *Show 'n' Shine Hot Rod Exhibition:* Oct. *Hinterland Spring Festival:* Oct.

Matilda's: seafood and steak; 6 Wellington Dr; (02) 6568 6024.

White Albatross Holiday Centre: waterfront, family-friendly accommodation; 1 Wellington Dr; (02) 6568 6468 or 1800 152 505. *Scared Mountain Retreat:* luxurious romantic retreat; Burkes La, Valla; (02) 6569 5026.

Valla Beach Apart from secluded beaches and rainforest surrounds, Valla Beach is a hive of activity. Attractions include an art and craft gallery, the Valla Smokehouse (specialising in smoked products), the Australiana Workshop and the Gallery of Hidden Treasures. The Valla Beach Fair is held each Jan; 10 km N.

Swiss Toymaker: visitors can view wooden toys being crafted; closed Sun; 5 km N.

See also HOLIDAY COAST, p. 27

Narooma

Pop. 3100
Map ref. 565 F8 | 567 L10

i Princes Hwy; (02) 4476 2881 or 1800 240 003; www.eurobodalla.com.au

104.3 Power FM, 810 AM ABC Local

Narooma is a tranquil resort and fishing town at the mouth of Wagonga Inlet, well known for its natural beauty. The stunning beaches and waterways continue to draw people back to enjoy the excellent boating, aquatic sports and big-game fishing. Excellent fresh local seafood is a specialty in many of the restaurants.

 Wagonga Princess This environmentally friendly, electronically powered boat is a converted huon pine ferry offering scenic cruises most days, taking in mangroves, forests and birdlife. The tour includes Devonshire tea. Commentary and tales (both tall and true) of local history, flora and fauna are provided by a third-generation local. Bookings (02) 4476 2665.

Walking tracks: several walking tracks incorporate places such as the Mill Bay Boardwalk, Australia Rock and lookout and numerous foreshore paths; maps from visitor centre. *Whale-watching cruises:* humpback and killer whales can be seen migrating, often with calves, Sept–Nov; bookings at visitor centre. *Scuba-diving cruises:* to shipwrecks; bookings at visitor centre.

Narooma Oyster Festival: May. *Great Southern Blues and Rockabilly Festival:* Oct.

Casey's Wholefood Cafe: healthy snacks, great coastal views; Cnr Wagonga and Canty sts; (02) 4476 1241. *Quarterdeck Cafe:* retro cafe; Riverside Dr; (02) 4476 2723. *The Whale Restaurant:* modern Australian; Whale Motor Inn, 104 Wagonga St; (02) 4476 2411. *Anton's at Kianga:* seaside cafe; 65 Dalmeny Dr, Kianga; (02) 4476 1802.

Anchors Aweigh B&B: homely 4-star accommodation; 5 Tilba St; (02) 4476 4000. *Whale Motor Inn:* stunning views, comfortable accommodation; 104 Wagonga St; (02) 4476 2411.

Montague Island Nature Reserve This isolated island, with access only by guided tours (bookings at visitor centre), is a major shearwater breeding site and home to little penguins and Australian and New Zealand fur seals. Whales can be viewed off the coast Sept–Nov. The tour includes historic buildings such as the Montague Lighthouse, which was first lit in 1881, but is now fully automated. Guides also explain the history of the island (known as Barunguba) as a fertile hunting ground for the Walbanga and Djiringanj tribes. 9 km SE.

Central Tilba Classified as an 'unusual mountain village' by the National Trust, Central Tilba was founded in 1895 and has many quality arts and craft shops. It has several old buildings worth a visit, including the ABC Cheese Factory in original 19th-century condition. The Tilba Festival is held here each Easter. 17 km SW. Tilba Tilba, a further 2 km S, features Foxglove Spires, a historic cottage surrounded by a beautiful 3.5 ha garden.

Mystery Bay: popular spot with strange-looking stones, snorkelling and access to Eurobodalla National Park; 17 km S.

See also SOUTH COAST, p. 32

Narrabri

Pop. 6104
Map ref. 556 F7

 Newell Hwy; (02) 6799 6760 or 1800 659 931; www.narrabri.nsw.gov.au

91.3 MAX FM, 648 AM ABC New England North West

The fledgling town of Narrabri was devastated by a flood in 1864, but was rebuilt and grew in regional importance from 1865 when the newly constructed courthouse took over local services from Wee Waa. Cotton was introduced to the area in 1962 and the region now enjoys one of Australia's largest yields. This success has brought prosperity to Narrabri and surrounding towns. The town is located between the Nandewar Range and Pilliga scrub country in the Namoi River Valley.

Australian Cotton Centre: outstanding interactive displays and a 3D cinema experience; Newell Hwy. *Narrabri Old Gaol and Museum:* historic museum with local artefacts. Night tours of the gaol on offer; Barwan St. *Riverside park:* pleasant surroundings next to the Namoi River with barbecue and picnic facilities; Tibbereena St. *Self-guide town walk:* historic buildings including the original courthouse (1865) and police residence (1879); leaflet from visitor centre.

Rodeo: Mar. *Nosh on the Namoi:* food and wine festival; Mar.

The Bush Coffee House: relaxed cafe; Shop 5, 111 Maitland St; (02) 6792 5747.

Dawsons Spring Cabins: basic self-contained cabins; Mt Kaputar National Park; (02) 6792 7300. *Nandewar Motor Inn:* central, traditional motel accommodation; Newell Hwy; (02) 6792 1155.

Paul Wild Observatory Here you'll find an impressive line of 22 m diameter antennas all facing the sky. They are connected on a rail track and are moved around to get full coverage. A sixth antenna lies 3 km away, and all 6 are sometimes connected with telescopes at Coonabarabran and Parkes. The visitor centre features a video, displays and an opportunity to view the telescope; open Mon–Fri (weekends during school holidays); 25 km W.

Yarrie Lake: birdwatching, waterskiing and windsurfing; 32 km W. *Scenic drive:* includes Mount Kaputar National Park (*see Barraba*) and cotton fields; leaflet from visitor centre.

See also NEW ENGLAND, p. 29

Narrandera

Pop. 3960
Map ref. 554 A8 | 559 N8

 Narrandera Park, Newell Hwy; (02) 6959 1766 or 1800 672 392; www.narrandera.nsw.gov.au

92.3 FM, 549 AM ABC Central West

This historic town on the Murrumbidgee River in the Riverina district is an urban conservation area with several National Trust–classified buildings. It has been home to two Australian writers. Local magistrate Thomas Alexander Browne used the nom de plume Rolf Boldrewood to write early Australian novels such as *Robbery Under Arms.* Father Patrick Hartigan, parish priest of St Mel's Catholic Church, was better known as poet John O'Brien.

Parkside Cottage Museum Displays include the scarlet Macarthur Opera Cloak, made from the first bale of merino wool the Macarthur family sent to England in 1816. Also on display are a snow shoe and ski from Scott's Antarctic expedition, a valuable collection of shells from around the world and a set of silver ingots commemorating 1000 years of the British monarchy. Open 2–5pm daily; Newell Hwy.

Lake Talbot: boating, waterskiing, fishing and canoeing. Also scenic walking trails around the lake; Lake Dr. *Lake Talbot Holiday Complex:* water slides, swimming and barbecue facilities. Aquatic facilities open Oct–Mar; Lake Dr. *NSW Forestry Tree Nursery:* seedlings of a huge range of native trees for sale; open Mon–Fri; Broad St. *Narrandera Park and Tiger Moth Memorial:* beautiful park that houses the restored DN82 Tiger Moth commemorating the WW II pilots who trained in the district; Cadell St. *Visitor Centre:* features a 5.8 m playable guitar; Narrandera Park. *Lavender Farm:* tours and product sales; Bells Rd. *Two-foot town heritage tour:* sights include the Royal Mail Hotel (1868) and the former police station (c. 1870); brochure from visitor centre. *Antique Corner and Objects d'Art:* beautifully restored historic home which now houses fine antiques; Larmer St. *Bundidgerry Walking Track:* track passes through the koala regeneration reserve; best viewing time is at dawn; brochure from visitor centre. *Blue Arrow scenic drive:* historic sites, cemetery and lake; brochure from visitor centre.

Rodeo: Jan. *John O'Brien Bush Festival:* Mar. *Hot Rod Rally:* Easter. *National Cavy Show:* guinea pig show; Aug. *National Model Aeroplane Championships:* Apr. *Camellia Show:* Aug. *Narrandera Cup:* horse racing; Aug.

Narrandera Bakery: fantastic bakery; 108 East St; (02) 6959 3677.

Farrellee House: luxury 1920s guesthouse; 53 Douglas St; 0427 533 682. *Midtown Motor Inn:* comfortable, affordable, centrally located; 110 Larmer St; (02) 6959 2122. *Narrandera Club Motor Inn:* budget-friendly accommodation; 38 Bolton St; (02) 6959 3123 or 1800 422 225

John Lake Centre: fisheries visitor centre with live exhibits, audiovisual presentations and guided tours; open Mon–Fri; 6 km SE. *Craigtop Deer Farm:* deer raised for venison and velvet with presentation on deer-farming and a tour of the deer-handling facility; 8 km NW. *Robertsons Gladioli Farm:* produces flowers for Sydney and regional markets; 8 km W. *Berembed Weir:* picnicking, fishing and boating; 40 km SE.

See also RIVERINA, p. 34

 RADIO STATIONS
 IN TOWN
 WHAT'S ON
 WHERE TO EAT
 WHERE TO STAY
 NEARBY

NEWCASTLE

Pop. 493 465

Map ref. 543 H3 | 548 | 549 D9 | 550 B12 | 555 M4

ⓘ 361 Hunter St; (02) 4974 2999 or 1800 654 558;
www.visitnewcastle.com.au

📻 105.3 New FM, 1233 AM ABC Local

Newcastle began as a penal settlement and coalmining town, with a shipment of coal to Bengal in 1799 noted as Australia's first export. It soon became an industrial city, known for its steel works and port. As the steel industry is phased out, Newcastle is developing a reputation for being an elegant and cosmopolitan seaside city. The spectacular harbour is the largest export harbour in the Commonwealth and the town is bordered by some of the world's finest surfing beaches.

🏠 **Fort Scratchley** This fascinating fort was built in 1882 amid fears of Russian attack. Soldiers' barracks and officers' residences were built in 1886. It is one of the few gun installations to have fired on the Japanese in WW II and it remains in excellent condition. Explore networks of tunnels, gun emplacements and fascinating military and maritime museums, all perched high above Newcastle Harbour. Nobbys Rd; (02) 4929 3066.

Queens Wharf: centre point of foreshore redevelopment with restaurants, boutique brewery and observation tower linked by a walkway to City Mall; Hunter St. *Newcastle Regional Art Gallery:* broad collection of Australian art including works by Arthur Streeton, Brett Whiteley, William Dobell, Sidney Nolan and Russell Drysdale, as well as changing exhibitions; closed Mon; Laman St; (02) 4974 5100. *Darby Street:* Newcastle's bohemian enclave has vibrant restaurants and cafes, giftshops, galleries and young designer boutiques. *King Edward Park:* waterfront recreation reserve since 1863 featuring sunken gardens, ocean views, band rotunda (1898), Soldiers Baths (public pool) and Bogey Hole, a hole cut in rocks by convicts; Shortland Espl. *Merewether Baths:* largest ocean baths in the

Southern Hemisphere; Scenic Dr. *Blackbutt Reserve:* 182 ha of bushland with duck ponds, native animal enclosures, walking trails, and picnic and barbecue facilities; New Lambton, off Carnley Ave. *Hunter Wetlands Centre:* 45 ha wetlands reserve 10 min from the city centre, with bike trails, playground, treasure hunt, guided eco-tours, canoe hire, picnic areas and cafe. *Self-guide walks:* include Town Walk and Shipwreck Walk; maps from visitor centre. *Cruises:* on the river and harbour; bookings at visitor centre.

🌴 *Street Performers' Festival:* Mar. *Surfest:* Apr. *Newcastle Jazz Festival:* Aug. *Cathedral Flower Festival:* Aug/Sept. *Newcastle Music Week:* Oct. *Maritime Festival:* Oct. *Mattara Festival:* celebration of the culture and beauty of Newcastle; Oct. *King Street Fair:* arts and crafts; Dec.

🍴 *Bacchus:* modern European; 141 King St; (02) 4927 1332. *Queens Wharf Brewery:* seafood; 150 Wharf Rd; (02) 4929 6333. *Restaurant II:* modern Australian; 8 Bolton St; (02) 4929 1233. *Silo Restaurant & Lounge:* modern Australian, harbourside; 18/1 Honeysuckle Dr, The Boardwalk; (02) 4926 2828.

🛏 *Ashiana:* Federation B&B; 8 Helen St, Merewether; (02) 4929 4979. *Cooks Hill Cottage:* luxury self-contained house; 102 Dawson St; 0401 269 863. *Crowne Plaza Newcastle:* chic, contemporary hotel; cnr Merewether St and Wharf Rd; (02) 4907 5000.

🚙 **Lake Macquarie** The enormous saltwater lake provides a huge aquatic playground with secluded bays and coves, sandy beaches and well-maintained parks lining its foreshore. Lake cruises leave from Toronto Wharf and Belmont Public Wharf. Dobell House, on the shore at Wangi Wangi, was the home of artist Sir William Dobell and has a collection of his work and memorabilia. Open to the public Sat and Sun 1–4pm and public holidays; (02) 4975 4115. The Lake Macquarie Heritage Afloat Festival is held here every Apr. 20 km s.

Munmorah State Recreation Area: coastal wilderness area including Shortland Wetlands, a bird and reptile habitat with walking, cycling and canoeing trails; 15 km w. *Eraring Power Station:* regular tours include access to cooling towers and a simulator used to train operators; bookings essential (02) 4973 0700; 22 km s. *Swansea:* modern resort town enjoying both lake and ocean exposure. It is popular with anglers and has excellent surf beaches; 24 km s. *Surf beaches:* many with world-class breaks, including Newcastle, Merewether and Nobbys; details from visitor centre.

See also HUNTER VALLEY & COAST, p. 26

[NEWCASTLE WATERFRONT]

Nelson Bay

Pop. 8153
Map ref. 549 G7 | 550 C12 | 555 N4

 Port Stephens Visitor Information Centre, Victoria Pde; (02) 4980 6900 or 1800 808 900; www.portstephens.org.au

 1233 AM ABC Newcastle

Nelson Bay is a coastal tourist centre that has remained small enough to maintain its charm. With outstanding white beaches and gentle waters, it is a superb spot for all aquatic activities and enjoys close proximity to Tomaree National Park. The attractive bay is the main anchorage of Port Stephens.

Inner Lighthouse This 1872 lighthouse, originally lit with 4 kerosene lamps, has been restored by the National Trust and is now completely automated. The adjacent museum features a display of the area's early history, souvenirs and a teahouse. Views of Nelson Bay are stunning. Nelson Head.

Community Art Centre: oil and watercolour paintings, pottery china and quilting; Shoal Bay Rd. *Self-guide heritage walk:* from Dutchmans Bay to Little Beach; brochure from visitor centre. *Cruises:* dolphin-watching (all year-round) and whale-watching (May–July and Sept–Nov); on the harbour, Myall River and to Broughton Island. Also dive charters; bookings at visitor centre. *4WD tours:* along coastal dunes; bookings at visitor centre.

Craft markets: Neil Carroll Park, Shoal Bay Rd, 1st and 3rd Sun each month; Lutheran Church grounds, Anna Bay, 1st Sat each month. *Tomaree Markets:* Tomaree Sports Complex, Nelson Bay Rd, Salamander Bay; 2nd and 4th Sun each month. *Medowie market:* Bull 'n' Bush Hotel; 2nd Sat each month. *Jazz Wine and Food Festival:* Sept. *Port Stephens Whale Festival:* Sept–Oct. *Tastes of the Bay Food, Wine and Jazz Festival:* Nov.

Fishermen's Wharf Seafoods: fish and chips; 1 Teramby Rd; (02) 4984 3330. *Ritual Organics:* modern Australian; Shops 1 and 2, Austral St Shopping Village, Austral St; (02) 4981 5514. *Zest Restaurant:* modern Australian; 16 Stockton St; (02) 4984 2211.

Oaks Lure: self-contained apartments, motel rooms; 20 Tomaree St; (02) 4980 4888. *The Landmark Nelson Bay:* resort accommodation; Dowling St; (02) 4984 4633. *Thurlows at the Bay:* luxury guesthouse; 60 Thurlow Ave; (02) 4984 3722.

Tomaree National Park This park consists of bushland, sand dunes, heathland, native forest and over 20 km of rocky coastline and beaches. There is a signposted walk around the headland and another up to Fort Tomaree Lookout for breathtaking 360-degree views. Yacaaba Lookout across the bay (70 km by road) also offers great views. The park is a popular spot for bushwalking, swimming, surfing, snorkelling, fishing and picnicking. The park stretches from Shoal Bay (3 km NE) to Anna Bay (10 km SW).

Little Beach: white beach with native flora reserve behind; 1 km E. *Gan Gan Lookout:* spectacular views south to Newcastle and north to Myall Lakes; Nelson Bay Rd; 2 km S. *Shoal Bay:* popular and protected bay with spa resort; 3 km NE. *Shell Museum:* diverse display of shells, some rare; Sandy Point Rd; 3 km SW. *Toboggan Hill Park:* toboggan runs, minigolf and indoor wall-climbing; 5 km SW. *Oakvale Farm and Fauna World:* 150 species of native and farm animals, with visitor activities and feeding shows; 16 km SW. *Tomago House:* 1843 sandstone villa with family chapel and 19th-century gardens; open 11am–3pm Sun; Tomago Rd; 30 km SW. *Stockton Sand Dunes:* huge dune area

popular for sand-boarding and whale-watching. Access is from Anna Bay or Williamtown by 4WD or safari (bookings at visitor centre); 38 km SW. *Port Stephens wineries:* several in area, with Stephens Winery featuring Jazz at the Winery in Mar; brochure from visitor centre.

See also HUNTER VALLEY & COAST, p. 26

Nimbin

Pop. 351
Map ref. 551 F4 | 557 O3

 80 Cullen St; (02) 6689 1388; www.visitnimbin.com.au

102.3 NIM FM, 738 AM ABC Local

Situated in a beautiful valley, Nimbin is a place of healing and initiation for the Bundjalung people. When its original industry of timber faltered, the cleared land was put to use for dairy and banana farming, but Nimbin hit a depression in the late 1960s when the dairy industry collapsed. It took the 1973 Aquarius Festival to establish Nimbin as the alternative-culture capital of Australia and resurrect its fortunes. Today Nimbin is a blend of hippie counter-culture, artists' community and cottage industries amid a backdrop of farmland and forests.

Nimbin Museum: dedicated to hippie culture and Aboriginal heritage; Cullen St; (02) 6689 1123. *Nimbin Candle Factory:* produces stunning, environmentally friendly candles sold throughout Australia and the world; Butter Factory, Cullen St; (02) 6686 6433. *The Rainbow Cafe:* infamous cafe with gorgeous courtyard and colourful paintings; Cullen St. *Town hall:* features mural of Aboriginal art; Cullen St. *Rainbow Power Company:* take a tour of this alternative power supplier, now exporting power products such as solar water pumps and hydro-generators to over 20 countries; Alternative Way; (02) 6689 1430. *Local art, craft and psychedelia:* brochure from visitor centre.

Market: local craft; Nimbin Community Centre, Cullen St; 3rd and 5th Sun each month. *Rainbow Lane Markets:* next to museum, Sat mornings. *Artist Gallery Autumn Extravaganza:* Mar/Apr. *Mardi Grass Festival:* organised by the Nimbin HEMP (Help End Marijuana Prohibition) Embassy; May.

Rainbow Cafe: healthy and delicious food; 70 Cullen St; (02) 6689 1997.

Black Sheep Farm Rainforest Guest House: cosy, contemporary rainforest retreat; 449A Gungas Rd; (02) 6689 1095.

Nightcap National Park This lush World Heritage–listed forest offers signposted bushwalks from easy to very difficult, requiring a map and compass. The dramatic Protestors Falls is the site of the 1979 anti-logging protest that led to the area being gazetted as a national park. Rocky Creek Dam has a platypus-viewing platform and views of Mt Warning. 5 km NE.

Nimbin Rocks: spectacular remnants of an ancient volcano overlooking the town. This is a sacred initiation site for the Bundjalung people, so viewing is from the road only; Lismore Rd; 3 km S. *The Channon:* town featuring an alternative-craft market, 2nd Sun each month; Opera at the Channon in Aug; and Music Bowl Live Band Concert in Nov. 15 km SE.

See also TROPICAL NORTH COAST, p. 28

Nowra

Pop. 30 953
Map ref. 553 D9 | 555 I10 | 565 G4 | 567 O1

(i) Shoalhaven Visitors Centre, cnr Princes Hwy and Pleasant Way, Nowra; (02) 4421 0778 or 1300 662 808; www.shoalhavenholidays.com.au

94.9 Power FM, 104.5 Triple U FM, 603 AM ABC Radio National

Nowra is the principal town in the Shoalhaven district and is popular with tourists for its attractive river and water activities. The racehorse Archer began his famous 550-mile (880-kilometre) walk from Terara, on the outskirts of Nowra, to compete in the Melbourne Cup. He was led and ridden by his jockey, Dave Power. The two went on to be the first winners of the Melbourne Cup in 1861 and returned for a second win in 1862.

Meroogal Said to be the most intact 19th-century home in NSW, this 1885 property was passed down through 4 generations of women. Furniture, household objects, diaries, letters, scrapbooks, photographs and even clothes have been saved so visitors can see relics from each generation of its occupation. Open Sat afternoon and Sun; Cnr Worrigee and West sts; (02) 4421 8150.

Shoalhaven Historical Museum: old police station exhibiting the history of the town in records, photographs, household items and tools; Cnr Plunkett and Kinghorne sts; (02) 4421 8150. *Shoalhaven River:* fishing, waterskiing, canoeing and sailing. *Shoalhaven River Cruises:* departing from Nowra Wharf, Riverview Rd; bookings and times 0429 981 007. *Hanging Rock:* 46 m above the river with scenic views; off Junction St. *Nowra Animal Park:* native animals, reptiles and birds plus pony rides and opportunities to pat a koala; Rockhill Rd. *Scenic walks:* include Bens Walk along the river and Bomaderry Creek Walk from Bomaderry; leaflets from visitor centre.

Market: Nowra Greyhound Track; 4th Sun each month.

River Deli: excellent cafe and provedore; 84 Kinghorne St; (02) 4423 1344. *The Boatshed:* modern Australian, beautiful setting; 10 Wharf Rd; (02) 4421 2419.

The White House Heritage Guest House: rustic, contemporary comfort; 30 Junction St; (02) 4421 2084.

Kangaroo Valley This town of historic buildings has the National Trust–classified Friendly Inn, a Pioneer Settlement Reserve (a reconstruction of an 1880s dairy farm) and the Hampden Bridge, built in 1898 and is the oldest suspension bridge in Australia. Kangaroo Valley Fruit World is a working fruit farm open to visitors. Canoeing and kayaking safaris to Kangaroo River and Shoalhaven Gorge can be booked at the visitor centre. There is also beautiful rural scenery along Nowra Rd. 23 km NW.

Fleet Air Arm Museum Australia's largest aviation museum with displays and planes over 6000 sq m. The Wings Over Water exhibition tells the story of Australian naval aviation and the Royal Australian Navy's Fleet Air Arm; (02) 4424 1999; 8 km SW.

Marayong Park Emu Farm: group tours include the emu incubation room, brooder area, chick-rearing shed and breeding pen. Chicks hatch Aug–Oct; bookings required (02) 4447 8505; 11 km S. *Cambewarra Lookout:* spectacular views of the Shoalhaven River and Kangaroo Valley; 12 km NW. *Greenwell Point:* fresh fish and oyster sales; 14 km E. *Bundanon:* National Estate–listed homestead donated to the nation by artist Arthur Boyd and his wife Yvonne. The Bundanon collection and Boyd's studio are open Sun; (02) 4423 5999; 21 km W. *Culburra:* nearby

Lake Wollumboola and coastal beaches are good for surfing, swimming, prawning and fishing. Culburra also holds the Open Fishing Carnival each Jan; 21 km SE. *Morton National Park:* the Nowra section features the Tallowa Dam water-catchment area, a popular spot for picnics; via Kangaroo Valley; 38 km NW. *For the Ulladulla section of the park see Ulladulla. Beaches:* many beautiful beaches in the vicinity for swimming and surfing; maps at visitor centre. *Wineries:* several in region offering cellar-door tastings; brochure from visitor centre.

See also SOUTH COAST, p. 32

Nundle

Pop. 290
Map ref. 557 I10

(i) Fossickers Tourist Park, Jenkins St; (02) 6769 3355.

92.9 2TTT FM, 648 AM ABC New England North West

A thriving gold town in the 1850s, Nundle drew prospectors from California, Jamaica, China and Europe. Today the town is a quiet place nestled between the Great Dividing Range and the Peel River, but traces of gold can still be found and it is known as 'the town in the hills of gold'. The Peel River is well known for its fishing, with yellow-belly, trout and catfish being common catches.

Woollen Mill: Australia's famous wool mill offers a fascinating insight into one of the country's largest industries. View the inner workings of the mill from the observation deck or take the factory tour. Retail store also on site; Oakenville St. *Courthouse Museum:* built in 1880, now housing a history of Nundle and the gold-rush era; Jenkins St. *Peel Inn:* 1860s pub with meals and accommodation; Jenkins St. *Mount Misery Gold Mine:* walk back in time through a re-created goldmine evoking life on the Nundle goldfields 150 years ago; Gill St.

Go for Gold Chinese Festival: Easter. *Nundle Dog Race:* May.

Nundle Country Cafe: tranquil cafe; 96 Jenkins St; (02) 6789 3158.

The Rose and Willow Guest House: charming self-contained cottage; 53 Jenkins St; (02) 6765 7433.

 Hanging Rock The area is popular for mineral fossicking, with good samples of scheelite and an excellent site for gold panning on the Peel River. Sheba Dams Reserve is home to numerous birds and animals. Activities include picnicking, bushwalking, camping and fishing, with regular stockings of trout and salmon. 11 km W.

Chaffey Reservoir: enjoy good swimming, fishing, sailing and picnicking. Dulegal Arboretum, an attractive garden of native trees and shrubs, is on the foreshore; 11 km N. *Fossicker's Way tour:* through scenic New England countryside; brochure from visitor centre.

See also NEW ENGLAND, p. 29

Nyngan

Pop. 1975
Map ref. 561 O10

(i) Nyngan Leisure and Van Park, 12 Old Warren Rd; (02) 6832 2366; www.nyngan.com

95.1 FM ABC Local, 96.7 Rebel FM, 100.7 FM Outback Radio

Nyngan is a pleasant country town on the Bogan River, on the edge of the outback. It was largely unknown to the rest of the country until 1990, when the worst floods of the century struck here, doing damage worth $50 million. A helicopter was called in to airlift 2000 people – almost the whole town – to safety. Today the town is at the centre of a sheep, wheat and wool district.

 Nyngan Museum: local memorabilia, photographs, an audio room with local stories, an 1800s kitchen and remnants from the 1990 flood; at railway station, Railway Sq. *Mid-state Shearing Shed:* informative displays of the continuing importance of shearing to the region, with work of local artists in murals; Mitchell Hwy. *Historical town drive and Levee Tour:* includes historic buildings in Cobar and Pangee sts, the Bicentennial Mural Wall and the heritage-listed railway overbridge with a lookout over town. The levee was built after the 1990 floods; brochure from visitor centre.

ANZAC Day Race Meeting: horserace; Apr. *Nyngan Show:* highlights the produce of the area; May.

Beancounters House: B&B; 103 Pangee St; (02) 6832 1610. *Country Manor Motor Inn:* comfortable, affordable accommodation; 145 Pangee St; (02) 6832 1447 or 1800 819 913.

Macquarie Marshes This mosaic of semi-permanent wetlands includes two major areas: the south marsh and the north marsh. The wetlands expand and contract, depending on recent rainfall, and provide a waterbird sanctuary and breeding ground. It is thought that the Macquarie Marshes contributed to the early myth of an inland sea, which led explorers – most notably Charles Sturt – on many ill-fated journeys. NSW National Parks & Wildlife Service has discovery rangers available to take visitors on tours of the reserve. Bookings in advance (02) 6842 1311. Marsh Meanders offers a range of activities including kayaking and bushwalking. Inquiries (02) 6824 2070. Both tours are seasonally dependant on water levels. 64 km N.

Cairn: marking the geographic centre of NSW. It is on private property but visible from the road; 65 km s. *Richard Cunningham's grave:* botanist with explorer Major Mitchell's party, Cunningham was killed by Aboriginal people in 1835 and buried here; 70 km s.

See also CENTRAL WEST, p. 30

Oberon
Pop. 2475
Map ref. 554 H6

137–139 Oberon St; (02) 6336 0666; www.oberonweb.com

549 AM ABC Central West

This picturesque farming town is 1113 metres above sea level, which gives Oberon a mountain climate of cool summers, crisp winters and occasional snow. The town was named after the king in *A Midsummer Night's Dream* at the suggestion of a local Shakespeare enthusiast, after it was decided that the original name Glyndwr was unpleasant to the ear.

Oberon Museum Almost 1 ha of displays including early farming equipment, a fully furnished early settlers' house, a blacksmith shop and a functioning forge. A wide collection of artefacts and memorabilia are housed in the town's original 1920s railway station. Open 2–5pm Sat or by appt; Lowes Mount Rd.

Lake Oberon: good spot for trout fishing (both brown and rainbow). Boats and swimming are not permitted, but there are barbecue and picnic facilities; Jenolan St. *The Common:* green park with a small lake and picnic facilities; Edith Rd. *Reef Reserve:* natural bushland with access to the lake foreshore;

Reef Rd. *Cobweb Craft Shop:* 8 tapestries on show depicting the town's landscape and buildings; Oberon St.

Market: Anglican Church; 1st Sat each month. *Rodeo:* Feb. *Kowmung Music Festival:* chamber music in caves; Mar. *Sheep Show:* Aug. *Daffodil Festival:* Sept.

McKeown's Rest: contemporary B&B; 5194 Jenolan Caves Rd; (02) 6335 6252.

Kanangra–Boyd National Park This is a rugged and dramatic piece of Australia with vast gorges, spectacular lookouts and scenic rivers. Sandstone formations of Thurat Spires, Kanangra Walls and Mt Cloudmaker are breathtaking and the park is excellent for bushwalking, rock climbing and camping. The Jenolan Caves are just outside the park border and are justifiably the country's best known cluster of caves. Tours of the majestic caverns feature fascinating flowstone deposits, helictites, columns and lakes. On the south-east edge of the park is Yerranderie, a restored silver-mining town with accommodation and walking trails. Inquiries (02) 6336 1972; Jenolan Caves 30 km SE; Kanangra Walls 52 km SE; Yerranderie 85 km SE.

Evans Crown Nature Reserve: bushwalking area with diverse flora and fauna and granite tors. Crown Rock was an initiation and corroboree site for the Wiradjuri people and is now popular for abseiling; 21 km N. *Abercrombie River National Park:* low eucalypt forest ideal for bushwalks, with kangaroos, wallaroos and wallabies. Abercrombie River, Retreat River and Silent Creek are havens for platypus and great for fishing, swimming and canoeing; (02) 6336 1972; 40 km s. *Driving tours:* routes taking in caves, national parks and surrounding towns; brochure from visitor centre. *Wood mushrooms:* delicacies that grow in Jenolan, Vulcan and Gurnang state forests Jan–early May. Mushrooms should be correctly identified before picking. Brochure from visitor centre.

See also BLUE MOUNTAINS, p. 23

Orange
Pop. 35 338
Map ref. 554 G4

Cnr Byng and Peisley sts; (02) 6393 8226 or 1800 069 466; www.orange.nsw.gov.au

105.9 Star FM, 549 AM ABC Central West

Before European occupation this area was home to the Wiradjuri people, who thrived on the plentiful bush tucker resulting from the fertile volcanic soil and the abundant kangaroos and wallabies. The town was named by explorer Sir Thomas Mitchell after the Dutch Prince of Orange – they had fought together in a war in Spain. Today the prosperous 'colour city' on the slopes of Mount Canobolas enjoys a reputation for excellent food, wine, parks and gardens. It is also known for its goldmining history and as the birthplace of renowned Australian poet A. B. (Banjo) Paterson.

Civic Square This is Orange's cultural hub and also the first stop for visitors, with the visitor centre (incorporating a wine-tasting facility), the City Library, the Civic Theatre and a monument to Banjo Paterson. The Orange Regional Gallery (open Tues–Sun) is one of the busiest in the country. It has touring exhibitions as well as permanent collections that focus on jewellery, ceramics and clothing. Cnr Byng and Peisley sts.

Cook Park: colourful in any season with a begonia house (flowers Feb–May), duck pond, fernery, native bird aviary, Cook Park Guildry (for arts and crafts) and a picnic area; Summer St.

Botanic Gardens: 17 ha parklands with an impressive exotic and native plant collection and a signposted walk through billabongs, rose gardens, orchards and woodlands; Kearneys Dr. *Banjo Paterson Memorial Park:* remains of Narambla Homestead, Paterson's birthplace, and a memorial obelisk; Ophir Rd. *Self-guide historical walk:* 90 min stroll past historic homes and buildings; brochure from visitor centre.

Market: Kmart carpark; Sun. *Farmers market:* showgrounds; 2nd Sat each month. *Slow Food Festival:* Feb. *Orange Cup:* horseracing; Mar. *FOOD (Food of Orange District) Week:* Apr. *Music Week:* Aug. *Orange Region Winefest:* Oct.

Blue Wren Restaurant: modern Australian, located at beautiful winery; 433 Cassilis Rd; (02) 6372 6205. *Lolli Redini:* modern Australian; 48 Sale St; (02) 6361 7748. *Selkirks:* modern Australian; 179 Anson St; (02) 6361 1179. *Tonic Resaurant:* modern Australian; cnr Pym and Victoria sts, Millthorpe; (02) 6366 3811.

Arancia B&B: luxury retreat; 69 Moulder St; (02) 6365 3305 *Cloudgap B&B:* romantic retreat; 224 Strathnook La; (02) 6365 1231. *de Russie Suites:* boutique hotel; 72 Hill St; (02) 6360 0973.

Ophir goldfields This was the site of the first discovery of payable gold in Australia (1851). The 1850s saw an influx of immigrants from Britain, Germany and China, all hoping to strike it rich. Features today include a fossicking centre, picnic area, walking trails to historic tunnels and tours of a working goldmine. There is still plenty of gold to be found in the area; the gold medals at the 2000 Sydney Olympic Games were made of Ophir gold. Brochure from visitor centre; 27 km N.

Campbell's Corner: cool-climate gardens and popular picnic spot; Pinnacle Rd; 8 km s. *Lake Canobolas Reserve:* recreation area with trout fishing in the lake, diving pontoons, children's playground and picnic and barbecue facilities; 9 km sw. *Lucknow:* old goldmining town and site of Australia's second gold discovery, now with historic bluestone buildings and craft shops; 10 km se. *Mt Canobolas Park:* 1500 ha bird and animal sanctuary; 14 km sw. *Borenore Caves:* undeveloped caves with evidence of fossils. Outside are walking trails, and picnic and barbecue facilities. Torch required if entering the caves; brochure from visitor centre; 22 km w. *Cadia Mines:* largest goldmine and coppermine in NSW; check with visitor centre for open days; 25 km se. *Mitchell's Monument:* site of Sir Thomas Mitchell's base camp; 33 km w. *Molong:* charming rural town with Yarn Market, Craft Cottage and Coach House Gallery; 35 km nw. Grave of Yuranigh, Mitchell's Aboriginal guide, lies 2 km e of Molong. *Wineries:* over 30 cellar doors can be found in surrounding wine region; brochure from visitor centre.

See also CENTRAL WEST, p. 30

Parkes

Pop. 9825
Map ref. 554 E4

 Kelly Reserve, Newell Hwy; (02) 6863 8860; www.visitparkes.com.au

📻 95.5 ROK FM, 549 AM ABC Local

Parkes is most famous for its huge telescope. It originated as a tent city, which grew into a town named Bushmans, built almost overnight when gold was found in the area in 1862. The name of the town changed following visits from New South Wales Colonial Secretary Henry Parkes in 1873. The main street, Clarinda Street, was named after Mrs Parkes the following year.

Pioneer Park Museum Set in a historic school and church, displays include early farm machinery and transport. The museum incorporates the collection of the previously separate Henry Parkes Historical Museum, which specialises in memorabilia from the gold rush, and includes the fascinating 1000-volume personal library of Sir Henry Parkes. Pioneer St, North Parkes; (02) 6862 3509.

Motor Museum: displays of vintage and veteran vehicles and local art and craft; Cnr Bogan and Dalton sts. *Memorial Hill:* excellent views of the town and surrounds; Bushman St, North Parkes. *Kelly Reserve:* playground and picnic and barbecue facilities in bush setting; Newell Hwy, North Parkes. *Bushmans Hill Reserve:* take the walking trail to a lookout, passing mining relics and a memorial to those who lost their lives in local mines; Newell Hwy, North Parkes. *Tyndalls Lavender Farm:* visitors welcome to watch distillation process; also includes shop; Wellington Rd. *Self-guide historical town walk and drive:* highlights include the police station (1875), post office (c. 1880) and Balmoral, one of the town's oldest homes, noted for its iron lace, Italian marble and stained-glass windows; brochure from visitor centre.

Elvis Festival: Jan. *Parkes National Marbles Championships:* Mar. *Parkes Astrofest:* July. *Trundle Bush Tucker Day:* Sept. *Country Music Spectacular:* Oct.

Dish Cafe: homemade lunches; Parkes Radio Telescope; (02) 6862 1566. *Parkes International Restaurant:* diverse menu; Parkes International Comfort Inn, Newell Hwy; (02) 6862 5222. *Station Hotel:* modern Australian; 82 Peak Hill Rd; (02) 6862 8444.

Kadina B&B: friendly, traditional B&B; 22 Mengarvie Rd; (02) 6862 3995 or 0412 444 452. *The Old Parkes Convent:* rustic B&B; 33 Currajong St; (02) 6862 5385.

Parkes CSIRO Radio Telescope Commissioned in 1961, the telescope is the largest and oldest of the 8 antennae making up the Australian Telescope National Facility. It has been used for globally important work such as identifying the first quasar in 1963, mapping important regions of the Milky Way, and tracking the NASA Apollo moon missions. It was most famously instrumental in transmitting images of Neil Armstrong's first steps on the moon to the world. The story of the events on the ground at Parkes is portrayed in the film *The Dish* (2000). The visitor centre explains the uses of the telescope and has 3D displays. Inquiries (02) 6861 1777; 23 km N.

Condobolin This country town is where the first *Australian Idol* runner-up Shannon Noll has his roots. A lookout on Reservoir Hill gives views over the town, which is at the junction of 2 rivers and surrounded by red-soil plains. Mt Tilga, 8 km N, is said to be the geographical centre of NSW, and Gum Bend Lake, 5 km w, is a good spot for fishing and watersports. 95 km w.

Macusani Alpaca Farm and Shop: includes workshops throughout the year; Tichborne, 10 km s. *Peak Hill:* working goldmine with lookout offering views of Parkes; 48 km N.

See also CENTRAL WEST, p. 30

Picton

Pop. 3025
Map ref. 544 F12 | 553 D2 | 555 J7 | 565 G1

 Old Post Office, cnr Argyle and Menangle sts; (02) 4677 8313; www.visitwollondilly.com.au

📻 C91.3 FM Campbelltown, 603 AM ABC Radio National

Located in the foothills of the Southern Highlands, Picton was once a thriving town, but since the re-routing of the Hume Highway it has become a peaceful and well-preserved village. Originally gazetted as Stonequarry, the town was renamed after Thomas Picton, one of Wellington's generals at the battle of Waterloo.

 George IV Inn and Scharer's Brewery This is one of Australia's oldest operating inns. It only serves beer from its own brewery made from its own original German recipe (one of only a few pub breweries in the country) and has meals and regular entertainment. Argyle St; (02) 4677 1415.

Picton Botanical Gardens: quiet rural park with views over the farmland, barbecues and picnic facilities; Regreme Rd. *Self-guide historical walk:* includes the splendid railway viaduct (1862) over Stonequarry Creek, and St Mark's Church (1848). *Ghost tours:* local pioneer ghost tour and tales with supper or 2-course meal. Bookings essential (02) 4677 2044.

Brush with the Bush: art festival; Oct.

 Dreamcatcher Lodge B&B: B&B plus self-contained cottage; 2330 Remembrance Dr; (02) 4683 3232. *White Waratah Retreat:* country guesthouse; 1665 Remembrance Dr; (02) 4677 2121.

 Thirlmere This quiet and attractive town is best known for its NSW Rail Transport Museum. The complex offers steam-train rides on the 1st and 3rd Sun of each month (except in summer when the diesel trains run). The Festival of Steam is held here in Mar, and includes market stalls and street parade. 5 km sw. Thirlmere Lakes National Park (a further 3 km sw) protects 5 reed-fringed freshwater lakes that are home to waterbirds and other wildlife. This is a great place for swimming, picnicking and canoeing, and there is a scenic walk around the lakes.

Jarvisfield Homestead: 1865 home of pioneer landowners, now the clubhouse of Antill Park Golf Club; Remembrance Dr; 2 km n. *Sydney Skydiving Centre:* catering for beginners and experienced skydivers with video-viewing facilities and a picnic and barbecue area; (02) 9791 9155; 5 km e. *Maldon Suspension Bridge:* bungee jumping; 5 km se. *Wirrimbirra Sanctuary:* native flora and fauna including Dingo Sanctuary, with regular events and twilight tours. Overnight cabins are available. Closed Mon; inquiries (02) 4684 1112; 13 km sw.

See also SOUTHERN HIGHLANDS, p. 24

Port Macquarie

see inset box on next page

Queanbeyan

Pop. 38 593
Map ref. 554 F11 | 563 G7 | 564 F6 | 565 D5 | 566 H3

i Cnr Farrer Pl and Lowe St; (02) 6299 7307; www.visitqueanbeyan.com.au

106.3 Mix FM, 549 AM ABC Local

Queanbeyan is a growing city adjoining Canberra. Even though most of the city is in New South Wales, the outskirts sprawl into the ACT. Queanbeyan takes its name from a squat ex-convict Timothy Beard inhabited near the Molonglo River. He called 'Quinbean' after an Aboriginal word meaning 'clear waters'.

 History Museum: documented history of the city in restored police sergeant's residence; open 1–4pm Sat and Sun; Farrer Pl. *Queanbeyan Printing Museum:* includes memorabilia from the first newspaper in Queanbeyan; open 2pm–4pm Sat and Sun; Farrer Pl. *Queanbeyan Art Society Inc:* exhibits local art

and craft; Trinculo Pl. *Railway Historical Society:* steam-train rides depart from station in Henderson St; check times (02) 6284 2790. *Self-guide town walks:* include Byrne's Mill (1883), now a restaurant, and St Benedict's Convent, built in the 1800s for the Sisters of the Good Samaritan; now home to an art and bead gallery; brochure available from visitor centre.

 Queanbeyan Gift: footrace; Nov.

Basil at Byrne's Mill Restaurant: modern Australian; 55 Collett St; (02) 6297 8283.

Hamiltons Townhouse Motel: comfortable contemporary accommodation; 53 Tharwa Rd, cnr Canberra Ave; (02) 6297 1877. *Quality Inn Country Plaza:* well-appointed country motel; 147 Uriarra Rd; (02) 6297 1211.

 Bungendore This historic country village is set in a picturesque valley near Lake George and still consists of old stone, brick and timber buildings that have been there since the 19th century. The town square contains charming colonial-style shops selling crafts and antiques, and there are several hobby farms in the area. There is a Country Muster in Feb and a rodeo in Oct. 26 km NE. Lark Hill Winery, 7 km N of Bungendore, has cellar-door tastings and sales.

Molonglo Gorge: scenic drive and 3 km walking trail provide spectacular views of Molonglo River; 2 km N. *Googong Dam:* fishing, bushwalking and picnicking; 10 km s. *London Bridge Woolshed and Shearers' Quarters:* visual history of turn-of-the-century farming and settlement life. Take the easy 1 km walk to a remarkable limestone arch. 24 km s. *Captains Flat:* tiny mining town, ideal for walking around, with historic buildings; 45 km s.

See also CAPITAL COUNTRY, p. 31

Raymond Terrace

Pop. 12 700
Map ref. 543 H2 | 549 D7 | 550 A12 | 555 M3

i Shop 7, 42 Williams St; (02) 4987 5276; www.portstephens.org.au

102.9 KO FM, 1233 AM ABC Newcastle

Situated on the banks of the Hunter and William rivers just outside Newcastle, Raymond Terrace was an important wool-shipping area in the 1840s. Many historic buildings from that era remain today. The town is in the middle of a koala corridor thanks to the vast remaining eucalypt forests in the region.

 Sketchley Cottage: built in 1840 and rebuilt after being destroyed by fire in 1857. Displays include early Australian farming equipment, wine casks, furniture, handicrafts and photography; Pacific Hwy. *Self-guide historical town walk:* includes courthouse (1838) and an 1830s Anglican church built of hand-hewn sandstone; map from visitor centre.

Golden Terrace Chinese Restaurant: takeaway available; Pacific Gardens Caravan Park, 278 Pacific Hwy; (02) 4983 1515.

Motto Farm Motel: spacious budget-friendly accommodation; 2285 Pacific Hwy; (02) 4987 1211.

Tanilba House Home to the first white settler in Tanilba Bay, Lieutenant Caswell, Tanilba House was convict-built in 1831. Features of the house include decorative quoins defining the building edge, door and window openings, and high ceilings, archways and large rooms. There is said to be a resident ghost, thought to be an 1830s governess; 36 km NE.

Hunter Region Botanic Gardens: over 2000 native plants and several theme gardens; Pacific Hwy; 3 km s. *Grahamstown Lake:* beautiful serene lake with picnic facilities; 12 km n. *Fighter World:* hands-on displays of old fighter planes, engines and equipment; RAAF base, Williamtown; 16 km ne. *Clarence Town:* this historic village was one of the first European settlements in Australia; 27 km nw. *Tilligerry Habitat:* ecotourism centre with art and craft and guided walks to see koalas; 34 km ne. *Koala Reserve:* boardwalk through koala colony; 40 km n.

See also HUNTER VALLEY & COAST, p. 26

Richmond

Pop. 25 011
Map ref. 544 H4 | 547 O7 | 555 J6

ℹ Hawkesbury Visitor Information Centre, Ham Common, Hawkesbury Valley Way, Clarendon; (02) 4578 0233 or 1300 362 874; www.hawkesburytourism.com.au

📻 89.9 FM Hawkesbury Radio, 94.5 FM ABC Local

Richmond provides a peaceful country atmosphere on the Hawkesbury River, but is close enough to Sydney to enjoy the best of both worlds. Many residents commute to the city each day. The township was settled in 1794 because of the rich Hawkesbury River flats. Richmond was soon being used as a granary to supply half of Sydney's grain and is still important agriculturally. There are magnificent views of the Blue Mountains.

🏠 *Bowman's Cottage:* restored c. 1815 cottage, now National Parks & Wildlife office; Windsor St. *Pugh's Lagoon:* pleasant picnic spot with plentiful waterbirds; Kurrajong Rd. *Self-guide historical town walks:* features many heritage buildings including St Peter's Church (1841) and adjacent pioneer graves; brochure from visitor centre.

🌴 *Bellbird Craft Markets:* March St; 2nd Sat each month. *Fruits of the Hawkesbury Festival:* throughout region; Sept–Nov.

✕ *Red Rum Italian Restaurant:* modern Italian; 39 Bells Line of Road, North Richmond; (02) 4571 3148.

⊗ **Bilpin** This tiny town is known for its apples and apple juice. It was originally named Belpin after Archibald Bell Jnr, who was the first European to cross the mountains from Richmond (Bells Line of Road is also named after him). The fact that he did this with the help of local Aboriginal people, who had been doing it for thousands of years, did not seem to detract from the achievement. Bilpin now has many orchards that are part of the Hawkesbury Farm Gate Trail. Brochures are available from the visitor centre. In keeping with the Australian penchant for 'big' attractions, Bilpin has the Big Bowl of Fruit. There are markets every Sat. 31 km nw.

RAAF base: oldest Air Force establishment in Australia, used for civilian flying from 1915; Windsor–Richmond Rd; 3 km e. *Kurrajong:* quaint mountain village that's home to shops, cafes and galleries, and the Scarecrow Festival held in Oct. Just off Bells Line of Rd; 10 km nw. *Bellbird Hill Lookout:* clear views across to Sydney skyline; Kurrajong Heights; 13 km nw. *Hawkesbury Lookout:* great views of Sydney over the Cumberland plain; 15 km sw. *Avoca Lookout:* stunning views over Grose Valley; 20 km w. *Mountain Lagoon:* mountain bushland setting with walking trails leading down to the pristine Colo River; brochure from visitor centre; 40 km nw.

See also CENTRAL COAST & HAWKESBURY, p. 25

Robertson

Pop. 1207
Map ref. 553 D6 | 555 J9 | 565 G3

ℹ Southern Highlands Visitor Information Centre, 62–70 Main St, Mittagong; (02) 4871 2888 or 1300 657 559; www.southern-highlands.com.au

📻 102.9 2ST FM, 603 AM ABC Radio National

Robertson sits high atop Macquarie Pass with some points in town enjoying spectacular views all the way across to the Pacific Ocean. The region's rich red soil has made Robertson the centre of the largest potato-growing district in New South Wales and there is a 'big potato' on the main street, although it is not signposted and visitors could be forgiven for thinking it is merely a large brown cylinder. The undulating hills create a picturesque setting and were featured in the film *Babe* (1996).

🏠 **Kev Neel's Old Time Music Machines** This music museum displays antique gramophones (some still in working condition) and music memorabilia from as early as the 1800s. Outside are deer, birds and views of the Illawarra Escarpment. Tour the grounds and use the picnic facilities. Illawarra Hwy.

Cockatoo Run Heritage Railway: steam train (when available) to Port Kembla. Robertson Railway Station. For running times call 1300 653 801. *Art and craft shops:* several in town featuring local work; details from visitor centre.

🌴 *Market:* Robertson School of Arts; 2nd Sun each month. *Springtime Festival:* Oct.

✕ *Pizzas in the Mist:* Italian/modern Australian; 42 Hoddle St; (02) 4885 1799.

🛏 *Greetham B&B:* traditional B&B; 2 Meryla St; (02) 4885 1220. *Sentinel Farm Cottage:* large self-contained cottage; 116 Illawarra Hwy; (02) 4885 1571.

⊗ **Morton National Park, Robertson section** This section of the park has two attractive features: Belmore Falls (10 km sw) and Fitzroy Falls (15 km sw). Belmore Falls plunges into 2 separate rockpools, which then cascade down to the valley below. The area also features walking tracks and pleasant picnic facilities. At Fitzroy Falls is the National Parks & Wildlife Service visitor centre, which has maps and information about the entire national park and offers guided tours. The falls drop 80 m over sandstone cliffs onto black rocks and then another 40 m into the valley below. The walking trail around the falls has excellent lookouts. *For other sections of the park see Bundanoon, Nowra and Ulladulla.*

Illawarra Fly Tree Top Walk Visitors can experience the Southern Highlands' native flora and fauna from 25 m above ground. The 600 m walkway has 2 cantilevered arms stretching to the forest fall line, with expansive views of Lake Illawarra and the South Pacific Ocean. For those who want to get even higher, a spiralling tower reaches 45 m above ground. The environmentally friendly visitor centre has a cafe. Knights Hill Rd; 1300 362 881; 15 km se.

Robertson Rainforest: 5 ha portion of what was the 2500 ha Yarrawah Brush. It is home to abundant birdlife and features an attractive bushwalk; 2 km s. *Fountaindale Grand Manor:* c. 1924 with over 80 rooms and uninterrupted views of the surrounding hills and valley. Deer and peacocks roam the immaculate, landscaped grounds. It is now a guesthouse and function centre; Illawarra Hwy; (02) 4885 1111; 3 km e. *Burrawang:* 19th-century village with an excellent historic pub; 6 km w. *Macquarie Pass National Park:* preserved section of the Illawarra Escarpment with bushwalks through eucalypt forest and picnic facilities; 10 km e. *Budderoo National Park:* Robertson section features

PORT MACQUARIE

Pop. 39 508
Map ref. 550 G6 | 557 M11

[SUNSET OVER PORT MACQUARIE]

i Cnr Gordon and Gore sts; (02) 6581 8000 or 1300 303 155; www.portmacquarieinfo.com.au

102.3 Star FM, 684 AM ABC Local

Port Macquarie, one of the oldest towns in the state, was established in 1821 as a self-sufficient penal settlement. Convicts chosen for their skills and good behaviour maintained the fledgling town, doing everything from farming, boatbuilding and blacksmithing to teaching, baking and clerical duties. Today the city is a major holiday resort at the mouth of the Hastings River. It provides a fascinating history and features historic buildings, nature reserves, excellent surf and fishing beaches, an outstanding museum and scenic coastal walking tracks.

Historical Society Museum This award-winning museum has over 20 000 items in its ever-increasing collection. It specialises in letters, photographs and documents covering convict and free settlement and the evolution of the town from penal colony to coastal metropolis. The museum is in one of the town's beautifully restored older buildings (c. 1836). Clarence St; (02) 6583 1108.

St Thomas' Church: third oldest surviving church in Australia (1824–28), designed by convict architect Thomas Owen; Hay St. *Port Macquarie Historic Courthouse:* built in 1869, it served the community for 117 years; tours of the restored building by appt; closed Sun; Cnr Hay and Clarence sts; (02) 6584 1818. *Mid-north Coast Maritime Museum:* shipwreck relics, model ships and early photographs; William St; (02) 6583 1866. *Kooloonbung Creek Nature Reserve:* 50 ha of nature reserve with boardwalks and picnic area. Visit the historic cemetery nearby dating from 1842; Horton St. *Koala Hospital:* Koala rehabilitation and adoption centre, the only one of its kind in NSW. Daily walks and feeding tours from 3pm; Lord St. *Roto House and Macquarie Nature Reserve:* adjacent to the koala hospital and built in 1890, classified by the National Trust; off Lord St. *Port Macquarie Observatory:* planetarium, telescope and solar system display; call for opening times (02) 6582 2397; William St. *Billabong Koala and Aussie Wildlife Park:* wide variety of Australian and exotic wildlife with kangaroo-feeding and koala photo sessions each day; Billabong Dr. *Town beach:* patrolled swimming and surfing beach with sheltered coves at one end. *Cruises:* depart daily; bookings at visitor centre. *Scenic walks:* 9 km coastal walk from

Westport Park in the town centre to Tacking Point Lighthouse; traverses beaches and subtropical rainforest with picnic spots, interpretative signs and viewing platforms along the trail; look out for the dolphins of Hastings River and a variety of birdlife; walk takes 3 hrs 30 min one way; brochure from visitor centre.

Market: Findlay Ave; 2nd and 4th Sun each month. *Golden Lure Tournament:* deep-sea fishing; Jan. *Australian Ironman Triathlon:* Apr. *Heritage Festival:* Apr. *FreshArt:* youth arts festival; June. *Aquasculpture:* odd-numbered years, Oct. *Tastings of the Hastings:* food and wine festival; Oct. *Festival of the Sun:* music festival; Dec.

Bliss Restaurant: modern Australian; Level 1, 74 Clarence St; (02) 6584 1422. *Ca Marche:* modern Australian; Cassegrain Winery, 764 Fernbank Creek Rd; (02) 6582 8320. *The Breakwall:* modern Australian, relaxed ambience; The Observatory Resort, 40 William St; (02) 6583 9300.

Quality Inn HW Boutique: beautiful accommodation, stunning location; 1 Stewart St; (02) 6583 1200. *Woodlands B&B:* traditional B&B; 348 Oxley Hwy; (02) 6581 3913.

Lake Innes Nature Reserve This reserve is home to koalas, kangaroos and bats, but was once the location of the grand Lake Innes House. Major Innes was an early settler and had fantastic visions for the future of Port Macquarie. He built his stately home and invested his money in property in the fledgling town. Unfortunately, he had overstretched himself and was forced to declare himself bankrupt. The house was left to decay, and the ruins are all that remain. Guided tours are available; brochure at visitor centre. 7 km sw.

Sea Acres Rainforest Centre: elevated 1.3 km boardwalk through canopy; tours available; 4 km s. *Lighthouse Beach:* 16 km of white sand with camel rides, dolphin-watching from shore and breathtaking views from the grounds of Tacking Point Lighthouse at the northern end of the beach (lighthouse not open to public); 10 km s. *Lake Cathie:* holiday town between surf beach and tidal lake for swimming and fishing; 16 km s. *Wineries:* several in the area offering cellar-door tastings including Lake Innes Vineyard (7 km w) and Cassegrain Winery (13 km w). *Skydiving, sea plane flights, trike tours, golf:* brochures from visitor centre.

See also HOLIDAY COAST, p. 27

Carrington Falls, a 50 m waterfall with adjacent walking tracks, lookouts and picnic facilities; 10 km SE. *Manning Lookout:* views over Kangaroo Valley; 16 km SW.

See also SOUTHERN HIGHLANDS, p. 24

Rylstone
Pop. 616
Map ref. 555 I3

ⓘ Council offices, Louee St; (02) 6379 4318; www.rylstone.com

📻 98.7 KRR FM, 549 AM ABC Central West

Visitors are drawn to Rylstone for its rural tranquillity. This old stone village is on the Cudgegong River and is a popular spot for birdwatching and fishing.

🏠 **Jack Tindale Park** This park is a pleasant green reserve, perfect for swimming, picnics and barbecues. Platypus are sometimes spotted in the water here and in the river below the showground. Cox St.

Olive Press: see how fresh olives are pressed, and sample or purchase some of the region's best olive oil. Open Sat and Sun Apr–Oct; Lue Rd. *Self-guide historical walk:* includes the Bridge View Inn (restaurant, formerly a bank) and the post office; brochure from visitor centre. *Art and craft outlets:* several featuring local work; details at visitor centre.

🌴 *Agricultural Show:* Feb. *Great Escapade Bike Ride:* Apr. *StreetFeast:* highlight is the Long Lunch, with gourmet regional food served to 350 people on long tables; Nov.

🍴 *Jessie's Steakhouse:* steaks, pub bistro; Rylstone Hotel, 62 Louee St; (02) 6379 1118.

🛏 *Above the Clouds:* self-contained accommodation; 1710 Nullo Mountain Rd; (02) 6379 6253.

⊚ *Kandos:* industrial town known for its cement. It features the Bicentennial Industrial Museum (open weekends) and holds the Kandos Street Machine and Hot Rod Show each Jan; 3 km S. *Fern Tree Gully:* tree ferns in subtropical forest with walking trails and lookouts; 16 km N. *Dunn's Swamp:* camping, fishing, bushwalking; 18 km E. *Windermere Dam:* watersports, fishing, camping, picnic and barbecue facilities. Also home of fishing competition each Easter; 19 km W. *Military Vehicle Museum:* vehicles from WW II and the Korean and Vietnam wars; 20 km N. *Turon Technology Museum:* power museum with restored steam engines; 20 km S. *Glen Davis:* this fascinating shale oil ghost town is at the eastern end of the Capertee Valley. The valley is almost 30 km across and is surrounded by sheer sandstone cliffs, which makes it the largest enclosed valley in the Southern Hemisphere; 56 km SE. *Wineries:* several in the area, including De Beaurepaire and Louee Winery; brochure from visitor centre.

See also CENTRAL WEST, p. 30

Scone
Pop. 4628
Map ref. 555 K1 | 556 H12

ⓘ Cnr Susan and Kelly sts; (02) 6545 1526; www.upperhuntertourism.com.au

📻 98.1 Power FM, 549 AM ABC Local

Set among rolling green hills in the Hunter Valley, Scone (rhymes with stone) is a pleasant rural town with tree-lined streets. It is known as the 'horse capital of Australia' and is actually the world's second largest thoroughbred and horse-breeding centre.

🏠 *Australian Stock Horse Museum:* photographs and displays on stockhorse history, and the headquarters of the Australian Stock Horse Society; open Mon–Fri; Kelly St. *Mare and Foal:* life-size sculpture by Gabriel Sterk; Kelly St. *Historical Society Museum:* large collection of local photographs and household furniture and appliances in an old lock-up (1870); open 9.30am–2.30pm Wed, 2.30–4.30pm Sun; Kingdon St.

🌴 *Horse Festival:* May.

🍴 *Kerv Espresso Bar:* excellent coffee, light meals; 108 Liverpool St; (02) 6545 3111. *The Larda:* gourmet cafe plus homewares; 122 Kelly St; (02) 6545 9533.

🛏 *Belltrees Country House:* working ranch retreat; Gundy Rd; (02) 6546 1123. *Segenhoe View B&B:* beautiful French Provincial–style B&B; Pages Row, 429 Glenbawn Rd; (02) 6545 2081. *Strathearn Park Lodge:* elegant guesthouse; New England Hwy; (02) 6545 3200.

⊚ **Moonan Flat** This small town sits at the base of the Barrington Tops. It has a beautiful suspension bridge, a small post office and the Victoria Hotel (1856). The hotel was a Cobb & Co coach stop during the gold-rush era and was reputedly patronised by bushranger Captain Thunderbolt. It is small but friendly, and has accommodation and an adjoining restaurant. 50 km NE. *For Barrington Tops National Park, see Gloucester.*

Lake Glenbawn: watersports, bass fishing, picnic, barbecue and camping facilities and a rural life museum; 15 km E. *Burning Mountain:* deep coal seam that has been smouldering for at least 5000 years. Take the 4.6 km track through the bush; 20 km N. *Wineries:* several offering cellar-door tastings; brochure from visitor centre. *Tours:* thoroughbred stud and sheep station; bookings at visitor centre. *Trail rides:* throughout area, and mustering opportunities for experienced riders; bookings at visitor centre.

See also HUNTER VALLEY & COAST, p. 26

Shellharbour
Pop. 64 296
Map ref. 553 F6 | 555 J9 | 565 H3

ⓘ Lamerton House, Lamerton Cres; (02) 4221 6169; www.tourismshellharbour.com.au

📻 97.3 FM ABC Illawarra, 99.8 Wave FM

Shellharbour was a thriving port in the 1830s when development could not keep up with demand. The first shops did not appear until the 1850s and the courthouse and gaol were erected in 1877. Prior to this the local constable had to tie felons to a tree. Today the town is an attractive holiday resort close to Lake Illawarra and one of the oldest settlements on the South Coast.

🏠 **Illawarra Light Railway Museum** The museum offers tram rides, displays of steam trains and vintage carriages and a miniature railway. The ticket office and kiosk are in an original 1890s rail terminus and the volunteer staff are knowledgeable. Open Tues, Thurs and Sat. Steam-train rides 2nd Sun each month and Sun during public holiday weekends. Russell St.

Historical walk: take in the historical buildings of the town, beginning at the Steampacket Inn, parts of which date back to 1856. Contact visitor centre for more information. *Snorkelling and scuba diving:* at Bushranger's Bay; details from visitor centre or Shellharbour Scuba Centre; (02) 4296 4266.

🌴 *Craft market:* Shellharbour Public School, Mary St; 2nd Sun each month. *Gamefishing Tournament:* Feb. *City Festival:* 3-day local sports extravaganza; Mar. *Festival in the Forest:* Sept.

Relish on Addison: modern Australian; Shop 1, 31A Addison St; (02) 4295 5191.

Joylaine Beach House: luxury self-contained beach house; 5 Darley St; (02) 9550 5525. *Seascape Beach House:* large self-contained house; Addison St; (02) 4297 3574.

Lake Illawarra This large tidal estuary was once a valuable source of food for the Wadi Wadi people. It is home to waterbirds such as black swans, pelicans and royal spoonbills, and has picnic and barbecue areas. The lake is excellent for boating, swimming, waterskiing, windsurfing, fishing and prawning. 7 km N.

Blackbutt Forest Reserve: remnant of coastal plain forest in urban area. Walking trails offer views of Lake Illawarra and Illawarra Escarpment; 2 km w. *Killalea Recreation Park:* foreshore picnic area with an ideal beach for surfing, diving, snorkelling and fishing; 3 km s. *Bass Point Aquatic and Marine Reserve:* top spot for scuba diving, snorkelling, fishing and surfing, with a nice picnic area on the shore; 5 km sE. *Tongarra Museum:* shows area's history through photographs, maps and sketches; 11 km w. *Crooked River Wines:* specialty is Chardonnay White Port, with gorgeous restaurant also on-site; 20 km s.

See also SOUTHERN HIGHLANDS, p. 24

Singleton

Pop. 13 665
Map ref. 555 K3

 39 George St; (02) 6571 5888 or 1800 449 888; www.singleton.nsw.gov.au

98.1 Power FM, 1044 AM ABC Upper Hunter

Singleton is a pleasant and sleepy town set next to the Hunter River among beautiful pasturelands, mountains and national parks. It is the geographical heart of the Hunter Valley and is known for its excellent wines, with several famous vineyards.

Singleton Mercy Convent The Sisters of Mercy arrived from Ireland in 1875 and set up this convent. Set in manicured gardens is the prominent convent, a chapel with an impressive marble altar, and the Sisters of Mercy Museum in an old Georgian cottage. Tours are conducted by the sisters at 2pm on weekends Mar–Nov; Queen St.

James Cook Park: riverside park with picnic facilities and the largest monolithic sundial in the Southern Hemisphere; Ryan Ave. *Singleton Historical Museum:* memorabilia in Singleton's first courthouse and gaol from the town's pioneer days; Burdekin Park, New England Hwy. *Town walk:* enjoyable walk passing a historic Anglican church and lush parklands; brochure from visitor centre.

Market: Burdekin Park, New England Hwy; 4th Sun each month. *Countryfest:* includes the Australian Wife Carrying Race; Apr.

Charades Restaurant and Bar: modern Australian; Quality Inn Charbonnier Hallmark, 44 Maitland Rd; (02) 6572 2333. *Henri's Brasserie:* modern Australian; Level 1, 85 John St; (02) 6571 3566. *Roberts:* modern Australian, in National Trust cottage; Halls Rd, Pokolbin; (02) 4998 7330. *Terroir:* winery restaurant; Hungerford Hill, 1 Broke Rd, Pokolbin; (02) 4990 0711.

Glen-Nevis B&B: Victorian guesthouse; 399 Westbrook Rd; (02) 6577 5612.

Yengo National Park Mt Yengo is of cultural significance to local Aboriginal communities and there are extensive carvings and paintings in the area. The park is a rugged area of steep gorges and rocky ridges with several walking tracks and lookouts. Old Great North Rd, along the south-east boundary, is an intact example of early 19th-century convict roadbuilding. There are picnic and barbecue areas and campsites throughout the park. Inquiries (02) 6574 5555; 15 km s.

Royal Australian Military Corps Museum: traces history of the infantry corps in Australia; 5 km s. *Wollemi National Park:* Singleton section features picturesque walking trails, lookouts and campsites; (02) 6372 7199; 15 km sw. *For further details on the park see Lithgow. Hillside Orange Orchard:* pick your own oranges; Windsor–Putty Rd; 25 km sw. *Lake St Clair:* extensive recreational and waterway facilities and you can camp onshore. Nearby lookouts offer magnificent views of Mount Royal Range; 25 km N. *Broke:* tiny township with breathtaking national park views and village fair in Sept; 26 km s. *Mt Royal National Park:* rainforest area with scenic walking tracks and lookouts with spectacular 360-degree views from Mt Royal over the entire region; (02) 6574 5555; 32 km N. *Local Hunter Valley wineries:* wineries with cellar-door tastings including Wyndham Estate, Australia's oldest winery, and Cockfighters Ghost; tours available; brochure from visitor centre.

See also HUNTER VALLEY & COAST, p. 26

Stroud

Pop. 669
Map ref. 549 F4 | 550 B10 | 555 M3

 Forster Visitor Information Centre, Little St; Forster; (02) 6554 8799 or 1800 802 692; www.greatlakes.org.au

93.1 Breeze FM, 1512 AM ABC Radio National

This delightful town is nestled in the green Karuah Valley and seems to be from another era. The absence of tourist facilities combined with the plethora of historic buildings gives Stroud an unaffected charm. The annual International Brick and Rolling Pin Throwing Competition sees residents competing against towns called Stroud in the United States, England and Canada.

St John's Anglican Church This convict-built church was made with bricks of local clay in 1833 and features beautiful stained-glass windows and original cedar furnishings. The church is noted as the place where bushranger Captain Thunderbolt married Mary Ann Bugg. Cowper St.

Underground silo: one of 8 brick-lined silos built in 1841 for grain storage, it can be inspected by descending a steel ladder; Silo Hill Reserve, off Broadway St. *Self-guide town walk:* covers 32 historic sites including Orchard Cottage (1830s) and St Columbanus Catholic Church (1857), which is still in original condition; brochure from visitor centre.

International Brick and Rolling Pin Throwing Competition: July. *Rodeo:* Sept/Oct.

Lizzie's Cafe Brasserie: golf course brasserie; Bucketts Way; (02) 4994 5113. *Terra Cottage Gallery and Cafe:* great coffee and desserts; 17 Bucketts Way; (02) 4994 5338.

Orchard Cottage Accommodation: cosy self-contained accommodation; 3 Broadway St; (02) 4994 5608. *Telegherry Estate:* huge estate, beautiful accommodation options; 524 Bucketts Way; (02) 4994 5100.

 RADIO STATIONS IN TOWN WHAT'S ON WHERE TO EAT WHERE TO STAY NEARBY

Dungog In 1838 this town, nestled in the Williams River valley, was established as a military outpost to prevent bushranging by local villains such as Captain Thunderbolt. North of Dungog is Chichester Dam, with its blue-gum surrounds, and east of the dam is Chichester State Forest. In the foothills of the Barrington Tops, the forest has picnic spots, camping, lookouts and walking trails. 22 km w.

See also HOLIDAY COAST, p. 27

Tamworth

Pop. 42 496
Map ref. 556 H9

561 Peel St; (02) 6755 4300; www.visittamworth.com

92.9 FM Tamworth's Hit Music Station, 648 AM ABC New England North West

Tamworth is a prosperous city and the self-proclaimed country music capital of Australia, an image that has been carefully cultivated since the late 1960s. There is no question that Tamworth has increased country music's credibility and acceptance in Australia, with local events helping to launch the international careers of several stars. Thousands of fans flock to the Tamworth Country Music Festival every year.

Walk a Country Mile Interpretive Centre From the air this building is guitar-shaped, and it features various displays including one that cleverly documents the history of country music through lyrics. This is also Tamworth's visitor centre, and the first port of call for information on the festival. Peel St.

Hands of Fame Park: Country Music Hands of Fame Cornerstone features handprints of over 200 country music stars; Cnr New England Hwy and Kable Ave. *Australian Country Music Foundation:* features the Legends of Australian Country Music exhibition, a display on the Country Music Awards and a theatrette playing films and documentaries; Brisbane St. *Calala Cottage:* National Trust–classified home of Tamworth's first mayor with antique household items and original shepherd's slab hut; Denson St. *Tamworth Regional Gallery:* houses over 700 works including some by Hans Heysen and Will Ashton, and the National Fibre Collection; closed Mon; Peel St. *Powerhouse Motorcycle Museum:* collection of immaculate motorbikes from the 1950s through to the 1980s; Armidale Rd. *Oxley Park:* sanctuary for kangaroos and other marsupials, with picnic and barbecue facilities; off Brisbane St. *Oxley Lookout:* views of the city and beautiful Peel Valley. It is also the starting point for the Kamilaroi walking track (6.2 km); brochure from visitor centre; top of White St. *Powerstation Museum:* traces Tamworth's history as the first city in the Southern Hemisphere to have electric street lighting (installed in 1888); Peel St. *Joe Maguire's Pub:* features Noses of Fame, nose imprints of country music stars; Peel St. *Anzac Park:* attractive picnic and barbecue spot with playground; bordered by Brisbane, Napier, Fitzroy and Upper sts. *Bicentennial Park:* fountains, granite sculptures and period lighting; Kable Ave. *Regional Botanic Gardens:* 28 ha of native flora and exotic displays; top of Piper St. *Line dancing:* various venues; lessons offered; brochure from visitor centre. *Historical town walks:* two available of 90 min each, visiting churches, theatres and hotels; brochure from visitor centre. *Art and craft:* several shops and galleries; brochure from visitor centre.

Market: Showground Pavilion; 2nd Sun each month. *Main St Market:* Peel St Blvd; 3rd Sun each month. *Tamworth Country Music Festival:* Jan. *National Pro Rodeo:* Jan. *Gold*

Cup Race Meeting: horserace; Apr/May. *Australian Line Dance Festival:* May. *Hats Off to Country Festival:* July. *Bush Poets and Balladeers:* traditional Australian variety show with poets and country singers; July. *National Cutting Horse Association Futurity:* competition and entertainment; Sept–Oct. *North-West Craft Expo:* Dec.

Bellepoque Restaurante: Mediterranean; Cnr Darling and Marius sts; (02) 6766 3495. *Golden Guitar Coffee Shop:* cafe and tourist attraction; The Big Golden Guitar Tourist Centre, 2 Ringers Rd; (02) 6765 2688.

Jacaranda Cottage B&B: secluded retreat; 105 Carthage St; (02) 6766 4281. *Paradise Tourist Park:* excellent facilities; 575 Peel St; (02) 6766 3120 or 1800 330 133. *The Retreat at Froog-Moore Park:* luxurious unique retreat; 78 Bligh St; (02) 6766 3353.

Big Golden Guitar Tourist Centre The 12 m golden guitar is a giant replica of the country music award and an Australian icon. Inside the complex is the Gallery of Stars Wax Museum, which features wax models of Australian country music legends alongside current stars. Opposite is the outdoor Country Music Roll of Renown, which is said to be Australia's highest honour in country music. There are special tributes to, among others, Tex Morton, Smoky Dawson and Slim Dusty. 6 km s.

Oxley anchor: the original anchor from John Oxley's ship marks the point where he crossed the Peel River on his expedition to the coast; 9 km NW. *Birdwatching routes:* great birdwatching walks and drives in and around Tamworth; brochure from visitor centre.

See also NEW ENGLAND, p. 29

Taree

Pop. 16 519
Map ref. 550 E8 | 555 O1 | 557 L12

Manning Valley Visitor Information Centre, 21 Manning River Dr, Taree North; (02) 6592 5444 or 1800 182 733; www.gtcc.nsw.gov.au

107.3 MAX FM, 684 AM ABC Local

Taree is a big modern town on the Manning River and the commercial hub of the Manning River district. It is well known for its handicrafts and its beautiful parklands and nature reserves.

Fotheringham Park and Queen Elizabeth Park These parklands make an ideal riverside picnic spot to watch the boats go by. To mark the bicentenary in 1988, an unusual herb and sculpture garden was established – the herbs are available to locals for cooking. There are also several memorials throughout the park. Between Pacific Hwy and Manning River.

Taree Craft Centre: huge craft centre featuring local work and picnic facilities; Manning River Dr, Taree North; (02) 6551 5766. *Manning Regional Art Gallery:* changing exhibitions always include some local works; Macquarie St; (02) 6592 5455. *Self-guide historical walks:* through eastern and western sections of town; brochure from visitor centre. *Manning Valley River cruises:* offering a variety of cruises on the Manning River; bookings at visitor centre.

Weekly markets: at various venues in the region; contact visitor centre for details. *Manning River Summer Festival:* Jan. *Powerboat racing:* Easter. *Envirofair:* June. *Manning Valley Festival of the Arts:* even-numbered years, June.

Raw Sugar Cafe: traditional cafe favourites; 214 Victoria St; (02) 6550 0137. *Rio's Churrascaria:* Brazilian, waterfront setting; Jolly Swagman Motel, 1 Commerce St; (02) 6552 3511.

 Nundoobah Retreat: luxury romantic retreat; 200 Woola Rd; (02) 6552 2818. *Kiwarrak Country Retreat:* self-contained accommodation; 239 Half Chain Rd, Old Bar; (02) 6553 7391.

Coorabakh National Park The park features the volcanic plug outcrops of Big Nellie, Flat Nellie and Little Nellie. The Lansdowne escarpment is made up of sandstone cliffs and also has spectacular views. From Newbys Lookout you might see sea eagles and wedge-tailed eagles. 20 km NE.

Ellenborough Falls: One of the longest single-drop waterfalls in the Southern Hemisphere at 200 m. Viewing platforms and a boardwalk to the bottom of the falls. Bulga Plateau, via Elands; 50 km NW. *Joy-flights and tandem skydiving:* flights over the Manning Valley depart from the airport on the northern outskirts of town; Lansdowne Rd; (02) 6551 7776. *Deep Water Shark Gallery:* Aboriginal art and craft; Peverill St; 8 km SW. *Ghinni Wines:* boutique winery; Pacific Hwy, Ghinni Ghinni; 10 km NE. *The Big Buzz Funpark:* toboggan run, water slides and go-karts; Lakes Way; (02) 6553 6000; 15 km S. *Beaches:* excellent surfing conditions; 16 km E. *Hallidays Point:* features a rainforest nature walk; brochure from visitor centre; 25 km SE. *Manning River:* 150 km of navigable waterway with beaches, good fishing and holiday spots. *Art and craft galleries:* several in the area; brochure from visitor centre. *Nature reserves:* numerous in the area with abundant wildlife in rainforest settings and walking trails; map from visitor centre.

See also HOLIDAY COAST, p. 27

Tathra

Pop. 1622
Map ref. 565 E9

ⓘ Andy Poole Dr; (02) 6494 1436; www.sapphirecoast.com.au

📻 87.6 Hot Country FM, 810 AM ABC South East

Tathra is an idyllic family holiday location with a 3-kilometre surf beach, frequented by dolphins, that is safe for swimming and excellent for fishing. The town started as a small jetty that served as a shipping outlet for a group of local farmers. It is now the only sea wharf on the east coast. The region is abundant with prawns from November to May.

Sea wharf Deterioration of the 1860s wharf led to a demolition order in 1973. Only strenuous local action and the intervention of the National Trust saved the wharf. It has always been a popular fishing platform and there is also a seafood cafe. Above the wharf is the Maritime Museum, which traces the history of the wharf and steam shipping in the area and has replicas of early vessels. Fur seals and little penguins can often be seen.

Tathra Beach: 3 km patrolled beach with excellent surfing conditions. *Fishing spots:* several good spots for salmon and tailor; map from visitor centre.

Wharf to Waves Weekend: includes 1200 m swim; Jan.

Tathra Beachhouse Apartments: award-winning contemporary accommodation; 57 Andy Poole Dr; (02) 6499 9900.

Mimosa Rocks National Park This beautifully rugged coastal park features surf beaches, caves, offshore rock stacks, lagoons, patches of rainforest and incredible volcanic sculptures. It is excellent for snorkelling, surfing, bushwalking, birdwatching and foreshore fossicking. The name of the park comes from the steamship *Mimosa*, which was wrecked on volcanic rock in 1863; (02) 4476 2888; 17 km N.

Kianinny Bay: known fossil site with steep cliffs and rugged rocks, and diving and deep-sea fishing charters available. The 9 km Kangarutha track follows the coast with spectacular scenery; 1 km S. *Mogareeka Inlet:* safe swimming ideal for small children; northern end of Tathra Beach; 2 km N. *Bournda National Park:* picturesque conservation area for great camping and bushwalking. Wallagoot Lake has a wetland area with birdwatching, fishing, prawning, swimming, watersports and boat hire; (02) 6495 5000; 11 km S.

See also SOUTH COAST, p. 32

Temora

Pop. 4082
Map ref. 554 C7 | 559 P7

ⓘ 294–296 Hoskins St; (02) 6977 1511; www.temora.com.au

📻 89.1 FM ABC Radio National, 549 AM ABC Local

In 1879 gold was discovered in the area and in 1880 the town site was chosen. By 1881 the Temora district was producing half of the state's gold. Of course this could not be maintained, and the population of around 20 000 dwindled quickly. What is left now is a quiet rural Riverina town with several historic buildings. It is also a harness-racing centre with numerous studs in the district.

Temora Rural Museum This award-winning museum has several impressive displays on rural life. There are fashions from the mid-1800s ranging from baby clothes to wedding dresses, and a replica flour mill and display explaining the history of wheat since 3000 BC. Don Bradman's first home, a hardwood slab cottage, has been moved to the grounds from Cootamundra. There is also an impressive rock and mineral collection with an emphasis on the local gold industry. Wagga Rd; (02) 6977 1291.

Skydive Centre: instruction and adventure jumps; weekends; Aerodrome Rd. *Aviation Museum:* This claims to be the world's finest collection of flying historic aircraft. The museum is home to the country's only 2 flying spitfires, the oldest Tiger Moth still flying in Australia, a WW II Hudson, the only flying Gloster Meteor F.8 in the world and many more. The museum holds regular flying weekends throughout the year; Menzies St; (02) 6977 1088. *Heritage walk and drives:* include Edwardian and Federation buildings around town; brochure from visitor centre.

Quota Markets: Pale Face Park; last Sat each month. *Temora Rural Museum Exhibition Day:* Mar.

Waratah Cafe: takeaway/burgers; 222 Hoskins St; (02) 6977 2054.

Courthouse Cottage B&B: restored Federation B&B; 158 Deboos St; (02) 6978 0418.

Lake Centenary: boating, swimming and picnicking; 4 km N. *Ingalba State Forest:* 10 000 ha of state forest featuring flora and fauna native to the area; 10 km W. *Paragon Goldmine:* working mine until 1996; 15 km N. *Ariah Park:* town known as 'Wowsers, Bowsers and Peppercorn Trees', with beautiful historic streetscape lined with peppercorn trees. Hosts the Mary Gilmore Country Music Festival in Oct; 35 km W.

See also RIVERINA, p. 34

 RADIO STATIONS IN TOWN WHAT'S ON WHERE TO EAT WHERE TO STAY NEARBY

Tenterfield

Pop. 3129
Map ref. 551 A5 | 557 L4 | 653 L12

ℹ️ 157 Rouse St; (02) 6736 1082; www.tenterfield.com

📻 89.7 Ten FM, 738 AM ABC North Coast

Tenterfield is a town of four seasons with many deciduous trees making it particularly spectacular in autumn. It is perhaps best known from Peter Allen's song 'Tenterfield Saddler', which he wrote about his grandfather George Woolnough. But Tenterfield is also the self-proclaimed 'birthplace of the nation', as it is where Sir Henry Parkes delivered his famous Federation speech in 1889.

🏠 **Sir Henry Parkes Museum** Sir Henry Parkes made his Federation speech in this National Trust–classified building built in 1876. Today it stands as a monument to Parkes. Memorabilia includes a life-size portrait by Julian Ashton and Parkes' scrimshaw walking-stick made of whale ivory and baleen. Guided tours available. Cnr Manners and Rouse sts.

Centenary Cottage: 1871 home with local history collection. Open Wed–Sun; Logan St. *Railway Museum:* railway memorabilia in a beautifully restored station; Railway Ave. *Tenterfield Saddler:* handmade saddles at the place that inspired the Peter Allen song; High St. *Stannum House:* stately mansion built in 1888 for John Holmes Reid, a tin-mining magnate. Homestay and group tours; Rouse St. *Self-guide historical town walk:* includes early residential buildings in Logan St, St Stephens Presbyterian (now Anglican) Church where Banjo Paterson married Alice Walker in 1903 and the grand National Trust–classified post office; brochure from visitor centre.

🎪 *Railway Market:* railway station; 1st Sat every second month. *Tenterfield Show:* Feb. *Bavarian Beerfest:* odd-numbered years, Mar. *Oracles of the Bush:* Australian culture and bush poetry festival; Apr. *Food and Wine Affair:* Nov.

🍴 *Kurrajong Downs Wines:* international, wine tastings; Casino Rd; (02) 6736 4590.

🛏️ *Best Western Henry Parkes Motel:* stylish 4-star accommodation; 144 Rouse St; (02) 6736 1066. *Rover Park:* family tourist park; Bruxner Hwy; (02) 6737 6862. *Wangrah Wilderness Lodge:* vast mountain retreat; Bluff River Rd, Sandy Flat via Tenterfield; (02) 6737 3665.

🔘 **Bald Rock National Park** There are excellent 360-degree views from the summit of Bald Rock, the largest granite monolith in Australia. The park is full of canyons and stone arches, and kangaroos abound. Guided tours are available daily to Bald Rock with information on the park's Aboriginal and European heritage. Bookings at visitor centre; (02) 6736 4298; 35 km N.

Mt McKenzie Granite Drive: 30 km circuit from Molesworth St in town including Ghost Gully and Bluff Rock, an unusual granite outcrop; 10 km s. *Thunderbolt's Hideout:* reputed haunt of bushranger Captain Thunderbolt; 11 km NE. *Drake:* old goldmining town now popular for fossicking and fishing; 31 km NE. *Boonoo Boonoo National Park:* several bushwalks include an easy 30 min stroll to the spectacular 210 m Boonoo Boonoo Falls. Pleasant swimming area above the falls; (02) 6736 4298; 32 km NE. *Wineries:* several offering cellar-door tastings; tours available; brochure and bookings at visitor centre.

See also NEW ENGLAND, p. 29

Terrigal

Pop. 9746
Map ref. 543 E8 | 545 P3 | 555 L5

ℹ️ Gosford Visitor Information, 200 Mann St; Gosford; (02) 4343 4444 or 1300 130 708; www.visitcentralcoast.com.au

📻 101.3 Sea FM, 1512 AM ABC Radio National

Terrigal is a scenic and peaceful coastal town well known for its outstanding beaches, which are popular for surfing, swimming and surf-fishing. The Norfolk pines along the beachfront add to the relaxed feel and the boutique shops and restaurants add a sophisticated touch.

🏠 *Rotary Park:* pleasant for picnics and barbecues, backing onto Terrigal Lagoon, a good family swimming spot; Terrigal Dr.

🎪 *Artisans Market:* Rotary Park; 2nd Sat each month. *Terrigal Food and Wine Festival:* July.

🍴 *Onda Ristorante Italiano:* Italian; 150 Terrigal Dr; (02) 4384 5554. *Seasalt:* seafood and stunning views; Crowne Plaza Terrigal, Pine Tree La; (02) 4384 9133. *The Reef Restaurant:* modern Australian; The Haven; (02) 4385 3222. *Blue Bar and Restaurant:* modern Australian; 3/85 Avoca Dr, Avoca; (02) 4381 0707. *Lamiche:* modern Australian; 80 Oceanview Dr, Wamberal; (02) 4384 2044.

🛏️ *Beach Hut Terrigal:* Balinese-style guesthouse; 6 Ash St; (02) 4385 3950. *Clan Lakeside Lodge:* absolute waterfront accommodation; 1 Ocean View Dr; (02) 4384 1566. *Terrigal Pacific Resort:* relaxing resort; 224 Terrigal Dr; (02) 4385 1555.

🔘 **Bouddi National Park** This park ranges from secluded beaches beneath steep cliffs to lush pockets of rainforest, with several signposted bushwalks. Maitland Bay is at the heart of a 300 ha marine park extension to protect marine life, one of the first in NSW, and contains the wreck of the PS *Maitland*. Fishing is allowed in all other areas. Putty Beach is safe for swimming and Maitland Bay is good for snorkelling. Tallow Beach is not patrolled and is recommended for strong swimmers only. 17 km s.

The Skillion: headland offering excellent coastal views; 3 km SE. *Erina:* pretty town with St Fiacre Distillery; 4 km w. *Ken Duncan Gallery:* largest privately owned photographic collection in Australia; 8 km NW. *Several excellent beaches:* Wamberal Beach, a safe family beach with rockpools (3 km N), Avoca Beach (7.5 km s) and Shelly Beach (13 km N), both popular for surfing. *Sea-kayaking tours:* various routes available; bookings (02) 4342 2222.

See also CENTRAL COAST & HAWKESBURY, p. 25

The Entrance

Pop. 2632
Map ref. 543 E7 | 545 P2 | 555 L5

ℹ️ Memorial Park, Marine Pde; (02) 4334 4444 or 1300 130 708; www.theentrance.org

📻 101.3 Star FM, 1233 AM ABC Local

This immaculate seaside and lakeside town is named for the narrow channel that connects Tuggerah Lake to the Pacific Ocean. Given its proximity to Sydney and Newcastle, it has become a popular aquatic playground for residents of both cities.

🏠 *Memorial Park:* pelican-feeding with informative commentary at 3.30pm daily; Marine Pde. *The Waterfront:* town mall with shops, pavement eateries and children's playground.

🎪 *Markets:* Waterfront Plaza, Sat; Bayview Ave, Sun. *Art and craft market:* Marine Pde; Sun. *Central Coast Country Music Festival:* Mar. *Tuggerah Lakes Mardi Gras Festival:* Dec.

🍴 *Ocean Restaurant:* seafood; 102 Ocean Pde, Blue Bay; (02) 4334 4600.

🛏️ *Lavender House By The Sea:* traditional B&B; 66 Dening St; (02) 4332 2234. *El Lago Waters Resort:* comfortable,

THREDBO

Pop. 477
Map ref. 565 A8 | 566 C10 | 581 B4

i Thredbo Resort Centre, Friday Flat Dr, 1800 020 589; or
Snowy Region Visitor Centre, Kosciuszko Rd, Jindabyne,
(02) 6450 5600; www.thredbo.com.au

📻 88.9 FM ABC Local, 97.7 Snow FM

Thredbo, a mountain village in Kosciuszko National Park
(*see Adaminaby*), is a unique year-round resort, with some of
Australia's best skiing and winter sports in the colder months and
angling, bushwalking and mountain-biking in summer.

🏠 **Ski fields** Thredbo has 480 ha of skiing terrain and the
longest ski runs in Australia (up to 5.9 km). Night skiing is
a feature in July and Aug. There are slopes for beginners to
advanced skiers and snowboarders, with lessons and equipment
hire available. The ultimate skiing and scenic experience for
intermediate skiers is the Dead Horse Gap run. If skiing's
not your game, plunge down the 700 m luge-style track on a
bobsled, or go in-line skating along paths threading through
town. Thredbo Snowsports Outdoor Adventures offers off-piste
skiing, freeheeling, cross-country and snowshoeing lessons and
excursions; bookings (02) 6459 4044.

Thredbo Alpine bobsled: 700 m luge-style track; adjacent to
ski lifts; closed in winter. *Australian Institute of Sport Alpine
Training Centre:* quality sporting facilities used by athletes for
high-altitude training; northern end of the village. *Thredbo
River:* excellent trout fishing. *Village walks:* include the Meadows
Nature Walk through tea trees and the Thredbo Village Walk for
diversity of alpine architecture; brochure from visitor centre.
Mountain-biking: several tracks including the Village Bike Track;
all bike and equipment hire available from Thredbo Service
Station; bookings (02) 6457 6282.

🎪 *Blues Festival:* Jan. *Jazz Festival:* May. *SNOWYfest: film
festival;* June. *Top to Bottom Ski Race:* July/Aug. *Food and Wine
Festival:* Sept.

🍴 *Credo:* modern Australian; Riverside Cabins, Diggings Tce;
(02) 6457 6844. *Santé:* modern Australian bistro, bar, live music;
Shop 4, Squatter Run, Village Square; (02) 6457 6083. *Terrace:*
modern Australian; Denman Hotel, Diggings Tce; (02) 6457
6222. *Crackenback Cottage Restaurant:* modern Australian;
902 Alpine Way, Crackenback; (02) 6456 2198.

[CARVING UP THREDBO'S SLOPES]

🛏 *Alpine Habitats:* luxury eco-retreat; cnr Alpine Way and
Wollondibby Rd; (02) 6457 2228. *Squatter's Run:* luxurious
self-contained accommodation; Diggings Tce; (02) 6457 6066.
Crackenback Cottage: award-winning guesthouse; 902 Alpine
Way, Crackenback; (02) 6456 2601.

⊗ *Pilot Lookout:* the magnificent view is dominated by
the Pilot (1828 m) and the Cobberas (1883 m) in Victoria;
10 km SE. *Skitube:* access to Perisher and Mt Blue Cow ski fields
via this European-style train from Bullocks Flat. This winter-only
service passes through Australia's largest train tunnel; 15 km NE.
Charlotte Pass: tucked away past Perisher and accessible in winter
over snow only, Australia's highest snow resort is perfect for
beginner and intermediate skiers; it's popular with families who
enjoy being able to ski in and out of their lodgings. 69 km NE.
Tom Groggin Station: horseriding and accommodation at the
historic station where Banjo Paterson met Irish brumby-hunter
and horse-breaker Jack Riley, the inspiration for *The Man
from Snowy River;* (02) 6076 9510; 24 km SW. *Mt Kosciuszko:*
Australia's highest mountain, with easy access via chairlift from
Thredbo and 13 km walk; contact visitor centre for more details.

See also SNOWY MOUNTAINS, p. 33

---

affordable accommodation; 41 The Entrance; 1300 664 554.
Al Mare Beachfront Retreat: luxury getaway for couples;
42 Werrina Pde, Blue Bay; (02) 4333 7979.

⊗ **Wyrrabalong National Park** With sections lying north and
south of town, this park conserves the last significant coastal
rainforest on the Central Coast. Signposted walking tracks lead
along rocky cliffs and beaches with lookouts and picnic spots
along the way providing stunning coastal views. 5 km N and S.

Shell Museum: extensive shell collection; Dunleith Caravan Park;
1 km N. *Crabneck Point Lookout:* magnificent coastal views;
6 km S. *Nora Head Lighthouse:* attractive automated lighthouse
built in 1903 after several ships were wrecked on the coast; 8 km N.

Toukley: unspoiled coastal hamlet with breathtaking scenery.
Holds markets each Sun in the shopping centre carpark and
the Gathering of the Clans (Scottish festival) in Sept; 11 km N.
Munmorah State Recreation Area: signposted bushwalking trails
with magnificent coastal scenery; 21 km N. *Lakes:* 80 sq km lake
system, on average less than 2 m deep and shark-free. The linked
Tuggerah Lake, Budgewoi Lake and Lake Munmorah all empty
into the ocean at The Entrance and are fabulous for fishing and
prawning (in summer), as well as watersports.

See also CENTRAL COAST & HAWKESBURY, p. 25

 RADIO STATIONS   IN TOWN   WHAT'S ON   WHERE TO EAT   WHERE TO STAY   NEARBY

Tibooburra

Pop. 161
Map ref. 560 D2 | 662 H11

i National Parks and Wildlife Service, Briscoe St;
(08) 8091 3308.

999 AM ABC Local

Tibooburra is one of the hottest and most isolated towns in
New South Wales. Its name means 'heaps of rocks' in the local
Aboriginal language and refers to the 450-million-year-old granite
tors that surround the town. In a similar tale to the creation of the
Blue Mountains' Three Sisters, three brothers were turned to stone
after marrying women from another tribe, creating three large
rocks (only one remains today). Gold was discovered in 1881 but a
poor yield, outbreaks of typhoid and dysentery and a lack of water
meant the population explosion did not last.

Pioneer Park: features a replica of the whaleboat Charles
Sturt carried with him on his 1844–46 expedition to find an
inland sea; Briscoe St. *Courthouse Museum:* history of the region
told with photographs, relics and documents in the restored 1887
courthouse; Briscoe St. *Tibooburra Aboriginal Land Council
Keeping Place:* photographs and Indigenous artefacts on display
include a cockatoo-feather headdress; check opening times
(08) 8091 3435; Briscoe St. *School of the Air:* most remote school
in NSW servicing students of Tibooburra and the Cameron
Corner region. Tours during school terms; Briscoe St. *Family
Hotel:* pub walls have been painted on by artists including Russell
Drysdale, Clifton Pugh and Rick Amor; Briscoe St.

Gymkhana and Rodeo: Oct.

Sturt National Park This semi-desert park that begins on
the edge of town is noted for its wildlife – wedge-tailed eagles,
kangaroos and myriad reptiles. The landscape is diverse, ranging
from ephemeral lakes to jump-ups, grassy plains and the rolling
dunes of the Strzelecki Desert. Temperatures range from well over
40°C in summer to below 0°C at night in winter. Lake Pinaroo in
the west is the site where Charles Sturt once built a fort to protect
his party's supplies and sheep. There is an outdoor pastoralist
museum and camping and homestead accommodation at Mt
Wood, and short walking trails that lead from here and the park's
three other campsites. Details from visitor centre.

Milparinka The Albert Hotel continues to do business in this
small settlement, now almost a ghost town; (08) 8091 3863.
Historic buildings include a restored courthouse, the remains
of an old police station, a bank, a general store and a post office;
40 km s. Depot Glen Billabong, 14 km NW of Milparinka, is where
Charles Sturt was marooned for 6 months in 1845 while searching
for an inland sea. One of the worst droughts in Australia's history
kept the party there due to diminishing water supplies. The grave
of James Poole, Sturt's second-in-command who died of scurvy,
is 1 km further east under a grevillea tree. Poole's initials and the
year of his death were carved into the tree and can still be seen.
Poole's Cairn, commemorating the disastrous expedition, is
located at Mt Poole, 7 km N of Depot Glen.

Cameron Corner: where Queensland, NSW and SA meet. The
Dog Fence, the longest fence in the world, runs through here
from Jimbour in Queensland to the Great Australian Bight;
133 km NW.

See also OUTBACK, p. 36

Tocumwal

Pop. 1863
Map ref. 559 L11 | 584 F4

i 41 Deniliquin St; (03) 5874 2131 or 1800 677 271;
www.toconthemurray.com.au

102.5 Classic Rock FM, 675 AM ABC Riverina

This picturesque town ('Toc' to the locals) is on the northern
bank of the Murray River. The region is a popular holiday spot
due to its pleasant river beaches and laid-back lifestyle.

Foreshore Park: peaceful green park shaded by tall gum
trees, and featuring a large fibreglass Murray cod. Foreshore
markets are held 11 times during the year (dates from visitor
centre); Deniliquin Rd. *River cruises, walks, drives and bike
tracks:* self-guide and guided tours of town and the river;
brochures from visitor centre. *Art and craft shops:* several in
town featuring local work; brochure from visitor centre.

Foreshore market: Foreshore park; 3rd Sat each month
(not July). *Farmers market:* 3rd Sat each month. *Tocumwal
Classic:* fishing competition; Jan. *Horseraces:* Easter.

The Big Strawberry: cafe with strawberry picking;
Goulburn Valley Hwy, Koonoomoo; (03) 5871 1300.

Kingswood Motel & Apartments: budget-friendly,
traditional motel; cnr Barooga Rd and Kelly St; (03) 5874 2444.

Blowhole and the Rocks This area is sacred to the Ulupna
and Bangaragn people. The Rocks change colour according to
weather conditions, and the Blowhole is a 25 m deep hole that
legend says was home to a giant Murray cod that ate young
children who fell into it. One young boy escaped the cod and was
chased into the crevice, only to emerge in the Murray, suggesting
that the Blowhole and the river are linked. Strangely, water has
been known to flow from the Blowhole in times of drought.
Adjacent to it is a working granite quarry. Rocks Rd; 8.5 km NE.

Tocumwal Aerodrome: largest RAAF base in Australia during
WW II, now home to international Sportavia Soaring Centre
(glider joy-flights and learn-to-glide packages); 5 km NE. *Beaches:*
around 25 attractive river beaches in the vicinity, some with
picnic areas; map from visitor centre. *Wineries:* there are several
wineries in the area; brochure from visitor centre.

See also MURRAY, p. 35

Tumbarumba

Pop. 1487
Map ref. 554 D12 | 565 A6 | 566 B5 | 585 P5

i 10 Bridge St; (02) 6948 3333; www.visittumbashire.com.au

107.7 FM Radio Upper Murray, 675 AM ABC Local

This former goldmining town in the foothills of the Snowy
Mountains remains seemingly untouched by the modern world
with old-style charm and well-preserved buildings. This has
been helped by the fact that it has been bypassed by major road
and rail routes. It experiences four distinct seasons and enjoys
European-style vistas of snow-capped mountains, forested hills,
rolling green pastures and a crystal-clear creek. Tumbarumba's
name comes from the Wiradjuri language and is thought to mean
'sounding ground'. This relates to the suggestion that there are
places in the region where the ground sounds hollow.

Bicentennial Botanic Gardens: mix of native and exotic
trees, especially striking in autumn; Prince St. *Artists on Parade
Gallery:* run by local artists, exhibitions change regularly; The

Parade. *Tumbarumba Museum and Information Centre:* includes working model of a water-powered timber mill; Bridge St.

Campdraft: Jan. *Tumbafest:* food, wine and music festival; Feb. *Heritage Week:* Nov. *Christmas Street Carnival:* Dec.

Four Bears Cafe and Accommodation: cabin-style guest rooms; 32 The Parade; (02) 6948 3228. *Sunnyside Lodge:* heritage-listed homestead; Albury Close; (02) 6948 3200. *Lazy Dog B&B:* boutique guesthouse, country location; 235 Moody's Hill Rd (off Elliott Way); (02) 6948 3664.

Site of Old Union Jack Mining Area: memorial to the students of the Union Jack school who died in WW I; 3 km N. *Henry Angel Trackhead:* starting point for a 12 km section of the Hume and Hovell Walking Track along Burra Creek. It includes waterfalls and the place where Hume and Hovell first saw the Snowy Mountains. The full walking trail is a 23-day, 440 km trek from Albury to Yass. For a kit (including maps), contact Department of Lands, Sydney (02) 6937 2700; Tooma Rd; 7 km SE. *Pioneer Women's Hut:* fascinating domestic and rural museum focusing on women's stories. The National Quilt Register was an initiative of the women who run this museum. Open Wed, Sat and Sun; Wagga Rd; (02) 6948 2635; 8 km NW. *Paddy's River Falls:* the waterfall cascades over a 60 m drop in a beautiful bush setting with a scenic walking track and picnic area. A concreted walkway is at the bottom and lookouts are at the top; 16 km S. *Tooma:* historic town with old hotel (c. 1880); 34 km SE. *Wineries:* several with cellar doors including Glenburnie Vineyard; brochure from visitor centre; (02) 6948 2570.

See also RIVERINA, p. 34

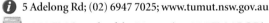

Tumut

Pop. 5926
Map ref. 554 D10 | 565 A4 | 566 C2

5 Adelong Rd; (02) 6947 7025; www.tumut.nsw.gov.au

96.3 FM Sounds of the Mountains, 97.9 FM ABC Riverina

Tumut (pronounced 'Tyoomut') is located in a fertile valley, surrounded by spectacular mountain scenery. The poplar and willow trees planted by early settlers make summer and autumn particularly striking. Prior to European settlement, Tumut was the seasonal meeting place for three Aboriginal tribes. Each summer the tribes would journey to the mountains to feast on Bogong moths.

Old Butter Factory Tourist Complex: local art and craft, and visitor centre; Snowy Mountains Hwy. *Millet Broom Factory:* 90 per cent of the state's broom millet comes from the region and visitors can see the factory in action; open Mon–Fri; Snowy Mountains Hwy. *Tumut Art Society Gallery:* specialises in work by local artists; open 10am–4pm Tues–Thurs and Sat; Cnr Tumut Plains Rd and Snowy Mountains Hwy. *Tumut Museum:* large collection of farm and domestic items and an excellent display of Miles Franklin memorabilia (the author was born in nearby Talbingo); open 1–4pm Sat and Sun; Cnr Capper and Merrivale sts. *River walk:* along Tumut River; from Elm Dr. *Historical and tree-identifying walks:* include Alex Stockwell Memorial Gardens with European trees and a WW I memorial; brochure from visitor centre.

Tumut Show: Mar. *Festival of the Falling Leaf:* autumn celebration; Apr/May. *Boxing Day Horse Races:* Dec.

Chit Chat: cafe with homemade treats; Shop 5, Wynyard Centre, Wynyard St; (02) 6947 1187. *The Coach House:* cafe with homemade bread; Tumut Connection, Russell St; (02) 6947 9143.

Nimbo Fork Lodge: luxurious fly-fishing lodge; 330 Nimbo Rd; (02) 6944 9099.

Blowering Reservoir This enormous dam is an excellent centre for watersports and fishing for rainbow trout, brown trout and perch. With the dam containing the largest trout hatchery in Australia, almost everyone catches a fish. There is a spectacular lookout over the dam wall, and the Blowering Cliffs walk (19 km S) is a pleasant 5 km stroll in Kosciuszko National Park along stunning granite cliffs; 10 km S.

Air Escape: powered hang-gliding; airport, off Snowy Mountains Hwy; 6 km E.

Tumut Valley Violets: largest African violet farm in Australia with over 1000 varieties; Tumut Plains Rd; 7 km S. *Snowy Mountains Trout Farm:* NSW's largest trout farm with fresh trout sales; 10 km SE. *Talbingo Dam and Reservoir:* dam in steep, wooded country; 40 km S. *Power station:* Tumut Power 3, tours available; 45 km S. *Kosciuszko National Park:* massive alpine park to the south-east includes nearby Yarrangobilly Caves; (02) 6947 7025; 60 km S. *For more details see Adaminaby.*

See also RIVERINA, p. 34

Tweed Heads

Pop. 84 325
Map ref. 557 O1 | 645 G11 | 646 H10 | 653 N11

Wharf St; (07) 5536 6737 or 1800 674 414; www.tweedtourism.com.au

94.5 FM ABC North Coast, 96.9 FM ABC Radio National

Tweed Heads is the state's northernmost town and – along with its twin town Coolangatta over the Queensland border – is a popular holiday destination at the southern end of the Gold Coast. The region has long been celebrated for its weather, surf beaches, night-life and laid-back atmosphere.

Point Danger This lookout is on the Queensland–NSW border and overlooks Duranbah Beach, which is popular for surfing. It was named by Captain James Cook to warn of the dangerous coral reefs that lay under the waves off the coast. The world's first laser-beam lighthouse is located here. Dolphins may be seen off the coast along the pleasant cliff-edge walk. There are several picnic spots with stunning ocean views.

Tweed Maritime and Heritage Museum: four original buildings house maritime, heritage and photographic collections; Pioneer Park, Kennedy Dr, Tweed Heads West. *Tweed Cruise Boats:* cruises visit locations along the Tweed River; River Tce. *Fishing and diving charters and houseboat hire:* guided and self-guide river excursions; bookings at visitor centre. *Tweed Snorkelling and Whale Adventures:* whale-watching adventures and snorkelling tours to Cook Island marine reserve; bookings (07) 5536 6737. *Catch a Crab Cruises, Birds Bay Oyster Farm, deep-sea fishing:* these tours depart daily, bookings from visitor centre.

Craft market: Florence St; Sun. *Tweed Harbour Fireworks Challenge:* Apr. *Wintersun Carnival:* festival and music; June. *Greenback Tailor Fishing Competition:* June. *Tweed River Festival:* Oct.

✖ *Ivory Tavern:* international; 156 Wharf St; (07) 5506 9988. *Signatures Restaurant:* seafood/modern Australian; Quality Resort Twin Towns, Wharf St; (07) 5536 2277.

🛏 *Cook's Endeavour Motor Inn:* traditional motel; 26–28 Frances St; (07) 5536 5399. *Penny Ridge Winery Resort:* luxurious bungalows, stunning location; 363 Carool Rd; (07) 5590 9033.

⊚ **Minjungbal Aboriginal Cultural Centre** The Aboriginal Heritage Unit of the Australian Museum is dedicated to self-determination and the importance of promoting, protecting and preserving Australian Indigenous cultures. The unit runs this museum, which features displays on all aspects of Aboriginal life on the north coast. There is also a walk encompassing a ceremonial bora ring and a mangrove and rainforest area. Located just over Boyds Bay Bridge.

Currumbin Wildlife Sanctuary: home to a huge range of Australian native wildlife; night tours available; Currumbin; (07) 5534 1266; 7 km N. *Beaches:* idyllic white sandy beaches for surfing and swimming, including Fingal (3 km S) and Kingscliff (14 km S). *Melaleuca Station:* re-created 1930s railway station in a tea-tree plantation with train rides, a tea-tree oil distillation plant and an animal nursery; Chinderah; 9 km S. *Tropical Fruit World:* home to the world's largest variety of tropical fruit with plantation safari, jungle riverboat cruise, fauna park and fruit tastings; 15 km S. *John Hogan Rainforest:* spectacular palm rainforest walks and picnic areas; 17 km SW.

See also TROPICAL NORTH COAST, p. 28

Ulladulla

Pop. 10 302
Map ref. 555 I11 | 565 G5 | 567 N4

ℹ Civic Centre, Princes Hwy; (02) 4455 1269; www.shoalhaven.nsw.gov.au

📻 94.9 Power FM, 702 AM ABC Local

This fishing town, built around a safe harbour, is surrounded by beautiful lakes, lagoons and white sandy beaches. It is a popular holiday destination, especially for surfing and fishing, and enjoys mild weather all year-round. Visitors flock here each Easter Sunday for the Blessing of the Fleet ceremony.

🏠 **Coomie Nulunga Cultural Trail** This 30 min signposted walk along the headland was created by the local Aboriginal Land Council. Along the path are hand-painted and hand-carved information posts incorporating names of local plants and animals. Dawn and dusk are the best times to experience the wildlife along the walk, but visitors are advised to stay on the path for the good of the local fauna and for their own protection (from snakes). Starts Deering St opposite Lighthouse Oval carpark.

Funland Timezone: large indoor family fun park; Princes Hwy; (02) 4454 3220. *Warden Head:* lighthouse views and walking tracks. *South Pacific Heathland Reserve:* walks among native plants and birdlife; Dowling St. *Ulladulla Wildflower Reserve:* 12 ha with walking trails and over 100 plant types including waratah and Christmas bush. Best in spring; Warden St.

🌴 *Royal Coastal Patrol Markets:* harbour wharf; 2nd Sun each month. *Blessing of the Fleet:* Easter. *Gamefishing Tournament:* June.

✖ *Carmelo's:* Italian; Shop 1, 2, 10 Wason St; (02) 4454 1443. *Elizans at Ulladulla Guest House:* modern Australian; 39 Burrill St; (02) 4455 1796. *Hayden's Pies:* excellent pies; 166 Princes Hwy;

(02) 4455 7798. *Bannisters:* modern Australian; Bannisters Point Lodge, 191 Mitchell Pde, Mollymook; (02) 4455 3044.

🛏 *Ulladulla Guest House:* luxurious variety of accommodation styles; 39 Burrill St; (02) 4455 1796. *Bannisters Point Lodge:* luxury contemporary waterfront accommodation; 191 Mitchell Pde, Mollymook; (02) 4455 3044.

⊚ **Pigeon House Mountain, Morton National Park** The Ulladulla section of Morton National Park features this eye-catching mountain, which Captain James Cook thought looked like a square dovehouse with a dome on top, hence its name. The local Aboriginal people obviously had a different viewpoint and named it Didhol, meaning 'woman's breast'. The mountain has now been assigned a dual name by the Geographic Names Board. The area is an Aboriginal women's Dreaming area. A 5 km return walk to the summit (for the reasonably fit) provides 360-degree views taking in the ocean, Budawang Mountains and Clyde River Valley. 25 km NW. *For the Nowra section of the park see Nowra.*

Mollymook: excellent surfing and beach fishing; 2 km N. *Narrawallee Beach:* popular surf beach; nearby Narrawallee Inlet has calm shallow water ideal for children; 4 km N. *Lakes:* good swimming, fishing and waterskiing at Burrill Lake (5 km SW) and Lake Conjola (23 km NW). *Milton:* historic town with art galleries and outdoor cafes. Village markets are held on the highway 1st Sat each month, the Scarecrow Festival in June and the Escape Arts Festival in Sept; 7 km NW. *Pointer Gap Lookout:* beautiful coastal views; 20 km NW. *Sussex Inlet:* coastal hamlet with fishing carnival in July; 47 km N.

See also SOUTH COAST, p. 32

Uralla

Pop. 2270
Map ref. 550 B1 | 557 J8

ℹ 104 Bridge St; (02) 6778 4496; ww.uralla.com

📻 100.3 Box FM, 819 AM ABC Local

This charming New England town is famous for its connection with bushranger Captain Thunderbolt, who lived and died in the area. It is no coincidence that this was a rich goldmining district at the time. Uralla's name comes from the Anaiwan word for 'ceremonial place'. Uralla is at its most striking when the European deciduous trees change colour in autumn.

🏠 **McCrossin's Mill** This restored 3-storey granite and brick flour mill (1870) is now a museum of local history. The ground floor and gardens are used for functions, but the upper levels have fascinating exhibitions, including the Wool Industry, Gold Mining (featuring a replica Chinese joss house) and an Aboriginal diorama. The Thunderbolt exhibition contains a set of 9 paintings depicting the events leading up to his death, painted by Phillip Pomroy. Inquiries (02) 6778 3022; Salisbury St.

Hassett's Military Museum: large and impressive collection features displays on military history and memorabilia, including war vehicles, uniforms and a field kitchen. Many of the displays were donated by local families; Bridge St; (02) 6778 4600. *Thunderbolt statue:* of 'gentleman' bushranger Fred Ward dominates the corner of Bridge St and Thunderbolt's Way. *Thunderbolt's grave:* he was hunted by police for over 6 years before being shot dead at nearby Kentucky Creek in 1870. His grave is clearly identified among some other magnificent Victorian monumental masonary headstones; Old Uralla Cemetery, John St. *New England Brass and Iron Lace Foundry:* beginning in 1872, it is the oldest of its kind still operating in Australia. Visitors are welcome and tours available; East St; (02) 6778 3297. *Self-guide heritage walk:* easy 2 km walk that includes 30 historic buildings, most built in the late 1800s; brochure from visitor centre.

Get off your Arts: Mar/Apr. *Thunderbolt Country Fair:* Nov.

Stokers Restaurant and Bar: bistro in heritage building; Bushranger Motor Inn, 37 Bridge St; (02) 6778 3777. *Thunderbolt Inn:* bistro-style country fare; Cnr Bridge and Hill sts; (02) 6778 4048. *White Rose Cafe:* traditional cafe; 82 Bridge St; (02) 6778 4159.

Cruickshanks Farmstay and B&B: working cattle farm; 313 Mihi Rd, off Tourist Dr 19; (02) 6778 2148.

Mt Yarrowyck Nature Reserve This dry eucalypt reserve has plentiful wildlife including kangaroos, wallaroos and wallabies, and is ideal for bushwalking and picnics. The highlight is the 3 km Aboriginal cultural walk – about halfway along the trail is a large overhang of granite boulders under which is a set of red-ochre paintings of circles and bird tracks. 23 km NW.

Dangars Lagoon: bird sanctuary and hide; 5 km SE. *Gold fossicking:* gold and small precious stones can still be found; map and equipment hire from visitor centre; 5 km SW. *Thunderbolt's Rock:* used by the bushranger as a lookout. Climb with care; 6 km S. *Tourist Drive 19:* signposted drive includes historic Gostwyck Church (11 km SE) and Dangars Falls and Gorge (40 km S); brochure from visitor centre.

See also NEW ENGLAND, p. 29

Urunga

Pop. 2685
Map ref. 550 H2 | 551 D12 | 557 M8

Pacific Hwy; (02) 6655 5711; www.bellingen.com

 738 AM ABC North Coast

Urunga is a sleepy, attractive town at the junction of the Bellinger and Kalang rivers and is regarded by locals as one of the best fishing spots on the north coast. Because it is bypassed by the Pacific Highway, the town has remained relatively untouched by tourism. A large percentage of the population are retirees and there are some beautiful walks around the foreshore.

Oceanview Hotel: refurbished with original furniture. Meals and accommodation are available; Morgo St. *Urunga Museum:* in historic building with photographs, documents and paintings from the local area; Morgo St. *Anchor's Wharf:* riverside restaurant and boat hire. *The Honey Place:* huge concrete replica of an old-style straw beehive with glass beehive display, honey-tasting, gallery and gardens; Pacific Hwy. *Watersports and fishing:* both on the rivers and beach; brochures from visitor centre.

Anchors Wharf Cafe: seafood/steak and boat hire; 4–6 Bellingen St; (02) 6655 5588.

Aquarelle B&B: self-contained guesthouses; 152 Osprey Rd, Hungry Head; (02) 6655 3174. *Maino Gabuna:* rustic accommodation options; Wollumbin Dr, Hungry Head; (02) 6655 6017.

Bongil Bongil National Park This stunning park is 10 km of unspoilt coastal beaches, pristine estuaries, wetlands, rainforest and magnificent views. The estuaries are perfect for canoeing and birdwatching, with abundant protected birdlife. The beaches provide outstanding fishing, surfing and swimming, as well

as important nesting areas for a variety of wading birds and terns. There are signposted bushwalks and scenic picnic spots; (02) 6651 5946; 15 km N.

Hungry Head: beautiful beach for surfing and swimming; 3 km S. *Raleigh:* charming town with Prince of Peace Anglican Church (1900), winery, horseriding and a go-kart complex; 4 km N.

See also HOLIDAY COAST, p. 27

Wagga Wagga

Pop. 52 491
Map ref. 554 B9 | 559 P9 | 585 M1

Tarcutta St; (02) 6926 9621 or 1300 100 122; www.waggawaggaaustralia.com.au

91.3 Star FM, 102.7 FM ABC Local

Wagga Wagga ('place of many crows' in the Wiradjuri language) is the largest inland city in New South Wales and is regarded as the capital of the Riverina. In 1864 Wagga Wagga received international attention when a man arrived claiming to be Roger Tichborne, a baronet who was believed drowned when his ship disappeared off South America. While Tichborne's mother believed him, the trustees of the estate were not so sure. What followed is believed to be the longest court case in England's history. The man was found to be Arthur Orton, a butcher, and sentenced to 14 years for perjury. Mark Twain found this story so fascinating that he insisted on visiting Wagga Wagga when he visited Australia in the 1890s.

Museum of the Riverina The museum is divided into 2 locations, one at the historic Council Chambers (Baylis St) and the other at the Botanic Gardens Wagga Wagga (Lord Baden Powell Dr). The chambers museum has a regular program of travelling exhibitions (inquiries on (02) 6926 9655). The museum at the botanic gardens focuses on the people, places and events that have been important to Wagga Wagga and incorporates the Sporting Hall of Fame, which features local stars such as former Australian cricket captain Mark Taylor.

Botanic Gardens: themed gardens, mini-zoo, free-flight aviary, miniature railway; picnic and barbecue facilities; Willans Hill. *Wagga Wagga Regional Art Gallery:* offers an extensive and changing exhibition program and includes the National Art Glass Collection; closed Mon; Cnr Baylis and Morrow sts; inquiries (02) 6926 9660. *Lake Albert:* watersports, fishing, bushwalking and birdwatching; Lake Albert Rd. *Charles Sturt University Winery and Cheese Factory:* open daily for tastings with a range of premium wines and handmade cheeses; off McKeown Dr. *Bikeways:* along Lake Albert, Wollundry Lagoon, Flowerdale Lagoon and the Murrumbidgee River.

Farmers market: Wollundry Lagoon; 2nd Sat each month. *Wagga Wagga Wine and Food Festival:* Mar. *Gold Cup Racing Carnival:* May. *Jazz and Blues Festival:* Sept.

Clancy's Restaurant: modern Australian; Quality Inn Carriage House Motel, cnr Sturt Hwy and Eunony Bridge Rd; (02) 6922 7374. *Three Chefs Restaurant:* modern Australian; Townhouse International Motel, 70 Morgan St; (02) 6921 5897.

Comfort Inn Prince of Wales: 32 comfortable guest rooms; 143 Fitzmaurice St; (02) 6921 1922. *Little Bunda Cottages:* self-contained cottages; 221 Coolamon Rd; (02) 6931 7016. *The Manor:* 4-star mansion; 38 Morrow St; (02) 6921 2958.

Junee This important railhead and commercial centre is located on Olympic Way. It has several historic buildings and museums. Monte Cristo Homestead is a restored colonial mansion with an impressive carriage collection. The Roundhouse Museum in Harold St contains an original workshop, locomotives, a model train and memorabilia. The visitor centre is located in Railway Sq in 19th-century railway refreshment rooms. 41 km NE.

Lake Albert: watersports, fishing, bushwalking and birdwatching; 7 km S. *Kapooka:* self-drive tours of the military base; brochure from visitor centre; 9 km SW. *RAAF Museum:* indoor and outdoor exhibits and barbecue facilities; open 10am–3pm; 10 km E. *The Rock:* small town noted for its unusual scenery. Walking trails through the reserve lead to the summit of the Rock; 32 km SW. *Aurora Clydesdale Stud and Pioneer Farm:* encounters with Clydesdales and other farm animals on a working farm; closed Thurs and Sun; 33 km W. *Lockhart:* historic town with National Trust–listed Green St for an impressive turn-of-the-century streetscape. Also several pleasant walking tracks in the area, and picnic races in Oct; 65 km W. *Wineries:* several in the area offering cellar-door tastings. Wagga Wagga Winery's tasting area and restaurant have an early-Australian theme; brochure from visitor centre. *River cruises and walking tracks:* guided and self-guide tours of the city sights; brochures from visitor centre.

See also RIVERINA, p. 34

Walcha
Pop. 1625
Map ref. 550 B3 | 557 J9

i 51W Fitzroy St; (02) 6774 2460; www.walchansw.com.au

88.5 FM ABC Local, 90.1 FM ABC Radio National

Walcha (pronounced 'Wolka') is an attractive service town to the local farming regions on the eastern slopes of the Great Dividing Range. Modern sculptures are featured throughout the town and the beautiful Apsley Falls are a must-see for visitors.

 Amaroo Museum and Cultural Centre This unique centre features Aboriginal art and craft with the artists working on-site; visitors are invited to watch them at work. The artists use traditional designs combined with contemporary flair to make original clothing, homewares, gifts, jewellery and art. Also on display is a collection of local Aboriginal artefacts. Open Mon–Fri; Derby St; (02) 6777 1111.

Open-Air Sculptures Situated throughout town, the works include street furniture created by local, national and international artisans; brochure from visitor centre.

Pioneer Cottage and Museum: includes a blacksmith's shop and the first Tiger Moth used for crop dusting in Australia; Derby St. *Walcha Bushmans Carnival and Campdraft:* Jan. *Timber Expo:* May. *Walcha Garden Festival:* Nov. *Cafe Graze:* great food and coffee; 21N Derby St; (02) 6777 2409. *Walcha Road Hotel Restaurant:* modern Australian; Walcha Rd; (02) 6777 5829. *Anglea House B&B:* beautiful self-contained guesthouse; Cnr Thunderbolts Way and Hill St; (02) 6777 2187. *Arran Eco-Farmstay:* European-influenced working vineyard; Winterbourne Rd; (02) 6777 9181.

Oxley Wild Rivers National Park This national park encompasses a high plateau, deep gorges and numerous waterfalls. The Walcha section of the park features Apsley Falls (20 km E), where 7 platforms and a bridge provide access to both sides of the gorge and waterfall. Tia Falls (35 km E) has beautiful

rainforest scenery. Campsites at Riverside and Youdales Hut are accessible by 4WD.

Trout fishing: several good locations; brochure from visitor centre.

See also NEW ENGLAND, p. 29

Walgett
Pop. 1734
Map ref. 556 B5

i 88 Fox St; (02) 6828 6139; www.walgett.nsw.gov.au

102.7 Power FM, 105.9 FM ABC Local

Walgett is the service centre to a large pastoral region. The name Walgett, which means 'the meeting of two waters', is apt, as the town is at the junction of the Barwon and Namoi rivers. The rivers provide excellent Murray cod and yellow-belly fishing. The area is rich in Aboriginal history, and archaeological digs in the shire have demonstrated that human life existed here up to 40 000 years ago.

Norman 'Tracker' Walford Track: signposted 1.5 km scenic walk includes the first European settler's grave on the banks of the Namoi River; from levee bank at end of Warrena St. *Dharriwaa Elders Group:* Aboriginal arts and craft with local work including paintings, carved emu eggs and wooden items; Fox St. *Hot artesian springs:* relaxing and therapeutic baths at swimming pool; Montekeila St.

Campdraft and rodeo: Aug. *Bulldust to Bitumen Festival:* Sept.

Caloola B&B: traditional working sheep and cattle farm; Gwydir Hwy; (02) 6828 1124. *Nolans on the Barwon:* relaxing accommodation and holiday park; cnr Brewarina and Cumborah rds; (02) 6828 1154. *Nomads Cryon:* picturesque working farm; Weetonga, Kamilaroi Hwy; (02) 6828 5237.

Come-by-Chance This town 'came by chance' to William Colless when all of the land in the area was thought to be allocated, but it was discovered that some had been missed. Colless came to own most of the buildings, including the police station, post office, hotel, blacksmith shop and cemetery. It is now an attractive and quiet town with riverside picnic spots, bushwalks and abundant wildlife. There are picnic races in Sept. 65 km SE.

Grawin, Glengarry and Sheepyard opal fields: go fossicking, but be warned that water is scarce so an adequate supply should be carried. Brochure from visitor centre; 70 km NW. *Macquarie Marshes:* 100 km SW; *see Nyngan.*

See also NEW ENGLAND, p. 29

Warialda
Pop. 1204
Map ref. 556 H5

i Heritage Centre, Hope St; (02) 6729 0046.

102.9 Gem FM, 648 AM ABC New England North West

Warialda is a historic town in a rich farming district. Its location on Warialda Creek gives the town a charm and contributes to its lush greenery. The origin of Warialda's name is uncertain but is thought to mean 'place of wild honey' and is presumed to be in the language of the original inhabitants, the Weraerai people.

Carinda House: historic home, now a craft shop featuring local work; Stephen St. *Pioneer Cemetery:* historic graves from as early as the 1850s in a bushland setting; Queen and Stephen sts. *Heritage Centre:* visitor centre and Well's Family Gem and Mineral collection; Hope St. *Koorilgur Nature Walk:* 3.6 km stroll through areas of wildflowers and birdlife; self-guide brochure from visitor centre. *Self-guide historical walk:* historic town buildings in Stephen and Hope sts; brochure from visitor centre.

Agricultural Show: May. *Warialda Off-Road 200:* motor race; Sept. *Honey Festival:* Nov.

Rose Cottage Guest House: self-contained cottage; 69 Queen St; (02) 6729 1238.

Cranky Rock Nature Reserve It is rumoured that during the gold rush a 'cranky' Chinese man, after being challenged about a wrongdoing, jumped to his death from the highest of the balancing granite boulders. Today you'll find picnic spots, camping, fossicking, wildflowers and wildlife. A suspension bridge leads to an observation deck above Reedy Creek for breathtaking views. 8 km E.

See also NEW ENGLAND, p. 29

Wauchope

Pop. 5499
Map ref. 550 F6 | 557 M11

High St; (02) 6586 4055.

100.7 2MC FM, 684 AM ABC Local

Wauchope (pronounced 'Waw-hope') is the centre of the local dairy and cattle industries, and the gateway to over 40 000 hectares of national parks and state forests. Bursting with country hospitality, its popularity with visitors has vastly increased since the introduction of the fascinating Timbertown.

Historical town walk: self-guide walk past historic buildings such as the old courthouse and the bank; brochure from visitor centre.

Hastings Farmers Markets: Wauchope Showground; 4th Sat each month. *Community Markets:* Hastings St; 1st Sat each month. *Lasiandra Festival:* community festival; Mar. *Jazz in the Vines:* Bago Vineyards; 2nd Sun each month.

Cooking with Company: cooking classes; The Company Farm, 3470 Oxley Hwy, Gannons Creek; (02) 6585 6495.

Jaspers Peak Holiday Retreat: versatile farmstay accommodation; Oxley Hwy; (02) 6587 7155. *Timbertown Resort and Motel:* comfortable accommodation options; 230 High St; (02) 6585 1355.

Timbertown This re-created 1880s sawmillers' village demonstrates the struggles and achievements of early pioneers. It features steam-train rides, Cobb & Co horserides and carriage rides, blacksmith, wood turner, art gallery, farmyard patting pen, bullock demonstrations, whip cracking, boutique winery, old-fashioned lolly shop and saloon bar with bush ballads. Oxley Hwy; (02) 6586 1940; 2 km w.

Billabong Koala and Nature Park: 2.5 ha of lush parkland and waterways with exotic and native animals and birds, and koala patting 3 times daily; 10 km E. *Bellrowan Valley Horse Riding:* relaxing horserides through the Australian bush with experienced guides. Daily trail rides and overnight packages; Beechwood; 5 km NW. *Old Bottlebutt:* the largest known bloodwood tree in NSW; 6 km s. *Bago Winery:* cellar-door tastings and sales with regular Jazz in the Vines concerts; 8 km sw. *Bago Bluff National Park:* signposted bushwalks (various fitness levels) through rugged wilderness; 12 km w. *Werrikimbie National Park:* magnificent World Heritage–listed wilderness with rainforests, rivers and wildflowers (best viewed in spring). Also several excellent sites for camping and picnics; 80 km w. *4WD tours and abseiling:* bookings at visitor centre.

See also HOLIDAY COAST, p. 27

Wee Waa

Pop. 1692
Map ref. 556 E6

Narrabri Shire Visitor Information Centre, Newell Hwy, Narrabri; (02) 6799 6760 or 1800 659 931; www.weewaa.com

91.3 Max FM, 648 AM ABC New England North Coast

Wee Waa is a dynamic rural community near the Namoi River and also the base for the Namoi Cotton Cooperative, the largest grower-owned organisation in the country. Cotton has only been grown here since the 1960s, but the town claims to be the 'cotton capital of Australia'. Wee Waa, meaning 'fire for roasting', comes from the local Aboriginal language.

Wee Waa Museum: fascinating display of machinery, artefacts and documents pertaining to the history of the Wee Waa district. Open Wed–Sat at various times; Rose St; (02) 6796 1760.

Wee Waa Show: May. *Village Fest:* food, music and games; June. *Rodeo:* Sept. *Christmas Mardi Gras:* Dec.

Wee Waa Chinese Restaurant: traditional Chinese; Bowling Club, Alma St; (02) 6795 4108. *Wee Waa Hot Bread Shop:* bakery cafe with freshly baked bread; 82 Rose St; (02) 6795 4393.

Wee Waa Motel: comfortable accommodation options; 148 Rose St; (02) 6795 4522.

Guided cotton gin and farm tour First the tour visits a local cotton farm to view the picking and pressing of cotton into modules ready for transporting to the cotton gin. At the gin the cotton is transformed from modules into bales and then goes to the classing department for sorting. Runs Mar–Aug; bookings (02) 6799 6760.

Cuttabri Wine Shanty The slab-construction shanty was built in 1882 and was once a Cobb & Co coach stop between Wee Waa and Pilliga. It was issued the second liquor licence in Australia and is the only wine shanty still operating in the country. 25 km sw.

Yarrie Lake: boating, swimming and birdwatching; 24 km s. *Cubbaroo Cellars:* cellar-door tastings and sales; 48 km w. *Barren Junction:* hot artesian bore baths (over 100 years old) in a pleasant location surrounded by tamarind trees; 51 km w.

See also NEW ENGLAND, p. 29

Wellington

Pop. 4660
Map ref. 554 F2

Cameron Park, Nanima Cr; (02) 6845 1733 or 1800 621 614; www.visitwellington.com.au

89.5 Zoo FM, 549 AM ABC Central West

Wellington is a typical Australian country town with a wide main street, numerous monuments to significant local people and attractive parklands. Sitting at the foot of Mount Arthur, it is best known for the nearby Wellington Caves.

Oxley Museum: the history of Wellington is told with photographs and artefacts; in the old bank (1883); open 1.30–4.30pm Mon–Fri, other times by appt; Cnr Percy and Warne sts. *Orana Aboriginal Corporation:* authentic Aboriginal ceramics, paintings, clothing and artefacts; open Mon–Fri; Swift St. *Cameron Park:* known for its rose gardens and suspension bridge over the Bell River, it also has picnic and barbecue facilities; Nanima Cres. *Self-guide town walk:* taking in historic buildings including hotels and churches; brochure from visitor centre.

Market: Cnr Percy St and and Nanima Cres; last Sat each month. *Vintage Fair:* with street parade and swap meet; Mar.

 RADIO STATIONS   IN TOWN   WHAT'S ON   WHERE TO EAT   WHERE TO STAY   NEARBY

The Wellington Boot: horseraces; Mar. *Wellington Show:* Apr. *Festivale:* week of celebrations; Oct. *Carols in the Cave:* Dec.

Keston Rose Garden Cafe: light lunches and cakes; Mudgee Rd; (02) 6845 3508. *Kimbells Bakery and Coffee Shop:* cafe in heritage building; 44 Warne St; (02) 6845 4647. *The Grange Restaurant:* modern Australian; Hermitage Hill, 35 Maxwell St; (02) 6845 4469.

Carinya B&B: quaint traditional B&B; 111 Arthur St; (02) 6845 4320. *Wellington Caves Holiday Complex:* secluded, relaxed holiday park; Caves Rd; (02) 6845 2970.

Wellington Caves These fascinating limestone caves include Cathedral Cave, with a giant stalagmite, and Gaden Cave, with rare cave coral. There are guided tours through the old phosphate mine (wheelchair-accessible). Nearby is an aviary, an opal shop, Japanese gardens, picnic facilities, kiosk and the bottle house, a structure made from over 9000 wine bottles. 9 km s.

Mt Arthur Reserve: walks to the lookout at the summit of Mt Binjang; maps from visitor centre; 3 km w. *Angora Tourist Farm:* demonstrations of shearing angora rabbits and alpacas; 20 km sw. *Eris Fleming Gallery:* original oil paintings and watercolours by the artist; 26 km s. *Nangara Gallery:* Aboriginal art and craft with artefacts dating back over 20 000 years; 26 km sw. *Lake Burrendong State Park:* watersports, fishing, campsites and cabins, and spectacular lake views from the main wall. Burrendong Arboretum is a beautiful spot for birdwatching and features several pleasant walking tracks. Also excellent camping, picnic and barbecue sites at Mookerawa Waters Park; 32 km se. *Stuart Town:* small gold-rush town formerly known as Ironbark, made famous by Banjo Paterson's poem 'The Man from Ironbark'; 38 km se. *Wineries:* several in the area offering cellar-door tastings and sales. Glenfinlass Wines sell exclusively through cellar door; brochure from visitor centre.

See also CENTRAL WEST, p. 30

Wentworth

Pop. 1305
Map ref. 558 D5 | 588 F5

ⓘ 66 Darling St; (03) 5027 3624; www.wentworth.nsw.gov.au

 90.7 Hot FM, 999 AM ABC Broken Hill

At the junction of the Murray and Darling rivers, Wentworth was once a busy and important town. With the introduction of the railways it became quieter and is now an attractive and peaceful holiday town with a rich history.

Old Wentworth Gaol The first Australian-designed gaol by colonial architect James Barnett. The bricks were made on-site from local clay, and bluestone was transported from Victoria. Construction took from 1879 to 1891. Closed as a gaol in 1927, the building is in remarkably good condition. Beverley St.

Pioneer World Museum: over 3000 historic artefacts including space junk, prehistoric animals and the country's largest collection of paddleboat photos; Beverley St. *Sturt's Tree:* tree on the riverbank marked by explorer Charles Sturt when he weighed anchor and identified the junction of the Murray and Darling rivers in 1830; Willow Bend Caravan Park, Darling St. *Fotherby Park:* PS *Ruby,* a historic paddlesteamer (1907), and statue of 'The Possum', a man who became a hermit during the Depression and lived in trees for 50 years; Wentworth St. *Lock 10:* weir and park for picnics; south-west edge of town. *Historical town walk:* self-guide walk includes the town courthouse (1870s) and Customs House (1 of 2 original customs houses still standing in Australia); brochure from visitor centre.

Market: Inland Botanic Gardens; 1st and 3rd Sat each month. *National Trust Festival Week:* Apr. *Country Music Festival:* Sept/Oct. *Wentworth Cup:* horserace; Nov.

Perry Sandhills These magnificent orange dunes are estimated to have originated during the last Ice Age, around 40 000 years ago. Skeletal remains of mega-fauna (kangaroos, wombats, emus and lions) have been found here. In WW II the area was used as a bombing range, but recently it has been used in film and television. The Music Under the Stars concerts are held here each Mar. Off Silver City Hwy; 5 km nw.

Mungo National Park: 157 km n; *see Balranald. Yelta:* former Aboriginal mission, now a Victorian town with model aircraft display; 12 km se. *Australian Inland Botanic Gardens:* the desert blooms with some exotic and colourful plant life. There are tractor/train tours of the gardens and a light lunch the last Sun each month; 28 km se. *Pooncarie:* 'outback oasis' with natural two-tier wharf, weir, museum and craft gallery; 117 km n. *Harry Nanya Aboriginal Cultural Tours:* travel to Mungo National Park with a Barkindji guide; brochure and bookings at visitor centre. *Heritage and nature driving tours:* various sites include Mildura and Lake Victoria; brochure from visitor centre. *Houseboat hire:* short- or long-term river holidays; brochure from visitor centre.

See also MURRAY, p. 35

West Wyalong

Pop. 3189
Map ref. 554 B6 | 559 P6

ⓘ 89–91 Main St; (02) 6972 3645; www.visitwestwyalong.com.au

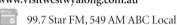 99.7 Star FM, 549 AM ABC Local

John Oxley was the first European explorer to visit West Wyalong. He disliked the region, claiming 'these desolate areas would never again be visited by civilised man'. He was proved wrong when squatters moved in, and the discovery of gold in 1893 meant the town became inundated with settlers. West Wyalong is now in one of the state's most productive agricultural regions.

West Wyalong Local Aboriginal Land Council Arts and Crafts The craft shop features local Aboriginal work. Handcrafted items are on display and for sale and include boomerangs, didgeridoos, hand-woven baskets, clothing, and traditional beauty and skin-care products. The library features a collection of historic and contemporary titles relating to Aboriginal heritage, culture and modern issues. Open Mon–Fri; Main St; (02) 6972 3493.

Bland District Historical Museum: displays of goldmining including a scale model of a goldmine and records from mines such as the Black Snake, the Blue Jacket and the Shamrock and Thistle; Main St.

West Wyalong Campdraft: Sept.

Cameo Inn Motel: traditional motel accommodation; 263 Neeld St; (02) 6972 2255. *Club Inn Resort:* beautiful accommodation nestled on golf course; Newell Hwy; (02) 6972 2000.

Lake Cowal When it is full, this is the largest natural lake in NSW and a bird and wildlife sanctuary. There are over 180 species of waterbird living in the area, with many rare or endangered. The lake is also excellent for fishing. No visitor facilities are provided. Via Clear Ridge; 48 km ne.

Barmedman: mineral-salt pool believed to help arthritis and rheumatism; 32 km se. *Weethalle Whistlestop:* Devonshire teas, art and craft; Hay Rd; 65 km w.

See also RIVERINA, p. 34

White Cliffs

Pop. 120
Map ref. 560 F7

 White Cliffs General Store, Keraro Rd; (08) 8091 6611.

 107.7 FM ABC Broken Hill, 1584 AM ABC Local

White Cliffs is first and foremost an opal town. The first mining lease was granted in 1890, and a boom followed with an influx of 4500 people. The area is still known for its opals, particularly the unique opal 'pineapples' and the opalised remains of a plesiosaur, a 2-metre-long 100-million-year-old fossil found in 1976. The intense heat has forced many people to build underground, often in the remains of old opal mines. The buildings left on the surface are surrounded by a pale and eerie moonscape with an estimated 50 000 abandoned opal digs.

 Solar Power Station The country's first solar power station was established by the Australian National University in 1981 at White Cliffs because it receives the most solar radiation in NSW. The row of 14 giant mirrored dishes is a striking sight between the blue sky and red earth. Next to council depot.

Outback Treasures: opal jewellery and Aboriginal art; Smith's Hill. *Jock's Place:* dugout home and museum with an opal seam along one wall; Turley's Hill. **Wellington's Underground Art Gallery:** paintings and polished opals by local artist; The Blocks. *Otto Photography:* gallery of outback landscape photos; Smith's Hill. *Self-guide and guided historical walks and fossicking:* include the old police station (1897) and school (1900) and several fossicking sites; brochures and maps from visitor centre. *Underground accommodation:* various standards available in dugout premises. Underground temperatures come as a relief at 22°C; details from visitor centre. *Opal shops:* several in town sell local gems; details from visitor centre.

Ironman Cliffhanger: 4WD challenge; July.

PJ's Underground B&B: luxury underground B&B; Dugout 72, Turley's Hill; (08) 8091 6626. *White Cliffs Underground Motel:* simple underground accommodation; Smiths Hill; (08) 8091 6647.

Paroo–Darling National Park: section 20 km E of town contains magnificent Peery Lake, part of the Paroo River overflow, where there is birdlife, Aboriginal cultural sites and walking trails. Southern section of park has camping along the Darling River. *Wilcannia:* small town with many fine sandstone buildings, an opening bridge across the Darling River and an old paddlesteamer wharf. Also a self-guide historical walk available; brochure from council offices in Reid St; 93 km s. *Mutawintji National Park:* 150 km sw; *see Broken Hill.*

See also OUTBACK, p. 36

Windsor

Pop. 1899
Map ref. 542 A2 | 545 I5 | 547 P7 | 555 J6

 Hawkesbury Visitor Information Centre, Ham Common, Hawkesbury Valley Way, Clarendon; (02) 4578 0233 or 1300 362 874; www.hawkesburytourism.com.au

 89.9 FM Hawkesbury Radio, 702 AM ABC Local

Windsor, located on a high bank of the Hawkesbury River, is the third oldest European settlement on mainland Australia, after Sydney Cove and Parramatta. There are still many old buildings standing and the surrounding national parks make for breathtaking scenery.

 Hawkesbury Regional Museum Built as a home in the 1820s, the building became the Daniel O'Connell Inn in 1843. In the late 1800s it was used to print *The Australian*, a weekly newspaper. Today it houses the history of the local area in photographs, documents and artefacts, with special displays on riverboat history and the Richmond Royal Australian Air Force base. Thompson Sq.

Hawkesbury Regional Gallery: displays contemporary and traditional works by national and international artists; George St. *St Matthew's Church:* designed by convict architect Francis Greenway and built in 1817, St Matthews is the oldest Anglican church in the country. The adjacent graveyard dates back to 1810; Moses St. *Self-guide tourist walk/drive:* historic sites include the original courthouse and doctor's house; brochure from visitor centre.

Market: Windsor Mall; Sun. *Bridge to Bridge Powerboat Classic:* May. *Bridge to Bridge Water Ski Race:* Nov. *Hawkesbury Canoe Classic:* Nov. *Hawkesbury Wine, Food and Music Affair Raceday:* Nov.

Clydesdale Horse Drawn Restaurant: modern Australian; 61 Hawkesbury Valley Way; (02) 4577 4544. *The Harvest Restaurant:* modern Australian/international; The Sebel Resort & Spa, 61 Hawkesbury Valley Way; (02) 4577 4222.

Windsor Terrace Motel: rustic motel accommodation; 47 George St; (02) 4577 5999.

Cattai National Park First Fleet assistant surgeon Thomas Arndell was granted this land and today the park features his 1821 cottage. There are also grain silos and the ruins of a windmill believed to be the oldest industrial building in the country. The old farm features attractive picnic and barbecue areas and campsites. In a separate section nearby, Mitchell Park offers walking tracks and canoeing on Cattai Creek. 14 km NE.

Ebenezer: picturesque town with Australia's oldest church (1809), colonial graveyard and schoolhouse; 11 km N. *Wollemi National Park:* Windsor section features the spectacular Colo River and activities including abseiling, canoeing (bring your own), bushwalking and 4WD touring; via Colo; 26 km N.

See also CENTRAL COAST & HAWKESBURY, p. 25

Wingham

Pop. 4813
Map ref. 550 D8 | 555 N1 | 557 K12

 Manning Valley Visitor Information Centre, 21 Manning River Dr, Taree North; (02) 6592 5444 or 1800 182 733; www.gtcc.nsw.gov.au

 107.3 MAX FM, 756 AM ABC Local

Heritage-listed Wingham is the oldest town in the Manning Valley. It has many Federation buildings surrounding the enchanting town common, which was based on a traditional English square. The wonderful Manning River and Wingham Brush bring nature to the centre of town. The Chinese Garden at the town's entrance marks the importance of the early Chinese settlers to the town's heritage. Best-selling Australian author Di Morrissey's book *The Valley* is based on the pioneering characters and places of the Manning Valley. It is largely set in and around Wingham where she was born.

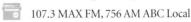 **Wingham Brush** The unique brush is part of the last 10 ha of subtropical flood-plain rainforest in NSW. It is home to 195

species of native plants including giant Moreton Bay fig trees, a large population of endangered grey-headed flying foxes and 100 bird species. The brush includes a boardwalk, picnic and barbecue facilities and a boat-launching area on the Manning River. Farquar St.

Manning Valley Historical Museum: housed in an old general store (1880s), this has one of the most extensive collections of historical memorabilia on the north coast. Includes displays on local farming, commercial and timber history; part of an attractive square bounded by Isabella, Bent, Farquar and Wynter sts. *Manning River:* picturesque waterway with several locations for swimming, boating, fishing and waterskiing. *Self-guide historical town walk:* tour of the town's Federation buildings; brochure from museum.

Market: Wynter St; 2nd Sat each month. *Wingham Farmers Market:* Wingham Showground, Gloucester Rd; 1st Sat each month. *Summertime Rodeo:* Jan. *Wingham Beef Week and Scottish Heritage Festival:* May. *Junior Rodeo and Bute Ute Show:* July. *All Breeds Horse Spectacular and A-Koo-Stik Festival:* Oct. *Killabakh Day in the Country:* country fair; Nov.

Bent on Food: cafe and provedore; 95 Isabella St; (02) 6557 0727.

Wingham Motel: traditional motel accommodation; 13 Bent St; (02) 6553 4295.

Tourist Drive 8 This enjoyable drive begins in Taree and passes through Wingham, Comboyne and Bybarra before finishing in Wauchope (36 km is unsealed; not suitable for motorists towing caravans). The highlight is Ellenborough Falls, 40 km N, one of the highest single-drop falls in NSW, with easy walking trails, lookouts and barbecue facilities. Red Tail Wines in Marlee (13 km N) has free tastings. Brochure from visitor centre.

See also HOLIDAY COAST, p. 27

Wisemans Ferry

Pop. 80
Map ref. 543 A7 | 545 K2 | 555 K5

ⓘ Hawkesbury River Tourist Information Centre; 5 Bridge St, Brooklyn; (02) 9985 7064; www.hawkesburyaustralia.com.au

89.9 FM Hawkesbury Radio, 702 AM ABC Local

Wisemans Ferry is a sleepy town built around what was once an important crossing on the Hawkesbury River. The mainland route from Sydney to Newcastle had always gone via this region, but when people started using the Castle Hill route, Solomon Wiseman, who had been granted a parcel of land and opened an inn, built a ferry to take people and cargo across the river. Today car ferries still cross at this point.

Wisemans Ferry Inn Before it was an inn, this was the home of Solomon Wiseman; he called it Cobham Hall. Wiseman later opened a section of the building as an inn and it is said to be haunted by his wife, whom he allegedly pushed down the front steps to her death. The inn provides food and accommodation. Old Northern Rd; (02) 4566 4301.

Cemetery: early settlers' graves include that of Peter Hibbs, who travelled on the HMS *Sirius* with Captain Phillip in 1788; Settlers Rd.

Riverbend Restaurant: modern Australian; Retreat at Wisemans, 5564 Old Northern Rd; (02) 4560 0593. *Wiseman's Steakhouse Bistro:* steakhouse, traditional pub; Wiseman's Inn Hotel, Lot 1, Old Northern Rd; (02) 4566 4739.

Retreat at Wisemans: luxury resort; 5564 Old Northern Rd; (02) 4566 4422.

Dharug National Park The multicoloured sandstone provides striking scenery on this historic land. The convict-built Old Great North Road is a great example of early 19th-century roadbuilding. Convicts quarried, dressed and shifted large sandstone blocks to build walls and bridges, but the road was abandoned before it was finished because of poor planning. Signposted walking tracks lead through beautiful bushland and to Aboriginal rock engravings. The clear-water tributaries are popular for swimming, fishing and canoeing. North side of the river.

Yengo National Park and Parr State Conservation Area: rugged land of gorges, cliffs and rocky outcrops. Discovery walks, talks and 4WD tours are conducted by NPWS; north-east side of the river (accessible by ferry); bookings (02) 4784 7301. *Marramarra National Park:* undeveloped park with wetlands and mangroves for canoeing, camping, bushwalking (experienced only) and birdwatching; 28 km s.

See also CENTRAL COAST & HAWKESBURY, p. 25

Woolgoolga

Pop. 4358
Map ref. 551 E11 | 557 N7

ⓘ Cnr Beach and Boundary sts; (02) 6654 8080; www.coffscoast.com.au

105.5 Star FM, 738 AM ABC Radio National

'Woopi' (as it is affectionately known to locals) is a charming and relaxed seaside town with a significant Sikh population. Punjabi migrants who were working on the Queensland cane fields headed south for work on banana plantations, many settling in Woolgoolga. Today Indians make up between a quarter and a half of the town's population, providing a unique cultural mix. The beaches are popular for fishing, surfing and swimming.

Guru Nanak Sikh Temple: spectacular white temple with gold domes; River St. *Woolgoolga Art Gallery:* exhibits local works; Turon Pde.

Market: Beach St; 2nd Sat each month.

Possum's Cafe: light meals; Shop 4, 53 Beach St; (02) 6654 2807.

Halcyon Retreat: self-contained suites; 237 Woolgoolga Creek Rd; (02) 6654 7750. *Waterside Cabins at Woolgoolga:* resort-style accommodation; cnr Pacific Hwy and Hearnes Lake Rd; (02) 6654 1644.

Yarrawarra Aboriginal Cultural Centre The focus of this centre is to help Aboriginal and Islander peoples maintain their heritage while teaching others about it. Visitors are encouraged to browse through the rooms of locally produced art, craft, books and CDs. The Bush Tucker Cafe offers meals with an Indigenous twist. Tours offered through the local area explore middens, ochre quarries and campsites while teaching about bush tucker and natural medicines. Stone and tool workshops and accommodation are also offered. Red Rock Rd; (02) 6649 2669; 10 km N.

Yuraygir National Park: Woolgoolga section is excellent for bushwalking, canoeing, fishing, surfing, swimming, picnicking and camping on unspoiled coastline; 10 km N. *Wedding Bells State Forest:* subtropical and eucalypt forest with walking trails to Sealy Lookout and Mt Caramba Lookout; 14 km NW.

See also TROPICAL NORTH COAST, p. 28

WOLLONGONG

Pop. 263 537

Map ref. 552 | 553 F5 | 555 J8 | 565 H2

i 93 Crown St; (02) 4227 5545 or 1800 240 737; www.tourismwollongong.com

96.5 Wave FM, 1431 AM ABC Radio National

As a major iron and steel producer, Wollongong has an undeserved reputation for being an unattractive industrial city. In fact, Wollongong enjoys some of the best coastal scenery and beaches in the state, superbly positioned with mountains to the west and ocean to the east. It has the facilities and sophistication missing in many smaller towns and has been awarded the title of 'Australia's most liveable regional city'.

Wollongong Botanic Garden The magnificent gardens encompass 27 ha of undulating land and feature a sunken rose garden, a woodland garden, rainforests, and flora representing a range of plant communities. Guided walks and bus tours are available. Various workshops including crafts and gardening throughout the year. Inquiries (02) 4225 2636. The adjacent Glennifer Brae Manor House is a Gothic-style 1930s house now home to the Wollongong Conservatorium of Music and used for music recitals. Northfields Ave; Keiraville.

Illawarra Historical Society Museum: highlights include handicraft room and Victorian parlour; open weekends and 12–3pm Thurs; Market St. *Wollongong City Gallery:* collection of 19th- and 20th-century art including Aboriginal art; cnr Burelli and Kembla sts. *Mall:* soaring steel arches and water displays; Crown St. *Rhododendron Park:* rhododendrons and azaleas, with rare companion plants. A section of rainforest has walking trails; Parrish Ave, Mount Pleasant. *Flagstaff Point:* fish market and historic lighthouse (1872); Endeavour Dr. *Five Islands Brewing Company:* locally brewed beers; Crown St. *Wollongong Harbour:* home to a huge fishing fleet and Breakwater Lighthouse. *Surfing beaches and rockpools:* to the north and south, with excellent surfing and swimming conditions. *Foreshore parks:* several with superb coastal views and picnic facilities.

Market: Harbour St; Sat. *Viva La Gong:* street arts festival; Oct.

Caveau: French; 122–124 Keira St; (02) 4226 4855. *Lagoon Seafood Restaurant:* seafood, incredible views; Stuart Park, cnr George Hanley Dr and Kembla St, North Wollongong; (02) 4226 1677. *Lorenzo's Diner:* modern Italian; 119 Keira St; (02) 4229 5633.

Above Wollongong at Pleasant Heights B&B: boutique B&B; 77 New Mount Pleasant Rd; (02) 4283 3355.

Royal National Park Established in 1879, this is the second oldest national park in the world after Yellowstone in the USA. There is much natural diversity packed into a compact parkland. Highlights include walking and cycling along Lady Carrington Dr through rich forest, swimming at Wattamolla, enjoying the Victorian-park atmosphere at Audley (with causeway, picnic lawns and rowboats) and walking the magnificent 26 km Coast Track. 35 km N. Grand Pacific Dr, a new tourist route along the coast, links Royal National Park with Wollongong. The 70 km drive takes in spectacular scenery and the Sea Cliff Bridge.

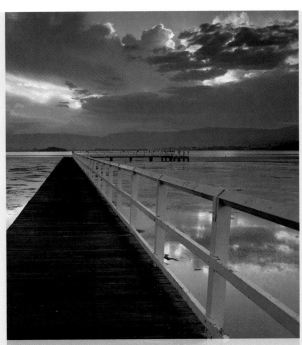

[LAKE ILLAWARRA]

Illawarra Escarpment: forms the western backdrop to the city and has spectacular lookouts at Stanwell Tops, Sublime Pt, Mt Keira and Mt Kembla. *University of Wollongong Science Centre and Planetarium:* hands-on displays and activities for all ages; 2 km N. *Nan Tien Temple:* largest Buddhist temple in the Southern Hemisphere with a range of programs available; closed Mon; 5 km SW. *Lake Illawarra:* stretching from the southern Pacific Ocean to the foothills of the Illawarra Range, the lake offers good prawning, fishing and sailing. Boat hire is available; 5 km S. *Port Kembla:* up-close view of local industry and the steel works at Australia's Industry World with tours; bookings (02) 4275 7023. *Mt Kembla:* site of horrific 1902 mining disaster. Also here are several historic buildings and a historical museum featuring a pioneer kitchen, a blacksmith's shop and a reconstruction of the Mt Kembla disaster. The Mt Kembla Mining Heritage Festival is held each winter in memory of those lost; 10 km W. *Bulli Pass Scenic Reserve:* steep scenic drive with stunning coastal views. Bulli Lookout at the top of the escarpment has great views and a walking path leads to Sublime Pt Lookout, which enjoys stunning views over Wollongong and has a restaurant; 16 km N. *Symbio Wildlife Gardens:* koalas, eagles, wombats and reptiles, as well as cow and goat milking; 32 km N. *Dharawal State Recreation Area:* swimming and canoeing in peaceful creeks and rockpools; 35 km N. *Lawrence Hargrave Memorial and Lookout:* on Bald Hill, this was the site of aviator Hargrave's first attempt at flight in the early 1900s. Now popular for hang-gliding; 36 km N. *Garawarra State Conservation Area:* undisturbed rainforest and spring wildflowers, with basic picnic facilities; 38 km N. *Heathcote National Park:* excellent for bushwalks through rugged bushland, past hidden pools and gorges; 40 km N. *Guided walks and 4WD, canoe and kayak tours:* bookings at visitor centre.

See also SOUTHERN HIGHLANDS, p. 24

Woy Woy

Pop. 9985
Map ref. 542 H1 | 543 D8 | 545 N4 | 555 K6

i Shop 1, 18–22 The Boulevard; (02) 4341 2888 or 1300 130 708; www.visitcentralcoast.com.au

101.3 Sea FM, 702 AM ABC Local

Woy Woy is the largest of the numerous holiday villages clustered around Brisbane Water, a shallow but enormous inlet. Along with nearby Broken Bay, the Hawkesbury River and Pittwater, it draws visitors looking for aquatic holidays. The nearby national parks encompass breathtaking wilderness and lookouts.

Woy Woy Hotel: historic 1897 hotel offering meals and accommodation; The Boulevard. *Waterfront reserve:* picnic facilities with Brisbane Water view.

Agweil: modern bistro; Everglades Country Club, Dunban Rd; (02) 4341 1866. *Riley's Brasserie:* international; Ettalong Beach Club, 52 The Esplanade, Ettalong Beach; (02) 4343 0111. *Bells at Killcare:* modern Italian; 107 The Scenic Rd, Killcare; (02) 4360 2411. *Lizotte's:* modern Australian, with live music; Lot 3, Avoca Dr, Kincumber; (02) 4368 2017. *Pearls on the Beach:* modern Australian; 1 Tourmaline Ave, Pearl Beach; (02) 4342 4400. *Stillwaters:* modern Australian; 1 Restella Ave, Davistown; (02) 4369 1300 *Yum Yum Eatery:* modern Australian; 60 Araluen Dr, Hardys Bay; (02) 4360 2999.

Glades Motor Inn: peaceful country accommodation; 15 Dunban Rd; (02) 4341 7374.

Brisbane Water National Park A beautiful park of rugged sandstone with spring wildflowers, bushwalks and birdlife. Staples Lookout has superb coastal views. Warrah Lookout enjoys a sea of colour in spring when the wildflowers bloom. A highlight is the Bulgandry Aboriginal engravings on Woy Woy Rd. 3 km sw.

Ettalong Beach: great swimming beach with seaside markets each Sat and Sun (Mon on long weekends); 3 km s. *Milson Island:* recreation reserve once used as an asylum and then as a gaol. *HMAS* Parramatta: a WW I ship, it ran aground off the northern shore and the wreck is still there today; 5 km s. *Mt Ettalong Lookout:* stunning coastal views; 6 km s. *Pearl Beach:* chic holiday spot favoured by the rich and famous, with magnificent sunsets; 12 km s. *Boating, fishing and swimming:* excellent conditions on Brisbane Water, Broken Bay and Hawkesbury River.

See also CENTRAL COAST & HAWKESBURY, p. 25

Wyong

Pop. 149 382
Map ref. 543 E6 | 545 P1 | 549 A12 | 555 L5

i Rotary Park, Terrigal Dr, Terrigal; (02) 4343 4444 or 1300 130 708; www.visitcentralcoast.com.au

101.3 Sea FM, 1512 AM ABC Radio National

Wyong is an attractive holiday town surrounded by Tuggerah Lakes and the forests of Watagan, Olney and Ourimbah. After World War II it became a popular area for retirees and it retains a relaxed atmosphere today.

District Museum Features displays of local history, including early ferry services across the lakes and records of the logging era. It is situated in historic Alison Homestead, with picnic and barbecue facilities on 2 ha of rolling lawns. Cape Rd; (02) 4352 1886.

Wyong Shire Festival of the Arts: Feb–Mar.

Karinyas Restaurant and Bar: modern Australian; Kooindah Waters Residential Golf & Spa Resort, 40 Kooindah Blvd; (02) 4355 5777 or 1800 705 355.

Olney State Forest This native rainforest has several scenic walks. The Pines picnic area has an education shelter and Mandalong and Muirs lookouts have sensational views. 17 km NW.

Burbank Nursery: 20 ha of azaleas (flowering in Sept); 3 km s. *Fowlers Lookout:* spectacular forest views; 10 km sw. *Yarramalong Macadamia Nut Farm:* offers tours, talks and sales in beautiful Yarramalong Valley; 18 km w. *Frazer Park:* recreational park in natural bush setting; 28 km NE.

See also CENTRAL COAST & HAWKESBURY, p. 25

Yamba

Pop. 5515
Map ref. 551 F8 | 557 O5

i Lower Clarence Visitor Centre, Ferry Park, Pacific Hwy, Maclean; (02) 6645 4121; www.yambansw.com.au

100.3 Yamba Radio FM, 738 AM ABC North Coast

This quiet holiday town at the mouth of the Clarence River offers excellent sea, lake and river fishing. It is the largest coastal resort in the Clarence Valley, with excellent facilities for visitors, but it manages to maintain a peaceful atmosphere. Fishing fleets from Yamba, Iluka and Maclean catch approximately 20 per cent of the state's seafood, so this is a great spot for lovers of fresh seafood.

Story House Museum This quaint museum tells the story of the development of Yamba from the time it was merely a point of entry to the Clarence River. The collection of photographs and records tells a compelling tale of early development of a typical Australian coastal town. River St.

Clarence River Lighthouse: coastal views from the base; via Pilot St. *Yamba Boat Harbour Marina:* departure point for daily ferry service to Iluka, river cruises, deep-sea fishing charters and whale-watching trips. Also houseboat hire; off Yamba Rd. *arthouse australia:* showcase of local artwork; Coldstream St. *Whiting Beach:* sandy river beach ideal for children. *Coastal beaches:* several in town with excellent swimming and surfing conditions; map from visitor centre.

River Market: Ford Park; 4th Sun each month. *Easter Yachting Regatta:* Easter. *Family Fishing Festival:* Oct. *Hot Rod Run:* Nov.

Beachwood Cafe: Mediterranean; 22 High St; (02) 6646 9781. *Pacific Hotel Bistro:* international; Pacific Hotel, 18 Pilot St; (02) 6646 2125.

Angourie Rainforest Resort: contemporary self-contained luxury; 166 Angourie Rd; (02) 6646 8600. *Moby Dick Waterfront Resort Motel:* waterfront accommodation; 27–29 Yamba Rd; (02) 6646 2196.

Maclean This quirky village is known as the 'Scottish town' because of the many Scots who first settled here. Some street signs are in Gaelic as well as English. Highlights in the town include Scottish Corner, Bicentennial Museum and a self-guide historical walk with a brochure available from the visitor centre. There is a market on the 2nd Sat each month and a Highland Gathering each Easter. A 24 hr ferry service crosses the river to Lawrence; 17 km w.

Lake Woolooweyah: fishing and prawning; 4 km s. *Yuraygir National Park:* Yamba section offers sand ridges and banksia heath, and is excellent for swimming, fishing and bushwalking; (02) 6627 0200; 5 km s. *The Blue Pool:* deep freshwater pool 50 m from the ocean, popular for swimming; 5 km s.

See also TROPICAL NORTH COAST, p. 28

Yass

Pop. 5330
Map ref. 554 F9 | 565 C3

 Coronation Park, Comur St; (02) 6226 2557 or 1300 886 014; www.yass.nsw.gov.au

100.3 Yass FM, 549 AM ABC Central West

Yass is set in rolling countryside on the Yass River. Explorers Hume and Hovell passed through on their expedition to Port Phillip Bay. Hume returned in 1839. Yass is also the end of the Hume and Hovell Walking Track, which begins in Albury.

Cooma Cottage The National Trust has restored and now maintains this former home of explorer Hamilton Hume. He lived with his wife in the riverside house from 1839 until his death in 1873. It now operates as a museum with relics and documents telling of Hume's life and explorations. Open Thurs–Sun, closed winter; Yass Valley Way.

Yass Cemetery: contains the grave of explorer Hamilton Hume; via Rossi St. *Yass and District Museum:* historical displays including a war exhibit encompassing the Boer War, WW I and WW II. Open Sat and Sun, or by appt, archive open Tues; Comur St. *Railway Museum:* history of the Yass tramway; open Sun; Lead St. *Aingeal Ridge Alpacas:* alpaca farm. *Self-guide town walk and drive:* highlight is the National Trust–listed main street; brochure from visitor centre.

Picnic races: Mar. *Yass Show and Rodeo:* Mar. *Wine Roses and all that Jazz:* food, wine and music festival in the Murrumbateman area; Oct. Rodeo: Nov.

Cafe Dolcetto: cakes, sandwiches; 129 Comur St; (02) 6226 1277. *Ewe'n Me:* steak, seafood; Thunderbird Motel, 264 Comur St; (02) 6226 1158. *Swaggers Restaurant:* steakhouse; Sundowner Motor Inn, cnr Laidlaw and Castor sts; (02) 6226 3188. *Smokehouse Cafe:* lovely cafe in restored farm cottage, gourmet produce available for purchase; Poachers Pantry, 'Marakei', Nanima Rd, Hall; (02) 6230 2487.

Kerrowgair B&B: popular rustic B&B; 24 Grampian St; (02) 6226 4932.

Wee Jasper This picturesque village, where Banjo Paterson owned a holiday home, is set in a valley at the foot of the Brindabella Ranges. The Goodradigbee River is excellent for trout fishing. Carey's Caves are full of limestone formations and were the site of the 1957 discovery of the spine of a large extinct wombat. 50 km sw.

Bookham: village with historic cemetery, markets 2nd Sun each month and Sheep Show and Country Fair in Apr; 30 km w. *Binalong:* historic town with Motor Museum, Southern Cross Glass and the grave of bushranger Johnny Gilbert; 37 km nw. *Burrinjuck Waters State Park:* bushwalking, cruises, watersports and fishing. Burrinjuck Ski Classic is held each Nov (water level permitting); off Hume Hwy; 54 km sw. *Brindabella National Park:* birdwatching, camping and bushwalking in alpine surrounds. 4WD access only; via Wee Jasper; (02) 6122 3100; 61 km sw. *Wineries:* in Murrumbateman area with cellar-door tastings. Follow the signs on Barton Hwy; brochure from visitor centre. *Hume and Hovell Walking Track:* 23-day, 440 km trek from Albury to Yass. For a kit (including maps), contact Department of Infrastructure, Planning and Natural Resources, Sydney (02) 9762 8044.

See also CAPITAL COUNTRY, p. 31

Young

Pop. 7139
Map ref. 554 E7 | 565 B1

 2 Short St; (02) 6382 3394 or 1800 628 233; www.visityoung.com.au

93.9 Star FM, 96.3 FM ABC Local

Young is an attractive town in the western foothills of the Great Dividing Range with a fascinating history of goldmining. The Lambing Flat goldfields were rushed after a discovery was announced in 1860. Within a year there were an estimated 20 000 miners in town, 2000 of whom were Chinese. A combination of lawlessness and racism boiled over in the Lambing Flat riots in 1861, which gave rise to the Chinese Immigration Restriction Act, the first legislation to herald the infamous White Australia Policy. Today the town is the peaceful centre of a cherry-farming district.

Lambing Flat Folk Museum This museum is recognised as one of the finest in the country. Meticulously maintained photographs and relics tell the story of the town during the 1800s and 1900s. The full horrific story of the Lambing Flat riots is covered. Items on display include a 'roll-up' flag carried by miners during the riots. Campbell St; (02) 6382 2248.

Burrangong Art Gallery: hosts changing exhibitions from guest and local artists; at visitor centre; Short St. *J. D.'s Jam Factory:* tours, tastings and Devonshire teas; Henry Lawson Way; (02) 6382 4060.

Hilltops Flavours of the Harvest Festival (Young): Feb. *Lambing Flat Festival:* Apr. *National Cherry Festival:* Nov/Dec.

Doves Restaurant: modern Australian; Youngs Services Club, Cloete St; (02) 6382 1944. *Hilltops Restaurant:* modern Australian; Hilltops Retreat Motor Inn, Olympic Hwy; (02) 6382 3300. *Young Cafe de Jour:* modern Australian; 4/21 Lovell St; (02) 6382 1413.

Adrianna's B&B: romantic B&B; 4484 Olympic Hwy; (02) 6382 2231. *Hilltops Retreat Motor Inn:* traditional motel with impressive restaurant; 4662 Olympic Hwy; (02) 6382 3300. *Young Federation Motor Inn:* simple, comfortable, affordable motel; 109–119 Main St; (02) 6382 5644.

Chinaman's Dam Recreation Area: scenic walks, playground, and picnic and barbecue facilities. Includes Lambing Flat Chinese Tribute Gardens with Pool of Tranquility; Pitstone Rd; 4 km se. *Yandilla Mustard Seed Oil Enterprises:* tours by appt; bookings (02) 6943 2516; 20 km s. *Murringo:* historic buildings, a glassblower and engraver; 21 km e. *Hilltops:* cool-climate wine region; cellar-door information at visitor centre. *Cherries and stone fruit:* sales and pick-your-own throughout the area Nov–Dec. Cherries blossom in Sept/Oct.

See also CAPITAL COUNTRY, p. 31

AUSTRALIAN CAPITAL TERRITORY

[HORSERIDING IN TIDBINBILLA NATURE RESERVE]

CANBERRA is...

A picnic in the AUSTRALIAN NATIONAL BOTANIC GARDENS / A visit to PARLIAMENT

HOUSE / Fine dining in one of MANUKA'S many restaurants / A wander through the

NATIONAL GALLERY OF AUSTRALIA's Sculpture Garden / Fun science activities at

QUESTACON – The National Science and Technology Centre / City views from the top

of MOUNT AINSLIE / A trip to the NATIONAL MUSEUM OF AUSTRALIA / Viewing

portraits of well-known Australians at the AUSTRALIAN PORTRAIT GALLERY

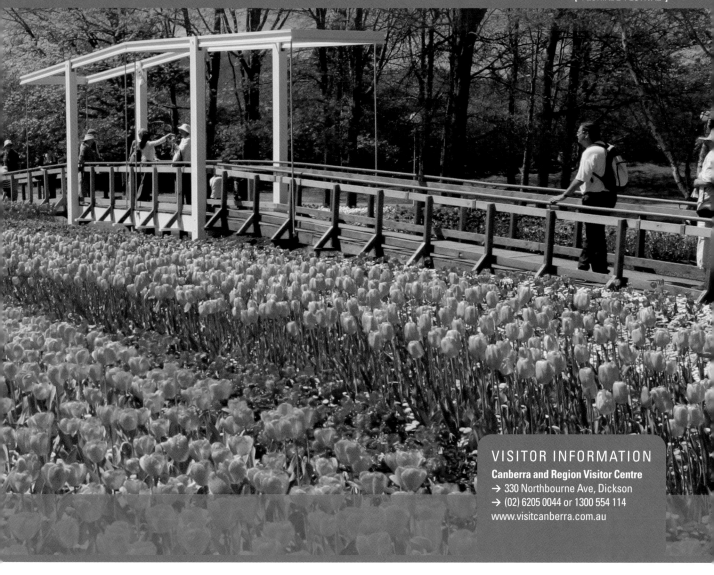

VISITOR INFORMATION
Canberra and Region Visitor Centre
→ 330 Northbourne Ave, Dickson
→ (02) 6205 0044 or 1300 554 114
www.visitcanberra.com.au

Canberra really is the bush capital – kangaroo-dotted nature reserves are scattered throughout the city, and the Brindabella mountain range bounds the south-western edge. As the national capital, Canberra claims some of Australia's most significant institutions, including a magnificent art gallery and a remarkable war museum. Grand public buildings and monuments complement the order and beauty of the city's original design, and the landmark flagpole of Parliament House can be seen from many parts of the city.

Many visitors are attracted by Canberra's impressive national collections or the experience of witnessing federal politics, but the city has much more to offer. The capital also boasts cool-climate wineries, top-class restaurants and bars, an annual balloon festival, attractions for children and a full calendar of vibrant cultural and sporting events.

With a population of about 346 000, life in Canberra moves at a comfortable pace; and with the snow and the sea both only two hours away, the locals have the best of both worlds. The city's creation solved the debate between Sydney and Melbourne over the location of Australia's capital, and Canberra is now one of the world's few completely planned cities.

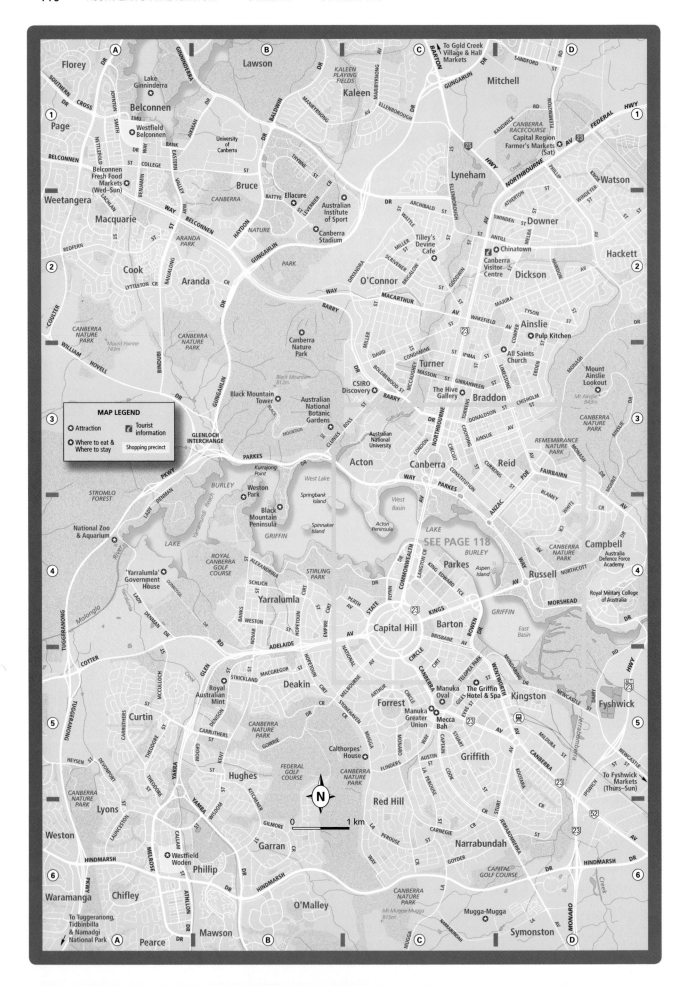

Parliamentary Triangle & War Memorial

The vision of Canberra's architect, Walter Burley Griffin, can be seen in the tree-lined avenues, spectacular lake views and spacious parks of central Canberra. The focal point is Parliament House, atop Capital Hill, situated at the apex of the Parliamentary Triangle. An integral part of Burley Griffin's plan was the vista from Capital Hill, extending to Lake Burley Griffin, bounded by Commonwealth and Kings avenues, up the broad sweep of Anzac Parade to the Australian War Memorial.

National Capital Exhibition 118 B2

The National Capital Exhibition tells the story of Canberra through interactive displays, rare photographs, a laser model of the city and various audiovisual material. Learn about the area's Indigenous inhabitants, European settlement and Walter Burley Griffin's design for the city. *Regatta Point, Barrine Dr, Commonwealth Park; (02) 6257 1068; open 9am–10pm Mon–Fri, 10am–4pm Sat–Sun; admission free.*

Parliament House 118 A5

Designed by the American-based architects Mitchell/Giurgola & Thorp, Parliament House was officially opened by the Queen in 1988. It is home to both houses of Federal Parliament (the Senate and the House of Representatives). If your visit coincides with the sitting of parliament, you can see democracy in action from the public galleries (check parliament's website, www.aph. gov.au, for sitting dates). The permanent displays include an extensive collection of Australian art, the Great Hall Tapestry and one of only four surviving 1297 copies of the Magna Carta. Once inside, take the lift to the roof for magnificent views of the city. It is worth noting that the flag flying atop the 81-metre flagpole is roughly the size of the side of a double-decker bus. Guided tours of the complex are recommended; brochures also give visitors the option of self-guide tours. Those with a keen eye may spot the fossils in the main foyer's marble floor. Those who prefer outdoor attractions can walk through the 23 hectares of landscaped gardens. *Parliament Dr, off State Circle; (02) 6277 5399; open 9am–5pm daily; admission free.*

Reconciliation Place 118 B4

Reconciliation Place, adjacent to Commonwealth Place on Lake Burley Griffin, symbolises the journey of reconciliation between Indigenous and white Australians, in the past, present and future. The location of Reconciliation Place within the Parliamentary Zone places the reconciliation process physically and symbolically at the heart of Australian democratic and cultural life. A series of public artworks, known as slivers, surround a central circular mound, while pathways link Reconciliation Place and Commonwealth Place, national institutions and Lake Burley Griffin.

climate

Canberra has a climate of extremes and seasons of beauty. Summer in the capital is hot and very dry, with temperatures sometimes reaching the mid to high 30s. Winter is cold and frosty, thanks to Canberra's altitude of roughly 600 metres, its inland location and its proximity to the Snowy Mountains. Don't let this stop you, though – Canberra winter days are breathtakingly crisp and usually fine, with cloudless, bright blue skies after the early morning fogs lift. Spring is Canberra at its most pleasant – the city is awash with colour and flowers abound – although some say that it is in autumn that Canberra is at its most beautiful.

J	F	M	A	M	J	J	A	S	O	N	D	
28	28	24	20	15	12	11	13	16	19	23	26	MAX °C
13	13	11	7	4	1	0	1	4	6	9	11	MIN °C
59	51	55	49	47	37	52	47	65	61	58	46	RAIN MM
5	4	4	5	5	5	6	7	7	7	7	5	RAIN DAYS

AUSTRALIAN CAPITAL TERRITORY

[PARLIAMENT HOUSE]

Museum of Australian Democracy at Old Parliament House 118 B4

Home to Australia's Federal Parliament from 1927 to 1988, this heritage-listed building captivates its audiences with its rich history as well as several innovative and vibrant exhibitions. It's now home to the Museum of Australian Democracy, Canberra's newest cultural attraction, which provides insights into the stories and events that have shaped Australia's democracy. Wander through the corridors of power or take a free guided tour. In summer enjoy Friday night drinks and music in the lower house courtyard. Flanking the building are the **Old Parliament House Rose Gardens**, while across the road are the **Aboriginal Tent Embassy**, established in 1972 to protest against a lack of land rights for the country's Indigenous peoples, and the **National Rose Gardens**. *18 King George Tce, Parkes; (02) 6270 8222; open 9am–5pm daily.*

National Portrait Gallery 118 B4

The National Portrait Gallery opened in December 2008, in a new building next door to the High Court of Australia and the National Gallery of Australia in Parkes. The National Portrait Gallery has a permanent display of over 450 portraits that represent the human face of Australia – those who have contributed to Australian society or whose lives have set them apart. Included are paintings, sculptures, photographs and multimedia works. The gallery also hosts changing exhibitions as well as those online. *King Edward Tce, Parkes; (02) 6102 7000; open 10am–5pm daily; general admission free.*

National Archives of Australia 118 B4

The National Archives occupy what was Canberra's first GPO, opened in 1927. The permanent exhibition, 'Memory of a Nation', highlights the extent and diversity of the treasures contained within the National Archives' collection, including ASIO surveillance photos, wooden balls used in National Service ballots to conscript young men to the Vietnam War and an 1897 draft of the Constitution complete with Australia's first prime minister Edmund Barton's edits. Learn how to search for war service and migration records to trace your family history. The Federation Gallery displays Australia's 'birth certificate'– Queen Victoria's Royal Commission of Assent and Australia's original Constitution. *Queen Victoria Tce, Parkes; (02) 6212 3600; open 9am–5pm daily; admission free.*

National Library of Australia 118 B3

Collecting since 1901, this is the country's largest reference library. The present building contains over six million books as well as newspapers, periodicals, photographs and other documents. There are free tours every hour and if you are there on Thursday take the free behind-the-scenes weekly tour. The Library cafe, bookplate, is a good spot for lunch or coffee. *Parkes Pl, Parkes; (02) 6262 1111; open 9am–9pm Mon–Thurs, 9am–5pm Fri–Sun; admission free.*

Questacon – The National Science and Technology Centre 118 B4

Making science fun and relevant for everyone, Questacon has many interactive exhibits – you can experience an earthquake and a cyclone, see lightning created and free-fall 6 metres on the vertical slide. *King Edward Tce, Parkes; (02) 6270 2800; open 9am–5pm daily.*

High Court of Australia 118 C4

Located between Questacon and the National Gallery of Australia, the High Court is notable for its glass-encased public

getting around

Canberra is an easy city to get around if you have a car and a map. The road infrastructure is probably the best in Australia, with wide, well-planned roads, and visitors will find that they can cover long distances in a short time. Certainly in the central area of the city it is very easy to travel from one attraction to the next by car or public transport. Walking between the attractions in the Parliamentary Triangle is also very pleasant.

Buses are the only public transport available in Canberra, but these services can be variable at off-peak times. For a convenient way to get around the main attractions, catch one of the sightseeing buses that depart from the Melbourne Building on Northbourne Avenue.

Canberra is a city full of cyclists and major roads have on-road cycling lanes, often marked with green where roads merge. Take care, as cyclists have right of way on the green lanes.

Public transport ACTION Buses 13 1710.

Motoring organisation NRMA 13 1122, roadside assistance 13 1111.

Car rental ACT Car Rentals (02) 6282 7272; Avis 13 6333; Budget 13 2727; Hertz 13 3039; Rumbles (02) 6280 7444; Thrifty 1300 367 227.

Taxis Canberra Cabs 13 2227.

Bicycle hire Mr Spokes Bike Hire (02) 6257 1188.

monuments

Anzac Parade Memorials Eleven dramatic monuments set along the striking red gravel of Anzac Parade commemorate Australian involvement in military conflicts, and the Australians who served in the various defence forces. 118 C2

Australian–American Memorial Celebrates America's World War II contribution to Australia's defence in the Pacific. 118 D4

Captain Cook Memorial Jet An impressive 150-metre water jet – hire a paddleboat to cruise under the spray. 118 B3

National Carillon The largest carillon in Australia, with 53 bells, it was a gift from the British government to celebrate Canberra's 50th anniversary. Regular recitals can be heard. 118 C4

See also Australian War Memorial, p. 120, Reconciliation Place, p. 117

gallery and timber courtrooms. Murals by artist Jan Senbergs reflect the history and functions of the court, and the role of the states in Federation. Visitors can explore the building, talk to the knowledgeable attendants and view a short film on the court's work. *Parkes Pl, Parkes; (02) 6270 6811; open 9.45am–4.30pm Mon–Fri; admission free.*

National Gallery of Australia 118 C4

Established in 1911, the gallery has been housed across the road from the High Court since 1982. With over 100 000 works, the collection provides a brilliant overview of Australian art. The

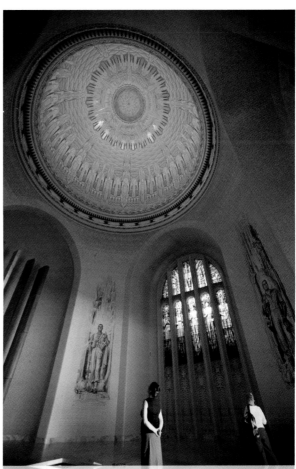

[HALL OF MEMORY, AUSTRALIAN WAR MEMORIAL]

AUSTRALIAN CAPITAL TERRITORY

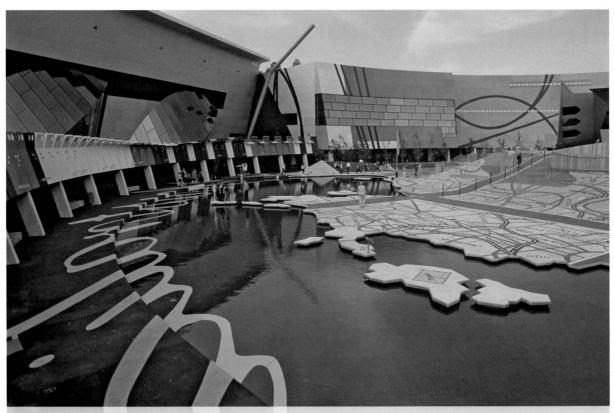

[NATIONAL MUSEUM OF AUSTRALIA]

international collection is just as impressive and includes Jackson Pollock's *Blue Poles* and Australian-born Ron Mueck's *Pregnant Woman*. Enjoy a picnic lunch in the tranquil **Sculpture Garden**, which comprises a series of native gardens and contains over 50 sculptures set between the gallery and the lake. *Parkes Pl, Parkes; (02) 6240 6411; open 10am–5pm daily; general admission free.*

Blundell's Cottage 118 C3

Built in the 1860s, the historic Blundell's Cottage was part of the Campbell family's 32 000-acre (12 800-hectare) estate and home to tenant farm workers. The cottage is now a museum that offers a close encounter with the region's early farming history. *Wendouree Dr, off Constitution Ave, Parkes; (02) 6257 1068; open 10am–3pm Sat.*

Australian War Memorial 118 D1

The War Memorial, set at the foot of Mount Ainslie and at the end of Anzac Parade, commemorates and honours the Australian men and women who have served in war. The memorial has undergone redevelopment, culminating in the opening of Aircraft Hall, the Second World War Gallery and ANZAC Hall. Free guided tours run daily. Visitors can browse over 20 exhibition galleries or find moments of silent contemplation at the Hall of Memory, the Tomb of the Unknown Australian Soldier, the Pool of Reflection and the Roll of Honour, which lists the names of over 102 000 Australian servicemen and servicewomen who died in war. *Treloar Cres, Campbell; (02) 6243 4211; open 10am–5pm daily; admission free.*

National Zoo & Aquarium 116 A4

This modern zoo, with naturalistic enclosures rather than cages, has a strong commitment to breeding endangered species and conservation. Animals range from the big cats to bears, otters and monkeys. Wander through the aquarium to see colourful marine life in the Great Barrier Reef exhibit and visit the shark-filled Predators of the Deep exhibit. Special tours include handfeeding the big cats and bears, meeting a cheetah and going on a ZooVenture. (These tours can cost significantly more than general admission, but include all-day zoo entry.) *Scrivener Dam, Lady Denman Dr, Yarralumla; (02) 6287 8400; open 10am–5pm daily.*

Royal Australian Mint 116 B5

Opened in 1965, the mint has the capacity to produce two million coins per day. You can learn how coins are made and see

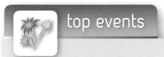

top events

Summernats Car Festival Canberra becomes a 'cruise city' full of street machines. January.

National Multicultural Festival A showcase of cultures in food, art and performance. February.

National Autumn Balloon Spectacular An eight-day festival with over 50 hot-air balloons launched daily from the lawns of the Museum of Australian Democracy at Old Parliament House. March.

National Folk Festival Hundreds of performers and thousands of spectators create one of Canberra's biggest parties. Easter.

Rally of Canberra Car rally as part of the Australian Rally Championship. June.

Fireside Festival Warm up winter with fireside food, wine and arts. August.

Floriade A celebration of spring, flowers and fun. September–October.

Wine, Roses and All That Jazz Open weekend of the cool-climate vineyards, with music, food and much wine-tasting. November.

the production floor from an elevated gallery. There are displays of old coins, a video on coin production, and visitors can even make their own coins. *Denison St, Deakin; (02) 6202 6800; open 9am–4pm Mon–Fri, 10am–4pm Sat–Sun; admission free.*

City Centre & Surrounds

The modest size of Canberra's city centre, Civic, is a reminder that Canberra's population is only just over 340 000 people. There are many attractions in the centre, along with excellent shopping, the peaceful Glebe Park, great cafes and Casino Canberra.

Garema Place 118 B1

The top end of Civic, this open public space is encircled by cafes and restaurants, and features a large movie screen (which shows movies at night during summer). Garema Place is a popular meeting place and is next to the Civic bus interchange. On Friday and Saturday evenings the Irish pub King O'Malley's is usually bursting at the seams, and the outdoor cafes are full of relaxed diners. If you head south from Garema Place down the tree-lined City Walk towards the large Canberra Centre mall, you will find Civic's landmark carousel. Built in 1914 in Melbourne, its hand-carved horses and two elephants were imported from Germany.

Canberra Museum and Gallery 118 B1

CMAG's permanent collection reflects the history, environment, culture and community of the Canberra region. Dynamic exhibitions and diverse community events celebrate Canberra's social history and visual arts. It is also playing host to the Nolan Collection, works by the renowned Australian painter Sidney Nolan, while the Nolan Gallery at Lanyon is refurbished. *Cnr London Circuit and Civic Sq, Civic; (02) 6207 3968; open 10am–5pm Tues–Fri, 12–4pm Sat–Sun; admission free.*

National Film and Sound Archive 118 A2

Housed in the former Institute of Anatomy next to the landscaped grounds of the Australian National University, Australia's national screen and sound archive collects, preserves and shares Australia's film and sound heritage. The displays include film memorabilia, special exhibitions and interactive activities. *McCoy Circuit, Acton; (02) 6248 2000; open 9am–5pm Mon–Fri, 10am–5pm Sat–Sun; admission free.*

National Museum of Australia 118 A3

Opened in 2001, this thoroughly modern museum uses state-of-the-art technology and hands-on interactive displays to show stories about Australia's past, present, people, issues and future. Begin your experience in Circa, a rotating cinema, to get an overview of the three main themes of the museum: land, nation, people. The permanent displays include 'First Australians', an amazing display of Indigenous culture, experience, dance and music; and 'Nation', where you can celebrate Australian icons such as the Hills hoist, *Play School* and Vegemite. 'Old New Land' takes you through 20 000 years of environmental change, and in 'Eternity' you can share the joy and sorrow of ordinary and extraordinary Australians. Children will love 'KSpace', a virtual-reality experience, and 'Our Place', with four different cubbyhouses

shopping

Canberra Centre, City Recently expanded, this stylish mall has department stores, a wide variety of smaller shops and specialty stores, in the heart of the CBD. 118 C1

Kingston Old-fashioned specialty shopping and restaurants. 116 C5

Manuka Up-market fashion and homewares, streets lined with cafes, and a supermarket open until midnight. 116 C5

Westfield Woden One of Canberra's largest shopping malls with department stores, over 200 specialty shops, Hoyts 8 cinemas and plenty of parking. 116 A6

Other suburban malls These include Westfield Shopping Centre in Belconnen, the Tuggeranong Hyperdome and two factory outlet centres in Fyshwick. 116 A1, 574 D6, E5

to explore. Fascinating temporary exhibitions change throughout the year. Guided tours available. *Lawson Cres, Acton Peninsula; (02) 6208 5000; open 9am–5pm daily; general admission free.*

CSIRO Discovery 116 C3

The centre showcases Australia's scientific research and innovation with exhibitions and interactive displays. Take part in the hands-on experiments, experience the virtual-reality theatre and find out about the latest research breakthroughs. *Off Clunies Ross St, Acton; (02) 6246 4601; open 9am–5pm Mon–Fri, 11am–3pm Sun.*

St John the Baptist Church and St John's Schoolhouse Museum 118 C2

Visit Canberra's oldest church and first schoolhouse, built in the 1840s. The buildings have been restored and now form an interesting museum. The adjoining cemetery has some of Canberra's oldest headstones. *Constitution Ave, Reid; (02) 6249 6839; open 10am–12pm Wed, 2–4pm Sat–Sun and public holidays; general admission free, museum entry by donation.*

where to eat

Ellacure Great cafe with a good, casual menu in the pizza and pasta mode. Cnr Braybrook and Battye sts, Bruce; (02) 6251 0990; open Tues–Sun for lunch and Tues–Sat for dinner. 116 B2

Iori Japanese Inner-city Japanese restaurant where the emphasis is on really exciting food. 41 East Row; (02) 6257 2334; open Mon–Fri for lunch and Mon–Sat for dinner. 118 B1

Mecca Bah Buzzing Middle Eastern bazaar with a fun menu and a great feel. Shop 25–29, Manuka Terrace, cnr Flinders Way and Franklin St, Manuka; (02) 6260 6700; open daily for lunch and dinner. 116 C5

Mezzalira Top-notch Italian restaurant in the city where you'll get serious and very good food. Melbourne Building, cnr London Circuit and West Row; (02) 6230 0025; open Mon–Fri for lunch and Mon–Sat for dinner. 118 B1

Pulp Kitchen Classy, simple brasserie-style restaurant that offers some of the best, most uncluttered food in town. Shop 1, Wakefield Gardens, Ainslie shops; (02) 6257 4334; open Tues–Fri for lunch and Tues–Sat for dinner. 116 D2

[GINNINDERRA CREEK]

Inner North

Incorporating some of the oldest suburbs in Canberra, this area is an enjoyable mix of relaxed cafes, interesting attractions and nature reserves with excellent walking and mountain-bike tracks.

Belconnen Fresh Food Markets Fresh fruit, vegetables, produce and home to one of Australia's 'big things' – the Giant Mushroom. Wed–Sun. 116 A1

Fyshwick Markets Fresh produce markets with a great atmosphere and excellent value. Thurs–Sun. 564 E5

Gorman House Markets, Braddon Arts and crafts, home-baked treats, plants, clothes and a great up-beat atmosphere, near the city centre. Sat. 118 C1

Hall Markets Set in the historic showgrounds of Hall village on the outskirts of Canberra, with up to 500 stalls of crafts, home produce, plants and homemade stylish clothing. 1st Sun each month (closed Jan). 564 D3

Old Bus Depot Markets, Kingston A local favourite, showcasing the creativity of the Canberra region, with handcrafted and home-produced arts, crafts and jewellery, gourmet food, New Age therapies, kids' activities and musical entertainment. Sun. 118 C5

Capital Region Farmer's Markets, Exhibition Park Farmers and growers from the coast to the capital bring their food to these markets off Northbourne Ave. Sat. 116 D1

Mount Ainslie Lookout 116 D3

Drive to the top of Mount Ainslie for a stunning view of the city and the surrounding mountain ranges. From here you will clearly see the geometry of the capital's design. During autumn this is the best place to see the capital's stunning array of natural colours. *Mt Ainslie Dr, off Fairbairn Ave, Campbell.*

Ainslie, Braddon and Dickson 116 C3, D2

If you are in need of a good coffee, a tasty Chinese meal or a beer in the sun, head to the inner north-eastern suburbs. This is an area with an 'alternative' atmosphere, traditionally populated by Canberra's students. The shopping precincts of these suburbs offer small art galleries, interesting fashion and street cafes. **Ainslie** and **Braddon** have some of Canberra's earliest houses, and make for pleasant walking. In Braddon, browse the Hive Gallery (on Lonsdale Street) for one-of-a-kind gifts. Ainslie is also home to the historic **All Saints Church** (on Cowper Street). Further north, **Dickson** is a hive of activity and home to Canberra's small version of Chinatown (on Woolley Street).

North-west

The inner north-west of Canberra is a hub of activity, with the leafy suburbs of Turner, O'Connor and Lyneham particularly popular with students from the nearby Australian National University. Canberra Nature Park's Mount Ainslie and Mount Majura lie on the edge of the city centre. Further out is Belconnen, which is the main centre for northern Canberra. It offers a large shopping mall, a top-quality sports and aquatic centre, and many other facilities. Also in Belconnen you will find Lake Ginninderra, a favourite recreational and picnic spot.

Australian National Botanic Gardens 116 B3

At the base of Black Mountain, these magnificent gardens (roughly 90 hectares, with 40 hectares developed and the remainder bushland) have the largest collection of Australian native flora in the world. The gardens are organised into sections representing Australia's various climatic zones and ecosystems. Follow the Aboriginal Plant Use Walk for an understanding of the species used for foods and medicines by the country's Indigenous inhabitants. In summer, people flock here for evening picnics and weekend twilight jazz. *Clunies Ross St, Acton; (02) 6250 9540; open 8.30am–5pm daily; admission free.*

Black Mountain Tower 116 B3

One of Canberra's landmarks, the communications tower rises 195 metres above the summit of Black Mountain and offers superb views of Canberra. It has two open viewing platforms, an exhibition gallery and **Alto**, a revolving restaurant with a growing reputation. *Black Mountain Dr, Acton; (02) 6219 6111; open 9am–10pm daily.*

Australian Institute of Sport 116 C2

Providing world-class facilities across a broad range of disciplines, the AIS is the training ground for many elite athletes. The Sports Visitors Centre is the entrance point for visitors and has exhibitions and displays of sporting memorabilia. Tours of the AIS are led by athletes and give visitors an insight into the life of an elite athlete. The tours include Sportex, an interactive exhibition where you can test your sporting skills against those recorded by our Olympians and see the latest in sport technology. *Leverrier Cres, Bruce; (02) 6214 1010; open 9am–5pm daily; general admission free.*

North

In Canberra's north is Gold Creek Village, a tourist attraction that takes its name from an old property established in the area in the mid-1800s. To make matters confusing, there is no Gold Creek, and no history of goldmining in this area – Gold Creek Station was apparently named after a racehorse. The station, north of the village, is still a large working merino property and is open to visitors wanting a taste of Australian rural life (groups only; bookings (02) 6230 9208). However, Gold Creek Village is the real drawcard here, with specialty shops, galleries, cafes, historic buildings and a host of modern attractions.

walks & tours

Anzac Parade Walk Follow the war memorials set along the regal Anzac Parade on this self-guide walk (2.5 kilometres). Brochure available from the visitor centre or download a tour podcast (www.nationalcapital.gov.au).

Australians of the Year Walk On the lake foreshore in front of the National Library, this walk honours the award's recipients, with plaques for each year of the award.

Balloon Aloft! Experience the beauty of Canberra as you float above the city in a hot-air balloon. Bookings on (02) 6285 1540.

Burley Griffin Walk or Ride A self-guide walk takes in the north-eastern shores of Lake Burley Griffin, from the National Capital Exhibition to the National Carillon (4.6 kilometres). Brochure available from the visitor centre.

Canberra Tracks Drive one, or all three, of these fascinating, signed road trips. Track 1 explores the path of Canberra's original Indigenous peoples; Track 2 takes you through the pastoral era; and Track 3 gives you an overview of Canberra's layout, via lookouts. Brochures available from the visitor centre.

Lakeside Walk This self-guide walk begins at Commonwealth Place and passes the National Gallery, the High Court and the National Library (1.8 kilometres). Brochure available from the visitor centre.

where to stay

Diamant Sleek, ultra-modern hotel with bright splashes of modern art close to the CBD. 15 Edinburgh Ave; (02) 6175 2222. 118 B2

Hyatt Canberra A grand Art Deco hotel offering old-world luxury in the shadow of Parliament. Commonwealth Ave; (02) 6270 1234. 118 B3

Redbrow Garden Luxury lakeside B&B set in a wildlife haven and country property just 20 minutes from the city. 1143 Nanima Rd, Murrumbateman; (02) 6226 8166. 564 D1

The Griffin Hotel & Spa Stylish boutique apartment hotel in the trendy cafe neighbourhood of Kingston. 15 Tench St; 1800 622 637. 116 C5

Hotel Realm Canberra's newest five-star hotel. Modern luxury in the heart of the Parliamentary Triangle. 18 National Circuit; (02) 6163 1888. 118 B5

entertainment

Cinema The big suburban malls of Woden and Belconnen have Hoyts multiplexes, but for arthouse and independent cinema try the Dendy Canberra Centre in the city or Limelight Cinemas in Tuggeranong. Manuka Greater Union has a wide range of interesting new releases. See the *Canberra Times* for details of current films.

Live music Canberra has a surprisingly busy music scene and there is usually a good selection of live music around town, ranging from rock gigs at the ANU Union Bar to mellow jazz or soul at Tilley's Devine Cafe in Lyneham. Big acts play at the Canberra Theatre Centre or the Royal Theatre, both in the city centre. You will find nightclubs aplenty in Civic,

Kingston, Manuka and Braddon. For gig details pick up a copy of the *Canberra Times* on Thursday for its lift-out entertainment guide 'Fly' or look for the free street magazine *BMA*.

Classical music and performing arts The main venue for performing arts is the Canberra Theatre Centre. A couple of smaller venues around town, such as Gorman House Arts Centre in Braddon and the Street Theatre on Childers Street, cater to more eclectic tastes. Classical music concerts most often take place at Llewellyn Hall, part of the ANU's Canberra School of Music, in Acton. See the *Canberra Times* for details of what's on.

sport

If a visit to the Australian Institute of Sport leaves you wanting more, then there is plenty of sport to see in Canberra. Watch a game of **basketball** as the two Canberra WNBL teams, the Capitals and the AIS, go head-to-head or play interstate teams. The Capitals play their home games at Southern Cross Stadium in Tuggeranong and the AIS team at the AIS.

See Canberra's **Rugby League** side, the Raiders, take on the rest of the nation at Canberra Stadium. The ACT Brumbies, the capital's **Rugby Union** team, also play at Canberra Stadium, to partisan capacity crowds. Canberra doesn't have an **AFL** (Australian Football League) team of its own, but one Melbourne team plays a couple of 'home' games a year at the picturesque Manuka Oval.

If **cricket** is more your thing, visit in summer to see the Prime Minister's XI take on one of the touring international sides at Manuka Oval.

If you like dust, mud and excitement, try the Rally of Canberra **car rally** in June.

National Dinosaur Museum 564 E3

The museum has an extensive display of fossilised dinosaur remains, full skeletons and full-size replicas. During school holidays there are plenty of activities for children as well as guided tours. *Cnr Gold Creek Rd and Barton Hwy, Gold Creek Village; (02) 6230 2655; open 10am–5pm daily.*

Cockington Green 564 E3

Journey through a magical world of miniatures, from a Stonehenge replica to a village cricket match amid beautifully manicured gardens, or take a ride on a miniature steam train. A heritage rose walk links the miniatures with the steam train. *11 Gold Creek Rd, Gold Creek Village; (02) 6230 2273; open 9.30am–5pm daily.*

Canberra Reptile Sanctuary 564 E3

Dedicated to research, conservation and education, this is the place for all things reptilian. Both Australian and exotic species are on display, including a boa constrictor, the giant day gecko from Madagascar and local favourites such as the blue-tongue lizard and children's python. The collection is continually increasing

so there will be something new each time you visit. *O'Hanlon Pl, Gold Creek Village; (02) 6253 8533; open 10am–5pm daily.*

The Bird Walk 564 E3

Walk among over 500 birds representing 54 species from Australia and around the world in this aviary, which measures 1000 square metres. You can photograph and handfeed the colourful creatures, which fly free in the landscaped 9-metre-high enclosure. *Federation Sq, Gold Creek Village; (02) 6230 2044; open 10am–4.30pm daily in summer, 11am–3pm daily in winter.*

Ginninderra Village 564 E3

The old village of Ginninderra predates **Hall**, the nearby town that began life as a village well before the city of Canberra was created. Ginninderra serviced the surrounding farming districts, including the property of Gold Creek Station. The Ginninderra Village that is today part of Gold Creek Village contains the old Ginninderra schoolhouse and the township's old Roman Catholic church. They can be found among giftware stores, craft studios and galleries. *O'Hanlon Pl, Gold Creek Village; open daily.*

Inner South

Drive around Canberra's leafy inner-south suburbs to see official residences, Art Deco bungalows, carefully tended gardens and the diplomatic precinct. Most of the embassies are located in the suburbs of Yarralumla and Forrest, between State Circle and Empire Circuit. The Lodge, the prime minister's Canberra residence, next to Parliament House, is noticeable by the large cream brick wall that surrounds it. It is not open to the public, but occasional open days are held. Likewise, Government House, the governor-general's residence at Yarralumla, a grand 1920s building, is only open to the public once or twice a year. There are views of the grounds from a lookout on Lady Denman Drive.

Manuka and Kingston 116 C5, D5

Over the years many of the original homes in these two suburbs have been replaced by townhouses and apartments – their proximity to both Lake Burley Griffin and the city centre has

[HOT-AIR BALLOONS OVER LAKE BURLEY GRIFFIN]

made them sought-after addresses. Both Manuka and Kingston have vibrant shopping precincts, with a fabulous variety of cafes, restaurants, nightclubs, bars and pubs. Up-market shops and public squares add to the vibe, and the lovely **Telopea Park** is only a few minutes away from both suburbs. On the Kingston Foreshore you'll find the **Canberra Glassworks**, nestled in an old powerhouse next to the weekly Old Bus Depot Markets. The nearby suburb of **Griffith** has some of Canberra's best organic and alternative shopping, along with a couple of excellent restaurants and cafes.

Calthorpes' House 116 C5

Built in 1927 in Spanish Mission style, the house contains the original furnishings and photos, offering glimpses into what domestic life was like in the then-fledgling capital. Explore the 1920s garden or hide in the World War II air-raid shelter. There are guided tours during the week (group bookings only) and open house on the weekend. *24 Mugga Way, Red Hill; (02) 6295 1945; open 1–4pm Sat–Sun.*

Mugga-Mugga 116 C6

Set on 17 hectares of grazing land, Mugga-Mugga is a collection of buildings and cultural objects dating from the 1830s to the 1970s. The highlight is the 1830s shepherd's cottage, which has been carefully preserved and furnished with household belongings from the early 1900s. The option of combined admission fees with Calthorpes' House and Lanyon Homestead *(see Day tours, below)* offers good value. *Narrabundah La, Symonston; (02) 6239 5607; open 1.30–4.30pm Sat–Sun.*

South

Tuggeranong Homestead 564 D6

Sitting on 31 hectares, this historic homestead started life as an 1830s cottage, was added to between 1890 and 1903, then was

waterside retreats

Black Mountain Peninsula A picnic and barbecue spot on the edge of the lake in the shadow of Black Mountain. 116 B4

Casuarina Sands Where the Cotter and Murrumbidgee rivers meet. 564 C5

Commonwealth Park Formal gardens, parkland and public art on the edge of the lake. 118 C3

Commonwealth Place Promenade on the shores of the lake, with the International Flag Display and vistas of the Australian War Memorial and Parliament House. 118 B3

Jerrabomberra Wetlands A refuge for wildlife, including 77 bird species. 118 D5

Weston Park A woodland and lakeside recreation area with play equipment for children. 116 B4

rebuilt in 1908 (part of the old cottage was incorporated into the drawing room). A stone barn built by convicts in the 1830s is still standing. The property was bought by the Commonwealth government in 1917 for military purposes. War historian Charles Bean lived here from 1919 to 1925 while he wrote the official history of the Australian involvement in World War I. A cafe and markets are held on the site every second Sunday of the month. *Johnson Dr, opposite Calwell Shops, Richardson; (02) 6292 8888; open Sat–Sun or by appt.*

Lake Tuggeranong 564 D6

Artificial Lake Tuggeranong offers waterside recreation for Canberra's inhabitants, who come here to ride the cycle path, enjoy a picnic, have a swim or go fishing, sailing or windsurfing.

day tours

Namadgi National Park Namadgi is part of the Australian Alps and the informative visitor centre is only a 45-minute drive from the city centre. Walking the 160 kilometres of marked trails is a popular way to explore the park. Beautiful scenery can be enjoyed in the rugged Bimberi Wilderness in the western part of the park. Namadgi has a wide range of natural environments, an abundance of native wildlife and a rich Aboriginal heritage with the evidence of several rock art sites in the park. For more details see p. 31

Lanyon Homestead South of Canberra is one of Australia's most historic grazing properties and a beautiful 19th-century homestead. On the banks of the Murrumbidgee River, the homestead and its gardens provide a glimpse of the 1850s. The homestead's outbuildings (the kitchen, dairy, storerooms and workers' barracks) were built from wood and stone – the stone was cut and quarried by convict labour. Parts of the homestead have been restored and furnished in the style of the period.

Tidbinbilla Nature Reserve South-west of Canberra is the Tidbinbilla Nature Reserve, which includes dry and wet forests, subalpine areas and wetlands. Enjoy a bushwalk or picnic, play with the kids in the Playground at Tidbinbilla, or marvel at the free-ranging wildlife at The Sanctuary. Near the reserve is the Canberra Deep Space Communication Complex, one of three facilities in the world that form NASA's Deep Space Network.

Here you can view a genuine piece of moon rock that is 3.8 billion years old, astronaut suits, space food, spacecraft models and photographs. Just south of the Tidbinbilla Nature Reserve is Corin Forest, which has an 800-metre bobsled alpine slide, a flying fox, a waterslide and some great bushwalks and picnic areas. Admission is free to all attractions.

Wine district Canberra district wineries have established a sound reputation for their cool-climate wines. With 140 vineyards and 33 wineries within 35 minutes' drive from the city centre, making a winery tour is a must. You can pick up a guide to the wineries from the visitor centre or from cellar doors around the region. In addition to cellar-door sales, some wineries offer excellent dining facilities and entertainment, with the annual Wine, Roses and all that Jazz Festival proving popular each November. For more details see p. 31

Historic towns A number of towns within easy driving distance of Canberra are noted for their heritage buildings and are filled with a sense of the area's farming and goldmining history. These towns include Captains Flat, Goulburn, Braidwood, Bungendore, Yass and Young; most are within an hour or so of the capital. Historic Bungendore, full of craft galleries and antique shops, is a great daytrip, although at only 30 minutes away it is easy enough to visit just for a fine meal or an enjoyable shopping expedition. For more details see p. 31

VICTORIA is...

Barracking for your team at a footy match at the MCG / Watching penguins waddle

from the sea to their burrows on PHILLIP ISLAND / Taking a paddlesteamer ride on the

Murray River from ECHUCA / Panning for gold and enjoying traditional hard-boiled

lollies at SOVEREIGN HILL in Ballarat / Soaking in a mineral spa in DAYLESFORD

VICTORIA

[MOUNTAIN ASH TREES, YARRA RANGES NATIONAL PARK]

or HEPBURN SPRINGS / Driving along the spectacular GREAT OCEAN ROAD
to see the TWELVE APOSTLES / Bushwalking in a timeless mountain landscape in
GRAMPIANS NATIONAL PARK / A daytrip to the DANDENONGS, stopping off at
some cellar doors in the YARRA VALLEY / Hitting the slopes at MOUNT BULLER

VICTORIA

is possibly Australia's most diverse state. In a half-hour drive from Melbourne you could be taking in mist-laden mountain ranges and fern gullies. In an hour you could be lying on a sandy beach in a sheltered bay, or surfing in the rugged Southern Ocean. In around four hours you could be standing on the edge of the immense desert that stretches away into Australia's interior. In a country full of mind-numbing distances, nothing seems far away in Victoria.

More than five million people live in Victoria, with 3.8 million in Melbourne. The city was only founded in 1835, as a kind of afterthought to Sydney and Hobart, but by the 1850s Victoria was off to a racing start. A deluge of people from all corners of the world fanned out across the state in response to the madness that was gold. It brought prosperity to Victoria and it also brought the certain wildness treasured in the state's history – uprisings like the Eureka Rebellion and bushrangers like Ned Kelly.

Two centuries later, Victoria has also recognised the richness of its natural landscape. To the west of Melbourne, beyond Geelong, a tract of cool-temperate rainforest unravels on its way to

[MOUNT HOTHAM AT SUNSET, ALPINE NATIONAL PARK]

the vivid green Cape Otway, where a lighthouse stands on the cliff-top. The Great Ocean Road winds past here, en route to the state's iconic limestone stacks, the Twelve Apostles.

On the other side of Melbourne, the land falls away into a series of peninsulas, islands and isthmuses. One leads to Wilsons Promontory, an untouched landscape of forested hills, tea-brown rivers and beaches strewn with enormous rust-red boulders.

[GEELONG WATERFRONT]

The amber-hued Yarra Valley produces some of the country's finest cool-climate wines, and from here the landscape begins its gradual climb up into the High Country, which becomes a vista of snowfields in winter.

Perhaps Victoria's most cherished place is the Grampians, an offshoot of the Great Dividing Range. With a quarter of the state's flora and 80 per cent of its Aboriginal rock art, the Grampians is a living gallery and a superb place for bushwalking and camping.

fact file

Population 5 473 300
Total land area 227 010 square kilometres
People per square kilometre 22.1
Sheep per square kilometre 94
Length of coastline 1868 kilometres
Number of islands 184
Longest river Goulburn River (566 kilometres)
Largest lake Lake Corangamite (209 square kilometres)
Highest mountain Mount Bogong (1986 metres), Alpine National Park
Hottest place Mildura (77 days per year above 30°C)
Wettest place Weeaproinah (1900 millimetres per year), Otway Ranges
Oldest permanent settlement Portland (1834)
Most famous beach Bells Beach, Torquay
Tonnes of gold mined 2500 (2 per cent of world total)
Litres of milk produced on Victorian dairy farms per year 7 billion
Quirkiest festival Great Vanilla Slice Triumph, Ouyen
Famous people Germaine Greer, Barry Humphries, Kylie Minogue
Original name for the Twelve Apostles The Sow and Piglets
Best invention Bionic ear
First Ned Kelly film released *The Story of the Kelly Gang*, 1906 (also believed to be the world's first feature film)
Local beer Victoria Bitter

gift ideas

Raspberry drops (Sovereign Hill, Ballarat) Delicious, old-fashioned lollies from the gold-rush days are still made and sold at Charles Spencer's Confectionery Shop in Main Street and at the Sovereign Hill Gift Shop. See Ballarat p. 166, 579 C10

Replica of Melbourne tram (Best of Souvenirs, Melbourne) Prince Christian of Denmark received a real tram on the occasion of his birth, but you can take home a smaller – and beautifully crafted – version of Melbourne's distinctive transportation. Melbourne Visitor Information Centre, Federation Square, cnr Flinders and Swanston sts, Melbourne. 134 C4

Football souvenirs (National Sports Museum, Richmond) Scarves, beanies and jerseys with team colours and souvenirs from the home of Australian Rules Football. See MCG and National Sports Museum p. 145, 132 E3

Bread, pastries and provisions (Phillippa's, Armadale and Brighton, Melbourne) A small business that produces delicious baked goods. Highly recommended are the chocolate brownie and caramel, date and walnut blondie. 1030 High St, Armadale; 608 Hampton St, Brighton. 133 F5, 570 D7

Beach boxes souvenirs (The Esplanade Market St Kilda, Melbourne) Victoria's famous beach boxes are represented on fridge magnets, key holders, coasters and prints. See Markets p. 137, 132 D6

Stefano's products (Mildura) Dine at the acclaimed Stefano's restaurant and then take home jams, chutneys, pasta and pasta sauces. See Mildura p. 195, 558 E6

Wine (Yarra Valley and Mornington Peninsula) Fantastic chardonnay, pinot noir and sparkling varieties from these two wine-producing regions. See Yarra & Dandenongs p.148, 571 C6 and Mornington Peninsula p. 149, 573 I10

Red Hill muesli (Red Hill Market) This popular muesli comes in five different varieties including roast hazelnut, tropical and Wicked (with chocolate). See Flinders p. 179, 570 D12

Ned Kelly memorabilia (Glenrowan) Victoria's famous bushranger is remembered through everything from replicas of his head armour to belt buckles and T-shirts. See Glenrowan p. 180, 586 E5

Spa and skincare products (Hepburn Springs and Daylesford) The heart of Victoria's Spa Country offers a range of locally made beauty, spa and skincare products from shops and spa centres. See Spa & Garden Country p. 151, 579 E8

MELBOURNE is...

A footy match at the MCG / Admiring architecture and art in

FEDERATION SQUARE / Shopping for produce at the QUEEN VICTORIA

MARKET / A stroll along the ST KILDA foreshore / Taking a ferry trip to

WILLIAMSTOWN / Moonlight Cinema in the ROYAL BOTANIC GARDENS during

summer / Sweating it out in the crowd at the AUSTRALIAN OPEN / Stopping

for coffee in DEGRAVES STREET, one of the city's laneways / Live music at a

pub in FITZROY / Waterside dining at SOUTHGATE or NewQuay, DOCKLANDS

VISITOR INFORMATION
Melbourne Visitor Information Centre
→ Federation Sq, cnr Flinders and
Swanston sts
→ (03) 9658 9658
www.visitmelbourne.com

Melbourne is renowned as Australia's cultural capital. The city has a decidedly European feel, with neo-Gothic banks and cathedrals, much-loved department stores, art galleries and theatres around every corner. And hidden among these buildings is a string of vibrant laneways given over to cafe culture and boutique shopping. Yet Melbourne wouldn't be Melbourne without sport – seeing a footy match at the MCG is a must.

Melbourne was born in 1835, and quickly became a city. With the boom of Victoria's goldfields, unbelievable wealth was poured into public buildings and tramways, grand boulevards and High Victorian masterpieces.

Today Melbourne's population of around 3 893 000 still enjoys the good life, at the very centre of which is a love of good food and fine dining. You can find comfort food in a cosy corner pub or meals with a view and a waterfront setting – a trend in so many of the country's coastal cities. Southbank, the shopping and eating precinct on the Yarra River, has become an extension of the city centre, while Docklands is the city's latest waterside area.

You might come to Melbourne for the dining and the shopping; the gardens and the architecture; the arts and music; the football, cricket and tennis. The city has as much diversity as it has suburbs, and at last check these were marching right down the Mornington Peninsula.

MAP LEGEND

✪ Attraction

◆ Where to eat &
Where to stay

ℹ Tourist
information

Shopping precinct

PORT PHILLIP BAY

HOBSONS BAY

N

0   1 km

CBD Central

Melbourne's central business district (CBD) lies on the north bank of the Yarra River. The train system runs a ring around the CBD and trams amble up and down most of its main streets. Melbourne's heart is bounded by Flinders, Elizabeth, Little Bourke and Russell streets. This central core takes in the eclectic corner of Swanston and Flinders streets, and further in there's a charming network of arcades and backstreets.

A station, a pub and a cathedral 134 C4

As the major train station in the CBD, **Flinders Street Station** is the first port of call for many people travelling in from the suburbs.

On the three corners facing the station are three other landmarks: Federation Square *(see next entry)*, St Paul's Cathedral and the **Young and Jackson Hotel**. Across Swanston Street, the grandiose **St Paul's Cathedral** was built in 1891. Its mosaic interior is well worth a look.

Federation Square 134 C4

Federation Square is the biggest building project to occur in Melbourne in decades – if not in actual size, then at least in terms of its public significance and architectural ambition. The central piazza is paved with 7500 square metres of coloured Kimberley sandstone. Surrounding it are bars, cafes, restaurants and shops, many of them with unique views over Flinders Street Station and the Yarra. Down by the river, Federation Wharf is home to Rentabike *(see Getting around, p. 135)* and a departure point for river cruises *(see Walks & tours, p. 142)*. Fed Square's must-visit attractions are the Ian Potter Centre: NGV Australia and the Australian Centre for the Moving Image *(see below)*.

Ian Potter Centre: NGV Australia 134 C4

Australian art has finally found a home of its own at this gallery. On the ground floor is a large space dedicated to Indigenous art – from traditional sculptures and bark paintings to the bright and expressive works of modern Aboriginal artists. Also in the gallery are the best of the colonial artists, such as Tom Roberts and Arthur Streeton. The new NGV Kids Corner is one of the city's best destinations for pre-schoolers. *Federation Sq; (03) 8620 2222; open 10am–5pm Tues–Sun; general admission free. The National Gallery of Victoria's international collection can be found on St Kilda Rd (see p. 140).*

Australian Centre for the Moving Image (ACMI) 134 C4

ACMI is a museum of the 21st century and an Australian first, exploring all current guises of the moving image. Here you will find cinemas screening films and darkened galleries with screen-based art, as well as temporary exhibitions. Check the newspapers for details of films running or visit the website (www.acmi.net.au). *Federation Sq; (03) 8663 2200, bookings (03) 8663 2583; open 10am–6pm daily, open later for scheduled film screenings; general admission free.*

Swanston Street 134 C3, C4

Your experience of Swanston Street can be totally different depending on which side of the road you walk on. One side of the street is a grand boulevard lined with trees, and dotted with significant buildings and quirky public sculptures. The other side (the west side) seems overcrowded with discount stores, souvenir shops and fast-food outlets. Swanston Street is closed to cars other than taxis.

On the corner of Swanston and Collins streets is the prominent **Melbourne Town Hall**, a venue for various public events including the Melbourne International Comedy Festival. Opposite is a statue of **Burke and Wills**, the two explorers who set out on a doomed journey to find the fabled inland sea. On the corner of Bourke Street is the quirky sculpture, *Three Businessmen Who Brought Their Own Lunch*. Swanston Street also boasts some fine historic buildings *(see Grand old buildings, p. 139)*, and further north is the State Library of Victoria *(see p. 138)*.

Collins Street 134 C4, D3

This is Melbourne's most dignified street. The top end near Spring Street has been dubbed the 'Paris end' with its European ambience and designer boutiques. Near Elizabeth Street is

VICTORIA

climate

'Four seasons in one day' is a familiar phrase to all Melburnians. It might reach 38°C in the morning then drop to 20°C in the afternoon – and the weather the next day is anyone's guess. Generally though, winter is cold – daytime temperatures of 11–12°C are not unusual – and spring is wet. January and February are hot, with temperatures anywhere between the mid-20s and high 30s. The favourite season of many locals is autumn, when the weather is usually dry and stable.

J	F	M	A	M	J	J	A	S	O	N	D	
25	25	23	20	16	14	13	14	17	19	21	24	MAX °C
14	14	13	10	8	6	5	6	7	9	11	12	MIN °C
48	47	50	57	56	49	47	50	58	66	59	59	RAIN MM
5	5	6	8	9	9	9	9	10	10	8	7	RAIN DAYS

Australia on Collins, where you will find all the big names in Australian fashion as well as a ground-floor food court. Towards Spencer Street are impressive buildings, such as the Old ANZ Bank (*see Grand old buildings, p. 139*).

Laneways and arcades 134 C3, C4

From Flinders Street Station to Bourke Street Mall, you can slip through a world of cafes, fashion boutiques and jewellers, many of them selling one-off items that you just won't find in malls and department stores. But it is also worth it for the walk alone – narrow, darkened and usually bustling, these laneways seem to be a completely separate world to the rest of the city.

The section of **Degraves Street** closest to Flinders Lane is closed to cars and is full of cafes spilling onto the paved street. Across from Degraves Street is **Centre Place**, with more cafes as well as bars and designer-fashion outlets. Towards Collins Street, Centre Place becomes a covered arcade.

Block Arcade runs between Collins and Little Collins streets. It boasts Italian mosaic floors, ornate glass ceilings, tearooms and exclusive clothing boutiques. Follow the arcade to Elizabeth Street, or to the laneway that joins it to Little Collins Street, where there are yet more cafes.

Over Little Collins Street is **Royal Arcade**, Australia's oldest surviving arcade. Above the Little Collins Street entrance stand two giants, **Gog and Magog**, of the ancient British legend. You can take Royal Arcade to either Bourke Street Mall or Elizabeth Street. (To get to the mall you can also take the adjacent, cafe-lined **Causeway**.)

Recent building works in the city, such as the GPO development in Bourke Street Mall (*see next entry*), the renovation of Melbourne Central (*see p. 139*) and the QV site (*see p. 138*), have opened up more of the old laneways, restoring the original vision of Melbourne's designer, Robert Hoddle.

Bourke Street Mall 134 C3

Bourke Street Mall is the heart of Melbourne's shopping district, with big department stores and brand-name fashion outlets. Between Elizabeth and Swanston streets the mall is closed to cars, making it the territory of trams and pedestrians.

The **Myer** and **David Jones** department stores both have entrances on the mall. Myer, in particular, is renowned for its fine window displays at Christmas. At the west end of the mall is **Melbourne's GPO**, once the city's post office but now a smart shopping complex showcasing a who's who of fashion labels, cafes and bars. If you fancy a break from shopping, grab a seat along the mall and watch life wander by. More often than not there will be a busker performing for your entertainment.

Art spaces 134 C4

Flinders Lane is home to a terrific array of art galleries (*see Flinders Lane galleries, p. 137*), including the **Anna Schwartz Gallery**. With exhibitions that draw on a wide variety of art forms and often push the envelope, expect to be surprised and delighted, especially if you're into conceptual art. On the corner of Flinders Lane and Swanston Street, the **Nicholas Building** is an important address in the Melbourne arts scene, home to numerous, small, artist-run spaces. *Anna Schwartz Gallery: 185 Flinders La; (03) 9654 6131; open 12–6pm Tues–Fri, 1–5pm Sat; admission free.*

CBD West

This part of Melbourne stretches from the Queen Victoria Market down to the Yarra River, taking in the city's legal district including the Supreme Court of Victoria on William Street. Bounded by Spencer Street to the west, the old Spencer Street train station was replaced in 2006 with the architecturally superb Southern Cross Railway Station. It is worth a visit even if you're not planning a train ride.

 getting around

Melbourne's trams are an icon, but also a very good way of getting around the city. The City Circle tram is free and extends to Docklands. Trams depart every 12 minutes between 10am and 6pm from Sunday to Wednesday, and till 9pm from Thursday to Saturday. Other (paid) services head out into the suburbs, with especially good coverage of the eastern, south-eastern and northern suburbs. A map of the different services can be found inside most trams.

Trains are generally a faster option if there is a service that goes to your destination. Details of services can be found at each of the five stations in the CBD (*see map on p. 134*).

Buses tend to cover the areas that trains and trams don't service. The free Melbourne City Tourist Shuttle is a hop-on, hop-off bus service stopping at 13 key city destinations. The service runs every 30 minutes between 9.30am and 4.30pm daily and includes an informative on-board commentary. Details of routes and stops can be found at www.thatsmelbourne.com.au, or pick up a brochure from the Melbourne Visitor Information Centre at Federation Square.

Melbourne's public transport system is progressively moving from Metcard tickets to plastic myki smart cards. Initially, myki will only be available for train travel. While this is happening you will notice two types of ticketing equipment on the train, tram and bus networks. The price of your journey will depend on which of the two 'zones' you need to travel to. For an update on ticketing and an excellent journey planner facility, see www.metlinkmelbourne.com.au

For drivers, the much-talked-about feature of Melbourne's roads is the hook-turn, a process of moving to the left of the road in order to turn right, and therefore getting out of the way of trams. If you wish to use the tollways CityLink or the new EastLink, either an e-TAG or a day pass is required (there are no tollbooths, but day passes can be purchased over the phone either before or after making a journey).

Public transport Tram, train and bus information line 13 1638.

Airport shuttle bus Skybus (03) 9335 2811.

Tollways CityLink 13 2629; EastLink 13 5465.

Motoring organisation RACV 13 7228, roadside assistance 13 1111.

Car rental Avis 13 6333; Budget 1300 362 848; Hertz 13 3039; Thrifty 1300 367 227.

Taxis 13CABS 13 2227; Silver Top 13 1008; West Suburban (03) 9689 1144.

Water taxi Melbourne Water Taxis 0416 068 655.

Tourist buses AAT Kings (03) 9663 3377; Australian Pacific Tours 1300 655 965.

Bicycle hire Rentabike @ Federation Square 0417 339 203; Bike Now (South Melbourne) (03) 9696 8588; St Kilda Cycles (03) 9534 3074.

VICTORIA

top events

Australian Open One of the world's four major tennis Grand Slams. January.

Australian Grand Prix The first round of the FIA World Championships. March.

Melbourne Food and Wine Festival Eat your way through Melbourne and regional Victoria. March–April.

Melbourne International Comedy Festival Just as many laughs as in Edinburgh and Montreal. April.

Melbourne International Film Festival Features, shorts and experimental pieces from around the world. July–August.

AFL Grand Final The whole city goes footy-mad. September.

Melbourne International Arts Festival Visual arts, theatre, dance and music in indoor and outdoor venues. The alternative Melbourne Fringe Festival is held around the same time. October.

Melbourne Cup The pinnacle of the Spring Racing Carnival. November.

Boxing Day Test Boxing Day in Melbourne wouldn't be the same without this cricket match. December.

Hardware Lane 134 B3

Sitting between Bourke and Lonsdale streets, west of Bourke Street Mall, Hardware Lane comes alive at lunchtime and in the evening when office workers and bar seekers crowd the outdoor tables. The cobblestone paving, the window boxes and the brightly painted facades of the old buildings add to the atmosphere.

Former Royal Mint 134 B3

Two blocks north-west of the Supreme Court of Victoria, the Old Royal Mint was built in Renaissance Revival style, set off by a dazzling coat of arms. Originally constructed to mint the bounty from Victoria's goldfields, it operated until 1968 and is now home

shopping

Bourke Street Mall, City With department stores Myer and David Jones as well as the swish Melbourne's GPO. 134 C3

Collins Street, City Glamorous shopping strip with the big names in high-end fashion. Check out the boutique-style shopping on adjacent Flinders Lane and Little Collins Street too. 134 C4, D3

Melbourne Central and QV, City These two nearby precincts are a shopper's paradise. 134 C3

Chapel Street, South Yarra Where shopping is an event to dress up for. 132 E5

DFO, South Warf Shopping mall of factory outlets for bargain hunters. 134 A5

Southgate, Southbank A classy range of clothing, art and gifts. 134 C4

Bridge Road, Richmond Back-to-back factory outlets and designer warehouses. 133 F3

Brunswick Street, Fitzroy Unique fashion boutiques and giftshops. 132 E2, E3

to the **Hellenic Museum**, which holds items from the Byzantine period and displays related to Greek migration to Australia. *Cnr William and Latrobe sts; (03) 8615 9016; open 10am–3pm Tues–Thurs.*

Melbourne Aquarium 134 B5

Beside the Yarra River, take a journey into the depths of the ocean, past rockpool and mangrove habitats and a surreal display of jellyfish, then into a tunnel and the 'fishbowl' for a close-up encounter with sharks, stingrays and multitudes of fish. The **Antarctica** exhibition, featuring King and Gentoo penguins among other Antarctic creatures, is a must-see. *Cnr King and Flinders sts; (03) 9923 5999; open 9.30am–6pm daily.*

Immigration Museum 134 B4

At first glance this might seem like a specialist museum, but no subject could be more generally relevant in Australia, where migration has been constant since the first days of European settlement. The Immigration Museum is about journeys, tumultuous new beginnings, and people coming from all corners of the world and bringing their traditions with them. It also investigates Australia's changing government policies on immigration, and how they continue to shape the country. *400 Flinders St; (03) 9927 2700; open 10am–5pm daily.*

Koorie Heritage Trust Cultural Centre 134 A3

As you walk through this centre you realise the drastic, violent and totally irreversible changes made to a culture over 40 000 years old. Displays take you through the local traditions and lifestyle, including food and crafts, as well as events that have occurred in the last two centuries. There are also changing exhibitions by local Aboriginal artists. *295 King St; (03) 8622 2600; open 10am–4pm daily; entry by donation.*

Queen Victoria Market 134 B2

This famous market is spread across 7 hectares under the shelter of a massive shed. The meat hall is at the Elizabeth Street end, while outside all manner of fruit, vegetable and herb stalls extend towards the horizon. On weekends, Saturdays in particular, the aisles are crammed with shoppers from all over Melbourne, and the wide range of clothing and souvenirs make this a hot spot for tourists as well. *Main entrance cnr Elizabeth and Victoria sts; (03) 9320 5822; open 6am–2pm Tues and Thurs, 6am–5pm Fri, 6am–3pm Sat, 9am–4pm Sun.*

On Wednesday evenings during summer, the 'Queen Vic' takes on a whole new character with the **Suzuki Night Market**. At these times it feels more like a festival than a market, with live music, international food and a healthy dose of alternative-clothing and craft stalls.

Flagstaff Gardens 134 A2

Originally known as Burial Hill – many of Melbourne's early settlers ended up here –Flagstaff Gardens were Melbourne's first public gardens and once served as a signalling station for ships arriving from Britain. With open lawns, mature trees (including several lovely Moreton Bay fig trees and avenues of elms), a rose garden, public barbecues and tennis/netball/handball/volleyball courts, it is a lovely space in which to enjoy some time out from the city bustle. *Bounded by William, Latrobe, King and Dudley sts; sports bookings (03) 9663 5888.*

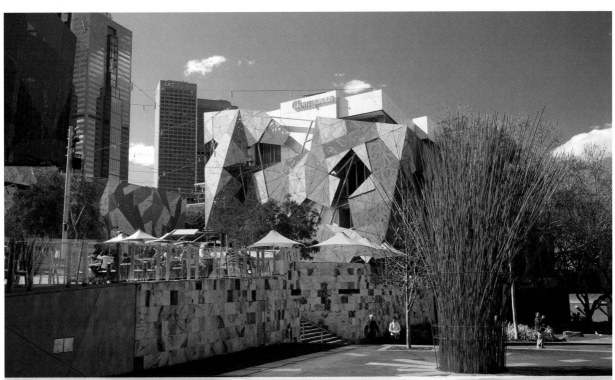

[RED CENTRE SCULPTURE, FEDERATION SQUARE]

CBD East

This is Melbourne's most distinguished quarter, taking in some fine old buildings and the government district. The Parliament of Victoria occupies a suitably prominent position on Spring Street at the top of a hill. At the top end of Collins Street is the Melbourne Club, where Melbourne's male elite have been socialising and doing business since the city's earliest days.

Parliament of Victoria 134 D3

The Parliament of Victoria is perched atop a grand run of steps, which are a popular spot for wedding photos. Built in stages between 1856 and 1929, the building remains incomplete – an ornate dome in the centre was originally supposed to be double its height. From 1901 to 1927 this was the seat of federal government before it moved to Canberra. Free tours of the building run on days when parliament is not sitting; sitting dates are published on the parliament's website (www.parliament.vic.gov.au). *Spring St, facing Bourke St; (03) 9651 8911.*

The imposing structure just south of parliament facing Collins St is the **Old Treasury Building**. In a similar style and often mistaken for the parliamentary building, it is now home to the Victorian Marriage Registry and glamorous wedding parties can often be seen posing for photos on the steps.

Flinders Lane galleries 134 C4, D3

This laneway boasts the highest concentration of commercial galleries in Australia, mainly in the section between Spring and Swanston streets. There is a strong focus on Indigenous and contemporary art, with standout galleries including **Flinders Lane Gallery**, exhibiting emerging and established Australian contemporary artists; **Gallery Gabrielle Pizzi**, with Aboriginal

art from many of Australia's lesser known regions; and **Craft Victoria**, with an excellent gallery and retail space fostering creativity in craft and design. *Flinders Lane Gallery: 137 Flinders La; (03) 9654 3332; open 11am–6pm Tues–Fri, 11am–4pm Sat. Gallery Gabrielle Pizzi: Level 3, 75 Flinders La; (03) 9654 2944; open 10am–5.30pm Tues–Fri, 12–4pm Sat. Craft Victoria: 31 Flinders La; (03) 9650 7775; open 12–5pm Mon, 10am–5pm Tues–Sat; admission free.*

markets

Sunday Market, Southbank Crafts galore, leading from the Arts Centre. 134 C4

The Esplanade Market St Kilda Melbourne's oldest art and craft market, with over 150 artisans. Sun. 132 D6

Collingwood Children's Farm – Farmers' Market Victorian produce, from free-range eggs to fresh fruit and vegetables, in a lovely bushland setting on the Yarra. 2nd Sat each month. 133 F3

South Melbourne Market Produce, deli items, clothing and homewares. Wed and Fri–Sun. 132 D4

Flemington Racecourse Market Art, craft and regional produce. 3rd Sun each month. 132 B2

CERES Market Count your organic food miles as you shop at this community-run environmental park in Brunswick East. Cafe, nursery and inspiration for greening your life. Wed and Sat. 132 E1

Camberwell Market Melbourne's best trash and treasure event. Sun. 573 J6

St Andrews Market Laid-back market with alternative crafts, foods, music and clothing, an hour's drive from the city. Sat. 573 K4

See also Queen Victoria Market, p. 136, and Prahran Market, p. 142

VICTORIA

entertainment

Cinema The major cinemas in the city are Hoyts in Melbourne Central's On3 entertainment floor and Greater Union in Russell Street. For arthouse films, try Kino Cinemas in Collins Place. Standout cinemas in the inner-city area include: Cinema Nova in Carlton for a great range of popular and arthouse films; Village Jam Factory in South Yarra or Village in the Crown Entertainment Complex for a Hollywood-style experience; the Rivoli in Camberwell for an old-world cinema experience; and the Astor in St Kilda East, where they play re-runs of the classics and recent releases. See daily newspapers for details.

Live music Melbourne is renowned for its live-music scene. Fitzroy is one of the major centres of original music, with venues like Bar Open and the Evelyn hosting bands most nights. Further north is the Northcote Social Club, venue for local and international acts. On the south side of town is The Esplanade Hotel in St Kilda, one of Melbourne's best original rock venues, and in Richmond there's the Corner Hotel, showing many local acts. Other venues dabble in jazz but Bennetts Lane Jazz Club, off Little Lonsdale Street, is the real deal. For a boogie to anything from reggae to funk, try the relaxed and lamplit Night Cat in Johnston Street, Fitzroy. Bigger local and international acts play at other venues around town. Pick up one of the free street publications, *Beat* or *Inpress*, or get the 'EG' lift-out from *The Age* on Fridays.

Classical music and performing arts The Theatres Building at the Arts Centre is Melbourne's premier venue for theatre, opera and ballet, and Hamer Hall, next door, is the venue for classical music concerts. The new Melbourne Recital Centre is a world-class chamber music venue. Popular musicals and theatrical productions are held at the Regent, Her Majesty's and Princess theatres. The Malthouse Theatre company and the Melbourne Theatre Company (MTC) host plays, and La Mama in Carlton is the venue for more experimental works. Check out the arts section of *The Age* for details. Most performances are booked through Ticketmaster and Ticketek.

where to eat

Chocolate Buddha Quick and delicious modern Japanese served at long communal tables overlooking Federation Square's piazza. Federation Square, cnr Flinders and Swanston sts; (03) 9654 5688. 134 C4

Degraves Espresso Excellent coffee, breakfasts and lunches served amidst stylishly 'distressed' decor or outside at a laneway table. 23–25 Degraves St; (03) 9654 1245. 134 C4

Flower Drum Melbourne's iconic Cantonese restaurant, with dishes such as crayfish with ginger and their famous Peking duck. 17 Market La; (03) 9662 3655. 134 C3

Pellegrini's Espresso Bar The city's original Italian eatery, where the pasta arrives only minutes after ordering and the ice-cold granitas are always good. 66 Bourke St; (03) 96621885. 134 D3

Vue de monde Watch super-chef Shannon Bennett and staff prepare some of the best food in Australia in this chic city dining room. 430 Little Collins St; (03) 9691 3888; open Tues–Fri for lunch and Tues–Sat for dinner. 134 B4

CBD North

This part of town is occupied mainly by office buildings, but there are some interesting places among them, such as the Old Melbourne Gaol, the State Library of Victoria, Chinatown, and the QV shopping and food precinct.

QV 134 C3

Occupying the block between Swanston, Lonsdale, Russell and Little Lonsdale streets, QV is divided up into a series of laneways. You can weave through here at your leisure, maybe stopping in at one of the cafes or go shopping with a purpose: high-end fashion stores line Albert Coates Lane, while Artemis Lane is a wonderland of homewares. You can also explore Red Cape and Jane Bell lanes. (The medical-themed lane names relate to the site's history – QV was once the site of the Queen Victoria Women's Hospital, a part of which still remains.) When you've finished shopping, step into one of QV's various eateries. *Open 10am–6pm Mon–Wed and Sat, 10am–7pm Thurs, 10am–9pm Fri, 10am–5pm Sun.*

State Library of Victoria 134 C2

The State Library of Victoria's front steps and lawn make a great spot for soaking up the sun. In fact, pre–Fed Square, this was the city centre's biggest public space and the main meeting spot for demonstrations. On the third floor of the Roman-style building is an impressive five-storey octagonal reading room, restored to its original sky-lit splendour. The library also incorporates several art galleries and is now home to the Wheeler Centre: Books, Writing and Ideas, the centerpiece of Melbourne's UNESCO City of Literature Initiative. This new hub for Victoria's literary community hosts a year-round program of talks, readings and debates. *Cnr Lonsdale and Swanston sts; (03) 8664 7000; open 10am–9pm Mon–Thurs, 10am–6pm Fri–Sun.*

Old Melbourne Gaol 134 C2

Melbourne Gaol was the setting for the execution of some of early Victoria's most notorious criminals. Discover the horrifying reality of death masks and the *Particulars of Execution*, a how-to book on this gruesome subject. If you are brave enough, join a candle-lit Hangman's Night Tour (conducted four times weekly at 8.30pm, 7.30pm in winter) or a ghost hunt (held monthly); contact Ticketek (13 2849) for bookings. *Russell St, between Victoria and Latrobe sts; (03) 8663 7228; open 9.30am–5pm daily; at 12.30pm and 2pm Sat the story of Ned Kelly, 'Such a Life', is performed (free with entry).*

Chinatown 134 C3

Chinatown has prospered and flourished since the first Chinese migrated to Victoria at the beginning of the gold rush. Decorated archways herald the entrance to the Little Bourke Street strip at the Swanston, Russell and Exhibition street ends. Like Chinatowns around the world, Melbourne's Chinatown is distinctive, with lanterns decorating the street at night and exotic aromas drifting out through the doorways of small restaurants.

The **Chinese Museum**, in Cohen Place off Little Bourke Street, tells the tale of the Chinese who migrated to Australia in search of the 'New Gold Mountain', and is also the resting place of Dai

Loong (Big Dragon), which roams the streets during Chinese New Year. *22 Cohen Pl; (03) 9662 2888; open 10am–5pm daily.*

Lonsdale Street 134 C3

The section of Lonsdale Street between Russell and Swanston streets is the centre of Melbourne's Greek community. On the southern side are Greek bookshops, music stores and, of course, cafes and restaurants.

Melbourne Central 134 C3

The Melbourne Central shopping complex has undergone a major facelift, with some serious thought given to the way Melburnians like to shop. The central shot tower and pointed glass ceiling remain, but it now offers less of a one-stop shopping experience and more of an adventure through a network of arcades and laneways. But this is not so much an innovation as a restoration of Melbourne as it was intended to be. An underground shopping concourse leads from the Lonsdale Street entrance to Melbourne Central Station. *Open 10am–6pm Mon–Thurs and Sat, 10am–9pm Fri, 10am–5pm Sun.*

Southbank

This inner-city suburb takes in some of Melbourne's best leisure and dining precincts, as well as a concentration of public arts institutions. Behind Flinders Street Station is Southgate, a stylish shopping and dining area on the Yarra River. On the riverbanks here are also some interesting public sculpture pieces.

Eureka Tower 134 C5

Standing 300 metres and 92 storeys high, the Eureka Tower is Melbourne's tallest building and boasts the Southern Hemisphere's highest viewing platform. This structure is a particularly prominent feature of Melbourne's city skyline due to the 24-carat, gold-plated glass across the top ten levels. On the 88th floor, **Eureka Skydeck 88** offers the ultimate 360-degree view of the city, bay and mountains. Viewfinders placed around the deck pinpoint major attractions. For a heart-stopping experience, step inside The Edge, a 3-metre glass cube that projects out of the side of the building. On the ground floor is the Serendipity Table, with information on the history of Melbourne. *7 Riverside Quay, Southbank; (03) 9693 8888; open 10am–10pm daily.*

Southgate 134 C4

Over 15 years ago, Southgate was just like Docklands *(see p. 142)* – an industrial site being slowly reinvented. Apartments, office blocks, shops, restaurants and a tree-lined promenade have been added to form what is today an essential part of Melbourne.

On the ground floor of the complex is a food court and shops. As you make your way to the top, the restaurants and bars become increasingly exclusive and the shops become boutiques selling glassware, art and jewellery. Some of Melbourne's finest restaurants are located on the top floors.

grand old buildings

Old ANZ Bank Known as the Gothic Bank, with an incredible, gold-leafed interior and a banking museum. 380 Collins St.

Manchester Unity Building Chicago-style building with stark vertical lines, once the city's tallest skyscraper. Cnr Collins and Swanston sts.

Capitol Theatre Designed by the architects of Canberra with a ceiling that will amaze you. 109–117 Swanston St.

St Patrick's Cathedral Victoria's largest church building, built with tonnes of Footscray bluestone. Cnr Gisborne St and Cathedral Pl, East Melbourne.

Princess Theatre The dramatic exterior culminates in three domes with cast-iron tiaras. 163 Spring St.

Forum Theatre Moorish domes, and a starry night sky on the inner ceiling of the main theatre. Cnr Russell and Flinders sts.

St Paul's Cathedral Gothic cathedral made of sandstone. Cnr Flinders and Swanston sts.

Old Melbourne Magistrates' Court The rough sandstone exterior and deeply set archways make for a grim atmosphere. Cnr Russell and Latrobe sts.

Olderfleet Building An intricate Gotham City facade. Nearby is The Rialto, designed by the same architect. 477 Collins St.

Regent Theatre Melbourne's most glamorous theatre, with an interior of Spanish-style lattice and red carpet. 191 Collins St.

St James' Old Cathedral A humble relic of Melbourne's founding years. 419–435 King St.

University of Melbourne More historic buildings than you can count. Parkville.

Hotel Windsor Layered like a wedding cake and fit for a queen. 111 Spring St.

City Baths A feast of domes on the skyline, this building dates back to the days when bathrooms were a luxury few could afford. Cnr Swanston and Victoria sts.

See also Royal Exhibition Building, p. 144

where to stay

Langham Hotel Located riverside on Southbank Promenade, this world-class hotel enjoys spectacular city and river views with a superlative in-house Chuan Spa. 1 Southgate Ave; (03) 8696 8888. 134 C5

The Como In the heart of trendy South Yarra's fashion shopping strip, this intimate and discreet hotel is regarded by visiting celebrities as their 'home away from home'. 630 Chapel St, South Yarra; (03) 9825 2222. 133 F4

The Lyall Hotel A chic intimate property of just 40 suites in tree-lined fashionable South Yarra, it boasts a champagne bar, in-house spa and a plethora of restaurants nearby. 14 Murphy St, South Yarra; (03) 9868 8222. 132 E4

The Prince This glamorous hotel in bayside St Kilda dazzles with its innovative rooms, highly acclaimed restaurant, Circa, The Prince, and adjacent pampering Aurora Spa Retreat. 2 Acland St, St Kilda; (03) 9536 1111. 132 D6

The Westin Melbourne Situated centrally on City Square, the Westin enjoys the best location in town. It also boasts the chic Martini Bar, Wellness Centre and Allegro restaurant. 205 Collins St; (03) 9635 2222. 134 C4

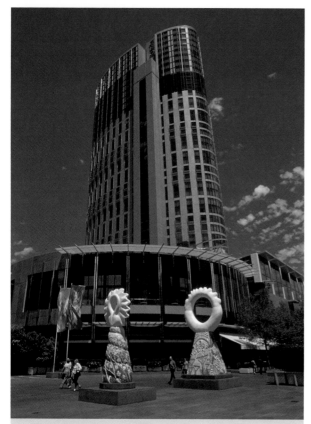

[SCULPTURES OUTSIDE CROWN CASINO]

Crown Entertainment Complex 134 B5

This huge complex begins just over Queensbridge Street. As well as a casino, Crown contains shops, a food court, nightclubs and cinemas. Restaurants include world-class dining such as Neil Perry's Rockpool Bar and Grill, Japanese restaurant Nobu and Silks for Chinese banquets. The big names in fashion such as Versace and Prada reside here too, and items regularly top the $1000 mark.

Melbourne Convention and Exhibition Centre 134 A5

Over Clarendon Street from Crown is the **Melbourne Convention and Exhibition Centre**, with its striking entrance angled upwards over the water. This is the venue for most of Melbourne's major expos, from car shows to wedding exhibitions. *2 Clarendon St, South Wharf; (03) 9235 8000.*

Next to the centre in Dukes Dock is the 1885 tall ship **Polly Woodside**. Following renovations in 2010, visitors will be able to step aboard the tall ship for a journey into Melbourne's maritime history. *See www.nattrust.com.au for opening details.*

The Arts Centre 134 C5

The Arts Centre, on St Kilda Road over Princes Bridge from Flinders Street Station, consists of two main buildings – **Hamer Hall** and the **Theatres Building**, with its distinctive lattice spire intended to resemble a ballerina's tutu. The Theatres Building plunges six levels below St Kilda Road and includes three theatres: the State Theatre, with seating for 2000 and a venue for opera, ballets and musicals; the Playhouse, for drama; and the George Fairfax Studio, a smaller drama venue.

If you are not heading to a concert or a theatre show, you can still visit **Gallery 1**, also under the spire. This is the main exhibition space for the **Performing Arts Collection**, which preserves a variety of Australian performing-arts memorabilia. *100 St Kilda Rd; (03) 9281 8000; open 8am–end of last performance daily; admission free.*

NGV International 134 C5

The large grey building next to the Arts Centre has been the home of the National Gallery of Victoria since 1968. After recent renovations, it now houses the gallery's highly regarded international component, including permanent and touring exhibitions. There are more than 30 galleries, a water curtain at the entrance that has become a Melbourne icon, and a magnificent stained-glass roof by Leonard French towards the back of the building. *180 St Kilda Rd; (03) 8620 2222; open 10am–5pm Wed–Mon; general admission free. NGV Australia can be found at Federation Square (see p. 133).*

museums

Jewish Museum of Australia   A record of the experiences of Australia's many Jewish migrants. 26 Alma Rd, St Kilda; (03) 8534 3600; open 10am–4pm Tues–Thurs, 10am–5pm Sun.

Montsalvat   An artists' colony that began in 1934; magnificent French provincial buildings and artworks for view in the gallery. 7 Hillcrest Ave, Eltham; (03) 9439 7712; open 9am–5pm daily.

ANZ Banking Museum   Old money boxes, staff uniforms, historic displays and an interactive ATM exhibit in the glorious Gothic setting of the Old ANZ Bank. 380 Collins St; open 10am–3pm Mon–Fri; admission free.

Ian Potter Museum of Art   An extensive art collection, including cultural artefacts and contemporary artworks. University of Melbourne, Swanston St, between Faraday and Elgin sts, Parkville; (03) 8344 5148; open 10am–5pm Tues–Fri, 12–5pm Sat–Sun; admission free.

Victoria Police Museum   Victoria's life of crime revealed, from the capture of Ned Kelly to the Hoddle Street shootings. Lower Concourse Level, World Trade Centre, 637 Flinders St; (03) 9247 5214; open 10am–4pm Mon–Fri; admission free.

Fire Services Museum   Huge collection of fire brigade memorabilia, including vintage vehicles and historic photos. 39 Gisborne St, East Melbourne; (03) 9662 2907; open 9am–3pm Thurs–Fri, 10am–4pm Sun.

ARHS Railway Museum   Open-air museum with historic locomotives. Champion Rd, North Williamstown; (03) 9397 7412; 12–5pm Sat, Sun and public holidays.

See also Melbourne Museum, p. 145, Melbourne Cricket Ground (MCG) and National Sports Museum, p. 145, Sturt Street arts, p. 141, Immigration Museum, p. 136, Koorie Heritage Trust Cultural Centre, p. 136, ACCA, p. 141, Heide Museum of Modern Art, p. 146, Ian Potter Centre: NGV Australia, p. 133, NGV International, this page, Australian Centre for the Moving Image, p. 133, Chinese Museum, p. 138, Flinders Lane galleries, p. 137, and Arts Centre, this page

Sturt Street arts 134 C5, C6

Behind St Kilda Road is Sturt Street, home to four arts institutions – the CUB Malthouse, the Australian Centre for Contemporary Art (ACCA) and the new Melbourne Recital Centre (MRC)/Melbourne Theatre Company (MTC) complex.

Once a malt factory, the **CUB Malthouse** has four theatres and is home to the Malthouse Theatre company, dedicated to contemporary theatre. Next door, the **ACCA** is housed in a rusted-steel building that is intended to resemble the colour of Uluṟu against a blue sky. Inside the stark structural forms are changing contemporary Australian and international exhibitions, quite often confronting and interactive. *CUB Malthouse: 113 Sturt St; bookings on (03) 9685 5111. ACCA: 111 Sturt St; (03) 9697 9999; open 10am–5pm Tues–Fri, 11am–6pm Sat–Sun and public holidays; admission free.*

Resembling a giant beehive in parts, the stunning new **Melbourne Recital Centre** gives ACCA a run for its money in the architectural stakes. Comprising the 1001-seat Elisabeth Murdoch Hall for chamber music, the 150-seat Salon for more intimate performances and public spaces including a cafe-bar, it's an exciting addition to Melbourne's arts precinct. The adjacent new home of the **Melbourne Theatre Company** is an equally fascinating, cutting-edge structure. *Cnr Sturt St and Southbank Blvd, Southbank; MRC bookings on (03) 9699 3333, MTC bookings on (03) 8688 0800.*

CBD South-east

Sidney Myer Music Bowl 134 D5

Set in the Kings Domain gardens, the iconic Sidney Myer Music Bowl is a massive grassy amphitheatre leading down to a stage, above which floats a soaring, tent-like roof. Much-loved by Melburnians for its annual Christmas extravaganza, Carols by Candlelight, it also hosts numerous other summertime events, including free concerts by the Melbourne Symphony Orchestra. Just fabulous for a champagne picnic on a starry summer's eve. *Linlithgow Ave, Kings Domain; (03) 9281 8000.*

Gardens 134 C6, 132 E4

Bordered by the curve of the Yarra and the bitumen of St Kilda Road is a series of public gardens, including Kings Domain and the Royal Botanic Gardens. In **Kings Domain** is the Sidney Myer Music Bowl *(see previous entry)* and the imposing **Shrine of Remembrance**. Deep within the shrine stands a statue of two soldiers, representing the generations of Australians who have fought in various wars around the world. You access the shrine from the chambers below, through the visitor centre. From the balcony at the top there are views straight down St Kilda Road. The shrine is the centre for ANZAC Day commemorations. *Birdwood Ave, South Yarra; (03) 9661 8100; open 10am–5pm daily; admission free.*

To the east of the shrine is **La Trobe's Cottage**, a prefabricated house built in England and brought to Australia for the residence of Victoria's first lieutenant governor. Tours of this structure and magnificent **Government House**, located nearby but hidden behind a tangle of vegetation, run from here on Mondays and Wednesdays. *Tour bookings (03) 8663 7260.*

Directly opposite the shrine, across Birdwood Avenue, is Observatory Gate, behind which are the renowned **Royal Botanic Gardens**. Inside the gate is a cafe and the Old Melbourne

parks and gardens

Birrarung Marr   Melbourne's newest park, with sculptural displays, a colourful playground and a bike track leading up to Federation Square. City. 134 D4

Albert Park   A great spot for exercising around the lake, and the site for the Australian Formula One Grand Prix. Albert Park. 132 D5

Gasworks Arts Park   Sculptures, native gardens, barbecues, a cafe and artist studios in the former South Melbourne Gasworks. Albert Park. 132 C5

Yarra Bend Park   Closest bushland to the city, with boats for hire, a golf course, great views and a strong Aboriginal heritage. Kew/Fairfield. 133 F2

Eltham Lower Park   Featuring the Diamond Valley Miniature Railway, which offers rides for kids on Sunday 11am–5pm. Eltham. 570 F5

Brimbank Park   With wetlands, a children's farm, a visitor centre with a cafe and walking trails along the Maribyrnong River. Keilor. 570 D5

Jells Park   A haven for waterbirds and a great place for a stroll through the bush. Wheelers Hill. 570 F7

Wattle Park   Native bush and birds, a nine-hole golf course and accessible by tram. Surrey Hills. 570 F6

Westerfolds Park   On the Yarra and popular for canoeing and cycling, with the Mia Mia Aboriginal Art Gallery on top of the hill. Templestowe. 570 F5

See also Royal Botanic Gardens, this page, Fitzroy Gardens, p. 145

Observatory. The visitor centre here has information on walks and activities in the gardens, including night tours at the observatory and the Aboriginal Heritage Walk *(see Walks & tours, p. 142)*. The **Children's Garden**, open from Wednesday to Sunday (daily during school holidays), was created as a fun and interactive space for kids, with a program of hands-on activities. In summer the botanic gardens also host **Moonlight Cinema**; programs are available around town, and the films on offer range from new releases to the classics.

If you are after a riverfront picnic spot, look just outside the botanic gardens across Alexandra Avenue. Free gas barbecues dot the Yarra bank from Swan Street Bridge to Anderson Street.

Melbourne and Olympic parks 132 E4

Between the city and the suburbs of Richmond and Abbotsford are Melbourne's biggest sporting venues, scattered on either side of the rail yards like giant resting UFOs. The two major ones are the **MCG** *(p. 145)* and **Melbourne Park**, incorporating the **Rod Laver** and **Hisense** arenas, and home of the Australian Open and big-ticket concerts. Heading towards Richmond, **AAMI Park** in the **Olympic Park** precinct is the home of Melbourne Rebels (Rugby Union), Melbourne Storm (Rugby League) and Melbourne Victory (soccer). *Olympic Blvd; (03) 9286 1600.*

Docklands

Melbourne's CBD is once again on the move, this time west across Spencer Street and the rail yards to Docklands. Until the 1960s this was a busy shipping port; now it is being transformed into a residential, business, entertainment and retail precinct, with nine mini neighbourhoods including NewQuay, Waterfront City and Victoria Harbour.

NewQuay and Waterfront City 132 C3

At the northern end of Docklands, the adjacent waterfront neighbourhoods of NewQuay and Waterfront City comprise high-rise apartments, offices, retail outlets, galleries, marinas and the bulk of Docklands' bars and restaurants. The precinct is home to **Wonderland Park**, with a host of rides for kids, and the impressive new **Icehouse**, a world-class ice sports and entertainment venue designed to resemble the fault line in a glacier. The Icehouse features a public skating rink with spectacular sound and lights, and a huge stadium for events such as ice hockey and figure skating. *1300 756 699; open daily; session times and events www.icehouse.com.au.*

The new **Harbour Town** shopping centre is home to a large range of brand outlets and fashion stores, while trash-and-treasure lovers will want to check out the weekly **Sunday Market** (10am–5pm).

Etihad Stadium 132 C3

A major venue for Australian Football League (AFL) games, other sporting events and concerts, Etihad Stadium is a Colosseum-like stadium with a retractable roof (very handy for when the weather is inclement). You can go on a 'Behind the Scenes' tour to inspect, among other things, the AFL players' change rooms and the coaches' box. The one-hour tours leave at 11am, 1pm and 3pm Monday to Friday from the Customer Service Centre opposite Gates 2 and 3. *Bounded by Bourke and Latrobe sts, Wurundjeri Way and Harbour Esplanade; tour bookings (03) 8625 7277.*

Art Journey 132 C3, C4

A self-guide urban art tour, the Art Journey takes you past more than 30 superb, large-scale public artworks, including the whimsical wind-powered **Blowhole**, the sublimely sculptural **Webb Bridge** for pedestrians and cyclists, and the amusing **Cow Up A Tree** (which is exactly that). You can also make use of the facilities along the way, including barbecues, recreation areas and a terrific children's playground. Pick up a copy of the Art Journey brochure from the Melbourne Visitor Information Centre, or download one from the Melbourne Docklands website (www.docklands.com.au).

Fox Classic Car Collection 132 C3

With its incredible collection of vintage cars, including Bentley, Jaguar, Rolls Royce and some ultra-cool Porsche and Mercedes Benz makes, the Fox Classic Car Collection has up to 50 vehicles on display at any given time. Located in the historic Queen's Warehouse building (originally built as a customs house). *Cnr Batmans Hill Dr and Collins St; (03) 9620 4086; open 10am–2pm Tues Feb–Nov.*

Inner South-east

Beyond the gardens south-east of the CBD are some of the city's most exclusive suburbs: South Yarra, Toorak, Malvern and Armadale. South Yarra and Toorak centre around Toorak Road, where exclusive clothing and footwear stores, as well as cafes and food shops, line the street. Chapel Street runs in the other direction, from South Yarra into St Kilda, and is virtually non-stop shops for three major blocks, from Toorak Road to Dandenong Road.

Chapel and Greville streets 132 E5

The northern end of Chapel Street, between Toorak and Commercial roads, is the place to come for the latest in fashion. About halfway down this stretch is the **Jam Factory**, a shopping complex and food court inside the old premises of the Australian Jam Company. Inside is a cinema complex that screens most of the new releases as well as some arthouse titles.

Just around the corner from Chapel Street on Commercial Road is the **Prahran Market**, Australia's oldest continually running market. *163 Commercial Rd, South Yarra;*

walks & tours

Golden Mile Heritage Trail   Walk with a guide or navigate this trail on your own. It leads from the Immigration Museum to Melbourne Museum, taking in historic buildings and heritage attractions along the way (walkers gain discounted entry to various places). Bookings on 1300 780 045, or buy a self-guide brochure from the Melbourne Visitor Information Centre at Federation Square. 10am daily.

Aboriginal Heritage Walk   With an Aboriginal guide and a gum leaf for a ticket, stroll through the Royal Botanic Gardens and learn about the bushfoods, medicines and traditional lore of the Boonerwrung and Woiwurrung people, whose traditional lands meet here. Bookings on (03) 9252 2429; 11am Thurs–Fri and some Sundays.

Hidden Secrets Tours   Various tours focusing on the city's innovative fashion, design and gourmet food culture. Bookings on (03) 9663 3358.

Haunted Melbourne Ghost Tours   Get the adrenaline pumping as you traipse down dark alleys and enter city buildings that the ghosts of early Melbourne are known to haunt. Bookings on (03) 9670 2585.

Chocoholic Tours   A range of tours to get you drooling, taking in Melbourne's best chocolatiers, candy-makers, ice-creameries and cafes. Bookings on (03) 9686 4655.

Harley Rides   Take the Introduction to Melbourne Tour, exploring the bay and over the West Gate Bridge with the wind whistling through your hair. Bookings on 1800 182 282; tours daily.

Foodies' Tours   Get tips on picking the best fresh produce, meet the specialist traders and taste samples from the deli at Queen Victoria Market. Bookings on (03) 9320 5822; 10am Tues and Thurs–Sat.

Carlton & United Brewery Tours   Free tastings of CUB draught beers are preceded by a tour around Abbotsford Brewery, the home of Fosters. Bookings (03) 9420 6800. 10am and 2pm Mon–Fri.

River Cruises   A trip down the Yarra or the Maribyrnong or across to Williamstown will give you new views of Melbourne. Melbourne River Cruises (03) 8610 2600, City River Cruises (03) 9650 2214, Williamstown Ferry (03) 9517 9444, Maribyrnong River Cruises (03) 9689 6431.

(03) 8290 8220; open dawn–5pm Tues, Thurs and Sat, dawn–6pm Fri, 10am–3pm Sun.

A little further up Chapel Street, Greville Street runs off to the west. The narrow strip is lined with cafes, bars, hip clothing shops and original occupants such as **Greville Records**.

Just south of Greville Street is **Chapel Street Bazaar**, a treasure trove for collectors. If the northern end of Chapel Street is the fashion darling, the Prahran/Windsor end, south of Commercial Road, is its more down-to-earth, homely sibling. Lined with dozens of interesting cafes, restaurants and shops, it is a fantastic stretch to browse and graze.

Como House and Herring Island 132 F4

Como House is a National Trust–listed mansion at the end of Williams Road. Stroll around the gardens and take a tour of the house, complete with the original furnishings of the Armytage family. You can visit the gorgeous cafe (open Wednesday to Sunday) without paying admission. Nearby is Como Landing, where you can take a punt across to Herring Island in the middle of the Yarra. This artificial island boasts a sculpture park and picnic/barbecue facilities. *Como House: cnr Williams Rd and Lechlade Ave, South Yarra; (03) 9827 2500; open 10am–4pm daily. Herring Island punt: 11am–5pm Sat–Sun during daylight saving.*

Inner North

Carlton and Fitzroy are two lively inner suburbs to the north and north-east of the city. Carlton is the heart of Victorian terrace territory, while Fitzroy is where many young Melburnians would choose to live if they could afford it. Smith Street, a major street to the east, is blossoming with cafes, health-food shops and independent fashion designers.

sport

Melbourne is possibly Australia's most sporting city, with hardly a gap in the calendar for the true sports enthusiast. **AFL** (Australian Football League) is indisputably at the top of the list. The season begins at the end of March and as it nears the finals in September, footy madness eclipses the city. Victoria has ten teams in the league, and the blockbuster matches are played at the **MCG** and **Etihad Stadium**.

After the football comes the **Spring Racing Carnival**, as much a social event as a horseracing one. October and November are packed with events at racetracks across the state, with the city events held at Caulfield, Moonee Valley, Sandown and Flemington racetracks. The Melbourne Cup, 'the race that stops the nation', is held at Flemington on the first Tuesday in November, and is a local public holiday.

Cricket takes Melbourne through the heat of summer. One Day International and Test matches are usually played at the MCG, and the popular Boxing Day Test gives Christmas in Melbourne a sporting twist.

In January Melbourne hosts the Australian Open, one of the world's four major **tennis** Grand Slams. The venue is **Melbourne Park**, home to the Rod Laver Arena and the Hisense Arena, both of which host other sporting events and concerts throughout the year.

Come March, and the **Australian Formula One Grand Prix** comes to town, attracting a large international crowd. The cars race around Albert Park Lake, which for the rest of the year is the setting for rather more low-key sporting pursuits such as jogging and rollerblading.

See also Melbourne Cricket Ground (MCG) and National Sports Museum, p. 145, and Melbourne and Olympic parks, p. 141

[ETERNAL FLAME, SHRINE OF REMEMBRANCE]

VICTORIA

[ST KILDA PIER AT SUNSET]

other suburbs

Brunswick Sydney Road is the place to come to for cheap fabrics, authentic Turkish bread and a healthy dose of Middle Eastern culture. 132 D1

Footscray A mini-Saigon that is the lesser-known version of Victoria Street, Abbotsford, now with a growing African flavour. Jam-packed with cheap eateries and one of Melbourne's best produce markets. 132 A2

Camberwell and Canterbury Melbourne's eastern money belt, with fashion outlets lining Camberwell's Burke Road, and the elegant Maling Road shopping precinct in Canterbury. 570 E6

Yarraville A gem tucked away in a largely industrial sweep of suburbs, with cafes and a superb Art Deco cinema. 132 A3

Hawthorn With a strong student culture from the nearby university, and a strip of shops on Glenferrie Road offering everything from Asian groceries to smart fashion. 570 E6

Balaclava Kosher butchers mixed with an emerging cafe culture. Here and neighbouring Elwood are the affordable alternatives to St Kilda. 133 F6

Black Rock One of many bayside suburbs shifting from a sleepy village into sought-after real estate, fronting two of Melbourne's best beaches. 573 J7

Dandenong The base for Melbourne's Indian community – with food stores galore and also one of Melbourne's oldest markets. 573 K7

Eltham All native trees and mud-brick architecture, this suburb feels like a piece of the country only 30 minutes from the city. 570 F5

Lygon Street, Carlton 132 D2

This is Carlton's main artery and the centre of Melbourne's Italian population, with many restaurants, cafes, bookstores, clothing shops and the excellent **Cinema Nova**. Stop for authentic pasta, pizza, gelato and good coffee at places such as **Brunetti**, on Faraday Street, an institution that is always crowded with Italian pastry lovers. You can also head to **Rathdowne Street**, parallel to Lygon Street, which has more cafes, restaurants and food stores.

Brunswick Street, Fitzroy 132 E2

Brunswick Street offers an eclectic mix of cafes, pubs and shops. Anything goes in Brunswick Street – young professionals come here for leisurely weekend breakfasts at cafes such as **Babka** and **Mario's**. This is a hot spot in Melbourne's live-music scene (*see Entertainment, p. 138*).

Royal Exhibition Building 134 D1

The Royal Exhibition Building is Melbourne's most significant historic building – and arguably the country's now that it has become Australia's first man-made structure to achieve World Heritage status. The building and the adjacent Carlton Gardens were admitted to the list in 2004, joining the likes of Uluṟu and the Great Barrier Reef.

A vast hall topped with a central dome, it is considered an enduring monument to the international exhibition movement that began in the mid-19th century. No comparable 'great halls' survive from other international exhibitions held elsewhere in the world.

At dusk each night the building is illuminated, creating a vista that harks back to the heady days of 1880s Melbourne. Tours to view its interior run from the adjacent Melbourne Museum *(see next entry)* at 2pm daily whenever the building is not in use (bookings 13 1102). The area comes alive during the Melbourne International Flower & Garden Show (March–April). *11 Nicholson St, Carlton.*

Melbourne Museum 134 D1

Melbourne Museum is housed in the spaceship-like structure of metal and glass next to the Royal Exhibition Building. It is the home of Phar Lap, Australia's champion racing horse, standing proud and tall in a dimly lit room. Bunjilaka is an Aboriginal cultural centre telling the Koorie story from the Koorie perspective. Other features of the museum include dinosaur skeletons, a living rainforest and impressive displays on science, the mind and the body. Located in the same building is the **IMAX Theatre**, screening films in 2D and 3D. *Melbourne Museum: Nicholson St, Carlton; 13 1102; open 10am–5pm daily.*

Melbourne Zoo 132 D2

This is Australia's oldest zoo, and the single iron-barred enclosure that remains is a testimony to the days when animals were kept in minuscule cages. Today things are rather different – take the Trail of the Elephants, for instance, where elephants live in a re-creation of an Asian rainforest, complete with an elephant-sized plunge pool (and Asian hawker stalls for visitors). Another perennial favourite here is the Butterfly House, where butterflies are quite happy to land on you as you pass through. From mid-January to mid-March the zoo runs a popular program of open-air, evening jazz sessions called Zoo Twilights. *Elliott Ave, Parkville; (03) 9285 9300; open 9am–5pm daily, to 9.30pm for Zoo Twilights.*

Inner East

Richmond and Abbotsford lie to the east of the city, and for both food and clothing the combination of quality and price here is hard to beat. Further out is a stretch of parkland that follows the winding path of the Yarra River.

Bridge Road, Richmond 133 F3

Bridge Road is Richmond's main artery, and between Hoddle and Church streets it is a shopper's heaven. Many a tour bus pulls up here, with shoppers pouring into the designer-clothing stores and factory outlets. In the next block, between Church and Burnley streets, is a strip of reasonably priced restaurants offering various cuisines. Swan Street, south of Bridge Road, is another good spot for wining and dining, and features the **Corner Hotel**, staging local bands.

Victoria Street, Abbotsford 133 F3

Victoria Street, north of Bridge Road, is a living, breathing piece of Vietnam. From Hoddle Street to Church Street it overflows with Asian grocery stores and Vietnamese restaurants, where the focus is on authentic food, fast.

Melbourne Cricket Ground (MCG) and National Sports Museum 132 E3

A footy or cricket match at the MCG (or the 'G' as it is locally called) would have to be one of Melbourne's top experiences. But if you visit in the off-season or simply can't get enough sport in your system, then you can take a tour on non-event days, 10am–3pm, from Gate 3 in the Olympic Stand. Tour prices can include entry to the MCG's interactive National Sports Museum. Some of the 3500 artefacts include swimmer Ian Thorpe's swimsuit, the inaugural Brownlow Medal, legendary cricketer Sir Don Bradman's baggy green cap and Bart Cummings' 12 Melbourne Cups. Visitors can also try out their own sporting skills in the 'Game On' room. *Brunton Ave, Richmond; open 10am–5pm daily; (03) 9657 8879.*

Fitzroy Gardens 132 E3

Fitzroy Gardens, bounded by Albert, Clarendon and Lansdowne streets and Wellington Parade, are one of a handful of public gardens surrounding the CBD, but the only one that can boast **Cooks' Cottage**, a fairy tree and a model Tudor village. *Cook's Cottage: (03) 9419 4677; open 9am–5pm daily.*

Yarra Bend Park 133 F2

Yarra Bend Park is a bushland sanctuary that feels far, far away from the city even though it is, in fact, just a few minutes' drive from it. It features walking tracks and a golf course, and boat-hire facilities at the historic **Studley Park Boathouse**. Go boating on the river, then dock for a spot of Devonshire tea. *Off Studley Park Rd, Kew; (03) 9853 1828; boathouse and kiosk open 9am–5pm daily.*

Bayside

Melbourne's eastern bayside suburbs sprawl down towards the Mornington Peninsula. At the top of the bay is Port Melbourne, once the entry point for many thousands of migrants and now the docking point for Spirit of Tasmania ferries. Port Melbourne's Bay Street has a range of pubs, shops and cafes, as does Clarendon Street, South Melbourne. On Coventry Street is the South Melbourne Market and south of here is Albert Park, the venue for the Australian Formula One Grand Prix each March as well as a spot for jogging and boating. Various other sports are also on offer in Albert Park's Melbourne Sports and Aquatic Centre. Further south again is St Kilda.

St Kilda 132 D6

St Kilda began life as a seaside holiday destination, so separate from the city that on the sandy track that was then St Kilda Road, travellers ran the risk of a run-in with a bushranger.

Fitzroy Street is a long line of shoulder-to-shoulder cafes, restaurants, bars and pubs. Straight ahead is the palm-lined foreshore and the beach, and around the corner is the much-loved **St Kilda Pier** with its historic kiosk that offers great views and quality food.

The path along the foreshore goes from Port Melbourne in the north to beyond Brighton in the south and is often busy with cyclists, rollerbladers and walkers. **The Esplanade Hotel** is an integral part of Melbourne's live-music scene, and **The Palais**, a grand, French-style theatre, is the venue for concerts. Luna Park *(see next entry)* is next door to The Palais, and there is an arts and crafts market on The Esplanade every Sunday *(see Markets, p. 137).*

Just around the corner from The Esplanade are the continental cake shops that have made **Acland Street** famous.

South from St Kilda is a string of swimming beaches, including **Brighton Beach** with its trademark colourful bathing boxes and views of the city. **Rippon Lea Estate**, on Hotham Street in Elsternwick, is a grand Romanesque mansion set in beautiful gardens and open daily.

Luna Park 132 E6

While it is now appropriately modernised, Luna Park still feels like a chunk of the early 20th century, when a ride on the Scenic Railway rollercoaster was a big night out. Since it opened in 1912, many things about the park have lived on, including the huge and famous (and much-renovated) face that forms its entrance. Among the traditional rides such as the carousel, Ferris wheel and rollercoaster are the more modern Shock Drop, Enterprise and G Force. *Lower Esplanade, St Kilda; (03) 9525 5033; see www.lunapark.com.au for monthly operating hours.*

Western Bayside

Williamstown 132 A6

Travel over the West Gate Bridge and you'll find a landscape of factories and new suburbs. But south of the bridge, on the western arm of Hobsons Bay, is Williamstown – one of Melbourne's true gems. Bobbing up and down in its harbour are a fleet of yachts, and along Nelson Place are restaurants, bars and cafes in old maritime buildings. Williamstown's main beach is around the other side of the bay. For those after an alternative to driving, there is a ferry service to Williamstown from St Kilda and Southgate, with an optional stop at Scienceworks *(see next entry)*. For information on the ferry, see Walks and tours, p. 142.

Scienceworks 132 A4

This is the place to come to 'push it, pull it, spin it, bang it', and inadvertently get a grasp on science. It is a great place to bring the kids, with interactive exhibitions on all things science-related. Also in the complex is the **Melbourne Planetarium**, with simulated night skies and 3D adventures through space. A historic pumping station is located on site, and tours are available. *2 Booker St, Spotswood; 13 1102; open 10am–5pm daily.*

North-east

Heide Museum of Modern Art 573 J5

Surrounded by beautiful parklands and intriguing sculptures, this complex was formerly home to museum founders John and Sunday Reed. The Reeds emerged as patrons of the arts in the 1930s and 40s, and today the support for modern art continues in the museum, which has changing exhibitions in its three galleries. Sunday Reed's original kitchen garden lives on and supplies produce to the new restaurant, Café Vue at Heide, operated by renowned chef Shannon Bennett of Vue de monde. *7 Templestowe Rd, Bulleen; (03) 9850 1500; open 10am–5pm Tues–Sun and public holidays; restaurant open Thurs–Sat for dinner and Tues–Sun for breakfast and lunch; admission free to gardens and sculpture park.*

 day tours

The Dandenongs   These scenic hills at the edge of Melbourne's eastern suburbs are a popular daytrip. Native rainforests of mountain ash and giant ferns, cool-climate gardens, the popular steam train Puffing Billy, and galleries, craft shops and cafes, many serving Devonshire tea, are among the many attractions. For more details see p. 148

Yarra Valley and Healesville   High-quality pinot noir and sparkling wines are produced across one of Australia's best-known wine areas. Pick up a brochure from the information centre in Healesville and map out your wine-tasting tour. Worthy of its own daytrip is Healesville Sanctuary, featuring around 200 species of native animals in a bushland setting. For more details see p. 148

Mornington Peninsula   This holiday centre features fine-food producers, around 40 cool-climate vineyards, historic holiday villages, quiet coastal national parks, 18 golf courses and many attractions for children. For more details see p. 149

Phillip Island   The nightly Penguin Parade on Phillip Island is one of Victoria's signature attractions. For the avid wildlife-watcher, seals and koalas are the other stars of the show, though the island also boasts magnificent coastal scenery and great surf breaks. For more details see p. 150

Sovereign Hill   Ballarat's award-winning re-creation of a 19th-century goldmining village conjures up the detail and drama of life during one of the nation's most exciting periods of history. You can even stay the night at a new accommodation complex within the village, with full period costume thrown in! For more details see Ballarat, p. 154

Bellarine Peninsula   The Bellarine Peninsula separates the waters of Port Phillip from the famously rugged coastline of Victoria's south-west. Beyond the historic buildings, streets and Geelong's waterfront are quaint coastal villages, excellent beaches, golf courses and wineries. For more details see p. 152

Mount Macedon and Hanging Rock   Country mansions and superb 19th- and 20th-century European-style gardens sit comfortably in the native bushland. Here you'll find wineries, cafes, nurseries, galleries and the mysteriously beautiful Hanging Rock. For more details see p. 151

Spa country   For a few hours of health-giving indulgence, visit the historic spa complex at Hepburn Springs. Explore Daylesford, enjoy a meal at one of the region's excellent eateries, or take a peaceful forest drive. For more details see p. 151

REGIONS
victoria

[OTWAY FLY, SOUTH-WEST COAST]

[SUNSET OVER MOUNT BUFFALO, HIGH COUNTRY]

Mallee Country
156

NEW SOUTH WALES

SOUTH AUSTRALIA

Grampians &
Central-West
155

Goldfields
154

Goulburn
& Murray
157

High Country
158

SOUTH

151

148

East Gippsland
159

pa & Garden
Country

South-West Coast
152

MELBOURNE

Phillip
Island &
Gippsland

Yarra &
Dandenongs

153

150

149
Mornington
Peninsula

Werribee
& Bellarine

YARRA & DANDENONGS

A daytrip to the Dandenongs, stopping off at cellar doors in the Yarra Valley, combines native forest landscapes with indulgent wining and dining on Melbourne's doorstep.

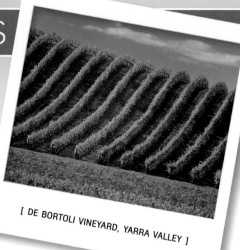

[DE BORTOLI VINEYARD, YARRA VALLEY]

Healesville Sanctuary Spread across 32 hectares of bushland, this world-renowned native animal sanctuary has over 200 species, most roaming in natural settings. Special features include talks by keepers, a nocturnal viewing area, the bird-of-prey displays and the platypus exhibit.

Yarra Valley wineries The 50 or so wineries of this district produce high-quality chardonnay, cabernet sauvignon and pinot noir. Visit Domaine Chandon, built by French champagne makers Moët & Chandon; the magnificent tasting-room offers fine views across the vine-covered valley. TarraWarra Estate features an impressive art gallery with temporary exhibitions of work by artists such as Brett Whiteley, Sidney Nolan and Arthur Boyd, and De Bortoli is home to a restaurant serving fine Italian-style fare. While touring the region for wines, follow the Yarra Valley Regional Food Trail, a self-guide tour taking in the many gourmet food outlets in the region.

Marysville and Lake Mountain
For 100 years, the beautiful subalpine village of Marysville was a much-frequented holiday destination for Melburnians. Providing access to the magnificent 84-metre Steavenson Falls nearby, the town charmed visitors with its cafes, galleries and popular guesthouses. In February 2009, Marysville was destroyed by bushfire, and many people lost their lives. The surviving residents have vowed to rebuild their much-loved town. Nearby Lake Mountain also suffered in the bushfires but it remains a popular tobogganing and cross-country skiing resort in winter, and a great bushwalking destination in summer.

Gardens of the Dandenongs Mountain ash forests and fern gullies frame the historic cool-climate gardens of one of Australia's best-known gardening regions. Many of the private gardens are open daily. Public gardens include the National Rhododendron Gardens and the R. J. Hamer Forest Arboretum (both near Olinda), the William Ricketts Sanctuary (Mount Dandenong) and the Alfred Nicholas Memorial Gardens (Sherbrooke).

Puffing Billy Steam Train This magical little steam train takes you on a 25-kilometre journey through lush forest and tree ferns from Belgrave to Gembrook and back again. A genuine relic of Victoria's early rail days, kids love the two-hour round trip, dangling their legs out the windows. Stopping at Emerald Lake along the way, a lovely tranquil spot ideal for picnics, paddleboating and walks, you can alight here to spend the day before returning on the train in the late afternoon.

TOP EVENTS

FEB	Grape Grazing Festival (throughout Yarra Valley wine region)
MAY	Great Train Race (Emerald)
JULY	Winterfest (Warburton)
AUG–NOV	Rhododendron and Daffodil Festivals (Olinda)
SEPT–OCT	Tesselaar's Tulip Festival (Silvan, near Olinda)

CLIMATE

HEALESVILLE

J	F	M	A	M	J	J	A	S	O	N	D	
26	26	24	19	16	12	12	14	16	19	22	24	MAX °C
11	12	11	9	7	4	4	5	6	8	9	11	MIN °C
58	68	64	91	96	82	87	98	94	106	93	86	RAIN MM
7	7	8	11	14	14	16	17	15	14	12	10	RAIN DAYS

TOURS OF THE FOREST

This area has some of the state's best forest scenery. Bushwalkers, horseriders and cyclists can travel the 38-kilometre Warburton Rail Trail, starting in Lilydale. The Beeches, an area of rainforest near Marysville, has a 5-kilometre stroll through forests of ancient beech and mountain ash. The less energetic can take a forest drive through or around Yarra Ranges National Park, choosing from the Black Spur Drive (between Healesville and Marysville), Acheron Way (from Warburton to Marysville) and the Lady Talbot Forest Drive (a shorter drive in the Marysville region). For something special, visit Mount Donna Buang Rainforest Gallery (near Warburton), which includes a viewing platform and a raised walkway through the rainforest.

→ For more detail see maps 570, 571, 573, 575 & 582. For descriptions of ⊕ towns see Towns from A–Z (p. 160).

MORNINGTON PENINSULA

This region's well-serviced seaside towns are popular during summer, while in winter wineries in the beautiful hinterland have welcoming cellar doors.

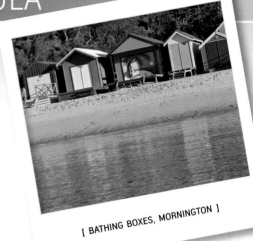

[BATHING BOXES, MORNINGTON]

Sorrento sojourns The Queenscliff–Sorrento car ferry crosses Port Phillip several times a day, offering visitors a tour of the two peninsulas – Bellarine and Mornington – without a long drive by land. Dolphin cruises, some including a swim with Port Phillip's bottlenose dolphins, operate in summer.

Arthurs Seat Just inland from Dromana, Arthurs Seat offers superb views across Melbourne and the bay. The 300-metre summit is reached by foot or vehicle – at the top are picnic facilities and a restaurant. Nearby is Arthurs Seat Maze with a series of themed gardens and mazes, where the large Maize Maze Festival is held each autumn.

Portsea Near the north-west tip of the peninsula, this village has long been favoured by Melbourne's wealthy. It has large houses (some with private boathouses), elegant hotels, B&Bs, good restaurants and a legendary pub. Further west, don't miss Fort Nepean, once an important defence site, and London Bridge, a rock formation off Portsea Surf Beach.

Mornington Peninsula National Park This park extends along the south-west coast of the peninsula, where the Bass Strait surf pounds windswept beaches and headlands. A 32-kilometre walking track runs from Portsea Surf Beach right down to Cape Schanck, with its historic 1858 lighthouse (offering accommodation).

Red Hill Market The small town of Red Hill, in the scenic undulating landscape of the Mornington Peninsula, is famous for its market held on the first Saturday of each month (from September to May). Affectionately known as the 'grand dame' of Victoria's craft market scene, the market has featured exceptional local produce, clothing and crafts for over 30 years. A visit to this much-lauded community event is a real treat.

TOP EVENTS

JAN	Portsea Swim Classic (Portsea)
FEB	Rye Beach Sand Sculpting Championship (Rye)
FEB–APR	Maize Maze Festival (Arthurs Seat)
MAR	Colour the Sky Kite Festival (Rosebud)
OCT	Pinot Week (throughout wine region)
OCT	Mornington Food and Wine Festival (throughout wine region)

CLIMATE

MORNINGTON

	J	F	M	A	M	J	J	A	S	O	N	D	
	25	25	23	19	16	14	13	14	16	18	20	23	MAX °C
	13	14	13	11	9	7	7	7	8	10	11	12	MIN °C
	45	42	50	63	70	71	69	71	72	71	59	54	RAIN MM
	7	7	8	11	14	15	15	16	14	13	10	8	RAIN DAYS

WINERIES

The grape came relatively late to the peninsula: the oldest vineyard, Elgee Park, north of Merricks, was established early in the 1970s. Viticulture exploded during the 1980s and 90s; now there are nearly 40 wineries in this cool-climate region, most clustered around Red Hill and many set in postcard-perfect landscapes. The vineyards tend to be small and concentrate on the classic varieties of pinot noir and chardonnay. Stonier, Tucks Ridge and Main Ridge Estate are a few of the names to look out for.

→ For more detail see maps 570, 572–3, 574–5 & 582. For descriptions of ⓣ towns see Towns from A–Z (p. 160).

VICTORIA

PHILLIP ISLAND & GIPPSLAND

This diverse area features historic towns, snowfields, the remote beauty of Wilsons Promontory and the famous Phillip Island penguins.

Gourmet Deli Trail   Central Gippsland is home to producers of trout, venison, cheese, berries, potatoes, herbs and wine. The trail covers the area north and south of Warragul, and annotated maps are available from visitor centres.

Korumburra's Coal Creek Heritage Village   A delightful re-creation of a 19th-century coalmining village on the site of the original Coal Creek mine (1890s), this heritage village has over 30 historic buildings. Visitors can take a guided tour through a coalmine, go on a carriage ride or board a small locomotive for a meander through tranquil bushland.

Phillip Island   Phillip Island is best known for its little penguins, but visitors can also walk around Cape Woolamai, drive across the bridge to Churchill Island to see a historic homestead, or immerse themselves in motor-racing history at the Phillip Island Grand Prix Circuit Visitor Centre.

[WILSONS PROMONTORY COASTLINE]

Baw Baw National Park   The highest part of the park, Mount Baw Baw (via Moe), has ski facilities and, unlike many other slopes, is seldom crowded. The eastern section (via Erica and Walhalla) is popular in summer with bushwalkers, wildflower enthusiasts and campers.

Walhalla   The perfectly preserved former goldmining town of Walhalla is set in a steep valley. Take the signposted town walk or a 45-minute ride on the Walhalla Goldfields Railway, or inspect the Long Tunnel Mine.

Wilsons Promontory   The Prom is a remote and beautiful landscape supporting diverse native flora and fauna in a near-wilderness. Around 150 kilometres of walking tracks along bays and through bush begin at Tidal River and other points along the access road.

Port Albert   Today Port Albert is a quaint fishing village, but as the state's first official port, it was once the gateway to Gippsland and Victoria. About 40 old buildings survive. For anglers, plentiful snapper, whiting, flathead, bream and trevally are found in the protected waters offshore.

TOP EVENTS

FEB–MAR	World Superbike Championships (Phillip Island)
MAR	Jazz Festival (Inverloch)
MAR	Blue Rock Classic (multi-sport race, Moe)
MAR	Fishing Contest (Port Albert)
EASTER	Tarra Festival (Yarram)
OCT	Australian Motorcycle Grand Prix (Phillip Island)

CLIMATE

WARRAGUL

J	F	M	A	M	J	J	A	S	O	N	D	
26	26	24	20	16	13	13	14	16	19	21	23	MAX °C
13	13	12	9	7	5	4	5	6	8	9	11	MIN °C
62	52	69	84	94	93	91	103	104	109	89	80	RAIN MM
8	7	10	13	15	16	16	17	16	15	13	11	RAIN DAYS

PHILLIP ISLAND WILDLIFE

The Penguin Parade on Summerland Beach is a major international tourist attraction. Just after sunset, the world's smallest penguins, at 33 centimetres tall, come home to their burrows in the sand dunes after a day in the sea. To protect the penguins, visitors are restricted to designated viewing areas and cameras are prohibited. Bookings are essential during peak holiday periods. The visitor centre also offers a simulated underwater tour showing the penguins foraging for food and avoiding predators. On the island's western tip you can walk along a cliff-top boardwalk for views across to Seal Rocks, 2 kilometres offshore, where thousands of Australian fur seals live. For an up-close view of the frolicking animals, take a cruise from Cowes or watch them on cameras that you control yourself at the Nobbies Centre. Also visit the Koala Conservation Centre near Cowes, where you can see the delightful marsupials snoozing in the treetops.

→ For more detail see maps 573, 575 & 582–3. For descriptions of ⓣ towns see Towns from A–Z (p. 160).

SPA & GARDEN COUNTRY

Grand European-style gardens and historic spa towns feature in this district, which retains the air of a 19th-century hill retreat.

[PARMA VILLA, HEPBURN SPRINGS]

Daylesford and Hepburn Springs The spa complex at Hepburn Springs offers heated mineral spas, flotation tanks, saunas and massages. The adjacent town of Daylesford is an attractive weekend destination with galleries, antique shops, heritage buildings, B&Bs and fantastic restaurants and cafes. The Convent Gallery, a 19th-century former convent, houses local artwork, sculpture and jewellery.

Hanging Rock This impressive rock formation north-east of Woodend was created by the erosion of solidified lava. The spot was the inspiration for Joan Lindsay's novel *Picnic at Hanging Rock*, and a setting for the subsequent film. Walking tracks lead up to a superb view, with glimpses of koalas along the way, and the Discovery Centre tells the story of the site.

Lake House Daylesford's beloved Lake House is regarded as one of regional Victoria's best restaurants, if not the best. Opened in 1984, it is partly responsible for the town's transformation into a gourmet destination. The white, light-filled restaurant overlooks picturesque Lake Daylesford, and the menu might feature local yabbies, free-range pork and dishes that tip their hat to the owner's Russian heritage. Luxury accommodation is also available, as is pampering at the on-site Salus Day Spa.

Organ Pipes National Park Lava flows have created a 20-metre wall of basalt columns in this small park near Sunbury. The 'organ pipes', within a gorge, can be seen close-up via an easy walking trail. A regeneration program is gradually bringing this formerly denuded area back to its native state.

Lerderderg State Park The Lerderderg River has cut a deep gorge through sandstone and slate in this 14 250-hectare park. Rugged ridges enclose much of the river, and there are also some interesting relics of old goldmining days. Explore on foot, or take a scenic drive via O'Briens Road (turn off south of Blackwood).

VICTORIA

TOP EVENTS

JAN	New Year's Day and Australia Day races (Hanging Rock, near Woodend)
APR–MAY	Hepburn Springs Swiss–Italian Festival (Hepburn Springs)
JUNE	Winter Arts Festival (Woodend)
SEPT	Daffodil and Arts Festival (Kyneton)
OCT	Macedon Ranges Budburst Food and Wine Festival (throughout wine region)
DEC	Highland Gathering (Daylesford)

CLIMATE

KYNETON

	J	F	M	A	M	J	J	A	S	O	N	D	
	27	27	24	18	14	11	10	12	15	18	22	25	MAX °C
	10	10	8	6	4	2	2	2	3	5	7	9	MIN °C
	37	39	47	54	75	90	82	84	74	69	52	50	RAIN MM
	5	5	6	9	12	15	16	16	13	11	9	7	RAIN DAYS

COUNTRY GARDENS

Gardens flourish in the volcanic soil and cool, moist climate of the spa country. There are botanic gardens in Daylesford and Malmsbury. Around the beautiful village of Mount Macedon, classic mountain-side gardens surround large houses; check with a visitor centre for their spring and autumn open days. Cope-Williams Winery at Romsey is well known for its English-style garden and cricket green, while at Blackwood the beautiful Garden of St Erth offers 2 hectares of exotic and native species (closed Wednesday and Thursday). For something special, visit the Lavandula Swiss Italian Farm at Shepherds Flat, where lavender sits beside other cottage-style plants.

→ For more detail see maps 572–3, 579, 582, 584 & 593. For descriptions of ⬤ towns see Towns from A–Z (p. 160).

WERRIBEE & BELLARINE

Beyond the regional centre of Geelong, diverse attractions beckon: watersports, wineries, Victorian-era hotels and even an African-style safari park.

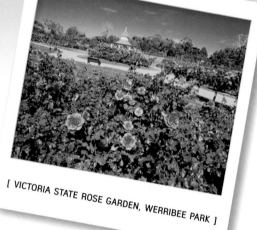

[VICTORIA STATE ROSE GARDEN, WERRIBEE PARK]

The You Yangs These granite tors rise abruptly from the Werribee Plains. There is a fairly easy walk (3.2 kilometres return) from the carpark to the top of Flinders Peak. On a clear day the view extends to Mount Macedon, Geelong and the skyscrapers of Melbourne.

Werribee Park Built in Italianate style during the 1870s, Werribee Mansion is now preserved in all its splendour, grandly furnished to re-create the lifestyle of a wealthy family in Victoria's boom years. Take a tour through the house, then visit the Victoria State Rose Garden before heading off on a safari at the Werribee Open Range Zoo.

Geelong wine region Vines were first planted around Geelong in the 1850s, but were uprooted during the 1870s phylloxera outbreak. Today's industry was established in the 1960s and there are now around 20 wineries, including eight on the Bellarine Peninsula. Scotchmans Hill, near Drysdale, has views to the coast and a growing reputation for pinot noir and chardonnay.

Geelong Victoria's second largest city is a bustling port that grew with the state's wool industry. The redeveloped Eastern Beach Waterfront district features cafes, restaurants and colourful sculptures, with the historic Cunningham Pier as a centrepiece. Take a stroll along the promenade or cool off in the restored 1930s sea baths.

TOP EVENTS

JAN	Skandia Geelong Week (Geelong)
FEB–MAR	Spray Farm Estate summer concert series (Bellarine)
MAR	Highland Gathering (Geelong)
JUNE	National Celtic Folk Festival (Geelong)
OCT	Geelong Cup (horseracing, Geelong)
NOV	Queenscliff Music Festival (Queenscliff)

CLIMATE

GEELONG

J	F	M	A	M	J	J	A	S	O	N	D	
25	26	24	20	17	14	14	15	17	19	21	24	MAX °C
14	14	13	10	8	6	5	6	7	8	10	12	MIN °C
44	38	35	39	47	43	42	47	53	63	52	48	RAIN MM
8	6	9	12	14	16	16	17	16	15	13	10	RAIN DAYS

HOLIDAY HAVENS

Just an hour or so from Melbourne, this district is enormously popular for weekend getaways. Queenscliff offers luxurious accommodation and fine dining, and the Maritime Centre and Museum in town displays the region's historic relationship with the sea. The tiny historic town of Point Lonsdale has great views of the turbulent entrance to Port Phillip. Ocean Grove, the peninsula's biggest town, is popular with retirees, surfers and scubadivers. A bridge across the estuary leads to Barwon Heads, which was the setting for the television series *SeaChange*. This is a small town with an excellent surfing beach and good accommodation and restaurants.

→ For more detail see maps 570, 572, 574, 582 & 593. For descriptions of ⊤ towns see Towns from A–Z (p. 160).

SOUTH-WEST COAST

The breathtaking coastal landscape and charming holiday towns of the Great Ocean Road are world renowned, while inland lies a volcanic landscape.

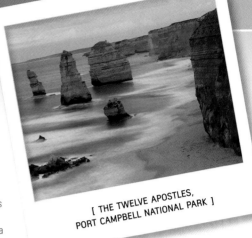

[THE TWELVE APOSTLES, PORT CAMPBELL NATIONAL PARK]

Mount Eccles National Park This park is at the far edge of the 20 000-year-old volcanic landscape that extends west from Melbourne. There are excellent walking trails, and camping is available.

Cape Bridgewater A two-hour walk leads to a viewing platform overlooking one of the country's largest Australian fur seal colonies; take a boat trip into the mouth of a cave for a closer look at these charming creatures.

Warrnambool's southern right whales Each year from June to September, southern right whales can be spotted from Warrnambool's Logans Beach; they return annually to these waters from Antarctica to give birth and raise their young. There's a purpose-built viewing platform at the beach (binoculars or a telescope are recommended), and the local visitor centre releases daily information on whale sightings.

Surf coast Torquay is Victoria's premier surfing town. Factory outlets offer great bargains on surf gear and the local Surfworld Australia museum celebrates the wonders of the wave. Bells and Jan Juc beaches are just around the corner.

Port Fairy Port Fairy is a superbly preserved whaling port, with historic bluestone buildings lining the main street. In summer it offers lazy beachside holidays, and in winter, a refuge from the cold in one of the many cosy restaurants and B&Bs.

The Twelve Apostles These spectacular limestone stacks were part of the cliffs until wind and water left them stranded in wild surf off the shore. Preserved in Port Campbell National Park, they are one of Australia's most photographed sights.

The Otways The contrast between rugged coastline and tranquil, temperate rainforest is at its most impressive in Great Otway National Park. In the north, the Otway Fly takes visitors on a suspended walkway to a treetop lookout; in the south, at Cape Otway, a lighthouse offers views over the sea. Another highlight is Melba Gully, where, at dusk, visitors can witness a show of twinkling lights from glow worms.

Lorne This popular resort village could be called the capital of the south-west coast, with excellent cafes and restaurants and a lively summertime crowd. Nearby, in Great Otway National Park, beautiful forests and waterfalls provide time-out for bushwalkers and nature lovers.

VICTORIA

TOP EVENTS

JAN	Pier to Pub Swim and Mountain to Surf Foot Race (Lorne)
FEB	Go Country Music Festival and Truck Show (Colac)
FEB	Wunta Fiesta (Warrnambool)
MAR	Port Fairy Folk Festival (Port Fairy)
EASTER	Rip Curl Pro (Bells Beach, near Torquay)
DEC–JAN	Falls Festival (Great Otway National Park)

CLIMATE

WARRNAMBOOL

J	F	M	A	M	J	J	A	S	O	N	D	
23	24	22	19	16	14	13	14	15	17	19	21	MAX °C
11	12	11	9	7	6	5	6	7	7	9	10	MIN °C
49	35	53	69	75	101	96	107	109	82	66	63	RAIN MM
11	9	12	15	17	20	20	20	19	16	15	13	RAIN DAYS

SHIPWRECKS

There are about 80 wrecks along the vital yet treacherous south-west-coast shipping route. Victoria's Historic Shipwreck Trail, between Moonlight Head (in Port Campbell National Park) and Port Fairy, marks 25 sites with plaques telling the history of the wrecks. Not to be missed is the evocative *Loch Ard* site, near Port Campbell. On a direct route from London to Melbourne, the *Loch Ard* ran into trouble while negotiating the entrance to Bass Strait; fog and haze prevented the captain from seeing that the ship was only a short distance from the cliffs. In the struggle to change direction the ship hit the cliffs and soon sank – only two people managed to swim ashore to the now well-known Loch Ard Gorge. At Flagstaff Hill Maritime Village in Warrnambool you can see a magnificent statue of a peacock, which was being transported on the *Loch Ard* for display in Melbourne's International Exhibition of 1880 and was washed ashore after the wreck. You can also watch the sound-and-laser spectacular 'Shipwrecked', which brings the tale of the *Loch Ard* to life.

→ For more detail see maps 572, 574, 580 & 592–3. For descriptions of ❶ towns see Towns from A–Z (p. 160).

GOLDFIELDS

This region is an historic jewel of rural Australia with an intense concentration of Victorian architecture in grand public buildings and parks.

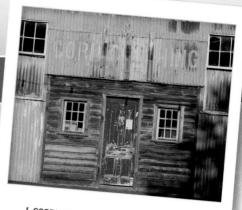

[CORRUGATED-IRON BUILDING, MALDON]

Backblocks of the goldfields   Quieter gold towns are tucked away north-west of Bendigo. In Dunolly 126 nuggets were found – see replicas of some of the most impressive finds at the Goldfields Historical and Arts Society. St Arnaud boasts the beautiful Queen Mary Gardens and a number of old pubs and verandah-fronted shops. There are eucalyptus distilleries at Inglewood and Wedderburn.

Maryborough Old Railway Station
Grand for the size of the town, the former railway station now houses a tourist complex that includes an antique emporium, a woodworking shop and a restaurant and cafe.

Maldon   The 1860s streets of Maldon are shaded by European trees and lined with old buildings of local stone. Declared a Notable Town by the National Trust, Maldon has historic B&Bs and a tourist steam train.

Sovereign Hill   One of Victoria's top tourist attractions, Ballarat's Sovereign Hill is a living museum. Blacksmiths, bakers and storekeepers in period dress ply their trades amid the tents, while miners pan for gold.

Bendigo's Chinese sites   The restored Joss House on the city's northern outskirts and the Golden Dragon Museum in Bridge Street are reminders of the substantial presence of Chinese immigrants on the goldfields. A ceremonial archway leads from the museum to the Garden of Joy, built in 1996 to represent the Chinese landscape in miniature.

Pall Mall   The tree-lined, French-style boulevard of Pall Mall in Bendigo is probably country Australia's most impressive street. Many of its buildings date back to the gold rush and vintage trams continue to operate.

Castlemaine   This historic goldmining town's original market building, with its classical Roman facade, now houses visitor information and a gold-diggings interpretive centre. Visit the 1860s Buda Historic Home, with its heritage-listed garden, and the Castlemaine Art Gallery with its impressive collection of local and international art.

Ballarat Begonia Festival   Every year in early March for the past 100-odd years, Ballarat's 40-hectare Botanic Gardens have been awash with colour during the city's annual Begonia Festival. Apart from stunning floral displays, the 20 000-plus people who come to the festival enjoy gardening forums, street parades, fireworks, art shows, kids' activities and much more.

Map labels

Wedderburn
St Arnaud
Inglewood
GREATER BENDIGO NP
ST ARNAUD RANGE NP
Dunolly
Laanecoorie Reservoir
BENDIGO
GREATER BENDIGO NP
Lake Eppalock
Maryborough
Maldon
Avoca
Tullaroop Reservoir
Cairn Curran Reservoir
Castlemaine
Clunes
Creswick
N
0   20 km
Lake Burrumbeet
BALLARAT

TOP EVENTS

JAN	Organs of the Ballarat Goldfields (Ballarat)
MAR	Country Food and Wine Race Meeting (Avoca)
MAR	Ballarat Begonia Festival (Ballarat)
EASTER	Easter Festival (Bendigo)
OCT–NOV	Folk Festival (Maldon)
NOV	Festival of Gardens (Castlemaine)

CLIMATE

BENDIGO

	J	F	M	A	M	J	J	A	S	O	N	D	
	29	29	26	21	16	13	12	14	16	20	24	26	MAX °C
	14	15	13	9	7	4	3	5	6	8	11	13	MIN °C
	33	32	36	41	55	61	56	59	54	52	37	33	RAIN MM
	5	4	5	7	10	12	13	13	11	10	7	6	RAIN DAYS

GOLD-RUSH HISTORY

Sovereign Hill in Ballarat is one of the country's best historic theme parks. It offers a complete re-creation of life on the 1850s goldfields. The nearby Gold Museum, part of the Sovereign Hill complex, features displays of gold nuggets and coins, and changing exhibits on the history of gold. The Eureka Stockade Centre offers interpretive displays on Australia's only armed insurrection, which took place in 1854. See the original Eureka Flag at the Ballarat Fine Art Gallery, which also houses an excellent collection of work by artists such as Tom Roberts, Sidney Nolan, Russell Drysdale and Fred Williams. In Eureka Street is the tiny Montrose Cottage (1856), an ex-miner's house furnished in the style of the period; here a museum display movingly recalls the lives and contribution of women in the gold-rush era. In Bendigo, the Central Deborah Gold Mine offers tours 80 metres down a reef mine, and excellent displays on goldmining techniques.

→ For more detail see maps 572, 579, 591 & 593. For descriptions of ❶ towns see Towns from A–Z (p. 160).

GRAMPIANS & CENTRAL WEST

Ancient mountains, semi-arid plains and farming landscapes typify this area, while Aboriginal rock-art sites are remnants of life before white settlement.

[VIEW FROM MOUNT ARAPILES]

Little Desert National Park During spring, more than 600 varieties of wildflowers and over 40 types of ground orchids flourish in this 132 647-hectare park. With nearly 600 kilometres of tracks, it is ideal for four-wheel driving, but perhaps the best way to appreciate the colourful spring display is on foot: for keen hikers, there is the 84-kilometre Desert Discovery Walk.

Mount Arapiles Mount Arapiles is regarded as Australia's best rock climbing venue, attracting interstate and international enthusiasts with its 2000 rock climbing routes marked out across 365 metres of sandstone cliffs.

Hamilton Hamilton is the commercial hub of the wool-rich Western District. Gracious houses and churches on its tree-lined streets testify to over a century of prosperity. Close to town are historic homesteads in magnificent gardens.

The olive groves of Laharum Mount Zero Olives at Laharum is the largest olive plantation in the Southern Hemisphere, with 55 000 trees on 730 hectares. The first trees were planted in 1943, after World War II stopped olive oil imports. You can buy oil, vinegar and lentils, and stay overnight.

Grampians day drive and balloon flights From Halls Gap, drive to Boroka Lookout, Reed Lookout and MacKenzie Falls. Break for lunch at Zumsteins, home to a large kangaroo population. Dawn hot-air balloon flights over the Grampians leave from Stawell.

Wines of Great Western Grapevines were first planted at Seppelt's Great Western vineyards in 1865. Today the winery is best known for its red and white sparkling wines. Other wineries in the area include Best's and Garden Gully.

Byaduk Caves These caves, located in Mount Napier State Park, are part of a giant, 24-kilometre lava flow stretching to Mt Eccles in the south-west, evidence of the volcanic activity that shaped the region's landscape. The caves, one of which is open, are a wonderland of ropey lava, columns, stalactites and stalagmites.

**Map labels:**
Jeparit • Wycheproof • Warracknabeal • Lake Buloke • Nhill • WIMMERA • Dimboola • Donald • LITTLE DESERT NATIONAL PARK • Mount Arapiles • HORSHAM • MOUNT ARAPILES–TOOAN STATE PARK • Natimuk • Laharum • Lake Lonsdale • Edenhope • Toolondo Reservoir • Wartook Reservoir • Stawell • Great Western • Halls Gap • Rocklands Reservoir • GRAMPIANS NATIONAL PARK • Ararat • THE GRAMPIANS • Lake Muirhead • Casterton • Coleraine • Hamilton • Dunkeld • Lake Bolac • MOUNT NAPIER STATE PARK • AUSTRALIA • SOUTH • N • 0 20 km

TOP EVENTS

JAN	Picnic Races (Great Western)
FEB	Grampians Jazz Festival (Halls Gap)
MAR	Jailhouse Rock Festival (Ararat)
EASTER	Stawell Easter Gift (professional footrace, Stawell)
MAY	Grampians Grape Escape (Halls Gap)
JUNE–JULY	Australian Kelpie Muster and Kelpie Working Dog Auction (Casterton)

CLIMATE

STAWELL

	J	F	M	A	M	J	J	A	S	O	N	D	
	27	28	25	20	16	13	12	14	16	19	22	26	MAX °C
	13	13	12	9	7	5	4	5	6	8	9	11	MIN °C
	36	28	33	41	57	60	67	67	64	58	36	29	RAIN MM
	6	5	7	9	12	16	18	18	14	12	9	7	RAIN DAYS

ABORIGINAL CULTURE

The Djab Wurrung and Jardwadjali people shared the territory they called Gariwerd for at least 5000 years before European settlement, although some evidence suggests up to 30 000 years of habitation. Brambuk – The National Park and Cultural Centre near Halls Gap, run by five Koorie communities, is an excellent first stop for information about the region's Indigenous heritage. There is a ceremonial ground for everything from dance performances to boomerang-throwing, while bush tucker–inspired meals are served in the cafe. The region contains 100 recorded rock-art sites, representing more than 80 per cent of all sites in Victoria. A Brambuk-guided tour of some of the sites (most are in Grampians National Park) is probably the most rewarding way to experience the meaning and nature of the art. Notable sites include Gulgurn Manja, featuring over 190 kangaroo, emu and handprint motifs, and Ngamadidj, a site decorated with 16 figures painted in white clay. Bunjil's Shelter is just outside the park near Stawell, and is the only site in the area where more than one colour is used and a known figure is represented. Bunjil was a creator spirit from the Dreaming, responsible for the people, the land and the law.

VICTORIA

→ For more detail see maps 590–1 & 592–3. For descriptions of ⊕ towns see Towns from A–Z (p. 160).

MALLEE COUNTRY

The Murray River is the lifeblood of this region, allowing the cultivation of fruit crops and the development of various riverside settlements.

[EMU AND CHICKS, HATTAH–KULKYNE NATIONAL PARK]

Mildura   With its museums and galleries, excellent dining and surrounding wineries and orchards, Mildura is like a colourful Mediterranean oasis. Go to the zoo, visit the Mildura Arts Complex and the Rio Vista museum (once the home of William Chaffey), or book a day tour with Indigenous guides to Mungo National Park in New South Wales.

Stefano's   The star of Mildura is Stefano's, the kind of place you dine at one night and love so much you go again the next. This may have something to do with the restaurant's beautiful setting in a historic hotel cellar – and celebrity chef Stefano de Pieri's food. The menu is degustation, with five different courses nightly, each focusing on the best local and seasonal produce; you can expect handmade pastas and dishes featuring the finest quality beef, pork and lamb.

River district wines   The wine-producing areas of Mildura and Swan Hill are an unrecognised heartland of the Australian wine industry, producing 37 per cent of the total output – most for the bulk market, although prestige production is rising. The dozen or so wineries include the large Lindemans Karadoc estate, with cellar-door tastings and sales.

Swan Hill Pioneer Settlement
This 7-hectare park offers a lively experience of river-port life in early Australia. Wander through the 19th-century-style streets, complete with staff in period dress. Ride on a paddlesteamer or book for the popular Sound and Light Tour. Also in the park is an Aboriginal canoe tree.

Wyperfeld National Park   A park of brilliant sunsets, huge open spaces and spring wildflowers, Wyperfeld is explored via walks from Wonga Campground and Information Centre, 50 kilometres west of Hopetoun. The park is home to the endangered mallee fowl, a turkey-size bird that makes nesting mounds up to 5 metres across.

TOP EVENTS

MAR	Arts Festival (Mildura)
AUG–SEPT	Great Australian Vanilla Slice Triumph (Ouyen)
SEPT	Vintage Tractor Pull (Mildura)
SEPT–OCT	Country Music Festival (Mildura)

CLIMATE

MILDURA

J	F	M	A	M	J	J	A	S	O	N	D	
32	32	28	23	19	16	15	17	20	24	27	30	MAX °C
17	16	14	10	8	5	4	5	7	10	12	15	MIN °C
21	22	19	19	27	23	26	28	29	31	24	23	RAIN MM
4	3	4	4	7	8	9	9	8	7	6	4	RAIN DAYS

MURRAY AND MALLEE WILDLIFE

This landscape of rivers and plains is home to abundant wildlife. Most notable is the birdlife: spoonbills, herons, eagles, mallee fowl, harriers and kites are to be found in the parks and on the roadsides and riverbanks. Hattah–Kulkyne National Park protects around 200 bird species as well as the red kangaroo. Murray–Sunset National Park – true desert country in parts – includes riverine plains. It supports an array of native fauna, including mallee fowl and the rare black-eared miner. To see the kangaroos and birdlife of Wyperfeld National Park, follow the Brambruk Nature Trail.

→ For more detail see maps 588–9 & 591. For descriptions of ❶ towns see Towns from A–Z (p. 160).

GOULBURN & MURRAY

The Goulburn Valley contains Victoria's richest farm land, while the Murray has historical attractions, particularly the paddlesteamers of Echuca.

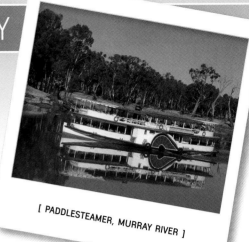

[PADDLESTEAMER, MURRAY RIVER]

Echuca The historic port of Echuca, with its impressive red-gum wharf, recalls the late 19th century, when the Murray carried wool and other goods from farms and stations. A number of beautifully restored paddlesteamers are moored here, including some offering cruises up the river.

Barmah State Park and State Forest
These neighbouring areas form the state's biggest river red gum forest. This is a popular area for bushwalking, canoeing and camping. Walking trails take in various Aboriginal sites, and the Dharnya Centre interprets the culture of the local Yorta Yorta people.

Cobram This lovely fruit-growing town is surrounded by peach, nectarine, pear and orange orchards. It also offers access to a number of wide, sandy beaches on the Murray, perfect for swimming, fishing, picnicking and watersports. Camping facilities are available, and across the river in New South Wales is the renowned 36-hole Cobram Barooga golf course.

Tahbilk winery Tahbilk was established in 1860 on the sandy loam of the Goulburn River north of Nagambie. One of Australia's most beautiful wine properties, it has a National Trust–classified cellar, which – along with other buildings – is a timepiece of the early Australian wine industry. Tahbilk wines have won over 1000 awards.

Seymour's Royal Hotel Dating from 1848, this classic old pub on Emily Street in Seymour is a great spot to stop for a beer and counter meal. If the hotel looks vaguely familiar, it is because you might have seen it before in the famous, haunting painting *The Cricketers* (1948), by one of Australia's most notable artists, Russell Drysdale.

VICTORIA

TOP EVENTS

JAN	Peaches and Cream Festival (Cobram, odd-numbered years)
FEB	Southern 80 Ski Race (Torrumbarry Weir to Echuca)
FEB	Riverboats, Jazz, Food and Wine Festival (Echuca)
MAR	Bridge to Bridge Swim (Cohuna)
APR	Barmah Muster (Barmah State Forest)
JUNE	Steam, Horse and Vintage Rally (Echuca)

CLIMATE

ECHUCA

	J	F	M	A	M	J	J	A	S	O	N	D	
	31	31	27	22	18	14	13	15	18	22	26	29	MAX °C
	15	15	13	9	7	5	4	5	6	9	11	14	MIN °C
	27	27	31	33	42	43	41	43	40	43	32	28	RAIN MM
	4	4	5	6	9	10	11	11	10	9	6	5	RAIN DAYS

FOOD AND WINE

Irrigation has transformed the once-dusty Goulburn Valley into the fruit bowl of Victoria. Orchards, market gardens and farms supply the canneries in Shepparton, which are among the largest in the Southern Hemisphere. The valley is dotted with outlets for venison, poultry, smoked trout, berries, organic vegetables, honey, jams, preserves, fruit juices, mustards, pickles, vinegar and liquored truffles. The region's nine wineries make reliable reds and distinctive whites. Near Nagambie, Tahbilk Winery and Mitchelton Wines are both must-visit cellar doors, not only for their superb wines but also for their scenic surrounds. Tahbilk is set next to a wetlands and wildlife reserve, while Mitchelton offers great views of the region from its famous tower. At nearby Avenel, Plunkett Fowles is another excellent cellar door with various wines available for tasting, including their 490m range inspired by the grapes grown at high altitude in the Strathbogie Ranges.

→ For more detail see maps 584 & 586. For descriptions of ⊤ towns see Towns from A–Z (p. 160).

HIGH COUNTRY

The Victorian Alps offer challenging skiing; beyond the foothills lie charming old gold towns and Rutherglen wineries.

[ALPINE LAKE, BOGONG HIGH PLAINS]

Wines of Rutherglen   The vines on the alluvial flats in a shallow loop of the Murray produce some of the world's great fortified wines. The region is known for tokays and muscats, big reds and – more recently – lighter reds such as gamay. There are over a dozen wineries near Rutherglen; look out for All Saints, with its historic building, and Pfeiffer, Chambers, Gehrig Estate and Campbells.

Kelly country   A giant effigy of Ned Kelly greets visitors to Glenrowan. After killing three local policemen in 1878, the Kelly Gang hid for two years in the Warby Range, raiding nearby towns. Visit the Ned Kelly Memorial Museum and Homestead in Gladstone Street.

Historic Beechworth
The National Trust has classified over 30 buildings in what is now one of Australia's best-preserved gold-rush towns. Dine in a stately former bank, visit the powder magazine, wander through an evocative cemetery for Chinese goldminers, and sample the delectable goods from Beechworth Bakery.

Mount Buffalo National Park   This 31 000-hectare national park is the state's oldest, declared in 1898. A plateau of boulders and tors includes The Horn, the park's highest point and a great place for views at sunrise. Walking tracks are set among streams, waterfalls, stunning wildflowers, and snow gum and mountain ash forest. There is summer camping, swimming and canoeing at Lake Catani. In winter, the Mount Buffalo ski area is popular with families.

Lake Eildon   Created by damming the Goulburn River in the 1950s, this lake is popular with watersports enthusiasts, anglers and houseboat holiday-makers. The surrounding Lake Eildon National Park offers bushwalking, camping and four-wheel-drive tracks through the foothills of the Victorian Alps.

Horseback riding   Jack Riley, believed to be the original Man from Snowy River, is buried in Corryong's pretty hillside cemetery. Each year, at an annual festival honouring his memory, horseriding competitions are held to find his modern-day equivalent. A gentle trail ride through this stunning countryside is a great way to appreciate this High Country legend.

TOP EVENTS

MAR	The High Country Autumn Festival (Mansfield)
MAR	Tastes of Rutherglen (district wineries)
APR	The Man from Snowy River Bush Festival (Corryong)
APR–MAY	Autumn Festival (Bright)
OCT–NOV	Festival of Jazz (Wangaratta)
NOV	Celtic Festival (Beechworth)

CLIMATE

MOUNT BULLER

	J	F	M	A	M	J	J	A	S	O	N	D	
	16	17	14	10	7	3	2	2	5	8	12	14	MAX °C
	8	8	6	4	1	–1	–3	–2	–1	1	4	6	MIN °C
	83	66	79	136	161	160	190	185	156	185	155	124	RAIN MM
	7	5	8	12	14	14	15	16	14	16	13	11	RAIN DAYS

SKI COUNTRY

Victoria's ski resorts are within easy reach of Melbourne. They include, in order of their distance from the city: Mount Buller (via Mansfield), Mount Buffalo (via Myrtleford), Mount Hotham (via Bright) and Falls Creek (via Mount Beauty). The ski season starts officially on the Queen's Birthday weekend, early in June, and ends on the first weekend in October. Snowsport conditions, however, depend on the weather. All resorts offer a range of skiing, from protected runs for beginners to cross-country ski trails. Mount Hotham, known as the 'powder snow capital' of Australia, has the most challenging runs for experienced downhill skiers and snowboarders. After the snow melts a range of summer activities come in to play. The adventurous can try mountain-bike riding, tandem paragliding, abseiling or caving. Mountain lakes and streams offer trout fishing, swimming, sailing and canoeing. Trails across the mountains, ablaze with wildflowers in summer, can be explored on horseback or on foot. The less energetic can just breathe the crystalline air and gaze across the hazy blue ridges.

→ For more detail see maps 573, 582–3, 584–5 & 586–7. For descriptions of ⊤ towns see Towns from A–Z (p. 160).

EAST GIPPSLAND

Natural wonders and outdoor activities abound in this region, which is blessed with some magnificent national parks and inland waterways.

[POINT HICKS, CROAJINGOLONG NATIONAL PARK]

Snowy River National Park The much-celebrated Snowy River begins as a trickle near Mount Kosciuszko and passes through wild limestone gorges and forest country before reaching a coastal lagoon. McKillops Bridge (via Buchan) is a beautiful area with camping and barbecue facilities, swimming spots and some good short walks.

Buchan Caves Reserve This spectacular limestone cave system comprises more than 350 caves, of which the Royal and Fairy caves are the most accessible. Fairy Cave is over 400 metres long, with impressive and elaborate stalactites and stalagmites, while Royal Cave impresses with pretty calcite-rimmed pools. Tours of both caves are run daily. After exploring the caves, you can cool off in a spring-fed swimming pool.

Mallacoota Surrounded by the remote ocean beaches, estuarine waterways and unspoiled bush of Croajingolong National Park, this old-fashioned resort offers one of the best nature-based holidays in the state, with excellent fishing, walking, boating and swimming. Hire a boat in town and explore Mallacoota Inlet.

Large lakes and a long beach The Gippsland Lakes are fed by five major rivers and contained on the coastal side by Ninety Mile Beach. At the system's centre, The Lakes National Park offers birdwatching, walking, swimming and camping. Access is via boat from Paynesville or road and foot from Loch Sport.

Lakes Entrance Lakes Entrance, at the head of the lakes, is a great base for fishing and boating, and offers accommodation to suit all budgets. For a holiday afloat, book a self-drive cruiser from nearby Metung. There are several wineries in the area – Wyanga Park Winery offers a lakes cruise from town to its cellar door and restaurant.

VICTORIA

TOP EVENTS

JAN	Foothills Festival (Buchan)
FEB	Jazz Festival (Paynesville)
FEB	Blues and Arts Festival (Bruthen)
MAR	Marlay Point–Paynesville Overnight Yacht Race
MAR	Line Dancing Championships (Bairnsdale)
EASTER	Rodeo (Buchan)

CLIMATE

LAKES ENTRANCE

J	F	M	A	M	J	J	A	S	O	N	D	
24	24	22	20	17	15	15	16	17	19	20	22	MAX °C
15	15	13	11	9	7	6	6	8	9	11	13	MIN °C
56	41	56	63	67	65	54	51	59	64	71	70	RAIN MM
9	7	10	10	11	13	12	14	13	13	12	11	RAIN DAYS

FISHING

Fishing is a huge drawcard in East Gippsland. Fish for trout in the mountain streams and rivers – such as the Delegate River – or head for the coast. The lakes, rivers and inlets around Paynesville, Marlo, Bemm River and Mallacoota are great for bream, trevally and flathead. Boat angling is the best choice here, although land-based angling also yields results. Ninety Mile Beach and the remote beaches of The Lakes National Park provide some of the best surf-fishing in Victoria, with salmon, tailor and flathead among the prospects.

→ For more detail see maps 565, 581 & 583. For descriptions of ⊕ towns see Towns from A–Z (p. 160).

LEGEND

🛈 VISITOR INFORMATION

📻 RADIO STATIONS

🏠 IN TOWN

🌴 WHAT'S ON

🍴 WHERE TO EAT

🛏 WHERE TO STAY

🧭 NEARBY

[COAST NEAR LOCH ARD GORGE, PORT CAMPBELL NATIONAL PARK]

Alexandra
Pop. 2142
Map ref. 571 F1 | 573 N1 | 582 F1 | 584 F12 | 586 B10

🛈 36 Grant St; (03) 5772 1100 or 1800 652 298;
www.alexandratourism.com

📻 102.9 FM ABC Local Radio, 106.9 UGFM Upper Goulburn
Community Radio

Alexandra was apparently named after Alexandra, Princess of
Wales, although, coincidentally, three men named Alexander
discovered gold here in 1866. Situated in the foothills of the Great
Dividing Range, Alexandra is supported primarily by agriculture.
Nearby, the Goulburn River is an important trout fishery.

🏠 *Alexandra Timber Tramways:* museum housed in the
original railway station that offers an insight into the timber
industry around Alexandra; open 2nd Sun each month;
Station St. *Art and craft galleries:* many outlets around town
displaying and selling local art, pottery and glassware.

🌴 *Bush market:* Perkins St; 3rd Sat each month (excluding
winter). *Picnic Races:* Jan, Mar, Oct and Nov. *Truck, Ute and Rod
Show:* June. *Open Gardens Weekend:* Oct. *Rose Festival:* Nov.

🍴 *Mia Mia Tea Rooms:* good country fare; 79 Grant St;
(03) 5772 2122. *Stonelea Country Estate:* excellent food in a
country-house setting; Connellys Creek Rd, Acheron; (03) 5772
2222. *Tea Rooms at Yarck:* regional Italian; 6585 Maroondah
Hwy, Yarck; (03) 5773 4233.

🛏 *Athlone Country Cottages:* 3 well-equipped cottages;
266 UT Creek Rd; (03) 5772 2992. *Mittagong Homestead
and Cottages:* 3 well-appointed cottages; 462 Spring Creek Rd;
(03) 5772 2250. *Stonelea Country Estate:* cottage and homestead
accommodation; Connellys Creek Rd, Acheron; (03) 5772 2222.

🧭 *McKenzie Nature Reserve:* in virgin bushland, with orchids
and wildflowers during winter and spring. *Self-guide tourist
drives:* the Skyline Rd from Alexandra to Eildon features lookouts
along the way; information from visitor centre. *Taggerty:* home
to the Willowbank Gallery and a bush market; open 4th Sat each
month; 18 km s. *Trout fishing:* in the Goulburn, Acheron and
Rubicon rivers. *Lake Eildon National Park:* excellent walking
trails in the north-west section of the park; *for more details see
Eildon. **Bonnie Doon:*** a good base for exploring the lake region.
Activities include trail-riding, bushwalking, watersports and
scenic drives; 37 km NE near Lake Eildon.

See also HIGH COUNTRY, p. 158

Anglesea
Pop. 2292
Map ref. 572 E10 | 580 F3 | 593 N9

🛈 Off Great Ocean Rd; or ring Torquay Information Centre,
(03) 5261 4219 or 1300 614 219; www.visitsurfcoast.com

📻 94.7 The Pulse FM, 774 AM ABC Local Radio

A pretty and sheltered part of the surf coast, Anglesea is one
of the smaller holiday hamlets along the Great Ocean Road.

The main beaches are patrolled from Christmas through to Easter, making it a favourite destination for both swimmers and beginner surfers.

Coogoorah Reserve Set on the Anglesea River, the name of this park means 'swampy reed creek'. Coogoorah was established after the 1983 Ash Wednesday fires and now features a network of boardwalks weaving through the distinctive wetland vegetation. Keep an eye out for local birdlife, including the peregrine falcon.

Anglesea Golf Course: golfers share the greens with kangaroos; Golf Links Rd. *Melaleuca Gallery:* open daily 11am–5.30pm; Great Ocean Rd. *Viewing platform:* overlooks open-cut brown-coal mine and power station; behind town in Coalmine Rd. *Paddleboats:* for hire on the banks of the Anglesea River.

Markets: local crafts and produce, held over summer, Easter and Melbourne Cup weekend; by the Anglesea River. *Rock to Ramp Swim:* Jan. *Anglesea Art Show:* June. *ANGAIR Wildflower and Art Show:* Sept.

Locanda Del Mare: a slice of Italy; 5 Diggers Pde; (03) 5263 2904. *Pete's Place:* cosy seafood cafe; 113 Great Ocean Rd; (03) 5263 2500. *A La Grecque:* modern Greek cuisine; 60 Great Ocean Rd, Aireys Inlet; (03) 5289 6922.

Aireys-on-Aireys: 3 luxury villas; 19 Aireys St, Aireys Inlet; (03) 5289 6844.

Aireys Inlet This pretty little town is overlooked by a lighthouse built to guide passing ships along this treacherous coastline. Painkalac Creek flows out to the ocean here, creating the inlet of the town's name and a safe swimming spot. Horseriding and fishing are favourite activities along the sheltered beaches. South of town is the Great Ocean Road Memorial Arch, built in 1939. 11 km sw.

J. E. Loveridge Lookout: 1 km w. *Pt Roadknight Beach:* a shallow, protected beach, popular with families; 2 km sw. *Ironbark Basin Reserve:* features ocean views, local birdlife and good bushwalking. The Pt Addis Koorie Cultural Walk leads through the park, highlighting sites of Indigenous significance; 7 km NW, off Pt Addis Rd. *Great Otway National Park:* the park begins near Anglesea and stretches to the south and west. The section near Anglesea features unique heathland flora and good walking trails; access via Aireys Inlet, 11 km sw. *For more details see Apollo Bay.* *Surf Coast Walk:* 30 km from Torquay to Moggs Creek (south of Aireys Inlet). The track passes through Anglesea. *Surf schools:* learn to surf on one of the beginner courses available at nearby beaches; details from visitor centre.

See also SOUTH-WEST COAST, p. 153

Apollo Bay

Pop. 1373
Map ref. 572 B12, | 580 C5 | 593 L10

 Great Ocean Road Visitor Information Centre, 100 Great Ocean Rd; 1300 689 297; www.visitgreatoceanroad.org.au

89.5 FM ABC Local Radio, 104.7 Otway FM

Named after a local schooner, Apollo Bay has become the resting place of many shipwrecks, yet it maintains an appeal for all lovers of the ocean. The town is situated near Otway National Park with a wonderful contrast between rugged coastline and tranquil green hills. The seaside town is popular with fishing enthusiasts and, like many other coastal towns, its population swells significantly over summer as visitors flock here for the holidays.

Old Cable Station Museum: features artefacts from Australia's telecommunications history and informative displays exploring the history of the region; open 2–5pm weekends and school and public holidays; Great Ocean Rd. *Bass Strait Shell Museum:* holds an impressive array of shells and provides many facts about the marine life along the Victorian south-west coast; Noel St. *Great Ocean Walk:* enjoy stunning views on this 91 km walk between Apollo Bay and Glenample Homestead, near the Twelve Apostles. Walkers must register to use campgrounds en route. Further information available at www.greatoceanwalk.com.au

Foreshore Market: each Sat. *Apollo Bay Music Festival:* Apr.

Bay Leaf Cafe: substantial cafe food; 131 Great Ocean Rd; (03) 5237 6470. *Chris's Beacon Point Restaurant & Villas:* Mediterranean/Greek; 280 Skenes Creek Rd; (03) 5237 6411. *Great Ocean Road Hotel:* modern Australian and bar menu; 29 Great Ocean Rd; (03) 5237 6240. *La Bimba Restaurant & Cafe:* modern Mediterranean; 125 Great Ocean Rd; (03) 5237 7411.

Captain's at the Bay: stylish accommodation options; 21 Pascoe St; (03) 5237 6771. *Chocolate Gannets:* villas with views; 6180 Great Ocean Rd; 1300 500 139. *Chris's Beacon Point Restaurant & Villas:* villas and studios with views; 280 Skenes Creek Rd; (03) 5237 6411. *Point of View:* villas for couples; 165 Tuxion Rd; 0427 376 377.

Great Otway National Park Formerly named Otway National Park, this section of the 103 000 ha park includes some of the most rugged coastline in Victoria, particularly around Cape Otway and the stretch of coast towards Princetown. It is an ideal location for a bushwalking adventure taking in sights through the park to the sea, from the scenic Elliot River down to adjacent Shelly Beach. Many species of wildlife inhabit the park, including koalas and the rare tiger quoll. Also look out for the historic Cape Otway Lighthouse, built in 1848. The Great Ocean Rd, west of Apollo Bay, passes through the park. Contact Parks Victoria on 13 1963; 13 km sw.

Otway Fly The consistently popular Otway Fly is a steel-trussed walkway perched high among the temperate rainforest treetops of the Otway Ranges. The 'Fly' is 25 m high and stretches for 600 m. It is accessible to all ages and levels of mobility. Get a bird's-eye view of ancient myrtle beech, blackwood and mountain ash while looking out for a variety of wildlife, including pygmy possums and the raucous yellow-tailed black cockatoo. A springboard bridge takes you over Youngs Creek, where you might spot a shy platypus. Inquiries on 1800 300 477; 62 km NW via Lavers Hill.

Marriners Lookout: with views across Skenes Creek and Apollo Bay; 1.5 km NW. *Barham Paradise Scenic Reserve:* in the Barham River Valley, it is home to a variety of distinctive moisture-loving trees and ferns; 7 km NW. *Tanybryn Gallery:* displays and sells art and craft work in the magnificent surrounds of the Otway Ranges; Skenes Creek Rd; 20 km NE. *Forests and Waterfall Drive:* 109 km loop drive featuring spectacular Otway Ranges scenery. Waterfalls include Beauchamp, Triplet and Houptoun falls. Drive starts at Apollo Bay, travels west to Lavers Hill and around to Skenes Creek. Map from visitor centre. *Charter flights:* views of the Twelve Apostles, the Bay of Islands and the 'Shipwreck Coast'; details from visitor centre.

See also SOUTH-WEST COAST, p. 153

VICTORIA

Ararat

 Railway Station Complex, 91 High St; (03) 5355 0281 or 1800 657 158; www.visitararat.com.au

99.9 VoiceFM, 107.9 FM ABC Local Radio

Ararat is a city with a vibrant history. Once inhabited by the Tjapwurong Aboriginal people, the promising lands soon saw squatters move in, and the area really started to boom when gold was discovered in 1854. Thousands of prospectors arrived, and Ararat finally came into existence when Chinese immigrants rested on the town's site in 1857, after walking from South Australian ports in order to avoid Victorian poll taxes. One member of the party discovered alluvial gold, and Ararat was born. Today Ararat is a service centre to its agricultural surrounds.

J Ward The town's original gaol, 'J Ward' served as an asylum for the criminally insane for many years and offers an eerie glimpse into the history of criminal confinement. Now guided tours reveal in chilling detail what life was like for the inmates. Girdlestone St; daily tours (03) 5352 3357.

Gum San Chinese Heritage Centre Gum San means 'hill of gold', a fitting name for this impressive centre built in traditional Southern Chinese style and incorporating the principles of feng shui. The centre celebrates the contribution of the Chinese community both to Ararat, which is said to be the only goldfields town founded by Chinese prospectors, and to the surrounding Goldfields region. The experience is brought to life with interactive displays and an original Canton lead-mining tunnel, uncovered during the building of the centre. Western Hwy; (03) 5352 1078.

Alexandra Park and Botanical Gardens: an attractive formal garden featuring ornamental lakes, fountains and an orchid glasshouse; Vincent St. *Historical self-guide tours (walking or driving):* of particular note are the bluestone buildings in Barkly St, including the post office, town hall, civic square and war memorial; details from visitor centre. *Ararat Art Gallery:* a regional gallery specialising in wool and fibre pieces by local artists; Barkly St. *Langi Morgala Museum:* displays Aboriginal artefacts; Queen St.

Jailhouse Rock Festival: Mar. *Australian Orchid Festival:* Sept. *Golden Gateway Festival:* held over 10 days; Oct.

Nectar Ambrosia: smart eatery in old pub; 157–159 Barkly St; (03) 5352 7344.

Mt Buangor State Park The park features the Fern Tree Waterfalls and the 3 impressive peaks of Mt Buangor, Mt Sugarloaf and Cave Hill. Its diverse terrain with many varieties of eucalypts offers great sightseeing, bushwalking and picnicking. There are more than 130 species of birds, as well as eastern grey kangaroos, wallabies and echidnas. Contact Parks Victoria on 13 1963. Access to the southern section is via Ferntree Rd off the Western Hwy; 30 km E. Mt Buangor and Cave Hill can be accessed from the main Mt Cole Rd in the Mt Cole State Forest.

Garden Gully Winery: hosts a scarecrow competition each Apr, with ingenious entries from across the state scattered through the vineyard; 17 km N on Western Hwy. Many more of the region's wineries can be accessed on the Great Grape Rd, a circuit through Ballarat and St Arnaud. This region is famous for sparkling whites and traditional old shiraz varieties; brochure and map from visitor centre. *Green Hill Lake:* great for fishing and water activities; 4 km E. *McDonald Park Wildflower Reserve:* an extensive display of flora indigenous to the area, including wattles and banksias, impressive during the spring months; 5 km N on Western Hwy. *One Tree Hill Lookout:* 360-degree views across the region; 5 km NW. *Langi Ghiran State Park:* Mt Langi Ghiran and Mt Gorrin form the key features of this park. A popular walk starts at the picnic area along Easter Creek, then goes to the Old Langi Ghiran Reservoir and along the stone water race to a scenic lookout; access via Western Hwy, Kartuk Rd; 14 km E. *Mt Cole State Forest:* adjoins Mt Buangor State Park, with bushwalking, horseriding, 4WD tracks and trail-bike riding. The Ben Nevis Fire Tower offers spectacular views; 35 km E.

See also GRAMPIANS & CENTRAL WEST, p. 155

Avoca

122 High St; (03) 5465 1000 or 1800 206 622; www.pyreneestourism.com.au

91.1 FM ABC Local Radio, 96.5 Radio KLFM

Avoca was built during the gold boom of the 19th century and is renowned for its wide main street, divided by a stretch of park with trees and a war memorial. Avoca is set in the picturesque Pyrenees Ranges, with the Avoca River flowing by the town.

Historic walk: takes in the original courthouse, one of the oldest surviving courts in Victoria, as well as the powder magazine and Lalor's, one of the state's earliest pharmacies; map from visitor centre. *Cemetery:* Chinese burial ground from the goldmining period; on outskirts of town.

Avoca Fine Wine, Arts and Craft Market: 3rd Sun each month. *Blue Pyrenees Pink Lamb and Purple Shiraz Race Meeting:* country race meeting; Mar. *Petanque Tournaments (French Bowls):* Mar and Dec. *Mt Avoca Anzac Day Races:* Apr. *Taltarni Cup Races:* Oct.

Warrenmang Vineyard & Resort: regional food; 188 Mountain Creek Rd, Moonambel; (03) 5467 2233.

eco-luxe @ Mount Avoca: eco-friendly luxury lodges; Mount Avoca Winery, Moates La, Avoca; (03) 5465 3282. *Warrenmang Vineyard & Resort:* chalets and luxury suites; 188 Mountain Creek Rd, Moonambel; (03) 5467 2233.

Pyrenees Ranges State Forest Covering a large stretch of bushland, these ranges are great for bushwalking and picnics and camping. Visitors can see a variety of wildlife, including koalas, wallabies, kangaroos and goannas. Orchids and lilies can be found growing around the base of the ranges in season. An 18 km walking track starts at The Waterfall camping area and finishes at Warrenmang–Glenlofty Rd. Access via Sunraysia or Pyrenees hwys. For further information contact the Department of Sustainability and Environment Customer Sevice Centre on 13 1186.

Blue Pyrenees Estate: with underground cellar, petanque piste and gourmet lunches on weekends; 7 km W. *Mt Lonarch Arts:* displays and sells fine bone china made on the premises; Mt Lonarch; 10 km S. *Warrenmang Vineyard Resort:* with cottage-style accommodation and a restaurant specialising in regional produce. The vineyard is also the venue for A Sparkling Affair each Nov, an event celebrating the release of sparkling wines; 22 km NW. *Wine-tasting tours:* including self-guide Great Grape Rd; details from visitor centre.

See also GOLDFIELDS, p. 154

Bacchus Marsh

Pop. 13 258
Map ref. 572 G4 | 579 G12 | 582 A3 | 593 O5

 156 Main St; (03) 5367 7488;
www.discoverbacchusmarsh.org

98.5 3APL Apple FM, 774 AM ABC Local Radio

Bacchus Marsh shares part of its name with the Roman god of wine, but is actually better known for the apples that grow so well in the fertile valley region between the Werribee and Lerderg rivers. Considered a satellite town within commuting distance of Melbourne, Bacchus Marsh retains a certain charm with stunning heritage buildings and a rural atmosphere.

Avenue of Honour Visitors to the town are greeted by the sight of the renowned Avenue of Honour, an elm-lined stretch of road built in honour of the Australian soldiers who fought in WW I. Eastern approach to town.

Big Apple Tourist Orchard: fresh produce market; Avenue of Honour. *Historic buildings:* include The Manor, the original home of the town's founder, Captain Bacchus (now privately owned), and Border Inn, built in 1850, thought to be the state's first stop for Cobb & Co coaches travelling to the goldfields; details from visitor centre. *Local history museum:* connected to the blacksmith cottage and forge; open Sat–Sun; Main St. *Naturipe Fruits, Strawberry, Peach and Nectarine Farm:* pick-your-own fruits and roadside sales; Avenue of Honour.

Rotary Art Show: June.

Lerderg State Park Featuring the imposing Lerderg Gorge, the park is a great venue for picnics, bushwalking and swimming, while the Lerderg River is ideal for trout fishing. The area was mined during the gold rush, and remnants from the water races used for washing gold can still be found upstream from O'Brien's Crossing. Late winter and spring are good times to see wildflowers and blossoming shrubs. Look out for koalas nestled in giant manna gums and for the magnificent sulphur-crested cockatoo and the wedge-tailed eagle. Contact Parks Victoria on 13 1963. Access via Western Fwy to Bacchus Marsh–Gisborne and Lerderg Gorge rds; 10 km N.

Werribee Gorge State Park Over time the Werribee River has carved through ancient seabed sediment and lava flows to form a spectacular gorge. The name 'Werribee' comes from the Aboriginal word 'Wearibi', meaning 'swimming place' or 'backbone', perhaps in reference to the snake-like path of the river. Rock climbing is permitted at Falcons Lookout and a popular walk follows the Werribee River from the Meikles Pt picnic area, providing views of the river and the gorge cliff-faces. Contact Parks Victoria on 13 1963. Access via Western Fwy and Pentland Hills Rd to Myers Rd, or via Ironbark Rd (the Ballan–Ingliston Rd) from the Bacchus Marsh–Anakie Rd; 10 km W.

Long Forest Flora Reserve: a great example of the distinctive mallee scrub that once covered the region; 2 km NE. *St Anne's Vineyard:* with a bluestone cellar built from the remains of the old Ballarat Gaol; Western Fwy; 6 km W. *Merrimu Reservoir:* attractive park area with picnic facilities; about 10 km NE. *Melton:* now virtually a satellite suburb of Melbourne, this town has a long and rich history of horse breeding and training. Visit the Willow Homestead to see exhibits detailing the life of early settlers (open Wed, Fri and Sun), picnic on the Werribee River at Melton Reservoir, or taste the fine wines in the nearby Sunbury Wine Region; 14 km E. *Brisbane Ranges National Park:* with good walking tracks, wildflowers during spring and the imposing, steep-sided Anakie Gorge; 16 km SW. *Ballan:* try the refreshing mineral-spring water at Bostock Reservoir, or join in the festivities at the Vintage Machinery and Vehicle Rally in Feb, and an Autumn Festival held each Mar; 20 km NW. *Blackwood:* visit the Mineral Springs Reserve and Garden of St Erth (closed Wed and Thurs). Blackwood is also the start of the 53 km return scenic drive through the Wombat State Forest; 31 km NW.

See also SPA & GARDEN COUNTRY, p. 151

Bairnsdale

Pop. 11 284
Map ref. 583 M5

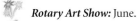 240 Main St; (03) 5152 3444 or 1800 637 060;
www.lakesandwilderness.com.au

100.7 FM ABC Local Radio, 105.5 3REG Radio East Gippsland FM

An attractive rural centre situated on the Mitchell River Flats and considered to be the western gateway to the lakes and wilderness region of East Gippsland. The area has a rich Koorie history brought to life through local landmarks, especially in Mitchell River National Park, where a fascinating piece of Aboriginal folklore is based around the Den of Nargun.

Aboriginal culture The Krowathunkoolong Keeping Place, on Dalmahoy St, details the cultural history of the region's Kurnai Aboriginal people and provides an insight into the impact of white settlement. To explore local Aboriginal history further, visit Howitt Park, Princes Hwy – a tree here has a 4 m scar where bark has been removed to make a canoe. The Bataluk Cultural Trail from Sale to Cann River takes in these and other Indigenous sites of East Gippsland. Details of the trail from Krowathunkoolong.

Historical Museum: built in 1891, contains relics from Bairnsdale's past; Macarthur St. *Jolly Jumbuck Country Craft Centre:* wool spinning and knitting mills, plus woollen products for sale; edge of town. *Self-guide heritage walks:* take in St Mary's Church, with wall and ceiling murals by Italian artist Francesco Floreani, and the Court House, a magnificent, castle-like construction; details from visitor centre.

Howitt Park Market: 4th Sun each month. *Line Dancing Championships:* Mar. *East Gippsland Agricultural Field Days:* popular event with family entertainment; Apr. *Bairnsdale Easter Races:* Easter. *Bairnsdale Cup:* Sept.

Paper Chase: modern bookshop cafe; 168 Main St; (03) 5152 5181.

Comfort Inn Riversleigh: spacious rooms in heritage building; 1 Nicholson St; (03) 5152 6966. *Tara House:* 3 ensuite rooms; 37 Day St; (03) 5153 2253. *Waterholes Guest House:* rooms each with own verandah; 540 Archies Rd; (03) 5157 9330.

Mitchell River National Park Set in the remnants of temperate rainforest, this park has its own piece of mythology. According to Koorie history, Nargun was a beast made all of stone except for his hands, arms and breast. The fierce creature would drag the unwary to his den, a shallow cave beneath a waterfall on the Woolshed Creek. This Den of Nargun can be found in the park, as can giant kanooka trees, wildflowers and over 150 species of birds. There is a circuit walk to Bluff Lookout and Mitchell River, and Billy Goat Bend is good for picnics. Contact Parks Victoria on 13 1963; Princes Hwy; 15 km W near Lindenow.

 RADIO STATIONS   IN TOWN   WHAT'S ON   WHERE TO EAT   WHERE TO STAY   NEARBY

VICTORIA

McLeods Morass Wildlife Reserve: a boardwalk extends over the freshwater marshland, allowing a close-up view of the many species of waterbirds found here; southern outskirts of town, access via Macarthur St; 2 km s. *Wineries:* include Nicholson River Winery, for tastings and sales; 10 km E. *Bruthen:* hosts a Blues Bash each Feb; 24 km NW. *Dargo:* historic township in Dargo River valley and major producer of walnuts. Dargo Valley Winery has accommodation and cellar-door sales. The road beyond Dargo offers a scenic drive through high plains to Hotham Heights, stunning in spring when wattles bloom (unsealed road, check conditions); 93 km NW.

See also EAST GIPPSLAND, p. 159

Ballarat

see inset box on next page

Beechworth

Pop. 2644
Map ref. 585 J7 | 586 H4

i Ford St; (03) 5728 3233 or 1300 366 321; www.beechworth.com

101.3 Oak FM, 106.5 FM ABC Local Radio

Set in the picturesque surrounds of the Australian Alps, Beechworth is one of the state's best preserved 19th-century gold towns, with over 30 buildings listed by the National Trust. The grandeur of Beechworth's buildings can be explained by the fact that during the 1850s over four million ounces of gold were mined here. There is a delightful tale about Beechworth's heyday: the story goes that Daniel Cameron, a political candidate vying for support from the Ovens Valley community, rode at the head of a procession through the town on a horse shod with golden shoes. Sceptics claim they were merely gilded, but the tale offers a glimpse into the wealth of Beechworth during the gold rush.

 Historic and cultural precinct This fantastic precinct provides a snapshot of 19th-century Beechworth. Featuring fine, honey-coloured granite buildings, the area incorporates the telegraph station, gold office, Chinese prospectors' office, town hall and powder magazine. Of particular interest is the courthouse, site of many infamous trials including Ned Kelly's, and where Sir Isaac Isaacs began his legal career. Also in the precinct is the Robert O'Hara Burke Memorial Museum, with the interesting 'Strand of Time' exhibition where 19th-century Beechworth shops are brought to life.

Beechworth Gaol Built in 1859, the original wooden gates of this gaol were replaced with iron ones when it was feared prisoners would break out in sympathy with Ned Kelly during his trial. The gaol is located in William St but not presently open to the public.

Walking tours: Ned Kelly and Gold Rush walking tours operate daily, and Ghost Tours are available at the former Mayday Hills Asylum; bookings at visitor centre. *Carriage Museum and Australian Light Horse Exhibition:* National Trust horse-drawn carriage display and Australian Light Horse Exhibition housed at the historic Murray Breweries, which also offers turn-of-the-century gourmet cordial made to time-honoured recipes; 29 Last St. *Beechworth Honey Experience:* interpretive display on the history of honey; includes a glass-fronted live bee display. A wide range of premium Australian honey is on offer in the concept shop; Cnr Ford and Church sts. *Harry Power's Cell:* under the shire offices, where the 'gentleman bushranger' was once briefly held; Albert Rd. *The Beechworth Pantry:* gourmet cafe and centre for produce of the north-east; Ford St. *Beechworth Bakery:* famous for its pastries and cakes; Camp St.

Country Craft Market: Queen Victoria Park, 4 times a year; details from visitor centre. *Golden Horseshoes Festival:* a celebration of the town's past, with street parades and a variety of market stalls; Easter. *Beechworth Harvest Celebration:* May; details from visitor centre. *Drive Back in Time:* vintage car rally; May. *Celtic Festival:* music festival; Nov.

Provenance Restaurant: contemporary regional food; 86 Ford St; (03) 5728 1786. *The Green Shed Bistro:* European-influenced; 37 Camp St; (03) 5728 2360. *The Ox and Hound:* contemporary bistro; 52 Ford St; (03) 5728 2123. *Wardens Food & Wine:* modern Italian; 32 Ford St; (03) 5728 1377.

1860 Luxury Accommodation: original slab hut relocated; 4 Surrey La; 0408 273 783. *Black Springs Bakery:* charming provincial-style barn; 464 Wangaratta Rd; (03) 5728 2565. *Provenance Restaurant & Luxury Suites:* 4 contemporary suites; 86 Ford St; (03) 5728 1786. *Stone Cottage:* 1-bedroom cottage, 2-bedroom barn; 6 Tanswell St; (03) 5728 2857. *The Stanley:* boutique rooms at country pub; 1 Wallace St, Stanley; (03) 5728 6502.

Beechworth Cemetery This cemetery is a fascinating piece of goldfields history. More than 2000 Chinese goldminers are buried here. Twin ceremonial Chinese burning towers stand as a monument to those who died seeking their fortune far from home. Northern outskirts of town.

Beechworth Historic Park: surrounds the town and includes Woolshed Falls Historical Walk through former alluvial goldmining sites. *Gorge Scenic Drive (5 km):* starts north of town. *Beechworth Forest Drive:* takes in Fletcher Dam; 3 km SE towards Stanley. *Kellys Lookout:* at Woolshed Creek; about 4 km N. *Mt Pilot Lookout:* views of Murray Valley, plus signposted Aboriginal cave paintings nearby; 5 km N. *Stanley:* a historic goldmining settlement with fantastic views of the alps from the summit of Mt Stanley; 10 km SE. *Wineries:* 5 cellar doors in and around Beechworth for tastings and sales; map from visitor centre.

See also HIGH COUNTRY, p. 158

Benalla

Pop. 9128
Map ref. 584 G8 | 586 D5

i 14 Mair St; (03) 5762 1749; www.benallaonline.com.au

97.7 FM ABC Local Radio, 101.3 Oak FM

Motorists from Melbourne entering Benalla will notice the Rose Gardens positioned beside the highway a short distance before Lake Benalla – gardens for which the city has become known as the 'Rose City'. The town is Sir Edward 'Weary' Dunlop's birthplace and proudly advertises the fact with a museum display and a statue in his honour at the Benalla Botanical Gardens.

 Benalla Art Gallery Set beside Lake Benalla, the gallery has an impressive collection including contemporary Australian art, works by Sidney Nolan, Arthur Streeton, Tom Roberts and Arthur Boyd, and a substantial collection of Indigenous art. Built in 1975, the gallery is a striking work of modern architecture. There is a permanent exhibition featuring the works of Laurie Ledger, a local resident, and examples of the Heidelberg School and early colonial art. Bridge St; (03) 5762 3027.

Benalla Ceramic Art Mural: a Gaudi-inspired community construction, this fascinating 3D mural is opposite the art gallery on Lake Benalla. *The Creators Gallery:* paintings, pottery and craft; at the information centre. *Benalla Costume and Pioneer Museum:* has period costumes, a Ned Kelly exhibit (including Kelly's cummerbund) and a feature display of Benalla's 'famous sons', in particular, Sir Edward 'Weary' Dunlop; Mair St. *Lake Benalla:* created in Broken River, it has good recreation and picnic facilities and is a haven for waterbirds. Take the self-guide walk around the lake. *Botanical Gardens:* features a splendid collection of roses and memorial statue of Sir Edward 'Weary' Dunlop; Bridge St. *Aeropark:* centre for the Gliding Club of Victoria, offering hot-air ballooning and glider flights; northern outskirts of town; bookings on (03) 5762 1058.

Lakeside Craft and Farmers Market: near the Civic Centre; 3rd Sat each month. *Benalla Festival:* Feb/Mar.

Benalla Gallery Cafe: contemporary local produce menu; Benalla Art Gallery, Bridge St East; (03) 5762 3777. *Georgina's:* modern Australian menu; 100 Bridge St East; (03) 5762 1334. *North Eastern Hotel:* regional contemporary dishes; 1–3 Nunn St; (03) 5762 7333. *Raffety's Restaurant:* homemade modern Australian dishes; 55 Nunn St; (03) 5762 4066.

Merriollia: 3 B&B rooms; 17–19 Cecil St; (03) 5762 3786. *Nillahcootie Estate:* 3-bedroom guesthouse; 3630 Midland Hwy, Lima South; (03) 5768 2685.

Reef Hills State Park Features grey box, river red gum, wildflowers in spring and wattle blossom in winter. The park offers scenic drives, bushwalks, picnics and horseriding. There are more than 100 species of birds, including gang-gang cockatoos and crimson rosellas, plus animals such as eastern grey kangaroos, sugar gliders, brush-tailed possums, echidnas and bats. Contact Parks Victoria on 13 1963; 4 km sw, western side of the Midland Hwy.

Lake Mokoan: depending on water levels, great for fishing, boating and waterskiing; 10 km NE. *1950s-style cinema:* showing classic films at Swanpool; 23 km s.

See also HIGH COUNTRY, p. 158

Bendigo *see inset box on page 168*

Bright *see inset box on page 171*

Buchan

Pop. 326
Map ref. 565 A11 | 581 A10 | 583 P4

ⓘ General Store, Main St; (03) 5155 9202 or 1800 637 060; www.lakesandwilderness.com.au

📻 90.7 FM 3REG Radio East Gippsland, 828 AM ABC Local Radio

Situated in East Gippsland, Buchan is primarily an agricultural town renowned for offering some of the best caving in Victoria. Although the origin of the town's name is disputed, it is said to be derived from the Aboriginal term for either 'smoke-signal expert' or 'place of the grass bag'.

Foothills Festival: Jan. *Canni Creek Races:* Jan. *Rodeo:* Easter. *Flower Show:* Nov.

Parks Victoria Wilderness Retreat Buchan Caves: 5 comfortable tents; Buchan Caves Reserve; 13 1963.

Buchan Caves Reserve The reserve features more than 350 limestone caves, of which the Royal and Fairy caves are the most accessible – the Fairy Cave alone is over 400 m long, with impressive stalactites. Europeans did not discover the caves until 1907, but from then on they became a popular tourist

destination. Now visitors can cool off in the spring-fed swimming pool after exploring the caves. Tours of the Royal and Fairy caves run daily. Off Buchan Rd, north of town; (03) 5162 1900.

Snowy River Scenic Drive The drive takes in the Buchan and Snowy rivers junction and runs along the edge of Snowy River National Park to Gelantipy. Beyond Gelantipy is Little River Gorge, Victoria's deepest gorge. A short walking track leads to a cliff-top lookout. Near the gorge is McKillops Bridge, a safe swimming spot, a good site to launch canoes, and the starting point for 2 walking tracks. Care is required on the road beyond Gelantipy; 4WD is recommended. Details from visitor centre.

Suggan Buggan: this historic townsite, surrounded by Alpine National Park, features an 1865 schoolhouse and the Eagle Loft Gallery for local art and craft; 64 km N.

See also EAST GIPPSLAND, p. 159

Camperdown

Pop. 3164
Map ref. 580 H7 | 593 J7

ⓘ Old Courthouse, Manifold St; (03) 5593 3390; www.greatoceanrd.org

📻 104.7 Otway FM, 594 AM ABC Local Radio

Located at the foot of Mount Leura, a volcanic cone, Camperdown is more famous for its natural attractions than for the town itself, being situated on the world's third largest volcanic plain. But that should not detract from Camperdown – National Trust–listed Finlay Avenue features 2 kilometres of regal elm trees, while in the town centre the Gothic-style Manifold Clock Tower proudly stands as a tribute to the region's first European pioneers.

Manifold Clock Tower: an imposing structure built in 1896; open 1st Sun each month; Cnr Manifold and Pike sts. *Historical Society Museum:* displays Aboriginal artefacts, local historical photographs, and household and farming implements; Manifold St. *Courthouse:* built in 1886–87, described as one of the most distinctive courthouses in Australia; Manifold St. *Buggy Museum:* collection of 30 restored horse-drawn buggies; Ower St.

Craft market: Finlay Ave or Theatre Royal; 1st Sun each month. *Heritage Festival:* Nov.

Purrumbete Homestead: perfect for an indulgent holiday; 3551 Princes Hwy; (03) 5594 7374. *Timboon House & Stables B&B:* 3 rooms in historic house; 320 Old Geelong Rd; (03) 5593 1003.

Crater lakes Surrounding Camperdown are spectacular crater lakes that provide an interesting history of volcanic activity over the past 20 000 years, as well as opportunities for watersports and excellent fishing. Travelling west of town, take the scenic drive around the rims of lakes Bullen Merri and Gnotuk, and join in the watersports and swimming at South Beach. The lakes are regularly stocked with Chinook salmon and redfin. For a scenic picnic spot, and some of the best fishing, visit Lake Purrumbete; 15 km SE. By far one of the most impressive lakes is Lake Corangamite, the Southern Hemisphere's largest permanent salt lake. This lake lies 25 km E, but the best viewing spot is Red Rock Lookout; *see Colac.*

Derrinallum and Mt Elephant Mt Elephant rises to almost 200 m behind the small township of Derrinallum – it doesn't sound like a lot, but across the plains of the Western District you can see it from up to 60 km away. A gash in the elephant's western side is

 RADIO STATIONS   IN TOWN   WHAT'S ON   WHERE TO EAT   WHERE TO STAY   NEARBY

VICTORIA

BALLARAT

Pop. 85 196

Map ref. 572 D3 | 527 | 579 C10 | 593 M4

i The Eureka Centre, cnr Rodier and Eureka sts; 1800 446 633; www.ballarat.com

99.9 VoiceFM, 107.9 FM ABC Local Radio

Ballarat is Victoria's largest inland city and features grand old buildings and wide streets that create an air of splendour. Built on the wealth of the region's goldfields, Ballarat offers activities ranging from fine dining in the many restaurants to real-life experiences of the area's goldmining past. Although dry in recent years, Lake Wendouree provides a beautiful backdrop for picnics. Ballarat was the site of the infamous Eureka Rebellion of 3 December 1854. When goldfields police attempted to quell the miners' anger over strict mining-licence laws, a bloody massacre eventuated. The Eureka Rebellion is viewed by many as a symbol of the Australian workers' struggle for equity and a 'fair go'. The best place to get a feel for this historic event is at Sovereign Hill.

Sovereign Hill This is the main destination for visitors to Ballarat and a good place to get a taste for what life was like on the Victorian goldfields. Spread over 60 ha, Sovereign Hill is a replica goldmining town, complete with authentically dressed townspeople. Panning for gold is a popular activity, while in the evening the 'Blood on the Southern Cross' show re-enacts the Eureka Rebellion. Bradshaw St; (03) 5337 1100.

Eureka Stockade Centre: a uniquely designed building, with information about the infamous battle; Eureka St. *Ballarat Botanic Gardens:* an impressive collection of native and exotic plants; Prime Minister Ave features busts of all of Australia's prime ministers. *Ballarat Wildlife Park:* houses native Australian animals such as koalas, kangaroos, quokkas and crocodiles; Cnr Fussel and York sts. *Ballarat Fine Art Gallery:* holds a significant collection of Australian art. The original Eureka Rebellion flag is also on display; 40 Lydiard St. *Gold Museum:* details the rich goldmining history of the area; opposite Sovereign Hill. *Historic buildings:* include Her Majesty's Theatre, built in 1875 and Australia's oldest intact, purpose-built theatre, and Craig's Royal and the George hotels, with classic old-world surroundings;

[PANNING FOR GOLD, SOVEREIGN HILL]

Lydiard St. *Vintage Tramway:* via Wendouree Pde; rides weekends, and public and school holidays. *Avenue of Honour and Arch of Victory:* honours those who fought in WW I; western edge of city.

Pleasant St Market: 4th Sun each month. *Ballarat Lakeside Farmers Market:* Lake Wendouree foreshore; 2nd Sat each month. *Organs of the Ballarat Goldfields:* music festival held in historic venues; Jan. *Begonia Festival:* popular event for garden lovers; Mar. *Royal South Street Eisteddfod:* music festival; Sept–Nov. *Ballarat Cup:* Nov.

Europa Cafe: cafe with all-day breakfast; 411 Sturt St; (03) 5338 7672. *L'espresso:* Italian cafe; 417 Sturt St; (03) 5333 1789. *Masons Cafe & Foodstore:* excellent blackboard specials; 32 Drummond St North; (03) 5333 3895. *Phoenix Brewery:* hearty, contemporary food; 10 Camp St; (03) 5333 2686.

Abena's Boutique Accommodation: 3-bedroom cottage; 210 Grant St; (03) 5338 7397. *Craig's Royal Hotel:* restored historic hotel rooms; 10 Lydiard St South; (03) 5331 1377. *Cumberland Villa:* 4-bedroom villa; 332 Lydiard St North; (03) 5331 6216. *Montrose of Ballarat:* heritage cottage; 111 Eureka St; 0429 439 448.

Enfield State Park Great for bushwalking or horseriding, the park has many species of orchids and numerous animals including echidnas, koalas, bats and frogs. There is a pretty picnic ground and walking tracks at Remote Long Gully. Also featured are the remnants of early goldmining settlements, including the Berringa Mines Historic Reserve. Contact Parks Victoria on 13 1963; access via Incolls and Misery Creek rds; 16 km s.

Buninyong Buninyong features many fine art and craft galleries. Ballarat Bird World, home to many species of parrots, has raised walkways through the aviaries. Visit in Mar for the Gold King Festival, which celebrates the early history of the town, and in May for the Buninyong Film Festival. The Mt Buninyong Lookout east of town offers great views. 13 km SE.

Kirks and Gong Gong reserves: ideal for picnics and bushwalking, these parks include many unique, indigenous plants; on opposite sides of Daylesford Rd; 5 km NE. *Kryal Castle:* replica of a medieval castle, with daily tours and family entertainment; 9 km E. *Yuulong Lavender Estate:* set in scenic landscaped gardens, the estate produces and sells lavender products; 15 km SE at Yendon. *Lal Lal Falls:* plunge 30 m into the Moorabool River; 18 km SE. *Lal Lal Blast Furnace:* fascinating 19th-century archaeological remains; 18 km SE. *Lake Burrumbeet:* this 2100 ha lake is a popular fishing spot, especially for redfin in spring and summer. Watersports and family activities are available on the lake; various boat ramps provide access. Caravan parks are set on the lakeside and are popular with holiday-makers; 22 km NW. *Skipton:* in town is an eel factory selling smoked eel and other products; 51 km SW. South of town are the Mt Widderin Caves – one has been named the Ballroom, as it was once a venue for dances and concerts. The caves are on private property; tours by appt (03) 5340 2081. *Beaufort:* a small town on the shores of Lake Beaufort, an artificial lake surrounded by gardens, providing a picturesque location for picnics and leisurely walks; 54 km w. South of town is Lake Goldsmith, home of a major rally of steam-driven machinery and vehicles each May and Nov. **Mooramong Homestead:** built in the 1870s and then altered during the 1930s by its ex-Hollywood owners. It is surrounded by beautiful gardens and a flora and fauna reserve, and is open for tours 3rd Sun each month; 56 km nw via Skipton. **Great Grape Rd:** circuit through Avoca, St Arnaud and Stawell, visiting local wineries.

See also GOLDFIELDS, p. 154

the result of decades of quarrying. The mountain is actually the scoria cone of an extinct volcano, and inside is a 90 m deep crater. Now owned by the community, there is a walking trail to the top, and the Music on the Mount festival is held here in Nov. Lake Tooliorook on the other side of town offers good fishing for trout and redfin, and watersports. 40 km n.

Camperdown–Timboon Rail Trail: walking or riding track through bush, following historic railway line. **Mt Leura:** extinct volcano close to the perfect cone of Mt Sugarloaf. A lookout offers excellent views over crater lakes and volcanoes, and north across the plains to the Grampians; 1 km s. **Camperdown Botanic Gardens:** feature rare examples of Himalayan oak and a lookout over lakes Bullen Merri and Gnotuk; 3 km W. **Cobden Miniature Trains:** operates 3rd Sun each month; Cobden; 13 km s.

See also SOUTH-WEST COAST, p. 153

Cann River

Pop. 223
Map ref. 565 C11 | 581 E10

ⓘ Parks Victoria Cann River office, (03) 5158 6351; or East Gippsland Visitor Information Centre, 1800 637 060; www.lakesandwilderness.com.au

101.7 FM 3MGB Wilderness Radio, 106.1 FM ABC Local Radio

Cann River is situated at the junction of the Princes and Cann Valley highways, and is notable for its proximity to several spectacular national parks. The area boasts excellent fishing, bushwalking and camping in the rugged hinterland, with nearby Point Hicks notable for being the first land on the east coast of Australia to be sighted by Europeans.

Point Hicks Lighthouse: 2 cottages, each sleeps 6; Point Hicks Rd; (03) 5156 0432.

Lind National Park The park includes the Euchre Valley Nature Drive through temperate rainforest gullies. It also supports open eucalypt forests with grey gum, messmate and silvertop ash. Watch for wildlife such as the pretty masked owl and the elusive long-footed potoroo. Has picnic facilities. 15 km w.

Coopracambra National Park This park is in one of the most remote sections of Victoria. Ancient fossil footprints have been found in the red sandstone gorge of the Genoa River, and the surrounding granite peaks create a spectacular scene. The 35 000 ha area protects unique ecosystems and rare flora and fauna. Only experienced and well-equipped hikers should undertake walks in the rugged and remote parts of this park. A 'trip intentions' form needs to be lodged at the Cann River or Mallacoota office of Parks Victoria prior to departure, and parks staff must be notified upon return. 30 km n near NSW border.

Croajingolong National Park: the road travelling south of Cann River leads to Pt Hicks and its historic 1890 lighthouse (daily tours offered); *for further details on the park see Mallacoota.*

See also EAST GIPPSLAND, p. 159

Casterton

Pop. 1654
Map ref. 592 C3 | 601 H11

ⓘ Shiels Tce; (03) 5581 2070; www.castertonnow.org.au

94.1 FM ABC Local Radio, 99.3 Coastal FM

Casterton is a Roman name meaning 'walled city', given to the town because of the natural wall of hills surrounding the valley where it lies. These hills, and the Glenelg River that flows through town, create an idyllic rural atmosphere. The region is colloquially known as 'Kelpie Country' as it is the birthplace of this world-famous breed of working dog. In the mid-1800s a prized Scottish collie female pup from nearby Warrock Homestead was sold to a stockman named Jack Gleeson, who named her 'Kelpie' – she was bred out with various 'black and tan' dogs, and so began the long line of the working man's best friend.

Historical Museum: housed in the old railway station, the museum displays local artefacts; open by appt; Cnr Jackson and Clarke sts. **Alma and Judith Zaadstra Fine Art Gallery:** Henty St. **Mickle Lookout:** a great view across the town; Moodie St, off Robertson St on the eastern edge of town.

Vintage Car Rally: Mar. **Polocrosse Championships:** Mar. **Casterton Cup:** June. **Australian Kelpie Muster and Kelpie Working Dog Auction:** June/July.

Dergholm State Park The park features a great diversity of vegetation, including woodlands, open forests, heaths and swamps. An abundance of wildlife thrives, including echidnas, koalas, kangaroos, reptiles and the endangered red-tailed black cockatoo. A key attraction is Baileys Rocks, unique giant green-coloured granite boulders. Contact Parks Victoria on 13 1963; 50 km n.

Long Lead Swamp: waterbirds, kangaroos, emus and a trail-bike track; Penola Rd; 11 km w. **Geological formations:** in particular, The Hummocks, 12 km ne, and The Bluff, viewable from Dartmoor Rd, 20 km sw. Both rock formations are around 150 million years old. **Warrock Homestead:** a unique collection of 33 buildings erected by its founder, George Robertson. The homestead was built in 1843 and is National Trust–classified; open day on Easter Sun; 26 km n. **Bilston's Tree:** 50 m high and arguably the world's largest red gum; Glenmia Rd; 30 km n.

See also GRAMPIANS & CENTRAL WEST, p. 155

 RADIO STATIONS   IN TOWN   WHAT'S ON   WHERE TO EAT   WHERE TO STAY   NEARBY

BENDIGO

Pop. 81 941

Map ref. 578 | 579 F3 | 584 A9 | 591 O10

ⓘ Post Office, 51–67 Pall Mall; (03) 5434 6060 or 1800 813 153; www.bendigotourism.com

📻 89.5 The Fresh FM, 91.1 FM ABC Local Radio, 96.5 Radio KLFM

Bendigo was the place of one of the world's most exciting gold rushes, with more gold found here between 1850 and 1900 than anywhere else in the world. Elaborate buildings and monuments from the golden past line the main streets, offering an ever-present reminder of the riches from the goldfields. Today modern life weaves itself around this legacy with a vibrant pace. The town's new wealth can be seen in many areas including art, culture, dining, wine and shopping.

🏛 **Golden Dragon Museum** The museum commemorates the contribution of the Chinese community to life on the goldfields. On display are exhibitions depicting the daily life and hardships of Chinese immigrants and an impressive collection of Chinese memorabilia and processional regalia, including what is said to be the world's oldest imperial dragon, 'Loong' (which first appeared at the Bendigo Easter Fair in 1892), and the world's longest imperial dragon, 'Sun Loong'. Adjacent to the museum is the Classical Chinese Garden of Joy. Bridge St; (03) 5441 5044.

Central Deborah Gold Mine To get a feel for life in a goldmining town is to take a trip down this mine, where you can still see traces of gold in the quartz reef 20 storeys below the ground. The Central Deborah Gold Mine was the last commercial goldmine to operate in Bendigo. From 1939 to 1954 around a tonne of gold was excavated. Violet St; tour details (03) 5443 8322.

Bendigo Art Gallery: well regarded for contemporary exhibitions plus an extensive permanent collection with a focus on Australian artists, including Arthur Boyd, Tom Roberts and Arthur Streeton. Guided tours daily; View St; (03) 5434 6088. *Self-guide heritage walk:* takes in landmarks including The Hotel Shamrock, built in 1897, cnr Pall Mall and Williamson St; Sacred Heart Cathedral, the largest outside Melbourne, Wattle St; Alexandra Fountain, built in 1881, one of the largest and most ornate fountains in regional Victoria, at Charing Cross; and the Renaissance-style post office and law courts at Pall Mall; details from visitor centre. *Bendigo Pottery:* Australia's oldest working pottery, with potters at work, a cafe and sales; Midland Hwy, Epsom. *Dudley House:* National Trust–classified building; View St. *Vintage Trams:* run from Central Deborah Gold Mine on 8 km city trip, including a stop at the Tram Depot Museum; taped commentary provided. *Chinese Joss House:* National Trust–classified temple built by Chinese miners; included on the vintage tram trip; Finn St, North Bendigo. *Rosalind Park:* majestic parklands that sit beautifully in the centre of Bendigo, offering stately gardens for leisure and relaxation; includes a lookout tower, Cascades water feature and Conservatory Gardens; Pall Mall. *Discovery Science and Technology Centre:* features more than 100 hands-on displays; Railway Pl. *Making of a Nation Exhibition:* permanent interpretive display providing details about Bendigo's role in Federation; at the visitor centre, Pall Mall.

🌳 *Bridge Street Market:* Bendigo's newest market features local produce and handmade arts and crafts; Bridge St near

[THE HISTORIC BENDIGO POST OFFICE, NOW HOME TO THE BENDIGO VISITOR INFORMATION AND INTERPRETIVE CENTRE]

Golden Dragon Museum; 8am–2pm 3rd Sat each month. *Large undercover market:* Prince of Wales Showgrounds, Holmes St; 8.30am–3pm each Sun. *Bendigo Summer Fiesta:* a full summer program of arts and entertainment in Bendigo's most stunning locations. *Bendigo International Madison:* major cycling event; Mar long weekend. *Bendigo Easter Festival:* first held in 1871, the festival spans 4 days and is a major event on the town's calendar, with free music and entertainment, craft markets, art exhibits, food, wine and the famous procession featuring 'Sun Loong'. *Australian Sheep and Wool Show:* showcases everything from farming to fashion; July. *Bendigo Heritage Uncorked:* wine event in the historic streets; 2nd weekend Oct. *National Swap Meet:* Australia's largest meet for vintage cars and bikes; Bendigo Showgrounds; Nov. *Bendigo Cup:* horseracing; Nov.

🍴 *GPO Bendigo:* cafe-bar; 60–64 Pall Mall; (03) 5443 4343. *The Bridge:* contemporary gastropub; 49 Bridge St; (03) 5443 7811. *The Dispensary:* European menu; 9 Chancery La; (03) 5444 5885. *Whirrakee Restaurant:* contemporary French; 17 View St; (03) 5441 5557. *Wine Bank on View:* Mediterranean wine bar; 45 View St; (03) 5444 4655.

🛏 *Anchorage by the Lake:* apartments decorated in French or oriental style; 300–302 Napier St; (03) 5442 4777. *Fountain View*

Suites: boutique suites; 10–12 View St; (03) 5435 2121. ***The Hotel Shamrock:*** historic hotel rooms; Cnr Pall Mall and Williamson St; (03) 5443 0333. ***Byronsvale Vineyard B&B:*** 3 converted-stable apartments; 51 Andrews Rd, Maiden Gully; (03) 5447 2790.

Greater Bendigo National Park The park, which extends to the north and south of town, protects some high-quality box-ironbark forest and is popular for scenic driving, cycling, walking and camping. Relics of the region's goldmining and eucalyptus-oil industries can be found within. Fauna includes over 170 species of birds including the grey shrike-thrush, a pretty songbird. In the early morning and later in the evening, look out for eastern grey kangaroos, black wallabies and echidnas. Detailed maps of the park are available at the visitor centre.

Contact Parks Victoria on 13 1963; access via Loddon Valley Hwy through Eaglehawk; 8 km N.

One Tree Hill observation tower: panoramic views; 4 km S. ***Eaglehawk:*** site of the gold rush in 1852, it features remnants of goldmining days and fine examples of 19th-century architecture; details of self-guide heritage tour from visitor centre; 6.5 km NW. ***Mandurang:*** features historic wineries and is the exact centre of Victoria; 8 km SE. ***Bendigo Wine Region:*** more than 30 wineries are located around Bendigo, producing award-winning wines and offering welcoming cellar-door experiences with tastings and sales; wine booklet with map available from visitor centre.

See also GOLDFIELDS, p. 154

Castlemaine

Pop. 7250
Map ref. 579 F6 | 591 O12 | 593 N1

Castlemaine Market Building, 44 Mostyn St; (03) 5471 1795 or 1800 171 888; www.maldoncastlemaine.com

91.1 FM ABC Local Radio, 106.3 Radio KLFM

Castlemaine is a classic goldmining town known for its grand old buildings and sprawling botanical gardens. This area was the site of the greatest alluvial gold rush that the world has ever seen. Now the town relies largely on agriculture and the manufacturing sectors, as well as being home to a thriving artistic community that takes inspiration from the area's red hills.

Castlemaine Art Gallery Housed in an elegant Art Deco building, the gallery was designed in 1931 by Peter Meldrum and is renowned for its collection of Australian art. Along with the permanent collection, many exhibitions appear here. Works by Rembrandt, Francisco Goya and Andy Warhol have all been displayed at this delightful gallery. 14 Lyttleton St; (03) 5472 2292.

Buda Historic Home and Garden Buda is considered to have one of the most significant examples of 19th-century gardens in Victoria. The house itself is furnished with period pieces and art and craft created by the Leviny family, who lived here for 118 years. Ernest Leviny was a silversmith and jeweller. Five of his 6 daughters never married, but remained at Buda and pursued woodwork, photography and embroidery. Open 12–5pm Wed–Sat, 10am–5pm Sun; 42 Hunter St; (03) 5472 1032.

Victorian Goldfields Railway This historic railway runs from Castlemaine to Maldon. The steam train journeys through box-ironbark forest in a region that saw some of the richest goldmining in the country. As well as the regular timetable, it also hosts special events throughout the year. Castlemaine Railway Station, Kennedy St; recorded information (03) 5475 2966, inquiries (03) 5470 6658.

Diggings Interpretive Centre: housed in the restored 19th-century Castlemaine Market building, the centre features interactive displays about the area's many goldmines as well as various exhibitions; Mostyn St. ***Theatre Royal:*** hosts live shows and films and also offers luxurious backstage accommodation; Hargraves St. ***Castlemaine Botanic Gardens:*** one of Victoria's oldest and most impressive 19th-century gardens; cnr Walker and Downes rds. ***Old Castlemaine Gaol:*** restored gaol now offers tours; Bowden St. ***Food and wine producers:*** dotted throughout the area; food and wine trail brochures from visitor centre.

Castlemaine Farmers Market: 1st Sun each month. ***Wesley Hill Market:*** each Sat; 2.5 km E. ***Castlemaine State Festival:*** odd-numbered years, Apr. ***Festival of Gardens:*** Nov.

Bold Cafe Gallery: Asian-influenced nursery cafe; 146 Duke St; (03) 5470 6038. ***Saffs Cafe:*** casual cafe food; 64 Mostyn St; (03) 5470 6722. ***The Empyre:*** modern gastropub; 68 Mostyn St; (03) 5472 5166. ***Togs Place:*** popular breakfast/lunch spot; 58 Lyttleton St; (03) 5470 5090.

The Empyre: 6 beautiful suites; 68 Mostyn St; (03) 5472 5166. ***The Hermitage B&B:*** 2nd floor of sandstone cottage; 181 Blakeley Rd; (03) 5472 2008. ***Tuckpoint:*** historic 2-bedroom cottage; 60 Kennedy St; 0439 035 382. ***Sage Cottage:*** 2-bedroom miners cottage; 25 Castlemaine St, Fryerstown; (03) 5473 4322. ***Shack 14 @ Prospect House:*** eco-friendly hideaway, sleeps 4; Hooper Rd, Chewton; (03) 5472 1677.

Castlemaine Diggings National Heritage Park The wealth on Castlemaine's streets springs from the huge hauls of gold found on the Mt Alexander Diggings, east and south of town. Thousands of miners worked the fields. Towns such as Fryerstown, Vaughan and Glenluce, now almost ghost towns, supported breweries, schools, churches and hotels. Today visitors can explore Chinese cemeteries, mineral springs, waterwheels and old townsites. Fossicking is popular. Details of self-guide walks and drives from visitor centre. 4 km S.

Chewton: historic buildings line the streets of this former gold town; 4 km E. *Harcourt:* this town is known for its many wineries, including Harcourt Valley Vineyard and Blackjack Vineyards, with tastings and cellar-door sales. Also at Harcourt is the Skydancers Orchid and Butterfly Gardens. The town hosts the Apple Festival in Mar and spring, and the Orchid Festival in Oct; 9 km NE. *Big Tree:* a giant red gum over 500 years old; Guildford; 14 km SW. *Koala Reserve:* Mt Alexander; 19 km NE.

See also GOLDFIELDS, p. 154

Chiltern

Pop. 1067
Map ref. 559 N12 | 585 J6 | 586 H2

 30 Main St; (03) 5726 1611; www.chilternvic.com

101.3 Oak FM, 106.5 FM ABC Local Radio

Now surrounded by rich pastoral farmland, Chiltern was once at the centre of a goldmining boom and had as many as 14 suburbs. After the Indigo gold discovery in the 1850s, there was a major influx of miners and settlers, but the boom was brief and farming was soon prominent in the town's economy. Today the rich heritage of the 19th century can be seen in the streetscapes, a vision not lost on Australian filmmakers keen for that 'authentic' 1800s scene.

Athenaeum Museum: historic building with heritage display; Conness St. *Dow's Pharmacy:* old chemist shop with original features; Conness St. *Star Theatre and Grapevine Museum:* the quaint theatre still operates and the museum, formerly the Grapevine Hotel, boasts the largest grapevine in Australia, planted in 1867 and recorded in the Guinness World Records; Main St. *Federal Standard newspaper office:* open by appt for groups; Main St. *Lakeview House:* former home of author Henry Handel Richardson; open afternoons on weekends and public and school holidays; Victoria St. *Lake Anderson:* picnic and barbecue facilities; access via Main St.

Antique Fair: Aug. *Ironbark Festival:* heritage fair with woodchopping, live music and markets; Oct.

The Mulberry Tree: 2 rooms in former bank; 28 Conness St; (03) 5726 1277. *Koendidda Country House:* elegant B&B; 79 Pooleys Rd, Barnawartha; (02) 6026 7340.

Chiltern–Mt Pilot National Park This park stretches from around Chiltern south to Beechworth and protects remnant box-ironbark forest, which once covered much of this part of Victoria. Also featured are significant goldmining relics, including the impressive Magenta Goldmine (around 2 km E). Of the park's 21 000 ha, 7000 were exposed to bushfire in Jan 2003. But its regeneration is evidence of the hardiness of the forest, and there are now upgraded visitor facilities. An introduction to the forest scenery and goldmining history is on the 25 km scenic drive signposted from Chiltern. Other activities include canoeing and rafting, fishing, and cycling and walking trips along the many marked trails. Contact Parks Victoria on 13 1963; access via Hume Hwy and the road south to Beechworth.

See also HIGH COUNTRY, p. 158

Clunes

Pop. 1024
Map ref. 572 C1 | 579 C8 | 593 M2

 Old School Complex, 70 Bailey St; (03) 5345 3896; www.visitclunes.com.au

99.9 VoiceFM, 107.9 FM ABC Local Radio

The first registered gold strike in the state was made at Clunes on 7 July 1851. The town, north of Ballarat, is said to be one of the most intact gold towns in Victoria, featuring historic buildings throughout. Surrounding the town are a number of extinct volcanoes. A view of these can be obtained 3 kilometres to the south, on the road to Ballarat. The town was used as a location for the film *Ned Kelly*, starring Heath Ledger.

Clunes Museum: local history museum featuring displays on the gold-rush era; open weekends and school public holidays; Fraser St. *Bottle Museum:* in former South Clunes State School; open Wed–Sun; Bailey St. *Queens Park:* on the banks of Creswick Creek, the park was created over 100 years ago.

Market: Fraser St; 2nd Sun each month. *Booktown:* large-scale book fair; May. *Words in Winter Celebration:* Aug.

Talbot This delightful, historic town has many 1860–70 buildings, particularly in Camp St and Scandinavian Cres. Attractions include the Arts and Historical Museum in the former Methodist Church; the Bull and Mouth Restaurant in an old bluestone building, formerly a hotel; and a market (holds the honour of being the first farmers market in the region) selling local produce, 3rd Sun each month. 18 km NW.

Mt Beckworth Scenic Reserve: popular picnic and horseriding reserve with panoramic views from the summit; 8 km W.

See also GOLDFIELDS, p. 154

Cobram

Pop. 5061
Map ref. 559 L12 | 584 F4

 Cnr Station St and Punt Rd; (03) 5872 2132 or 1800 607 607

101.3 Oak FM, 106.5 FM ABC Local Radio

At Cobram and nearby Barooga (across the New South Wales border) the Murray River is bordered by sandy beaches, making it a great spot for fishing, watersports and picnics. The stretch of land between the township and the river features river red gum forests and lush wetlands, with tracks leading to various beaches, the most accessible of which is Thompsons Beach, located near the bridge off Boorin Street. The town is supported by orchards and dairies, earning it the nickname 'peaches and cream country'. A biennial festival is held in honour of these industries.

Historic log cabin: built in Yarrawonga in 1875, then moved piece by piece to its current location; opposite the information centre on Station St. *Station Gallery:* at the railway station, displays a collection of art by local artists.

Market: Punt Rd; 1st Sat each month. *Peaches and Cream Festival:* free peaches and cream, a rodeo, fishing competitions and other activities; odd-numbered years, Jan. *Rotary Art Show:* May. *Antique Fair:* June. *Open Gardens Display:* Oct.

Tokemata Retreat: 4 cottages by golf range; 100 Cemetery Rd, Cobram East; (03) 5873 5332.

Quinn Island Flora and Fauna Reserve: home to abundant birdlife and Aboriginal artefacts, including scar trees, flint tools and middens, the island can be explored on a self-guide walk; on the Murray River, accessed via a pedestrian bridge off River Rd. *Binghi Boomerang Factory:* large manufacturer and exporter of boomerangs. Free demonstrations are offered with purchases; Tocumwal Rd, Barooga, across the river. *Scenic Drive Strawberry Farm:* strawberry-picking during warmer months; Torgannah Rd, Koonoomoo; 11 km NW. *Cactus Country:* Australia's largest cacti gardens; Strathmerton; 16 km W. *Ulupna Island:* part of Barmah State Park; turn-off after Strathmerton; *see Echuca for details. Murray River Horse Trails:* a fantastic way to explore the Murray River beaches; (03) 5868 2221.

See also GOULBURN & MURRAY, p. 157

Cohuna

Pop. 1891
Map ref. 559 I11 | 584 A3 | 591 O5

 Gannawarra Shire Council, 49 Victoria St, Kerang; (03) 5450 9333; www.gannawarra.vic.gov.au

99.1 Smart FM, 594 AM ABC Local Radio

A peaceful, small service centre located on the Murray River. Cohuna's claim to fame is that its casein factory developed

BRIGHT

Pop. 2113
Map ref. 585 K9 | 587 I7

ℹ 119 Gavan St; 1300 551 117; www.brightescapes.com.au

📻 89.7 FM ABC Local Radio, 101.3 Oak FM

Bright is situated in the Ovens Valley in the foothills of the Victorian Alps. A particularly striking element of the town is the avenues of deciduous trees, at their peak during the autumn months. The Bright Autumn Festival is held annually in celebration of the spectacular seasonal changes. The Ovens River flows through the town, providing a delightful location for picnics or camping. The town also offers off-the-mountain accommodation for nearby Mount Hotham and Mount Buffalo.

🏠 **Old Tobacco Sheds** You could easily spend half a day here – wandering through the sheds filled with antiques and bric-a-brac and through the makeshift museums, which give an insight into the local tobacco industry and the gold rush. Also on-site is a historic hut, and the Sharefarmers Cafe serves Devonshire tea. Great Alpine Rd.

Gallery 90: local art and craft; at the visitor centre. *Centenary Park:* with a deep weir, children's playground and picnic facilities; Gavan St. *Bright Art Gallery and Cultural Centre:* community-owned gallery, displays and sells fine art and handicrafts; Mountbatten Ave. *Bright Brewery:* enjoy award-winning beers or brew your own; 121 Great Alpine Rd. *Bright and District Historical Museum:* in the old railway station building, with artefacts and photographs from the town's past; open by appt (contact visitor centre); Cnr Gavan and Anderson sts. *Walking tracks:* well-marked tracks around the area include Canyon Walk along the Ovens River, where remains of gold-workings can be seen; details from visitor centre. *Murray to the Mountains Rail Trail:* Bright sits at one end of this 94 km track suitable for cycling and walking; links several townships.

🌺 *Craft market:* Burke St; 3rd Sat each month. *Autumn Festival:* activities include craft markets and entertainment; Apr/May. *Alpine Spring Festival:* free entertainment, displays and open gardens, celebrating the beauty of Bright in spring; Oct.

🍴 *Poplars:* French-inspired menu; Shop 8, Star Rd; (03) 5755 1655. *Simone's of Bright:* excellent Italian cuisine; 98 Gavan St; (03) 5755 2266. *Villa Gusto:* Tuscan-style regional menu; 630 Buckland Valley Rd, Buckland; (03) 5756 2000.

🛏 *Centenary Peaks:* stylish apartments; 1 Delany Ave; (03) 5750 1433. *The Buckland Studio Retreat:* luxury eco-retreats; 116 McCormacks La, Buckland; 0419 133 318. *The Odd Frog:* architecturally designed studios; 3 McFadyens La; 0418 362 791. *The Kilns:* 3-bedroom corrugated-iron homestead; Cavedons La, Porepunkah; 0408 553 332. *Villa Gusto:* Tuscan-style suites; 630 Buckland Valley Rd, Buckland; (03) 5756 2000.

🧭 **Wandiligong** A National Trust–classified hamlet, the area contains well-preserved historic buildings from the town's goldmining days. The tiny village is set in a rich green valley, with an enormous hedge maze as the dominant feature and over 2 km of walkways surrounded by lush gardens. The maze is well signposted. Open 10am–5pm Wed–Sun; 6 km s.

Mt Buffalo National Park This is not a large park, but it is one of Victoria's favourites. In winter it is a haven for skiers. In summer bushwalkers and campers descend on the park, taking in the superb views from the granite peaks, the gushing waterfalls and the display of alpine wildflowers. Lake Catani is a popular spot for canoeists, and rock climbing and hang-gliding are also popular. Contact Parks Victoria on 13 1963; 10 km NW.

Tower Hill Lookout: 4 km NW. *Boyntons/Feathertop Winery:* open for sales and tastings; at junction of Ovens and Buckland rivers, Porepunkah; 6 km NW. *The Red Stag Deer and Emu Farm:* Hughes La, Eurobin; 16 km NW. *Harrietville:* a former goldmining village located just outside the Alpine National Park. Attractions include Pioneer Park, an open-air museum and picnic area; Tavare Park, with a swing bridge and picnic and barbecue facilities; and a lavender farm; 20 km SE. *Alpine National Park: see Mount Beauty;* to the south-east of town.

See also HIGH COUNTRY, p. 158

[THE COLOURS OF AUTUMN CREATE A PICTURESQUE SETTING]

VICTORIA

produce that became part of the diet of the astronauts flying the Apollo space missions. East of town is Gunbower Island, at the junction of the Murray River and Gunbower Creek. The island is home to abundant wildlife, including kangaroos and emus, plus breeding rookeries for birdlife during flood years.

Cohuna Historical Museum: housed in the former Scots Church, the museum features memorabilia relating to explorer Major Mitchell; Sampson St.

Murray River International Music Festival: Feb. *Bridge to Bridge Swim:* Mar. *Austoberfest:* Oct.

Gunbower Family Hotel: excellent steakhouse; Murray Valley Hwy, Gunbower; (03) 5487 1214.

Gunbower Island This island, surrounded by Gunbower Creek and the Murray River, is an internationally recognised wetland, with a great variety of waterbirds and stands of river red gum forest. A 5 km canoe trail flows through Safes Lagoon and bushwalking is another highlight.

Grove Patchwork Cottage and Tearooms: for local art and craft; Murray Valley Hwy; 4 km SE. *Mathers Waterwheel Museum:* features waterwheel memorabilia and outdoor aviary; Brays Rd; 9 km W. *Murray Goulburn Factory:* cheese factory; Leitchville; 16 km SE. *Kow Swamp:* bird sanctuary with picnic spots and fishing at Box Bridge; 23 km S. *Section of Major Mitchell Trail:* 1700 km trail that retraces this explorer's footsteps from Mildura to Wodonga via Portland. From Cohuna, follow the signposted trail along Gunbower Creek down to Mt Hope; 28 km S. *Torrumbarry Weir:* during winter the entire weir structure is removed, while in summer waterskiing is popular; 40 km SE.

See also GOULBURN & MURRAY, p. 157

Colac

Pop. 10 859

Map ref. 572 B9 | 580 B2 | 593 L8

ⓘ Cnr Murray and Queen sts (Princes Hwy); (03) 5231 3730; www.visitotways.com

104.7 Otway FM, 594 AM 3WV ABC Local Radio

Colac was built by the shores of Lake Colac on the volcanic plain that covers much of Victoria's Western District. The lake was once the largest freshwater body in Victoria, but harsh drought has seen it almost depleted. Still, the town acts as the gateway to the Otways. The area was once described by novelist Rolf Boldrewood as 'a scene of surpassing beauty and rural loveliness … this Colac country was the finest, the richest as to soil and pasture that I had up to that time ever looked on'.

Colac Heritage Walk: self-guide tour of the history and architectural wonders of Colac; details from visitor centre. *Performing Arts and Cultural Centre:* incorporates the Colac Cinema, open daily; and the Historical Centre, open 2–4pm Thurs, Fri and Sun; Cnr Gellibrand and Ray sts. *Botanic Gardens:* unusual in that visitors are allowed to drive through the gardens. Picnic, barbecue and playground facilities are provided; by Lake Colac. *Barongarook Creek:* prolific birdlife, and a walking track leading from Princes Hwy to Lake Colac; on the northern outskirts of town.

Lions Club Market: Memorial Sq, Murray St; 3rd Sun each month. *Go Country Music Festival and Truck Show:* Feb. *Colac Cup:* Feb. *Kana Festival:* community festival with family entertainment, music and displays; Mar. *Garden Expo:* Colac Showgrounds; Oct.

Old Lorne Road Olives: Mediterranean-inspired cafe; 45 Old Lorne Rd, Deans Marsh; (03) 5236 3479. *Otway Estate Winery and Brewery:* tasting plates and more; 10–30 Hoveys Rd, Barongarook; (03) 5233 8400.

Elliminook Heritage B&B: charming garden B&B; 585 Warncoort Rd, Birregurra; (03) 5236 2080.

Red Rock Lookout The lookout features a reserve with picnic and barbecue facilities, plus spectacular views across 30 volcanic lakes, including Lake Corangamite, Victoria's largest saltwater lake. At the base of the lookout is the Red Rock Winery. Near Alvie; 22 km N. The Volcano Discovery Trail goes from Colac to Millicent in SA, and follows the history of volcanic activity in the region; details from visitor centre.

Old Beechy Rail Trail: 45 km trail that follows one of the state's former narrow-gauge railway lines from Colac to Beech Forest, suitable for walkers and cyclists. The trail starts at Colac railway station; details from visitor centre. *Art and craft galleries:* at Barongarook (12 km SE); details from visitor centre. *Burtons Lookout:* features Otway Estate Winery and Brewery with its well-known Prickly Moses ale range, views of the Otways; 13 km S. *Tarndwarncoort Homestead:* wool displays and sales; off Warncoort Cemetery Rd; 15 km E. *Birregurra:* township located at the foot of the Otway Ranges and the edge of volcanic plains; 20 km E. *Forrest:* old timber and logging town in the Otway Ranges; 32 km SE. Attractions nearby include fishing, walking and picnics at the West Barwon Reservoir (2 km S), or spotting a platypus at Lake Elizabeth, formed by a landslide in 1952 (5 km SE).

See also SOUTH-WEST COAST, p. 153

Coleraine

Pop. 992

Map ref. 592 E3

ⓘ Lonsdale St, Hamilton; 1800 807 056; www.sthgrampians.vic.gov.au

 94.1 FM ABC Local Radio, 99.3 Coastal FM

Situated in Victoria's Western District, Coleraine is a small, picturesque town supported by wool and beef industries. A chocolate factory, the ultimate native garden and vintage cars are just a few of the intriguing prospects that await in Coleraine.

Peter Francis Points Arboretum Two thousand species of native flora are found here, including 500 species of eucalyptus. 'The Points' sprawls up the hillside behind the town, with great views from the top, on Portland–Coleraine Rd. In town is the Eucalyptus Discovery Centre, designed to complement the arboretum and give an insight into the natural history and commercial applications of eucalypts. Whyte St.

Glenelg Fine Confectionery: immerse yourself in the rich aroma of German-style continental chocolates; tastings available; Whyte St. *Historic Railway Station:* also site of the visitor centre, it displays and sells local arts and crafts; Pilleau St. *Coleraine Classic Cars:* open by appt; Whyte St.

Tour of Southern Grampians Cycling: Apr. *Coleraine Cup:* Sept.

Bochara Wines: wine-tasting available Fri–Sun; Glenelg Hwy. *Glacier Ridge Redgum:* gallery of wooden products for sale; open by appt. *Balmoral:* historic township west of the Grampians; 49 km N. Nearby features include the Glendinning Homestead, just east of town, with gardens and a wildlife sanctuary. The town is also the gateway to Rocklands Reservoir, for watersports and fishing, and Black Range State Park, for bushwalking. It also holds the Balmoral Annual Show in Mar.

See also GRAMPIANS & CENTRAL WEST, p. 155

Corryong

Pop. 1229
Map ref. 566 A8 | 585 O7 | 587 O3

i 50 Hanson St; (02) 6076 2277; www.pureuppermurrayvalleys.com

📻 88.7 FM Radio Upper Murray, 99.7 FM ABC Local Radio

Welcome to authentic 'Man from Snowy River' country. This district offers superb mountain scenery and excellent trout fishing in the Murray River and its tributaries, with the town being known as the home and final resting place of Jack Riley, the original 'Man from Snowy River'. A life-size statue depicting 'that terrible descent' made famous by Banjo Paterson's poem sits in the town. An annual festival honours Riley's memory with a feature event called the 'Challenge' to find his modern-day equivalent. Corryong is also the Victorian gateway to Kosciuszko National Park across the New South Wales border.

🏠 **The Man from Snowy River Folk Museum** Banjo Paterson's poem evoked the lives of the High Country's settlers. This charming museum proudly does the same, with local exhibits, memorabilia and photos depicting the hardships of local life, as well as a unique collection of historic skis. Hanson St.

Jack Riley's grave: Corryong cemetery. *Man from Snowy River Statue:* Hanson St. *Large wooden galleon:* Murray Valley Hwy. *Playle's Hill Lookout:* for a great view of the township; Donaldson St.

🌴 *Towong Cup:* Sat long weekend in Mar. *The Man from Snowy River Bush Festival:* music, art and horsemanship challenges; Apr. *Upper Murray Challenge:* 1st Sat in Oct. *Corryong Pro Rodeo:* New Year's Eve.

🧭 **Burrowa–Pine Mountain National Park** Pine Mountain is one of Australia's largest monoliths. Mt Burrowa is home to wet-forest plants and unique wildlife, including wombats and gliders. Both mountains provide excellent and diverse opportunities for bushwalkers, campers, climbers and birdwatchers. The Cudgewa Bluff Falls offer fabulous scenery and bushwalking. Contact Parks Victoria on 13 1963; main access is from the Cudgewa–Tintaldra Rd, which runs off Murray Valley Hwy; 27 km W.

Khancoban This NSW town was built by the Snowy Hydro for workers on the hydro-electric scheme. Its willow- and poplar-lined streets, historic rose garden and mountains give the town a European feel. Huge trout are caught in Khancoban Pondage. Nearby, Murray 1 Power Station Visitor Centre reveals the workings of this 10-turbine station. South, along Alpine Way through Kosciuszko National Park, is the spectacular Scammell's Spur Lookout and historic Geehi Hut. 32 km E.

Nariel: Nariel Creek is a good spot for trout fishing. The town hosts the Nariel Creek Folk Music Festival each Dec; 8 km SW. *Towong:* historic Towong Racecourse is where scenes from *Phar Lap* were filmed. Gangster Squizzy Taylor also once stole the takings; 12 km E. *Lookouts:* lookout with views over Kosciuszko National Park at Towong, 12 km NE; Embery's Lookout over Mt Mittamatite, 16 km N. *Walwa:* hire canoes and mountain bikes from Upper Murray Holiday Resort and Winery; 47 km NW.

Touring routes: Murray River Rd, Lakeside Loop, Mitta Valley Loop; details from visitor centre.

See also HIGH COUNTRY, p. 158

Cowes

see inset box on next page

Creswick

Pop. 2487
Map ref. 572 D2 | 579 C9 | 593 M3

i 1 Raglan St; (03) 5345 1114; www.creswick.net

📻 99.9 VoiceFM, 107.9 FM ABC Local Radio

Creswick is an attractive and historic town, a symbol of the rich and heady life of the gold-rush days of the 1850s. Unfortunately, the goldmining also meant that the surrounding forests were decimated. Today the town is surrounded by pine plantations over 100 years old; they exist thanks to the initiative and foresight of local pioneer John La Gerche and – while they are no replacement for the Australian bush – they have given Creswick the title of 'the home of forestry'. Creswick was the birthplace of renowned Australian artist Norman Lindsay, many of whose paintings can be seen in the local historical museum.

🏠 *Historic walk:* self-guide tour, map from visitor centre. *Giant Mullock Heaps:* indicate how deep mines went; Ullina Rd. *Creswick Museum:* photos and memorabilia from the town's goldmining past as well as an exhibition of Lindsay paintings; open Sun, public holidays or by appt; Albert St. *Gold Battery:* est. 1897; Battery Cres. *Creswick Woollen Mills:* last coloured woollen mill of its type in Australia; offers product sales, regular demonstrations and exhibitions; Railway Pde.

🌴 *Creswick Makers Market:* 1st Sun each month. *Creswick CALCAN Market:* 3rd Sat each month. *Forestry Fiesta:* Oct.

🍴 *Harvest 383:* regional produce menu; Novotel Forest Resort Creswick, 1500 Midland Hwy; (03) 5345 9600.

🛏 *Novotel Forest Resort Creswick:* luxury rooms; 1500 Midland Hwy; (03) 5345 9600. *Rossmore Cottage:* 2-bedroom miners cottage; 12 Bald Hills Rd; (03) 5345 2759.

🧭 **Creswick Regional Park** After La Gerche replanted the denuded hills around Creswick in the 1890s, the state established a nursery that it continues to operate today. Further natural history can be explored on the various walking trails, including the 30 min Landcare Trail or the longer La Gerche Forest Walk. Visit St Georges Lake, once a mining dam and now popular for picnics and watersports, and Koala Park, an old breeding ground for koalas that was highly unsuccessful (they escaped over the fences). Slaty Creek is great for gold panning or picnics, with abundant birdlife. The park stretches east and south-east of town. Contact Parks Victoria on 13 1963 or the Creswick Landcare Centre, located within the park, on (03) 5345 2200.

Tangled Maze: a maze formed by climbing plants; 5 km E. *Smeaton:* pretty little town with the historic Smeaton House, the Tuki Trout Farm and Anderson's Mill; 16 km NE.

See also GOLDFIELDS, p. 154

Daylesford

see inset box on page 177

 RADIO STATIONS IN TOWN WHAT'S ON WHERE TO EAT WHERE TO STAY NEARBY

VICTORIA

COWES

Pop. 4217

Map ref. 573 K11 | 575 L10 | 582 D8

ⓘ 895 Phillip Island Tourist Rd, Newhaven; (03) 5956 7447 or 1300 366 422; www.visitphillipisland.com

89.1 3MFM South Gippsland, 774 AM ABC Local Radio

Situated on the north side of Phillip Island, Cowes is the island's major town. It is linked to the Mornington Peninsula by a ferry service to Stony Point and by road to Melbourne via the San Remo bridge. The foreshore offers coastal walks, safe swimming beaches and fishing from the jetty. Seal-watching cruises to Seal Rocks operate from the jetty and are the best way to see the fur seals close-up. There are many activities and events that attract 3.5 million visitors to Phillip Island each year. All are within easy reach of Cowes.

Seal-watching cruises: depart from the jetty to Seal Rocks; bookings on 1300 763 739.

Market: crafts and second-hand goods; Settlement Rd; each Sun. *Farmers market:* Churchill Island; 4th Sat each month. *World Superbike Championships:* Grand Prix Circuit; Mar/Apr. *Churchill Island Working Horse Festival:* farm show; Easter. *Australian Motorcycle Grand Prix:* Grand Prix Circuit; Oct. *V8 Supercars:* Grand Prix Circuit; Nov/Dec.

Harry's on the Esplanade: waterfront dining; Shop 5, 17 The Esplanade; (03) 5952 6226. *Hotel:* casual bistro dining; 11–13 The Esplanade; (03) 5952 2100. *Infused:* modern Australian; 115 Thompson Ave; (03) 5952 2655. *Foreshore Bar and Restaurant:* rustic dining; 11 Beach Rd, Rhyll; (03) 5956 9520.

All Seasons Eco Resort Phillip Island: villas on acreage; 2128 Phillip Island Rd; (03) 5952 8000. *Holmwood Guesthouse:* 3 B&B rooms, 2 cottages; 37 Chapel St; (03) 5952 3082. *Quest Phillip Island:* centrally located apartments; Cnr Bass Ave and Chapel St; (03) 5952 2644. *Silverwater Resort:* apartments and hotel rooms; 17 Potters Hill Rd, San Remo; (03) 5671 9300 or 1800 033 403.

Penguin Parade The nightly penguin parade is Phillip Island's most popular attraction. During this world-famous event, little penguins emerge from the sea after a tiring fishing expedition and cross Summerland Beach to their little homes in the dunes. Tours run at sunset each night, and the penguins can be spotted from the boardwalks and viewing platforms. The site also has an interactive visitor centre with fascinating details about these adorable creatures. Note that no cameras are allowed beyond the visitor centre. Bookings on (03) 5951 2800; 12 km sw.

The Nobbies Centre and Seal Rocks An interactive centre gives visitors an insight into local marine life, including Australia's largest colony of Australian fur seals via cameras that you can control yourself. Outside, the island features a cliff-side boardwalk with views of the fantastic natural landmark The Nobbies and out to Seal Rocks. Walk around to the Blowhole to hear the thunderous noise of huge waves and look out for the nesting sites of vast colonies of seagulls and short-tailed shearwaters that migrate to the island annually. Informative displays explain each natural attraction. Ventnor Rd; 15 km sw.

[LITTLE PENGUINS COMING ASHORE AT DUSK]

Phillip Island Wildlife Park: features native fauna, with visitors able to handfeed kangaroos and wallabies; 3 km s. *Koala Conservation Centre:* view these lovely creatures in their natural habitat from an elevated boardwalk; Phillip Island Rd; 5 km se. *Grand Prix Circuit:* the circuit is steeped in both old and recent history, which is detailed thoroughly in the visitor centre. You can also go go-karting on a replica of the Grand Prix track; Back Beach Rd; 6 km s. *A Maze 'N Things:* family fun park featuring a large timber maze, optical-illusion rooms and 'maxigolf'; Phillip Island Rd; 6 km se. *Rhyll Inlet:* wetlands of international significance, with the marshes and mangroves providing an important breeding ground for wading birds. There are various loop walks, as well as an excellent view from the Conservation Hill Observation Tower; 7 km e. *Rhyll Trout & Bush Tucker Farm:* fish for rainbow trout in the indoor Rainforest Pool, take a fishing lesson or wander around the self-guide bush tucker trail; open 10am–5pm; 36 Rhyll–Newhaven Rd, Rhyll; (03) 5956 9255. *Wineries:* Phillip Island Vineyard and Winery offers tastings, sales and casual dining; Berrys Beach Rd; 7 km sw. Purple Hen Wines also offers tastings and light meals; McFees Rd, Rhyll; 9 km se. *Churchill Island:* a road bridge provides access to this protected parkland, which features a historic homestead, a walking track and abundant birdlife; 16 km se. *National Vietnam Veterans Museum:* details the history of Australian involvement in the Vietnam War, displaying around 6000 artefacts; 25 Veterans Dr, Newhaven; 16 km se. *Phillip Island Chocolate Factory:* visit Panny's Amazing World of Chocolate with information on the chocolate-making process and a model of Dame Edna made from 12 000 chocolate pieces; visitors can even make their own chocolate; Newhaven; 16 km se. *Pelicans:* see these unusual birds up close, with feeding time daily at 12pm; San Remo Pier (opposite the Fishing Co-op); 17 km se. *Cape Woolamai:* the beach is renowned for its fierce and exciting surf (patrolled in season). From the beach there are a number of 2–4 hr loop walks, many to the southern end of the cape and passing the Pinnacles rock formations on the way. South of Cape Woolamai township; 18 km se. *Wildlife Wonderland:* centre includes the Earthworm Museum, a giant earthworm and Wombat World; 31 km e.

See also Phillip Island & Gippsland, p. 150

Dimboola   Pop. 1493
                                                   Map ref. 590 F8

ℹ️ **Dim E-Shop, 109–111 Lloyd St; (03) 5389 1588;
www.dimboola.com.au**

📻 96.5 Triple H FM, 594 AM ABC Local Radio

Dimboola, on the Wimmera River, is a key access point to the
Little Desert National Park. The area was home to the Wotjobaluk
Aboriginal people until the first European settlers arrived. The
district was known as 'Nine Creeks' because of the many little
streams that appear when the river recedes after floods. Many of
the early white settlers were German.

🏠 *Historic buildings:* include the mechanics institute in
Lloyd St and the Victoria Hotel, a grand 2-storey structure
with grapevines hanging from the verandahs (cnr Wimmera
and Victoria sts). *Walking track:* follows a scenic stretch of the
Wimmera River. The track can be followed all the way to the
Horseshoe Bend camping ground in the Little Desert National
Park 7 km away; details of walks from visitor centre.

 Little Desert National Park This park covers 132 647 ha. The
eastern block (the section nearest to Dimboola) has picnic and
camping facilities and good walking tracks. The park does not
resemble the typical desert – it contains extensive heathlands and,
during spring, more than 600 varieties of wildflowers and over
40 types of ground orchids. The park is home to the distinctive
mallee fowl, and the large ground-nests built by the male birds
can be seen during breeding season. Kangaroos, possums and
bearded dragons are just some of the other wildlife that inhabit
the park. 6 km sw. *See also Nhill.*

Pink Lake: a salt lake that reflects a deep pinkish colour,
particularly impressive at sunset, but has dried up in recent
years; 9 km NW. *Ebenezer Mission Station:* founded in 1859 in
an attempt to bring Christianity to the local Aboriginal people.
The site contains fascinating ruins of the original buildings, a
cemetery and a restored limestone church; off the Dimboola–
Jeparit Rd; 15 km N. *Kiata Lowan Sanctuary:* the first part of
Little Desert National Park to be reserved, in 1955. Home to the
mallee fowl; Kiata; 26 km w.

See also **GRAMPIANS & CENTRAL WEST, p. 155**

Donald   Pop. 1429
                                                  Map ref. 558 F12 | 591 J7

ℹ️ **Council Offices, cnr Houston and McCulloch sts;
(03) 5497 1300.**

📻 96.5 Triple H FM, 99.1 FM ABC Local Radio

Donald is on the scenic Richardson River and referred to by locals
as 'Home of the Duck', owing to the many waterbirds that live in
the region. The town also features Bullocks Head, a tree on the
riverbank with a growth that looks like its namesake. The 'bull'
is also used as a flood gauge – according to how high the waters
are, the 'bull' is either dipping his feet, having a drink or, when the
water is really high, going for a swim.

🏠 *Bullocks Head Lookout:* beside Richardson River; Byrne
St. *Steam Train Park:* a restored steam locomotive, an adventure
playground and barbecue facilities; Cnr Hammill and Walker sts.
Historic Police Station: dates back to 1865; Wood St. *Shepherds
hut:* built by early settlers; Wood St. *Agricultural Museum:* an
impressive collection of agricultural machinery; Hammill St.
Scilleys Island: reserve on the Richardson River featuring

wildlife, walking tracks and picnic facilities; access by footbridge
from Sunraysia Hwy. *Kooka's Country Cookies:* tours and sales;
Sunraysia Hwy.

🌴 *Scottish Dancing Country Weekend:* June.
Donald Cup: Nov.

🧭 **Lake Buloke** The lake is filled by the floodwaters of the
Richardson River, so its size varies greatly with the seasons.
This extensive wetland area is home to a variety of birdlife and is
a popular venue for fishing, picnicking and bushwalking. The end
of the park closest to town is a protected bird sanctuary. 10 km N.

Fishing There is good fishing for redfin and trout in the many
waterways close to town. Good spots include Lake Cope Cope,
10 km s; Lake Batyo Catyo and Richardson River Weir, both
20 km s; Watchem Lake, 35 km N; and the Avoca River, which
runs through Charlton, 43 km NE.

Mt Jeffcott: flora, kangaroos and views over Lake Buloke;
20 km NE.

See also **GRAMPIANS & CENTRAL WEST, p. 155**

Drysdale   Pop. 10 217
                                    Map ref. 570 A9 | 572 G8 | 574 D4 | 582 A6 | 593 O7

ℹ️ **Queenscliff Visitor Information Centre, 55 Hesse St,
Queenscliff; (03) 5258 4843; www.visitgreatoceanroad.org.au**

📻 94.7 The Pulse FM, 774 AM ABC Local Radio

Drysdale, situated on the Bellarine Peninsula, is primarily a
service centre for the local farming community. The town is
close to the beaches of Port Phillip Bay and there are a number of
wineries in the area, including the delightful Spray Farm Winery.
Drysdale is now considered a satellite town of Geelong, yet retains
a charming, holiday-resort atmosphere.

🏠 *Old Courthouse:* home of the Bellarine Historical Society;
High St. *Drysdale Community Crafts:* High St.

🌴 *Celtic Festival:* June. *Community Market:* at the reserve
on Duke St; 3rd Sun each month Sept–Apr.

🍴 *Loam Restaurant:* local produce menu; Lighthouse
Olive Grove, 650 Andersons Rd; (03) 5251 1101. *Port Pier Cafe:*
casual Spanish; Portarlington Foreshore, Pier St, Portarlington;
(03) 5259 1080. *The Ol' Duke Hotel:* contemporary cuisine;
40 Newcombe St, Portarlington; (03) 5259 1250.

🛏️ *The Ol' Duke Hotel:* 6 bedrooms, 2 self-catering
apartments; 40 Newcombe St, Portarlington; (03) 5259 1250.

🧭 **Wineries** For over 150 years vines have been grown on
the Bellarine Peninsula, and most vineyards here today remain
family owned and operated. Owing to the peninsula's varying soil
conditions, a range of white and red wines are produced. Many
wineries in the area offer cellar-door tastings and sales. These
include the historic Spray Farm Winery, which runs the summer
concert series each Feb and Mar, known as A Day on the Green,
in a natural amphitheatre. Great views to the sea can be had from
Scotchmans Hill Winery. Winery map from visitor centre.

Bellarine Peninsula Railway: steam-train rides from Queenscliff
to Drysdale and return; *see Queenscliff. Lake Lorne picnic area:*
1 km sw. *Portarlington:* a popular seaside resort town with a
restored flour mill featuring displays of agricultural history, a safe
bay for children to swim in and fresh mussels for sale near the pier.
There is a market at Parks Hall, last Sun each month; 10 km NE.

St Leonards: a small beach resort, which includes Edwards Point Wildlife Reserve, a memorial commemorating the landing of Matthew Flinders in 1802 and of John Batman in 1835; 14 km E.

See also WERRIBEE & BELLARINE, p. 152

Dunkeld

Pop. 400
Map ref. 592 G4

ℹ️ Lonsdale St, Hamilton; 1800 807 056; www.sthgrampians.vic.gov.au

📻 94.1 FM ABC Local Radio, 99.3 Coastal FM

Dunkeld is considered the southern gateway to the Grampians, and its natural beauty has long been recognised since the explorer Major Thomas Mitchell camped here in 1836. It was originally named Mount Sturgeon after the mountain that towers over the town. Both Mount Sturgeon and Mount Abrupt (to the north of town) have been renamed to recognise the ancient Aboriginal heritage of the landscape; they are now known as Mount Wuragarri and Mount Murdadjoog respectively.

Dunkeld Arboretum Exotic species from all over the world have been planted. Ideal for walking, cycling, fishing and picnics. Old Ararat Rd.

Historical Museum Housed in an old church, the museum features displays on the history of the local Aboriginal people, the wool industry and the journeys of explorer Major Mitchell. It also offers dining and accommodation. Open weekends or by appt; Templeton St.

Corea Wines: open by appt. *Varrenti Wines:* open 12–5pm; Blackwood Rd. *Sandra Kranz Art Studio:* Glass St. *Waiting Room Art Gallery:* Parker St. *Bushwalking:* walking trails include Mt Abrupt, Mt Sturgeon and the Piccaninny Walk.

Dunkeld Cup: Nov. *Dunkeld Arts Festival:* biennial, Nov.

Gourmet Pantry: cafe and provedore; 109 Parker St (Glenelg Hwy); (03) 5577 2288. *Royal Mail Hotel:* outstanding contemporary menu, exceptional wine list; 98 Parker St (Glenelg Hwy); (03) 5577 2241.

Aquila Eco Lodges: 2 tree houses and 2 loft houses; Manns Rd; (03) 5577 2582. *Griffins Hill:* stylish yoga retreat; Victoria Valley Rd; (03) 5577 2499. *Royal Mail Hotel:* rooms and shearers' cottages; 98 Parker St (Glenelg Hwy); (03) 5577 2241. *Southern Grampians Cottages:* log cabins; 33–35 Victoria Valley Rd; (03) 5577 2457.

Grampians National Park The southern section of the park includes Victoria Valley Rd, a scenic drive that stops at Freshwater Lake Reserve (8 km N), popular for picnics. Also near Dunkeld are various hiking destinations and the Chimney Pots, a formation popular for rock climbing; access via Henty Hwy. *For further details on the park see Halls Gap.*

Grampians Pure Sheep Dairy: sample some of the sheep milk, yoghurts and cheeses while also watching how they are made; Glenelg Hwy.

See also GRAMPIANS & CENTRAL WEST, p. 155

Dunolly

Pop. 605
Map ref. 579 C4 | 591 M10

ℹ️ 109 Broadway; (03) 5468 1205.

📻 91.1 FM ABC Local Radio, 99.1 Goldfields FM

The towns of Dunolly, Wedderburn and Inglewood formed the rich goldfield region colloquially known in the 1850s as the 'Golden Triangle'. The district has produced more gold nuggets than any other goldfield in Australia, with 126 unearthed in Dunolly itself. The 'Welcome Stranger', considered to be the largest nugget ever discovered, was found 15 kilometres north-west of Dunolly, at Moliagul.

Restored courthouse: offers a display relating to gold discoveries in the area; open Sat afternoons; Market St. *Original lock-up and stables:* viewable from street only; Market St. *Gold-themed tours of the region:* include gold panning in local creeks; details from visitor centre.

Market: with local produce, crafts and second-hand goods; Market St; 3rd Sat each month. *Community Street Market:* Broadway; 4th Sat each month.

Moliagul: the Welcome Stranger Discovery Walk leads to a monument where the Welcome Stranger nugget was found in 1869. Moliagul is also the birthplace of Rev. John Flynn, founder of the Royal Flying Doctor Service; 15 km NW. *Laanecoorie Reservoir:* a great spot for swimming, boating and waterskiing, water levels permitting, with camping and picnic facilities; 16 km E. *Tarnagulla:* a small mining town with splendid Victorian architecture and a flora reserve nearby; 16 km NE. *Bealiba:* hosts a market 2nd Sun each month; 21 km NW.

See also GOLDFIELDS, p. 154

Echuca

Pop. 12 361
Map ref. 559 J12 | 584 C5

ℹ️ 2 Heygarth St; (03) 5480 7555 or 1800 804 446; www.echucamoama.com

📻 91.1 FM ABC Local Radio, 104.7 Radio EMFM

Visitors to this delightful town are transported back in time by the sight of beautiful old paddleboats cruising down the Murray River. The town is at the junction of the Murray, Campaspe and Goulburn rivers. Once Australia's largest inland port, its name comes from an Aboriginal word meaning 'meeting of the waters'. A historic iron bridge joins Echuca to Moama, over the river in New South Wales.

Port of Echuca The massive red-gum wharf has been restored to the grandeur of its heyday, with huge paddlesteamers anchored here. Cruises are available on many boats, including the paddlesteamer *Pevensey*, renamed *Philadelphia* for the TV miniseries *All the Rivers Run*; the D26 logging barge; PS *Alexander Arbuthnot*; and PS *Adelaide*. Cruises are also available on PS *Canberra*, *Pride of the Murray* and PS *Emmylou*. The MV *Mary Ann* also features a fine restaurant.

Historic buildings: many along Murray Espl include the Star Hotel, with an underground bar and escape tunnel, and the Bridge Hotel, built by Henry Hopwood, the founder of Echuca, who ran the original punt service. *Red Gum Works:* wood-turning demonstrations; Murray Espl. *Sharp's Magic Movie House and Penny Arcade:* award-winning attractions; Murray Espl. *Echuca Historical Society Museum:* housed in former police station; open 11am–3pm daily; High St. *Billabong Carriages:* Murray Espl. *National Holden Museum:* Warren St.

Southern 80 Ski Race: from Torrumbarry Weir to Echuca; Feb. *Riverboats, Jazz, Food and Wine Festival:* Feb. *Steam, Horse and Vintage Rally:* June. *Winter Blues Festival:* July. *Port of Echuca Steam Heritage Festival:* Oct.

Ceres: appealing modern menu; 2 Nish St; (03) 5482 5599. *Left Bank:* modern bistro; 551 High St; (03) 5480 3772. *Oscar W's Wharfside:* modern Australian; 101 Murray Espl, Port of

DAYLESFORD

Pop. 3071

Map ref. 572 E1 | 579 E8 | 593 N3

 98 Vincent St; (03) 5321 6123; www.visitdaylesford.com

99.9 VoiceFM, 107.9 FM ABC Local Radio

Daylesford is at the centre of Victoria's spa country. The area developed with the discovery of gold, which lured many Swiss-Italian settlers, but it was the discovery of natural mineral springs that proved a more lasting attraction. Of the 72 documented springs in the area, the most famous are nearby Hepburn Springs. The water is rich with minerals that dissolve into it as it flows from the crest of the Great Dividing Range through underground rocks, and it is known for its rejuvenating and healing qualities. Daylesford has grown as a destination in itself, complete with beautiful gardens, interesting shopping, great eating and a huge range of accommodation. The streets are lined with trees that blaze with colour in autumn, and inside the attractive old buildings are restaurants, cafes, galleries, bookshops, bakeries and chocolate shops. Overlooking the lake is one of regional Victoria's most highly regarded restaurants, the Lake House.

Convent Gallery A magnificent building surrounded by delightful cottage gardens, this former convent and girls school has been restored and features an impressive collection of artwork, sculptures and jewellery. A cafe serves local produce and Devonshire tea. Daly St.

[LAKE HOUSE RESTAURANT]

Historical Museum: features a collection of photographs from the region's past and artefacts from the local Djadja Wurrung people; open weekends and public and school holidays; Vincent St. **Lake Daylesford:** a lovely spot for picnics, with paddleboats and rowboats for hire in the warmer months. The Tipperary walking track starts here and ends at the Mineral Springs Reserve; access to the lake is from Bleakly Rd. **Wombat Hill Botanical Gardens:** est. 1861, these lovely gardens are situated on the hill overlooking town. **Daylesford Spa Country Train:** leaves railway station for Bullarto (11 km SE) each Sun.

Market: for arts, crafts and local produce; near railway station; each Sun morning. **Silver Streak Champagne Train:** train journey with gourmet food; 1st Sat each month. **Hepburn Swiss–Italian Festival:** Apr/May. **Highland Gathering:** Dec.

Frangos & Frangos: city-chic European menu; 82 Vincent St; (03) 5348 2363. **Lake House:** exceptional regional dining; King St; (03) 5348 3329. **Mercato @ Daylesford:** modern Italian; 32 Raglan St; (03) 5348 4488. **The Farmers Arms Hotel:** hearty rustic dishes; 1 East St; (03) 5348 2091. **Cosy Corner:** quaint eatery; 3 Tenth St, Hepburn Springs; (03) 5348 2576.

Lake Daylesford Lodge: luxurious lakeside villas; 32 King St; (03) 5348 4422. **Lake House:** waterfront suites and lodge rooms; King St; (03) 5348 3329. **Latte Cottage:** contemporary 2-bedroom cottage; 33 Fulcher St; 0416 264 165. **Peppers Springs Retreat & Spa:** luxury hotel and villas; 124 Main Rd, Hepburn Springs; (03) 5348 2202.

Hepburn Springs spas The Hepburn Spa and Bathhouse Wellness Retreat offers pure mineral water spas and hydrotherapy, massage therapies and an extensive range of relaxation, health and beauty treatments. Mineral Springs Cres, Hepburn Springs; (03) 5348 8888. Dating back to 1894, the recently renovated Hepburn Bathhouse has state-of-the-art communal and private mineral bathing, spas and therapies utilising the renowned local mineral springs, plus a day spa for massage, facials and indulgent beauty treatments. Mineral Springs Reserve Rd, Hepburn Springs; (03) 5321 6000; 4 km N.

Lavandula Swiss Italian Farm A sprawling estate featuring fields of lavender, cottage gardens and sales of lavender-based products. The Lavandula Harvest Festival is a popular event with a variety of family entertainment, held in Jan. Open daily, winter months weekends only; Shepherds Flat; (03) 5476 4393; 10 km N.

Hepburn Regional Park: located around Daylesford and Hepburn Springs, this park features goldmining relics, mineral springs and the impressive Mt Franklin, an extinct volcano, with panoramic views from the summit and picnic, barbecue and camping facilities around the base. There are good walking tracks. **Waterfalls:** several in area, including Sailors Falls, 5 km S; Loddon Falls, 10 km NE; Trentham Falls, 21 km SE. **Breakneck Gorge:** early goldmining site; 5 km N. **Glenlyon:** small town that hosts the popular Glenlyon Sports Day on New Year's Day, and the Fine Food and Wine Fayre in July; 8 km NE. **Lyonville Mineral Springs:** picnic and barbecue facilities; 15 km SE. **Yandoit:** historic Swiss-Italian settlement; 18 km NW.

See also SPA & GARDEN COUNTRY, p. 151

VICTORIA

Echuca; (03) 5482 5133. **PS *Emmylou:*** set-price 3-course dinner; 57 Murray Espl; (03) 5482 5244.

🛏 **PS *Emmylou:*** 2-berth cabins; 57 Murray Espl; (03) 5482 5244. ***Quest Echuca:*** stylish serviced apartments; 25–29 Heygarth St; (03) 5481 3900. ***Bright on the Murray:*** 5 B&B homestead rooms; 93 Goldsborough Rd, Moama; (03) 5483 6264. ***Perricoota Vines Retreat:*** spa villas; 400 Perricoota Rd, Moama; (03) 5482 6655 or 1800 826 655.

🧭 **Barmah State Park** This park combines with Barmah State Forest to contain the largest river red gum forest in Victoria. Nearby are Barmah Lakes, a good location for fishing and swimming. Canoes and barbecue pontoons are available for hire. Ulupna Island, in the eastern section of the park (near Strathmerton), has river beaches, camping and a large population of koalas. Barmah Muster, a cattle muster, is held in the state forest in Apr. Contact Parks Victoria on 13 1963; 39 km NE.

Moama: attractions include the Silverstone Go-Kart Track and the Horseshoe Lagoon nature reserve; 2 km N. ***Mathoura:*** set among the mighty red gums, Mathoura is a charming Murray town over the NSW border. Fishing is popular, with sites including Gulpa Creek and the Edward and Murray rivers. To see the forest in its splendour, take the Moira Forest Walkway or, for that authentic Murray River experience, visit nearby Picnic Pt, popular for camping, picnics, waterskiing and fishing; 40 km N. ***Nathalia:*** a town on Broken Creek with many historic buildings. Walking tracks along the creek take in fishing spots, old homesteads and a lookout; 57 km E.

See also GOULBURN & MURRAY, p. 157

Edenhope
Pop. 787
Map ref. 590 C11 | 601 H9

ℹ **96 Elizabeth St; (03) 5585 1509; www.westwimmera.vic.gov.au**

📻 94.1 FM ABC Local Radio, 96.5 Triple H FM

Just 30 kilometres from the South Australian border, Edenhope is set on the shores of Lake Wallace, a haven for waterbirds. The town is renowned as the site where, in 1868, Australia's first all-Aboriginal cricket team trained – their coach was T. W. Wills, who went on to establish Australian Rules football. A cairn in Lake Street honours the achievements of this early cricket team.

🏠 ***Edenhope Antiques:*** offers an extensive variety of antique wares; Elizabeth St. ***Bennetts Bakery:*** Elizabeth St. ***Lake Wallace:*** walking tracks and birdwatching hides; Wimmera Hwy.

🌴 ***Henley-on-Lake Wallace Festival:*** with market and family entertainment; Feb. ***Races:*** Mar long weekend.

🧭 **Harrow** One of Victoria's oldest inland towns, Harrow has many historic buildings in Main St, including the Hermitage Hotel, the police station and an early log gaol. The Johnny Mullagh Cricket Centre, a celebration of the first Australian Aboriginal cricketer to travel overseas, is also located in town. Kelly's Garage and Transport Museum in Main St is popular with car enthusiasts, and the National Bush Billycart Championship is held here in Mar. 32 km SE.

Dergholm State Park: 26 km S; *see Casterton.* ***Naracoorte Caves National Park:*** World Heritage site of fabulous caves with extensive fossil history to explore; around 50 km W over SA border. ***Fishing:*** redfin, trout and yabbies in many lakes and swamps nearby. Availability depends on water levels; contact visitor centre for locations.

See also GRAMPIANS & CENTRAL WEST, p. 155

Eildon
Pop. 742
Map ref. 571 H1 | 573 O1 | 582 G1 | 584 G12 | 586 C11

ℹ **High St; (03) 5774 2909; www.murrindinditourism.com.au**

📻 97.3 FM ABC Local Radio, 106.9 UGFM Upper Goulburn Community Radio

Eildon established itself as a town to service dam workers, and later holiday-makers, when the Goulburn River was dammed to create Lake Eildon. This is the state's largest constructed lake, irrigating a vast stretch of northern Victoria and providing hydro-electric power. In recent years low water levels have revealed homesteads that were submerged when the dam was constructed. The lake and the surrounding national park are popular summer holiday destinations, especially for watersports, fishing and boating.

🌴 ***Lions Club Monster Market:*** Easter. ***Opening of Fishing Season Festival:*** Sep.

🛏 ***Robyns Nest B&B:*** retreat for 2 couples; 13 High St; (03) 5779 1064.

🧭 **Lake Eildon National Park** Comprising the lake and surrounding woodlands, hills and wilderness areas, this national park provides a venue for many water- and land-based activities. When full, Lake Eildon has 6 times the capacity of Sydney Harbour. Hire a kayak, boat or houseboat from the outlets in Eildon to explore the waters, or enjoy the thrills of waterskiing with the picturesque foothills of the Australian Alps providing a backdrop. In the surrounding hills and woodlands there are various nature walks, scenic drives and panoramic lookout points. Many of the walks start at the campgrounds; details from visitor centre, or from Parks Victoria on 13 1963.

Lake Eildon Wall Lookout: 1 km N. ***Eildon Pondage and Goulburn River:*** for excellent fishing – there is no closed season for trout in Lake Eildon. ***Mt Pinniger:*** for views of Mt Buller, the alps and the lake; 3 km E. ***Freshwater Discovery Centre:*** native-fish aquariums and displays; Snobs Creek; 6 km SW. ***Waterfalls:*** include Snobs Creek Falls and Rubicon Falls; 18 km SW via Thornton. ***Eildon Trout Farm:*** towards Thornton on Back Eildon Rd.

See also HIGH COUNTRY, p. 158

Emerald
Pop. 6317
Map ref. 570 H7 | 571 C10 | 573 L7 | 575 O1 | 582 E5

ℹ **Dandenong Ranges Information Centre, 1211 Burwood Hwy, Upper Ferntree Gully; (03) 9758 7522; www.dandenongrangestourism.com.au**

📻 97.1 FM 3MDR Mountain District Radio, 774 AM ABC Local Radio

Emerald is a delightful little town set in the Dandenong Ranges, which lie behind Melbourne's eastern suburbs. Over the weekend people come from the city into 'the hills' to take in the scenic forests and visit the cafes, galleries, and antique and craft stores.

🏠 **Emerald Lake** The lake is a lovely, tranquil spot ideal for picnics and walks. Attractions include the largest model railway display in the Southern Hemisphere, paddleboats, cafe and tearooms, fishing, free wading pool (summer months) and a variety of walking trails. Picnic shelters are available for hire throughout the year. Puffing Billy stops at Emerald Lake and many passengers spend a day here before returning on the train in the late afternoon. Emerald Lake Rd.

Galleries and craft shops: a wide variety, specialising in locally made products; along Main St.

PAVE (Performing and Visual Arts in Emerald) Festival: Apr. *Great Train Race:* runners attempt to race Puffing Billy from Belgrave to Emerald Lake Park; 1st Sun in May.

Elevation at Emerald: casual dining with views; 374 Main Rd; (03) 5968 2911.

Fernglade on Menzies: self-contained and B&B suites; 11 Caroline Cres; (03) 5968 2228. *Fernhem Cottages:* 3 country-style cottages; 109 Emerald–Monbulk Rd; (03) 5968 5462.

Puffing Billy Victoria's favourite steam train runs between Belgrave and Gembrook, stopping at Emerald Lake. The views from the train are of tall trees and ferny gullies, and if you time your trip for the last Sat of the month you could catch the local craft and produce market at Gembrook station. Also at Gembrook is the Motorist Cafe and Museum. Puffing Billy operates every day of the year, except Christmas Day; 24 hr recorded timetable and fare information on 1900 937 069, all other inquiries (03) 9757 0700; Belgrave 9 km w, Gembrook 14 km E.

Menzies Creek This town is home to Cotswold House, where visitors enjoy gourmet food amid fantastic views. Nearby is Cardinia Reservoir Park, where picnic spots are shared with free-roaming kangaroos, and Lake Aura Vale, a popular spot for sailing. Belgrave–Gembrook Rd; 4 km NW.

Sherbrooke Equestrian Park: trail-rides; Wellington Rd; 3 km w. *Australian Rainbow Trout Farm:* Macclesfield; 8 km N. *Sherbrooke Art Gallery:* impressive collection of local artwork; Monbulk Rd, Belgrave; 11 km NW. *Bimbimbie Wildlife Park:* Mt Burnett; 12 km SE.

See also YARRA & DANDENONGS, p. 148

Euroa

Pop. 2773
Map ref. 584 F9 | 586 A7

 Strathbogie Ranges Tourism Information Service, BP Service Centre, Tarcombe St; 1300 134 610; www.strathbogieregion.com.au

97.7 FM ABC Local Radio, 98.5 FM

Euroa was the scene of one of Ned Kelly's most infamous acts. In 1878 the notorious bushranger staged a daring robbery, rounding up some 50 hostages and making off with money and gold worth nearly £2000. The Strathbogie Ranges, once one of the Kelly Gang's hideouts, now provide a pretty backdrop to the town, and the region really comes to life in spring, when stunning wildflowers bloom. During this time and in autumn a number of private gardens are open to the public.

Farmers Arms Historical Museum The museum features displays explaining the history of Ned Kelly and Eliza Forlonge; Eliza and her sister are said to have imported the first merino sheep into Victoria. Open Fri–Mon afternoons; Kirkland Ave.

Walking trail: self-guide trail to see the rich history and architecture of the town, including the National Bank building and the post office, both in Binney St; brochure available from visitor centre. *Seven Creeks Park:* good freshwater fishing, particularly for trout; Kirkland Ave.

Miniature steam-train rides: Turnbull St; last Sun each month. *Wool Week:* Oct.

Ruffy Produce Store: excellent regional produce store; 26 Nolans Rd, Ruffy; (03) 5790 4387.

Forlonge B&B: 2 air-conditioned suites; 76 Anderson St; (03) 5795 2460.

Faithfull Creek Waterfall: 9 km NE. *Longwood:* includes the delightful White Hart Hotel and horse-drawn carriage rides; 14 km SW. *Gooram Falls:* a scenic drive takes in the falls and parts of the Strathbogie Ranges; 20 km SE. *Locksley:* popular for gliding and parachuting; 20 km SW. *Polly McQuinns Weir:* historic river crossing and reservoir; Strathbogie Rd; 20 km SE. *Mt Wombat Lookout:* spectacular views of surrounding country and the Australian Alps; 25 km SE. *Blue Wren Lavender Farm:* lavender products and Devonshire tea; Boho South; 28 km E. *Avenel Maze:* Ned Kelly–themed maze; open Thurs–Mon, school and public holidays; 37 km SW.

See also GOULBURN & MURRAY, p. 157

Flinders

Pop. 575
Map ref. 573 I11 | 575 I10 | 582 C8

ℹ️ **Nepean Hwy, Dromana; (03) 5987 3078 or 1800 804 009.**

📻 98.7 3RPP FM, 774 AM ABC Local Radio

Flinders is set on the south coast of the Mornington Peninsula, a region famous for its wineries. During the 1880s, Flinders became known as a health and recreation resort and a number of guesthouses and hotels began to emerge. Today Flinders remains a popular holiday spot, with its renowned cliff-top golf course and gastropub. Heritage buildings have wide verandahs, often shading antique and curio shops or excellent cafes, giving the town an enchanting and historic air. This, combined with taking in the view across the bay to The Nobbies and Seal Rocks, makes it easy to understand the town's perennial appeal.

Foreshore Reserve: popular for picnics and fishing from the jetty. *Studio @ Flinders:* small but unique art gallery with emphasis on ceramics, also exhibits handcrafted jewellery, glass, textiles, wood and paintings; Cook St. *Historic buildings:* 'Bimbi', built in the 1870s, is the earliest remaining dwelling in Flinders; King St. 'Wilga' is another fine Victorian-era home; King St. *Flinders Golf Links:* great views across Bass Strait; West Head, Wood St.

Peninsula Piers and Pinots: the region's winemakers showcase their pinots with local food and produce at Flinders Pier; Mar long weekend.

Foxeys Hangout: casual winery cafe; 795 White Hill Rd, Red Hill; (03) 5989 2022. *Merricks General Store:* wine-friendly rustic fare; 3458 Frankston–Flinders Rd, Merricks; (03) 5989 8088. *Montalto:* slick vineyard restaurant; 33 Shoreham Rd, Red Hill South; (03) 5989 8412. *Ten Minutes by Tractor:* cellar-door restaurant, dishes matched with wines; 1333 Mornington–Flinders Rd, Main Ridge; (03) 5989 6080.

Flinders B&B: 1-bedroom fisherman's cottage; 94 Cook St; (03) 5989 0301. *Cape Schanck Light Station:* 4 cottages; 420 Cape Schanck Rd, Cape Schanck; (03) 5968 6411. *Lindenderry:* luxury country house; 142 Arthurs Seat Rd, Red Hill; (03) 5989 2933. *Shoreham Beach House:* beach house, sleeps 10; 20 Myers Dr, Shoreham; (03) 5989 8433.

Red Hill This is fine wine country, where vineyards are interspersed with noted art galleries, farm gates, cafes and restaurants. The Red Hill Market is legendary and held on the first Sat of each month from Sept to May. It specialises in local

VICTORIA

crafts, clothing and fresh produce. The town also features a number of galleries and The Cherry Farm, where you can 'pick your own' cherries and berries in a pleasant setting (in season); Arkwells La. The Mornington Peninsula Winter Wine Fest is held annually on the Queen's Birthday weekend (June) and the Cool Climate Wine Show is in Mar.

Mornington Peninsula National Park The park covers 2686 ha and features a diverse range of vegetation, from the basalt cliff-faces of Cape Schanck to banksia woodlands, coastal dune scrubs and swampland. One of the park's many attractions is the Cape Schanck Lighthouse, built in 1859, which provides accommodation in one of the lighthouse keepers' houses. Historic Pt Nepean retains its original fortifications and has information displays and soundscapes. Also available here is a 'hop-on, hop-off' tractor train with commentary, and bicycle hire. There are ocean beaches for swimming and surfing, while the Bushranger Bay Nature Walk, starting at Cape Schanck, and the Farnsworth Track at Portsea are just 2 of the many walks on offer. Contact Parks Victoria on 13 1963; access to Cape Schanck from Rosebud–Flinders Rd; 15 km w.

French Island National Park French Island once served as a prison where inmates kept themselves entertained with their own 9-hole golf course. This unique reserve features a range of environments from mangrove saltmarsh to open woodlands. During spring more than 100 varieties of orchids come into bloom. The park is home to the most significant population of koalas in Victoria. Long-nosed potoroos and majestic sea-eagles can also be spotted. There is a variety of walking tracks on the island and bicycles can be hired from the general store. There are also guesthouses, and camping and picnic facilities. Contact Parks Victoria on 13 1963; access is via a 30 min ferry trip from Stony Pt, 30 km NE of Flinders.

Ashcombe Maze and Lavender Gardens: a large hedge maze surrounded by beautifully landscaped gardens; closed Aug; Red Hill Rd, Shoreham; 6 km N. *Ace Hi Horseriding and Wildlife Park:* beach and bush trail-rides and a native-animal sanctuary; Cape Schanck; 11 km w. *Main Ridge:* Sunny Ridge Strawberry Farm – pick your own berries in season; Mornington–Flinders Rd. Also The Pig and Whistle, English-style pub, Purves Rd; 11 km NW. *Pt Leo:* great surf beach; 12 km NE via Shoreham. *Balnarring:* hosts a market specialising in handmade crafts; 3rd Sat each month Nov–May; 17 km NE. Nearby is Coolart Homestead, an impressive Victorian mansion with historical displays, gardens, wetlands and a bird-observation area.

See also Mornington Peninsula, p. 149

Foster

Pop. 1039
Map ref. 582 G9

ⓘ Stockyard Gallery, Main St; 1800 630 704; www.visitpromcountry.com.au

📻 89.5 3MFM South Gippsland, 100.7 FM ABC Local Radio

Foster was originally a goldmining town settled in the 1870s. The town boasts close access to Wilsons Promontory – affectionately called 'the Prom' – and is a popular base for visitors. Set in the centre of a rich agricultural area, Foster is the main shopping precinct for the Prom, Corner Inlet and Waratah Bay.

🏛 *Historical Museum:* in old post office; Main St. *Stockyard Gallery:* Main St. *Hayes Walk:* view the site of Victory Mine, Foster's largest goldmine; starts in town behind the carpark. *Pearl Park:* picturesque picnic spot.

🎪 *Tastes of Prom Country:* Jan. *Great Southern Portrait Prize:* Jan. *Prom Coast Seachange Festival:* Apr. *Mt Best Art Show:* Apr. *Prom Country Challenge:* fun run; Aug. *Promontory Home Produce and Craft Market:* Nov–Apr.

🛏 *Basia Mille Luxury Apartments:* Tuscan-inspired accommodation; 1 Taylor Crt, Fish Creek; (03) 5687 1453

⊙ **Wilsons Promontory National Park** The Prom is well loved across the state for its wild and untouched scenery. Its 130 km coastline is framed by granite headlands, mountains, forests and fern gullies. Bordered on all sides by sea, it hangs from Victoria by a thin, sandy isthmus. Limited road access means opportunities for walking are plentiful. The park features dozens of walking tracks, ranging from easy strolls to more challenging overnight hikes that take visitors to one of 11 campsites only accessible by foot. Hikes range from beginner to intermediate, and permits are required. Detailed information is provided at the park's own visitor centre: the remnants of a commando training camp from WW II. Contact Parks Victoria on 13 1963; 32 km s.

Toora An internationally recognised wetland site located on Corner Inlet, it is renowned for the huge variety of migratory birds that nest in the area. Toora is also home to Agnes Falls, a wind farm, a lavender farm and the Bird Hide where you can watch migratory and indigenous birdlife. 12 km E.

Foster North Lookout: 6 km NW. *Wineries:* Windy Ridge Winery; 10 km s. *Fish Creek:* A rural village, which attracts many visitors en route to the Prom. From the novelty of the giant mullet on top of the Promontory Gate Hotel to the fish-shaped seats around town, there is more to this unusually themed town than meets the eye. Galleries and vineyards are located in the area. Access the Great Southern Trail and walk, ride or cycle your way to Foster. Nearby Mt Nicol offers a lookout with spectacular views; 13 km sw. *Turtons Creek Reserve:* features mountain ash, blackwood and tree ferns, and a small waterfall. Bush camping is available; 18 km N. *Coastal towns:* popular bases during summer months; Sandy Pt, 22 km s; Waratah Bay, 34 km sw; Walkerville, 36 km sw. *Cape Liptrap:* views over rugged coastline and Bass Strait; 46 km sw.

See also Phillip Island & Gippsland, p. 150

Geelong

see inset box on next page

Glenrowan

Pop. 324
Map ref. 584 H8 | 586 E5

ⓘ Wangaratta Visitor Information Centre, 100 Murphy St, Wangaratta; 1800 801 065; www.visitwangaratta.com.au

📻 101.3 Oak FM, 106.5 FM ABC Local Radio

Glenrowan is a town well known to most Victorians as the site of Ned Kelly's final showdown with the police in 1880. Most of the attractions in Glenrowan revolve around the legends surrounding Kelly's life – a giant statue of Kelly himself towers over shops in Gladstone Street. Almost as legendary as Ned Kelly are the numerous wineries and fruit orchards in the area.

🏠 *Kate's Cottage Museum:* with an extensive collection of Kelly memorabilia as well as a replica of the Kelly homestead and blacksmith shop; Gladstone St. *Cobb & Co Museum:* an underground museum featuring notorious stories of Kelly and other bushrangers; Gladstone St. *Kellyland:* a computer-animated show of Kelly's capture; Gladstone St. *Kelly Gang*

Siege Site Walk: discover the sites and history that led to the famous siege on this self-guide walk (brochure available). *Wine and produce outlets:* over 22 local wines are offered for tastings and sales at the Buffalo Mountain Wine Centre; Gladstone St. Gourmet jams and fruit products are also available at Smiths Orchard and The Big Cherry; Warby Range Rd. *White Cottage Herb Garden:* herb sales; Hill St.

 Trails, Tastings and Tales wine and food event: June.

Baileys Old Block Cafe: weekend platters and grazing food; Baileys of Glenrowan, Taminick Gap Rd; (03) 5766 2392.

Warby Range State Park The 'Warbys', as they are known locally, extend for 25 km north of Glenrowan. The steep ranges provide excellent viewing points, especially from Ryans Lookout. Other lookouts include the Pangarang Lookout near the Pine Gully Picnic Area and the Mt Glenrowan Lookout, the highest point of the Warbys at 513 m. There are well-marked tracks for bushwalkers and a variety of pleasant picnic spots amid open forests and woodlands, with wildflowers blossoming during the warmer months. Access from Taminick Gap Rd.

See also HIGH COUNTRY, p. 158

Halls Gap

see inset box on page 185

Hamilton

Pop. 9379
Map ref. 592 F4

ⓘ Lonsdale St; (03) 5572 3746 or 1800 807 056; www.sthgrampians.vic.gov.au

📻 94.1 FM ABC Local Radio, 99.3 Coastal FM

Hamilton is a prominent rural centre in the heart of a sheep-grazing district. This industry is such an important part of the town's economy that it has been dubbed the 'Wool Capital of the World'. It is both the geographical and business hub of the Western District. A thriving country city, Hamilton is filled with cultural experiences, whether gazing at botanical, artistic or architectural beauty, browsing through great shops or putting in a bid as part of a 50 000-head sheep sale.

Hamilton Art Gallery This gallery is said to be one of regional Australia's finest, featuring a diverse collection of fine arts and museum pieces dating back to the earliest European settlements in Australia. Many trinkets and treasures of the region's first stately homes are on display, as well as English and European glass, ceramic and silver work. There is also a good collection of colonial art from the Western District. Guided heritage tours of the gallery and district are available. Brown St.

Botanic Gardens First planted in 1870 and classified by the National Trust in 1990, these gardens have long been regarded as one of the most impressive in rural Victoria. Designed by the curator of the Melbourne Botanic Gardens, William Guilfoyle, the gardens feature his 'signature' design elements of sweeping lawns interrupted by lakes, islands, and contrasting plant and flower beds. Keep an eye out for the free-flight aviary, enormous English oaks and historic band rotunda. French St.

Lake Hamilton: attractive landscaped man-made lake used for swimming, sailing, yachting and rowing, and featuring an excellent walking/bike track; off Ballarat Rd. *Sir Reginald Ansett Transport Museum:* birthplace of Ansett Airlines, the museum tells the story of Ansett and our aviation history in one

of the airline's original hangars; Ballarat Rd. *Hamilton Pastoral Museum:* features farm equipment, tractors, engines, household items and small-town memorabilia; Ballarat Rd. *Big Wool Bales:* built in the shape of 5 giant wool bales and surrounded by native red gums, the Wool Bales tell the fascinating story of Australia's wool industry; Coleraine Rd. *Mt Baimbridge Lavender:* set on 12 acres. Wander through gardens and browse the gallery; Mt Baimbridge Rd; tours available by appt (03) 5572 4342. *Hamilton History Centre:* features the history of early Western District families and town settlement; Gray St.

 Hamilton Farmer's Market: last Sat each month. *Harvest Rally:* Jan. *Beef Expo:* Feb. *Hamilton Cup:* Apr. *Promenade of Sacred Music:* Apr. *Plough and Seed Rally:* May. *Sheepvention:* promotes the sheep and wool industries; Aug.

Darriwill Farm: produce/wine store and cafe; 169 Grey St; (03) 5571 2088. *Hamilton Strand Restaurant:* modern Italian; 100 Thompson St; (03) 5571 9144. *Roxburgh House:* wine-bar-cum-cosy-cafe; 64 Thompson St; (03) 5572 4857. *Cafe Catalpa:* game-heavy menu; 7921 Hamilton Hwy, Tarrington; (03) 5572 1888.

 Garland Cottage: 1-bedroom cottage; 18 Skene St; (03) 5572 1054. *Seven Palmer Street:* ultra-chic 2-bedroom house; 7 Palmer St; 0408 212 100.

Grampians National Park See Halls Gap. 35 km NE.

Mt Eccles National Park The key feature of this park is a large volcanic crater lake. A range of walks let visitors explore the scoria cones and caves formed thousands of years ago by volcanoes. The 3 main craters hold a 700 m long lake, Lake Surprise, fed by underground springs. Contact Parks Victoria on 13 1963; near Macarthur; 40 km S.

Tarrington: established by German settlers and originally named Hochkirch, this area is fast becoming a well-known 'pinot noir' grape-producing area; 12 km SE. *Waterfalls:* Nigretta Falls has a viewing platform; 15 km NW. Also Wannon Falls; 19 km W. *Mt Napier State Park:* features Byaduk Caves (lava caves) near the park's western entrance. Only 1 cave is accessible to the public; 18 km S. *Cavendish:* a small town en route to the Grampians, notable for the 3 beautiful private gardens open during the Southern Grampians Open Gardens Festival each Oct; 25 km N. *Penshurst:* a lovely historic town at the foot of Mt Rouse. Excellent views from the top of the mountain, where there is a crater lake. Country Muster each Feb; 31 km SE.

See also GRAMPIANS & CENTRAL WEST, p. 155

Healesville

Pop. 7357
Map ref. 573 L4 | 582 E4

ⓘ Yarra Valley Visitor Information Centre, Old Courthouse, Harker St; (03) 5962 2600; www.visityarravalley.com.au

📻 99.1 Yarra Valley FM, 774 AM ABC Local Radio

To the west of Yarra Ranges National Park and within easy reach of Melbourne, Healesville has a charming rural atmosphere. There are good restaurants and cafes in town, all focusing on quality local produce, especially the world-class Yarra Valley wines. On top of this is a host of art and craft boutiques and two major attractions – TarraWarra Museum of Art and the famous Healesville Sanctuary, one of the best places in Victoria to experience Australia's unique wildlife close-up.

VICTORIA

GEELONG

Pop. 160 989

Map ref. 572 F8 | 574 B4 | 576 | 580 H1 | 582 A6 | 593 O7

ℹ️ **Cnr Princes Hwy and St Georges Rd, Corio; (03) 5275 5797 or 1800 620 888; www.visitgreatoceanroad.org.au**

📻 94.7 The Pulse FM, 774 AM ABC Local Radio

Situated on Corio Bay, Geelong is the largest provincial city in Victoria. Geelong was traditionally a wool-processing centre, and the National Wool Museum in Brougham Street details its early dependence upon the industry. The town was first settled by Europeans in the 1830s, but Geelong and its surrounds were originally home to the Wathaurong people, with whom the famous convict escapee William Buckley lived for many years. Buckley later described the unique culture of the Aboriginal tribes who welcomed him into their lives, and his writing is now one of the most priceless historical records of Indigenous culture in southern Australia. Geelong is a beautifully laid-out city, and a drive along the scenic Esplanade reveals magnificent old mansions built during its heyday.

🏠 **Waterfront Geelong** This superbly restored promenade stretches along Eastern Beach and offers a variety of attractions. Visitors can relax in the historic, 1930s-built sea-baths, enjoy fine dining in seaside restaurants and cafes or stroll along the famous Bollards Trail featuring colourful sculptures. The Waterfront district is on Eastern Beach Rd, with the beautiful old Cunningham Pier as a centrepiece.

National Wool Museum Housed in a historic bluestone woolstore, the centre features audiovisual displays plus re-created shearers' quarters and a mill-worker's cottage. There is a licensed restaurant and bar in the cellar, and a souvenir shop selling locally made wool products. Cnr Moorabool and Brougham sts; (03) 5227 0701.

Geelong Art Gallery: this regional gallery is considered one of the finest in the state. The focus is on late-19th- and early-20th-century paintings by British artists and members of the Royal Academy, such as Tom Roberts and Arthur Streeton; Little Malop St. ***Historic buildings:*** there are over 100 National Trust classifications in Geelong, including Merchiston Hall, Osborne House and Corio Villa. 'The Heights' is a 14-room prefabricated timber mansion set in landscaped gardens; contact visitor centre for details of open days; Aphrasia St, Newtown. Christ Church, still in continuous use, is the oldest Anglican Church in Victoria; Moorabool St. ***Ford Discovery Centre:*** Geelong has long been a major manufacturing centre for Ford and this centre details the history of Ford cars with interactive displays; closed Tues; Cnr Brougham and Gheringhap sts. ***Wintergarden:*** a historic building housing a gallery, a nursery, antiques and a giftshop; McKillop St. ***Botanic Gardens:*** overlooking Corio Bay and featuring a good collection of native and exotic plants; part of Eastern Park; Garden St. ***Johnstone Park:*** picnic and barbecue facilities; Cnr Mercer and Gheringhap sts. ***Queens Park:*** walks to Buckley Falls; Queens Park Rd, Newtown. ***Balyang Bird Sanctuary:*** Shannon Ave, Newtown. ***Barwon River:*** extensive walking tracks and bike paths in parkland by the river. ***Norlane Water World:*** water slides and fun park (summer only); Princes Hwy, Norlane. ***Corio Bay beaches:*** popular for swimming, fishing and sailing; boat ramps provided.

[COLOURFUL BOLLARDS ALONG GEELONG'S WATERFRONT]

Steampacket Gardens Market: on foreshore at Eastern Beach; 1st Sun each month. *Geelong Farmers Market:* Little Malop St; 2nd Sat each month. *Skandia Geelong Week:* Jan. *Pako Festa:* Victoria's premier multicultural event; Pakington St; last Sat in Feb. *Highland Gathering:* Mar. *National Celtic Folk Festival:* June. Geelong Show: Oct. *Geelong Cup:* Oct. *Christmas Carols by the Bay:* Eastern Beach; Dec. *Geelong New Year Waterfront Festival:* New Year's Eve, New Year's Day.

2 Faces: contemporary cuisine; 8 Malop St; (03) 5229 4546. *Fishermen's Pier:* seafood; Yarra St, Eastern Beach; (03) 5222 4100. *Pettavel Winery & Restaurant:* gastronomic winery; 65 Pettavel Rd, Waurn Ponds; (03) 5266 1120. *The Beach House:* contemporary beachside; Eastern Beach Reserve, Waterfront Bay; (03) 5221 8322.

Chifley on the Esplanade: hotel rooms and apartments; 13 The Esplanade; (03) 5244 7700 or 1300 650 464. *Four Points by Sheraton Geelong:* waterfront rooms/studios; 10–14 Eastern Beach Rd; (03) 5223 1377. *Haymarket Boutique Hotel:* 6 centrally located suites; 244 Moorabool St; (03) 5221 1174. *Mercure Hotel Geelong:* variety of room types; Cnr Gheringhap and Myers sts; (03) 5223 6200.

You Yangs Regional Park These granite outcrops that rise 352 m above Werribee's lava plains have an ancient link to the Wathaurong people as they provided a much-needed water source – rock wells were created to catch water, and many of them can still be seen at Big Rock. The park's activities include the 12 km Great Circle Drive and the climb to Flinders Peak for fantastic views of Geelong, Corio Bay, Mt Macedon and Melbourne's skyline. Contact Parks Victoria on 13 1963; 24 km N.

Werribee Park and Open Range Zoo The key feature of Werribee Park is a beautifully preserved 1870s mansion with the interior restored to its original opulence. The mansion is surrounded by 12 ha of gardens, including a grotto and a farmyard area, complete with a blacksmith. Within the grounds is the Victoria State Rose Garden with over 500 varieties of flowers. Next to the park is the Werribee Open Range Zoo, developed around the Werribee River. The zoo covers 200 ha and has a variety of animals native to the grasslands of Africa, Asia, North America and Australia, including giraffes, rhinos, meerkats, cheetahs and vervet monkeys. Guided safaris through the replicated African savannah are a must. Access from the Princes Hwy; Werribee Park 13 1963; Open Range Zoo (03) 9731 9600; 40 km NE.

Fyansford: one of the oldest settlements in the region, with historic buildings including the Swan Inn, Balmoral Hotel and Fyansford Hotel. The Monash Bridge across the Moorabool River is thought to be one of the earliest reinforced-concrete bridges in Victoria; outskirts of Geelong; 4 km w. *Adventure Park:* Victoria's first waterpark, with 22 attractions and rides; open Oct–Apr; Bellarine Hwy, Wallington; 15 km SE. *Avalon Airfield:* hosts the Australian International Air Show in odd-numbered years; off Princes Hwy; 20 km NE. *Serendip Sanctuary:* a wildlife research station that includes nature trails, bird hides and a visitor centre; just south of the You Yangs. *Fairy Park:* features miniature houses and scenes from fairytales; north of Anakie (29 km N). *Steiglitz:* once a gold town, Steiglitz is now almost deserted. The restored courthouse is open on Sun; 37 km NW. *Little River Earth Sanctuary:* 200 animals live here in the open grassy woodland, including species that had been extinct in Victoria for over 100 years and were reintroduced right here. Take the Wildlife Adventure Walk at sunset to see such creatures as potoroos and pademelons. Also on-site is the set used in the film *Ned Kelly*; guided tours only, bookings on (03) 5283 1602; 45 km NE. *Geelong Wine Region:* stretching north past Anakie, around Geelong and south along the Bellarine Peninsula, this region produces a diverse range of red and white wines. Cellar doors offer tastings and sales; map from visitor centre.

See also WERRIBEE & BELLARINE, p. 152

Silvermist Studio Gallery: handmade gold and silver jewellery; Maroondah Hwy. *Open-air trolley rides:* from Healesville railway station; open Sun and public holidays. *Giant Steps/Innocent Bystander Winery:* thoroughly modern cellar door in the town centre with an excellent bakery, bistro serving mouth-watering pizzas, and cheese room; 336 Maroondah Hwy; (03) 5962 6111 or 1800 661 624.

Market: River St; 1st Sun each month. *Grape Grazing Festival:* events held throughout wine district to celebrate the harvest; Feb. *Australian Car Rally Championship:* Sept.

3777: contemporary with views; Mt Rael Retreat, 140 Healesville–Yarra Glen Rd; (03) 5962 1977. *Giant Steps/ Innocent Bystander:* modern bakery, cafe and cellar door; 336 Maroondah Hwy; (03) 5962 6111 or 1800 661 624. *Healesville Hotel:* country gastropub; 256 Maroondah Hwy; (03) 5962 4002. *Bella Vedere:* bakery, cafe-cum-restaurant; 874 Maroondah Hwy, Coldstream; (03) 5962 6161.

Healesville Hotel: 7 hotel rooms; 256 Maroondah Hwy; (03) 5962 4002. *Mt Rael Retreat:* modern suites with views, adult guests only; 140 Healesville–Yarra Glen Rd; (03) 5962 1977. *RACV Healesville Country Club:* recently renovated club with modern rooms, RACV club members and guests only; Healesville–Yarra Glen Rd; (03) 5962 4899.

Healesville Sanctuary Australia's unique animal species are on show at this 32 ha reserve. The sanctuary is also one of the few places in the world to have successfully bred platypus in captivity. Allow at least half a day to visit and see the animal hospital or go on a behind-the-scenes keeper tour (bookings on (03) 5957 2800). Badger Creek Rd; 4 km s.

TarraWarra Museum of Art TarraWarra Estate has been operating as a vineyard since 1983, producing a selection of fine chardonnay and pinot noir. Now there is a striking building housing an extensive private collection of modern art. The collection focuses on the 3 key themes of Australian Modernism – landscape, figuration and abstraction – and works by artists such as Howard Arkley, Arthur Boyd and Brett Whiteley can be found within. Healesville–Yarra Glen Rd; (03) 5957 3100.

 RADIO STATIONS   IN TOWN   WHAT'S ON   WHERE TO EAT   WHERE TO STAY   NEARBY

VICTORIA

Hedgend Maze: giant maze and fun park; Albert Rd; 2.5 km s. *Corranderrk Aboriginal Cemetery:* once the burial ground for an Aboriginal mission, and the final resting place of well-known Wurundjeri leader William Barak; 3 km s. *Maroondah Reservoir Park:* a magnificent park set in lush forests with walking tracks and a lookout nearby; 3 km NE. *Donnelly's Weir Park:* starting point of the 5000 km Bicentennial National Trail to Cooktown (Queensland). The park also has short walking tracks and picnic facilities; 4 km N. *Badger Weir Park:* picnic area in a natural setting; 7 km SE. *Mallesons Lookout:* views of Yarra Valley to Melbourne; 8 km s. *Mt St Leonard:* good views from the summit; 14 km N. *Toolangi:* attractions include the Singing Gardens of C. J. Dennis, a beautiful, formal garden; the Toolangi Forest Discovery Centre, for a fascinating insight into the local forests and how they were formed; and Toolangi Pottery; 20 km NW. *Wineries:* around 85 in the area open for tastings and sales. Tours available; details from visitor centre. *See also Yarra Glen.*

See also YARRA & DANDENONGS, p. 148

Heathcote
Pop. 1572
Map ref. 584 B10 | 591 P11

i Cnr High and Barrack sts; (03) 5433 3121; www.heathcote.org.au

 91.1 FM ABC Local Radio, 100.7 Highlands FM

Heathcote is located near the outskirts of the scenic Heathcote–Graytown National Park, with the McIvor Creek flowing by the town. Heathcote was established during the gold rush, but is now known as a prominent wine region with good red wines produced from a number of new vineyards.

🏠 *Courthouse Crafts:* displays relating to the gold rush, plus arts and crafts; High St. *Pink Cliffs:* eroded soil from gold sluices gave the cliffs their remarkable pink colour; Pink Cliffs Rd, off Hospital Rd. *McIvor Range Reserve:* walking tracks; off Barrack St; details of walks from visitor centre. *Heathcote Winery:* this winery, in the old Thomas Craven Stores building, has an art gallery and cellar-door sales; High St.

🌴 *World's Longest Lunch:* Mar. *Rodeo:* Mar long weekend. *Heathcote Wine and Food Festival:* 1st weekend in Oct.

🍴 *Emeu Inn:* regional produce; 187 High St; (03) 5433 2668.

🛏 *Emeu Inn:* 6 suites, 1 cottage; 187 High St; (03) 5433 2668. *Hut on the Hill:* 2-bedroom luxury cottage; 720 Dairy Flat Rd; (03) 5433 2329. *Olive Grove Retreat:* chic guesthouse with pool; Travers La; 0403 876 988.

🧭 **Heathcote–Graytown National Park** Compared with many of Victoria's national parks, Heathcote–Graytown was declared quite late as part of a statewide plan to preserve box-ironbark forest. Now protecting the largest forest of this type in the state, the park is not only an important nature reserve but also has a long history of settlement. Take one of the many walks or scenic drives to explore evidence of Aboriginal, goldmining and pioneering history, or take in scenic views from the lookouts at Mt Black, Mt Ida and Viewing Rock (just near Heathcote). Contact Parks Victoria on 13 1963; access from Northern Hwy and Heathcote–Nagambie Rd.

Wineries: Heathcote shiraz makes wine lovers go weak at the knees. Its depth is the result of the dark, red Cambrian soil and the continental climate. Jasper Hill is the most exclusive name in the area. Its elegant red wines can be hard to come by, so if you manage to find a bottle, it is worth purchasing it on the spot.

Other good wineries include Heathcote Winery with its cellar door located on the town's main street, Shelmerdine Vineyards, Wild Duck Creek Estate and Red Edge. To find most of the region's wines under one roof, head to Cellar and Store, which also stocks a full range of local gourmet produce.

Lake Eppalock: one of the state's largest lakes, great for fishing, watersports and picnics; 10 km w.

See also GOULBURN & MURRAY, p. 157

Hopetoun
Pop. 591
Map ref. 558 E10 | 590 H4

i Gateway Beet, 75 Lascelles St; (03) 5083 3001; www.hopetounvictoria.com.au

📻 92.9 3MBR-FM Mallee Border Radio, 594 AM ABC Local Radio

This small Mallee town, south-east of Wyperfeld National Park, was named after the first governor-general of Australia, the Earl of Hopetoun. The Earl was a friend of Edward Lascelles, who played a major role in developing the Mallee Country by eradicating vermin, developing water strategies to cope with the dry conditions, and enticing settlers to the region.

🏠 *Hopetoun House:* the residence of Lascelles, this majestic building is now National Trust–classified; Evelyn St. *Mallee Mural:* depicts history of the region; wall of Dr Pete's Memorial Park, cnr Lascelles and Austin sts. *Lake Lascelles:* good for boating, swimming and fishing when filled, presently dry. Camping facilities available; access from end of Austin St.

🌴 *Hopetoun Bowl Club Annual Carnival:* Apr. *Hopetoun A & P Society Annual Show:* Oct.

🧭 **Wyperfeld National Park** Outlet Creek connects the network of lake beds that are the main highlight for visitors to this park. They fill only when Lake Albacutya overflows, which in turn fills only when Lake Hindmarsh overflows. Once a corroboree ground, the main lake bed, Wirrengren Plain, has flooded only once in the last 100 years. Eastern grey kangaroos can be seen grazing on Wirrengren and the other lake beds, and the Eastern Lookout Nature Drive is a great way to see the range of vegetation in the park – river red gums, black box, mallee and cypress pine, and wildflowers in spring. A variety of walking trails leave from the 2 campgrounds – Wonga Campground in the south and Casuarina Campground in the north, near the lakes. Contact Parks Victoria on 13 1963; 50 km NW.

Patchewollock: the northern gateway to the Wyperfeld National Park, and also home of the Patchewollock Outback Pub; 35 km NW.

See also MALLEE COUNTRY, p. 156

Horsham
Pop. 14 120
Map ref. 590 G9

i 20 O'Callaghan Pde; (03) 5382 1832 or 1800 633 218; www.grampianslittledesert.com.au

 96.5 Triple H FM, 594 AM ABC Local Radio

Horsham is an important centre for the Wimmera district. Prior to European settlement, Horsham and its surrounds were occupied by the Jardwa and Wotjobaluk Aboriginal people, who referred to the region as 'Wopetbungundilar'. This term is thought to have meant 'place of flowers', a reference to the flowers that grow along the banks of the Wimmera River. Flowers continue to play an important role in Horsham, which is

HALLS GAP

Pop. 279
Map ref. 590 H12 | 592 H1

i **Grampians Rd; (03) 5356 4616 or 1800 065 599;
www.grampianstravel.com.au**

94.1 FM ABC Local Radio, 99.9 VoiceFM

The little village of Halls Gap is set in the heart of the Grampians. It was named after Charles Browing Hall, who discovered the gap and valley in 1841. The valley was later developed by cattle-station owners, but the town really took off in the early 1900s when tourists, nature lovers and botanists caught on to the beauty and diversity of the mountain ranges that would later become Grampians National Park. The town itself has its own charm – shops, galleries and cafes lend a laid-back atmosphere that befits the location, while in the evening long-billed corellas arrive to roost opposite the shops in the main street.

Grampians Jazz Festival: Feb. **Grampians Grape Escape:** wine and food festival; May. **Wildflower Exhibition:** Oct.

Boroka Downs: 5 contemporary retreats; 51 Birdswing Rd; (03) 5356 6243. **DULC Cabins:** 3 environmentally friendly cabins; 9 Thryptomene Crt; (03) 5356 4711. **Lakuna Retreat:** architect-designed 3-bedroom home; 81 High Rd; (03) 5221 1606. **Kangaroos in the Top Paddock:** adults-only bushland retreat; Northern Grampians Rd, Wartook; (03) 9497 2020.

Grampians National Park Aboriginal occupation of the area known as the Grampians dates back over 5000 years (some evidence suggests up to 30 000 years). To local Koorie communities, this magnificent mountain range is known as Gariwerd. Within the 168 000 ha park is a startling array of vegetation and wildlife, including 200 bird species and a quarter of Victoria's native flora species. The heathlands abound in colourful shows of wildflowers including Grampians boronia, blue pincushion lily and Grampians parrot-pea. Twenty of the park's 800 plant species are not found anywhere else in the world. Brambuk – The National Park and Cultural Centre, a short walk or drive south of Halls Gap, is an excellent first stop in the park. It features interactive displays and written information about the park's attractions, bringing to life the culture of the local Jardwadjali and Djab Wurrung people. Natural highlights of the Grampians include MacKenzie Falls, the largest of the park's many waterfalls; Zumsteins picnic ground, a beautiful spot with tame and friendly kangaroos; and the Balconies, a rock ledge once known as the Jaws of Death, offering views over Victoria Valley. The most popular section of the park is the Wonderland Range, true to its name with features including Elephants Hide, Grand Canyon, Venus Baths and Silent Street. There are over 90 bushwalks available in the park, all varying in length and degree of difficulty. Visitors are advised to consult a ranger before embarking on one of the longer treks. For further information, contact Brambuk – The National Park and Cultural Centre on (03) 5361 4000.

The Gap Vineyard: cellar-door tastings and sales of award-winning white and red wine varieties, as well as port; closed Mon and Tues; Pomonal Rd; 2 km E. **Grampians Adventure Golf:** world-class minigolf, 18-hole course set on 2 acres; 481 Grampians Rd; 4 km s near Lake Bellfield. **Halls Gap Zoo:** explore the park's nature track and view the animals, many of which are free-range; (03) 5356 4668; 7 km SE. **Grampians Horse Riding Adventures:** morning and afternoon rides lasting 2 hrs, also has on-site accommodation; Brimpaen; (03) 5383 9225; 44 km W.

See also GRAMPIANS & CENTRAL WEST, p. 155

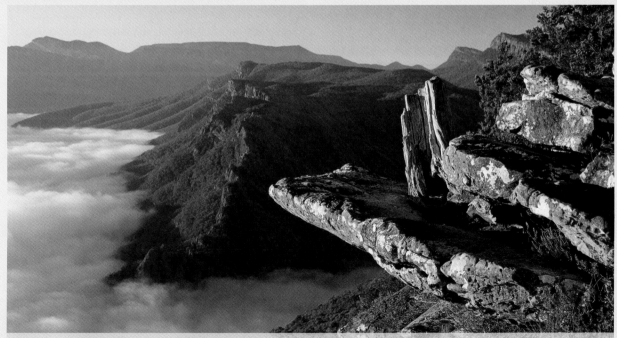

[BOROKA LOOKOUT, GRAMPIANS NATIONAL PARK]

VICTORIA

considered to be one of the prettiest regional towns in Victoria – the town prides itself on its clean streets and picturesque gardens. Although the Wimmera is a renowned wheat-growing region, Horsham is also a centre for fine wool production.

Horsham Regional Art Gallery This is one of Victoria's key regional galleries, with an extensive collection housed in a 1930s Art Deco building. Most of the artwork is centred on the Mack Jost collection of Australian art, with contemporary Australian photography another specialty. 80 Wilson St; (03) 5362 2888.

Botanic Gardens: picturesquely set on the banks of the Wimmera River; Cnr Baker and Firebrace sts. *The Wool Factory:* produces extra-fine wool from Saxon-Merino sheep, with tours daily; Golf Course Rd. *Wimmera River:* key attraction for the town, with scenic picnic spots along the river's edges. Visit the river at dusk for spectacular sunsets.

Market: showgrounds on McPherson St; 2nd Sun each month. *Haven Recreation Market:* 1st Sat each month. *Wimmera Machinery Field Days:* Longerenong; Mar. *Art Is:* community festival; Apr. *Awakenings Festival:* largest Australian festival involving disabled patrons; Oct. *Spring Garden Festival:* Oct. *Horsham Show:* Oct. *Kannamaroo Rock 'n' Roll Festival:* Nov. *Karkana Strawberry Festival:* Nov.

Cafe Chickpea: hearty breakfasts and light lunches; 30A Pynsent St; (03) 5382 3998.

Orange Grove B&B: mud-brick cottage or modern unit; 123 Keatings Rd; (03) 5382 0583. *Sylvania Park Mohair Farm:* 2 farm homesteads; 808 East Rd, Wimmera; (03) 5382 2811.

Murtoa This town lies on the edge of Lake Marma, which has dried out in recent times. The Water Tower Museum (open Sun) displays the history of the area as well as James Hill's 1885–1930 taxidermy collection of some 500 birds and animals. On the eastern side of town, among the grain silos, is an unusual relic called the Stick Shed. The roof of this now empty storage shed is held up with 640 unmilled tree trunks, and the interior is an evocative sight (open once a year in Oct); 31 km NE.

Jung: market on last Sat each month; 10 km NE. *Fishing:* redfin and trout in local lakes, depending on water levels. Reasonable levels at Taylors Lake; 18 km SE. *Mount Zero Olives:* the largest olive grove in the Southern Hemisphere, with tastings and sales of olive oil; Laharum; 30 km s.

See also GRAMPIANS & CENTRAL WEST, p. 155

Inglewood
Pop. 684
Map ref. 579 D1 | 591 M9

ⓘ **Loddon Visitor Information Centre, Wedderburn Community Centre, 24 Wilson St, Wedderburn; (03) 5494 3489; www.loddonalive.com.au**

89.5 The Fresh FM, 91.1 FM ABC Local Radio

North along the Calder Highway from Bendigo is the 'Golden Triangle' town of Inglewood. Sizeable gold nuggets were found in this area during the gold rush and are still being unearthed. Inglewood is also known as Blue Eucy town, due to the once vigorous blue mallee eucalyptus oil industry. The town is also the birthplace of Australian aviator Sir Reginald Ansett.

Old eucalyptus oil distillery: not in operation but can be viewed; Calder Hwy, northern end of town. *Old courthouse:* local historical memorabilia; open by appt; Southey St. *Streetscape:* historic buildings are evidence of the town's goldmining history.

Kooyoora State Park The park sits at the northern end of the Bealiba Range and features extensive box-ironbark forests. The Eastern Walking Circuit offers a great opportunity for bushwalkers, passing through strange rock formations and giant granite slabs. The Summit Track leads to Melville Caves Lookout. The caves were once the haunt of the notorious bushranger Captain Melville. Camping is allowed around the caves. Contact Parks Victoria on 13 1963; 16 km w.

Bridgewater on Loddon: fishing and watersports, Old Loddon Vines Vineyard, Water Wheel Vineyards and horse-drawn caravans for hire; 8 km SE. *Loddon Valley wineries:* the warm climate and clay soils of this region are known for producing outstanding red varieties and award-winning chardonnays. Taste the wines at cellar doors like Pandalowie at Bridgewater on Loddon (8 km SE) and Kingower (11 km SW); winery map from visitor information centre.

See also GOLDFIELDS, p. 154

Inverloch
Pop. 3682
Map ref. 573 M12 | 582 F9

ⓘ **A'Beckett St; 1300 762 433; www.visitbasscoast.com**

88.1 3MFM South Gippsland, 100.7 FM ABC Local Radio

Inverloch is a small seaside resort set on the protected waters of Anderson Inlet, east of Wonthaggi. It is characterised by long stretches of pristine beach that offer good surf and excellent fishing.

Bunurong Environment Centre: natural history displays with special focus on dinosaur diggings; also sales of natural products; The Esplanade. *Shell Museum:* The Esplanade.

Inverloch Food and Wine Festival: Feb. *Annual Dinosaur Dig:* Feb/Mar. *Inverloch Jazz Festival:* Mar. *Inverloch Billy Cart Derby:* Nov.

Tomo: sophisticated Japanese; Shop 1, 23 A'Beckett St; (03) 5674 3444. *Vella 9:* modern Australian/Mediterranean; 9 A'Beckett St; (03) 5674 1188.

RACV Inverloch Resort: hotel rooms, villas and caravan sites; 70 Cape Paterson–Inverloch Rd; (03) 5674 0000.

Bunurong Coastal Drive Stretching the 14 km of coastline between Inverloch and Cape Paterson is this spectacular coastal drive with magnificent views to Venus Bay and beyond. Carparks offer access to beaches and coastal walks along the drive. The waters offshore are protected within Bunurong Marine National Park, and offer opportunities to surf, snorkel, scuba dive or simply explore the numerous rockpools that are dotted along the coast.

Anderson Inlet: the most southerly habitat for mangroves in Australia. This calm inlet is popular for windsurfing and watersports, and nearby Townsend Bluff and Maher's Landing offer good birdwatching; adjacent to town. *Fishing:* in nearby waterways such as the Tarwin River; 20 km SE.

See also PHILLIP ISLAND & GIPPSLAND, p. 150

Jeparit
Pop. 374
Map ref. 558 D12 | 590 F6

ⓘ **Wimmera–Mallee Pioneer Museum, Charles St; (03) 5397 2101.**

 96.5 Triple H FM, 594 AM ABC Local Radio

This little town in the Wimmera is 5 kilometres south-east of Lake Hindmarsh, which was once the largest natural freshwater lake in

Victoria. Sadly, it has been empty for the past several years. Former prime minister Sir Robert Menzies was born here in 1894.

 Wimmera–Mallee Pioneer Museum This unique museum details what life was like for early settlers in the Wimmera through a collection of colonial buildings furnished in the style of the period. The buildings on display are spread over a 4 ha complex and include log cabins, a church and a blacksmith's shop. The museum also features displays of restored farm machinery. Southern entrance to town, Charles St; (03) 5397 2101.

Menzies Sq: site of the dwelling where Menzies was born; Cnr Charles and Roy sts. *Wimmera River Walk:* 6 km return; starts at museum.

 Lake Hindmarsh Victoria's largest freshwater lake has seen dire water levels for the past several years. It was fed by the Wimmera River. Boating, waterskiing and fishing were all popular pastimes (Schulzes Beach has a boat ramp), with pelicans and other waterbirds existing at the lake in breeding colonies. Picnic and camping spots are available on the lake's shores. A historic fisherman's hut can also be seen. Contact the visitor centre for an update on water levels. 5 km NW.

Rainbow: a charming little Wimmera township, with Pasco's Cash Store, an original country general store, and Yurunga Homestead, a beautiful Edwardian home with a large collection of antiques and original fittings (northern edge of town, key available); 35 km N. *Pella:* former German settlement with Lutheran church and old schoolhouse; 40 km NW via Rainbow. *Lake Albacutya:* fills only when Lake Hindmarsh overflows; 44 km N. *Wyperfeld National Park:* great for bushwalking; known for its birdlife, including the endangered mallee fowl, and wildflowers in spring; 60 km NW via Rainbow; *for details see Hopetoun.*

See also GRAMPIANS & CENTRAL WEST, p. 155

Kerang
Pop. 3780
Map ref. 558 H11 | 591 N4

 Sir John Gorton Library, cnr Murray Valley Hwy and Shadforth St; (03) 5452 1546; www.gannawarra.vic.gov.au

 99.1 Smart FM, 102.1 FM ABC Local Radio

Kerang, situated on the Loddon River just south of the New South Wales border, lies at the southern end of the Kerang wetlands and lakes. They extend from Kerang 42 kilometres north-west to Lake Boga and offer a wonderland for watersports enthusiasts and birdwatchers; the lakes contain what are reputedly the world's largest ibis breeding grounds. The town itself is a service centre for its agricultural surrounds.

Lester Lookout Tower: town views; Cnr Murray Valley Hwy and Shadforth St. *Historical Museum:* focuses on cars and antique farm machinery; Riverwood Dr.

Races: Easter and Boxing Day. *Tour of the Murray River:* cycling race; late Aug/early Sept.

Reedy Lakes: a series of 3 lakes. Apex Park, a recreation reserve for swimming, picnicking and boating, is set by the first lake, and the second features a large ibis rookery. Picnic facilities are available at the third lake; 8 km NW. *Leaghur State Park:* on the Loddon River flood plain, this peaceful park is a perfect spot for a leisurely walk through the black box woodlands and wetlands; 25 km SW. *Murrabit:* a historic timber town on the Murray surrounded by picturesque forests, with a country

market 1st Sat each month; 27 km N. *Quambatook:* hosts the Australian Tractor Pull Championship each Easter; 40 km SW. *Lake Boga:* popular for watersports, with good sandy beaches; 42 km NW. *Fishing:* Meran, Kangaroo and Charm lakes all offer freshwater fishing; details from visitor centre.

See also GOULBURN & MURRAY, p. 157

Kilmore
Pop. 4720
Map ref. 573 J1 | 582 C1 | 584 C12

 Library, 12 Sydney St; (03) 5781 1319.

 97.1 OKR FM, 774 AM ABC Local Radio

Kilmore is Victoria's oldest inland town, known for its historic buildings and many horseracing events. Like many towns in the central goldfields, Kilmore was the scene of a Kelly family saga. In this case, it was Ned Kelly's father who had a run-in with the law. In 1865 John 'Red' Kelly was arrested for killing a squatter's calf to feed his family, and was locked away in the Kilmore Gaol for six months. It was a crime that Ned had actually committed. Soon after Red's release, he died of dropsy and was buried in the small town of Avenel, where the Kelly family lived for some time.

 Old Kilmore Gaol An impressive bluestone building, established in 1859, that is now a privately owned auction house; Sutherland St.

Hudson Park: picnic/barbecue facilities; Cnr Sydney and Foote sts. *Historic buildings:* Whitburgh Cottage, Piper St, and a number of 1850s shops and hotels along Sydney St; brochure from visitor centre.

Kilmore Celtic Festival: June. *Kilmore Cup:* harness racing; Oct.

 Bindley House B&B: 2 self-contained suites; 20–22 Powlett St; (03) 5781 1142. **Laurel Hill Cottage:** 2-bedroom cottage; 12 Melrose Dr; (03) 5782 1630. **Woodbury Estate B&B:** 2 luxury in-house rooms; 110A Butlers Rd; (03) 5782 0307.

 Tramways Heritage Centre at Bylands: extensive display of cable cars and early electric trams, with tram rides available; open Sun only; just south of town. *Broadford:* a small town featuring a historic precinct on High St; 17 km NE. *Mt Piper Walking Track:* wildlife and wildflowers can be spotted along the way (1 hr return); near Broadford. *Strath Creek:* walks to Strath Creek Falls and a drive through the Valley of a Thousand Hills; starts at outskirts of Broadford.

See also SPA & GARDEN COUNTRY, p. 151

Koo-wee-rup
Pop. 1423
Map ref. 570 H10 | 573 L9 | 575 O6 | 582 E7

 Newsagency, 277 Rossiter Rd; (03) 5997 1456.

 103.1 3BBR FM West Gippsland Community Radio, 774 AM ABC Local Radio

Koo-wee-rup and the surrounding agricultural area exist on reclaimed and drained swampland. It has given rise to Australia's largest asparagus-growing district. The town's name derives from the Aboriginal name meaning 'blackfish swimming', a reference to the fish that were once plentiful in the swamp.

 Historical Society Museum: local history; open Sun; Rossiter Rd.

VICTORIA

Swamp Observation Tower: views of remaining swampland and across to Western Port. A market with local produce operates regularly at the base; South Gippsland Hwy; 2 km SE. *Bayles Fauna Reserve:* native animals; 8 km NE. *Harewood House:* restored 1850s house with original furnishings; South Gippsland Hwy towards Tooradin. *Tooradin:* offers good boating and fishing on Sawtells Inlet; 10 km W. *Caldermeade Farm:* originally a premier beef cattle property but now a fully operational modern dairy farm focused on educating and entertaining visitors; 10 km SE. *Pakenham:* now considered a suburb of Melbourne, Pakenham is home to the Military Vehicle Museum, Army Rd, and the Berwick Pakenham Historical Society Museum, John St; 13 km N. *Tynong:* attractions include Victoria's Farm Shed, featuring farm animals and shearing, and Gumbaya Park, a family fun park; 20 km NE. *Royal Botanic Gardens Cranbourne:* renowned, wonderfully maintained native gardens; 22 km NW. *Grantville:* hosts a market 4th Sun each month; 30 km S.

See also PHILLIP ISLAND & GIPPSLAND, p. 150

Korumburra

Pop. 3145
Map ref. 573 N11 | 582 F8

ℹ Prom Country Information Centre, South Gippsland Hwy; (03) 5655 2233 or 1800 630 704; www.visitpromcountry.com.au

📻 88.1 3MFM South Gippsland, 100.7 FM ABC Local Radio

Established in 1887, Korumburra stands firmly as the heritage centre of South Gippsland. The township was a primary producer of black coal for Victoria's rail industry until the last mine closed in 1958. Korumburra is set in the rolling green hills of South Gippsland, with scenic drives found in any direction.

Coal Creek Heritage Village Coal Creek is an open-air museum that offers all the fascination of life in a 19th-century coalmining village, including history and memorabilia of the area. The village contains beautiful picnic areas, bush tramway and cafe, and community events are held throughout the year. South Gippsland Hwy; (03) 5655 1811.

Korumburra Federation Art Gallery: South Gippsland Hwy. *Whitelaw Antiques & Collectibles:* 9 Mine Rd.

Korumburra Farmers Market: Railway Siding; 3rd Sat each month. *Korumburra Agricultural Show:* Feb. *Rotary Club of Korumburra Art Show:* Feb.

Cypress Hill B&B: 3 Mediterranean-style guesthouse suites; 75 Korumburra–Bena Rd, Whitelaw; (03) 5657 2240.

South Gippsland Tourist Railway This railway travels to Leongatha, Korumburra, Loch and Nyora, and provides a scenic way to view the ever-changing South Gippsland landscape. Trains operate Sun and public holidays with a Wed service during school holidays. The grand Edwardian Railway Station behind the main street is also worth a visit. (03) 5658 1111.

Loch: a thriving art and craft village with cosy eateries, antique stores and galleries; 14 km NW. *Poowong:* beautiful country town nestled among the rolling hills of South Gippsland with Poowong Pioneer Chapel, est. 1878; 18 km NW.

See also PHILLIP ISLAND & GIPPSLAND, p. 150

Kyneton

Pop. 4286
Map ref. 572 G1 | 579 G8 | 582 A1 | 584 A11 | 593 O2

ℹ Jean Haynes Reserve, High St; (03) 5422 6110; www.visitmacedonranges.com

📻 91.1 FM ABC Local Radio, 100.7 Highlands FM

Part of Victoria's picturesque spa and garden country, Kyneton is a well-preserved town with many attractive bluestone buildings. Caroline Chisholm, who helped many migrants find their feet in this country, lived in Kyneton, where her family owned a store and her husband worked as a magistrate. While living in the town, she established a series of affordable, overnight shelters for travellers on the Mount Alexander Road (now the Calder Highway), a road frequented by gold prospectors. Remnants of the shelters can be seen at the historic township of Carlsruhe, south-east of Kyneton.

Kyneton Museum: in a former bank building, with a drop-log cottage in the grounds; open Fri–Sun; Piper St. *Wool on Piper:* features a spinning mill, with yarns and handmade garments for sale; Piper St. *Botanic Gardens:* 8 ha area scenically located above Pipers Creek. The gardens feature rare varieties of trees; Clowes St. *Historic buildings:* many in town, including mechanics institute on Mollison St and old police depot, Jenning St. *Campaspe River Walk:* scenic walk with picnic spots; access from Piper St.

Farmers market: farmgate produce; Piper St; 2nd Sat each month. *Kyneton Daffodil and Arts Festival:* Sept. *Kyneton Cup:* Nov.

Annie Smithers' Bistrot: French Provincial–style; 72 Piper St; (03) 5422 2039. *Little Swallow Cafe:* European-style cafe; 58A Piper St; (03) 5422 6241. *Pizza Verde:* city-smart pizzeria; 62 Piper St; (03) 5422 7400. *Royal George Hotel:* contemporary dining room; 24 Piper St; (03) 5422 1390. *Star Anise Bistro:* modern bistro; 29A Piper St; (03) 5422 2777.

Rockville: chic, spacious house; 59 Ebden St; (03) 5422 2617. *St Agnes Homestead:* 3 rooms and 1 apartment; 30 Burton Ave (continuation of Piper St); (03) 5422 2639. *Tilwinda B&B and Woolshed Barn:* 2 rooms, 1 barn; 1793 Kyneton–Trentham Rd; (03) 5422 2772.

Trentham and Wombat State Forest This picturesque spa-country town has a mixed history of gold, timber and farming. It has a charming streetscape and attractions include a historic foundry and Minifie's Berry Farm, where you can pick your own berries in season. Just north-east of town is Wombat State Forest – deep within is Victoria's largest single-drop waterfall, Trentham Falls. Cascading 32 m onto a quartz gravel base, the falls are an impressive backdrop for a picnic. 22 km SW.

Reservoirs: several offering scenic locations for walks and picnics. Upper Coliban, Lauriston and Malmsbury reservoirs all nearby. *Paramoor Farm and Winery:* a former Clydesdale horse farm, now winery and B&B; Carlsruhe; 5 km SE. *Malmsbury:* a town noted for its old bluestone buildings. It features historic Botanic Gardens and The Mill, National Trust–classified, not open to the public. Also wineries in the area; 10 km NW. *Turpins and Cascade Falls:* with picnic area and walks; near Metcalfe; 22 km N.

See also SPA & GARDEN COUNTRY, p. 151

Leongatha

Pop. 4501
Map ref. 573 N11 | 582 G8

ℹ Michael Place Complex; (03) 5662 2111; www.visitpromcountry.com.au

 88.1 3MFM South Gippsland, 100.7 FM ABC Local Radio

LAKES ENTRANCE

Pop. 5545
Map ref. 583 06

i **Lakes and Wilderness Tourism, cnr Esplanade and Marine Pde; (03) 5155 1966 or 1800 637 060; www.discovereastgippsland.com.au**

90.7 FM 3REG Radio East Gippsland, 100.7 FM ABC Local Radio

Lakes Entrance is a lovely holiday town situated at the eastern end of the Gippsland Lakes, an inland network of waterways covering more than 400 square kilometres. The artificially created 'entrance' of the town's name allows the Tasman Sea and the lakes to meet, creating a safe harbour that is home to one of the largest fishing fleets in Australia. While many of the attractions in Lakes Entrance are based around the water, there is also the opportunity for gourmets to indulge themselves with a variety of cafes and restaurants lining The Esplanade, plus sales of fresh fish and local wines.

Seashell Museum: The Esplanade.

Markets: Lakes Entrance Primary School, Myer St; 3rd Sat each month. *Arts Festival:* Forest Tech Living Resource Centre; Mar long weekend. *Lakes Motor Fest:* biannual; Apr. *New Year's Eve Entertainment and Fireworks*: Dec.

Boathouse Restaurant: local seafood; 201 The Esplanade; (03) 5155 3055. *Ferryman's Seafood Cafe:* super fresh fish; Middle Boat Harbor, The Esplanade; (03) 5155 3000. *Miriam's:* European, local seafood; Level 1, cnr The Esplanade and Bulmer St; (03) 5155 3999. *The Metung Galley:* excellent local-produce-driven menu; 3/59 Metung Rd, Metung; (03) 5156 2330.

Goldsmith's in the Forest: 4-room private retreat; 191 Harrisons Track; (03) 5155 2518. *The Lakes Apartments:* contemporary apartments; 35 Church St; (03) 5155 6100.

Waverley House Cottages: cottages with modern furnishings; 205 Palmers Rd; (03) 5155 1257. *5 Knots:* high-tech waterfront apartments; 42 Metung Rd, Metung; (03) 5156 2462.

Gippsland Lakes Five rivers end their journey to the sea here, forming a vast expanse of water tucked in behind Ninety Mile Beach. The lakes are a true playground for anyone with an interest in water activities, especially fishing and boating. Explore the lakes on a sightseeing cruise, including one to Wyanga Park Winery, or on the ever-popular houseboats that can be hired over summer. Details from visitor centre.

Jemmys Point: great views of the region; 1 km w. *Lake Bunga:* nature trail along foreshore; 3 km E. *Lake Tyers:* sheltered waters ideal for fishing, swimming and boating. Cruises depart from Fishermans Landing in town. Lake is 6–23 km NE, depending on access point. Lake Tyers Forest Park is great for bushwalking, wildlife-spotting, picnicking and camping; 20 km NE. *Nyerimilang Heritage Park:* 1920s homestead, with original farm buildings and the wonderfully maintained East Gippsland Botanic Gardens. Rose Pruning Day, with demonstrations, is held in July; 10 km NW. *Swan Reach:* Rosewood Pottery; Malcolm Cameron Studio Gallery, open weekends; 14 km NW. *Metung:* a scenic town on Lake King with boat hire, cruises and a marina regatta each Jan. Chainsaw Sculpture Gallery has chainsaw sculpture and a display of Annemieke Mein's embroidery art; 15 km w. *Nicholson River Winery:* 22 km NW. *East Gippsland Carriage Co:* restored horse-drawn carriages and tours; 30 km E. *Bataluk Cultural Trail:* driving tour taking in Aboriginal cultural sites in the East Gippsland region; self-guide brochure from visitor centre.

See also EAST GIPPSLAND, p. 159

VICTORIA

[SCRUB, SAND AND SEA IN LAKES ENTRANCE]

Leongatha is a thriving town, considered the commercial centre of South Gippsland. Idyllically positioned as a gateway to Gippsland destinations and attractions, any major road departing Leongatha provides access to popular attractions, all within an easy one hour's drive.

Historical Society Museum: McCartin St. *Leongatha Gallery:* Cnr McCartin St and Michael Pl. *Mushroom Crafts:* craft sales and gallery; 40 Blair St. *Great Southern Rail Trail:* commencement of 50 km rail trail that winds between Leongatha and Foster.

South Gippsland Golf Classic: Feb. *Music for the People Concert:* Mossvale Park; Feb. *Mossvale Music Festival:* Mar. *Raw Vibes Youth Festival:* Mar. *Daffodil Festival:* Sept. *Garden and Lifestyle Expo:* Nov.

Koonwarra Fine Food & Wine Store: excellent regional fare, courtyard setting; South Gippsland Hwy, Koonwarra; (03) 5664 2285.

Lamont House: 3-bedroom historic cottage; 19 Long St; (03) 5662 4510. *Lyre Bird Hill Winery:* 3 B&B rooms, family cottage; 370 Inverloch Rd, Koonwarra; (03) 5664 3204.

Koonwarra Situated between Leongatha and Meeniyan on the South Gippsland Hwy, Koonwarra became the first eco-wise town in Australia. The town prides itself on its commitment to sustainable lifestyles. Drop in to the Koonwarra Fine Food & Wine Store to purchase local wines, cheese and pantry items. On the first Sat of each month, Koonwarra holds a farmers market. The town also boasts an organic cooking school, day spa, specialty shops, pottery and winery nearby. 8 km SE.

Meeniyan: great place to visit for the art and craft enthusiast. Places of interest include Meeniyan Art Gallery, South Gippsland Craft Merchants, Beth's Antiques and Lacy Jewellery. Meeniyan hosts an annual art and craft exhibition over the Melbourne Cup weekend; 16 km SE. *Mossvale Park:* tranquil setting for a picnic or barbecue. Music concerts and festivals are held here in Feb and Mar; 16 km NE. *Mirboo North:* situated among the picturesque Strzelecki Ranges, the township is decorated with murals depicting the history of the area. Grand Ridge Brewery, Lyre Bird Forest Walk and the Grand Ridge Rail Trail are also located here; 26 km NE.

See also PHILLIP ISLAND & GIPPSLAND, p. 150

Lorne

Pop. 971
Map ref. 572 D11 | 580 E4 | 593 M9

ⓘ 15 Mountjoy Pde; (03) 5289 1152; www.visitgreatoceanroad.org.au

 94.7 The Pulse FM, 774 AM ABC Local Radio

Lorne is one of Victoria's most attractive and lively coastal resorts. The approach into town along the Great Ocean Road is truly spectacular, with the superb mountain scenery of the Otways on one side and the rugged Bass Strait coast on the other. The village of Lorne was established in 1871 and quickly became popular with pastoralists from inland areas, leading to its development around the picturesque Louttit Bay. When the Great Ocean Road opened in 1932 Lorne became much more accessible; however, the area has remained relatively unspoiled with good beaches, surfing, fishing and bushwalking in the hills – activities made all the more enjoyable by the area's pleasant, mild climate.

Teddys Lookout: excellent bay views; behind the town, at the end of George St. *Shipwreck Walk:* walk along the beach taking in sites of the numerous shipwrecks along this stretch of coast; details from visitor centre. *Foreshore Reserve:* great spot for a picnic, with paddleboats available for hire. *Qdos:* contemporary art gallery; Allenvale Rd. *Lorne Fisheries:* on the recently opened new pier with daily supplies.

Pier to Pub Swim: Jan. *Mountain to Surf Foot Race:* Jan. *Great Ocean Road Marathon:* May. *Anaconda Adventure Race:* Dec. *Falls Festival:* Dec–Jan.

Ba Ba Lu Bar and Restaurant: Spanish-style menu; 6A Mountjoy Pde; (03) 5289 1808. *Bistro C Bar & Restaurant:* mainly local seafood; Cumberland Lorne Resort, 150 Mountjoy Pde; (03) 5289 2455. *Lorne Ovenhouse:* modern wood-fired menu; 46A Mountjoy Pde; (03) 5289 2544. *Qdos:* cafe-bar next to gallery; 35 Allenvale Rd; (03) 5289 1989.

Acacia Villas: 4 bushland villas; 9 Fletcher St; (03) 5289 2066. *Cumberland Lorne Resort:* apartments and penthouses; 150 Mountjoy Pde; (03) 5289 4444. *Grand Pacific Hotel:* rooms and apartments; 268 Mountjoy Pde; (03) 5289 1609. *Mantra Erskine Beach Resort:* apartments and hotel rooms; 1–35 Mountjoy Pde; (03) 5228 9777.

 Great Otway National Park This park covers 103 000 ha and includes a range of environments, from the timbered ridges of the eastern Otways to fern gullies, waterfalls and a coastline with tall cliffs, coves and sandy beaches. Around Lorne there are more than 100 walking tracks and the rock platforms along the coast provide ideal spots for ocean fishing. The Falls Festival, a major rock-music festival, is held over New Year's Eve at a property near the Erskine Falls, 9 km NW. These popular falls are a peaceful location and drop 30 m over moss-covered rocks. As well as driving, you can walk to the falls from Lorne along the river. The park surrounds Lorne and can be accessed from various points along the Great Ocean Rd. Contact Parks Victoria on 13 1963.

Cumberland River Valley: walking tracks and camping; 4 km SW. *Mt Defiance Lookout:* 10 km SW. *Wye River:* a small coastal village, good for rock and surf fishing, surfing and camping; 17 km SW. *Old Lorne Road Olives:* olive grove, cafe and gallery; closed Tues and Wed; Deans Marsh Rd; 22 km N. *Gentle Annie Berry Gardens:* pick your own; open Nov–Apr; 26 km NW via Deans Marsh. *Scenic drives:* west through the Otway Ranges, and south-west or north-east on the Great Ocean Rd.

See also SOUTH-WEST COAST, p. 153

Maffra

Pop. 4151
Map ref. 583 K6

ⓘ 96 Johnson St; (03) 5141 1811; www.tourismwellington.com.au

94.7 100.7 FM ABC Local Radio, 104.7 Gippsland FM

Maffra, settled in the 1840s, has the charm and old-style hospitality of another era. Named after Maffra in Portugal because many of the early Gippsland settlers had fought in that area of Europe during the Peninsula War, the town's early days were fraught with drought until a sugar beet industry established in the 1890s provided a major boost. The Glenmaggie Irrigation Scheme of 1919 also signalled a new heyday and ensured the viable and lengthy success of today's dairy industry. The sugar beet factory closed in 1948 owing to World War II's labour shortages and the competing dairy industry, but Maffra continues to support its rich agricultural surrounds. It also holds a great sense of history in its original shop verandahs and grand homesteads.

Maffra Sugar Beet Historic Museum: local history museum with special interest in the sugar beet industry; open Sun afternoon; River St. *Mineral and gemstone display:* large collection of rare gemstones and fossils at the information centre; Johnson St. *All Seasons Herb Garden:* Foster St. *Gippsland Vehicle Collection:* outstanding rotating display of interesting vehicles; located in a historic vegetable dehydrating factory; Maffra–Sale Rd; (03) 5147 3223. *Gippsland Plains Rail Trail:* recreational trail for cycling and walking that passes through town; still under development but when complete will link Stratford in the east to Traralgon in the west by traversing dairy country.

Gippsland Harvest Festival: Mar. *Mardi Gras:* Mar.

Stratford: the scenic Avon River flows through town. Knobs Reserve is a site where the local Aboriginal people once sharpened axe heads on sandstone grinding stones – it is part of the Bataluk Cultural Trail, which takes in significant Indigenous sites throughout East Gippsland. Stratford hosts the Shakespeare Celebration in May; 9 km E. *Australian Wildlife Art Gallery and Sculpture:* Princes Hwy near Munro; 25 km E. *Robotic Dairy:* the first Australian dairy farm to install 4 'Astronaut Milking Robots' where the cows decide when to be milked; open on public visitor days or by appt; Toongabbie Rd, Winnindoo; (03) 5199 2212; 26 km W. *Lake Glenmaggie:* popular watersports venue; 42 km NW via Heyfield. *Alpine National Park:* sprawls from Licola, 75 km NW, to the NSW border. Near Licola is Lake Tali Karng, which lies 850 m above sea level and is a popular bushwalking destination during the warmer months. *Scenic drives:* the Traralgon to Stratford Tourist Route highlights attractions of the area. For stunning scenery, drive north along Forest Rd, through the Macalister River Valley to Licola and Mt Tamboritha in Alpine National Park; or to Jamieson (166 km NW via Heyfield), with access to snowfields or Lake Eildon.

See also EAST GIPPSLAND, p. 159

Maldon

Pop. 1222
Map ref. 579 E5 | 591 N11 | 593 N1

High St; (03) 5475 2569; www.maldon.org.au

91.1 FM ABC Local Radio, 106.3 Radio KLFM

Maldon is one of Victoria's best-known gold towns and a popular weekend getaway for Melburnians. The town has been wonderfully preserved, with the wide, tree-lined main street featuring old buildings and shopfronts. Aside from the cafes and galleries, the town seems unchanged from the gold rush days. Maldon was declared Australia's first 'notable town' by the National Trust in 1966.

Historic town walk: grab a brochure from the visitor centre and take to the wide, old footpaths to discover the historic delights of Maldon. See preserved 19th-century shopfronts and old stone cottages. Highlights include the restored Dabb's General Store in Main St, and the Maldon Hospital in Adair St. *Museum:* displays on mining as well as domestic memorabilia from Maldon's past, in heritage building; open 1.30–4pm daily; High St. *The Beehive Chimney:* southern end of Church St. *Anzac Hill:* the walk to the top is rewarded with magnificent views of the area; southern end of High St.

Fair: Easter. *Vintage Car Hill Climb:* Oct. *Folk Festival:* Oct–Nov.

Penny School Gallery/Cafe: international cuisine; 11 Church St; (03) 5475 1911. *Zen Eden Produce:* vegetarian cafe and produce store; 6 Main St; 0408 319 188.

Clare House: 3 B&B rooms; 99 High St; (03) 5475 2229. *Heatherlie:* romantic cottage with pool; High St; 0413 123 650. *Mount Hawke of Maldon:* 3 B&B rooms in historic house; 24 Adair St; (03) 5475 1192. *Wywurri B&B:* in-house accommodation for a couple; 3 Templeton St; (03) 5475 2794.

Porcupine Township This award-winning tourist attraction is a reconstruction of an early 1850s goldmining town, with an array of slab, shingle and mudbrick buildings moved here from other goldfields. The village, complete with a blacksmith's, a doctor's surgery and even a bowling alley, is located in rugged bushland on the site of the original Porcupine diggings, where the first gold discovery between Castlemaine and Bendigo was made. Visitors to the township can pan for gold, handfeed emus or take a ride on the Little Toot train, which does a circuit through the diggings. Cnr Maldon–Bendigo and Allans rds; (03) 5475 1000; 3 km NE.

Mt Tarrangower Lookout Tower: town views; 2 km W. *Carman's Tunnel Mine:* guided mine tours feature relics from goldmining days; 2 km SW. *Nuggetty Ranges and Mt Moorol:* 2 km N. *Cairn Curran Reservoir:* great for watersports and fishing, water levels permitting; features picnic facilities and a sailing club near the spillway; 10 km SW. *Victorian Goldfields Railway:* historic steam trains run from Maldon Railway Station (Hornsby St) through scenic forest to Castlemaine; operates Wed, Sun and public holidays; bookings on (03) 5470 6658.

See also GOLDFIELDS, p. 154

Mallacoota

Pop. 973
Map ref. 565 D12 | 581 G11

Visitor Information Shed, Main Wharf; (03) 5158 0800; www.visitmallacoota.com

101.7 FM 3MGB Wilderness Radio, 104.9 FM ABC Local Radio

Mallacoota is a popular holiday centre in far East Gippsland, surrounded by the scenic Croajingolong National Park, which features Point Hicks, notable for being the first land on the east coast of Australia to be sighted by Europeans. There are spectacular surf beaches near the town, with Mallacoota Inlet offering great fishing.

WW II bunker and museum: restored and located at the airport. *Information shed:* a mural depicting Mallacoota's history is painted on the external walls; Main Wharf. *The Spotted Dog Gold Mine:* established in 1894, this was the most successful goldmine in the Mallacoota district.

Holiday markets: Easter and Christmas. *Bream Fishing Classic:* Mar (round 1) and June (round 2). *Tour of Gippsland Cycling Event:* July/Aug. *Flora and Fauna weekend:* 1st weekend in Nov.

Lucy's Noodles: authentic noodles with home-grown produce; 64 Maurice Ave; (03) 5158 0666.

Karbeethong Lodge: stylish historic guesthouse; 16 Schnapper Point Dr; (03) 5158 0411. *Gipsy Point Lodge:* guesthouse and 3 cottages; 35 Macdonald St, Gipsy Point; (03) 5158 8205 or 1800 063 556.

Croajingolong National Park This park takes up a vast portion of what has been dubbed the Wilderness Coast. It protects remote beaches, tall forests, heathland, rainforest, estuaries and granite peaks, as well as creatures such as wallabies, possums, goannas and lyrebirds. Offshore, you might be lucky enough to spot dolphins, seals or southern right and humpback whales. Pt Hicks Lighthouse is a popular spot to visit, and Tamboon and Mallacoota inlets are good spots for canoeing. Access the park via a track west of town or various roads south of the Princes Hwy; contact Parks Victoria on 13 1963.

Surf beaches: Bastion Point, 2 km s; Bekta, 5 km s. *Gabo Island Lightstation Reserve:* take a scenic daytrip or stay in the Lightkeeper's Residence; 11 km E (offshore). *Gipsy Pt:* a quiet holiday retreat overlooking the Genoa River; 16 km NW.

See also East Gippsland, p. 159

Mansfield

Pop. 2846
Map ref. 584 H11 | 586 D9

i The Station Precinct, 173 Maroondah Hwy; 1800 039 049; www.mansfield-mtbuller.com.au

99.7 FM Radio Mansfield, 103.7 FM ABC Local Radio

Mansfield is located in Victoria's High Country at the junction of the Midland and Maroondah highways. It is within easy reach of Lake Eildon's network of rivers, Alpine National Park and Mansfield State Forest. Activities ranging from hiking to horseriding to skiing make it an ideal destination for anyone with a love of outdoor adventure, no matter what the season.

Troopers' Monument: monument to police officers shot by Ned Kelly at Stringybark Creek; Cnr High St and Midland Hwy. *Mansfield Mullum Wetlands Walk:* along reclaimed railway line; starts from behind the visitor centre. *Self-guide town walk:* take in many buildings of historical significance.

The High Country Autumn Festival and Merrijig Rodeo: Mar long weekend. *High Country Spring Arts Festival:* 24 Oct – 4 Nov.

Mansfield Hotel: pizzas and DIY barbecue; 86 High St; (03) 5775 2101. *Mansfield Regional Produce Store:* popular local cafe, great coffee; 68 High St; (03) 5779 1404. *The Magnolia Restaurant:* modern Australian; 190 Mt Buller Rd; (03) 5779 1444. *Jamieson Brewery:* menu complements house-crafted ales; Eildon Rd, Jamieson; (03) 5777 0515.

Burnt Creek Cottages: luxurious cottages; 68 O'Hanlons Rd; (03) 5775 3067. *Highton Manor:* manor house plus motel-style units; 140 Highton La; (03) 5775 2700. *Magnolia Gourmet Country House:* 2 attic rooms; 190 Mount Buller Rd; (03) 5779 1444. *Wombat Hills Cottages:* 3 romantic stone cottages; 55 Lochiel Rd, Barwite; (03) 5776 9507.

Mt Buller Victoria's largest and best alpine skiing resort is Mt Buller, whose summit stands 1804 m above sea level. The 24 lifts, including the new 6-seater Holden chairlift (first of its kind in Australia), give access to 180 ha of ski trails, from gentle 'family runs' to heart-stopping double black diamond chutes. If you are a beginner, take on the friendly Bourke Street (Green Run) to find your 'ski legs', or join one of the ski schools there. There is also a half pipe at Boggy Creek and Terrain Park, or cross-country skiing at nearby Mt Stirling. Mt Buller Village offers resort accommodation, and the ski season runs between early June and late Sept. (03) 5777 6077; 47 km E.

Craig's Hut The High Country is synonymous with courageous and hardy cattlemen, transformed into Australian legends by Banjo Paterson's iconic ballad 'The Man from Snowy River'. The men would build huts on the high plains for shelter during summer cattle drives. Craig's Hut on Mt Stirling is a replica of one such shelter, used as a set on the 1983 film *The Man from Snowy River*. It burnt down in the 2006 bushfires, but was rebuilt and reopened in January 2008. The last 2 km of the track to the hut is 4WD or 1.5 km via a fairly steep walking track. 50 km E.

Delatite Winery: Stoneys Rd; 7 km SE. *Mt Samaria State Park:* scenic drives, camping and bushwalking; 14 km N. *Lake Eildon:* houseboat hire, fishing and sailing; 15 km s; *see Eildon for further details. Lake Nillahcootie:* popular for boating, fishing and watersports; 20 km NW. *Jamieson:* an old goldmining town on the Jamieson River with historic buildings; 37 km s. *Alpine National Park:* begins around 40 km SE (*see Mount Beauty*). *Scenic drive:* take the road over the mountains to Whitfield (62 km NE), in the King River Valley, passing through spectacular scenery, including Powers Lookout (48 km NE) for views over the valley. *Lake William Hovell:* for boating and fishing; 85 km NE. *Mt Skene:* great for bushwalking, with wildflowers in summer; 85 km SE via Jamieson. *Fishing:* good spots include the Delatite, Howqua, Jamieson and Goulburn rivers. *Horse trail-riding:* a different way to explore the region, from 2 hr rides to 10-day treks; details from visitor centre. *Mountain-biking:* summer months reveal an expanding network of downhill and cross-country trails at Mt Buller and Mt Stirling.

See also High Country, p. 158

Maryborough

Pop. 7690
Map ref. 579 C5 | 591 M11 | 593 M1

i Cnr Alma and Nolan sts; (03) 5460 4511 or 1800 356 511; www.visitmaryborough.com.au

99.1 Goldfields FM, 107.9 FM ABC Local Radio

Maryborough is a small city set on the northern slopes of the Great Dividing Range. Its historic 19th-century buildings, particularly around the civic square, are a testament to the riches brought by the gold rush of the 1850s. Stroll through the streets to enjoy the cafes, craft shops and magnificent buildings, such as the National Trust–listed courthouse, post office and town hall.

Maryborough Railway Station So immense and impressive is this building that Mark Twain, on his visit to the town, remarked that Maryborough was 'a station with a town attached'. Rumour has it that the building was actually intended for Maryborough in Queensland. The beautifully preserved station houses the visitor centre, the extensive Antique Emporium, the Woodworkers Gallery (open weekends only), and Twains Wood and Craft Gallery. Station St.

Pioneer Memorial Tower: Bristol Hill. *Worsley Cottage:* a historical museum featuring local relics; open Sun; Palmerston St. *Central Goldfields Art Gallery:* features an impressive collection of local artworks, housed in the old fire station; Neill St. *Phillips Gardens:* Alma St.

Maryborough Highland Gathering: New Year's Day. *Energy Breakthrough:* energy expo; Nov.

Paddys Ranges State Park This park offers the chance to enjoy red ironbark and grey box vegetation on a scenic walk or drive. The majority of walks start from the picnic area – see old goldmines and relics or keep an eye out for the rare painted

honeyeater and other birdlife. There is also fossicking within the park, but in designated areas only. Access to the park is just south of Maryborough. Contact Parks Victoria on 13 1963.

Aboriginal wells: impressive rock wells; 4 km s. *Carisbrook:* holds a popular tourist market 1st Sun each month; 7 km E.

See also GOLDFIELDS, p. 154

Marysville

Pop. 516
Map ref. 571 F5 | 573 N3 | 582 F3

ℹ️ 49 Darwin St; 0429 000 394; www.marysvilletourism.com

📻 98.5 UGFM Upper Goulburn Community Radio, 774 AM ABC Local Radio

The historic town of Marysville was almost totally destroyed by bushfire on 7 February 2009. With the help of the community, state and federal governments, this once idyllic township is slowly being rebuilt.

🏠 *Uncle Fred & Aunty Val's Lolly Shop & Produce Store:* old-fashioned candy store; 8 Murchison St; (03) 5963 3644; *Bruno's Art & Sculpture Garden:* gardens featuring sculptures by artist Bruno Torfs; open 10am–5pm daily; (03) 5963 3513.

🎪 *Marysville Community Market:* 2nd Sun each month. *Marysville Farmers Market:* 4th Sun each month. *Taggerty 4 Seasons Market:* Apr.

🍴 *Fraga's Cafe:* stop for lunch or a coffee; 1/19 Murchison St; (03) 5963 3216. *Marysville Country Bakery:* country-style bakery and cafe; 17 Murchison St; (03) 5963 3477. *My Chef Mike:* restaurant serving excellent pizzas; 49 Darwin St; (03) 5963 4512. *Black Spur Inn:* country-style restaurant; 436 Maroondah Hwy, Narbethong; (03) 5963 7121.

🛏️ *Delderfield:* 2 private suites; 1 Darwin St; (03) 5963 4345. *Black Spur Inn:* country-style suites; 436 Maroondah Hwy, Narbethong; (03) 5963 7121. *Woodlands Rainforest Retreat:* 4 luxurious bungalows; 137 Manby Rd, Narbethong; (03) 5963 7150.

🧭 *Cathedral Range State Park* The word 'imposing' does not do justice to the 7 km rocky ridge that forms the backbone of this park. Challenging hikes up the ridge to lookout points offer unparalleled views to the valley below. Walks can include overnight stays at the Farmyard, so named because lyrebirds imitate the noises of the domestic animals in the farmyards below. Contact Parks Victoria on 13 1963; 15 km N.

Lake Mountain Renowned for first-rate cross-country skiing, the area is also great for tobogganing, snow tubing and sled rides. When the snow melts and the wildflowers bloom, hikers can take the Summit Walk (4 km return) over the mountain. Ski and walk brochure available from visitor centre.

Lady Talbot Forest Drive: this 46 km route begins east of town. Stop en route to enjoy picnic spots, walking tracks and lookouts. *Buxton Trout & Salmon Farm:* drop a line in one of the well-stocked ponds, purchase smoked fish or enjoy a barbecue lunch; open 9am–5pm daily; 2118 Maroondah Hwy, Buxton; (03) 5774 7370; 12 km SE. *Scenic walks:* many tracks in the area, including a short walk to Steavenson Falls, from Falls Rd; 4 km loop walk in Cumberland Memorial Scenic Reserve, 16 km E; 4 km Beeches Walk through ancient beech and mountain ash forests (accessed via Lady Talbot Forest Dr). *Big River State Forest:* camping, fishing and gold fossicking; 30 km E.

See also YARRA & DANDENONGS, p. 148

Milawa

Pop. 202
Map ref. 585 I8 | 586 H6

ℹ️ Wangaratta Visitor Information Centre, 100 Murphy St, Wangaratta; 1800 801 065; www.visitwangaratta.com.au

📻 97.7 FM ABC Local Radio, 101.3 Oak FM

Milawa is the perfect destination for lovers of fine food and wine. The Milawa gourmet region boasts over 13 wineries, including the renowned Brown Brothers vineyard. Other fresh local produce outlets sell olives, honey, cheese, chocolates and berries.

🏠 *Milawa Mustards:* a wide range of locally produced mustards; set in attractive cottage gardens; Snow Rd. *Milawa Cheese Company:* sales and tastings of specialist, gourmet cheeses; Factory Rd. *Milawa Muse Gallery:* ever-changing collection of various art mediums complementing the fine quality of the region; Milawa Cheese Factory complex. *Brown Brothers:* cellar-door tastings and sales; Bobinawarrah Rd. *EV Olives:* working olive grove open for tastings and sales; Everton Rd, Markwood.

🎪 *A Weekend Fit for a King:* be treated like a king at the King Valley wineries festival; Queen's Birthday weekend, June. *Beat the Winter Blues and Jazz Festival:* July. *King Valley Shed Show:* Oct. *La Dolce Vita:* wine and food festival at the Milawa/King Valley wineries; Nov.

🍴 *Restaurant Merlot:* contemporary Australian; Lindenwarrah Country House Hotel, Milawa–Bobinawarrah Rd; (03) 5720 5777. *The Ageing Frog Bistrot:* French-influenced menu; Milawa Cheese Company, Factory Rd; (03) 5727 3589. *The Epicurean Centre:* rustic dishes to match wines; Brown Brothers Vineyard, 239 Milawa–Bobinawarrah Rd; (03) 5720 5540.

🛏️ *Lindenwarrah Country House Hotel:* boutique hotel rooms; Milawa–Bobinawarrah Rd; (03) 5720 5777. *Casa Luna Gourmet Accommodation:* 2 stylish rooms; 1569 Boggy Creek Rd, Myrrhee; (03) 5729 7650. *Willoaks Boutique Accommodation:* farmstay with 2 guest rooms; 31 Tetleys La, Oxley; (03) 5727 3292.

🧭 *King Valley Wine Region* This region produces wines with a distinctly Italian influence. Taste cabernet sauvignon, merlot, pinot noir, riesling and chardonnay at various cellar doors, as well as the Italian varieties of sangiovese, pinot grigio and nebbiolo.

Oxley: home to many wineries as well as the Blue Ox Blueberry Farm and King River Cafe; 4 km W.

See also HIGH COUNTRY, p. 158

Mildura

see inset box on next page

Moe

Pop. 15 581
Map ref. 573 P9 | 582 H7

ℹ️ Latrobe Visitor Information Centre, The Old Church, Southside Central, Princes Hwy; 1800 621 409; www.visitlatrobevalley.com

📻 100.7 FM ABC Local Radio, 104.7 Gippsland FM

Like many of the towns in this region, Moe is supported by the power industry, but it has managed to avoid becoming a grim industrial centre. Instead there is a small-town feel and a number of pretty gardens and public parks.

VICTORIA

Gippsland Heritage Park Also known as Old Gippstown, this is a re-creation of a 19th-century community with over 30 restored buildings and a fine collection of fully restored horse-drawn carriages. Lloyd St; (03) 5127 8709.

Cinderella Dolls: Andrew St. *Race track:* picturesque country horse track with regular meetings; Waterloo Rd.

Old Gippstown Market: at Gippsland Heritage Park, with local crafts and produce; last Sat each month Sept–May. *Fairies in the Park:* Feb. *Jazz Festival:* Mar. *Blue Rock Classic:* cross-country horserace; Mar. *Moe Cup:* horserace; Oct.

Baw Baw National Park The landscape of Baw Baw ranges from densely forested river valleys to alpine plateaus and the activities on offer are equally varied – from canoeing river rapids and fishing for trout to skiing, horseriding and bushwalking. Wildflowers carpet the alpine areas in spring. Baw Baw Alpine Resort is located 90 km north of Moe, while the popular Aberfeldy picnic and camping area is accessed via a track north of Walhalla. Contact Parks Victoria on 13 1963.

Edward Hunter Heritage Bush Reserve: 3 km s via Coalville St. *Trafalgar Lookout and Narracan Falls:* near Trafalgar; 10 km w. *Old Brown Coal Mine Museum:* explore the history and memorabilia of the original township known as 'Brown Coal Mine' and the establishment of the power industry in the Latrobe Valley; Cnr Third St and Latrobe River Rd, Yallourn North; 10 km E. *Blue Rock Dam:* fishing, swimming and sailing; 20 km NW. *Thorpdale:* a town renowned for its potatoes. A bakery sells potato bread and a potato festival is held each Mar; 22 km sw. *Walhalla Mountain River Trail:* leads to the picturesque old mining township of Walhalla; Tourist Route 91; details from visitor centre. *See Walhalla.*

See also PHILLIP ISLAND & GIPPSLAND, p. 150

Mornington

Pop. 20 821
Map ref. 570 D10 | 573 J9 | 575 J5 | 582 C7

ⓘ **Mornington Peninsula Visitor Information Centre,** Point Nepean Rd, Dromana; (03) 5987 3078 or 1800 804 009; www.visitmorningtonpeninsula.org

📻 98.7 3RPP FM, 774 AM ABC Local Radio

Mornington was once the hub of the Mornington Peninsula, which is the reason this long arm of land was eventually given the same name. Today Melbourne's urban sprawl has just about reached the town, and it has virtually become a suburb. It still retains a seaside village ambience, particularly with a historic courthouse and post office museum that provide a glimpse of the past. The Rocks restaurant on the harbour provides a stunning view over the famous yachts. In the distance, colourful bathing boxes line Mills Beach.

Historic Mornington Pier: built in the 1850s, the pier remains popular today for walks and fishing. *Mornington Peninsula Regional Gallery:* print and drawing collection, including works by Dobell, Drysdale and Nolan; open Tues–Sat; Dunns Rd. *World of Motorcycles Museum:* Tyabb Rd. *Old post office:* now home to a local history display; Cnr Main St and The Esplanade. *Mornington Tourist Railway:* 10 km journey on steam train; departs from cnr Yuilles and Watt rds; 1st, 2nd and 3rd Sun each month, with additional trips running on Thurs in Jan.

Street Market: Main St; each Wed. *Mornington Racecourse Craft Market:* 2nd Sun each month. *RACV Vintage Car Rally:* Jan. *Mornington Food and Wine Festival:* Oct.

🍴 *Afghan Marco Polo:* Afghan cuisine; 9–11 Main St; (03) 5975 5154. *Brass Razu Wine Bar:* modern European; 13 Main St; (03) 5975 0108. *The Rocks:* seafood with yachts; Mornington Yacht Club, 1 Schnapper Point Dr; (03) 5973 5599.

🏨 *Glynt Manor:* boutique hotel; 10 Greenslade Crt, Mount Martha; (03) 5974 8400. *George's Boutique B&B & Culinary Retreat:* 4 luxury suites; 776 Arthurs Seat Rd, Arthurs Seat; (03) 5981 8700. *Morning Star Estate:* boutique hotel; 2 Sunnyside Rd, Mount Eliza; (03) 9787 7760. *Woodman Estate:* boutique hotel and spa retreat; 136 Graydens Rd, Moorooduc; (03) 5978 8455.

Arthurs Seat State Park At 309 m, Arthurs Seat is the highest point on the Mornington Peninsula. The summit can be reached by foot or vehicle and offers panoramic views of the bay and surrounding bushland. Picnic facilities and a restaurant are on the summit. There are many short walks, plus the historic Seawinds Park with gardens and sculptures. The Enchanted Maze Garden is set in superb gardens, with a variety of mazes and the Maize Maze Festival in Feb–Apr. Contact Parks Victoria on 13 1963; Arthurs Seat Rd, near Dromana; 16 km sw.

Mornington Peninsula Wine Region Although the first vines were planted in 1886, the wine industry on the peninsula did not truly take off until the 1970s. Comprising over 170 vineyards, the region consists predominantly of boutique wineries, with more than 50 cellar doors. While enjoying the sunshine, beaches and coastal resorts, it seems appropriate to try the crisp chardonnay that is famed in this region – or even a pinot noir or cabernet sauvignon as the chilly sea breeze kicks in of an evening. Wine festivals include Pinot Week each Mar, Queen's Birthday Wine Weekend each June and the Cool Whites Festival each Nov. Winery map from visitor centre.

Mount Martha: here is The Briars with a significant collection of Napoleonic artefacts and furniture. The town also features many gardens, plus wetlands great for birdwatching and bushland walks; 7 km s. *Ballam Park:* historic, French-farmhouse-style homestead built in 1845; open Sun; Cranbourne Rd, Frankston; 14 km NE. *Mulberry Hill:* former home of artist Sir Daryl Lindsay and author Joan Lindsay, who wrote *Picnic at Hanging Rock*; open Sun afternoons; Golf Links Rd, Baxter; 14 km NE. *Tyabb Packing House Antique Centre:* Australia's largest collection of antiques and collectibles; Mornington–Tyabb Rd, Tyabb; 16 km E. *Hastings:* coastal town on Western Port with 2 km walking trail through wetlands and mangrove habitat; 21 km SE. *Moonlit Sanctuary Wildlife Conservation Park:* wildlife park featuring endangered native Australian animals; visit 11am–5pm or take an evening tour; night tour bookings on (03) 5978 7935; 550 Tyabb–Tooradin Rd, Pearcedale; 24 km E. *Beaches:* the stretch of coast between Mornington and Mount Martha features sheltered, sandy bays popular with holiday-makers.

See also MORNINGTON PENINSULA, p. 149

Morwell

Pop. 13 398
Map ref. 582 H7

ⓘ **Latrobe Visitor Information Centre, The Old Church,** Southside Central, Princes Hwy, Traralgon; 1800 621 409; www.visitlatrobevalley.com

📻 100.7 FM ABC Local Radio, 104.7 Gippsland FM

Morwell is primarily an industrial town and Victoria's major producer of electricity. Nestled in the heart of the Latrobe Valley, it contains one of the world's largest deposits of brown coal. Among all the heavy machinery is the impressive Centenary Rose

MILDURA

Pop. 46 035

Map ref. 558 E6 | 588 G6

[AERIAL VIEW OF THE MURRAY RIVER]

i **Alfred Deakin Centre**, 180–190 Deakin Ave; (03) 5018 8380 or 1800 039 043; www.visitmildura.com.au

104.3 FM ABC Local Radio, 106.7 HOTFM Sunraysia Community Radio

Mildura offers a Riviera lifestyle, with the Murray River flowing by the town and sunny, mild weather throughout the year. One of Victoria's major rural cities, Mildura's development has been aided by the expansion of irrigation, which has allowed the city to become a premier fruit-growing region.

Mildura Arts Centre Complex The complex is set on the banks of the Murray River and includes an art gallery, an amphitheatre and the Rio Vista museum. Rio Vista was the home of the town's founders, the Chaffey brothers, and is now preserved as a museum displaying colonial household items. The art gallery houses an impressive permanent collection and includes Australia's largest display of Brangwyn and Orpen paintings, as well as frequent temporary exhibitions. Outside, a delightful Sculpture Trail winds through the landscaped gardens surrounding the centre. Cureton Ave; (03) 5018 8330.

The Alfred Deakin Centre: interactive exhibitions and displays of the region; Deakin Ave. *Mildura Brewery:* produces natural and specialty beers inside the former Astor Theatre; view the brewing process or eat at the Brewery Pub; Langtree Ave; (03) 5021 5399. *Langtree Hall:* Mildura's first public hall now contains antiques and memorabilia; open Tues–Sun; Walnut Ave. *Mildura Wharf:* paddlesteamers departing here for river cruises include PS *Melbourne*, PS *Avoca* for lunch cruises on Sun, and PV *Rothbury* for daytrips to Trentham Winery each Thurs. Access from Madden Ave. *Snakes and Ladders:* fun park featuring 'dunny' collection; Seventeenth St. *Aquacoaster waterslide:* Cnr Seventh St and Orange Ave. *Stefano's:* Italian restaurant in the majestic Grand Hotel, featuring the culinary skills of television chef Stefano di Pieri; Seventh St.

Arts Festival: Mar. *Cup Carnival:* May. *Writers Festival:* July. *Golf Week:* July. *Country Music Festival:* Sept. *Vintage Tractor Pull:* Sept. *Jazz Food and Wine Festival:* Nov.

Spanish Bar and Grill: up-market steakhouse; Quality Hotel Mildura Grand, Seventh St; (03) 5021 2377. *Stefano's:* excellent Italian; Quality Hotel Mildura Grand, Seventh St; (03) 5023 0511. *The Gol Gol Hotel:* good pub dining; Sturt Hwy, Gol Gol; (03) 5024 8492. *Trentham Estate Restaurant:* modern Australian; Sturt Hwy, Trentham Cliffs; (03) 5024 8888.

Murray Haven: beautifully renovated 4-bedroom house; 118A Thirteenth St; 0408 213 404. *Pied-à-terre:* luxury 5-bedroom home; 97 Chaffey Ave; (03) 5022 9883. *Quality Hotel Mildura Grand:* refurbished rooms; Seventh St; (03) 5023 0511 or 1800 034 228. *Adventure Houseboats:* slick solar-powered vessels; 16 Sturt Hwy, Buronga; (03) 5023 4787.

Murray Darling Wine Region The Mediterranean-style climate mixed with irrigated lands has contributed to making this wine region Victoria's largest. The region is well regarded for its varieties of chardonnay, cabernet sauvignon and shiraz. Among the large-scale wineries such as Lindemans Karadoc, smaller boutique wineries offer specialty wines for tastings and sales. Brochure available from visitor centre.

Orange World: tours of citrus-growing region; 6 km N. *Australian Inland Botanic Gardens:* farmers market held 1st and 3rd Sat each month; garden tour with lunch last Sun each month; open daily; 8 km N. *Kings Billabong Wildlife Reserve:* situated on the Murray River flood plain, home to river red gums and abundant birdlife. Attractions include Psyche Pump Station, Bruce's Bend Marina and Kings Billabong Lookout; 8 km SE. *Angus Park:* dried fruits and confectionery; 10 km SE. *Red Cliffs:* an important area for the citrus and dried fruit industries. The town features the 'Big Lizzie' steam traction engine; 15 km S. *Hattah–Kulkyne National Park:* 70 km S; *see Ouyen. Murray–Sunset National Park:* attractions near Mildura include Lindsay Island, for boating, swimming and fishing; access from Sturt Hwy, about 100 km W of Mildura. *See Murrayville for further details on park. Mungo National Park:* 104 km NE over NSW border (*see Balranald, NSW*).

See also MALLEE COUNTRY, p. 156

VICTORIA

Garden, featuring over 4000 rose bushes and regarded as one of the finest rose gardens in the Southern Hemisphere.

PowerWorks: dynamic displays on the electrical industries; tours of mines and power stations daily; Ridge Rd. **Centenary Rose Garden:** off Commercial Rd. **Latrobe Regional Gallery:** hosts outstanding works of contemporary Australian art by local and national artists; Commercial Rd. **Gippsland Immigration Wall of Recognition:** acknowledges all immigrants who contributed to the development of the Gippsland region.

Market: Latrobe Rd; each Sun.

Morwell National Park This park protects some of the last remnant vegetation of the Strzelecki Ranges, including pockets of rainforest and fern gullies. The area was once occupied by the Woollum Woollum people, who hunted in the ranges. In the 1840s European settlers cleared much of the surrounding land. On the Fosters Gully Nature Walk, keep your eyes peeled for orchids (over 40 species are found here) and native animals. Contact Parks Victoria on 13 1963; 16 km s.

Hazelwood Pondage: warm water ideal for year-round watersports; 5 km s. **Arts Resource Collective:** housed in an old butter factory; Yinnar; 12 km sw. **Lake Narracan:** fishing and waterskiing; 15 km nw. **Narracan Falls:** 27 km w. **Scenic drives:** routes along the Strzelecki Ranges and Baw Baw mountains offer impressive views over the Latrobe Valley.

See also **Phillip Island & Gippsland, p. 150**

Mount Beauty

Pop. 1705
Map ref. 585 L10 | 587 J7

i **Alpine Discovery Centre, 31 Bogong High Plains Rd; (03) 5754 1962 or 1800 111 885; www.visitalpinevictoria.com.au**

92.5 Alpine Radio FM, 720 AM ABC Local Radio

At the foot of Mount Bogong, Victoria's highest mountain at 1986 metres, Mount Beauty was originally an accommodation town for workers on the Kiewa Hydro-electric Scheme. Today, the town is regarded as an adventure mecca and a focal point for a variety of adventure activities, with mountain-biking, hang-gliding and bushwalking just a few on offer. The pairing of adventure with more leisurely outdoor activities like golf, swimming and fishing makes Mount Beauty an ideal holiday destination.

Mt Beauty Pondage: for watersports and fishing; just north of Main St. **Wineries:** cool-climate vineyards at Annapurna Estate, Bogong Estate and Recline. **Scenic walks:** several scenic walking tracks; details from visitor centre.

Markets: Hollands St; 1st Sat each month. **Bogong Cup:** Jan. **MTBA National Series:** mountain-biking championships; Jan. **Music Muster:** Apr. **Mitta Mitta to Mount Beauty Mountain Bike Challenge:** Oct.

 Alpine National Park Covering 646 000 ha in 4 sections, this is Victoria's largest park, containing the highest mountains in the state. Most of Australia's south-east rivers, including the mighty Murray, have their source here. The area is known for its outstanding snowfields during winter, and bushwalking and wildflowers in summer. Other activities include horseriding, canoeing, rafting and mountain-bike riding. 30 km se.

Falls Creek Surrounded by Alpine National Park, Falls Creek is a winter playground for downhill and cross-country skiers. When the snow is falling, the ski resort caters for skiers and snowboarders with a variety of runs and terrain, including some to suit beginners. Novelty tours are also available, such as the

Snowmobile Tours. Each Aug, Falls Creek hosts the Kangaroo Hoppet cross-country ski race. In spring and summer, take a walk on the Bogong High Plains or fly-fish in one of the lakes and rivers nearby; 30 km se.

Tawonga Gap: features a lookout over valleys; 13 km nw. **Bogong:** scenic walks around Lake Guy and nearby Clover Arboretum for picnics; 15 km se. **Scenic drives:** to Falls Creek and the Bogong High Plains (not accessible in winter beyond Falls Creek); details from visitor centre.

See also **High Country, p. 158**

Murrayville

Pop. 210
Map ref. 558 B9 | 588 C11 | 590 C1 | 603 O10

i **Ouyen Information Centre, 17 Oke St, Ouyen; (03) 5092 2006; www.visitmildura.com.au/murrayville**

103.5 3MBR-FM Mallee Border Radio, 594 AM ABC Local Radio

Murrayville is a small town on the Mallee Highway near the South Australia border. It is near three major, remote national parks: Murray–Sunset National Park; Wyperfeld National Park; and Big Desert Wilderness Park, one of Victoria's largest wilderness zones.

Historic buildings: include the restored railway station and the old courthouse. **Walking tracks:** several, including the Pine Hill Walking Trail in the town.

Murray–Sunset National Park Millions of years ago this area was submerged beneath the sea. When the sea retreated, large sand ridges and dunes were left. Now there is a variety of vegetation including grasslands, saltbush and mallee eucalypts. In spring, wildflowers abound; look out for Victoria's largest flower, the Murray lily. Access roads to the park are off Mallee Hwy. The Pink Lakes saltwater lakes, with a distinctive, pinkish hue, are a key attraction and are especially remarkable at sunset. There are many good walking tracks near the lakes, as well as excellent camping facilities. Lakes access via Pink Lakes Rd (turn-off at Linga, 50 km e); contact Parks Victoria on 13 1963. *For north section of park see Mildura.*

Cowangie: a small, historic town with several 19th-century buildings, including Kow Plains Homestead; 19 km e. **Big Desert Wilderness Park:** a remote park with no access other than by foot. True to its name, this park has remained relatively untouched by Europeans and includes many reptile species and plants adapted to arid conditions; the track south of town takes you close to the park boundary. **Wyperfeld National Park:** access via Underbool or by 4WD track south of Murrayville; *for further details see Hopetoun.*

See also **Mallee Country, p. 156**

Myrtleford

Pop. 2726
Map ref. 585 J8 | 586 H6

i **Post Office Complex, Great Alpine Rd; (03) 5752 1044; www.visitalpinevictoria.com.au**

91.7 FM ABC Local Radio, 101.3 Oak FM

Myrtleford is a pretty town in Victoria's alpine High Country. Originally called Myrtle Creek Run in the early 1800s, it is a thriving agricultural district and gateway to Mount Hotham.

 The Phoenix Tree: a sculpture created by Hans Knorr from the trunk of a red gum; Lions Park. **The Big Tree:** a huge old red gum; Smith St. **Old School:** the town's original school, now fully restored; open Thurs, Sun or by appt; Albert St. *Swing Bridge over Myrtle Creek:* Standish St. *Reform Hill Lookout:* a scenic walking track from Elgin St leads to the lookout, which has great views across town; end of Halls Rd. *Parks:* Rotary Park in Myrtle St and Apex Park in Standish St are both delightful picnic spots. *Michelini Wines:* Great Alpine Rd. *Murray to the Mountains Rail Trail:* the cycle touring loop from Bright to Wangaratta runs through the town.

Market: local produce; Great Alpine Rd; each Sat Jan–Apr. *Alpine Classic Bike Ride:* to Bright; Jan. *Myrtleford Festival:* Mar. *Golden Spurs Rodeo:* Dec.

Plump Harvest: regional produce store/cafe; 72 Great Alpine Rd; (03) 5752 2257. *The Butter Factory:* produce store/cafe; 15 Great Alpine Rd; (03) 5752 2300.

Motel on Alpine: range of motel rooms; 258 Great Alpine Rd; (03) 5752 1438.

Mt Buffalo National Park: 7 km s; *see Bright.* *Wineries:* several in the region, including Rosewhite Vineyards and Winery; open weekends, public holidays and throughout Jan; Happy Valley Rd; 8 km se. *Gapsted:* home to the Victorian Alps Winery, offers tours and sales; 8 km nw. *Eurobin:* a number of farms near the town with sales of local produce, including Red Stag Deer Farm and Bright Berry Farm, offering homemade jams and berries Dec–Mar; 16 km se. *Fishing:* in the Ovens and Buffalo rivers and Lake Buffalo (25 km s).

See also HIGH COUNTRY, p. 158

Nagambie

Pop. 1381
Map ref. 584 D9

319 High St; (03) 5794 2647 or 1800 444 647; www.nagambielakestourism.com.au

97.7 FM ABC Local Radio, 98.5 FM

Nagambie is found between Seymour and Shepparton on the Goulburn Valley Highway. The town is on the shores of Lake Nagambie, which was created by the construction of the Goulburn Weir in 1891. Activities such as waterskiing, speedboating and especially rowing are popular on this man-made lake.

The Jetty: fine dining, lakeside apartments and spa; High St. *The Grapevine by the Lake:* sales of nuts and local produce; High St. *Nagambie Lakes Entertainment Centre:* renovated 1890s building with bars, gaming lounge and non-motorised boat hire; High St.

Rowing Regatta: Jan–Mar. *Head of the River:* Mar. *Nagambie On Water Festival:* Mar long weekend. After *Vintage Festival:* May. *Shiraz Challenge:* a search for the best shiraz in the region; Nov. *Fireworks over the Lake:* New Year's Eve.

Mitchelton Wines: regional produce menu; Mitchells Town Rd; (03) 5736 2221. *Tahbilk Wetlands Cafe:* casual cafe food; Tahbilk Winery, 254 O'Neils Rd, Tabilk; (03) 5794 2555. *The Jetty:* modern Australian; 317 High St; (03) 5794 1964.

Blackwood Park Country House: 3-bedroom house; Mitchelton Wines, Mitchells Town Rd; (03) 5736 2221. *Nagambie Lakes Leisure Park:* cabins and caravan sites; 69 Loddings La; (03) 5794 2373.

Goulburn Valley Wine Region The top wine here is shiraz, but also look out for marsanne at the area's 2 main players,

Tahbilk Winery and Mitchelton Wines. Tahbilk's vineyard features a 3-tiered chateau, a museum detailing the estate's history, and a wetland and wildlife reserve. Mitchelton offers a 55-metre lookout tower with views of Goulburn River, and an excellent restaurant.

Goulburn Weir The construction of this weir resulted in the creation of Lake Nagambie. It is the diversion weir on the Goulburn River for the Goulburn Valley Irrigation area and feeds water by channel and pipeline to Bendigo, among other places. A walkway runs across the weir offering views of the structure and lake. Picnic and barbecue facilities are available; 12 km n.

See also GOULBURN & MURRAY, p. 157

Natimuk

Pop. 445
Map ref. 590 F9

National Hotel, Main St; (03) 5387 1300.

96.5 Triple H FM, 594 AM ABC Local Radio

Natimuk is popular for its proximity to Mount Arapiles, a 369-metre sandstone monolith that has been described as 'Victoria's Ayers Rock'. The mountain was first climbed by Major Mitchell in 1836, and today is a popular rock-climbing destination with over 2000 marked climbing routes.

Arapiles Historical Society Museum: housed in the old courthouse; open by appt; Main St. *Arapiles Craft Shop:* features local arts and crafts; Main St. *The Goat Gallery:* showcases works of local and regional artists; Main St. *Self-guide heritage trail:* details from visitor centre.

Nati Frinj: biennial arts festival; Oct/Nov.

Mt Arapiles–Tooan State Park This park is divided into 2 blocks, the larger Tooan block and the smaller Mt Arapiles block; Mt Arapiles offers rock climbing and is by far the most popular. Mitre Rock presents a smaller climbing challenge if required. Should you choose not to scale one of the various rock faces, great views are still available from the walking tracks, or you can drive to the summit. Nature study is another possibility – a huge 14% of the state's flora is represented in the Mt Arapiles section alone. Contact Parks Victoria on 13 1963; access is from the Wimmera Hwy; 12 km sw.

Banksia Hill Flower Farm: 10 km e. *Duffholme Museum:* 21 km w.

See also GRAMPIANS & CENTRAL WEST, p. 155

Nhill

Pop. 1919
Map ref. 558 C12 | 590 E7

Victoria St; (03) 5391 3086.

96.5 Triple H FM, 594 AM ABC Local Radio

The name of this town may be derived from the Aboriginal word 'nyell', meaning 'white mist on water'. Nhill is exactly halfway between Melbourne and Adelaide, and claims to have the largest single-bin silo in the Southern Hemisphere. The town is a good starting point for tours of Little Desert National Park.

Historical Society Museum: open Thurs, Fri or by appt; McPherson St. *Cottage of John Shaw Neilson (lyric poet):* open by appt; Jaypex Park, Victoria St. *Boardwalk:* scenic walk from Jaypex Park to Nhill Lake. *Lowana Craft Shop:* local crafts; Victoria St. *Self-guide historical walk:* details from visitor centre.

VICTORIA

 RADIO STATIONS   IN TOWN   WHAT'S ON   WHERE TO EAT   WHERE TO STAY   NEARBY

Boxing Day Races: Dec.

 Little Desert National Park: the Little Desert Lodge is in the central section of the park, south of Nhill, and is a departure point for day tours and a popular place to stay. There are walking trails in the central and western sections. 15 km s. *See also Dimboola.* *Mallee Dam:* lately dry, once offered fantastic birdwatching with bird hides provided; 20 km sw.

See also GRAMPIANS & CENTRAL WEST, p. 155

Ocean Grove
Pop. 14 351
Map ref. 572 G9 | 574 D6 | 580 H2 | 582 A7 | 593 O8

ⓘ Geelong Visitor Information Centre, Stead Park, Princes Hwy, Corio; (03) 5275 5797 or 1800 620 888; www.visitgreatoceanroad.org.au

📻 94.7 The Pulse FM, 774 AM ABC Local Radio

Ocean Grove is a popular summer-holiday destination near the mouth of the Barwon River. The beaches around the town offer great surfing and safe swimming, with surf patrols operating during the summer months.

Ocean Grove Nature Reserve This reserve contains the only significant example of woodland on the Bellarine Peninsula, preserved virtually as it was prior to European settlement. A bird hide lets visitors look out for any number of the 130 different species that live here. Contact Parks Victoria on 13 1963; Grubb Rd.

Ti-Tree Village: peaceful cottages, some with a spa; 34 Orton St; (03) 5255 4433.

HMAS *Canberra* Dive Site Opened to the public in December 2009, this purposely sunken warship is Victoria's first artificial site created specifically for diving. Divers can visit every area of the ship's 138 m length, from the captain's cabin to the galley. Bookings must be made with a charter boat operator or dive shop to be taken to the dive site. For details, call 0414 922 916. 4 km SE.

Barwon Heads This is a pretty seaside town on the Barwon River, made famous as the location for the television series *SeaChange*. There are several good restaurants in the area, including one right on the Barwon River that provides a scenic environment for fine dining. The Barwon Heads Golf Club is one of the top 3 public courses in the state. The Jirrahlinga Koala and Wildlife Reserve on Taits Rd lets visitors encounter the delightful, yet often elusive, koala in a natural environment. Barwon Heads is a short drive from Ocean Grove. 3 km s.

Lake Connewarre State Game Reserve: with mangrove swamps and great walks, the game reserve is home to a variety of wildlife, including wallabies; 7 km N. *Wallington:* the town is home to A Maze'N Games, a timber maze with minigolf, picnic/barbecue facilities and a cafe, Koombahla Park Equestrian Centre, Adventure Park and Bellarine Adventure Golf. A strawberry fair is held in Wallington in Nov; 8 km N.

See also WERRIBEE & BELLARINE, p. 152

Olinda
Pop. 1568
Map ref. 570 H6 | 571 B9 | 573 L6 | 582 E5

ⓘ Dandenong Ranges Information Centre, 1211 Burwood Hwy, Upper Ferntree Gully; (03) 9758 7522; www.olindavillage.com.au

📻 98.1 Radio Eastern FM, 774 AM ABC Local Radio

Olinda is in the centre of the Dandenong Ranges, a landscape of towering mountain ash forests, lush fern gullies, waterfalls,

English gardens and picnic spots. The ranges have been a retreat for Melburnians since the 1800s. Olinda and nearby Sassafras are known for their many galleries and cafes, particularly the numerous tearooms serving traditional Devonshire teas.

 Rhododendron and Daffodil Festivals: Aug–Nov.

🍴 *Wild Oak Restaurant and Wine Bar:* French-influenced modern Australian menu; Cnr Ridge and Mt Dandenong Tourist rds; (03) 9751 2033. *Ladyhawke Cafe:* Middle Eastern cafe; 1365–1367 Mt Dandenong Tourist Rd, Mount Dandenong; (03) 9751 1104. *Miss Marple's Tea Room:* traditional tea room fare; 382 Mt Dandenong Tourist Rd, Sassafras; (03) 9755 1610. *Ripe – Australian Produce:* foodie cafe/produce store; 376–378 Mt Dandenong Tourist Rd, Sassafras; (03) 9755 2100.

🛏 *Folly Farm Rural Retreat:* 1-bedroom country cottage; 192 Falls Rd; (03) 9751 2544. *Lochiel Luxury Accommodation:* contemporary cottages; 1590–1594 Mt Dandenong Tourist Rd; (03) 9751 2300. *Woolrich Retreat:* executive garden retreat; 7–9 Monash Ave; (03) 9751 2464 or 1300 553 011. *Japanese Mountain Retreat:* traditional Japanese accommodation; 14 Mountain Cres, Montrose; (03) 9737 0086.

🧭 **Dandenong Ranges National Park** This park offers great walking tracks and picnic facilities. Visitors may be lucky enough to spot an elusive lyrebird, a species renowned for its ability to mimic sounds – from other bird calls to human voices and even chainsaws. Most walking tracks leave from picnic grounds, such as the Thousand Steps Track from Ferntree Gully Picnic Ground (south-west via the Mt Dandenong Tourist Rd) and the walk to Sherbrooke Falls from the Sherbrooke Picnic Ground (via Sherbrooke Rd from the Mt Dandenong Tourist Rd). The park extends to the east and west of town. Contact Parks Victoria on 13 1963; 2 km NE, 6 km SW.

William Ricketts Sanctuary William Ricketts was a well-known artist and conservationist whose intricate sculptures focus on Aboriginal people and the complexities of Australia's native vegetation. Many sculptures are displayed in a bushland setting on the scenic Mt Dandenong Tourist Rd. Contact Parks Victoria on 13 1963; 3 km N.

National Rhododendron Gardens: the gardens begin just east of town and are something of a mecca for garden enthusiasts, with superb displays of rhododendrons and azaleas in season. *R. J. Hamer Arboretum:* good walking tracks through 100 ha of rare and exotic trees; Olinda–Monbulk Rd, shortly after turn-off to Rhododendron Gardens. *Cloudehill Gardens:* twilight concerts are held here in summer; south of R. J. Hamer Arboretum. *Mt Dandenong Lookout:* spectacular views over Melbourne; picnic/barbecue facilities; 3 km N. *Alfred Nicholas Gardens:* an ornamental lake with the original boathouse and the George Tindale Memorial Garden, with flowering plants beneath mountain ash trees. The original Nicholas family home (built 1920s) is here; Sherbrooke; 4 km SE. *Kawarra Australian Plant Garden:* an impressive collection of native plants; Kalorama; 4.5 km N. *Markets:* art, craft, plants and homemade goods; nearby markets include Kallista Market, 6 km s, 1st Sat each month, and Upper Ferntree Gully Market, 12 km SE, every Sat and Sun. *Burrinja Gallery:* a memorial to artist Lin Onus, with Aboriginal and Oceanic sculptures and paintings; Upwey; 10 km sw. *Silvan:* prominent flower-growing region with many tulip farms. The famous Tesselaar's Tulip Farm hosts a popular festival each Sept–Oct with sales of flowers and bulbs, and traditional Dutch music and food; Monbulk Rd; 15 km NE. *Silvan Dam:* an area to the north of this major Melbourne water supply has walking tracks and picnic/barbecue facilities; turn-off after Silvan. *Mont De Lancey:* wonderfully preserved house, built in 1882 and set in landscaped gardens; includes a museum and a chapel; open 2nd Sat each month; Wandin North; 22 km NE via Mt Evelyn.

See also YARRA & DANDENONGS, p. 148

Omeo

Pop. 226
Map ref. 583 M1 | 585 M12 | 587 M11

 152 Great Alpine Rd; (03) 5159 1679; www.omeoregion.com.au

90.9 FM High Country Radio, 720 AM ABC Local Radio

Omeo is an Aboriginal word meaning mountains – appropriate for this picturesque town in the Victorian Alps. Today Omeo is a peaceful farming community, but it wasn't always so. During the 1800s gold rush, Omeo was an unruly frontier town, which early Australian novelist Rolf Boldrewood described as the roughest goldfield in Australia. Despite taking damage in the 1939 Black Friday bushfires, several historic buildings still remain.

A. M. Pearson Historical Park The park preserves a piece of Omeo's rich history in a peaceful, bushland setting. Buildings on display include the old courthouse, which now houses a museum, a log gaol, stables and a blacksmith's. Day Ave (Great Alpine Rd).

Historic buildings: many distinctive structures from the 19th century can be seen in town, including the post office, primary school and shire offices; Day Ave. *Shops:* several unique stores, including the German Cuckoo Clock Shop, Petersen's Gallery, High Country Paintings and Octagon Bookshop; Day Ave.

High Country Calf Sales: Mar. *Alpine Discovery Festival and Picnic Races:* Mar. *Rodeo, Easter Market and Easter Egg Hunt:* Easter. *Cobungra Polo Match:* Apr.

The Golden Age Hotel Motel: up-market country fare; 189 Day Ave; (03) 5159 1344.

Oriental Claims The Claims was a major goldmining area, and remains the highest alluvial goldfield in Australia. French-Canadians, Americans and Europeans all worked alongside Australians and Chinese during the gold boom. The word 'Oriental' in the mine's name may conjure an image of Chinese workers, but 'Oriental Claims' was actually the name of a European company. The Omeo Sluicing Company, however, was Chinese. There are a variety of walks around the site and visitors should look out for the variety of flora, including wild orchids. High cliffs, left by the hydraulic sluicing process, offer impressive views across town, and signs throughout the Parks Victoria– managed site explain the history of the Claims. Contact Parks Victoria on 13 1963; 1.5 km w on Great Alpine Rd.

Mt Hotham This popular downhill ski resort is suited to both budding and experienced skiers. Skiing areas range from the beginners' Big D Playground through to the more advanced slopes around Mary's Slide and the black diamond chutes of Heavenly Valley. In summer, the mountain is a popular hiking and mountain-bike-riding destination. (03) 5759 3550; 56 km w.

Livingstone Park and Creek: walking tracks and swimming area adjacent to the Oriental Claims. *Mt Markey Winery:* on the site of the old Cassilis Hotel, on the touring loop from Omeo to Swifts Creek; Cassilis Rd, Cassilis; 15 km s. *Lake Omeo:* scenic natural landscape, dry for most parts of the year; Benambra;

21 km NE. *Benambra:* gateway to the Alpine National Park; 24 km N. *Anglers Rest:* historic Blue Duck Inn, a good base for horseriding, whitewater rafting and fly-fishing; 29 km NW. *Swifts Creek:* this town situated at the junction of Swifts Creek and Tambo River has the Great Alpine Art Gallery; 40 km s. *Taylors Crossing suspension bridge:* part of the scenic Australian Alps Walking Track and also a great base for camping and fishing the Mitta Mitta River; off Tablelands Rd; 44 km NE. *Dinner Plain:* relaxed village surrounded by the Alpine National Park that offers many activities such as skiing, walking, horseriding and Australia's first indoor-outdoor alpine spa; 46 km w. *Ensay:* small but picturesque town that is home to the well-known Ensay Winery; 70 km s. *Great Alpine Rd:* covers over 300 km from the High Country to Gippsland Lakes and offers 6 individual self-guide touring routes with a diverse combination of scenery; details from visitor centre. Note that some drives cross state forests or alpine areas, so be alert for timber trucks and check conditions in winter. Omeo is located on this road. *Mitta Mitta and Cobungra rivers:* great trout fishing, waterskiing and whitewater rafting (only available in spring); details from visitor centre. *High Country tours:* explore the high plains around Omeo – on horseback, by 4WD or, for keen hikers, on challenging bushwalks; details from visitor centre.

See also HIGH COUNTRY, p. 158

Orbost

Pop. 2096
Map ref. 565 A12 | 581 B11

 Slab Hut, 39 Nicholson St; (03) 5154 2424; www.lakesandwilderness.com.au

90.7 FM 3REG Radio East Gippsland, 97.1 FM ABC Local Radio

Situated on the banks of the legendary Snowy River, Orbost is on the Princes Highway and surrounded by spectacular coastal and mountain territory. For those who love arts and crafts, there are many shops in the area supplying and displaying local products.

Visitor Information Centre: display explains complex rainforest ecology; Slab Hut, 39 Nicholson St. *Old Pump House:* behind relocated 1872 slab hut; Forest Rd. *Historical Museum:* details local history with displays of artefacts; Ruskin St. *Snowy River Country Craft:* Forest Rd. *Netherbyre Gemstone and Art Galley:* Cnr Browning and Carlyle sts. *Exhibition Centre:* equipped with 2 galleries, one dedicated to the National Collection of Australian Wood Design, the other presenting monthly exhibitions; Nicholson St. *Mirrawong Woolworks:* sells wool and felt handmade items; 295 Nicholson St. *The Paddle Boat Shed:* community project rebuilding the paddle steamer *Curlip*. *Heritage walk:* weaves its way through town with storyboards, fingerboards and plaques explaining the historic buildings; begins at Slab Hut.

Australian Wood Design Exhibition: Jan.

A Lovely Little Lunch: local produce cafe menu; 125A Nicholson St; (03) 5154 1303. *PS Curlip II:* lunches and snacks on a paddlesteamer; PS *Curlip* Centre, 1 Browning St; (03) 5154 1699.

Errinundra National Park The park is one of the largest remaining stands of cool temperate rainforest in Victoria, and features giant eucalypt forests. There is the rainforest boardwalk and for keen hikers there are walking tracks, as well as camping

VICTORIA

and picnic facilities. Enjoy superb views from Ellery View, Ocean View Lookout and the peak of Mt Morris. In winter, snow and rain can make access difficult. Errinundra Rd, off Princes Hwy; contact Parks Victoria on 13 1963; 54 km NE.

Marlo: a popular fishing spot also known for its galleries and Bush Races in Jan; 14 km s. *Cape Conran Coastal Park:* rugged coastal scenery and excellent walks. Turn south after Cabbage Tree Creek (26 km E) or take the coastal route from Marlo. *Cabbage Tree Palms Flora Reserve:* 27 km E. *Bemm River Scenic Reserve:* a 1 km signposted rainforest walk and picnic facilities; off Princes Hwy; 40 km E. *Snowy River National Park:* in the south of the park is Raymond Creek Falls. A 40 min return walk leads to the falls, with a further 1 hr walk leading to the Snowy River; 42 km N; 2WD access, check road conditions. McKillops Bridge, 148 km N via Deddick, is one of the most accessible parts of this park; *for more details see Buchan. Sydenham Inlet:* a good spot for bream fishing; 58 km E. *Tranquil Valley Tavern:* on the banks of the Delegate River near the NSW border; about 115 km NE. *Baldwin Spencer Trail:* a 262 km scenic drive following the route of this explorer, taking in old mining sites and Errinundra National Park; details from visitor centre.

See also EAST GIPPSLAND, p. 159

Ouyen

Pop. 1058
Map ref. 558 E8 | 588 H11

ℹ️ 17 Oke St; (03) 5092 2006; www.visitmildura.com.au/ouyen

📻 92.9 3MBR-FM Mallee Border Radio, 594 AM ABC Local Radio

Ouyen was once little more than a station on the Melbourne–Mildura train route, but it has since grown to become an important service town. Ouyen is at the centre of the Mallee region, which was developed in the early 1900s – relatively late when compared with other regions of rural Victoria. This was mainly due to the difficulties in clearing the land as well as the harsh climate. The current success of agriculture in the region, in particular wheat-growing, is a testament to the hardiness of early farmers and settlers.

🏠 *Roxy Theatre:* newly restored and functioning tropical-style theatre, only one of its type in southern Australia; Oke St.

🌿 *Great Australian Vanilla Slice Triumph:* 1st Fri in Sept.

🧭 **Hattah–Kulkyne National Park** This park protects an area of 48 000 ha that includes typical mallee country with both low scrub and open native pine woodlands. The freshwater Hattah Lakes are seasonally filled by creeks connected to the Murray River, which brings the area to life with plants and waterbirds. Activities within the park include bushwalking, canoeing, fishing and scenic drives. There are picnic and camping facilities at Mournpall and Lake Hattah. Contact Parks Victoria on 13 1963; off the Calder Hwy; 35 km N.

Speed: Mallee Machinery Field Days held here in Aug; 39 km s.

See also MALLEE COUNTRY, p. 156

Paynesville

Pop. 3455
Map ref. 583 N6

ℹ️ Community Craft Centre, Esplanade; (03) 5156 7479; www.lakesandwilderness.com.au

📻 90.7 FM 3REG Radio East Gippsland, 100.7 FM ABC Local Radio

Paynesville is a popular tourist resort close to the rural city of Bairnsdale, on the McMillan Straits. The town is set on the Gippsland Lakes and the beaches of the Tasman Sea, making it a favourite destination for fishing and waterskiing.

🏠 *St Peter-by-the-Lake Church:* built in 1961, this unique structure incorporates seafaring images in its design; The Esplanade. *Community Craft Centre:* displays and sells local arts and crafts; The Esplanade.

🌿 *Market:* Gilsenan Reserve; 2nd Sun each month. *Jazz Festival:* Feb. *Marlay Pt Paynesville Overnight Yacht Race:* Mar long weekend.

🍴 *Cafe Espas:* contemporary seafood; Raymond Island; (03) 5156 7275.

🏨 *Captain's Cove:* smart nautical units; 13 Mitchell St; (03) 5156 7223.

🧭 **Gippsland Lakes** This area incorporates The Lakes National Park, Gippsland Lakes Coastal Park and the famous Ninety Mile Beach – an incredible stretch of scenic coastline offering great swimming beaches. Lake cruises, boat charters and organised scenic tours of the region are all available; details from visitor centre.

Eagle Pt: a small fishing community set by Lake King. The Mitchell River empties here, where it forms curious silt jetties that stretch out into the distance. The town hosts the annual Australian Powerboat Racing Championships at Easter; 2 km NW. *Raymond Island:* Koala Reserve and Riviera Meadows, an animal farm that specialises in miniature breeds; the island is just east of Paynesville and can be accessed by a ferry that departs from the foreshore.

See also EAST GIPPSLAND, p. 159

Phillip Island

see Cowes

Port Albert

Pop. 253
Map ref. 583 I10

ℹ️ Old Courthouse, 9 Rodgers St, Yarram; (03) 5182 6553.

📻 100.7 FM ABC Local Radio, 104.7 Gippsland FM

Port Albert is a tranquil port on the south-east coast. Looking at this peaceful village now, it is hard to believe that it was the first established port in Victoria, with ships from Europe and America once docking at its jetty. Ships from China arrived here during the gold rush, bringing thousands of prospectors to the Gippsland goldfields. Still a commercial fishing port, the sheltered waters of Port Albert are popular with anglers and boat owners, which sees its population swell considerably during summer.

🏠 **Port Albert Hotel** This attractive old building has wide verandahs, and offers genuine country hospitality and a glimpse into the area's past. The hotel was first licensed in 1842, which makes it one of the oldest hotels in Victoria still operating. Wharf St.

Historic buildings: include original government offices and stores, and the Bank of Victoria, which now houses a maritime museum with photographs and relics from the town's past. Georgian and Victorian architectural styles are evident in over 40 buildings; Tarraville Rd. *Warren Curry Art:* a gallery featuring country-town streetscapes; Tarraville Rd.

🌿 *Fishing Contest:* Mar.

🍴 *Wildfish:* waterfront dining, freshest local seafood; 40 Wharf St; (03) 5183 2007.

Nooramunga Marine and Coastal Park Surrounding Port Albert and comprising the waters and sand islands offshore, this marine park is a fishing enthusiast's delight. Snapper, flathead and Australian salmon can be caught from the surf beaches or from a boat. The Aboriginal middens that dot the shorelines prove that fishing has been carried on here for many thousands of years. This park is an important reserve for migratory wading birds. Camping is allowed but permits must be obtained. Contact Parks Victoria on 13 1963.

Christ Church: built in 1856, this was the first church to be established in Gippsland; Tarraville; 5 km NE. *Beaches:* Manns, for swimming, 10 km NE; and Woodside, on Ninety Mile Beach, for good surfing, 34 km NE. Note that both beaches are patrolled during summer. *St Margaret Island:* a protected area featuring a wildlife sanctuary; 12 km E.

See also PHILLIP ISLAND & GIPPSLAND, p. 150

Port Campbell

Pop. 258
Map ref. 580 F10 | 593 I9

i 12 Apostles Visitor Information Centre, 26 Morris St; 1300 137 255; www.visit12apostles.com.au

103.7 3WAY-FM, 774 AM ABC Local Radio

This peaceful seaside resort – the base of a small crayfishing industry – is in the centre of Port Campbell National Park on the Great Ocean Road. The Twelve Apostles, one of Victoria's most famous attractions, can be found nearby.

Historical Museum: open Wed, Thurs and Sat; Lord St. *Fishing:* good from rocks and pier; boat charters available.

Market: Lord St; each Sun in summer and Easter.

Room Six Cafe Restaurant: Mediterranean- and Japanese-influenced menu; 28 Lord St; (03) 5598 6242. *The Craypot Bistro:* great-value food, seasonal crayfish; Port Campbell Hotel, 40 Lord St; (03) 5598 6320. *Timboon Railway Shed Distillery:* local-produce-driven menu; The Railway Yard, Bailey St, Timboon; (03) 5598 3555.

Daysy Hill Country Cottages: cottage, suite and cabin accommodation; 2585 Cobden–Port Campbell Rd; (03) 5598 6226. *Loch Ard Motor Inn:* motel rooms and apartments; 18–24 Lord St; (03) 5598 6328. *Sea Foam Villas:* stylish apartments; 14 Lord St; (03) 5598 6413.

Port Campbell National Park The park is a major attraction on the Great Ocean Rd, with magnificent rock formations jutting out into the ocean. Particularly impressive when viewed at dusk (when penguins can be seen) and dawn, the key coastal features are The Arch, 5 km W; London Bridge, 6 km W; Loch Ard Gorge, 7 km SE; and the world-famous Twelve Apostles, which begin 12 km SE of Port Campbell and stretch along the coast. Other notable features are The Grotto, Bay of Islands and Bay of Martyrs. There are walking tracks throughout the park, and the Historic Shipwreck Trail marks 25 sites along the coast between Moonlight Head and Port Fairy (sites are also popular with divers – a charter company is based in Port Campbell; details from visitor centre). For the ultimate view of this coastline, take an ever-popular scenic flight (details from visitor centre).

Mutton Bird Island: attracts short-tailed shearwaters, best viewed at dawn and dusk Sept–Apr; just off coast. *Great Ocean Walk:* between Apollo Bay and the Twelve Apostles. The 91 km walk

offers stunning views; walkers must register to use campgrounds en route; further information available at greatoceanwalk.com.au *Timboon:* a pretty town in the centre of a dairy district. Timboon Farmhouse Cheese offers tastings and sales of gourmet cheeses, while Timboon Railway Shed Distillery offers a variety of spirits. A scenic drive goes from Port Campbell to the town. It is also on one end of the Camperdown–Timboon (Crater to Coast) Rail Trail. Pick your own berries in season at nearby Berry World; 16 km N. *Otway Deer and Wildlife Park:* 19 km SE. *Gourmet Food and Wine Loop:* map from visitor centre.

See also SOUTH-WEST COAST, p. 153

Port Fairy

Pop. 2597
Map ref. 580 B8 | 592 F8

i Railway Place, Bank St; (03) 5568 2682; www.visitportfairy.com

103.7 3WAY-FM, 1602 AM ABC Local Radio

Port Fairy was once a centre for the whaling industry and one of the largest ports in Australia. Today many visitors are attracted to it for its charming old-world feel, its legacy of historic bluestone buildings, the small fleet of fishing boats that line the old wharf, and its great beach and lively atmosphere in summer. The town truly comes alive in March, when the Port Fairy Folk Festival is held. International folk and blues acts play, and tickets are best booked well in advance.

History Centre: displays relating to local history housed in the old courthouse; Gipps St. *Battery Hill:* old fort and signal station at the river mouth; end of Griffith St. *Port Fairy Wharf:* sales of fish and crayfish when in season. *Historic buildings:* many are National Trust–classified, including the splendid timber home of Captain Mills, Gipps St; Mott's Cottage, Sackville St; Caledonian Inn, Bank St; Seacombe House, Cox St; St John's Church of England, Regent St; and the Gazette Office, Sackville St.

Port Fairy Folk Festival: Mar. *Spring Music Festival:* Oct. *Moyneyana Festival:* family entertainment; Dec.

Merrijig Inn: innovative food using fresh produce; 1 Campbell St; (03) 5568 2324. *Portofino on Bank:* contemporary Mediterranean; 26 Bank St; (03) 5568 2251. *Saltra Brasserie:* modern Australian; 20 Bank St; (03) 5568 3058. *Time & Tide:* gallery-cum-cafe; 21 Thistle Pl; (03) 5568 2134.

Hearn's Beachside Villas: waterside spa villas; 13–17 Thistle Pl; (03) 5568 3150. *Merrijig Inn:* historic B&B rooms; 1 Campbell St; (03) 5568 2324. *Moyne Mill Townhouse:* riverside accommodation; Unit 4, 25 Gipps St; (03) 5568 2229. *Oscars Waterfront Boutique Hotel:* French Provincial–style rooms; 41B Gipps St; (03) 5568 3022.

Griffiths Island Connected to town by a causeway, this island is home to a large colony of short-tailed shearwaters. Each year they travel across the Pacific Ocean from North America to nest in the same burrows (Sept–Apr). Also on the island is a much-photographed lighthouse.

The Crags: rugged coastal rock formations; 12 km W. *Yambuk:* a small township centred on an old inn with Yambuk Lake, a popular recreation area, nearby; 17 km W. *Lady Julia Percy Island:* home to a fur seal colony; charters can be arranged from Port Fairy Wharf; 22 km off coast. *Codrington Wind Farm:* Victoria's first wind-power station; 27 km W. *Mahogany Walk to Warrnambool:* a 6–7 hr walk (one way, can return by bus) taking

VICTORIA

in a magnificent stretch of coastline; details from visitor centre. *Historic Shipwreck Trail:* between Port Fairy and Moonlight Head with 25 wreck sites signposted along the way.

See also SOUTH-WEST COAST, p. 153

Portland

Pop. 9824
Map ref. 592 D8

i Lee Breakwater Rd; (03) 5523 2671 or 1800 035 567; www.visitgreatoceanroad.org.au

96.9 AM ABC Local Radio, 99.3 Coastal FM

Portland is the most westerly of Victoria's major coastal towns and the only deep-water port between Melbourne and Adelaide. It was also the first permanent settlement in Victoria, founded in 1834 by the Hentys. The township, which features many National Trust–classified buildings, overlooks Portland Bay. The Kerrup–Tjmara people, who once numbered in the thousands, were the original inhabitants of the district and referred to it as 'Pulumbete' meaning 'Little Lake' – a reference to the scenic lake now known as Fawthorp Lagoon.

Portland Maritime Discovery Centre The centre features a 13 m sperm whale skeleton, and the lifeboat used to rescue 19 survivors from the *Admella* shipwreck in 1859. Another wreck, the *Regia*, is displayed in 2 m of water. The centre shares the building with the information centre. Lee Breakwater Rd.

Botanical Gardens: established in 1857, with both native and exotic plant life. A restored 1850s bluestone worker's cottage is within the grounds and open to the public; Cliff St. *Historical buildings:* more than 200 around town, many National Trust–classified. The best way to explore buildings such as the courthouse, Steam Packet Inn and Mac's Hotel is to take either a guided or self-guide walk; details from visitor centre. *History House:* a historical museum and family research centre in the old town hall; Charles St. *Burswood:* a bluestone, regency-style mansion that was once the home of pioneer settler Edward Henty. The house is set amid 5 ha of gardens; Cape Nelson Rd. *Fawthorp Lagoon:* prolific birdlife; Glenelg St. *Powerhouse Car Museum:* Percy St. *Watertower Lookout:* displays of WW II memorabilia on the way up the 133 steps to magnificent 360-degree views across Portland and the ocean, where whales and dolphins can sometimes be spotted; Percy St. Another good spot for whale-watching is Battery Hill.

Anzac Day Floral Display: Apr. *Portland Bay Festival:* Nov. *3 Bays Marathon:* Nov.

Clock by the Bay: contemporary Australian; Cnr Cliff and Bentinck sts; (03) 5523 4777. *Lido Larder:* modern cafe; 5 Julia St; (03) 5521 1741. *Bridgewater Bay Beach Cafe:* views and food worthy of detour; 1661 Bridgewater Rd, Cape Bridgewater; (03) 5526 7155.

Clifftop Accommodation Portland: 3 studio apartments; 13 Clifton Crt; (03) 5523 1126. *Sheoak Tinntean:* 2 studio apartments; 22 Cavendish St; (03) 5523 2296.

Cape Bridgewater This cape is home to a 650-strong colony of Australian fur seals. A 2 hr return walk leads to a viewing platform, or you can take a 45 min boat ride that leads into the mouth of a cave to see them up close (bookings essential, (03) 5526 7247). Across the cape towards Discovery Bay are the Petrified Forest and the Blowholes – spectacular during high seas. 21 km sw.

Lower Glenelg National Park The Glenelg River is a central feature of the park. It has cut an impressive 50 m deep gorge through a slab of limestone. Watch for platypus, water rats, moorhens and herons around the water's edge. Bushwalking, camping, fishing and canoeing are all popular, and Jones Lookout and the Bulley Ranges offer great views. Also in the park are the Princess Margaret Rose Caves on the north side of the river – you can drive there via Nelson or Dartmoor. Alternatively, boat tours operate from Nelson. Contact Parks Victoria on 13 1963; 44 km NW.

Cape Nelson: here a lighthouse perches on top of tall cliffs and lightstation tours are available; 11 km SW. *Narrawong State Forest:* a short walk leads to Whalers Pt, where Aboriginal people once watched for whales; 18 km NE. *Discovery Bay Coastal Park:* Cape Bridgewater is included in this park, though the majority of it is remote and relatively untouched. The Great South West Walk *(see below)* offers the best chance to take in the park's scenery. Behind Cape Bridgewater are the Bridgewater Lakes (19 km W) – popular for waterskiing and fishing. A walking track leads from here to the beach. *Mt Richmond National Park:* a 'mountain' formed by an extinct volcano. The area has abundant spring wildflowers and native fauna, including the elusive potoroo; 25 km NW. *Heywood:* home to the Bower Birds Nest Museum, and the Wood, Wine and Roses Festival in Feb. Budj Bim National Heritage Landscape, the traditional lands of the Gunditjmara people, is located here also. Visitors can experience the aquaculture system including stone eel traps, permanent stone houses and smoking trees; Budj Bim Tours (03) 5527 1699; 28 km N. *Nelson:* a charming hamlet near the mouth of the Glenelg River. There is good waterskiing in the area; 70 km NW. *Great South West Walk:* this epic 250 km walking trail takes in the full range of local scenery – the Glenelg River, Discovery and Bridgewater bays and Cape Nelson are some of the highlights. It is possible to do just small sections of the walk; maps and details from visitor centre.

See also SOUTH-WEST COAST, p. 153

Pyramid Hill

Pop. 467
Map ref. 559 I12 | 591 N6

i Loddon Visitor Information Centre, Wedderburn Community Centre, 24 Wilson St, Wedderburn; (03) 5494 3489; www.pyramidhill.net.au

91.1 FM ABC Local Radio, 104.7 Radio EMFM

Pyramid Hill's namesake is an unusually shaped, 187-metre-high hill. The town, which is located in a wheat-growing district about 30 kilometres from the New South Wales border, was a source of inspiration to notable Australian author Katherine Susannah Pritchard, who based a character in her book *Child of the Hurricane* on a woman she met while staying in Pyramid Hill during World War I.

Pyramid Hill A climb to the top of this eerily symmetrical hill reveals views of the surrounding irrigation and wheat district. There are abundant wildflowers in spring.

Historical Museum: features local story displays; open Sun afternoons or by appt; McKay St.

Terrick Terrick National Park The park is a large Murray pine forest reserve with granite outcrops, including Mitiamo Rock. There is a variety of good walking tracks, and the park is a key nesting area for the distinctive brolga. Contact Parks Victoria on 13 1963; access is via the Pyramid Hill–Kow Swamp Rd; 20 km SE.

Mt Hope: named by explorer Major Mitchell, who 'hoped' he would be able to spot the sea from the mountain's peak. Now known for its wildflowers; 16 km NE. *Boort:* nearby lakes provide a habitat for swans, ibis, pelicans and other waterbirds, and a place for watersports, fishing and picnics; 40 km W.

See also GOULBURN & MURRAY, p. 157

Queenscliff
Pop. 3892
Map ref. 570 A10 | 572 H9 | 574 E6 | 582 B7 | 593 P8

ⓘ 55 Hesse St; (03) 5258 4843; www.queenscliffe.vic.gov.au

 94.7 The Pulse FM, 774 AM ABC Local Radio

Queenscliff is a charming seaside town on the Bellarine Peninsula. It began life as a resort for wealthy Victorians in the 1800s, as testified by lavish buildings such as the Queenscliff Hotel, with its ornate lattice work and plush interiors. The town's wide main street is lined with cafes and restaurants, plus an array of art galleries, and the nearby beaches become a playground for holiday-makers during summer. A ferry runs between Queenscliff and Sorrento, a resort town across Port Phillip Bay.

Queenscliff Maritime Museum The museum explores the town's long association with ships and the sea through a collection of maritime memorabilia. It features a re-created fisherman's cottage, a diving-technology display and an array of navigational equipment. Weeroona Pde; (03) 5258 3440.

Marine Discovery Centre This is a great family destination where visitors can learn all about the local marine life. It has a number of aquariums and touch-tanks. The centre also runs various tours, including boat cruises off Port Phillip and 'rockpool rambles'. Adjacent to the Maritime Museum, Weeroona Pde; (03) 5258 3344.

The Blues Train An incredibly popular attraction that provides a unique dining and entertainment experience on board a steam train. Round trips provide 4 carriages, each with a different blues musician. Guests can change carriages at stops on the journey and purchase drinks from the mobile bar at each station platform. Operates Sat nights Oct–May. Departs from and returns to Queenscliff Railway Station; bookings at Ticketek on 132 849, or contact visitor centre for more information.

Fort Queenscliff: built during the Crimean War, it includes the unique 'Black Lighthouse'. Tours of the fort run most days; details from visitor centre. *Queenscliff Historical Museum:* open daily 2–4pm; Hesse St. *Bellarine Peninsula Railway:* beautifully restored steam trains run between Queenscliff and Drysdale. There are many engines on display around the station. Trains run Sun, public holidays and other times during school holidays; Symonds St. *Bellarine Rail Trail:* 32.5 km track that extends from South Geelong to Queenscliff; on reaching Drysdale it runs along the Bellarine Peninsula Railway and ends in the town.

Market: with crafts and second-hand goods; Princes Park, Gellibrand St; last Sun each month except winter. *Queenscliff Music Festival:* major event attracting local and international music acts; Nov.

Apostle Queenscliff: modern Australian; 79 Hesse St; (03) 5258 3097. *Athelstane House:* contemporary Australian; 4 Hobson St; (03) 5258 1024. *Vue Grand Hotel:* classic menu, impressive dining room; 46 Hesse Street; (03) 5258 1544.

Athelstane House: 8 rooms and 1 apartment; 4 Hobson St; (03) 5258 1024. *Lathamstowe:* B&B rooms, 3-bedroom cottage;

44 Gellibrand St; (03) 5258 4110. *Queenscliff Hotel:* vintage ensuite bedrooms; 16 Gellibrand St; (03) 5258 1066. *Vue Grand Hotel:* grand hotel rooms; 46 Hesse St; (03) 5258 1544.

 Pt Lonsdale This peaceful holiday town offers gorgeous beaches suitable for either surfing or swimming. A lookout from the cliff-top provides a great view of the treacherous entrance to Port Phillip known as 'The Rip'. A market is held here on the 2nd Sunday of each month. 6 km SW.

Lake Victoria: an important waterbird habitat; 7 km SW via Pt Lonsdale. *Harold Holt Marine Reserve:* incorporates Mud Island and coastal reserves. Guided boat tours can be arranged from the Marine Discovery Centre.

See also WERRIBEE & BELLARINE, p. 152

Robinvale
Pop. 2216
Map ref. 558 F7 | 589 J8

ⓘ Kyndalyn Park Information Centre, Bromley Rd; (03) 5026 1388; www.murrayriver.com.au/html/towns/robinvaleeuston.html

 90.7 HOTFM Sunraysia Community Radio

Robinvale is set on the New South Wales border by a pretty stretch of the Murray River. The Robinswood Homestead, built in 1926, was home to the town's founder, Herbert Cuttle (you can find the homestead in River Road). Herbert's son, Robin, was killed during World War I, so he named both the homestead and the town in Robin's honour. As another form of remembrance, the town has a sister city in France, near where young Robin died.

Rural Life Museum: housed in the information centre, with locally grown almonds for sale; open by appt; Bromley Rd. *Murray River:* the beaches around Robinvale are popular for picnics and fishing, while in the river waterskiing and swimming are favourite summer pastimes.

Ski Race: Mar. *Tennis Tournament:* Easter. *Almond Blossom Festival:* Aug.

Euston Weir and Lock on Murray: created as an irrigation water store, it features a 'fish ladder' that enables fish to jump over the weir. Picnic and barbecue facilities are provided; Pethard Rd, south-west edge of town. *Robinvale Organic and Bio-dynamic Wines:* tastings and sales of these distinctive, preservative-free wines. Also a children's playground; Sea Lake Rd; 5 km S. *Olive oil:* this region is renowned for its award-winning olive oil. Robinvale Estate offers farmgate sales and tastings; Tol Tol Rd; 8 km SE. There is also Boundary Bend Estate; Boundary Bend; Murray Valley Hwy; 1 km S of the Murray River. *Robinvale Indigenous Arts and Crafts:* learn about the local bush tucker; River Rd. *Hattah–Kulkyne National Park:* 66 km SW; *see Ouyen.*

See also MALLEE COUNTRY, p. 156

Rochester
Pop. 2827
Map ref. 584 C7

ⓘ Council offices, 43 Mackay St; (03) 5484 4500; www.rochester.org.au

 91.1 FM ABC Local Radio, 104.7 Radio EMFM

On the Campaspe River, near Echuca, Rochester is the centre of a rich dairying and tomato-growing area. There are several lakes and waterways near town, making Rochester a popular destination for freshwater fishing.

 RADIO STATIONS   IN TOWN   WHAT'S ON   WHERE TO EAT   WHERE TO STAY   NEARBY

VICTORIA

The 'Oppy' Museum The museum details the history of Sir Hubert Opperman, affectionately known as Oppy, a champion cyclist who competed in the Tour de France. There is a collection of memorabilia related to Oppy's career as a cyclist, as well as artefacts from the town's past. A statue of Oppy is opposite the museum. Moore St.

Heritage walk: take in the town's attractive old buildings. *Campaspe River Walk:* a pleasant, signposted walk by the river.

Kyabram Fauna Park This park, owned by the Kyabram community, is home to over 140 animal species – everything from wombats to waterfowl. It has been built from the ground up on a piece of degraded farmland, and is now heavily involved in breeding programs for endangered species such as the eastern barred bandicoot. There is a walk-through aviary and Australia's first energy-efficient reptile house. (03) 5852 2883; 35 km NE.

Campaspe Siphon: an impressive engineering feat, where the Waranga–Western Main irrigation channel was redirected under the Campaspe River; 5 km N. *Fishing:* nearby channels, rivers and lakes are popular with anglers for redfin and carp. Lakes include Greens Lake and Lake Cooper (14 km SE), also good for picnicking and watersports. *Elmore:* here is the Campaspe Run Rural Discovery Centre, which explains Koorie and colonial history and heritage. Elmore Field Days are held each Oct; 17 km S.

See also GOULBURN & MURRAY, p. 157

Rushworth

Pop. 1041
Map ref. 584 D8

i 33 High St; (03) 5856 1117; www.campaspe.vic.gov.au/community/rushworth/main.htm

97.7 FM ABC Local Radio, 98.5 FM 98.5

Situated in central Victoria off the Goulburn Valley Highway, this delightful little town was once a goldmining settlement. The original site of the township was known as Nuggetty owing to the numerous gold nuggets found during the 19th century. Rushworth has retained much of its original character, with well-preserved early buildings lining the main street.

Historic buildings: many along High St are National Trust–classified, including the Church of England, the Band Rotunda, the former Imperial Hotel, the Glasgow Buildings and the Whistle Stop. Take the High St Heritage Walk to see these and others; map from visitor centre. *History Museum:* housed in the old mechanics institute with displays relating to the town's goldmining heritage; Cnr High and Parker sts. *Growlers Hill Lookout Tower:* views of the town, Rushworth State Forest and the surrounding Goulburn Valley; Reed St.

Rushworth State Forest The largest natural ironbark forest in the world, Rushworth State Forest is also renowned for the orchids and wildflowers that blossom here in spring. Picnics and bushwalks are popular activities in this attractive reserve where over 100 species of birds, along with echidnas and kangaroos, can be seen. Access via Whroo Rd; 3 km S.

Jones's Eucalyptus Distillery: eucalyptus oil is extracted from blue mallee gum; Parramatta Gully Rd, just south of town. *Waranga Basin:* an artificial diversion of the Goulburn weir constructed in 1916, now a haven for boating, fishing, swimming and watersports; 6 km NE. *Whroo Historic Reserve:* Balaclava Hill, an open-cut goldmine, along with camping and picnic facilities, the Whroo cemetery and an Aboriginal waterhole; 7 km S. *Murchison:* a small town picturesquely set on the

Goulburn River. Town attractions include the Italian war memorial and chapel; Meteorite Park, the site of a meteorite fall in 1969; Longleat Winery; and Campbell's Bend Picnic Reserve; 19 km E. *Days Mill:* a flour mill with buildings dating from 1865; 39 km NE via Murchison. *Town ruins:* goldmining played a huge role in the development of this region, but not all towns survived the end of the gold rush. Ruins of Angustown, Bailieston and Graytown are all to the south of Rushworth.

See also GOULBURN & MURRAY, p. 157

Rutherglen

Pop. 1991
Map ref. 559 N12 | 585 J6 | 586 G1

i 57 Main St; (02) 6033 6300 or 1800 622 871; www.rutherglenvic.com

101.3 Oak FM, 106.5 FM ABC Local Radio

Rutherglen is the centre of one of the most important winegrowing districts in Victoria, with a cluster of vineyards surrounding the town. Many of the local wineries are best known for their fortified wines. Rutherglen's main street features preserved late-19th-century architecture.

Rutherglen Wine Experience: interpretive displays of Rutherglen's wine history; visitor centre, Main St. *Common School Museum:* local history displays and a re-creation of a Victorian-era schoolroom; behind Main St. *Historic tours:* take a self-guide walk, bike ride or drive, following maps provided at the visitor centre. *Lake King:* originally constructed in 1874 as Rutherglen's water storage, it is now a wildlife sanctuary and offers a scenic walk.

Tastes of Rutherglen: celebration of the region's gourmet food and wine; Mar. *Rutherglen and District Art Society Show:* Mar. *Easter in Rutherglen:* Easter. *Winery Walkabout:* June. *Country Fair:* June. *Wine Show:* Sept. *Tour de Rutherglen:* cycling and wine event; Oct. *Young Bloods and Bloody Legends:* food and wine event; Oct.

Beaumont's Cafe: contemporary fare; 84 Main St; (02) 6032 7428. *Vintara Winery, Brewery & Cafe:* modern menu matched to beers, wines; 105 Fraser Rd; 0447 327 517. *Pickled Sisters Cafe:* local produce cafe; Cofield Wines, Distillery Rd, Wahgunyah; (02) 6033 2377. *Terrace Restaurant:* regional vineyard menu; All Saints Estate, All Saints Rd, Wahgunyah; (02) 6035 2209.

Bank on Main: 2 B&B rooms; 80 Main St; (02) 6032 7000. *Ready Cottage B&B:* original 3-room family homestead; 92 High St; (02) 6032 7407. *The House at Mount Prior:* elegant rooms; 1194 Gooramadda Rd; (02) 6026 5256. *Vineyards at Tuileries:* spa units; 13–35 Drummond St; (02) 6032 9033.

Rutherglen Wine Region At many of the fantastic wineries in this region the appeal extends beyond cellar-door tastings and sales, such as at the All Saints Estate, 10 km NW, which features a National Trust–classified, castle-like building and a fine restaurant. A Day on the Green concert is held here in Feb. In the grounds of the Bullers Calliope Vineyard, 6 km W, is a bird park, with over 100 native and exotic species. Gehrig Estate, 21 km E, is Victoria's oldest continuously operating vineyard. It displays historic farming implements and has a charming restaurant.

Great Northern Mine: marked by mullock heaps associated with the first alluvial goldmine in the district. Historical details are provided on-site; Great Northern Rd, 5 km E. *Lake Moodemere:* found near the winery of the same name, the lake is popular for

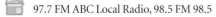

watersports and features ancient Aboriginal canoe trees by the shores; 8 km w. **Old customs house:** a relic from the time when a tax was payable on goods from NSW; 10 km NW.

See also HIGH COUNTRY, p. 158

St Arnaud

Pop. 2274
Map ref. 591 K9

 4 Napier St; (03) 5495 1268 or 1800 014 455.

91.1 FM ABC Local Radio, 99.1 Goldfields FM

A former goldmining town surrounded by forests and scenic hill country, St Arnaud is a service centre for the district's farming community, yet retains a peaceful rural atmosphere. The main street is lined with well-preserved historic buildings, many of which feature impressive ornate lacework. Together, these buildings form a nationally recognised historic streetscape.

 Self-guide historic tour: brochure available from visitor centre. **Queen Mary Gardens:** great spot for a picnic; Napier St. **Old Post Office:** now a B&B and restaurant; Napier St. **Police lock-up:** built in 1862; Jennings St.

Heritage Festival: Nov.

St Arnaud Range National Park The park protects an oasis of dense box-ironbark forest and woodland surrounded by agricultural land. Over 270 different species of native flora have been recorded here and provide a glimpse of what the area would have looked like before the land-clearing that occurred during and after the gold rush. Within the park are the Teddington Reservoirs, popular for brown trout and redfin fishing. The rugged terrain throughout provides a great opportunity for keen bushwalkers or 4WD enthusiasts. Wedge-tailed eagles can be seen soaring above the steep, forested ranges. Contact Parks Victoria on 13 1963; Sunraysia Hwy; 15 km s.

Great Grape Rd: wine-themed circuit through Stawell and Ballarat; details from visitor centre.

See also GOLDFIELDS, p. 154

Sale

Pop. 13 335
Map ref. 583 K7

 Wellington Visitors Information Centre, Princes Hwy; (03) 5144 1108 or 1800 677 520; www.tourismwellington.com.au

104.7 Gippsland FM, 828 AM ABC Local Radio

Situated by the Thomson River near the Latrobe River junction, Sale grew on the back of the gold rush and became Gippsland's first city in 1950. Although largely considered an industrial town, with the nearby Bass Strait oilfields providing a large part of the town's economy, Sale has a lot more to offer. The Port of Sale is being redeveloped and there are many good cafes and restaurants, and a number of fine-art galleries and craft outlets. The lakes near Sale are home to the unique Australian black swan – the bird that has become a symbol for the town.

Gippsland Arts Gallery The gallery promotes the work of artists and craftspeople in central Gippsland. Works range from traditional landscapes to visual statements on environmental and cultural issues, and may be in any medium from painting and photography to film and video. Foster St; (03) 5142 3372.

Lake Guthridge Parklands This major recreational area within Sale comprises the Lake Guthridge and Lake Guyatt precincts, the Sale Botanic Gardens and the Regional Aquatic Complex. The precinct showcases over 35 ha of historically significant botanic gardens, walking trails, Indigenous artworks and a contemporary fauna park. It also provides sensory gardens, abundant seating, an adventure playground for children and tennis courts. Foster St.

Historical Museum: local history memorabilia; Foster St. **Ramahyuck Aboriginal Corporation:** offers local arts and crafts and is part of the Bataluk Cultural Trail, which takes in sites of Aboriginal significance in the region; Foster St. **Historical buildings:** include Our Lady of Sion Convent in York St; Magistrates Court and Supreme Court, Foster St; St Paul's Anglican Cathedral featuring fine stained-glass windows, Cunninghame St; St Mary's Cathedral, Foster St. Bicentennial clock tower in the mall utilises the original bluestone base, ironwork and clock mechanisms; Raymond St. **RAAF base:** home of the famous Roulettes aerobatic team; Raglan St. **Sale Common and State Game Refuge:** protected wetland area with a boardwalk; south-east edge of town. **Textile art:** Sale is the home of internationally recognised textile artist Annemieke Mein. Her work is on permanent display in the foyer of the Port of Sale Civic Centre, ESSO BHP Billiton Wellington Entertainment Centre and St Mary's Cathedral; Foster St.

Sale Cup: Greenwattle Racecourse; Oct.

Bis Cucina: contemporary menu; 100 Foster St; (03) 5144 3388. **Il Nido:** modern Italian; 29 Desailly St; (03) 5144 4099. **Relish @ the Gallery:** modern cafe; Gippsland Art Gallery, 68–70 Foster St; (03) 5144 5044.

Minnies B&B: groovy 2-bedroom country house; 202 Gibsons Rd; (03) 5144 3344. **Quest Sale:** modern studios and apartments; 180–184 York St; (03) 5142 0900. **Frog Gully Cottages:** 2 contemporary cottages; Lot 2419 Rosedale Rd, Longford; (03) 5149 7242.

Holey Plains State Park The open eucalypt forests in this park are home to abundant wildlife, while swamps provide a habitat for many frog species. There is a good swimming lake, and a series of fascinating fossils can be seen nearby in a limestone quarry wall. Bushwalking, picnicking and camping are all popular activities, particularly around Harriers Swamp. Access from Princes Hwy; 14 km sw.

Fishing: good fishing for trout in the Avon River near Marlay Pt and also in the Macalister, Thomson and Latrobe rivers, especially at Swing Bridge; 5 km s. **Marlay Pt:** on the shores of Lake Wellington with boat-launching facilities provided. The yacht club here sponsors an overnight yacht race to Paynesville each Mar; 25 km E. **Seaspray:** a popular holiday spot on Ninety Mile Beach; offers excellent surfing and fishing; 32 km s. **Golden and Paradise beaches:** 2 more townships on Ninety Mile Beach with great surfing and fishing; 35 km SE. **Loch Sport:** set on Gippsland Lakes and popular for camping and fishing; 65 km SE. *For details on Gippsland Lakes see Lakes Entrance and Paynesville.* **Howitt Bike Trail:** 13-day round trip beginning and ending in Sale; details from visitor centre. **Bataluk Cultural Trail:** takes in sites of Indigenous significance from Sale to Cann River; brochure from visitor centre.

See also EAST GIPPSLAND, p. 159

VICTORIA

 RADIO STATIONS IN TOWN WHAT'S ON WHERE TO EAT WHERE TO STAY NEARBY

Seymour

Pop. 6062
Map ref. 584 D10

 Old Courthouse, Emily St; (03) 5799 0233.

 87.6 Seymour FM, 97.7 FM ABC Local Radio

Seymour is a commercial, industrial and agricultural town on the Goulburn River. The area was recommended for a military base by Lord Kitchener during his visit in 1909. Nearby Puckapunyal became an important training place for troops during World War II, and remains a major army base today.

Royal Hotel: featured in Russell Drysdale's famous 1941 painting *Moody's Pub*; Emily St. *Old Courthouse:* built in 1864, it now houses local art; Emily St. *Fine Art Gallery:* in the old post office; Emily St. *Goulburn River:* a walking track goes by the river and the Old Goulburn Bridge has been preserved as a historic relic. *Goulburn Park:* for picnics and swimming; Cnr Progress and Guild sts. *Seymour Railway Heritage Centre:* restored steam engines and carriages; open by appt; Railway Pl. *Australian Light Horse Memorial Park:* Goulburn Valley Hwy.

Market: Kings Park; 3rd Sat each month. *Alternative Farming Expo:* Feb. *Tastes of the Goulburn:* food and wine festival; Oct. *Seymour Cup:* Oct.

Plunkett Fowles Cellar Door and Cafe: local-produce-driven menu; Cnr Hume Hwy and Lambing Gully Rd, Avenel; (03) 5796 2150. *The Trough:* modern Australian; 2 Queen St, Avenel; (03) 5796 2122. *Trawool Shed Cafe:* slick contemporary cafe; 8447 Goulburn Valley Hwy, Trawool; (03) 5799 1595.

Rosehill Cottages: 2 cosy cottages; 8447 Goulburn Valley Hwy, Trawool; (03) 5799 1595. *Trawool Valley Resort:* picturesque country resort; 8150 Goulburn Valley Hwy, Trawool; (03) 5792 1444.

Tallarook State Forest Tallarook is a popular destination for bushwalking, camping, rock climbing and horseriding. The key features are Mt Hickey, the highest point in the park and the location of a fire-lookout tower, and Falls Creek Reservoir, a scenic picnic spot. Warragul Rocks offers great views over the Goulburn River. 10 km s.

Travellers note: Lookout from Warragul Rocks can only be accessed via private property. The landowner requests that any visitor contact him first to arrange access: Ron Milanovic, 0413 402 744.

Wineries: several in the area, including Somerset Crossing Vineyards, 2 km s; Plunkett Fowles, 21 km NE; Tahbilk, 26 km N; Mitchelton, 28 km N. *RAAC Memorial and Army Tank Museum:* Puckapunyal army base; 10 km w.

See also GOULBURN & MURRAY, p. 157

Shepparton

Pop. 44 598
Map ref. 584 E7

 534 Wyndham St; (03) 5831 4400 or 1800 808 839; www.greatershepparton.com.au

 97.7 FM ABC Local Radio, 98.5 FM

Shepparton has recently become a popular destination for conferences and sporting events, and so has plenty of modern accommodation and good restaurants in town. Indeed, Shepparton is a thriving city and is considered the 'capital' of the Goulburn Valley. It is home to many orchards irrigated by the Goulburn Irrigation Scheme.

Art Gallery: features Australian paintings and ceramics; Welsford St. *Bangerang Cultural Centre:* displays and dioramas on local Aboriginal culture; Parkside Dr. *Historical Museum:* in the Historical Precinct; open even-dated Sun afternoons; High St. *Emerald Bank Heritage Farm:* displays of 1930s farming methods; Goulburn Valley Hwy. *Victoria Park Lake:* scenic picnic spot; Tom Collins Dr. *Reedy Swamp Walk:* prolific birdlife; at the end of Wanganui Rd. *Moooving Art:* mobile interactive public art of life-size 3-D cow sculptures; various parks in Shepparton including Monash Park, Queens Gardens and Murchison riverbank. *Factory sales:* Pental Soaps and Campbells Soups.

Trash and treasure market: Melbourne Rd; each Sun. *Craft market:* Queens Gardens, Wyndham St; 3rd Sun each month. *International Dairy Week:* Jan. *Bush Market Day:* Feb. *Shepparton Fest:* major local arts festival with family entertainment; Mar. *Spring Car Nationals:* car competitions; Nov.

Bohjass: contemporary menu with tapas; Level 1, 276B Wyndham St; (03) 5822 0237. *Cellar 47 Restaurant & Wine Bar:* top regional restaurant; 166–170 High St; (03) 5831 1882. *Letizia's:* innovative cross-cultural menu; 67 Fryers St; (03) 5831 8822. *Teller:* modern Australian; 108 McLennan St, Mooroopna; (03) 5825 3344.

Central Shepparton Apartments: 2-bedroom serviced apartments; 507 Wyndham St; (03) 5821 4482. *The Carrington:* boutique and traditional motel accommodation; 505 Wyndham St; (03) 5821 3355. *The Churches:* beautifully renovated century-old church; Woodlands Estate Lavender, 325 Poplar Ave, Orrvale; (03) 5829 1019.

 SPC Ardmona KidsTown: a fun attraction with a maze, flying fox, enormous playground and miniature railway, and camel rides on the weekends; Midland Hwy; (03) 5831 4213; 3 km w. *Mooroopna:* a small town in the fruit-growing district. It hosts the Fruit Salad Day in Feb. SPC Ardmona also has a factory sales supermarket here; 5 km w. *Kialla:* Ross Patterson Gallery, with displays and sales of local artwork. Also here is Belstack Strawberry Farm, where you can pick your own berries; Goulburn Valley Hwy; 9 km s. *Tatura:* a museum with displays on local WW II internment camps. Taste of Tatura is held each Mar; 17 km sw. *Wunghnu:* the town (pronounced 'one ewe') is centred on the well-known Institute Tavern in the restored mechanics institute building. A tractor-pull festival is held each Easter; 32 km N.

See also GOULBURN & MURRAY, p. 157

Stawell

Pop. 5879
Map ref. 591 I11 | 593 I1

 Stawell and Grampians Visitor Information Centre, 50–52 Western Hwy; (03) 5358 2314 or 1800 330 080.

 96.5 Triple H FM, 594 AM ABC Local Radio

Pastoral runs were established in the Stawell region in the 1840s, but it was the discovery of gold in 1853 by a shepherd at nearby Pleasant Creek that was the catalyst for creating a town. Stawell remains a goldmining centre with Victoria's largest mine. However, it is actually better known as the home of the Stawell Gift, Australia's richest footrace, and the gateway to the Grampians.

 Stawell Gift Hall of Fame Museum In 1878 the Stawell Athletic Club was formed by local farmers and businessmen who were keen to have a sports day each Easter. The club put up the prize pool of £110, and the race was on. The annual Stawell Gift has run almost continuously since and is now one of the most prestigious races in the world. The race has been run at Central

SORRENTO

Pop. 1530

Map ref. 570 B11 | 572 H9 | 574 F7 | 593 P8

[POINT KING]

ℹ️ Mornington Peninsula Visitor Information Centre, 359B Pt Nepean Rd, Dromana; (03) 5987 3078 or 1800 804 009.

📻 98.7 3RPP FM, 774 AM ABC Local Radio

Just inside Port Phillip Heads on the Mornington Peninsula, in 1803 Sorrento was the site of Victoria's first European settlement. The town is close to historic Point Nepean and major surf and bayside beaches. Its population swells significantly over summer as visitors flock to soak up the holiday-resort atmosphere. A ferry links Sorrento to Queenscliff on the Bellarine Peninsula.

🏠 **Collins Settlement Historic Site:** marks the state's first European settlement and includes early graves; on Sullivan Bay. **Historic buildings:** include Sorrento Hotel on Hotham Rd and Continental Hotel on Ocean Beach Rd. Both are fine examples of early Victorian architecture, with the latter reputed to be the largest limestone building in the Southern Hemisphere; the visitor centre can give details of self-guide historical walks. **Nepean Historical Society Museum and Heritage Gallery:** a collection of local artefacts and memorabilia in the National Trust–classified mechanics institute. Adjacent is Watt's Cottage and the Pioneer Memorial Garden; Melbourne Rd. **Dolphin and seal cruises:** depart from the pier; not in winter months.

🌴 **Craft market:** primary school, cnr Kerferd and Coppin rds; last Sat each month. **Street Festival:** Oct.

🍴 **Acquolina:** Italian trattoria; 26 Ocean Beach Rd; (03) 5984 0811. **Loquat Restaurant & Bar:** modern Mediterranean; 3183 Point Nepean Rd; (03) 5984 4444. **Smokehouse Sorrento:** pizzas and Mediterranean fare; 182 Ocean Beach Rd; (03) 5984 1246. **The Baths:** iconic beachside eatery; 3278 Point Nepean Rd; (03) 5984 1500.

🛏️ **Oceanic Sorrento:** original guesthouse and new apartments; 231 Ocean Beach Rd; (03) 5984 4166. **Sorrento Beach Motel:** beach-style studios; 780 Melbourne Rd; (03) 5984 1356. **Aquabelle Apartments:** 3 architect-designed apartments; Level 1, 2331–2335 Point Nepean Rd, Rye; 1300 880 319. **Lakeside Villas at Crittenden Estate:** 3 contemporary villas; Crittenden Estate, Harrisons Rd, Dromana; (03) 5987 3275. **Peppers Moonah Links Resort:** modern golf resort; 55 Peter Thomson Dr, Fingal; 5988 2000.

⊚ **Mornington Peninsula National Park** The park incorporates Sorrento, Rye and Portsea back beaches and stretches south-east to Cape Schanck and beyond (see Flinders). Walks, picnics and swimming are the main attractions, but there is also the unique rock formation of London Bridge, at Portsea. The rugged coastline offers good surfing. Pt Nepean and historic Fort Nepean can be accessed by a daily transport service departing from Portsea. A former Quarantine Station on Pt Nepean has recently been opened to the public (after being closed for 150 years) and offers a self-guide walking tour through the Boiler House. Walking tracks also link up with other attractions like London Bridge. Contact Parks Victoria on 13 1963.

Portsea: an opulent holiday town with good, safe swimming beaches. It hosts the Portsea Swim Classic each Jan; 4 km NW. **Popes Eye Marine Reserve:** an artificially created horseshoe-shaped island and reef, now a popular spot for diving. Gannets nest here. Cruises available; details from visitor centre; 5 km offshore at Portsea. **Rye:** a beachside holiday spot with horseriding trips on offer and the annual Beach Sand Sculpting Championship each Feb; 8 km E. **Peninsula Hot Springs:** relaxing, outdoor, naturally heated pools. Private mineral pools, baths and massage therapies available; Springs La, Rye. **Moonah Links Golf Course:** 2 fantastic 18-hole golf courses, one designed specifically for the Australian Open; Peter Thompson Dr, Fingal. **Rosebud:** a bayside resort town with gorgeous, safe swimming beaches. Summer fishing trips depart from Rosebud pier. A film festival is held here each Nov; 15 km E. **McCrae Homestead:** National Trust–classified drop-slab property built in 1844; open afternoons; McCrae; 17 km E.

See also **MORNINGTON PENINSULA, p. 149**

VICTORIA

Park since 1898. Visit the museum to discover the glory and heartbreak of the race since its inception. Open 9–11am Mon–Fri; Main St; (03) 5358 1326.

Big Hill Lookout and Stawell Gold Mine viewing area: the Pioneers Lookout at the summit of this local landmark presents magnificent 360-degree views of the surrounding area. Continue down Reefs Rd to Stawell Gold Mine viewing area to hear about the daily operations of Victoria's largest gold-producing mine. ***Casper's Mini World:*** miniature tourist park with working models of famous world attractions such as the Eiffel Tower and including dioramas and commentaries; London Rd. ***Fraser Park:*** displays of mining equipment; Main St. ***Pleasant Creek Court House Museum:*** local history memorabilia; Western Hwy. ***Stawell Ironbark Forest:*** spring wildflowers, including rare orchids; northern outskirts of town, off Newington Rd.

SES Market: Drill Hall, Sloane St; 1st Sun each month. ***Farmer's Market:*** Harness Racing Club, Patrick St; last Sun each month. ***Stawell Gift:*** Easter.

Bunjil's Shelter This is Victoria's most important Aboriginal rock-art site. It depicts the creator figure, Bunjil, sitting inside a small alcove with his 2 dingoes. Bunjil created the geographical features of the land, and then created people, before disappearing into the sky to look down on the earth as a star. The site is thought to have been used for ceremonies by the local Djab Wurrung and Jardwadjali people. Off Pomonal Rd; 11 km s.

The Sisters Rocks: huge granite tors; beside Western Hwy; 3 km SE. ***Great Western:*** picturesque wine village with Seppelt Great Western Winery, est. 1865, featuring National Trust–classified underground tunnels of cellars and Champagne Picnic Races in Jan; 16 km SE. ***Tottington Woolshed:*** rare example of a 19th-century woolshed; road to St Arnaud; 55 km NE. ***Great Grape Rd:*** circuit through Ballarat and St Arnaud, stopping at wineries; details from visitor centre.

See also GRAMPIANS & CENTRAL WEST, p. 155

Swan Hill

Pop. 9684
Map ref. 558 G9 | 589 M12 | 591 L2

ⓘ Swan Hill Region Information Centre, cnr McCrae and Curlewis sts; (03) 5032 3033 or 1800 625 373; www.swanhillonline.com

99.1 Smart FM, 102.1 FM ABC Local Radio

In 1836, explorer Thomas Mitchell named this spot Swan Hill because of the black swans that kept him awake all night. The town's swans remain, but there are many other attractions in this pleasant city on the Murray Valley Highway.

Swan Hill Pioneer Settlement This museum re-creates the Murray and Mallee regions from the 1830s to the 1930s. There are barber shops and chemists, and rides available on the PS *Pyap* or horse-drawn carts. There is also the Sound and Light Tour; bookings required. End of Gray St on Little Murray River.

Swan Hill Regional Art Gallery: an impressive permanent collection plus touring exhibitions; opposite the Pioneer Settlement Museum.

Market: Curlewis St; 3rd Sun each month. ***Racing Cup Carnival:*** June. ***Australian Inland Wine Show:*** Oct.

Carriages Restaurant: hospitality students prepare international menu; 423 Campbell St; (03) 5033 2796. ***Java Spice:*** South-East Asian; 17 Beveridge St; (03) 5033 0511.

Quo Vadis: Italian restaurant and pizza parlour; 255–259 Campbell St; (03) 5032 4408. ***Yutaka Sawa:*** Japanese; 107 Campbell St; (03) 5032 3515.

BIG 4 Swan Hill: holiday park cabins; 186 Murray Valley Hwy; (03) 5032 4372 or 1800 990 389. ***Best's Riverbed and Breakfast:*** 5 in-house rooms; 7 Kidman Reid Dr, Murray Downs; (03) 5032 2126. ***Burrabliss B&B:*** B&B and self-catering options; 169 Lakeside Dr, Lake Boga; (03) 5037 2527. ***Murray Downs Resort:*** hotel rooms and apartments; Lot 5 Murray Downs Dr, Murray Downs; (03) 5033 1966 or 1800 807 574.

 Swan Hill Wine Region The region, which starts around Tresco to the south-east and ends around Piangil to the north-west, takes advantage of the Murray River and the Mediterranean-style climate. The first vines were planted here in 1930, but the proliferation of vineyards really began when Sicilian immigrants arrived on the Murray after WW II. Today cellar doors offer tastings and sales of predominantly shiraz, colombard and chardonnay varieties. Winery map from visitor centre.

Lake Boga The town has an interesting history as an RAAF flying-boat repair depot during WW II. The depot serviced over 400 flying boats, one of which can be seen at the Flying Boat Museum. The underground museum is in the original communications bunker in Willakool Dr. At Lake Boga, the water mass is popular for watersports, fishing and camping, and is home to a variety of bird species that can be seen on the various walks. A yachting regatta is held here each Easter. 17 km SE.

Lakeside Nursery and Gardens: over 300 varieties of roses; 10 km NW. ***Tyntyndyer Homestead:*** built in 1846; open Tues and Thurs 10am–4pm or by appt; Murray Valley Hwy; 20 km NW. ***Nyah:*** good market with local produce; 2nd Sat each month; 27 km NW. ***Tooleybuc:*** situated in NSW, it has a tranquil riverside feel and good fishing, picnicking and riverside walks. The Bridgekeepers Cottage has sales and displays of dolls and crafts; 46 km N.

See also MALLEE COUNTRY, p. 156

Tallangatta

Pop. 955
Map ref. 585 L7 | 587 K3

ⓘ 50 Hanson St, Corryong; (02) 6076 2277; www.pureuppermurrayvalleys.com

101.3 Oak FM, 106.5 FM ABC Local Radio

When the old town of Tallangatta was going to be submerged in 1956 after the level of the Hume Weir was raised, the residents simply moved the entire township 8 kilometres west. Tallangatta now has an attractive lakeside location and sits directly north of Victoria's beautiful alpine region.

The Hub: local art and craft, and Lord's Hut, the only remaining slab hut in the district; Towong St.

Farm and Water Festival: Apr. ***Fifties Festival:*** Oct. ***Garage Sale Festival:*** Oct.

Lake Hume Tallangatta is on the shores of this enormous and attractive lake, formed when the then largest weir in the Southern Hemisphere was constructed. It is now a picturesque spot for swimming, waterskiing, windsurfing and fishing. The foreshore reserves are perfect for barbecues.

Eskdale: craft shops, and trout fishing in the Mitta Mitta River; 33 km s. ***Lake Dartmouth:*** great for trout fishing and boating; hosts the Dartmouth Cup Fishing Competition over the June long weekend. Also here is The Witches Garden featuring unique medicinal plants; 58 km SE. *Mitta Mitta:* remnants of a large open-cut goldmine. Also a gallery, Butcher's Hook Antiques and Bharatralia Jungle Camp. Hosts the Mitta Muster on Sun on the long weekend in Mar; 60 km S. *Australian Alps Walking Track:* passes over Mt Wills; 108 km S via Mitta Mitta. *Scenic drives:* to Cravensville, to Mitta Mitta along Omeo Hwy and to Tawonga and Mount Beauty.

See also HIGH COUNTRY, p. 158

Terang
Pop. 1830
286 C4 | 288 C4

i Old Courthouse, 22 High St; (03) 5592 1984.

103.7 3WAY-FM, 774 AM ABC Local Radio

Terang is in a fertile dairy-farming district. It is a well-laid-out town with grand avenues of deciduous trees, and is known throughout the state for its horseracing carnivals.

Cottage Crafts Shop: in the old courthouse on High St. *District Historical Museum:* old railway station and memorabilia; open 3rd Sun each month; Princes Hwy. *Lions Walking Track:* 4.8 km, beside dry lake beds and majestic old trees; begins behind Civic Centre on High St. *Historic buildings:* many examples of early-20th-century commercial architecture. A Gothic-style Presbyterian church is in High St.

Terang Cup: Nov.

Demo Dairy: demonstrates dairy-farming practices; Princes Hwy, 4 km W. *Lake Keilambete:* 2.5 times saltier than the sea and reputed to have therapeutic properties; must obtain permission to visit as it is surrounded by private land; 4 km NW. *Model Barn Australia:* collection of model cars, boats and planes; open by appt; Robertson Rd; 5 km E. *Noorat:* birthplace of Alan Marshall, author of *I Can Jump Puddles.* The Alan Marshall Walking Track here involves a gentle climb to the summit of Mt Noorat, an extinct volcano, with excellent views of the crater, the surrounding district and the Grampians; 6 km N.

See also SOUTH-WEST COAST, p. 153

Torquay
Pop. 9848
Map ref. 572 F9 | 574 A7 | 580 G2 | 593 N8

i Surfworld Australia, Surf City Plaza, cnr Surfcoast Hwy and Beach Rd; (03) 5261 4219 or 1300 614 219; www.visitsurfcoast.com

94.7 The Pulse FM, 774 AM ABC Local Radio

Torquay was one of the first resort towns on Victoria's coast, and remains one of the most popular today. It was named in honour of the famous English resort, but its heritage is very different. Not only does Torquay and its coast have some of the best surf beaches in the world, it was also the birthplace of world leaders in surfboards, wetsuits and other apparel, including Rip Curl and Quiksilver, founded here in the 1960s and 70s.

Surf City Plaza This modern plaza houses some of the biggest names in surfing retail alongside smaller outlets. The complex boasts the world's biggest surfing museum, Surfworld. See how board technology has developed over the last century, find out exactly what makes a good wave, and learn about the history of surfing at Bells Beach. A theatre here screens classic 1960s and 70s surf flicks and the latest surf videos. Beach Rd.

Fishermans Beach: good spot for fishing, with a sheltered swimming beach and a large sundial on the foreshore. *Tiger Moth World:* theme park based around the1930s Tiger Moth biplane. Joy-flights available; Blackgate Rd. *Surf schools:* programs available to suit all abilities, with many courses run during summer school holidays; details from visitor centre.

Cowrie Community Market: foreshore; 3rd Sun each month Sept–Apr. *Danger 1000 Ocean Swim:* Jan. *Surf for Life Surfing Contest:* Jan. *Kustom Jetty Surf Pro:* Jan. *Rip Curl Pro:* Easter. *Hightide Festival:* fireworks display; Dec.

Growlers: cafe-bar and restaurant; 23 The Esplanade; (03) 5264 8455. *Scorched:* modern Australian; 17 The Esplanade; (03) 5261 6142. *The Surf Rider:* modern fusion menu; 26 Bell St; (03) 5261 6477. *Sunnybrae Restaurant and Cooking School:* regionally inspired weekend lunches; Cnr Cape Otway and Lorne rds, Birregurra; (03) 5236 2276.

Crowne Plaza Torquay: beachfront rooms and apartments; 100 The Esplanade; (03) 5261 1500 or 1800 007 697. *Peppers The Sands Resort:* golf resort; 2 Sands Blvd; (03) 5264 3333.

Surf coast It is no wonder the coast that runs from Torquay through to Eastern View (past Anglesea) has dubbed itself the Surf Coast. Submerged reefs cause huge waves that are a surfer's paradise. Most famous is Bells Beach, around 5 km SW of Torquay. The clay cliffs provide a natural amphitheatre for one of the best surf beaches in the world and the longest running surf competition, the Rip Curl Pro, which started in 1973 and attracts top competitors. Other good surf beaches include Jan Juc, Anglesea and Fairhaven. To see the coast on foot, take the 30 km Surf Coast Walk, starting at Torquay and travelling south to Moggs Creek.

Hinterland: delightful towns like Bellbrae, Deans Marsh and Birregurra are dotted along the vista of the Surf Coast hinterland; starts 8 km W. *Bicycle lane:* runs along Surfcoast Hwy from Grovedale to Anglesea.

See also SOUTH-WEST COAST, p. 153

Traralgon
Pop. 21 960
Map ref. 583 I7

i Latrobe Visitor Information Centre, The Old Church, Southside Central, Princes Hwy; 1800 621 409; www.visitlatrobevalley.com

100.7 FM ABC Local Radio, 104.7 Gippsland FM

Traralgon is one of the Latrobe Valley's largest towns; a commerical hub located on the main Gippsland rail and road routes. Primarily a service centre for neighbouring agricultural communities, timber and electricity production, it also retains a certain village atmosphere with historic buildings in its wide streets and attractive public gardens.

Historic buildings: include the old post office and courthouse; Cnr Franklin and Kay sts. *Victory Park:* a great spot for picnics. Also here is a band rotunda and miniature railway; Princes Hwy.

Farmers market: 4th Sat each month. *International Junior Tennis Championships:* Jan. *Traralgon Cup:* Nov.

Cafe Aura: cafe-deli-cum-restaurant; Shop 3, 19–25 Seymour St; (03) 5174 1517. *Iimis Cafe:* good Mediterranean/Greek; 28 Seymour St; (03) 5174 4577. *Neilsons:* contemporary

Australian; 13 Seymour St; (03) 5175 0100. *Terrace Cafe:* modern fare; Century Inn, 5 Airfield Rd; (03) 5173 9400.

Walhalla Mountain Rivers Trail: this scenic drive (Tourist Route 91) winds through pretty hills to the north of town. *Loy Yang power station:* tours available; 5 km s. *Toongabbie:* a small town that hosts the Festival of Roses each Nov; 19 km NE. *Hazelwood Cooling Pond:* year-round warm water makes this a popular swimming spot; outskirts of Churchill; 20 km SW. *Tarra–Bulga National Park:* temperate rainforest; 30 km s.

See also PHILLIP ISLAND & GIPPSLAND, p. 150

Walhalla

Pop. 15
Map ref. 583 I5

i Latrobe Visitor Information Centre, The Old Church, Southside Central, Princes Hwy, Traralgon; 1800 621 409.

100.7 FM ABC Local Radio, 104.7 Gippsland FM

This tiny goldmining town is tucked away in dense mountain country in Gippsland – in a steep, narrow valley with sides so sheer that some cemetery graves were dug lengthways into the hillside. The town has a tiny population and is a relic from a long-gone era – it was only connected to electricity in 1998.

Long Tunnel Gold Mine One of the most prosperous goldmines in the state during the 19th century with over 13 tonnes of gold extracted here. Guided tours take visitors through sites such as Cohen's reef and the original machinery chamber 150 m below the ground. Tours operate daily at 1.30pm; Main St.

Historic buildings and goldmining remains: include the old post office, bakery and Windsor House, now a B&B. *Walks:* excellent walks in the town area, including one to a cricket ground on top of a 200 m hill. Another walk leads to a historic cemetery with graves of early miners; details from visitor centre. *Old Fire Station:* with hand-operated fire engines and firefighting memorabilia; open weekends and public holidays. *Museum and Corner Store:* local history displays plus goldmining artefacts; Main St. *Walhalla Goldfields Railway:* wonderfully restored old steam engine; departs from Thomson Station on Wed, Sat, Sun and public holidays. *Gold panning:* try your luck along pretty Stringers Creek, which runs through town. *Ghost tours:* spook yourself with a night-time guided ghost tour of Walhalla using old-fashioned lanterns; details from visitor centre.

Parker's Restaurant: contemporary hotel dining room; Walhalla's Star Hotel, Main Rd; (03) 5165 6262.

Walhalla's Star Hotel: modern hotel suites; Main Rd; (03) 5165 6262.

Deloraine Gardens: terraced gardens; just north of town. *Thomson River:* excellent fishing and canoeing; 4 km s. *Rawson:* a town built to accommodate those who helped construct the nearby Thomson Dam. Mountain trail-rides are available; 8 km SW. *Erica:* visit this small timber town to see a timber-industry display at the Erica Hotel. The King of the Mountain Woodchop is held in town each Jan; 12 km SW. *Baw Baw National Park:* park areas accessible from Walhalla include the Aberfeldy River picnic and camping area; 12 km N. *See Moe. Moondarra State Park:* great for walks and picnics. Moondarra Reservoir is nearby; 30 km s. *4WD tours:* to gold-era 'suburbs' such as Coopers Creek and Erica. Tours can be organised through Mountain Top Experience, (03) 5134 6876. *Australian Alps Walking Track:* starts at Walhalla and goes for an incredible 655 km. It can be done in sections; details from visitor centre.

See also PHILLIP ISLAND & GIPPSLAND, p. 150

Wangaratta

Pop. 16 846
Map ref. 585 I7 | 586 F4

i 100 Murphy St; 1800 801 065; www.visitwangaratta.com.au

101.3 Oak FM, 106.5 FM ABC Local Radio

Wangaratta lies in a rich agricultural district in north-eastern Victoria that produces a diverse range of crops including kiwifruit, wine grapes, walnuts and wheat. An entry for both the Murray to the Mountains Rail Trail and the Great Alpine Road, it offers the services of a rural city while retaining a country-town warmth. A short drive in any direction will lead to world-class wineries, gourmet food and some spectacular views.

Self-guide historical walk: historic sites and buildings, such as the majestic Holy Trinity cathedral, Vine Hotel Cellar Museum and the Wangaratta Historical Museum; details from visitor centre. *Wangaratta Cemetery:* headless body of infamous bushranger Daniel 'Mad Dog' Morgan is buried here; Tone Rd. *Wangaratta Exhibitions Gallery:* changing exhibitions by national and regional artists; Ovens St. *Brucks Textile Factory:* a factory outlet for Sheridan sheets; Sicily Ave. *Australian Country Spinners:* an outlet for local wool products; Textile Ave.

Wangaratta Trash and Treasure Market: Olympic Swimming Pool carpark, Swan St; each Sun. *Wangaratta Stitched Up Festival:* textile displays; June/July. *Wangaratta Show:* agricultural show; Oct. *Festival of Jazz:* well-known jazz festival; Oct/Nov.

Quality Hotel Wangaratta Gateway: imaginative dining room; 29–37 Ryley St; (03) 5721 8399. *Rinaldo's:* Italian; 8–10 Tone Rd; (03) 5721 8800. *Tread:* tapas-style menu; 56–58 Faithful St; (03) 5721 4635.

King River Stables: 3 bedrooms, sleeps 8; 170 Oxley Flats Rd; (03) 5721 8195. *Quality Hotel Wangaratta Gateway:* refurbished suites and apartments; 29–37 Ryley St; (03) 5721 8399.

Warby Range State Park The steep ranges of the 'Warbys', as they are known locally, provide excellent viewing points, especially from Ryan's Lookout. Other lookouts include the Pangarang Lookout, near Pine Gully Picnic Area, and Mt Glenrowan Lookout, the highest point of the Warbys at 513 m. There are well-marked tracks for bushwalkers and a variety of pleasant picnic spots amid open forests and woodlands, with wildflowers blossoming during the warmer months. 12 km W.

Eldorado Eldorado is a fascinating old goldmining township named after the mythical city of gold. The main relic of the gold era is a huge dredge, the largest in the Southern Hemisphere, which was built in 1936. There is a walking track with information boards around the lake where the dredge now sits. The Eldorado Museum provides details of the town's mining past, alongside WW II relics and a gemstone collection. 20 km NE.

Wombi Toys: old-fashioned, handmade toys for sale; Whorouly; 25 km SE. *Reids Creek:* popular with anglers, gem fossickers and gold panners; near Beechworth; 28 km E. *Newton's Prickle Berry Farm:* pick your own blackberries and buy organic berry jams; Whitfield; 45 km s. *Scenic drives:* one goes for 307 km along the Great Alpine Rd through the alps to Bairnsdale. The road south leads through the beautiful King Valley and to Paradise Falls. A network of minor roads allows you to fully explore the area, including a number of tiny, unspoiled townships such as Whitfield, Cheshunt and Carboor. *Murray to the Mountains Rail Trail:* following historical railway lines with 94 km of bitumen sealed track, the trail ventures into pine forests, natural bushland and open valleys. It links several townships. Suitable for both cycling and walking; a gentle gradient makes the track appropriate for all ages and levels of fitness.

See also HIGH COUNTRY, p. 158

Warburton

Pop. 1949
Map ref. 571 F8 | 573 M5 | 582 F4

 Water Wheel Visitor and Information Centre, 3400 Warburton Hwy; (03) 5966 9600; www.warburtononline.com

99.1 Yarra Valley FM, 774 AM ABC Local Radio

Warburton was established when gold was discovered in the 1880s, but its picturesque location and proximity to Melbourne meant it quickly became a popular tourist town, with many guesthouses built over the years. There are fine cafes and antique and craft shops in town.

Information Centre: local history display and an old-style, operating water wheel, 6 m in diameter. A wood-fired bakery is adjacent to the centre; Warburton Hwy. *River Walk:* 9 km return walk, following a pretty stretch of the Yarra River; starts at Signs Bridge on Warburton Hwy. *Upper Yarra Arts Centre:* cinema with regular screenings and a variety of live performances held during the year; Warburton Hwy. *Warburton Golf Course:* with great views across the river valley; Dammans Rd. *O'Shannassy Aqueduct Trail:* good walking and cycling track that follows the historic open channelled aqueduct; details from visitor centre.

Film Festival: Upper Yarra Arts Centre; June. *Winterfest:* wood festival; July.

Wild Thyme: bohemian cafe for music lovers; 3391 Warburton Hwy; (03) 5966 5050. *Bulong Estate Winery & Restaurant:* modern French menu; 70 Summerhill Rd, Yarra Junction; (03) 5967 1358.

Charnwood Cottages: 3 luxurious country cottages; 2 Wellington Rd; (03) 5966 2526. *Forget Me Not Cottages:* cottages and apartment for couples; 18 Brett Rd; (03) 5966 5805. *3 Kings B&B:* contemporary apartments; 2482 Warburton Hwy, Yarra Junction; 0409 678 046.

Yarra Ranges National Park Here, tall mountain ash trees give way to pockets of cool temperate rainforest. Mt Donna Buang, a popular daytrip destination – especially during winter, when it is often snow-covered – is 17 km NW of Warburton. The Rainforest Gallery on the southern slopes of the mountain features a treetop viewing platform and walkway. Night walk tours here reveal some of Victoria's unique nocturnal creatures. Acheron Way is a scenic 37 km drive north through the park to Marysville. Along the way are views of Mt Victoria and Ben Cairn. Drive starts 1 km E of town.

Yarra Centre: indoor sports and swimming; Yarra Junction, Warburton Hwy; 9 km SW. *Yarra Junction Historical Museum:* local history displays; open 1–5pm Sun or by appt; Warburton Hwy; 10 km SW. *Upper Yarra Reservoir:* picnic and camping facilities; 23 km NE. *Walk into History:* takes in the goldmining and timber region from Warburton East to Powelltown (25 km s); details from visitor centre. *Ada Tree:* a giant mountain ash over 300 years old; access from Powelltown. *Yellingbo State Fauna Reserve:* good for nature spotting. Home to the helmeted honeyeater, a state emblem; 25 km SW. *Vineyards:* several in the region, many with tastings and sales. They include the Yarra Burn Winery, the Five Oaks Vineyard and the Brahams Creek Winery. *Rail trails:* former railway tracks now used for walking, bikeriding or horseriding, the main one being the Lilydale to Warburton trail; details from visitor centre.

See also YARRA & DANDENONGS, p. 148

Warracknabeal

Pop. 2491
Map ref. 558 E12 | 590 H7

 119 Scott St; (03) 5398 1632; www.wag.wimmera.com.au

96.5 Triple H FM, 594 AM ABC Local Radio

The town's Aboriginal name means 'the place of the big red gums shading the watercourse', a name that is both beautifully descriptive and accurate, especially for the part of town around Yarriambiack Creek. Warracknabeal is a major service town at the centre of a wheat-growing district.

Historical Centre: includes a pharmaceutical collection, clocks, and antique furnishings of child's nursery; open afternoons; Scott St. *Black Arrow Tour:* a self-guide driving tour of historic buildings. *Walks:* including the Yarriambiack Creek Walk; details from visitor centre. *National Trust–classified buildings:* include the post office, the Warracknabeal Hotel and the original log-built town lock-up. *Lions Park:* by the pleasant Yarriambiack Creek with picnic spots and a flora and fauna park; Craig Ave.

Y-Fest: golf, horseracing, machinery and country music; Easter.

North Western Agricultural Machinery Museum: displays of farm machinery from the last 100 years; Henty Hwy; 3 km s.

See also GRAMPIANS & CENTRAL WEST, p. 155

Warragul

Pop. 11 501
Map ref. 573 N9 | 582 G6

 Gippsland Food and Wine, 123 Princes Hwy, Yarragon; 1300 133 309; www.bawbawcountry.com.au

99.1 Yarra Valley FM, 104.7 Gippsland FM

Warragul is a thriving rural town with a growing commuter population, being the dairying centre that supplies much of Melbourne's milk. An excellent base to explore the delightful countryside including the Baw Baw snowfields and 'Gippsland Gourmet Country', the town itself showcases 19th-century architecture, especially in the ornate facades and arched windows of Queen Street.

West Gippsland Arts Centre Part of the town's fantastic, architect-designed civic centre complex, the centre is a mecca for art lovers from across the state. It houses a good permanent collection of contemporary visual arts and is known for the variety of theatre productions and events held here throughout the year. Ask inside for a full program of events. Civic Pl; (03) 5624 2456.

Harvest of Gippsland: Mar. *Gippsland Field Days:* Mar/Apr.

The Grange Cafe and Deli: local-produce menu; 15 Palmerston St; (03) 5623 6698. *Jack's at Jindivick:* modern Australian; 1070 Jacksons Track, Jindivick; (03) 5628 5424. *Sticcado Cafe:* features local Gippsland beef; Shop 6, The Village Walk, Yarragon; (03) 5634 2101. *The Outpost Retreat:* modern regional fare; 38 Loch Valley Rd, Noojee; (03) 5628 9669.

VICTORIA

WARRNAMBOOL

Pop. 30 393

Map ref. 580 C8 | 592 G8

i Adjacent Flagstaff Hill Maritime Museum, Merri St; (03) 5564 7837; www.warrnamboolinfo.com.au

103.7 3WAY-FM, 594 AM ABC Local Radio

Warrnambool lies at the end of the Great Ocean Road on a notorious section of coastline that has seen over 80 shipwrecks. The best known was the *Loch Ard* in 1878, which claimed the lives of all but two of those on board. While the wreck site itself is closer to Port Campbell, impressive relics from the ship are held at the Flagstaff Hill Maritime Museum in town. Warrnambool, as Victoria's fifth largest city, offers first-rate accommodation and dining as well as a fantastic swimming beach. The southern right whales that migrate here in winter are another major drawcard.

Flagstaff Hill Maritime Village This reconstructed 19th-century maritime village is complete with a bank, hotel, schoolhouse and surgery. There are also 2 operational lighthouses and an authentic keeper's cottage, now housing the Shipwreck Museum, where relics retrieved from the *Loch Ard* – including the famous earthenware Loch Ard Peacock – are kept. On display is the Flagstaff Hill tapestry, depicting themes of Aboriginal history, sealing, whaling, exploration, immigration and settlement. At night, visitors can watch the sound-and-light show 'Shipwrecked', which details the story of the *Loch Ard*. Merri St; (03) 5559 4600.

[SHEEP OUTSIDE THE FLAGSTAFF HILL MARITIME MUSEUM]

Main beach: a safe swimming beach, with a walkway along the foreshore from the Breakwater to near the mouth of the Hopkins River. *Lake Pertobe Adventure Playground:* a great spot for family picnics; opposite main beach, Pertobe Rd. *Art Gallery:* local artwork, plus European and avant-garde collections; Timor St. *Customs House Gallery:* Gilles St. *Botanic Gardens:* pretty regional gardens designed by Guilfoyle (a curator of Melbourne's Royal Botanic Gardens) in 1879; Botanic Rd. *Fletcher Jones Gardens/Mill Markets:* award-winning landscaped gardens and market in front of former Fletcher Jones factory; Raglan Pde, eastern approach to town. *History House:* local history museum; open 1st Sun each month or by appt; Gilles St. *Portuguese Padrao:* monument to early Portuguese explorers; Cannon Hill, southern end of Liebig St. *Heritage walk:* 3 km self-guide walk taking in historic buildings around town; details from visitor centre. *Hopkins River:* great for fishing and boating. Blue Hole is a popular swimming spot with rockpools. Cruises are available; east of town. *Proudfoots Boathouse:* National Trust–classified boathouse on the Hopkins. *Wollaston Bridge:* an unusual bridge, built over 100 years ago; northern outskirts of town. *Tours and charters:* fishing, whale-watching and diving tours (including shipwreck sites); details from visitor centre.

Trash and treasure market: showgrounds on Koroit St; each Sun. *Hillside market:* Flagstaff Hill; operates throughout summer. *Wunta Fiesta:* family entertainment, food stalls and music; Feb. *Tarerer Festival:* Indigenous culture and music; Mar. *Racing Carnival:* May. *Fun 4 Kids:* children's festival; June. *Melbourne–Warrnambool Cycling Classic:* Oct. *Flower Shows:* held in spring.

Donnelly's Restaurant: contemporary regional fare; 78 Liebig St; (03) 5561 3188. *Kermond's Hamburgers:* excellent old-fashioned hamburgers; 151 Lava St; (03) 5562 4854. *Nonna Casalinga:* up-market Italian; 69 Liebig St; (03) 5562 2051. *Pippies by the Bay:* contemporary food with a view; 91 Merri St; (03) 5561 2188.

104 on Merri Apartments: luxury 2-bedroom apartments; 104 Merri St; 0448 668 738. *Aqua Ocean Villas:* 4 contemporary apartments; 72 Merri St; (03) 5562 5600. *Logans Beach Spa and Fitness:* 2 comfortable apartments; 7 Logans Beach Rd; (03) 5561 3750. *The Sebel Deep Blue Warrnambool:* hotel rooms and apartments; 16 Pertobe Rd; (03) 5559 2000.

Tower Hill State Game Reserve This is a beautiful piece of preserved bushland featuring an extinct volcano and a crater lake, with tiny islands. Nature walk starts at the Worn Gundidj Visitor Centre in the reserve. For further information contact (03) 5561 5315; 12 km NW, just after the turn-off to Koroit.

Logans Beach Each year in June, southern right whales return to the waters along the south coast of Australia to give birth, raise their young and start the breeding cycle again. Each female seems to have a favourite spot to give birth, which means that many familiar faces keep reappearing at Warrnambool's Logans Beach. The beach features a purpose-built viewing platform above the sand dunes (binoculars or telescopes are recommended), and the local visitor centre releases information on whale sightings daily.

Allansford Cheeseworld: for cheese tastings and sales; 10 km E.
Hopkins Falls: scenic picnic spot, particularly spectacular in winter after heavy rain. In spring hundreds of baby eels migrate up the falls, creating a most unusual sight; 16 km NE. *Cudgee Creek Wildlife Park:* deer, crocodiles and other native fauna, plus an aviary. Picnic and barbecue facilities are provided; Cudgee; 18 km E. *Koroit:* National Trust–classified buildings, good local arts and crafts shops, botanic gardens and an Irish festival in Apr; 19 km NW.

See also SOUTH-WEST COAST, p. 153

 Mt Worth State Park This park protects a rich variety of native flora including the silver wattle and the Victorian Christmas bush. The Giant's Circuit is a walk that takes in a massive old mountain ash that is 7 m in circumference. Other walks include the Moonlight Creek and MacDonalds tracks, both of which are easily accessible. No camping is permitted. Contact Parks Victoria on 13 1963; access via Grand Ridge Rd; 22 km SE.

Yarragon Nestled in the foothills of the Strzelecki Ranges and with views of green rolling hills, Yarragon is a wonderful destination with an abundance of delightful shops and accommodation options. It boasts one of Gippsland's leading antique stores and a unique gallery renowned for its quality original artwork, exquisite jewellery, beautiful handblown glass and much more. Sample local wines and gourmet produce, including award-winning cheeses from Tarago River and Jindi Cheese. 13 km SE.

Gippsland Gourmet Country: the renowned 'Gippsland Gourmet Country' takes in lush green pastures and state forests to reveal a diverse range of superb gourmet delights. Previously known as 'Gourmet Deli Country', Gippsland Gourmet encompasses some of the best food and wine producers in the region. Sure to tempt your tastebuds and tantalise the senses; details from visitor centre. *Darnum Musical Village:* a complex of buildings housing a collection of musical instruments dating back to the 1400s; Princes Hwy; 8 km E. *Oakbank Angoras and Alpacas:* sales of yarn and knitted goods; near Drouin, 8 km w. *Waterfalls:* Glen Cromie, Drouin West (10 km NW); Glen Nayook, south of Nayook; and Toorongo Falls, just north of Noojee. *Neerim South:* visit Tarago Cheese Company for tastings and sales of top-quality cheeses, or enjoy a picnic or barbecue at the pleasant reserve near the Tarago Reservoir. Scenic drives through mountain country start from town; 17 km N. *Grand Ridge Road:* 132 km drive that starts at Seaview, 17 km s, and traverses the Strzelecki Ranges to Tarra–Bulga National Park *(see Yarram for park details).* *Nayook:* good fresh produce, a fruit-and-berry farm, and the Country Farm Perennials Nursery and Gardens; 29 km N. *Childers:* Sunny Creek Fruit and Berry Farm, and Windrush Cottage; 31 km SE. *Noojee:* a mountain town featuring a historic trestle bridge and the Alpine Trout Farm; 39 km N.

See also PHILLIP ISLAND & GIPPSLAND, p. 150

Wedderburn
Pop. 702
Map ref. 591 L8

ⓘ **Loddon Visitor Information Centre, Wedderburn Community Centre, 24 Wilson St; (03) 5494 3489; www.loddonalive.com.au**

📻 91.1 FM ABC Local Radio, 99.1 Goldfields FM

Wedderburn, part of the 'Golden Triangle', was once one of Victoria's richest goldmining towns. Many large nuggets have been unearthed here in the past and – for some lucky people – continue to be discovered today. The town's annual Detector Jamboree, with music, historical re-enactments and family entertainment, is growing every year and recognises the importance of gold in the development of so many towns.

🏠 **Hard Hill Tourist Reserve** Hard Hill is a fascinating former mining district with original gold diggings and Government Battery. There is a good walking track through the site, where old mining machinery can be seen. Hard Hill is in a pleasant bushland setting, and picnic facilities are provided. Nearby is a fully operational eucalyptus distillery offering tours and selling eucalyptus products. Northern outskirts of town.

Coach House Cafe and Museum: a 1910 building restored to its original appearance, with authentic, old-fashioned stock and coach-builders quarters; High St. *Bakehouse Pottery:* old bakery now used as a pottery, also home to gold pistachio nuts; High St. *Nardoo Creek Walk:* takes in the key historic buildings around town; map from visitor centre.

🌴 *Wedderburn Detector Jamboree:* gold festival; Mar long weekend. *Historic Engine Exhibition:* Sept.

🧭 *Mt Korong:* bushwalking; 16 km SE. *Wychitella Forest Reserve:* wildlife sanctuary set in mallee forest, home to mallee fowl; 16 km N. *Kooyoora State Park:* see Inglewood for details. *Fossickers Drive:* takes in goldmining sites, places of Aboriginal significance, local wineries and the Melville Caves; details from visitor centre.

See also GOLDFIELDS, p. 154

Welshpool
Pop. 200
Map ref. 582 H9

ⓘ **Old Courthouse, 9 Rodgers St, Yarram; (03) 5182 6553.**

📻 89.5 3MFM South Gippsland, 828 AM ABC Local Radio

Welshpool is a small dairying community in South Gippsland. On the coast nearby, Port Welshpool is a deep-sea port servicing the local fishing and oil industries. Barry Beach Marine Terminal, a short distance west of Port Welshpool, services the offshore oil rigs in Bass Strait.

🧭 **Port Welshpool** This popular coastal town has all the natural attractions that a seaside village could want. It is frequented by families who enjoy the safe beaches and fabulous coastal walks, and has fantastic views across to Wilsons Promontory. Fishing enthusiasts should drop a line from the historic jetty, or try from a boat. The port's long link with the sea is detailed in the

 VICTORIA

Port Welshpool and District Maritime Museum, which exhibits shipping relics and local history displays as well. 2 km s.

Franklin River Reserve: great bushwalking with well-marked tracks; near Toora; 11 km w. ***Agnes Falls:*** the highest single-span falls in the state, spectacular after heavy rain; 19 km nw. ***Scenic drive:*** head west to see magnificent views from Mt Fatigue; off South Gippsland Hwy. ***Fishing and boating:*** excellent along the coast.

See also Phillip Island & Gippsland, p. 150

Winchelsea
Pop. 1336
Map ref. 572 D8 | 580 E1 | 593 M8

 Old Library, Willis St (Princes Hwy); open 11am–4pm Fri–Sun; 1300 614 219; www.historicwinchelsea.com.au

94.7 The Pulse FM, 774 AM ABC Local Radio

This charming little town on the Barwon River west of Geelong was first developed with cattle runs in the 1830s. Many of the historic buildings that grew from this development can still be seen around town, the most impressive being the nearby Barwon Park Homestead – a mansion built by famous settlers of the district, Thomas and Elizabeth Austin. Winchelsea soon became a key stopover for travellers taking the road from Colac to Geelong, and it still serves that purpose for travellers on the Princes Highway.

Barwon Bridge: an impressive arched bridge, built from stone in 1867; Princes Hwy. ***Antiques and collectibles:*** many shops in town that outline its history; Main St and Princes Hwy. ***Winchelsea Historical Trail:*** map available from visitor information centre, or check township information boards. ***Barwon Hotel:*** known locally as the 'bottom pub' of the town, offers country style; Main St. ***Winchelsea Tavern:*** recently renovated Art Deco 'top pub'; Princes Hwy. ***Old Shire Hall:*** beautifully restored bluestone building, now housing popular tearooms; Princes Hwy. ***Old Library:*** houses the visitor information centre; Princes Hwy. ***Marjorie Lawrence Trail:*** details the life of one of the world's most adored dramatic sopranos from the 1900s; details from visitor centre.

Winchelsea Festival: wool shearing, dog trials, wool classing, children's activities, local produce and market stall, plus more; Nov.

Barwon Park Homestead Only the greatest estate would satisfy Elizabeth Austin, and her husband, Thomas, acquiesced. Barwon Park, built in 1869, was the biggest mansion in the Western District. Featuring 42 rooms furnished largely with original pieces, the bluestone building is an impressive example of 19th-century design. The name Austin might be familiar: Thomas Austin reputedly imported the first of Australia's devastating rabbit population and Elizabeth Austin contributed to major charities, and established the Austin Hospital in Melbourne. Open 11am–4pm Wed and Sun; Inverleigh Rd; (03) 5267 2209; 3 km n.

Country Dahlias Gardens: beautiful gardens, best viewed during spring, with sales of dahlia plants; open Feb–Apr; Mathison Rd; 5 km s. ***Killwarrie Cottage:*** rose garden display, home-grown vegetables; open Nov–Mar; 7 km sw.

See also South-West Coast, p. 153

Wodonga
Pop. 29 713
Map ref. 554 A12 | 559 N12 | 585 K6 | 587 I2

 Gateway Visitor Information Centre, Lincoln Causeway; 1300 796 222; www.destinationalburywodonga.com.au

106.5 FM ABC Local Radio, 107.3 Ten-73 Border FM

Wodonga and its twin town, Albury (in New South Wales), sit astride the Murray River. There are many attractions around the Murray and nearby Lake Hume, making the region a popular holiday destination.

Gateway Village: includes woodwork shops and cafes. Also houses the visitor centre; Lincoln Causeway. ***Huon Hill Lookout:*** maps from visitor centre. ***Sumsion Gardens:*** a pretty lakeside park with walking track, picnic and barbecue facilities; Church St. ***Tennis Centre:*** the largest grass court centre of its kind in Australia; Melrose Dr.

Wodonga Craft Market: Woodland Gr; 1st Sat each month. ***Farmers market:*** Gateway Village; 2nd Sat each month. ***Wodonga Show:*** Mar. ***In My Backyard Festival:*** raises environmental awareness; Mar. ***Wine and Food Festival:*** Oct.

Zilch Food Store: friendly modern cafe; 8/1 Stanley St; (02) 6056 2400.

Mt Granya State Park This landscape contrasts between steep, rocky slopes and open eucalypt forests. Bushwalking is a popular pastime and the display of wildflowers in spring is magnificent. There is a pleasant picnic spot at Cottontree Creek, and a short walk leads to the Mt Granya summit, which offers spectacular views of the alps. Murray River Rd; 56 km e.

Military Museum: Bandiana; 4 km se. ***Hume Weir:*** good spot for walks and picnics; 15 km e. ***Tours:*** winery and fishing tours, as well as scenic drives through the Upper Murray region, the mountain valleys of north-east Victoria and the Riverina; details from visitor centre.

See also High Country, p. 158

Wonthaggi
Pop. 6528
Map ref. 573 L12 | 582 E9

 Watt St; 1300 854 334; www.visitbasscoast.com

88.1 3MFM South Gippsland, 100.7 FM ABC Local Radio

Once the main supplier of coal to the Victorian Railways, Wonthaggi, near the beachside town of Cape Paterson, is South Gippsland's largest town. There are good tourist facilities in town and a number of pretty beaches nearby.

Bass Coast Rail Trail: 16 km trail that runs between Wonthaggi and Anderson. Suitable for walking and cycling, it is the only coastal rail trail in Victoria with landscape that varies from flat farmland and bushland to rugged coastline.

Energy and Innovation Festival: Mar.

State Coal Mine The demand for black coal created a thriving industry in Wonthaggi from 1909 until 1968, and the mine site has been retained to show visitors the lifestyle and working conditions of the miners. Daily underground tours offer close-up views of the coalface, a short walk into the East Area Mine and a cable-hauled skip ride to the surface. Above ground, visit the museum for an introduction to the history of the mine and of Wonthaggi itself, or take a walk around the historic buildings. Inquiries (03) 5672 3053 or Parks Victoria on 13 1963; Cape Paterson Rd; 1.5 km s.

Cape Paterson: waters offshore are protected by Bunurong Marine and Coastal Park and are good for surfing, swimming, snorkelling and scuba diving; 8 km s. **George Bass Coastal Walk:** starts at Kilcunda; 11 km NW. Ask at visitor centre for details of other walks. **Gippsland Gourmet Country:** takes in central Gippsland's gourmet food and wine producers; details from visitor centre.

See also PHILLIP ISLAND & GIPPSLAND, p. 15

Woodend

Pop. 3166
Map ref. 572 G2 | 579 H9 | 582 B2 | 584 A12 | 593 P3

 High St, beside Five Mile Creek; (03) 5427 2033 or 1800 244 711; www.visitmacedonranges.com

100.7 Highlands FM, 774 AM ABC Local Radio

During the gold rushes of the 1850s, travellers sought refuge from mud, bogs and bushrangers at the 'wood's end' around Five Mile Creek, where a town eventually grew. In the late 19th century Woodend became a resort town, and its lovely gardens and proximity to spectacular natural sights, such as Hanging Rock and Mount Macedon, still make it a popular daytrip and weekend getaway for visitors from Melbourne.

Bluestone Bridge: built in 1862, the bridge crosses Five Mile Creek on the northern outskirts of town. **Clock Tower:** built as a WW I memorial; Calder Hwy. **Courthouse:** historic structure built in 1870; Forest St.

Craft market: 3rd Sun each month Sept–May. **Woodend Winter Arts Festival:** June. **Macedon Ranges Budburst Festival:** held throughout the wine district; Nov.

Campaspe Country House: lovely regional dining room; Goldies La; (03) 5427 2273. **Holgate Brewhouse:** modern menu; 79 High St; (03) 5427 2510.

Campaspe Country House: rooms and a cottage; Goldies La; (03) 5427 2273. **Holgate Brewhouse:** ensuite rooms; 79 High St; (03) 5427 2510. **Woodbury Cottage B&B:** charming converted stables; 18 Jason Dr; (03) 5427 1876.

Hanging Rock A massive rock formation made famous by *Picnic at Hanging Rock*, the novel by Joan Lindsay that was later made into a film. The story, about schoolgirls who mysteriously vanished while on a picnic in the reserve, became something of a legend. There is certainly something eerie about Hanging Rock with its strange rock formations and narrow tracks through dense bushland. Hanging Rock is renowned for the annual races held at its base, especially the New Year's Day and Australia Day races. Other events include a Vintage Car Rally and Harvest Picnic, both held in Feb. The reserve also has a discovery centre and cafe. Access from South Rock Rd, off Calder Hwy; 8 km NE.

Macedon: a town at the foot of Mt Macedon. Home to the Church of the Resurrection, with stained-glass windows designed by Leonard French, and excellent plant nurseries; 8 km SE. **Mt Macedon:** a township located higher up the mountain, 2 km from Macedon, renowned for its beautiful gardens, many open to the public in autumn and spring. **Macedon Regional Park:** bushwalking and scenic drives. The Camels Hump marks the start of a signposted walk to the summit of the mountain where there stands a huge WW I memorial cross. Access via turn-off after Mt Macedon township. **Wineries:** several in region include Hanging Rock Winery at Newham; 10 km NE; details from

visitor centre. **Gisborne:** a variety of craft outlets. Gisborne Steam Park holds a steam-train rally each May; 16 km SE. **Glen Erin at Romsey/Cope-Williams Winery:** tastings and sales, surrounded by charming English-style gardens, tennis courts and a cricket green; Romsey; 19 km E. **Lancefield:** historic buildings and wineries. Mad Gallery and Bankart Gallery offer contemporary and fine art, respectively. The town is also home to a woodchopping competition in Mar and a farmers market, for local produce, 4th Sat each month; 25 km NE. **Monegeetta:** in town is the Mintaro Homestead, a smaller replica of Melbourne's Government House, but not open to the public; 27 km E via Romsey.

See also SPA & GARDEN COUNTRY, p. 151

Wycheproof

Pop. 686
Map ref. 558 G12 | 591 K6

 Wycheproof Community Resource Centre, 280 Broadway; (03) 5493 7455; www.wycheproof.vic.au

99.1 Goldfields FM, 102.1 FM ABC Local Radio

Wycheproof is renowned for the long wheat trains that travel down the middle of the main street, towing up to 60 carriages behind them. There are many historic buildings in town, as well as rare, old peppercorn trees. Mount Wycheproof, at a mere 43 metres, has been named the smallest mountain in the world.

Mt Wycheproof A walking track leads up and around the mountain. Emus and kangaroos can be seen up close in a fauna park at the mountain's base.

Willandra Museum: farm machinery, old buildings and historical memorabilia; open by appt; Calder Hwy. **Centenary Park:** aviaries, 2 log cabins and barbecue facilities; Calder Hwy.

Music on the Mount: Oct. **Racing Carnival:** Oct/Nov.

Tchum Lakes: artificially created lakes, great for fishing and watersports dependent on water levels; 23 km W. **Birchip:** visitors to town are greeted by the town's beloved 'Big Red' mallee bull in the main street. Also in town is the Soldiers Memorial Park with large, shady Moreton Bay fig trees, a great spot for a picnic; 31 km W.

See also GRAMPIANS & CENTRAL WEST, p. 155

Yackandandah

Pop. 663
Map ref. 585 K7 | 587 I4

 The Athenaeum, High St; (02) 6027 1988; www.uniqueyackandandah.com.au

101.3 Oak FM, 106.5 FM ABC Local Radio

Yackandandah, with its avenues of English trees and traditional buildings, is so rich with history that the entire town is National Trust–classified. It is situated south of Wodonga in the heart of the north-east goldfields region. In fact, many of the town's creeks still yield alluvial gold.

Historic buildings: the post office, several banks and general stores, with the Bank of Victoria now preserved as a museum, open Sun and school holidays. Explore these and other buildings on a self-guide walk; details from visitor centre; High St. **Ray Riddington's Premier Store and Gallery:** displays and sales of local art; High St. **The Old Stone Bridge:** a beautiful old structure, built in 1857; High St. **Arts and crafts:** many outlets in town, including Yackandandah Workshop, cnr Kars and

Hammond sts, and Wildon Thyme, High St. **Antiques:** Finders Bric-a-Brac and Old Wares, High St; Frankly Speaking, High St; and Vintage Sounds Restoration, specialising in antique gramophones, radios and telephones, Windham St. **Rosedale Garden and Tea Rooms:** Devonshire teas; Kars St.

Folk Festival: 3rd weekend Mar. **Spring Migration Festival:** Sept. **Flower Show:** Oct.

Star Hotel: pub classics; 30 High St; (02) 6027 1493. **Sticky Tarts Cafe:** charming casual cafe; 26 High St; (02) 6027 1853.

Creek Haven Cottage: cosy 3-bedroom cottage; 281 Osbornes Flat Rd; (02) 6027 1389. **Karalilla B&B:** 4 rooms in Victorian homestead; 271 Ben Valley La; (02) 6027 1788.

Kars Reef Goldmine: take a tour of this fascinating old goldmine, or try your hand at gold panning (licence required); details of tours from visitor centre; Kars St. **Lavender Patch Plant Farm:** sales of plants and lavender products; Beechworth Rd; 4 km w. **Kirbys Flat Pottery and Gallery:** Kirbys Flat Rd; open weekends or by appt; 4 km s. **Indigo Valley:** a picturesque area with a scenic drive leading along the valley floor to Barnawatha; 6 km NW. **Allans Flat:** a great destination for food lovers, with The Vienna Patisserie for coffee, ice-cream and delicious Austrian cakes (closed Tues). Also here are Parks Wines and Schmidt's Strawberry Winery, both with tastings and sales; 10 km NE. **Wombat Valley Tramways:** a small-gauge railway; open Easter or by appt for groups; Leneva; 16 km NE.

See also HIGH COUNTRY, p. 158

Yarra Glen

Pop. 1901
Map ref. 570 H4 | 571 C6 | 573 L4 | 582 E4

ⓘ **Yarra Valley Visitor Information Centre, Old Courthouse, Harker St, Healesville; (03) 5962 2600; www.yarraglen.com.au**

99.1 Yarra Valley FM, 774 AM ABC Local Radio

Yarra Glen is in the heart of the Yarra Valley wine region, nestled between the Yarra River and the Great Dividing Range. A gorgeous area featuring lush, vine-covered hills and fertile valleys; all within easy reach of Melbourne. Fine wines and top-quality local produce; fascinating antique, specialty gift and clothing shops; and not forgetting restaurants; are all in town to entice. For the more adventurous, Yarra Glen is home to hot-air ballooning, scenic helicopter flights over the valley and even skydiving at nearby Coldstream airfield. The bushfire of February 2009 came very close to the township of Yarra Glen, and some businesses and townsfolk were directly affected.

 Yarra Glen Grand Hotel: imposing heritage-listed and National Trust–classified hotel, built in 1888 with a recently refurbished restaurant, stands like a sentinel in the main street; Bell St. **Hargreaves Hill Brewing Co:** the old Colonial Bank building houses a fine-dining restaurant specialising in local produce and an extensive choice of Yarra Valley and European boutique beers; Bell St. **Tea Leaves:** a treasure chest containing Melbourne's largest range of premium-quality teas, novelty teapots and tea accessories; Bell St. **Den of Antiquities and Yarra Valley Antique Centre:** boasts large collections of genuine antique furniture, china and glass, vintage radios and other collectibles; Bell St. **Yarra Glen Railway Station:** old station on the 1888 Healesville–Lilydale railway line, rebuilt in 1915 and now being restored as part of the Yarra Valley Tourist Railway; King St.

Yarra Valley Farmers Market: Historic Barn at Yering Station; 3rd Sun each month. **Gulf Station Farmers Market:**

Gulf Station Historic Farm; 4th Sun each month. **Craft market:** racecourse; 1st Sun each month Sept–June. **Grape Grazing Festival:** wine, food and music throughout the valley; Feb. **Shortest Lunch:** midwinter fine food and wine at the smaller boutique wineries; June. **Melba Festival and Melba Wine Trail:** arts, culture, food and wine event; Oct.

Hargreaves Hill Brewing Company Restaurant: Mediterranean-style dishes; 25 Bell St; (03) 9730 1905. **TarraWarra Estate Wine Bar Cafe:** rustic European fare; 311 Healesville–Yarra Glen Rd; (03) 5957 3510. **Eleonore's Restaurant at Chateau Yering:** elegant dining room; Chateau Yering, 42 Melba Hwy, Yering; (03) 9237 3333 or 1800 237 333. **Yering Station Wine Bar Restaurant:** modern Australian; 38 Melba Hwy, Yering; (03) 9730 0100.

Art at Linden Gate: 3-suite country escape; 899 Healesville–Yarra Glen Rd; (03) 9730 1861. **Valley Guest House:** garden suites; 319 Steels Creek Rd; (03) 9730 1822. **Chateau Yering:** historic luxury hotel; 42 Melba Hwy, Yering; (03) 9237 3333 or 1800 237 333.

Yarra Valley Wine Region Victoria's first vines were planted in the Yarra Valley by the Ryrie brothers in 1838 – these plantings would develop into Yering Station, today home to one of the region's finest wineries and restaurants. It produces excellent shiraz viognier as well as award-winning pinot noir. With over 55 cellar door outlets and around 100 wineries, the Yarra Valley is also home to other exceptional names. The De Bortoli Winery in Dixons Creek is Australia's oldest family-owned winery; Domaine Chandon, owned by the legendary Moët & Chandon, makes sophisticated sparkling wines that can be enjoyed in the glass-walled tasting room overlooking the vines. To combine wine with art, head to TarraWarra Estate, well known for its chardonnay and pinot noir, and its modern gallery that holds exhibitions of work by Australian greats from Arthur Boyd to Peter Booth; *see Healesville.* Excellent restaurants abound throughout the valley, many at wineries. Tour companies offer bus tours and personalised winery tours by car through the Yarra Valley region. The ever-popular Grape Grazing Festival is celebrated each Feb, and the smaller wineries' Shedfest wine festival is held in Oct. Winery map available from visitor centre.

Kinglake National Park Kinglake's beautiful messmate forests, fern gullies, panoramic lookouts and bushwalking tracks were devastated by the bushfire of February 2009, and the park is closed until further notice. Phone Parks Victoria on 13 1963 for an update on progress on the park's reopening.

Gulf Station: this National Trust–owned pastoral property, preserved as it was during pioneering days, features old-fashioned farming implements and early animal breeds; open Wed–Sun and public holidays; 2 km NE. **Yarra Valley Dairy:** a working dairy with sales of specialty cheeses, clotted cream and local produce; 4 km s. **Ponyland Equestrian Centre:** trail-rides and riding lessons; 7 km w. **Sugarloaf Reservoir Park:** sailing, fishing and walking, with barbecue and picnic facilities available; 10 km w. **Yarra Valley Regional Food Trail:** a self-guide tour, taking in the many gourmet food outlets in the region; details from visitor centre.

See also YARRA & DANDENONGS, p. 148

Yarram

Pop. 1716
Map ref. 583 I9

 i Old Courthouse, 9 Rodgers St; (03) 5182 6553;
www.tourismwellington.com.au

89.5 3MFM South Gippsland, 100.7 FM ABC Local Radio

Yarram is deep in the dairy country of South Gippsland, and at the heart of some of its most beautiful locales, from the splendour of Ninety Mile Beach to the refreshingly cool atmosphere of Tarra–Bulga National Park. Yarram was originally settled on a swamp, and its name is derived from an Aboriginal word meaning 'plenty of water'. In town are some notable examples of early architecture, including the recently restored Regent Theatre and the historic courthouse.

Regent Theatre: built in 1930, this theatre has been wonderfully restored. Cinemas operate on weekends and school holidays; Commercial Rd.

Tarra Festival: Easter.

Tarra–Bulga National Park Tarra–Bulga is a tranquil park with spectacular river and mountain views. Fern Gully Walk, starting from the Bulga picnic ground, takes in the dense temperate rainforests of mountain ash, myrtle and sassafras. The walk leads across a suspension bridge high among the treetops. A walk to Cyathea or Tarra falls, surrounded by lush fern gullies, completes the rainforest experience. Keep an eye out for rosellas, lyrebirds and the occasional koala. The Tarra–Bulga Visitor Centre is on Grand Ridge Rd near Balook; from Yarram, access the park from Tarra Valley Rd; 20 km NW.

Won Wron Forest: great for walks, with wildflowers in spring; Hyland Hwy; 16 km N. **Beaches:** there are many attractive beaches in the region, including Manns, for fishing, 16 km SE; McLoughlins, 23 km E; and Woodside Beach, which is patrolled in summer; 29 km E. **Tarra Valley:** there are many great gardens, including Eilean Donan Gardens and Riverbank Nursery; located just north-west of Yarram. **Scenic drive:** a 46 km circuit goes from Yarram through Hiawatha and takes in Minnie Ha Ha Falls on Albert River, where picnic and camping facilities are provided.

See also PHILLIP ISLAND & GIPPSLAND, p. 150

Yarrawonga

Pop. 5726
Map ref. 559 M12 | 584 H5 | 586 D1

 i Irvine Pde; (03) 5744 1989 or 1800 062 260;
www.yarrawongamulwala.com.au

101.3 Oak FM, 106.5 FM ABC Local Radio

Yarrawonga and its sister town Mulwala, across the New South Wales border, are separated by a pleasant stretch of the Murray River and the attractive Lake Mulwala. The 6000-hectare lake was created in 1939 during the building of the Yarrawonga Weir, which is central to irrigation in the Murray Valley. Yarrawonga's proximity to such great water features has made it a popular holiday resort. The sandy beaches and calm waters are ideal for watersports, and are also home to abundant wildlife.

Yarrawonga and Mulwala foreshores: great locations for walks and picnics, with shady willows, water slides, barbecue facilities and boat ramps. **Canning A.R.T.S Gallery:** work by local artists; Belmore St. **Tudor House Clock Museum:** Lynch St. **Cruises:** daily cruises along the Murray on paddleboats *Paradise Queen* or *Lady Murray*; depart from Bank St.

Rotary Market: local crafts and second-hand goods; showgrounds; 3rd Sun each month. **Powerboat Racing:** May. **Murray Marathon:** Dec.

Lady Murray Cruises: barbecue lunches, 3-course dinners; Yarrawonga foreshore; (03) 5744 2005.

Fyffe Field Wines: tastings and sales; Murray Valley Hwy; 19 km W. **Fishing:** Murray River for Murray cod and yellow-belly. **Guided tours:** local wineries; book at visitor centre.

See also GOULBURN & MURRAY, p. 157

Yea

Pop. 1051
Map ref. 571 D1 | 573 L1 | 582 E1 | 584 E12

i Old Railway Station, Station St; (03) 5797 2663;
www.murrindinditourism.com.au

88.9 UGFM Upper Goulburn Community Radio, 97.7 FM ABC Local Radio

This town sits by the Yea River, a tributary of the Goulburn River. Hume and Hovell, the first explorers through the region, discovered this wonderfully fertile area – a discovery that led in part to the settlement of the rest of Victoria. Near the Yea–Tallarook Road there are beautiful gorges and fern gullies, a reminder of what Yea looked like thousands of years ago.

Historic buildings: Beaufort Manor, High St; General Store, now a restaurant, High St. **Wetlands Walk:** sightings of abundant birdlife and glider possums; eastern outskirts of town.

Market: local craft and produce; Main St; 1st Sat each month Sept–May. **Autumn Fest:** Mar.

Marmalades: hearty country food; 20 High St; (03) 5797 2999.

Cheviot Glen Cottages: 2 country cottages; 175 Limestone Rd, Cheviot Hills; (03) 5797 2617.

Murrindindi Reserve: see the impressive Murrindindi Cascades and a variety of wildlife including wombats, platypus and lyrebirds; 11 km SE. **Ibis Rookery:** Kerrisdale; 17 km W. **Flowerdale Winery:** Whittlesea–Yea Rd; 23 km SW. **Grotto:** a beautiful old church set in the hillside; Caveat; 27 km N. **Berry King Farm:** pick your own fruit; Two Hills Rd, Glenburn; 28 km S. **Wilhelmina Falls:** spectacular falls and a great spot for walks and picnics; access via Melba Hwy; 32 km S. **Kinglake National Park:** 32 km S; *see Yarra Glen*. **Mineral springs:** Dropmore, off back road to Euroa; 47 km N. **Scenic drives:** many in the region. Best time is Aug–Sept when wattles are in bloom; maps from visitor centre.

See also GOULBURN & MURRAY, p. 157

 VICTORIA

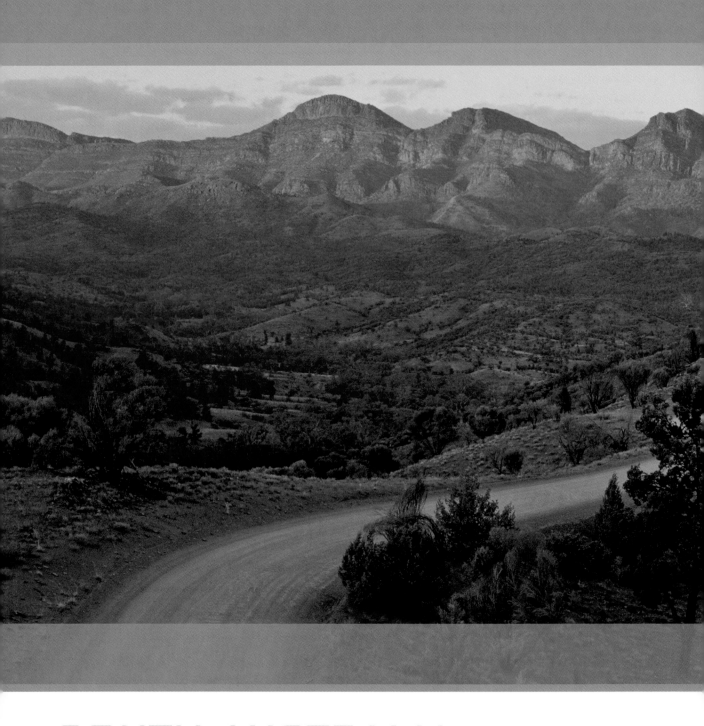

SOUTH AUSTRALIA is...

Seeing a performance at the ADELAIDE FESTIVAL OF ARTS / A walk along

NORTH TERRACE, Adelaide / A glittering, panoramic night view from WINDY

POINT, Belair / Enjoying excellent wine and gourmet food in the BAROSSA

VALLEY / Birdwatching in COORONG NATIONAL PARK / Taking a scenic flight

SOUTH AUSTRALIA

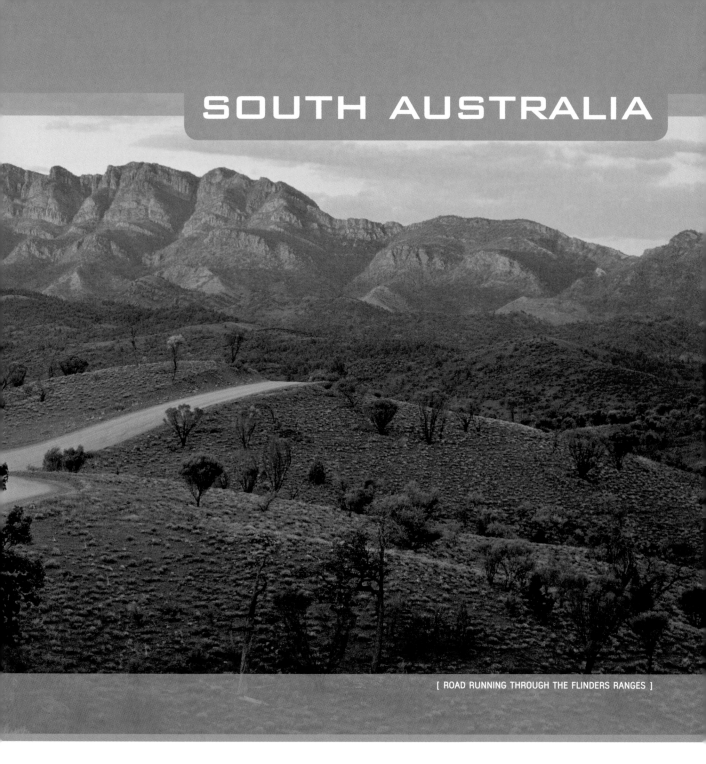

[ROAD RUNNING THROUGH THE FLINDERS RANGES]

over WILPENA POUND in the Flinders Ranges / A tour of one of the NARACOORTE

CAVES / Visiting historic towns, wineries and galleries in the ADELAIDE HILLS / Sleeping

underground and searching for opals in COOBER PEDY / Discovering pristine vegetation

and native fauna on KANGAROO ISLAND / Driving along the NULLARBOR PLAIN

SOUTH AUSTRALIA

is a million square kilometres of ancient Dreamtime landscapes and wild coastal beauty. It is also a land of incredible contrast: the endless desert of the north and the fertile vales of the south-east are a world apart.

In 1836 Colonel William Light chose the site for the capital of South Australia on Kaurna land beside the River Torrens. The settlement's early days were far from ideal as the first colonists huddled in squalid mud huts, perhaps regretting they had no convict labour to call on. But today the world's first planned city is a gracious capital of wide streets and generous public parks.

In the 1840s German Lutherans fleeing persecution in Europe settled in the Adelaide Hills and the Barossa Valley, bringing traditions of wine-growing and social liberty that have flourished here ever since. In the early 1970s the election of flamboyant rebel Don Dunstan as premier launched a decade of social reform unmatched in any other state. South Australians are proud of their history of social innovation, and their state has a well-earned reputation for tolerance and cultural diversity.

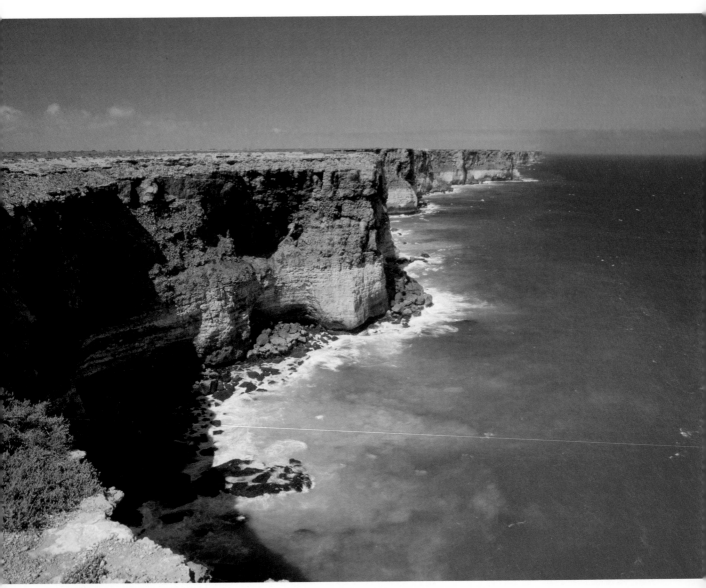

[BUNDA CLIFFS, HEAD OF BIGHT]

For travellers, South Australia is the perfect place to get off the beaten track. This is the nation's most urbanised state, so the outback begins just an hour or two up the road from Adelaide.

The Flinders Ranges are one of the oldest mountain ranges on earth. At its centre, is the natural amphitheatre Wilpena Pound (Ikara), a lost world of cypress pines and hidden creeks, its gorges created by Akurra the serpent as he travelled north with a grumbling belly full of salt water.

The state's Southern Ocean coastline includes the sheer cliffs of the Great Australian Bight and the sheltered wetlands of the Coorong. This refuge for native and migratory birds begs you to sit quietly with a pair of binoculars.

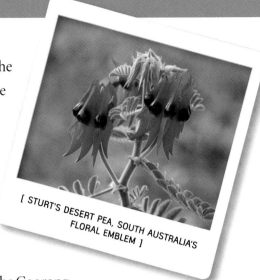

[STURT'S DESERT PEA, SOUTH AUSTRALIA'S FLORAL EMBLEM]

fact file

Population 1 629 500
Total land area 984 377 square kilometres
People per square kilometre 1.6
Sheep per square kilometre 13.25
Length of coastline 3816 kilometres
Number of islands 346
Longest river Murray River (650 kilometres)
Largest lake Lake Eyre (9500 square kilometres)
Highest mountain Mount Woodroffe (1440 metres), Musgrave Ranges, Pitjantjatjara Land
Lowest place Lake Eyre, 15 metres below sea level (Australia's lowest point)
Hottest place 50.7°C – Australia's hottest recorded temperature – was reached in Oodnadatta in 1960
Driest place Lake Eyre is Australia's driest place with a mere 125 millimetres of rainfall per year
Longest place name Nooldoonooldoona, a waterhole in the Gammon Ranges
Best surf Cactus Beach, near Ceduna
Best discoveries and inventions Penicillin by Howard Florey (he describes the discovery as 'a terrible amount of luck'); the wine cask by Tom Angove
Most dangerous coast There are 80 shipwrecks around Kangaroo Island
Best political stunt Premier Don Dunstan wore pink hot pants into parliament to campaign for gay law reform in the 1970s
Favourite takeaway food Adelaide's pie floater (a meat pie floating in a bowl of pea soup – with or without tomato sauce)
Local beer Coopers
Interesting fact Adelaide boasts a higher ratio of restaurants to residents than any other state

gift ideas

Leather boots (R. M. Williams Outback Heritage Museum, Adelaide) This iconic bushman began making saddlery and leather boots while camping in South Australia's Gammon Ranges. 5 Percy St, Prospect. 596 D4

Strawberry jam (Beerenberg, Hahndorf) Now world famous, but the original signature product can still be bought from the pioneer farm. Mt Barker Rd, Hahndorf. See Hahndorf p. 256, 596 F9

Ligurian honey (Kangaroo Island) The purest organic honey of its type in the world. See Kangaroo Island p. 236, 599 C11

Glass art (JamFactory, Adelaide) Pick up a finely crafted, unique piece of glass or ceramic art from an emerging or established artist. See JamFactory p. 229, 226 B2

Wine (Barossa and Clare valleys) Take home some cases of wine from two of Australia's eminent wine regions, particularly famous for shiraz and riesling. See Barossa Valley p. 238 and Clare p. 252, 597 F4, 603 J6

Jewellery (Zu design, Adelaide Arcade, Adelaide) Distinctive contemporary objects of adornment from Adelaide artists. 226 C2

Shiraz-filled chocolates (David Medlow, McLaren Vale) Delightfully rich shiraz liqueur encased in dark chocolate. McLarens on the Lake, Kangarilla Rd, McLaren Vale. See McLaren Vale p. 263, 597 B12

Premium oysters (Coffin Bay) Pure from the nutrient-rich water currents of the Southern Ocean. See Coffin Bay p. 252, 602 C8

King George whiting (South Australian waters) Sweet, delicate and always fresh from stores around the state.

Opals (Coober Pedy) Although available around the country, purchase these beautiful stones directly from this mining town. See Coober Pedy p. 255, 609 O10

ADELAIDE IS...

Coffee at Lucia's in ADELAIDE CENTRAL MARKET / A Popeye cruise along the

RIVER TORRENS / A tram trip to GLENELG / Surveying the city from LIGHT'S

VISION / A visit to the Australian Aboriginal Cultures Gallery at the SOUTH

AUSTRALIAN MUSEUM / Shopping at Adelaide's historic RUNDLE MALL / HENLEY

SQUARE on a Sunday afternoon, for lunch and a walk by the sea / A night out

in EAST END / A stroll around the JAMFACTORY craft and design gallery

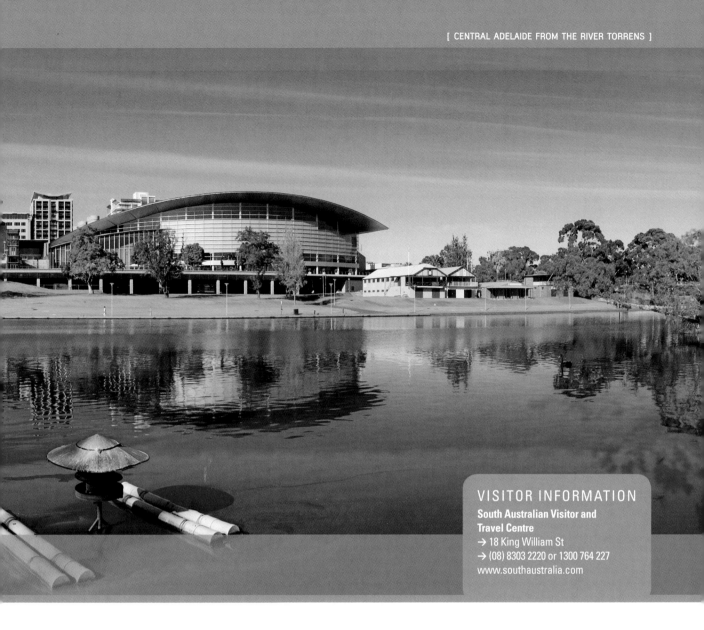

VISITOR INFORMATION
South Australian Visitor and Travel Centre
→ 18 King William St
→ (08) 8303 2220 or 1300 764 227
www.southaustralia.com

One of the best-planned cities in the world, Adelaide remains testament to the work of its first surveyor, Colonel William Light, whose statue stands on Montefiore Hill, overlooking Adelaide Oval.

Settled in 1836, Adelaide was Australia's first free settlement. Like other well-planned cities around the world, Adelaide has few skyscrapers and its architecture blends both heritage and contemporary styles, retaining a 'human scale'.

Since the 1970s Adelaide has been famous for food and wine. The state is the powerhouse of the booming Australian wine industry, producing almost 60 per cent of the total output, while Adelaide Central Market is possibly the finest fresh-produce market in Australia. The city is renowned for its restaurants – from the fish cafes of Gouger Street to the many gourmet eateries dotted around the CBD, and tucked away in quiet corners.

Adelaide also knows how to throw a party, and with a population of 1 173 000 the city is compact enough to generate a feeling of all-over revelry. First on the calendar is the Adelaide Festival of Arts, one of the world's great arts festivals. During February and March every second year, the festival and the now annual Adelaide Fringe take over the city.

CBD North

The northern section of central Adelaide is based around North Terrace and Rundle Mall. North Terrace, a wide, tree-lined boulevard with a university located at either end, hosts three of South Australia's most important cultural institutions: the state library, the museum and the art gallery. Rundle Mall lies one block south.

Rundle Mall 226 C2

Rundle Mall was Australia's first shopping mall and forms the city's shopping heart, with major department stores, specialty clothing outlets, souvenir and craft stores, food outlets and music shops. Public sculptures dot the mall, including two silver balls colloquially known as the 'Malls Balls'. While you're here, visit **Haigh's Chocolates** on historic Beehive Corner (*you can also visit the Haigh's factory in Parkside, see p. 231*).

Rundle Mall runs parallel to Grenfell Street, and they are joined by two treasures of old Adelaide – Adelaide Arcade and Regent Arcade. Opened in 1885, **Adelaide Arcade** was the first retail establishment in the country to have electric lights. It is a thoroughly Victorian affair, lined with small shops of every kind on the ground floor and charming balcony level.

East End 226 C2

The east end of Rundle Mall, beyond the main shopping zone, is the hub of Adelaide's nightlife. Friday and Saturday nights in the East End throb with longstanding pubs – such as the Austral and the Exeter – among newer bars and clubs, all of them bursting with revellers. With over 50 cafes and restaurants, this is also a superb place to come for food, and the shopping is great too. **Mary Martin Bookshop**, 'purveyors of fine literature since 1945', is Adelaide's oldest bookseller. On Sundays Rundle Street is transformed into an exciting craft and fashion street market.

climate

Adelaide's weather is described as temperate Mediterranean, with temperatures in summer rising to around 40°C on a number of days, and falling to a minimum near zero a couple of times in winter. The in-between seasons are near-perfect, with maximum temperatures in the mid-20s for much of March, April, September and October.

J	F	M	A	M	J	J	A	S	O	N	D	
28	28	26	22	18	15	14	16	18	21	24	26	MAX °C
16	16	15	12	10	8	7	8	9	11	13	15	MIN °C
20	20	24	44	68	71	66	61	51	44	30	26	RAIN MM
2	2	3	6	10	11	12	11	9	7	5	4	RAIN DAYS

SOUTH AUSTRALIA

[SOUTH AUSTRALIAN MUSEUM]

getting around

Adelaide has a wide range of public transport. First there is the city's tram service, which runs from Glenelg, all the way to the city, through Victoria Square and City West, to the newly renovated Entertainment Centre on Port Road, Hindmarsh. Then there is the Adelaide O-Bahn – the longest and fastest guided bus service in the world. It travels along Currie and Grenfell streets in the city, then heads out to Westfield Tea Tree Plaza in Modbury.

The City Loop Bus and the Terrace to Terrace Tram are two free services that operate around the city centre. The City Loop bus runs every 15 minutes and takes in North Terrace and Light, Hindmarsh and Victoria squares; the Terrace to Terrace Tram runs every ten minutes and includes Victoria Square, King William Street and the railway station. Board either the Glenelg or South Terrace tram anywhere between South Terrace and North Terrace during shopping hours.

The Adelaide Metroticket JetBus is a daily service linking the airport to the city, Glenelg, West Beach and the north-eastern suburbs.

Four train routes operate from the CBD to Adelaide's suburbs: to Gawler in the north, Outer Harbour in the north-west, Noarlunga in the south and Belair in the Adelaide Hills. There are also plenty of bus services operating around the suburbs. All public transport in Adelaide is covered by one ticketing system, and tickets can be purchased at train stations and on buses and trams, as well as newsagents and convenience stores displaying the Metroticket signage, and the Adelaide Metro InfoCentre, corner King William and Currie streets in the City centre.

Public transport Passenger Transport InfoLine 1300 311 108 or 1800 182 160.

Airport shuttle bus Skylink Airport Shuttle (08) 8413 6196.

Motoring organisation RAA (08) 8202 4600, roadside assistance 13 1111.

Car rental Avis 13 6333; Budget 13 2727; Europcar 13 1390; Hertz 13 3039; Thrifty 1300 367 227.

Taxis Independent Taxis 13 2211; Suburban Taxis 13 1008; Yellow Cabs 13 2227.

Tourist bus Adelaide Explorer (replica tram) (08) 8293 2966.

Bicycle hire Contact Bicycle SA for operators (08) 8168 9999.

The **Rundle Lantern**, on the corner of Rundle and Pulteney streets, uses computer-controlled LEDs to deliver a platform for digital art. It operates each night from dusk until midnight, with extended hours for special events.

Hindley Street 226 B2

At the other end of Rundle Mall, Hindley Street, sometimes known as the West End, is another lively part of Adelaide. The ornate Wests Coffee Palace building, constructed in 1903 as the Austral Stores and serving as a coffee palace from 1908 onwards, is now the home of **Arts SA**.

Parliament House & Government House 226 B2

These impressive buildings adorn the northern intersection of North Terrace and King William Road. Government House, the oldest in Australia, is set on a sweep of manicured lawns and was the meeting place of the first council of government. As the council expanded, new buildings were constructed, including what is now **Old Parliament House**. These buildings, along with several statues and monuments – including the **War Memorial** at the corner of Kintore Avenue – make for an interesting and informative walk. Government House normally has two open days a year; phone (08) 8203 9800 for details. Guided tours of Parliament House run on non-sitting days (Monday and Friday) at 10am and 2pm; sitting days are published on the website (www.parliament.sa.gov.au).

State Library of South Australia 226 C2

The State Library complex is a wonderful blend of charming 19th-century buildings and modern technology, bringing the history of South Australian culture to the people, as well as showcasing the library's collection. It also includes the Bradman Digital Library and Trail, based on the life of cricketer Sir Donald Bradman, who lived in Adelaide for much of his life. The archives are the ultimate research source covering his career. *North Tce; open daily; admission free.*

Migration Museum 226 C2

This museum details immigrant life from pioneering days up to today. The museum building was once Adelaide's Destitute Asylum, where many of the city's aged, homeless and underprivileged lived (and died). The stories of the women and children who lived there from the 1850s to 1918 are told in the 'Behind the Wall' exhibition. *82 Kintore Ave; open 10am–5pm Mon–Fri, 1–5pm Sat–Sun and public holidays; admission free.*

top events

Schützenfest Traditional German folk festival with music, food and frivolity in Bonython Park. January.

Jacobs Creek Tour Down Under Bike riders descend on Adelaide for this race into the hills. January.

Carnevale Adelaide Italian culture, food, song and dance in Rymill Park. February.

Adelaide Festival of Arts The city's defining event, and one of the world's highest regarded arts festivals. February–March (even-numbered years).

Adelaide Fringe Alongside the Festival of Arts, the edgy performances of this world-renowned annual festival are great entertainment. February–March.

WOMADelaide A huge festival of world music and dance in Botanic Park. March.

Clipsal 500 Adelaide V8 supercars race on city streets in what is said to be Australia's best motor event. March.

Glendi Festival Greek culture, food, song and dance in Ellis Park, West Terrace. March.

Tasting Australia International event celebrating food, wine and beer as well as chefs and writers. October (odd-numbered years).

Feast Festival One of the country's top gay and lesbian events, with theatre, film, dance and more. November.

Credit Union Christmas Pageant An Adelaide institution since 1933 welcomes Father Christmas to the city streets. November.

shopping

Rundle Mall The CBD's main shopping area, with major department stores as well as individual offerings of clothing, chocolates and much more. 226 C2

Melbourne Street, North Adelaide Adelaide's most exclusive shopping strip, with designer fashion boutiques. 225 G2

The Parade, Norwood Very cosmopolitan, with an array of stores and plenty of places to stop for a coffee, a meal or a drink. 225 H3

King William Road, Hyde Park Hip fashion outlets sprinkled among cafes, and furniture and homewares stores. 225 F4

Jetty Road, Glenelg A great mix of stores, and food and drink outlets. 224 B6

Harbour Town This complex offers seconds and discount stores. 224 B4

Magill Road, Stepney For antiques and second-hand treasures. 225 H2

See also Adelaide Central Market, p. 230, and Gouger Street, p. 230

markets

Fisherman's Wharf Market, Port Adelaide Fresh seafood and other produce are the main drawcards, but other food stalls and bric-a-brac make up the mix. Sun. 597 B8

Torrens Island Open Air Market, Port Adelaide Buy fish direct from the boat. Other food stalls also showcase quality local produce. Sun. 597 B7

Brickworks Market, Torrensville Located in an old kiln, the market's 100 stalls offer a wide range of wares, including clothing and crafts, as well as produce. Fri–Sun. 224 E2

Junction Markets, Kilburn Popular market offering fresh produce and specialty stores. Thurs–Sun. 596 C6

Adelaide Showgrounds Farmers' Market, Goodwood Fresh produce and gourmet goods. 9am–1pm Sun. 225 F4

See also Adelaide Central Market, p. 230

[ADELAIDE FESTIVAL CENTRE]

South Australian Museum 226 C2

For over a century, the South Australian Museum has played a crucial role in researching, documenting and exhibiting every facet of Aboriginal culture. The excellent **Australian Aboriginal Cultures Gallery** contains over 3000 objects and is the world's most comprehensive Aboriginal cultural exhibition.

In the **Origin Energy Fossil Gallery** is a fascinating collection of opalised fossils – look up to see the impressive model skeleton of the *Addyman plesiosaur*, a marine animal over 100 million years old.

Australia's richest natural history art exhibition, the Waterhouse Natural History Art Prize is held each year in the **ETSA Utilities Gallery** at the museum from July to September. *North Tce; open daily.*

Art Gallery of South Australia 226 C2

This gallery has grouped its permanent collection in three major categories. The Australian collection includes some fine works from distinguished South Australian artists Margaret Preston and Stella Bowen. An impressive display of contemporary British artwork is housed in the European collection, as is an array of major works by French sculptor Auguste Rodin.

The Asian collection includes delicate Japanese artworks and South-East Asian ceramics. There is also a program of changing exhibitions. *North Tce; open daily; general admission free.*

Ayers House 226 C2

North Terrace was the home of wealthy and prestigious figures such as Premier Henry Ayers, whose name identified the country's most recognisable landmark (Ayers Rock) until it was changed back to its Indigenous name, Uluṟu. After years in the hands of the Royal Adelaide Hospital, the original decorations of the building have now been painstakingly restored, and one wing has been transformed into a luxurious restaurant. *288 North Tce; open 10am–4pm Tues–Fri, 1–4pm Sat–Sun.*

Tandanya – National Aboriginal Cultural Institute 226 C2

This is a vibrant meeting place of cultures with a strong emphasis on the culture of the Kaurna people, the traditional owners of the land on which Adelaide stands. In the gallery, see the exciting work of emerging artists, or taste modern versions of traditional bush tucker in the cafe. Indigenous tours are also offered, encompassing both the centre and the grounds. *253 Grenfell St; open daily.*

Botanic Gardens of Adelaide 226 C2

The gardens were laid out in the mid-1800s and retain a northern-European style. The **Palm House**, imported in 1875, is a fine example of German engineering. The impressive **Bicentennial Conservatory** is considered to be the largest single-span conservatory in the Southern Hemisphere. Inside, walkways guide visitors through a lush rainforest environment, past endangered native and exotic plant species. **Amazon Waterlily Pavilion** is the most recent addition, opened in 2007. The fully licensed restaurant overlooking the Main Lake serves some of South Australia's finest wines and innovative cuisine. *North Tce; open daily, guided walks 10.30am.*

National Wine Centre of Australia 226 D2

Here visitors can take a Wine Discovery Journey through the different stages of wine-production, meet winemakers and try winemaking – all through virtual technology. The centre has its own vineyard and a retail centre for wine-tasting. *Cnr Botanic and Hackney rds; open daily; admission free.*

Adelaide Zoo 226 C1

The preservation of the zoo's 19th-century buildings and landscaped gardens has led many to call it the most attractive zoo in Australia. The **Elephant House** is a highlight of 1900s architecture – the enclosure's design was based on an Indian temple, and is now classified by the National Trust. The zoo's newest residents – giant pandas Wang Wang and Funi – are also very popular. *Frome Rd; open daily.*

The River Torrens 226 B1

The river provides a scenic setting for a host of leisure activities including enjoying a ride on Adelaide's **Popeye** cruises and motor launches. From the Elder Park Wharf, Popeye cruises operate every hour, on the hour, on weekdays, and every 20 minutes on weekends. Paddleboats can be hired on weekends from **Jolleys Boathouse** under the Adelaide Bridge on King William Road. You can also take a romantic Venetian gondola ride from Red Ochre restaurant day or night. Alternatively, enjoy good food and lovely views at the boathouse restaurant.

Adelaide Festival Centre 226 B2

In the 1970s, South Australia had a premier who was determined to turn the arts into a viable industry rather than just a pastime. Don Dunstan's accomplishments include developing the South Australian Film Corporation and increasing support for the state's other major arts groups. Overlooking Elder Park and the River Torrens, his Festival Centre consists of four theatres and is an architectural landmark. Visitors can take in a show or wander through the foyer to view the centre's collection of artworks as well as the changing displays of the **Performing Arts Collection of South Australia**, with its costumes, props and photographs. Visit the website (www.adelaidefestivalcentre.com.au) to find out what's on.

JamFactory – Contemporary Craft and Design 226 B2

Each year a rigorous application process sifts through hopefuls keen on becoming a Design Associate of the JamFactory. The pieces produced here are said to be some of the most innovative

where to stay

Adelaide Luxury Beach House A stunning beachfront residence with designer interiors, gulf views and outdoor living options. Esplanade, Henley Beach; 0418 675 339. 224 A3

Adelaide Shores Holiday Village Self-contained seafront bungalows offering relaxed family accommodation just metres from the beach. Military Rd, West Beach; (08) 8355 7360. 224 B4

Bishops Garden Hotel A lavish three-bedroom apartment in a historic villa with open living spaces and private garden. Molesworth St, North Adelaide; (08) 8272 1355. 225 F2

Majestic Old Lion Apartments Stylish courtyard units with self-contained comforts and close to cafes and parkland attractions. 9 Jerningham St, North Adelaide; (08) 8334 7799. 226 C1

Sebel Playford Adelaide A welcoming, boutique-style luxury hotel, acclaimed for its exceptional service and Art Nouveau flair. 120 North Tce; (08) 8213 8888. 226 B2

where to eat

Chianti Classico A welcoming family-run trattoria serving Italian regional fare with dash and rustic charm. 160 Hutt St; (08) 8232 7955; open daily for breakfast, lunch and dinner. 226 C3

Jasmin Perennial favourite for authentic Indian dishes brought to life by quality ingredients and spices. 31 Hindmarsh Sq; (08) 8223 7837; open Thurs–Fri for lunch and Tues–Sat for dinner. 226 C2

Jolleys Boathouse Smart, bistro-style dining featuring contemporary flavours in a relaxing riverside setting. Jolleys La; (08) 8223 2891; open Sun–Fri for lunch and Mon–Sat for dinner. 226 B1

Magill Estate Glorious city and vineyard views complement the artful marriage of fine cuisine with Penfolds wines. 78 Penfold Rd, Magill; (08) 8301 5551; open Fri for lunch and Tues–Sat for dinner. 597 C9

T Chow A diverse, crowd-pleasing menu of southern Chinese fare, including famed duck dishes. 68 Moonta St; (08) 8410 1413; open daily for lunch and dinner. 226 B3

entertainment

Cinema Those who want an atmospheric cinema-going experience should head for the Wallis Piccadilly Cinema in North Adelaide, which screens mainstream and arthouse films. A similar line-up is available at the Palace Nova cinemas in Rundle Street's East End. Adelaide's main alternative cinema is the Mercury at the Lion Arts Centre – it shows cult classics, foreign language and arthouse movies, and holds short film festivals. The Capri Theatre, in Goodwood, is notable for the live organ recitals that introduce film screenings on Tuesday, Saturday and Sunday nights. Check the *Adelaide Advertiser* for daily listings.

Live music The best live-music venue in Adelaide, without question, is the Governor Hindmarsh Hotel on Port Road, opposite the Adelaide Entertainment Centre. Offering everything from Irish fiddlers in the front bar to major international acts in the large, barn-like concert room at the back, The Gov (as it's known to the locals) has been the top venue in town for at least a decade. Plenty of other pubs also offer live music, like the Grace

Emily on Waymouth Street, an intimate venue that also boasts an excellent beer garden. The best way to find out what's on is to pick up a copy of *Rip It Up*, the local contemporary-music paper.

Classical music and performing arts The Adelaide Festival Centre is the hub of mainstream performing arts activity in Adelaide, hosting the three major and highly regarded state companies: State Theatre SA, State Opera of South Australia and Adelaide Symphony Orchestra (ASO). The ASO also holds small recitals at its Grainger Studio in Hindley Street. Adelaide nurtures a diverse range of theatre companies – look out for performances by the Australian Dance Theatre (contemporary dance), Vitalstatistix (women's theatre) and Windmill Performing Arts (children's theatre). The Lion Arts Centre is the venue for two innovative companies: Nexus (cabaret) and Doppio Teatro (multicultural). Indigenous dance is also on display in daily performances at Tandanya. The *Adelaide Advertiser* publishes a listing of entertainment events each Thursday.

grand old buildings

Barracks and Armoury Built in 1855, these magnificent examples of colonial architecture were the local Australian Army headquarters from 1857 to 1870. Behind South Australian Museum.

Adelaide Railway Station Built in 1856, the main feature is the Great Hall, with marble floors, Corinthian columns and a domed ceiling. SKYCITY Adelaide casino now occupies much of the station's upper floors. North Tce.

Edmund Wright House Wright was the architect of some of Adelaide's grandest buildings, including Parliament House, the GPO and the Adelaide and Glenelg town halls. This elaborate Italianate creation was completed in 1878 and used as a banking chamber. 59 King William St.

Adelaide Town Hall Opened in 1866, this building is much admired for its magnificent tower and classic portico, and its equally grand interior. Free tours run on Monday at 10am; bookings essential (08) 8203 7590. Regular classical music concerts and recitals. 128 King William St.

Bonython Hall Part of the University of Adelaide, the hall has an unusual sloping floor. This was insisted upon by benefactor Langdon Bonython, a strict Methodist, to prevent dancing. North Tce.

Elder Hall This church-like building in the grounds of the University of Adelaide is in fact a concert venue with a spectacular pipe organ. Next to Bonython Hall.

Churches As well as St Francis Xavier's Cathedral near Victoria Square, there's St Peter's Cathedral in North Adelaide and the Holy Trinity Church on North Terrace.

Old Adelaide Fruit and Produce Exchange The charming facade of this old wholesale market still stands on East Terrace. The rear has been converted into apartments.

Queens Theatre For a theatre, this is a surprisingly humble affair – perhaps because it is the oldest theatre on the mainland, built in 1840. Cnr Gilles Arcade and Playhouse La.

The Grange (Sturt House) The home of Charles Sturt, the man who sailed into South Australia on a whaleboat down the Murray, which led to the settlement of the state. Many original furnishings remain. Jetty St, Grange; open Fri–Sun and public holidays.

See also Ayers House, p. 228, Migration Museum, p. 227, Parliament House & Government House, p. 227, and Carrick Hill, p. 233

and impressive craft designs on the Australian market. Changing exhibits of international and JamFactory works are showcased in the gallery, and many one-off designs are available for purchase in the store. Nearby is another Adelaide arts institution, the **Experimental Art Foundation** at the Lion Arts Centre. This centre has some of the best in new media, such as video and installation art. *JamFactory: 19 Morphett St; open daily; admission free. There is also a JamFactory outlet in Rundle Plaza, open Mon–Fri.*

Historic Adelaide Gaol 226 A2

Today you can tour the cells and yards of this complex – which operated as a gaol from 1841 to 1988 – and imagine the days when Sister Mary MacKillop visited the prisoners, or take a night tour (bookings required) or a Ghost Tour. *Gaol Rd; tour bookings (08) 8231 4062; open 11am–4pm Mon–Fri and Sun.*

CBD South

The southern part of central Adelaide is home to some stellar attractions – the Adelaide Central Market is an absolute must-see, and there is superb dining on Gouger Street.

Adelaide Central Market 226 B3

Located just off Victoria Square, the market fills the block between Grote and Gouger streets. A showcase for South Australia's fresh produce, the market has evolved into a significant shopping and social centre. It's a wonderland of fruit, vegetables, fish, breads, cheeses, meats and nuts, with rows of stalls surrounded by alleys and arcades crammed with shops and cafes. Grab lunch at Zuma's, Malacca Corner or Lucia's, or just wander the aisles of the market and experience its sensory delights. *Open Tues and Thurs–Sat.*

Gouger Street 226 B3

Originally a spin-off from Central Market, Gouger Street has grown into an attraction in its own right with its restaurants, cafes, bars and clubs. Gouger Street winds down earlier than East End, but has its own character and appeal.

There are several Chinese restaurants on Gouger Street, but Adelaide's **Chinatown** is centred on Moonta Street between Gouger and Grote streets. Among the noodle bars and Chinese shops look for T Chow, an Adelaide institution.

Inner North

North Adelaide is one of the city's most exclusive residential addresses. It is also rich in history, with a mix of stately mansions and humble workers' cottages. From Light's Vision you can take a walk through Lower North Adelaide to get the full picture. Take Palmer Place (the section that runs parallel to Jeffcott Street) into Brougham Place to see old mansions with commanding views across the city.

Brougham Place continues into Stanley Street. Down the hill you'll find small stone cottages that formed part of South Australia's first subdivision. Melbourne Street is the heart of this area and is Adelaide's classiest street, with art galleries, boutiques, restaurants and the restored Lion Hotel.

To find the true cafe heart of North Adelaide, head to O'Connell Street – it has old pubs bedecked with Victorian iron lace, as well as restaurants and cafes. Tynte Street, which runs off O'Connell Street and was once North Adelaide's main street, has many fine 19th-century buildings.

R. M. Williams Outback Heritage Museum 597 A9

Reginald Murray Williams was a classic example of the 1930s battler. He made his first pair of boots in outback South Australia and later started up a 'factory' in his father's shed. Out of this grew an Australian legend. This museum, on the site of that shed, charts the story of his life in fascinating photographs, objects and displays. *5 Percy St, Prospect; open Mon–Fri; admission free.*

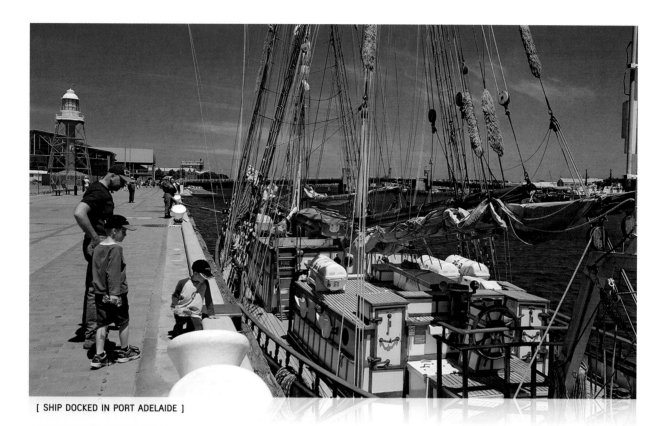

[SHIP DOCKED IN PORT ADELAIDE]

Inner South

Haigh's Chocolates 226 C4

Australia's oldest chocolate-maker is located just south of
Adelaide's CBD. The visitor centre includes a viewing area,
displays of original factory machinery and a delightful old-
world shop with a tempting array of chocolates. You'll be sure
to find your favourites after taking a tour (bookings essential).
*154 Greenhill Rd, Parkside; tour bookings (08) 8372 7077; free tours
11am, 1pm and 2pm Mon–Sat.*

Inner West

South Australian Brewing Company 224 E2

Not to be outdone in Australia's premier wine state, this company,
which makes a range of brands including Tooheys, XXXX, Hahn,
Lion Red, Steinlager and Speight's, offers tours of its premises.
Learn all about making beer by taking a tour (bookings essential),
from the raw materials through to brewing, canning and bottling.
*107 Port Rd, Thebarton; tour bookings (08) 8354 8888; tours
10.30am Mon–Thurs.*

Southern Bayside

Glenelg 224 B6

One of Adelaide's great features is its long frontage to Gulf St
Vincent. Glenelg is South Australia's best-known beach and
its most developed piece of coastal real estate. It spills with
shops, restaurants, high-rise apartments and people strolling,
sunbaking, cycling and rollerblading. It's around 20 minutes from
the city centre, on the sweep of Holdfast Bay.

Since the late 1800s Adelaidians have flocked to Glenelg to
partake of the sea air – the Glenelg tram, which was once the main
mode of transport, still runs to the suburb from Victoria Square in
the city. Other relics of the era have survived too, most notably the
grandiose 1875 town hall. Housed within it is the **Bay Discovery
Centre**, where an exhibition details the rich history of the area.

walks & tours

Adelaide Oval Tours Get an up-close view of this Adelaide icon
as well as access to the Adelaide Oval Museum. Weekdays at 10am,
departing from the southern gate (no bookings required). (08) 8300 3800.

Market Adventures Follow the experts through Adelaide's famous
Central Market. The same company also runs a 'Grazing on Gouger'
tour, giving people the chance to eat five courses at five of Gouger
Street's best restaurants. Bookings on (08) 8336 8333.

Wineries at your doorstep Visit McLaren Vale, one of Australia's
greatest wine regions, just 40 minutes from Adelaide. Enjoy the local
tasty foods too. Check out www.mclarenvale.info

City of Adelaide Historical Walking Trails Pick up a brochure from
the visitor centre and head out on themed walks covering everything
from the grand buildings of North Adelaide to the places of interest
around Rundle Mall and Adelaide's historic cinemas and theatres.

Port Walks Take a walk through historic Port Adelaide. Contact the Port
Adelaide Visitor Centre for details. 66 Commercial Rd; (08) 8405 6560.

Yurrebilla Trail Take in the magnificent bushland on Adelaide's
doorstep on this 52-kilometre trail that links Black Hill and Morialta
conservation parks in the north with Belair National Park in the south.
The scenery includes unsurpassed views of the city. Walkers can try
smaller sections of the hike. Contact the visitor centre for details or visit
the website (www.environment.sa.gov.au/parks/sanpr/yurrebilla).

parks and gardens

Rymill Park The centrepiece is Rymill Lake, with rowboats for hire, but there is also a large rose garden. City. 226 D2

Himeji Gardens Created in conjunction with Himeji, Adelaide's sister city, this garden blends classic Japanese styles. City. 226 C4

Veale Gardens For some years the green belt around Adelaide was more paddock than parkland, but a town clerk named William Veale started beautifying the gardens in the mid-1900s. Veale Gardens were his pièce de résistance. City. 226 B4

Bonython Park A park with native style. The river attracts birdlife, and there is also a children's playground and a popular picnic area. Thebarton. 226 A1

Linear Park This park follows the curves of the Torrens all the way from West Beach to Paradise, and is great for bike riding. The sections near the city offer fantastic views, while further out the track runs through a thick corridor of bushland. 224 B3, 225 G1

sport

Adelaide has been passionate about **cricket** from its earliest beginnings. Until his death in 2001, Adelaide was the proud home of Australia's greatest cricketer, Sir Donald Bradman. The city is also home to the Adelaide Oval, regarded as one of the most beautiful sporting arenas in the world. Adelaide's cricket test, usually in December, is a great event. Drop in and visit the famed Bradman Collection, featuring many items donated by the legendary player. *Open 9.30am–4.30pm Mon–Fri.*

With two local **AFL** (Australian Football League) teams, Adelaide and Port Adelaide, football is the city's other sporting passion. Showdown is the twice-yearly match between the two teams, and the whole city stops to watch what is considered Adelaide's own grand final. AAMI Stadium at West Lakes is the city's home of AFL.

In March there is a **motor race** that literally takes over the city. Sections of the Clipsal 500 Adelaide track, centring on Victoria Park Racecourse, are run on Wakefield Road and East Terrace in the south-east of the city. This V8 event was created after Adelaide lost the Australian Formula One Grand Prix to Melbourne and, interestingly, is more popular than Formula One ever was.

Also on the calendar is the AAPT Championships, the international **tennis** tournament held at Memorial Drive near the Adelaide Oval in early January. Adelaide's United **soccer** team matches are held at Hindmarsh Stadium, and the NBL 36ers play **basketball** on their home court at Beverley.

Each Year, on a public holiday Monday early in March, Adelaide comes alive with **horseracing** fever for the SKYCITY Adelaide Cup at Allan Scott Park, Morphettville. Held annually in November at Rymill Park, the Adelaide International Three Day Event is Australia's premier equestrian competition. It is the only CCI four-star event held in the Southern Hemisphere and one of only six held across the world.

Staged annually on the last Sunday in September, the Bay to Birdwood **vintage car rally** takes place. More than 1500 vehicles drive the 70-kilometre route from Adelaide Shores, West Lakes to the National Motor Museum Birdwood, watched by over 100 000 spectators.

History is re-created along the foreshore where a replica of the HMS *Buffalo* – the ship that carried the first South Australian settlers – now stands. Unlike the original, it has an onboard restaurant offering fine seafood dining, along with a small museum. Nearby is **Holdfast Shores**, a recent development with restaurants, boutique shopping and a massive marina.

Walking trails lead up and down the coast (for information call into the Bay Discovery Centre), and the calm water is perfect for swimming, fishing and sailing. And there is, of course, the long, iconic South Australian pier – this is the spot to dine on fish and chips at sunset. Experience swimming with dolphins from the *Temptation* catamaran (0412 811 838; www.dolphinboat.com.au), or simply enjoy a relaxing cruise.

Hallett Cove Conservation Park 597 A10

The southern suburbs of Adelaide begin to blur into the Fleurieu Peninsula just south of Brighton. Here you'll find Hallett Cove Conservation Park, which protects an incredible record of glaciation. A walking trail takes visitors on a guided geological tour to see some spectacular ochre- and sand-coloured rock formations. For the energetic, take the Marino Rocks to Hallett Cove boardwalk and reward yourself with refreshments at the Marino Rocks Café.

Western Bayside

Henley Beach to Semaphore 224 A2

At Henley Beach another long wooden jetty extends into Gulf St Vincent, flanked on either side by a long strip of sand and lapping waters. Set just back from the sea is **Henley Square**, a drawcard especially on weekends with restaurants, bars and cafes often humming with live music.

Straight up Seaview Road is the suburb of **Grange**, which has its own combination of beach and jetty. Relax and enjoy the view over coffee or a cafe meal at the Grange Jetty Kiosk.

Further along is **Semaphore**, a suburb with fine heritage buildings, many cafes and uninterrupted sea views. The Art Deco **Semaphore Palais** offers dining right on the waterfront, while the Semaphore Waterslide Complex has activities for the kids. A walking and bike-riding track heads north to Largs Bay and North Haven Marina, and visitors can also take a 40-minute ride aboard a tourist train to Fort Glanville, built in 1878 in response to fears of a Russian invasion. *Train operates 11am–4pm Sat–Sun (Oct–April), school and public holidays.*

North-west

Port Adelaide 597 B8

Without being overly commercialised, 'the Port', established in 1840, retains the charm of its maritime history and serves as an interesting destination in its own right, with weekend wharf markets, pubs and cafes, and galleries and antique shops. This was South Australia's first State Heritage Area, with historic buildings and a sense of the days when the old ports were busy trading and social centres.

This is, however, still very much a working port, with a grain terminal, a tug-base, and fishing and pleasure boats in the inner port – on the upper reaches of the Port River – and a container terminal and wharves for large ships in the outer harbour, at the mouth of the river.

The Port Adelaide Visitor Information Centre has information about attractions, events and cruises. *66 Commercial Rd; (08) 8405 6560; open daily.*

South Australian Maritime Museum 597 B8

Behind the red-and-white lighthouse in the middle of Port Adelaide, on Queens Wharf, visitors can immerse themselves in South Australia's beach-going lifestyle, climb aboard a replica ketch, or learn about the tentative beginnings of the state's rock-lobster industry. This is a first-class centre with a program of permanent and changing exhibitions. *126 Lipson St, Port Adelaide; open daily.*

Port Adelaide's dolphins 597 B8

The environment of thick mangroves, mud and mosquitoes didn't endear the Port Adelaide area to the early settlers and they named it Port Misery. Today this environment is known as a haven for birdlife and the home of animals including a pod of playful bottlenose dolphins. Visitors can drive along the Dolphin Trail to the six hot spots where dolphins are commonly sighted (maps are available from the visitor centre) or take a cruise from Queens Wharf near the lighthouse – the dolphins often swim alongside the boat. For a special outing, book a cruise on one of the tall ships docked at the wharf. *Port Adelaide Visitor Centre, 66 Commercial Rd.*

Ships' Graveyard 597 B8

Many shipwrecks and other sunken vessels around Australia provide magnificent sites for divers – but the one in Port Adelaide can be accessed from land. Around 25 wrecks were abandoned on the south side of Garden Island, including barges, sailing ships and steamers – their disintegrating skeletons create an eerie skyline above the water. Visitors can view this watery graveyard from the Garden Island Bridge, or – for a closer look – on a kayak tour with Adventure Kayaking SA, (08) 8295 8812.

North

St Kilda 597 B7

St Kilda is more of an outer village than an outer suburb, even though it is only a short distance (as the crow flies) from Port

Adelaide and the Lefevre Peninsula. The access road crosses vast salt crystallisation pans, but beyond them is an idyllic little marina and other attractions that make this an excellent daytrip destination. First is the **Mangrove Trail and Interpretive Centre**, which gives a fascinating insight into this little-understood ecosystem and its inhabitants. Then there is the **Tramway Museum**, open afternoons on Sundays and public holidays, which has 20 historic trams and provides tram rides to the nearby adventure playground. The playground is St Kilda's showcase attraction, with a range of unique play equipment that includes a wooden ship, giant slides and a monorail.

South

Carrick Hill 225 H6

This 1930s house was once the home of Edward and Ursula Hayward – Edward was the son of wealthy retailers, and Ursula was the daughter of wealthy pastoralists. On their year-long honeymoon they collected many of the fittings for their house, including 16th- to 18th-century windows, doors, staircases and panelling. When they returned, their house was built in the style of a 17th-century English manor. The gardens surrounding the house contain a citrus orchard, a pleached pear arbour and avenues of poplars. The house also has an impressive collection of art. The **Children's Literary Trail** is an enchanting walk encompassing scenes from 10 popular children's classics throughout the grounds. *46 Carrick Hill Dr, Springfield; open Wed–Sun and public holidays.*

East

Penfolds Magill Estate 597 C9

This winery, located between the city and the hills, was the first venture of Penfolds, one of Australia's best-known winemakers. Established in 1844, the vintage cellar is still used for making shiraz, and the Still House, once used for making brandy, is now used for cellar-door tastings and sales. The Magill Estate Restaurant has views over the Adelaide Plains, fine food and an incredible wine list – including Grange by the glass! *78 Penfold Rd, Magill; (08) 8301 5551; tours 11am and 3pm daily, lunch Fri, dinner Tues–Sat.*

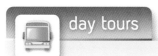
day tours

Adelaide Hills The hills directly east of Adelaide have long been a retreat for citysiders including, most famously, 19th-century governors. Today the attractions of this beautiful semi-rural area include cool-climate wineries, gourmet produce, forests and lookouts over the city. For more details see p. 237

Barossa Valley Australia's best-known winegrowing region is a landscape of rolling yellow hills carpeted with vines. It boasts around 50 wineries, including some of the top names in the business. The district owes much to its strong German heritage, which is also expressed in the local food, architecture and many cultural events. For more details see p. 238

Clare Valley Boutique wineries, attractive 19th-century buildings and magnificent food and accommodation make the scenic Clare Valley a favourite weekend retreat. Just east of Clare is another world altogether – the old mining region of Burra, with landmarks that recall the immense copper boom. For more details see p. 239

Fleurieu Peninsula The small seaside villages along Gulf St Vincent and the historic maritime town of Victor Harbor are irresistible seaside destinations close to the capital. En route to the peninsula, visitors can stop in at one of the cellar doors around McLaren Vale, one of the country's top wine regions. For more details see p. 235

Murraylands Before ending its long journey at Lake Alexandrina and onto the rich wetlands of the Coorong, the Murray River passes through diverse landscapes of rugged cliffs, mallee scrub, river red gum forests and pastoral lands. Visitors can relive the river's rich history as a bustling trade route and take a relaxing cruise from one of the ports of yesterday. For more details see p. 241

REGIONS
south australia

[FLINDERS RANGES]

[REMARKABLE ROCKS, KANGAROO ISLAND]

NORTHERN   TERRITORY   QUEENSLAND

WESTERN

AUSTRALIA

Flinders Ranges & Outback
243

NEW   SOUTH   WALES

Eyre Peninsula
& Nullarbor
244

Mid-North

239

Barossa Valley
238

Yorke Peninsula
240

ADELAIDE

Murray
241

VICTORIA

236
Kangaroo Island

242 Limestone
Coast

Fleurieu
Peninsula
235

Adelaide
Hills
237

FLEURIEU PENINSULA

This region is South Australia's most popular and accessible holiday destination, also known for its wineries and gourmet produce.

[ALMOND BLOSSOM AT MCLAREN VALE WINERY]

McLaren Vale While wineries are a major feature of this area, vines are not the only side to agriculture here – olives, almonds, avocados and stone fruits are also grown in the fertile surrounds. In town, visit the Almond and Olive Train and the McLaren Vale Olive Grove for local produce, and head to Medlow Confectionery for high-quality gels and chocolates.

Mount Compass Gourmet Trail Mount Compass is the centre of gourmet food production in the region, with trout, berry, deer, pheasant and marron farms open for viewing and sales. Pick up a touring map from the visitor centre in McLaren Vale.

Gulf St Vincent coast The Fleurieu Peninsula's western coastline includes spectacular scenery and popular holiday towns. Go snorkelling at Port Noarlunga, dive off Aldinga Beach, bathe at one of a number of family beaches or visit the heritage-listed sand dunes at Normanville.

Victor Harbor Historic Victor Harbor on Encounter Bay began as a whaling port in the 1830s, later becoming the ocean port for trade along the Murray River. Today visitors can soak up the relaxed atmosphere of this popular holiday resort town. Take a walk around the many heritage sites, jump on a horse-drawn tram to Granite Island to see penguins, dolphins and maybe even whales, or ride around the bay to Goolwa on the historic Cockle Train, in operation since 1887.

Map labels

Port Noarlunga
ONKAPARINGA RIVER NATIONAL PARK
McLaren Vale
Strathalbyn
Langhorne Creek
Angas
Aldinga Beach
Willunga
GULF ST VINCENT
Bremer R.
Mount Compass
N
0   10 km
Normanville
Yankalilla
Lake Alexandrina
FLEURIEU PENINSULA
Port Elliot
Goolwa
Victor Harbor
Encounter Bay
Granite Island
COORONG NATIONAL PARK
Cape Jervis
SOUTHERN OCEAN

TOP EVENTS

JAN	Milang to Goolwa Freshwater Sailing Classic
JUNE	Sea and Vines Festival (McLaren Vale)
JUNE	Playtime Festival and Whale Season Launch (Victor Harbor)
JULY–AUG	Almond Blossom Festival (Willunga)
OCT	Glenbarr Highland Gathering (Strathalbyn)
OCT	Fiesta! (McLaren Vale)

CLIMATE

VICTOR HARBOR

J	F	M	A	M	J	J	A	S	O	N	D	
25	25	23	21	19	16	15	16	18	20	22	24	MAX °C
15	15	14	12	10	8	8	8	9	10	12	14	MIN °C
21	20	23	43	62	71	75	67	56	46	28	24	RAIN MM
5	4	6	10	14	15	17	16	14	11	8	7	RAIN DAYS

WINE DISTRICTS

The Fleurieu Peninsula has two main wine-producing districts: McLaren Vale and Langhorne Creek. The McLaren Vale district is set against a landscape of weathered hills and rolling acres. With a viticulture history dating back to 1838, the region is highly regarded particularly for its full-bodied reds, most notably its shiraz. Over 50 wineries, ranging from boutique outfits to big players, are located in the district – Tourist Route 60 is an excellent way to explore both the wineries and the region. The second district is based around the highly productive Langhorne Creek area on the floodplains of the Bremer and Angas rivers. Vines have been grown here since the 1850s, but only five cellar doors offer tastings and sales. Many of the grapes grown here are sold to wine producers in other regions around the country.

→ For more detail see maps 596, 597, 598, 599, 601 & 603. For descriptions of ⊤ towns see Towns from A–Z (p. 245).

SOUTH AUSTRALIA

KANGAROO ISLAND

Australia's third largest island is a relatively untouched paradise with a large population of native creatures that live undisturbed in pristine, natural habitats.

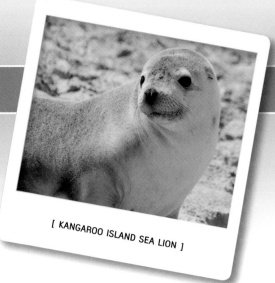

[KANGAROO ISLAND SEA LION]

Cape Borda Lighthouse This unusually shaped lighthouse – squat and square rather than tall and round – was built in 1858 and converted to automatic operation in 1989. Guided tours are conducted regularly and accommodation is available in the old lighthouse keeper's residence.

Gourmet produce Fast developing as an authentic, grassroots foodie destination, 'KI' is deservedly proud of its 'clean and green' status. The island offers flapping-fresh seafood, superb cheese and honey. Try Ferguson Australia in Kingscote for fresh rock lobster and crab, Island Pure Sheep Dairy in Cygnet River (for its haloumi, in particular) and Clifford's Honey Farm in MacGillivray. Cafe-style eateries showcasing local produce are dotted across the island; Rockpool Cafe in remote Stokes Bay is one favourite.

Flinders Chase National Park This park is the location of the Remarkable Rocks, enormous weathered boulders that are perched precariously on a cliff. It is also known for its wonderfully varied springtime wildflowers and for its wildlife – including the New Zealand fur seal colony at Cape du Couedic and the Cape Barren geese often seen wandering around the visitor centre. Walking trails lead into the wilderness.

Seal Bay Conservation Park Some 700 Australian sea lions feed their young and rest between fishing expeditions at Seal Bay. See the creatures from a boardwalk or up-close on a ranger-guided tour, which takes you down onto the beach.

Kingscote The island's largest town, Kingscote is situated on the Bay of Shoals. It was the site of the state's first European settlement (1836), and its long pioneering history is presented in the excellent National Trust Museum. Other attractions include tours to see the nearby colony of little penguins.

TOP EVENTS

FEB	Racing Carnival (Kingscote)
FEB	Street Party (Kingscote)
EASTER	Art Exhibition (Penneshaw)
OCT	Kangaroo Island Art Feast (Penneshaw)

CLIMATE

KINGSCOTE

J	F	M	A	M	J	J	A	S	O	N	D	
24	24	22	20	18	15	15	15	17	19	21	22	MAX °C
15	15	14	13	11	9	8	8	9	10	12	14	MIN °C
15	17	18	35	58	73	77	65	47	37	23	19	RAIN MM
4	4	5	9	13	16	18	17	13	10	7	5	RAIN DAYS

WILDLIFE-WATCHING

As a result of its isolation from the mainland, Kangaroo Island has one of Australia's most impressive concentrations of wildlife. Seal Bay is home to a colony of Australian sea lions, while at Cape du Couedic in Flinders Chase National Park there is a 600-strong colony of New Zealand fur seals. This national park is also the best place to see land animals like kangaroos, tammar wallabies, brush-tailed possums and the occasional koala or platypus. Little penguins can be seen on tours operating from Kingscote or Penneshaw. There is a large and varied bird population (240 species) across the island, with Murray Lagoon (en route to Seal Bay) home to many waterbirds.

→ For more detail see maps 598, 599, 601, 602 & 603. For descriptions of ⊕ towns see Towns from A–Z (p. 245).

ADELAIDE HILLS

An interesting mix of Australian bushland and European-style farmland is the setting for this region's historic villages, gardens, museums, galleries and wineries.

[GERMAN-STYLE CRAFT SHOP, HAHNDORF]

Cleland Wildlife Park   Within Cleland Conservation Park, this excellent wildlife park has a large collection of everybody's favourite animals, including kangaroos, emus and wallabies. Nocturnal walks reveal some of the rarer species, including bettongs and bandicoots. Daytime visits could be combined with a picnic in the adjacent Mount Lofty Botanic Gardens.

Belair National Park   South Australia's oldest national park, established in 1891, offers a natural landscape of eucalypt forests and brilliant flowering plants. Green thumbs will enjoy a stroll through the gardens of the governor's old summer residence, which dates back to 1859.

Birdwood National Motor Museum   This impressive museum has the largest collection of vintage vehicles in the Southern Hemisphere, with more than 300 classic cars, motorcycles and commercial vehicles housed in an 1852 flour mill. Learn about the history of motoring and visit the workshop complex to see the vehicles being lovingly restored by coach builders and mechanics.

Hahndorf   This distinctive town was settled in the 1830s by Prussian refugees. Its heritage is preserved in the village architecture and German-style shops, museums and cafes. Visit The Cedars, former home of artist Hans Heysen, and see contemporary artworks at the Hahndorf Academy.

Mount Lofty Lookout   Enjoy spectacular views of Adelaide and the hills from the lookout at the 727-metre summit of Mount Lofty. Drop in to the information centre to plan your day, and enjoy 'food with a view' in the adjacent restaurant and cafe.

TOP EVENTS

EASTER	Oakbank Easter Racing Carnival (Oakbank)
APR	Rock and Roll Rendezvous (Birdwood)
MAY	Jazz and Heritage Festival (Mount Barker)
SEPT	Bay to Birdwood Run (vintage vehicles, even-numbered years)
SEPT–OCT	Heysen Festival (Hahndorf)
DEC	Lights of Lobethal Festival (Lobethal)

CLIMATE

MOUNT BARKER

J	F	M	A	M	J	J	A	S	O	N	D	
27	27	25	20	17	14	13	14	16	19	22	25	MAX °C
12	12	10	8	7	5	5	5	6	7	9	10	MIN °C
26	26	31	59	89	100	105	103	86	68	40	34	RAIN MM
6	5	7	11	15	16	17	18	15	13	9	7	RAIN DAYS

FOOD AND WINE

The Adelaide Hills are becoming increasingly well known as a touring destination for those with gourmet inclinations. Highlights include a visit to Petaluma's Bridgewater Mill, an old flour mill, for tastings and sales of Petaluma wines or lunch at the attached restaurant. In Hahndorf try German-style produce, including breads and smallgoods, at the many outlets. Here you can also buy full-flavoured berry produce at Beerenberg Strawberry Farm or go wine-tasting at Hahndorf Hill Winery or Hillstowe Wines. There is an excellent introduction to South Australia's regional wine and cheese at the Birdwood Wine and Cheese Centre, which offers tastings. Fine boutique wineries are also found around Birdwood.

SOUTH AUSTRALIA

→ For more detail see maps 596, 597, 598, 601 & 603. For descriptions of ⓣ towns see Towns from A–Z (p. 245).

BAROSSA VALLEY

Australia's best-known wine region offers a landscape of vine-covered hills dotted with historic villages, stone cottages and the grand buildings of old wine estates.

[CHATEAU DE KARLSBURG, BAROSSA VALLEY]

Seppeltsfield   The Seppelts estate, established in the 1850s, is one of the grandest in the country. Elegant bluestone buildings are surrounded by superb gardens, and the property is accessed by an avenue of 2000 date palms. Don't miss the hill-top mausoleum built in the style of a Doric temple.

Barossa wineries   In this famed region is a landscape of old, gnarled shiraz vines planted as early as the 1840s, adding character to the newer vines and varieties. The Barossa is best known for its shiraz, semillon and chardonnay. The biennial Barossa Vintage Festival is a time of great activity and colour.

Kaiserstuhl Conservation Park   This rugged mountain-side park offers a view of what the Barossa would have looked like before European settlement. A couple of excellent walking trails allow visitors to explore the varied terrain and glimpse the local wildlife.

Eden Valley wineries   This elevated wine-producing area is regarded as a distinct region, with a small number of wineries are open for tastings. In Springton stands the Herbig Tree, a giant, hollow red gum that was the temporary home of a German family in the 1850s.

TOP EVENTS

FEB	Barossa under the Stars (Tanunda)
EASTER	Gawler Gourmet and Heritage Festival (Gawler)
APR	Barossa Vintage Festival (throughout region, odd-numbered years)
OCT	Barossa International Music Festival (throughout region)
OCT	Barossa Band Festival (Tanunda)

CLIMATE

NURIOOTPA

	J	F	M	A	M	J	J	A	S	O	N	D	
	29	29	26	21	17	14	13	14	17	20	24	26	MAX °C
	14	14	12	9	7	5	4	5	6	8	10	12	MIN °C
	19	19	22	38	55	56	66	64	60	49	29	24	RAIN MM
	5	4	5	8	12	13	16	16	13	11	8	6	RAIN DAYS

GOURMET TRADITION

While many parts of Australia have developed gourmet credentials over the last decade or so, the Barossa has a culinary heritage that dates back to the mid-1800s. German-style baking is a highlight: try the Lyndoch Bakery, or the Apex Bakery in Tanunda, established 70 years ago. Old-fashioned ice-cream is made and served at Tanunda's Nice Ice and in Angaston you'll find the shopfront for Australia's biggest processor of dried fruit – the Angas Park Fruit Company. Maggie Beer's Farm Shop at Nuriootpa sells the cook's renowned products – everything from quince paste to verjuice – while Angaston Gourmet Foods is a one-stop shop for all the best local foods.

→ For more detail see maps 596, 597, 601 & 603. For descriptions of ⊕ towns see Towns from A–Z (p. 245).

MID-NORTH

Clare Valley wineries and the historically important coppermining sites of Burra make this a great place for a weekend away.

[FARMHOUSE BESIDE THE BARRIER HIGHWAY]

Clare Valley wineries This wine-producing district extends for 35 kilometres across the fertile valley, including big names as well as charming boutique establishments. Well-known names include Annie's Lane, Taylors, Pikes and Mount Horrocks. Although the climate is generally Mediterranean in style, many Clare Valley wines have cool-climate characteristics. Clare Valley rieslings are regarded as among the best in Australia.

Clare Valley produce The Clare Valley is famed for its gourmet food producers, who embrace the slow-food philosophy in their lovingly created offerings, such as chutneys, jams, olive oils and sausages, available at Wild Saffron in Clare and other outlets throughout the region.

Riesling Trail Running through the picturesque Clare Valley wine region between Clare and Auburn, this scenic 27-kilometre route is the perfect way to visit the surrounding villages and wineries on foot or by bicycle. One of the first rail trails to be commissioned in South Australia, it traverses the old Riverton to Spalding railway line, passing by several cellar doors on the way.

Burra Located in the sparse landscape of the Bald Hills Range, this former coppermining centre is a timepiece of the mid-19th century. Pick up a Burra Heritage Passport and visit mine shafts, museums and heritage buildings. Marvel at the creek-bed dugouts that were home to over 1800 miners, and see the working conditions on a guided mine tour.

Sevenhill Cellars Austrian Jesuit priests established the Clare Valley's first winery here in 1851 to ensure a steady supply of altar wine. The winery continues to be run by Jesuits, and now offers a range of table wines. Drop into St Aloysius Church (1875), next to the cellars.

Mintaro Mintaro is an almost-intact 19th-century village, with many attractive stone buildings incorporating the region's unique slate. It was the first town in South Australia to be declared a State Heritage Area. Just south-east is Martindale Hall, an 1879 mansion used in the film *Picnic at Hanging Rock* (1975) and now open to the public.

Map:
Peterborough
Jamestown
Spalding
Burra
Clare
Sevenhill
Mintaro
Auburn
Balaklava
Riverton
Kapunda
GULF ST VINCENT
N 0 20 km

→ For more detail see maps 597, 599, 601, 603 & 605. For descriptions of ⊕ towns see Towns from A–Z (p. 245).

TOP EVENTS

FEB	Jailhouse Rock Festival (Burra)
MAR	Music in the Monster Mine (Burra)
EASTER	Clare Races (horseracing, Clare)
MAY	Antique and Decorating Fair (Burra)
MAY	Gourmet Weekend (Clare)
SEPT	Celtic Music Festival (Kapunda, dates vary)

CLIMATE

CLARE

J	F	M	A	M	J	J	A	S	O	N	D	
30	29	27	22	17	14	13	15	18	21	25	27	MAX °C
13	13	12	8	6	4	3	4	5	7	10	12	MIN °C
25	24	25	47	73	80	82	80	73	57	37	29	RAIN MM
4	4	5	8	12	14	15	15	13	11	7	6	RAIN DAYS

MID-NORTH HISTORY

Historically, this is one of the most interesting and well-preserved areas of rural South Australia. In 1839 Edward Eyre explored the Clare Valley and his favourable reports led quickly to pastoral settlement. Jesuit priests planted the first Clare Valley vines at Sevenhill in 1851, and a booming wine industry followed. Copper deposits found at Burra and Kapunda in the 1840s drove a huge mining industry, but this fell into decline in the 1870s. The community's perseverance in preserving Burra's history led to the town's State Heritage Area listing in 1993. Kapunda had a change of direction after mining, with cattle baron Sir Sidney Kidman initiating an agricultural industry that has since grown exponentially. This mixture of viticulture, agriculture and mining history is a Clare Valley attraction in itself – endless stories of survival and success can be found in the museums and displays throughout the region.

SOUTH AUSTRALIA

YORKE PENINSULA

This long, boot-shaped peninsula is a popular beachside holiday destination with the surrounding waters offering excellent fishing, diving and surfing.

[WOOL BAY, NEAR STANSBURY]

Little Cornwall   The Cornish miners that flocked to Wallaroo, Moonta and Kadina in the early 1860s prompted the colloquial name for this triangle of towns – Little Cornwall. The discovery of substantial copper deposits led to a prosperous mining industry, revealed in the heritage architecture of the three towns. Visit the Moonta Mines State Heritage Area, with walking trails to mining ruins.

Innes National Park   At the southern tip of the peninsula, Innes National Park protects salt lakes, low mallee scrub, wildflowers, sandy beaches and rugged cliffs. Browns Beach, West Cape and Pondalowie Bay are popular for surfing, diving and fishing. A 1904 shipwreck can be glimpsed from Ethel Beach, and the interesting remains of Inneston mining town are found in the southern area of the park.

Port Victoria   This town was once the main port of call for the clippers and windjammers that transported grain to the Northern Hemisphere, a period of history recorded in the local Maritime Museum. Port Victoria is now a resort town, offering access to swimming beaches and Wardang Island, a popular diving spot with an underwater heritage trail featuring eight wrecks.

Edithburgh   The town's jetty was once the site of a large shipping operation, when tonnes of salt harvested from the nearby lakes were exported from here. Edithburgh is now a popular resort town. Attractions include a tidal pool for safe swimming, good diving locations and access to Troubridge Island, home to populations of little penguins, black-faced shags and crested terns.

Map labels:
PORT PIRIE · Crystal Brook · Port Broughton · Wallaroo · Bumbunga Lake · Kadina · Moonta Bay · Moonta · SPENCER GULF · YORKE PENINSULA · Maitland · Goose Island · Wardang Island · Port Victoria · Ardrossan · GULF ST VINCENT · Minlaton · Stansbury · Edithburgh · Troubridge Island · Yorketown · Browns Beach · Pondalowie Bay · West Cape · Inneston · INNES NATIONAL PARK · INVESTIGATOR STRAIT · N · 0   20 km

TOP EVENTS

MAY	Kernewek Lowender (Cornish festival, odd-numbered years, Kadina, Moonta and Wallaroo)
JUNE	Winter Fun Fishing Contest (Port Broughton)
SEPT	Blessing of the Fleet (Port Pirie)
OCT	Garden Fair (Moonta)
OCT	Yorke Surfing Classic (Innes National Park)
OCT	Festival of Country Music (Port Pirie)

CLIMATE

KADINA

	J	F	M	A	M	J	J	A	S	O	N	D	
	31	30	28	24	19	16	15	17	20	23	26	28	MAX °C
	16	16	14	11	9	7	6	6	8	10	12	14	MIN °C
	15	19	19	33	46	52	49	45	39	34	23	18	RAIN MM
	3	3	4	6	10	12	13	13	10	8	6	4	RAIN DAYS

FISHING

The Yorke Peninsula is one of South Australia's top fishing destinations, with jetties at Wallaroo, Moonta Bay, Edithburgh, Stansbury and Port Victoria, and rocky points and sandy coves all through the region, providing excellent opportunities for land-based anglers. Snapper, squid, tommy ruff, garfish and whiting are among the more commonly caught species. Reef-fishing is also popular. Browns Beach, on the western side of Innes National Park, is renowned for its big hauls of salmon. Near Goose Island, just north of Wardang Island on the west coast, are two reefs that offer excellent boat fishing for a variety of species.

→ For more detail see maps 599, 601, 602–3 & 604. For descriptions of ⊕ towns see Towns from A–Z (p. 245).

MURRAY

Rich in history, this region encompasses cliff-lined river valleys, mallee scrub, river red gum forests, lagoons, orchards and vineyards.

[BANDSTAND IN RIVERSIDE PARK, MANNUM]

Morgan Morgan's days as a busy river port may be over, but a rich legacy of sites and buildings preserves something of the excitement of the 19th-century river trade. Look out for the wharves (built in 1877), the customs house and the courthouse. For a thorough look at the history of Morgan, drop in to the Port of Morgan Historical Museum in the old railway buildings.

Camping and watersports From Murray Bridge to Renmark there are caravan parks and camping grounds with river frontage and access to a wide range of watersports, including canoeing, fishing and swimming. Murray River National Park provides a couple of quiet spots at the north-east end of the river for those who like their recreation in a park setting.

Houseboat on the Murray River A terrific way to discover the secrets of the mighty Murray is to captain your own houseboat. Slow down and take in the captivating landscapes of river red gums, limestone cliffs, plains and mallee scenery; at times you may have this beautiful river all to yourself. Houseboats are for hire at numerous places along the South Australian, Victorian and New South Wales stretches of the river, at towns such as Murray Bridge, Renmark, Mildura and Echuca–Moama.

Riverland produce The Riverland is the fruit bowl of South Australia, producing over 90 per cent of the state's citrus fruit, stone fruit and nuts. Wine is also produced here; tastings and sales are available at half a dozen estates, including Angoves near Renmark, Berri Estates Winery near Berri, and Banrock Station Wine and Wetland Centre at Kingston-on-Murray.

The Coorong The Coorong, a shallow lagoon protected within Coorong National Park, is one of Australia's most significant wetlands. It stretches 135 kilometres along the coast, separated from the Southern Ocean by the dunes of the Younghusband Peninsula. The Coorong is best known for its abundant birdlife (and for birdwatching). Over 240 species have been recorded, including many migratory species.

TOP EVENTS

FEB	Riverland Greek Festival (Renmark)
FEB	Mardi Gras (Loxton)
MAR	Rotary Food Fair (Waikerie)
JUNE	South Australian Country Music Festival (Barmera)
JUNE	Riverland Balloon Fiesta (Renmark)
OCT	Rose Festival (Renmark)

CLIMATE

RENMARK

J	F	M	A	M	J	J	A	S	O	N	D	
33	32	29	24	20	17	16	18	21	24	28	30	MAX °C
17	17	14	11	8	6	5	6	8	11	13	15	MIN °C
16	19	14	18	25	25	23	25	28	28	21	18	RAIN MM
3	3	3	4	6	8	8	9	7	6	4	4	RAIN DAYS

PADDLESTEAMERS

Paddlesteamers were first used in South Australia when PS *Mary Ann* was launched at Mannum in 1853. Carrying goods and passengers, they were vital in the development of the all-important trade route that ran from the mouth of the Murray River into New South Wales and Victoria (and vice versa). Two of the original boats, PS *Mayflower* and PS *Marion*, operate as day-cruisers, departing from Morgan and Mannum respectively. Longer tours are available from Mannum on PS *River Murray Princess* – the largest paddleboat ever built in the Southern Hemisphere.

→ For more detail see maps 597, 601 & 603. For descriptions of ⊕ towns see Towns from A–Z (p. 245).

SOUTH AUSTRALIA

LIMESTONE COAST

A major holiday region, the Limestone Coast features the World Heritage— listed Naracoorte Caves, Mount Gambier and the prestigious wineries of the Coonawarra.

[COASTAL SCENERY NEAR BEACHPORT]

Bool Lagoon Game Reserve One of southern Australia's largest and most diverse freshwater lagoon systems, Bool Lagoon was declared a reserve in 1967 and is on the Ramsar List of Wetlands of International Importance. These wetlands rarely dry out, creating a refuge for over 150 bird species, including brolgas, black swans, magpie geese and tiny fairy-wrens. A network of boardwalks, trails and observation hides, such as a 500-metre boardwalk to an ibis rookery, allows close-up views of the wetland activity.

Robe Settled in the 1840s, Robe is one of the state's oldest and best-preserved towns. It boasts a fine collection of stone cottages, shops, public buildings and hotels, many of them National Trust–classified. Set around Guichen Bay along a beautiful stretch of coast, Robe combines a quaint fishing-village atmosphere with excellent facilities for holiday-makers.

Naracoorte Caves Along with Queensland's Riversleigh Fossil Site, this is one of Australia's most significant cave systems, a fact reflected by its World Heritage listing. There are 60 known caves, several of which are open to the public. At the excellent Wonambi Fossil Centre, displays show how the fossils found in these caves have played a key role in charting the continent's evolutionary history.

The Coonawarra The Coonawarra is Australia's most valuable piece of wine real estate. The first vines were planted by John Riddoch in the late-1800s. Since then this 12-kilometre-long and 2-kilometre-wide stretch of terra rossa soil has continually produced wine of the highest quality, chiefly bold red varieties. The region's cabernet sauvignon is outstanding. Over 20 wineries offer cellar-door tastings and sales.

Mount Gambier This major regional centre is set on the slopes of an extinct volcano – its crater contains the intensely coloured Blue Lake. Beneath the town, stretching from the coast all the way to Bordertown in the north, is an enormous wedge of limestone that has given rise to many caves. Nearby examples include Engelbrecht Cave (popular with divers) and the Umpherston Sinkhole.

Map labels

Kingston S.E.
Cape Jaffa
Naracoorte
NARACOORTE CAVES NATIONAL PARK
Lake Hawdon North
Guichen Bay
Robe
BOOL LAGOON GAME RESERVE
Bool Lagoon
Lake Eliza
Lake Hawdon South
Lake St Clair
Coonawarra
Lake George
Penola
Beachport
VICTORIA
Millicent
CANUNDA NATIONAL PARK
Lake Bonney S.E
MOUNT GAMBIER
SOUTHERN OCEAN
Port MacDonnell
0   20 km
N

TOP EVENTS

JAN	Cape Jaffa Seafood and Wine Festival (Cape Jaffa)
FEB	Blue Lake City Muster (country music event, Mount Gambier)
FEB	Taste the Limestone Coast (Naracoorte)
MAY	Penola Coonawarra Arts Festival (Penola)
MAY	Mount Gambier Gold Cup Carnival (Mount Gambier)
OCT	Cabernet Celebrations (Coonawarra/Penola)

CLIMATE

MOUNT GAMBIER

	J	F	M	A	M	J	J	A	S	O	N	D	
	25	25	23	19	16	14	13	14	16	18	20	23	MAX °C
	11	12	10	9	7	6	5	5	6	7	8	10	MIN °C
	26	25	35	55	72	84	99	94	73	63	47	37	RAIN MM
	9	8	11	14	18	19	21	21	19	17	14	12	RAIN DAYS

SEASIDE TOWNS

In summer, the Limestone Coast's quiet fishing towns transform into busy holiday centres, offering great beaches and fantastic seafood. Visit Kingston S.E., a major lobster port at the southern end of Coorong National Park – nearby lakes and lagoons are havens for birdlife. Head further south to Robe, with its lovely combination of maritime history and windswept scenery, or to Beachport, settled as a whaling station in the 1830s. Today the town's long jetty is a popular spot for fishing. For more fishing, don't miss Port MacDonnell, where you'll find South Australia's largest lobster fleet.

→ For more detail see map 601. For descriptions of ⊤ towns see Towns from A–Z (p. 245).

FLINDERS RANGES & OUTBACK

This vast region covers around 70 per cent of South Australia. Here you'll find some of the country's most legendary landscapes and the quintessential outback town of Coober Pedy.

[WINDMILL IN CARRIETON, NEAR QUORN]

Coober Pedy   Coober Pedy is considered the opal capital of the world, producing an incredible 80 per cent of the world's gem-quality supply. It is also Australia's most famous underground town, with homes, churches and art galleries all set into the hills to keep cool. Visit the museums and mines, and try your hand at prospecting.

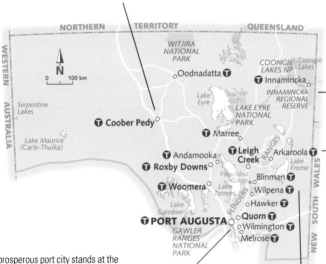

Innamincka Regional Reserve   Four-wheel-drive enthusiasts flock to this remote reserve to tackle the terrain, but there is more here than just adventure driving. The area's wetlands are internationally significant, particularly Coongie Lakes, which provide a vital refuge for waterbirds. Closer to Innamincka is the Cullyamurra Waterhole on Cooper Creek, where visitors can see Aboriginal rock carvings.

Ridgetop Tour   The signature attraction of the northern Flinders Ranges, this four-hour, four-wheel drive tour in an open-top vehicle takes you along an insanely steep track, originally built for mining exploration. The guided tour, run by Arkaroola Wilderness Sanctuary, scales heart-stoppingly hairy ridges to reward passengers with panoramic views featuring red granite mountains and the desert beyond.

Port Augusta   This prosperous port city stands at the northern tip of Spencer Gulf. It has some excellent attractions for visitors – the award-winning Wadlata Outback Centre provides an Indigenous, natural and social history of the outback and ranges, while the Australian Arid Lands Botanic Garden offers an in-depth look at the country's little-understood arid environments.

Wilpena Pound   The Pound, part of Flinders Ranges National Park, is one of the most extraordinary geological formations in Australia. It is a vast natural amphitheatre, surrounded by sheer cliffs and jagged rocks that change colour according to the light. An old homestead within the pound, built by the Hill family in 1902 and abandoned after floods in 1914, stands as a reminder of the difficulties of farming in this environment.

TOP EVENTS

FEB	Wilpena under the Stars (Wilpena)
EASTER	Opal Festival (Coober Pedy)
MAY	Races and gymkhana (Oodnadatta)
JULY	Pichi Richi Marathon (Quorn)
JULY	Australian Camel Cup (Marree)
NOV	Outback Surfboat Carnival (Port Augusta)

CLIMATE

HAWKER

	J	F	M	A	M	J	J	A	S	O	N	D	
	34	33	30	25	20	16	16	18	22	26	29	32	MAX °C
	18	18	15	11	7	5	4	4	7	10	13	16	MIN °C
	19	21	17	20	31	39	35	33	28	25	22	21	RAIN MM
	3	3	2	3	5	7	7	7	6	5	4	3	RAIN DAYS

TRAILS AND TRACKS

Beginning (or ending) in the Flinders Ranges are two long-distance trails for bushwalkers and bikeriders. The longest track is the 1200-kilometre Heysen Trail, which begins at Cape Jervis and follows the mountain ranges to Parachilna Gorge north of Flinders Ranges National Park, taking in the best of the scenery of the Fleurieu Peninsula, Adelaide Hills and Barossa Valley en route. The 900-kilometre Mawson Trail is a bike track that runs between Adelaide and Blinman, named after explorer Sir Douglas Mawson. The trail explores the lesser known parts of the Mount Lofty and Flinders ranges, travelling along unmade and rarely used roads, farm-access tracks and national-park trails. Beyond the ranges are some of Australia's premier four-wheel-drive treks, including the Oodnadatta Track – taking in hot springs, old railway sidings and sections of the Dog Fence – and the Birdsville Track, crossing impressive sandhills and Cooper Creek.

SOUTH AUSTRALIA

→ For more detail see maps 604–5, 606–7 & 608–9. For descriptions of ⊤ towns see Towns from A–Z (p. 245).

EYRE PENINSULA & NULLARBOR

This diverse region features a coastline that's ideal for surfing and fishing, as well as the vast, treeless plain of the Nullarbor.

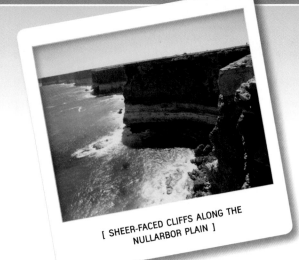

[SHEER-FACED CLIFFS ALONG THE NULLARBOR PLAIN]

Nullarbor Plain   The Nullarbor, Latin for 'treeless', is a plain of 250 000 square kilometres, resting on a massive area of limestone riddled with caves. Along the coast, a long line of sheer-faced cliffs drop suddenly into the foaming waters of the Great Australian Bight. Head of Bight offers some of the country's best whale-watching, between June and October.

Murphy's Haystacks   Located some 40 kilometres south-east of Streaky Bay, these ancient wind-worn granite inselbergs (from the German words for 'island' and 'mountain') have stood sentinel over the surrounding plains for nearly 34 000 years. The Stonehenge-like arrangement of pink-tinted pillars and boulders is one of the most photographed attractions on the Eyre Peninsula, and is a lovely (if unusual) location for a picnic (undercover facilities are available).

Surf coast   This 73-kilometre stretch of coast between Ceduna and the tiny settlement of Penong justifiably promotes itself as a surfing paradise. There are renowned surf beaches along the remote coastline, the most famous being Cactus Beach, just south of Penong, which boasts three world-famous breaks.

WARNING: Sharks have been known to frequent these waters – seek local advice before entering.

Spencer Gulf coast   Here calm waters lap against the shores of peaceful holiday villages and the northern regional centre of Whyalla. At Port Lincoln, the huge natural harbour is home to Australia's foremost tuna fleet. Beaches, museums, golf, walks and drives all feature, but the biggest drawcard is fishing – jetty-fishing or gamefishing – in some of the best waters in Australia.

Coffin Bay National Park   This park protects a pristine coastal wilderness of exposed cliffs, small coves and beaches. Bush camping, surfing, walking and fishing are all popular activities. Many of the vehicle tracks are four-wheel-drive only, but for conventional vehicles there is a popular scenic tour called the Yangie Trail, beginning at Coffin Bay township.

Map labels: NULLARBOR PLAIN · NULLARBOR NATIONAL PARK · WA · GREAT AUSTRALIAN BIGHT · Penong · Cactus Beach · Ceduna · Streaky Bay · Point Labatt · Wudinna · Elliston · Kimba · Whyalla · Cowell · EYRE PENINSULA · SPENCER GULF · Coffin Bay · Tumby Bay · COFFIN BAY NP · SIR JOSEPH BANKS GROUP CP · PORT LINCOLN · LINCOLN NATIONAL PARK · 0 60 km

TOP EVENTS

JAN	Tunarama Festival (Port Lincoln)
FEB–MAR	Adelaide to Lincoln Yacht Race and Lincoln Week Regatta (Port Lincoln)
EASTER	Australian Snapper Championship (Whyalla)
APR	Sculptures on the Cliff (Elliston)
JUNE–AUG	Australian Salmon Fishing Competition (Elliston)
OCT	Oysterfest (Ceduna)

CLIMATE

PORT LINCOLN

	J	F	M	A	M	J	J	A	S	O	N	D	
	25	26	24	22	19	17	16	17	18	20	22	24	MAX °C
	15	16	15	13	11	9	8	8	9	11	12	14	MIN °C
	13	15	20	37	57	75	79	69	50	36	22	19	RAIN MM
	4	4	5	10	14	16	18	17	13	11	7	6	RAIN DAYS

WILDLIFE

This sparsely settled region remains a wildlife haven. Rare and endangered bird species find refuge in many of the parks and reserves; at Nullarbor National Park look out for Major Mitchell cockatoos, or see migrating birds land at Lincoln National Park after their journey from the chilly Arctic Circle. Lolling about on the sands after days of fishing far out at sea are the rare and endangered Australian sea lions of Point Labatt Conservation Park – they are Australia's only resident mainland colony. One of the most important parks in the region is the Sir Joseph Banks Group Conservation Park, on islands offshore from Tumby Bay. This park is Australia's largest breeding ground for Cape Barren geese, and is home to dolphins, New Zealand fur seals and Australian sea lions.

→ For more detail see maps 602, 604 & 610–1. For descriptions of ⊕ towns see Towns from A–Z (p. 245).

TOWNS A-Z

south australia

[PIPI SHELLS ON THE BEACH, THE COORONG]

LEGEND

i VISITOR INFORMATION

RADIO STATIONS

IN TOWN

WHAT'S ON

WHERE TO EAT

WHERE TO STAY

NEARBY

Aldinga Beach
Pop. 5979
Map ref. 597 A12 | 598 E6 | 599 H9 | 601 B4 | 603 J10

i **McLaren Vale and Fleurieu Visitor Centre, Main Rd,
McLaren Vale; (08) 8323 9944 or 1800 628 410;
www.mclarenvale.info**

94.7 5EFM, 639 AM ABC North and West

The rolling hills of the southern Mount Lofty Ranges form the
backdrop to Aldinga Beach, a long curve of white sand facing
Gulf St Vincent. One and a half kilometres off the coast is
one of the state's best diving spots – the Aldinga Drop Off, an
underwater cliff where divers say the marine life has to be seen to
be believed. The township – to the west of the original Aldinga,
which grew as a small farming centre in the mid-1800s – is a
popular holiday spot.

Gnome Caves: 5 theme 'caves', great for kids;
Aldinga Beach Rd.

Lake Coolangatta Cafe: casual beachfront seafood;
1 Norman Rd, Silver Sands; (08) 8557 4000.

Cockleshell Cottage: beachside, country-style comfort;
10 Boomerang Ave; 0409 702 208. *Silver Sands B&B:* elevated
waterfront apartment with views; 277 Esplanade;
(08) 8557 4002.

Star of Greece In 1888 the *Star of Greece* plunged to the
ocean floor in a wild storm. The ship was only a short distance
from land, but at 3am, and in gigantic swells, 17 of the 28 people
on board drowned. Today a portion of the vessel can be seen from
shore at low tide. A plaque lies on the seabed for the benefit of

divers, but for those wanting to stay dry, pictures of the wreck line
the walls of the Star of Greece Cafe. Port Willunga; 3 km N.

Aldinga Scrub Conservation Park: walk through remnant
coastal vegetation; the park is ablaze with colourful wildflowers
in spring; end of Dover St, off Aldinga Beach Rd; 1 km S. *Aldinga:*
Uniting Church cemetery has the graves of those who died in
the *Star of Greece* shipwreck. Community Market held 1st Sat
each month in Institute Hall, Old Coach Rd; 4 km NE. *Beaches:*
many north and south of Aldinga Beach including Port Willunga
Beach, with the remains of an old jetty and caves built in the cliff
by anglers (3 km N); Sellicks Beach, with boat access and good
fishing (8 km S); and Maslin Beach, Australia's first official nudist
beach (10 km N). *Lookouts:* one south of Sellicks Beach (11 km S)
and another over the Myponga Reservoir (23 km S).

See also FLEURIEU PENINSULA, p. 235

Andamooka
Pop. 528
Map ref. 604 F3

i **Dukes Bottlehouse Motel (incorporating post office),
275 Opal Creek Blvd; (08) 8672 7007;
www.andamookaopal.com.au**

105.9 FM ABC North and West

If Queen Elizabeth II had ever been to Andamooka, perhaps she
would have thought differently about the Andamooka Opal given
to her as a gift in 1954 on her first visit to Australia. The opal
weighed 203 carats and glistened in blues, reds and greens. It was
the result of an extensive search for the most beautiful opal in the

state, yet Andamooka itself is a misshapen collection of tin sheds, dugouts and fibros in the middle of the desert. With constant water shortages, no local council and an all-consuming drive to find opals, residents have become experts in making do. The town offers old-fashioned outback hospitality to an increasing number of tourists.

Opal showrooms: showrooms in town include Andamooka Gems and Trains, attached to Dukes Bottlehouse Motel, with opals and a model railway. *Historic miners huts:* a handful of old semi-dugouts line the creek bed in the centre of town, complete with old tools and furnishings. Access is by tour, which includes a visit to an underground mine; details from post office. *Cemetery:* with miners' nicknames on the headstones.

Market and barbecue: local art and craft; Sat long weekends (Easter, June and Oct).

Fossicking: noodling in unclaimed mullock dumps surrounding town; details from post office. *Lake Torrens:* one of the state's largest salt lakes stretches away to the south-east; 4WD recommended for access.

See also FLINDERS RANGES & OUTBACK, p. 243

Angaston

Pop. 1865

Map ref. 597 F4 | 601 C2 | 603 K8

ⓘ Barossa Visitor Information Centre, 66–68 Murray St, Tanunda; (08) 8563 0600 or 1300 852 982; www.barossa.com

📻 89.1 Triple B FM, 1062 AM ABC Riverland

Angaston takes its name from George Fife Angas who purchased the original plot of land on which the town now stands. He was a prominent figure in the South Australian Company and one of the shareholders who used his substantial buying power to get the best plots of land and dictate the terms of purchase. Many of the town's public buildings were funded by him, even before he emigrated. In a sense, the town's strong German heritage was also funded by him as he sponsored many Lutherans to make the journey to South Australia. Angaston still has strong ties with its history. In town is a German butchers that has been making wursts for more than 60 years, a blacksmith shop over a century old and a cafe and specialty food shop named the South Australian Company Store. Jacarandas and Moreton Bay figs line the main street.

A. H. Doddridge Blacksmith Shop This is the town's original blacksmith, started by Cornish immigrant William Doddridge. The shop closed in 1966 and 15 years later it was purchased by local townspeople. On Sat and Sun it operates as a working smithy, complete with the original bellows that Doddridge brought out from England. Murray St.

Angas Park Fruit Co: retail outlet for Angas Park dried fruits and nuts; Murray St. *The Abbey:* second-hand clothing and period pieces inside the old church; open Thurs–Sun; Murray St. *The Lego Man:* one of Australia's largest Lego collections; Jubilee Ave. *Food outlets:* include Angaston Gourmet Foods, famous for their baguettes, and the Barossa Valley Cheese Company, which makes cheese on the premises; Murray St. *Angaston Heritage Walk:* brochure from visitor centre.

Farmers market: behind Vintners Bar and Grill, Nuriootpa Rd; Sat mornings. *Angaston Show:* Feb/Mar. *Barossa Vintage Festival:* celebration of locally produced food and wine in various locations; odd-numbered years, Apr. *Barossa Gourmet Weekend:* Aug.

Blond Coffee: homemade snacks and lunches; 60 Murray St; (08) 8564 3444. *Vintners Bar & Grill:* robust Mediterranean flavours; Nuriootpa Rd; (08) 8564 2488.

Caithness Manor: hosted heritage suites; 12 Hill St; (08) 8564 2761. *Collingrove Homestead:* stately historic residence; Eden Valley Rd; (08) 8564 2061. *Naimanya Cottage:* secluded stone cottage; Pohlner Rd; (08) 8565 3275. *Strathlyn B&B:* gracious hosted and self-contained suites; Nuriootpa Rd; (08) 8564 2430.

Wineries: Barossa Valley wineries surrounding Angaston include Yalumba, with its cellar door on Eden Valley Rd, (08) 8561 3200, and Saltram, Nuriootpa Rd, (08) 8561 0200. *For more information on the Barossa Valley, see Nuriootpa, Lyndoch and Tanunda. Collingrove Homestead:* the old Angas family home, now owned by the National Trust and open for tours, boutique accommodation and dining; 7 km SE. *Mengler Hill Lookout:* views over the Barossa Valley; 8 km SW. *Kaiserstuhl Conservation Park:* a small pocket of native flora and fauna, with walking trails; 10 km S. *Butcher, Baker, Winemaker Trail:* between Lyndoch and Angaston, taking in wineries and gourmet-food producers along the way. Smartcard available for purchase, which allows you VIP experiences and rewards points; details and brochure from visitor centre.

See also BAROSSA VALLEY, p. 238

Ardrossan

Pop. 1125

Map ref. 599 F5 | 601 A1 | 603 I7

ⓘ Ardrossan Bakery, 39 First St, (08) 8837 3015; or Harvest Corner Visitor Information Centre, 29 Main St, Minlaton, (08) 8853 2600 or 1800 202 445; www.yorkepeninsula.com.au

📻 89.3 Gulf FM, 639 AM ABC North and West

A cluster of bright white grain silos sit atop the red clay cliffs at Ardrossan, an industrial town on Yorke Peninsula. The town has two jetties – one for the export of grain, salt and dolomite, and the other for the benefit of local anglers. Ardrossan is well known for its blue swimmer crabs that are found under the jetty or in the shallows at low tide. The best season for crabbing is between September and April.

Stump Jump Plough A lonely stump-jump plough stands in the cliff-top park opposite East Tce. Mallee scrub once covered much of this area and caused endless grief to early farmers because it was so difficult to clear. The invention of the stump-jump plough made it possible to jump over stumps left in the ground and plough on ahead. The plough's design was perfected in Ardrossan. The original factory, on Fifth St, now houses a historical museum. Open 2.30–4.30pm Sun.

Kalinda Shores: beachfront family holiday home; 108 Black Point Dr, Black Point; (08) 8838 2208.

Zanoni wreck South Australia's most complete shipwreck is 15 km south-east of Ardrossan off Rogues Point. The wreck was lost for over 100 years, but was eventually rediscovered by some local fishermen. It lies virtually in one piece on the seabed. Some artefacts from the ship can be found at the Ardrossan historical museum, but divers wanting to see the wreck in situ need a permit from Heritage South Australia. (08) 8204 9245.

Walking trail: 3 km track along cliff-tops to Tiddy Widdy Beach; begins at the boat ramp in town. *BHP Lookout:* view of Gulf St Vincent and dolomite mines; 2 km S. *Clinton Conservation Park:*

mangrove swamps and tidal flats with an array of birdlife; begins after Port Clinton, 25 km N, and stretches around the head of Gulf St Vincent.

See also YORKE PENINSULA, p. 240

Arkaroola

Map ref. 600 F2 | 605 K3

 Arkaroola Village reception; (08) 8648 4848 or 1800 676 042; www.arkaroola.com.au

999 AM ABC Broken Hill

Arkaroola is set in an incredible landscape of ranges laced with precious minerals, waterholes nestled inside tall gorges and places with songful names like Nooldoonooldoona and Bararranna. What's more, the Flinders Ranges are still alive, rumbling with up to 200 small earthquakes a year. It was a place that geologist Reg Sprigg found fascinating, and worth conserving. He purchased the Arkaroola property in 1968 and created a wildlife sanctuary for endangered species. Today a weather station, seismograph station and observatory (tours available) add to its significance and the spectacular four-wheel-drive tracks entice many visitors. The village has excellent facilities for such a remote outpost.

Arkaroola Wilderness Sanctuary: famed resort in rugged terrain; (08) 8648 4848 or 1800 676 042. *Grindell's Hut:* remote, rustic bush hut; Wortupa Loop Rd, Vulkathunha–Gammon Ranges National Park, via Balcanoona; (08) 8648 0049.

Ridgetop Tour This, the signature attraction of the northern Flinders Ranges, is a 4WD tour along an insanely steep track. The original track, built for mining exploration, wound through the creek beds, but run-off from the ridges washed the road away in just a few years. The idea was formed to create a track along the ridges themselves. A few bulldozers later, the track was complete. This is a guided tour, but Arkaroola Wilderness Sanctuary also has 100 km of self-guide 4WD tracks, including the popular Echo Camp Backtrack.

Vulkathunha–Gammon Ranges National Park This park is directly south of Arkaroola, taking in much of the distinctive scenery of the northern Flinders Ranges. The Adnyamathanha people believe that the Dreamtime serpent, Arakaroo, drank adjacent Lake Frome dry and carved out Arkaroola Gorge as he dragged his body back to his resting spot, inside Mainwater Pound. His restlessness is the cause of the earthquakes. Features include the surprisingly lush Weetootla Gorge, fed by a permanent spring, and Italowie Gorge, the unlikely spot where an impoverished R. M. Williams began making shoes. Park Headquarters at Balcanoona; (08) 8648 0048; 32 km S.

Waterholes: many picturesque waterholes along Arkaroola Creek and tributaries west and north-east of the village. *Bolla Bollana Smelter ruins:* where the ore from surrounding mines was once treated. It includes a Cornish beehive-shaped kiln; 7 km NW. *Paralana Hot Springs:* the only active geyser in Australia, where water heated by radioactive minerals bubbles through the rocks. Swimming or extended exposure is not recommended; 27 km NE. *Big Moro Gorge:* rockpools surrounded by limestone outcrops. The gorge is on Nantawarrina Aboriginal Land; obtain permit from Nepabunna Community Council, (08) 8648 3764; 59 km S. *Astronomical Tours:* boasts some of the best star-watching

conditions in the Southern Hemisphere at 3 magnificent observatories; (08) 8648 4848. *Scenic flights:* over the ranges or further afield; details from village reception.

See also FLINDERS RANGES & OUTBACK, p. 243

Balaklava

Pop. 1627
Map ref. 599 H4 | 603 J7

 Council offices, Scotland Pl; (08) 8862 0800.

 90.9 Flow FM, 1062 AM ABC Riverland

Balaklava is set on the Wakefield River in an area dominated by traditional wheat and sheep farms. It sprang up as a stopping point between the Burra copper fields and Port Wakefield, but a grain merchant from Adelaide, Charles Fisher, soon turned the focus to agriculture. He built grain stores here before there was any sign of grain. This proved a canny move, as it lured farmers to the area. The town features old sandstone buildings and a 'silent cop', a curious keep-left sign in the middle of a roundabout.

Courthouse Gallery The arts are alive and well in Balaklava, as shown by this community-run art gallery that has a changing program of local and visiting exhibitions, plus a popular art prize in July. Open 2–4pm Thurs, Fri and Sun; Edith Tce.

Balaklava Museum: old household items and local memorabilia; Old Centenary Hall, May Tce. *Urlwin Park Agricultural Museum:* old agricultural machinery, 2 old relocated banks and a working telephone exchange; open 2–4pm, 2nd and 4th Sun each month or by appt; Short Tce; (08) 8862 1854. *Walking trail:* scenic 3 km track along the riverbank.

Adelaide Plains Cup Festival: arts and crafts exhibitions, as well as golf and clay-shooting competitions; 1st Sun in Mar. *Balaklava Cup:* major regional horserace; Aug. *Balaklava Show:* Sept.

Port Wakefield Behind the highway's long line of takeaways and petrol stations is a quiet town that began life as a cargo port to carry the copper mined in Burra's Monster Mine back to Port Adelaide. It is set on the mangrove-lined Wakefield River at the top of Gulf St Vincent. The wharf, which has a floor of mud at low tide, is now used by the local fishing industry. A historical walk brochure is available from the Port Wakefield/Rivergum Information Centre. This is a popular spot for fishing, crabbing and swimming. 25 km W.

Devils Garden: a picnic spot among river box gums, once a 'devil of a place' for bullock wagons to get through as the black soil quickly turned to mud; 7 km NE. *Rocks Reserve:* walking trails and unique rock formations by the river; 10 km E. *Balaklava Gliding Club:* offers weekend 'air experience flights' with an instructor; Whitwarta Airfield; (08) 8864 5062; 10 km NW.

See also MID-NORTH, p. 239

Barmera

Pop. 1927
Map ref. 558 A6 | 601 G1 | 603 N7

 Barwell Ave; (08) 8588 2289; www.berribarmera.sa.gov.au

93.1 MAGIC FM, 1062 AM ABC Riverland

Barmera lies in the middle of a swooping hairpin bend of the Murray River, close to the Victorian border, but it is hard to tell where the river stops and where the flood plains and tributaries begin in the area to the west of town. The wetlands eventually

SOUTH AUSTRALIA

flow into Lake Bonney, a large body of water to the north of Barmera. Swimming, waterskiing, sailing and fishing are some of the activities popular on the lake. The town was established in 1921 as a settlement for returned World War I soldiers, who were all promised a patch of well-irrigated farmland.

Rocky's Country Music Hall of Fame Dean 'Rocky' Page established Barmera's famous country music festival and was a well-known musician in his own right. Within the centre is an array of country music memorabilia and a display of replica guitars with the handprints of the legends who used them. The pièce de résistance is Slim Dusty's hat. Open Wed–Fri; Barwell Ave; (08) 8588 1463.

Donald Campbell Obelisk: commemorates an attempt in 1964 to break the world water-speed record, but 347.5 km/h was not quite enough to make the books; Queen Elizabeth Dr. *Bonneyview Winery:* cosy atmosphere with award-winning reds and light pastries; Sturt Hwy; (08) 8588 2279.

5RM Barmera Main Street Market: 1st Sun each month Sept–Dec. *Lake Bonney Yachting Regatta:* Easter. *South Australian Country Music Festival:* June. *Riverland Field Days:* Sept. *Barmera Bonnie Sheepdog Trials:* Oct.

Banrock Station Wine & Wetland Centre: stylish eco-cafe; Holmes Rd, Kingston on Murray; (08) 8583 0299. *The Overland Corner Hotel:* historic bush pub; Old Coach Rd, Overland Corner; (08) 8588 7021.

Banrock Station Wine & Wetland Centre Fruity wines mix with a cacophony of birds and frogs at Banrock Station. In these new times of sensitive agriculture, Banrock is working with environmental organisations to breathe life back into a pocket of wetland that was ruined by irrigation (almost 70% of all Murray wetlands have been affected). The natural cycles of flooding and drying have seen the return of black swans, native fish and ibis, and a boardwalk gives visitors a close-up look. Kingston-on-Murray; (08) 8583 0299; 10 km w.

Overland Corner This was the first settlement in the area, a convenient stop en route for drovers and people travelling to the goldfields. By 1855 a police post had been established to deal with the odd bushranger and quell the problems flaring between drovers and the indigenous inhabitants. In 1859 the Overland Corner Hotel opened its doors. Its thick limestone walls and red gum floors have seen many floods. An 8 km walking track into the adjacent Herons Bend Reserve leaves from the hotel. 19 km nw.

Cobdogla Irrigation and Steam Museum: has the world's only working Humphrey Pump, used in the early days of irrigation. Also local memorabilia and steam-train rides; open Sun long weekends; 5 km w. *Highway Fern Haven:* garden centre featuring an indoor rainforest; 5 km e. *Napper's Old Accommodation House:* ruins of a hotel built in 1850 on the shores of the lake; turn east over Napper Bridge; 10 km nw. *Loch Luna Game Reserve:* linking Lake Bonney and the Murray, these wetlands form an important refuge for waterbirds and one of the few inland nesting sites for sea eagles. Chambers Creek, which loops around the reserve, is popular for canoeing; turn west over Napper Bridge; 16 km nw. *Moorook Game Reserve:* these wetlands surround Wachtels Lagoon; 16 km sw. *Loveday Internment Camps:* guided tour or self-guide drive to the camps where Japanese, Italian and German POWs were held during WW II; details from visitor centre.

See also MURRAY, p. 241

Beachport

Pop. 342
Map ref. 601 E10

i Millicent Rd; (08) 8735 8029; www.wattlerange.sa.gov.au

107.7 5THE FM, 1161 AM ABC South East

Beachport started out as a whaling port. Today the crayfish industry has taken over and the town has South Australia's second-longest jetty, favoured by anglers young and old with regular catches including whiting, flathead and garfish. People flock here for summer holidays to relax on the beautiful sandy beaches and swim in the bay. The Bowman Scenic Drive provides stunning views over the Southern Ocean with access to sheltered coves and rocky headlands for the adventurous to explore. It is also a great place for whale-watching.

Old Wool and Grain Store Museum The old store contains a whaling and fishing display including harpoons and whaling pots, as well as relics from shipwrecks off the coastline. Upstairs rooms are furnished in the style of the day. Natural history display features local and migratory seabirds. Open 10am–4pm daily over holiday period, 10am–1pm Sun at other times; Railway Tce.

Lanky's Walk: a short walk through bushland to Lanky's Well, where the last full-blood member of the Boandik tribe camped while working as a police tracker; begins on Railway Tce North; details on this and other walks from visitor centre. *Pool of Siloam:* this small lake, 7 times saltier than the sea, is said to be a cure for all manner of ailments. Also a popular swimming spot; end of McCourt St. *Lighthouse:* the original lighthouse was located on Penguin Island, a breeding ground for seals and penguins offshore from Cape Martin, where the current lighthouse now stands. It offers good views of the island from the cape; south of town.

Market: Sat long weekends (Jan, Easter and Oct). *Duck Race:* Jan. *Festival by the Sea:* stalls and entertainment; odd-numbered years, Feb/Mar.

Beachport Harbourmasters: trendy beachfront apartment; 1 Beach Rd; (08) 8735 8197. *Beachport Retreat:* spacious holiday home; 10 Ethel St; (08) 8735 7211.

Beachport Conservation Park This park is a succession of white beaches, sand dunes and rugged limestone cliffs, with the southern shore of Lake George lying inland. The coast is dotted with ancient shell middens and is accessed primarily by 4WD or on foot. Five Mile Drift, a beach on Lake George, is a good base for swimming, sailing and windsurfing. Access to the coast side is via Bowman Scenic Dr, which begins at the lighthouse. Access to the Lake George side is via Railway Tce North. 4 km nw.

Woakwine Cutting: an incredible gorge, cut through Woakwine Range by one man to drain swampland and allow farming, with viewing platform, information boards and machinery exhibit; 10 km n.

See also LIMESTONE COAST, p. 242

Berri

Pop. 4009
Map ref. 558 A6 | 588 A6 | 601 G1 | 603 N7

i Riverview Dr; (08) 8582 5511; www.berribarmera.sa.gov.au

 93.1 MAGIC FM, 1062 AM ABC Riverland

Orange products and wine are big business in this Riverland town, which has Australia's largest winery and is one of the major growing and manufacturing centres of the country's biggest

orange-juice company. The Big Orange, on the north-west outskirts of town, makes this rather clear. The name 'Berri' has nothing to do with fruit, though. It comes from the Aboriginal 'Bery Bery', thought to mean 'bend in the river'. The town was established in 1911, the year after irrigation of the Murray began.

 Berri Direct: makers of Berri fruit juice and other products, with sales and a video presentation detailing production history of the Riverland; Old Sturt Hwy. *Riverlands Gallery:* local and touring art exhibitions; open Mon–Fri; Wilson St. *Gilbert Street Gallery:* artwork by local artists, including some amazing glassware and woodwork; Gilbert St. *Berri Community Mural:* enormous community-painted mural commemorating the past and present fruit industry; Old Sturt Hwy next to Berri Direct. *Berri Lookout Tower:* panoramic views of river, town and surrounds from a converted water tower; cnr Fiedler St and Vaughan Tce. *Lions Club Walking Trail:* 4 km riverfront walk from Berri Marina to Martin Bend Reserve, a popular spot for picnics and waterskiing; an Aboriginal mural and totems are under the bridge and further along are monuments to famous Aboriginal tracker Jimmy James. *Birdwatching safaris:* to Bookmark Biosphere Reserve; tours offered by Jolly Goodfellows Birding; (08) 8583 5530. *Berri Air Tours:* offering scenic flights over the Riverland; (08) 8582 2799.

 Farmers Market: Sat. *Speedboat Spectacular:* Mar (subject to river conditions). *Riverland Renaissance:* Oct. *Craft Fair:* Nov.

 Cragg's Creek Cafe: smart waterfront tapas and snacks; Riverview Dr; (08) 8582 4466.

 Riverbush Cottages: roomy, relaxed, riverfront homes; Old Sturt Hwy; (08) 8582 3455 or 1800 088 191.

 Berri Estates Winery This impressive winery was founded in 1922 and has grown to be the largest winery and distillery in Australia. The Murray River and the temperate climate have much to do with the quality of the wines here, including reds, whites and fortified wines, as well as brandy. Between Berri and Glossop.

Murray River National Park, Katarapko section In this park, see the merging of 2 distinct vegetations – of the famous Murray River flood plains and the equally renowned Mallee region. The 6 km Mallee Drive takes the visitor into the heart of the park and to the distinctive mallee terrain. There are also walking trails to see some of the park's inhabitants, including the ever-popular kangaroo. Just south of Berri; (08) 8595 2111.

Angas Park Fruit Company: dried fruits and other products; open 8.30am–5pm Mon–Fri, 10am–12pm Sat and public holidays; Old Sturt Hwy; (08) 8561 0800; 3 km w. *Monash:* a small irrigation town best known for the free family attractions at the Monash Adventure Park on Morgan Rd. Enjoy delicate handmade chocolates at the Chocolates and More store opposite the park, or taste the wines at nearby Thachi Wines; 12 km NW.

See also MURRAY, p. 241

Birdwood

Pop. 733

Map ref. 596 H5 | 597 E8 | 601 C3 | 603 K9

 Shannon St; (08) 8568 5577.

98.7 Power FM, 1062 AM ABC Riverland

The small town of Birdwood is set picturesquely in the Torrens Valley in the northern part of the popular Adelaide Hills district.

The region's beauty would have been a welcome sight for German settlers escaping religious persecution in the 1840s. Like many of the German-settled towns in the area, Birdwood was originally named after a Prussian town, Blumberg. However, anti-German sentiment during World War I created a feeling of unrest and the town's name was changed to Birdwood after the commander of the ANZAC forces in Gallipoli, Sir William Birdwood.

 National Motor Museum The largest in the Southern Hemisphere, this impressive collection of over 300 vintage cars, motorcycles and commercial vehicles is housed in the 1852 flour mill. The vehicles are lovingly restored, often from simply a shell. Visit the workshop complex to see the process of restoration as coach builders and mechanics work tirelessly on these old machines. The building's original history as a flour mill can be seen in the Mill Building. Shannon St; (08) 8568 5006.

Birdwood Wine and Cheese Centre: introduces visitors to boutique wines and cheeses of regional SA with tastings and sales; open Wed–Sun; Shannon St. *Blumberg Inn:* imposing 1865 inn harking back to German-settler days; Main St.

 Rock and Roll Rendezvous: Apr. *Bay to Birdwood Run:* vintage motoring event attracting more than 1600 vehicles; even-numbered years, Sept.

 Chain of Ponds Vineyard Cottage: large stone residence with vistas; Mannum Rd, Gumeracha; (08) 8389 1415. *Stoneybank Settlement Cottages:* quaint, rural heritage hideaways; Lot 100 Stoneybank La, Mount Pleasant; (08) 8568 2075.

 Lobethal The quaint town of Lobethal features historic German-style cottages and an 1842 Lutheran seminary. Fairyland Village takes the visitor into the world of fairytales; open weekends. The National Costume Museum houses a collection of dresses, suits and accessories dating from 1812 (closed Mon). The town lights up each Christmas in the 'Lights of Lobethal' festival. 13 km sw.

The Toy Factory: a family business manufacturing wooden toys from a shop adjacent to an 18 m giant rocking horse; Gumeracha; 7 km w. *Chain of Ponds Wine:* boutique winery with tastings, sales, viewing platform, restaurant and B&B (1880s cottage); 9 km w. *Herbig Tree:* an extraordinary insight into Friedrich Herbig and the hollow red gum tree where he raised a family in the 1850s. School museum and pioneer cemetery also on-site; Springton; group bookings only (08) 8568 2287; 15km NE. *Malcolm Creek Vineyard:* boutique winery with cellar door and friendly deer; open weekends and public holidays; Bonython Rd, Kersbrook; 20 km NW. *Roachdale Reserve:* self-guide nature trail with brochure; 23 km NW via Kersbrook. *Torrens Gorge:* spectacular cliffs and streams make this a popular spot for picnics; 25 km w. *Samphire Wines and Pottery:* a small boutique winery and handmade pottery shop; cnr Watts Gully and Robertson rds; 27 km NW via Kersbrook. *Warren Conservation Park:* difficult trails, including part of the long-distance Heysen Trail, lead to spectacular views over countryside and Warren Gorge; adjacent to Samphire Wines and Pottery. *Mt Crawford Forest:* walkers, horseriders and cyclists will enjoy the forest tracks of this park, which is scattered in various locations north, west and south-west of Birdwood; visit the information centre on Warren Rd (signposted turn-off between Kersbrook and Williamstown) for a map.

See also ADELAIDE HILLS, p. 237

SOUTH AUSTRALIA

Blinman

Pop. 151
Map ref. 600 C7 | 605 I5

ⓘ General store, Mine Rd; (08) 8648 4370.

During the 19th century numerous mining townships dotted the northern Flinders Ranges. Blinman is the sole surviving town surveyed at the time. The discovery of copper here in 1859 was accidental; the story goes that a shepherd, Robert Blinman, used to watch his sheep from a boulder. One day he absentmindedly broke off a chunk and discovered it was copper. Historic buildings in the main street are reminders of those rich (and temporary) days.

Land Rover Jamboree: Easter. **Cook Outback:** food/wine festival with camp oven competition; Oct long weekend.

Blinman Hotel: rustic bush pub; Mine Rd; (08) 8648 4867. **Prairie Hotel:** innovative outback cuisine; Cnr High St and West Tce, Parachilna; (08) 8648 4844.

Alpana Station: historic station accommodation; Wilpena Rd; (08) 8648 4626. **Blinman Cottage:** cosy, heritage character; 201 Hancock St; 0417 084 003. **Gum Creek Station:** basic, homestead-style accommodation; Wilpena Rd; (08) 8648 4883. **Moolooloo Station:** rustic and remote shearers quarters; Glass Gorge Rd; (08) 8648 4861. **Prairie Hotel:** innovative outback luxury; Cnr High St and West Tce, Parachilna; (08) 8648 4844.

Blinman Mine Historic Site: a 1 km self-guide walk explains the history and geology of the site. Contact the caretaker on (08) 8648 4874 for a guided tour; just north-east of Blinman. **Great Wall of China:** impressive limestone ridge; Wilpena Rd; 10 km s. **Angorichina Tourist Village:** Start point for 4 km walk along creek bed to Blinman Pools, permanent spring-fed pools in scenic surrounds. Accommodation ranges from tents to cabins; (08) 8648 4842; 14 km w. **Glass and Parachilna gorges:** 10 km NW and 15 km w of town are these 2 beautiful gorges. Parachilna Gorge is the end point of the 1200 km Heysen Trail (bushwalking trail), which begins at Cape Jervis; for information contact Parks SA, (08) 8124 4792. **Flinders Ranges National Park:** see Wilpena for more details; 26 km s; **Prairie Hotel:** a historic hotel at Parachilna offering cuisine with a bush-tucker twist as well as first-rate accommodation. Hotel staff can arrange activities including 4WD tours, scenic flights and visits to nearby Nilpena Station on the edge of Lake Torrens to sample the outback life; (08) 8648 4844; 32 km w. **Scenic drive:** travel east through Eregunda Valley (around 20 km E), then north-east to Mt Chambers Gorge (around 75 km NE), with its rockpools and Aboriginal carvings; further north is Vulkathunha–Gammon Ranges National Park; see Arkaroola. **Mawson Trail:** this 900 km bike trail from Adelaide ends in Blinman. It is named after famous Australian explorer Sir Douglas Mawson and traverses the Mt Lofty and Flinders ranges; for details contact Bicycle SA, (08) 8411 0233.

See also FLINDERS RANGES & OUTBACK, p. 243

Bordertown

Pop. 2584
Map ref. 558 A12 | 590 A7 | 601 G7

ⓘ 81 North Tce; (08) 8752 0700; www.tatiara.sa.gov.au

 106.1 5TCB FM, 1062 AM ABC Riverland

In spite of its name, Bordertown is actually 18 kilometres from the South Australia–Victoria border in the fertile country of the Tatiara District. Thought to be the Aboriginal word for 'good country', Tatiara's name is justified by the region's productive wool and grain industries. For a different native-animal experience, look out for Bordertown's famous white kangaroos,

Australia's only known colony. Former Australian prime minister Robert (Bob) J. L. Hawke was born here.

 Robert J. L. Hawke's childhood home: includes memorabilia. Visit by appt only, contact visitor centre for details; Farquhar St. **Bordertown Wildlife Park:** native birds and animals, including pure-white kangaroos; Dukes Hwy. **Hawke Gallery:** in foyer of council chambers; Woolshed St. **Bordertown Recreation Lake:** popular spot for fishing, canoeing and walking, with artwork on display; northern outskirts of town.

Bordertown Show: Oct.

Dunalan Cottage: roomy farmstay residence; Dukes Hwy; (08) 8753 2323. **Curlew Park:** contemporary country homestead; Lot 146 Chark Rd, Mundulla; (08) 8753 4133.

 Padthaway The Padthaway district has long been regarded as a leader in Australian wine production. An excellent place to start the tasting of such wines is the Padthaway Estate Winery, where meals and wine-tastings enrich the palate. Adjacent is the historic Padthaway Homestead, an 1882 building rising regally above the surrounding region. After indulging in gastronomic delights, walk among the magnificent red gums and stringybarks at nearby Padthaway Conservation Park. 42 km sw.

Clayton Farm: incorporates the Bordertown and District Agricultural Museum and features vintage farm machinery and a National Trust–classified thatched-roof building and woolshed; 3 km s. **Mundulla:** a historic township featuring the heritage-listed Mundulla Hotel; 10 km sw. **Bangham Conservation Park:** a significant habitat for the red-tailed black cockatoo; 30 km SE.

See also MURRAY, p. 241

Burra

Pop. 976
Map ref. 603 K5

ⓘ 2 Market Sq; (08) 8892 2154; www.vistburra.com.au

 105.1 Trax FM, 1062 AM ABC Riverland

The Burra region exploded into activity when copper was found by two shepherds in 1845. Settlements were established based on the miners' country of origin: Aberdeen for the Scottish, Hampton for the English, Redruth for the Cornish and Llwchwr for the Welsh. The combined settlement grew to be the second largest in South Australia, but the miners were fickle – with riches promised on the Victorian goldfields, they did not stay for long. In 1877 the Monster Mine closed. Luckily, Burra did not turn into a ghost town. Instead, the rich heritage of its past has been carefully preserved by the community, resulting in the town being declared a State Heritage Area in 1993. Burra is in the Bald Hill Ranges, named for the 'naked' hills around the town.

Burra Heritage Passport This 'passport' allows visitors to discover the major heritage sites of Burra – armed with an unlimited-access 'key' and a brief history of each site outlined in the pamphlet *Discovering Historic Burra*. Included in the passport is the Burra Historic Mine Site (off Market St), with an ore dressing tower and powder magazine offering views of the open-cut mine and town. At the site is Morphetts Enginehouse Museum (additional entry fee), featuring an excavated 30 m entry tunnel and engine displays. Another site is the Burra Creek Miners' Dugouts (alongside Blyth St) – these dugouts cut into the creek beds housed 1800 people in the boom. Visit the Unicorn Brewery Cellars (Bridge Tce) that date back to 1873, the police lock-up and stables (Tregony St) – these were the first built outside Adelaide – and Redruth Gaol (off Tregony St), which served as a gaol, then a girls reformatory from 1856 to 1922. You can also visit the ruins of a private English township called Hampton, on the northern outskirts of town. Passports are available from the visitor centre and can be upgraded to provide access to the town's museums.

Bon Accord Mine Complex: National Trust interpretive centre with working forge and model of Burra Mine. Guided tours available; closed Mon and Fri; Railway Tce. **Market Square Museum:** an old-style general store, post office and family home returned to its heyday; opposite visitor centre. **Malowen Lowarth Cottage:** restored 1850s Cornish miners cottage; Kingston St. **Burra Regional Art Gallery:** local and touring exhibitions; Market St. **Thorogoods:** enjoy some of Australia's best apple wine and cider; John Barker St. **Antique shops:** in Commercial and Market sts. **Burra Creek:** canoeing and picnicking.

 Jailhouse Rock Festival: Feb. **Music in the Monster Mine:** Mar. **Antique and Decorating Fair:** May. **Burra Show:** Oct.

 Burra Bakery: classic Cornish fare; 16 Commercial St; (08) 8892 2070. **Burra Hotel:** hearty country fare; 5 Market Sq; (08) 8892 2389.

 Birch Cottage: quaint, homely country retreat; 10 Thames St; (08) 8892 2210. **Burra Heritage Cottages:** charming and historic miners digs; 8–18 Truro St; (08) 8892 2461.

 Burra Trail Rides: horseriding adventures in Bald Hills Range; bookings 0427 808 402. **Burra Gorge:** picnics, camping and walking tracks around gorge and permanent springs; 23 km SE. **Dares Hill Drive:** scenic 90 km drive with lookout; begins 30 km N near Hallett; map available from visitor centre.

See also MID-NORTH, p. 239

Ceduna

Pop. 2304
Map ref. 611 M8

 58 Poynton St; (08) 8625 2780 or 1800 639 413; www.cedunatourism.com.au

 94.5 5CCR FM, 693 AM ABC Eyre Peninsula and West Coast

The name Ceduna is derived from the Aboriginal word 'chedoona', meaning resting place, which is apt for those who have just traversed the Nullarbor. Ceduna is also the last major town for those about to embark on the journey west – the place to check your car and stock up on food and water. The difficulty of obtaining supplies and provisions has a long history around Ceduna. Denial Bay, where the original settlement of McKenzie was situated, was where large cargo ships brought provisions for the early pioneers. Ceduna was established later, in 1896, and is situated on the shores of Murat Bay with sandy coves, sheltered bays and offshore islands. In the 1850s there was also a whaling station on St Peter Island (visible from Thevenard).

 Old Schoolhouse National Trust Museum: pioneering artefacts, including those from British atomic testing at Maralinga; closed Sun; Park Tce. **Ceduna Arts Cultural Centre:** original paintings, local pottery and ceramics; open Mon–Fri; cnr Eyre Hwy and Kuhlmann St. **Oyster tours:** offered to Denial Bay, Thevenard and Smoky Bay; book at visitor centre. **Ceduna Oyster Bar:** fresh oysters year-round; western outskirts, on Eyre Hwy. **Local beaches:** swimming, boating, waterskiing and fishing. The foreshore is an ideal spot for walks and picnics (sharks have been known to frequent these waters – seek local advice). **Encounter Coastal Trail:** 3.8 km interpretive trail from the foreshore to Thevenard.

Oysterfest: community festival including street parade and fireworks; Oct long weekend. **Ceduna Races:** horseracing; Dec and Jan.

Great Australian Bight Marine Park The park preserves the fragile ecosystem of the Great Australian Bight. It has spectacular wildlife sights, including the breeding and calving of southern right whales from June to Oct. Spend a day observing these giant creatures from the viewing platform at Head of Bight. There are also spectacular views of the Bunda Cliffs, which begin at the head and trail all the way to the WA border. Whale-watching permits are purchased from the visitor centre on-site. Interpretive centre also on-site. 300 km W.

Nullarbor National Park Aboriginal culture is closely linked with this park's network of caves, part of the largest karst landscape in the world (Murrawijinie Caves north of Nullarbor Roadhouse are the only caves accessible to the public). Vast and mainly flat, the park's most beautiful scenery is along the coast where the cliffs stretch for 200 km overlooking the Southern Ocean. Visitors should take care along the unstable cliff edges. Rare and endangered species such as the Major Mitchell cockatoo and the peregrine falcon are often sighted. Watch out for the southern hairy-nosed wombat. 300 km W.

Thevenard: a deep-sea port that handles bulk grain, gypsum and salt, as well as a large fishing fleet noted for whiting hauls. Bill's Seafood Tours gives an insight into the commercial fishing industry; contact visitor centre for details. A 3.6 km interpretive trail, 'Tracks Along the Coast', runs from the Sailing Club to Pinky Point; 4 km SW. **Denial Bay:** visit the McKenzie ruins to see an early pioneering home and the heritage-listed landing where cargo was brought to shore. Denial Bay jetty is good for fishing and crabbing; 14 km W. **Davenport Creek:** see pure-white sandhills and swim in the sheltered creek. Beyond the sandhills is excellent surfing and waterskiing; 40 km W. **South-east towns and beaches:** Decres Bay for swimming, snorkelling and rock-fishing (10 km SE); Laura Bay with cove-swimming near the conservation park (18 km SE); Smoky Bay for safe swimming, fishing and boating (40 km SE); Point Brown for surf beaches, salmon fishing and coastal walks (56 km SE). **Penong:** more than 40 windmills draw the town's water from underground. See historical memorabilia and local crafts at the Penong Woolshed Museum. Camel day rides and safaris on offer; 73 km W. **Cactus Beach:** renowned for its 'perfect' surfing breaks; 94 km W. **Fowlers Bay:** this town, surrounded by a conservation park, offers long, sandy beaches and excellent fishing; 139 km SW. **North-east conservation parks and reserves:** comprising Yellabinna, Yumbarra, Pureba, Nunnyah and Koolgera, an extensive wilderness area of dunes and mallee country. Rare species of wildlife live here, including dunnarts and mallee fowl. 4WD is essential, and visitors must be experienced in outback travel; north of Ceduna. **Googs Track:** 4WD trek from Ceduna to the Trans-Australia railway track (154 km N) through Yumbarra Conservation Park and Yellabinna Regional Reserve; contact visitor centre for details.

See also EYRE PENINSULA & NULLARBOR, p. 244

Clare

Pop. 3061
Map ref. 599 H2 | 603 J6

i Cnr Main North and Spring Gully rds; (08) 8842 2131 or 1800 242 131; www.clarevalley.com.au

105.1 Trax FM, 639 ABC North and West

Clare is known as the 'Garden of the North'. In the mid-1800s, Edward John Eyre reported favourably on the area and pastoral settlement followed; the town came to be known as Clare after the county in Ireland. The land has proved as favourable as Eyre claimed and Clare continues to boast a rich agricultural industry, including the famous Clare Valley wine region. The first vines were planted by Jesuit priests at Sevenhill in 1851. The Sevenhill Cellars are still operated by Jesuit brothers and the monastery buildings, including the historic St Aloysius Church, are of special interest.

Old Police Station Museum: once a prison, a casualty hospital and housing for government employees, it is now a National Trust museum with historic artefacts and photographs; open weekends and public holidays, other times by appt; Neagles Rock Rd; (08) 8842 2376. *Lookouts:* Billy Goat Hill from Wright St and Neagles Rock Lookout on Neagles Rock Rd. *Town walk:* self-guide trail; brochure from visitor centre.

Clare Races: horseraces among the vines; Easter. *Spanish Festival:* Apr. *Clare Gourmet Weekend:* May. *Clare Show:* Oct.

Salt n Vines Restaurant: seafood and steaks; Wendouree Rd; (08) 8842 1796. *Wild Saffron Gourmet Food & Catering:* snacks and foodie treats; 288 Main North Rd; (08) 8842 4255. *Penna Lane Wines:* cellar-door platters; Penna La, Skilly Hills; (08) 8843 4364. *Sevenhill Hotel:* sturdy pub tucker; Main North Rd, Sevenhill; (08) 8843 4217. *Skillogalee Winery Restaurant:* stylish country fare; Trevarrick Rd, Sevenhill; (08) 8843 4311.

Brice Hill Country Lodge: elegant country resort; 56–66 Warenda Rd; (08) 8842 2925. *Molly's Chase:* secluded log cabins; Leighton Rd, Sevenhill; 0413 550 225. *Mundawora Mews:* historic bluestone cottages; Main North Rd; (08) 8842 3762. *Skillogalee:* luxury winery retreat; Trevarrick Rd, Sevenhill; (08) 8843 4311. *Thorn Park by the Vines:* heritage flair, graciously hosted; Quarry Rd, Sevenhill; (08) 8843 4304.

Clare Valley Wine Region The Clare Valley wine region consists of 12 valleys of undulating hills and lowlands, home to over 30 boutique and commercial wineries. The area is most famous for producing a fine riesling, grown to perfection because of the high terrain and continental climate. The wineries are around Clare, Polish Hill River, Mintaro, Sevenhill, Penwortham, Watervale and Auburn. For those wanting to see the villages and wineries on foot or bicycle, the 27 km Riesling Trail is a good option. It starts from either Clare or Auburn and follows an old railway line. Contact the visitor centre for a winery map.

Watervale: a historic town with a self-guide walk leaflet available from the visitor centre; 12 km s. *Blyth:* a little country town overlooking the western plains. Take a short walk on the interpretive botanical trail or picnic at Brooks Lookout. Medika Gallery, originally a Lutheran church, offers an art gallery and Australian craft sales; 13 km w. *Auburn:* the birthplace in 1876 of poet C. J. Dennis. Take a self-guide walk through National Trust historic precinct in St Vincent St; 26 km s. *Scenic drive:* travel south to Spring Gully Conservation Park with its walking tracks and rare red stringybarks.

See also Mid-North, p. 239

Coffin Bay

Pop. 582
Map ref. 602 D8

i Beachcomber Agencies, Esplanade; (08) 8685 4057; www.coffinbay.net

89.9 Magic FM, 1485 AM ABC Eyre Peninsula and West Coast

A picturesque holiday town and fishing village on the shores of a beautiful estuary, Coffin Bay is popular particularly in summer, when the population quadruples. The bay offers sailing, waterskiing, swimming and fishing. The town was originally known as Oyster Town because of the abundant natural oysters in the bay, but they were dredged to extinction last century. Today the cultivated oysters are among the best in the country. The bay – in spite of what some locals will try to tell you – was named by Matthew Flinders in 1802 in honour of his friend Sir Isaac Coffin.

Fishing: in the bay or in game fishing areas; boat hire and charters available. *Oyster Walk:* 12 km walkway along foreshore and bushland from a lookout (excellent view of Coffin Bay) to Long Beach; brochure from visitor centre. *Coffin Bay Explorer:* catamaran offering a 3 hr cruise on Coffin Bay, visiting oyster leases and greeting dolphins and other spectacular sea life; bookings essential, 0428 880 621.

The Oysterbeds Restaurant: bayside seafood; 61 Esplanade; (08) 8685 4000.

Railway Shack 1: basic waterfront cottage; The Esplanade; 0427 844 568. *Sheoak Eastside Apartment:* elevated family beach house; 257 Esplanade; 0427 844 568. *Mt Dutton Bay Woolshed:* historic waterfront stone house; 1 Woolshed Dr, Mt Dutton Bay; (08) 8685 4031.

Coffin Bay National Park A mixture of rugged coastal landscapes, calm bays and waterways makes this diverse park a pleasure to wander and drive through. Conventional vehicles can access the eastern part of the park where walks through she-oak and samphire swamps reveal incredible birdlife. The beaches and lookouts provide a different perspective on this remote wilderness. 4WD vehicles and bushwalkers can access the western part, which includes Gunyah Beach, Point Sir Isaac and the Coffin Bay Peninsula. The park extends south and west of town; (08) 8688 3111.

Kellidie Bay Conservation Park: a limestone landscape popular for walking and canoeing; eastern outskirts of Coffin Bay. *Yangie Trail:* the 10 km trail starts at Coffin Bay and travels south-west via Yangie Bay Lookout, which offers magnificent views to Point Avoid and Yangie Bay. *Mt Dutton Bay:* features the restored heritage-listed jetty and woolshed, the latter now a shearing and farming museum; 40 km N. *Farm Beach:* popular swimming spot; 50 km N. *Gallipoli Beach:* location for the film *Gallipoli* (1981); 55 km N. *Scenic coastal drive:* between Mt Hope and Sheringa; 105 km N.

See also Eyre Peninsula & Nullarbor, p. 244

Coober Pedy

see inset box on next page

Coonawarra

Pop. 310
Map ref. 590 A12 | 592 A2 | 601 G10

 27 Arthur St, Penola; (08) 8737 2855; www.wattlerange.sa.gov.au

96.1 Star FM, 1161 AM ABC South East

Unlike many other Australian wine regions, Coonawarra was a planned horticulture scheme – and a very successful one at that. John Riddoch, a Scottish immigrant, acquired extensive lands in South Australia's south-east in the late 1800s. He subdivided 800 hectares of his landholding specifically for orchards and vineyards. Prominent wine professionals such as Wolf Blass damned this region as a place that could never produce decent wine, and the original John Riddoch wine estate was nearly sold to the Department of Forestry and Lands (thankfully, David Wynn purchased the property and it is now Wynns Coonawarra). In the 1950s, large wine companies such as Penfolds and Yalumba finally began recognising the depth of the region's reds, and opinions began to change. Coonawarra's famed terra rossa (red earth) combined with the region's particular climate is now known to create some of the best cabernet sauvignon in the country, as well as excellent shiraz, merlot, riesling and chardonnay. Wynns Coonawarra produces world-class shiraz and cabernet sauvignon, some for purchase at reasonable prices. Other excellent wineries to visit are Balnaves of Coonawarra, Brands of Coonawarra, Majella and Zema Estate.

 Coonawarra Cup: Jan. *Coonawarra After Dark:* cellar doors open in the evenings; Apr. *Penola Coonawarra Festival:* arts, food and wine; May. *Coonawarra Cellar Dwellers:* July. *Cabernet Celebrations:* Oct.

Kitchen @ The Poplars: tasty breakfasts and lunches; The Poplars Winery, Riddoch Hwy; (08) 8736 3065. *Upstairs at Hollick:* elegant winery dining; Ravenswood La; (08) 8737 2752.

Punters Vineyard Retreat: contemporary vineyard escape; Punters Corner Vineyard, cnr Riddoch Hwy and Racecourse Rd; (08) 8737 2007. *The Menzies Retreat:* stylish modern vineyard accommodation; Yalumba Winery, Riddoch Hwy; (08) 8737 3603.

See also LIMESTONE COAST, p. 242

Cowell

Pop. 883
Map ref. 599 B1 | 602 G5

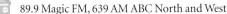

ℹ Main St; (08) 8629 2588.

89.9 Magic FM, 639 AM ABC North and West

This pleasant Eyre Peninsula township is on the almost land-locked Franklin Harbour – its entrance is merely 100 metres wide. Matthew Flinders sailed past here in 1802 and, understandably, mistook the harbour for a large lagoon. The sandy beach is safe for swimming and the fishing is excellent. Oyster farming is a relatively new local industry, and fresh oysters can be purchased year-round. The world's oldest and perhaps largest jade deposit is in the district. Discovered in the Minbrie Range in 1965, the deposit is believed to have been formed around 1700 million years ago by the shifting of the earth's surface.

Franklin Harbour Historical Museum: in the old post office and its attached residence (1888), now operated by the National Trust and featuring local history displays; closed Mon and Tues; Main St; (08) 8629 2686. *Ruston Proctor Steam Tractor Museum:* open-air agricultural museum; Lincoln Hwy. *Cowell Jade Motel:* showroom and sales of local jade jewellery; Lincoln Hwy. *Turner Aquaculture:* tours of an oyster factory; Oyster Dr. *Foreshore and Mangrove Boardwalk*: ideal for a picnic, with barbecue area and adventure playground for the kids; The Esplanade. *Boat hire:* from the caravan park.

Fireworks Night: includes street party; Dec.

Franklin Harbour Hotel: old-style pub with views; 1 Main St; (08) 8629 2015 or 1800 303 449.

Scenic drive: 20 km drive south to Port Gibbon along a coast renowned for its history of wrecked and sunken ketches; interpretive signs detail the history at each site. *Franklin Harbour Conservation Park:* coastal peninsula park of sand dunes and mangrove habitat, popular for bush camping and fishing; 5 km s. *May Gibbs Memorial:* marks the location of children's author May Gibbs' first home; Cleve Rd; 10 km s. *The Knob:* good fishing from sheltered beach and rocks; 13 km s. *Lucky Bay:* safe swimming for children and the start of a 4WD track to Victoria Point with excellent views of the harbour. Sea SA operates a ferry from here to Wallaroo on the Yorke Peninsula 4 times a day on weekdays and twice a day on weekends; bookings (08) 8823 0777; 16 km E. *Port Gibbon:* old shipping port with remains of original jetty. Sea lions are visible from the short walk to the point; 25 km s. *Yeldulknie Weir and Reservoir:* picnics and walking; 37 km w. *Cleve:* a service town with murals depicting its early days and an observation point at Tickleberry Hill; 42 km w. *Arno Bay:* a holiday town with sandy beaches and a jetty for fishing. Regular yacht races are held on Sun in summer; 44 km sw.

See also EYRE PENINSULA & NULLARBOR, p. 244

Crystal Brook

Pop. 1188
Map ref. 603 I4 | 604 H12

ℹ Port Pirie Regional Tourism and Arts Centre, 3 Mary Elie St, Port Pirie; (08) 8633 8700 or 1800 000 424.

105.1 Trax FM, 639 AM ABC North and West

Crystal Brook serves the sheep and wheat country at the southern point of the Flinders Ranges. It once formed part of a vast sheep station, Crystal Brook Run, which extended from the current town to Port Pirie in the north-west. The country feel of the town begins on entering the tree-lined main street.

National Trust Old Bakehouse Museum: local history collection in the town's first 2-storey building; open 2–4pm Sun and public holidays, or by appt; Brandis St; (08) 8636 2328. *Crystal Crafts:* local craft; Bowman St. *Creekside parks:* popular spots for picnics.

Crystal Brook Show: Aug.

The Big Goanna: we love our things big, be it fruit, rocking horses, or in this case, reptiles; 3 km N. *Bowman Fauna Park:* enjoyable walks, including part of the Heysen Trail, around ruins of the Bowman family property, Crystal Brook Run (1847); 8 km E. *Koolunga:* a small community, home to the mythical bunyip – in 1883 2 attempts to capture the beast were unsuccessful. Also craft outlets and the Bunyip River Walk on the banks of Broughton River; 10 km E. *Gladstone:* set in rich rural country in the Rocky River Valley. Heritage-listed Gladstone Gaol offers daily tours. Try traditional soft drinks, including Old Style Ginger Beer, at the Trends Drink Factory in Sixth Ave (open Mon–Fri) or discover the town's history on foot by picking up a map from the caravan park; 21 km NE. *Redhill:* riverside walk, museum, craft shop and antique shop; 25 km s. *Laura:* boyhood home of C. J. Dennis, author of *The Songs of a Sentimental Bloke*, known for its cottage crafts, art galleries and historic buildings. Leaflet available for self-guide walking tour from Biles Art

 SOUTH AUSTRALIA

Gallery, Herbert St. The Folk Fair each Apr brings thousands of visitors to the town; 32 km N. West of town is the Beetaloo Valley and Reservoir, a pleasant picnic spot in cooler months. *Snowtown:* surrounded by large salt lakes that change colour according to weather conditions. Lake View Drive is a scenic 6 km drive around the lakes. Lochiel–Ninnes Rd Lookout provides panoramic country and lake views; 50 km S.

See also Yorke Peninsula, p. 240

Edithburgh

Pop. 394
Map ref. 599 E8 | 602 H9

 Cnr Weaver and Towler sts, Stansbury; (08) 8852 4577; www.yorkepeninsula.com.au

98.9 Flow FM, 1044 5CS AM

Edithburgh is located on the foreshore at the south-eastern tip of Yorke Peninsula. This is an area synonymous with shipwrecks and, although reflecting tragic maritime days of old, it is a source of excitement for the diving enthusiast. Despite the construction of a lighthouse in 1856, over 26 vessels were wrecked on the coast between West Cape in Innes National Park and Troubridge Point just south of Edithburgh. Today Edithburgh is a popular coastal holiday destination overlooking Gulf St Vincent and Troubridge Island.

Edithburgh Museum: a community museum with local history of the town and region featuring a historical maritime collection; open 2–4pm Sun and public holidays, or by appt; Edith St; (08) 8852 6187. *Native Flora Park:* walk through eucalypts and casuarinas and see a variety of birdlife; Ansty Tce. *Bakehouse Arts and Crafts:* local handcrafts and produce in a historic 1890 building; Blanche St. *Town jetty:* built in 1873 to service large shipments of salt found inland, it offers views to Troubridge Island and is popular with anglers; end of Edith St. *Natural tidal pool:* excellent for swimming; foreshore. *Nature walks:* south to Sultana Point or north to Coobowie.

Gala Day: family day of entertainment and stalls; Oct.

Faversham's Restaurant: fine dining; Edithburgh House, 7 Edith St; (08) 8852 6373.

Edithburgh House: gracious heritage B&B; 7 Edith St; (08) 8852 6373. *Tipper's Edithburgh:* renovated rustic hideaway; 35 Blanche St; (08) 8852 6181. *Troubridge Island Hideaway:* offshore lighthouse keeper's cottage; Troubridge Island; (08) 8852 6290.

 Dive sites Discover the south coast of Yorke Peninsula with *The Investigator Strait Maritime Heritage Trail* brochure that includes the history and maps of 26 dive sites. By far the worst recorded shipwreck was that of the *Clan Ranald*, a huge steel steamer that, through incompetence and greed, was wrecked in 1909 just west of Troubridge Hill. The disaster claimed 40 lives – 36 bodies were later buried in the Edithburgh Cemetery.

Wattle Point Wind Farm: currently Australia's largest wind farm with 55 turbines; free viewing area 3km SW of Edithburgh. *Sultana Point:* fishing and swimming; 2 km S. *Coobowie:* a coastal town popular for swimming; 5 km N. *Troubridge Island Conservation Park:* home to penguins, black-faced shags and crested terns; tours available (30 min by boat) from town. *Scenic drive:* west along the coast to Innes National Park; *see Yorketown.*

See also Yorke Peninsula, p. 240

Elliston

Pop. 199
Map ref. 602 B5

Town Hall, 6 Memorial Dr; (08) 8687 9200.

89.5 Magic FM, 693 AM ABC Eyre Peninsula and West Coast

Nestled in a range of hills on the shores of picturesque Waterloo Bay is the small community of Elliston. The waters of the bay used to have rich abalone beds, but fierce exploitation in the 1960s decimated them. Thanks to a hatchery and rehabilitation, the abalone population is now back on the increase. The rugged and scenic coastline is spectacular and – with its excellent fishing and safe swimming beaches – Elliston is becoming a popular holiday destination. The 12-kilometre stretch of coast north of Elliston, known as Elliston's Great Ocean View, is said to rival the landscape of Victoria's Great Ocean Road, but on a smaller scale.

Town Hall Mural: the Southern Hemisphere's largest mural, which represents the history of the town and district; Main St. *Jetty:* the heritage-listed 1889 jetty has been restored and is lit by night.

Sculptures on the Cliff: Anzac Day weekend Apr. *Australian Salmon Fishing Competition:* June–Aug.

Elliston's Great Ocean View: scenic cliff-top drive north of town to adjacent Anxious Bay, with fabulous coastal views. Along the way is Blackfellows, reputedly one of the best surfing beaches in Australia. *Anxious Bay:* good fishing from beach and ledges for King George whiting. The boat ramp here provides access to Waldegrave Island (4 km offshore) and Flinders Island (35 km offshore), both good for fishing and seal-spotting (seek local advice about conditions before departing). *Locks Well:* a long stairwell down to a famous salmon-fishing and surf beach with coastal lookout; 12 km SE. *Walkers Rock:* good beaches for swimming and rock-fishing; 15 km N. *Lake Newland Conservation Park:* significant dunes separate the park's salt lakes and wetlands from the sea. Walk along bush tracks or try a spot of fishing; 26 km N. *Scenic drive:* to Sheringa (40 km SE). From Sheringa Beach, a popular fishing spot, see whales, dolphins and seals offshore. *Talia Caves:* spectacular scene of caves with waves crashing on edge. Another good spot for beach-fishing; 45 km N.

See also Eyre Peninsula & Nullarbor, p. 244

Gawler

Pop. 20 002
Map ref. 596 E2 | 597 D5 | 601 C2 | 603 J8

2 Lyndoch Rd; (08) 8522 9260; www.gawler.sa.gov.au

89.1 BBB FM, 639 AM ABC North and West

Set in the fork of the North and South Parra rivers and surrounded by rolling hills, it is no wonder that Gawler was picked, in 1839, as the site of South Australia's first country town. The grand architecture of that era can be seen in its stately homes and buildings, especially in the Church Hill State Heritage Area. Gawler is today a major service centre to a thriving agricultural district and has a growing Adelaide commuter population.

Historical walking trail The excellent trail brochure guides the visitor past stately buildings and homes, many with original cast-iron lacework. The Church Hill State Heritage Area provides a fascinating snapshot of town planning in the 1830s, and the 2.4 km walk around it includes a look at several churches, the old school, the courthouse, and cottages of the Victorian era. Also on the way are Gawler Mill, Eagle Foundry (now a popular B&B), the

COOBER PEDY

Pop. 1470
Map ref. 606 A10 | 609 O10

Council offices, Hutchison St; (08) 8672 4617 or 1800 637 076; www.opalcapitaloftheworld.com.au

104.5 Dusty Radio FM, 106.1 FM ABC Local

On 1 February 1915 a group of gold prospectors discovered opal in the area surrounding Coober Pedy. It was to become the biggest opal field in the world, which today provides around 80 per cent of the world's gem-quality opals. The name Coober Pedy is derived from the Aboriginal phrase 'Kupa Piti', loosely translating to 'white man's hole in the ground'. The town's unique underground style of living was first established by soldiers returning from World War I who were used to trench life. Today much of the population call the 'dugouts' home – as ideal places to escape the severe summer temperatures and cold winter nights. The landscape of Coober Pedy is desolate and harsh, dotted with thousands of mines.

Umoona Underground Mine and Museum This award-winning underground centre provides an all-round look at Coober Pedy. A detailed town history and an Aboriginal interpretive centre comprehensively document Coober Pedy's evolution. Experience 'dugout' life in an underground home or mine life on an on-site mine tour. An excellent documentary on Coober Pedy is shown in the underground cinema. Hutchison St; (08) 8762 5228.

Old Timers Mine: museum in an original 1916 mine featuring 3 large opal seams and interpretive centre with self-guide walk; Crowders Gully Rd. *Underground churches:* St Peter and St Pauls was the first underground church in the world; Hutchison St. Other interesting churches include the Catacomb Church on Catacomb Rd and the Serbian Orthodox Church with its 'ballroom' style. *Desert Cave:* international underground hotel with shopping complex and display gallery detailing the early hardships of miners in Coober Pedy; open 8am–8pm daily; Hutchison St. *Underground Art Gallery:* works of central Australian artists, including Aboriginal pieces; Hutchison St. *Opal retailers:* outlets offer jewellery and stone sales; many demonstrate the skill required to cut and polish opals. *Big Winch Lookout:* monument and lookout over town; Italian Club Rd. *Outback scenic and charter flights:* both local and outback tours; depart from airport; bookings (08) 8672 3067. *Mine tours:* to local mines; contact visitor centre.

Opal Festival: Easter. *Coober Pedy Greek Glendi:* celebration of Greek culture; July. *Horseracing:* Aug.

Tom & Mary's Greek Taverna: famous Greek cafe; Hutchinson St; (08) 8672 5622.

Desert Cave Hotel: full-service outback luxury; Hutchison St; (08) 8672 5688 or 1800 088 521. *Down to Erth B&B:* underground 2-bedroom apartment; Lot 1795 Wedgetail Cres; (08) 8672 5762.

Moon Plain and the Breakaways The rocky landscape of Moon Plain (15 km NE) has been the backdrop for many movies, especially those with a science-fiction bent. Likewise, the 40 sq km reserve of the Breakaways (30 km N). The unique arid landscape of flat-topped outcrops and stony gibber desert

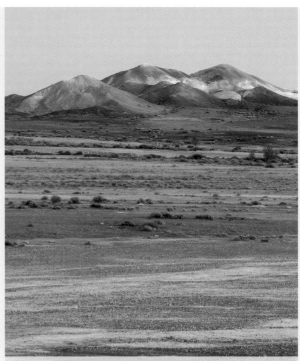

[THE BREAKAWAYS, NEAR COOBER PEDY]

is breathtaking, as is the wildlife that has adapted to these harsh conditions. Passes to the reserve are available from the visitor centre and other outlets in town. Return via the road past part of the Dog Fence, a 5300 km fence built to protect sheep properties in the south from wild dogs.

The Mail Run This overland adventure is a unique way of discovering the remote outback of SA. Travelling with Coober Pedy's mailman, the tour travels past waterholes and through scenic landscapes on its delivery run to Oodnadatta, William Creek and the remote cattle stations in between. Travelling 600 km over outback roads and the renowned Oodnadatta Track, the mailman offers up fascinating stories and history of the landscape and people. Tours depart from the Underground Bookshop at 9am on Mon and Thurs; bookings (08) 8672 5226 or 1800 069 911.

Underground Pottery: handmade pottery depicting the colours and landscape of the desert; 2 km w. *William Creek:* the smallest town in SA, situated in Anna Creek station, the world's largest cattle station. A race meeting is held the weekend before Easter each year. Flights offered over Lake Eyre; 166 km E. *Painted Desert:* rich colours paint the Arckaringa Hills, also noted for flora and fauna; 234 km N.

Travellers note: Opal fields are pocked with diggings. Beware of unprotected mine shafts. Avoid entering any field area unless escorted. For safety reasons, visitors to the mines are advised to join a tour. Trespassers on claims can be fined a minimum of $1000. Coober Pedy is the last stop for petrol between Cadney Homestead (151 km N) and Glendambo (252 km S).

See also FLINDERS RANGES & OUTBACK, p. 243

SOUTH AUSTRALIA

HAHNDORF

Pop. 1806

Map ref. 596 F9 | 597 D10 | 598 H3 | 603 K9

ⓘ Adelaide Hills Visitor Information Centre, 41 Main St; (08) 8388 1185; www.visitadelaidehills.com.au

📻 639 AM ABC North and West

In the heart of the Adelaide Hills is Hahndorf, Australia's oldest surviving German settlement. Prussian Lutheran refugees fleeing religious persecution in their homelands settled the area in the late 1830s. The town has retained a distinctly Germanic look and many local businesses and attractions are still operated by descendants of the original German pioneers. The surrounding countryside with its rolling hills, historic villages, vineyards, gourmet-produce farms and native bushland is renowned as a tourist destination.

🏠 *Main Street:* a mix of historic buildings, German-style bakeries, delis, cafes, restaurants and art and craft shops. *The Cedars:* historic paintings, gardens and home of famous landscape artist Hans Heysen; closed Sat; Heysen Rd. *Hahndorf Academy:* displays work of local artists in SA's largest regional gallery; Main St. *Model Train Land:* housed in a historic butcher shop with a model railway in miniature Bavarian countryside; Mt Barker Rd. *Hahndorf Farm Barn:* interactive farm animal shows, with petting and feeding; Mt Barker Rd. *Hillstowe Wines:* wine and cheese tastings; Main St. *Hahndorf Hill Winery:* boutique cool-climate winery with tastings and sales; open weekends; Pains Rd. *Beerenberg Strawberry Farm:* balcony viewing of the farm and packing area, jam and condiment sales, and berry-picking Oct–May; Mt Barker Rd. *Historic Hahndorf:* obtain *A Guide to Historic Hahndorf*, which lists 42 historic properties; available from visitor centre.

[THE CEDARS, HOME OF ARTIST HANS HEYSEN]

🌴 *Heysen Festival:* major 10-day event celebrating the life of Hans Heysen, with the Heysen Art Prize, food, wine and entertainment; Sept–Oct. *Oktoberfest:* Oct.

🍴 *Hahndorf Hill Winery:* sophisticated cellar-door lunches; Lot 10 Pains Rd; (08) 8388 7512. *The Lane Vineyard:* chic menu and fine views; Ravenswood La; (08) 8388 1250. *Udder Delights Cheese Cellar:* snacks, platters and cheese tastings; 91A Main Rd; (08) 8388 1588. *The Organic Market & Cafe:* famed hills fare; 5 Druids Ave, Stirling; (08) 8339 7131. *Petaluma Restaurant:* sublime modern cuisine; Bridgewater Mill, Mt Barker Rd, Bridgewater; (08) 8339 9200.

🛏 *The Manna:* sleek modern motel units; 25 Main St; (08) 8388 1000 or 1800 882 682. *Adelaide Hills Country Cottages:* romantic, rural hideaways; Oakwood Rd, Oakbank; (08) 8388 4193. *Hannah's Cottage:* secluded country haven; 'Botathan', Lot 14 Jones Rd, Balhannah; (08) 8388 4148. *Mount Lofty House:* gracious boutique hotel; 74 Mt Lofty Summit Rd, Crafers; (08) 8339 6777. *Thorngrove Manor Hotel:* authentic baronial-themed luxury; 2 Glenside La, Stirling; (08) 8339 6748.

◉ **Cleland Conservation Park** This park protects a variety of vegetation, from the stringybark forests in the highlands to the woods and grasses of the lowlands. It also includes panoramic views from the Mt Lofty Summit viewing platform. A highlight is the award-winning Cleland Wildlife Park where native animals wander freely about. Kids will enjoy the daily animal-feeding shows and the guided night tours. Bookings on (08) 8339 2444. For a rich cultural experience, take the guided Aboriginal tour on the Yurridla Trail. Mt Lofty Summit Rd; 14 km NW.

Belair National Park The oldest national park in SA was declared in 1891. There are plenty of activities, including 5 defined bushwalks ranging from the easy Wood Duck Walk to the more challenging 6.5 km Waterfall Walk, and cycling and horseriding tracks. Visitors can also visit Old Government House, built in 1859 to serve as the governor's summer residence; open Sun and public holidays; (08) 8278 5477. 19 km W.

Mount Barker: a historic town renowned for its gourmet outlets. The *SteamRanger* tourist train operates from here, including regular trips to Strathalbyn and on to the coastal section from Goolwa to Victor Harbor (this section is known as the Cockle Train; *see Goolwa*). For *SteamRanger* information and bookings contact 1300 655 991. Local events include the Highland Gathering and Heritage Festival in Feb; 6 km SE. *Bridgewater:* a historic town with excellent gardens and Petaluma's Bridgewater Mill, which has wine-tastings, sales and an up-market restaurant for lunch in a historic flour mill; 6 km W. *Oakbank:* craft shops and historic buildings with self-guide heritage-walk brochure available from local businesses. The Oakbank Easter Racing Carnival, held each Apr, is the Southern Hemisphere's biggest picnic race meeting and brings thousands of visitors to the town each year; 7 km N. *Aldgate:* a historic village featuring art and craft shops and historic sites that include the Aldgate Pump and the National Trust–listed Stangate House with its extensive camellia garden; 8 km W. *Stirling:* renowned for its European gardens and architecture, including the National Estate–listed

Beechworth Heritage Garden (Snows Rd). See colourful parrots in the aviaries at Stirling Parrot Farm (Milan Tce); 10 km w. **Warrawong Sanctuary:** large native animal reserve for reintroduced and endangered species, with walking trails and a boardwalk around Platypus Lakes. Guided dawn and evening tours are available; bookings (08) 8370 9197; 10 km sw via Mylor. **Jupiter Creek Goldfields:** walking trails with interpretive signs across historic fields discovered in 1852; 12 km sw. **Woodside**

Heritage Village: includes Melba's Chocolate Factory (with guided tours and sales) as well as craft studios with artisans at work; Woodside; 13 km ne. **Mt Lofty Botanic Gardens:** Australia's largest botanic gardens, with walking trails past cool-climate garden species, on the eastern face of Mt Lofty; access via Summit or Piccadilly rds; 14 km nw. **Wittunga Botanic Gardens:** native plants; Shepherds Hill Rd; 21 km w at Blackwood.

See also ADELAIDE HILLS, p. 237

Anglican Church with its pipe organ (open Sun) and Para Para Mansion (1862), a grand mansion that features a domed ballroom and has had British royalty as its guests (closed to public).

Gawler Museum: located in the Old Telegraph Station, this National Trust museum displays the history of Gawler's pioneer past; closed Sat–Mon; Murray St. **Historic main street walking tour:** the town is filled with some of South Australia's oldest and most historic hotels, pubs and churches; brochure available from visitor centre. **The Food Forest:** award-winning permaculture farm producing 160 varieties of organically certified food; tours available; on the Gawler River. **Fielke Cricket Bats:** the only cricket bat maker in South Australia, visit the workshop and see how the English Willow bats are meticulously handcrafted; Crown St. **Dead Man's Pass Reserve:** so named because an early pioneer was found dead in the hollow of a tree. It has picnic facilities and a walking trail; southern end of Murray St. **Community Art Gallery:** local artwork on display; 23rd Street. **Adelaide Soaring Club:** glider flights over Gawler and region; Wells Rd; (08) 8522 1877.

Markets: Gawler Railway Station; Sun mornings. **Antique and Collectors Auction:** Gawler Greyhound Pavillion; 1st Sun each month. **Band Festival:** Mar. **Gawler Gourmet and Heritage Festival:** even-numbered years, Apr. **Barossa Cup:** horseracing; May. **Gawler Show:** Aug. **Christmas Street Festival:** Dec.

The Garden Pavilion: sumptuous French Provincial–style garden rooms; AL-RU Farm, One Tree Hill Rd, One Tree Hill; (08) 8280 7353. **The Miner's Cottage:** secluded heritage charm; Goldfields Rd, Cockatoo Valley; (08) 8524 6213 or 1800 646 213.

Roseworthy Agricultural Museum: a dryland farming museum featuring vintage farm equipment, located at the Roseworthy campus of the University of Adelaide; open every Wed and 3rd Sun each month; (08) 8303 7739; 15 km n. **Freeling:** a rural town with a self-guide historical walk; 17 km ne. **Two Wells:** named for 2 Aboriginal wells found by original settlers, forgotten, then recovered in 1967. It has craft shops with local crafts; Main Rd; 24 km w. **Stockport Astronomical Facility:** run by the Astronomical Society of SA, featuring impressive observatory with public viewing nights; (08) 8338 1231; 30 km n.

See also BAROSSA VALLEY, p. 238

Goolwa

Pop. 5881

Map ref. 598 G8 | 601 C4 | 603 J11

ⓘ Signal Point River Murray Interpretive Centre, Goolwa Wharf; (08) 8555 3488; www.alexandrina.sa.gov.au

87.6 Alex FM, 639 AM ABC North and West

Goolwa is a rapidly growing holiday town on the last big bend of the Murray River before it reaches open waters. In 2007 Goolwa became the first town in Australia to be declared a Cittaslow, or 'slow town', joining a network of other towns in Europe and throughout the world which aim to improve the quality of life in towns. Goolwa was originally surveyed as the capital of South Australia, but Adelaide was later thought to be a better option. Goolwa did, however, boom as a river port from the 1850s to the 1880s – in the golden days of the riverboats. The area is excellent for fishing, with freshwater fishing in the Murray and saltwater fishing in the Southern Ocean and the Coorong, as well as boating, surfing, watersports, birdwatching and photography.

Signal Point River Murray Interpretive Centre Learn about the river and district before European settlement and see the impact of later development. There is also a detailed history on Goolwa's river port, the paddlesteamers and local Aboriginal people. A highlight is the 3D model showing how the Murray River interacts with the SA landscape. The Wharf.

National Trust Museum: documents the history of Goolwa and early navigation of the Murray River; Porter St. **South Coast Regional Arts Centre:** explore the restored old court and police station and see exhibitions by local artists; Goolwa Tce. **Goolwa Barrage:** desalination point to prevent salt water from reaching the Murray River; open Mon–Fri; Barrage Rd. **Armfield Slipway:** a working exhibition of wooden boatbuilding and restoration; open Tues mornings and Fri afternoons; Barrage Rd. **Horse-Drawn Railway Carriage:** first carriages used in SA between Goolwa and Port Elliot from 1854; Cadell St. **Goolwa Beach:** popular surfing and swimming beach with large cockles to be dug up (in season); end of Beach Rd. **Cockle Train:** journey around Encounter Bay from Goolwa Wharf to Victor Harbor, stopping at Port Elliot. The train has been operating since 1887, and its name comes from the abundance of large cockles found on Goolwa's surf beach. It forms part of the longer *SteamRanger* tourist railway from Mount Barker; *see* Hahndorf; operates most weekends and public/school holidays; bookings (08) 8231 4366. **Cruises:** day tours to the mouth of the Murray, the Coorong, the Barrages and the Lower Murray; details and bookings at visitor centre. **Scenic flights:** over the region; contact visitor centre for details. **Goolwa Heritage Walk:** a self-guide tour to see the 19th-century architecture of the river port's boom days; brochure available from visitor centre.

Goolwa Wharf Markets: 1st and 3rd Sun each month. **Milang to Goolwa Freshwater Sailing Classic:** Jan. **Wooden Boat Festival:** odd-numbered years, Mar.

Aquacaf Gourmet Cafe: innovative riverside fare; Barrage Rd; (08) 8555 1235. *Blues Restaurant:* relaxed snacks and seafood; Main Goolwa Rd, Middleton; (08) 8554 1800.

Jackling Cottage: updated heritage retreat; 18 Oliver St; 0433 571 927. *The Yellow House:* colourful waterfront family escape; 3 Barrage Rd; 0417 861 940. *Boatman's Cabin:* relaxed lakefront boathouse; Island View Dr, Clayton Bay; (08) 8537 0372. *Coorong Beach House:* stylish waterfront family escape; 1 Goolwa Channel Dr, Hindmarsh Island; (08) 8383 0504.

Hindmarsh Island: Captain Sturt located the mouth of the Murray River from here in 1830 – visit the Captain Sturt Lookout and monument. The island is now popular for both freshwater and saltwater fishing and is home to the kid-friendly Narnu farm, which offers horseriding, cottage accommodation and the opportunity to milk a cow; east of town; farm bookings (08) 8555 2002. *Currency Creek Game Reserve:* feeding grounds, breeding rookeries and hides for many waterbirds; access by boat only; 3 km E. *Currency Creek:* Lions Park is a popular picnic spot with a walking track along the creek. Near town is an Aboriginal canoe tree (a eucalypt carved to make a canoe) and also the Currency Creek Winery with a restaurant and fauna park; 7 km N.

See also FLEURIEU PENINSULA, p. 235

Hahndorf

see inset box on previous page

Hawker

Pop. 225
Map ref. 600 A12 | 604 H8

i Hawker Motors, cnr Wilpena and Cradock rds; (08) 8648 4022 or 1800 777 880; www.hawkersa.info

 105.9 Magic FM, 639 AM ABC North and West

This small outback town was once a thriving railway centre, and historic buildings are still well preserved in its streets. Hawker was also once an agricultural region producing bumper crops of wheat. Serious drought sent the crops into decline and the industry died. Today Hawker is the place to begin exploring the fantastic natural attractions of the southern Flinders Ranges.

Fred Teague's Museum: local history displays; Hawker Motors, cnr Wilpena and Cradock rds. *Jeff Morgan Gallery:* including a 30 m painting of the view from Wilpena Pound; Cradock Rd. *Heritage walk:* self-guide walk on numbered path; brochure from visitor centre. *Scenic flights and 4WD tours:* contact visitor centre for details.

Horseracing: May. *Art Exhibition:* Sept/Oct.

Meaney's Rest: quaint sandstone cottage; 68 Craddock Rd; (08) 8648 4022 or 1800 777 880. *Arkaba Station:* stylish homestead B&B; Wilpena Rd; (02) 9571 6399 or 1300 790 561.

Jarvis Hill Lookout: walking trail with views over the countryside; 7 km sw. *Yourambulla Caves:* Aboriginal rock paintings in hillside caves; 12 km sw. *Willow Waters:* popular picnic spot with a short walk to Ochre Wall; 20 km E off Cradock Rd. *Moralana Scenic Drive:* 22 km drive with superb views of Wilpena Pound and the Elder Range; leaves Hawker–Wilpena Rd 23 km N. *Cradock:* a tiny town with National Heritage–listed St Gabriel's Church (1882); 26 km SE. *Kanyaka Homestead Historic Site:* ruins of the homestead, stables and woolshed once part of a large sheep run, with informative

displays explaining the history of each ruin; 28 km sw. *Kanyaka Death Rock:* once an Aboriginal ceremonial site, it overlooks a permanent waterhole; near Kanyaka Homestead ruins. *Long-distance trails:* close to Hawker you can pick up sections of the Heysen (walking) and Mawson (cycling) trails; information from visitor centre.

See also FLINDERS RANGES & OUTBACK, p. 243

Innamincka

Pop. 15
Map ref. 607 N7 | 662 F8

i Inland Mission; (08) 8675 9909.

 1602 AM ABC North and West

This tiny settlement is built around a hotel and trading post on Cooper Creek. The first European explorer to visit the area was Charles Sturt, who discovered the Cooper in 1846 while vainly searching for an inland sea. It was also the final destination of the ill-fated Burke and Wills expedition. In 1860 all but one of Burke and Wills' party perished near the creek. John King survived owing to the outback skills of the Aboriginal people who found him. Innamincka was once a customs depot and service centre for surrounding pastoral properties, but now mainly services travellers, many of whom come from the south via the intrepid Strzelecki Track (for four-wheel-drive vehicles only).

Australian Inland Mission Built in 1928 to service the medical needs of remote pastoral properties, this mission was attended by a rotating staff of 2 nurses on horseback. Injured workers, flood victims and even fallen jockeys from the races called on their expertise. The mission was abandoned in the early 1950s when the Royal Flying Doctor Service began providing services. The restored classic outback building now houses the national parks headquarters as well as a tribute museum to the nurses who faced the trials of this isolated region.

Boat hire and tours: fishing and cruising trips; contact hotel for details on (08) 8675 9901.

Picnic Race Meeting: Aug.

Innamincka Regional Reserve This isolated but spectacular reserve is popular with 4WD enthusiasts and nature lovers. It covers 13 800 sq km and comprises important wetland areas, the most impressive being Coongie Lakes (112 km NW). This internationally significant wetland area is a haven for wildlife, particularly waterbirds. Closer to Innamincka is Cullyamurra Waterhole, on Cooper Creek (16 km NE), for bush camping and fishing. Aboriginal rock carvings and the Cullyamurra Choke are accessible by foot at the eastern end of the waterhole. 4WD is essential in parts of the park; after heavy rains roads become impassable. A Desert Parks Pass is required; visit the Inland Mission in Innamincka or phone 1800 816 078.

Memorial plaques: to Charles Sturt and Burke and Wills; 2 km N. *Burke and Wills Dig Tree:* famous Dig Tree where supplies were buried for their expedition; 71 km across border in Qld. *Strzelecki Regional Reserve:* sand-dune desert country with birdwatching and camping at Montecollina Bore; 167 km sw.

Travellers note: Motorists intending to travel along the Strzelecki Track should ring the Northern Roads Condition Hotline on 1300 361 033 to check conditions before departure. There are no supplies or petrol between Lyndhurst and Innamincka.

See also FLINDERS RANGES & OUTBACK, p. 243

Jamestown

Pop. 1408
Map ref. 603 J4 | 605 I11

i Country Retreat Caravan Park, 103 Ayr St; (08) 8664 0077; www.clarevalley.com.au

105.1 Trax FM, 639 AM ABC North and West

Jamestown survived the demise of wheat crops in the late 1800s to become an important service town to the thriving agricultural farmlands of the Clare Valley. John Bristow Hughes took up the first pastoral lease in 1841 and the strength of stud sheep and cattle farms, cereals, dairy produce and timber grew rapidly. A look at the names of towns in South Australia will reveal that the governors, politicians and surveyors of the day were bent on commemorating themselves or people they liked. Jamestown followed this trend, named after Sir James Fergusson, then state governor.

Railway Station Museum: a National Trust museum detailing local rail and Bundaleer Forest history and featuring the Both-designed iron lung (invented at Caltowie); Mannanarie Rd; (08) 8664 0522. **Heritage murals:** on town buildings. **Belalie Creek:** parks for picnics along the banks; floodlit at night. **Town and cemetery walks:** self-guide tours; brochure available from caravan park.

Producers Market: 1st Sun each month. **Bundaleer Forest Weekend:** fine music, food and wine in the autumn; Mar. **Jamestown Show:** largest 1-day show in SA; Oct. **Christmas Pageant:** Dec.

North Bundaleer: lavish, luxurious heritage homestead; RM Williams Way; (08) 8665 4024.

Bundaleer Forest Reserve This plantation forest, established in 1876, was the first in the world. Walking tracks start from the Arboretum, Georgetown Rd and the picnic area, and range from botanic walks to historic trails past building ruins and extensive dry-stone walls. The longer Mawson (cycling) and Heysen (walking) trails also travel through the reserve, as does a scenic drive from Jamestown, which then continues towards New Campbell Hill, Mt Remarkable and The Bluff. Each Easter Sunday the Bilby Easter Egg Hunt is held in the reserve. Spalding Rd; 9 km s.

Appila Springs: scenic picnic and camping spot; 31 km NW via Appila. **Spalding:** a town in the Broughton River valley. Picnic areas and excellent trout fishing; 34 km s.

See also MID-NORTH, p. 239

Kadina

Pop. 4026
Map ref. 599 E3 | 602 H6

i The Farm Shed Museum and Tourist Centre, 50 Moonta Rd; (08) 8821 2333 or 1800 654 991; www.yorkepeninsula.com.au

89.3 Gulf FM, 639 AM ABC North and West

Kadina exists solely as a result of the digging habits of wombats. In 1860 upturned ground from wombat diggings revealed copper. This was the starting point of coppermining on Yorke Peninsula. The wombats were commemorated by the naming of Kadina's 1862 hotel: Wombat Hotel. Kadina, along with Wallaroo and Moonta, formed part of a copper triangle colloquially named Little Cornwall because of the number of Cornish immigrants recruited to work in the mines. Kadina is now the commercial centre and largest town on Yorke Peninsula.

The Farm Shed Museum and Tourist Centre: home to the Dry Land Farming Interpretative Centre; Matta House, former home to the mining manager's family; a 1950s style schoolroom; Kadina story, a display of the town's history; and the visitor information centre; Moonta Rd; (08) 8821 2333. **Ascot Theatre Gallery:** cultural centre exhibiting local artists' work, with sales; closed Sun; Graves St. **Victoria Square Park:** historic band rotunda and Wallaroo Mine Monument; Main St. **Heritage walk:** self-guide walk includes historic hotels such as the Wombat and the Royal Exchange with iron-lace balconies and shady verandahs; brochure from visitor centre.

Kernewek Lowender: Cornish festival held with Wallaroo and Moonta; odd-numbered years, May. **Kadina Show:** Aug.

Yorke Peninsula Field Days: Australia's oldest field days, started in 1884, are held each Sept (odd-numbered years); Paskeville; 19 km SE.

See also YORKE PENINSULA, p. 240

Kangaroo Island
see Kingscote

Kapunda

Pop. 2479
Map ref. 597 E2 | 601 C1 | 603 K7

i Cnr Hill and Main sts; (08) 8566 2902; www.clarevalley.com.au

99.5 Flow FM, 1062 AM ABC Riverland

Kapunda is between two wine districts – the Barossa Valley and the Clare Valley – but its history is very different. Copper was discovered here by Francis Dutton, a sheep farmer, in 1842. It was to be the highest-grade copper ore found in the world. Settlement followed, and Kapunda came into existence as Australia's first coppermining town. When the mines closed in 1878, Australia's 'cattle king' Sir Sidney Kidman moved in, eventually controlling 26 million hectares of land across Australia.

Kapunda Museum: excellent folk museum with a short Kapunda history film and displays of old agricultural machinery, an original fire engine and other vehicles in the pavilion. Detailed mining history is in Bagot's Fortune interpretive centre; open 1–4pm daily; Hill St; (08) 8566 2286. **Community Gallery:** significant regional gallery with local and touring art exhibitions; cnr Main and Hill sts. **'Map Kernow':** 8 m bronze statue commemorating early miners, many of whom migrated from Cornwall in England; end of Main St at southern entrance of town. **High school's main building:** former residence of Sir Sidney Kidman; West Tce. **Gundry's Hill Lookout:** views over township and surrounding countryside; West Tce. **Heritage trail:** 10 km self-guide tour through town and historic Kapunda Copper Mine; *Discovering Historic Kapunda* brochure available at visitor centre.

Farm Fair: including fashion, craft and antiques; odd-numbered years, Apr/May. **Celtic Music Festival:** Sept (can vary). **Kapunda Show:** Nov.

Wheatsheaf Hotel: revamped pub, hearty food; Burra Rd, Allendale North; (08) 8566 2198.

Anlaby Homestead: historic pastoral estate; Anlaby Rd; (08) 8566 2465. **Oldham House:** lavish, stately country house; 14 Jeffs St; (08) 8566 3503.

SOUTH AUSTRALIA

Pop. 1691

KINGSCOTE

Map ref. 597 A11 | 599 C11 | 602 G12

ⓘ **Kangaroo Island Gateway Visitor Information Centre,** Howard Dr, Penneshaw; (08) 8553 1185; www.tourkangarooisland.com.au

🖻 90.7 KIX FM

In the early days of Australia's European settlement, Kangaroo Island was a haven for some of the country's most rugged characters – escaped convicts and deserters from English and American whaleboats. These men formed gangs, hunted more than their fair share of whales, seals, kangaroos, wallabies and possums, and went on raids to the mainland to kidnap Aboriginal women. It was an island truly without law. Two centuries on, the only ruggedness to speak of is found along the island's southern coast, where the surf is Southern Ocean–style and the seals are now left in peace. The north shore is a rippling line of bays and coves, with grass-covered hills sweeping down into Investigator Strait. On the shores of the resplendent Nepean Bay is Kingscote, the island's capital and the state's first official settlement (est. 1836). Amidst the beautiful scenery and wildlife, Kinsgscote is also the island's main commercial and business hub.

🏠 **Kangaroo Island Marine Centre** This interpretive marine centre is a must to visit. The size and shape of the aquariums allow visitors to get up close and personal with the vast array of sea life, which includes big bellied seahorses and giant cuttles. The Penguin Tour is the ultimate highlight, where you can observe the little penguins interact with each other. The penguins' breeding season is Mar–Dec, which is the best time to visit. There are 2 tours every night; times vary during the year. Pelican feedings and aquarium tours also on offer. The Wharf; (08) 8553 3112.

Hope Cottage Museum: this National Trust museum exhibits the town's long pioneering and maritime history through memorabilia and photographs; open 1–4pm daily; Centenary Ave; (08) 8553 3017. *St Alban's Church:* view the impressive stained-glass windows and pioneer memorials; Osmond St.

Kangaroo Island Gallery: beautiful local artworks from ceramics and glassworks to paintings and woodcrafts; Murray St. *Cemetery:* SA's oldest cemetrey; Seaview Rd. *Fishing:* the jetty is a hot spot for keen anglers.

🎪 *Racing Carnival:* Feb. *Ozone Street Party:* Feb. *Art Exhibition:* Penneshaw; Easter. *Kangaroo Island Art Feast:* Penneshaw; Oct. *Kangaroo Island Speed Shears:* Parndana; Nov. *Kingscote Show:* Nov.

🍴 *Marron Cafe:* island fare; Harriet Rd, Parndana; (08) 8559 4114. *Sorrento's Restaurant:* contemporary fine dining; Kangaroo Island Seafront Resort, 49 North Tce, Penneshaw; (08) 8553 1028 or 1800 624 624. *The Rockpool Cafe:* laid-back beachfront seafood; Stokes Bay; (08) 8559 2277.

🛏 *Blue Seas Beach House:* modern oceanfront hideaway; D'Estrees Bay; (08) 8553 8268. *Cape Borda Lighthouse:* remote lighthouse keepers cottages; Cape Borda; (08) 8559 7235. *Kangaroo Island Beach House:* beachfront family retreat; Island Beach; 0403 986 007. *Sea Dragon Lodge:* dramatic, secluded coastal haven; Willoughby Rd, Cape Willoughby; (08) 8553 1449. *Southern Ocean Lodge:* stunning, stylish wilderness resort; Hanson Bay; (02) 9918 4355.

⊙ **Seal Bay Conservation Park** This park protects the habitat of the rare Australian sea lion, which faced extinction on the SA coast during the 1800s. Guided beach tours provide close-up encounters with the snoozing creatures. There are also views down to the beach from the 400 m boardwalk that runs through dunes to an observation deck. (08) 8559 4207; 58 km sw.

Flinders Chase National Park On the south coast of this vast park are the precariously positioned granite boulders called the Remarkable Rocks, gradually being eroded by wind and sea to form spectacular shapes. Nearby is the Cape du Couedic lighthouse, and a colony of New Zealand fur seals that can be seen from the boardwalk down to Admirals Arch, a sea cave.

[VIVONNE BAY, POPULAR FOR SURFING AND FISHING]

There are many walking trails and a detailed map is available from the visitor centre at Rocky River. Watch for the Cape Barren geese around the visitor centre. (08) 8559 7220; 93 km sw.

Island Pure Sheep Dairy: tasting and sales of produce, and milking demonstrations; open 1–5pm daily; Cygnet River; 12 km sw. ***Emu Bay:*** excellent swimming at the beach with fishing from the jetty; 17 km sw. ***Emu Ridge Eucalyptus Oil Distillery:*** sales of eucalyptus-oil products; open 9am–2pm daily; Wilsons Rd, off South Coast Rd; 20 km s. ***Clifford's Honey Farm:*** sales and free tasting of honey produced by pure Ligurian bees; Hundred Line Rd; 30 km s. ***Prospect Hill Lookout:*** spectacular views from the spot where Matthew Flinders surveyed Kangaroo Island; on the narrow neck to Dudley Peninsula; 35 km se. ***American River:*** a fishing village overlooking Eastern Cove and Pelican Lagoon, havens for birdlife; 40 km se. ***Parndana:*** a small town known as the Place of Little Gums, featuring the Soldier Settlement Museum; 40 km sw. ***Murray Lagoon:*** well-known waterbird area with tea-tree walk; 40 km sw. ***Stokes Bay:*** natural

rock tunnel leads to a rockpool, ideal for swimming; 50 km w. ***Little Sahara:*** large sand dunes surrounded by bush; 55 km sw. ***Penneshaw:*** a small town on Dudley Peninsula where the vehicular ferry arrives from Cape Jervis. The town features a National Trust folk museum and nightly penguin tours from the Penguin Interpretive Centre at Hog Bay Beach; 60 km e. ***Vivonne Bay:*** popular beach for surfing and fishing (beware of strong undertow – safe swimming near the jetty, boat ramp and Harriet River); 63 km sw. ***Antechamber Bay:*** picturesque beach and area, excellent for bushwalking, fishing and swimming; 72 km se. ***Kelly Hill Conservation Park:*** sugar gum forest walks and guided tours of limestone caves; 85 km sw. ***Western River Wilderness Protection Area:*** 2.5 km track to winter waterfall; 85 km e. ***Scott Cove:*** from here you can view SA's highest coastal cliffs, at 263 m; near Cape Borda; 100 km w. ***Cape Borda Lightstation:*** historical tours offered of 1858 lighthouse. Also here is the Cape Borda Heritage Museum. Cannon is fired at 12.30pm; 105 km w.

See also **KANGAROO ISLAND**, p. 236

 Pines Reserve: nature and wildlife reserve; 6 km nw on road to Tarlee. ***Anlaby Station:*** historic Dutton Homestead and gardens, once a setting for large prestigious parties. Also a coach collection and historic station buildings; open 10am–4pm Wed–Sun; Anlaby Rd; 16 km ne. ***Tarlee:*** historic local-stone buildings; 16 km nw. ***Riverton:*** a historic town in the Gilbert Valley, once a stopover point for copper-hauling bullock teams. Many historic buildings remain, including the heritage-listed railway station and Scholz Park Museum, which incorporates a cottage, blacksmith and wheelwright shop; open 1–4pm weekends; 30 km nw. ***Scenic drive:*** 28 km drive north-east through sheep, wheat and dairy country to Eudunda.

See also **MID-NORTH**, p. 239

Pop. 1089
Map ref. 601 F6

 Mobil Roadhouse, cnr Riddock and Dukes hwys; (08) 8755 1700; www.tatiara.sa.gov.au

 104.5 5TCB FM, 1062 AM ABC Riverland

Keith is a farming town in the area formerly known as the Ninety Mile Desert. Settlers found the original land unpromising, but the area has since been transformed from infertile pasture to productive farmland with the addition to the soil of missing trace elements and water piped from the Murray.

 Congregational Church: National Trust church with 11 locally made leadlight windows depicting the town's life and pioneering history; Heritage St. ***Early Settler's Cottage:*** limestone pioneer cottage; open by appt; Heritage St; (08) 8755 1118. ***Keith Water Feature:*** water sculpture; Heritage St.

 Keith Show: Oct.

 McIntyre Cottage: romantic Mediterranean-style villa; 3 Tolmer Tce; (08) 8755 1126.

 Ngarkat group of conservation parks Protecting 262 700 ha of sand dunes, mallee and heath are the 4 adjacent conservation parks – Ngarkat, Scorpion Springs, Mt Rescue and Mt Shaugh. The walking trails are an excellent introduction to the region's vegetation. Birdwatching is particularly good at Rabbit Island (Mt Rescue) and Comet Bore (Ngarkat). For panoramic views, try walking to the summit of Mt Rescue, Goose Hill or Mt Shaugh. Visitors can drive through the parks on the Pinaroo–Bordertown Rd. The main entrance is via Snozwells Rd near Tintinara.

Monster Conservation Park: scenic views and picnic spots; 10 km s. ***Tintinara Homestead:*** one of the first homesteads in the area, with woolshed, shearers quarters and pioneer cottage; caters for visitors; 38 km nw. ***Mt Boothby Conservation Park:*** mallee scrub, granite outcrops and wildflowers in spring; 58 km nw via Tintinara.

See also **MURRAY**, p. 241

Pop. 636
Map ref. 602 F4 | 604 D11

 Kimba Mobil Roadhouse, Eyre Hwy; (08) 8627 2040; www.kimba.sa.gov.au

 89.9 Magic FM, 1485 AM ABC Eyre Peninsula and West Coast

A small town on the Eyre Peninsula, Kimba is 'halfway across Australia' according to the huge sign on the Eyre Highway. It is the gateway to the outback, a fact that explorer Edward John Eyre confirmed when he traversed the harsh landscape in 1839. Early settlers thought the country too arid for settlement and it wasn't until demand for wheat production grew, and rail services were extended to the area in 1913, that the Kimba region developed. It is now major sheep- and wheat-farming country.

 Kimba and Gawler Ranges Historical Museum: a 'living' museum featuring local history and a Pioneer House (1908), a

SOUTH AUSTRALIA

blacksmith's shop and 'Clancy' the fire truck; open 1.30–4pm Sat (closed Jan) or by appt; Eyre Hwy; (08) 8627 2349. *Halfway Across Australia Gem Shop and the Big Galah:* standing 8 m high, the Big Galah is in front of the gem shop, which offers sales of local gemstones, carved emu eggs, opal and locally mined jade, including rare black jade; Eyre Hwy. *Pine 'n' Pug Gallery:* local craft; High St. *Roora Walking Trail:* meanders through 3 km of bushland to White Knob Lookout; starts at north-eastern outskirts of town.

Kimba Show: Sept.

Lake Gilles Conservation Park: habitat for mallee fowl; 20 km NE. *Caralue Bluff:* popular for rock climbing; 20 km SW. *Carappee Hill Conservation Park:* bush camping and walking; 25 km SW. *Darke Peak:* excellent views from the summit and a memorial at the base to John Charles Darke, an explorer who was speared to death in 1844; 40 km SW. *Pinkawillinie Conservation Park:* the largest mallee vegetation area on the peninsula and a habitat for small desert birds, emus and western grey kangaroos; turn-off 50 km W.

See also EYRE PENINSULA & NULLARBOR, p. 244

Kingscote

see inset box on previous page

Kingston S.E.

Pop. 1632
Map ref. 601 E8

i BP Roadhouse, 1 Princes Hwy; (08) 8767 2404; www.thelimestonecoast.com

107.7 5THE FM, 1161 AM ABC South East

Known as the 'Gateway to the South East', Kingston S.E. is at the southern end of Coorong National Park on Lacepede Bay. The area was once home to the Ngarrindjeri, river people who mastered the waterways of the Coorong and the Murray River. This famous lobster town was established in 1858 and its shallow lakes and lagoons are a haven for birdlife and a delight for photographers.

  National Trust Museum: pioneer museum; open 2–4.30pm daily during school holidays, or by appt; Cooke St; (08) 8767 2114. *Cape Jaffa Lighthouse:* built in the 1860s on the Margaret Brock Reef, it was dismantled and re-erected on its current site in the 1970s; open 2–4.30pm daily during school holidays, or by appt; Marine Pde; (08) 8767 2591. *Analematic Sundial:* an unusual sundial, 1 of only 8 in the world; on an island in the creek adjacent to Apex Park in East Tce. *Aboriginal burial ground:* Dowdy St. *Power House engine:* historic engine that produced the town's energy until 1974; Lions Park, Holland St. *The Big Lobster:* 17 m high 'Larry Lobster' has sales of cooked lobster; Princes Hwy.

Fishing Contest: Jan.

  Kingston Shore Villas: modern 2-storey beachfront villas; 99 Marine Pde; 0417 886 329.

Butchers Gap Conservation Park: this important coastal park provides a winter refuge for bird species. Follow the walking trail from the carpark; 6 km SW. *The Granites:* rocky outcrops, a striking sight from the beach; 18 km N. *Cape Jaffa:* scenic drive south-west from Kingston S.E. leads to this small fishing village popular with anglers and divers. The Cape Jaffa Seafood and Wine Festival is held here each Jan; 18 km SW. *Mt Scott Conservation Park:* part of a former coastal dune system, with walks through stringybark forest; 20 km E. *Jip Jip Conservation Park:* features a prominent outcrop of unusually shaped granite boulders; 50 km NE.

See also LIMESTONE COAST, p. 242

Leigh Creek

Pop. 547
Map ref. 600 B4 | 604 H4

i 13 Black Oak Dr; (08) 8675 2723.

1602 AM ABC North and West

Located in the Flinders Ranges, Leigh Creek is a modern coalmining town that services a huge open-cut mine to the north. The original township (13 kilometres north) was unfortunately placed, as it was situated over a large coal seam. The lure of the dollar led to the town's relocation in 1982 to its current site. A tree-planting scheme has transformed the town from a barren landscape to an attractive oasis.

Copley Bush Bakery & Quandong Cafe: great pies and cakes; Railway Tce, Copley; (08) 8675 2683.

Warraweena Conservation Park: rustic, remote shearers quarters; via Beltana Roadhouse; (08) 8675 2770.

Coal mine tours: tours to the open-cut mine each Sat from Mar to late Oct and during school holidays; contact visitor centre for details. *Aroona Dam:* in a steep-sided valley with coloured walls; picnic area near gorge; 4 km W. *Coalmine viewing area:* turn-off 14 km N (area is 3 km down road to coalmine). *Beltana:* almost a ghost town, it has a historic reserve and holds a Picnic Race Meeting and Gymkhana each Sept; 27 km S. *Lyndhurst:* starting point of the famous Strzelecki Track. It also features a unique gallery of sculptures by well-known talc-stone artist 'Talc Alf'; tours by appt (08) 8675 7781; 39 km N. *Ochre Cliffs:* here Aboriginal people used to dig for ochre. The colours range from white to reds, yellows and browns; 44 km N via Lyndhurst. *Sliding Rock Mine ruins:* access track is rough in places; 60 km SE. *Vulkathunha–Gammon Ranges National Park:* 64 km E; *see Arkaroola.*

Travellers note: Care must be taken on outback roads. Check road conditions with Northern Roads Condition Hotline on 1300 361 033 before departure.

See also FLINDERS RANGES & OUTBACK, p. 243

Loxton

Pop. 3432
Map ref. 558 A6 | 588 A7 | 601 G2 | 603 N8

i Bookpurnong Tce; (08) 8584 7919; www.riverland.info

93.1 Magic FM, 1062 AM ABC Riverland

Although the area around Loxton was originally settled largely by German immigrants, the town's boom began when servicemen returned from World War II. The enticement of irrigated allotments brought a great number of them to town and the success of current-day industries, such as the production of citrus fruits, wine, dried fruit, wool and wheat, was due to their skill on the land. Loxton's delightful setting on the Murray River has made the town the 'Garden City of the Riverland'.

Loxton Historical Village The Riverland's pioneering history comes to life in the 30 historic buildings, all fully furnished in the styles of late 1880s to mid-1900s. A highlight is the pine-and-pug building, Loxtons Hut, built by the town's namesake, boundary rider William Loxton. Visit on one of the Village Alive days held thrice yearly in the village. Locals dress up in period costume and the whole village steps back 100 years. Allan Hosking Dr; (08) 8584 7194.

Terrace Gallery: local art and pottery displays and sales; part of visitor centre; Bookpurnong Tce. *The Pines Historical Home:* resplendent gardens and historic home filled with antique furniture and fine china. Tours of home every Sun followed by afternoon tea; Henry St; (08) 8584 4646. **Pepper tree:** grown from a seed planted by Loxton over 110 years ago; near the historical village. **Nature trail:** along riverfront; canoes for hire. **Heritage walk:** brochure from visitor centre.

Mardi Gras: Feb. **Nippy's Loxton Gift:** SA's largest and richest footrace; Feb. **Riverland Harvest Festival & Great Grape Stomp:** Apr. **Loxton Annual Spring Show:** Oct. **Loxton Lights Up:** Christmas lights throughout town; self-guide tour map available; Nov–Dec.

Mill Cottage: inviting stone home and garden; 2 Mill Rd; 0439 866 990. **Thiele's Heritage B&B:** evocative cliff-top farmhouse; Casson Ave, Loxton North; 0402 837 012.

McGuigan Simeon Wines Loxton Cellars: wine-tasting and sales; Bookpurnong Rd, Loxton North; (08) 8584 7236; 4 km N. **Torambre Nissen Hut Wines:** boutique winery with award-winning shirazes and merlots; Balfour–Ogilvy Rd, Loxton North; (08) 8584 1530; 6 km NE. **Lock 4:** picnic/barbecue area; 14 km N on Murray River. **MV Loch Luna Eco Cruise:** relaxing 3 hr cruise around the Nockburra and Chambers creeks; departs daily from Kingston at 9am and 1.30pm; 0449 122 271. **Banrock Station Wine and Wetland Centre:** magnificently restored wetlands and mallee woodlands, with 250 ha of picturesque vineyards and a wine centre; Holmes Rd, Kingston-on-Murray; (08) 8583 0299; 35km NW.

See also MURRAY, p. 241

Lyndoch

Pop. 1419
Map ref. 596 G2 | 597 E5 | 601 C2 | 603 K8

Kies Family Wines, Lot 2, Barossa Valley Hwy; (08) 8524 4110; www.barossa-region.org

89.1 Triple B FM, 639 AM ABC North and West

Lyndoch is one of the oldest towns in South Australia. The first European explorers, led by Colonel Light in 1837, described the area around Lyndoch as 'a beautiful valley'. The undulating landscape and picturesque setting attracted Lutheran immigrants and English gentry, who began growing grapes here. By 1850 Johann Gramp had produced his first wine from the grapes at Jacob's Creek.

Spinifex Arts & Crafts: retail shop selling exclusive quality hand-crafted goods including pottery, quilts, folk art and paintings of local scenes. All goods are locally made in the Barossa region; Barossa Valley Way. **Helicopter and balloon flights:** scenic flights over the Barossa region; contact visitor centre for details. **Historic Lyndoch Walk:** self-guide walk featuring buildings from the mid-1800s, including many built from locally quarried hard ironstone; brochure from visitor centre.

Barossa under the Stars: food, wine and music; Tanunda; Feb. **Barossa Vintage Festival:** celebration of food and wine in various locations; odd-numbered years, Apr. **Barossa Gourmet Weekend:** Aug.

Abbotsford Country House: gracious hosted suites; Yaldara Dr; (08) 8524 4662. **Bandicoot Nest:** stone cottage with modern makeover; address provided on booking; (08) 8524 5353. **Barossa Country Cottages:** easygoing garden cottages; 55 Gilbert St; (08) 8524 4426. **Barossa Pavilions:** dashing, designer hilltop retreats; 461 Yaldara Dr; (08) 8524 5497 or 1800 990 055.

Para Wirra Recreation Park Para Wirra comes from the Aboriginal words for 'river with scrub'. The park has a large recreational area with extensive facilities including tennis courts, picnic and barbecue areas, and walking trails ranging from short 800 m walks to more extensive 7.5 km trails. The park consists of mostly eucalypts and is home to a large variety of native birds – including inquisitive emus that meander around the picnic areas. The historic Barossa Goldfield Trails (1.2 km or 5 km loop walks) cover the history of the old goldmines. 12 km SW.

Barossa Wine Region: wineries and cellar doors lie around Lyndoch and Rowland Flat, just north-east, with rich red varieties as well as crisp whites. At Rowland Flat is the Jacob's Creek Visitor Centre where viticulture history is on display. For a total Barossa experience, take the self-drive Butcher, Baker, Winemaker trail from Lyndoch to Angaston and Eden Valley; brochure available from visitor centre. *For more information on the region see Tanunda, Angaston and Nuriootpa.* **Sandy Creek Conservation Park:** on undulating sand dunes, with walking trails and birdlife. See western grey kangaroos and echidnas at dusk; 5.5 km W. **Lyndoch Lavender Farm and Cafe:** wander through rows of over 60 lavender varieties. The nursery and farm shop offer lavender-product sales; open daily Sept–Feb, Mon–Fri Mar–April; cnr Hoffnungsthal and Tweedies Gully rds; 6 km SE. **Barossa Reservoir and Whispering Wall:** acoustic phenomenon allowing whispered messages at one end to be audible at the other end, 140 m away; 8 km SW.

See also BAROSSA VALLEY, p. 238

McLaren Vale

Pop. 2907
Map ref. 596 B12 | 597 B12 | 598 E5 | 599 H9 | 601 B4 | 603 J10

Main Rd; (08) 8323 9944 or 1800 628 410; www.mclarenvale.info

94.7 5EFM, 639 AM ABC North and West

McLaren Vale is recognised as a region of vineyards, orchards and gourmet-produce farms. The first grape vines were planted here in 1838, just two years after Adelaide was settled, and McLaren Vale has remained a prominent wine region ever since. Shiraz is the most transcendent drop and is known for its overtones of dark chocolate. Cabernet sauvignon, grenache, chardonnay and sauvignon blanc are also very respectable. Coriole makes wonderful shiraz as well as olive oil, while d'Arenberg has many interesting varieties and a good restaurant, d'Arry's Verandah. Other wineries to visit include Geoff Merrill Wines and two of the oldest and biggest names in the district: Hardys Tintara and Rosemont Estate. The best time to visit the region is late winter, when almond blossoms provide a gentle pink blush. The town is also known for its coastal vistas to the west, which provide subject matter for the artists who exhibit in the galleries.

McLaren Vale Visitors Centre: picturesque landscaped grounds with a vineyard and a centre that features changing art exhibitions, sales of local craft and produce, and a cafe; Main Rd; (08) 8323 9944. **The Old Bank Artel:** community cooperative of local crafts including pottery, jewellery and metalwork; Main Rd. **Almond and Olive Train:** sales of local produce, including almonds, in a restored railway carriage; Main Rd. **McLaren Valley Bakery:** produces unique 'wine pies'; Central Shopping Centre, Main Rd. **McLaren Vale Olive Grove:** grows over 26 varieties of olives and sells olive products, arts and crafts, and local gourmet produce; Warners Rd. *Medlow Confectionery and FruChocs Showcase:* tastings and sales of gourmet chocolate and other confectionery. Interactive confectionery machine for kids; Main Rd. *McLaren Vale Heritage Trail:* self-guide trail of historic sites, including wineries, with audio CD available; starts at visitor centre.

Sea and Vines Festival: music, food and wine; June. *Fiesta!:* month-long food and wine festival; Oct.

d'Arry's Verandah Restaurant: glorious cellar-door views, regional cuisine; d'Arenberg Wines, Osborn Rd; (08) 8329 4848. *Red Poles:* arty cafe; McMurtrie Rd; (08) 8323 8994. *Salopian Inn:* creative contemporary cooking; Cnr McMurtrie and Main rds; (08) 8323 8769. *The Kitchen Door:* stylish rustic fare; Penny's Hill Winery, Main Rd; (08) 8556 4000.

Bellevue B&B: comfortable suites, impeccably hosted; 12 Chalk Hill Rd; 0432 868 402. *McLaren Ridge Log Cabins:* hilltop vineyard havens; Whitings Rd; (08) 8383 0504. *Aunt Amanda's Cottage:* cute, secluded farmhouse retreat; Peters Creek Rd, Kangarilla; (08) 8383 7122.

Onkaparinga River National Park The Onkaparinga River, SA's second longest river, travels through valleys and gorges to Gulf St Vincent. The walks in Onkaparinga Gorge are impressive, but very steep. More regulated walking trails are on the northern side of the gorge. The estuary section of the park is an altogether different environment and is best explored on the 5 km interpretive trail. Look out for the 27 species of native orchids. Access is via Main South Rd, Old Noarlunga; (08) 8278 5477; 7 km NW.

Old Noarlunga: self-guide tour of historic colonial buildings (brochure available). Walks into Onkaparinga National Park start from here; 7 km NW. *Port Noarlunga:* popular holiday destination with historic streetscapes. A marked underwater trail along the reef is provided for divers and snorkellers; 11 km NW. *Coastal beaches:* safe family beaches to the north-west include O'Sullivan, Christies and Moana.

See also FLEURIEU PENINSULA, p. 235

Maitland	Pop. 1055
	Map ref. 599 E5 | 602 H7

ⓘ Council offices, 8 Elizabeth St; (08) 8832 0000; www.yorkepeninsula.com.au

📻 89.3 Gulf FM, 639 AM ABC North and West

Maitland represents a much smaller version of the city of Adelaide, with the town layout in the same pattern of radiating squares. It is in the heart of Yorke Peninsula and is central to a rich agricultural region. In recent years tourism has grown dramatically on the peninsula, but barley and wheat industries remain strong.

Maitland Museum: located in the former school, this National Trust museum documents local indigenous and settlement history; open 2–4pm Sun, public/school holidays, other times by appt; cnr Gardiner and Kilkerran tces; (08) 8832 2220. *White Flint Olive Grove:* range of olive oil products produced from own trees, great food and tea on offer; appt only; South Tce; (08) 8832 2874. *St John's Anglican Church:* stained-glass windows depict biblical stories in an Australian setting; cnr Alice and Caroline sts. *Aboriginal cultural tours:* a range of tours through Adjahdura Land (Yorke Peninsula), with an Aboriginal guide; bookings and inquiries 0429 367 121. *Heritage town walk:* interpretive walk; brochure from council in Elizabeth St.

Maitland Show: Mar. *Maitland Art/Craft Fair:* June and Nov.

Gregory's Wines: Yorke Peninsula's only commercial vineyard. Cellar-door tastings and sales 10am–5pm weekends or by appt; Lizard Rd; (08) 8834 1258; 13 km s. *Balgowan:* this town has safe, sandy beaches and is popular with anglers; 15 km w.

See also YORKE PENINSULA, p. 240

Mannum	Pop. 2037
	Map ref. 597 H9 | 601 D3 | 603 L9

ⓘ 6 Randell St; (08) 8569 1303; www.murraylands.info

📻 98.7 Power FM, 1062 AM ABC Riverland

Mannum is one of the oldest towns on the Murray River, at the romantic heart of the old paddlesteamer days. In 1853 the 'Father of Mannum', William Randell, built the first Murray River paddlesteamer, *Mary Ann* (named after his mother), in order to transport his flour to the Victorian goldfields. The paddlesteamer set out from Mannum in 1853 and started a boom in the river transport industry. Another first for Mannum was Australia's first steam car, built in 1894 by David Shearer.

Mannum Dock Museum This excellent museum documents the changing history of the Mannum region from ancient days through Indigenous habitation, European settlement and river history to the present day. Outside is the renowned Randell's Dry Dock, where the grand lady of the Murray, PS *Marion*, is moored. Passenger cruises on the restored paddlesteamer still operate. Randell St; (08) 8569 2733.

Mary Ann Reserve: popular recreation reserve on the riverbank with a replica of PS *Mary Ann's* boiling engine. PS *River Murray Princess* is moored here between cruises. *Ferry service:* twin ferries operate to the eastern side of the river. *River cruises and houseboat hire:* afternoon, day and overnight cruises are available from the town wharf, including the Murray Expedition Captain's Dinner. Alternatively, hire a houseboat to discover the Murray River your own way. Contact visitor centre for details. *Town lookout:* off Purnong Rd to the east. *Scenic and historical walks:* brochures from visitor centre.

Mannum Show: Mar. *Houseboat Hirers' Open Days:* May. *Christmas Pageant:* Dec.

Baseby House: ultra-modern riverfront B&B; 152 River La; (08) 8569 2495. *River Dream Boatel:* opulent, architect-designed cruising; Mannum Waterfront, 16 Randell St; (08) 8223 3030. *Riverview Rise Retreats:* glamorous getaway for couples; Bowhill Rd; 0400 310 380. *Unforgettable Houseboats:* 11-strong fleet, multi-award-wining operator; 69 River La; (08) 8569 2559 or 1800 656 323.

Mannum Falls: picnics and scenic walks, best visited in winter (after rains) when the waterfall is flowing; 6 km SE. *Kia Marina:* the largest river marina in SA; boats and houseboats for hire; 8 km NE. *Lowan Conservation Park:* mallee vegetation park with varied wildlife, including fat-tailed dunnarts, mallee fowl and western grey kangaroos; turn-off 28 km E at Bowhill. *Purnong:* scenic drive north-east, runs parallel to excellent Halidon Bird Sanctuary; 33 km E.

See also MURRAY, p. 241

Marree	Pop. 300
	Map ref. 604 H1 | 606 H12 | 662 A12

ⓘ Marree Outback Roadhouse and General Store; (08) 8675 8360.

📻 105.7 AM ABC Local

Marree is the perfect image of a tiny outback town. It is frequented by four-wheel-drive enthusiasts taking on the legendary Birdsville and Oodnadatta tracks. The settlement was established in 1872 as a camp for the Overland Telegraph Line as it was being constructed, and also became a railhead for the Great Northern Railway (which was later known as the *Ghan*). The town soon serviced all travellers and workers heading north, including the famous Afghan traders who drove their camel trains into the desert and played a significant role in opening up the outback.

 Aboriginal Heritage Museum: features artefacts and cultural history; in Arabunna Aboriginal Community Centre. *Marree Heritage Park:* includes Tom Kruse's truck that once carried out the famous outback mail run on the Birdsville Track in the 1950s. *Camel sculpture:* made out of railway sleepers. *Scenic flights:* including over Lake Eyre and the Marree Man, a 4 km long carving in a plateau of an Aboriginal hunter. The carving, visible only from the air, appeared mysteriously in 1998, and is slowly fading; contact visitor centre for details.

Australian Camel Cup: July.

Lake Eyre National Park Of international significance, Lake Eyre is dry for most of the time – it has filled to capacity on only 3 occasions in the last 150 years. When water does fill parts of the lake (usually due to heavy rains in Queensland funnelled south via creeks and rivers), birds flock to it. Avoid visiting in the hotter months (Nov–Mar). Lake Eyre North is accessed via the Oodnadatta Track, 195 km w of Maree. Lake Eyre South is accessed via the 94 km track north of Marree (along this track is Muloorina Station, which offers camping alongside the Frome River). Both access routes are 4WD only. Lake Eyre South also meets the Oodnadatta Track about 90 km w of Marree, where there are good views. A Desert Parks Pass is required for the park and is available from Marree Post Office or by contacting the Desert Parks Hotline on 1800 816 078. Scenic flights are perhaps the most rewarding option, from both Marree and William Creek.

Oodnadatta Track: a 600 km 4WD track from Marree to Marla. Highlights along the track include the Dog Fence (around 40 km w) and the railway-siding ruins at Curdimurka Siding and Bore (90 km w) from the original Great Northern Railway line to Alice Springs. A short distance beyond Curdimurka is Wabma Kadarbu Mound Springs Conservation Park, with a series of springs – fed by water from the Great Artesian Basin – supporting a small ecosystem of plants and animals. Between Marree and Marla, fuel is available only at William Creek (202 km NW) and Oodnadatta (405 km NW). *Birdsville Track:* famous 4WD track from Marree to Birdsville (in Queensland) of just over 500 km, once a major cattle run. Highlights on the track include the failed date palm plantation at Lake Harry Homestead (30 km N) and the meeting of the Tirari and Strzelecki deserts at Natterannie Sandhills (140 km N, after Cooper Creek crossing). Cooper Creek may have to be bypassed if flooded (with a 48 km detour to a ferry). Between Marree and Birdsville, fuel is available only at Mungerannie Roadhouse (204 km N).

Travellers note: Care must be taken when attempting the Birdsville and Oodnadatta tracks. These tracks are unsealed, with sandy patches. Heavy rain in the area can cut access for several days. Motorists are advised to ring the Northern Roads Condition Hotline on 1300 361 033 before departure.

See also FLINDERS RANGES & OUTBACK, p. 243

Melrose

Pop. 450
Map ref. 603 I3 | 604 H10

i Melrose Caravan and Tourist Park, Joes Rd; (08) 8666 2060; www.mountremarkable.com.au

105.1 Trax FM, 639 AM ABC North and West

Melrose, a quiet settlement at the foot of Mount Remarkable, is the oldest town in the Flinders Ranges. Indigenous groups who occupied the southern Flinders Ranges around Mount Remarkable and Melrose resisted European settlement in the 1840s, but after just a few decades the population was reduced to a handful. Pastoral properties were established on the mountainous slopes of the ranges, but Melrose truly took off when copper deposits were found nearby in 1846. Bushwalking through Mount Remarkable National Park is a highlight of any visit to this area. The arid north country meets the wet conditions of southern regions to provide a diverse landscape to explore.

 National Trust Museum: documents local history, with particular focus on early law enforcement. Original stone buildings include the courthouse and lock-up; open 2–5pm; Stuart St. *Bluey Blundstone Blacksmith Shop:* a restored shop with a cafe and B&B; closed Tues; Stuart St. *Serendipity Gallery:* Australiana arts and crafts; Stuart St. *War Memorial and Lookout Hill:* views over surrounding region. *4WD tours:* to local landmarks; contact visitor centre for operators. *Heritage walk:* self-guide walk includes ruins of Jacka's Brewery and Melrose Mine; brochure from visitor centre.

Melrose Show: Oct.

The North Star Hotel: rejuvenated landmark pub; Nott St; (08) 8666 2110. *The Old Bakery Stone Hut:* classic English-style pies; 1 Main North Rd, Stone Hut; (08) 8663 2165

Mount Remarkable Cottage: private, self-contained bush retreat; Diocesan Rd; (08) 8666 2173. *The North Star Hotel:* heritage pub with hip makeover; Nott St; (08) 8666 2110.

Mt Remarkable National Park Part of the southern Flinders Ranges and popular with bushwalkers. Marked trails through the park's gorges and ranges vary in scope from short scenic walks to long 3-day hikes. Highlights include pretty Alligator Gorge and the tough but worthwhile 5 hr return walk from Melrose to the summit of Mt Remarkable (960 m), with breathtaking views from the top. Access to the park by vehicle is via Mambray Creek or Wilmington. Foot access is from carparks and Melrose. (08) 8634 7068; 2 km w.

Cathedral Rock: an impressive rock formation on Mt Remarkable Creek; just west of Melrose. *Murray Town:* a farming town with nearby scenic lookouts at Box Hill, Magnus Hill and Baroota Nob. Remarkable View Wines offers tasting and sales on weekends. Starting point for a scenic drive west through Port Germein Gorge; 14 km s. *Booleroo Centre:* this service town to a rich farming community features the Booleroo Steam Traction Preservation Society's Museum. Annual Rally Day is held in Mar/Apr; open by appt; (08) 8667 2193; 15 km SE. *Wirrabara:* you could easily lose half a day in this town's bakery-cum-antiques shop, wandering through the rooms of relics and antiques just to work up an appetite for another homemade pastry; 25 km s.

See also FLINDERS RANGES & OUTBACK, p. 243

SOUTH AUSTRALIA

Meningie

Pop. 939
Map ref. 601 D5 | 603 L11

 The Chambers, 14 Princes Hwy; (08) 8575 1770; www.thelimestonecoast.com

98.7 Power FM, 1161 AM ABC South East

Today Meningie is an attractive lakeside town, but it was once a wilderness area, home to the Ngarrindjeri people, who had a self-sufficient lifestyle on the water. They made canoes to fish on the waterways and shelters to protect themselves from the weather. However, European settlement – after Captain Charles Sturt's journey down the Murray from 1829 to 1830 – soon wiped out much of the population, largely through violence and the introduction of smallpox. Stretching south from the mouth of the Murray and located just south of Meningie, the Coorong, with its lakes, birdlife, fishing and deserted ocean beaches, attracts visitors year-round.

The Cheese Factory Museum Restaurant: a restaurant and separate community museum with special interest in the changing population of Meningie and the Coorong; closed Mon; Fiebig Rd. *Coorong Cottage Industries:* local craft and produce; The Chambers, Princes Hwy.

Campbell Park Cottage: stylish, exclusive homestead accommodation; Campbell Park Rd; 0412 887 910. *Poltalloch Station:* heritage lakefront estate; Poltalloch Rd, Narrung; (08) 8574 0043.

Coorong National Park Listed as a 'wetland of international importance', this park's waterways, islands and vast saltpans demonstrate a diverse ecological environment invaluable for the refuge and habitat of migratory and drought-stricken birds. Throughout the park are reminders of the long history of habitation by the Ngarrindjeri people. There are ancient midden heaps and burial grounds, and the Ngarrindjeri people continue to have strong links with the Coorong. There are a number of ways to see the park: take a boat, canoe or cruise on the waterways; walk one of the varied tracks offered; drive your 4WD onto the Southern Ocean beach; or simply sit and soak up the park's atmosphere. Walking is the best way to access great coastal views, birdwatching spots and historic ruins. The most comprehensive walk in the park is the Nukan Kungun Hike. This 27 km hike starts at Salt Creek and includes smaller, side trails, including the informative walk to Chinaman's Well, the ruins of a temporary settlement that sprang up en route to the goldfields. The hike ends at the 42 Mile Crossing Sand Dune Walk, which leads to the wild Southern Ocean; (08) 8575 1200; 10 km s.

Scenic drive: follows Lake Albert to the west, adjacent to Lake Alexandrina, which is the largest permanent freshwater lake in the country (50 000 ha). Ferry crossing at Narrung. *Camp Coorong:* cultural centre offering bush-tucker tours and other traditional Aboriginal experiences; (08) 8575 1557; 10 km s. *Coorong Wilderness Lodge:* operated by the Ngarrindjeri people, this accommodation lodge offers Aboriginal heritage tours of the Coorong as well as traditional bush tucker and other cultural experiences; Hacks Point; (08) 8575 6001; 25 km s. *Poltalloch Station:* a historic pastoral property established in the 1830s as a sheep station. Guided tours take in a heritage-listed farm village and museum, historic farm machinery, and past and present farm life. Cottage accommodation available; Poltalloch Rd near Narrung; (08) 8574 0043; 30 km NW.

See also MURRAY, p. 241

Millicent

Pop. 4768
Map ref. 601 F11

 1 Mt Gambier Rd; (08) 8733 0904; www.wattlerange.sa.gov.au

107.7 5THE FM, 1161 AM ABC South East

Millicent, a prosperous, friendly and vibrant community located in the heart of the Limestone Coast region, is named after Millicent Glen, wife of one of the early pioneers and daughter of the first Anglican Bishop of Adelaide. In 1876 the barque *Geltwood* was wrecked off Canunda Beach, with debris, bodies and cargo littering the sands. Relics from the *Geltwood* can be found in the award-winning National Trust Living History Museum. The town's distinctive aroma can be attributed to the surrounding pine forests, which support a pulp mill, a paper mill and sawmill.

Visitor Centre and National Trust Living History Museum: centre provides extensive information on the region and surrounding areas. Souvenirs, arts and crafts, and local produce available. History museum includes a shipwreck room, farm machinery shed, Aboriginal and natural history rooms, a T-Class locomotive and the largest collection of restored horse-drawn vehicles in SA; Mt Gambier Rd; (08) 8733 0904. *Lake McIntyre:* boardwalks and bird hides to view the lake's prolific birdlife, native fish and yabbies; northern edge of town.

Nangula Market Days: 2nd Sun each month (excluding Jan). *Tall Timbers Wood Work Exhibition:* pine and red-gum craft; Mar–May. *Geltwood Craft Festival:* Mar/Apr. *Pines Enduro Off-Road Championships:* Sept. *Millicent Show:* Sept.

Canunda National Park The massive sand-dune system of the southern part of the park rises to cliffs and scrublands in the north. These 2 sections provide quite different experiences. In the north (accessed via Southend and Millicent) the walking trails pass along cliff-tops and through the scrubland. In the south (accessed via Carpenter Rocks and Millicent) the beaches and wetlands provide picturesque coastal walks. You can surf, 4WD, birdwatch, bushwalk and fish (excellent from the beaches and rocks). (08) 8735 1177; 10 km w.

Woakwine Range Wind Farms: dozens of giant turbines dominate the Woakwine Range skyline, comprising the largest wind farm development in the Southern Hemisphere. Take a drive along the Wind Farm Tourist Drive. Maps available at the Visitor Centre; 2 km s. *Mt Muirhead Lookout:* a large viewing platform provides views of Millicent, pine plantations and Mt Burr Range. It is also the start of the Volcanoes Discovery Trail (brochure from visitor centre); 6 km NE. *Mount Burr:* a historic timber town, the first to plant pines for commercial use on the Limestone Coast; 10 km NE. *Tantanoola:* home of the famous 'Tantanoola Tiger', a Syrian wolf shot in the 1890s, now stuffed and displayed in the Tantanoola Tiger Hotel; 20 km SE. *Tantanoola Caves Conservation Park:* daily tours of an imposing dolomite cavern in an ancient limestone cliff. Also walks and picnic areas; 21 km SE. *Glencoe Woolshed:* National Trust limestone woolshed once occupied by 38 shearers; 29 km SE.

See also LIMESTONE COAST, p. 242

Minlaton

Pop. 772
Map ref. 599 E6 | 602 H8

 Harvest Corner Visitor Information Centre, 29 Main St; (08) 8853 2600 or 1800 202 445; www.yorkepeninsula.com.au

98.9 Flow FM, 639 AM ABC North and West

MOUNT GAMBIER

Pop. 23 494
Map ref. 592 A5 | 601 G11

i Lady Nelson Visitor Information and Discovery Centre, Jubilee Hwy East; (08) 8724 9750 or 1800 087 187; www.mountgambiertourism.com.au

 96.1 Star FM, 1476 AM ABC South East

Mount Gambier is set on an extinct volcano – the area boasts a fascinating network of volcanic craters above sea level and one of limestone caves beneath. Lieutenant James Grant named the volcano in 1800 – he sighted it from HMS *Lady Nelson*, off the coast. The original settlement was known as Gambier Town. Today Mount Gambier is at the centre of the largest softwood pine plantation in the Commonwealth and is surrounded by farming, viticulture and dairy country.

Blue Lake The lakes formed in the craters of the extinct volcano have become an important recreational area for locals and visitors alike. The most spectacular is Blue Lake, so-called because the water's dull, blue-grey winter colour changes to a vibrant blue each Nov and stays that way until Mar the following year. Discover the area on the 3.6 km walking track around the shores. Aquifer Tours offers a trip in a lift down an old well shaft. The area also includes a wildlife park and an adventure playground; southern outskirts of town; (08) 8723 1199.

Old Courthouse: a National Trust dolomite building with a local history museum; open by appt; Bay Rd; (08) 8725 5284. *Lady Nelson Visitor Information and Discovery Centre:* full-scale replica of HMS *Lady Nelson*, interactive displays on the region's history and geography, and free local information packs; Jubilee Hwy East. *Riddoch Art Gallery:* changing exhibitions of local and touring art and sculpture; open Tues–Sun; Commercial St

East. *Cave Garden:* a cave used as a water supply for early settlers, now a rose garden with a suspended viewing platform; Bay Rd. *Umpherston Sinkhole:* a sunken garden on the floor of a collapsed cave; floodlit at night; Jubilee Hwy East. *Engelbrecht Cave:* guided tour of the limestone cave system under the city; contact visitor centre for details. *Centenary Tower:* views of the city, the lakes area and surrounding countryside; top of Mt Gambier, 190 m above sea level. *Heritage walk:* self-guide tour of historic buildings, many constructed of white Mt Gambier stone; brochure from visitor centre.

Mount Gambier Market: behind Harvey Norman; Sat. *World Series Sprintcars:* Jan. *Blue Lake City Muster:* Feb. *Mount Gambier Gold Cup Carnival:* May. *Mount Gambier Show:* Oct. *Christmas Parade:* Nov.

Sage & Muntries Restaurant: imaginative, regional dishes; 78 Commercial St West; (08) 8724 8400. *Sorrento's Cafe:* relaxed all-day eatery; 6 Bay Rd; (08) 8723 0900. *The Barn Steakhouse:* excellent steaks and grills; Punt Rd; (08) 8726 8250.

Clarendon Chalets: self-contained garden units; Clarke Rd; (08) 8726 8306. *Colhurst House:* graceful, historic mansion suites; 3 Colhurst Pl; (08) 8723 1309. *Eliza Cottage:* cosy, restored town residence; 30 Wehl St South; 0407 422 877.

Haig's Vineyards: wine-tastings and sales; 4 km SE. *Mt Schank:* excellent views of the surrounding district from the summit of an extinct volcano. Note that the 2 summit walks are very steep; 17 km S. *Nelson and Lower Glenelg National Park:* over the Victorian border; *see Portland (Vic).*

See also LIMESTONE COAST, p. 242

[BLUE LAKE]

 RADIO STATIONS   IN TOWN   WHAT'S ON   WHERE TO EAT   WHERE TO STAY   NEARBY

This small rural centre on Yorke Peninsula was originally called Gum Flat, because of the giant eucalypts in the area, but was later changed to Minlaton – from the Aboriginal word 'minlacowrie', thought to mean 'sweet water'. Aviator Captain Harry Butler, pilot of the *Red Devil*, a 1916 Bristol monoplane, was born here.

Butler Memorial: in a hangar-like building stands the *Red Devil*, a fighter plane – thought to be the only one of its type left in the world – that fought in France and, less romantically, flew mail between Adelaide and Minlaton; Main St. **Minlaton Museum:** National Trust museum in the historic general store features a local history display and Harry Butler memorabilia; open 9.30am–1pm Tues–Fri, 9.30am–12pm Sat; Main St. **Harvest Corner Yorke Peninsula Visitor Information Centre:** accredited visitor centre with tourist information, craft and local produce sales, a gallery featuring local artists and tearooms; Main St. **The Creamery:** crafts, ceramics and art exhibitions in a historic building; Maitland Rd. **Gum Flat Gallery:** art workshop and gallery; open 10am–2pm Wed; Main St. **Minlaton Fauna Park:** popular spot for picnics, with kangaroos, emus and up to 43 species of birds; Maitland Rd. **Minlaton Walking Trail:** a trail to the only naturally occurring stand of river red gums in the Yorke Peninsula. See a number of historic landmarks including an old horse dip and ancient Aboriginal wells, catch a local glimpse of the birdlife at the bird hide, and learn about the area through interpretive signs; contact visitor centre for details.

Minlaton Show: Oct.

Red Devil Cafe: smart pub dining; Minlaton Hotel, 26 Main St; (08) 8853 2014.

Ramsay Park: native flora and fauna park; between Minlaton and Port Vincent to the east. **Port Rickaby:** quiet swimming and fishing spot; 16 km NW.

See also YORKE PENINSULA, p. 240

Mintaro

Pop. 223
Map ref. 603 J6

i **Cnr Main North and Spring Gully rds; (08) 8842 2131 or 1800 242 131; www.clarevalley.com.au**

105.1 Trax FM, 639 AM ABC North and West

Although it is in the Clare Valley region, Mintaro's prosperity is not linked with the valley's booming wine industry. Instead, its buildings date back to the 1840s and '50s, when bullock drays carried copper from the Monster Mine at Burra to Port Wakefield in the south. Many of the buildings use local slate. In 1984 Mintaro became the first town in South Australia to be classified a State Heritage Area.

Timandra Garden: one of the town's fine garden displays; enter via Timandra Nursery, Kingston St. **Mintaro Garden Maze:** kids will love getting lost in the maze, comprising over 800 conifers; open 10am–4pm Thurs–Mon; Jacka St. **Reillys Wines:** wine-tastings, cellar-door sales and a restaurant; Burra Rd. **Mintaro Cellars:** wine-tastings and sales; Leasingham Rd. **Mintaro Slate Quarries:** fine-quality slate, produced since the quarry opened in 1854, is used world-wide for billiard tables; open 7.30am–3pm Mon–Fri; viewing platform in Kadlunga Rd. **Heritage walk:** self-guide trail includes 18 heritage-listed colonial buildings and 2 historic cemeteries; brochure available.

Reilly's Wines & Restaurant: satisfying country meals; Cnr Burra and Hill sts; (08) 8843 9013. **The Station Cafe:** weekend snacks and platters; Mount Horrocks Wines, Curling St, Auburn; (08) 8849 2202.

Reilly's Country Retreat: quaint vineyard cottages; Reilly's Wines; Cnr Burra and Hill sts; (08) 8843 9013. **William Hunt's Retreat:** stylish converted barn; Lot 32 Burra St; 0447 008 135. **Dennis Cottage:** well-appointed garden haven; St Vincent St, Auburn; (08) 8843 0048. **Martindale Hall:** magnificent heritage mansion; Manoora Rd, Martindale; (08) 8843 9088.

 Martindale Hall This 1879 mansion was built for Edmund Bowman who, the story goes, commissioned it for his bride-to-be from English high society. The lady declined his offer of marriage, and Bowman lived there on his own until 1891. Today visitors can explore the National Trust, Georgian-style home with its Italian Renaissance interior. A room in the mansion was used in the 1975 film *Picnic at Hanging Rock* as a girls' dormitory. Accommodation and dining are available. Open 11am–4pm Mon–Fri, 12–4pm weekends; Manoora Rd; (08) 8843 9088; 3 km SE.

Polish Hill River Valley: a subregion of the Clare Valley wine region, with cellar doors offering tastings and sales; between Mintaro and Sevenhill. **Waterloo:** features the historic Wellington Hotel, once a Cobb & Co staging post; 23 km SE.

See also MID-NORTH, p. 239

Moonta

Pop. 3353
Map ref. 599 E3 | 602 H6

i **Railway Station, Blanche Tce; (08) 8825 1891; www.yorkepeninsula.com.au**

89.3 Gulf FM, 639 AM ABC North and West

The towns of Moonta, Kadina and Wallaroo form the 'Copper Coast' or 'Little Cornwall', so called because of abundant copper finds and the significant Cornish population. Like so many other copper discoveries in South Australia, Moonta's was made by a local shepherd – in this case, Paddy Ryan in 1861. It was to prove a fortunate find: Moonta Mining Company paid over £1 million in dividends. Thousands of miners, including experienced labourers from Cornwall, flocked to the area. The mines were abandoned in the 1920s because of the slump in copper prices and rising labour costs. Moonta has survived as an agricultural service town with an increasing tourist trade.

All Saints Church of England: features a locally constructed copper bell; cnr Blanche and Milne tces. **Queen Square:** park for picnics, with the imposing town hall opposite; George St. **Heritage walks and drives:** self-guide trails to see heritage stone buildings and historic mine sites; brochure from visitor centre.

Kernewek Lowender: prize-winning Cornish festival held with Kadina and Wallaroo; odd-numbered years, May. **Moonta Garden Fair:** Oct. **Moonta Antiques and Collectible Fair:** Nov.

Moonta Mines State Heritage Area Take a historical walk or drive from Moonta to this significant heritage area. Interpretive walking trails guide the visitor to the major sites, including the Hughes Pump House, shafts, tailing heaps and ruins of mine offices. A 50 min historical railway tour runs from the museum (tours depart Wed 2pm, Sat and Sun 1–3pm on the hour, public/ school holidays daily 11–3pm on the hour). Also on the site is a historic 1880 pipe organ in the Moonta Mines Heritage Uniting Church; Cornish lifestyle history and memorabilia at the Moonta Mines Museum; and the National Trust furnished Miners Cottage and Heritage Garden. Open 1–4pm daily. Enjoy old-style sweets at the Moonta Mines Sweet Shop. Via Verran Tce; 2 km SE.

Wheal Hughes Copper Mine: underground tour of one of the modern mines; tours Wed, Sat and Sun; Wallaroo Rd;

(08) 8825 1891; 3 km N. **Moonta Bay:** a popular seaside town for fishing and swimming. See native animals at the Moonta Wildlife Park; 5 km W.

See also YORKE PENINSULA, p. 240

Morgan

Pop. 425
Map ref. 603 L6

 Shell Morgan Roadhouse, 14–18 Fourth St; (08) 8540 2354; www.riverland.info

93.1 Magic FM, 1062 AM ABC Riverland

This Murray River town was once a thriving port and a stop on the rail trade route to Adelaide. Settlers saw the potential of the region, and Morgan boomed as soon as it was declared a town in 1878. Now it is a quiet holiday destination, but evidence of its boom days can still be seen in the streetscapes and the historic wharf and rail precinct.

Port of Morgan Museum This comprehensive museum is dedicated to the rail- and river-trade history of Morgan. In the old railway buildings are museum exhibits focusing on the paddlesteamers and trains that were the lifeblood of the town. The Landseer Building has vintage vehicles and a 12 m mural depicting the old Murray River lifestyle. Other highlights are the restored wharf and permanently moored PS *Mayflower*. Open 2–4pm Wed, Sat and Sun; Riverfront; (08) 8540 2085.

Houseboats: for hire; contact visitor centre for details. **Heritage walk:** self-guide trail covers 41 historic sites, including the impressive wharves (1877) standing 12 m high, the customs house and courthouse, the sunken barge and steamer, and the rail precinct; brochure from visitor centre.

Mallyons on the Murray: home-grown and handmade delights; Morgan–Renmark Rd; (08) 8543 2263.

Bessie's of Morgan: charming, historic settler's cottage; 16 Seventh St; (08) 8541 9096.

Morgan Conservation Park: a diverse landscape of river flats, sand dunes and mallee scrub with abundant birdlife; across the Murray River from Morgan. **White Dam Conservation Park:** well known for red and western grey kangaroo populations; 9 km NW. **Cadell:** scenic 12 km drive east from Morgan via a ferry crossing (operates 24 hrs) to Cadell, a major citrus-growing region.

See also MURRAY, p. 241

Mount Gambier

see inset box on previous page

Murray Bridge

Pop. 14 048
Map ref. 597 H11 | 601 D3 | 603 L10

 3 South Tce; (08) 8539 1142 or 1800 442 784; www.murraybridge.sa.gov.au

98.7 Power FM, 1062 AM ABC Riverland

Murray Bridge, just as its name suggests, is all about bridges. The town was established in 1879 when a road bridge was built over the Murray River. The plan to make the river a major trade route from east to west and back had become a reality. In 1886 the construction of a railway line between Adelaide and Melbourne cemented the town's importance. Now watersports, river cruises and a relaxed river atmosphere make Murray Bridge South Australia's largest river town, a perfect holiday spot.

Captain's Cottage Museum: local history museum; open 10am–4pm weekends; Thomas St. **Dundee's Wildlife Park:** crocodiles, koalas and a bird sanctuary; Jervois Rd. **Murray Bridge Regional Gallery:** regular art exhibitions from local artists; closed Sat; Sixth St. **Heritage and Cultural Community Mural:** depicts significant aspects of Murray Bridge; Third St. **Sturt Reserve:** offers fishing, swimming, picnic and playground facilities, as well as the mythical Aboriginal creature, the Bunyip (coin-operated); Murray Cod Dr. **Long Island Marina:** houseboat hire and recreational facilities; Roper Rd. **Thiele Reserve:** popular for waterskiing; east of the river. **Avoca Dell:** a popular picnic spot with boating, waterskiing, minigolf and caravan facilities. **Swanport Wetlands:** recreational reserve with raised walkways and bird hides; adjacent to Swanport Bridge. **Charter and regular cruises:** on the Murray River; contact visitor centre. **Town and riverside walks:** brochure from visitor centre.

AutoFest: Australia Day weekend Jan. **International Pedal Prix:** novelty bikes and endurance event; Sept. **Murray Bridge Show:** Sept. **Waterski Race:** over 110 km; Nov. **Christmas Pageant and Fireworks:** Nov.

Balcony On Sixth Lodge: suites, basic to deluxe; 6 Sixth St; (08) 8531 1411. **Childsdale The Udder Place:** dairy converted to rural retreat; Long Flat Rd; (08) 8531 1153. **Oz Houseboats:** huge fleet, budget to luxury craft; Long Island Marina; (08) 8365 7776. **Rainforest Retreat:** self-contained house in garden oasis; 19A Torrens Rd; (08) 8532 6447.

Monarto Zoological Park This open-range 1000 ha zoo features Australian, African and Asian animals. It also runs a breeding program for rare and endangered species. Jump on a safari bus tour to see the animals up close. On the way you might encounter the huge giraffe herd or some cheetahs, zebras or rhinoceroses. Tours depart hourly 10.30am–3.30pm. There are also walking tracks through native bushland and mallee country. Princes Hwy; (08) 8534 4100; 10 km W.

Sunnyside Reserve Lookout: views across the wetlands and Murray River; 10 km E. **Willow Point Winery:** cellar-door tastings and sales of famous ports, sherries and muscats; closed Sun; Jervois Rd; 10 km S. **Ferries–McDonald and Monarto conservation parks:** walking trails through important mallee conservation areas, prolific birdlife, and blossom in spring; 16 km W. **Tailem Bend:** a historic railway town with views across the Murray River. A children's playground features an old steam locomotive, and over 90 historic buildings are displayed at the Old Tailem Town Pioneer Village; 25 km SE. **Wellington:** situated where Lake Alexandrina meets the Murray River. A museum is in the restored courthouse. Wellington and nearby Jervois have free 24 hr vehicle ferries; 32 km S. **Karoonda:** the heart of the Mallee, Karoonda is well known for the 1930 meteorite fall nearby (monument at RSL Park). Natural attractions include the limestone caves of Bakara Plains and walking trails in Pioneer Historical Park; 66 km E.

See also MURRAY, p. 241

Naracoorte

Pop. 4889
Map ref. 590 A10 | 601 G9

 MacDonnell St; (08) 8762 1399 or 1800 244 421; www.naracoortelucindale.sa.gov.au

89.7 5TCB FM, 1161 AM ABC South East

NURIOOTPA

Pop. 4415

Map ref. 597 F4 | 601 C1 | 603 K8

ⓘ Barossa Visitor Information Centre, 66–68 Murray St, Tanunda; (08) 8563 0600 or 1300 812 662; www.barossa-region.org

📻 89.1 BBB FM, 639 AM ABC North and West

The long history of winemaking in this Barossa town is apparent when travelling down the main street. Old vines that glow red in autumn drape the verandahs of equally old buildings. Surprisingly, the town actually began life as a pub. As a trade route was being established northwards to the Kapunda coppermines, William Coulthard foresaw the demand for rest and refreshment. He built the Old Red Gum Slab Hotel in 1854 and the town developed around it. The Para River runs through Nuriootpa, its course marked by parks and picnic spots.

🏡 **Coulthard Reserve:** popular recreation area; off Penrice Rd. **Barossa Trike Tours:** provides chauffeured Barossa tours aboard an Oztrike Chopper 4 with seating for 3 as you take in the beauty and splendour of Australia's most famous wine region; South Tce; 0438 623 342.

🎪 **Barossa Vintage Festival:** celebration of food and wine in various locations; odd-numbered years, Apr. **Barossa Gourmet Weekend:** Aug. **Barossa International Music Festival:** various venues; Oct.

🍴 **Maggie Beer's Farm Shop:** snacks and goodies; Pheasant Farm Rd; (08) 8562 4477. **The Branch:** versatile country cafe; 15 Murray St; (08) 8562 4561. **Appellation:** benchmark regional fine dining; The Louise, cnr Seppeltsfield and Stonewall rds, Marananga; (08) 8562 4144.

🛏 **The Lodge Country House:** elegant, heritage homestead; Seppeltsfield Winery, Seppeltsfield; (08) 8562 8277. **The Louise:** opulent resort-style vineyard suites; Cnr Seppeltsfield and Stonewell rds, Marananga; (08) 8562 2722. **Seppeltsfield Vineyard Cottage:** exquisite, secluded vineyard retreat; Gerald Roberts Rd, Seppeltsfield; (08) 8563 4059.

🍷 **Barossa Wine Region** The Barossa is Australia's eminent wine region, a landscape of historic villages panning out to vine-swept hills and grand buildings on old wine estates. Shiraz is the premier drop, with semillon the star of the whites. Some of the shiraz vines date back to the 1840s, and several winemaking families, many with German backgrounds, are into their sixth generation. Senior names include Yalumba (which is officially part of the Eden Valley), Penfolds and Seppelt. You can sample the iconic Penfolds Grange at Penfolds Barossa Valley, and visit the Winemakers' Laboratory to blend your own wine to take home in a personlised bottle. Seppelt is a must-visit winery with its elegant bluestone buildings and gardens. Its range of fortified wines includes Spanish styles and classic tawny wines – the jewel is Para Liqueur, a tawny released when it is 100 years old. Peter Lehmann and Wolf Blass are other well-known wineries in the area. Smaller gems include Charles Melton, known for its Nine Popes blend of shiraz, grenache and mourvedre and for the Rose of Virginia; the nearby Rockford, with fantastic wines seldom seen in other Australian states; Torbreck Vintners, offering excellent shiraz and shiraz viognier; and Langmeil. For some history on the Barossa and winemaking, the Jacob's Creek Visitor Centre has a gallery with displays next to its wine-tasting area, where you can sample some of this well-known label's varieties; *for more information on the region see Tanunda, Lyndoch and Angaston.*

Light Pass: a small, historic township with notable Lutheran churches and Luhrs Pioneer German Cottage, displaying German artefacts; 3 km E. **Maggie Beer's Farm Shop:** tastings and sales of gourmet farm produce from renowned chef and writer Maggie Beer, as well as Pheasant Farm and Beer Brothers wines. Enjoy a gourmet lunch (bookings essential, (08) 8562 4477); Pheasant Farm Rd; 5 km SW. **Wolf Blass Visitor Centre:** an opportunity to discover your own unique and memorable Wolf Blass experience, be it through learning about one of Australia's most storied winemakers or enjoying the tasting room; Sturt Hwy; (08) 8568 7311.

See also BAROSSA VALLEY, p. 238

[PENFOLDS WINERY, BAROSSA VALLEY]

Naracoorte dates from the 1840s, but its growth has been slow. In the 1850s it was a stopover for Victorian gold escorts and miners. Since then it has developed a rich agricultural industry. Today it is renowned for its natural attractions, including the parks and gardens but more significantly the Naracoorte Caves, protected within South Australia's only World Heritage area.

 The Sheep's Back: a comprehensive museum in the former flour mill (1870) details the history and community of the wool industry, with a craft and souvenir shop and information centre; MacDonnell St. **Naracoorte Art Gallery:** local and touring exhibitions; open Tues–Fri; Ormerod St. **Mini Jumbuk Centre:** display gallery and sales of woollen products; Smith St. **Pioneer Park:** restored locomotive on display; MacDonnell St. **Walking trail:** starts at the town centre and winds 5 km along the Naracoorte Creek.

 Taste the Limestone Coast: wine and gourmet food festival; Feb. **Naracoorte Horse Trials:** May. **Swap Meet:** May. **Limestone Coast Children's Expo:** Oct. **Naracoorte Show:** Oct. **Christmas Pageant:** Dec.

Sherwood Cottages Country Retreat: endearing, luxury stone cottage; McMillan Rd; (08) 8762 1652. **Willowbrook Cottages:** restful home and garden; 5 Jenkins Tce; (08) 8762 0259.

Naracoorte Caves National Park For thousands of years the 26 Naracoorte Caves – today protected by national park and World Heritage listing – have acted as a natural trap for animals, providing an environment that was just right for fossilisation. Twenty fossil deposits have been found – an incredible record of Australia's evolution over the last 500 000 years. Guided walking tours take in the chambers, extensive stalagmite and stalactite deposits and fossil collections. The Victoria Fossil Cave Tour is an introduction to the ancient animal history of Australia, while the natural delights of the caves, including helictites and fabulous domed ceilings, are accessed on the 30 min Alexandra Cave Tour. The world of bats is celebrated on the Bat Tour, the highlight being unhindered views of the bats' activity from infra-red cameras. Adventure caving allows visitors to see the caves in their raw state, while also providing an opportunity for exciting squeezes and crawls through some very tight spaces. For caving beginners, try the Blackberry and Stick-Tomato tours. For the more experienced cavers, enjoy the crawls and sights on the Starburst Chamber Tour. The Fox Cave Tour is the ultimate caving experience, with access to the cave system by a small entrance, leading to great fossil collections, vast speleothem development and incredible scenery. You can get details on these tours from Wonambi Fossil Centre, located within the park; (08) 8762 2340; 12 km SE.

Wrattonbully Wine Region: a recently established wine region focusing mainly on red wine varieties; 15 km SE. **Bool Lagoon Game Reserve:** wetland area of international significance, a haven for ibis and over 100 waterbird species. It includes boardwalks and a bird hide; 17 km S. **Frances:** a historic railway town that each Mar holds the Frances Folk Gathering; 38 km NE. **Lucindale:** a small country town featuring a Historical Society Museum and Jubilee Park with a lake, island and bird haven. It holds mammoth South East Field Days each Mar; 41 km W. **Padthaway:** prominent wine region; 47 km NW; see Bordertown.

See also LIMESTONE COAST, p. 242

Oodnadatta

Pop. 277
Map ref. 606 B6

 Pink Roadhouse, Ikaturka Tce; (08) 8670 7822 or 1800 802 074.

95.3 FM ABC North and West

Oodnadatta is a gutsy outback town on the legendary Oodnadatta Track. It was once a major railway town, but the line's closure in 1981 left it largely deserted. Local Aboriginal people have successfully kept the town operating since then. Today many travellers use it to refuel and gather supplies before heading out to the major desert parks to the north. It is believed that the name Oodnadatta originated from an Aboriginal term meaning 'yellow blossom of the mulga'.

 Pink Roadhouse: a town icon, and also the place to go for information on local road conditions and outback travel advice; Ikaturka Tce. **Railway Station Museum:** well-preserved sandstone station (1890), now a local museum; key available from roadhouse.

 Races and gymkhana: May. **Bronco Branding:** July.

Witjira National Park This arid park is famous for the Dalhousie Springs. These thermal springs emerge from the Great Artesian Basin deep below the surface and are said to be therapeutic (visitors can swim in the main spring). They are also a habitat for many fish species that can adapt to the changing water conditions. A Desert Parks Pass is required; they are available from Mt Dare Homestead (which has fuel and supplies), the Pink Roadhouse or Parks SA (1800 816 078); 180 km N.

Oodnadatta Track: runs from Marree (404 km SE) through Oodnadatta and joins the Stuart Hwy at Marla (212 km NW); see Marree. **Neales River:** swim in permanent waterholes. **The Painted Desert:** superb desert scenery of richly coloured hills; 100 km SW. **Simpson Desert Conservation Park and Regional Reserve:** 4WD tracks across enormous dune desert east of Witjira. Travellers must be totally self-sufficient; details from visitor centre.

See also FLINDERS RANGES & OUTBACK, p. 243

Penola

Pop. 1315
Map ref. 592 A2 | 601 G10

 The John Riddoch Centre, 27 Arthur St; (08) 8737 2855; www.wattlerange.sa.gov.au

107.7 5THE FM, 1161 AM ABC South East

Penola is one of the oldest towns in south-east South Australia, and has some excellent wineries nearby. The town is noted for its association with Mary MacKillop, a Josephite nun who in 1866 established Australia's first school to cater for children regardless of their family's income or social class. In 2010 she was canonised by the Vatican, making her the first Australian to be declared a saint. Penola is also noted for its literary roots – several Australian poets have been inspired by the landscape and lifestyle.

 Mary MacKillop Interpretive Centre and Woods MacKillop Schoolhouse: details the lives of Mary MacKillop and Father Julian Tenison (who shared Mary's dream) through photos, memorabilia and displays in this 1860s-style schoolhouse; Portland St. **Petticoat Lane:** heritage area of original cottages, including Sharam Cottage, the first built in

SOUTH AUSTRALIA

town; many are now retail outlets. *The John Riddoch Centre:* incorporates the Local History Exhibition and Hydrocarbon Centre, featuring hands-on and static displays on natural gas; Arthur St. *Toffee and Treats:* old-fashioned sweet sales; Church St. *Heritage walk:* details from visitor centre.

Vigneron Cup: Jan. *Petanque Festival:* Feb. *Penola Coonawarra Arts Festival:* arts, food and wine; May. *Cellar Dwellers:* July. *Cabernet Celebrations:* Oct. *Penola Show:* Oct/Nov.

Pipers of Penola: exquisite contemporary cuisine; 58 Riddoch St; (08) 8737 3999.

Merlot and Verdelho: adjoining luxury townhouses; 14 Arthur St; (08) 8737 3035 or 0413 512 559. *must @ Coonawarra:* cutting-edge designer apartments; 126 Church St; (08) 8737 3444. *Sarah's Cottage:* intimate, refurbished cottage; 24 Julian St; (03) 5571 9030.

Yallam Park: a magnificent 2-storey Victorian home with original decorations; by appt (08) 8737 2435; 8 km w. *Penola Conservation Park:* signposted woodland and wetland walk; 10 km w. *Coonawarra Wine Region:* more than 20 wineries, most open for tastings and cellar-door sales; north to Coonawarra. *Nangwarry Forestry & Logging Museum:* features a fascinating array of mill machinery, firefighting equipment, photographs and other artefacts from a bygone era; 18 km s. *Glencoe Woolshed:* built in 1863, this shed is unique as it was never converted to mechanised shearing. Now a museum with relics of the period; via Nangwarry; 50km s.

See also LIMESTONE COAST, p. 242

Peterborough

Pop. 1689
Map ref. 603 K3 | 605 I11

i Main St; (08) 8651 2708; www.peterborough.au.com

105.1 Trax FM, 639 AM ABC North and West

Peterborough is a town obsessed with the railway. Its very existence and growth can be claimed by that industry. In 1881 the line to Jamestown was opened and over the next few years the town became a key intersection between all the major South Australian towns. Locals boast about how, in a mammoth one-day effort, 105 trains travelled the Broken Hill to Port Pirie line. The rail passion continued even after many of the lines closed, and today each town entrance has a welcoming model steam train.

Steamtown With a 100-year-old rail history this dynamic museum, located around the old locomotive workshops, is a collection of historic rolling stock, including a converted Morris car that rides the tracks. Also on display is Australia's only 3-gauge roundhouse and turntable. Main St; (08) 8651 3355.

Town hall: a beautiful, ornate 1927 building with its original theatre and a Federation wall hanging in the foyer; Main St. *The Gold Battery:* ore-crushing machine; contact visitor centre; end Tripney Ave. *Meldonfield:* view a world of miniature horse-drawn carriages modelled on the style used in the 1800s; Lloyd St. *Dragons Rest Habitat Garden:* reptiles and exotic plant life; Watkins Rd. *Victoria Park:* features a lake and islands with deer and kangaroo enclosure and a playground; Queen St. *Bus tour:* guided tour of sights and history of town; contact visitor centre. *Town walk and drive:* self-guide tour; brochure from visitor centre.

Rodeo: Feb.

Terowie: an old railway town with well-preserved 19th-century main street. Self-guide drive or walk tour; brochure *A Tour of Terowie* available from tearooms; 24 km SE. *Magnetic Hill:* park the car, turn off the engine and watch it roll uphill; 32 km NW via Black Rock.

See also MID-NORTH, p. 239

Pinnaroo

Pop. 587
Map ref. 558 B9 | 588 B11 | 590 B1 | 601 H4 | 603 O10

i Mallee Tourist and Heritage Centre, Railway Tce Sth; (08) 8577 8644.

107.5 3MBR FM, 1062 AM ABC Riverland

In the 19th century the harshness of the land prevented settlers from properly establishing a farming community here. Instead, they chose the more fertile conditions south-west. The arrival of rail in 1906 and the influx of farming families allowed the community to grow. Although conditions remained tough, the now-renowned Mallee spirit of the farmers allowed the region's agricultural industry to strengthen to what it is today.

Mallee Tourist and Heritage Centre Established in 1999, the centre dwarfs its former home in the old railway station which is now a Pioneer Women's Museum. The new building comprises the D. A. Wurfel Grain Collection, featuring the largest cereal collection in Australia (1300 varieties); working letter presses in the Printing Museum; dioramas, interpretive displays and photos depicting local history in the Heritage Museum; and a collection of restored farm machinery in the Gum Family Collection. Open 10am–1pm or by appt; Railway Tce Sth; (08) 8577 8644.

Animal Park and Aviary: South Tce.

Pinnaroo Show: Oct.

Karte Conservation Park: includes a walking trail through low scrub and 40 m high sand dunes; 30 km NW. *Billiatt Conservation Park:* the 1 km walk through mallee scrub and dune country ends with panoramic views from Trig Point; 37 km NW. *Lameroo:* Mallee town with historic 1898 Byrne pug-and-pine homestead (Yappara Rd) and railway station (Railway Tce); 40 km w. *Ngarkat group of conservation parks:* south-west of town; *see Keith. Peebinga Conservation Park:* important reserve for the rare western whipbird; Loxton Rd; 42 km N.

See also MURRAY, p. 241

Port Augusta

Pop. 13 255
Map ref. 602 H2 | 604 G9

i Wadlata Outback Centre, 41 Flinders Tce; (08) 8641 9193 or 1800 633 060; www.wadlata.sa.gov.au

105.9 Magic FM, 639 AM ABC North and West

Port Augusta is the most northerly port in South Australia. The difficulty of land transportation in the 1800s prompted the town's establishment in 1854. It was a major wool and wheat shipping depot until its closure in 1973 – luckily the power stations built by the State Electricity Trust were already generating the city's chief income. Fuelled by coal from the huge open-cut mines at Leigh Creek, the stations generate more than a third of the state's electricity. Port Augusta is also a supply centre for outback areas, an important link on the *Indian–Pacific* railway and a stopover for the Adelaide to Darwin *Ghan* train.

Wadlata Outback Centre This award-winning complex (recently upgraded) covers the natural history of the outback and Flinders Ranges, as well as the people that have called it home throughout the ages. There are hands-on interpretive displays, audiovisual presentations and artefacts. Discover the landscape of 15 million years ago in the Tunnel of Time, and hear ancient Dreamtime stories. The centre is a place in which to learn – Wadlata is an Aboriginal word for communicating. 41 Flinders Tce.

Homestead Park Pioneer Museum: picnic areas, re-creation of a blacksmith's shop, miniature steam and diesel train rides (1st and 3rd Sun each month), and the restored 130-year-old pine-log Yudnappinna homestead; Elsie St; (08) 8642 2035. **Fountain Gallery:** local and touring art and cultural exhibitions; open Mon–Fri; Flinders Tce. **Gladstone Square:** landscaped square surrounded by historic sites, including the courthouse, barracks and Presbyterian church; cnr Jervois and Marryatt sts. **Australian Arid Lands Botanic Garden:** walks through 200 ha of arid-zone vegetation. Guided tours 10am weekdays; northern outskirts, on the Stuart Hwy; (08) 8641 1049. **McLellan Lookout:** site of Matthew Flinders' landing in 1802; Whiting Pde. **Water Tower Lookout:** spectacular views from the balcony of the 1882 tower; Mitchell Tce. **Matthew Flinders Lookout:** excellent view of Spencer Gulf and the Flinders Ranges; end of McSporran Cres. **Boat cruises and adventure tours:** contact visitor centre. **Heritage walk:** self-guide town walk includes courthouse and the magnificent stained glass in St Augustine's Church; brochure from visitor centre. **Curdnatta Art and Pottery Gallery:** high-quality painting, pottery and fabric art; Flinders Tce.

Cup Carnival: horseracing; June. **Outback Surfboat Carnival:** Nov.

Majestic Oasis Apartments: smart serviced units; Marryatt St; (08) 8648 9000 or 1800 008 648.

Spencer Gulf: watersports, yachting and fishing for King George whiting in northern waters. **Scenic drive:** north-east to the splendid Pichi Richi Pass, historic Quorn and Warren Gorge. See the same sights by train on Pichi Richi Railway, a 33 km round trip operating from Quorn; *see Quorn.*

See also FLINDERS RANGES & OUTBACK, p. 243

Port Broughton

Pop. 910
Map ref. 599 F1 | 603 I5 | 604 G12

 Bay St; (08) 8635 2261; www.yorke peninsula.com.au

87.6 Easy FM, 639 AM ABC North and West

This Yorke Peninsula holiday town has a quiet coastal feel in winter and bustles with sun-seeking holiday-makers in summer. Set on a quiet inlet on Spencer Gulf, it has a long fishing history. In the 1900s the fishing fleets and ketches operated from the jetty. Today the town is still a major port for fishing boats and each week truckloads of blue swimmer crabs depart for city restaurants.

Heritage Centre: local history museum in the old school; Edmund St. **Sailboat hire and fishing charters:** from foreshore. **Town jetty:** popular fishing spot. **Historical walking trail:** grab a *Walk Around Port Broughton* booklet from the visitor centre and navigate the historical sights of the town, including the Heritage Plaques on the foreshore.

Winter Fun Fishing Competition: June. **Rubber Duck Race:** Oct.

Fisherman Bay: fishing, boating and holiday spot with over 400 holiday shacks; 5 km N along the coast.

See also YORKE PENINSULA, p. 240

Port Elliot

Pop. 1750
Map ref. 598 F8 | 599 H10 | 601 B5 | 603 J11

Goolwa Wharf; (08) 8555 3488; www.visitalexandrina.com

89.3 5EFM, 639 AM ABC North and West

Port Elliot is a charming historic town set on scenic Horseshoe Bay. Its popularity as a holiday destination lies in the fabulous beaches and the relaxed coastal atmosphere. The town was established in 1854, the year Australia's first public (horse-drawn) railway began operating between Goolwa and the town. Port Elliot's intended purpose as an ocean port for the Murray River was, however, unsuccessful. The bay proved less protected than was first thought and the port was moved to Victor Harbor.

National Trust Historical Display: interpretive centre detailing local history in the old railway station; The Strand. **The Strand:** historic street of art and craft shops, cafes and restaurants. **Cockle Train:** stops at the railway station on Henry St on its journey from Goolwa Wharf to Victor Harbor, so you can do a section of the journey from here; *for more details see Goolwa.* **Freeman Nob:** spectacular views and coastal walks; end of The Strand. **Encounter Bikeway:** scenic coastal route between Goolwa and Victor Harbor. **Horseshoe Bay:** safe family beach with fishing from jetty. **Boomer Beach:** popular surfing beach; western edge of town. **Maritime Heritage Trail:** the town's story illustrated in foreshore displays. **Heritage walk:** brochure from railway station.

Market: Lakala Reserve; 1st and 3rd Sat each month. **Port Elliot Show:** Oct.

Flying Fish Cafe: popular seafood destination; 1 The Foreshore, Horseshoe Bay; (08) 8554 3504. **Stranded Mexican:** versatile Mexican fare; 12 The Strand; (08) 8554 2022.

Brooklands Heritage B&B: snug, restored settler's cottage, Heysen Rd; (08) 8554 3808. **The Summer House:** contemporary luxury home; 7 Charlotte St; (08) 8363 4510. **Trafalgar House:** majestic 19th-century guesthouse; 25 The Strand; (08) 8554 3888.

Basham Beach Regional Park: scenic coastal trails with interpretive signage and southern right whale sightings during their migration season, June–Sept; just north-east of Port Elliot. **Middleton:** coastal town with heritage bakery, the old flour mill and fabulous beaches; 3 km NE. **Crows Nest Lookout:** excellent views of the coast; 6 km N.

See also FLEURIEU PENINSULA, p. 235

Port Lincoln

Pop. 13 046
Map ref. 602 D8

3 Adelaide Pl; (08) 8683 3544 or 1300 788 378; www.visitportlincoln.net

89.9 Magic FM, 1485 AM ABC Eyre Peninsula and West Coast

Each January this township on the Eyre Peninsula celebrates the life of the tuna – one of the few festivals in Australia devoted to a fish and a fair indication of the reign tuna has over this town. Lincoln Cove, the marina, is the base for Australia's largest tuna fleet and tuna-farming industry. Port Lincoln is set on attractive Boston Bay, which is three times the size of Sydney Harbour. The townsite was reached by Matthew Flinders in his expedition of 1802 and he named it in honour of his home, Lincolnshire, in

England. Sheltered waters, a Mediterranean climate and scenic coastal roads make this a popular holiday spot.

Mill Cottage: National Trust museum with early pioneering artefacts and paintings; open 10am–2pm Wed, 2–4pm Sun or by appt; Flinders Hwy. *Railway Museum:* relics of the railway past displayed in a historic 1926 stone building; open 1–4pm Wed, Sat and Sun; Railway Pl. *Axel Stenross Maritime Museum:* features original boatbuilding tools and working slipway; open 9.30–11.30am and 1–4.30pm Tues, Thurs and Sun, 1–4.30pm Sat or by appt; Lincoln Hwy. *Settler's Cottage:* stone cottage with early pioneer photos and documents; open 2–4.30pm Sun (closed July and Aug) or by appt; in Flinders Park, Flinders Hwy. *Kotz Stationary Engines:* museum collection of oil and petrol engines; Baltimore St. *Nautilus Theatre:* features 2 galleries of local and touring art, a gallery shop and a wine bar; Tasman Tce. *Kuju Arts and Crafts:* Aboriginal craft sales; closed Sat and Sun; Ravendale Rd. *Mayne Gallery:* local arts and crafts; open 12.30–4.30pm daily; King St. *Lincoln Cove:* includes marina, leisure centre with water slide, holiday charter boats and the base for the commercial fishing fleet (tastings of local catches available). Guided walking tours of the marina are available from the visitor centre; off Ravendale Rd. *Boston Bay:* swimming, waterskiing, yachting and excellent fishing. *Yacht and boat charters:* for gamefishing, diving, day fishing and for viewing sea lions, dolphins and birdlife around Sir Joseph Banks Group Conservation Park and Dangerous Reef; contact visitor centre for details. *Aquaculture Cruise:* offers you a chance to view the working tuna farms (when in season) and to taste some mouth-watering local sashimi; a sea lion colony can also be visted; contact visitor centre for details. *Boston Island boat tours:* cruises around bay and island; contact visitor centre for details. *Adventure tours and safaris:* offshore and land adventure offered, including close-up tuna tours, shark expeditions and 4WD safaris; contact visitor centre for details. *Old Mill Lookout:* panoramic views of town and bay; Dorset Pl. *Parnkalla Walking Trail:* 14 km trail with coastal views and abundant wildlife. It forms part of the longer Investigator Walking Trail from North Shields to Lincoln National Park; brochure from visitor centre.

Tunarama Festival: Jan. *Adelaide to Lincoln Yacht Race and Lincoln Week Regatta:* Feb/Mar. *Port Lincoln Show:* Aug.

Del Giorno's Cafe Restaurant: wonderful Italian-inspired seafood; 80 Tasman Tce; (08) 8683 0577. *The Marina Bistro:* seafood and grills; The Marina Hotel, 13 Jubilee Dr; (08) 8682 6141.

Bay 10 Holiday House: neatly renovated foreshore villa; 24 Lincoln Hwy; (08) 8682 1010. *Belle Vista:* smartly restored stone bungalow; 12 Normandy Pl; (08) 8683 0180. *The Anchorage Holiday Apartment:* spacious marina accommodation; 6/33 South Point Dr; (08) 8683 0992. *Donington Cottage:* rustic and remote lighthouse keeper's residence; Donington Rd, Lincoln National Park; (08) 8683 3544 or 1300 788 378.

Lincoln National Park This spectacular coastal park has a network of walking trails through rugged wilderness areas to fantastic coastal scenery. The park is an important sanctuary for migrating birds. To see the park from a height, take the 1.1 km return hike up Stamford Hill. At the top is the Flinders Monument and panoramic views of the coast. For a true, uninterrupted wilderness experience, grab a key and permit from the visitor centre and head on to Memory Cove, a calm bay with a fantastic beach. There is also a replica of the plaque placed by Matthew Flinders in 1802 in memory of 8 crew members lost in

seas nearby. 4WD enthusiasts would enjoy the challenges of the Sleaford Bay coast. (08) 8688 3111; 20 km s.

Delacolline Estate Wines: well known for blended variety of sauvignon blanc/semillon; tastings and sales; open 1.30–4pm weekends; Whillas Rd; 1 km w. *Winters Hill Lookout:* views to Boston Bay, Boston Island and Port Lincoln; Flinders Hwy; 5 km NW. *Boston Bay Winery:* tastings and sales; closed Tues and Wed; Lincoln Hwy; 6 km N. *Roseview Emu Park and Rose Gardens:* picturesque gardens in bush setting, with sales of emu produce; Little Swamp La; 10 km NW. *Glen-Forest Tourist Park:* native animals, bird-feeding and miniature golf course; Greenpatch; 15 km NW. *Poonindie Church:* quaint old church built in 1850 with the unique feature of 2 chimneys; 20 km N. *Mikkira Station and Koala Park:* historic 1842 homestead, with bushwalks to see native wildlife. Permit required, available from Port Lincoln Visitor centre; off Fishery Bay Rd; 26 km sw. *Constantia Designer Craftsmen:* guided tours of world-class furniture factory and showroom; open Mon–Fri; on road to Whalers Way. *Whalers Way:* cliff-top drive through privately owned sanctuary inhabited by seals, ospreys, kangaroos and emus. Permit from visitor centre; 32 km s.

See also EYRE PENINSULA & NULLARBOR, p. 244

Port MacDonnell

Pop. 624
Map ref. 592 A6 | 601 G12

7 Charles St; (08) 8738 2576; www.thelimestonecoast.com.au

96.1 Star FM, 1476 AM ABC South East

Port MacDonnell is a quiet fishing town that was once a thriving port. The establishment of the breakwater in 1975 has ensured the southern rock lobster trade many more years of fruitful operation. The fleet is now the largest in Australia. While fishing is the main focus of the area, the rich maritime history, fascinating crystal pools and coastal scenery attract visitors year-round.

 Port MacDonnell and District Maritime Museum The long maritime history of this stretch of coast is littered with stories of shipwrecks and bravery. Here photos and salvaged artefacts bring the old days to life. A particularly tragic story is the crash of the *Admella* on an off-coast reef in 1859. Only 24 of the 113 people aboard survived. The ship's bell and cannon are on display in the museum. There is also a focus on community history and on the rock lobster industry. Open 12.30–4.30pm Wed, Fri and Sun; Meylin St; (08) 8738 7259.

Clarke's Park: popular picnic spot with natural spring; northern outskirts. *Fishing:* anglers will enjoy fishing from the jetty and landing. Boat charters available for deep-sea catches of tuna; details from visitor centre. *Heritage walk:* includes historic cemetery with hidden headstones; contact visitor centre.

Bayside Festival: Jan.

Ewens Ponds and Piccaninnie Ponds conservation parks For a unique snorkelling or diving experience, visit the crystal-clear waters of these parks. At Ewens Ponds (7 km E) there are 3 ponds, connected via channels. Snorkel on the surface to see the amazing plant life underwater, or go diving for the ultimate experience. The deep caverns in Piccaninnie Ponds (20 km E) offer visitors an insight into the underwater world. Snorkellers can gaze into the depths of the Chasm, while divers can explore the limestone-filtered waters of the Cathedral, so named because of its regal white walls. While no experience is necessary for snorkelling, divers require qualifications. Inquiries and bookings to SA Parks and Wildlife; (08) 8735 1177.

Cape Northumberland Heritage and Nature Park: a coastal park famous for sunrises and sunsets. Other highlights include a historic lighthouse, a penguin colony and unusual rock formations; just west of town. ***Dingley Dell Conservation Park:*** the historic 1862 restored cottage that is located here was once the home of Australian poet Adam Lindsay Gordon and features displays on his life and work; tours 10am–4pm daily; 2 km w. ***Germein Reserve:*** 8 km boardwalk (loop track) through wetlands; opposite Dingley Dell. ***Southern Ocean Shipwreck Trail:*** over 89 vessels came to grief on the section of coast from the Victorian border to the Murray River mouth. The drive trail includes 10 interpretive sites; brochure from visitor centre.

See also Limestone Coast, p. 242

Port Pirie
Pop. 13 204
Map ref. 603 I4 | 604 H11

 Regional Tourism and Arts Centre, 3 Mary Elie St; (08) 8633 8700 or 1800 000 424; www.pirie.sa.gov.au

105.1 Trax FM, 639 ABC North and West

Industry in its splendour greets the visitor at this major industrial and commercial centre. The oil tanks, grain silos and 250-metre-high smokestack all tower over the city, while on the waterfront huge local and overseas vessels are loaded and discharged. Broken Hill Proprietary Company (BHP) began mining lead in 1889 and various South Australian ports at that time vied for BHP's smelting business. Port Pirie eventually won, and created what is today the largest lead-zinc smelter in the world. Wheat and barley from the mid-north are also exported from here. Port Pirie shows great character in its old buildings and attractive main street, and Spencer Gulf and the Port Pirie River offer swimming, waterskiing, fishing and yachting.

Regional Tourism and Arts Centre This award-winning centre comprises an eclectic mix of exhibitions, art and information. A lifelike fibreglass model of the largest white pointer shark taken from SA's waters is on display. Local and regional history is presented through a series of art pieces and on the miniature railway, Pirie Rail Express, which replicates the journey from Port Pirie to Broken Hill (runs 1st and 3rd Sun each month). There are local and touring art exhibitions in the art gallery and the centre runs tours to the Pasminco smelter. Mary Elie St; (08) 8633 8700.

National Trust Museum: located in historic town buildings, including the old customs house (1882) and the Victorian pavilion-style railway station, the museum houses a local history display and rooms furnished in early-1900s style; Ellen St. ***Memorial Park:*** features the John Pirie anchor, memorials, and the Northern Festival Centre; Memorial Dr. ***Fishing:*** good local spots include the main wharf. ***Self-guide walks:*** including National Trust Walking Tours and The Journey Landscape, a 1.6 km nature trail representing changes in vegetation from Broken Hill to Port Pirie; brochures from visitor centre.

State Masters Games: even-numbered years, Apr. ***Blessing of the Fleet:*** celebrates the role of Italians in establishing the local fishing industry; Sept. ***Festival of Country Music:*** Oct.

Sampsons Cottage: landmark shop, now self-contained B&B; 66 Ellen St; (08) 8632 3096.

Weeroona Island: good fishing and holiday area accessible by car; 13 km n. ***Port Germein:*** a quiet beachside town with a tidal beach safe for swimming. At 1.7 km, the town's jetty is one of the longest in Australia; 23 km n. ***Telowie Gorge Conservation Park:*** follow the marked Nukunu Trail from the park's entrance to the breathtaking Telowie Gorge on the south-west edge of the Flinders Ranges. Care should be taken on less-formal tracks in the park; 24 km ne.

See also Yorke Peninsula, p. 240

Port Victoria
Pop. 344
Map ref. 599 D5 | 602 H8

 Port Victoria Kiosk, Esplanade; or The Farm Shed Museum and Tourist Centre, 50 Moonta Rd, Kadina; (08) 8821 2333 or 1800 654 991; www.yorkepeninsula.com.au

89.3 Gulf FM, 639 AM ABC North and West

A tiny township on the west coast of Yorke Peninsula, Port Victoria was tipped to be a thriving port town after James Hughes travelled up the coast in 1840. Hughes, a land surveyor, studied the coastline from his schooner, *Victoria*, and reported favourably on the region. It became an important port for grain exports, with windjammers transporting wheat from here to Europe. The town still proudly proclaims that it is the 'last of the windjammer ports'.

Maritime Museum: displays, relics and artefacts of the great era of the windjammer; open 2–4pm weekends and public holidays; Main St. ***Jetty:*** original 1888 jetty with good swimming and fishing; end of Main St. ***Geology trail:*** 4 km interpretive track along the foreshore explains the coast's ancient volcanic history; brochure from visitor centre.

Goose Island Conservation Park: important breeding area for several bird species and the Australian sea lion; 13 km offshore; access by private boat. ***Wardang Island:*** this large island is an Aboriginal reserve, and permission for access is required from Goreta (Point Pearce) Aboriginal Community Council; (08) 8836 7205; near Goose Island. ***Wardang Island Maritime Heritage Trail:*** this scuba-diving and overland trail includes 8 shipwreck sites with underwater plaques around Wardang Island and 6 interpretive signs at Port Victoria; waterproof self-guide leaflet available from visitor centre.

See also Yorke Peninsula, p. 240

Quorn
Pop. 1073
Map ref. 603 I1 | 604 H9

 3 Seventh St; (08) 8648 6419; www.flindersranges.com

89.1 5UMA FM, 1242 5CS AM

Nestled in a valley in the Flinders Ranges, Quorn was established as a town on the Great Northern Railway line in 1878. The line was built by Chinese and British workers and operated for over 45 years (it closed in 1957). Part of the line through Pichi Richi Pass has been restored as a tourist railway, taking passengers on a scenic 33-kilometre round trip via Port Augusta. The town's old charm has not been lost on movie producers – the historic streetscapes and surrounding landscapes have been used in many films.

Railway Workshop Tours: guided tours of the workshop where locomotives travelling on the Pichi Richi line are maintained and restored. Tours by appt; book at visitor centre. ***Junction Art Gallery:*** local art exhibition; Railway Tce. ***Outback Colours Art Gallery:*** Seventh St. ***Town walks:*** the Walking Tour of Quorn and the Quorn Historic Buildings walk; brochures from visitor centre.

Flinders Ranges Bush Festival: Apr. **Taste of the Outback:** Apr. **Race Meeting:** June. **Pichi Richi Marathon:** July. **Quorn Show:** Sept. **Spring Craft Fair:** Oct. **Christmas Pageant and Party:** Dec.

Quandong Cafe: heritage cafe; 31 First St; (08) 8648 6155.

Endilloe Lodge: luxurious, contemporary stone cottage; 319 Schmidt Rd; (08) 8648 6536. **Wilderness Cabin:** remote bush retreat; Horseshoe Range via Quorn; (08) 8648 6438.

Pichi Richi Railway: historical tourist train travels through dramatic countryside from Quorn to Port Augusta and back; tours by arrangement; bookings 1800 440 101 or through visitor's centre. **Quorn Native Flora Reserve:** stone reserve, once the town's quarry, with informative brochure available that details the reserve's flora; Quarry Rd; 2 km NW. **Pichi Richi Camel Tours:** award-winning camel tours through the gorgeous native bushland, with candlelit dinners and moonlight rides on offer; Devils Peak Rd; (08) 8648 6640; 6 km SE. **The Dutchmans Stern Conservation Park:** colourful rocky outcrops observed on 2 trails through the park. The Ridge Top Trail (8.2 km return) offers spectacular views of the Flinders Ranges and Spencer Gulf; 8 km W. **Devil's Peak Walking Trail:** panoramic views up steep climb to the summit; closed Nov–Apr (fire season); 10 km S. **Mt Brown Conservation Park:** mixed landscape of ridges and woodland. The loop trail, starting at Waukarie Falls, offers a side climb to the Mt Brown summit; Richman Valley Rd; 15 km S. **Warren Gorge:** imposing red cliffs popular with climbers. Also the habitat of the rare yellow-footed rock wallaby; 23 km N. **Buckaringa Gorge Scenic Drive:** drive past Buckaringa Sanctuary and Proby's Grave (he was the first settler at Kanyaka Station) to a lookout accessed via a short walk; begins 35 km N.

See also FLINDERS RANGES & OUTBACK, p. 243

Robe

Pop. 1249
Map ref. 601 E9

i The Robe Institute, Mundy Tce; (08) 8768 2465 or 1300 367 144; www.council.robe.sa.gov.au

 107.7 5THE FM, 1161 AM ABC South East

Guichen Bay and Robe's coastline would have been a welcome sight to the Chinese immigrants arriving in the mid-1800s. During the Victorian gold rush, around 16 500 Chinese disembarked here and travelled overland to the goldfields to avoid the Poll Tax enforced at Victorian ports. Robe had a thriving export trade before rail was introduced, which has left a legacy of historic buildings, from quaint stone cottages to the Caledonian Inn, with internal doors salvaged from shipwrecks. Today Robe is one of the state's most significant historic towns, but also a fishing port and holiday centre, famous for its crayfish and its secluded beaches.

The Robe Institute: incorporates the visitor centre, library and Historic Interpretation Centre with photographic and audiovisual displays on Robe's history; Mundy Tce. **Robe Customs House:** historic 1863 building, once the hub of Robe's export trade, now a museum featuring Chinese artefacts and displays; open 2–4pm Tues, Sat and daily in Jan; Royal Circus. **Art and craft galleries:** throughout town, especially in Smillie and Victoria sts. **Deep Sea Fishing charter:** sightseeing cruise also on offer; bookings (08) 8768 1807. **Crayfish fleet:** anchors in Lake Butler (Robe's harbour); sells fresh crayfish and fish Oct–Apr.

Walk and scenic drive tours: self-guide tours available. Take the town walk past 81 historic buildings and sites; brochures from visitor centre.

Robe Easter Surfing Classic: Easter. **Blessing of the Fleet:** celebrates the role of Italians in establishing the local fishing industry; Sept. **Robe Village Fair:** last full weekend in Nov.

Caledonian Inn: historic pub, smart food; 1 Victoria St; (08) 8768 2029. **The Gallerie Restaurant & Wine Bar:** stylish seafood; 2 Victoria St; (08) 8768 2256.

Caledonian Inn: historic pub and seafront suites; 1 Victoria St; (08) 8768 2029. **Cricklewood:** tranquil, relaxed lakefront cottage; 24 Woolundry Rd; (08) 8768 2137. **Grey Masts:** historic seaside cottages; Smillie St; 0411 627 146. **Honeyfield:** French Provincial–style cottage hideaway; Robe Rd; 1300 760 629. **The Shore:** spacious luxury beachfront residence; 11 Wrattonbully Rd; 1300 760 629.

Lake Fellmongery: popular spot for waterskiing; 1 km SE. **Long Beach:** 17 km pristine beach for surfing and swimming. Cars are allowed on the sand; 2 km N. **Little Dip Conservation Park:** features a complex, moving sand-dune system, salt lakes, freshwater lakes and abundant wildlife. Drive or walk through native bush to beaches for surfing and beach-fishing; some areas 4WD only; 2 km S. **Beacon Hill:** panoramic views of Robe, lakes and coast from lookout tower; Beacon Hill Rd; 2 km SE. **The Obelisk:** navigational marker at Cape Dombey. Scenic access via cliff walk from the Old Gaol at Robe; 2 km W. **Mt Benson Wine Region:** young wine region specialising in shiraz and cabernet sauvignon. Eight cellar doors offer tastings and sales; 18 km N.

See also LIMESTONE COAST, p. 242

Roxby Downs

Pop. 3848
Map ref. 604 E4

i Roxby Downs Cultural Precinct; (08) 8671 2001; www.roxbydowns.com

 102.7 AM ABC Local, 105.5 ROX FM

In 1975 Roxby Downs station was a hard-working property on the red sand dunes of central South Australia. That was until a body of copper and uranium, the largest in the world, was discovered near a dam. Roxby Downs, the township, was built to accommodate the employees of the Olympic Dam mining project and has many modern facilities.

Cultural Precinct: incorporates the visitor centre, cinema, cafe, art gallery with local and touring exhibitions, and interpretive display on town and dam history; Richardson Pl. **Arid Discovery:** area of native landscape with sunset tours to see reintroduced native animals, including bilbies and burrowing bettongs. A highlight is the close viewing of animals in the observation hide; contact visitor centre for tour details. **Emu Walk:** self-guide flora walk through town; contact visitor centre.

Market: Richardson Pl; closest Sat to the 15th each month. **Outback Fringe Festival:** Apr.

Olympic Dam Mining Complex: an extensive underground system of roadways and trains services the mine that produces refined copper, uranium oxide, gold and silver. The mine is 9 km N, but limited views are available at the site. Olympic Dam Tours run surface tours 3 days a week; times and bookings through the visitor centre.

See also FLINDERS RANGES & OUTBACK, p. 243

RENMARK

Pop. 4342
Map ref. 558 A5 | 588 B5 | 601 G1 | 603 O7

[ERODED RED CLIFFS ALONG THE MURRAY RIVER]

i 84 Murray Ave; (08) 8586 6704;
www.renmarkparinga.sa.gov.au

93.1 Magic FM, 1062 AM ABC Riverland

It is hard to imagine that the lush lands around Renmark, thriving with orchards and vineyards, were once a veritable wasteland. In 1887 the Canadian-born Chaffey brothers were granted 30000 acres (12 000 hectares) by the South Australian government to test their irrigation scheme. Theirs was the first of its type to succeed in Australia and today the farmlands are still irrigated with water piped from the Murray River.

Olivewood: National Trust historic building, formerly the Chaffey homestead, dressed in period furnishings, set in the grounds of a still-operating orangery and with famous olive trees in the orchard; closed Wed; cnr Renmark Ave and Twenty-first St. *PS Industry:* 1911 grand lady of the river still operates on steam when taking visitors on her monthly cruises; 90 min tours run at 11am and 1.30pm first Sun each month; bookings at visitor centre. *Renmark Hotel:* historic community-owned and -run hotel; Murray Ave. *Nuts About Fruit:* sales of local dried fruit, nuts and other produce; closed Sun; Renmark Ave. *Renmark North Lookout:* views of town and Murray River; northern outskirts of town. *Murray River cruises:* houseboat hire or paddlesteamer tours to cruise the mighty Murray; contact visitor centre for details.

Riverland Greek Festival: Feb. *Riverland Balloon Fiesta:* June. *Rose Festival:* Oct. *Renmark Rose Run:* race along the riverfront; Oct. *Renmark Show:* Oct.

River's Edge Restaurant: regional cuisine; Renmark Club, Murray Ave; (08) 8586 6611.

Liba Liba Houseboats: 14 paddlewheel boats, 4–12 berth; Jane Eliza Landing; (08) 8586 6734 or 1800 810 252. *Willows & Waterbirds:* large, convenient family home; 41 Murray Ave; (08) 8295 8836. *Customs House Houseboats:* secluded boating

along Victorian border; Customs House Marina, via Renmark; 1300 557 706. *Paringa House B&B Stone Cottages:* romantic riverfront getaways; 1 Museum Dr, Paringa; (08) 8595 5217. *Riverfun Houseboat Hire:* 10 vessels, classic to ultra-modern; Lock 5 Rd, Paringa; (08) 8595 5537.

Bookmark Biosphere Reserve This reserve incorporates the mallee country and arid outback landscapes of Chowilla Regional Reserve and Danggali Conservation Park. In Chowilla (50 km N) are stretches of flood plains interspersed with native woodland and scrubland. Fishing, canoeing and birdwatching are popular and the history of the flood plains is explained on the Old Coach Road Vehicle Trail. Danggali (90 km N) is a vast wilderness area with interesting trails to explore. The 2 drive tours, Nanya's Pad Interpretive Drive (100 km circuit, 2WD accessible) and Tipperary Drive (100 km circuit, 4WD only), are both excellent introductions to the mallee scrub region, while the 10 km Target Mark Walking Trail passes through native vegetation to the dam.

Lock and Weir No. 5: picnic in surrounding parklands; 2 km SE. *Paringa:* small farming community featuring a historic suspension bridge (1927), Bert Dix Memorial Park and nearby Headings Cliffs Lookout; 4 km E. *Angove's:* producers of St Agnes Brandy as well as wine, with cellar-door tastings and sales; Bookmark Ave; 5 km SW. *Bredl's Wonder World of Wildlife:* unique fauna, particularly reptiles. Handling and feeding times between 11am and 3pm; (08) 8595 1431; 7 km SW. *Ruston's Rose Garden:* the Southern Hemisphere's largest rose garden with over 50 000 bushes and 4000 varieties; open Oct–May; Moorna St, off Sturt Hwy; (08) 8586 6191; 7 km SW. *Dunlop Big Tyre:* spans the Sturt Hwy at Yamba Roadhouse and marks the fruit-fly inspection point (no fruit allowed between Victoria and SA); 16 km SE. *Murray River National Park, Bulyong Island section:* popular park for water-based activities, fishing and birdwatching; just upstream from Renmark on the Murray River.

See also MURRAY, p. 241

Stansbury

Pop. 521
Map ref. 599 E7 | 602 H9

i Cnr Weaver and Towler sts; (08) 8852 4577;
www.stansburysa.com

98.9 Flow FM, 639 AM ABC North and West

Situated on the lower east coast of Yorke Peninsula and with
views of Gulf St Vincent, Stansbury was originally known as
Oyster Bay because of its claim to the best oyster beds in the state.
The town has always serviced the farms inland, but its mainstay
today is tourism. The bay is excellent for fishing and watersports,
including diving and waterskiing.

Schoolhouse Museum: this local history museum in
Stansbury's first school features cultural and environmental
displays as well as the headmaster's rooms furnished in early-
1900s style; open 2–4pm Wed and Sun, daily in Jan; North Tce.
Oyster farms: see daily operations of local oyster farms and try
fresh oysters. *Fishing:* popular spots include the jetty, rocks and
beach. *Mills' Gully Lookout:* popular picnic spot with panoramic
views of bay, town and Gulf St Vincent; northern outskirts of
town. *Coastal trails:* walking and cycling trails past reserves,
lookouts and a historic cemetery; start at foreshore caravan park;
brochure from visitor centre.

Stansbury Seaside Markets: monthly Oct–May; check
dates with visitor centre. *Stansbury and Port Vincent Wooden
and Classic Boat Regatta:* even-numbered years, Apr. *Sheepdog
Trials:* odd-numbered years, May.

Musgrave Manor: extravagant, high-tech seaside home;
Lot 2 Musgrave La; 0417 855 064.

Kleines Point Quarry: SA's largest limestone quarry;
5 km s. *Lake Sundown:* one of the many salt lakes in the area
and a photographer's delight at sunset; 15 km NW. *Port Vincent:*
popular holiday destination with good swimming, yachting and
waterskiing; 17 km N.

See also YORKE PENINSULA, p. 240

Strathalbyn

Pop. 3894
Map ref. 597 E12 | 598 H5 | 601 C4 | 603 K10

i Old Railway Station, South Tce; (08) 8536 3212;
www.visitalexandrina.com

94.7 5EFM, 639 AM ABC North and West

This heritage town has some of the most picturesque and historic
streetscapes in country South Australia. It has a predominantly
Scottish heritage, first settled by Dr John Rankine, who emigrated
with 105 other Scotsmen in the late 1830s. The town is set on the
Angas River, with the Soldiers Memorial Gardens following the
watercourse through the town. Strathalbyn is renowned for its
antique and craft shops.

National Trust Museum: history display in the courtroom,
Victorian-era relics in the courthouse, and a historical room and
photographic displays in the Old Police Station; open 2–5pm
Wed, Thurs, Sat and Sun; Rankine St. *Old Railway Station:*
complex includes the visitor centre, the Station Master's Gallery
with local and touring art exhibitions (open Wed–Sun), and
the station for the tourist railway from Mount Barker, the
SteamRanger (*see Hahndorf*); South Tce. *St Andrew's Church:*
impressive church with castle-like tower; Alfred Pl. *Original Lolly
Shop:* old-fashioned lollies and fudge; High St. *Antiques, art and
craft shops:* outlets in High St. *Heritage walk:* self-guide trail
featuring over 30 heritage buildings and the architectural delights
of Albyn Tce; brochure available from visitor centre.

Collectors, Hobbies and Antique Fair: Aug. *Strathalbyn
Show:* Oct. *Glenbarr Highland Gathering:* Oct. *Rotary Duck
Race:* plastic ducks; Nov.

Victoria Hotel: creative pub meals; 16 Albyn Tce;
(08) 8536 2202.

Gasworks B&B: charming heritage cottages; 12 South Tce;
(08) 8536 4291. *Longview Lodge Apartments:* designer vineyard
retreats; Longview Vineyard, Pound Rd, Macclesfield; (08) 8388
9694. *The Old Oak B&B:* secluded rural homestead; Bald Hill Rd,
Bull Creek; (08) 8536 6069.

Milang This old riverboat town is now a popular holiday
destination on the shores of Lake Alexandrina, Australia's largest
freshwater lake. The lake offers fishing, sailing and windsurfing.
In town, visit the Port Milang Railway for its local history display
and pick up a Heritage Trail brochure for a self-guide walk. Each
Australia Day weekend the Milang–Goolwa Freshwater Classic
fills the town with visitors who come to watch hundreds of yachts
begin the race. 20 km SE.

Lookout: views over town and district; 7 km SW. *Ashbourne:* buy
local produce at roadside stalls and at the country market held
3rd Sun each month; 14 km w. *Langhorne Creek wine region:*
on the Bremer and Angas rivers flood plains, the first vines
were planted in the 1850s. This winemaking region has always
specialised in red varieties, particularly cabernet sauvignon
and shiraz. Five cellar doors offer tastings and sales; 15 km E.
Meadows: features Pottery at Paris Creek and Iris Gardens (open
Oct–Mar) nearby. The Country Fair is held each Oct; 15 km NW.

See also FLEURIEU PENINSULA, p. 235

Streaky Bay

Pop. 1059
Map ref. 602 A3 | 611 N10

i Rural Transaction and Visitor Information Centre,
21 Bay Rd; (08) 8626 7033; www.streakybay.sa.gov.au

99.3 Flow FM, 693 AM ABC Eyre Peninsula and
West Coast

A holiday town, fishing port and agricultural centre for the
cereal-growing hinterland. The bay was first sighted in 1627 by
Dutch explorer Peter Nuyts, but it wasn't fully explored until
1802 by Matthew Flinders. Flinders named the bay after the
'streaky' colour of the water, caused by seaweed oils. While this
town is pretty, it is the surrounding bays and coves, sandy beaches
and towering cliffs that bring the visitors.

National Trust Museum: early pioneer history displays in
the old school, as well as a restored pioneer cottage and a doctor's
surgery; open 2–4pm Tues and Fri, or by appt; Montgomerie Tce;
(08) 8626 1443. *Powerhouse Restored Engine Centre:* display of
old working engines; open 2–5pm Tues and Fri; Alfred Tce. *Shell
Roadhouse:* Great White Shark replica (original caught with rod
and reel); Alfred Tce. *Fishing:* for King George whiting, southern
rock lobster, salmon, mullaway, garfish, abalone and shark (check
with PIRSA & Fisheries centre).

Perlubie Sports Day: Jan. *Streaky Bay Cup:*
horseracing; Apr.

Mocean Cafe: innovative seafront dining; 34B Alfred Tce;
(08) 8626 1775.

Scenic drives: include Westall Way Scenic Drive, which
starts 9 km S, taking in rock formations, high cliffs, quiet pools
and the Yanerbie Sand Dunes. Also the drive west of town to
Cape Bauer and the Blowhole (20 km NW), for views across the

Bight. *Calpatanna Waterhole Conservation Park:* bushwalking in coastal park to an important Aboriginal waterhole; excellent birdwatching; 28 km SE. *Murphy's Haystacks:* a much-photographed cluster of pink granite boulders, with interpretive signage and paths; 40 km SE. *Baird Bay:* a small coastal town with an attractive beach for swimming, boating and fishing. Baird Bay Charters and Ocean Ecotours offer swims with sea lions and dolphins; (08) 8626 5017; 45 km SE. *Point Labatt Conservation Park:* from the cliff-top viewing platform, see the rare and endangered Australian sea lions sleeping on the beach (this colony is the only permanent one on the Australian mainland). Parts of access road unsealed; 50 km SE. *Venus Bay Conservation Park:* important reserve for breeding and reintroduction of native species. The park includes the peninsula and 7 islands with beach-fishing and swimming. Peninsula access is 4WD only; turn-off 50 km SE. *Acraman Creek Conservation Park:* this mangrove and mallee park is an important refuge for coastal birds. Popular activities include canoeing and fishing. 2WD access to beach, 4WD to Point Lindsay; turn-off 53 km N. *Port Kenny:* this small township on Venus Bay offers excellent fishing, boating and swimming, with sea lion and dolphin tours available; 62 km SE. *Venus Bay:* fishing village renowned for catches of King George whiting, trevally, garfish and many more. Its waters are safe for swimming and watersports, and nearby beaches are good for surfing. Needle Eye Lookout close by provides fantastic views, with southern right whale sightings June–Oct; 76 km S.

See also EYRE PENINSULA & NULLARBOR, p. 244

Swan Reach

Pop. 237
Map ref. 601 E2 | 603 L8

 General Store, 47 Anzac Ave; (08) 8570 2036 or 1800 442 784; www.murraylands.info

 93.1 Magic FM, 1062 AM ABC Riverland

This quiet little township on the Murray River was once one of five large sheep stations; the original homestead is now the Swan Reach Hotel. Established as one of the first river ports for Murray River trade, the introduction of rail, and Morgan's rise as one of the state's busiest ports, saw the era of paddlesteamers in Swan Reach decline. Today the picturesque river scenery and excellent fishing make the town a popular holiday destination.

 Swan Reach Museum: local history displays with special interest in Swan Reach's flood history, the waters having devastated the town in the early 1900s; Nildottie Rd.

 Griffens Marina Houseboats: luxury 10–12 berth boats; Griffens Marina, Blanchetown; (08) 8540 5250.

 Yookamurra Sanctuary This sanctuary represents an initiative to restore 1100 ha of land to its original state. Fittingly, the sanctuary is named Yookamurra after the Aboriginal word for 'yesterday'. The mallee vegetation that was found here before European habitation has been replanted; keep an eye out for the rare and endangered numbat or the bilby and woylie. Walking tours and overnight stays are available. Bookings are essential, (08) 8562 5011; Pipeline Rd, Sedan; 21 km W.

Murray Aquaculture Yabby Farm: catch your own yabbies; 1.5 km E. *Ridley and Swan Reach conservation parks:* both parks represent typical western Murray vegetation and protect the habitat of the hairy-nosed wombat; 7.5 km S and 10 km W respectively. *Ngaut Ngaut Boardwalk:* guided tours of

archaeological site, established when an ancient skeleton was discovered; Nildottie; 14 km S. *Big Bend:* imposing Murray cliffs, the tallest found on the river, home to diverse flora and fauna. Spectacular nightly tours are available; inquiries (08) 8570 1097; 20 km downstream. *Bakara Conservation Park:* mallee-covered plains and sand dunes, important habitat for the mallee fowl; 32 km E. *Brookfield Conservation Park:* bushwalking in limestone country to see hairy-nosed wombats, red kangaroos and a variety of bird species; 40 km NW.

See also MURRAY, p. 241

Tanunda

Pop. 4152
Map ref. 597 E4 | 601 C2 | 603 K8

 Barossa Visitor Information Centre, Murray St; (08) 8563 0600 or 1300 812 662; www.barossa-region.org

 89.1 BBB FM, 639 AM ABC North and West

Tanunda is at the heart of the Barossa and surrounded by vineyards. The modern-day township grew out of the village of Langmeil, which was the focal point for early German settlement. The German Lutherans found it only natural to plant vines, as it was a basic part of their lifestyle. Many of the Barossa's shiraz vines date back to those early days. Tanunda has a boisterous German spirit and fine examples of Lutheran churches.

 Barossa Historical Museum: situated in the former post and telegraph office (1865), its collections specialise in German heritage; Murray St. *Gourmet produce:* specialty stores include Tanunda Bakery for German breads (Murray St), Tanunda's Nice Ice for homemade ice-cream (Kavel Arcade) and Apex Bakery for traditional pastries (Elizabeth St). *Heritage walk:* includes many historic Lutheran churches; brochure available from visitor centre.

 Barossa Under the Stars: Feb. *Tanunda Show:* Mar. *Barossa Vintage Festival:* celebration of locally produced food and wine in various locations; odd-numbered years, Apr. *Barossa Gourmet Weekend:* Aug. *Barossa Band Festival:* Oct.

 1918 Bistro & Grill: modern Australian; 94 Murray St; (08) 8563 0405. *Apex Bakery:* traditional German bakery; 1A Elizabeth St, (08) 8563 2483. *Krondorf Road Cafe:* authentic German recipes; Krondorf Rd; (08) 8563 0889. *Jacob's Restaurant:* sleek cellar-door dining; Jacob's Creek Visitor Centre, Barossa Valley Way, Rowland Flat; (08) 8521 3000.

 Goat Square Cottages: quaint heritage town houses; 33 John St; (08) 8524 5353 or 1800 227 677. *Jacob's Creek Retreat:* opulent, European-themed resort; Nitschke Rd; (08) 8563 1123. *Lawley Farm:* beautifully restored settler's cottages; Krondorf Rd; (08) 8563 2141. *Stonewell Cottages:* dreamy lakefront retreats; Stonewell Rd; 0417 848 977. *Sonntag House:* peaceful heritage cottage; Bethany Rd, Bethany; 0419 814 349.

 Barossa Wine Region The Mediterranean-style climate, varying soils, specialised winemakers and long history (dating back to the 1840s) have created a world-renowned wine region in the Barossa Valley. Nearly all outfits offer cellar-door tastings and sales. Close to Tanunda is the Barossa Small Winemakers Centre, housed in the cellar door at Chateau Tanunda, Basedow Rd, and showcasing the rare and handmade varieties of the Barossa's small producers. At the Chateau Dorrien Winery Tourism Centre in Barossa Valley Way there is an interesting mural depicting Barossa heritage. Winery map available from visitor centre. *For more information see Angaston, Lyndoch and Nuriootpa.*

VICTOR HARBOR

Pop. 10 377

Map ref. 598 F9 | 599 H10 | 601 B5 | 603 J11

i Causeway Building, Esplanade; (08) 8551 0777; www.tourismvictorharbor.com.au

89.3 5EFM, 639 AM ABC North and West

In the 1830s the crystal waters of Encounter Bay – and the Southern Ocean beyond – throbbed with the whalers and sealers of the south. Granite Island housed a whaling station, Victor Harbor was its port, and life revolved around the ocean slaughters. Today the whalers and sealers are gone, Granite Island is a recreation park and Victor Harbor is a holiday town. The naming of Encounter Bay comes from the unexpected meeting in the bay between explorers Matthew Flinders and Nicolas Baudin.

South Australian Whale Centre This unique centre focuses on the 25 species of whale and dolphin, and other marine life found in the southern Australian waters, with an aim to educate and conserve these species. Past atrocities are displayed alongside interactive displays and presentations that reveal the wonders of the amazing creatures. Between June and Sept each year, southern right whales mate and breed in Encounter Bay. The centre offers whale cruises and sighting information, as well as a Whale Info Hotline for the latest sightings (in season). Open 9.30am–5pm daily; Railway Tce; 1900 931 223.

Encounter Coast Discovery Centre: National Trust museum that covers Aboriginal, whaling, settler and recent local history. A museum walk finishes at the Old Customs House, which has period furnishings; open 1–4pm daily; Flinders Pde. *Cockle Train:* departs from Railway Tce for return journey to Goolwa; bookings 1300 655 991; *for more details see Goolwa. Camel and pony rides:* on foreshore; start near Causeway entrance from 11am weekends and school holidays (weather permitting). *Amusement Park:* family fun fair on the beach with the state's biggest Ferris wheel, dodgem cars and an inflatable slide; open long weekends and school holidays; the Causeway; 0418 845 540. *SteamRanger Heritage Railway:* heritage steam and diesel

[THE COCKLE TRAIN, TRAVELLING FROM GOOLWA TO VICTOR HARBOR]

tourist trains run to Port Elliot, Goolwa, Strathalbyn and Mount Barker; phone 1300 655 991. *Scenic flights:* helicopter joy-flights over Victor Harbor, Granite Island, local vineyards and the mouth of the Murray; (08) 8552 8196.

Regional Art Show: Jan. *Triathlon:* Mar. *Whaletime, Playtime Festival and Whale Season Launch:* June.

Ocean Grill Restaurant: steaks and seafood; Anchorage Seafront Hotel, 21 Flinders Pde; (08) 8552 5970. *Waterside Restaurant:* contemporary bayside dining; Whalers Inn Resort, 121 Franklin Pde, Encounter Bay; (08) 8552 4400.

Anchorage Seafront Hotel: affordable foreshore suites; 21 Flinders Pde; (08) 8552 5970. *Riverhouse:* engaging country retreat, 447 Waggon Rd; (08) 8552 5657. *Whalers Inn Resort:* self-contained suites with spectacular views; 121 Franklin Pde, Encounter Bay; (08) 8552 4400.

Granite Island Recreation Park Granite Island has a long and varied history. It has significance in the Ramindjeri people's Dreamtime; in 1837 a whaling station was established; and today the island is a recreation park. This history is detailed on the Kaiki Trail, a 1.5 km walk around the island. A highlight is the Below Decks Oceanarium, just off the Screwpile Jetty, with close-up views of marine life and tours daily; at dusk, take a guided Penguin Discovery Tour to see the penguins scuttle in and out of their burrows (all tour bookings (08) 8552 7555). The island is linked to the mainland by a 630 m causeway. Walk or take the horse-drawn tram, the last one remaining in the Southern Hemisphere; tram departs from entrance to Causeway at 10am daily. Tickets available at visitor centre or on the Horse Tram.

Hindmarsh River Estuary: peaceful picnic and fishing spot with boardwalk through coastal scrub; 1 km NE. *Greenhills Adventure Park:* family-fun activities including go-karts, jumping castle and water slide; Waggon Rd; 3.5 km N. *Victor Harbor Winery:* cellar-door tastings and sales of cool-climate reds, whites and fortified wines; open Wed–Sun; Hindmarsh Valley; 4 km N. *Urimbirra Wildlife Park:* popular fauna park with a wetland bird sanctuary, crocodile-feeding and children's farmyard; Adelaide Rd; 5 km N. *Wild Rose Garden and Miniature Village:* minute replicas of SA's historical attractions in landscaped gardens, with tearooms and fruit sales (in season) at the Apple Shed; next to Urimbirra Wildlife Park. *Nangawooka Flora Reserve:* tranquil walks through native bushlands with over 1250 native plant varieties on show; opposite Urimbirra Wildlife Park. *The Bluff (Rosetta Head):* 500-million-year-old mass of granite, well worth the 100 m climb for the views; 5 km SW. *Newland Head Conservation Park:* known for its wild surf and coastal vegetation, this park protects the headland and Waitpinga and Parsons beaches, which offer surf-fishing opportunities and beach walks; turn-off 15 km SW. *Hindmarsh Falls:* pleasant walks and spectacular waterfall (during winter); 15 km NW. *Mt Billy Conservation Park:* mallee and forest park renowned for its rare orchid species; 18 km NW. *Inman Valley:* features Glacier Rock, said to be the first recorded discovery of glaciation in Australia; 19 km NW.

See also FLEURIEU PENINSULA, p. 235

Norm's Coolies: see performances by a unique breed of sheepdog, Norm's coolie, at 2pm Mon, Wed and Sat; just south on Barossa Valley Way. *Bethany:* this pretty village was the first German settlement in the Barossa. The creekside picnic area, pioneer cemetery, attractive streetscapes and walking trail along Rifle Range Rd make it well worth a visit; 3 km SE. *The Keg Factory:* makers of American and French oak kegs, as well as barrel furniture and wine racks; St Halletts Rd; 4 km SW.

See also BAROSSA VALLEY, p. 238

Tumby Bay

Pop. 1348
Map ref. 602 E7

ℹ️ Hales MiniMart, 1 Bratten Way; (08) 8688 2584; www.tumbybay.sa.gov.au

📻 89.9 Magic FM, 1485 AM ABC Eyre Peninsula and West Coast

Tumby Bay is a pretty coastal town on the east coast of Eyre Peninsula. Its development was slow – Matthew Flinders discovered the bay in 1802, settlers arrived in the 1840s and the jetty was built in 1874 to ship the grain produce, but still there was no town. It took until the early 1900s for any official settlement to be established. Now the famous long, crescent beach, white sand and blue water attract holiday-makers.

🏠 *C. L. Alexander National Trust Museum:* depicts early pioneer history in an old timber schoolroom; open 10–11am Wed, 2.30–4.30pm Sun or by appt; West Tce; (08) 8688 2760. *Rotunda Art Gallery:* local art display and a fantastic mural on the outside of the rotunda; open 10am–12pm Mon and Wed or by appt; Tumby Tce; (08) 8688 2678. *Excell Blacksmith and Engineering Workshop Museum:* original workshop and equipment dating from the early 1900s; open 1.30–4.30pm 4th Sun each month, or by appt; Barraud St; (08) 8688 2101. *Mangrove boardwalk:* 70 m walkway with interpretive signs explaining ecology of mangroves; Berryman St. *Fishing:* from the recreational jetty, beach, rocks or boats (hire and charters available).

🏡 *Tumby Bay Beach House:* smart, revived waterfront shack; 1 Elfrieda Dr; 0429 830 328.

🧭 *Koppio Smithy Museum* The early 1900s come to life in this extensive National Trust museum in the Koppio Hills. Consisting of the restored Blacksmith's Shop (1903), historic log cottage 'Glenleigh' (1893) and schoolrooms, the museum houses an eclectic collection of Aboriginal artefacts, early pioneer furniture, firearms and early machinery. Closed Mon; 30 km SW.

Trinity Haven Scenic Drive: travels south from town along the coast and offers scenic coastal views and secluded beaches and bays. *Island Lookout Tower and Reserve:* views of town, coast and islands. Enjoy a picnic in the reserve; Harvey Dr; 3 km S. *Lipson Cove:* popular spot for anglers. Walk to the coastal sanctuary on Lipson Island at low tide; 10 km NE. *Ponta and Cowleys beaches:* fishing catches include snapper and bream; 15 km NE. *Moody Tanks:* State Heritage–listed water-storage tanks once used to service passing steam trains; 30 km W. *Cummins:* rich rail heritage celebrated each Apr at the World Championship Kalamazoo Classic; 37 km NW. *Port Neill:* an old port town with a safe beach for fishing and watersports. Also Ramsay Bicentennial Gardens, and vintage vehicles at Vic and Jill Fauser's Living

Museum. Port Neill Lookout, nearby, provides fantastic views of the coast; 42 km NE. *Sir Joseph Banks Group Conservation Park:* comprising around 20 islands and reefs, this park is a breeding area for migrating coastal birds and the Australian sea lion colony at Dangerous Reef; boat access is from Tumby Bay, Port Lincoln and 250 m north of Lipson Cove.

See also EYRE PENINSULA & NULLARBOR, p. 244

Waikerie

Pop. 1744
Map ref. 601 E1 | 603 M7

ℹ️ Orange Tree Giftmania, Sturt Hwy; (08) 8541 2332.

📻 93.1 Magic FM, 1062 AM ABC Riverland

Waikerie, the citrus centre of Australia, is surrounded by an oasis of irrigated orchards and vineyards in the midst of the mallee-scrub country of the Riverland. Owing to its position on cliff-tops, the area around Waikerie was not a promising settlement. However, in an experiment by the South Australian government in 1894 that attempted to alleviate unemployment and decentralise capital, 281 people were relocated from Adelaide. It was an instant town. Waikerie has beautiful views of the river gums and sandstone cliffs along the Murray River, which is a popular spot for fishing, boating and waterskiing – and the skies above are a glider's paradise due to the fantastic thermals and flat landscape.

🏠 *Rain Moth Gallery:* local art exhibitions; open 10.30am– 2.30pm Mon–Fri, 10am–1pm Sat; Peake Tce. *Waikerie Murray River Queen:* unique floating motel, restaurant and cafe; moored near the ferry. *Harts Lagoon:* wetland area with bird hide; Ramco Rd. *Houseboat hire:* scenic trips along the Murray; contact visitor centre for details. *Bush Safari:* camel or 4WD tours to the river and outback country north-east of Waikerie; bookings (08) 8543 2280. *Scenic walk:* along cliff-top to lookout; northern outskirts of town.

🌴 *Rotary Food Fair:* Mar. *Horse and Pony Club Easter Horse Show:* Easter. *Music on the Murray:* odd numbered years, Apr. *Riverland Rock 'n' Roll Festival:* May. *Hit n Miss Tractor Pull:* odd-numbered years, Sept.

🧭 *Orange Tree Giftmania:* local produce sales – including citrus and dried fruits – and souvenirs. Enjoy Murray River views from the viewing platform; Sturt Hwy. *Waikerie Gliding Club:* offers recreational flights, beginner courses and cross-country training; Waikerie Aerodrome, off Sturt Hwy, east side of town; inquiries (08) 8541 2644. *Maize Island Conservation Park:* this waterbird reserve has fantastic cliffs and lagoons. Beware of strong currents when swimming; 2 km N. *Pooginook Conservation Park:* both dense and open mallee country, home to kangaroos, hairy-nosed wombats and the ever-busy mallee fowl; 12 km NE. *Stockyard Plain Disposal Basin Reserve:* varied plant and birdlife – over 130 bird species identified; key available from visitor centre; 12 km SW. *Broken Cliffs:* popular fishing spot; Taylorville Rd; 15 km NE. *Birds Australia Gluepot Reserve:* important mallee area that forms part of the Bookmark Biosphere Reserve (*see Renmark*). Also significant bird refuge, with over 17 threatened Australian species to be seen on the 14 walking trails; access key from Shell Service Station in Waikerie; 64 km N.

See also MURRAY, p. 241

Wallaroo

Pop. 3050
Map ref. 599 E3 | 602 H6

ℹ️ The Farm Shed Museum and Tourist Centre,
50 Moonta Rd, Kadina; (08) 8821 2333 or 1800 654 991;
www.yorkepeninsula.com.au

📻 89.3 Gulf FM, 639 AM ABC North and West

Vast grain silos greet visitors to Wallaroo, a coastal town and shipping port on the west coast of Yorke Peninsula. The town is an interesting mix of tourism and industry. The safe beaches and excellent fishing prove popular with holiday-makers, while the commercial port controls exports of barley and wheat. Wallaroo exists thanks to a lucky shepherd's discovery of copper in 1859. Vast deposits were uncovered and soon thousands of Cornish miners arrived. The area boomed until the 1920s, when copper prices dropped and the industry slowly died out. Wallaroo's buildings and old Cornish-style cottages are a reminder of its colourful past. Wallaroo and nearby towns Moonta and Kadina are part of the 'Copper Coast' or 'Little Cornwall'.

🏠 **Wallaroo Heritage and Nautical Museum** This National Trust museum in Wallaroo's original 1865 post office features shipwreck displays, maps, charts, model ships and records, as well as local cultural and religious history. Meet George, the unlucky giant squid eaten then recovered from a whale's belly 30 years ago. Open 10.30am–4pm Mon–Fri, 2–4pm Sat–Sun; Jetty Rd; (08) 8823 3015.

Yorke Peninsula Railway: historical diesel-train journey from Wallaroo to Bute; runs 2nd Sun each month and school holidays; contact visitor centre for details. *Ausbulk:* informative drive through grain-handling facility; Lydia Tce. *Boat hire and charters:* for the ultimate gulf-fishing experience. *Self-guide historical walk:* highlight is the 1865 Hughes chimney stack, which contains over 300 000 bricks and measures more than 7 sq m at its base; brochure available from museum or town hall.

🎭 *Kernewek Lowender:* Cornish festival held in conjunction with Moonta and Kadina; odd-numbered years, May.

🍴 *The Boatshed Restaurant:* waterfront seafood specialists; 1 Jetty Rd; (08) 8823 3455.

🛏️ *The Cornucopia Hotel:* updated heritage hotel; 49 Owen Tce; (08) 8823 3457. *Tipara:* modern waterfront apartment; 7 Tipara Crt, Moonta Bay; (08) 8843 0187. *Top Deck Cliff House:* beachfront family retreat; 1 Queen Pl, Moonta Bay; (08) 8636 2343.

⚫ *Bird Island:* crabbing; 10 km s.

Travellers note: To avoid the extra driving distance to the Eyre Peninsula, Sea SA runs a ferry service between Wallaroo and Lucky Bay 4 times a day on weekdays, and twice a day on weekends. Bookings (08) 8823 0777.

See also YORKE PENINSULA, p. 240

Whyalla

Pop. 21 123
Map ref. 602 H3 | 604 G11

ℹ️ Lincoln Hwy; (08) 8645 7900 or 1800 088 589;
www.whyalla.com

📻 107.7 5YYY FM, 639 AM ABC North and West

Whyalla, northern gateway to Eyre Peninsula, has grown from the small settlement of Hummock Hill to the largest provincial city in South Australia. It has become known for its heavy industry since iron ore was found in the 1890s around Iron Knob and the steel works opened in 1964. Whyalla also has an interesting natural attraction. Each year, from May to August, an incredible number of cuttlefish spawn on the rocky coast just north – a must-see for diving and snorkelling enthusiasts. The city is modern and offers safe beaches, excellent fishing and boating.

🏠 **Whyalla Maritime Museum** The central attraction is HMAS *Whyalla*, a 650-tonne corvette, the largest permanently land-locked ship in Australia. It was the first ship built in the BHP shipyards. Guided tours of the ship are included in the entry price and run on the hour 11am–3pm Apr–Oct, 10am–2pm Nov–Mar. The lives of the 4 wartime corvettes built by BHP are documented, as are histories of the shipbuilding industry and maritime heritage of Spencer Gulf. Lincoln Hwy; (08) 8645 8900.

Mt Laura Homestead Museum: National Trust museum featuring the original homestead with progressive city-history displays, period furnishings in the 1914 Gay St Cottage, and the Telecommunications Museum; open 10am–12pm Mon–Fri, 2–4pm Sun; Ekblom St. *Tanderra Craft Village:* art and craft shops, market and tearooms; open 10am–4pm last weekend each month; next to Maritime Museum. *Whyalla Wetlands:* park and wetlands area with walking trails and a picnic/barbecue area; Lincoln Hwy. *Foreshore and marina:* safe beach, jetty for recreational fishing, picnic/barbecue area, access to Ada Ryan Gardens, and a marina with boatlaunching facilities. *Ada Ryan Gardens:* mini-zoo with picnic facilities under shady trees; Cudmore Tce. *Murray Cod Tour:* see a fully operational inland freshwater aquaculture venture, and learn about recycling water and the various growth stages of the Murray cod. Closed footwear required; book at visitor centre. *Steelworks Tour:* 2 hr guided tour explains steelmaking process; departs 9.30am Mon, Wed and Fri; book at visitor centre. *Hummock Hill Lookout:* views of city, gulf, steel works and coast from WW II observation post; Queen Elizabeth Dr. *Flinders and Freycinet Lookout:* Farrel St; *Whyalla Visitor Guide* from visitor centre.

🌴 *Australian Snapper Championship:* Easter. *Whyalla Show:* family activities, rides and stalls; Aug.

⚫ *Whyalla Conservation Park:* 30 min walking trail through typical semi-arid flora and over Wild Dog Hill; 10 km N off Lincoln Hwy. *Port Bonython and Point Lowly:* this area of coast offers beautiful views of Spencer Gulf, fishing from rocks, and dolphin sightings. Lowly Beach is a popular swimming beach and the Freycinet Trail is a scenic drive from just before Port Bonython along Fitzgerald Bay to Point Douglas (parts are gravel); 34 km E. *Iron Knob:* a mining town with museum and mine lookout tours (depart from the museum at 10am and 2pm Mon–Fri); 53 km NW.

See also EYRE PENINSULA & NULLARBOR, p. 244

Willunga

Pop. 2103
Map ref. 597 B12 | 598 E6 | 599 H9 | 601 B4 | 603 J10

ℹ️ McLaren Vale Visitors Centre, Main Rd, McLaren Vale; (08) 8323 9944 or 1800 628 410; www.mclarenvale.info

📻 94.7 5EFM, 639 AM ABC North and West

The historic town of Willunga grew rapidly around the slate quarries, which drove the town's economy until the late 1800s. Fortunately, by that time Willunga already had a thriving new industry – almonds. The town sits at the southern edge of the McLaren Vale wine region and is surrounded by farmlands and olive groves. Its name is derived from the Aboriginal word 'willa-unga', meaning 'the place of green trees'.

🏠 *Willunga Courthouse Museum:* National Trust museum with local history displays in the original 1855 courtroom, cells

WILPENA

Map ref. 600 B10 | 605 I7

ⓘ Wilpena Rd, via Hawker; (08) 8648 0048;
www.wilpenapound.com.au

Wilpena consists of a resort and caravan/camping park on the edge of Wilpena Pound, in Flinders Ranges National Park. In 1902 the Hill family, wheat farmers, built a homestead inside the pound, but abandoned it after a flood washed away the access road in 1914. The pound is a vast natural amphitheatre surrounded by peaks that change colour with the light, and is a fantastic destination for bushwalking.

🏠 *Wilpena Pound Resort:* partly powered by the largest solar-power system in the Southern Hemisphere (viewing area accessed by a walking trail). The visitor centre at the resort has extensive information on 4WD and organised tours, self-guide drives, scenic flights, bushwalking and hiking; (08) 8648 0004.

🌴 *Wilpena Under the Stars:* black-tie dinner and dance to raise funds for the Royal Flying Doctor Service; Feb. *Tastes of the Outback:* Apr. *Flinders Ranges Event Program:* events run in autumn and spring, including guided walks, tours and cultural activities; details from visitor centre.

🛏 *Rawnsley Park Station:* multi-faceted bush resort; Wilpena Rd, (08) 8648 0030. *Willow Springs:* rustic station accommodation: Wilpena Rd, (08) 8648 4022. *Wilpena Pound Resort:* famed outback holiday destination; Wilpena Pound, (08) 8648 0004.

◎ **Flinders Ranges National Park** For thousands of years the ancient landscapes of the Flinders Ranges were home to the Adnyamathanha people – the 'people of the rocks'. Their Muda (Dreamtime) stories tell of the creation of the slopes and gorges that ripple across the landscape for over 400 km, from south-east of Port Augusta to north of Arkaroola. In the 1850s stock runs were established at Arkaba, Wilpena and Aroona. Foreign plant and animal species were introduced and the natural balance of

the ranges was altered. Within 50 years of European settlement many endemic animals had been pushed to extinction. Today conservationists are trying to recover the natural balance of the area, and have had success in the recovery of yellow-footed rock wallabies. The central ranges are a fabulous place for hikers. There are 17 walks and hikes to choose from and the choice is difficult. All provide a different historical, geological or scenic look at the ranges. For a look into early European settlement take the 5.4 km return Hills Homestead Walk into the extraordinary natural rock formation of Wilpena Pound. Impressive rock paintings depicting the creation of the ranges can be seen on the Arkaroo Rock Hike (3 km loop track). And for nature lovers there is the Bunyeroo Gorge Hike, a 7.5 km return trail that follows the gorge and reveals fantastic wildlife and rock formations. There are also driving tours that reveal some of the park's most spectacular scenery. The popular Brachina Gorge Geological Trail is a 20 km drive that details the long physical history of the ranges, from when the hills were layers of sediment beneath an ocean, to when they were compressed and pushed up into the shape of mountains. Look out for the yellow-footed rock wallaby in the rocky upper slopes of this beautiful gorge. All the roads north of Wilpena are unsealed, but are generally 2WD accessible. Among all of this, at Wilpena, is some of the best accommodation and facilities north of Adelaide. Drop into the Wilpena Pound Visitor Information Centre for a park guide; (08) 8648 0048.

Sacred Canyon: Aboriginal rock carvings and paintings; 19 km E. *Rawnsley Park Station:* camping and holiday-unit accommodation, scenic flights, horseriding and 4WD tours; (08) 8648 0030; 20 km s on Hawker Rd. *Moralana Scenic Drive:* 22 km route between Elder Range and south-west wall of Wilpena Pound with lookouts and picnic spots en route; drive starts 25 km s.

See also FLINDERS RANGES & OUTBACK, p. 243

[WILPENA POUND'S NATURAL AMPHITHEATRE]

and stables; guided 'Willunga Walks and Talks' tours; open 11am–4pm Tues, 1–5pm weekends; High St; (08) 8556 2195. *Quarry:* operated for 60 years (1842–1902), now a National Trust site; Delabole Rd. *Historical walk:* self-guide walk featuring historic pug cottages, colonial architecture and an Anglican church with an Elizabethan bronze bell; brochure from museum.

Willunga Farmers Market: Hill St; Sat mornings. *Willunga Quarry Market:* country market with local produce and crafts; Aldinga Rd; 2nd Sat each month. *Almond Blossom Festival:* running since 1970, celebrates the blooming of almond trees; July. *Fleurieu Folk Festival:* Oct.

Fino Restaurant: rustic regional cuisine; 8 Hill St; (08) 8556 4488. *Star of Greece:* stunning cliff-top seafood; The Esplanade, Port Willunga; (08) 8557 7420. *Victory Hotel:* popular pub and cellar; Main South Rd, Sellicks Beach; (08) 8556 3083.

Citrus Cottage: immaculate heritage cottage; 37 High St; (08) 8557 8516. *Sea & Vines Cottage:* secluded historic farmhouse; Culley Rd; (08) 8295 8659. *Saltaire:* easy-going seaside holiday home; 4 Marlin Rd, Port Willunga; (08) 8339 4151. *The Blue Grape:* vineyard hideaway; Newman Cl, Willunga South; (08) 8556 4078.

Mt Magnificent Conservation Park: explore virtually untouched rocky landscapes and vegetation popular for picnics and scenic walks. The highlight is the walk to the Mt Magnificent summit for coastal views; 12 km SE. *Mount Compass:* a small farming town featuring the Wetlands Boardwalk and many farms open for viewing and sales, offering both primary products and gourmet food. Australia's only Cow Race is held here each Jan or Feb; 14 km S. *Fleurieu Big Shed:* local produce, art and craft sales; 15 km S. *Kyeema Conservation Park:* completely burnt out in the 1983 Ash Wednesday fires and then again in the fires of 1994 and 2001, this park is evidence of nature's ability to constantly regenerate. It is home to over 70 species of birdlife and offers good hiking and camping. Part of the Heysen Trail passes through it; 14 km NE.

See also FLEURIEU PENINSULA, p. 235

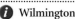 Wilmington
Pop. 217
Map ref. 603 I2 | 604 H10

 Wilmington General Store, Main North Rd; (08) 8667 5155.

105.9 Magic FM, 639 AM ABC North and West

Robert Blinman had the foresight to build an inn, called the Roundwood Hotel, at the base of Horrocks Pass in 1861, and soon the Cobb & Co coaches were stopping there on their passenger routes. The town was built around the first hotel, and before long the farming community was thriving. Originally named Beautiful Valley by European explorers, the name was changed to Wilmington in 1876, although the original name still persists in many local establishments. Today the town retains much of its old-time feel and is renowned for its stone buildings.

Wilmington Hotel: built around 1876, the hotel is one of the town's oldest buildings and was first called The Globe Hotel. Original Cobb & Co coach stables are at the rear of the building; Main North Rd. *Mt Maria Walking Trail:* 2 km walking trail starting from town leads to vantage point over Wilmington; brochure available from general store.

Night Rodeo: Jan. *Wilmington Show:* Sept.

 Alligator Lodge: bushland holiday retreat; Alligator Gorge Rd, Mt Remarkable National Park; (08) 8634 7068.

Spring Creek Mine Drive: 24 km scenic loop beginning south of town, passing mountain and farm scenery and an old copper mine, now the town's water supply; brochure from general store. *Horrocks Pass and Hancocks Lookout:* this historic pass was named after explorer John Horrocks who traversed the pass in 1846. Hancocks Lookout, at the highest point of the pass, offers magnificent views to Spencer Gulf; 8 km W off road to Port Augusta. *Mt Remarkable National Park:* 13 km S; *see Melrose.* *Winninowie Conservation Park:* coastal park of creeks and samphire flats, home to abundant birdlife; 26 km SW. *Hammond:* historic ghost town; 26 km NE. *Bruce:* historic railway town featuring 1880s architecture; 35 km N. *Carrieton:* historic buildings and Yanyarrie Whim Well in town. A rodeo is held here each Dec; 56 km NE. See Aboriginal carvings a further 9 km along Belton Rd.

See also FLINDERS RANGES & OUTBACK, p. 243

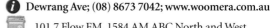

Wilpena
see inset box on previous page

Woomera
Pop. 294
Map ref. 604 E5

Dewrang Ave; (08) 8673 7042; www.woomera.com.au

101.7 Flow FM, 1584 AM ABC North and West

Woomera and its testing range were established in 1947 as a site for launching British experimental rockets during the Cold War era. The town was a restricted area until 1982. The Woomera Prohibited Area remains today and is still one of the largest land-based rocket ranges in the world.

Woomera Heritage and Visitor Information Centre: provides a detailed history of the area through videos, exhibitions, rocket relics and photographic displays. It also includes a bowling alley. Tours of the Rocket Range can be booked and depart here; Dewrang Ave. *Missile Park:* open-air defence display of rockets, aircraft and weapons; cnr Banool and Dewrang aves. *Baker Observatory:* viewing the night sky through a computer-controlled telescope; contact visitor centre for details.

See also FLINDERS RANGES & OUTBACK, p. 243

Wudinna
Pop. 517
Map ref. 602 C3 | 604 B11

44 Eyre Hwy; (08) 8680 2969; www.lehunte.sa.gov.au

89.5 Magic FM, 693 AM ABC Eyre Peninsula and West Coast

The enormous silos in Wudinna are indicative of the town's major grain industry, predominantly wheat and barley, grown here since the first pastoral lease was granted in 1861. Wudinna was proclaimed a town in 1916 and has since grown as a service centre to the Eyre Peninsula. A little travelling in the surrounding countryside will reveal unusually shaped granite outcrops – the area is known as granite country.

Gawler Ranges Cultural Centre: dedicated to the exhibition of artwork with a ranges theme; Ballantyne St.

Wudinna Show: Sept.

Gawler Ranges National Park This rugged national park offers fantastic gorge and rocky-outcrop scenery, spectacular when the spring wildflowers are in bloom. There are no marked trails, but highlights of drive tours include the Organ Pipes, a large and unique formation of volcanic rhyolite, the Kolay Mirica Falls and Yandinga Gorge. Some areas are accessible by 2WD, but

4WD is generally recommended. Roads may be impassable after rain. Guided tours into the ranges are offered by 2 operators: Gawler Ranges Wilderness Safaris (1800 243 343) and Nullarbor Traveller (1800 816 858). 40 km N.

Wudinna Granite Trail: signposted 25 km tourist drive to all major rock formations in the area. **Mt Polda Rock Recreation Reserve:** walking trail for excellent birdwatching with views from the top of Polda Rock; 7 km NE. **Mt Wudinna Recreation Reserve:** the mountain is thought to be the second-largest granite outcrop in the Southern Hemisphere. At its base is a picnic area, a 30 min return interpretive walking trail, and original stone walls used as water catchments. Enjoy scenic views at the mountain's summit. On the road to the reserve look out for Turtle Rock; 10 km NE. **Ucontitchie Hill:** isolated and unique granite formations, similar to Kangaroo Island's Remarkable Rocks; 32 km S. **Minnipa:** home to the Agricultural Centre, which provides invaluable research into sustainable dryland farming. Nearby are granite formations of geological significance, including Yarwondutta Rock (2 km N), Tcharkuldu Rock (4 km E) and the wave-like formation of Pildappa Rock (15 km N); 37 km NW. **Koongawa:** memorial to explorer John Charles Darke; 50 km E.

See also EYRE PENINSULA & NULLARBOR, p. 244

Yankalilla

Pop. 552
Map ref. 598 D8 | 599 G10 | 603 J10

 104 Main South Rd; (08) 8558 2999; www.yankalilla.sa.gov.au

89.3 5EFM, 639 AM ABC North and West

Since the first land grant in 1842, Yankalilla has been the centre of a thriving farming industry. It is a growing settlement just inland from the west coast of the Fleurieu Peninsula, but it still retains its old country flavour. It has even adopted the slogan 'Yankalilla Bay – you'll love what we haven't done to the place'. In recent times it has seen an influx of visitors keen to see the apparition at Our Lady of Yankalilla Shrine. The Blessed Virgin Mary was first sighted here in 1996.

Yankalilla District Historical Museum: local history and interpretive trail; open 1–4pm Sun; Main South Rd. **Anglican Church:** historic and known for apparition of Mary; Main St.

Leafy Sea Dragon Festival: arts and cultural festival; odd-numbered years, Apr. **Yankalilla Show:** Oct long weekend.

Lilla's Cafe: creative cafe fare; 117 Main South Rd; (08) 8558 2525.

Rattleys at Pear Tree Hollow: secluded farm cottage; 9 Nosworthy Rd, Inman Valley; (08) 8558 8234. **Ridgetop Retreats:** contemporary bush pavilions; Deep Creek Conservation Park; (08) 8598 4169. **The Beach House:** family-sized retreat; 21A Ronald St, Normanville; (08) 8558 3223.

Deep Creek Conservation Park Take one of the many walks along rugged coastal cliffs, tranquil creeks, majestic forests and scenic waterfalls. Walks range from easy and short to more challenging long-distance hikes. Keep an eye out for the western grey kangaroos at dusk on the Aaron Creek Hiking Trail or drop a line at Blowhole Creek and Boat Harbour beaches. Permits are required in the park (self-registration). 26 km SW.

Normanville: a seaside town with beach and heritage-listed sand dunes. Shipwrecks are popular with divers; 3 km W. **Myponga Conservation Park:** popular bushwalking and birdwatching park;

9 km NE. **Myponga:** a historic town with fantastic views from the Myponga Reservoir; 14 km NE. **Second Valley:** a peaceful picnic spot with a jetty for fishing; 17 km SW. **Rapid Bay:** this seaside town offers excellent fishing and diving opportunities. Sightings of the endangered leafy sea dragon in the bay make diving a must for any enthusiast; 27 km SW. **Talisker Conservation Park:** an interpretive trail explains the old silver-mine workings in the park; 30 km SW. **Cape Jervis:** breathtaking sea and coastal views on entering town. Vehicular ferries to Kangaroo Island depart from here, and it is also the starting point of the 1200 km Heysen Trail (bushwalking trail) to the Flinders Ranges. Morgan's and Fishery beaches nearby have good fishing; 35 km S.

See also FLEURIEU PENINSULA, p. 235

Yorketown

Pop. 687
Map ref. 599 E8 | 602 H9

 SYP Telecentre, Yorketown or Harvest Corner Visitor Information Centre, 29 Main St; (08) 8853 2600 or 1800 202 445; www.yorkepeninsula.com.au

98.9 Flow FM, 639 AM ABC North and West

Yorketown is a small rural community at the southern end of Yorke Peninsula. The surrounding landscape is dotted with many inland salt lakes, some of which are still mined. In the late 1840s farmers were eager to take up land here as it was prime crop-producing land. The town was settled in 1872 and has remained an important service centre on the peninsula since.

Courthouse Photographic Display: photographs of the area's pioneering days; open Fri mornings or by appt.

Marion Bay Tavern: relaxed beachside meals; Stenhouse Bay Rd, Marion Bay; (08) 8854 4141.

Innes National Park Heritage Accommodation: roomy, rustic cottages; Inneston, Innes National Park; (08) 8854 3200. **Marion Bay Holiday Villas:** peaceful seaside cottages; Cnr Waratah Ave and Templetonia Cres, Marion Bay; (08) 8854 4142.

Innes National Park In summer, soak up the sun at beaches or bays with excellent (but challenging) surf breaks at Chinamans Reef, Pondalowie Bay and West Cape. In winter, keep an eye out at Stenhouse Bay and Cape Spencer for migrating southern right whales. Diving is popular, especially near the Gap, an eroded gap in a 60 m high cliff. Other activities include beach and jetty fishing, and walking on coastal and inland tracks. Accommodation is something special in this park – enjoy fabulous coastal camping in the mallee scrub or stay at the heritage lodge in the old mining township of Inneston. The annual Yorke Surfing Classic is held here each Oct. (08) 8854 3200; 81 km SW.

Ballywire Farm and Tearooms: Experience a fully working farm by joining in farming activities. Tearooms and a licensed restaurant on-site, as well as farm produce for sale, interactive displays and a games area for kids; open 10am–5pm Wed–Sun (daily school holidays); (08) 8852 1053; 11km S. **Bublacowie Military Museum:** personal stories, memorabilia and documents, and also a craft centre; closed Mon; 25 km N. **Corny Point:** coastal town featuring a lighthouse and lookout, and fishing and camping; 69 km NW. **Daly Head:** great surfing spot with nearby blowhole; 75 km W. **Marion Bay:** popular with surfers and visitors to nearby Innes National Park; 79 km SW.

See also YORKE PENINSULA, p. 240

 RADIO STATIONS   IN TOWN   WHAT'S ON   WHERE TO EAT   WHERE TO STAY   NEARBY

 SOUTH AUSTRALIA

WESTERN AUSTRALIA is...

Spending a day at Perth's beaches, including COTTESLOE / Eating fish and chips on

FREMANTLE'S WHARF / Seeing magnificent beaches and searching for quokkas on

ROTTNEST ISLAND / Taking a camel ride along CABLE BEACH, Broome / Sampling

wines at cellar doors in MARGARET RIVER / Feeding dolphins at MONKEY MIA /

WESTERN AUSTRALIA

[FISHING ALONG SHARK BAY, PERON PENINSULA]

A scenic flight over the Bungle Bungles in PURNULULU NATIONAL PARK / Walking

through giant stands of karri and tingle trees in the VALLEY OF THE GIANTS /

A visit to NAMBUNG NATIONAL PARK, home to the moonscape of limestone pillars

known as the PINNACLES / Swimming with whale sharks in NINGALOO REEF

WESTERN AUSTRALIA

is defined by its size. Spanning an area of 2.5 million square kilometres, it covers one-third of the Australian continent. In dramatic contrast to its size, its population is just over two million, around one-tenth of Australia's total population. Over 72 per cent of Western Australians live in or around the capital city of Perth.

Within this great state are incredibly diverse landscapes – an ancient terrain of rugged ranges and dramatic gorges to the north, towering forests to the south, arid deserts to the east and 12 889 kilometres of the world's most pristine coastline to the west. To match the huge variety in landscape are huge differences in climate, from the tropical humidity of the north and the dryness of the desert to the temperate Mediterranean-style climate of the South-West.

After driving for hours along empty highways, you'll get a true feeling for the state's vastness. But you will be amply rewarded when you reach your destination. Western Australia boasts precious natural features, including the 350-million-year-old Bungle Bungle Range, the limestone sentinels of the Pinnacles Desert and the majestic karri forests of the South-West.

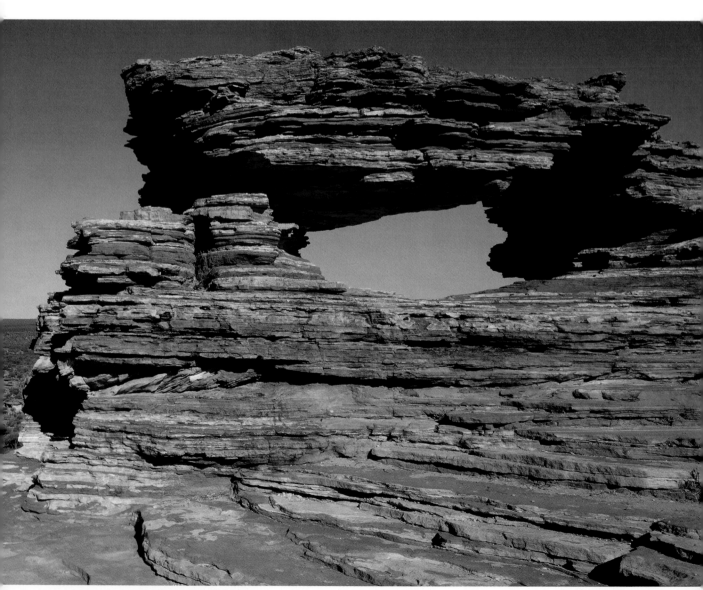

[NATURE'S WINDOW, KALBARRI NATIONAL PARK]

There is the extraordinary marine life of Ningaloo Reef, the friendly dolphins of Monkey Mia and Rottnest Island's famous quokkas.

Western Australia's historic sites are also a highlight. The Aboriginal people who first inhabited the land up to 65 000 years ago left a legacy of distinctive rock art. Albany, the site of the state's first European settlement in 1826, boasts well-preserved heritage buildings, while gracious 19th-century buildings in the capital city of Perth and its nearby port of Fremantle hark back to the days of the Swan River Colony. Remnants of great gold discoveries remain around Coolgardie and Kalgoorlie from the 1890s, which transformed Western Australia into one of the world's great producers of gold, iron ore, nickel, diamonds, mineral sands and natural gas.

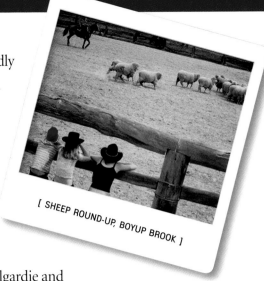

[SHEEP ROUND-UP, BOYUP BROOK]

fact file

Population 2 259 500
Total land area 2 529 875 square kilometres
People per square kilometre 0.8
Sheep and cattle per square kilometre 9.8
Nearest interstate city Adelaide, 2700 kilometres east
Length of coastline 12 889 kilometres
Number of islands 3747
Longest river Gascoyne River (760 kilometres)
Largest constructed reservoir Lake Argyle (storage volume 10 760 million cubic metres)
Highest mountain Mount Meharry (1253 metres), Karijini National Park
Highest waterfall King George Falls (80 metres), northern Kimberley
Highest town Tom Price (747 metres)
Hottest place Marble Bar (160 days a year over 37.5°C)
Coldest place Bridgetown (33 days a year begin at below 2°C)
Most remote town Warburton
Strangest place name Walkaway
Most famous person Rolf Harris
Quirkiest festival Milk Carton Regatta, Hillarys Boat Harbour
Number of wildflowers 12 500 species
Most challenging road Gibb River Road, the Kimberley
Best beach Cable Beach, Broome
Most identifiable food Pavlova (created at Perth's Esplanade Hotel)
Local beer Swan Lager

gift ideas

Gold nuggets (Kalgoorlie–Boulder)
Visit the Australian Prospectors and Mining Hall of Fame to find gold nuggets in presentation cases and on chains as pendants.
See Kalgoorlie–Boulder p. 338, 620 H5

Cricket merchandise (WACA, East Perth)
Cricket lovers will be thrilled to receive a memento from the world-famous Western Australian Cricket Association grounds.
See Museums p. 298, 292 E3

Ugg boots (Uggs-N-Rugs, Kenwick, Perth) These iconic sheepskin footwear are available around Australia, but in January 2006, Uggs-N-Rugs won a legal battle to remove an American company's trademark for 'ugh boots' from the Australian Trademarks Registry – a major victory for Australian manufacturers.
9 Royal St, Kenwick. 614 E7

Arts and crafts (Fremantle Markets, Fremantle) Over 150 stalls sell everything from local arts, crafts and clothes to fresh produce. See Fremantle Markets p. 302, 301 B2

Argyle diamonds (The Kimberley)
Diamonds of unique brilliance in various colours, including the world's only intense pink diamonds. See Kimberley p. 314, 625 K5

Freshwater pearls (Broome) With its unique pearling heritage, exquisite pearl jewellery is available all over Broome. Willie Creek Pearls also has a showroom in Sorrento Quay, Hillarys Boat Harbour, north of Perth.
See Broome p. 320, 624 H8

Wine (Margaret River) There is an abundance of fine wine to choose from in this top wine-producing region. See Margaret River p. 346, 616 B8

Jarrah, karri and marri woodwork (South-West region) Western Australia's unique woods are turned into handcrafted furniture, boxes, bowls, platters, salt and pepper grinders, to name but a few.
See The South-West p. 307, 616

Wood-fired bread, biscuits and nut cake (New Norcia) Made by New Norcia's Benedictine monk community. Their rich, intensely flavoured, panforte-style nut cake is also available at the New Norcia Bakeries at 163 Scarborough Beach Rd, Mount Hawthorn, and Bagot Rd, Subiaco. See New Norcia p. 352, 618 C2

Quokka soft toy (Rottnest Island) Get a soft toy version of this small marsupial, which famously lives on 'Rotto', from the general store or gift shop. See Rottnest Island p. 305, 615 A6

PERTH is...

Views across the city from KINGS PARK / SWIMMING at any of Perth's beaches / Eating fish 'n' chips on FREMANTLE'S WHARF / Sipping a coffee on the 'cappuccino strip' of SOUTH TERRACE, Fremantle / Seeing black swans at LAKE MONGER / A cricket match at the WACA / A picnic on the MATILDA BAY foreshore / A visit to the WESTERN AUSTRALIAN MUSEUM / Eating out in NORTHBRIDGE / Browsing the eclectic offerings at the FREMANTLE MARKETS / A footy match at SUBIACO OVAL / Touring the forbidding FREMANTLE PRISON

VISITOR INFORMATION
Western Australian Visitor Centre
→ Cnr Forrest Pl and Wellington St
→ 1300 361 351 or 1800 812 808
www.westernaustralia.com;
www.wavisitorcentre.com

Perth is the most isolated capital city in the world, closer to Singapore than it is to Sydney. Its nearest neighbour, Adelaide, is 2700 kilometres away by road. Yet it is exactly this isolation that has allowed Perth to retain a feeling of space and relaxed charm.

Claimed to be the sunniest state capital in Australia, Perth has a Mediterranean climate: hot and dry in summer, cool and wet in winter. This climate, and the city's proximity to both river and ocean, fosters a relaxed lifestyle for the population of 1 603 000. One of Perth's great attributes is that its water frontages are public land, accessible to everyone. Picnicking is a popular pastime, while cafes and bars spill their tables and chairs out onto pavements to make the most of the glorious weather.

Yet for all Perth's coastal beauty, it is the Swan River that defines the city. North of the river is Kings Park and the old-money riverside suburbs with their grand homes; further on are the beaches and the newer northern beach suburbs stretching up the coast. At the mouth of the Swan is the historic port city of Fremantle, with its rich maritime history, creative community and street-cafe culture. Upstream from Perth – where the river dwindles to a meandering waterway – is the Swan Valley, the state's oldest wine district.

City Centre

Perth's city centre is a compact mix of towering skyscrapers and elegant colonial buildings. It is bordered to the south and east by the Swan River, with stretches of grassy parkland fringing the riverbank. Perth's central business district (CBD) harbours the city's large pedestrian-only shopping precinct, made up of a series of malls and arcades. This is connected northwards to the Perth train station by an overhead walkway across Wellington Street. To the west, the ultra-hip King Street is renowned for its gourmet cafes, galleries and fashion houses. On the south side of the city is St Georges Terrace, the main commercial street, a strip of high-rise buildings interspersed with remnants of Perth's early British heritage. Just beyond it is the main bus depot, the Esplanade Busport, and at the river end of Barrack Street is the city's jetty at Barrack Square.

Malls, arcades & a touch of old England 294 B2

Perth's central shopping precinct is in the blocks bounded by St Georges Terrace and William, Wellington and Barrack streets. These three main shopping blocks encompass the vehicle-free zones of **Hay Street Mall**, **Murray Street Mall** and **Forrest Place**. Between them, the two malls contain a swag of brand-name fashion outlets, bookstores and homewares shops. The big department stores of Myer and David Jones both have entrances on Murray Street Mall, and the western side of Forrest Place is home to the GPO. A series of arcades and underground walkways run from Murray Street Mall through to Hay Street Mall and on to St Georges Terrace, making it possible to shop in the city without ever crossing a street. **Carillon City** is a modern shopping centre between the malls, while **London Court**, an arcade with the appearance of a quaint Elizabethan street, runs from Hay Street Mall to St Georges Terrace, and is Perth's only open-air arcade. At the mall end, knights joust above a replica of Big Ben every 15 minutes, while St George and the Dragon do battle above the clock at the St Georges Terrace end.

King Street 294 B2

This historic precinct of commercial buildings between Hay and Wellington streets dates from the 1890s gold rush. While the street has been restored to its turn-of-the-century character, its commercial interests are entirely modern: designer fashion houses, specialist bookstores, art galleries and gourmet cafes, such as the ever-popular **No 44 King Street**, with its homemade bread and extensive wine list.

St Georges Terrace 294 A2, B2

The city's main commercial street is lined with modern office towers that overshadow a number of historic buildings. At the western end of the terrace is the **Barracks Archway**, the only remains of the Pensioners' Barracks, a structure that originally had two wings and 120 rooms. This building housed the retired British soldiers who guarded convicts in the mid-1800s. The **Central Government Building** on the corner of Barrack Street marks the spot where Perth was founded with a tree-felling ceremony in 1829. Around 50 years later, convicts and hired labour commenced work on the building that stands there today. At one stage it housed the GPO, and a plaque on the building's east corner marks the point from which all distances in the state are measured. Other historic buildings along the terrace include the Cloisters, the Old Perth Boys' School, the Deanery, St George's Cathedral, Government House and the Old Court House *(see Grand old buildings, p. 298).* As you're walking along the Terrace, look out for the commemorative plaques inlaid in the footpath which celebrate the achievements of over 170 notable Western Australians. This was a sesquicentennial project in 1979 celebrating 150 years since the foundation of the Swan River Colony.

City gardens 294 C2, C3

Two delightful city gardens are located in the block bounded by St Georges Terrace, Riverside Drive, Barrack Street and Victoria Avenue. **Stirling Gardens** offer ornamental trees, well-kept lawns and plenty of shady spots. Along the footpath on the St Georges Terrace side there are large statues of kangaroos – a great photo opportunity. Just nearby within the gardens is an ore obelisk, a memorial acknowledging the state's role as one of the world's foremost producers of minerals. Look carefully in the garden beds from the footpath on the Barrack

climate

Perth is Australia's sunniest capital, with an annual average of eight hours of sunshine per day. All this sunshine gives Perth a Mediterranean climate of hot, dry summers and mild, wet winters. The average maximum temperature in summer is 31°C; however, heat waves of temperatures in the high 30s and low 40s are not unusual. Fortunately, an afternoon sea breeze affectionately known as 'the Fremantle Doctor' eases the heat of summer.

J	F	M	A	M	J	J	A	S	O	N	D	
30	31	29	25	22	19	18	18	20	22	26	28	MAX °C
17	17	16	13	10	8	7	8	9	11	14	16	MIN °C
8	12	19	45	123	184	173	136	80	54	21	14	RAIN MM
3	3	4	8	14	17	18	17	14	11	6	4	RAIN DAYS

Street side of the gardens and you'll find small statues of May Gibbs' 'Gumnut Babies' nestled amongst the ferns. The gardens also house the oldest public building in Perth, now the Francis Burt Law Museum (*see Museums, p. 298*). The **Supreme Court Gardens**, further towards Riverside Drive, are a popular location for concerts on warm summer evenings, including the annual Carols by Candlelight.

Bells & a jetty 294 B3

Barrack Square, at the water's edge south of the city, is where you'll find the Swan Bells and the ferry jetty. The Barrack Street Jetty is the departure point for ferry services to Fremantle, South Perth, Rottnest Island and Carnac Island, along with various leisure cruises on the Swan River and to the vineyards of the Swan Valley. Behind Jetty 6 is the Willem de Vlamingh Memorial, which features a sundial indicating Amsterdam time and many historical references.

The Swan Bells consist of 18 'change-ringing' bells, which form the largest set in the world. Twelve of the bells, given to the state in 1988 by the British government, come from London's St Martin-in-the-Fields church. The bell tower – which cost $6 million to build amid great controversy – offers galleries from which you can view the bellringers and the bells in action. A viewing platform at the top of the bell tower provides excellent views of the river and city. *Barrack Sq, cnr Barrack St and Riverside Dr; (08) 6210 0444; open from 10am daily, closing times vary*

seasonally (check the website, www.swanbells.com.au); full bell ringing 12–1pm Mon, Tues, Thurs and Sat–Sun.

Northbridge

Northbridge, which lies north of the city centre across the train line, is Perth's centre for the arts and the heart of the city's nightlife. This inner-city suburb is connected to the city centre via a walkway that crosses Perth Railway Station and leads directly to the Perth Cultural Centre. Bounded by Roe, Francis, Beaufort and William streets, the Perth Cultural Centre includes the state museum, art gallery, state library and Perth's institute of contemporary arts. William Street and the streets further west are packed with restaurants and bars that offer great eating, drinking and nightclubbing.

Art Gallery of Western Australia 294 C1

The state's principal public art gallery, founded in 1895, houses collections of Australian and international paintings, sculpture, prints, craft and decorative arts. The gallery's collection of Aboriginal art is one of the finest in Australia. *Perth Cultural Centre, James St Mall; (08) 9492 6622 (24-hour information line) or (08) 9492 6600; open 10am–5pm Wed–Mon; general admission free; free guided tours available.*

Western Australian Museum 294 C1

At this comprehensive museum you can see a 25-metre whale skeleton, the 11-tonne Mundrabilla meteorite and 'Megamouth', a rare species of shark. There are exhibitions concerning the state's Aboriginal people; the origins of the universe; and dinosaur, bird, butterfly, mammal and marine galleries. The interactive Discovery Centre is great for children. Within the museum complex is the **Old Gaol**, built in 1856 and used by the Swan River Colony until 1888. *Perth Cultural Centre, James St Mall; (08) 9212 3700; open 9.30am–5pm Thurs–Tues; admission by donation; free guided tours available.*

Perth Institute of Contemporary Arts 294 B1

Commonly referred to by its acronym, PICA, the Perth Institute of Contemporary Arts is where you can sample the latest in visual and performance art. There is an ever-changing program of exhibitions. *Perth Cultural Centre, James St Mall; (08) 9228 6300; open 11am–6pm Tues–Sun; general admission free.*

East Perth

East Perth is where you'll find the Western Australian Cricket Association oval, known colloquially as the WACA (pronounced 'Wacka'), where cricket matches entertain the crowds over the summer months. Gloucester Park Raceway, with night harness horseracing on Friday nights, is nearby. Once the dead end of town – except when night matches or race meets lit up the night sky – East Perth is now an enclave of offices and hip inner-city apartments. There are two historically significant sites in this precinct, the Perth Mint and Queens Gardens.

The Perth Mint 294 D2

The Mint's imposing facade was built in 1899 from Rottnest Island limestone, and is one of the best examples of Perth's gold-boom architecture. Here at Australia's oldest operating mint you can see the world's largest collection of natural gold specimens, including the 'Golden Beauty', a 11.5-kilogram nugget. Visitors can hold a 400-ounce gold bar, mint their own coins, take a guided tour and watch gold being poured. *310 Hay St (cnr Hill St), East Perth; (08) 9421 7277; open 9am–5pm Mon–Fri, 9am–1pm Sat–Sun and public holidays.*

Queens Gardens 292 E3

The serene, English-style Queens Gardens feature a tranquil water garden complete with a replica of the famous Peter Pan statue that graces London's Kensington Gardens. These gardens were originally clay pits, where bricks were kilned for use in early colonial buildings such as the Perth Town Hall. *Cnr Hay and Plain sts.*

WACA 292 E3

Across Hale Street from Queens Gardens is the WACA, the home of the state's cricket team, the Western Warriors. True lovers of the sport should visit the WACA's cricket museum *(see Museums, p. 298).*

getting around

The city is compact and easy to explore. A free bus service known as the CAT (Central Area Transit) System operates regular services, every five–ten minutes, around central Perth. The blue CAT runs in a north–south loop, the red CAT operates in an east–west loop, and the yellow CAT travels to the city centre from East Perth. (Note that a CAT bus also services Fremantle.) You can also travel free on Transperth buses or trains within the Free Transit Zone in the city centre, but only on trips that start and finish within the zone.

Trains run from the city out to the northern suburbs and down to Fremantle while the Southern Suburbs Railway links Perth to Mandurah. Ferries and cruise boats depart regularly from Barrack Street Jetty to various destinations, including Fremantle, South Perth, Rottnest Island and the Swan Valley wine region. (Transperth runs the ferry to South Perth, while private operators travel further afield.) Perth, with its largely flat landscape, is also excellent for cycling; maps of the city's 700-kilometre bike network are available at bike shops or online at the Department of Transport website, www.transport.wa.gov.au.

Public transport Transperth (bus, train and ferry) 13 6213.

Airport shuttle bus Airport–city shuttle 1300 666 806.

Swan River and Rottnest ferries and cruises Captain Cook Cruises (08) 9325 3341; Oceanic Cruises (08) 9325 1191.

Motoring organisation RAC of WA (08) 9301 3113 or 13 1703.

Car rental Avis 13 6333; Budget 13 2727; Hertz 13 3039; Thrifty 13 6139.

Taxis Black and White Taxis 13 1008; Swan Taxis 13 1330.

Bicycle hire About Bike Hire (08) 9221 2665.

See also Getting to Fremantle, p. 301

top events

Hopman Cup Prestigious international tennis event. January.

Perth Cup Western Australia's premier horseracing event. January.

Australia Day Skyworks A day-long party of events, culminating in a spectacular fireworks display. January.

Perth International Arts Festival Music, theatre, opera, dance, visual arts and film. February.

City of Perth Winter Arts Festival A three-month program of locally created arts and culture. June–August.

Kings Park Wildflower Festival Australia's premier native plant and wildflower exhibition. September.

Perth Royal Show Showcases the state's primary and secondary resources. September–October.

Red Bull Air Race A weekend of jaw-dropping, low-level aerial racing over the Swan River. November.

See also Top events in Fremantle, p. 302

shopping

London Court Mock-Tudor arcade with souvenir, jewellery and antique stores. 294 B2

Hay Street Mall, Murray Street Mall and Forrest Place
The CBD's main shopping precinct with brand-name fashion outlets and major department stores Myer and David Jones. 294 B2

King Street High fashion, galleries and cafes with style. 294 B2

Rokeby Road, Subiaco Funky local designers sit alongside more established labels. 292 C3

Bay View Terrace, Claremont Perth's up-market fashion hot spot. 292 B5

Napoleon Street, Cottesloe Cafes, boutiques and designer homewares. 292 B5

[THE FUTURISTIC SWAN BELLS TOWER]

markets

The Markets @ Perth Cultural Centre The only regular weekend market in the city with produce, flowers and arts and crafts. 8.30am–5pm Sat–Sun. 294 C1

Subiaco Pavilion Markets Art and craft stalls with large food hall in restored warehouse adjacent to station. Cnr Rokeby and Roberts rds, Subiaco; 10am–9pm Thurs–Fri, 10am–5pm Sat–Sun. 292 C3

Subiaco Station Street Markets A colourful outdoor and undercover market with an eclectic array of goods and live entertainment. 41 Station St, Subiaco; (08) 9382 2832; 9am–5.30pm Fri–Sun. 292 C3

Scarborough Fair Markets Specialty stalls and a food hall on Scarborough Beach. 9am–5.30pm Sat–Sun. 292 A1

Canning Vale Markets Huge undercover flea markets, and the primary fruit and vegetable wholesale market for the state. Cnr South St and Bannister Rd; 7am–1pm Sun. 615 C6

Wanneroo Markets Huge undercover markets with food court selling everything from locally grown fruit and vegetables to footwear and jewellery. 33 Prindiville Dr, Wangara; (08) 9409 8397; 9am–5pm Fri–Sun. 615 B4

See also Fremantle Markets, p. 302

Inner East

Burswood Entertainment Complex 293 F3

Built on an artificial island on the southern banks of the Swan River, this complex includes a casino, hotel, convention centre, tennis courts, golf course and Burswood Dome indoor stadium (the venue for the Hopman Cup). The Atrium Lobby has an impressive 47-metre-high pyramid of shimmering glass containing a tropical garden and waterfall. Burswood Park, the beautifully landscaped gardens that surround the complex, offers paths for walkers, cyclists and joggers, a heritage trail and a children's playground. *Great Eastern Hwy, Burswood; (08) 9362 7777.*

Inner North

Tranby House 293 F3

Just beyond East Perth in the suburb of Maylands is historic Tranby House. Built in 1839 overlooking the picturesque Swan River, Tranby is one of the oldest surviving buildings from the early settlement of the Swan River Colony and is a unique example of colonial farmhouse architecture. A major attraction is the property's gardens which feature two century-old oak trees. The house has been beautifully restored by the National Trust. *Johnson Rd, Maylands; (08) 9272 2630; open 10am–4pm Wed–Sun (closed 24 Dec – 6 Feb).*

Inner West

Just minutes from the city centre, Kings Park is visited by millions of people each year. Beyond it at the end of Kings Park Road is the suburb of Subiaco, with its popular shopping, cafe and market precinct. Below Kings Park, Mounts Bay Road winds its way along the river's edge to the suburb of Crawley, passing the Old Swan Brewery site, now a riverside complex of up-market offices, apartments and restaurants. The distinctive clock tower of the University of Western Australia's Winthrop Hall is an easily spotted landmark. Across Matilda Bay Road from the university is the grassy Matilda Bay shoreline, with shady spots and views back up the river towards the city.

Kings Park & Botanic Garden 292 D4

The first stop for any visitor to Perth has to be Kings Park. Standing on top of Mount Eliza, you enjoy sweeping views of the city and the Swan River, with the Darling Range in the distance. Within this huge 400-hectare natural bushland reserve there are landscaped gardens and walkways, lakes, playgrounds, a restaurant and cafes.

Fraser Avenue, the main entrance road into the park, is lined with towering lemon-scented gums, honouring those who perished in war. The clock tower and bronze portrait bust at this entrance is a memorial to Edith Cowan, the first woman elected to an Australian parliament. A tireless advocate for women's rights and children's welfare, she now lends her name to one of Perth's universities.

Opened in 2003, the Lotterywest Federation Walkway is a combination of on-ground pathways, elevated walkway and spectacular steel-and-glass bridge, extending 620 metres through the Botanic Garden. It is a snapshot of Western Australia's famed flora; at ground level you'll pass boabs, boronias and tuart trees, while the walkway through the treetops takes you close to karri, marri, tingle and jarrah trees. The Botanic Garden itself is spread over 17 hectares and planted with more than 1700 native species.

The Botanic Garden's newest attraction arrived in July 2008 when a giant boab tree weighing 36 tonnes and estimated to be 750 years old was transported 3200 kilometres from the Kimberley town of Warnum and transplanted in the garden opposite Forrest Carpark. It joins long-time favourite attractions such as the State War Memorial precinct; the Pioneer Women's Memorial, with its water fountains which periodically shoot skywards; the nearby DNA Tower, offering spectacular views; the fantastic dinosaur and fossil creations at Synergy Parkland; and the child-friendly Lotterywest Family Area.

In spring the annual Kings Park Festival showcases the best of the state's wildflowers, attracting over 500 000 visitors from around the world. This month-long event showcases all aspects of the park, with myriad spectacular events and activities. During summer the park is a favourite venue for live outdoor entertainment and moonlight movies (www.bgpa.wa.gov.au). *Fraser Ave; (08) 9480 3600; open daily; free guided walks from the visitor centre at 10am and 2pm daily.*

University of Western Australia 292 C4

With its distinctive Mediterranean-style architecture and landscaped gardens, the University of Western Australia is renowned as one of Australia's most beautiful campuses. Here you'll find **Winthrop Hall**, with its majestic clock tower and reflection pond, and the **Sunken Garden**, backdrop for many a wedding photo. The **Lawrence Wilson Art Gallery**, home to the university's extensive collection of Australian art, includes works by Sidney Nolan, Arthur Boyd, Fred Williams and Rupert Bunny.

where to eat

Aquarium Chinese restaurant with an emphasis on fresh seafood and only a few minutes from the CBD. 202 Great Eastern Hwy, Ascot; (08) 9478 1868; open Tues–Sat for lunch and dinner. 614 E6

Ha-Lu Relatively new and already an award finalist offering Japanese cuisine served in the Japanese pub style. Shop 4/401 Oxford St, Mt Hawthorn; (08) 9444 0577; open Wed–Sun for dinner. 292 D2

Must Winebar Bistro-style French Provincial cuisine with impressive wine list and always busy. 519 Beaufort St, Highgate; (08) 9328 8255; open daily for lunch and dinner. 292 E3

New Norcia Bakeries Authentic sourdough and yeasted breads baked in a traditional wood-fired oven; also many other tempting delights. 163 Scarborough Beach Rd, Mt Hawthorn; (08) 9442 4114; open daily for breakfast and lunch. 292 D2

Restaurant Amusé Michelin-star trained chef Hadleigh Troy brings an innovative degustation menu to his awaiting fans. 64 Bronte St, East Perth; (08) 9325 4900; open Tues–Sat for dinner. 292 E3

See also Where to eat in Fremantle, p. 303

35 Stirling Hwy, Crawley; (08) 6488 3707; open 11am–5pm Tues–Fri, 12–5pm Sun; admission free.

Also within the university grounds is the **Berndt Museum of Anthropology**, which houses one of Australia's finest collections of traditional and contemporary Australian Aboriginal art and artefacts. Currently in the process of relocating, the museum will be closed until the end of 2010. It will then temporarily reopen in the Lawrence Wilson Art Gallery building until its new, purpose-built home is finished. *www.berndt.uwa.edu.au*

entertainment

Cinema After once reigning supreme in town, Hoyts and Greater Union have moved out to the suburbs, leaving the city centre bereft of any major cinemas. There is, however, the Piccadilly Cinema in Piccadilly Arcade in the Hay Street Mall, which screens new-release films in Perth's only surviving grand old Art Deco cinema. The most easily accessible Hoyts cinemas are in Fremantle at the Queensgate on William Street and the Millennium on Collie Street. The closest Greater Union cinema to the city is in Innaloo. Subiaco has an independent cinema, the Ace at 500 Hay Street on the corner of Alvan. There's also Cinema Paradiso in Northbridge, the Luna Palace in Leederville, the Windsor in Nedlands, the Cygnet in Como and, in Fremantle, Luna on SX (Essex Street). In summer, there are a number of outdoor cinemas that operate; favourites are the Moonlight Cinema in Kings Park and the Somerville Auditorium at the University of Western Australia. The latter, which screens films for the Perth International Arts Festival from December through March, is defined by a cathedral of Norfolk pine trees and patrons sit on deckchair-style seats under the stars. Programs and session times, including those for the open-air cinemas over summer, are listed daily in *The West Australian.*

Live music Northbridge, Leederville and Subiaco are the places to go for live music, as a healthy pub scene supports local musicians. In Northbridge popular venues include the Brass Monkey, the Mustang Bar, the Paramount, the Elephant & Wheelbarrow and Rosie O'Grady's. The Leederville Hotel on Oxford Street has a legendary Sunday afternoon session; the Ocean Beach Hotel in Cottesloe (known locally as the 'OBH') adds sunset views from the bar. In Fremantle, the premier live music venues are the Fly by Night Musicians Club on Parry Street, Kulcha on South Terrace and Mojos in North Freo. Pick up the free street publication *Xpress* for gig guides or visit www.xpressmag.com.au. Jazz venues include the Hyde Park Hotel in Bulwer Street, North Perth; the Navy Club in High Street, Fremantle; and the Ellington Jazz Club at 191 Beaufort Street, Perth. Aficionados should visit www.jazzwa.com or phone the recorded information Jazzline on (08) 9357 2807.

Classical music and performing arts His Majesty's Theatre, Australia's only remaining Edwardian theatre, is Perth's premier venue for high-end theatre, opera and ballet. Black Swan State Theatre Company is Western Australia's flagship theatre company; there is also the Perth Theatre Company, based at the Playhouse Theatre in Pier Street. Other local productions can be seen at the Subiaco Arts Centre and the Regal Theatre, while Fremantle is home to Deckchair Theatre in High Street and Spare Parts Puppet Theatre in Short Street. The Perth Concert Hall in St Georges Terrace is the fine music venue for concerts by local and international musicians. The Burswood Entertainment Complex hosts touring shows and musicals; ME Bank Stadium in East Perth is the venue for big international acts. In the warmer months, outdoor concerts are held in the Supreme Court and Queens Gardens, and in Kings Park. Check *The West Australian* for details.

grand old buildings

Government House Gothic arches and turrets reminiscent of the Tower of London. St Georges Tce (opposite Pier St).

His Majesty's Theatre 'The Maj', built in 1904, features an opulent Edwardian exterior. 825 Hay St; free foyer tours 10am–4pm Mon–Fri.

Kirkman House In front of this gracious edifice is an immense Moreton Bay fig tree, planted in the 1890s and now classified by the National Trust. 10 Murray St.

Old Court House Perth's oldest surviving building (1836), now home to the Francis Burt Law Museum. Cnr St Georges Tce and Barrack St.

Old Perth Boys' School Perth's first purpose-built school was made from sandstone ferried up the Swan River by convict labour. 139 St Georges Tce.

Perth Town Hall Built by convict labour (1867–70) in the style of an English Jacobean market hall. Cnr Hay and Barrack sts.

St George's Cathedral This 1879 Anglican church features an impressive jarrah ceiling. 38 St Georges Tce.

St Mary's Cathedral Grand Gothic-style cathedral, one end of which was built in 1865. Victoria Sq.

The Cloisters Check out the decorative brickwork of this 1858 building, originally a boys' school. The old banyan tree adjoining it is something special too. 200 St Georges Tce.

See also Fremantle's grand old buildings, p. 302

museums

Fire and Emergency Services Education and Heritage Centre Refurbished in 2009, this limestone building dating from 1900 houses exhibitions on the history of the Perth fire brigade, including fire rescue and old Big Red engines. Cnr Murray and Irwin sts; (08) 9323 9353; 10am–4pm Tues–Thurs; admission free.

Francis Burt Law Museum The history of the state's legal system is housed in the Old Court House. Stirling Gardens, cnr St Georges Tce and Barrack St; (08) 9325 4787; open 10am–2.30pm Wed–Fri; admission free.

Museum of Performing Arts Entertainment history brought to life through exhibitions of costumes and memorabilia taken from backstage archives. His Majesty's Theatre, 825 Hay St; (08) 9265 0900; open 10am–4pm Mon–Fri; admission by gold coin donation.

WACA Museum Offers cricket memorabilia for fans of the sport. Gate 2, Nelson Cres, East Perth; (08) 9265 7222; open 10am–3pm Mon–Fri except match days; tours of ground and museum run at 10am and 1pm Mon–Thurs.

Army Museum of Western Australia Houses WA army memorabilia dating from colonial times to the present day. Artillery Barracks, Burt St, Fremantle; (08) 9430 2535; open 11am–4pm Wed–Sun.

See also The Perth Mint, p. 295, Western Australian Museum, p. 295, Western Australian Maritime Museum, p. 302, Shipwreck Galleries, p. 302, and Fremantle Arts Centre, p. 303

Foreshore suburbs 292 C4, C5

Extending along the river foreshore from Matilda Bay towards the ocean is a series of exclusive waterfront suburbs with charming village-style shopping areas, fashionable galleries and foreshore restaurants. **Nedlands** is the suburb closest to the University of Western Australia. **Dalkeith's** Jutland Parade takes you to Point Resolution, with magnificent views of the river to the south and west. Follow the walking paths down the hillside to White Beach on the foreshore, a popular recreational spot.

Subiaco 292 C3

Beyond West Perth is the popular shopping, cafe and market precinct of Subiaco, with its village-style main street, Rokeby Road (pronounced 'Rock-a-bee'). 'Subi', as it is known to the locals, is one of Perth's oldest suburbs, and there are some fine old homes in the back streets behind Rokeby Road. The word Subiaco rings a bell for AFL supporters too, as it is the home of **Subiaco Oval**.

Parliament House 292 D3

Go inside the corridors of power on a free, 45-minute guided tour. *Harvest Tce, West Perth; (08) 9222 7259; tours 10.30am Mon and Thurs.*

Scitech Discovery Centre 292 D3

This interactive science and technology centre has more than 160 hands-on exhibits. You can touch, switch, climb, crank and explore – all in the name of science. There's also **Horizon**, a state-of-the-art planetarium screening extraordinary journeys into space on the largest dome screen in the Southern Hemisphere. *City West, cnr Sutherland and Railway sts, West Perth; (08) 9215 0700; open 9.30am–4pm Mon–Fri, 10am–5pm Sat–Sun, school holidays and public holidays.*

Inner North-west

Lake Monger 292 C3

Lake Monger, a large urban wetland 5 kilometres north of Perth's CBD in the suburb of Wembley, is the best place in Perth to see Western Australia's famous black swans. Ever since 1697, when Dutch explorer Willem de Vlamingh named the Swan River after the numerous black swans he found on its waters, the majestic waterbirds have been inextricably linked with Western Australia. The first settlement was named the Swan River Colony, and the black swan became the official State Bird Emblem of Western Australia in 1973.

South-western Beachside

With pristine white-sand beaches stretching northwards up the coast, swimming and surfing are a way of life in Perth. Several stunning beaches, including Cottesloe, are close to the city. Scattered along these beach-fronts are lovely cafes, restaurants and bars. Enjoy the sublime Perth experience of sipping a glass of Western Australian wine as you watch the sun sink into the Indian Ocean.

Cottesloe 292 A5

Cottesloe is distinguished by its towering Norfolk Island pines and the **Indiana Cottesloe Beach Restaurant**, a neo-colonial

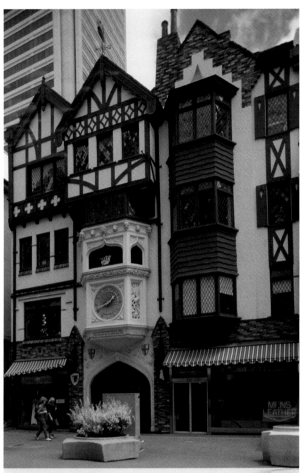

[LONDON COURT]

building of grand proportions that sits right on the beach. *91 Marine Pde, Cottesloe; (08) 9385 5005.*

The Spanish-style **Cottesloe Civic Centre**, once the private mansion of flamboyant millionaire Claude de Bernales, boasts magnificent gardens with sweeping views of the Indian Ocean. *109 Broome St; (08) 9285 5000; open daily; admission free.*

Claremont 292 B4

This up-market suburb is home to Perth's swankiest shopping area, centred around Bay View Terrace. The **Claremont Museum**, on Victoria Avenue, was built in 1862 by convicts and the Pensioner Guards as the Freshwater Bay School. It now offers an interesting social history display of more than 9000 items related to the district, including artefacts, photographs, oral history tapes and documents. The main exhibitions are housed in the schoolhouse, which has been carefully preserved to provide a glimpse into the colonial education system. Nearby is a children's playground and picnic area. *66 Victoria Ave, Claremont; (08) 9340 6983; open 12–4pm Mon–Fri; admission free.*

Peppermint Grove 292 B5

Peppermint Grove boasts some of Perth's grandest homes. A drive along The Esplanade takes you past grass-backed riverside beaches, natural bushland and shady picnic areas. Follow the road around to Bay View Park – another great place for picnicking – in Mosman Park, and up the hill for sweeping views of Mosman Bay, the Swan River and Perth city skyline.

galleries

Aspects of Kings Park Contemporary Australian craft and design, with a focus on local artists. Fraser Ave, Kings Park and Botanic Garden, West Perth; (08) 9480 3900; open 9am–5pm daily.

Indigenart Mossenson Galleries One of Australia's foremost Aboriginal art galleries.115 Hay St, Subiaco; (08) 9388 2899; open 10am–5pm Mon–Fri, 11am–4pm Sat.

Greenhill Galleries New York–style gallery features works of leading Australian artists. 16 Gugeri St, Claremont; (08) 9383 4433; open 10am–5pm Tues–Fri, 10am–4pm Sat.

Holmes à Court Gallery Changing display of works from Australia's finest private art collection. Level 1, 11 Brown St, East Perth; (08) 9218 4540; open 12–5pm Wed–Sun; general admission free.

Kailis Australian Pearls Perfectly matched strands and handcrafted pieces made from exquisite cultured and seedless pearls. 29 King St; (08) 9422 3888; cnr Marine Tce and Collie St, Fremantle; (08) 9239 9330.

See also Art Gallery of Western Australia, p. 294, and Perth Institute of Contemporary Arts, p. 295

North-western Beachside

Scarborough 292 A2

Renowned for its beachside cafe society, the beach here is a top spot for surfers and sailboarders. The five-star Rendezvous Observation City Hotel dominates the landscape, reminiscent of the Gold Coast resorts. On weekends the Scarborough Fair Markets set up stalls just opposite the hotel, where you can shop for antiques, bric-a-brac, arts and crafts plus – of course – surf gear and hippie wear. *Cnr Scarborough Beach Rd and West Coast Hwy; open 9am–5.30pm Sat–Sun.*

where to stay

Burswood Entertainment Complex Complex includes five-star resort, 24-hour casino, golf course, day-spa, bars and many restaurants. Great Eastern Hwy, Burswood; (08) 9362 7777. 293 F3

Medina Apartments Situated in two locations in the CDB, both complexes include self-contained studios, one- and two-bedroom apartments. 33 Mounts Bay Rd and 138 Barrack St; 1300 633 462. 294 A2

Pension of Perth Romantic and historic B&B, each room has been restored to its former glory and includes an en-suite. 3 Throssell St; (08) 9228 9049. 292 D3

The Old Swan Barracks Built in 1896, the converted barracks offer budget accommodation close to nightlife and the CBD. 2–8 Francis St, Northbridge; (08) 9428 0000. 294 C1

The Outram One of the city's most luxurious places to stay and situated in the elite West Perth district. 32 Outram St; (08) 9322 4888. 292 D3

See also Where to stay in Fremantle, p. 303

sport

AFL (Australian Football League) is the most popular spectator sport in Perth, with crowds flocking to Subiaco Oval from April through September to support their local teams, the West Coast Eagles and the Fremantle Dockers. Subiaco Oval is also home to Western Australia's **Rugby Union** team, the Western Force, which plays in the Super 14 international rugby union competition.

The **cricket** season takes up where the footy leaves off, with the famous WACA hosting both interstate and international test matches over the summer months.

Perth's **soccer** club, the Perth Glory, play at ME Bank Stadium (formerly Members Equity Stadium) in East Perth. **Basketball** fans can catch the popular Perth Wildcats from September to February at Challenge Stadium in Mount Claremont, while their female counterparts, the Perth Lynx, play nearby at the new $44 million WA Basketball Centre.

In January, Perth's Burswood Dome hosts the Hopman Cup, a prestigious international **tennis** event.

Horseracing is a year-round event, split between two venues: Ascot racecourse in summer and Belmont Park in winter. Events such as the Perth Cup (held on New Year's Day), the Easter Racing Carnival and the Opening Day at Ascot draw huge crowds. Night harness racing can be seen at Gloucester Park every Friday night.

Hillarys Boat Harbour 615 B4

This ocean-side complex houses a marina, a world-class aquarium *(see next entry)*, and Sorrento Quay, a 'village' of shops, cafes, restaurants and resort apartments. If the beautiful sandy beaches are too tame for you, try The Great Escape, a leisure park with water slides, miniature golf and trampolines. Ferries to Rottnest Island run from Hillarys, and there are whale-watching cruises from September to November. If you visit in March, be sure to attend the Milk Carton Regatta, a fundraising event for the local telethon. Competitors in this wacky boatrace build their craft entirely from milk cartons, then dress up to coordinate with their creative craft and paddle for glory. The day also includes a sand sculpture competition that produces amazing results and plenty of other beachside entertainment. *Southside Dr, Hillarys; Boat Harbour, (08) 9448 7544; Sorrento Quay, (08) 9246 9788.*

Aquarium of Western Australia (AQWA) 615 B4

The highlight of this attraction, housing five different aquariums, is an incredible 98-metre underwater tunnel aquarium, surrounded by approximately 3 million litres of the Indian Ocean. Here you'll see thousands of marine creatures including sharks, stingrays, seals, crocodiles, sea dragons and turtles. For the ultimate underwater sensation, visitors can snorkel or swim with sharks. *Hillarys Boat Harbour, 91 Southside Dr, Hillarys; (08) 9447 7500; open 10am–5pm daily.*

Inner South

Perth Zoo 292 D4

Perth Zoo, with its shady gardens, walkways and picnic areas, is just a short ferry ride across the river from the city. Visit the Australian Walkabout for a close-up look at native animals in a bush setting. Other exhibits include the Penguin Plunge, African Savannah, Reptile Encounter and Rainforest Retreat. *20 Labouchere Rd, South Perth; (08) 9474 0444 or (08) 9474 3551 (recorded information line); open 9am–5pm daily.*

Old Mill 292 D4

This picturesque whitewashed windmill at the southern end of the Narrows Bridge is one of the earliest buildings in the Swan River Colony – the foundation stone was laid by Captain James Stirling, the first governor, in 1835. The mill, the adjacent miller's cottage and the recently established Education Centre review the development of flour milling in the early days of the colony. Coloured lights turn the huge Norfolk Island pine next to the Old Mill into a giant Christmas tree every December, making a festive display in the summer night sky. *Mill Point Rd, South Perth; (08) 9367 5788; open 10am–4pm Tues–Fri, 1–4pm Sat–Sun.*

South

Wireless Hill Park 292 D6

This natural bushland area boasts a magnificent springtime wildflower display. Three lookout towers provide views of the Swan River and the city skyline. A **Telecommunications**

walks & tours

Perth Walking Tours Take a free city orientation tour at 11am Monday to Saturday and noon on Sunday, or learn about Perth's history and culture on a free guided tour at 2pm weekdays. City of Perth Information Kiosk, Murray St Mall (near Forrest Pl).

Swan Brewery Tour This state-of-the-art brewery in Canning Vale is renowned for its Swan and Emu beers. 25 Baile Rd, Canning Vale; bookings on (08) 9350 0222.

Swan Valley Wine Cruise Choose from full- or half-day cruises up the Swan River to the Swan Valley, with wine-tastings included. Captain Cook Cruises, bookings on (08) 9325 3341.

Kings Park Walks Free guided walks, including the Botanic Garden Discovery, Bushland Nature Trail and the Memorials Walk, among others. (08) 9480 3600; 10am and 2pm daily.

Kings Park Indigenous Heritage Tour Learn about bush medicines, bush tucker and Indigenous history in this 1.5-hour tour. (08) 9480 3600; 1.30pm daily.

Fremantle Prison Tours Choose from a range of tours including the fascinating 'Doing Time Tour', every 30 minutes between 10am and 5pm, and the spooky 'Torchlight Tour' on Wednesdays and Fridays at 7pm. 1 The Terrace, Fremantle; (08) 9336 9200.

Perth–Fremantle River Cruise Enjoy informative on-board commentary as you cruise from Perth to Fremantle and back again. Or take the Triple Tour, which adds an Open Top Bus Tour in Perth and a Tram Tour in Fremantle. (08) 9325 1191.

Pedal Oz City Discovery Tour Gentle bicycle tour from Perth to Fremantle, with coffee at Cottesloe Beach, lunch and beer tasting at Fremantle then river cruise back to Perth. 1300 784 864.

Museum is housed in the original Wireless Station and is open by appointment only. *Almondbury Rd, Ardross; (08) 9364 0158.*

Point Walter Reserve 292 B6

This recreation area on the river is a pleasant spot for a picnic. Pick a shady peppermint tree by the water's edge to sit under and watch children paddling in the river. A kiosk, cafe, free barbecue facilities and children's playground area are nearby. Stroll out on the jetty to see what's biting, and walk out on the huge sandbar for great views both up and down river. *Honour Ave, Bicton.*

Point Heathcote Reserve 292 D5

Cross the Canning River – a large tributary of the Swan River – via Canning Bridge and wind your way through the affluent suburb of Applecross to Point Heathcote Reserve on Duncraig Road. This hilltop playground and parkland area, which includes a local museum, art gallery, restaurant, kiosk and free barbecue facilities, is the best spot south of the Swan for sweeping views of the river and city.

Outer South

Adventure World 615 C6

The state's biggest amusement park offers over 30 thrill rides and water slides, including the Turbo Mountain Rollercoaster, the Power Surge, the Shotgun and the Tunnel of Terror that corkscrews its way down Water Mountain. Nearby Bibra Lake is a great place to see black swans and other waterbirds. *179 Progress Dr, Bibra Lake; (08) 9417 9666; open 10am–5pm Thurs–Mon, daily in Jan and school holidays.*

Fremantle

VISITOR INFORMATION

Fremantle Visitor Centre
→ Town Hall, Kings Sq, High St
→ (08) 9431 7878
www.fremantlewa.com.au

Although now linked to Perth by a sprawl of suburbs, Fremantle ('Freo' to the locals) has a feel that is quite different in both architecture and atmosphere. Today it is a major boat and fishing centre at the mouth of the Swan River, but it also has the streetscape of a 19th-century port. It is a place to stay, unwind and watch the world go by. You can shop at the famous Fremantle Markets, or rest at a cafe on **South Terrace** and wait for the arrival of 'the Fremantle Doctor', the refreshing afternoon wind that blows in off the Indian Ocean.

European settlers arrived at Fremantle in 1829. The settlement developed gradually, its existence dependent on whaling and fishing. The population was boosted with the arrival in 1850 of British convicts, who constructed the forbidding Fremantle Prison (now open to the public) and the imposing lunatic asylum, now the Fremantle Arts Centre. Many heritage houses and terraces with cast-iron balconies from this period have survived.

Fremantle was at the centre of the world stage in 1987 when it hosted the America's Cup series of yacht races, following the win by *Australia II* – a Fremantle yacht – in 1983. Preparations for this huge event included the restoration of many old buildings in Fremantle, and the boost to its tourist economy has lasted to the present day.

getting to fremantle

By car A drive of 20–30 minutes, either via Stirling Highway on the north bank of the Swan River or via Canning Highway on the south.

By train A 30-minute journey from Perth Railway Station, Wellington Street. Trains depart every 15 minutes on weekdays and less frequently on weekends.

By bus Many buses and routes link both cities. Timetables and route details from Transperth 13 6213.

By ferry Various ferry operators travel twice daily between Perth and Fremantle, departing Barrack Street Jetty, Perth. *See Getting around, p. 295*

Combined travel packages For combined ferry, train and 'tram' tours of Perth and Fremantle, contact either Fremantle Tram Tours (08) 9433 6674 or Perth Tram Company (08) 9322 2006.

Once you've arrived Look out for the free orange CAT bus, which runs regular services from Victoria Quay, through the city centre and down to South Fremantle. 'Tram' tours are another option, departing hourly between 10am and 5pm from the town hall.

top events in fremantle

St Patrick's Day Parade and Concert   Celebrates the Irish national holiday with much gusto. March.

Fremantle Street Arts Festival   Local, national and international buskers perform on the streets. Easter.

Freo's West Coast Blues 'n Roots Festival   Day-long celebration of blues, roots, reggae and rock, with many big-name acts. April.

Blessing of the Fleet   Traditional Italian blessing of the fishing fleet. October.

Fremantle Festival   Performing arts and community activities culminating in a street parade and dance party. November.

Shipwreck Galleries 301 A2

Part of the Western Australian Maritime Museum, the galleries are one of three sites showcasing Western Australia's maritime history. The state's treacherous coastline has doomed many ships to a watery grave. The Shipwreck Galleries, housed in the restored convict-built Commissariat building, document this chapter of maritime history. The most popular exhibit is the stern of the *Batavia*, wrecked in 1629, which has been reconstructed from recovered timbers. *Cliff St; www.museum.wa.gov.au/oursites/ shipwreckgalleries; open 9.30am–5pm Thurs–Tues; admission by donation.*

Grand old buildings

Fremantle has a compact cluster of lovely old buildings, beginning with the Georgian-style **Elder's Building** at 11 Cliff Street. Made of brick and Donnybrook stone, it was once the hub of Fremantle's overseas trade. At 31–35 Cliff Street, the **Lionel Samson Building**'s rich facade epitomises the opulent style of gold-rush architecture. The **Esplanade Hotel**, on the corner of Marine Terrace and Essex Street, dates from the 1890s and its newer extension blends in seamlessly with the original facade. Now the Challenger TAFE e-Tech, the **Fremantle Technical College** displays Art Nouveau decorative touches and boasts Donnybrook stone facings and plinth. It's on the corner of South Terrace and Essex Street. On the corner of Ellen and Ord streets, the grand old **Samson House** dates from 1900 and was originally built for Michael Samson, who later became mayor of Fremantle.

where to stay in fremantle

Esplanade Hotel   Impressive heritage building is centrally located to the town centre and each room is elegantly decorated. Cnr Marine Tce and Essex St; (08) 9432 4000. 301 B2

Newport House   Executive house with stunning views. 4 Trafford St, Beaconsfield; Fremantle Visitor Centre (08) 9431 7878. 614 C8

Oceanic Apartment Fremantle   Three-bedroom apartment. 3/8 Collie St; 0420 309 030. 301 B2

Port Mill B&B   Converted historic flour mill. 3/17 Essex St; (08) 9433 3832. 301 B2

Terrace Central B&B Hotel   Refurbished heritage hotel located on South Terrace's vibrant 'Cappuccino Strip'. 79–85 South Tce; (08) 9335 6600. 614 C8

Finally, there's the stone bell-tower and large stained-glass window of **St John's Anglican Church**, on the corner of Adelaide and Queen streets, and Henderson Street's **Warders' Quarters**, a row of convict-built cottages built in 1851, and until recently used to house warders from Fremantle Prison. *(See also the Round House and Fremantle Prison, on this page.)*

Fremantle Markets 301 B2

One of the city's most popular attractions are these National Trust–classified markets, with their ornate gold-rush era architecture, which were opened in 1897. They offer a diversity of stalls: fresh produce, food, books, clothes, bric-a-brac, pottery and crafts. There is also a great tavern bar where buskers often perform. *Cnr South Tce and Henderson St; (08) 9335 2515; open 9am–8pm Fri, 9am–6pm Sat–Sun.*

The Round House 301 A2

Its name a misnomer, the Round House is actually a dodecahedron, with its 12 sides erected around a central yard. Built in 1831 by the first settlers as a prison, it is the oldest public building in the state. At 1pm each day, the Round House's signal station fires a cannon – the time gun – and this activates a time ball (an instrument once used to give accurate time readings to vessels out at sea). The Whalers' Tunnel underneath the Round House was cut by a whaling company in 1837 for access to Bathers Bay. *10 Arthur Head; (08) 9336 6897; open 10.30am– 3.30pm daily; admission by gold coin donation.*

Western Australian Maritime Museum 301 A2

This stunning, nautically inspired building perched on the waterfront has six galleries, each of which explores a different theme in the state's maritime history. Highlights of the collection of historic and significant boats include the yacht that won the America's Cup – *Australia II* – and the *Parry Endeavour*, in which Western Australian Jon Sanders circumnavigated the world three times. Outside the museum are the Welcome Walls, a series of engraved panels that list the names of thousands of migrants who arrived in Western Australia through the port of Fremantle, while next door to the museum is another of its prize exhibits, the submarine HMAS *Ovens*, which was in service during World War II. Take the tour to see what conditions are like inside a real submarine. *Victoria Quay; (08) 9431 8334; open 9.30am–5pm Thurs–Tues.*

Leeuwin Ocean Adventure 301 A2

The *Leeuwin II* – a 55-metre, three-masted barquentine – is rated as the largest ocean-going tall ship in Australia. It is available for half-day or twilight sails and for longer voyages along the coast of Western Australia and the Northern Territory. When in Fremantle, it is open to the public. *B Berth, Victoria Quay; (08) 9430 4105.*

Fremantle Prison 301 B2

The first convicts arrived in Fremantle in 1850. Built with their own hands, this complex of buildings was initially used as a barracks and became a prison in 1867. Huge, forbidding and full of history, it was in use until 1991. Now visitors can experience the atmosphere on a guided tour, running every half-hour and taking in the isolation chamber and the gallows. The entrance can be reached via steps and a walkway around Fremantle Oval from Parry Street. *1 The Terrace; (08) 9336 9200; open 10am–5pm daily; Tunnels Tours daily and Torchlight Tours Wed and Fri (bookings essential).*

Fremantle Arts Centre 301 B1

This magnificent limestone building, with its steeply pitched roofs and Gothic arches, was also built by convicts. The colony's first lunatic asylum, it now offers an interesting display on the history of Fremantle, contemporary art exhibitions, a craft shop with a range of wares made by Western Australian artists, a ghost walk and a garden area with a cafe. *1 Finnerty St; (08) 9432 9555; open 10am–5pm daily; admission free.*

Fishing Boat Harbour 301 B3

This popular restaurant strip for locals and tourists alike overlooks the boats of the local fishermen. Sample the fresh catch of the day at restaurants such as **Cicerello's**, famous for its fish and chips. On the footpath in front of Cicerello's is a statue of AC/DC's Bon Scott, unveiled in October 2008. Across the railway line is the **Esplanade Reserve**, an ideal spot to relax under the giant Norfolk Pines.

where to eat in fremantle

Cicerello's The epitome of fish and chip dining on Fremantle's Fishing Boat Harbour. 2/1 Howard St; (08) 9335 9811; open daily for lunch and dinner. 301 A2

Little Creatures Harbour-side brewery, bar and restaurant serves hearty fare to its enormous following. 40 Mews Rd; (08) 9339 9500; open daily for lunch and dinner, and Sun for breakfast. 301 A2

Ruocco's Has been serving delicious wood-fired pizzas for so long that it's now run by the second generation of the Ruocco family. 213 South Tce; (08) 9335 6939; open Tues–Sun for lunch and dinner. 301 B3

Sala Thai A local favourite, serves Thai cuisine comparable to its country of origin. 22 Norfolk St; (08) 9335 7749; open daily for dinner. 301 B2

The Red Herring Restaurant Up-market seafood restaurant boasts a magical setting right on the river. 26 Riverside Rd, East Fremantle; (08) 9339 1611; open daily for lunch and dinner, and Sun for breakfast. 292 A5

day tours

Rottnest Island Just off the coast of Perth, the low-key island resort of Rottnest makes for a perfect day tour. Access is via ferry from Fremantle, Perth or Hillarys Boat Harbour. No private cars are permitted: island transport is by foot, bicycle or bus. Visitors to Rottnest can divide their time between the beach and the scenic and historic attractions of the island. For more details see p. 305

Darling Range Follow the Great Eastern Highway for a tour of the Darling Range and its 80 000 hectares of escarpment and jarrah forest in the Hills Forest area. Highlights include a scenic drive through John Forrest National Park and a visit to the huge, forest-fringed Mundaring Weir. For more details see p. 306

Swan Valley A premier winegrowing district, with vineyards along the scenic Swan River. Other attractions include the historic town of Guildford; Woodbridge House, a Victorian mansion in West Midland; Walyunga National Park; and Whiteman Park, a 2500-hectare area that includes Caversham Wildlife Park. For more details see p. 306

Yanchep National Park On the coast north of Perth, Yanchep has long been one of the city's favourite recreation areas. Have your photo taken with a koala; see didgeridoo and dance performances; or take a guided tour of Crystal Cave, where stalactites hang above the inky waters of an underground pool.

[WESTERN AUSTRALIAN MARITIME MUSEUM]

REGIONS
western australia

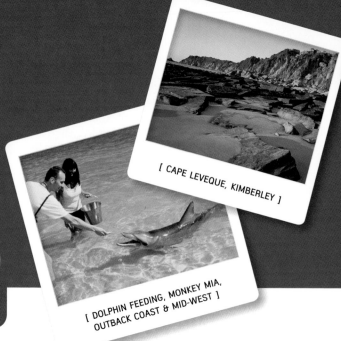

[CAPE LEVEQUE, KIMBERLEY]

[DOLPHIN FEEDING, MONKEY MIA,
OUTBACK COAST & MID-WEST]

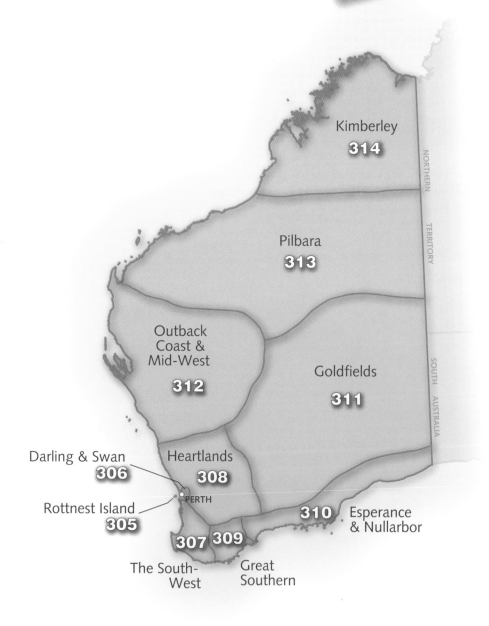

Kimberley
314

Pilbara
313

NORTHERN TERRITORY

Outback
Coast &
Mid-West
312

Goldfields
311

SOUTH AUSTRALIA

Darling & Swan
306

Heartlands
308

Rottnest Island
305

PERTH

310   Esperance
& Nullarbor

307 **309**

The South-
West

Great
Southern

ROTTNEST ISLAND

In azure waters only 18 kilometres from Perth, Rottnest Island's white, sandy beaches are perfect for a range of aquatic pleasures. The island is also home to the famous quokka.

[ROTTNEST ISLAND QUOKKA]

The Basin An outer reef surrounds Rottnest, protecting the clear waters and creating calm conditions for family swimming. The Basin is one of a number of beautiful sandy beaches on the eastern end of the island. It is within easy walking distance of Thomson Bay and has basic facilities.

Underwater wonderland The diversity of fish and coral species, and the numerous shipwrecks, found around the island make Rottnest a favourite site for scubadivers and snorkellers. Dive charters and snorkelling tours are popular; if you prefer not to get wet, enjoy the underwater scenery aboard the glass-bottomed Underwater Explorer.

Quokka country The quokka is a native marsupial found primarily on Rottnest Island. It is semi-nocturnal and furry, and grows to the size of a hare. Find the interpretive signs about a kilometre south of Thomson Bay, just before Kingstown Barracks; if you don't see one of the 10 000 quokkas on the island here, then there are good viewing spots along the boardwalk at Garden Lake.

West End The 'West End' of Rottnest can be reached on an 11-kilometre bike ride along a sealed road, or on a bus tour. There are stunning ocean views from Cape Vlamingh (where you may also spot a humpback whale in winter) and a 1-kilometre heritage trail that affords sightings of wedge-tailed shearwaters, fairy terns, quokkas and bottlenose dolphins.

TOP EVENTS

FEB	Rottnest Channel Swim
MAR	The Big Splash (watersports race, Fremantle–Rottnest Island)
JUNE	The State Open Surfing Series
OCT	Marathon and Fun Run
DEC	Rottnest Swim Thru

CLIMATE

ROTTNEST ISLAND

J	F	M	A	M	J	J	A	S	O	N	D	
26	27	25	23	20	18	17	17	18	20	22	24	MAX °C
18	19	18	16	14	13	12	12	12	13	15	17	MIN °C
7	13	14	37	106	156	149	104	61	39	17	10	RAIN MM
2	2	4	8	15	18	20	18	14	11	6	3	RAIN DAYS

ISLAND HERITAGE

Known as Wadjemup to the Nyungar people, Rottnest Island was unoccupied when Europeans arrived, although there is evidence of Aboriginal occupation around 7000 years ago when the island was linked to the mainland. The island was given the unflattering name Rotte-nest, meaning 'rats' nest', in 1696 by explorer Willem de Vlamingh, who mistook the island's quokkas for large rats. Europeans settled on the island in 1831. From 1838 to 1903 it was used as a prison for Aboriginal people. During World War I it became an internment camp and in 1917 it was declared an A-class reserve. World War II saw it used as a military post. Many heritage sites can be found, including an original 1840s streetscape – Thomson Bay's Vincent Way. Other interesting sites are the Chapel (1858), the octagonal prison building known as the Quad (1864), the Oliver Hill Gun Battery (1930s) and Rottnest Lighthouse (1859) on Wadjemup Hill.

DARLING & SWAN

Barely half an hour from the centre of Perth are two distinct country landscapes perfect for picnicking, walking, sampling local produce and looking for wildflowers.

[SWAN VALLEY VINEYARD]

John Forrest National Park   Declared a national park in 1947, John Forrest is one of the oldest and best-loved picnic spots in the Perth Hills. A drive through the park has vantage points with superb views across Perth and the coastal plain. A popular walk is the Heritage Trail on the western edge, past waterfalls and an old rail tunnel.

Swan Valley wineries   The Swan Valley region is renowned for its chardonnay, shiraz, chenin blanc and verdelho. It boasts over 40 wineries; of these, Houghton and Sandalford are the best known. For a treat that offers scenery as well as wine-tasting, take a Swan River wineries cruise from Perth.

Mundaring Weir   The rolling lawns and bush-clad surrounds of this weir reserve make it ideal for picnics. At the foot of the weir, the Number 1 Pump Station commemorates C. Y. O'Connor's extraordinary engineering feat in piping water to the goldfields some 600 kilometres east. Nearby, at the Hills Forest Discovery Centre, you can sign up for nature-based activities such as bushcraft.

Araluen Botanic Park   Tall forest trees (jarrah, eucalypt and marri) frame the rockpools, cascades and European-style terraces of these beautiful 59-hectare gardens. Established in the 1930s by the Young Australia League, the gardens have picturesque walking trails, picnic and barbecue areas, and, in spring, magnificent tulip displays.

TOP EVENTS

MAR–APR	Taste of the Valley (food, wine and art festival, throughout Swan Valley)
AUG	Avon Descent (whitewater race down Avon and Swan rivers, from Northam to Perth)
OCT	Spring in the Valley (wine festival, throughout Swan Valley)
NOV	Darlington Arts Festival (Darlington)

CLIMATE

GUILDFORD

	J	F	M	A	M	J	J	A	S	O	N	D	
	32	32	30	27	22	19	18	19	21	23	27	30	MAX °C
	17	17	15	13	10	8	7	8	9	10	13	15	MIN °C
	8	10	17	43	122	177	172	139	86	56	20	13	RAIN MM
	2	2	4	7	14	17	19	17	14	11	6	4	RAIN DAYS

HERITAGE SITES

In historic Guildford, roam among yesteryear's farm tools, fashions and household items at the Old Courthouse, Gaol and Museum. Then enjoy a drink at the nearby Rose and Crown Hotel (1841), the oldest trading hotel in the state. The faithfully restored Woodbridge House (1885), picturesquely located on the banks of the Swan River, is a fine example of late-Victorian architecture. And just south of Upper Swan, at Henley Brook on the western bank of the river, All Saints Church (1839–41) is the state's oldest church.

→ For more detail see maps 614, 615, 618 & 620. For descriptions of ⊕ towns see Towns from A–Z (p. 315).

THE SOUTH-WEST

This region is renowned for its world-class wines, excellent surf breaks, towering old-growth forests and the 963-kilometre Bibbulmun Track.

[MEELUP BEACH, DUNSBOROUGH]

Swim with dolphins In Bunbury's Koombana Bay you can swim under ranger guidance with wild bottlenose dolphins. Learn about the dolphins and other marine life at the Dolphin Discovery Centre's interpretive museum and theatre.

Busselton Jetty Stretching a graceful 2 kilometres into Geographe Bay, this wooden jetty is the longest in the Southern Hemisphere. Built in 1865, the jetty originally serviced American whaling ships. Today a small tourist train takes you from the Interpretive Centre at one end to the Underwater Observatory at the other.

Lake Cave One of hundreds of limestone caves in Leeuwin–Naturaliste National Park, magnificent Lake Cave is centred on the incredibly still, eerie waters of an underground lake, which reflects the cave's stunning crystal formations. Its other highlight is the Suspended Table, a huge column hanging precariously from the cave's ceiling.

Margaret River This beautiful area has long had a reputation as one of Australia's best wine-producing regions, a reputation that rests principally on its cabernet sauvignon and chardonnay grapes grown on grey-brown, gravelly sandy soils. Try the cabernet from Vasse Felix, Moss Wood and Cullen, and the chardonnay from Leeuwin, Voyager and Ashbrook.

Valley of the Giants Gain a unique perspective on the majestic southern forests as you walk through the upper branches of giant tingle and karri trees. East of Walpole, this walkway, 38 metres above the forest floor, is one of the highest and longest of its kind in the world.

Blackwood Valley The Blackwood River meanders for 500 kilometres through wheat-belt plains and forested valleys to its broad estuary at Augusta. Secluded spots along the river between Nannup and Alexandra Bridge offer tranquil camping, fishing, swimming and canoeing. The Sheoak Walk is a one-hour loop through the forest close to Nannup.

Map labels: ROCKINGHAM; MANDURAH; Peel Inlet; SERPENTINE NP; Pinjarra; YALGORUP NP; Harvey Estuary; Lake Clifton; Dwellingup; Lake Pollard; Lake Preston; Preston Beach; INDIAN OCEAN; Harvey; Lake Ballingall; Koombana Bay; Australind; Collie; BUNBURY; WELLINGTON NP; Geographe Bay; Cape Naturaliste; Donnybrook; Dunsborough; Yallingup; BUSSELTON; Boyup Brook; Balingup; LEEUWIN–NATURALISTE; Margaret River; Margaret; Bridgetown; Gnarabup; Redgate; Blackwood; Nannup; Manjimup; NATIONAL PARK; Alexandra Bridge; BEEDELUP NP; Augusta; SCOTT NP; Cape Leeuwin; Pemberton; GLOUCESTER NP; WARREN NP; Lake Muir; MT ROE–MT LINDESAY NP; Northcliffe; SHANNON NP; MOUNT FRANKLAND NP; D'ENTRECASTEAUX; Walpole; NATIONAL PARK; SOUTHERN OCEAN; WALPOLE–NORNALUP NP; 0 30 km; N

→ For more detail see maps 614, 615, 616, 617, 618 & 620. For descriptions of Ⓣ towns see Towns from A–Z (p. 315).

TOP EVENTS

FEB–MAR	Leeuwin Estate Concert (near Margaret River)
MAR–APR	Margaret River Pro (surfing competition)
MAY	Margaret River Wine Region Festival (Margaret River)
NOV	Blues at Bridgetown Festival (Bridgetown)
DEC	Ironman Western Australia Triathlon (Busselton)
DEC	Cherry Harmony Festival (Manjimup)

CLIMATE

BUSSELTON

	J	F	M	A	M	J	J	A	S	O	N	D	
	29	28	26	23	19	17	16	17	18	20	24	27	MAX °C
	14	14	13	11	9	8	8	8	8	9	11	13	MIN °C
	10	11	22	42	118	175	167	117	75	52	24	13	RAIN MM
	3	2	4	8	15	19	22	19	16	13	7	4	RAIN DAYS

JARRAH, KARRI, TUART AND TINGLE

Western Australia's only forests are in the cool, well-watered South-West. The grey-barked tuart tree grows only on coastal limestone; just outside Busselton is the largest remaining pure tuart forest in the world. Jarrah, a beautifully grained, deep-red hardwood, flourishes between Dwellingup and Collie. The Forest Heritage Centre at Dwellingup has interpretive displays on the issues of forest management, and a treetop walk. Forests of karri – one of the world's tallest trees, that can reach 90 metres in 100 years – are found in the wetter areas, from Manjimup to Walpole. Near Pemberton, 4000 hectares of old-growth karri forest are protected by Warren and Beedelup national parks. In Gloucester National Park, right outside the town, is the 61-metre Gloucester Tree, with a spiral ladder to the top. The Valley of the Giants, east of Walpole, is home to towering red tingle trees. Nearby is the 25-metre-wide Giant Red Tingle, a huge fire-hollowed tree that is regarded as one of the ten largest living things on the planet.

HEARTLANDS

Dominated by the wheat belt, this region features the Avon Valley, New Norcia and the extraordinary Pinnacles Desert.

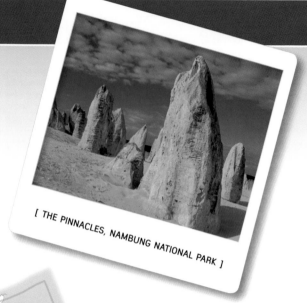

[THE PINNACLES, NAMBUNG NATIONAL PARK]

The Pinnacles   Thousands of limestone pillars, the eroded remnants of what was once a thick bed of limestone, create a weirdly beautiful landscape in Nambung National Park. Other park attractions include a beautiful coastline with superb beaches where visitors can fish, swim, snorkel, walk or picnic.

New Norcia   This town, with its Spanish Colonial architecture, was built in 1846 by Benedictine monks who established a mission for the local Indigenous population. It remains Australia's only monastic town. Visitors can tour the buildings and visit the fascinating museum and art gallery.

Avon Valley   In the 1860s, bushranger Moondyne Joe hid in the forests, caves and wildflower fields of this lush valley. Now Avon Valley National Park preserves much of the landscape. In the valley's heart, and marking the start of the wheat belt, are the historic towns of Northam and York.

Wave Rock and Mulka's Cave   Wave Rock, east of Hyden, is a 2.7-billion-year-old piece of granite, 15 metres high and 100 metres long. It looks like a giant wave frozen at the moment of breaking and has vertical bands of colour created by algal growth. To the north is Mulka's Cave, decorated with Aboriginal rock art.

TOP EVENTS

JAN	Lancelin Ocean Classic (windsurfing competition)
MAY	Moondyne Festival (Toodyay)
AUG	Avon Descent (whitewater race down Avon and Swan rivers, from Northam to Perth)
SEPT–OCT	Jazz Festival (York)
OCT	Kulin Bush Races (Kulin)
NOV	Blessing of the Fleet (Jurien Bay)

CLIMATE

NORTHAM

	J	F	M	A	M	J	J	A	S	O	N	D	
	34	34	31	26	21	18	17	18	20	24	28	32	MAX °C
	17	17	15	12	9	7	5	6	7	9	12	15	MIN °C
	10	13	19	23	57	83	84	62	37	25	12	9	RAIN MM
	2	2	3	6	11	15	16	14	11	7	4	2	RAIN DAYS

WILDFLOWERS

Western Australia is home to some 12 500 kinds of wildflowers, and the Heartlands is one of the most accessible areas to see magnificent wildflower displays. Top spots include the Chittering Valley near Gingin, Lesueur and Badgingarra national parks near Jurien Bay, and the sand plains around Southern Cross. Up to 20 species of native orchids flourish around Hyden in spring; yellow wattles light up the countryside around Dalwallinu; and massed displays of white, pink and yellow everlastings line the road from Moora to Wubin.

→ For more detail see maps 614, 615, 618 & 620. For descriptions of ⊤ towns see Towns from A–Z (p. 315).

GREAT SOUTHERN

This varied region encompasses sheep country, parts of the wheat belt, wineries, surf beaches and the historic town of Albany.

[LILY WINDMILL, STIRLING RANGE]

Great Southern wineries   This region has over 40 wineries, extending from Frankland east through Mount Barker to Porongurup. Since the first plantings in 1967, the region has gained an international reputation for its aromatic rieslings. More recently, premium chardonnay, shiraz, cabernet sauvignon and pinot noir are also proving popular. Many of the wineries are open for tastings and sales.

Stirling Range National Park   The Stirling Range rises abruptly above the surrounding plains; its rock-faces are composed of the sands and silts laid down in the delta of an ancient river. The highest peaks can be veiled in swirling mists, which creates a cool and humid environment that supports a proliferation of flowering plants. Bluff Knoll, at 1073 metres, is one of the state's premier hiking challenges.

The Old Farm at Strawberry Hill   The Old Farm, near Albany, is a delightful stone cottage on Western Australia's oldest cultivated farm. Originally home to the first government resident in the state, the 1836 building at Strawberry Hill, as it was known, was the centre of Albany's social life in its day. These days the property welcomes swarms of visitors to its picturesque heritage buildings and stunning gardens.

Albany Whaleworld   The bloody realities of whaling are displayed at the old Cheynes Beach Whaling Station on Frenchman Bay, 25 kilometres south-east of Albany. Visitors can explore *Cheynes IV*, a restored whalechaser, and relive the sights and sounds of the hunt. A 3D theatrette occupies one of the old whale-oil storage tanks.

Torndirrup National Park   Located 15 minutes from Albany, this park features the Blowholes, the Gap and Natural Bridge, all sculpted into their current form by the treacherous Southern Ocean. Granite outcrops and cliffs alternate with dunes, and sandy heath supports peppermint, banksia and karri. Easy walking trails take in some of the spectacular sights.

Map labels: Lake Grace South · Chinocup Lake · Katanning · Kojonup · Cranbrook · Bluff Knoll · STIRLING · STIRLING RANGE NP · Frankland · Mount Barker · PORONGURUP NP · Bremer Bay · Cheyne Bay · SOUTHERN OCEAN · WAYCHINICUP NP · Denmark · ALBANY · Frenchman Bay · TORNDIRRUP NP · WILLIAM BAY NP · WEST CAPE HOWE NP · 0 20 km · N

TOP EVENTS

JAN	Mount Barker D'Vine Wine Festival (Mount Barker)
JAN	Vintage Blues Festival (Albany)
MAR	Wine Summer Festival (Porongurup)
EASTER	Brave New Works (new performance art, Denmark)
SEPT	Wildflower Display (Cranbrook)
SEPT–OCT	Great Southern Wine Festival (Albany)

CLIMATE

ALBANY

	J	F	M	A	M	J	J	A	S	O	N	D	
	25	25	24	22	19	17	16	16	17	19	21	24	MAX °C
	14	14	13	12	10	8	8	7	8	9	11	12	MIN °C
	27	24	28	63	102	103	124	106	82	78	48	25	RAIN MM
	8	9	11	14	18	19	21	21	18	15	13	10	RAIN DAYS

ALBANY HERITAGE

Albany, the oldest white settlement in Western Australia, was officially founded on 21 January 1827. The founders were a party of soldiers and convicts, under the command of Major Edmund Lockyer, who had arrived on the *Amity* a month earlier. Albany's magnificent harbour, once commanding the sea lanes running between Europe, Asia and eastern Australia, became a whaling station and later a coaling port for steamships. Museums now occupy several of the town's historic buildings, and a full-size replica of the *Amity* stands next to one of them, the Residency Museum. Stirling Terrace has some evocative Victorian shopfronts, while Princess Royal Fortress on Mount Adelaide has restored buildings and gun emplacements, and offers fine views.

→ For more detail see maps 617, 618 & 620. For descriptions of ⊤ towns see Towns from A–Z (p. 315).

ESPERANCE & NULLARBOR

Esperance's beaches are famed for their white sand and turquoise waters, while to the north-east lies the vast Nullarbor Plain.

[TURQUOISE WATERS AND WHITE SAND, CAPE ARID NATIONAL PARK]

90-mile straight   Four kilometres west of Caiguna, be sure to have your photo taken beside the signpost marking the eastern end of the longest straight stretch of road in Australia, which runs for 90 miles (146.6 kilometres) between Caiguna and a point east of Balladonia.

Cape Le Grand National Park   Swimming beaches, sheltered coves, heathlands, sand plains and the Whistling Rock are all features of this park, 56 kilometres east of Esperance. There are easy walking trails and two camping areas. Scenic spots include Thistle Cove, Hellfire Bay and Lucky Bay (where luck might have you spot a kangaroo on the beach).

Eucla   This isolated outpost was established in 1877 as a telegraph station; today coastal dunes partially obscure the station's ruins. On the beach, a lonely jetty stretches out into startlingly blue waters, and in Eucla National Park you can wander among the rippling Delisser Sandhills.

Great Ocean Drive   A 38-kilometre circuit drive explores the coast west of Esperance. Attractions include Australia's first wind farm, sheltered swimming at Twilight Cove, and Pink Lake, rendered lipstick-colour by algae. There are coastal lookouts, and sightings of southern right whales from June to October.

Archipelago of the Recherche   This group of 105 granite islands and 1500 islets stretches for 250 kilometres along the Esperance coast. Boat tours, available from Esperance, may provide sightings of fur seals, sea lions, dolphins and, in season, southern right whales. Visitors can stay overnight in safari huts or camp on Woody Island.

TOP EVENTS

JAN	Summer Festival (Hopetoun)
SEPT	Wildflower Show (Ravensthorpe)
SEPT	Wildflower Show (Esperance)
OCT	Agricultural Show (Esperance)

CLIMATE

ESPERANCE

J	F	M	A	M	J	J	A	S	O	N	D	
26	26	25	23	20	18	17	18	19	21	23	25	MAX °C
16	16	15	13	11	9	8	9	10	11	13	14	MIN °C
22	27	31	43	76	82	98	84	58	50	36	17	RAIN MM
6	6	8	11	14	16	17	17	14	12	10	7	RAIN DAYS

THE NULLARBOR

The Nullarbor is one of the country's essential touring experiences. This 250 000-square-kilometre treeless limestone slab was initially part of the seabed, and has been formed in part by deposits of marine fossils. The terrain is riddled with sinkholes, caverns and caves, only some of which are open to the public. Murrawijinie Caves include Koonalda Cave, which is open to the public and contains rock art that dates back 20 000 years. Although it can seem featureless, the country is far from monotonous, particularly where the highway veers to the coast for a view of dramatic cliffs and the wild Southern Ocean, and perhaps a lucky sighting of migrating southern right whales.

→ For more detail see maps 620–1. For descriptions of ⦿ towns see Towns from A–Z (p. 315).

GOLDFIELDS

Gold continues to be mined in this region, while sheep stations the size of small nations produce fine wool. The area offers an excellent opportunity to delve into its fascinating heritage.

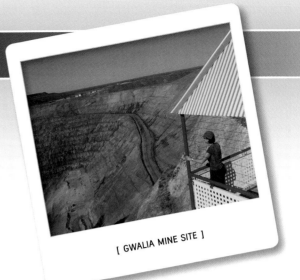

[GWALIA MINE SITE]

North of Kalgoorlie The town of Menzies has 130 people and several intact old buildings, while Kookynie has retained its spacious 1894 Grand Hotel. Gwalia, almost a ghost town, has a museum, the restored State Hotel and tin houses preserved in their lived-in state. Laverton, 100 kilometres east, has historic buildings saved by the nickel industry.

Coolgardie The 100-plus street markers scattered through Coolgardie are a good introduction to this town, the first settlement in the eastern goldfields. Coolgardie's splendid historic buildings include the Marble Bar Hotel, now the RSL, and the 1898 Warden's Court. The latter is an architectural treasure and houses the comprehensive Goldfields Exhibition Museum and the visitor centre.

Kalgoorlie–Boulder Kalgoorlie–Boulder produces half of Australia's gold. Take a circuit of the open-cut Superpit on the Loopline Railway, see the gold vault at the Museum of the Goldfields, and sample the rigours of 1890s mining at the Australian Prospectors and Miners Hall of Fame.

Peak Charles National Park In this park south-west of Norseman, granite mountains rise in wave-cut platforms to a height of 651 metres. Walking trails to the summit of Peak Charles and its twin, Peak Eleanora, should only be attempted in favourable weather, but at the top are fantastic views across saltpans, sand plains and dry woodlands.

TOP EVENTS

FEB	Undies 500 Car Rally (Kalgoorlie–Boulder)
MAR	Norseman Cup (horseracing, Norseman)
MAY–JUNE	Leonora Golden Gift and Festival (Leonora)
SEPT	Race Round (horseracing, Kalgoorlie–Boulder)
SEPT–OCT	Metal Detecting Championships (Coolgardie, odd-numbered years)
OCT	Balzano Barrow Race (Kanowna to Kalgoorlie–Boulder)

GOLDFIELDS HISTORY

The discovery of gold in the region in 1892 secured the economic success of Western Australia. Since then, goldmines from Norseman to Laverton have yielded well over 1000 tonnes. A railway from Perth in 1896 and a water pipeline in 1903 helped Kalgoorlie and Boulder sustain a population of 30 000, the liquor requirements of which were met by 93 hotels. By 1900, surface gold was exhausted and big companies went underground. Exhausted mines have left a belt of ghost towns north of Kalgoorlie, while nickel mining since the 1960s has allowed towns such as Kambalda, Leonora and Laverton to survive.

CLIMATE

KALGOORLIE–BOULDER

	J	F	M	A	M	J	J	A	S	O	N	D	
	34	32	30	25	20	18	17	18	22	26	29	32	MAX °C
	18	18	16	12	8	6	5	5	8	11	14	17	MIN °C
	22	28	19	19	28	31	26	20	15	16	18	15	RAIN MM
	3	4	4	5	7	8	9	7	5	4	4	3	RAIN DAYS

→ For more detail see maps 620–1 & 623. For descriptions of ⊕ towns see Towns from A–Z (p. 315).

OUTBACK COAST & MID-WEST

This vast area is known for the richness and rarity of its natural features, from colourful Ningaloo Reef to the eroded cliffs and gorges of Kalbarri National Park.

[AN UNDERWATER LANDSCAPE OF FISH AND CORAL, NINGALOO REEF]

Ningaloo Reef Ningaloo Marine Park protects the state's largest reef, a stunning underwater landscape of fish and coral located directly off the beach. For a quintessential Ningaloo experience, take a swim with the whale sharks – this is one of the few places in the world where they come close to shore. These gentle giants migrate to the reef between March and June; tours can be arranged in Exmouth.

Monkey Mia The wild bottlenose dolphins of Monkey Mia are world famous for their daily morning ritual of swimming into the shallows to be handfed with fish. Under the guidance of rangers, visitors can wander into the water and witness this rare event. For a total marine encounter, dugong-watching cruises can also be arranged from here.

Kalbarri National Park This park is best known for its 80 kilometres of gorges carved out by the Murchison River. Watersports are popular on the river's lower reaches. The park is also one of the world's richest wildflower areas. Dolphins, whale sharks and whales frequent the coastal waters, and the fishing is excellent.

Geraldton Geralton is surrounded by superb swimming and surfing beaches, but if you prefer architecture to aquatics follow the Hawes Heritage Trail, which highlights the remarkable church buildings (1915–39) of architect-priest Monsignor John Cyril Hawes. In Geraldton, the Byzantine-styled St Francis Xavier Cathedral is considered to be one of Hawes' masterpieces.

TOP EVENTS

MAR	Sport Fishing Classic (Kalbarri)
MAR	Gamex (gamefishing competition, Exmouth)
APR–MAY	Whale Shark Festival (Exmouth)
AUG–SEPT	Mullewa Wildflower Show (Mullewa)
OCT	Airing of the Quilts (Northampton)
OCT	Sunshine Festival (Geraldton)

SHARK BAY

World Heritage–listed Shark Bay is a sunny paradise of bays, inlets and shallow azure waters, blessed with a great number of unusual features. It boasts the world's most diverse and abundant examples of stromatolites – the world's oldest living fossils – which dot the shores of Hamelin Pool in rocky lumps. The bay region supports the largest number and greatest area of seagrass species in the world. Covering 4000 square kilometres, these vast underwater meadows are home to around 14 000 dugongs, 10 per cent of the world's total number. The bay's extraordinary marine population also includes humpback whales resting on their long migrations, manta rays, green and loggerhead turtles and, most famously, the dolphins that regularly visit Monkey Mia.

CLIMATE

CARNARVON

J	F	M	A	M	J	J	A	S	O	N	D	
31	33	31	29	26	23	22	23	24	26	27	29	MAX °C
22	23	22	19	15	12	11	12	14	16	19	21	MIN °C
12	21	16	14	38	48	47	19	6	6	4	2	RAIN MM
2	3	2	3	5	7	7	5	3	2	1	1	RAIN DAYS

Map labels

EXMOUTH GULF
Exmouth
Ningaloo Reef
NINGALOO MARINE PARK
CAPE RANGE NP
Coral Bay
INDIAN OCEAN
KENNEDY RANGE NP
MOUNT AUGUSTUS NP
COLLIER RANGE NP
Lake MacLeod
Gascoyne Junction
Carnarvon
Shark Bay
River
FRANCOIS PERON NP
Monkey Mia
Denham
Hamelin Pool
Murchison
Meekatharra
Lake Way
Lake Austin
Cue
Mount Magnet
KALBARRI NP
Kalbarri
Yalgoo
Lake Noondie
Northampton
Mullewa
GERALDTON
Greenough
Morawa
Dongara-Denison
0   80 km   N

→ For more detail see maps 619, 620 & 622. For descriptions of ⊤ towns see Towns from A–Z (p. 315).

PILBARA

Home to the ochre-hued Hamersley Range, this region is characterised by rust-red landscapes and vast tidal flats broken by mangroves.

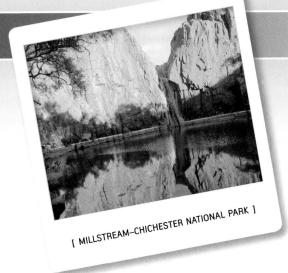

[MILLSTREAM–CHICHESTER NATIONAL PARK]

Pilbara islands The Dampier Archipelago and the Montebello and Mackerel islands seem a far-flung beach paradise from the industrial ports of the Pilbara. In reality, the nearest islands – those of the Dampier Archipelago – are just 20 minutes by boat from Dampier. These islands are a haven for marine life, including turtles, dolphins and migrating humpback whales, and are a renowned location for fishing.

Cossack This first port in the north-west was built between 1870 and 1898, and is now a ghost town. Many buildings have been restored. The old post office houses a gallery and the courthouse has a museum, while the police barracks offer budget accommodation.

Marble Bar The mining town of Marble Bar has gained the dubious reputation as the hottest town in Australia. For 161 consecutive days in 1923–24, the temperature in town did not drop below 37.8° Celsius. The heart of the town is the Ironclad Hotel, a classic outback pub where you can enjoy a counter meal and that cold beer you're going to need. You can also experience Marble Bar's goldmining past at Comet Gold Mine, a museum and tourist centre.

Millstream–Chichester National Park
Located within the arid beauty of Millstream–Chichester National Park, spring-fed Chinderwarriner Pool has an almost mirage-like quality. Encircled by remnant rainforest, the oasis is a haven for a range of plants and animals, many of them rare. Visit historic Millstream homestead, and take a refreshing dip in the pool.

Karijini National Park Karijini was the name given to this area by the original inhabitants, the Banjima. It is renowned for extraordinary gorges, multicoloured walls, and hidden pools and waterfalls. Brilliant wildflowers carpet the rust-red hills in spring. Camping is available inside the park.

TOP EVENTS

MAR	Campdraft and Rodeo (Newman)
MAY	Welcome to Hedland Night (Port Hedland)
JULY	Roebourne Cup (horseracing, Roebourne)
AUG	FeNaCING Festival (Karratha)
SEPT	Pilbara Music Festival (Port Hedland)

CLIMATE

ROEBOURNE

	J	F	M	A	M	J	J	A	S	O	N	D	
	39	38	38	35	30	27	27	29	32	35	38	39	MAX °C
	26	26	25	22	18	15	14	15	17	20	23	25	MIN °C
	59	67	63	30	29	30	14	5	1	1	1	10	RAIN MM
	3	5	3	1	3	3	2	1	0	0	0	1	RAIN DAYS

HAMERSLEY RANGE RESOURCES

One of the world's richest deposits of iron ore was discovered in Hamersley Range in 1962, spearheading the Hamersley Iron Project. Towns with swimming pools, gardens and golf courses then sprang up in this landscape of mulga scrub, spinifex and red mountains. Visitors can inspect open-cut mines at Tom Price and Newman. At Dampier and Port Hedland there are iron-ore shipping ports; the latter boasts the largest iron-ore export centre in Australia. Offshore from Karratha is the massive North West Shelf Gas Project; a visitor centre at the processing plant on Burrup Peninsula explains its operations.

→ For more detail see maps 619, 622, 624 & 626–7. For descriptions of ⊤ towns see Towns from A–Z (p. 315).

KIMBERLEY

Covering more than 420 000 square kilometres, this is an ancient landscape of mighty ranges, spectacular gorges and arid desert.

[BUNGLE BUNGLE RANGE, PURNULULU NATIONAL PARK]

Gibb River Road   One of Australia's premier four-wheel-drive destinations, the Gibb River Road is a 649-kilometre outback adventure between Derby and Kununurra, traversing some of the most spectacular gorge country of the Kimberley. Highlights of the rugged and diverse landscape include the many gorges, where waterfalls and crystal-clear pools are fringed by palms and pandanus.

Port of pearls
Broome's attractions include its tropical climate, cosmopolitan character and world-famous pearling industry. Enjoy a camel ride at sunset along Cable Beach, renowned as one of the most beautiful beaches in the world.

Lake Argyle   Lake Argyle was formed in the 1960s as part of the Ord River Scheme, the success of which is evident in the lush crops within its irrigation area. It has transformed a dusty, million-acre cattle station into a habitat for waterbirds, fish and crocodiles; the hills and ridges of the former station have become islands.

Purnululu National Park
A rough track off the Great Northern Highway leads to the spectacular Bungle Bungle Range in Purnululu National Park, on the Ord River. A fantastic landscape of huge black-and-orange sandstone domes is intersected by narrow, palm-lined gorges where pools reflect sunlight off sheer walls.

Geikie Gorge   The Fitzroy River cuts through the Geikie Range to create a 7-kilometre gorge just north-east of Fitzroy Crossing. The riverbanks are inhabited by freshwater crocodiles, fruit bats and many bird species, and the only way to see the gorge is by boat – during the Dry.

Wolfe Creek Crater   Two hours south of Halls Creek by unsealed road is the world's second largest meteorite crater. It is 850 metres across and was probably formed by a meteorite weighing at least several thousand tonnes crashing to earth a million years ago. It is most impressive from the air; scenic flights run from Halls Creek.

Map labels

TIMOR SEA
INDIAN OCEAN
ADMIRALTY GULF
JOSEPH BONAPARTE GULF
LAWLEY RIVER NP
Kalumburu
DRYSDALE RIVER NATIONAL PARK
MITCHELL RIVER NP
Wyndham
HIDDEN VALLEY NP
Kununurra
BUCCANEER ARCHIPELAGO
Montgomery Reef
Cape Leveque
Lombadina
Beagle Bay
King Sound
WINDJANA GORGE NP
Derby
DAMPIER PENINSULA
TUNNEL CREEK NP
Geikie Gorge
GEIKIE RANGE
KIMBERLEY
Lake Argyle
NORTHERN TERRITORY
BUNGLE BUNGLE RA
PURNULULU NATIONAL PARK
Halls Creek
Cable Beach
BROOME
Fitzroy Crossing
GEIKIE GORGE NP
WOLFE CREEK METEORITE CRATER NP
TANAMI DESERT
N
0   50 km
GREAT SANDY DESERT

TOP EVENTS

APR–MAY	King Tide Day (celebrating Australia's highest tide, Derby)
MAY	Ord Valley Muster (Kununurra)
JULY	Boab Festival (mardi gras, mud football and Stockmen and Bushies weekend, Derby)
JULY	Rodeo (Fitzroy Crossing)
AUG	Opera Under the Stars (Broome)
AUG–SEPT	Shinju Matsuri (Festival of the Pearl, Broome)

CLIMATE

HALLS CREEK

	J	F	M	A	M	J	J	A	S	O	N	D	
	37	36	36	34	30	27	27	30	34	37	38	38	MAX °C
	24	24	23	20	17	14	13	15	19	23	25	25	MIN °C
	153	137	74	22	13	5	6	2	4	17	37	77	RAIN MM
	13	13	8	3	2	1	1	1	1	3	6	11	RAIN DAYS

ABORIGINAL ART

The Kimberley is one of Australia's most important regions for Aboriginal rock art. It is renowned for two styles – the Bradshaw and the Wandjina. The Bradshaw figures, as they are known, are painted in red ochre. According to one Aboriginal legend, birds drew the figures using their beaks. One rock-face frieze shows figures dancing and swaying; another depicts figures elaborately decorated with headdresses, tassels, skirts and epaulets. Significant Bradshaw sites have been found on the Drysdale River. The more recent Wandjina figures, depictions of ancestor spirits from the sky and sea who brought rain and fertility, are in solid red or black, outlined in red ochre, and sometimes on a white background. Wandjina figures are typically human-like, with pallid faces and wide, staring eyes, halos around their heads and, for reasons of religious belief, no mouths. Good examples of Wandjina art have been found near Kalumburu on the King Edward River and at the burial site known as Panda-Goornnya on the Drysdale River.

TOWNS A–Z
western australia

[FITZROY BLUFF, THE KIMBERLEY]

LEGEND

ℹ️ VISITOR INFORMATION

📻 RADIO STATIONS

🏠 IN TOWN

🌴 WHAT'S ON

🍴 WHERE TO EAT

🛏️ WHERE TO STAY

🧭 NEARBY

Albany

see inset box on next page

Augusta

Pop. 1072
Map ref. 616 C11 | 618 B11 | 620 B11

ℹ️ Blackwood Ave; (08) 9758 0166; www.margaretriver.com

📻 98.3 FM ABC South West Radio, 99.1 FM ABC Radio National

The town of Augusta lies in the south-west corner of Western Australia. The state's third-oldest settlement sits high on the slopes of the Hardy Inlet, overlooking the mouth of the Blackwood River and the waters of Flinders Bay. Just beyond it lies Cape Leeuwin with its unforgettable signpost dividing the oceans: the Southern Ocean to the south and the Indian Ocean to the west.

🏠 **Augusta Historical Museum** Augusta's difficult beginning in 1830 is documented in this collection of artefacts and photographs. An exhibit details the 1986 rescue of whales that beached themselves near the town. Blackwood Ave; (08) 9758 0465.

Crafters Croft: locally made handcrafts, jams, emu-oil products; Ellis St.

🌴 *Augusta River Festival:* Mar. *Spring Flower Show:* Sept/Oct.

🍴 *The Colourpatch Cafe:* modern Australian; 98 Albany Tce; (08) 9758 1295.

🛏️ *Augusta Sheoak Chalets:* chalets with panoramic views; 298 Hillview Rd; 0419 555 072. *Baywatch Manor:* budget B&B;

9 Heppingstone View (rear of 88 Blackwood Ave); (08) 9758 1290. *Blackwood River Houseboats:* houseboats along the Blackwood River; Lot 450 Bussell Hwy, Westbay; (08) 9758 0181. *Brilea Cottages and B&B:* self-contained cottages and B&B; Bussell Hwy, Karridale; (08) 9758 5001. *Molloy Island Hideaway:* self-contained house; Fairlawn Pl, Molloy Island; 0403 338 813.

🧭 **Leeuwin–Naturaliste National Park** This park extends 120 km from Cape Naturaliste in the north to Cape Leeuwin in the south. Close to Augusta are 3 major attractions: Cape Leeuwin, Jewel Cave and Hamelin Bay. Cape Leeuwin (8 km sw) marks the most south-westerly point of Australia. Climb 176 steps to the top of the limestone lighthouse, mainland Australia's tallest. Nearby is the Old Water Wheel, built in 1895 from timber that has since calcified, giving it the appearance of stone. Jewel Cave (8 km nw on Caves Rd) is renowned for its limestone formations, including the longest straw stalactite found in any tourist cave. At Hamelin Bay (18 km nw) a windswept beach and the skeleton of an old jetty give little indication of the massive amounts of jarrah and karri that were once transported from here. In the heyday of the local timber industry, the port's exposure to the treacherous north-west winds resulted in 11 wrecks. These now form the state's most unusual Heritage Trail: the Hamelin Bay Wreck Trail, for experienced divers. *See also Margaret River and Dunsborough.*

The Landing Place: where the first European settlers landed in 1830; 3 km s. *Whale Rescue Memorial:* commemorates the 1986 rescue of beached pilot whales; 4 km s. *Matthew Flinders Memorial:* Flinders began mapping the Australian coastline from

ALBANY

Pop. 25 197

Map ref. 617 D11 | 618 G11 | 620 E11

i Old Railway Station, Proudlove Pde; (08) 9841 9290 or 1800 644 088; www.albanytourist.com.au

100.9 FM Albany Community Radio, 630 AM ABC Local Radio

Albany, a picturesque city on Western Australia's south coast, is the site of the state's first European settlement. On Boxing Day 1826, Major Edmund Lockyer, with a party of soldiers and convicts from New South Wales, came ashore to establish a military and penal outpost. Ninety years later, Albany was the embarkation point for Australian troops during World War I and, for many, their last view of the continent. A whaling industry, which began in the 1940s, defined the town until the Cheynes Beach Whaling Company closed in 1978. Nowadays, whale-watching has taken its place. Lying within the protected shelter of the Princess Royal Harbour on the edge of King George Sound, Albany is one of the state's most popular tourist destinations.

Historic buildings Albany boasts more than 50 buildings of historical significance dating back to the early years of the settlement. Two of the oldest were built in the 1830s: Patrick Taylor Cottage on Duke St, which houses an extensive collection of period costumes and household goods, and the Old Farm at Strawberry Hill on Middleton Rd, site of the first government farm in WA. Other heritage buildings include the Old Gaol (1851), with its collection of social history artefacts, and the Residency Museum (1850s), a showcase of historical and environmental exhibits, both in Residency Rd. There are self-guide walks available, including the Colonial Buildings Historical Walk; contact visitor centre for brochures.

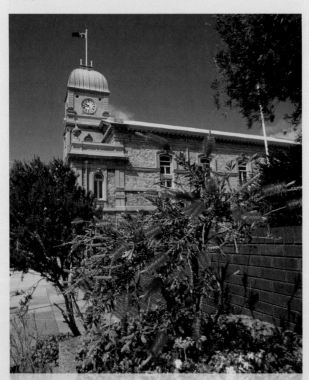

[ALBANY'S TOWN HALL]

The Amity: full-scale replica of the brig that brought Albany's first settlers from Sydney in 1826; Princess Royal Dr. *St. John's Church:* 1848 Anglican church is the oldest in the state; York St. *Vancouver Arts Centre:* gallery, craft shop, studio and workshop complex, originally the Albany Cottage Hospital (1887); Vancouver St. *House of Gems:* extensive range of gemstones and jewellery; cnr York St and Stirling Tce. *Dog Rock:* granite outcrop resembling the head of an enormous labrador is a photo opportunity not to be missed; Middleton Rd. *Princess Royal Fortress:* commissioned in 1893, Albany's first federal fortress was fully operational until the 1950s; off Forts Rd. *Tanglehead Brewing Company:* award-winning ales; Stirling Tce. *Spectacular views:* lookouts at the peaks of Mt Clarence and Mt Melville have 360-degree views. Near the top of Mt Clarence is the Desert Mounted Corps Memorial statue, a recast of the original statue erected at Suez in 1932; Apex Dr. John Barnesby Memorial Lookout at the top of Mt Melville is 23 m high, with observation decks; Melville Dr. *Bibbulmun Track:* 963 km walking track to Perth begins at Albany's Old Railway Station in Proudlove Pde; *see below. Whale-watching:* cruises daily from town jetty to see southern rights; June–Oct.

Farmers markets: Aberdeen St; Sat mornings. *Vintage Blues Festival:* Jan. *Great Southern Wine Festival:* Feb.

Earl of Spencer: pub fare in historic tavern; Cnr Earl and Spencer sts; (08) 9841 1322. *Lime 303:* contemporary, creative restaurant; The Dog Rock Motel, 303 Middleton Rd; (08) 9841 1400. *The Naked Bean:* for coffee addicts; 21 Sanford Rd; (08) 9841 4225. *The Wild Duck Restaurant:* sophisticated dining; 112 York St; (08) 9842 2554. *The Lily Railway Station Restaurant:* European fare; 9793 Chester Pass Rd, Amelup; (08) 9827 9205 or 1800 980 002.

Foreshore Apartments: harbour-view apartments; 81–89 Proudlove Pde; (08) 9841 1506. *Middleton Beach Holiday Park:* beachside holiday park; 28 Flinders Pde; (08) 9841 3593 or 1800 644 674. *Old Surrey:* self-contained manor; 55–59 Burt St, Mount Clarence; 0413 015 145. *The Priory:* elegant B&B; 55–59 Burt St, Mount Clarence; 0413 015 145. *The Rocks Albany:* stately B&B; 182–188 Grey St West; (08) 9842 5969. *Cape Howe Cottages:* self-contained cottages; 322 Tennessee Rd South, Lowlands Beach; (08) 9845 1295. *The Lily Dutch Windmill:* Nordic-style self-contained accommodation; 9793 Chester Pass Rd, Amelup; (08) 9827 9205 or 1800 980 002.

Bibbulmun Track At 963 km, this is WA's only long-distance walking trail and one of the longest continuously marked trails in Australia. It stretches from Kalamunda, a suburb on the outskirts of Perth, to Albany. On the way it passes through some of the state's most picturesque southern towns including Dwellingup, Collie, Balingup, Pemberton, Northcliffe, Walpole and Denmark. Named after a local Aboriginal language group, the track is marked by a stylised image of the 'Waugal' (rainbow serpent), a spirit being from the Aboriginal Dreaming. Whether taking a short walk or a 5-day hike, easy access points enable walkers of all ages and fitness levels to experience the Bibbulmun Track. Walk the track in springtime and see the bush at its best with WA's amazing array of wildflowers. Near Walpole you'll encounter the massive red tingle trees of the Valley of the Giants. Other well-known natural attractions on the track include Mt Cook, the highest point in the Darling Range, Beedelup Falls and the Gloucester Tree lookout. For maps and more information contact the Bibbulmun Track Office of DEC on (08) 9334 0265 or visit www.bibbulmuntrack.org.au

Torndirrup National Park Torndirrup is one of the most visited parks in the state, featuring abundant wildflowers, wildlife and bushwalking trails. The park is renowned for its rugged coastal scenery, including such features as the Gap, a chasm with a 24 m drop to the sea, and the Natural Bridge, a span of granite eroded by huge seas to form a giant arch. Exercise extreme caution on this dangerous coastline; king waves can rush in unexpectedly. 17 km s.

Whale World Even before the Cheynes Beach Whaling Company closed in 1978, Albany's oldest industry was a major tourist attraction. In its heyday, the company's chasers took up to 850 whales a season. View the restored whale-chaser *Cheynes IV*, whale skeletons, the old processing factory, an aircraft display and the world's largest collection of marine mammal paintings. This is the only whaling museum in the world created from a

working whaling station. Free guided tours are available on (08) 9844 4021. 25 km SE.

Albany Bird Park: undercover walk-in aviary with over 250 native and exotic birds; Frenchman Bay Rd; 3.5 km sw. *Deer-O-Dome:* showcases the Australian deer industry; 6 km N. *Mt Romance Sandalwood Factory:* skincare products, perfumes, therapeutics and free guided tours; (08) 9845 6888; 12 km N. *Albany Wind Farm:* 12 giant turbines, each 100 m high; 12 km sw. *Point Possession Heritage Trail:* views and interpretive plaques; Vancouver Peninsula; 20 km SE. *Fishing:* Emu Point (8 km NE), Oyster Harbour (15 km NE), Jimmy Newhill's Harbour (20 km s) and Frenchman Bay (25 km SE). *Diving:* former HMAS *Perth* was scuttled in 2001 as an artificial dive reef; Frenchman Bay; 25 km SE. *West Cape Howe National Park:* walking, fishing, swimming and hang-gliding; 30 km w. *Two Peoples Bay Nature Reserve:* sanctuary for the noisy scrub bird, thought to be extinct but rediscovered in 1961; 40 km E. *Tours:* include sailing, wineries, eco-tours, 4WD driving and national parks tours; contact visitor centre for more details.

See also GREAT SOUTHERN, p. 309

Cape Leeuwin in December 1801; 5 km s. *Alexandra Bridge:* picnic and camping spot with towering jarrah trees and beautiful wildflowers in season; 10 km N. *Boranup Maze and Lookout:* the maze offers a short walking track under trellis, while the lookout provides a picnic area with panoramic views towards the coast; 18 km N. *Augusta–Busselton Heritage Trail:* 100 km trail traces the history of the area through the pioneering Bussell and Molloy families, who settled in Augusta only to move further up the coast looking for suitable agricultural land; contact visitor centre for map. *Cruises:* Blackwood River and Hardy Inlet. *Marron in season:* fishing licence required and available at the post office; Blackwood Ave. *Whale-watching:* charter boats and coastal vantage points offer sightings of migrating humpback whales (June–Aug) and southern right whales (June–Oct), plus pods of dolphins and fur seals; contact visitor centre for details.

See also THE SOUTH-WEST, p. 307

Australind

Pop. 8716
Map ref. 616 E3 | 618 C8 | 620 C9

ℹ️ Henton Cottage, cnr Old Coast and Paris rds; (08) 9796 0122.

📻 95.7 Hot FM, 1224 AM ABC Radio National

Lying on the Leschenault Estuary and bordered by the Collie River, Australind offers a multitude of aquatic pleasures including fishing, crabbing, prawning, swimming, boating, sailing and windsurfing. The town's unusual name is a contraction of Australia and India, coined by its founders in the hope of a prosperous trade in horses between the two countries.

🏠 *St Nicholas Church:* built in 1840, reputedly the smallest church in Australia at only 3.6 m wide and 8.2 m long; Paris Rd. *Henton Cottage:* early 1840s heritage building now houses the

visitor centre and an art and craft gallery; cnr Old Coast and Paris rds. *Featured Wood Gallery:* fine furniture and craft made from the local timbers of jarrah, she-oak, marri, banksia and blackbutt. Also includes a museum of Australian and American West history; Piggott Dr; (08) 9797 2411. *Pioneer Memorial:* site of the first settlers' landing in 1840; Old Coast Rd. *Cathedral Ave:* scenic 2 km drive through arching paperbark trees with sightings of kangaroos and black swans, especially at sunset; off Old Coast Rd.

🌴 *Carols in the Park:* Dec.

🛏️ *Australind Tourist Park:* ideal crabbing location; Lot 9 Old Coast Rd; (08) 9725 1206. *Cook's Park on Australind Waters:* 2-bedroom house; 474 Cathedral Ave; (08) 9796 0505. *Leschenault Inlet Caravan Park:* shady caravan park; Lot 52 Cathedral Ave; (08) 9797 1095.

🧭 **Leschenault Inlet** Offers recreational attractions from the simple pleasure of fishing from the Leschenault Inlet Fishing Groyne to picnicking, camping and bushwalking in the Peninsula Conservation Park. The park is a haven for native wildlife with over 60 species of birds recorded. Only walking or cycling is permitted in the park except for 4WD beach access from Buffalo Rd (1 km s). The Leschenault Waterway Discovery Centre has an interpretive gazebo with information on the estuary environment. Old Coast Rd; 2 km s.

Pioneer Cemetery: graves dating back to 1842 and beautiful wildflowers in season; Old Coast Rd; 2 km N. *Binningup and Myalup:* pleasant beach towns north of Leschenault. *Australind–Bunbury Tourist Drive:* coastal scenery, excellent crabbing and picnic spots; contact visitor centre for brochure.

See also THE SOUTH-WEST, p. 307

 RADIO STATIONS   IN TOWN   WHAT'S ON   WHERE TO EAT   WHERE TO STAY   NEARBY

Balingup

Pop. 443
Map ref. 616 G6 | 618 C9 | 620 C10

ℹ️ Brockman St; (08) 9764 1818; www.balinguptourism.com.au

📻 93.3 ABC Classic FM, 1044 AM ABC Local Radio

This small town, nestled in the Blackwood River Valley, is surrounded by rolling hills, forests and orchards. Balingup is renowned for its glowing summer sunsets, amazing autumn colours and misty winter mornings.

🏠 *Birdwood Park Fruit Winery:* unique award-winning fruit wines, chutneys, jams and fruits; Brockman St; (08) 9764 1172. *Tinderbox:* herbal and natural products; South Western Hwy. *Old Cheese Factory Craft Centre:* the largest art and craft centre in WA, including pottery and timber products; Balingup–Nannup Rd; (08) 9764 1018.

🌴 *Opera in the Valley:* Jan. *Small Farm Field Day:* festival and roadside scarecrows; Apr. *Medieval Carnivale:* Aug. *Festival of Country Gardens:* Oct/Nov. *Balingup Jalbrook Concert:* Nov.

🍴 *Balingup Bronze Cafe:* healthy and tasty; Balingup Bronze Gallery, South Western Hwy; (08) 9764 1843. *Fre-Jac French Restaurant:* French cuisine; Forrest St; (08) 9764 1883.

🛏️ *Balingup Heights Hilltop Forest Cottages:* timber cottages; 65 Nannup Rd; (08) 9764 1283. *Balingup Jalbrook Cottages & Alpacas:* range of cottages; Lot 1 Jayes Rd; (08) 9764 1616. *Balingup Rose B&B:* historic B&B; 208 Jayes Rd; (08) 9764 1205.

🔘 **Golden Valley Tree Park** This 60 ha arboretum boasts a superb collection of exotic and native trees. Other attractions include a tree information gazebo, walk trails, lookout and the historic Golden Valley Homestead. Old Padbury Rd; 2 km s.

Jalbrook Alpacas and Knitwear Gallery: alpacas to feed and alpaca knitwear; accommodation also available; (08) 9764 1190; 2 km E. *Lavender Farm:* oil-producing lavender farm with open gardens, picnic area, art gallery and giftshop. Take a distillation tour; open Sept–Apr, Balingup–Nannup Rd; (08) 9764 1436; 2.5 km w. *Balingup Heights Scenic Lookout:* stunning views of town and orchards; off Balingup–Nannup Rd; 2.5 km w. *Greenbushes:* boasts WA's first metal-producing mine (1888), still in production and now the world's largest tantalum producer. The Discovery Centre has interactive displays and walking trails, and there is an excellent lookout at the mine; 10 km w. *Heritage Country Cheese:* cheese-producing factory with viewing window and tastings; 16 km w. *Wineries:* several in area; contact visitor centre for details. *Balingup–Nannup Rd:* enjoy wonderful scenery, interesting and historic landmarks and great marroning, fishing and picnic sites. *Bibbulmun Track:* sections of this trail pass through Balingup; *see Albany.*

See also THE SOUTH-WEST, p. 307

Balladonia

Pop. 20
Map ref. 621 K7

ℹ️ Balladonia Roadhouse, Eyre Hwy; (08) 9039 3453.

Balladonia lies on the Eyre Highway on the western edge of the Nullarbor Plain. Its closest towns are Norseman, 191 kilometres to the west, and Caiguna, 182 kilometres to the east. This arid desert shrubland is one of the world's oldest landscapes, containing seashells millions of years old from when the area was ocean floor. Balladonia made world headlines in 1979 when space debris from NASA's *Skylab* landed 40 kilometres east on Woorlba Station.

🏠 **Cultural Heritage Museum** Learn about the crash-landing of *Skylab*, local indigenous culture, early explorers, Afghan cameleers and other chapters in the area's history. Balladonia Roadhouse, Eyre Hwy.

🍴 *Balladonia Roadhouse:* light meals and hearty fare; Eyre Hwy; (08) 9039 3453.

🛏️ *Balladonia Caravan Facility:* caravan sites, dorms, motel rooms; Eyre Hwy; (08) 9039 3453.

🔘 **90-Mile Straight** Have your photo taken beside the signpost marking the western end of the longest straight stretch of road in Australia, which runs for 90 miles (146.6 km) between Balladonia and Caiguna. Begins 35 km E.

Newman Rocks: superb views from rocky outcrop, with picnic and camping areas on-site; 50 km w. *Cape Arid National Park and Israelite Bay:* great birdwatching and fishing; access via 4WD track, south of town; check track conditions at roadhouse.

See also ESPERANCE & NULLARBOR, p. 310

Beverley

Pop. 850
Map ref. 618 E5 | 620 D7

ℹ️ Aeronautical Museum, 139 Vincent St; (08) 9646 1555; www.beverleywa.com

📻 99.7 FM ABC News Radio, 531 AM ABC Local Radio

Beverley is a small town set on the banks of the Avon River 130 kilometres east of Perth. Its main street boasts some beautifully preserved buildings, representing Federation to Art Deco architectural styles. This farming community, while having long been associated with wheat and wool, also produces grapes, olives, emus, deer and yabbies.

🏠 **Aeronautical Museum** This museum presents a comprehensive display of early aviation in WA. The museum's star attraction is the *Silver Centenary*, a biplane built between 1928 and 1930 by local man Selby Ford and his cousin Tom Shackles. Ford designed the plane in chalk on the floor where he worked. The plane first flew in July 1930, but was never licensed because of the lack of design blueprints. Vincent St.

Station Gallery: art exhibitions and sales in the Tudor-style (1889) railway station; Vincent St. *Dead Finish Museum:* the oldest building in town (1872) houses memorabilia and historic items from wooden cotton wheels to washing boards; open 11am–3pm Sun Mar–Nov or by appt through visitor centre; Hunt Rd.

🌴 *Yabbie Races:* Apr. *Annual Quick Shear:* Aug.

🍴 *Freemasons Hotel:* classic Australian pub; 104 Vincent St; (08) 9646 1094.

🛏️ *Beverley B&B:* heritage B&B; 131 Forrest St; (08) 9646 0073.

🔘 **Avondale Discovery Farm** Avondale is an agricultural research station with displays of historic farming machinery and tools. The 1850s homestead is furnished in period style and set in traditional gardens. There is also an animal nursery, Clydesdale horses and a picnic area with barbecues and a children's playground. A land-care education centre houses interactive displays. The farm hosts the Clydesdale and Vintage Day in June. Waterhatch Rd; (08) 9646 1004; 6 km w.

Brookton: attractions of this nearby town include the Old Police Station Museum and the Brookton Pioneer Heritage Trail, which highlights places significant to the local Aboriginal people; 32 km s. *County Peak Lookout:* spectacular views from the summit; 35 km SE. *The Avon Ascent:* take a self-drive tour of the Avon Valley; contact visitor centre for map.

See also HEARTLANDS, p. 308

Boyup Brook

Pop. 531
Map ref. 618 D9 | 620 C10

 Cnr Bridge and Abel sts; (08) 9765 1444;
www.bbvisitor.mysouthwest.com.au

100.5 Hot FM, 1044 AM ABC Local Radio

Boyup Brook is on the tranquil Blackwood River in the heart of Western Australia's grass-tree country. The town's name is thought to derive from the Aboriginal word 'booyup', meaning 'place of big stones' or 'place of much smoke', which was given to the nearby Boyup Pool. Seasonal wildflowers are abundant during September and October.

Carnaby Beetle and Butterfly Collection Keith Carnaby was such a leading light in the field of entomology that beetles have been named after him. His collection of Jewel beetles, part of which is on display at the Boyup Brook Tourist Information Centre, is regarded as the best outside the British Museum of Natural History. Cnr Bridge and Abel sts.

Pioneers' Museum: displays of historic agricultural, commercial and domestic equipment; open 2–5pm Mon, Wed, Fri or by appt; Jayes Rd. *Sandakan War Memorial:* honours 1500 Australian POWs sent to Sandakan to build an airfield for the Japanese; Sandakan Park. *The Flax Mill:* built during WW II for processing flax needed for war materials. At its peak it operated 24 hrs a day and employed over 400 people. A scale model of the mill can be viewed on-site, which is now the caravan park; off Barron St. *Heritage walk:* follows 23 plaques around town centre; self-guide pamphlet available from visitor centre. *Bicentennial Walking Trail:* pleasant walk around town and beside the Blackwood River.

Country Music Festival and Ute Muster: Feb. *Blackwood Marathon:* running, canoeing, horseriding, cycling and swimming a 58 km course to Bridgetown; Oct.

Chudacud Estate: versatile vineyard restaurant; Lot 22 Wade Rd; (08) 9764 4053.

Scotts Brook: tranquil B&B; 201B Scotts Brook Rd; (08) 9765 3014. *Tulip Cottage:* restored cottage; 30 Bridge St; (08) 9765 1223.

Harvey Dickson's Country Music Centre This entertainment shed is decorated wall-to-wall and floor-to-rafter with music memorabilia spanning 100 years. The 'record room' containing hundreds of records also has Elvis memorabilia. There is a music show in Sept and a rodeo in Oct, with basic bush camping facilities. Open by appt; Arthur River Rd; (08) 9765 1125; 5 km N.

Roo Gully Wildlife Sanctuary: for injured and orphaned Australian wildlife, with a special focus on raising unfurred marsupial young; 1 km N. *Gregory Tree:* remaining stump of a tree blazed by explorer Augustus Gregory in 1845; Gibbs Rd; 15 km NE. *Norlup Homestead:* built in 1874, this is one of the district's first farms; to view contact (08) 9767 3034; off Norlup Rd; 27 km SE. *Wineries:* Scotts Brook Winery (20 km SE) and Blackwood Crest Winery (at Kilikup, 40 km E); both open daily. *Haddleton Flora Reserve:* displays of brown and pink boronia in season. Not suitable for campers or caravans; 50 km NE. *Boyup Brook flora drives:* self-guide maps available from visitor centre.

See also THE SOUTH-WEST, p. 307

Bremer Bay

Pop. 239
Map ref. 620 G10

 Community Resource Centre and Library, Mary St; (08) 9837 4171; www.bremerbay.com

103.5 WA FM, 531 AM ABC Local Radio

Bremer Bay on the south coast is a wide expanse of crystal-clear blue water and striking white sand. The main beach, only a ten-minute walk from the town, has a sheltered cove for swimming and fishing. Just north of Bremer Bay is the magnificent Fitzgerald River National Park with its four rivers, dramatic gorges, wide sand plains, rugged cliffs, pebbly beaches and spectacular displays of wildflowers between August and October.

Watersports: fishing, boating, swimming, surfing, waterskiing, scuba diving, bay cruises and seasonal whale-watching are the town's main attractions. *Rammed-earth buildings:* the Bremer Bay Hotel/Motel on Frantom Way and Catholic Church on Mary St are excellent examples of rammed-earth construction.

Mount Barren Restaurant: local produce; Bremer Bay Resort, 1 Frantom Way; (08) 9837 4133.

Bremer Bay Beaches Tourist Resort Caravan Park: 4-star holiday park; Wellstead Rd; (08) 9837 4290. *Bremer Bay Resort:* well-appointed resort; 1 Frantom Way; (08) 9837 4133. *Quaalup Homestead Wilderness Retreat:* range of simple accommodation; Fitzgerald River National Park; (08) 9837 4124.

Fitzgerald River National Park This huge 242 739 ha park, lying between Bremer Bay and Hopetoun to the east, is renowned for its scenery and flora. A staggering 1800 species of flowering plants have been recorded. Royal hakea, endemic to this region, is one of the most striking. Quaalup Homestead (1858), restored as a museum, offers meals and accommodation in the park. Point Ann has a viewing platform for whale-watching (southern rights, June–Oct). Campgrounds, barbecues and picnic areas available. 17 km N.

Wellstead Homestead Museum: the first residence in the area, now incorporating a gallery and museum with family heirlooms, historic farm equipment and vintage cars; Peppermint Grove, Wellstead Rd; (08) 9837 4448; 9 km SW. *Surfing:* nearby beaches include Native Dog Beach, Dillon Bay, Fosters Beach and Trigelow Beach; ask at visitor centre for directions.

See also GREAT SOUTHERN, p. 309

Bridgetown

Pop. 2321
Map ref. 616 H8 | 618 D9 | 620 C10

 154 Hampton St; (08) 9761 1740 or 1800 777 140; www.bridgetown.com.au

100.5 Hot FM, 1044 AM ABC Local Radio

Bridgetown is a picturesque timber town nestled among rolling hills on the banks of the Blackwood River. Crossing the river, Bridgetown boasts the longest wooden bridge in the state, made of the area's famous jarrah. In addition to tourism, timber milling and mining (lithium, tantalum and tin) are now the largest industries in the area.

Brierley Jigsaw Gallery The only public jigsaw gallery in the Southern Hemisphere, Brierley has over 170 jigsaws ranging from the world's smallest wooden puzzle to a huge 9000-piece jigsaw. A highlight is an 8000-piece jigsaw of the Sistine Chapel. Back of visitor centre, Hampton St.

BROOME

Pop. 11 547

Map ref. 624 H8 | 628 A11

i **Cnr Bagot St and Broome Rd; (08) 9192 2222;**
www.broomevisitorcentre.com.au

100.3 WA FM, 675 AM ABC Local Radio

Broome is distinguished by its pearling history, cosmopolitan character and startling natural assets: white sandy beaches, turquoise water and red soils. The discovery of pearling grounds off the coast in the 1880s led to the foundation of the Broome township in 1883. A melting pot of nationalities flocked to its shores in the hope of making a fortune. Japanese, Malays and Koepangers joined the Aboriginal pearl divers, while the Chinese became the shopkeepers in town. By 1910 Broome was the world's leading pearling centre. In those early, heady days, over 400 pearling luggers operated out of Broome. The industry suffered when world markets collapsed in 1914, but stabilised in the 1970s as cultured-pearl farming developed. Today remnants of Broome's exotic past are everywhere, with the town's multicultural society ensuring a dynamic array of cultural influences. Broome's beaches are ideal for swimming and there is good fishing year-round.

Pearl Luggers Experience Broome's pearling heritage by visiting 2 restored pearling luggers in Chinatown. Tours daily. Dampier Tce; (08) 9192 2059.

Japanese Cemetery The largest Japanese cemetery in Australia contains the graves of over 900 Japanese pearl divers, dating back to 1896. This is a sobering reminder of the perils of the early pearling days when the bends, cyclones and sharks claimed many lives. Cnr Port Dr and Savannah Way.

Staircase to the Moon This beautiful optical illusion is caused by a full moon reflecting off the exposed mudflats of Roebuck Bay at extremely low tides. Town Beach; 3 nights monthly from Mar–Oct; check dates and times at visitor centre.

Chinatown: an extraordinary mix of colonial and Asian influences, Chinatown was once the bustling hub of Broome where pearl sheds, billiard saloons and Chinese eateries flourished; now it is home to some of the world's finest pearl showrooms. *Buildings on Hamersley Street:* distinctive Broome-style architecture including the courthouse, made of teak inside and corrugated iron outside; Captain Gregory's House, a classic old pearling master's house, built in 1915, now an art gallery; and Matso's Cafe, once the Union Bank Building. *Historical Museum:* pearling display and collection of photographs and literature on Broome's past; Robinson St. *Bedford Park:* war memorial, replica of explorer William Dampier's sea chest and an old train coach; Hamersley St. *Shell House:* one of the largest shell collections in Australia; Guy St. *Sun Pictures:* the world's oldest operating outdoor cinema, opened in 1916; Carnarvon St. *St John of God Convent:* built in 1926 by a Japanese shipbuilder using traditional methods that emphasise the external framing of the building; cnr Barker and Weld sts. *Deep Water Jetty:* good for fishing; Port Dr. *Heritage trail:* 2 km walk introduces places of interest; contact visitor centre for self-guide pamphlet.

Courthouse Markets: Hamersley St; Sat and Sun mornings Apr–Oct. *Town Beach Markets:* Robinson St; 1st 2 nights of the Staircase to the Moon; check with visitor centre for dates and times. *Race Round:* horseracing; June–Aug. *Opera Under the Stars:* Aug. *Shinju Matsuri:* Festival of the Pearl, recalls Broome's heyday and includes Dragon Boat Regatta; Aug/Sept. *Mango Festival:* Nov.

Cafe Carlotta: rustic Italian; Jones Pl; (08) 9192 7606. *Matso's Broome Brewery:* laid-back brewery; 60 Hamersley St; (08) 9193 5811. *The Club Restaurant:* fine dining; Cable Beach Club Resort & Spa, Cable Beach Rd; 1800 199 099. *The Old Zoo Cafe:* alfresco cafe; 2 Challenor Dr; (08) 9193 6200. *The Wharf Restaurant:* casual seafood; On the Wharf, Port Dr; (08) 9192 5700.

Cable Beach Club Resort & Spa: outstanding resort; Cable Beach Rd; 1800 199 099. *Kimberley Klub Broome:* centrally

[CAMEL RIDE ON CABLE BEACH]

WESTERN AUSTRALIA

located hostel; 62 Fredrick St; (08) 9192 3233 or 1800 004 345. **McAlpine House:** historic restored house; 55 Herbert St; (08) 9192 0510 or 1800 746 282. **The Bungalow-Broome:** romantic bungalow; 3 McKenzie Rd; 0417 918 420. **The Courthouse B&B:** luxurious B&B; 10 Stewart St; (08) 9192 2733. **Kooljaman at Cape Leveque:** beach safari retreat; Cape Leveque; (08) 9192 4970.

Cable Beach With its 22 km of pristine white sands fringing the turquoise waters of the Indian Ocean, Cable Beach is one of the most stunning beaches in the world. Every day the beach is washed clean by 10 m high tides. It takes its name from the telegraph cable laid between Broome and Java in 1889. The $55 million Cable Beach Resort, which fronts onto the beach, is a popular tourist destination. While you're here, why not do that quintessential Broome activity and ride a camel along this famous beach? Contact visitor centre for details. 7 km NW.

Gantheaume Point Dinosaur footprints believed to be 130 million years old can be seen at very low tide. A plaster cast of the tracks has been embedded at the top of the cliff. Nearby, view the almost perfectly round Anastasia's Pool, built by a lighthouse keeper for his wife. 5 km NE.

Crocodile Park: home to some of Australia's biggest crocodiles; Cable Beach Rd; 7 km NW. **Reddell Beach:** enjoy the dramatic sight of Broome's distinctive red soils, known as 'pindan', meeting white sands and brilliant blue water; 7 km SW. **Buccaneer Rock:** at entrance to Dampier Creek, this landmark commemorates

Captain William Dampier and HMS *Roebuck*; 15 km E. **Broome Bird Observatory:** see some of the 310 species of migratory wader birds that arrive each year from Siberia; 17 km E. **Willie Creek Pearl Farm:** the Kimberley's only pearl farm open to the public, with daily tours; (08) 9192 0000; 35 km N. **Dampier Peninsula:** this remote area north of Broome boasts unspoiled coastline (4WD access only). Record-breaking game fish have been caught in the surrounding waters, which may account for the fact that the coastal towns of the Pilbara boast the highest rate of private vessel ownership in the country. Charters and tours leave from Dampier. The Sacred Heart Church at Beagle Bay (118 km NE) was built by Pallotine monks in 1917 and boasts a magnificent pearl-shell altar. Lombadina (200 km NE) is a former mission now home to an Aboriginal community that offers sightseeing, fishing and mudcrabbing tours; contact (08) 9192 4936. Cape Leveque, at the north of the peninsula, is well known for its pristine beaches and rugged pindan cliffs; 220 km NE. **Buccaneer Archipelago:** in Broome you can arrange scenic flights over this magnificent landscape that stretches north-east of the Dampier Peninsula. Also known as the Thousand Islands, this is a dramatic coastal area of rugged red cliffs, spectacular waterfalls and secluded white sandy beaches. Here you'll find whirlpools created by massive 11 m tides and the amazing horizontal two-way waterfall of Talbot Bay. **Hovercraft Spirit of Broome:** tours of Roebuck Bay; details from visitor centre.

See also KIMBERLEY, p. 314

Bridgedale: historic house owned by John Blechynden, one of the area's first European settlers, constructed in 1862 of local timber and bricks made from riverbank clay; South Western Hwy. **Memorial Park:** picnic area with a giant chessboard, 3 ft high pieces for hire from visitor centre; South Western Hwy.

Blackwood River Park Markets: Sun mornings each fortnight. **State Downriver Kayaking Championships:** Aug. **Blackwood Classic Powerboat Race:** Sept. **Blackwood Marathon:** between Boyup Brook and Bridgetown; Oct. **Blues at Bridgetown Festival:** Nov. **Festival of Country Gardens:** Nov.

Bridgetown Pottery Tearooms & Gallery: home-style cooking; 81 Hampton St; (08) 9761 1038. **Nelson's of Bridgetown:** country charm; 38 Hampton St; (08) 9761 1641 or 1800 635 565. **The 1896 Cafe:** wholesome cafe; 145–151 Hampton St; (08) 9761 1699. **The Bridgetown Hotel:** pub grub; 157 Hampton St; (08) 9761 1034.

Ford House Retreat: romantic B&B; Eedle Tce; (08) 9761 1816. **Maranup Ford:** range of accommodation; Maranup Ford Rd; (08) 9761 1200. **Nelson's of Bridgetown:** range of accommodation; 38 Hampton St; (08) 9761 1641 or 1800 635 565. **Tortoiseshell Farm:** cottages and B&B; Polina Rd; (08) 9761 1089.

The Cidery Discover the history of Bridgetown's apple industry and sample fresh juice, cider or award-winning beers. The orchard contains over 80 varieties of apple. Closed Tues; cnr Forrest St and Gifford Rd; (08) 9761 2204; 2 km N.

Geegelup Heritage Trail: 52 km walk retraces history of agriculture, mining and timber in the region. It starts at Blackwood River Park. **Scenic drives:** choose from 8 scenic drives in the district through green hills, orchards and valleys into karri and jarrah timber country; self-guide maps available at visitor centre. **Excellent views:** Sutton's Lookout, off Phillips St and Hester Hill, 5 km N. **Bridgetown Jarrah Park:** ideal place for a picnic or bushwalk. The Tree Fallers and Shield Tree trails commemorate the early timber history of the town; Brockman Hwy; 20 km W. **Karri Gully:** bushwalking and picnicking; 20 km W.

See also THE SOUTH-WEST, p. 307

Bunbury

see inset box on next page

Busselton

Pop. 15 385
Map ref. 616 C6 | 618 B9 | 620 B10

ⓘ 38 Peel Tce; (08) 9752 1288; www.geographebay.com

📻 96.5 FM Western Tourist Radio, 684 AM ABC Local Radio

First settled by Europeans in 1834, Busselton is one of the oldest towns in Western Australia. It is situated on the shores of Geographe Bay and the picturesque Vasse River. Sheltered from most prevailing winds, the tranquil waters of the bay are an aquatic playground edged with 30 kilometres of white sand beaches. Over the past three decades, the traditional industries of timber, dairying, cattle and sheep have been joined by grape-growing and

 RADIO STATIONS   IN TOWN   WHAT'S ON   WHERE TO EAT   WHERE TO STAY   NEARBY

winemaking. Fishing is also important, particularly crayfish and salmon in season. In spring, the wildflowers are magnificent.

 Busselton Jetty The longest timber jetty in the Southern Hemisphere was built over a 95-year period, beginning in 1865, principally for the export of timber. Over 5000 ships from all over the world docked here through the ages of sail, steam and diesel, before the port closed in 1972. The jetty stretches a graceful 1.8 km into Geographe Bay and has always been a popular spot for fishing, snorkelling and scuba diving because of the variety of marine life. An Interpretive Centre at the base of the jetty displays historical and environmental exhibits. At the seaward end is an Underwater Observatory featuring an observation chamber with viewing windows 8 m beneath the surface revealing vividly coloured corals, sponges and fish. Tours are available, bookings essential. End of Queen St.

Ballarat Engine: first steam locomotive in WA; Pries Ave. *St Mary's Anglican Church:* built in 1844 of limestone and jarrah, with a she-oak shingle roof. The churchyard has many pioneer graves, including John Garrett Bussell's, after whom Busselton was named; Peel Tce. *Nautical Lady Entertainment World:* family fun park with giant water slide, flying fox, minigolf, skate park, racing cars, lookout tower and nautical museum; on beachfront at end of Queen St; (08) 9752 3473. *Old Courthouse:* restored gaol cells and arts complex; Queen St. *Busselton Historical Museum:* originally a creamery, now houses historic domestic equipment; closed Tues; Peel Tce. *Vasse River Parkland:* barbecue facilities; Peel Tce.

Markets: Barnard Park, 1st and 3rd Sat each month; Railway Building Park, Causeway Rd, 2nd and 4th Sun each month. *Southbound:* music festival; Jan. *Festival of Busselton:* Jan. *Beach Festival:* Jan. *Busselton Jetty Swim:* Feb. *Geographe Bay Race Week:* yachting; Feb. *Bluewater Fishing Classic:* Mar. *Great Escapade:* cycling; Mar. *Busselton Agricultural Show:* one of the oldest and largest country shows in WA; Oct/Nov. *Smell the Roses, Taste the Wine:* Nov. *Ironman Western Australia Triathlon:* Dec.

Newtown House Restaurant: fine dining; 737 Bussell Hwy; (08) 9755 4485. *The Equinox:* beachside dining; 343 Queen St; (08) 9752 4641. *The Goose:* jetty-side longtime favourite; Geographe Bay Rd; (08) 9754 7700. *Vasse Bar Cafe:* funky Mediterranean; 44 Queen St; (08) 9754 8560.

Beachlands Holiday Park: well-appointed holiday park; 10 Earnshaw Rd; (08) 9752 2107 or 1800 622 107. *Mandalay Holiday Resort and Tourist Park:* beachside holiday park; off Bussell Hwy at Lockhart St, Broadwater; (08) 9752 1328 or 1800 248 231. *Martin Fields Beach Retreat:* beachside retreat; 24 Lockville Rd, Geographe; (08) 9754 2001.

Tuart Forest National Park The majestic tuart tree grows only on coastal limestone 200 km either side of Perth. Known locally as the Ludlow Tuart Forest, this 2049 ha park protects the largest natural tuart forest in the world. It also has the tallest and largest specimens of tuart trees on the Swan Coastal Plain, up to 33 m high and 10 m wide. Enjoy scenic drives, forest walks and picnics in a magnificent setting. 12 km SE.

Wonnerup House: built in 1859, now a National Trust museum and fine example of colonial architecture, furnished in period style; 10 km N. *Bunyip Craft Centre:* Ludlow; 15 km E. *Wineries:* numerous vineyards and wineries in the area. Many are open for cellar-door tastings; contact visitor centre for map. *Augusta–Busselton Heritage Trail:* contact visitor centre for map.

See also THE SOUTH-WEST, p. 307

Caiguna

Pop. 10
Map ref. 621 L7

i Caiguna Roadhouse; (08) 9039 3459.

The small community of Caiguna, on the Nullarbor Plain, consists of a 24-hour roadhouse, caravan park, motel, restaurant and service station. The nearest towns are Balladonia, 182 kilometres west, and Cocklebiddy, 65 kilometres east. To the south is the coastal wilderness of Nuytsland Nature Reserve. From immediately east of Caiguna until Border Village, locals operate on Central Western Time, 45 minutes ahead of the rest of Western Australia.

John Eyre Motel: comfortable motel rooms; Eyre Hwy; (08) 9039 3459.

 John Baxter Memorial In 1841, the explorer John Baxter, together with an Aboriginal guide known as Wylie and 2 other unnamed Aboriginal men, accompanied Edward John Eyre on his epic journey across the Nullarbor Plain. The party left Fowlers Bay in SA on 25 Feb and reached the site of modern-day Eucla on 12 Mar. Later, the 2 unnamed Aboriginal men killed Baxter and, taking most of the supplies, fled into the desert. Eyre and Wylie walked for another month and eventually reached Thistle Cove (near Esperance), where they were rescued by a French whaler. The Baxter memorial is on the Baxter Cliffs overlooking the Great Australian Bight; 4WD access only. 38 km S.

90-Mile Straight: have your photo taken beside the signpost marking the eastern end of the longest straight stretch of road in Australia, which runs for 90 miles (146.6 km) between Caiguna and a point east of Balladonia; 4 km w. *Caiguna Blowhole:* a hole in the flat limestone landscape where the earth seemingly breathes in and out; 5 km w.

See also ESPERANCE & NULLARBOR, p. 310

Carnamah

Pop. 358
Map ref. 620 B4

i Council offices, Macpherson St; (08) 9951 7000; www.carnamah.wa.gov.au

101.9 WA FM, 612 AM ABC Radio National

Carnamah is a typical wheat-belt town servicing the surrounding wheat and sheep properties. From late July through to December the shire of Carnamah and the rest of the wheat belt blossoms into a wildflower wonderland. This is one of Western Australia's richest areas of flowering plants, with more than 600 species.

Historical Society Museum: displays historic domestic equipment and old farm machinery; Macpherson St.

North Midlands Agricultural Show, Rodeo and Ute Parade: Sept.

Three Springs Tourist Lodge: B&B accommodation; Three Springs; (08) 9954 1065.

Tathra National Park This park, with its diverse range of spring wildflowers, is named after the Nyungar word for 'beautiful place'. 25 km SW.

Macpherson's Homestead: an excellent example of pioneering architecture (1869), once the home of Duncan Macpherson, the first settler in the area; open by appt; Bunjil Rd; (08) 9951 1690; 1 km E. *Yarra Yarra Lake:* this salt lake changes from pink in summer to deep blue in winter. View it from the Lakes Lookout; 16 km S. *Eneabba:* spectacular wildflowers surround this mining town; 74 km w. *Lake Indoon:* a freshwater lake popular for sailing,

BUNBURY

Pop. 54 967

Map ref. 616 D4 | 618 C8 | 620 C9

[VIEW OF BUNBURY FROM LESCHENAULT INLET]

i Old Railway Station, Carmody Pl; (08) 9792 7205 or 1800 286 287; www.visitbunbury.com.au

95.7 Hot FM, 684 AM ABC Local Radio

Bunbury is known as the 'city of three waters', surrounded by the Indian Ocean, Koombana Bay and the Leschenault Inlet. This is a water-lover's paradise with fishing, crabbing, diving, white sandy beaches, sailing and kayaking. Bunbury is also known for its wild dolphins that come close to the beach at Koombana Bay. Bunbury was settled by Europeans in 1838 and the Koombana Bay whalers were a source of initial prosperity. Today the port is the main outlet for the timber and mining industries.

Dolphin Discovery Centre Wild bottlenose dolphins regularly visit Koombana Bay. The centre has interpretative displays on dolphins and other marine life, and offers visitors the chance to swim with dolphins under ranger guidance. Dolphin visits usually occur in the mornings; however, times and days of visits are unpredictable. If you prefer not to get wet, take a dolphin-spotting cruise on the bay. Open daily 8am–5pm Sept–May, 9am–3pm June–Aug; Koombana Dr; (08) 9791 3088.

Historic buildings: many date back to the early decades of the settlement, including the 1865 Rose Hotel; Cnr Victoria and Stephen sts; contact visitor centre for details. **King Cottage:** this cottage was built in 1880 by Henry King using homemade bricks. It now displays items of domestic life from the early 20th century; open 2–4pm daily; Forrest Ave. **Sir John Forrest Monument:** born in Picton on the outskirts of Bunbury in 1847, Sir John Forrest was elected the first Premier of WA in 1890 and entered Federal Parliament in 1901; cnr Victoria and Stephen sts. **Victoria Street:** a 'cappuccino strip' of sidewalk cafes and restaurants. **Bunbury Regional Art Galleries:** built in 1887, formerly a convent for the Sisters of Mercy and now the largest art gallery in the South-West; Wittenoom St. **Miniature Railway Track:** take a ride on this 800 m track through the trees at Forrest Park; 3rd Sun each month; Blair St. **Lookouts:** Boulter's Heights, Haig Cres and Marlston Hill; Apex Dr. **Lighthouse:** painted in black-and-white check, this striking landmark has a lookout at the base; end of Ocean Dr. **Basaltic rock:** formed by volcanic lava flow 150 million years ago; foreshore at end of Clifton St, off Ocean Dr. **Mangrove boardwalk:** 200 m elevated boardwalk lets you view the southernmost mangrove colony in WA, estimated

to be 20 000 years old; Koombana Dr. **Big Swamp Wildlife Park:** handfeed kangaroos, see bettongs, wombats, swamp wallabies and more, and enjoy the South-West's largest walk-through aviary; Prince Phillip Dr. **Heritage trail:** 12 km walk from the Old Railway Station; contact visitor centre for brochure.

Bunbury Carnaval: Mar. **Bunbury International Jazz Festival:** May. **Geographe Crush:** Food and Wine Festival; Nov.

Alexanders Restaurant: modern Australian; Quality Hotel Lord Forrest, 20 Symmons St; (08) 9726 5777. **Aristos Waterfront:** casual seafood; 2/15 Bonnefoi Blvd; (08) 9791 6477. **Boardwalk Bar & Bistro:** local seafood; The Parade Hotel, 1 Austral Pde; (08) 9721 2933. **Mojo's Restaurant:** contemporary Australian; Grand Cinema Complex, Victoria St; (08) 9792 5900. **Vat 2:** harbour-side dining; 2 Jetty Rd; (08) 9791 8833. **Carlaminda Wines Bistro:** French fare; Carlaminda Wines, Richards Rd, Ferguson Valley; (08) 9728 3002. **Hackersley:** seasonal menu; Ferguson Rd, Ferguson Valley; (08) 9728 3033. **Truffles Restaurant:** fresh local produce; Meadowbrooke Estate, 33 Turner St, Boyanup; (08) 9731 5550.

All Seasons Sanctuary Golf Resort: golfing enthusiast resort; Cnr Old Coast Rd and Australind Bypass, Pelican Pt; (08) 9725 2777 or 1800 677 309. **Boathouse B&B:** harbour-side B&B; 11 Austral Pde; (08) 9721 4140. **Bunbury Silo Accommodation:** converted silo apartments; off Casurina Dr, Marlston Waterfront; 0439 973 285. **Quality Hotel Lord Forrest:** premier town accommodation; 20 Symmons St; (08) 9726 5777 or 1800 097 811.

St Marks Anglican Church: built in 1842, this is the second oldest church in WA. The churchyard contains the graves of many early Bunbury settlers; 5 km SE at Picton. **Lena Dive Wreck:** apprehended by the navy in 2002 for illegal fishing, the *Lena* was sunk 3 nautical miles from Bunbury as a dive wreck; suitable for snorkelling and diving for all levels of experience. **South West Gemstone Museum:** over 2000 gemstones; 12 km s. **Wineries:** at the heart of the Geographe Wine Region, many in the area offer cellar-door tastings, including Killerby Wines (10 km s) and Capel Vale Wines (27 km s); contact visitor centre for details. **Abseiling tours:** on the quarry face of the Wellington Dam; contact visitor centre for details. **Scenic flights:** over Bunbury and surrounds.

See also THE SOUTH-WEST, p. 307

CARNARVON

Pop. 5283

Map ref. 619 B7

i Civic Centre, 11 Robinson St; (08) 9941 1146;
www.carnarvon.org.au

99.7 Hot Hits FM, 846 AM ABC Local Radio

Carnarvon is a large coastal town at the mouth of the Gascoyne
River. The river and the fertile red earth surrounding it are crucial
to the town's thriving agricultural industry. Plantations stretching
for 15 kilometres along the riverbanks draw water from the
aquifer of the river basin to grow a host of tropical fruits such as
bananas, mangoes, avocados, pineapples, pawpaws and melons.
Carnarvon gained national prominence when a NASA tracking
station operated nearby at Browns Range from 1964 to 1974.

Robinson Street In 1876 the region's founding fathers,
Aubrey Brown, John Monger and C. S. Brockman, overlanded
4000 sheep from York. Carnarvon was gazetted in 1883 and
developed into the centre of an efficient wool-producing area.
Camel teams, driven by Afghan camel drivers, brought the wool
to Carnarvon from the outlying sheep stations. This is the reason
for the extraordinary width of the town's main street, which, at
40 m, gave the camel teams enough room to turn around.

Jubilee Hall: built in 1887 as the Roads Board building, now
used as a craft market. In 1960 a cyclone blew the roof off and
all the shire papers blew away; Francis St. *Pioneer Park:* good
picnic spot; Olivia Tce. *Murals:* up to 15 buildings in the town,
including the Civic Centre, are adorned with murals painted
by local artists. *Heritage walking trail:* 20 historic landmarks
around the town; contact visitor centre for map.

Growers' market: Civic Centre; Sat mornings May–Nov.
Courtyard Markets: Robinson St; every Sat May–Dec. *Fremantle–
Carnarvon Yacht Race:* odd-numbered years, May. *Carnarfin:*
fishing competition; June. *Carnarvon Festival:* Aug/Sept.

Kingsford Restaurant: popular, conveniently located
restaurant; Fascine Lodge, 34 David Brand Dr; (08) 9941 2411.
Sails Restaurant: international cuisine; Best Western Hospitality

Inn, 6 West St; (08) 9941 1600. *Schnappers:* international menu;
Gateway Motel, 379 Robinson St; (08) 9941 1532.

Carnarvon Central Apartments: 2-bedroom apartments;
120 Robinson St; (08) 9941 1317. *The Carnarvon Hotel:* motel
and backpacker accommodation; 121 Olivia Tce; (08) 9941
1181. *Wintersun Carnarvon Park:* range of accommodation;
546 Robinson St; (08) 9941 8150 or 1300 555 585. *Quobba
Station:* working sheep station; Gnarloo Rd, 80 km north-west of
Carnarvon; (08) 9948 5098.

Carnarvon Heritage Precinct On Babbage Island, and
connected to the township by a causeway, this heritage precinct
incorporates the One Mile Jetty. Built in 1897, this is the longest
jetty in WA's north, stretching for 1493 m into the Indian Ocean.
It offers excellent fishing and a jetty train runs its length. Other
attractions include the Lighthouse Keeper's Cottage museum,
prawning factory at the old whaling station (tours in season,
check times at visitor centre) and Pelican Point, for picnics,
swimming and fishing.

Blowholes Jets of water shoot up to 20 m in the air after being
forced through holes in the coastal rock. When you arrive at
the Blowholes, you are greeted by a huge sign declaring 'KING
WAVES KILL' – a cautionary reminder that this picturesque
coastline has claimed the lives of over 30 people in freak waves.
73 km N. Nearby, a sheltered lagoon provides good swimming
and snorkeling (1 km s). A further 7 km north of the blowholes is
a cairn commemorating the loss of HMAS *Sydney* in 1941.

'The Big Dish': a huge 29 m wide reflector, part of the old NASA
station, with views of town and plantations from the base; 8 km E.
Bibbawarra Artesian Bore: hot water surfaces at 65° C and
picnic area nearby; 16 km N. *Bibbawarra Trough:* 180 m long,
believed to be the longest in the Southern Hemisphere; adjacent
to bore; 16 km N. *Miaboolya Beach:* good fishing, crabbing and
swimming; 22 km N. *Rocky Pool:* picnic area and deep billabong
ideal for swimming (after rains) and wildlife watching; Gascoyne
Rd; 55 km E. *Red Bluff:* world-renowned
surfing spot with waves 1–6 m, depending on
the time of the year; 143 km N. *Mt Augustus:*
considered the biggest rock in the world,
twice the size of Uluṟu. It is known as
Burringurrah to the local Aboriginal people.
This 'monocline' is over 1750 million years
old, cloaked in thick scrub, and offers
many interesting rock formations, caves
and Indigenous rock art. Camping and
powered sites are available at Mt Augustus
Outback Tourist Resort; (08) 9943 0527;
road conditions vary; 450 km E; *see also
Gascoyne Junction.* *Fishing:* excellent fishing
for snapper or groper and game fishing for
marlin or sailfish; charter boats available
from Williams St. Also excellent fishing off
One Mile Jetty.

See also Outback Coast & Mid-West, p. 312

[POINT QUOBBA]

boating, camping, picnics and barbecues (swimming is forbidden due to poor water quality); 85 km w.

See also Heartlands, p. 308

Cervantes

Pop. 506
Map ref. 618 A2 | 620 A5

 Pinnacles Visitor Centre, Cadiz St; (08) 9652 7672 or 1800 610 660; www.visitpinnaclescountry.com.au

99.9 WA FM, 612 AM ABC Radio National

This small but thriving fishing town was established in 1962 and named after the American whaling ship *Cervantes*, which sank off the coast in 1844. The town's fishing fleet nearly doubles in rock lobster season, and in spring the town is surrounded by spectacular displays of wildflowers with vistas of wattles stretching from horizon to horizon. Not far from Cervantes is one of Australia's best-known landscapes, the Pinnacles Desert, lying at the heart of Nambung National Park.

Pinnacle Wildflowers: displays of native WA flora, dried flower arrangements, souvenirs. Flowers are visible year-round, but at their peak in Aug and Sept; Bradley Loop. *Thirsty Point:* lookout has superb views of the bay and Cervantes islands. A trail connects the lookouts between Thirsty Point and Hansen Bay. Popular in wildflower season; off Seville St.

Ronsard Bay Tavern: bistro dining; 219 Cadiz St; (08) 9652 7009. *The Europa Anchor Restaurant:* local seafood; Cervantes Pinnacles Motel, 7 Aragon St; (08) 9652 7145.

Cervantes Pinnacles Motel: comfortable motel; 7 Aragon St; (08) 9652 7145. *Pinnacles Caravan Park:* beachfront caravan park; 35 Aragon St; (08) 9652 7060.

Nambung National Park In the Pinnacles Desert, thousands of limestone pillars rise out of a stark landscape of yellow sand, reaching over 3 m in places. They are the eroded remnants of a bed of limestone, created from sea-shells breaking down into lime-rich sands. See formations like the Indian Chief, Garden Wall and Milk Bottles. The loop drive is one-way and not suitable for caravans. The park allows day visits only; tours departing morning and sunset can be arranged at the visitor centre. 17 km s.

Lake Thetis Stromatolites: one of WA's 6 known locations of stromatolites, the oldest living organism on earth; 5 km s. *Kangaroo Point:* good picnic spot; 9 km s. *Hangover Bay:* a stunning white sandy beach ideal for swimming, snorkelling, windsurfing and surfing; 13 km s.

See also Heartlands, p. 308

Cocklebiddy

Pop. 75
Map ref. 621 M6

Cocklebiddy Roadhouse; (08) 9039 3462.

107.3 FM ABC Radio National, 648 AM ABC Local Radio

This tiny settlement, comprising a roadhouse with motel units, caravan sites and camping facilities, lies between Madura and Caiguna on the Nullarbor Plain. Nuytsland Nature Reserve extends southwards, a 400 000-hectare strip running along the Great Australian Bight. Locals operate on Central Western Time, 45 minutes ahead of the rest of the state.

Cocklebiddy Wedgetail Inn: convenient motel; Eyre Hwy; (08) 9039 3462.

Eyre Bird Observatory Housed in the fully restored 1897 Eyre Telegraph Station, Australia's first bird observatory offers birdwatching, bushwalking and beachcombing in Nuytsland Nature Reserve. Over 240 species of birds have been recorded at Eyre, including Major Mitchell cockatoos, brush bronzewings, honeyeaters and mallee fowl. It is near the site where Edward John Eyre found water and rested during his Nullarbor journey in February 1841. Courses, tours and whale-watching (June–Oct) as well as accommodation can be arranged on (08) 9039 3450. 4WD access only. 50 km se.

Chapel Rock: picnic area; 4 km e. *Twilight Cove:* fishing and whale-watching spot with views of 70 m high limestone cliffs overlooking the Great Australian Bight; 4WD access only; 32 km s.

See also Esperance & Nullarbor, p. 310

Collie

Pop. 7084
Map ref. 616 G3 | 618 D8 | 620 C9

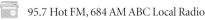 Old Collie Post Office, 63 Throssell St; (08) 9734 2051; www.collierivervalley.org.au

95.7 Hot FM, 684 AM ABC Local Radio

Collie is Western Australia's only coalmining town. The surrounding area was first explored in 1829 when Captain James Stirling led a reconnaissance party to the land south of Perth. The region was originally considered ideal for timber production and as pasturelands. However, the discovery of coal along the Collie River in 1883 changed the region's fortunes. In dense jarrah forest, near the winding Collie River, the town has many parks and gardens. The drive into Collie on the Coalfields Highway along the top of the Darling Scarp offers spectacular views of the surrounding forests, rolling hills and farms.

Tourist Coal Mine Step back in time and gain an insight into the mining industry and the working conditions in underground mines. This replica mine was constructed in 1983 to commemorate the 100-year anniversary of coal discovery. Tours by appt only; contact visitor centre for details. Throssell St.

Coalfields Museum: displays of historic photographs, coalmining equipment, rocks and minerals, woodwork by local miner Fred Kohler, a doll house and art housed in the historic Roads Board building; Throssell St. *Collie Railway Station:* the rebuilt station houses railway memorabilia, a scale model of the Collie township with model trains, tearooms and a giftshop; Throssell St. *Soldiers' Park:* bordering the Collie River, features include a war memorial, rose garden, gazebo and childrens' playground; Steere St. *All Saints Anglican Church:* impressive Norman-style church distinctive for its unusual stained-glass windows, extensive use of jarrah timbers and elaborate mural, which in 1922 took renowned stage artist Philip Goatcher 8 months to complete. Tours by appt; contact visitor centre; Venn St. *Old Collie Goods Shed:* restoration of rolling stock; Forrest St. *Central Precinct Historic Walk:* self-guide walk of historic buildings; contact visitor centre for map. *Collie River Walk:* pleasant walk along riverbank; contact visitor centre for map.

Market: Old Goods Shed, Forrest St; 1st and 3rd Sun each month (except winter). *Collie Rock and Coal Music Festival:* Mar. *Collie–Donnybrook Cycle Race:* Aug. *Collie River Valley Marathon:* Sept. *Griffin Festival:* Sept.

The Ridge: contemporary menu; Collie Ridge Motel, 185–195 Throssell St; (08) 9734 6666.

Peppermint Lane Lodge: charming B&B; 351 Wellington Mill Rd, Wellington Mill; (08) 9728 3138.

Wellington National Park Covering 4000 ha, this park is characterised by jarrah forest. Picnic, swim, canoe or camp at Honeymoon Pool or Potters Gorge, or go rafting in winter on the rapids below the Wellington Dam wall (note that work is being carried out on the wall until 2010, when the Quarry picnic area will reopen). 18 km w.

Minninup Pool: where the Collie River is at its widest, ideal for swimming, canoeing or picnicking; off Mungalup Rd; 3 km s. *Stockton Lake:* camping and waterskiing; 8 km E. *Brew 42:* microbrewery producing 6 different beers, especially traditional Irish and English ales. Tastings and sales Thurs–Sun or by arrangement; Allanson; (08) 97344784; 8km w. *Harris Dam:* beautiful picnic area; 14 km N. *Collie River Scenic Drive:* views of jarrah forest and wildflowers in season; contact visitor centre for map. *Munda Biddi Trail:* starting in the hills near Perth, this bike trail winds through scenic river valleys and forests south to Collie; details from visitor centre. *Bibbulmun Track:* sections of this trail pass through Collie; *see Albany.*

See also THE SOUTH-WEST, p. 307

Coolgardie

Pop. 801
Map ref. 620 H5

ⓘ Goldfields Exhibition Building, Bayley St; (08) 9026 6090; www.coolgardie.wa.gov.au

📻 97.9 Hot FM, 648 AM ABC Local Radio

After alluvial gold was found in 1892, Coolgardie grew in ten years to a town of 15 000 people, 23 hotels, six banks and two stock exchanges. The main street, lined with some magnificent buildings, was made wide enough for camel trains to turn around in. As in many outback towns, the heat and the isolation led to innovation, in this case that of the Coolgardie safe, which used water and a breeze to keep food cool before the days of electricity.

Historic buildings There are 23 buildings in the town centre that have been listed on the National Estate register, many of them on the main street, Bayley St. Over 100 markers are positioned at buildings and historic sites across the town, using stories and photographs to recapture the gold-rush days. The index to markers is in Bayley St next to the visitor centre.

Goldfields Exhibition Museum Local photographs and displays inside the old Warden's Court including a display on the famous Varischetti mine rescue. In 1907 Modesto Varischetti was trapped underground in a flooded mine for 9 days. Varischetti survived in an air pocket until divers eventually found him. The dramatic rescue captured world attention. Bayley St.

Ben Prior's Open-Air Museum: unusual collection of machinery and memorabilia; cnr Bayley and Hunt sts. *Warden Finnerty's House:* striking 1895 example of early Australian architecture and furnishings; open 11am–4pm daily except Wed; McKenzie St. *C. Y. O'Connor Dedication:* fountain and water course in memory of O'Connor, who masterminded the Goldfields Water Supply Scheme; McKenzie St. *Gaol tree:* used for prisoners in early gold-rush days, before a gaol was built; Hunt St. *Lindsay's Pit Lookout:* over open-cut goldmine; Ford St.

Coolgardie Day: Sept. *Metal Detecting Championships:* odd-numbered years, Sept/Oct.

Coolgardie Motel: comfortable, versatile motel; 49–53 Bayley St; (08) 9026 6080.

Coolgardie Cemetery The town cemetery gives you an inkling of the harshness of the early gold-rush years. The register of burials records that of the first 32 burials, the names of 15 were unknown, and many entries for 'male child' and 'female child' note 'fever' as the cause of death. One of the most significant graves is that of Ernest Giles, an Englishman whose name is associated with the exploration of inland Australia. 1 km w.

Coolgardie Camel Farm: offers rides on the 'ships of the desert'; (08) 9026 6159; 4 km w. *Gnarlbine Rock:* originally an Aboriginal well, then one of the few water sources for the early prospectors; 30 km sw. *Kunanalling Hotel:* once a town of over 800 people, the ruins of the hotel are all that remain; 32 km N. *Victoria Rock:* camping, and spectacular views from the summit; 55 km sw. *Burra Rock:* popular camping and picnic area (55 km s). Cave Hill, a similar destination, lies a further 40 km s (4WD only). *Rowles Lagoon Conservation Park:* picnicking and camping spots available although recently there has been no water; 65 km N. *Wallaroo Rocks:* 3 dams with scenic views and good bushwalking; 90 km w. *Golden Quest Discovery Trail:* Coolgardie forms part of this 965 km self-guide drive trail of the goldfields; book, map and CD available at visitor centre.

See also GOLDFIELDS, p. 311

Coral Bay

Pop. 192
Map ref. 619 B5

ⓘ Coastal Adventure Tours, Coral Bay Arcade, Robinson St; (08) 9948 5190; www.coralbaytours.com.au

📻 91.7 FM ABC Radio National, 104.9 FM ABC Local Radio

Coral Bay is famous for one thing: its proximity to Ningaloo Marine Park. Ningaloo Reef boasts an incredible diversity of marine life and beautiful coral formations. At Coral Bay the coral gardens lie close to the shore, which makes access to the reef as easy as a gentle swim. Lying at the southern end of Ningaloo Marine Park, Coral Bay has pristine beaches and a near-perfect climate: it is warm and dry regardless of the season, and the water temperature only varies from 18°C to 28°C degrees. Swimming, snorkelling, scuba diving, and beach, reef and deep-sea fishing (outside sanctuary areas) are available year-round.

Fin's Cafe: beachside cafe; People's Park Shopping Village; (08) 9942 5900. *Shades:* casual dining; Ningaloo Reef Resort, 1 Robinson St; (08) 9942 5934 or 1800 795 522. *The Reef Cafe:* Italian and seafood; Robinson St; (08) 9942 5882.

Bayview Coral Bay: range of accommodation options; Robinson St; (08) 9385 6655. *Ningaloo Reef Resort:* range of accommodation options; 1 Robinson St; (08) 9942 5934 or 1800 795 522. *The Ningaloo Club:* hostel; 46 Robinson St; (08) 9948 5100 or (08) 9385 6655.

Ningaloo Marine Park This park protects the 260 km long Ningaloo Reef, the longest fringing coral reef in Australia. It is the only large reef in the world found so close to a continental land mass: about 100 m offshore at its nearest point and less than 7 km at its furthest. This means that even novice snorkellers and children can access the coral gardens. The reef is home to over 500 species of fish, 250 species of coral, manta rays, turtles and a variety of other marine creatures, with seasonal visits from humpback whales, dolphins and whale sharks. Ningaloo Reef is famous for the latter, and from Apr to June visitors from around the world visit the reef to swim with these gentle giants.

Point Cloates: the wrecks of the *Zvir, Fin, Perth* and *Rapid* lie on the reef just off the point; 4WD access only; 8 km N. *Tours:*

glass-bottomed boat cruises, snorkel and dive tours, kayak tours, fishing charters, scenic flights and marine wildlife-watching tours to see whale sharks (Apr–June), humpback whales (June–Nov) and manta rays (all year); contact visitor centre for details.

See also OUTBACK COAST & MID-WEST, p. 312

Corrigin

Pop. 687
Map ref. 618 F5 | 620 E8

 Corrigin Resource Centre, Larke Cres; (08) 9063 2778; www.corrigin.wa.gov.au

92.5 ABC Classic FM, 100.5 Hot FM

Corrigin was established in the early 1900s and was one of the last wheat-belt towns to be settled. Today the town has a healthy obsession with dogs, as demonstrated by its Dog Cemetery and its national record for lining up 1527 utes with dogs in the back.

Corrigin Pioneer Museum Superb collection of old agricultural equipment including an original Sunshine harvester and some early steam-driven farm machinery. A small working steam train carries passengers on a short circuit around the museum and local rest area. Open Sun and by appt; Kunjin St.

RSL Monument: a Turkish mountain gun from Gallipoli; McAndrew Ave.

Dog in a Ute event: held in varying years in Apr; contact visitor centre for dates.

Corrigin Windmill Motel: motel rooms plus family lodge; Brookton Hwy; (08) 9063 2390.

Dog Cemetery Loving dog owners have gone to the considerable expense of having elaborate headstones placed over the remains of their faithful four-footed friends. There are over 80 dogs buried in the cemetery, with gravestones dedicated to Dusty, Rover, Spot et al. There is even one statue of a dog almost 2 m high. Brookton Hwy; 7 km W.

Wildflower scenic drive: signposted with lookout; 3 km W. *Gorge Rock:* large granite outcrop with picnic area; 20 km SE.

See also HEARTLANDS, p. 308

Cranbrook

Pop. 279
Map ref. 618 F10 | 620 E10

 Council offices, Gathorne St; (08) 9826 1008; www.cranbrook.wa.gov.au

95.3 Hot FM, 630 AM ABC Local Radio

The small town of Cranbrook greets travellers with a large sign announcing that it is the 'Gateway to the Stirlings'. A mere 10 kilometres away is Stirling Range National Park, a mecca for bushwalkers and climbers. The nearby Frankland area has gained a national reputation for its premium-quality wines.

Station House Museum: restored and furnished 1930s-style; Gathorne St. *Wildflower walk:* 300 m walk to Stirling Gateway with displays of orchids in spring; Salt River Rd.

Cranbrook Shire on Show: Apr. *Wildflower Display:* Sept. *Art trail and Photographic Competition:* Oct.

Stirling Range National Park Surrounded by a flat, sandy plain, the Stirling Range rises abruptly to over 1000 m, its jagged peaks veiled in swirling mists. The cool, humid environment

created by these low clouds supports 1500 flowering plant species, many unique to the area, earning the park recognition as one of the top-10 biodiversity hot spots in the world. This National Heritage–listed park is one of WA's premier destinations for bushwalking. Best time to visit is Oct–Dec. 10 km SE.

Sukey Hill Lookout: expansive views of farmland, salt lakes and Stirling Range; off Salt River Rd; 5 km E. *Lake Poorrarecup:* swimming and waterskiing; 40 km SW. *Wineries:* the nearby Frankland River region boasts several wineries, including Alkoomi, Frankland Estate and Ferngrove; 50 km W. *Wildflower drive and heritage trail:* contact visitor centre for brochure.

See also GREAT SOUTHERN, p. 309

Cue

Pop. 273
Map ref. 619 H10 | 620 D1 | 622 D11

 Golden Art Shop and Tourist Information Centre, Austin St; (08) 9963 1936; www.cue.wa.gov.au

102.9 WA FM, 106.1 FM ABC Local Radio

This town was once known as the 'Queen of the Murchison'. In 1891 Mick Fitzgerald and Ed Heffernan found large nuggets of gold not far from what was to become the main street. It was their prospecting mate, Tom Cue, who registered the claim on their behalf and when the town was officially proclaimed in 1894, it bore his name. Within ten years the population of this boom town had exploded to about 10 000 people. While Cue's population has dwindled, the legacy of those heady gold-rush days is evident in the town's remarkably grandiose buildings.

Heritage buildings Many early buildings still stand and are classified by the National Trust. A stroll up the main street takes in the elegant band rotunda, the former Gentleman's Club (now the shire offices, housing a photographic display of the region's history), the Old Gaol, the courthouse, the post office and the police station. One block west in Dowley St is the former Masonic Lodge built in 1899 and reputed to be the largest corrugated-iron structure in the Southern Hemisphere.

Murchison Club Hotel: hotel and motel accommodation; Austin St; (08) 9963 1020.

Walga Rock This monolith is 1.5 km long and 5 km around the base. It has several Aboriginal rock paintings. One of the most extraordinary paintings, considering that Cue is over 300 km from the sea, is of a white, square-rigged sailing ship. It is believed to depict one of the Dutch ships that visited WA's mid-west shores in the 17th century. 50 km W.

Day Dawn: once Cue's twin town, thanks to the fabulous wealth of the Great Fingall Mine. The mine office, a magnificent century-old stone building now perched precariously on the edge of a new open-cut mine, is all that remains of the town; 5 km W. *Milly Soak:* popular picnic spot for early Cue residents. A tent hospital was set up nearby during the typhoid epidemic; 3 lone graves are the only reminder of the thousands who died; 16km N. *Heritage trail:* includes the abandoned towns Big Bell and Day Dawn; contact visitor centre for brochure. *Fossicking:* areas surrounding the town; contact visitor centre for details.

See also OUTBACK COAST & MID-WEST, p. 312

Denham

Pop. 609
Map ref. 619 B9

i Knight Tce; (08) 9948 1590 or 1300 135 887; www.sharkbaywa.com.au

105.3 Hot Hits FM, 107.5 FM ABC Radio National

On the middle peninsula of Shark Bay, Denham is the most westerly town in Australia. Dirk Hartog, the Dutch navigator, landed on an island at the bay's entrance in 1616, the first known European to land on the continent. Centuries later, in 1858, Captain H. M. Denham surveyed the area and a town bearing his name was established. The Shark Bay region was once known for its pearling and fishing, and the streets of Denham were literally paved with pearl shells. In the 1960s, however, the local roads board poured bitumen over the pearl shells, and so destroyed what could have been a unique tourist attraction. Fortunately, several buildings made from coquina shell block still stand in the town. Today Shark Bay is renowned for the wild dolphins that come inshore at Monkey Mia (pronounced 'my-a'). As a World Heritage area, it also protects dugongs, humpback whales, green and loggerhead turtles, important seagrass feeding grounds and a colony of stromatolites, the world's oldest living fossils.

Shell block buildings: St Andrews Anglican Church, cnr Hughes and Brockman sts, and the Old Pearlers Restaurant, cnr Knight Tce and Durlacher St, were both built from coquina shell block. *Town Bluff:* popular walk for beachcombers; from town along beach to bluff. *Pioneer Park:* contains the stone on which Captain Denham carved his name in 1858; Hughes St.

Old Pearler Restaurant: maritime-themed seafood restaurant; 71 Knight Tce; (08) 9948 1373. *The Boughshed Restaurant:* international cuisine; Monkey Mia Dolphin Resort, Monkey Mia; (08) 9948 1320 or 1800 653 611.

Bay Lodge Economy Beachfront: beachfront budget accommodation; 113 Knight Tce; (08) 9948 1278 or 1800 812 780. *Denham Villas:* self-contained accommodation; 8 Durlacher St; 9948 1264. *Heritage Resort Shark Bay:* beachfront elegance; Cnr Knight Tce and Durlacher St; (08) 9948 1133. *Monkey Mia Dolphin Resort:* wide range of accommodation; Monkey Mia; (08) 9948 1320 or 1800 653 611.

Monkey Mia The daily shore visits by the wild bottlenose dolphins at Monkey Mia are a world-famous phenomenon. The dolphins swim into the shallows, providing a unique opportunity for humans to make contact with them. It began in the 1960s when a local woman started feeding the dolphins that followed her husband's fishing boat to the shoreline. Feeding still occurs, although now it is carefully monitored by rangers to ensure that the dolphins maintain their hunting and survival skills. Visiting times, and the number of dolphins, vary. 26 km NE.

Dirk Hartog Island The state's largest and most historically significant island, named after Dutchman Dirk Hartog who landed here in 1616 – 154 years before Captain Cook. Hartog left behind an inscribed pewter plate, which was removed in 1697 by his countryman Willem de Vlamingh and replaced with another plate. The original was returned to Holland; Vlamingh's plate is now housed in the Maritime Museum in Fremantle. Flights and cruises depart daily; bookings at visitor centre. 30 km W.

Hamelin Pool stromatolites The shores of Hamelin Pool are dotted with stromatolites, the world's largest and oldest living fossils. These colonies of micro-organisms resemble the oldest and simplest forms of life on earth, dated at around 3.5 million years old. The Hamelin Pool stromatolites are relatively new

colonies however, about 3000 years old. They thrive here because of the extreme salinity of the water, the occurrence of calcium bicarbonate and the limited water circulation. Visitors can view these extraordinary life forms from a boardwalk. Close by is the Flint Cliff Telegraph Station and Post Office Museum (1884) with a history of the region. 88 km SE.

Dugongs The Shark Bay World Heritage Area has the largest seagrass meadows in the world, covering about 4000 sq km. These meadows are home to around 10 000 dugongs, 10% of the world's remaining population. An endangered species, the dugong is nature's only vegetarian sea mammal. Also known as a sea cow, the dugong can live for up to 70 years and grow up to 3 m long. Tours are available offering visitors a unique opportunity to see dugongs in the wild. Contact visitor centre for details.

Little Lagoon: ideal fishing and picnic spot; 3 km N. *Francois Peron National Park:* Peron Homestead with its 'hot tub' of artesian water; 4WD access only; 7 km N. *Ocean Park:* marine park with aquarium and touch pool; 9 km S. *Eagle Bluff:* habitat of sea eagle and a good viewing spot for sharks and stingrays; 20 km S. *Blue Lagoon Pearl Farm:* working platform where black pearls are harvested; Monkey Mia; 26 km NE. *Shell Beach:* 120 km of unique coastline comprising countless tiny coquina shells; 45 km SE. *Steep Point:* western-most point on mainland with spectacular scenery; 4WD access only; 260 km W. *Zuytdorp Cliffs:* extend from beneath Shark Bay region south to Kalbarri; 4WD access only. *Tours:* boat trips and charter flights to historic Dirk Hartog Island, catamaran cruises, safaris and coach tours; contact visitor centre for details.

See also OUTBACK COAST & MID-WEST, p. 312

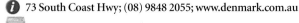

Denmark

Pop. 2735
Map ref. 617 A11 | 618 F11 | 620 E11

i 73 South Coast Hwy; (08) 9848 2055; www.denmark.com.au

92.1 FM ABC News Radio, 630 AM ABC Local Radio

Denmark lies at the foot of Mt Shadforth, overlooking the tranquil Denmark River and Wilson Inlet. It is surrounded by forests of towering karri trees that sweep down to meet the Southern Ocean. The Aboriginal name for the Denmark River is 'koorabup', meaning 'place of the black swan'. Originally a timber town, Denmark's economy is today sustained by a combination of dairying, beef cattle, fishing, timber and tourism. The town is close to some of the most beautiful coastline in the state.

Bert Bolle Barometer Huge water barometer that visitors can view by climbing the surrounding tower. Reputedly the world's largest, housed in the visitor centre.

Historical Museum: in old police station; Mitchell St. *Bandstand:* located on the riverbank with seating for the audience on the other side of the river; Holling Rd. *Arts and crafts:* galleries abound, including the Old Butter Factory in North St; contact visitor centre for details. *Mt Shadforth Lookout:* magnificent views; Mohr Dr. *Berridge and Thornton parks:* shaded picnic areas; along riverbank in Holling Rd.

Craft Market: Berridge Park; Jan, Easter and Dec. *Pantomime:* Civic Centre; Jan. *Brave New Works:* new performance art; Easter.

Che Sera Sera: modern Australian, water views; The Denmark Waterfront, 63 Inlet Dr; (08) 9848 3314. *Greenpool Restaurant:* slick fine dining; Forest Hill Vineyard, cnr Myers Rd and South Coast Hwy; (08) 9848 0091. *The Southern End*

Restaurant: local produce; Denmark Observatory Resort, 427 Mt Shadforth Rd; (08) 9848 2600.

 Chimes Spa Retreat: luxurious pampering; Mt Shadforth Scenic Dr; (08) 9848 2255. *Misty Valley Country Cottages:* cosy country cottages; 52 Hovea Rd; (08) 9840 9239. *Mt Lindesay View B&B:* well appointed with spectacular views; Cnr Mt Shadforth Tourist Dr and McNabb Rd; (08) 9848 1933. *Pensione Verde:* intimate guesthouse affiliated with organic cooking school; 31 Strickland St; (08) 9848 1700. *Tree Tops:* romantic getaway; 21 Payne Rd, Weedon Hill; (08) 9848 2055 or (08) 9364 1594.

William Bay National Park This relatively small 1867 ha park protects stunning coastline and forest between Walpole and Denmark on WA's south coast. It is renowned for its primeval windswept granite tors. Green's Pool, a natural rockpool in the park, remains calm and safe for swimming and snorkelling all year-round. Nearby are the Elephant Rocks, massive rounded boulders resembling elephants; Madfish Bay, a good fishing spot; and Waterfall Beach for swimming. 17 km sw.

Ocean Beach: one of the finest surfing beaches in WA; 8 km s. *Monkey Rock:* lookout with panoramic views; 10 km sw. *Bartholomew's Meadery:* honey, honey wines, gourmet honey ice-cream and other bee products, as well as a live beehive display; 20 km w. *Pentland Alpaca Stud and Tourist Farm:* diverse collection of animals, including alpacas, koalas, kangaroos, bison, water buffalo, llamas and many more; cnr McLeod and Scotsdale rds; (08) 9840 9262; 20 km w. *Eden Gate Blueberry Farm:* spray-free fruit, a range of blueberry products and blueberry wines; open Thurs–Mon Dec–Apr; 25 km E. *Whale-watching:* viewing platform above Lowlands Beach (southern rights June–Oct); 28 km E. *Fishing:* at Wilson Inlet, Ocean Beach (8 km s) and Parry Beach (25 km w). *West Cape Howe National Park:* Torbay Head, WA's most southerly point, and Cosy Corner, a protected beach perfect for swimming; 30 km sw. *Wineries:* many wineries open for cellar-door tastings, including Howard Park Winery, West Cape Howe and Tinglewood Wines; contact visitor centre for map. *Scenic drives:* the 25 km Mt Shadforth Scenic Drive and the 34 km Scotsdale Tourist Drive both feature lush forests, ocean views, wineries and galleries; contact visitor centre for maps. *Heritage trails:* 3 km Mokare trail, 5 km Karri Walk or 9 km Wilson Inlet trail; contact visitor centre for maps. *Bibbulmun Track:* a section of this world-class 963 km long-distance trail passes through Denmark; *see Albany. Valley of the Giants Tree Top Walk: see Walpole;* 65 km w.

See also GREAT SOUTHERN, p. 309

Derby

Pop. 3091
Map ref. 625 I7 | 628 D9

 2 Clarendon St; (08) 9191 1426 or 1800 621 426; www.derbytourism.com.au

 102.7 WA FM, 873 AM ABC Local Radio

It is said that Derby, known as the 'Gateway to the Gorges', is where the real Kimberley region begins. The first town settled in the Kimberley, it features some spectacular natural attractions nearby: the Devonian Reef Gorges of Windjana and Tunnel Creek are only a few hours' drive along the Gibb River Road, and the magnificent islands of the Buccaneer Archipelago are just a short cruise away. Although King Sound was first explored in 1688, it wasn't until the early 1880s that the Port of Derby was established as a landing point for wool shipments and Derby was proclaimed a townsite. The first jetty was built in 1885, the same year that gold was discovered at Halls Creek. Miners and prospectors poured into the port on their way to the goldfields but by the 1890s, as gold fever died, the port was used almost exclusively for the export of live cattle and sheep. In 1951 iron-ore mining began at Cockatoo Island, which revitalised the town. Derby is now a service centre for the region's rich pastoral and mining industries. Rain closes some roads in the area from November to March, so check conditions before setting out on any excursion.

 Old Derby Gaol: built in 1906, this is the oldest building in town; Loch St. *Wharfinger House Museum:* built in the 1920s for the local harbourmaster, the design is typical of the tropics. Now houses an extensive collection of historical memorabilia and Aboriginal artefacts. Key from visitor centre; Loch St. *Derby Jetty:* some of the highest tides in Australia, up to 12 m, can be seen from the jetty. Now used to export ore from various local mines.

 Market: Clarendon St; each Sat May–Sept. *King Tide Day:* festival celebrating highest tide in Australia; Apr/May. *Moonrise Rock Festival:* June. *Derby Races:* June/July. *Mowanjum Festival:* indigenous art and culture; July. *Boab Festival:* Mardi Gras, mud football, mud crab races and bush poets; July. *Derby Rodeo:* Aug. *Boxing Day Sports:* Dec.

 Derby Boab Inn: international cuisine; 100 Loch St; (08) 9191 1044. *Oasis Bistro:* bistro dining; King Sound Resort Hotel, 112 Loch St; (08) 9193 1044. *The Point Restaurant:* seaside seafood; 1 Jetty Rd; (08) 9191 1195.

 Jila Gallery Apartment: centrally located apartment; 18 Clarendon St; (08) 9193 2560. *Kimberley Cottages:* self-contained cottages; 18 Windjana Rd; (08) 9191 1114. *Kimberley Entrance Caravan Park:* shady caravan park; 2–12 Rowan St; (08) 9193 1055. *King Sound Resort Hotel:* central hotel accommodation; 112 Loch St; (08) 9193 1044.

Windjana Gorge National Park A 350-million-year-old Devonian reef rises majestically above the surrounding plains. An easy walking trail winds through the gorge, taking in primeval life forms fossilised within the gorge walls. 145 km E.

Tunnel Creek National Park Wear sandshoes, carry a torch and be prepared to get wet as you explore the 750 m long cave that runs through the Napier Range. Nearby Pigeon's Cave was the hideout of an 1890s Aboriginal outlaw, Jandamarra, also known as 'Pigeon'. Contact visitor centre for tour details. 184 km E.

Prison tree: 1000-year-old boab tree formerly used as a prison; 7 km s. *Myall's Bore:* beside the bore stands a 120 m long cattle trough reputed to be the longest in the Southern Hemisphere; 7 km s. *Gorges:* Lennard Gorge (190 km E), Bell Gorge (214 km E), Manning Gorge (306 km E), Barnett River Gorge (340 km NE) and Sir John Gorge (350 km E); 4WD access only. *Mitchell Plateau:* highlights include the Wandjina rock art and spectacular Mitchell Falls, King Edward River and Surveyor's Pool. In this remote region, visitors must be entirely self-sufficient; via Gibb River Rd and Kalumburu Rd; 580 km NE. Scenic flights can also be arranged from Drysdale River Station and Kununurra. *Pigeon Heritage Trail:* follow the story of the Aboriginal outlaw Jandamarra, nicknamed Pigeon, and his people, the Bunuba; contact visitor centre for map. *Gibb River Rd:* 4WD road between Derby and Wyndham traverses some of the most spectacular

 RADIO STATIONS IN TOWN WHAT'S ON WHERE TO EAT WHERE TO STAY NEARBY

gorge country of the Kimberley; contact visitor centre for guidebook and current road conditions. *Buccaneer Archipelago:* in Derby you can arrange a scenic flight or cruise around this archipelago which begins north of King Sound; *see Broome.*

See also KIMBERLEY, p. 314

Dongara–Denison

Pop. 3052
Map ref. 620 A4

 9 Waldeck St; (08) 9927 1404; www.irwin.wa.gov.au

96.5 WA FM, 828 AM ABC Local Radio

Dongara and its nearby twin town of Port Denison lie on the coast 359 kilometres north of Perth. Dongara–Denison is the self-proclaimed 'Lobster Capital' of the state, with its offshore reefs supporting a profitable industry. Dongara's main street is lined with magnificent Moreton Bay fig trees while Port Denison provides local anglers with a large marina and harbour.

Irwin District Museum Housed in Dongara's Old Police Station, Courthouse and Gaol (1870), the museum features exhibits on the history of the buildings, the invasion of rabbits into WA and the Irwin Coast shipwrecks. Open 10am–4pm Mon–Fri; Waldeck St; (08) 9927 1323.

Russ Cottage: a beautifully restored farm-worker's cottage (1870). The hard-packed material of the kitchen floor was made from scores of anthills, and the flood-level marker near the front door indicates how high the nearby Irwin River rose during the record flood of 1971; open 10am–12pm Sun or by appt; St Dominics Rd, Dongara. *The Priory Hotel:* this 1881 building has been an inn, a priory and a boarding college for girls and is now once again a hotel; St Dominics Rd, Dongara. *Church of St John the Baptist:* (1884) its pews were made from the driftwood of shipwrecks and its church bell is said to have come from Fremantle Gaol; cnr Waldeck and Church sts, Dongara. *The Royal Steam Flour Mill:* (1894) it served the local wheat-growing community until its closure in 1935; northern end of Waldeck St, Dongara. *Cemetery:* headstones dating from 1874 and a wall of remembrance to Dominican sisters; brochure from visitor centre; Dodd St, Dongara. *Town heritage trail:* 1.6 km walk that features 28 historic Dongara sites; contact visitor centre for map. *Fisherman's Lookout:* 1 remaining of 2 obelisks built in 1869, with panoramic views of Port Denison; Point Leander Dr, Port Denison.

Monthly Market: Priory Gardens; 1st Sat each month. *Craft Market:* old police station, Dongara; Easter and Christmas. *Dongara Races:* Easter. *Larry Lobster Community Festival and Blessing of the Fleet:* at the start of each rock lobster season; Nov.

The Season Tree: rustic cafe; 8 Moreton Tce; (08) 9927 1400.

Getaway Beach: contemporary beach houses; off Brand Hwy; (08) 9927 2458. *Port Denison Holiday Units:* self-contained holiday units; 14 Carnarvon St; (08) 9927 1104. *Sea Spray Beach Holiday Park:* beachside apartments; 79–81 Church St; (08) 9927 1165.

Silverdale Olive Orchards: olive oil products and tastings; open Sat Apr–Nov or by appt; 10 km N. *Mingenew:* small town in agricultural surrounds. Nearby is Fossil Cliff, filled with marine fossils over 250 million years old; 47 km E.

See also OUTBACK COAST & MID-WEST, p. 312

Donnybrook

Pop. 1932
Map ref. 616 F5 | 618 C9 | 620 C10

 Old Railway Station, South Western Hwy; (08) 9731 1720; www.donnybrook-balingup.wa.gov.au

95.7 Hot FM, 1224 AM ABC Radio National

Donnybrook is the centre of the oldest and largest apple-growing area in Western Australia. This is the home of the Granny Smith apple and where Lady William apples were developed. Gold was found here in 1897 but mined for only four years. Donnybrook is famous for its sandstone, which has been used in construction statewide since the early 1900s. In Perth, the GPO, St Mary's Cathedral and the University of Western Australia buildings have all been faced with Donnybrook stone. The quarry can be seen from the Upper Capel Road out of town.

Memorial Hall: built of Donnybrook stone; Bentley St. *Anchor and Hope Inn:* (1862) the oldest homestead in the district, now a private property; view outside from South Western Hwy. *Trigwell Place:* picnic and barbecue facilities, and canoeing on nearby Preston River; South Western Hwy.

Gourmet Wine and Food Fest: Feb. *Apple Festival Ball:* even-numbered years, Easter. *Marathon Relay:* Nov.

Old Goldfields Orchard & Cider Factory: country cosiness and international cuisine; 75 Goldfields Rd; (08) 9731 0311.

Boronia Farm: self-contained cottage on organic farm; 47 Williams Rd; (08) 9731 7154. *Country Charm Retreat B&B:* country B&B; 629 Hurst Rd; (08) 9731 2010. *Jarragon B&B:* centrally located cottage; 9 Collins St; (08) 9731 1930. *Kirup Kabins Farmstay:* self-contained cottages; Lot 3 Mailman Rd; (08) 9731 6272.

Old Goldfields Orchard and Cider Factory Combines goldfield history with a working orchard and restaurant. Climb the reconstructed poppet head over the mine, study the history of gold on the property and try your hand at gold prospecting. The orchard provides seasonal fruit for sale and you can enjoy tastings of cider, fruit juice and wines. Open 9.30am–4.30pm Wed–Sun and public/school holidays; Goldfields Rd; (08) 9731 0322; 6 km S.

Boyanup: features a transport museum; 12 km NW. *Ironstone Gully Falls:* barbecue area en route to Capel; 19 km W. *Gnomesville:* surprising roadside collection of garden gnomes; by the side of the Wellington Mills roundabout on the road between Dardanup and Lowden; 25 km SE.

See also THE SOUTH-WEST, p. 307

Dunsborough

Pop. 3373
Map ref. 616 B6 | 618 B9 | 620 B10

 Seymour Blvd; (08) 9752 1288; www.geographebay.com

98.4 FM Western Tourist Radio, 1224 AM ABC Radio National

Dunsborough is a picturesque coastal town on the south-western tip of Geographe Bay. Just west of the town is Leeuwin–Naturaliste National Park with its dramatic coastline and seasonal wildflower displays. Many of the wineries of the South-West region are only a short drive from the town.

Market: Dunsborough Hall, cnr Gibney St and Gifford Rd; 1st Sat each month. *Margaret River Wine Festival:* throughout region; Apr/May.

Dunsborough Bakery: renowned bakery; 243 Naturaliste Tce; (08) 9755 3137. *Other Side of the Moon Restaurant:* swanky fine dining; Quay West Resort, Bunker Bay Rd, Bunker Bay; (08) 9756 9159. *Wise Vineyard Restaurant:* seasonal international cuisine; 80 Eagle Bay Rd; (08) 9755 3331.

Dunsborough Rail Carriages & Farm Cottages: restored rail carriages; 123 Commonage Rd; (08) 9755 3865. *Newberry Manor:* character-filled B&B; 16 Newberry Rd; (08) 9756 7542. *Quay West Resort Bunker Bay:* sublime resort; Bunker Bay Rd, Bunker Bay; (08) 9756 9100 or 1800 010 449. *Whalers Cove:* contemporary self-contained accommodation; 3 Lecaille Crt; (08) 9755 3699.

Leeuwin–Naturaliste National Park Close to Dunsborough at the northern end of the park is Cape Naturaliste, with its lighthouse, museum and whale-watching platform (humpback whales linger offshore Sept–Nov). Walking tracks offer spectacular views of the coastline. Sugarloaf Rock is a dramatic formation just south of the lighthouse – it is also a habitat of the endangered red-tailed tropic bird. 13 km NW. *See also Margaret River and Augusta.*

Country Life Farm: animals galore, plus merry-go-round, giant slide and bouncing castles; Caves Rd; (08) 9755 3707; 1 km W. *Simmo's Icecreamery:* 39 flavours of homemade ice-cream made fresh daily; Commonage Rd; 5 km SE. *Quindalup Fauna Park:* specialises in birds, fish, tropical butterflies and baby animals; (08) 9755 3933; 5 km E. *Wreck of HMAS* Swan: the largest accessible dive-wreck site in the Southern Hemisphere; tour bookings and permits at visitor centre; off Point Picquet, just south of Eagle Bay; 8 km NW. *Beaches:* to the north-west, popular for fishing, swimming and snorkelling, include Meelup (5 km), Eagle Bay (8 km) and Bunker Bay (12 km). *Wineries:* as part of the Margaret River wine region, there are many wineries nearby; contact visitor centre for details. *Tours and activities:* whale-watching charters (Sept–Nov); deep-sea fishing charters; scuba diving, snorkelling and canoeing; wildflower displays in season.

See also THE SOUTH-WEST, p. 307

Dwellingup

Pop. 344
Map ref. 615 E10 | 618 C7 | 620 C8

i Marrinup St; (08) 9538 1108; www.murray.wa.gov.au

97.3 Coast FM, 684 AM ABC Local Radio

Set among pristine jarrah forest, this is a thriving timber town that was virtually destroyed in 1961 when lightning started a bushfire that lasted for five days, burnt 140 000 hectares of forest and destroyed several nearby towns. Dwellingup was the only town to be rebuilt, and is now a forest-management centre. The Hotham Valley Tourist Railway operates here.

Forest Heritage Centre This centre records WA's jarrah forest heritage and promotes fine wood design, training and education. The building is formed from rammed earth, and designed to represent 3 jarrah leaves on a bough. It includes an Interpretive Centre, a School of Wood and a Forest Heritage Gallery. Learn about conservation and walk among the treetops on an 11 m high canopy walkway. Acacia Rd; (08) 9538 1395.

Historical Centre: includes a photographic display depicting early 1900s life in the mill towns. Also a 1939 Mack Fire Truck, the only one in WA; visitor centre, Marrinup St. *Community Hotel:* last community hotel in WA; Marrinup St.

Log Chop and Community Fair: Feb. *Giant Pumpkin Competition:* Apr.

Dwellingup Community Hotel Motel: counter meals; Marrinup St; (08) 9538 1056. *Dwellingup Millhouse Restaurant:* cosy cafe; 41 McLarty St; (08) 9538 1122. *Lake Navarino Restaurant:* cosy restaurant, international cuisine; Lake Navarino Forest Resort, 147 Invarell Rd, Waroona; (08) 9733 3000 or 1800 650 626. *Newbliss Vineyard Cafe:* rustic lunches; Newbliss Winery, Lot 20 Irwin Rd; (08) 9538 1665.

Banksia Springs Cottages: well-appointed cottages; Banksiadale Rd; (08) 9538 1880. *Dwellingup Bunkhouses Outdoor Adventure Camp:* perfect for group adventurists; Lot 1379 Vandals Rd; (08) 9538 1314. *Dwellingup Chalet & Caravan Park:* peaceful accommodation; 23 Del Park Rd; (08) 9538 1157. *Lake Navarino Forest Resort:* variety of accommodation in country setting; 147 Invarell Rd, Waroona; (08) 9733 3000 or 1800 650 626.

Lane–Poole Reserve Provides opportunities for picnicking, swimming, canoeing, rafting, fishing, camping and walking. Walk trails include sections of the Bibbulmun Track, the 18 km King Jarrah Track from Nanga Mill, the 17 km Nanga Circuit and a 1.5 km loop from Island Pool. 10 km S.

Marrinup Forest Tour: unique 16 km vehicle and walk tour that features many aspects of the Darling Scarp including the Marrinup POW camp and remnants of old mills and towns of days gone by; contact visitor centre for map. *Hotham Valley Tourist Railway:* travel from Perth via Pinjarra to Dwellingup by train, taking in lush green dairy country before climbing the Darling Range, WA's steepest and most spectacular section of railway, and finishing in the heart of the jarrah forest; steam-hauled May–Oct, diesel-hauled Nov–Apr; bookings (08) 9221 4444; Dwellingup Railway Station. *Etmilyn Forest Tramway:* takes visitors 8 km through farms and old-growth jarrah forest to the pioneer settlement of Etmilyn. *Bibbulmun Track:* long-distance walk trail runs through the middle of the town; *see Albany. Munda Biddi Trail:* WA's first long-distance off-road bike track begins in Mundaring near Perth and winds 182 km through native forest to Dwellingup. It will eventually be extended to Albany; contact visitor centre for details.

See also THE SOUTH-WEST, p. 307

Esperance

Pop. 9536
Map ref. 621 I9

i Museum Village, Dempster St; (08) 9083 1555 or 1300 664 455; www.visitesperance.com

102.3 Hot FM, 837 AM ABC Local Radio

Esperance was a sleepy backwater until, in the 1950s, it was found that adding trace elements to the sandy soil made farming feasible. The town became a port and service centre for the agricultural and pastoral hinterland. However, it is the magnificent scenery, the pristine beaches and the proximity of many national parks that draw visitors to this town. Take the Great Ocean Drive, 38 kilometres of postcard-perfect scenery, and you'll understand why Esperance is a popular holiday spot.

Municipal Museum Visit one of WA's outstanding regional museums. See exhibits about shipwrecks, including the famous *Sanko Harvest*, and learn of Australia's only recorded pirate, the bloodthirsty Black Jack Anderson, who roamed the Recherche

Archipelago. There is also a comprehensive display about *Skylab*, which crashed and spread debris through the area in 1979. Open 1.30–4.30pm daily; James St; (08) 9071 1579.

Museum Village: collection of historic buildings housing craft shops, pottery shops, art gallery, cafe and visitor centre; Dempster St. *Cannery Arts Centre:* local exhibitions with wind garden and views behind; Norseman Rd. *Mermaid Leather:* unique range of leather products made from fish and shark skins; Wood St. *Aquarium:* 14 aquariums and touch pool; the Esplanade.

Market: Dempster St; Sun mornings. *Wildflower Show:* Sept. *Agricultural Show:* Oct.

Bonaparte Seafood Restaurant: traditional town favourite; 51 The Esplanade; (08) 9071 7727. *Loose Goose:* vibrant modern restaurant; 9A Andrews St; (08) 9071 2320. *Ocean Blues Restaurant:* simple seaside fare; 19 The Esplanade; (08) 9071 7107. *Taylor Street Cafe:* beachside cafe; Taylor St Jetty; (08) 9071 4317. *The Deck:* a favourite for ice-creams; Cnr Clarke and Veal sts, Hopetoun; (08) 9838 3303.

Bay of Islands B&B: seaview B&B; 73 Twilight Beach Rd; (08) 9072 1995. *Seascape Beach House:* holiday house set in bush surrounds; 11 Cornell St; (08) 9071 3150. *The Jetty Resort:* range of apartments; 1 The Esplanade; (08) 9071 3333. *Woody Island Ecostays:* safari huts, eco accommodation; via Mackenzie's Island Cruises, 71 The Esplanade; (08) 9071 5757.

Great Ocean Drive One of Australia's most spectacular scenic drives, this 38 km loop road passes wind farms, which supply 30% of the town's electricity, and some of the region's best-known natural attractions. Contact visitor centre for map.

Cape Le Grand National Park This spectacular coastline is lined with pristine beaches, including Hellfire Bay and Thistle Cove. At Lucky Bay, kangaroos can often be spotted lying on the beach. Visit Whistling Rock, which 'whistles' under certain wind conditions, and climb Frenchman's Peak for breathtaking views. There are magnificent displays of wildflowers in spring, and many bushwalks. Camping at Cape Le Grand and Lucky Bay. 56 km E.

Recherche Archipelago The Esperance region is known as the Bay of Isles because of this collection of 110 islands dotted along the coast that provide a haven for seals and sea lions. Cruises (3 hrs 30 min, subject to numbers and weather) take you around Cull, Button, Charlie, Woody and other islands; landing is permitted only on Woody Island. For an extraordinary camping experience, try a safari hut on Woody Island (open Sept–Apr). These canvas huts set high on timber decking overlook an idyllic turquoise bay framed by eucalyptus trees. Woody Island also has an interpretive centre to provide information to visitors.

Rotary Lookout: views of bay, town and archipelago; Wireless Hill; 2 km w. *Pink Lake:* a pink saltwater lake; 5 km w. *Twilight Cove:* sheltered swimming; 12 km w. *Observatory Point and Lookout:* dramatic views of bay and islands; 17 km w. *Monjingup Lake Nature Reserve:* walk trails, birdwatching and wildflowers in spring; 20 km w. *Dalyup River Wines:* the most isolated winery in WA; open weekends in summer; (08) 9076 5027; 42 km w. *Stokes National Park:* beautiful coastal and inlet scenery; 80 km w. *Cape Arid National Park:* birdwatching, fishing, camping and 4WD routes; 120 km E. *Whale-watching:* southern right whales visit bays and protected waters to calve (June–Oct); along the Great Ocean Drive and at Cape Arid. *Great Country Drive:* takes visitors 92 km inland; maps from visitor centre.

See also ESPERANCE & NULLARBOR, p. 310

Eucla

Pop. 50
Map ref. 610 C7 | 621 P6

i Eucla Motel; (08) 9039 3468.

97.1 FM ABC Radio National, 531 AM ABC Local Radio

Eucla is the largest settlement on the Nullarbor Plain, located just near the South Australian border. The ruins of a telegraph station exist at the original townsite and beyond the ruins are the remains of a jetty, a reminder of pioneering days when supplies were transported by boat. Eucla is today located on the Hampton Tableland and operates on Central Western Time, 45 minutes ahead of the rest of Western Australia.

Telegraph station ruins Opened in 1877 (just 33 years after Samuel Morse invented the telegraph), the Eucla Telegraph Station helped link WA with the rest of Australia and the world, often sending over 20 000 messages a year. The first message, sent to Perth in December 1877, stated simply, 'Eucla line opened. Hurrah.' 4 km s.

Eucla Museum: local history, including exhibits of the telegraph station, told through newspaper clippings and old photographs; Eucla Motel. *Travellers' Cross:* dedicated to travellers and illuminated at night; on the escarpment, west of town. *Bureau of Meteorology:* visitors welcome; east of town; (08) 9039 3444. *9-hole golf course:* site of the Golf Classic in May; north of town.

Eucla Amber Motor Hotel: counter meals; Eyre Hwy; (08) 9039 3468.

Eucla Amber Motor Hotel: hotel rooms, caravan park; Eyre Hwy; (08) 9039 3468.

Eucla National Park This small park extends between Eucla and Border Village. On the coast near the SA border is Wilsons Bluff Lookout, with views to the east following the Bunda Cliffs into the distance. Closer to Eucla are the enormous sculptural shapes of the Delisser Sandhills. Mark your footprints in the dunes.

Border Village: quarantine checkpoint for people entering WA (travellers should ensure they are not carrying fruit, vegetables, honey, used fruit and produce containers, plants or seeds). The Border Dash starts here every Oct; 13 km E.

See also ESPERANCE & NULLARBOR, p. 310

Exmouth

Pop. 1845
Map ref. 619 B3

i Murat Rd; (08) 9949 1176 or 1800 287 328; www.exmouthwa.com.au

107.7 ABC Radio National, 1188 AM ABC Local Radio

One of the newest towns in Australia, Exmouth was founded in 1967 as a support town for the Harold E. Holt US Naval Communications Station, the main source of local employment. Excellent year-round fishing and proximity to Cape Range National Park and Ningaloo Reef have since made Exmouth a major tourist destination. The town is the nearest point in Australia to the continental shelf.

 Mall Market: each Sun Apr–Sept. *Gamex:* world-class game-fishing competition; Mar. *Whale Shark Festival:* Apr/May. *Art Quest:* July. *Bill Fish Bonanza:* Oct/ Nov.

Mantaray's Restaurant: modern brasserie; Novotel Ningaloo Resort, Madaffari Dr; (08) 9949 0000. *Potshot Resort Restaurant:* relaxed dining; Potshot Resort, Murat Rd; (08) 9949 1200. *Sailfish Bar and Restaurant:* alfresco dining and

beer garden; Seabreeze Resort, 116 North C St; (08) 9949 1800. *Whaler's Restaurant:* local seafood; 5 Kennedy St; (08) 9949 2416.

Best Western Sea Breeze Resort: close access to Ningaloo Marine Park; 116 North C St; (08) 9949 1800. *Exmouth Cape Holiday Park:* range of accommodation; 3 Truscott Cres; (08) 9949 1101 or 1800 621 101. *Novotel Ningaloo Resort:* ideal for exploring Ningaloo Marine Park; Madaffari Dr; (08) 9949 0000. *Sal Salis Ningaloo Reef:* camping in style; North West Cape, Cape Range National Park; (02) 9571 6399 or 1300 790 561.

Cape Range National Park This rugged landscape of arid rocky gorges is edged by the stunning coastline of Ningaloo Marine Park. Wildlife is abundant, with emus, euros, rock wallabies and red kangaroos often sighted. In late winter there is a beautiful array of wildflowers including the Sturt's desert pea and the superb bird flower. Attractions within the park include Shothole Canyon, an impressive gorge; Mangrove Bay, a sanctuary zone with a bird hide overlooking a lagoon; and Mandu Mandu Gorge where you can walk along an ancient river bed. Yardie Creek is the only gorge with permanent water. Turquoise Bay is a popular beach for swimming and snorkelling (watch for currents). The Milyering Visitor Centre (54 km sw), made of rammed earth and run by solar power, is 52 km from Exmouth on the western side of the park and offers information on both Cape Range and Ningaloo. Contact (08) 9949 2808.

Ningaloo Marine Park: see Coral Bay. *Naval Communication Station:* the centre tower in its antenna field, at 388 m, is one of the tallest structures in the Southern Hemisphere; not open to public; 5 km N. *Vlamingh Head Lighthouse and Lookout:* built in 1912, Australia's only kerosene-burning lighthouse served as a beacon to mariners until 1967. The lookout offers panoramic 360-degree views; 19 km N. *Learmonth Jetty:* popular fishing spot, rebuilt after Cyclone Vance; 33 km S. *Wildlife-watching:* turtle-nesting (Nov–Jan); coral-spawning (Mar–Apr); boat cruises and air flights to see whale sharks (Mar–June); humpback whales (Aug–Nov) from lighthouse (17 km N) and from whale-watching boat tours. Snorkellers can swim with whale sharks and manta rays located by cruise boats. Coral-viewing boat cruises also available; contact visitor centre for details.

See also OUTBACK COAST & MID-WEST, p. 312

Fitzroy Crossing

Pop. 925
Map ref. 625 K8 | 628 H11

 Cnr Great Northern Hwy and Flynn Dr; (08) 9191 5355.

102.9 WA FM, 106.1 FM ABC Local Radio

Fitzroy Crossing is in the heart of the Kimberley region. As its name suggests, the original townsite was chosen as the best place to ford the mighty Fitzroy River. In the wet season, the river can rise over 20 metres and spread out up to 15 kilometres from its banks. Fitzroy Crossing's main attraction is its proximity to the magnificent 30-metre-deep Geikie Gorge with its sheer yellow, orange and grey walls. Check road conditions before any excursions from December to March, as this area is prone to flooding.

Crossing Inn First established in the 1890s as a shanty inn and trade store for passing stockmen, prospectors and drovers, it has operated on the same site ever since, and is one of the very few hotels in the state to retain a true outback atmosphere.

A stop-off and drink are a must for all travellers passing by. Skuthorp Rd; (08) 9191 5080.

Rodeo: July. *Garnduwa Festival:* sporting events; Oct.

Riverside Restaurant: traditional Australian fare; Fitzroy River Lodge, Great Northern Hwy; (08) 9191 5141.

Fitzroy River Lodge: range of accommodation; Great Northern Hwy; (08) 9191 5141. *Imintji Wilderness Camp:* wilderness camp with amazing views; Gibb River Rd; (08) 9277 8444 or 1800 889 389. *Mornington Wilderness Camp:* safari tents; Gibb River Rd; (08) 9191 7406 or 1800 631 946.

Geikie Gorge National Park Geikie Gorge has cliffs and sculptured rock formations carved by water through an ancient limestone reef. The Fitzroy River is home to sharks, sawfish and stingrays that have, over centuries, adapted to the fresh water. Freshwater crocodiles up to 3 m long and barramundi are plentiful, best seen on a guided boat tour. Aboriginal heritage and cultural tours are run by guides from the local Bunuba tribe; bookings essential. DEC rangers run tours on the geology, wildlife and history of the area. Entry to park is restricted during wet season (Dec–Mar). Contact visitor centre for details. 18 km NE.

Causeway Crossing: concrete crossing that was the only way across the river until the new bridge was built in the 1970s; Geikie Gorge Rd; 4 km NE. *Tunnel Creek National Park:* unique formation created by waters from the creek cutting a 750 m tunnel through the ancient reef; 4WD access only; 110 km NW. *Windjana Gorge National Park:* 350-million-year-old Devonian reef rising majestically above the surrounding plains. An easy walking trail takes you past primeval life forms fossilised within the gorge walls; 4WD access only; 145 km NW. *4WD tours:* to Tunnel Creek and Windjana Gorge; bookings essential, contact visitor centre for details.

See also KIMBERLEY, p. 314

Gascoyne Junction

Pop. 46
Map ref. 613 D7 | 622 A8

Shire offices, 4 Scott St; (08) 9943 0988; www.gascoyneonline.com.au

Lying at the junction of the Lyons and Gascoyne rivers, Gascoyne Junction is a small administration centre for the pastoral industry. Sheep stations in the area, ranging in size from around 36 000 to 400 000 hectares, produce a wool clip exceeding 1.5 million kilograms annually.

Junction Hotel: see the high-water mark from the 1982 floods on the wall of this Aussie pub; Carnarvon–Mullewa Rd. *Old Roads Board Museum:* memorabilia of the area; Scott St.

Bush Races: Sept/Oct. *Gascoyne Dash:* cross-country endurance; Oct.

The Junction Hotel: counter meals; Lot 27, Carnarvon Meekatharra Rd; (08) 9943 0504.

Bidgemia Station: working cattle station; Carnarvon Rd; (08) 9943 0501.

Kennedy Range National Park Along with spectacular scenery, the park is home to fossils of the earliest known species of banksia in Australia, and marine fossils that reflect the history of the region as an ocean bed. Ideal for sightseeing, hiking and bush camping, trails start from the camping area and pass through gorges where you can see honeycomb-like rock formations. 60 km N.

Mt Augustus National Park Mt Augustus is the world's largest monolith, twice the size of Uluṟu. It is also known as Burringurrah, named after a boy who, in Aboriginal legend, broke tribal law by running away from his initiation. On capture, he was speared in the upper right leg. The spear broke as the boy fell to the ground, leaving a section protruding from his leg. It is said that, as you look at Mt Augustus, you can see the shape of the boy's body with the stump of the spear being the small peak at the eastern end called Edney's Lookout. There are several walking and driving trails; maps available from visitor centre. 294 km NE; *see Carnarvon.*

See also OUTBACK COAST & MID-WEST, p. 312

Geraldton

Pop. 31 550
Map ref. 619 D12 | 620 A3

 Bill Sewell Complex, cnr Chapman Rd and Bayley St; (08) 9921 3999 or 1800 818 881; www.geraldtontourist.com.au

 94.9 ABC Classic FM, 96.5 WA FM

Situated on the spectacular Batavia Coast, Geraldton is the largest town in the mid-west region. As a port city, it is the major centre for the wheat belt and is renowned for its rock lobster industry. Geraldton is also regarded as one of the best windsurfing locations in the world. The nearby Houtman Abrolhos Islands are the site of 16 known shipwrecks. The most infamous is that of the Dutch ship *Batavia*, which foundered on a reef in 1629.

HMAS *Sydney* Memorial Built on Mt Scott overlooking the town to commemorate the loss of 645 men from HMAS *Sydney* on 19 November 1941. The ship sank after an encounter with the German raider HSK *Kormoran*. The wrecks of both ships were found in March 2008. Seven pillars representing the 7 seas hold aloft a 9 m high domed roof formed of 645 interlocking figures of seagulls. At night an eternal flame lights the cupola. Near the memorial is the bronze sculpture of a woman looking out to sea, representing the women left behind waiting for those who would not return. Tours of the memorial site are conducted daily at 10.30am. Cnr George Rd and Brede St.

WA Museum Geraldton Exhibits focus on the cultural and natural heritage of the Geraldton region. Maritime displays include finds from Australia's oldest shipwrecks, notably the original stone portico destined to adorn the castle gateway in the city of Batavia and lost to the sea when the *Batavia* sank in 1629. Museum Pl, Batavia Coast Marina; (08) 9921 5080. Adjacent in the Geraldton Marina is a replica of the *Batavia* longboat.

Historic buildings: explore the town's historic architecture dating back to the mid-1800s, with works by noted architect Monsignor John Cyril Hawes a highlight. Many of the buildings have been restored and are open to the public, including the Old Geraldton Gaol (1858), which is now a craft centre, and the Bill Sewell Complex (1884), which was built as a hospital and subsequently became a prison. In Cathedral Ave, St Francis Xavier Cathedral offers tours (10am Mon, Wed and Fri), and the Cathedral of the Holy Cross has one of the largest areas of stained glass in Australia. Self-guide walks are available, including the Heritage Trail; contact visitor centre for details. *Geraldton Regional Art Gallery:* the original Geraldton Town Hall (1907) converted to house art exhibitions and workshops; closed Mon; Chapman Rd. *Leon Baker Jewellers:* international jeweller works with Abrolhos

pearls and Argyle diamonds. Workshop tours are available; Marine Tce Mall. *Rock Lobster Factory:* take a tour and follow the journey of Geraldton's most famous export, the western rock lobster, from processor to plate; covered shoes required; tours 9.30am Mon–Fri Nov–June; Willcock Dr, Fisherman's Wharf. *Point Moore Lighthouse:* assembled in 1878 from steel sections prefabricated in England, and standing 34 m tall, this is the only lighthouse of its kind in Australia; Willcock Dr.

Sunshine Festival: Oct.

Boatshed Restaurant: modern Australian and seafood; 359 Marine Tce; (08) 9921 5500. *The Freemason's Hotel:* brasserie style; cnr Durlacher St and Marine Terrace Mall; (08) 9964 3457. *Tides of Geraldton:* contemporary dining with harbour views; 103 Marine Tce; (08) 9965 4999. *Chapman Valley Wines Restaurant:* vineyard platters; Chapman Valley Wines, Lot 14 Howatharra Rd, Nanson; (08) 9920 5148.

Drummond Cove Holiday Park: well-equipped caravan park; North West Coastal Hwy; (08) 9938 2524. *Mantra Geraldton:* self-contained studios and apartments; 221 Foreshore Dr; (08) 9956 1300 or 1300 987 604. *Marina Views:* harbour-view apartments; Foreshore Dr; (08) 9938 3848. *Ocean Centre Hotel:* boutique hotel; Cnr Foreshore Dr and Cathedral Ave; (08) 9921 7777.

Houtman Abrolhos Islands These 122 reef islands with a fascinating history span 100 km of ocean and are the main source of rock lobster for the local lobster fishing industry. There are 16 known shipwrecks in the Abrolhos Islands, the most infamous of which is that of the Dutch ship *Batavia* from 1629. Captain Pelsaert and 47 of the survivors sailed north to Batavia (modern-day Jakarta) for help. When they returned 3 and a half months later, they discovered that a mutiny had taken place and 125 of the remaining survivors had been massacred. All of the mutineers were hanged, except for 2 who were marooned on the mainland, becoming Australia's first white inhabitants. There is no record of their subsequent fate. The wreck was discovered in 1963 and some skeletons of victims of the mutiny have been found on Beacon Island. The islands now offer diving, snorkelling, surfing, windsurfing, fishing and birdwatching. Access is via boat or plane; tours and charters are available. Contact visitor centre for details and bookings. 65 km w.

Fishing: good fishing spots at Sunset Beach (6 km N) and Drummond Cove (10 km N). *Mill's Park Lookout:* excellent views over Moresby Range and coastal plain; 10 km NE. *Oakabella Homestead:* one of the region's oldest pioneering homesteads with a rare buttressed barn; tours available; 30 km N. *Chapman Valley:* an area of scenic drives and spectacular scenery, once home to the first coffee bean plantation in Australia. Also a huge diversity of wildflowers on display July–Oct. Wineries include Chapman Valley Wines, the northernmost winery in WA; enjoy free tastings; 35 km NE. *Scenic flights:* tours over nearby Abrolhos Islands, Murchison Gorges or the coastal cliffs of Kalbarri; contact visitor centre.

See also OUTBACK COAST & MID-WEST, p. 312

Gingin

Pop. 527
Map ref. 615 C1 | 618 B3 | 620 C7

 Council offices, Brockman St; (08) 9575 2211; www.gingin.wa.gov.au

720 AM ABC Local Radio, 810 AM ABC Radio National

Gingin is one of the oldest towns in Western Australia, having been settled in 1832, only 2 years after the establishment of the Swan River Colony. For tourists, it has the charm of old original stone buildings within a picturesque natural setting. Situated 84 kilometres north of Perth, it is an ideal destination for a daytrip from the city.

Historic buildings Enjoy a pleasant self-guide stroll around the town on the Gingin Walkabout Trail, which features many fine examples of early architecture including Philbey's Cottage and St Luke's Anglican Church, both made from local stone. Contact visitor centre for map.

Granville Park: in the heart of the town with free barbecue facilities, playground and picnic area. *Self-guide walks:* stroll along the Gingin Brook on the Jim Gordon VC Trail or try the Three Bridges Recreation Trail, rebuilt after being destroyed by fire in Dec 2002; contact visitor centre for maps.

Horticultural Expo: Apr. *British Car Club Day:* May. *Market Day Festival:* Sept.

Amirage Restaurant: European fare; 1654 Gingin Brook Rd; (08) 9575 7646. *Kyotmunga Estate:* platter lunches; 287 Chittering Valley Rd, Lower Chittering; (08) 9571 8001. *Stringybark Winery & Restaurant:* international cuisine; 2060 Chittering Rd, Chittering; (08) 9571 8069. *Willowbrook Farm Tearooms:* country tearooms; 1679 Gingin Brook Rd; (08) 9575 7566.

Brookside: chalets and shared accommodation; 1010 Chitna Rd, West Gingin; (08) 9575 7585. *Bindoon's Windmill Farm:* chalet and homestead accommodation; Great Northern Hwy, Bindoon; (08) 9576 1136. *Orchard Glory Farm Resort:* self-contained chalets; 41 Mooliabeenee Rd, Bindoon; (08) 9576 2888. *The Orchard Villa:* European-inspired home; Great Northern Hwy, Bindoon; (08) 9271 2270.

Gravity Discovery Centre Opened in 2003, this $4 million centre offers hands-on and static scientific displays on gravity, magnetism and electricity. It includes the biggest public astronomy centre in the Southern Hemisphere and the largest telescope in WA. Visitors can take a high-tech look at heavenly bodies in an evening presentation (bookings essential) and see a number of WA inventions relating to physics. Military Rd; (08) 9575 7577; 15 km sw.

Cemetery: with a spectacular display of kangaroo paws in early spring; northern outskirts of town. *Jylland Winery:* open to public, wine-tastings and cellar-door sales; 2 km s. *West Coast Honey:* live bee display, honey extraction, tastings, sales of honey and bee products; open 9am–4pm Wed–Sun, or Mon and Tues by appt; Gingin Brook Rd; 3 km w. *Moore River National Park:* special area for conservation featuring banksia woodlands and wildflower displays in spring; 20 km NW.

See also HEARTLANDS, p. 308

Greenough

Pop. 15 394
Map ref. 620 A3

Cnr Chapman Rd and Bayly St, Geraldton; (08) 9921 3999 or 1800 818 881; www.cgg.wa.gov.au

96.5 WA FM, 99.7 FM ABC Radio National

Lying 24 kilometres south of Geraldton, the Greenough Flats form a flood plain close to the mouth of the Greenough River.

At its peak in the 1860s and '70s, Greenough (pronounced 'Grennuff') was a highly successful wheat-growing area. However, the combined effects of drought, crop disease and floods led to the area's decline and from 1900 the population dropped dramatically. The historic hamlet that was once the centre of this farming community has been extensively restored and is classified by the National Trust.

Central Greenough Historic Settlement Precinct of 11 restored stone buildings dating from the 1860s including a school, police station, courthouse, gaol and churches. Fully re-created interior furnishings. Self-guide maps are available, or tours by appt. Cnr Brand Hwy and McCartney Rd; (08) 9926 1084.

Pioneer Museum: folk display located in an original limestone cottage; tours available; Brand Hwy. *Leaning trees:* these trees are a unique sight, having grown sideways in response to the harsh salt-laden winds that blow from the Indian Ocean; seen from Brand Hwy on the Greenough Flats. *Hampton Arms Inn:* fully restored historic inn (1863); Company Rd.

Abrolhos Restaurant: seafood; Greenough River Resort, Greenough River Rd; (08) 9921 5888.

Rock of Ages Cottage: charming heritage B&B; Phillips Rd; (08) 9926 1154.

Walkaway Railway Station: built in the style of a traditional British railway station, now housing a railway and heritage museum; closed Mon; Evans Rd; 10 km E. *Greenough River mouth:* ideal for swimming, canoeing, beach and rock fishing, birdwatching and photography; 14 km N. *Flat Rocks:* surfing, swimming and rock-fishing. A round of the State Surfing Championships is held here in June every year; 10 km S. *Ellendale Pool:* this deep, freshwater swimming hole beneath spectacular sandstone cliffs is an ideal picnic area; 23 km E. *Greenough River Nature Trail:* self-guide walk; contact visitor centre for brochure. *The Greenough/Walkaway Heritage Trail:* 57 km self-drive tour of the area; contact visitor centre for map.

See also OUTBACK COAST & MID-WEST, p. 312

Halls Creek

Pop. 1209
Map ref. 625 N7 | 629 L11

Hall St; (08) 9168 6262; www.hallscreek.wa.gov.au

102.9 WA FM, 106.1 FM ABC Local Radio

In the heart of the Kimberley region and on the edge of the Great Sandy Desert, Halls Creek is the site of the first payable gold discovery in Western Australia. In 1885 Jack Slattery and Charlie Hall (after whom the town is named) discovered gold, thereby sparking a gold rush that brought over 15 000 people to the area. In 1917 a seriously injured stockman named James 'Jimmy' Darcy was taken into Halls Creek. With neither doctor nor hospital in the town, the local postmaster carried out an emergency operation using a penknife as instructions were telegraphed by morse code from Perth. The Perth doctor then set out on the ten-day journey to Halls Creek via cattle boat, model-T Ford, horse-drawn sulky and, finally, on foot, only to discover that the patient had died the day before his arrival. The event inspired Reverend John Flynn to establish the Royal Flying Doctor Service in 1928, a development that helped to encourage settlement throughout the outback.

Russian Jack Memorial: tribute to a prospector who pushed his sick friend in a wheelbarrow to Wyndham for medical help; Thomas St. **Trackers Hut:** restored original hut of Aboriginal trackers; Robert St, behind police station.

Rodeo: July. **Picnic Races:** Oct.

Russian Jack's Restaurant: hearty fare; Best Western Halls Creek Motel, 194 Great Northern Hwy; (08) 9168 9600.

Best Western Halls Creek Motel: central Kimberley location; 194 Great Northern Hwy; (08) 9168 9600. **Kimberley Hotel:** motel units; Roberta Ave; (08) 9168 6101.

Wolfe Creek Crater National Park Wolfe Creek Crater is the second-largest meteorite crater in the world. Named after Robert Wolfe, a Halls Creek prospector, it is 870–950 m across and, in Aboriginal legend, said to be the site of the emergence of a powerful rainbow serpent from the earth. Scenic flights afford magnificent views; contact visitor centre for details.148 km s.

Purnululu National Park This World Heritage Area in the outback of the east Kimberley is home to the Bungle Bungle Range, a remarkable landscape of tiger-striped, beehive-shaped rock domes. A scenic flight is the best way to gain a perspective of the Bungle Bungles' massive size and spectacular scenery (details from visitor centre). The most visited site in Purnululu is Cathedral Gorge, a fairly easy walk. A couple of days and a backpack allow you to explore nearby Piccaninny Creek and Gorge, camping overnight. On the northern side of the park is Echidna Chasm, a narrow gorge totally different from those on the southern side. Purnululu is also rich in Aboriginal art, and there are many traditional burial sites within its boundaries. Purnululu is open to visitors (Apr–Dec) and is accessible by 4WD. There are few facilities and no accommodation; visitors must carry in all food and water and notify a ranger. 160 km E.

China Wall: white quartz formation said to resemble Great Wall of China; 6 km E. **Caroline's Pool:** deep pool ideal for swimming (in wet season) and picnicking; 15 km E. **Old Halls Creek:** remnants of original town including graveyard where James Darcy is buried; prospecting available; 16 km E. **Palm Springs:** fishing, swimming and picnicking; 45 km E. **Sawpit Gorge:** fishing, swimming, picnicking; 52 km E. **Billiluna Aboriginal Community:** fishing, swimming, camping, birdwatching and bushwalking, and bush tucker and cultural tours; 180 km s.

See also KIMBERLEY, p. 314

Harvey

Pop. 2602
Map ref. 616 F2 | 618 C7 | 620 C9

ⓘ James Stirling Pl; (08) 9729 1122; www.harveytourism.com

96.5 FM Harvey Community Radio, 810 AM ABC Radio National

On the Harvey River, 18 kilometres from the coast, the thriving town of Harvey is surrounded by fertile, irrigated plains. Beef production, citrus orchards and viticulture flourish in the region and intensive dairy farming provides the bulk of Western Australia's milk supply. Bordered by the Darling Range, Harvey offers a wealth of natural attractions, from the magnificent scenic drives through the escarpment to the pristine white beaches with excellent sunsets and fishing on the coast.

Tourist and Interpretive Centre: tourist information and display of local industries and May Gibbs characters; James Stirling Pl. **Big Orange:** lookout, one of Australia's big icons; Third St. **Harvey Museum:** memorabilia housed in renovated

railway station; open 2–4pm Sun or by appt; Harper St. **Stirling Cottage:** replica of the home of Governor Stirling, which later became the home of May Gibbs, author of *Snugglepot and Cuddlepie*; James Stirling Pl tourist precinct. **Heritage Gardens:** picturesque country gardens on the banks of the Harvey River; James Stirling Pl tourist precinct. **Internment Camp Memorial Shrine:** the only roadside shrine of its type in the world, built by prisoners of war in the 1940s; collect key from visitor centre; South Western Hwy. **Heritage trail:** 6.2 km self-guide walk includes historic buildings and sights of town; map available at visitor centre. **Mosaics and murals:** unique collection throughout the region. See Uduc Rd, South Western Hwy, and entrances to Myalup and Binningup.

Summer Series Concerts: Jan–Mar. **Harvest Festival:** Mar. **Spring Fair:** Sept.

Old Coast Road Brewery: tasting plates and pub fare; West Break Rd, Myalup; 1300 792 106.

Bluehills Farmstay Harvey: stylish chalets; Weir Rd; 0439 313 898. **Harvey Hills Farmstay Chalets:** family-friendly accommodation; Weir Rd; (08) 9729 1434. **Harvey Rainbow Caravan Park:** range of accommodation; 199 Kennedy St; (08) 9729 2239. **Highland Valley Homestead:** country luxury; 402 Collie River Rd, Burekup; (08) 9726 3080. **Top Paddock Cottage:** contemporary 4-star cottage; Vista Ridge Estate, 7 Newell St; (08) 9729 3240. **Indian Ocean Retreat & Caravan Park:** beachfront chalets; Myalup Beach Rd, Myalup; (08) 9720 1113.

Harvey Dam: landscaped park with viewing platform, amphitheatre, barbecues and playground. Fishing is allowed in season with permit; 3 km E. **HaVe Cheese:** tours and gourmet cheese tasting; (08) 9729 3949; 3 km s. **White Rocks Museum and Dairy:** founded in 1887. Compare current technology with display of machinery from the past; open 2–4pm or by appt for groups; 15 km s. **Beaches:** Myalup Beach provides good swimming, surfing and beach fishing; 21 km w. Binningup Beach is protected by a reef that runs parallel to shore and is ideal for sheltered swimming, snorkelling, beach fishing and boating; 25 km sw. **Wineries:** more than 10 wineries open to the public, only a short distance from town; contact visitor centre for details.

See also THE SOUTH-WEST, p. 307

Hyden

Pop. 281
Map ref. 618 H5 | 620 F8

ⓘ Wave Rock; (08) 9880 5182; www.waverock.com.au

648 AM ABC Local Radio, 1296 AM ABC Radio National

The small wheat-belt town of Hyden is synonymous with its famous nearby attraction, Wave Rock, originally known as Hyde's Rock in honour of a sandalwood cutter who lived in the area. A typing error by the Lands Department made it Hyden Rock, and the emerging town soon became known as Hyden. The area around the town boasts beautiful wildflowers in spring, including a wide variety of native orchids.

Wave Rock Weekender: music festival; Sept/Oct.

Wave Rock Motel Homestead: 3 restaurants on-site; 2 Lynch St; (08) 9880 5052.

Wave Rock Cabins & Caravan Park: 3-star park; Wave Rock Rd; (08) 9880 5022. **Wave Rock Lakeside Resort:** lakeside 2-bedroom cottages; Wave Rock Rd; (08) 9880 5022. **Wave Rock Motel Homestead:** units and suites; 2 Lynch St; (08) 9880 5052.

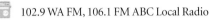

Wave Rock Resembling a breaking wave, this 100 m long and 15 m high granite cliff owes its shape to wind action over the past 2.7 billion years. Vertical bands of colour are caused by streaks of algae and chemical staining from run-off waters (4 km E). At Wave Rock Visitor Centre see the largest lace collection in the Southern Hemisphere with fine examples of antique lace, including lace worn by Queen Victoria. There are local wildflower species on display, an Australiana collection at the Pioneer Town, fauna in a natural bush environment and a walking trail.

Hippo's Yawn: rock formation; 5 km E via Wave Rock. *The Humps and Mulka's Cave:* Aboriginal wall paintings; 22 km N via Wave Rock. *Rabbit-Proof Fence:* see the fence where it meets the road; 56 km E.

See also HEARTLANDS, p. 308

Jurien Bay

Pop. 1175
Map ref. 620 A5

 Council offices, 110 Bashford St; (08) 9652 1020; www.dandaragan.wa.gov.au

103.1 WA FM, 107.9 FM ABC Radio National

Jurien Bay, settled in the mid-1850s, is the centre of a lobster fishing industry. The jetty was constructed in 1885 to enable a more efficient route to markets for locally produced wool and hides. Located within a sheltered bay protected by reefs and islands, the town has wide beaches and sparkling waters ideal for swimming, waterskiing, windsurfing, snorkelling, diving and surfing. The Jurien Bay boat harbour services the fishing fleet and has facilities for holiday boating and fishing. Anglers can fish from boat, jetty and beach.

Jurien Bay Charters: boat and fishing charters, scuba diving, sea lion tours; bookings at dive shop; Carmella St. *Old jetty site:* plaque commemorates site of original jetty. Remains of the jetty's timber piles have been discovered 65 m inland from high-water mark, which indicates the gradual build-up of coastline over time; Hastings St.

Market: Bashford St; usually last Sat each month. *Blessing of the Fleet:* Nov.

Leuseurs Gallery Cafe: relaxed cafe; 36 Bashford St; (08) 9652 2113. *Sandpiper Bar & Grill:* international cuisine; Cnr Roberts and Sandpiper sts; (08) 9652 1229.

Apex Camp Jurien: peaceful holiday park; 15 Bashford St; (08) 9652 1010. *Jurien Bay Tourist Park:* deluxe chalets, caravans and camping; Roberts St; (08) 9652 1595. *Ocean View Retreat:* 5-bedroom beach house; 6 Coubrough Pl; (08) 9255 2653. *Seafront Estate:* modern villa; Heaton St; (08) 9652 2055.

Jurien Bay Marine Park Established in August 2003, this marine park extends from Wedge Island to Green Head and encompasses major sea lion and seabird breeding areas. The reefs within the park are populated by a wide range of plants and animals including the rare Australian sea lion, and the seagrass meadows are a breeding ground for western rock lobsters.

Lions Lookout: spectacular views of town and surrounds; 5 km E. *Drovers Cave National Park:* rough limestone country with numerous caves, all of which have secured entrances limiting public access; 4WD access only; 7 km E. *Grigsons Lookout:* panoramic views of ocean and hinterland. Also wildflowers

July–Nov; 15 km N. *Lesueur National Park:* with over 900 species of flora, representing 10% of the state's known flora, Lesueur is an important area for flora conservation. Enjoy coastal views from a lookout; 23 km E. *Stockyard Gully National Park:* walk through 300 m Stockyard Gully Tunnel along winding underground creek; 4WD access only; 50 km N.

See also HEARTLANDS, p. 308

Kalbarri

Pop. 1329
Map ref. 619 C11

 Grey St; (08) 9937 1104 or 1800 639 468; www.kalbarriwa.info

102.9 WA FM, 106.1 FM ABC Local Radio

Kalbarri lies at the mouth of the Murchison River, flanked by Kalbarri National Park. Established in 1951, the town is a popular holiday resort, famous for the magnificent gorges up to 130 metres deep along the river. Just south of the township a cairn marks the spot where in 1629 Captain Pelsaert of the Dutch East India Company marooned two crew members implicated in the *Batavia* shipwreck and massacre. These were the first, albeit unwilling, white inhabitants of Australia.

Oceanarium: large aquariums and touch pools; Grey St; (08) 9937 2027. *Pelican feeding:* daily feeding by volunteers on the river foreshore; starts 8.45am; off Grey St. *Family Entertainment Centre:* trampolines, minigolf, bicycle hire; Magee Cres; (08) 9937 1105.

Sport Fishing Classic: Mar. *Canoe and Cray Carnival:* June.

Black Rock Cafe: cafe with emphasis on seafood; 80 Grey St; (08) 9937 1062. *The Grass Tree Cafe & Restaurant:* seafood with an Asian twist; 94–96 Grey St; (08) 9937 2288. *The Jetty Seafood Shack:* seafood restaurant with marina views; Shop 1, Marina Shopping Centre, 365 Grey St; (08) 9937 1067. *Zuytdorp Restaurant:* international cuisine; Kalbarri Beach Resort, Clotworthy St; (08) 9937 1061 or 1800 096 002.

Gecko Lodge: luxury B&B; 9 Glass St; (08) 9937 1900. *Kalbarri Palm Resort:* hotel and apartment accommodation; 8 Porter St; (08) 9937 2333 or 1800 819 029. *Kalbarri Seafront Villas:* spacious villas; 108 Grey St; (08) 9937 1025. *Kalbarri Tudor Holiday Park:* centrally located holiday park; 10 Porter St; (08) 9937 1077 or 1800 681 077.

Kalbarri National Park Gazetted in 1963, this park has dramatic coastal cliffs along its western boundary, towering river gorges and seasonal wildflowers, many of which are unique to the park. The Murchison River has carved a gorge through sedimentary rock known as Tumblagooda sandstone, creating a striking contrast of brownish red and purple against white bands of stone. Embedded in these layers are some of the earliest signs of animal life on earth. There are many lookouts including Nature's Window at the Loop, which overlooks the Murchison Gorge, and the breathtaking scenery at Z Bend Lookout. Along the 20 km coastal section of the park, lookouts such as Mushroom Rock, Pot Alley and Eagle Gorge offer panoramic views and whale-watching sites. Bushwalking, rock climbing, abseiling, canoeing tours, rafting, cruises, camping safaris, coach and wilderness tours, and barbecue facilities are all available. Contact visitor centre for details. 57 km E.

 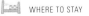

KALGOORLIE–BOULDER

Pop. 28 243

Map ref. 620 H5

(i) 250 Hannan St, (08) 9021 1966 or 1800 004 653; 106 Burt St, (08) 9093 1083; www.kalgoorlie.com

97.9 Hot FM, 648 AM ABC Local Radio

Kalgoorlie is the centre of Western Australia's goldmining industry. It was once known as Hannan's Find in honour of Paddy Hannan, the first prospector to discover gold in the area. In June 1893 Hannan was among a party of about 150 men who set out from Coolgardie to search for some lost prospectors near Yerilla. After a stop at Mount Charlotte, the main party continued on, leaving Hannan and two others behind as one of their horses had lost a shoe. Some idle 'specking' (looking on the ground for nuggets) led them to stumble on the richest goldfield the world had known – it soon grew to encompass the 'Golden Mile', which is reputedly the world's richest square mile of gold-bearing ore. Rapid development of Kalgoorlie and nearby Boulder followed, with thousands of men travelling to the field from all over the world, reaching a maximum population of about 30 000 in 1903. The shortage of water was always a problem, but in 1903 the genius of engineer C. Y. O'Connor enabled a pipeline to be opened that pumped water 560 kilometres from Perth. In its heyday Kalgoorlie and Boulder boasted eight breweries and 93 hotels. The two towns amalgamated in 1989 to form Kalgoorlie–Boulder, and today the population is again close to peak levels due to the region's second gold boom.

Historic buildings Although only a few kilometres apart, Kalgoorlie and Boulder developed independently for many years. The amalgamated towns now form a city with 2 main streets, each lined with impressive hotels and civic buildings. Built at the turn of the century, when people were flocking to the area, many of these buildings display ornamentation and fittings that reflect the confidence and wealth of the mining interests and are fine examples of early Australian architecture. In Hannan St, Kalgoorlie, the Kalgoorlie Town Hall (1908) displays a collection of memorabilia including some impressive furniture. Dame Nellie Melba performed in this building on several occasions. The offices of newspapers the *Kalgoorlie Miner* and *Western Argus* was the first 3-storey building in town. Burt St in Boulder is regarded as one of the most significant streetscapes in WA. Buildings to see include the Grand Hotel (1897), the Old Chemist (1900), which now houses a pharmaceutical museum, and the post office (1899), which was once so busy it employed 49 staff. The beautifully preserved Boulder Town Hall, built in 1908, is home to one of the world's last remaining Goatcher stage curtains, which elaborately depicts the Bay of Naples. Phillip Goatcher lived in Victorian times and was one of the greatest scenic painters of his era. His remarkable stage curtains could be found from London and Paris to New York. Public viewing of the curtain is on Tues, Wed and Thurs and Boulder Market Day (3rd Sun each month). Guided and self-guide heritage walks are available. Contact visitor centre for details.

Paddy Hannan's Statue: a monument to the first man to discover gold in Kalgoorlie; Hannan St. *St Mary's Church:* built in 1902 of Coolgardie pressed bricks, many of which are believed to contain gold; cnr Brookman and Porter sts, Kalgoorlie. *WA School of*

Mines Mineral Museum: displays include over 3000 mineral and ore specimens and many gold nuggets; open 8.30am–12.30pm Mon–Fri, closed on school holidays; Egan St, Kalgoorlie. *WA Museum Kalgoorlie–Boulder:* panoramic views of the city from the massive mining headframe at the entrance. Known locally as the Museum of the Goldfields, displays include a million-dollar gold collection, nuggets and jewellery. See the narrowest pub in the Southern Hemisphere, a re-created 1930s miner's cottage and other heritage buildings. Guided tours available; open 10am–4.30pm daily; 17 Hannan St, Kalgoorlie. *Goldfields Arts Centre:* art gallery and theatre; Cassidy St, Kalgoorlie. *Goldfields Aboriginal Art Gallery:* examples of local Aboriginal art and artefacts for sale; open 10.30am–4.30pm or by appt; Dugan St, Kalgoorlie. *Paddy Hannan's Tree:* a plaque marks the spot where Paddy Hannan first discovered gold; Outridge Tce, Kalgoorlie. *Red-light district:* view the few remaining 'starting stalls', in which women once posed as prospective clients walked by, and visit the only working brothel in the world that visitors can tour – Langtrees 181 (tours daily, bookings at visitor centre); Hay St, Kalgoorlie. *Superpit Lookout:* underground mining on the Golden Mile became singly owned in the 1980s and '90s and was converted into an open-cut operation – what is now known as the Superpit. Peer into its depths from the lookout off Goldfields Hwy, Boulder (can coincide visit with blasting; check times at visitor centre); daily tours (free on market day) and scenic flights are also available. *Mt Charlotte:* the reservoir holds water pumped from the Mundaring Weir in Perth via the pipeline of C. Y. O'Connor. A lookout provides good views of the city; off Goldfields Hwy, Kalgoorlie. *Hammond Park:* miniature Bavarian castle made from thousands of local gemstones. There is also a sanctuary for kangaroos and emus, and aviaries for a variety of birdlife; Lyall St, Kalgoorlie. *Arboretum:* a living museum of species of the semi-arid zone and adjacent desert areas, this 26.5 ha parkland has interpretive walking trails and recreation facilities; Hawkins St, adjacent Hammond Park. *Miners' Monument:* tribute to mine workers; Burt St, Boulder. *Goldfields War Museum:* war memorabilia and armoured vehicles on display; 106 Burt St, Boulder. *WMC Nickel Pots:* massive nickel pots and interpretive panels describe the story of the development of the nickel industry in the region; Goldfields Hwy. *Loopline Railway Museum:* view the steam train that once carried hundreds of miners to the surrounds of the Golden Mile; Boulder Station. *Royal Flying Doctor Visitor Centre:* climb on board an authentic RFDS plane; tours available; open 10am–3pm Mon–Fri; Airport, Hart Kerspien Dr. *Karlkurla Bushland:* pronounced 'gullgirla', this natural regrowth area of bushland offers a 4 km signposted walk trail, picnic areas and lookout over the city and nearby mining areas; Riverina Way. *Walks:* guided and self-guide heritage walks; details and maps at visitor centre.

Boulder Market Day: Burt St, Boulder; 3rd Sun each month. *Undies 500 Car Rally:* Feb. *Community Fair:* Mar/Apr. *Menzies to Kalgoorlie Cycle Race:* May. *Diggers and Dealers Mining Forum:* Aug. *Kalgoorlie and Boulder Cup:* Sept. *Back to Boulder Festival:* Oct. *Balzano Barrow Race:* Oct. *Art Prize Exhibition:* Dec. *St Barbara's Mining and Community Festival:* Dec.

Barista 202: funky cafe; 202 Hannan St, Kalgoorlie; (08) 9022 2228. *Saltimbocca:* Italian restaurant; 90 Egan St; (08) 9022 8028. *The Cornwall:* pub and bistro; 25 Hopkins St, Boulder; (08) 9093 0911. *The Exchange Hotel:* traditional Irish and Australian food; 135 Hannan St, Kalgoorlie; (08) 9021 2833.

All Seasons Kalgoorlie Plaza Hotel: centrally located hotel; 45 Egan St, Kalgoorlie; (08) 9080 5900. *Kalgoorlie Overland Motel:* range of motel rooms; 566 Hannan St, Kalgoorlie; (08) 9021 1433. *Palace Hotel:* centrally located historic pub; 137 Hannan St, Kalgoorlie; (08) 9021 2788. *Quest Yelverton Kalgoorlie:* premier town accommodation; 210 Egan St, Kalgoorlie; (08) 9022 8181. *Rydges Kalgoorlie:* studios and apartments; 21 Davidson St, Kalgoorlie; (08) 9080 0800 or 1300 857 922.

Australian Prospectors and Miners Hall of Fame Tour a historic underground mine, watch a gold pour or visit the Exploration Zone, which is designed specifically for young people. You will find interactive exhibits on exploration, mineral discoveries and surface and underground mining, including panning for gold. The Environmental Garden details the stages and techniques involved in mine-site rehabilitation. At Hannan's North Tourist Mine, historic buildings re-create an early gold-rush town and visitors can take a first-hand look at the cramped and difficult working conditions of the miners. Eastern Bypass Rd; (08) 9026 2700; 7 km N.

Bush 2-Up: visit the original corrugated-iron shack and bush ring where Australia's only legal bush 2-up school used to operate; off Goldfields Hwy; 8 km E. *Kanowna Belle Gold Mine lookouts:* wander the ghost town remains of Kanowna and see day-to-day mining activities from 2 lookouts over a previously mined open pit and processing plant; 20 km E. *Broad Arrow:* see the pub where scenes from the Googie Withers movie *Nickel Queen* were shot in the 1970s. Every wall is autographed by visitors; 38 km N. *Ora Banda:* recently restored inn; 54 km NW. *Kambalda:* nickel-mining town on Lake Lefroy (salt). Head to Red Hill Lookout for views across the expanse; 55 km S. *Prospecting:* visitors to the area may obtain a miner's right from the Dept of Mineral and Petroleum Resources in Brookman St, Kalgoorlie; strict conditions apply; details from the visitor centre. *Golden Quest Discovery Trail:* 965 km drive that traces the gold rushes of the 1890s through Coolgardie, Kalgoorlie–Boulder, Menzies, Kookynie, Gwalia, Leonora and Laverton; pick up the map, book and CD at the visitor centre. *Golden Pipeline Heritage Trail:* follow the course of the pipeline from Mundaring Weir to Mt Charlotte. Finding a reliable water supply to support the eastern goldfields' booming population became imperative after the 1890s gold rush. C. Y. O'Connor's solution was radically brilliant: the construction of a reservoir at Mundaring in the hills outside Perth and a 556 km water pipeline to Kalgoorlie. His project was criticised relentlessly by the press and public, which affected O'Connor deeply. On 19 Mar 1902 he went for his usual morning ride along the beach in Fremantle. As he neared Robb Jetty, he rode his horse into the sea and shot himself. The pipeline was a success, delivering as promised 22 million litres of water a day to Kalgoorlie, and continues to operate today. On the coast just

[AERIAL VIEW OF SALT LAKE NORTH-EAST OF KALGOORLIE]

south of Fremantle, a half-submerged statue of a man on a horse is a poignant tribute to this man of genius; guidebook available at visitor centre. *Tours:* self-drive or guided 4WD tours available to many attractions. Also fossicking, prospecting, camping and museum tours, and self-guide wildflower tours; details at visitor centre. *Scenic flights:* flights over Coolgardie, the Superpit, Lake Lefroy; details at visitor centre.

See also GOLDFIELDS, p. 311

Rainbow Jungle: breeding centre for rare and endangered species of parrots, cockatoos and exotic birds set in landscaped tropical gardens. Also here is the largest walk-in parrot free-flight area in Australia and an outdoor cinema featuring the latest movies; Red Bluff Rd; 3 km s. *Seahorse Sanctuary:* aquaculture centre focused on the conservation of seahorses and other tropical marine fish; Red Bluff Rd; 3 km s. *Wildflower Centre:* view over 200 species on display along a 1.8 km walking trail. Visit the plant nursery and herbarium, where you can purchase seeds and souvenirs; open July–Nov; Ajana–Kalbarri Rd; 3km E. *Murchison House Station:* tours available of one of the oldest and largest stations in WA, which includes historic buildings and cemetery, display of local arts and crafts, and wildflowers; seasonal, check with visitor centre; Ajana–Kalbarri Rd; 4 km E. *Big River Ranch:* enjoy horseriding through the spectacular countryside; Ajana–Kalbarri Rd; 4 km E. *Wittecarra Creek:* cairn marking the site where 2 of the mutineers from the Dutch ship *Batavia* were left as punishment for their participation in the murders of 125 survivors of the wreck; 4 km s. *Hutt River Province:* independant sovereign state founded in 1970; 50 km SE; *see Northampton.*

See also OUTBACK COAST & MID-WEST, p. 312

Kalgoorlie–Boulder

see inset box on previous page

Karratha

Pop. 11 727
Map ref. 619 E1 | 622 B2 | 624 B12 | 626 D5

 i 4548 Karratha Rd; (08) 9144 4600.

104.1 FM ABC News Radio, 106.5 WA FM

Karratha is the Aboriginal word for 'good country'. Founded in 1968 as a result of expansion of the iron-ore industry, Karratha was originally established for workers on the huge industrial projects nearby. For visitors, Karratha is an ideal centre from which to explore the fascinating Pilbara region.

TV Hill Lookout: excellent views over town centre and beyond; off Millstream Rd. *Jaburara Heritage Trail:* 3 hr walk features Aboriginal rock carvings; pamphlet available at visitor centre.

FeNaClNG Festival: this celebration takes its name from the town's mining roots (Fe is the chemical symbol for iron ore, NaCl is the symbol for salt, and NG is an abbreviation for natural gas); Aug. *Gamefishing Classic:* Aug.

Etcetera Brasserie: fine dining, Pilbara-style; Karratha International Hotel, cnr Hillview and Millstream rds; (08) 9187 3333. *Hearson's Bistro:* poolside fine dining; All Seasons Karratha, Lot 1079 Searipple Rd; (08) 9185 1155. *Whim Creek Pub:* counter meals; North West Coastal Hwy, Whim Creek; (08) 9176 4914.

Balmoral Holiday Park: long-term accommodation; Balmoral Rd; (08) 9815 3628. *Best Western Karratha Central Apartments:* modern self-contained accommodation; 27 Warambie Rd; (08) 9143 9888. *Pilbara Holiday Park:* variety of accommodation options; Rosemary Rd; (08) 9185 1855 or 1800 451 855. *Dampier Archipelago:* luxury yacht; contact Karratha Visitor Centre; (08) 9144 4600.

Millstream–Chichester National Park Rolling hills, spectacular escarpments and tree-lined watercourses with hidden rockpools characterise this park. The remarkable oasis of Millstream is an area of tropical palm-fringed freshwater springs, well known to the Afghan cameleers of Pilbara's past. Other notably scenic spots are Python, Deepreach and Circular pools, and Cliff Lookout. The Millstream Homestead Visitor Centre, housed in the Gordon family homestead (1919), has displays dedicated to the local Aboriginal people, early settlers and the natural environment. Popular activities include bushwalking, picnicking, camping, fishing, swimming and boating. Tours are available; contact visitor centre for details. 124 km s.

Salt Harvest Ponds: Australia's largest evaporative salt fields. Tours are available; details at visitor centre; 15 km N. *Dampier:* port facility servicing the iron-ore operations at Tom Price and Paraburdoo. Watersports and boat hire are available; 22 km N. *Hamersley Iron Port Facilities:* 3 hr tour and audiovisual presentation daily; bookings essential through visitor centre; 22 km N. *Cleaverville Beach:* scenic spot ideal for camping, boating, fishing and swimming; 26 km NE. *North-West Shelf Gas Project Visitor Centre:* displays on the history and technology of Australia's largest natural resource development, with panoramic views over the massive onshore gas plant; open 10am–4pm Mon–Fri Apr–Oct, 10am–1pm Mon–Fri Nov–Mar; Burrup Peninsula; 30 km N. *Aboriginal rock carvings:* there are more than 10 000 engravings on the Burrup Peninsula alone, including some of the earliest examples of art in Australia. A debate is currently raging over the damage being done to this magnificent outdoor gallery by the adjacent gas project; check with visitor centre for locations. *Dampier Archipelago:* 42 islands and islets ideal for swimming, snorkelling, boating, whale-watching and fishing; take a boat tour from Dampier. *Montebello Islands:* site of Australia's first shipwreck, the *Tryal*, which ran aground and sank in 1622. It is now a good spot for snorkelling, beachcombing, fishing and diving; beyond Dampier Archipelago. *Scenic flights:* over the Pilbara outback; details at visitor centre.

See also PILBARA, p. 313

Katanning

Pop. 3806
Map ref. 618 F8 | 620 E10

i Old Mill, cnr Austral Tce and Clive St; (08) 9821 4390; www.katanningwa.com

94.9 Hot FM, 612 AM ABC Radio National

Katanning lies in the middle of a prosperous grain-growing and pastoral area. A significant development in the town's history was the 1889 completion of the Great Southern Railway, which linked Perth and Albany. Construction was undertaken at both ends, and a cairn north of town marks the spot where the lines were joined.

Old Mill Museum: built in 1889, it features an outstanding display of vintage roller flour-milling processes; cnr Clive St and Austral Tce. *All Ages Playground and Miniature Steam Railway:* scenic grounds with playground equipment for all ages. Covered shoes required to ride the train, which runs on the 2nd and 4th Sun of each month; cnr Great Southern Hwy and Clive St. *Kobeelya:* a majestic residence (1902) with 7 bedrooms, ballroom, billiard room, tennis courts and croquet lawn, now a conference centre; Brownie St. *Old Winery Ruins:* inspect the ruins of the original turreted distillery and brick vats, with old ploughs and machinery on display; Andrews Rd. *Historical Museum:* the original school building has been converted into a museum of local memorabilia; open 2–4pm Sun, or by appt; Taylor St. *Sale Yards:* one of the biggest yards in Australia, sheep sales every Wed at 8am; viewing platform for visitors; Daping St. *Heritage Rose Garden:* with roses dating from 1830; Austral Tce. *Piesse Memorial Statue:* unveiled in 1916, this statue of Frederick H. Piesse, the founder of Katanning, was sculpted by

P. C. Porcelli, a well-known artist in the early days of WA; Austral Tce. *Art Gallery:* a changing display and local collection; closed Sun; Austral Tce.

Farmers markets: Pemble St; 3rd Sat each month. *Spring Lamb Festival:* Oct.

Kimberley Restaurant: intimate dining, Kimberley-style; New Lodge Motel, 170 Clive St; (08) 9821 1788. *Loretta @ Feddy:* seasonal menu; Federal Hotel, 111 Clive St; (08) 9821 7128.

New Lodge Motel: comfortable motel accommodation; 170 Clive St; (08) 9821 1788. *Woodchester B&B:* colonial B&B; 19 Clive St; (08) 9821 7007.

Police Pools (Twonkwillingup): site of the original camp for the district's first police officers. Enjoy swimming, picnicking, birdwatching and bushwalking; 3 km s. *Lake Ewlyamartup:* picturesque freshwater lake ideal for picnicking, swimming, boating and waterskiing, particularly in early summer when the water level is high; 22 km E. *Katanning-Piesse Heritage Trail:* 20 km self-drive/walk trail; map at visitor centre. *Watersports:* the lakes surrounding the town are excellent for recreational boating, waterskiing and swimming; details at visitor centre.

See also GREAT SOUTHERN, p. 309

Kellerberrin

Pop. 868
Map ref. 618 F4 | 620 D7

ℹ️ Shire offices, 110 Massingham St; (08) 9045 4006; www.kellerberrin.wa.gov.au

📻 107.3 FM ABC Radio National, 1215 AM ABC Local Radio

Centrally located in the wheat belt, Kellerberrin is 200 kilometres east of Perth. In springtime, magnificent displays of wildflowers adorn the roadsides, hills and plains around the town.

International Art Space Kellerberrin Australia This art gallery, built in 1998, is home to an ambitious art project. International artists are given the opportunity to live and work within the local community for a 3-month period. Workshops and mentoring programs provide collaboration between these established artists and emerging Australian talent. Many of the exhibitions created are then displayed in larger venues throughout Australia and the world. Massingham St; (08) 9045 4739.

Pioneer Park and Folk Museum: located in the old Agricultural Hall, displays include local artefacts, farming machinery and photographic records. Pick up the key from tourist information or Dryandra building next door; cnr Leake and Bedford sts. *Centenary Park:* children's playground, in-line skate and BMX track, maze, heritage walkway and barbecue facilities all in the centre of town; Leake St. *Golden Pipeline Lookout:* interpretive information at viewing platform with views of the countryside and pipeline; via Moore St. *Heritage trail:* self-guide town walk that includes historic buildings and churches; brochure available.

Keela Dreaming Cultural Festival: odd-numbered years, Mar. *Central Wheatbelt Harness Racing Cup:* May.

Kellerberrin Motor Hotel: hearty counter meals; 108 Massingham St; (08) 9045 5000.

Kellerberrin Caravan Park: 6 powered sites; Connelly St; 0428 138 474. *Kellerberrin Motor Hotel:* centrally located hotel; 108 Massingham St; (08) 9045 5000. *The Prev:* B&B with conference facilities; 1 George St; 0427 063 638.

Durokoppin Reserve: take a self-guide scenic drive through this woodland area, which is beautiful in the wildflower season; contact visitor centre for map; 27 km N. *Kokerbin Wave Rock:* the third largest monolith in WA. The Devil's Marbles and a historic well are also at the site. Restricted vehicle access to the summit, but the walk will reward with panoramic views; 30 km s. *Cunderdin:* museum housed in the No 3 pumping station has displays on the pipeline, wheat-belt farming and the Meckering earthquake; 45 km w. *Golden Pipeline Heritage Trail:* one of the main stops along the trail, which follows the water pipeline of C. Y. O'Connor from Mundaring Weir to the goldfields; guidebook available at visitor centre. *See Kalgoorlie–Boulder.*

See also HEARTLANDS, p. 308

Kojonup

Pop. 1124
Map ref. 618 F9 | 620 D10

ℹ️ 143 Albany Hwy; (08) 9831 0500; www.kojonupvisitors.com

📻 558 AM ABC Local Radio, 612 AM ABC Radio National

A freshwater spring first attracted white settlement of the town now known as Kojonup. In 1837 Alfred Hillman arrived in the area after being sent by Governor Stirling to survey a road between Albany and the Swan River Colony. He was guided to the freshwater spring by local Aboriginal people and his promising report back to Governor Stirling resulted in a military outpost being established. The Shire of Kojonup was the first shire in Western Australia to have a million sheep within its boundaries.

Kodja Place Visitor and Interpretative Centre: fascinating and fun displays about the land and its people, with stories of Aboriginal heritage and white settlement. It also includes the Australian Rose Maze, the only rose garden in the world growing exclusively Australian roses; 143 Albany Hwy. *Kojonup Museum:* in historic schoolhouse building with displays of local memorabilia; open by appt; Spring St. *A. W. Potts Kokoda Track Memorial:* a life-size statue of the brigadier facing towards his beloved farm 'Barrule'; Albany Hwy. *Centenary of Federation Wool Wagon:* commemorates the significance of the sheep industry to the Kojonup community; Albany Hwy. *Kojonup Spring:* grassy picnic area; Spring St. *Military Barracks:* built in 1845, this is one of the oldest surviving military buildings in WA and features historical information about the building; open by appt; Spring St. *Elverd's Cottage:* display of pioneer tools and farm machinery; open by appt; Soldier Rd. *Kodja Place Bush Tucker Walk:* follows the old railway line east where 3000 trees and shrubs indigenous to the area have been planted; map from visitor centre. *Town walk trail:* self-guide signposted walk of historic sights; map from visitor centre.

Wildflower Week: Sept. *Kojonup Show:* Oct.

Commercial Hotel: homely pub; 118 Albany Hwy; (08) 9831 1044.

Jacaranda Heights B&B: secluded residence; 14 Stock Rd; (08) 9831 1200. *Kemminup Farm Homestay:* country-style B&B; Kemminup Rd; (08) 9831 1286. *Kojonup B&B:* converted barn; 47 Newstead Rd; (08) 9831 1119.

Myrtle Benn Memorial Flora and Fauna Sanctuary: walk one of the numerous trails among local flora and fauna including many protected species; Tunney Rd; 1 km w. *Farrar Reserve:* scenic bushland and spectacular wildflower display in

 RADIO STATIONS   IN TOWN   WHAT'S ON   WHERE TO EAT   WHERE TO STAY   NEARBY

season; Blackwood Rd; 8 km w. *Australian Bush Heritage Block:* natural woodland featuring wandoo and species unique to the South-West; 16 km N. *Lake Towerinning:* boating, waterskiing, horseriding, camping; 40 km NW. *Aboriginal guided tours:* tours of Aboriginal heritage sites; details and bookings at visitor centre.

See also GREAT SOUTHERN, p. 309

Kulin

Pop. 354
Map ref. 618 G6 | 620 E8

 Resource Centre, Johnston St; (08) 9880 1021; www.kulin.wa.gov.au

720 AM ABC Local Radio

The sheep- and grain-farming districts surrounding Kulin provide spectacular wildflower displays in season. The flowering gum, *Eucalyptus macrocarpa*, is the town's floral emblem. A stand of jarrah trees, not native to the area and not known to occur elsewhere in the wheat belt, grows near the town. According to Aboriginal legend, two tribal groups met at the site and, as a sign of friendship, drove their spears into the ground. From these spears, the jarrah trees grew. The Kulin Bush Races event has expanded from horseracing to a major attraction including a weekend of live music, an art and craft show, foot races and Clydesdale horserides. In the months prior to the Kulin Races, tin horses appear in the paddocks lining the road on the way to the racetrack. These, along with the tin horses from past years, create an unusual spectacle.

Tin Horse Highway: starting in town and heading to the Jilakin racetrack, the highway is lined with horses made from a wide variety of materials. *Kulin Herbarium:* specialising in local flora; open by appt; Johnston St. *Butlers Garage:* built in the 1930s, this restored garage houses a museum of cars and machinery; open by appt; cnr Johnston and Stewart sts. *Memorial Slide and Swimming Pool:* the longest water slide in regional WA; pool open 12–7pm Tues–Fri, 10am–7pm weekends/public holidays, summer months; check for opening hours of water slide; Holt Rock Rd; (08) 9880 1222.

Charity Car Rally: Sept. *Kulin Bush Races:* Oct. *Longneck Roughneck Des Cook Memorial Quick Shears Shearing Competition:* Oct.

Kulin Hotel & Motel: Australian pub; Johnston St; (08) 9880 1201.

Kulin Caravan Park: includes railway carriages; Rankin St; (08) 9880 1204.

Macrocarpa Walk Trail: 1 km self-guide signposted walk trail through natural bush; brochure available at visitor centre; 1 km w. *Jilakin Rock and Lake:* granite monolith overlooking a 1214 ha lake; 16 km E. *Hopkins Nature Reserve:* important flora conservation area; 20 km E. *Buckley's Breakaways:* unusual pink and white rock formations; 70 km E. *Dragon Rocks Nature Reserve:* wildflower reserve with orchids and wildlife; 75 km E.

See also HEARTLANDS, p. 308

Kununurra

Pop. 3745
Map ref. 625 D4 | 629 M5 | 634 A11 | 636 A2

 75 Coolibah Dr; (08) 9168 1177 or 1800 586 868; www.kununurratourism.com

102.5 WA FM, 819 AM ABC Local Radio

Kununurra lies in the East Kimberley region not far from the Northern Territory border. It was established in the 1960s alongside Lake Kununurra on the Ord River at the centre of the massive Ord River Irrigation Scheme. Adjacent is the magnificent Mirima National Park. Lake Argyle to the south, in the Carr Boyd Range, was created by the damming of the Ord River and is the largest body of fresh water in Australia. Islands in the lake were once mountain peaks. The word 'Kununurra' means 'meeting of big waters' in the language of the local Aboriginal people. The climate in Kununurra and the East Kimberley is divided into 2 seasons, the Dry and the Wet. The Dry extends from April to October and is characterised by blue skies, clear days and cool nights. The Wet, from November to March, is a time of hot, humid days, when frequent thunderstorms deliver most of the annual rainfall to the region.

Historical Society Museum: artefacts and photos of the development of the town; Coolibah Dr. *Lovell Gallery:* art gallery exhibiting Kimberley artworks for sale; Konkerberry Dr. *Waringarri Aboriginal Arts:* large and varied display of Aboriginal art and artefacts for sale; open daily, weekends by appt; Speargrass Rd. *Red Rock Art:* a gallery and studio for Indigenous painters from across the Kimberley; open Mon–Fri; Coolibah Dr. *Kelly's Knob Lookout:* panoramic view of town and Ord Valley; off Speargrass Rd. *Celebrity Tree Park:* arboretum on the shore of Lake Kununurra where celebrities, including John Farnham, HRH Princess Anne, Harry Butler and Rolf Harris, have planted trees. Lily Creek Lagoon at the edge of the park is a good spot for birdwatching. The boat ramp was once part of the road to Darwin; off Victoria Hwy. *Historical Society walk trails:* choose between 2 trails of different lengths; maps available from the historical society.

Ord Valley Muster: May. *Kununurra Races:* Aug. *Rodeo and Campdraft:* Aug. *Night Rodeo:* Sept.

Gulliver's Tavern: typical pub fare; 186 Cottontree Ave; (08) 9168 1666. *Ivanhoes Gallery Restaurant:* international cuisine; All Seasons Kununurra, Messmate Way; (08) 9168 4000. *Kelly's Bar & Grill:* relaxed dining; Kununurra Country Club Resort, 47 Coolibah Dr; (08) 9168 1024 or 1800 808 999.

Diversion Cruises & Hire: houseboat on Lake Kununurra; 1 Lily Creek Dr; (08) 9168 3333. *Hidden Valley Tourist Park:* ideally located tourist park; Weaber Plains Rd; (08) 9168 1790. *Hotel Kununurra:* central and comfortable hotel; 37 Messmate Way; (08) 9168 0400. *Kununurra Country Club Resort:* centrally located resort; 47 Coolibah Dr; (08) 9168 1024 or 1800 808 999. *El Questro Wilderness Park:* featuring Aboriginal rock art, hot springs, spectacular scenery, camping, boating, fishing and a range of accommodation options; Gibb River Rd; (08) 9169 1777.

Mirima National Park Known by locals as the 'mini-Bungle Bungles', a striking feature of this park is the boab trees that grow on the rock faces, the seeds having been carried there by rock wallabies and left in their dung. There are walking trails within the park, and between May and Aug guided walks are available. Details at visitor centre; 2 km E.

Ivanhoe Farm: tastings and sales of melons and other local produce; open May–Sept; 1 km N. *Lake Kununurra:* formed after the completion of the Diversion Dam as part of the Ord River Scheme, the lake is home to a large variety of flora and fauna and is ideal for sailing, rowing, waterskiing and boat tours; details at visitor centre; 2 km S. *City of Ruins:* unusual sandstone formation of pinnacles and outcrops that resemble the ruins of an ancient city; off Weaber Plains Rd; 6 km N. *Ord River and Diversion Dam:* abundance of wildlife and spectacular scenery and a variety of watersports and cruises available; details at visitor centre; 7 km w. ***Top Rockz Gallery:*** exhibits gemstones and precious metals; open May–Sept; 10 km N. ***Ivanhoe Crossing:*** permanently flooded causeway is an ideal fishing spot; Ivanhoe Rd; 12 km N. ***Hoochery Distillery:*** visit a traditional old Country and Western Saloon Bar or take a tour of the only licensed distillery in WA; closed Sun; Weaber Plains Rd; 15 km N. ***Zebra Rock Gallery:*** view the amazing display of zebra rock, nearly 600 million years old and believed to be unique to the Kimberley, or feed fish from the lakeside jetty; Packsaddle Rd; 16 km S. ***Middle Springs:*** picturesque spot with diverse birdlife; 4WD access only; 30 km N. ***Black Rock Falls:*** spectacular waterfall during the wet season that spills over rocks stained by the minerals in the water; 4WD access only; Apr–Oct (subject to road conditions); 32 km N. ***Parry Lagoons Nature Reserve:*** enjoy birdwatching from a shaded bird hide at Marlgu Billabong or scan the wide vistas of the flood plain and distant hills afforded from the lookout at Telegraph Hill; 65 km NW. ***The Grotto:*** ideal swimming hole (in the wet season) at the base of 140 stone steps; 70 km NW. ***Argyle Downs Homestead Museum:*** built in 1884 and relocated when the lake was formed, the building is a fine example of an early station homestead; open 7am–4pm dry season, wet season by appt; Parker Rd; 70 km S. ***Lake Argyle:*** the view of the hills that pop out of the main body of water is said to resemble a crocodile basking in the sun and is known locally as Crocodile Ridge. Fishing, birdwatching, camping, bushwalking, sailing, canoeing and lake cruises are all available; 72 km S. ***Argyle Diamond Mine:*** the largest producing diamond mine in the world. Access is via tour only; details at visitor centre; 120 km S. ***Purnululu National Park:*** scenic flights available in town; 375 km S; *see Halls Creek*. ***Mitchell River National Park:*** one of the Kimberley's newest national parks protects this scenic and biologically important area. Mitchell Falls and Surveyor's Pool are the 2 main attractions for visitors. The area is remote with 4WD access to the park only, and is about 16 hours' drive from Kununurra; 680 km NW. ***Scenic flights:*** flights from town take visitors over the remarkable Bungle Bungles, Argyle Diamond Mine, Mitchell Plateau or Kalumburu; details and bookings at visitor centre. ***Tours:*** bushwalks, safaris, camping, canoeing, 4WD or coach; details at visitor centre.

See also KIMBERLEY, p. 314

Lake Grace

Pop. 503
Map ref. 618 H7 | 620 F9

 Stationmaster's house, Stubbs St; (08) 9865 2140; www.lakegrace.wa.gov.au

91.7 WA FM, 531 AM ABC Local Radio

The area around Lake Grace is a major grain-growing region for the state, producing wheat, canola, oats, barley, lupins and legumes. Sandy plains nearby are transformed into a sea of colour at the height of the wildflower season in September and October.

Inland Mission Hospital Museum: the only remaining inland mission hospital in WA, this fully restored building (est. 1926) is now a fascinating medical museum. Approach the building via Apex Park along the interpretive walkway; open daily by appt; Stubbs St. ***Mural:*** artwork depicting pioneering women was begun in 1912; Stubbs St. ***Memorial Swimming Pool:*** includes water playground for children; open 11am–6pm daily Oct–Apr; Bishop St.

Market: visitor centre; every Sat Oct–Mar. ***Art Exhibition:*** Oct.

Lake Grace Hotel: pub fare; Stubbs St; (08) 9865 1219.

Darean Farm Country Retreat: self-contained timber cottage; Lot 4126 South Rd; (08) 9865 1068.

Wildflower walk: easy walk through natural bushland with informative signage; details at visitor centre; 3 km E. ***Lake Grace:*** combination of 2 shallow salt lakes that gives the town its name; 9 km w. ***Lake Grace Lookout:*** ideal spot to view the north and south lakes system; 12 km w. ***White Cliffs:*** unusual rock formation and picnic spot on private property; details at visitor centre; 17 km S. ***Holland Track:*** in 1893 John Holland and his partners cut a track from Broomehill through bushland to Coolgardie in the goldfields. Hundreds of prospectors and their families trudged along this track in search of fortune, and cartwheel ruts are still evident today. A plaque marks the place where the track crosses the road; Newdegate Rd; 23 km E. ***Dingo Rock:*** now on private property, this reservoir for water run-off was built by labourers from Fremantle Gaol. Wildflowers are beautiful in season; details at visitor centre; 25 km NE. ***Newdegate:*** small town with a pioneer museum in the heritage-listed Hainsworth building. One of WA's major agricultural events, the Machinery Field Days, is held here in Sept each year; 52 km E.

See also HEARTLANDS, p. 308

Lake King

Pop. 219
Map ref. 620 G8

 Lake's Breaks, Church Ave; (08) 9874 4007; www.lakeking.com.au

92.5 WA FM, 531 AM ABC Local Radio

This small rural town lies on the fringe of sheep- and grain-farming country. With a tavern and several stores, Lake King is a stopping place for visitors travelling across the arid country around Frank Hann National Park to Norseman (adequate preparations must be made as there are no stops en route). Outstanding wildflowers in late spring include rare and endangered species.

Self-guide walks: signposted walk trails; maps from visitor centre.

Lake King Tavern & Motel: traditional meals; 165 Varley Rd; (08) 9874 4048.

Lake King Caravan Park: powered and unpowered sites; Critchley Ave; (08) 9838 0052. ***Lake King Tavern & Motel:*** rammed-earth motel; 165 Varley Rd; (08) 9874 4048.

Lake King and Causeway: 9 km road across the salt lake studded with native scrub and wildflowers. Lookout at eastern end; 5 km w. ***Pallarup Reserve:*** pioneer well and lake with abundant wildflowers in season; 15 km S. ***Mt Madden:*** cairn and lookout with picnic area that forms part of the Roe Heritage Trail; 25 km SE. ***Frank Hann National Park:*** good example of inland sand plain heath flora with seasonal wildflowers. The rabbit-proof fence forms a boundary to the park. Access is subject to weather conditions; 32 km E. ***Roe Heritage Drive Trail:*** begins south of Lake King and covers natural reserves and historic sites. It offers panoramic views from the Roe Hill lookout and retraces part of J. S. Roe's explorations in 1848; map available at visitor centre.

See also HEARTLANDS, p. 308

Laverton

Pop. 314
Map ref. 621 I2 | 622 I12

i Great Beyond Explorers Hall of Fame, Augusta St;
(08) 9031 1361; www.laverton.wa.gov.au

102.1 WA FM, 106.1 FM ABC Local Radio

Surrounded by old mine workings and modern mines, Laverton is on the edge of the Great Victoria Desert. In 1900 Laverton was a booming district of gold strikes and mines, yet gold price fluctuations in the late 1950s made it almost a ghost town. In 1969 nickel was discovered at Mount Windarra, which sparked a nickel boom. Early in 1995 a cyclone blew through Laverton, leaving it flooded and isolated for three months. Mines closed down and supplies were brought in by air. During this time, locals held a 'wheelie bin' race from the pub to the sports club, which is now an annual event. Today the town has two major gold mines and one of the world's largest nickel-mining operations. Wildflowers are brilliant in season.

Historic buildings Restored buildings include the courthouse, the Old Police Station and Gaol, and the Mt Crawford Homestead. The original Police Sergeant's House is now the local museum with displays of local memorabilia. Contact visitor centre for details.

Great Beyond Explorers Hall of Fame: uses cutting-edge technology to bring to life the characters and stories of the early explorers of the region. It also houses the visitor centre; Augusta St. *Cross-Cultural Centre:* houses the Laverton Outback Gallery, a collection of art and artefacts made and sold by the local Wongi people; Augusta St.

 Race Day: June. *Laverton Day and Wheelie Bin Race:* Nov.

The Desert Inn Hotel: traditional meals; 2 Laver St; (08) 9031 1188.

The Desert Inn Hotel & Motel: self-contained units; 2 Laver St; (08) 9031 1188.

Giles Breakaway: scenic area with interesting rock formation; 25 km E. *Lake Carey:* swimming and picnic spot exhibiting starkly contrasting scenery; 26 km W. *Windarra Heritage Trail:* walk includes rehabilitated mine site and interpretive plaques; Windarra Minesite Rd; 28 km NW. *Empress Springs:* discovered in 1896 by explorer David Carnegie and named after Queen Victoria. The spring is in limestone at the end of a tunnel that runs from the base of a 7 m deep cave. A chain ladder allows access to the cave. Enclosed shoes and torch required; 305 km NE. *Warburton:* the Tjulyuru Arts and Culture Regional Gallery showcases the art and culture of the Ngaanyatjarraku people; 565 km NE. *Golden Quest Discovery Trail:* Laverton forms part of the 965 km self-guide drive trail of the goldfields; book, map and CD available. *Outback Highway:* travel the 1200 km to Uluru from Laverton via the Great Central Rd. All roads are unsealed but regularly maintained.

Travellers note: Permits are required to travel through Aboriginal reserves and communities – they can be obtained from the Dept of Indigenous Affairs in Perth, and the Central Lands Council in Alice Springs. Water is scarce. Fuel, supplies and accommodation are available at the Tjukayirla, Warburton and Warakurna roadhouses. Check road conditions before departure at the Laverton Police Station or Laverton Shire Offices; road can be closed due to heavy rain.

See also GOLDFIELDS, p. 311

Leonora

Pop. 400
Map ref. 620 H2

i Rural Transaction Centre, cnr Tower and Trump sts;
(08) 9037 7016 ; www.leonora.wa.gov.au

102.5 WA FM, 105.7 FM ABC Local Radio

Leonora is the busy railhead for the north-eastern goldfields and the surrounding pastoral region. Mount Leonora was discovered in 1869 by John Forrest. Gold was later found in the area and, in 1896, the first claims were pegged. By 1908 Leonora boasted seven hotels and was the largest centre on the north-eastern goldfields. Many of the original buildings were constructed of corrugated iron and hessian, as these were versatile materials and light to transport. You can get a glimpse of these structures at nearby Gwalia, a town once linked to Leonora by tram.

 Historic buildings: buildings from the turn of the century include the police station, courthouse, fire station and Masonic Lodge; details at visitor centre. *Tank Hill:* excellent view over town; Queen Victoria St. *Miners Cottages:* miners camps, auctioned and restored by locals; around town.

Leonora Golden Gift and Festival: May/June.

White House Hotel: traditional pub; 120 Tower St; (08) 9037 6030.

Hoover House B&B: 3 antique-decorated rooms; Tower St; (08) 9037 7122.

Gwalia Gwalia is a mining ghost town that has been restored to show visitors what life was like in the pioneering gold-rush days. The original mine manager's office now houses the Gwalia Historical Museum with displays of memorabilia that include the largest steam winding engine in the world and a headframe designed by Herbert Hoover, the first mine manager of the Sons of Gwalia mine and eventually the 31st President of the United States. Self-guide heritage walk available. 4 km s.

Mt Leonora: sweeping views of the surrounding plains and mining operations; 4 km s. *Malcolm Dam:* picnic spot at the dam, which was built in 1902 to provide water for the railway; 15 km E. *Kookynie:* tiny township with restored shopfronts, and historic memorabilia on display at the Grand Hotel. The nearby Niagara Dam was built in 1897 with cement carried by camel from Coolgardie; 92 km SE. *Menzies:* small goldmining town with an interesting historic cemetery. View 'stick figure' sculptures, for which locals posed, about 55 km west of town on bed of Lake Ballard; 110 km s. *Golden Quest Discovery Trail:* self-guide drive trail of 965 km takes in many of the towns of the northern goldfields; maps, book and CD available at visitor centre, or visit www.goldenquesttrail.com

See also GOLDFIELDS, p. 311

Madura

Pop. 9
Map ref. 621 N6

i Madura Pass Oasis Motel and Roadhouse; (08) 9039 3464.

Madura, comprising a roadhouse, motel and caravan park on the Eyre Highway, lies midway between Adelaide and Perth on the Nullarbor Plain. It is remarkable, given the isolation of the area, that Madura Station was settled in 1876 to breed horses, which were then shipped across to India for use by the British Army. Now Madura is surrounded by private sheep stations. Locals operate on Central Western Time, 45 minutes ahead of the rest of Western Australia.

Blowholes: smaller versions of the one found at Caiguna. Look for the red marker beside the track; 1 km N. *Madura Pass Lookout:* spectacular views of the Roe Plains and Southern Ocean; 1 km W on highway.

See also ESPERANCE & NULLARBOR, p. 310

Mandurah

Pop. 67 783
Map ref. 615 C9 | 618 B6 | 620 C8

🛈 75 Mandurah Tce; (08) 9550 3999; www.visitmandurah.com

📻 97.3 Coast FM, 810 AM ABC Radio National

Mandurah has long been a popular holiday destination for Perth residents. The Murray, Serpentine and Harvey rivers meet at the town to form the vast inland waterway of Peel Inlet and the Harvey Estuary. This river junction was once a meeting site for Aboriginal groups who travelled here to barter. The town's name is derived from the Aboriginal word 'mandjar', meaning trading place. The river and the Indian Ocean offer a variety of watersports and excellent fishing and prawning. But the aquatic activity for which Mandurah is perhaps best known is crabbing. It brings thousands during summer weekends, wading the shallows with scoop nets and stout shoes.

🏠 **Christ's Church** Built in 1870, this Anglican church has hand-worked pews believed to be the work of early settler Joseph Cooper. Many of the district's pioneers are buried in the churchyard, including Thomas Peel, the founder of Mandurah. In 1994 the church was extended and a bell-tower added to house 8 bells from England. Cnr Pinjarra Rd and Sholl St.

Australian Sailing Museum: displays and models of vessels from the 1860s to Olympic yachts; Ormsby Tce. *Hall's Cottage:* (1832) restored home of one of the original settlers, Henry Hall; Leighton Rd. *Museum:* (1898) originally a school then a police station, now houses displays on Mandurah's social, fishing and canning histories; open Tues–Sun; Pinjarra Rd. *King Carnival Amusement Park:* fun-fair attractions including giant water slide, Ferris wheel and more; Leighton Rd. *Estuary Drive:* scenic drive along Peel Inlet and Harvey Estuary.

🎪 *Smart Street Markets:* off Mandurah Tce; each Sat. *Crab Fest:* Mar. *Boat and Fishing Show:* Oct.

🍴 *Cafe Pronto:* international cuisine; Cnr Pinjarra Rd and Mandurah Tce; (08) 9535 1004. *Red Manna Waterfront Restaurant:* waterfront seafood; upstairs, 5/9 Mandurah Tce; (08) 9581 1248. *Scusi:* fine dining; Shop 6, Lot 4 Old Coast Rd, Halls Head; (08) 9586 3479. *The Miami Bakehouse:* bakery cafe; Falcon Grove Shopping Centre, Old Coast Rd; (08) 9534 2705. *Millbrook Winery Restaurant:* innovative fresh produce; Millbrook Winery, Old Chestnut La, Jarrahdale; (08) 9525 5796. *Cafe on the Dam:* relaxed meals; Serpentine Dam, Kingsbury Dr, Jarrahdale; (08) 9525 9920.

🛏 *Dolphin House Boats:* variety of houseboats; Mandurah Ocean Marina; (08) 9535 9898. *Lakeside Holiday Apartments:* 2-bedroom apartments; 1 Lakes Cres, South Yunderup; (08) 9537 7634. *Peel Manor House:* elegant hotel; 164 Fletcher Rd, Karnup; (08) 9524 2838. *Seashells Resort Mandurah:* well-appointed apartments; 16 Dolphin Dr; (08) 9550 3000 or 1800 800 850.

🧭 *Coopers Mill:* the first flour mill in the Murray region, located on Cooleenup Island near the mouth of the Serpentine

River. Joseph Cooper built it by collecting limestone rocks and, every morning, sailing them across to the island. Accessible only by water; contact visitor centre for information. *Abingdon Miniature Village:* display of miniature heritage buildings and gardens from UK and Australia with maze, picnic area and children's playground; Husband Rd; 3 km E. *Marapana Wildlife Park:* handfeed and touch native and exotic animals; 14 km N at Karnup. *Yalgorup National Park:* swamps, woodlands and coastal lakes abounding with birdlife. Lake Clifton is 1 of only 3 places in Australia where the living fossils called thrombolites survive. A boardwalk allows close-up viewing; 45 km S. *Wineries:* several in the area; contact visitor centre for details. *Tours:* including estuary cruises and dolphin interaction tours; contact visitor centre for details.

See also THE SOUTH-WEST, p. 307

Manjimup

Pop. 4236
Map ref. 616 H10 | 617 B1 | 618 D10 | 620 C10

🛈 80 Giblett St; (08) 9771 1831; www.manjimupwa.com

📻 100.5 Hot FM, 738 AM ABC Local Radio

Manjimup is the gateway to the South-West region's tall-timber country. Magnificent karri forests and rich farmlands surround the town. While timber is the town's main industry, Manjimup is also the centre of a thriving fruit and vegetable industry that supplies both local and Asian markets. The area is well known for its apples and is the birthplace of the delicious Pink Lady apple.

🏠 **Timber and Heritage Park** A must-see for any visitor to Manjimup, this 10 ha park includes the state's only timber museum, an exhibition of old steam engines, an 18 m climbable fire-lookout tower and a historic village with an early settler's cottage, blacksmith's shop, old police station and lock-up, one-teacher school and early mill house. Set in natural bush and parkland, there are many delightful spots for picnics or barbecues. Cnr Rose and Edwards sts.

🎪 *Manjimup Motocross 15000:* June. *Festival of Country Gardens:* Oct/Nov. *Cherry Harmony Festival:* Dec.

🍴 *Cabernet Restaurant:* international cuisine; Kingsley Motel, 74 Chopping St; (08) 9771 1177 or 1800 359 177. *Déjà vu Cafe:* family-friendly cafe; 43A Giblett St; (08) 9771 2978. *Slice of Heaven Cafe:* home-style cooking; 31B Rose St; (08) 9777 1331.

🛏 *Dingup House B&B:* heritage homestead; 114 Dingup Rd; (08) 9772 4206. *Fonty's Pool & Caravan Park:* cottage, cabins and camping; Seven Day Rd; (08) 9771 2105. *Karri Glade Chalets:* contemporary chalets in lovely bush setting; Graphite Rd; (08) 9772 1120. *Diamond Tree Angus Stud:* cattle farmstay; Channybearup Rd; (08) 9776 1348.

🧭 **One Tree Bridge** In 1904 a single enormous karri tree was felled so that it dropped across the 25 m wide Donnelly River, forming the basis of a bridge. Winter floods in 1966 swept most of the bridge away; the 17 m piece salvaged is displayed near the original site with information boards. Nearby is Glenoran Pool, a scenic spot for catching rainbow trout and marron in season, with walking trails and picnic areas. Graphite Rd; 21 km W.

King Jarrah: estimated to be 600 years old, this massive tree is the centrepiece for several forest walks; Perup Rd; 3 km E. *Wine and Truffle Company:* tastings and information about truffle farming and dog training; (08) 9777 2474; 7 km SW.

MARGARET RIVER

Pop. 4413

Map ref. 616 B8 | 618 B10 | 620 B10

[CAPE MENTELLE VINEYARD]

ⓘ **Cnr Tunbridge St and Bussell Hwy; (08) 9780 5911; www.margaretriver.com**

100.3 Hot FM, 1224 AM ABC Radio National

One of the best-known towns in Western Australia, Margaret River is synonymous with world-class wines, magnificent coastal scenery, excellent surfing beaches and spectacular cave formations. A pretty township, it lies on the Margaret River near the coast, 280 kilometres south-west of Perth.

Wine Tourism Showroom Although the first grapevines were only planted in the area in 1967, Margaret River is now considered to be one of the top wine-producing regions in Australia. A huge 20% of Australia's premium wines are made here. The 'terroir' is perfect for grape-growing: cool frost-free winters, good moisture-retaining soils and low summer rainfall provide a long, slow ripening period. These conditions produce greater intensity of fruit flavour, the starting point for all great wines. There are now more than 100 wine producers in the region, many of which are open to the public for tastings and cellar-door sales. Others have restaurants and tours of their premises. A good place to start a wine tour is the Margaret River Wine Tourism Showroom at the visitor centre. It provides information about the regional wineries and vineyards, an interactive wineries screen, videos, a sensory display and wine-making paraphernalia. Bussell Hwy.

Rotary Park: picnic area on the riverbank with a display steam engine; Bussell Hwy. *St Thomas More Catholic Church:* one of the first modern buildings built of rammed earth; Wallcliffe Rd. *Fudge Factory:* fudge and chocolate made before your eyes; Bussell Hwy; (08) 9758 8881. *Arts and crafts:* many in town, including Margaret River Gallery on Bussell Hwy; contact visitor centre for details.

Town Square Markets: 11am–1pm Sun in summer, 2nd Sun each month rest of year. *Margaret River Pro:* surfing competition; Mar/Apr. *Great Escapade:* cycling; Mar/Apr.

Margaret River Wine Region Festival: May. *Margaret River Classic:* surfing competition; Oct/Nov.

🍴 *The Berry Farm Cottage Cafe:* charming cafe; 43 Bessell Rd; (08) 9757 5054. *Leeuwin Restaurant:* superb international cuisine; Leeuwin Estate Winery, Stevens Rd; (08) 9759 0000. *The Margaret River Chocolate Company:* chocolate-inspired cafe; Cnr Harman's Mill Rd and Harman's South Rd; (08) 9755 6555. *Brookwood Estate:* ploughman's lunches; Treeton Rd, Cowaramup; (08) 9755 5604. *Cullen Restaurant:* seasonal menu in a relaxed vineyard setting; Cullen Wines, Caves Rd, Cowaramup; (08) 9755 5656. *Sea Gardens Cafe:* tasty menu and magnificent views; 9 Mitchell Dr, Prevelly Park; (08) 9757 3074. *Udderly Divine Cafe:* dairy-themed cafe; 22 Bussell Hwy, Cowaramup; (08) 9755 5519.

🛏 *Basildene Manor:* old-world grandeur; Wallcliffe Rd; (08) 9757 3140. *Gilgara Retreat:* old station homestead replica; 300 Caves Rd; (08) 9757 2705. *Studio 9:* luxury retreat in town; Bussell Hwy; (08) 9757 2871. *Beach Barnacle:* traditional beach house; 25 Wooredah Cres, Prevelly; (08) 9757 3519. *Beckett's Flat Vineyard Cottage:* romantic cottage; 49 Beckett Rd, Metricup; (08) 9755 7402. *Craythorne Country House:* peaceful B&B; 180 Worgan Rd, Metricup; (08) 9755 7477. *Island Brook Estate:* well-appointed chalets; 7388 Bussell Hwy, Metricup; (08) 9755 7501. *Lake View Siesta:* motel-style accommodation; 30 Lake View Cres, Prevelly; (08) 9757 2579. *Prevelly Surf Shack:* architecturally designed beach house; Prevelly Park, Surfers Point Rd, Prevelly; 0439 971 054. *Redgate Farmstay:* pet-friendly cottages; 81 Redgate Rd, Witchcliffe; (08) 9757 6400. *The Grove Vineyard:* well-appointed chalets; Cnr Metricup and Carter rds, Wilyabrup; (08) 9755 7458. *The Noble Grape Guest House:* charming B&B; 29 Bussell Hwy, Cowaramup; (08) 9755 5538. *The Roozen Residence:* architecturally designed minimalist beach house; 4 Chapel Pl, Prevelly; 0407 479 004. *Villa Crisafina:* Mediterranean-style house; 45 Baudin Dr, Gnarabup; (08) 9757 1050.

Mammoth and Lake caves, Leeuwin–Naturaliste National Park Lying beneath the Leeuwin–Naturaliste Ridge that separates the hinterland from the coast is one of the world's most extensive and beautiful limestone cave systems. Mammoth Cave is home to the fossil remains of prehistoric animals. An audio self-guide tour lets you travel through the cave at your own pace (21 km sw). Only a few kilometres away is the beautiful Lake Cave with its delicate formations and famous reflective lake. The adjacent interpretive centre, CaveWorks, features a walk-through cave model, interactive displays and a boardwalk with spectacular views of a collapsed cavern (25 km sw). Further south, also in the national park, are Jewel and Moondyne caves; *see Augusta and Dunsborough.*

Eagles Heritage: the largest collection of birds of prey in Australia, with free-flight displays at 11am and 1.30pm daily; Boodjidup Rd; (08) 9757 2960; 5 km sw. *Surfer's Point:* the centre of surfing in Margaret River and home to the Margaret River Pro; 8 km w, just north of Prevelley. *Leeuwin Estate Winery:* the picturesque venue for the world-renowned open-air Leeuwin Estate Concert, held each Feb/Mar; 8 km s. *Cape Mentelle:* excellent cellar-door tastings; 331 Wallcliffe Rd; (08) 9757 0888; 5 km sw. *Prevelly Park:* huge waves attract surfers from around the world; detailed maps with surf spots available from visitor centre; 12 km w. *Margaret River Regional Wine Centre:* a one-stop centre for tastings and sales, offering in-depth information on local wines and wineries; Cowaramup; (08) 9755 5501; 13 km n. *Candy Cow:* free tastings of fudge, nougat and honeycomb, with demonstrations at 11am daily; Cowaramup; (08) 9755 9155; 13 km n.

Gnarabup Beach: safe swimming beach for all the family; 13 km w. *Cheese outlet:* Margaret River Cheese Factory; Bussell Hwy; 15 km n. *The Berry Farm:* jams, pickles, naturally fermented vinegars, fruit and berry wines; Bessell Rd; 15 km se. *Ellensbrook Homestead:* this wattle-and-daub homestead (1857) was once the home of Alfred and Ellen Bussell, the district's first pioneers; open weekends; (08) 9755 5173. Nearby is the beautiful Meekadarribee Waterfall, a place steeped in Aboriginal legend; 15 km nw. *Olio Bello:* boutique, handmade olive oil, with tastings available; Cowaramup; (08) 9755 9771; 17 km nw. *Grove Vineyard:* learn about and make your own sparkling wine. It also includes Yahava KoffeeWorks with coffee-appreciation sessions; Willyabrup; 20 km n. *Arts and crafts:* many in area, including Boranup Galleries, 20 km s on Caves Rd; contact visitor centre for details. *Margaret River Chocolate Company:* free chocolate tastings, interactive displays and viewing windows to watch the chocolate products being made; cnr Harmans Mill and Harmans South rds, Metricup; (08) 9755 6555; 30 km nw. *Bootleg Brewery:* enjoy naturally brewed boutique beers in a picturesque setting; Puzey Rd, Willyabrup; (08) 9755 6300; 45 km nw. *Bushtucker River and Winery Tours:* experience the Margaret River region through its wine, wilderness and food; open 12–5pm daily; bookings essential on (08) 9757 9084. *Land-based activities:* abseiling, caving, canoeing, coastal treks, horseriding and hiking; contact visitor centre for details. *Heritage trails:* including the Rails-to-Trails and Margaret River heritage trails; contact visitor centre for maps.

See also THE SOUTH-WEST, p. 307

Fonty's Pool: dammed in 1925 by Archie Fontanini for the irrigation of vegetables, it is now a popular swimming pool and picnic area in landscaped grounds; Seven Day Rd; 7 km s. *Dingup Church:* built in 1896 by the pioneer Giblett family and doubling as the school, this church is one of the few remaining local soapstone buildings; Balbarrup Rd; 8 km e. *Pioneer Cemetery:* poignant descriptions on headstones testify to the hardships faced by first settlers; Perup Rd; 8 km e. *Diamond Tree Lookout:* one of 8 tree towers constructed from the late 1930s as fire lookouts. Climb to the wooden cabin atop this 51 m karri, used as a fire lookout from 1941 to 1947; 9 km s. *Fontanini's Nut Farm:* gather chestnuts, walnuts, hazelnuts and fruit in season; open Apr–June; Seven Day Rd; 10 km s. *Nyamup:* old mill town redeveloped as a tourist village; 20 km se. *Four Aces:* 4 giant karri trees 220–250 years old and 67–79 m high stand in Indian file; Graphite Rd; 23 km w. *Great Forest Trees Drive:* self-guide drive through Shannon National Park; contact visitor centre for map; 45 km s. *Perup Forest Ecology Centre:* night spotlight walks to see rare, endangered and common native animals; contact DEC on (08) 9771 7988 for details; 50 km e. *Lake Muir Lookout/Bird Observatory:* boardwalk over salt lake to bird hide; 55 km e. *Wineries:* several in area; contact visitor centre for map.

See also THE SOUTH-WEST, p. 307

Marble Bar

Pop. 194
Map ref. 622 E2 | 624 E12 | 627 K5

 11 Francis St; (08) 9176 1375.

102.7 WA FM, 107.5 FM ABC Radio National

Marble Bar has gained a dubious reputation as the hottest town in Australia. For 161 consecutive days in 1923–24 the temperature in Marble Bar did not drop below 100°F (37.8°C). This mining town was named after a bar of mineral deposit that crosses the nearby Coongan River and was originally mistaken for marble. It proved to be jasper, a coloured variety of quartz.

Government buildings: built of local stone in 1895, now National Trust listed; General St.

Marble Bar Races: July.

Marble Bar Travellers Stop: seafood; Halse Rd; (08) 9176 1166.

Ironclad Hotel: heritage hotel; 15 Francis St; (08) 9176 1066. *Marble Bar Travellers Stop:* simple double rooms; Halse Rd; (08) 9176 1166.

Comet Gold Mine This mine operated from 1936 to 1955. The Comet is now a museum and tourist centre with displays of gemstones, rocks, minerals and local history. Also here is a 75 m high smoke stack, reputed to be the tallest in the Southern Hemisphere. Underground mine tours occur twice daily. (08) 9176 1015; 10 km s.

Marble Bar Pool: site of the famous jasper bar (splash water on it to reveal its colours) and a popular swimming spot; 4 km w. *Corunna Downs RAAF Base:* built in 1943 as a base for long-range attacks on the Japanese-occupied islands of the Indonesian archipelago; 40 km SE. *Doolena Gorge:* watch the cliff-face glow bright red as the sun sets; 45 km NW.

See also PILBARA, p. 313

Margaret River
see inset box on page 346

Meekatharra
Pop. 799
Map ref. 619 H9 | 622 D10

ⓘ Shire offices, 54 Main St; (08) 9981 1002; www.meekashire.wa.gov.au

📻 103.1 WA FM, 106.3 FM ABC Local Radio

The name Meekatharra is believed to be an Aboriginal word meaning 'place of little water' – an apt description for a town sitting on the edge of a desert. Meekatharra is now the centre of a vast mining and pastoral area. It came into existence in the 1880s when gold was discovered in the area. However, the gold rush was short-lived and it was only the arrival of the railway in 1910 that ensured its survival. The town became the railhead at the end of the Canning Stock Route, a series of 54 wells stretching from the East Kimberleys to the Murchison. The railway was closed in 1978, but the town continues to provide necessary links to remote outback areas through its Royal Flying Doctor Service.

 Royal Flying Doctor Service: operates an important base in Meekatharra; open to public 9am–2pm daily; Main St. *Old Courthouse:* National Trust building; Darlot St. *Meekatharra Museum:* photographic display and items of memorabilia from Meekatharra's past; open 8am–4.30pm Mon–Fri; shire offices, Main St. *State Battery:* relocated to the town centre in recognition of the early prospectors and miners; Main St. *Meeka Rangelands Discovery Trail:* walk or drive this trail for insight into the town's mining past, Aboriginal heritage and landscapes; maps at visitor centre.

🍴 *The Royal Mail Hotel:* counter meals; Main St; (08) 9981 1148.

🛏 *Auski Inland Motel:* best motel in town; Main St; (08) 9981 1433.

⚙ *Peace Gorge:* this area of granite formations is an ideal picnic spot; 5 km N. *Meteorological Office:* watch the launching of weather balloons twice daily at the airport; tours available on (08) 9981 1191; 5 km SE. *Bilyuin Pool:* swimming (but check water level in summer); 88 km NW. *Old Police Station:* remains of the first police station in the Murchison; Mt Gould; 156 km NW.

See also OUTBACK COAST & MID-WEST, p. 312

Merredin
Pop. 2556
Map ref. 618 G3 | 620 E6

ⓘ Barrack St; (08) 9041 1666; www.wheatbelttourism.com

📻 105.1 Hot FM, 107.3 FM ABC Radio National

Merredin started as a shanty town where miners stopped on their way to the goldfields. In 1893 the railway reached the town and a water catchment was established on Merredin Peak, guaranteeing the town's importance to the surrounding region. An incredible 40 per cent of the state's wheat is grown within a 100-kilometre radius of the town.

🏛 **Cummins Theatre** Heritage-listed theatre that was totally recycled from Coolgardie in 1928. Used regularly for local productions, events and visiting artists. Open 9am–3pm Mon–Fri; Bates St.

Military Museum: significant collection of restored military vehicles and equipment; closed Sat; Great Eastern Hwy. *Old Railway Station Museum:* prize exhibits are the 1897 locomotive that once hauled the *Kalgoorlie Express* and the old signal box with 95 switching and signal levers; open 9am–3pm daily; Great Eastern Hwy. *Pioneer Park:* picnic area adjacent to the highway including a historic water tower that once supplied the steam trains; Great Eastern Hwy. *Merredin Peak Heritage Walk:* self-guide walk that retraces the early history of Merredin and its links with the goldfields and the railway; contact visitor centre for map. *Merredin Peak Heritage Trail:* leads to great views of the countryside, and a rock catchment channel and dam from the 1890s. Adjacent to the peak is the interpretation site of a WW II field hospital that had over 600 patients in 1942; off Benson Rd. *Tamma Parkland Trail:* a 1.2 km walk around this 23 ha of bushland will give an insight into the flora and fauna of the area. Wildflowers in spring; South Ave.

🌴 *Community Show:* Oct.

🍴 *Denzil's Restaurant:* international cuisine; Merredin Olympic Motel, Lot 5 Great Eastern Hwy; (08) 9041 1588. *Merredin Motel & Gumtree Restaurant:* very decent meals; 10 Gamenya Ave; (08) 9041 1886.

🛏 *Merredin B&B:* converted bank residence; 30 Bates St; (08) 9041 4358. *Merredin Oasis Hotel Motel:* range of rooms; 8 Great Eastern Hwy; (08) 9041 1133. *Merredin Plaza All Suites:* town's premier accommodation; 149 Great Eastern Hwy; (08) 9041 1755. *Merredin Tourist Park:* self-contained units and camping; 2 Oats St; (08) 9041 1535.

⚙ *Pumping Station No 4:* built in 1902 but closed in 1960 to make way for electrically driven stations, this fine example of early industrial architecture was designed by C. Y. O'Connor; 3 km w. *Hunt's Dam:* one of several wells sunk by convicts under the direction of Charles Hunt in 1866. It is now a good spot for picnics and bushwalking; 5 km N. *Totadgin Conservation Park:* interpretive walk, Hunt's Well and mini rock formation similar to Wave Rock. Picnic tables and wildflowers in spring; 16 km SW. *Rabbit-Proof Fence:* roadside display gives an insight into the history of this feature; 25 km E. *Mangowine Homestead:* now a restored National Trust property, in the 1880s this was a wayside stop en route to the Yilgam goldfields. Nearby is the Billyacatting Conservation Park with interpretative signage; open 1–4pm Mon–Sat, 10am–4pm Sun (closed Jan); Nungarin; 40 km NW. *Shackelton:* Australia's smallest bank; 85 km SW. *Kokerbin Rock:* superb views from summit; 90 km SW. *Koorda:* museum and several wildlife reserves in area; 140 km NW.

See also HEARTLANDS, p. 308

Moora
Pop. 1606
Map ref. 618 B2 | 620 C6

ⓘ 34 Padbury St; (08) 9651 1401; www.moora.wa.gov.au

📻 90.9 WA FM, 612 AM ABC Radio National

On the banks of the Moore River, Moora is the largest town between Perth and Geraldton. The area in its virgin state was a large salmon gum forest. Many of these attractive trees can still be seen.

Historical Society Genealogical Records and Photo Display: open by appt; Clinch St. *Painted Roads Initiative:* murals by community artists on and in town buildings.

Moora Races: Oct.

Moora Hotel: traditional pub; 1 Gardiner St; (08) 9651 1177.

The Drovers Inn: hotel and motel accommodation; Cnr Dandaragan and Padbury sts; (08) 9651 1108.

The Berkshire Valley Folk Museum James Clinch, who came from England in 1839, created a village in the dry countryside of WA based on his home town in Berkshire. Over a 25-year period from 1847 Clinch built a homestead, barn, manager's cottage, stables, shearing shed and bridge. The elaborate buildings were made from adobe, pise, handmade bricks and unworked stone. Open by appt; 19 km E.

Western Wildflower Farm: one of the largest exporters of dried wildflowers in WA, with dried flowers, seeds and souvenirs for sale and an interpretive education centre; open 9am–5pm daily Easter–Christmas; Midlands Rd, Coomberdale; (08) 9651 8010; 19 km N. *Watheroo National Park:* site of Jingamia Cave; 50 km N. *Moora Wildflower Drive:* from Moora to Watheroo National Park, identifying flowers on the way; contact visitor centre for map.

See also HEARTLANDS, p. 308

Morawa

Pop. 594
Map ref. 620 B4

ℹ️ Winfield St (May–Oct), (08) 9971 1421; or council offices, cnr Dreghorn and Prater sts, (08) 9971 1204; www.morawa.wa.gov.au

📻 103.1 WA FM, 531 AM ABC Local Radio

Morawa, a small wheat-belt town, has the distinction of being home to the first commercial iron ore to be exported from Australia. In springtime the area around Morawa is ablaze with wildflowers.

Church of the Holy Cross and Old Presbytery From 1915 to 1939, the famous WA architect-priest Monsignor John C. Hawes designed a large number of churches and church buildings in WA's mid-west region. Morawa boasts 2 of them: the Church of the Holy Cross and an unusually small stone hermitage known as the Old Presbytery. The latter, which Hawes used when visiting the town, is reputed to be the smallest presbytery in the world with only enough room for a bed, table and chair. Both buildings are part of the Monsignor Hawes Heritage Trail. Church is usually open; if not, contact council offices; Davis St.

Historical Museum: housed in the old police station and gaol with displays of farm machinery, household items and a collection of windmills; open by appt; cnr Prater and Gill sts.

Everlastings Restaurant: buffet food; 10 Evan St; (08) 9971 1771.

Everlastings Guest Homes: modern hotel and cottage; 10 Evan St; (08) 9971 1771. *Morawa Chalets:* well-appointed chalets; White Ave; (08) 9971 1204. *Morawa Marian Convent B&B:* comfortable accommodation; Davis St; (08) 9971 1555.

Koolanooka Mine Site and Lookout: scenic views and a delightful wildflower walk in season; 9 km E. *Perenjori:* nearby

town has historic St Joseph's Church, designed by Monsignor Hawes, and the Perenjori–Rothsay Heritage Trail, a 180 km self-drive tour taking in Rothsay, a goldmining ghost town; 18 km SE. *Bilya Rock Reserve:* with a large cairn, reportedly placed there by John Forrest in the 1870s as a trigonometrical survey point; 20 km N. *Koolanooka Springs Reserve:* ideal for picnics; 26 km E.

See also OUTBACK COAST & MID-WEST, p. 312

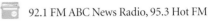

Mount Barker

Pop. 1760
Map ref. 617 C9 | 618 G11 | 620 E11

ℹ️ Old Railway Station, Albany Hwy; (08) 9851 1163; www.mountbarkertourismwa.com.au

📻 92.1 FM ABC News Radio, 95.3 Hot FM

Mount Barker lies in the Great Southern region of Western Australia, with the Stirling Range to the north and the Porongurups to the east. The area was settled by Europeans in the 1830s. Vineyards were first established here in the late 1960s. Today, Mount Barker is a major wine-producing area.

Old Police Station and Gaol: built by convicts in 1867–68, it is now a museum of memorabilia; open 10am–4pm Sat and Sun, daily during school holidays, or by appt; Albany Hwy, north of town. *Banksia Farm:* complete collection of banksia and dryandra species; guided tours daily, closed July; Pearce Rd; (08) 9851 1770.

Mount Barker D'Vine Wine Festival: Jan. *Mount Barker Wildflower Festival:* Sept/Oct.

Bluff Knoll Cafe: hillside cafe; Cnr Bluff Knoll and Chester Pass rds, Borden; (08) 9827 9293. *Galafrey Wines:* vineyard platters; 432 Quangellup Rd; (08) 9851 2022. *Porongurup Tearooms:* traditional tea rooms; 1972 Porongurup Rd, Porongurup; (08) 9853 1110. *The Vineyard Cafe:* hilltop cafe; Windrush Wines, cnr St Werburgh's and Hay River rds; (08) 9851 1353.

Karribank Country Retreat: range of accommodation options; 1983 Porongurup Rd, Porongurup; (08) 9853 1022. *Kendenup Lodge & Cottages:* charming cottages and lodge rooms; 217 Moorilup Rd, Kendenup; (08) 9851 4233. *The Sleeping Lady:* quality B&B; 2658 Porongurup Rd, Porongurup; (08) 9853 1113. *Cloud Nine Spa Chalets:* luxury chalets; 278 Moorilup Rd, East Porongurup; (08) 9853 1111. *Stirling Range Retreat:* range of accommodation and activities; Chester Pass Rd, Borden; (08) 9827 9229.

Porongurup National Park This is a park of dramatic contrasts, from stark granite outcrops and peaks to lush forests of magnificent karri trees. Many unusual rock formations, such as Castle Rock and Balancing Rock, make the range a fascinating place for bush rambles. The Tree in the Rock, a mature karri, extends its roots down through a crevice in a granite boulder. 24 km E.

Lookout and TV tower: easily pinpointed on the summit of Mt Barker by 168 m high television tower, it offers panoramic views of the area from the Stirling Ranges to Albany; 5 km SW. *St Werburgh's Chapel:* small mud-walled chapel (1872) overlooking Hay River Valley; 12 km SW. *Kendenup:* historic town, location of WA's first gold find; 16 km E. *Porongurup:* hosts Wine Summer Festival each Mar and boasts many small wineries; 24 km E. *Wineries:* several in the area, including Goundrey, Marribrook and Plantagenet; contact visitor centre for map. *Mount Barker Heritage Trail:* 30 km drive tracing the development of the

Mount Barker farming district; contact visitor centre for map. *Stirling Range National Park:* 80 km NE; *see Cranbrook.*

See also GREAT SOUTHERN, p. 309

Mount Magnet

Pop. 422
Map ref. 619 H11 | 620 D2 | 622 D12

ⓘ Hepburn St; (08) 9963 4172; www.mtmagnet.wa.gov.au

📻 102.5 WA FM, 105.7 FM ABC Local Radio

In 1854 the hill that rises above this Murchison goldmining town was named West Mount Magnet by surveyor Robert Austin after he noticed that its magnetic ironstone was playing havoc with his compass. Now known by its Aboriginal name, Warramboo Hill affords a remarkable view over the town and mines. Located 562 kilometres north-east of Perth on the Great Northern Highway, Mount Magnet offers visitors a rich mining history, rugged granite breakaway countryside and breathtaking wildflowers in season.

🏠 *Mining and Pastoral Museum:* collection of mining and pioneering artefacts includes a Crossley engine from the original State Battery; Hepburn St. *Heritage trail:* see the surviving historic buildings and sites of the gold-rush era on this 1.4 km walk; contact visitor centre for map.

🍴 *Mount Magnet Hotel:* traditional pub; 36 Hepburn St; (08) 9963 4002.

🛏 *Wondinong Pastoral Station:* working outback property; 72 km north-east of Mount Magnet; (08) 9963 5823.

 The Granites: rocky outcrop with picnic area and Aboriginal rock paintings; 7 km N. *Heritage drive:* 37 km drive of local historic and natural sights, including views of old open-cut goldmine. Also takes in the Granites and various ghost towns; contact visitor centre for map. *Fossicking for gemstones:* take care as there are dangerous old mine shafts in the area.

See also OUTBACK COAST & MID-WEST, p. 312

Mullewa

Pop. 419
Map ref. 619 E12 | 620 B3

ⓘ Jose St; (08) 9961 1500 ; www.mullewatourism.com.au

📻 107.5 FM ABC Radio National, 828 AM ABC Local Radio

Mullewa, 100 kilometres north-east of Geraldton, is in the heart of wildflower country. In spring, the countryside surrounding the town bursts forth with one of the finest displays of wildflowers in Western Australia. The wreath flower is the star attraction of the annual Mullewa Wildflower Show.

 Our Lady of Mt Carmel Church This small church is widely considered to be the crowning achievement of noted priest-architect Monsignor John C. Hawes. Built of local stone, this gem of Romanesque design took 7 years to build with Hawes as architect, stonemason, carpenter, modeller and moulder. The adjoining Priest House is now a museum in honour of Hawes, housing his personal belongings, books, furniture and drawings (cnr Doney and Bowes sts). Both of these buildings are part of the Monsignor Hawes Heritage Trail, which also features the Pioneer Cemetery (Mullewa–Carnarvon Rd; 1 km N) and a site at the old showground just outside town, where a rock carved by Monsignor Hawes was once a simple altar where he held mass for the local Aboriginal people (Mt Magnet Rd; 1.5 km E). Details and a map of the trail are available from the visitor centre.

🌸 *Mullewa Wildflower Show:* Aug/Sept.

🔘 **Butterabby Gravesite** This gravesite is a grim reminder of the harsh pioneering days. A stone monument recalls the spearing to death in 1864 of a convict labourer and the hanging in 1865 of 5 Aboriginal people accused of the crime. Mullewa–Mingenew Rd; 18 km S.

Tenindewa Pioneer Well: example of the art of stone pitching that was common at the time of construction, reputedly built by Chinese labourers en route to the Murchison goldfields. Also walking trails; 18 km W. *Bindoo Hill:* glacial moraine where ice-smoothed rocks dropped as the face of the glacier melted around 225 million years ago; 40 km NW. *Coalseam Conservation Park:* remnants of the state's first coal shafts, now a picnic ground; 45 km SW. *Tallering Peak and Gorges:* ideal picnic spot; Mullewa–Carnarvon Rd; check accessibility at visitor centre; 59 km N. *Wooleen Homestead:* stay on a working sheep and cattle station in the central Murchison district. Visit Boodra Rock and Aboriginal sites, and experience station life; (08) 9963 7973; 194 km N.

See also OUTBACK COAST & MID-WEST, p. 312

Mundaring

Pop. 3004
Map ref. 614 G5 | 615 E4 | 618 C5 | 620 C7

ⓘ The Old School, 7225 Great Eastern Hwy; (08) 9295 0202; www.mundaringtourism.com.au

📻 94.5 Mix FM, 720 AM ABC Local Radio

Mundaring is virtually an outer suburb of Perth, being only 34 kilometres east. Nearby, the picturesque Mundaring Weir is the water source for the goldfields 500 kilometres further east. The original dam opened in 1903. The hilly bush setting makes the weir a popular picnic spot.

🏠 *Mundaring Arts Centre:* contemporary WA fine art and design with comprehensive exhibition program; Great Eastern Hwy; (08) 9295 3991. *Mundaring District Museum:* displays on the diverse history of the shire; Great Eastern Hwy. *Mundaring Sculpture Park:* collection of sculptures by WA artists, set in natural bush park with grassed areas for picnics and children's playground; Jacoby St.

🌸 *Market:* Nichol St, 2nd Sun each month. *Truffle Festival:* Aug. *Perth Hills Wine Show:* Aug. *Trek the Trail:* Sept. *Darlington Arts Festival:* Nov.

🍴 *Little Caesars Pizzeria:* award-winning pizzeria; Shop 7, 7125 Great Eastern Hwy; (08) 9295 6611. *The Loose Box:* French cuisine at its best; 6825 Great Eastern Hwy; (08) 9295 1787. *Black Swan Winery & Restaurant:* up-market international cuisine; 8600 West Swan Rd, Henley Brook; (08) 9296 6090. *Darlington Estate Restaurant:* modern Australian; Darlington Estate Winery, 1495 Nelson Rd, Darlington; (08) 9299 6268. *Elmar's in the Valley:* German fare; 8731 West Swan Rd, Henley Brook; (08) 9296 6354. *Le Paris Brest Cafe & Patisserie:* French fare; Shop 9, Kalamunda Village Shopping Centre, 22 Haynes St, Kalamunda; (08) 9293 2752. *Little River Winery Restaurant:* provincial French fare; 2 Forest Rd, Henley Brook; (08) 9296 4462. *Sandalford Restaurant:* European food, vineyard setting; Sandalford Wines, 3210 West Swan Rd, Caversham; (08) 9374 9301. *Sittella Restaurant:* international cuisine with picturesque views; Sittella Winery, 100 Barrett St; Herne Hill; (08) 9296 2600. *Stewart's Restaurant:* award-winning European cuisine; Brookleigh Estate, 1235 Great Northern Hwy, Upper Swan; (08) 9296 6966.

🛏 *The Loose Box:* country chic–style cottages; 6825 Great Eastern Hwy; (08) 9295 1787. *Catton Hall Country Homestead:*

luxury cottage; Wilkins Rd, Mt Helena; (08) 9572 1375. **Chapel Farm Getaway:** uniquely designed rooms; 231 Toodyay Rd, Middle Swan; (08) 9250 4755. **Grandis Cottages:** self-contained cottages; 45 Casuarina Pl, Henley Brook; (08) 9296 3400. **Grandview B&B:** B&B with stunning views; 30 Girrawheen Dr, Gooseberry Hill; (08) 9293 2518. **Hidden Valley Eco Spa Lodges:** country luxury; 85 Carinyah Rd, Pickering Brook; (08) 9293 7337. **Settlers Rest Farmstay:** character 3-bedroom cottage; 90 George St, West Swan; (08) 9250 4540. **Strelley Brook Cottage:** historic mud-brick farmhouse; 90 Lefroy St, Herne Hill; (08) 9296 1876. **Tannamurra:** luxury home; off Great Northern Hwy, via Lynward Park Estate; (08) 9430 9933. **Vines Resort & Country Club:** resort for golf enthusiasts; Verdelho Dr, The Vines; (08) 9297 3000.

Mundaring Weir The Number 1 Pump Station, formerly known as the C. Y. O'Connor Museum, houses an exhibition on the mammoth project of connecting the weir to the goldfields (open 10am–4pm Mon–Sun and public holidays; Mundaring Weir Rd; 8 km s). This is also the starting point of the 560 km Golden Pipeline Heritage Trail to Kalgoorlie, which follows the route of O'Connor's water pipeline, taking in towns and heritage sites. Nearby, the Perth Hills National Park Centre includes Nearer to Nature who provide hands-on activities including bush craft, animal encounters, bush walks and information about Aboriginal culture; contact (08) 9295 2244. The Mundaring Weir Gallery, built in 1908 as a Mechanics Institute Hall, showcases the work of local craftspeople; open 10am–4pm Thurs, Sat, Sun and public holidays; cnr Hall and Weir Village rds.

John Forrest National Park: on a high point of the Darling Range with sensational views and lovely picnic spot beside a natural pool at Rocky Pool; 6 km w. **Karakamia Sanctuary:** native wildlife sanctuary with guided dusk walks; bookings essential on (08) 9572 3169; Lilydale Rd, Chidlow; 8 km NE. **Calamunnda Camel Farm:** camel rides; open Thurs–Sun; 361 Paulls Valley Rd; (08) 9293 1156; 10 km s. **Lake Leschenaultia:** swimming, canoeing, bushwalks and camping with picnic/barbecue facilities; 12 km NW. **Kalamunda National Park:** walking trails through jarrah forest, including the first section of the 963 km Bibbulmun Track; 23 km s; see Albany. **Kalamunda History Village:** collection of historic buildings; open Sat–Thurs; 23 km s. **Lesmurdie Falls National Park:** good views of Perth and Rottnest Island near spectacular falls over the Darling Escarpment; 29 km s. **Walyunga National Park:** beautiful bushland and wildflowers, and venue for the Avon Descent, a major whitewater canoeing event held each Aug; 30 km NW. **Wineries:** several in the area; contact visitor centre for Heart of the Hills Wine Trail map. **Munda Biddi Bike Trail:** passes through Mundaring; maps from visitor centre.

See also DARLING & SWAN, p. 306

Nannup
Pop. 503
Map ref. 616 F8 | 618 C10 | 620 C10

4 Brockman St; (08) 9756 1211; www.nannupwa.com

98.9 FM ABC Radio National, 684 AM ABC Local Radio

Nannup is a historic mill town in the Blackwood Valley south of Perth. Known as 'The Garden Village', it has beautiful private and public gardens, tulip farms, daffodils and wildflowers. The countryside is a series of lush, rolling pastures alongside jarrah forests and pine plantations.

Old Police Station: now a visitor centre, original cell block open for viewing; Brockman St. **Town Arboretum:** fine collection of old trees planted in 1926; Brockman St. **Kealley's Gemstone Museum:** displays of rocks, shells, gemstones, bottles and stamps; closed Wed; Warren Rd. **Marinko Tomas Memorial:** memorial to the local boy who was the first serviceman from WA killed in the Vietnam War; Warren Rd. **Blackwood Wines:** beautiful winery and restaurant overlooking an artificial lake; closed Wed; Kearney St; (08) 9756 0077. **Arts, crafts and antiques:** many in town, including Crafty Creations for quality timber goods on Warren Rd (closed June). **Heritage trail:** in 2 sections, with a 2.5 km town walk highlighting historic buildings, and a 9 km scenic drive; contact visitor centre for map.

Market: Warren Rd; 2nd Sat each month. **Art and Photography Exhibition:** Jan. **Music Festival:** Feb/Mar. **Forest Car Rally:** Mar. **Nannup Cup Boat Race:** June. **Flower and Garden Festival:** tulips; Aug. **Rose Festival:** Nov.

Blackwood Bistro: modern Australian; Blackwood Wines, Kearney St; (08) 9756 0077. **Mulberry Tree Restaurant:** home-style cooking; 62 Warren Rd; (08) 9756 3038. **Nannup Bridge Cafe:** cosy eatery; 1 Warren Rd; (08) 9756 1287. **Tathra Restaurant:** specialises in local produce; Tathra Winery, Blackwood River Tourist Dr (Route 251); (08) 9756 2040.

Beyonderup Falls: spa chalets; Balingup Rd; (08) 9756 2034. **Crabapple Lane B&B:** tasteful B&B; Barrabup Rd; (08) 9756 0017. **Redgum Hill Country Retreat:** B&B and self-contained accommodation; Balingup Rd; (08) 9756 2056. **Tathra Hill Top Retreat:** country adult retreat; Blackwood River Tourist Dr (Route 251); (08) 9756 2040.

Kondil Park: bushwalks and wildflowers in season; 3 km w. **Barrabup Pool:** largest of several pools, ideal for swimming, fishing and camping. Also has barbecue facilities; 10 km w. **Cambray Sheep Cheese:** award-winning cheeses, visitors can watch the milking and cheese-making; samples available. There are also guest cottages; 12 km N. **Carlotta Crustaceans:** marron farm; 14 km s off Vasse Hwy. **Tathra:** fruit winery and restaurant; open 11am–4.30pm daily; 14 km NE. **Mythic Mazes:** mazes including sculptures of myths from around the world; 20 km N. **Donnelly River Wines:** open daily for cellar-door tastings; (08) 9301 5555; 45 km s. **Blackwood River:** camping, swimming, canoeing and trout fishing. **Self-guide walks:** wildflower (in spring), waterfall (in winter) and forest walks; contact visitor centre for maps. **Scenic drives:** through jarrah forest and pine plantations, including 40 km Blackwood Scenic Drive; contact visitor centre for maps.

See also THE SOUTH-WEST, p. 307

Narrogin
Pop. 4240
Map ref. 618 E7 | 620 D9

Dryandra Country Visitor Centre, cnr Park and Fairway sts; (08) 9881 2064; www.dryandratourism.org.au

100.5 Hot FM, 918 AM Radio West

Narrogin, 192 kilometres south-east of Perth on the Great Southern Highway, is the commercial hub of a prosperous agricultural area. Sheep, pigs and cereal farms are the major industries. First settled in the 1870s, the town's name is derived from an Aboriginal word 'gnarojin', meaning waterhole.

 RADIO STATIONS IN TOWN WHAT'S ON WHERE TO EAT WHERE TO STAY NEARBY

Gnarojin Park This park is a national award winner for its original designs and artworks portraying local history and culture, which include the Centenary Pathway, marked with 100 locally designed commemorative tiles, Newton House Barbecue and Noongar Cultural Sites. Gordon St.

History Hall: local history collection; Egerton St. *Old Courthouse Museum:* built in 1894 as a school, it later became the district courthouse; open Mon–Sat; Egerton St. *Narrogin Art Gallery:* exhibitions; open 10am–4pm Tues–Fri, 10am–12pm Sat; Federal St. *Lions Lookout:* excellent views; Kipling St. *Heritage trail:* self-guide walk around the town's historic buildings; contact visitor centre for map.

State Gliding Championships: Jan. *Spring Festival:* Oct. *Rev Heads:* car rally; Nov/Dec.

Albert's Restaurant: international cuisine; Albert Facey Motor Inn, 78 Williams Rd; (08) 9881 1899.

Albert Facey Motor Inn: hotel accommodation; 78 Williams Rd; (08) 9881 1899. *Chuckem Farm B&B:* homestead B&B and self-contained cottage; 1481 Tarwonga Rd; (08) 9881 1188. *Eden Valley Farmstay:* 2-bedroom cottage; 3733 Williams–Kondinin Rd; (08) 9881 5864.

Dryandra Woodland One of the few remaining areas of virgin forest in the wheat belt, Dryandra is a paradise for birdwatchers and bushwalkers. The open, graceful eucalypt woodlands of white-barked wandoo, powderbark and thickets of rock she-oak support many species of flora and fauna including numbats (the state's animal emblem), woylies, tammar wallabies, brush-tailed possums and many others. Over 100 species of birds have been identified, including the mound-building mallee fowl. Tune your radio to 100FM for 'Sounds of Dryandra', a 25 km radio drive trail with 6 stops featuring tales of the local Nyungar people, early forestry days, bush railways and Dryandra's unique wildlife. There are day-visitor facilities and accommodation, walk trails, a weekend Ecology Course (runs in autumn and spring; try your hand at radio-tracking, trapping and spotlighting) and school holiday programs. 22 km NW.

Barna Mia Animal Sanctuary The sanctuary, within the Dryandra Woodland, has guided spotlight walks at night that reveal threatened marsupials, including the bilby and boodie. Bookings essential; contact DEC on (08) 9881 9200 or visitor centre which also has maps; Narrogin–Wandering Rd; 26 km NW.

Foxes Lair Nature Reserve: 60 ha of bushland with good walking trails, wildflowers in spring and 40 species of birds; maps and brochures from visitor centre; Williams Rd; 1 km SW. *Yilliminning and Birdwhistle Rocks:* unusual rock formations; 11 km E. *District heritage trail:* contact visitor centre for map.

See also HEARTLANDS, p. 308

New Norcia

Pop. 70
Map ref. 618 C2 | 620 C6

(i) **Museum and art gallery, Great Northern Hwy;** (08) 9654 8056; www.newnorcia.wa.edu.au

612 AM ABC Radio National, 720 AM ABC Local Radio

In 1846 Spanish Benedictine monks established a mission 132 kilometres north of Perth in the secluded Moore Valley in an attempt to help the local Aboriginal population. They named their mission after the Italian town of Norcia, the birthplace of the order's founder, St Benedict. The imposing Spanish-inspired buildings of New Norcia, surrounded by the gum trees and dry grasses of the wheat belt, provide a most unexpected vista. The town still operates as a monastery and is Australia's only monastic town. Visitors may join the monks at daily prayers.

Abbey Church This fine example of bush architecture was built using a combination of stones, mud plaster, rough-hewn trees and wooden shingles. It is the oldest Catholic church still in use in WA and contains the tomb of Dom Rosendo Salvado, the founder of New Norcia and its first Abbot. Hanging on a wall is the painting of Our Lady of Good Counsel, given to Salvado before he left for Australia in 1845 by Bishop (later Saint) Vincent Palotti. One of New Norcia's most famous stories relates how, in 1847, Salvado placed this revered painting in the path of a bushfire threatening the mission's crops. The wind suddenly changed direction and drove the flames back to the part already burnt, and the danger was averted.

Museum and art gallery: the museum tells the story of New Norcia's history as an Aboriginal mission, while the art gallery houses priceless religious art from Australia and Europe as well as Spanish artefacts, many of which were gifts from Queen Isabella of Spain. The Museum Gift Shop features New Norcia's own produce including bread, nutcake, pan chocolatti, biscotti, wine, honey and olive oil. *Monastery:* daily tours of the interior. A guesthouse allows visitors to experience the monastic life for a few days. *New Norcia Hotel:* this magnificent building, featuring a massive divided central staircase and high, moulded pressed-metal ceilings, was opened in 1927 as a hostel to accommodate parents of the children who were boarding at the town's colleges. *Old Flour Mill:* the oldest surviving building in New Norcia dates from the 1850s. *Heritage trail:* 2 km self-guide walk highlights New Norcia's historic and cultural significance and the role of the Benedictine monks in colonial history; contact visitor centre for map. *Guided tour:* 2 hr tour of the town with an experienced guide takes you inside buildings not otherwise open to the public; 11am and 1.30pm daily from museum.

New Norcia Hotel: town landmark; Great Northern Hwy; (08) 9654 8034.

Monastery Guesthouse: Benedictine hospitality; Great Northern Hwy; (08) 9654 8002. *New Norcia Hotel:* simple hotel accommodation; Great Northern Hwy; (08) 9654 8034. *Nirranda Farmstay:* spacious 4-bedroom homestead; 9236 Great Northern Hwy, Wannamal; (08) 9655 9046.

Mogumber: town with one of the state's highest timber-and-concrete bridges; 24 km SW. *Piawaning:* magnificent stand of eucalypts north of town; 31 km NE. *Bolgart:* site of historic hotel; 49 km SE. *Wyening Mission:* former mission, now a historic site; open by appt; 50 km SE.

See also HEARTLANDS, p. 308

Newman

Pop. 4247
Map ref. 622 E5 | 627 L11

(i) **Cnr Fortescue Ave and Newman Dr; (08) 9175 2888;** www.newman-wa.org

 88.9 Red FM, 567 AM ABC Local Radio

Located in the heart of the Pilbara, Newman was built in the late 1960s by the Mount Newman Mining Company to house the workforce required at nearby Mount Whaleback, the largest open-cut iron-ore mine in the world. At the same time a 426-kilometre railway was constructed between Newman and Port Hedland to transport the ore for export to Japan.

Mt Whaleback Mine Tours: the mine produces over 100 million tonnes of iron ore every year. Tours (minimum 4 people) run Mon–Sat Apr–Sept, Tues and Thurs Oct–Mar; book through visitor centre. *Mining and Pastoral Museum:* interesting display of relics from the town's short history, including the first Haulpak (giant iron-ore truck) used at Mt Whaleback and outback station life; located at visitor centre. *Radio Hill Lookout:* panoramic view of town and surrounding area; off Newman Dr.

Campdraft and Rodeo: Mar. *Fortescue Festival:* Aug.

Newman Hotel Motel: traditional pub food; Newman Dr; (08) 9175 1101.

Newman Hotel Motel: centrally located motel rooms; Newman Dr; (08) 9175 1101. *Seasons Hotel Newman:* variety of modern rooms; Newman Dr; (08) 9177 8666.

Ophthalmia Dam: swimming, sailing, barbecues and picnics (no camping); 20 km E. *Mt Newman:* excellent views; 25 km NW. *Eagle Rock Falls:* permanent pools and picnic spots nearby; 4WD access only; 80 km NW. *Wanna Munna:* site of Aboriginal rock carvings; 74 km W. *Rockpools and waterholes:* at Kalgans Pool (65 km NE), Three Pools (75 km N) and Weeli Wolli (99 km W). *Newman Waterholes and Art Sites Tour:* maps available at the visitor centre. *Karijini National Park:* 196 km N; *see Tom Price.*

See also PILBARA, p. 313

Norseman

Pop. 861
Map ref. 621 I7

ℹ️ 68 Roberts St; (08) 9039 1071; www.norseman.info

📻 105.7 FM ABC Goldfields, 107.3 FM ABC Radio National

Norseman is the last large town on the Eyre Highway for travellers heading east towards South Australia. Gold put Norseman on the map in the 1890s with one of the richest quartz reefs in Australia. The town is steeped in goldmining history, reflected in its colossal tailings dump. If visitors could stand atop this dump they could have up to $50 million in gold underfoot (although the rock has been processed, much residual gold remains). The story behind the town's name has become folklore. The settlement sprang up in 1894 when a horse owned by prospector Laurie Sinclair pawed the ground and unearthed a nugget of gold; the site proved to be a substantial reef. The horse's name was Norseman.

Historical Collection: mining tools and household items; open 10am–1pm Mon–Sat; Battery Rd. *Phoenix Park:* open-plan park with displays, stream and picnic facilities; Prinsep St. *Statue of Norseman:* bronze statue by Robert Hitchcock commemorates Norseman, the horse; cnr Roberts and Ramsay sts. *Camel Train:* corrugated-iron sculptures represent the camel trains of the pioneer days; Prinsep St. *Gem fossicking:* gemstone permits are available from the visitor centre.

Norseman Cup: Mar.

Norseman Hotel: traditional pub food; 90 Roberts St; (08) 9039 1023.

Norseman Great Western Motel and Great Western Travel Village: Norseman's premier motel; Prinsep St; (08) 9039 1633.

Beacon Hill Lookout: spectacular at sunrise and sunset, this lookout offers an outstanding 360-degree panorama of the salt lakes, Mt Jimberlana, the township, tailings dump and surrounding hills and valleys; Mines Rd; 2 km E. *Mt Jimberlana:* reputed to be one of the oldest geological areas in the world. Take the walking trail to the summit for great views; 5 km E. *Dundas Rocks:* barbecue and picnic area amid granite outcrops near old Dundas townsite, where the lonely grave of a 7-month-old child is one of the only signs that the area was once inhabited. Travel here via the highway (22 km S) or along the 33 km heritage trail that follows an original Cobb & Co route (map available from visitor centre). *Buldania Rocks:* picnic area with beautiful spring wildflowers; 28 km E. *Bromus Dam:* freshwater dam with picnic area; 32 km S. *Peak Charles National Park:* good-weather track for experienced walkers and climbers to Peak Eleanora, with a magnificent view from top; 50 km S, then 40 km W off hwy. *Cave Hill Nature Reserve:* a granite outcrop with a cave set in its side and a dam nearby. Popular spot for camping, picnicking and rock climbing; 4WD access only; 55 km N, then 50 km W. *Fraser Range Station:* working pastoral property that specialises in Damara sheep. The station has a range of available accommodation and opportunities to experience a remote working pastoral property; (08) 9039 3210; 100 km E.

See also GOLDFIELDS, p. 311

Northam

Pop. 6007
Map ref. 615 G2 | 618 D4 | 620 C7

ℹ️ Avon Valley Visitor Centre, 2 Grey St; (08) 9622 2100; www.visitnorthamwa.com.au

📻 96.5 Hot FM, 1215 AM ABC Local Radio

Northam lies in the heart of the fertile Avon Valley. The Avon River winds its way through the town and on its waters you'll find white swans, a most unusual sight in a state where the emblem is a black swan. White swans were brought to Northam from England in the 1900s and have flourished here. Northam is also synonymous with hot-air ballooning as it is one of the few areas in Western Australia ideally suited to this pastime. Northam is home to the famous Avon Descent, a 133-kilometre whitewater race down the Avon and Swan rivers to Perth.

Historic buildings Of the many historic buildings in Northam, 2 are particularly noteworthy: Morby Cottage (1836) on Avon Dr, the home of Northam's first settler, John Morrell, now a museum and open 10.30am–4pm Sun or by appt; and the National Trust–classified Sir James Mitchell House (1905), cnr Duke and Hawes sts, with its elaborate Italianate architecture. Take the 90 min self-guide walk for the full tour of the town. Contact visitor centre for map.

Old Railway Station Museum: displays include a steam engine and renovated carriages, plus numerous artefacts from the early 1900s; open 10am–4pm Sun or by appt; Fitzgerald St West. *Visitor centre:* exhibition showcasing the area's significant postwar migrant history; Grey St. *Suspension bridge:* the longest pedestrian suspension bridge in Australia crosses the Avon River adjacent to the visitor centre.

Vintage Car Swap Meet: Feb. *Avon Descent:* Aug. *Northam Cup:* Oct. *Motorcycle Festival:* Nov. *Wheatbelt Cultural Festival:* Dec.

3twotwo: charming country pub; Avon Bridge Hotel, 322 Fitzgerald St; (08) 9622 1023. *Cafe Yasou:* Mediterranean flavours of Cyprus and Greece; 175 Fitzgerald St; (08) 9622 3128.

Avon Bridge Hotel: hotel and motel rooms; 322 Fitzgerald St; (08) 9622 1023. *Brackson House B&B:* heritage B&B; 7 Katrine Rd; (08) 9622 5262. *Egoline Reflections:* heritage homestead; Northam–Toodyay Rd; (08) 9622 5811. *Uralia Cottage:* 1-bedroom cottage with pool; Cnr 59 Gordon St and Uralia Tce; (08) 9622 1742. *Mystique Maison:* ideal for group retreats; 10 Forrest St, Goomalling; (08) 9629 1673.

Mt Ommanney Lookout: excellent views of the township and agricultural areas beyond; 1.5 km w. *Hot-air ballooning:* Northam Airfield; Mar–Nov; bookings essential; 2 km NE. *Meckering:* small town made famous in 1968 when an earthquake left a huge fault line in its wake; 35 km E. *Cunderdin Museum:* The museum housed in the No 3 pumping station has displays on the pipeline, wheat-belt farming and the Meckering earthquake; 50 km E.

See also **HEARTLANDS**, p. 308

Northampton

Pop. 814
Map ref. 619 D12 | 620 A3

i Old police station, Hampton Rd; (08) 9934 1488; www.northamptonwa.com.au

96.5 WA FM

Northampton, nestled in the valley of Nokarena Brook, 51 kilometres north of Geraldton, was awarded Historic Town status by the National Trust in 1993. It was declared a townsite in 1864 and is one of the oldest settlements in Western Australia. A former lead-mining centre, its prosperity is now based on sheep- and wheat-farming.

 Chiverton House Historical Museum: unusual memorabilia housed in what was originally the home of Captain Samuel Mitchell, mine manager and geologist. Surrounding gardens include herbarium and restored farm machinery; open 10am–12pm and 2–4pm Fri–Mon; Hampton Rd. *Mary Street Railway Precinct:* railway memorabilia at the site of the town's 2nd railway station, built 1913; Eastern end. *Church of Our Lady in Ara Coeli:* designed in 1936 by Monsignor John Hawes, WA's famous architect-priest; Hampton Rd. *Gwalla Church and Cemetery:* ruins of town's first church (1864); Gwalla St. *Hampton Road Heritage Walk:* 2 km walk includes 37 buildings of historical interest including the Miners Arms Hotel (1868) and the Old Railway Station (1879); contact visitor centre for map.

Market: Kings Park, cnr Essex St and Hampton Rd; 1st Sat each month. *Airing of the Quilts:* quilts hung in main street; Oct.

Miners Arms Hotel: counter meals; Hampton Rd; (08) 9934 1281. *The Railway Tavern:* great pizzas, history displays; 71 North West Coastal Hwy; (08) 9934 1120.

Old Miners' Cottages B&B: restored cottages; Brook St; (08) 9934 1864.

Alma School House: built in 1916 as a one-teacher school; 12 km N. *Aboriginal cave paintings:* at the mouth of the Bowes River; 17 km w. *Oakabella Homestead:* one of the first farms in WA to plant canola, or rapeseed as it was then known. Take a guided tour of the historic homestead and outbuildings; open daily Mar–Nov; 18 km s. *Horrocks Beach:* beautiful bays, sandy beaches, good swimming, fishing and surfing; 20 km w. *Lynton Station:* ruins of labour-hiring depot for convicts, used in 1853–56; 35 km NW. *Lynton House:* squat building with slits for windows, probably designed as protection from hostile Aboriginal people; 35 km NW. *Principality of Hutt River:* visitors

are given a tour by the royals of this 75 sq km principality. With their own government, money and postage stamps, Hutt River exists as an independent sovereign state, seceded from Australia in 1970; 35 km NW. *Hutt Lagoon:* appears pink in midday sun; 45 km NW. *Port Gregory:* beach settlement, ideal for swimming, fishing and windsurfing; 47 km NW. *Warribano Chimney:* Australia's first lead smelter; 60 km N.

See also **OUTBACK COAST & MID-WEST**, p. 312

Northcliffe

Pop. 299
Map ref. 616 H12 | 617 C4 | 618 D11 | 620 C11

i Muirillup Rd; (08) 9776 7203; www.northcliffe.org.au

102.7 WA FM, 105.9 FM ABC Local Radio

Magnificent virgin karri forests surround the township of Northcliffe, 31 kilometres south of Pemberton in the state's South-West. Just a kilometre from the town centre is Northcliffe Forest Park, where you can see purple-crowned lorikeets, scarlet robins and, in spring, a profusion of wildflowers. Not far away is the coastal settlement of Windy Harbour, a popular swimming beach.

Pioneer Museum Northcliffe came into existence as a result of the Group Settlement Scheme, a WA government plan to resettle returned WW I soldiers and immigrants by offering them rural land to farm. The scheme was enthusiastically backed by English newspaper magnate Lord Northcliffe (hence the town's name). Unfortunately, by the 1920s, when the scheme began, all the good land in the state had already been settled. The group settlers were left to contend with inhospitable country and with only crosscut saws and axes, they were faced with the daunting task of clearing some of the world's biggest trees from their land. It is not surprising that by the mid-1930s all of the Group Settlement projects in the South-West timber country had failed. A visit to the Pioneer Museum with its excellent displays is the best way to understand the hardships the group settlers experienced. Open 10am–2pm daily Sept–May, 10am–2pm Sat, Sun and school holidays June–Aug; Wheatley Coast Rd; (08) 9775 1022.

Canoe and mountain-bike hire: contact visitor centre for details.

Great Karri Ride: Mar. *Mountain Bike Championship:* May/June. *Night-time Mountain Bike Race:* Nov.

The Dairy Lounge Cafe: dairy-inspired eatery; Bannister Downs Farm, Muirillup Rd; (08) 9776 6300.

Northcliffe Hotel: traditional hotel; Lot 8 Wheatley Coast Rd; (08) 9776 7089. *Riverway Chalets:* relaxing rammed-earth chalets; Riverway Rd; (08) 9776 7183. *Watermark Kilns:* kilns converted to self-contained accommodation; Karri Hill Rd; (08) 9776 7349.

Northcliffe Forest Park: follow the Hollow Butt Karri and Twin Karri walking trails or enjoy a picnic; Wheatley Coast Rd. *Warren River:* trout fishing and sandy beaches; 8 km N. *Mt Chudalup:* spectacular views of the surrounding D'Entrecasteaux National Park and coastline from the summit of this giant granite outcrop; 10 km s. *Moon's Crossing:* delightful picnic spot; 13 km NW. *Lane Poole Falls and Boorara Tree:* 3 km walking trail leads to the falls, passing the Boorara Tree with 50 m high fire-lookout cabin; 18 km SE. *Point D'Entrecasteaux:* limestone cliffs, popular with rock climbers, rise 150 m above the sea where 4 viewing platforms provide superb views; 27 km s. *Windy Harbour:* swimming, snorkelling, fishing, camping and whale-watching (from platform, best times Sept–Nov); 27 km s.

Cathedral Rocks: watch seals and dolphins; 27 km s. *Salmon Beach:* surf beach offers salmon fishing Apr–June; 27 km s. *The Great Forest Trees Drive:* 48 km self-guide scenic drive takes in the karri giants at Snake Gully Lookout, the Boardwalk and Big Tree Grove; contact visitor centre for map. *Bibbulmun Track:* section of this long-distance walking trail links the 3 national parks around Northcliffe: D'Entrecasteaux (5 km s), Warren (20 km NW) and Shannon (30 km E); *see Albany. Mountain-bike trails:* 4 permanent trails have been established around Northcliffe; contact visitor centre for details.

See also THE SOUTH-WEST, p. 307

Onslow

Pop. 574
Map ref. 619 C2 | 626 A8

 Second Ave (May–Oct), (08) 9184 6644; or council offices, Second Ave, (08) 9184 6001; www.ashburton.wa.gov.au

106.7 WA FM, 107.5 FM ABC Radio National

Onslow, on the north-west coast between Exmouth and Karratha, is the supply base for offshore gas and oil fields. This part of the coast is among the north's most cyclone-prone and Onslow has often suffered severe damage. The town was originally at the Ashburton River mouth and a bustling pearling centre. In the 1890s gold was discovered nearby. In 1925 the townsite was moved to Beadon Bay after cyclones caused the river to silt up. During World War II, submarines refuelled here and the town was bombed twice. In the 1950s it was the mainland base for Britain's nuclear experiments at Montebello Islands. In 1963 Onslow was almost completely destroyed by a cyclone. It is now an attractive tree-shaded town.

Goods Shed Museum: memorabilia from the town's long history and collections of old bottles, shells and rocks; in visitor centre; Second Ave. *Beadon Creek and Groyne:* popular fishing spot. *Ian Blair Memorial Walkway:* 1 km scenic walk; starts at Beadon Point and finishes at Sunset Beach. *Heritage trail:* covers sites of interest in town; contact visitor centre for map.

Beadon Bay Hotel: counter meals; Second Ave; (08) 9184 6002. *Nikki's Licensed Restaurant:* steak and seafood; 17 First Ave; (08) 9184 6121.

Onslow Mackerel Motel: 4-star motel; Cnr Second Ave and Third St; (08) 9184 6586. *Onslow Sun Chalets:* beachfront motel rooms and chalets; Second Ave; (08) 9184 6058. *Club Thevenard:* variety of accommodation; Thevenard Island; (08) 9184 6444. *Direction Island:* secluded beach cabin; Direction Island; (08) 9184 6444.

Termite mounds: with interpretive display; 10 km s. *Mackerel Islands:* excellent fishing destination. Charter boats are available for daytrips or extended fishing safaris; contact visitor centre for details; 22 km off the coast. *Ashburton River:* swimming, camping and picnicking; 45 km sw. *Old townsite heritage trail:* self-guide walk around original townsite including old gaol; contact visitor centre for map; 45 km sw.

See also PILBARA, p. 313

Pemberton

Pop. 757
Map ref. 616 H11 | 617 B2 | 618 D11 | 620 C11

 Brockman St; (08) 9776 1133 or 1800 671 133; www.pembertontourist.com.au

97.3 WA FM, 558 AM ABC Local Radio

Pemberton sits in a quiet valley surrounded by some of the tallest trees in the world and, in spring, brilliant wildflowers. This is the heart of karri country, with 4000 hectares of protected virgin karri forest in the nearby Warren and Beedelup national parks. Pemberton is a centre for high-quality woodcraft and is renowned for its excellent rainbow trout and marron fishing.

Karri Forest Discovery Centre: interpretive centre includes museum with collection of historic photographs and forestry equipment; at visitor centre. *Pioneer Museum:* utensils, tools and other memorabilia from pioneer days plus a full-scale settler's hut; at visitor centre. *Craft galleries:* many in town, including the Fine Woodcraft Gallery in Dickinson St and the Peter Kovacsy Studio in Jamieson St.

Mill Hall Markets: Brockman St; 2nd Sat each month and public holidays. *CWA Markets:* Brockman St; 4th Sat each month. *Autumn Festival:* May.

Hidden River Estate Restaurant: superb international cuisine; Mullineaux Rd; (08) 9776 1437. *Jarrah Jacks Brewery:* innovative brewery menu; Lot 2 Kemp Rd; (08) 9776 1333. *King Trout Restaurant and Marron Farm:* seafood; Cnr Northcliffe and Old Vasse rds; (08) 9776 1352. *The Shamrock Restaurant:* local fare; 18 Brockman St; (08) 9776 1186.

Clover Cottage: self-contained cottages; 251 Wheatley Coast Rd; (08) 9773 1262. *Peppermint Grove Retreat:* elegant chalets; Lot 5198 Channybearup Rd; (08) 9776 0056. *Pump Hill Farm Cottages:* rammed-earth cottages; Pump Hill Rd; (08) 9776 1379. *Salitage Suites:* adults-only suites; Salitage Winery, Vasse Hwy; (08) 9776 1195. *Warren River Resort:* cottages set in the forest; 713 Pemberton–Northcliffe Rd; (08) 9776 1400.

Gloucester National Park In this park is the town's most popular tourist attraction, the Gloucester Tree. With its fire lookout teetering 61 m above the ground and a spine-tingling 153 rungs spiralling upwards, this is not a climb for the faint-hearted. The Gloucester Tree is one of 8 tree towers constructed from the late 1930s as fire lookouts. As the extremely tall trees in the southern forests offered few vantage points for fire-lookout towers, it was decided to simply build a cabin high enough in one of the taller trees to serve the purpose. Also within the park are the Cascades, a scenic spot for picnicking, bushwalking and fishing. 1 km s.

Warren National Park This park boasts some of the most easily accessible virgin karri forest. The Dave Evans Bicentennial Tree has another fire lookout with picnic facilities and walking tracks nearby. 9 km sw.

Beedelup National Park Here you'll find the Walk Through Tree, a 75 m, 400-year-old karri with a hole cut in it big enough for people to walk through. The Beedelup Falls, a total drop of 106 m, are rocky cascades best seen after heavy rain. Nearby are walk trails and a suspension bridge. 18 km w.

Lavender & Berry Farm: enjoy berry scones, lavender biscuits and other unusual produce; Browns Rd; 4 km N. *Big Brook Dam:* the dam has its own beach, picnic and barbecue facilities, trout and marron fishing in season, and walking trails; 7 km N. *Big Brook Arboretum:* established in 1928 to study the growth of imported trees from around the world; 7 km N. *King Trout Restaurant and Marron Farm:* catch and cook your own trout;

closed Thurs; 8 km sw. *Founder's Forest:* part of the 100-Year-Old Forest, with karri regrowth trees over 120 years old; 10 km N. *Wineries:* more than 28 wineries in the area, many offering tours, tastings and sales; contact visitor centre for details. *Pemberton Tramway:* tramcars based on 1907 Fremantle trams operate daily through tall-forest country to the Warren River Bridge; (08) 9776 1322. *Fishing:* in rivers, inland fishing licence is required for trout and marron; contact post office for details and permits. *Tours:* river tours, scenic bus tours, 4WD adventure tours, self-guide forest drives, walking trails and eco-tours; contact visitor centre for details. *Drive trails:* include the Heartbreak Trail, a one-way drive through the karri forest of Warren National Park; contact visitor centre for maps. *Walk trails:* include the 1 hr return Rainbow Trail; contact visitor centre for maps. *Bibbulmun Track:* walking trail passes through Pemberton; *see Albany.*

See also THE SOUTH-WEST, p. 307

Pingelly

Pop. 817
Map ref. 618 E6 | 620 D8

ⓘ Council offices, 17 Queen St; (08) 9887 1066; www.pingelly.wa.gov.au

📻 99.7 FM ABC News Radio, 612 AM ABC Radio National

Located 158 kilometres south-east of Perth on the Great Southern Highway, Pingelly is part of the central-southern farming district. Sandalwood was once a local industry, but today sheep and wheat are the major produce.

 Courthouse Museum: built in 1907, now houses historic memorabilia and photographs; Parade St. *Apex Lookout:* fine views of town and surrounding countryside; Stone St.

Autumn Country Show and Ute Muster: Mar.

The Exchange Tavern: counter meals; 1 Pasture St; (08) 9887 0180.

 Pingelly Roadhouse and Motel: town's premier accommodation; 8 Quadrant St; (08) 9887 1015.

Pingelly Heights Observatory: audio tour and telescope viewing of the stars and constellations; bookings essential on (08) 9887 0088; 5 km NE. *Moorumbine Heritage Trail:* walk or drive through this old townsite featuring early settlers' cottages and St Patrick's Church, built in 1873; contact council office for map; 8 km E. *Tutanning Flora and Fauna Reserve:* botanist Guy Shorteridge collected over 400 species of plants from here for the British Museum between 1903 and 1906; 22 km E. *Boyagin Nature Reserve:* widely recognised as one of the few areas of original fauna and flora left in the wheat belt, this picnic reserve has important stands of powderbark, jarrah and marri trees and is home to numbats and tammar wallabies; 26 km NW.

See also HEARTLANDS, p. 308

Pinjarra

Pop. 3295
Map ref. 614 D10 | 618 C6 | 620 C8

ⓘ Pinjarra Heritage Train Station, Fimmel La; (08) 9531 1438; www.pinjarravisitorcentre.com.au

📻 97.3 Coast FM, 585 AM ABC News Radio

A pleasant 84-kilometre drive south of Perth along the shaded South Western Highway brings you to Pinjarra, picturesquely set on the Murray River. Predominantly a dairying, cattle-farming and timber-producing area, Pinjarra was also once known as the horse capital of Western Australia when horses were bred for the

British Army in India. Today horseracing, pacing and equestrian events are a major part of Pinjarra culture. The Alcoa Refinery north-east of town is the largest alumina refinery in Australia.

🏠 **Edenvale Complex** Built in 1888 with locally fired clay bricks, Edenvale was the home of Edward McLarty, member of the state's Legislative Council for 22 years. Nearby is Liveringa (1874), the original residence of the McLarty family, now an art gallery. There is a Heritage Rose Garden featuring 364 varieties of old-fashioned roses, a quilters' display in the Old School House, and a machinery museum. Cnr George and Henry sts.

Suspension bridge: across the Murray River, with picnic areas at both ends; George St. *Heritage trail:* 30 min river walk follows series of tiles explaining the heritage of the area; contact visitor centre for map.

🌴 *Railway Markets:* Lions Park; 2nd Sun morning each month Sept–June. *Community Markets:* Fimmel La; 4th Sat morning each month Sept–May. *Pinjarra Cup:* Mar. *Pinjarra Festival:* June. *Murray Arts and Craft Open Day:* Nov.

✕ *Edenvale Homestead & Heritage Tearooms:* light meals; 1 George St; (08) 9531 2223. *Raven Wines:* revolving menu concept; 41 Wilson Rd; (08) 9531 2774. *Redcliffe on the Murray:* modern Australian; 13 Sutton St; (08) 9531 3894.

🛏 *Lazy River Boutique B&B:* luxurious spa suites; 9 Wilson Rd; (08) 9531 4550. *Pinjarra Cabins & Caravan Park:* peaceful caravan park; 1716 Pinjarra Rd; (08) 9531 1374. *Nautica Lodge:* luxury marine-themed B&B; 203 Culeenup Rd, North Yunderup; (08) 9537 8000.

 Fairbridge Established by Kingsley Fairbridge in 1912 as a farm school for British children, many of them orphans. Over the years more than 8000 English children were educated here. The boarding houses, which are today used as holiday cottages, have famous British names such as Clive, Shakespeare, Nightingale, Exeter, Evelyn and Raleigh. South Western Hwy; 1800 440 770; 6 km N.

Peel Zoo: set in lush native flora, includes opportunities to feed and interact with the animals and has picnic area and barbecues; (08) 9531 4322; 2 km N. *Old Blythewood:* beautiful National Trust property built in 1859 by John McLarty, who arrived in Australia in 1839; open Sat 10.30am–3.30pm, Sun 12.30pm–3.30pm, or by appt; 4 km s. *Alcoa Mine and Refinery Tours:* includes the mining process, and the world's biggest bulldozer. Tours are free Wed and the last Fri of each month (except during the summer school holidays); bookings essential on (08) 9531 6752; 6km NE. *Alcoa Scarp Lookout:* good views of coastal plain, surrounding farming area and Alcoa Refinery; 14 km E. *North Dandalup Dam:* recreation lake, picnic area and coastal views from lookout; 22 km NE. *South Dandalup Dam:* barbecues and picnic areas; 30 km E. *Lake Navarino:* formerly known as Waroona Dam, it is good for watersports, fishing, walking and horseriding; 33 km s. *Coopers Mill:* first flour mill in the Murray region, located on Cooleenup Island near the mouth of the Serpentine River. It is accessible only by water; contact visitor centre for details. *Hotham Valley Tourist Railway:* travel from Pinjarra to Dwellingup by train, taking in lush green dairy country before climbing the steep and spectacular Darling Range and finishing in the heart of the jarrah forest. The train is steam-hauled May–Oct and diesel-hauled Nov–Apr; check times with visitor centre. *Ravenswood Adventures:* explore the Murray River by kayak, dinghy, canoe or pedal boat; Ravenswood; (08) 9537 7173.

See also THE SOUTH-WEST, p. 307

Port Hedland

Pop. 11 557
Map ref. 622 D1 | 624 D11 | 626 H3

 ⓘ 13 Wedge St; (08) 9173 1711.

 91.7 WA FM, 94.9 FM ABC News Radio

Port Hedland was named after Captain Peter Hedland, who reached this deep-water harbour in 1863. An iron-ore boom that began in the early 1960s saw the town grow at a remarkable rate. Today, Port Hedland handles the largest iron-ore export tonnage of any Australian port. Iron ore is loaded onto huge ore carriers; the 2.6-kilometre trains operated by BHP Iron Ore are hard to miss. Salt production is another major industry with about 2 million tonnes exported per annum.

Don Rhodes Mining Museum: open-air museum with displays of historic railway and mining machinery; Wilson St. **Pioneer and Pearlers Cemetery:** used between 1912 and 1968, it has graves of early gold prospectors and Japanese pearl divers; off Stevens St. **Town tour:** visit the town's many attractions; 11am Mon, Wed and Fri June–Oct; book through visitor centre. **BHP Iron Ore Tour:** see the enormous machinery required to run this industrial giant; departs 9.30am Mon–Fri from visitor centre. **Heritage trail:** 1.8 km self-guide walk around the town; contact visitor centre for map.

Australia Day Festival: Jan. **Port Hedland Cup:** Aug. **Pilbara Music Festival:** Sept. **Welcome to Hedland Night:** every few months.

Esplanade Hotel Port Hedland: hearty counter meals; 2–4 Anderson St; (08) 9173 2783. **Heddy's Bar & Bistro:** bistro by the sea; All Seasons Port Hedland, cnr Lukis and McGregor sts; (08) 9173 1511. **The Pilbara Room Restaurant:** best dining in town; Hospitality Inn Port Hedland, Webster St; (08) 9173 1044. **Wedge Street Coffee Shop:** light meals; 12A Wedge St; (08) 9173 2128.

All Seasons Port Hedland: hotel with ocean views; Cnr Lukis and McGregor sts; (08) 9173 1511. **Cooke Point Holiday Park:** family-friendly holiday park; 2 Taylor St; (08) 9173 1271 or 1800 459 999. **Hospitality Inn Port Hedland:** comfortable motel accommodation; Webster St; (08) 9173 1044. **The Lodge Motel:** hotel rooms and self-contained apartments; 5–13 Hawke Pl, South Hedlands; (08) 9172 2188.

Stairway to the Moon Like the Broome version, this beautiful illusion is created when a full moon rises over the ocean at low tide. The moon's rays hit pools of water left by the receding tide, creating the image of a stairway leading up to the moon. It lasts for about 15 minutes. Check with visitor centre for dates and times. Coastal side of Goode St; 7 km E.

Pretty Pool: picnic, fish and swim at this scenic tidal pool; 8 km NE. **Dampier Salt:** see giant cone-shaped mounds of salt awaiting export; 8 km S. **Royal Flying Doctor Service:** operates an important base in Port Hedland at the airport; open to public 8–11am Mon–Fri; closed public holidays, school holidays and weekends; 15 km S. **School of the Air:** experience schooling outback-style at the airport; open to public 8–11am Mon–Fri; closed public and school holidays; 15 km S. **Turtle-watching:** flatback turtles nest in the area Oct–Mar at Pretty Pool, Cooke Point and Cemetery Beach. **Cruises:** scenic harbour and sunset cruises; contact visitor centre for details.

Travellers note: Poisonous stonefish frequent this stretch of coast, especially Nov–Mar, so wear strong shoes when walking on rocky reef areas and make local inquiries before swimming in the sea.

See also Pilbara, p. 313

Ravensthorpe

Pop. 438
Map ref. 620 G9

 ⓘ Morgans St; (08) 9838 1277; www.ravensthorpe.wa.gov.au

101.9 WA FM, 105.9 FM ABC Local Radio

Ravensthorpe is encircled by the Ravensthorpe Range. This unspoiled bushland is home to many plants unique to the area such as the Qualup bell, warted yate and Ravensthorpe bottlebrush. Gold was discovered here in 1898 and by 1909 the population had increased to around 3000. Coppermining reached a peak in the late 1960s; the last coppermine closed in 1972. Many old mine shafts can be seen around the district and fossicking is a favourite pastime.

Historical Society Museum: local history memorabilia; in Dance Cottage near visitor centre, Morgans St. **Historic buildings:** many in town including the impressive Palace Hotel (1907) and the restored Commercial Hotel (now a community centre); both in Morgans St. **Rangeview Park:** local plant species, picnic and barbecue facilities; Morgans St.

Wildflower Show: Sept.

Ravensthorpe Palace Motor Hotel: traditional pub food; 28 Morgan St; (08) 9838 1005.

Ravensthorpe Palace Motor Hotel: historic building; 28 Morgan St; (08) 9838 1005.

WA Time Meridian: plaque on a boulder marks the WA time meridian; at first rest bay west of town. **Eremia Camel Treks:** offers rides along the beach; open by appt Dec–Apr; Hopetoun Rd; (08) 9838 1092; 2 km SE. **Old Copper Smelter:** in operation 1906–18, now site of tailings dumps and old equipment; 2 km SE. **Archer Drive Lookout:** extensive views over farms and hills; 3 km N in Ravensthorpe Range. **Mt Desmond Lookout:** magnificent views in all directions; Ethel Daw Dr; 17 km SE in Ravensthorpe Range. **Hopetown:** seaside village with pristine beaches ideal for swimming, surfing, windsurfing, fishing and boating. Summer Festival each June. Walk on the Hopetoun Trail Head Loop (part of the Hopetoun–Ravensthorpe Heritage Walk) or visit Fitzgerald River National Park to the west; *see* Bremer Bay; 49 km S. **Scenic drives:** include the 170 km circular Hamersley Drive Heritage Trail; contact visitor centre for maps. **Rock-collecting:** check locally to avoid trespass.

See also Esperance & Nullarbor, p. 310

Rockingham

Pop. 67 521
Map ref. 614 C11 | 615 B7 | 618 B6 | 620 B8

 ⓘ 43 Kent St; (08) 9592 3464; www.rockinghamvisitorcentre.com.au

97.7 FM ABC Classic Radio, 720 AM ABC Local Radio

Lying on the edge of Cockburn Sound just 47 kilometres south of Perth, the coastal city of Rockingham offers sheltered waters ideal for swimming, snorkelling, sailing, windsurfing, fishing and crabbing. Established in 1872 to ship timber from Jarrahdale to England, Rockingham was the busiest port in Western

WESTERN AUSTRALIA

Australia until the end of the 19th century, after which all port activities were shifted north to Fremantle. It was only because of the industrial area nearby at Kwinana in the 1950s and the development of the HMAS *Stirling* Naval Base on Garden Island in the 1970s that the town was revitalised. Today, its magnificent beaches and proximity to Perth are Rockingham's main attractions.

Rockingham Museum: folk museum featuring local history exhibits including displays on the Group Settlement farms, the timber industry, domestic items and antique photographic equipment; open 1–4pm Tues, Wed, Thurs and Sat, 10am–4pm Sun; cnr Flinders La and Kent St; (08) 9592 3455. *Art Gallery and Craft Centre:* features local artists, with market every 3rd Sun; Civic Blvd. **The Granary:** museum of artefacts celebrating the history of WA's grain industry; open for tours (minimum group size 4) by appt; northern end of Rockingham Rd; (08) 9599 6333. *Mersey Point Jetty:* departure point for cruises and island tours; Shoalwater. *Kwinana Beach:* hull of wrecked SS *Kwinana*. *Cape Peron:* the lookout was once the main observation post for a WW II coastal battery; Point Peron Rd. *Bell and Churchill Park:* family picnics and barbecues in shaded grounds; Rockingham Rd.

Swap Mart: opposite Churchill Park; each Sun. *Sunset Jazz Festival:* Mar. *Musslefest:* Oct. *Spring Festival:* Nov.

Bettyblue Bistro: generous portions, steak and seafood; Shop 3, 1 Railway Tce; (08) 9528 4228. *Emma's on the Boardwalk:* innovative with bay views; Shop 7–8, 1–3 Railway Tce; (08) 9592 8881. *Sunsets Cafe Bistro:* bay-side bistro; The Boardwalk, Palm Beach; (08) 9528 1910. *Y2K Cafe & Restaurant:* relaxed dining; 57B Rockingham Beach Rd; (08) 9529 1044.

5 Star @ Aria: beachfront penthouse; Rockingham Beach Rd; 0407 419 194. *Luxury @ Nautilus:* beachside apartment; 18–24 Kent St; Rockingham Visitor Centre (08) 9592 3464. *Manuel Towers:* spectacular Mediterranean-style B&B; 32A Arcadia Dr, Shoalwater; (08) 9592 2698. *Payne's Find:* tri-level waterfront house; 171 Rockingham Beach Rd; Rockingham Visitor Centre (08) 9592 3464.

Penguin Island Take a trip to this offshore island, which is home to a colony of little penguins. The Discovery Centre allows you to see the penguins up close in an environment similar to their natural habitat and to learn about them through daily feedings, commentaries and displays. The island also provides picnic areas, lookouts and a network of boardwalks, and you can swim, snorkel or scuba dive at any of the pristine beaches. The island is open to the public in daylight hours Sept–June. Ferries to the island leave regularly from Mersey Point, south of Rockingham. The ferry also provides bay cruises and snorkelling tours.

Sloan's Cottage: restored pioneer cottage; open Mon–Fri; Leda; 2 km w. *Lake Richmond:* walks, flora and fauna, and thrombolites (domed rock-like structures like the famous stromatolites of Hamelin Pool near Denham, built by ancient micro-organisms); 4 km sw. *Marapana Wildlife Park:* handfeed and touch native and exotic animals; Karnup; 15 km se. *Wineries:* in the area include Baldivis Estate (15 km se) and Peel Estate (17 km se); contact visitor centre for details. *Secret Harbour:* surfing, snorkelling and windsurfing; 20 km s. *Serpentine Dam:* major water storage with brilliant wildflowers in spring, bushland and the nearby Serpentine Falls; 48 km se. *Garden Island:* home to HMAS *Stirling* Naval Base, two-thirds of the island is open to the public but is accessible only by private boat during daylight hours. *Shoalwater Bay Islands Marine Park:* extends from just south of Garden Island to Becher Point. Cruises of the park

are available; contact visitor centre for details. *Dolphin Watch Cruises:* swim with dolphins between Point Peron and Garden Island; daily Sept–May; contact visitor centre for details. *Scenic drives:* including Old Rockingham Heritage Trail, a 30 km drive that takes in 23 points of interest in the Rockingham–Kwinana area, and Rockingham–Jarrahdale Timber Heritage Trail, a 36 km drive retracing the route of the 1872 timber railway; contact visitor centre for maps.

See also THE SOUTH-WEST, p. 307

Roebourne

Pop. 853
Map ref. 619 F1 | 622 B2 | 624 B12 | 626 E5

i Old Gaol, Queens St; (08) 9182 1060; www.roebourne.wa.gov.au

107.5 FM ABC Radio National, 702 AM ABC Local Radio

Named after John Septimus Roe, Western Australia's first surveyor-general, Roebourne was established in 1866 and is the oldest town on the north-west coast. As the centre for early mining and pastoral industries in the Pilbara, it was connected by tramway to the pearling port of Cossack and later to Point Samson. Now Cossack is a ghost town and Point Samson is known for its beachside pleasures.

Historic buildings: some original stone buildings remain, many of which have been classified by the National Trust. The Old Gaol, designed by the well-known colonial architect George Temple Poole, now operates as the visitor centre and museum; Queen St. *Mt Welcome:* offers views of the coastal plains and rugged hills surrounding town. Spot the railroad from Cape Lambert to Pannawonica, and the pipeline carrying water from Millstream to Wickham and Cape Lambert; Fisher Dr.

Roebourne Cup: July.

Moby's Kitchen: beachside dining; Bartley Crt, Point Samson; (08) 9187 1435. *TaTa's Restaurant:* international cuisine; Point Samson Resort, 56 Samson Rd, Point Samson; (08) 9187 1052. *Trawlers Tavern:* ocean views; Roebourne Port Samson Rd; (08) 9187 1503. *Red Rock Cafe:* steak, pizza, seafood; Mulga Way, Wickham; (08) 9187 1303.

Amani Cottage: self-contained cottage; 1 McLeod St, Point Samson; (08) 9187 1085. *Point Samson Resort:* seaside resort; 56 Point Samson Rd, Point Samson; (08) 9187 1052. *Samson Beach Chalets:* architect-designed chalets; 44 Bartley Crt, Point Samson; (08) 9187 0202. *Samson Hideaway:* self-contained apartment; 49 Meares Dr, Point Samson; (08) 9187 0330.

Cossack Originally named Tien Tsin after the boat that brought the first settlers there in 1863, Cossack was the first port in the north-west region. During its days as a pearling centre in the late 1800s the population increased dramatically. Although now a ghost town, the beautiful stone buildings have been restored and 9 are classified by the National Trust. Cruises are available from the wharf. 14 km N.

Wickham: the company town for Robe River Iron Ore offers a spectacular view from Tank Hill lookout; tours available; 12 km N. *Point Samson:* good fishing, swimming, snorkelling and diving. Boat hire, whale-watching and fishing charters are available; 19 km N. *Cleaverville:* camping and fishing; 25 km N. *Harding Dam:* ideal picnic spot; 27 km s. *Millstream–Chichester National Park:* 150 km s; *see Karratha*. *Emma Withnell Heritage Trail:* 52 km historic self-drive trail, named after the first European woman in the north-west, takes in Roebourne, Cossack, Wickham and Point Samson; map available at visitor centre. *Tours:* include historic Pearls and Past tour and trips to Jarman Island; contact visitor centre for details.

See also PILBARA, p. 313

Southern Cross

Pop. 709
Map ref. 620 F6

 Council offices, Antares St; (08) 9049 1001; www.yilgarn.wa.gov.au

100.7 WA FM, 106.3 FM ABC Local Radio

A small, flourishing town on the Great Eastern Highway, Southern Cross is the centre of a prosperous agricultural and pastoral region. Its claim to fame is as the site of the first major gold discovery in the huge eastern goldfields and, although it never matched the fever pitch of Kalgoorlie and Coolgardie, Southern Cross remains the centre for a significant gold-producing area. The town's wide streets, like the town itself, were named after stars and constellations.

 Yilgarn History Museum: originally the town courthouse and mining registrar's office, it now houses displays on mining, agriculture, water supply and military involvement; Antares St. *Historic buildings:* including the post office in Antares St, the Railway Tavern in Spica St and the restored Palace Hotel in Orion St.

King of the Cross: 2 days of motorcycle races; Aug.

Club Hotel: serves lunch and dinner; 21 Antares St; (08) 9049 1202. *Palace Hotel:* traditional pub; Great Eastern Hwy; (08) 9049 1555. *Southern Cross Motel:* international cuisine; Canopus St; (08) 9049 1144.

Southern Cross Caravan Park & Motor Lodge: sites, cabins, motel rooms; Great Eastern Hwy; (08) 9049 1212.

Hunt's Soak: once an important water source, now a picnic area; 7 km N. *Frog Rock:* large rock with wave-like formations. Popular picnic spot; 34 km S. *Baladjie Rock:* granite outcrop with spectacular views; 50 km NW. *Karalee Rock and Dam:* this dam was built to provide water for steam trains and is now popular for swimming and picnics; 52 km E.

See also HEARTLANDS, p. 308

Tom Price

Pop. 2721
Map ref. 619 G3 | 622 C5 | 626 G10

 Central Rd; (08) 9188 1112; www.tompricewa.com.au

103.3 WA FM, 567 AM ABC Local Radio

The huge iron-ore deposit now known as Mount Tom Price was discovered in 1962 in the heart of the Pilbara, after which the Hamersley Iron Project was established. A mine, two towns (Dampier and Tom Price) and a railway line between them all followed. Today, the town is an oasis in a dry countryside. On the edge of the Hamersley Range at an altitude of 747 metres, this is the state's highest town, hence its nickname of 'Top Town in WA'.

Tom Price Hotel Motel: international cuisine; Central Rd; (08) 9189 1101.

Karijini Eco Retreat: luxury eco-tents and traditional campsites; off Weano Rd, Karijini National Park; (08) 9425 5591.

Karijini National Park The second largest national park in Western Australia, this park features ochre-coloured rock faces

with bright-white snappy gums, bundles of spinifex dotting the red earth and chasms up to 100 m deep. The waterfalls and rockpools of Karijini offer some of the best swimming in the state. The park protects the many different wildlife habitats, plants and animals of the Pilbara. The landscape is dotted with huge termite mounds and the rock piles of the rare pebble mouse; other species include red kangaroos and rock wallabies, and reptiles from legless lizards to pythons. Kalamina Gorge and Pool is the most accessible gorge, while at Hamersley Gorge a wave of tectonic rock acts as a backdrop to a swimming hole and natural spa. Oxer Lookout reveals where the Joffre, Hancock, Weano and Red gorges meet. Mt Bruce, the second-tallest peak in the state, offers spectacular views and interpretive signs along the trail to the top. The Karijini Visitor Centre is located off the road to Dales Gorge and has information on camping. 50 km E.

Kings Lake: constructed lake with nearby park offering picnic and barbecue facilities (no swimming); 2 km W. *Mt Nameless Lookout:* stunning views of district around Tom Price; 6 km W via walking trail or 4WD track. *Aboriginal carvings:* thought to be 35 000 years old; 10 km S. *Mine tours:* marvel at the sheer enormity of Hamersley Iron's open-cut iron-ore mine; bookings essential, arrange through visitor centre. *Hamersley Iron Access Road:* this private road is the most direct route between Tom Price and Karratha via Karijini and Millstream national parks. It requires a permit to travel along it; available from visitor centre.

Travellers note: To the north-east is Wittenoom, an old asbestos-mining town. Although the mine was closed in 1966, there is still a health risk from microscopic asbestos fibres present in the abandoned mine tailings in and around Wittenoom. If disturbed and inhaled, blue asbestos dust may cause cancer. The Ashburton Shire Council advocates avoidance of the Wittenoom area.

See also PILBARA, p. 313

Toodyay

Pop. 1068
Map ref. 615 F2 | 618 D4 | 620 C7

 7 Piesse St; (08) 9574 2435; www.toodyay.com

558 AM ABC Local Radio, 612 AM ABC Radio National

This National Trust–classified town is nestled in the Avon Valley surrounded by picturesque farming country and bushland. The name originates from 'Duidgee', which means the 'place of plenty'. Founded in 1836, Toodyay was one of the first inland towns to be established in the colony. It was a favourite haunt of Western Australia's most famous bushranger, Joseph Bolitho Johns, who was more commonly known as 'Moondyne Joe'.

Historic buildings Some original buildings from the early settlement of Toodyay still stand, including Stirling House (1908), Connor's Mill (1870s) with displays of working flour-milling equipment, the Old Newcastle Gaol (1865) built by convict labour and where Moondyne Joe was imprisoned, and the Police Stables (1870) built by convict labour from random rubblestone. Self-guide walk available; pamphlet at visitor centre.

Duidgee Park: popular picnic spot on the banks of the river has a miniature railway and a walking track; check at visitor centre for running times; Harper Rd. *Newcastle Park:* contains a unique stone monument of Charlotte Davies, the first white female to set foot on the soil of the Swan River Colony. Also has a children's playground; Stirling Tce. *Pelham Reserve and Lookout:* nature walks, a lookout with views over the town and a memorial to James Drummond, the town's first resident botanist; Duke St.

Moondyne Festival: May. *Avon Descent:* whitewater rafting; Aug. *Kombi Konnection:* Sept. *Music Festival:* Sept.

Cola Cafe and Museum: with a huge selection of Coca-Cola memorabilia on display and music from the 1950s playing, this is a cafe with a difference; 128 Stirling Tce; (08) 9574 4407. *Victoria Hotel:* international cuisine; 116 Stirling Tce; (08) 9574 2206.

Avondale Estate: cosy country retreat; 9 Railway Rd; (08) 9574 4033. *Ipswich View Homestead:* heritage B&B; 45 Folewood Rd; (08) 9574 4038. *Mountain Park Retreat:* large Queenslander-style home; Cnr Dumbarton Rd and Nairn Dr; (08) 9255 2653. *Toodyay Farmstay:* 2-bedroom cottage; 51 Leeder St, West Toodyay; (08) 9385 8824.

Avon Valley National Park The park offers spectacular scenery with abundant wildflowers in season. Being at the northern limit of the jarrah forests, the jarrah and marri trees mingle with wandoo woodland. This mix of trees creates diverse habitats for fauna, including a wide variety of birdlife. The Avon River, which in summer and autumn is a series of pools, swells to become impressive rapids during winter and spring. These rapids provide the backdrop for the Avon Descent, a well-known annual whitewater race held every Aug, which begins in Northam and passes through the park. The park is ideal for camping, bushwalking, canoeing and picnicking, although all roads are unsealed. Whitewater rafting tours are available. 25 km sw.

Pecan Hill Tearoom Museum: tearoom and museum set in a pecan nut orchard with a lookout offering spectacular views over the Avon Valley; Julimar Rd; 4 km nw. *Coorinja Winery:* dating from the 1870s; open for tastings and sales; closed Sun; 4 km sw. *Ringa Railway Bridge:* constructed in 1888, this timber bridge has 18 spans, but is not readily accessible; details from visitor centre; 6 km sw. *Windmill Hill Cutting:* the deepest railway cutting in Australia; 6 km se. *Avonlea Park Alpaca Farm:* alpacas and other farm animals, and sales of alpaca wool products; 12 km se. *Emu Farm:* one of the oldest in Australia. Birds range free in natural bushland. Also crafts and emu products for sale; 15 km sw. *Cartref Park Country Garden:* 2 ha park of English-style landscaped gardens and native plants, with prolific birdlife; 16 km nw. *Oliomio Farm:* olive and lavendar farm offering tastings and sales; Parkland Dr; 20 km nw. *Wyening Mission:* this Benedictine farm and winery runs tours of their mission, cellars and grounds; by appt; (08) 9364 6463; 38 km n. *Toodyay Pioneer Heritage Trail:* honouring the pioneering spirit in the Avon Valley, this 20 km self-drive trail retraces the route of the first settlers; contact visitor centre for map. *Avon Valley Tourist Drive:* 95 km scenic drive includes Toodyay, Northam, York and Beverley; contact visitor centre for map. *Hotham Valley Steam Railway:* the famous steam-train service runs special trips including a monthly 'murder-mystery' night; contact visitor centre for details.

See also HEARTLANDS, p. 308

Wagin

Pop. 1424
Map ref. 618 F8 | 620 D9

ⓘ Historical Village, Kitchener St; (08) 9861 1232; www.wagintouristinfo.com.au

 96.3 FM ABC News Radio, 558 AM ABC Local Radio

Wagin, 177 kilometres east of Bunbury, is the sheep capital of Western Australia. The importance of the wool industry to the district is celebrated in its annual Wagin Woolorama, one of the largest rural shows in the state, and its Giant Ram, an enormous structure that visitors from around the country come to photograph.

Wagin Historical Village Explore 24 relocated or re-created historic buildings and machinery providing a glimpse of pioneering rural life. The buildings are furnished with original pieces, and audio commentaries are available. Open 10am–4pm; Kitchener St.

Giant Ram and Ram Park: 9 m high statue provides a photo opportunity not to miss; Arthur River Rd. *Wagin Heritage Trail:* self-guide walk around the town; contact visitor centre for map.

Wagin Woolorama: Mar. *Foundation Day:* June.

The Palace Hotel: traditional pub; 51 Tudhoe St; (08) 9861 1003.

Morans' Wagin Hotel: family-run hotel; 77 Tudor St; (08) 9861 1017.

Puntapin Rock: spectacular views over the town and surrounding farmlands from the top of the rock. Enjoy the picnic and barbecue facilities nearby; Bullock Hill Rd; 4 km se. *Mt Latham:* interesting rock formation with walk trails, a lookout and abundant wildflowers in season; Arthur River Rd; 8 km w. *Lake Norring:* swimming, sailing and waterskiing; picnic and barbecue facilities; water levels vary considerably; check conditions at visitor centre; 17 km sw. *Lake Dumbleyung:* where Donald Campbell established a world water-speed record in 1964. Swimming, boating and birdwatching are subject to water levels that vary considerably; check conditions at visitor centre; 18 km e. *Wait-jen Trail:* self-guide 10.5 km signposted walk that follows ancient Aboriginal Dreaming. The word 'wait-jen' means 'emu footprint' in the language of the local Aboriginal people; contact visitor centre for map. *Wheat Belt Wildflower Drive:* self-guide drive that includes the Tarin Rock Nature Reserve; contact visitor centre for map.

See also HEARTLANDS, p. 308

Walpole

Pop. 322
Map ref. 617 F6 | 618 E12 | 620 D11

ⓘ Pioneer Cottage, South Coast Hwy; (08) 9840 1111; www.walpole.com.au

102.9 WA FM, 106.1 FM ABC Local Radio

Walpole is entirely surrounded by national park and is the only place in the South-West where the forest meets the sea. The area is renowned for its striking ocean and forest scenery, which provides an idyllic setting for outdoor activities. The town of Walpole was established in 1930 through the Nornalup Land Settlement Scheme for city families hit by the Great Depression.

Pioneer Cottage: re-creation of a historic cottage to commemorate the district's pioneer settlers; South Coast Hwy.

Easter Markets: Apr.

Tree Top Restaurant: local produce; Tree Top Walk Motel, Nockolds St; (08) 9840 1444. *Slow Food Cafe:* local produce; Old Kent River Wines, Kent River, South Coast Hwy; (08) 9855 1589. *The Nornalup Teahouse Restaurant:* cottage cafe; 6684 South Coast Hwy, Nornalup; (08) 9840 1422. *Thurlby Herb Farm Cafe:* fresh produce; Lot 3 Gardiner Rd; (08) 9840 1249.

Ayr Sailean: self-contained farmstay accommodation; 1 Tindale Rd, Bow Bridge; (08) 9840 8098. *Che Sara Sara Chalets:* tranquil riverside chalets; 92 Nunn Rd, Hazelvale; (08) 9840 8004. *Houseboat Holidays:* well-appointed houseboats; Lot 660 Boronia St; (08) 9840 1310. *Tree Elle Retreat:* superbly appointed self-contained retreat; Lot 4, South Coast Hwy; (08) 9840 8471. *Walpole Wilderness Resort:* self-contained cottages; Gardiner Rd; (08) 9840 1481.

Walpole–Nornalup National Park The many forest attractions include the Valley of the Giants, the Hilltop Drive and Lookout, Circular Pool and the Knoll. The park is probably best known for its huge, buttressed red tingle trees, some more than 400 years old, which are unique to the Walpole area. The world-class Bibbulmun Track, between Perth and Albany, passes through the park. *See Albany;* 4 km SE.

Valley of the Giants Here visitors can wander over a walkway suspended 38 m above the forest floor, the highest and longest tree-top walkway of its kind in the world. The Ancient Empire interpretive boardwalk weaves its way through the veteran tingle trees. Twilight walks are available in holiday season. Contact (08) 9840 8263; 16 km E.

Giant Red Tingle: a 25 m circumference defines this tree as one of the 10 largest living things on the planet; 2 km E. *Hilltop Lookout:* views over the Frankland River out to the Southern Ocean; 2 km W. *John Rate Lookout:* panoramic views over the mouth of the Deep River and of the nearby coastline and forests; 4 km W. *Thurlby Herb Farm:* herb garden display with sales of herbal products; Gardiner Rd; 13 km N. *Mandalay Beach:* site of the 1911 shipwreck of the Norwegian *Mandalay*. A boardwalk has descriptive notes about the wreck. Also popular for fishing; 20 km W. *Dinosaur World:* a collection of native birds and reptiles, and exotic birds; 25 km E. *Mt Frankland National Park:* noted for its exceptional variety of birdlife, it also offers breathtaking views from the top of Mt Frankland, known as 'Caldyanup' to the local Aboriginal people; 29 km N. *Peaceful Bay:* small fishing village with an excellent beach for swimming; 35 km E. *Fernhook Falls:* ideal picnic spot with boardwalk, at its best in winter when it is popular for canoeing and kayaking; 36 km NW. *Walk trails:* many trails in the area, including self-guide Horseyard Hill Walk Trail through the karri forest and the signposted Coalmine Beach Heritage Trail from the coastal heathland to the inlets; contact visitor centre for maps. *Tours:* take a guided cruise through the inlets and rivers, hire a boat or canoe, or go on a forest tour or wilderness eco-cruise; contact visitor centre for details.

See also THE SOUTH-WEST, p. 307

Wickepin

Pop. 245
Map ref. 618 F6 | 620 D8

ⓘ District Resource and Telecentre, 24 Wogolin Rd; (08) 9888 1500; www.wickepin.wa.au

📻 100.5 Hot FM, 612 AM ABC Radio National

The first settlers arrived in the Wickepin area in the 1890s. Albert Facey's internationally acclaimed autobiography, *A Fortunate Life*, details these pioneering times. However, Facey is not the only major literary figure to feature in Wickepin's history. The poet and playwright Dorothy Hewett was born in Wickepin in 1923, and much of her work deals with life in the area.

Historic buildings in Wogolin Road: excellent examples of Edwardian architecture. *Facey Homestead:* the home of author Albert Facey has been relocated and restored with its original furniture; open 10am–4pm daily Mar–Nov, 10am–4pm Fri–Sun and public holidays Dec–Feb.

Wickepin Hotel: traditional pub; 34 Wogolin Rd; (08) 9888 1192.

Wickepin Hotel: standard hotel rooms; 34 Wogolin Rd; (08) 9888 1192.

Tarling Well: the circular stone well marks the original intended site for the town; 8 km W. *Malyalling Rock:* unusual rock formation; 15 km NE. *Toolibin Lake Reserve:* see a wide variety of waterfowl while you enjoy a barbecue; 20 km S. *Yealering and Yealering Lake:* historic photographs on display in town, and swimming, boating, windsurfing and birdwatching at lake; 30 km NE. *Harrismith Walk Path:* self-guide trail through wildflowers in season, including orchids and some species unique to the area; contact visitor centre for brochure. *Albert Facey Heritage Trail:* 86 km self-drive trail brings to life the story of Albert Facey and the harshness of life in the early pioneering days of the wheat belt; contact visitor centre for map.

See also HEARTLANDS, p. 308

Wyndham

Pop. 672
Map ref. 625 N4 | 629 C5

ⓘ Kimberley Motors, Great Northern Hwy; (08) 9161 1281; www.wyndham.wa.au

📻 102.9 WA FM, 1017 AM ABC Local Radio

Wyndham, in the Kimberley region, is the most northerly town and safe port in Western Australia. The entrance to the town is guarded by the 'Big Croc', a 20-metre-long concrete crocodile.

Historical Society Museum: in the old courthouse building, its displays include a photographic record of the town's history, artefacts and machinery; open Apr–Oct; O'Donnell St. *Warriu Dreamtime Park:* bronze statues representing the Aboriginal heritage of the area; Koolama St. *Zoological Gardens and Crocodile Park:* daily feeding of crocodiles and alligators; Barytes Rd; (08) 9161 1124. *Durack's Old Store:* has an informative plaque with details of its history; O'Donnell St. *Pioneer Cemetery:* gravestones of some of the area's original settlers; Great Northern Hwy. *Boat charters:* scenic, fishing and camping cruises; contact visitor centre for details.

Races: Aug. *Art and Craft Show:* Aug/Sept.

Wyndham Town Hotel: traditional pub; O'Donnell St; (08) 9161 1003.

Kimberley Coastal Camp: wilderness retreat; Admiralty Gulf, access by air; 0417 902 006.

Three Mile Valley On offer is spectacular scenery typical of the Kimberley region, with rough red gorges and pools of clear, cold water during the wet season. Walk trails lead the visitor through the brilliant displays of wildflowers in season. Three Mile Valley is the home of the 'Trial Tree', a sacred Aboriginal site into which, when a person died of unnatural causes, the body was placed. Rocks were placed around the base of the tree, each rock representing a relative of the deceased. When the body started to decompose, the first rock to be marked by the decomposition

 RADIO STATIONS   IN TOWN   WHAT'S ON   WHERE TO EAT   WHERE TO STAY   NEARBY

indicated the name of the person responsible for the death. This person was then banished from the tribe. 3 km N.

Afghan Cemetery: containing the graves of Afghan camel drivers who carried supplies throughout the Kimberley region. All the gravestones face towards Mecca; 1 km E. **Koolama Wreck Site:** the *Koolama* was hit by Japanese bombs near Darwin in 1942. After limping along the coast to Wyndham, it sank just 40 m from the jetty. The spot is marked by unusual swirling in the water; 5 km NW. **Five Rivers Lookout:** spectacular views of the Kimberley landscape from the highest point of the Bastion Range, particularly good for viewing the striking sunsets. Also a good picnic area with barbecue facilities; 5 km N. **Moochalabra Dam:** completed in 1971, the dam was constructed to provide an assured water supply to the Wyndham area. The construction is unique in Australia, designed to allow overflow to pass through the rock on the crest of the hill. 4WD access only; King River Rd; 18 km SW. **Aboriginal rock paintings:** 4WD access only; well signposted off the King River Rd; 18 km SW. **Parry Lagoons Nature Reserve:** visitors can enjoy birdwatching from a shaded bird hide at Marlgu Billabong or scan the wide vistas of the flood plain and distant hills afforded from the lookout at Telegraph Hill; 20 km SE. **Prison Tree:** 2000–4000-year-old boab tree once used by local police as a lock-up; King River Rd; 22 km SW. **The Grotto:** this rock-edged waterhole, estimated to be 100 m deep, is a cool, shaded oasis offering year-round swimming; 36 km E.

See also KIMBERLEY, p. 314

Yalgoo

Pop. 164
Map ref. 619 F11 | 620 C2

ℹ️ Old Railway Station, Geraldton–Mt Magnet Rd; (08) 9962 8157; www.yalgoo.wa.gov.au

📻 104.5 WA FM, 106.1 FM ABC Local Radio

Alluvial gold was discovered in the 1890s in Yalgoo, which lies 216 kilometres east of Geraldton. Today, gold is still found in the district and visitors are encouraged to try their luck fossicking in the area. The name Yalgoo is from the Aboriginal word meaning 'blood', a rather odd fact given that in 1993 a Yalgoo resident was the first person in Australia to be the victim of a parcel bomb.

🏛️ **Courthouse Museum:** exhibits of local artefacts; Gibbons St. **Gaol:** built in 1896 and recently relocated to the museum precinct, it has photographs illustrating the town's history; Gibbons St. **Chapel of St Hyacinth:** designed by Monsignor Hawes and built in 1919 for the Dominican Sisters who lived in a wooden convent school near the chapel; Henty St. **Heritage walk:** self-guide town walk; pamphlet available at visitor centre.

🛏️ **Tardie and Yuin Stations:** outback homestead; (08) 9963 7980.

⚙️ **Cemetery:** the history of Yalgoo as told through headstones; 5 km W. **Joker's Tunnel:** a tunnel carved through solid rock by early prospectors and named after the Joker's mining syndicate, it has panoramic views near the entrance; 10 km SE. **Meteorite crater:** discovered in 1961, a portion of the meteorite is held at the WA Museum in Perth; 100 km N. **Gascoyne Murchison Outback Pathways:** 3 self-drive trips exploring outback history: the Wool Wagon Pathway, the Kingsford Smith Mail Run and the Miners Pathway; see visitor centre or website for maps.

See also OUTBACK COAST & MID-WEST, p. 312

Yallingup

Pop. 300
Map ref. 616 A6

ℹ️ Seymour Blvd, Dunsborough; (08) 9752 1288; www.geographebay.com

📻 98.4 FM Western Tourist Radio, 684 AM ABC Local Radio

Yallingup, known for its limestone caves and world-class surf breaks, is also an ideal location for swimming, fishing and beachcombing. Nearby Leeuwin–Naturaliste National Park offers spectacular scenery, interesting bushwalks and beautiful wildflowers in season. Art and craft galleries abound and many of the wineries of the South-West region are only a short drive from the town. Yallingup continues to live up to its Aboriginal meaning of 'place of love', with nearby Caves House Hotel being a favourite destination for generations of honeymooners and holiday-makers.

🏠 **Caves House Hotel:** originally built in 1903 as a holiday hotel, the building was damaged by fire in 1938 and rebuilt; off Caves Rd; (08) 9755 2131. **Yallingup Beach:** surfing, scuba diving, whale-watching and salmon fishing in season.

🌴 **Amberley Estate Seafood and Semillon Weekend:** Feb. **Yallingup Malibu Surfing Classic:** Dec.

🍴 **Amberley Restaurant:** picturesque vineyard setting; Amberley Estate, cnr Thornton and Wildwood rds; (08) 9750 1112. **Cape Lodge Restaurant:** superb fine dining; 3341 Caves Rd; (08) 9755 6311. **Flutes Restaurant:** Asian-influenced menu in charming surrounds; Brookland Valley Winery, Caves Rd; Wilyabrup; (08) 9755 6250. **Lamont's Margaret River:** dishes made with love; Gunyulgup Valley Dr; (08) 9755 2434. **Caves House Hotel:** local produce; Yallingup Beach Rd; (08) 9750 1500.

🛏️ **Cape Lodge:** sublime world-class hotel; 3341 Caves Rd; (08) 9755 6311. **Fourwells:** well-appointed 4-bedroom house; address confirmed with booking; (08) 9385 5611. **Injidup Spa Retreat:** luxury 2-bedroom suites; Cape Clairault Rd, Injidup; (08) 9750 1300. **Seashells Resort Yallingup:** Art Deco–style beachside resort; Yallingup Beach Rd; (08) 9750 1500. **Smiths Beach Resort:** stylish beachfront resort; Smiths Beach Rd; (08) 9750 1200.

⚙️ **Leeuwin–Naturaliste National Park:** stretches north and south of town; *see Dunsborough, Margaret River and Augusta.* **Ngilgi Cave:** (pronounced 'Nillgee') semi-guided adventure tours are available for this stunning display of stalactite, stalagmite and shawl rock formations. An interpretive area details the history of the cave; 2 km E. **Canal Rocks and Smith's Beach:** interesting rock formation plus fishing, surfing, swimming, snorkelling and diving; 5 km SW. **Gunyulgup Gallery:** over 120 artists and craftspeople are represented, with paintings, prints, ceramics and sculpture on display and for sale; (08) 9755 2177; 9 km SW. **Yallingup Gallery:** specialises in custom-built furniture; 9 km SW. **Quinninup Falls:** falls that are particularly attractive in winter and can be reached only by 4WD or on foot; 10 km S. **Shearing Shed:** sales of wool products, and shearing demonstrations at 11am; closed Fri; Wildwood Rd; (08) 9755 2309; 10 km E. **Wineries and breweries:** many award-winning wineries and boutique breweries in the area offer tastings and sales; contact visitor centre for details.

See also THE SOUTH-WEST, p. 307

Yanchep

Pop. 2481
Map ref. 615 A2 | 618 B4 | 620 B7

 Information office, Yanchep National Park; (08) 9561 1004

94.5 Mix FM, 720 AM ABC Local Radio

Only 58 kilometres north of Perth, Yanchep is a rapidly developing recreational area and popular tourist destination. It provides safe, sandy beaches and good fishing areas, as well as natural attractions such as the series of caves found within Yanchep National Park. The town derives its name from the Aboriginal word 'yanjet', which means bullrushes, a feature of the area.

Yanchep Lagoon: good swimming and fishing beach; off Lagoon Dr.

Blue Dolphin Restaurant: relaxed setting; Two Rocks Shopping Centre, Two Rocks; (08) 9561 1469. *Chocolate Drops:* handmade chocolates, light meals; Yanchep National Park, Wanneroo Rd; (08) 9561 6699. *Lindsay's Restaurant:* buffet and à la carte; Club Capricorn, Two Rocks Rd; (08) 9561 1106. *The Tudor Manor Restaurant:* popular seafood platters; Yanchep Inn, Yanchep National Park; (08) 9561 1001.

Casa Del Mar: architecturally designed villa; 10B Arney Crt; (08) 9298 9367. *Oceanview Retreat:* modern holiday home; address confirmed with bookings; (08) 9276 4257. *Yanchep Holiday Village:* self-contained apartments in natural setting; St Andrews Dr; (08) 9561 2244. *Yanchep Inn:* hotel- and motel-style accommodation; Yanchep National Park; (08) 9561 1001.

Yanchep National Park On a belt of coastal limestone, this 2842 ha park has forests of massive tuart trees, underground caves and spring wildflowers. Within the park, attractions include the historic Tudor-style Yanchep Inn; the Crystal Cave featuring magnificent limestone formations (daily tours available); a koala boardwalk; rowing-boat hire on freshwater Loch McNess; self-guide walk trails; and Aboriginal cultural tours (available on weekends and public holidays). Boomerang Gorge follows an ancient collapsed cave system and has an interpretive nature trail with access for people with disabilities. Grassy areas with barbecues and picnic tables provide a perfect setting for a family outing. 5 km E.

Marina: charter fishing boat hire; 6 km NW at Two Rocks. *Guilderton:* peaceful town at the mouth of the Moore River. Estuary provides safe swimming, and upper reaches of the river can be explored by boat or canoe (hire on river foreshore). Also good fishing; 37 km N. *Ledge Point:* great destination for diving, with dive trail to 14 shipwrecks. Also the starting point for Lancelin Ocean Classic, a major windsurfing race each Jan; 62 km N. *Lancelin:* great base for fishing and boating because of a natural breakwater offshore. White sandy beaches provide safe swimming, and sand dunes at the edge of town have designated areas for off-road vehicles and sand-boarding; 71 km N.

See also HEARTLANDS, p. 308

York

Pop. 2091
Map ref. 615 H4 | 618 D4 | 620 C7

 Town Hall, 81 Avon Tce; (08) 9641 1301; www.yorkwa.org

101.3 York FM, 612 AM ABC Radio National

On the banks of the Avon River in the fertile Avon Valley, York is one of the best preserved and restored 19th-century towns in Australia. It is now classified by the National Trust as 'York Historic Town'. Settled in 1831, only two years after the establishment of the Swan River Colony, York was the first inland European settlement in Western Australia.

Historic buildings There are a significant number of carefully preserved historic buildings in York, many made from local stone and some built of mudbrick. The 3 remaining hotels are fine examples of early coaching inns, while the Romanesque-style Town Hall (1911) with its ornate facade reflects the wealth brought into the town by the gold rushes. Contact visitor centre for details.

Avon Park: picturesque park on the banks of the river with playground and barbecue facilities; Low St. *York Motor Museum:* vehicles on display represent the development of motor transport; Avon Tce. *Mill Gallery:* display and sales of unique and award-winning recycled jarrah furniture and craft; Broome St. *Residency Museum:* personal possessions, ceramics and silverware reflect aspects of civic and religious life in early York; open 1–3pm Tues–Thurs, 11am–3.30pm Sat, Sun and public holidays; Brook St. *Suspension bridge and walk trail:* built in 1906, the bridge crosses the Avon River at Avon Park. A 1.5 km nature and heritage walk starts at the bridge; Low St.

Antique Fair: Apr. *York Society Photographic Awards:* Apr. *Olive Festival:* June. *Jazz Festival:* Sept/Oct. *Spring Garden Festival:* Oct.

Cafe Bugatti: town favourite; 104 Avon Tce; (08) 9641 1583. *Restaurant Eboracum:* international cuisine; Imperial Hotel York, 83 Avon Tce; (08) 9641 1255. *York Mill Bakehouse:* arty cafe; 7–13 Broome St; (08) 9641 2447.

Old Albion B&B: heritage cottages; 19 Avon Tce; (08) 9641 2608. *Imperial Hotel York:* romantic heritage hotel; 83 Avon Tce; (08) 9641 1255. *Quellington School House Farmstay:* 1880s school converted to cottage; Sees Rd, Quellington; (08) 9641 1343. *Tipperary Church:* church converted into B&B; 2092 Northam Rd; 0439 965 275.

Mt Brown Lookout: provides 360-degree views over town; 3 km SE. *Gwambygine Park:* picturesque picnic area overlooking the river with boardwalk and viewing platform; 10 km S. *Skydive Express:* award-winning centre; (08) 9641 2905; 10 km N. *Toapin Weir and Mt Stirling:* panoramic views; 64 km E. *Self-drive trails:* 8 different routes including the Avon Ascent through Perth's scenic hinterland to a series of special places in the Avon Valley; contact visitor centre for maps.

See also HEARTLANDS, p. 308

THE NORTHERN TERRITORY is...

Shopping for arts and crafts at the MINDIL BEACH SUNSET MARKETS / Swimming

near a waterfall in LITCHFIELD NATIONAL PARK / Touring through billabongs and

Aboriginal rock-art galleries in KAKADU NATIONAL PARK / Seeing spectacular ULURU

at sunrise and sunset / A visit to ALICE SPRINGS' CULTURAL PRECINCT / Fishing

NORTHERN TERRITORY

[NOURLANGIE ROCK, KAKADU NATIONAL PARK]

for BARRAMUNDI in the Territory's west coast rivers / Boarding an ADELAIDE
RIVER JUMPING CROCODILES CRUISE / Learning about the Aboriginal legend
behind the DEVILS MARBLES (KARLU KARLU) / Enjoying a drink at the historic
DALY WATERS PUB / Climbing Kings Canyon in WATARRKA NATIONAL PARK

THE NORTHERN TERRITORY is Australia's least

settled state or territory, with vast tracts of desert and tropical woodlands. But to regard this country as empty is to do it a disservice; Aboriginal people have lived and travelled across the territory for thousands of years, and still do. Many non-Aboriginal Australians see it as the last great frontier because of its remoteness, spectacular landscapes and hardy outback characters.

Desert regions lie towards central Australia, while the tropical Top End is lapped by the Timor and Arafura seas. Although the diversity of landscape and wildlife makes it one of Australia's most inspiring destinations, visitors should expect a lot of distance between highlights.

The tropical coastline and offshore islands are places of special beauty – pearly white beaches interspersed with rocky red cliffs and rich mangrove habitats. The coastal rivers are home to thousands of bird and marine species, and their flood plains carry the annual wet season deluge out into the Timor and Arafura seas and the Gulf of Carpentaria. The rivers are also spawning grounds for barramundi, which attract anglers from around the world.

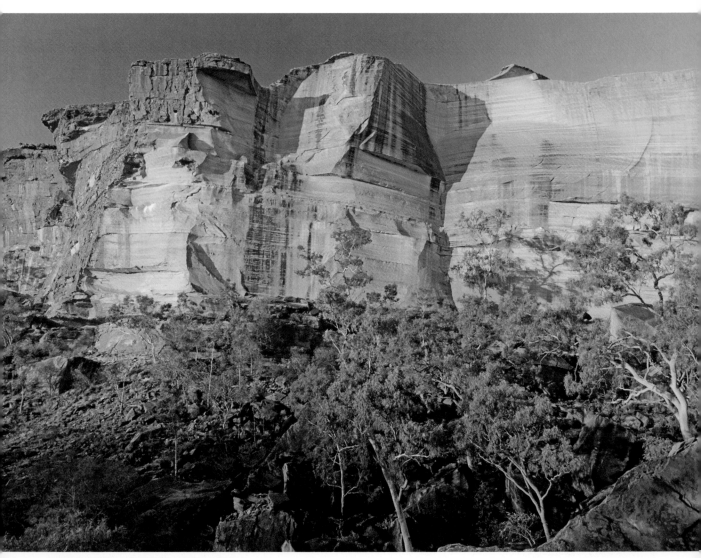

[KINGS CANYON, WATARRKA NATIONAL PARK]

The north-east includes Arnhem Land, the largest Aboriginal reserve in Australia, which saw the incredible trade and mingling of cultures that occurred between Yolngu people and Indonesian seafarers from the 1600s. Today it is home to many groups who still live a semi-traditional lifestyle. It is also the custodial land of Australia's most famous Indigenous instrument, the didgeridoo. Here visitors can explore parts of the Gove and Cobourg peninsulas, with their green vegetation, turquoise waters and great fishing.

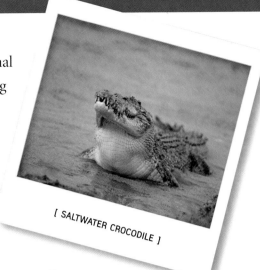

[SALTWATER CROCODILE]

The Red Centre is ancient and breathtaking, a land of intense as well as muted tones created by beautiful gorges, rock holes and vistas. While many travellers are drawn to Uluṟu and Kata Tjuṯa, the surrounding countryside is equally impressive – from the rolling red sandhills of the Simpson Desert to the undulating grasslands west of Glen Helen. North of Alice Springs, the Tanami Desert is incredibly remote and vastly interesting.

fact file

Population 227 000
Total land area 1 335 742 square kilometres
People per square kilometre 0.15
Beef cattle per square kilometre 1.3
Length of coastline 5437 kilometres
Number of islands 887
Longest river Victoria River (560 kilometres)
Highest mountain Mount Zeil (1531 metres), West MacDonnell National Park
Highest waterfall Jim Jim Falls (160 metres), Kakadu National Park
Highest town Areyonga (700 metres), west of Hermannsburg
Hottest place Aputula (Finke), 48.3°C in 1960
Strangest place name Humpty Doo
Quirkiest festival Henley-on-Todd Regatta with boat races in the dry riverbed, Alice Springs
Longest road Stuart Highway (approximately 2000 kilometres)
Most scenic road Larapinta Drive, from Alice Springs to Hermannsburg
Most famous pub Daly Waters Pub
Most impressive gorge Nitmiluk (Katherine) Gorge, Nitmiluk National Park
Most identifiable trees Pandanus palm and desert she-oak
Most impressive sight Electrical storms in the build-up to the wet season, Darwin
Favourite food Barramundi
Local beer NT Draught
Interesting fact Some 50 per cent of the Northern Territory is either Aboriginal land or land under claim

gift ideas

Aboriginal art and handmade baskets (Arnhem Land, Kakadu National Park & Darwin) Authentic pieces are best purchased from Aboriginal craft centres in places like Maningrida and Gunbalunya, Arnhem Land. Alternatively, visit Marrawuddi Gallery, Kakadu National Park, or Framed – The Darwin Gallery, 55 Stuart Hwy, Darwin. See Kakadu & Arnhem Land p. 379, 634–5

Barramundi-skin wallets and shoes (Barra Shack, Humpty Doo) Stop at this popular shop on the way to Kakadu National Park to pick up items that are true evidence of an outback experience. 41 Acacia Rd, Humpty Doo. 632 E4

Didgeridoos (The Didgeridoo Hut, Humpty Doo) Purchase an iconic Aboriginal item from this store owned and run by Indigenous people. 1 Arnhem Hwy, Humpty Doo. 632 E4

Handmade whips, crocodile-skin and kangaroo-skin products (Mindil Beach Sunset Markets, Darwin) A range of fantastic Top End products are on offer, from buffalo horns to necklaces with a crocodile tooth. In particular, visit Mick's Whips for various whips and handcrafted crocodile or kangaroo leather goods. See Mindil Beach Sunset Markets p. 374, 370 B5

Pukumani Poles (Bathurst & Melville islands) Aboriginal burial poles found only on the Tiwi Islands can be purchased at several arts and crafts centres. See Tiwi Islands p. 377, 634 D2

South Sea pearls (Paspaley & Bynoe Harbour Pearl Company, Darwin) Found in Australia's northern waters, the largest pearls in the world are made into elegant jewellery pieces. Paspaley, 19 The Mall; Bynoe Harbour Pearl Company, Shop 11, Darwin Wharf Precinct. See Shopping p. 375, 372 C2

Yothu Yindi CD (Arnhem Land) The most famous Indigenous band comes from the Yolngu people of Arnhem Land, and their well-known song 'Treaty' catapulted Indigenous music into the mainstream Australian music scene. The yearly Garma Festival of Traditional Culture, held during October in Gulkula, Arnhem Land, is organised by the Yothu Yindi Foundation. See Kakadu & Arnhem Land p. 379, 635

***Walkabout Chefs* book (Darwin)** With recipes by renowned outback chef Steve Sunk, available from any bookshop in Darwin.

DARWIN is...

Window-shopping for pearls in SMITH STREET MALL / A stroll along THE

ESPLANADE / Watching a movie at the DECKCHAIR CINEMA / A safe encounter

with reptiles at CROCOSAURUS COVE / A picnic at FANNIE BAY / Sunset drinks at

the DARWIN SAILING CLUB / Shopping for arts and crafts at the MINDIL BEACH

SUNSET MARKETS / Handfeeding fish at AQUASCENE / Exploring ABORIGINAL ART

GALLERIES / Learning about cyclones at the MUSEUM AND ART GALLERY OF THE

NORTHERN TERRITORY / Swimming in the wave lagoon at the DARWIN WATERFRONT /

Fishing off STOKES HILL WHARF / Watching a thunderstorm in the evening sky

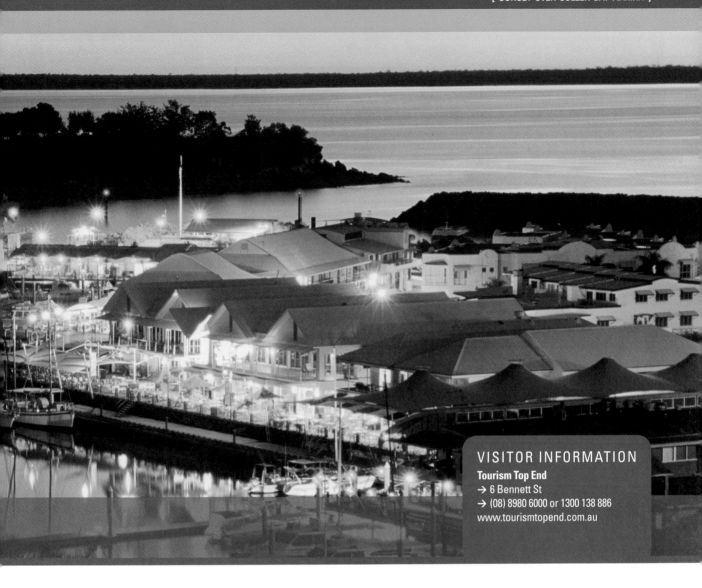

VISITOR INFORMATION
Tourism Top End
→ 6 Bennett St
→ (08) 8980 6000 or 1300 138 886
www.tourismtopend.com.au

Regarded as Australia's northern outpost, Darwin's proximity to Asia and its immersion in Aboriginal culture make it one of the world's most interesting cities. It retains a tropical, colonial feel despite having been largely rebuilt after the devastation wreaked by cyclone Tracy over 30 years ago.

The founding fathers of Darwin laid out the city centre on a small peninsula that juts into one of the finest harbours in northern Australia. Their names live on in the wide streets of the city centre, which is easy to get around and lacks the winding lanes of older Australian cities.

Built on the land of the Larrakia Aboriginal people, Darwin is a beautiful green city. Manicured lawns, and hedges of bougainvillea and frangipani adorn parks and roadways, while the waters of the Timor Sea lap three sides of the city.

The population of 121 000 comprises over 50 ethnic groups who live together harmoniously here. This diversity stretches back to the early days of Darwin's development when Aboriginal, European and Chinese people worked side by side. More recent arrivals include migrants from Greece, Timor, Indonesia and Africa.

Evidence of the early days remain, but Darwin is also a modern city. With so much natural beauty around its harbour, along the beaches and in its tropical parks, it remains one of the most attractive cities in the world.

SEE PAGE 372

City Centre

Like most of Darwin, the city centre is open and vibrant with wide streets, leafy parks, a cool mall and outdoor dining. Arching shade trees and towering palms are features of the lush parks and reserves, while stunning Aboriginal art and artefacts are characteristic of the retail areas. Tall, modern structures have begun to replace the old colonial-style buildings, but they still retain a fresh, tropical flavour with overhanging eaves, corrugated iron and lush vegetation.

Smith Street 372 B2, C2

Smith Street Mall is the retail heart of the central business district (CBD). Shady **Raintree Park** at the northern end is popular with tourists and locals at lunchtime, and many outdoor concerts are held here during the dry season. A walk down the mall between May and the end of August will reveal buskers from all over Australia who have travelled north to beat the southern winter. Plazas and small arcades reveal shops where visitors can buy Aboriginal art, locally made jewellery and tropical clothing. Halfway down the mall is the **Victoria Hotel**, a Darwin landmark and one of its oldest pubs. Almost directly opposite is the **Star Arcade**, which used to house the old open-air Star Theatre. At the southern end of the mall are some of the city's grandest buildings where it is possible to look at or buy South Sea pearls – one of northern Australia's most valued exports.

Across Bennett Street, Smith Street continues south towards the harbour past **Brown's Mart**, which was built in 1883 and is now home to the Darwin Theatre Company.

Behind Brown's Mart are the Darwin City Council Chambers, where an ancient banyan tree known as the **Tree of Knowledge** casts a huge umbrella of shade. Planted at the end of the 19th century, the tree has been a meeting place, dormitory and soapbox for generations who lived in or passed through Darwin. At the southern end of Smith Street is **Christ Church Cathedral**, built in 1902 and damaged by both Japanese bombers and cyclone Tracy.

Mitchell Street 372 A1, B2

One street to the west of Smith Street is Mitchell Street, a popular dining and entertainment area specialising in outdoor eateries. With backpacker accommodation, pubs and outdoor dining areas, Mitchell Street is the party precinct of Darwin. You'll find cinemas and the **Darwin Performing Arts Centre**, which hosts many exciting theatrical performances, particularly late in the dry season during the Festival of Darwin *(see Top events, p. 373)*. At **Crocosaurus Cove**, visitors can swim with crocodiles – safely protected inside a perspex cage!

Cavenagh Street 372 B1, C1

Cavenagh Street is one street east of Smith Street. Among the commercial buildings and government departments, it boasts a few art galleries and cafes. At the **Roma Bar**, which is popular with politicians, journalists, writers and artists, people from all walks of life rub shoulders over a coffee.

This street was Darwin's original Chinatown. In the late 1800s the southern end was full of ramshackle huts and shops with the occasional opium den. While some of the original stone buildings remain up near Darwin Post Office, a reminder of its Asian history is at nearby Litchfield Street where a modern

climate

Darwin has a constant temperature of around 30°C and the weather is always warm and humid – just how humid depends on the time of year. Most people visit during the dry season, which extends from May to the end of September. The 'build-up' period (between October and December) is famous for hot, stifling weather and massive electrical storms. During the wet season (which can last until late April), the Asian monsoon drops over Darwin, often bringing days of cleansing rain. When the inevitable cyclone comes, the streets of the city and surrounding landscape become waterlogged and flood-bound. The wet season may be uncomfortable, but it is the time when the landscape is green and lush. At the end of the season, native trees burst into flower and attract thousands of birds.

J	F	M	A	M	J	J	A	S	O	N	D	
32	32	32	33	32	31	30	31	33	34	34	33	MAX °C
25	25	24	24	22	20	19	20	23	25	25	25	MIN °C
393	329	258	102	14	3	1	1	12	52	124	241	RAIN MM
15	15	13	5	1	0	0	0	1	3	8	11	RAIN DAYS

Chinese Temple is built on the site of an older temple that was constructed in 1887. The **Northern Territory Chinese Museum** next door has displays taking visitors through the history of Chinese people in Darwin from the establishment of Chinatown and market gardens to the bombings in World War II. *Open during the dry season; admission by gold coin donation.*

getting around

Darwin is easy to get around – city streets are laid out in a grid, most attractions are within walking distance, and traffic is rarely heavy.

A regular public bus service covers many of the suburbs as well as the satellite town of Palmerston (the city terminus is on Harry Chan Avenue). Private minibuses can be found near the northern end of Smith Street Mall and taxis are available at either end of the mall.

The Tour Tub is an open-air bus service to the city's top sights, departing every hour from the northern end of Smith Street Mall.

Darwin's network of bicycle paths extends from the city out to the northern suburbs, and bikes can be hired from many backpacker lodges, most of which can be found on Mitchell Street.

Public transport Bus Service (08) 8924 7666.

Airport shuttle bus Darwin Airport Shuttle Bus 1800 358 945; Metro Minibus (08) 8983 0577.

Police road report 1800 246 199 (a good source of information for travel outside Darwin, particularly in the wet season).

Motoring organisation AANT (08) 8925 5901, roadside assistance 13 1111.

Car rental Avis 136 333; Britz Campervan Rentals 1800 331 454; Budget 132 727; Hertz 133 039; Sargent's four-wheel drive hire service 1800 077 353.

Taxis Radio Taxis 138 294 or (08) 8941 1258.

Bus tours Tour Tub (08) 8985 6322.

Bicycle and scooter hire Darwin Scooter Hire (08) 8941 2434.

The Esplanade 372 B2

Much of Darwin's up-market accommodation is built along The Esplanade, with balconies and windows looking out over Darwin Harbour and the new Darwin Waterfront development. Oil rigs can often be seen being towed out to the offshore fields of the Timor Sea, as can cattle boats lying at anchor, awaiting shipments. There are many Australian and American wrecks at the bottom of the harbour, sunk by the Japanese bombers that struck without warning in February 1942. There are memorial sites all around the harbour recording the hundreds of bombing raids that were made on the city during World War II.

Beautiful **Bicentennial Park** runs the length of The Esplanade and a walking/cycling track goes from Doctors Gully in the north to the Wharf Precinct in the south. The park is a great place to relax under a shady tree, enjoy lunch or simply watch the day go by; in the mornings and evenings, this is also a popular area for joggers and walkers. There is a children's playground halfway along the park, an eagle's nest lookout at the northern end and a **Cenotaph** honouring service men and women at the southern end. A branch of the walking/cycling track goes past Lameroo Beach and the **Deckchair Cinema**, showing current and popular films 'under the stars' every night during the dry season.

On the corner of Knuckey Street, at the southern end of The Esplanade, is **Old Admiralty House**, built in 1937. It shows off tropical design and living standards before the city was devastated in 1974, and is now incorporated into a restaurant. Further north is **Lyons Cottage**, the former British Australian Telegraph (BAT) headquarters for the Overland Telegraph. Built in 1925 for BAT staff, it now houses an excellent chronology of early Darwin life. *Lyons Cottage: cnr The Esplanade and Knuckey St; open daily; admission free.*

State Square

State Square is one of Darwin's most outstanding precincts. The thoroughly modern Parliament House and Supreme Court buildings are either loved or hated by locals, but most people agree that Government House, one of the few intact reminders of the city's colonial days, is utterly charming. The wide green lawns of Liberty Square and surrounding shade trees make this an ideal area in which to eat a sandwich or simply relax.

Palmerston Town Hall 372 C2

Darwin was initially named Palmerston, and the now-ruined Palmerston Town Hall was built in 1883. The building was partially destroyed by cyclone Tracy in 1974, and now stands as a memorial to the city's early colonial days and to the ferocity of the cyclone.

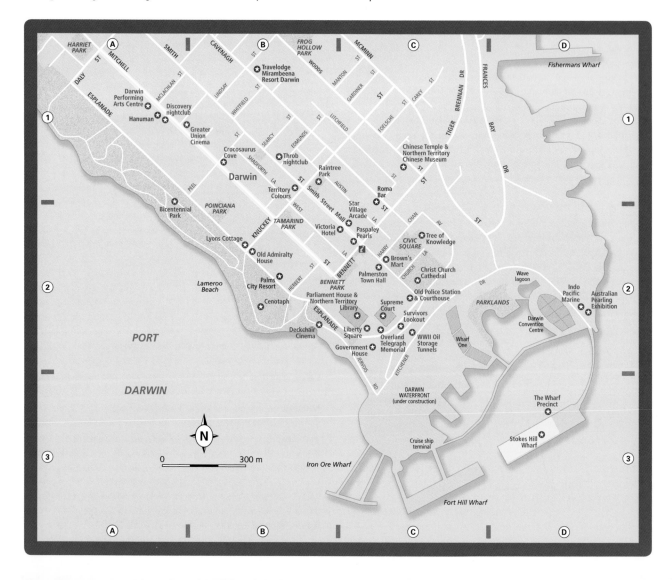

Parliament House, the Supreme Court & Liberty Square 372 C2

Parliament House is a large white rectangular building with one of the finest views of Darwin Harbour. Opened in 1994, this modern, imposing edifice also houses the **Northern Territory Library** and a cafe that opens out to an area of lawn, a large fountain and a great view. Visitors are encouraged to look through the grand hall that displays art and photographic exhibitions. *Guided tours (08) 8946 1434.*

Across the wide courtyard at the front of Parliament House is the Supreme Court building, which was built in 1990. High ceilings and an atmosphere of modern grandeur are also a feature of this building – it has a spectacular foyer with a giant mosaic floor designed by Aboriginal artist Norah Napaljarri Nelson, and a permanent exhibit of Arnhem Land burial poles. At the southern side of Parliament House, next to the Supreme Court, is an open, grassed area called Liberty Square. Edged by spreading rain trees, this is the place where unionists met early last century to protest against the administration of Dr John Gilruth, who was eventually forced to flee the city as a result of a popular uprising against him.

Government House, Old Police Station & Courthouse 372 C2

Across the road from Liberty Square is Government House, an elegant, gabled, colonial-style building built in 1879, which survived both cyclones and bombs. The building is open to the public once a year and is the venue for formal government occasions and ceremonies. Further along The Esplanade, on the corner of Smith Street, is the Old Police Station and Courthouse. They are now home to the offices for the Northern Territory administrator and staff. Directly opposite these buildings is **Survivors Lookout**. It surveys the Wharf Precinct and Darwin Harbour to East Arm Port and the terminus of the *Ghan*, a historic train that originally terminated in Alice Springs but now runs across the continent from Adelaide. The lookout also marks a spot where World War II battles were witnessed by journalists and photographers.

The Wharf Precinct

Steeped in history and perched upon one of the largest natural harbours in Australia, this precinct is the original base of the city of Darwin. Stokes Hill and Fort Hill wharves date back more than a century to a time when clippers and steam ships used to call in at Darwin to load exotic cargoes such as crocodile skins, buffalo hides and pearls. Today the port is used for luxury liners and warships, as a venue for outdoor dining, and as the home of Darwin's convention centre and new Waterfront recreation development.

World War II Oil Storage Tunnels 372 C2

A set of stairs leads from Survivors Lookout to the Wharf Precinct. At the bottom of the stairs are storage tunnels that were built underground after the above-ground tanks were bombed in early raids on Darwin. One of the five tunnels is open to the public and there are historical displays of the war years. *Kitchener Dr; open daily during the dry season.*

Indo Pacific Marine 372 D2

At this wonderful attraction, local coral ecosystems can be viewed without dipping a toe in the water. Find out what lies in Darwin Harbour – from deadly stone fish that can inflict terrible pain and even death, to the beautiful coral that lies hidden in the Top End's sometimes murky waters. Indo Pacific Marine is one of the few places in the world that has been able to transfer a living ecosystem from the water into a land-based exhibition. Also on show are creatures endemic to the Top End, such as the deadly box jellyfish. *Kitchener Dr, near the entrance to Stokes Hill Wharf; open daily.*

Australian Pearling Exhibition 372 D2

Housed in the same building as Indo Pacific Marine, this exhibition gives a detailed history of pearling in northern Australia and highlights the important contribution Aboriginal, Islander and Japanese people made to this multimillion-dollar industry. Also on display are some wonderful examples of South Sea pearls, which are found in northern waters and are the largest pearls in the world. Pearling makes a huge contribution to the northern Australian economy and is still an important source of employment. *Open daily.*

NORTHERN TERRITORY

markets

Parap Village Market This market is about waking up to the splendours of Asia. Colourful flowers, frozen-fruit ice-cream, silk-screened sarongs, Asian food, relaxing massages and exotic blended drinks are all on offer. Parap Shopping Centre; Sat mornings. 370 B4

Palmerston Night Market A community event with arts and crafts for sale. Frances Mall; Fri evenings May–Oct. 632 D3

Rapid Creek Markets Asian food, Top End craft and excellent fresh produce. Rapid Creek Shopping Centre; Sun mornings. 370 C1

Nightcliff Markets These markets are focused on relaxed Sunday mornings – visitors can drink coffee and read the newspapers – all in an outdoor setting. Nightcliff Shopping Centre; Sun mornings. 370 C2

See also Mindil Beach Sunset Markets, on this page.

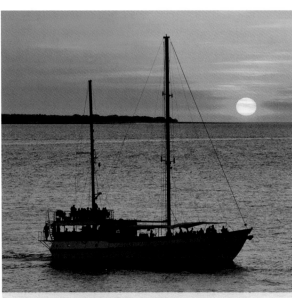

[SUNSET SAIL, PORT DARWIN]

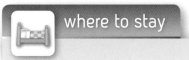

where to stay

Darwin Airport Resort Modern resort located 350 metres from Darwin Airport, and 10 minutes' drive from the CBD. 1 Henry Wrigley Dr, Marrara; (08) 8920 3333 or 1800 600 975. 370 D2

Feathers Sanctuary Luxury retreat for lovers of wildlife, particularly birds. Two minutes' drive from Darwin Airport and 10 minutes from the CBD. 49A Freshwater Rd, Jingili; (08) 8985 2144. 370 D2

Moonshadow Villas An award-winning complex with stylish indoor/outdoor living, within walking distance of the CBD. 6 Gardens Hill Cres, The Gardens; (08) 8981 8850. 370 B5

Palms City Resort Conveniently located on The Esplanade, a block from Mitchell Street and a short walk to Smith Street Mall. 64 The Esplanade; (08) 8982 9200. 372 B2

Travelodge Mirambeena Resort Darwin Centrally located with a good restaurant, two pools and beautifully landscaped gardens. 64 Cavenagh St; (08) 8946 0111 or 1300 886 886. 372 B1

Stokes Hill Wharf 372 D3

Once northern Australia's most important port catering to sailing vessels and steamers, Stokes Hill Wharf is now a berth for international cruise ships and a place for restaurants, bars and shops. Stokes Hill is popular with visitors and locals not only for dining, but also as a place to throw a line over. When the fish are biting, the wharf is one of the best places in Darwin to fish. During the build-up to the wet season, head here to watch one of the city's magnificent storms as it gathers across the harbour and travels towards Darwin. Often international naval vessels can be found berthed at Stokes Hill, with neighbouring Fort Hill Wharf used for commercial and cargo vessels.

The new Darwin Waterfront development is transforming the Wharf Precinct into a lively recreation and commercial zone, with a waterfront promenade, wave lagoon, apartments, restaurants and boutiques, parklands and picnic areas, and a new cruise ship terminal.

Inner North

The beaches of the inner north are idyllic in the dry season, but can be deadly during the build-up to the wet season when box jellyfish float in shallow waters along the shoreline (see Swimming, p. 373). Most visitors content themselves with sunbathing and only swim at the peak of the dry season.

Aquascene 370 B5

This is one of Darwin's most popular attractions, where visitors can handfeed fish that live in Darwin Harbour. Opening times depend on the high tide, but Aquascene publishes feeding times every day in the *Northern Territory News* and weekly timetables can be found at Tourism Top End. Aquascene not only offers the chance to interact with the marine life of the harbour, but also an opportunity to learn about northern Australian creatures through informative talks. *Doctors Gully Rd.*

Cullen Bay Marina 370 A5

Cullen Bay is a popular dining and recreational area where waterside mansions and berths for yachts are built alongside holiday apartments. A wide walking path fringes a gently sloping sandy beach, and a variety of restaurants and cafes overlook the blue waters of the marina. A regular ferry service crosses Darwin Harbour to Mandorah, departing from the front of the lock at Cullen Bay, while sunset and evening charters are based within the marina itself.

At about a kilometre north of central Darwin, the road down to the marina (Kahlin Avenue) passes **Myilly Point Heritage Precinct**. This small group of pre–World War II houses was constructed for senior public servants and survived cyclone Tracy; they are considered excellent examples of tropical residential architecture, with louvred windows and vibrant gardens. Burnett House is located here and is the headquarters of the National Trust. The buildings are open to the public at different times. *National Trust (08) 8981 2848.*

Mindil Beach Sunset Markets 370 B5

The Mindil Beach Sunset Markets are Darwin's most popular tourist attraction. Located off Gilruth Avenue, the markets operate on Thursday evenings (with a smaller version on Sunday evenings) from the end of April to the end of October, taking advantage of the superb dry-season weather. Up to 10 000 people enjoy the food of more than 30 nations and wander between stalls that offer everything from Aboriginal arts and Asian crafts to tarot-card readings, massages and kangaroo sausages. Live performances by theatrical and singing troupes are spiced with whip-cracking and poetry readings. Bands play at night and there is an occasional offshore fireworks display. At sunset, people often walk over the sand dunes to the beach to experience a quintessential Darwin moment.

SKYCITY 370 B5

Also on Mindil Beach, SKYCITY casino lies next to the market strips. As well as the attraction of gambling, the casino also frequently holds concerts on its lawns. With the beach only metres away, this is a very pleasant way to spend an afternoon or evening. There are several restaurants in the casino, and this is the hub of the horseracing scene in August when a gala ball is held on the lawns. *Gilruth Ave, Mindil Beach.*

George Brown Darwin Botanic Gardens 370 B5

The botanic gardens have paths that wind through one of the best collections of tropical plants in Australia. Established in the 1870s, the gardens cover an area of 42 hectares and contain attractions such as an extensive collection of tropical orchids and palms, and a self-guide Aboriginal plant-use trail. The gardens are popular with family groups and wedding parties. A wonderful tree house incorporated into a huge African mahogany is a hit with kids. *Geranium St, The Gardens.*

Museum and Art Gallery of the Northern Territory 370 B4

The Museum and Art Gallery of the Northern Territory is one of Darwin's main cultural icons. This institution houses one of the finest Aboriginal art collections in Australia, which is enhanced every year with the work of entrants in the Aboriginal and Torres Strait Islander Art Award. A spine-tingling cyclone Tracy gallery details what happened during and after that fateful Christmas in 1974. The museum also possesses an excellent natural history display of fauna and flora of the Top End and South-East Asia. The Maritime Boatshed, a vast room filled with all sorts of vessels that have travelled to northern Australia over the years, is impressive in its size and in the diversity of its exhibits from tiny jukung, with their slender outriggers and woven sails, to the large fishing vessels that limped to Australian shores overloaded with refugees. The nearby **Territory Craft Darwin** exhibits the work of local artists and craft producers. *Conacher St, Bullocky Point; open daily; general admission free.*

Sunset dining 370 B4

One of the pleasures of visiting Darwin is being able to enjoy a meal by the beach as the sun sets over Fannie Bay. There are several popular dining venues, such as the **Darwin Ski Club**, on the beach at Fannie Bay next to the Museum and Art Gallery of the Northern Territory, and the popular **Darwin Sailing Club**, just 200 metres further along the coast on Atkins Drive.

Fannie Bay Gaol Museum 370 B4

One of Darwin's most interesting destinations is Fannie Bay Gaol Museum, which served as Darwin's prison between 1883 and 1979. Located barely 300 metres from the Sailing Club, the gaol housed some of Darwin's most desperate criminals. The cells and gallows provide a sobering display for visitors, but are sometimes used as a backdrop for dinner parties and social events. *East Point Rd; open daily; admission free.*

shopping

Smith Street Mall, City Darwin's major shopping precinct with interesting shops that carry Aboriginal art and artefacts interspersed with outdoor eateries, five arcades and a galleria. Paspaley Pearls is a good place to buy pearls and there are several shops near the top of the mall and in Knuckey Street where you can buy Aboriginal art. Territory Colours, 21 Knuckey Street, has great examples of local art and craft, while Animale, in the Galleria, is a terrific frock shop. 372 B2, C2

Casuarina Square Every popular department and chain store is under one roof here, and there is also a huge eatery with more than 30 restaurants and cafes. 370 D1

Framed – The Darwin Gallery, City One of the oldest art galleries in Darwin, with some of the best Aboriginal and Islander art in northern Australia and also some of the best local craft. 370 B5

Cullen Bay Around the marina are some interesting shops and excellent outdoor dining venues. Shop, then eat; eat, then shop. Check out the Absolutely bookshop for a variety of local books, cards and alternative publications. 370 A5

North

Darwin is blessed with a particularly attractive coastline, lush parks and excellent walking paths that meander through a beautiful urban environment. The suburbs of Fannie Bay, Nightcliff and Casuarina all front onto the Timor Sea which is flat, calm and often like liquid gold at sunset. Tall palm trees sway in the breeze that blows onshore every afternoon, while parks full of fig trees provide shelter and food for the huge variety of birds that inhabit Darwin. The nature parks teem with wildlife and it is not unusual to see wallabies eating shoots of grass or goannas wandering the lawns and sandhills of the foreshore. Darwin is one of the few cities in Australia where sea turtles still come ashore to nest.

where to eat

Darwin Sailing Club There isn't a better view in town as the sun sets across the Arafura Sea; the food is good and reasonably priced. Atkins Dr, Fannie Bay; (08) 8981 1700; open daily for lunch and dinner. 370 B4

Hanuman Featuring excellent Thai, Nonya and Tamil cooking, Hanuman is a benchmark for dining in a truly multicultural city. Holiday Inn Esplanade, 93 Mitchell St; (08) 8941 3500; open daily for lunch and dinner. 372 A1

Pee Wee's at the Point On the beach at East Point, this eatery has one of the most magnificent views in Darwin. Alec Fong Lim Dr, East Point Reserve; (08) 8981 6868; open daily for dinner. 370 A3

Seadogs Pizza & Pasta Bar Traditional Italian family cooking by the beach, with Dean Martin crooning in the background. 1/57 Marina Blvd, Cullen Bay; (08) 8941 2877; open Tues–Sun for dinner. 370 A5

The Roma Bar Enjoy a traditional breakfast or try something a little tropical or Asian-inspired for dinner. 9–11 Cavenagh St; (08) 8981 6729; open daily for breakfast, lunch and dinner. 372 C1

entertainment

Cinema One of the first examples of entertainment infrastructure ever established in Darwin was the outdoor cinema that ran during the dry season – the nights were clear and balmy and the temperature perfect. That tradition continues to this day at the Deckchair Cinema (on the shores of Darwin Harbour just around from Lameroo Beach). There are also cinema complexes in Mitchell Street, Casuarina Shopping Square and The Hub in Palmerston. The Museum and Art Gallery of the Northern Territory also runs interesting documentaries, short films and movies at its theatrette. Check the *Northern Territory News* for daily showings.

Live music Darwin has a young population and is a regular stopover for naval and cruise vessels from many countries – an advantage of this is that Darwin is a city of many 'party' venues. There are plenty of clubs, pubs and restaurants in the centre of the city that provide live music. SKYCITY casino has regular entertainment on its lawns during the dry season, while there is a jazz program at Cullen Bay and Stokes Hill Wharf on weekends. Nightclubs such as Discovery and Throb have disc jockey commentaries interspersed with live music, while the Amphitheatre in the Botanic Gardens is a popular venue for touring musicians. Friday's edition of the *Northern Territory News* publishes a round-up of what's on in the Gig Guide, or visitors can check what's on by visiting Top End Tourism.

Classical music and performing arts Darwin has a vibrant arts community that has been deeply influenced by Aboriginal and Asian cultures. Local playwrights, dancers and artists are always producing some tropical gem that can be viewed at interesting venues such as Brown's Mart, the Palmerston Town Hall ruins in Smith Street or the Darwin Performing Arts Centre (DPAC) in Mitchell Street. During the dry season the Darwin Festival is particularly stimulating and includes a concert on The Esplanade. Check with Top End Tourism for the dates of the Darwin Festival as the timing changes each year. Otherwise, see the *Northern Territory News* for weekly programs.

walks & tours

The 'Discovering Trails' Walks Eight self-guided walks, including the Wharf Precinct, The Esplanade, the city centre, the northern suburbs, East Point and Fannie Bay. Brochure available from the visitor centre.

Heritage Carriage Tour A relaxed tour of the CBD in a horse-drawn carriage. Bookings on 0417 813 112.

George Brown Darwin Botanic Gardens Walks Self-guide walks through different habitats; pamphlets available from the visitor centre at the Geranium Street entrance. A guide can be organised if you book ahead. (08) 8981 1958.

Sunset Cruises Take a cruise on one of the charter boats at Cullen Bay Marina to see the sun slip below the horizon over the Timor Sea. City of Darwin Cruises 0417 855 829; Darwin Cruises and Charters (08) 8942 3131; Spirit of Darwin (08) 8981 3711.

Ferry to Mandorah Cast a line off the Mandorah Jetty and enjoy the views of Darwin. It's 130 kilometres by road, but only a 20-minute ferry ride from Cullen Bay Marina. Mandorah Ferry Service (08) 8941 1991.

[THE CAGE OF DEATH, CROCOSAURUS COVE]

East Point Reserve 370 A3

The cliff-top paths into and along East Point Reserve are spectacular and very popular with joggers, rollerbladers and cyclists. Early morning and sunset find a range of people taking a constitutional along these paths that meander between palm trees and parks, and around barbecue areas. The waters of Fannie Bay are enticing but, like all beaches in Darwin, are unsafe for swimming, particularly late in the year because of the presence of box jellyfish. **Lake Alexander**, at East Point Reserve, is an alternative swimming area, along with public baths at Parap, Nightcliff and Casuarina, and these are definitely the options preferred by the locals. A raised boardwalk on the northern side of the lake gives access to mangroves that are teeming with bird, fish and plant life.

East Point Military Museum, in the north of the reserve, sits in the shadow of two huge cement gun emplacements that were manned during World War II to protect the city. The museum highlights the role of Darwin in World War II and the parts played by service personnel in the defence of northern Australia. *Alec Fong Lim Dr, East Point; open daily.*

Nightcliff foreshore 370 B1

The Nightcliff foreshore provides an excellent cliff-top walkway that runs from Nightcliff boat ramp to a bridge over Rapid Creek, on to Casuarina Beach. Parks, play areas for children and fishing spots can be found all along here.

North-east

Australian Aviation Heritage Centre 632 D3

Darwin was the first port of call for many early aviators – Sir Charles Kingsford Smith touched down in present-day Parap on his historic flight between Britain and Australia. The Australian Aviation Heritage Centre houses an American B-52 bomber and the wreckage of a Japanese Zero shot down over Darwin in 1942. The city's rich aviation history is detailed at the centre, along with superbly restored exhibits. *Stuart Hwy, Winnellie; open daily.*

Casuarina Coastal Reserve 370 C1

This reserve boasts a magnificent white sandy beach that backs on to dunes and thickets of native she-oaks. Several hundred metres from Casuarina Beach is Free Beach, Darwin's only recognised nudist bathing area, popular with sunbathers and swimmers during the dry season.

Leanyer Recreation Park 632 D2

This popular family park offers bike-riding, skateboarding and basketball facilities; an all-abilities playground; shaded barbecues and picnic areas; and a water fun park with paddling pools, water cannons and a water playground. *Off Vanderlin Dr; open 8am–8pm daily; admission free.*

Outer North-east

Holmes Jungle Nature Park 632 D3

Off Vanderlin Drive in Karama, this nature park features a monsoonal rainforest full of native fauna and flora. Excellent walking trails meander through the jungle, and the reserve is home to many species of birds, mammals and reptiles. *Open 7am–7pm daily.*

South-east

Charles Darwin National Park 370 D4

Mangroves merge with tropical woodland at this national park, off Tiger Brennan Drive east of the city. There is an excellent view of the city from a lookout on the escarpment, and the park contains a number of Aboriginal shell middens and some World War II bunkers. It also incorporates some of the most pristine mangrove areas in northern Australia, and if accessed by boat there is excellent fishing.

East

Crocodylus Park 632 D3

Crocodylus Park is a research centre as well as a tourist attraction. Crocodiles emerge from the murky waters at feeding times (10am, 12pm and 2pm) to take pieces of meat that are dangled

sport

Darwinites love their sport. **AFL** (Australian Football League) is like a second religion in Darwin and the surrounding communities, particularly for Aboriginal and Torres Strait Islander players, many of whom go on to play for big clubs. In March the NTFL grand final is held at Marrara Stadium and the Tiwi Islands Football Grand Final is held on Bathurst Island – grand-final day is the only time Bathurst Island is open to visitors without a permit. Darwin and Territory teams often play a curtain-raiser to the Australian AFL season. Any match between the Aboriginal All Stars and an AFL team is a must-see game.

Rugby League and Rugby Union are also well supported in Darwin. **Rugby League** matches are played at Richardson Park in Fannie Bay, and **Rugby Union** is played at the headquarters at Marrara. The Marrara sporting complex is also home to hockey, basketball and gymnastics.

Fannie Bay and Darwin Harbour are great for **sailing**. The foreshore is also popular for recreational fishing, with the possibility of catching a barramundi at any beach or wharf.

The annual Darwin Cup **horseracing** carnival in August draws people from around the country, and Darwin's Fannie Bay track turns on perfect conditions and weather.

The Hidden Valley leg of the V8 supercar series in May brings **motorsport** to town. Three days of car racing is turned into a week of celebrations as Top Enders turn out in tens of thousands for this event.

over the side of their enclosures. Well-trained guides allow children – under supervision – to handle baby crocodiles that have their jaws taped shut to avoid any sharp teeth. Work by scientists at Crocodylus Park helped establish the Northern Territory's ground-breaking policies on crocodile preservation. There are other animals on show including monkeys and large cats, such as tigers. *End of McMillans Rd, past the airport, near the Police Centre; open daily.*

day tours

Palmerston   One of the nicest parts of Palmerston is Marlows Lagoon Nature Park. Gently sloping hills roll down to a beautiful lake surrounded by grassy open areas.

Howard Springs Nature Park   A pleasant, shaded swimming area south of Darwin with many native birds and animals and a crocodile-free pool. For more details see p. 380

Darwin Crocodile Farm   This working crocodile farm allows you to get up close to these remarkable reptiles. Feeding times are a highlight. For more details see p. 380

Territory Wildlife Park and Berry Springs Nature Park   This award-winning park showcases the Top End's flora and fauna. Many exhibits are connected by a 4-kilometre walk or shuttle train route. Berry Springs is next door with a swimming pool and picnic facilities. For more details see p. 380

Window on the Wetlands   Looking out over the Adelaide River flood plains, this centre not only has excellent interpretive displays of Top End ecology, but also has excellent views. Nearby, popular jumping crocodile cruises run on the Adelaide River. For more details see p. 380

Mary River   The river is a popular fishing area, with places such as Corroboree Billabong and Shady Camp popular for boating (houseboats can be hired at Corroboree) and fishing. But visitors should be careful: crocodiles are plentiful in these areas. For more details see p. 380

Litchfield National Park   A two-hour drive south of Darwin, this park is a wonderful place to visit or camp, with bubbling streams and gushing waterfalls that flow year-round. Visitors can take walks, admire the scenic views or take advantage of the picnic areas. While generally crocodile-free, you should still read the signs before venturing into any pools. For more details see p. 380

The Tiwi Islands   Bathurst and Melville islands lie 80 kilometres north of Darwin and are the traditional homes of the Tiwi Aboriginal people. 'Tiwi' is said to mean 'the people' or 'we, the chosen people'. Renowned artists, the Tiwi people produce beautiful silk-screened clothing, woven bangles, painted conch shells, carvings, pottery and elaborately decorated Pukumani burial poles. Tiwi Tours (part of Aussie Adventure Holidays) run one- and two-day tours to Bathurst Island from Darwin and arrange permits, accommodation and transport via light aircraft. 1300 721 36.

REGIONS
northern territory

[KATA TJUTA, ULURU–KATA TJUTA
NATIONAL PARK, RED CENTRE]

[FLOWER ALONG THE JATBULA TRAIL,
NITMILUK NATIONAL PARK, GULF TO GULF]

DARWIN

Around Darwin **380**

Kakadu & Arnhem Land **379**

Gulf to Gulf **381**

Red Centre **382**

WESTERN

AUSTRALIA

QUEENSLAND

SOUTH   AUSTRALIA

KAKADU & ARNHEM LAND

World Heritage–listed Kakadu National Park protects one-third of the country's bird species and is bordered by Aboriginal-owned Arnhem Land – visitors must apply for a permit before entering.

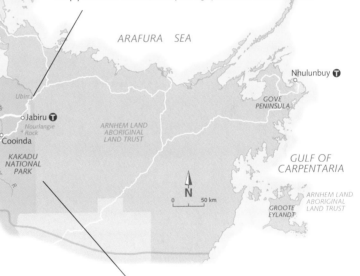

[JACANA SEARCHING FOR FOOD IN A BILLABONG, KAKADU NATIONAL PARK]

Cobourg Peninsula   Four Iwaidja clan groups are custodians of this peninsula, which is protected by Garig Gunak Barlu National Park. Here visitors can fish and explore the ruins of Victoria Settlement, set up by the British in Port Essington in 1838 to defend the north.

Walks at South Alligator River
Towards the end of the dry season, thousands of waterbirds congregate to feed in the Mamukala Wetlands. A short nature trail through the wetlands starts just east of South Alligator River crossing on the Arnhem Highway. The Gungarre Monsoon Rainforest Walk passes through a forest environment.

Yellow Water   Yellow Water (Ngurrungurrudjba) is a spectacular wetland area with prolific birdlife, especially in the dry season. Boat tours give visitors a close-up view of the birdlife and the Territory's crocodiles.

Nourlangie Rock   This is one of Kakadu's main Aboriginal rock-art areas. The Nourlangie Art Site walk takes visitors through a variety of rock-art styles, including prime examples of Kakadu X-ray art, which shows the anatomy of humans and animals in rich detail.

Sunset at Ubirr   Aboriginal people once camped in the rock shelters at Ubirr in Kakadu National Park, leaving the legacy of a spectacular rock-art site. A 1-kilometre circuit covers the main natural galleries, which feature portrayals of extinct animals and animated figures in motion. Another highlight is a shorter side track that climbs steeply to Nardab Lookout, a rocky vantage point with sensational views.

Jim Jim Falls and Twin Falls   Jim Jim Falls (Barrkmalam) and Twin Falls (Gungkurdul) are reached via a four-wheel-drive track off the Kakadu Highway. An incredible volume of water cascades over Jim Jim Falls in the wet season, when the falls can only be seen from the air.

Map labels: Port Essington, COBOURG PENINSULA, GARIG GUNAK BARLU NP., VAN DIEMEN GULF, ARAFURA SEA, Nhulunbuy, South, Ubirr, KAKADU NATIONAL PARK, Jabiru, Nourlangie Rock, Cooinda, GOVE PENINSULA, ARNHEM LAND ABORIGINAL LAND TRUST, Alligator R., KAKADU NATIONAL PARK, GULF OF CARPENTARIA, N, 0   50 km, GROOTE EYLANDT, ARNHEM LAND ABORIGINAL LAND TRUST

TOP EVENTS

MAR	Aurora Kakadu Klash fishing competition (Kakadu National Park)
AUG	Garma Festival of Traditional Culture (Nhulunbuy)
SEPT	Mahbilil Festival (Jabiru)

CLIMATE

JABIRU

	J	F	M	A	M	J	J	A	S	O	N	D	
	34	33	33	35	33	32	32	34	36	38	37	35	MAX °C
	25	24	24	24	22	19	18	19	21	24	25	25	MIN °C
	347	332	318	66	11	1	3	4	9	27	158	211	RAIN MM
	22	21	20	7	2	0	0	0	1	3	12	16	RAIN DAYS

YOLNGU CULTURE

The Yolngu people have lived in north-east Arnhem Land for over 40 000 years and, despite Australia's European settlement, have managed to keep their culture relatively intact. It was only from the 1930s that Yolngu people had steady contact with Balanda (white people). They were not truly affected by this contact until 1963, when a proposal to develop part of Arnhem Land for mining was put forth. In a famous response, the Yolngu sent their opposing petition to the House of Representatives on a piece of bark. While mining went ahead, the petition now hangs in Parliament House in Canberra, seen as having been instrumental in the fight for Aboriginal land rights. The Yolngu people are well known for their arts and crafts – particularly for their bark paintings – and for their skill at playing the didgeridoo. Most of the members of Australia's most prominent Indigenous band, Yothu Yindi, are of Yolngu descent.

→ For more detail see maps 633 & 634–5. For descriptions of 🅣 towns see Towns from A–Z (p. 383).

AROUND DARWIN

The attractions within easy reach of Darwin showcase extraordinary geological features and offer a glimpse of the local culture.

[WANGI FALLS, LITCHFIELD NATIONAL PARK]

Tiwi Islands   Bathurst and Melville islands, 80 kilometres offshore from Darwin, belong to the Tiwi people, whose unique culture results from their long isolation. The landscape includes escarpments, lakes, waterfalls, beaches and forests, but perhaps the biggest attraction is the renowned Tiwi art and craft.

Territory Wildlife Park   This award-winning park showcases northern Australia's native fauna and flora. Features include aviaries, raptor displays, an aquarium tunnel and a large nocturnal house. Nearby, Berry Springs Nature Park has a spring-fed pool – safe for swimming – in natural bushland.

Litchfield National Park   Two hours from Darwin, this is a world of waterfalls, gorges, pockets of rainforest, giant termite mounds and rock formations that resemble lost civilisations. Enjoy the scenic pools beneath the waterfalls – most offer crocodile-free swimming, but read the signs before you take the plunge.

Fogg Dam Conservation Reserve   Fogg Dam was built in the 1950s to provide irrigation to the Humpty Doo Rice Project; the agricultural scheme failed, but the dam became a dry-season refuge for an amazing range of wildlife, especially waterbirds. It's best to visit at sunrise or sunset, when there is the most activity. There are a few lovely walks through the park, such as the Monsoon Forest Walk, a 2.7-kilometre trail that traverses a variety of fascinating habitats; also inquire about ranger-guided nocturnal walks.

Window on the Wetlands Visitor Centre   With superb views over the Adelaide River flood plains, this interpretive centre offers an insight into the Top End's fascinating and unique wetland environments. Interactive displays detail the ecology of the wetlands, as well as local Aboriginal and European history. Time your visit for early morning or late afternoon, when the vistas are at their best.

TOP EVENTS

MAY	Races (horseracing, Pine Creek)
JUNE	Bush Race Meeting (horseracing, Adelaide River)
JUNE	Northern Territory Gold-panning Championships and Didgeridoo Festival (Pine Creek)
JUNE	Gold Rush Festival (Pine Creek)
JUNE	Rodeo and Campdraft (Adelaide River)
JUNE	Rodeo (Pine Creek)

CLIMATE

ADELAIDE RIVER

J	F	M	A	M	J	J	A	S	O	N	D	
32	31	32	33	32	31	30	31	33	33	33	33	MAX °C
25	25	25	24	22	20	19	21	23	25	25	25	MIN °C
429	353	322	103	21	1	1	6	16	73	141	250	RAIN MM
21	20	19	9	2	1	1	1	2	7	12	16	RAIN DAYS

CROCODILES

Crocodiles are both compelling and deadly creatures. Of the two types in northern Australia, the most dangerous is the estuarine crocodile ('saltie'). This well-camouflaged reptile is found out at sea, along the coastline, in creeks, and in rivers up to 100 kilometres from the coast. Never go swimming where salties have been seen. The freshwater crocodile ('freshie') inhabits rivers and lagoons; it is smaller, but can still inflict a serious wound. Both types nest and sun themselves near the water's edge. Always seek local advice before swimming, camping or boating. View these reptiles safely at Darwin Crocodile Farm, 40 kilometres south of the city; Crocodylus Park, an education and research centre in Darwin's north-eastern suburbs; and Crocosaurus Cove in the city centre.

→   For more detail see maps 632–3 & 634. For descriptions of ⊕ towns see Towns from A–Z (p. 383).

GULF TO GULF

Experience the natural riches of the Territory away from the crowds. Some of this region's attractions are well known, while others are scarcely on the map.

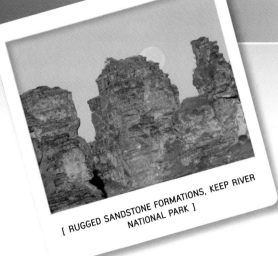

[RUGGED SANDSTONE FORMATIONS, KEEP RIVER NATIONAL PARK]

NORTHERN TERRITORY

Nitmiluk National Park The traditional home of the Jawoyn people, this park is world-renowned for its 13 stunning gorges, carved from red sandstone over a period of 20 million years. Visitors can navigate the gorges in canoes, take a boat tour with a Jawoyn guide, swim in the pools or explore the 100-kilometre network of walking tracks.

Never Never country Jeannie Gunn wrote *We of the Never Never* (1908) after living at Elsey Station. Now you can visit a faithful replica of Gunn's home on the property of Mataranka Homestead. Nearby in Elsey National Park visitors can enjoy the Mataranka thermal pool, which pumps out 20 million litres of water daily.

Keep River National Park This remote park includes the traditional land of the Miriwoong and Kadjerong peoples and contains many important rock-art sites, including the accessible Nganalam site. A major attraction is the rugged sandstone formations, similar to the Bungle Bungles over the Western Australian border. There are designated camping areas and good walking tracks.

Eastern frontiers The area adjoining the Gulf of Carpentaria is popular with four-wheel-drive travellers seeking new frontiers. The main settlement, Borroloola, is a popular spot for barramundi anglers and offers access to the waters around Barranyi (North Island) National Park.

Lost City The Lost City is an eerie landscape of free-standing sandstone pillars rising from the plains and suggesting a long forgotten civilisation. While there is a great walk among the towering formations, access is for experienced four-wheel drivers only, but there's always the much more civilised option of a helicopter ride from Cape Crawford.

Map labels: JOSEPH BONAPARTE GULF; Daly River; NITMILUK (KATHERINE GORGE) NATIONAL PARK; Nitmiluk (Katherine) Gorge; Katherine; Roper; Mataranka; ELSEY NATIONAL PARK; Roper Bar; GULF OF CARPENTARIA; KEEP RIVER NATIONAL PARK; GREGORY NATIONAL PARK; LIMMEN NATIONAL PARK (PROPOSED); Timber Creek; GREGORY NATIONAL PARK; Daly Waters; River; Borroloola; WESTERN AUSTRALIA; Victoria River; Cape Crawford; McArthur River; Elliott; Lake Woods; Tarrabool Lake; Corella Lake; Lake Sylvester; QUEENSLAND; N; 0 80 km

TOP EVENTS

EASTER	Barra Classic (Borroloola)
APR–MAY	Fishing competitions (Timber Creek)
MAY	Katherine Cup (horseracing, Katherine)
MAY	Back to the Never Never Festival (Mataranka)
AUG	Flying Fox Festival (Katherine)
AUG	Rodeo (Mataranka)

CLIMATE

KATHERINE

	J	F	M	A	M	J	J	A	S	O	N	D	
	35	34	35	34	32	30	30	33	35	38	38	37	MAX °C
	24	24	23	20	17	14	13	16	20	24	25	24	MIN °C
	234	215	161	33	6	2	1	1	6	29	89	195	RAIN MM
	15	14	10	2	1	0	0	0	1	3	8	12	RAIN DAYS

BARRAMUNDI FISHING

Barramundi, Australia's premier native sport fish, is nowhere as prolific or accessible to anglers as it is in the Northern Territory. There is good barra fishing along both east and west coasts. The rugged west features tropical wetlands and a network of waterways. Popular spots include the Daly River (known for the size of its barramundi and its fishing lodges), Nitmiluk (Katherine Gorge) National Park and Victoria River via Timber Creek. The numerous eastern rivers are smaller, with minimal tides but very clear water. Top spots east are Borroloola on the McArthur River and Roper Bar on the Roper River.

→ For more detail see maps 634–5 & 636–7. For descriptions of ⊕ towns see Towns from A–Z (p. 383).

RED CENTRE

The Red Centre is Australia's geographical, scenic and mythical heart, with spectacular landforms, deserts, blue skies and a monumental sense of scale.

[DEVILS MARBLES (KARLU KARLU)]

Devils Marbles (Karlu Karlu) This is one of the most iconic outback destinations, where massive red and orange boulders sit precariously atop each other in a broad desert playground; legend has it that they are the eggs of the Rainbow Serpent. A network of informal tracks meanders through the rock formations.

Kings Canyon Within Watarrka National Park, spectacular Kings Canyon has sandstone walls rising to 270 metres. A 6-kilometre return trail scales the side of the canyon and leads past beehive formations to the Garden of Eden.

Hermannsburg (Ntaria) This Aboriginal-owned site was established as a German Lutheran mission in 1877. Today the historic precinct displays preserved buildings from that time, as well as works of art from the acclaimed Hermannsburg School, of whom Albert Namatjira is the most famous.

Kata Tjuta Uluru's sister formation; comprising 36 magnificently domed and coloured shapes Kata Tjuta means 'many heads'. The three-hour Valley of the Winds walk winds through the crevices and gorges of the rock system.

Simpson Desert and Chambers Pillar The world's largest sand dune desert was formed around 18 000 years ago after the continent's central lakes dried up. The main attraction is Chambers Pillar, a sandstone obelisk towering 50 metres above the plain.

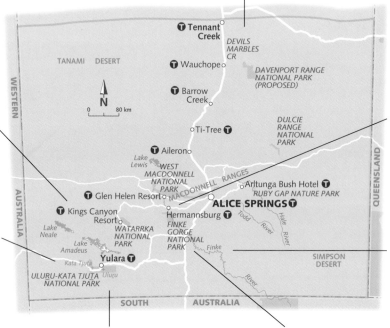

Exploring Uluru The Anangu prefer tourists not to climb Uluru. There are four guided walks as an alternative: a 9.4-kilometre walk around the base; the Mala walk to art sites; the Kuniya walk, which introduces creation stories; and the Liru walk, explaining the use of bush foods and materials, such as quandong fruit.

Finke Gorge National Park This park has four-wheel-drive access only. Its unique feature is Palm Valley, a 10 000-year-old oasis with 3000 red fan palms. The Finke River has maintained its course for over 100 million years and is possibly the world's oldest river.

TOP EVENTS

MAY	Bangtail Muster (Alice Springs)
JULY	Camel Cup (Alice Springs)
JULY	Alice Springs Show (Alice Springs)
AUG	Tennant Creek Cup (horseracing, Tennant Creek)
AUG	Henley-on-Todd Regatta (Alice Springs)
AUG–SEPT	Desert Harmony Festival (Tennant Creek)

CLIMATE

ALICE SPRINGS

J	F	M	A	M	J	J	A	S	O	N	D	
36	35	33	28	23	20	20	23	27	31	34	35	MAX °C
21	21	17	13	8	5	4	6	10	15	18	20	MIN °C
38	44	33	18	19	15	14	10	9	22	28	38	RAIN MM
5	5	3	2	3	3	3	2	2	5	6	6	RAIN DAYS

THE STORY OF ULURU

Uluru lies in the territory of the Anangu people. European explorer William Gosse named it Ayers Rock in 1873. Along with The Olgas (now Kata Tjuta) and surrounding land it became a national park in 1958, and was returned to its traditional owners and gazetted as Uluru. The rock is Australia's most identifiable natural icon. It is a massive, red, rounded monolith rising 348 metres above the plain, sitting 863 metres above sea level, and reaching 6 kilometres below the earth's surface. Uluru's circumference measures 9.4 kilometres. It has no joints – so despite its valleys, fissures and caves, it is a true monolith. Uluru attracts tourists because of its size and singularity. For the Anangu, however, the rock is not a single spiritual object but a thing of many parts; Uluru and Kata Tjuta were laid down during the Tjukurpa (creation period) and are joined by the iwara (tracks) of the ancestral beings that created all the land.

→ For more detail see maps 636–7, 638–9 & 640–1. For descriptions of ⊕ towns see Towns from A–Z (p. 383).

TOWNS A–Z
northern territory

[LOST CITY, CAPE CRAWFORD]

LEGEND

i VISITOR INFORMATION

📻 RADIO STATIONS

🏠 IN TOWN

🌴 WHAT'S ON

✕ WHERE TO EAT

🛏 WHERE TO STAY

◎ NEARBY

Adelaide River

Pop. 188
Map ref. 632 E8 | 634 D6

i Adelaide River Inn, Stuart Hwy; (08) 8976 7047.

📻 98.9 FM ABC Territory Radio

Adelaide River is a small town located near the headwaters of the river of the same name, known for its large population of saltwater crocodiles. A settlement was established here as a base for workers on the Overland Telegraph Line in the early 1870s. The population was boosted by gold discoveries at Pine Creek and the subsequent building of the Northern Australia Railway, which operated from 1888 to 1976. During World War II the relatively sheltered Adelaide River was a major military base for 30 000 Australian and US soldiers.

🏠 **Adelaide River Inn** The hotel was a favourite watering hole of soldiers during WW II and still has war photographs and memorabilia adorning the walls. Hard to ignore is the main attraction, Charlie the Buffalo, suitably stuffed, from the film *Crocodile Dundee*. Meals and accommodation are available. Stuart Hwy.

Adelaide River Railway Station: National Trust–classified station (1888), now a museum featuring relics of local history including the railway construction and WW II; open Apr–Sept, other times by appt; Stuart Hwy; (08) 8976 7101.

🌴 *Rodeo and Campdraft:* June. *Bush Race Meeting:* June and Aug.

✕ *Adelaide River Inn:* good pub food; 106 Stuart Hwy; (08) 8976 7047.

🛏 *Mount Bundy Station:* historic cattle station; Haynes Rd; (08) 8976 7009. *Daly River Mango Farm:* rustic accommodation; off Port Keats Rd, Daly River; (08) 8978 2464 or 1800 000 576. *Perry's on the Daly:* camping ground with 1 room and a house; Mayo Park, via Daly River Crossing; (08) 8978 2452. *Wooliana on the Daly:* group accommodation; Woolianna Rd, Daly River; (08) 8978 2478.

◎ **Daly River** Copper was discovered here in 1883 and mining began in 1884, which led to a bloody conflict between miners and Aboriginal people. Mining ceased about 1909. Daly River is now a sleepy riverside town with a roadside inn and local Aboriginal arts and crafts. It is said that the country's best barramundi are caught in the Daly River and the area teems with crocodiles and other reptiles, buffalo, cockatoos and wild pigs. The Merrepen Arts Festival is held here each June. 102 km sw.

War Cemetery This is Australia's only war cemetery on native soil. There are graves of 434 military personnel and 54 civilians killed in the 1942 Japanese air raids, along with memorials for those lost in Timor and other northern regions. 1 km E.

Mt Bundy Station: rural experience with fishing, walking, swimming and a wide range of accommodation; 3 km NE. *Robin Falls:* pleasant 15 min walk to falls that flow most of the year; 15 km s. *Snake Creek Armament Depot:* wartime military base and weapon storage area with 40 buildings still intact; 17 km N. *Grove Hill Heritage Hotel and Museum:* example of outback ingenuity made from recycled materials in a fashion designed to withstand the harsh weather of the Top End. Hotel offers meals and accommodation; Goldfields Rd; around 70 km SE.

See also AROUND DARWIN, p. 380

ALICE SPRINGS

Pop. 21 619
Map ref. 639 I7 | 641 J3

ℹ️ **Central Australian Tourism Industry Association,**
60 Gregory Tce; (08) 8952 5800 or 1800 645 199;
www.centralaustraliantourism.com

📻 96.9 Sun FM, 783 AM ABC Territory Radio

Located on the Todd River in the MacDonnell Ranges, Alice Springs is almost 1500 kilometres from the nearest capital city. In 1871 Overland Telegraph Line surveyor William Whitfield Mills discovered a permanent waterhole just north of today's city. Mills named the water source after Alice Todd, wife of South Australian Superintendent of Telegraphs Sir Charles Todd. A repeater station was built on the site. In 1888 the South Australian government gazetted a town 3 kilometres to the south. It was called Stuart until 1933, when the name Alice Springs was adopted. Supplies came to the slow-growing settlement by camel train from Port Augusta. The railway line from Adelaide, known as the Ghan after the original Afghan camel drivers, was completed in 1929. Today 'the Alice' is an oasis of modern civilisation in the middle of a vast and largely uninhabited desert, made all the more likeable by not taking itself too seriously (as some of its annual events testify).

🏠 **Alice Springs Cultural Precinct** This precinct includes some of Alice Springs' best cultural attractions. At the Araluen Centre are 4 galleries of Aboriginal art, with an emphasis on work from the central desert, and a magnificent stained-glass window by local artist Wenten Rubuntja. The Museum of Central Australia offers an insight into the geological and natural history of the Red Centre, with interpretive displays and impressive fossils. Also in the precinct are the Strehlow Research Centre, the Central Australian Aviation Museum, several memorials and the Yeperenye Sculpture, depicting a Dreamtime caterpillar. One ticket covers the entry to each attraction. Cnr Larapinta Dr and Memorial Ave.

Alice Springs Desert Park David Attenborough was so impressed by this desert park that he proclaimed, 'there is no museum or wildlife park in the world that could match it'. The park invites visitors to explore the arid lands and the relationship between its plants, animals and people. A walking trail leads through 3 habitats: Desert Rivers, Sand Country and Woodland. There are films, interactive displays, guided tours and talks about flora, fauna and the ability of Aboriginal people to survive in such harsh conditions. The park has a spectacular desert nocturnal house with native marsupials such as the bilby and mala, and there are free-flying birds of prey in daily shows. Larapinta Dr; (08) 8951 8788.

John Flynn Memorial Uniting Church: in memory of the founder of Royal Flying Doctor Service and Australian Inland Mission; Todd Mall. (Flynn's grave can be found 1 km beyond the entrance to Alice Springs Desert Park.) **Adelaide House:** originally a hospital designed by Rev Flynn, now a museum displaying pedal-radio equipment he used and other artefacts and photographs; open 10am–4pm Mon–Fri and 10am–12pm Sat Mar–Nov; Todd Mall. **Sounds of Starlight Theatre:** musical journey through Central Australia; open Apr–Nov; Todd Mall. **Aboriginal Australia Art and Culture Centre:** exhibits of local Arrernte culture and an Aboriginal music museum including the only didgeridoo university in the world. Activities include boomerang and spear throwing, damper and billy tea and a bush tucker experience; Todd St. **Royal Flying Doctor Service Base:** operational base since 1939, with daily tours and presentations and an interactive museum; Stuart Tce. **National Pioneer Women's Hall of Fame:** national project dedicated to preserving women's place in Australia's history; open Feb–mid-Dec; Old Alice Springs Gaol, 2 Stuart Terrace. **Minerals House:** fossicking, geological and mineral displays; closed weekends; Hartley St. **Old Stuart Town Gaol:** the harsh but functional design of stone and timber reflects the community attitude to prisoners at the time of construction (1907); open 10am–12.30pm Mon–Sat; Parsons St. **Technology, Transport and Communications Museum:** relics are used to demonstrate the methods pioneers devised to overcome the hardships of isolation; Memorial Dr. **Anzac Hill:** the most visited landmark in Alice Springs, this war memorial features panoramic views of town and the MacDonnell Ranges; Anzac Hill Rd. **Stuart Town Cemetery:** original town cemetery with graves of the earliest pioneers dating from 1889; George Cres. **School of the Air:** the first of its kind in Australia with a classroom size of 1.3 million sq km. See interpretive displays and hear lessons being broadcast; Head St. **Old Hartley Street School:** originally constructed in 1930 and closed in 1965, the school was added to several times as the population surged, reflecting the changing styles and requirements of school design through different periods; open 10am–2.30pm Mon–Fri; Hartley St. **The Juicy Rump:** part of Lasseters Casino complex, this bar offers 17 beers on tap and an impressive menu of surf and turf; Barrett Dr. **Olive Pink Botanic Gardens:** named for an anthropologist who worked with Central Desert people, this is Australia's only arid-zone botanic garden. Covering 16 ha, it contains over 300 Central Australian plant species in simulated habitats such as sand dunes, woodlands and creeks; Barrett Dr. **The Residency:** grand home completed in 1927 and housing Central Australia's regional administrator until 1973, it has welcomed many VIPs, including Queen Elizabeth II, and now showcases local history; Cnr Parsons and Hartley sts. **Red Centre Dreaming:** authentic, traditional and modern Aboriginal dance. Australian food is served including damper, kangaroo and barramundi; North Stuart Hwy. **Aboriginal art and artefacts:** many outlets with authentic products; brochure from visitor centre.

🌴 **Market:** Todd Mall; contact city council for dates and times. **Alice is Wonderland Festival:** gay and lesbian event; Mar. **Heritage Festival:** Apr. **Racing Carnival:** Apr/May. **Bangtail Muster:** street parade and sports day; May. **Finke Desert Race:** car and motorbike racing; June. **Beanie Festival:** June. **Camel Cup:** July. **Show:** cooking, crafts and camels; July. **Rodeo:** Aug. **Henley-on-Todd Regatta:** boats wheeled or carried along a dry riverbed; Aug. **Masters Games:** mature-age athletics carnival, even-numbered years; Oct. **Desert Festival:** Arts festival; Oct. **Bassinthedust:** youth music concert; Oct. **Christmas Carnival:** Dec.

🍴 **Alice Vietnamese Restaurant:** authentic Vietnamese; Heffernan Rd; (08) 8952 0745. **Bluegrass Restaurant:** modern Australian; Cnr Gap Rd and Stott Tce; (08) 8955 5188. **Casa Nostra Pizza Bar & Spaghetti House:** authentic Italian; Cnr Undoolya Rd and Sturt Tce; (08) 8952 6749.

NORTHERN TERRITORY

[BUSH TUCKER DISPLAY, ALICE SPRINGS DESERT PARK]

Hanuman Alice Springs: excellent modern Asian; Crowne Plaza, 82 Barrett Dr; (08) 8953 7188. *Keller's Restaurant:* Swiss and Indian cuisine; Diplomat Hotel, 20 Gregory Tce; (08) 8952 3188. *Oscar's Cafe & Restaurant:* Portuguese and Spanish; 86 Todd Mall; (08) 8953 0930. *The Lane:* a slice of the Mediterranean; 58 Todd St; (08) 8952 5522. *The Overlanders Steakhouse:* dares diners to try the 'Drover's Blowout', a multi-course meal of soup, emu, crocodile, camel, barramundi, beef, kangaroo and dessert; 72 Hartley Tce; (08) 8952 2159.

Alice on Todd: modern self-contained apartments; Cnr South Tce and Strehlow St; (08) 8953 8033. *Alice Springs Resort:* low-set quality accommodation; 34 Stott Tce; (08) 8951 4545. *Cavenagh Lodge B&B:* private, comfortable B&B; 4 Cavenagh Cres; (08) 8952 2257. *Lasseters Hotel Casino:* modern rooms in great setting; 93 Barrett Dr; (08) 8950 7777 or 1800 808 975. *The Swagmans Rest Motel:* budget self-contained rooms; 67–69 Gap Rd; (08) 8953 1333 or 1800 089 612. *White Gum Motel:* comfortable rooms close to CBD; 17 Gap Rd; (08) 8952 5144 or 1800 624 110. *Bond Springs Station:* historic cattle station; Bond Springs; (08) 8952 9888. *Gunya Titjikala Resort:* safari-style luxury: Old South Rd, Titjikala; (02) 9211 2322 or 1300 135 657. *Ooraminna Station Homestead:* historic cattle station; Old South Rd; (08) 8953 0170. *Ross River Resort:* caravan park; Ross Hwy; (08) 8956 9711 or 1800 241 711.

West MacDonnell National Park The majestic MacDonnell Ranges, once higher than the Himalayas, were formed over 800 million years ago. Over time the ancient peaks have been dramatically eroded so that what remains is a spectacular environment of rugged gorges, hidden waterholes, remnant rainforest and an unexpectedly large number of animal species and diversity of flora. The jewel of the ranges is Ormiston Gorge, one of the most beautiful in Australia, while the Ochre Pits are a natural quarry once mined by Aboriginal people for ochre which they used in rock art, painting and ceremonial decoration. The Larapinta Trail is a huge 230 km walk divided into 12 sections covering the major sites of the ranges and can be walked separately. Walkers are advised to use the Walker Registration Scheme prior to departure (1300 650 730), or contact the Parks & Wildlife Commission of the Northern Territory for maps and tour options on (08) 8951 8250. 17 km w

Emily and Jessie Gaps Nature Park Located in the East MacDonnells, Emily Gap (13 km E) and Jessie Gap (18 km E) both contain Aboriginal rock art and are important spiritual sites to the Eastern Arrernte people. The caterpillar beings of Mparntwe (Alice Springs) originated where Emily Gap lies today. They formed Emily Gap and other topographical features around Alice Springs and then spread across to the edge of the Simpson Desert. Both gaps are popular barbecue and picnic places. (08) 8951 8250.

Pitchi Richi Sanctuary: open-air museum with displays of William Ricketts' clay sculptures and lessons about the Dreamtime and bush tucker; 2 km E. *Alice Springs Telegraph Station Historical Reserve:* area protecting original stone buildings and equipment, with historical display, guided tours, bushwalking and wildlife (Alice Springs waterhole is located here); 3 km N. *Old Timers Traeger Museum:* unique museum set

ALICE SPRINGS   *continued from previous page*

in a retirement home and run by volunteer residents. It displays photographs and memorabilia from the early days of white settlement in Central Australia; 5 km s. *Frontier Camel Farm:* camel rides and tours, reptile house and museum with displays highlighting the importance of camels and Afghan workers to the area; 7 km E. *The Date Farm:* locally grown dates and a pleasant palm garden at Australia's first commercial date farm; 7 km E. *National Road Transport Hall of Fame:* impressive collection of old trucks, cars and motorbikes; 8 km s. *Ghan Railway Museum:* re-creation of a 1930s railway siding featuring the Old Ghan, which runs on 8 km of private line between MacDonnell Siding and Mt Ertiva; 10 km s. *Tropic of Capricorn Marker:* bicentennial project marking the Tropic of Capricorn; 30 km N. *Ewaninga Rock Carvings Conservation Reserve:* soft sandstone outcrops form natural galleries of sacred Aboriginal paintings. Custodians request that visitors do not climb on rocks or interfere with the paintings; 35 km SE. *Corroboree Rock Conservation Reserve:* significant Eastern Arrernte site for ceremonial activities with a short walk and information signs; 43 km E. *Standley Chasm:* spectacular narrow, sheer-sided gorge that is particularly striking at midday when sun lights up the rocks. An attractive 1 km creek walk leads to the chasm and picnic and barbecue facilities; 50 km w. *Camel Outback Safaris:*

1-day outback camel safaris; bookings on (08) 8956 0925; 93 km sw. *Rainbow Valley Conservation Reserve:* stunning freestanding sandstone cliffs that change colour at sunrise and sunset. Access by 4WD only; 101 km s. *Mud Tank zircon field:* prospecting for zircons, guided fossicking tours and gem-cutting at the caravan park; 135 km NE. *Henbury Meteorites Conservation Reserve:* contains 12 craters created when meteorites (comprising 90% iron) crashed to earth 4700 years ago. The largest of the meteorites was over 100 kg and is now at the Museum of Central Australia in Alice Springs; 147 km sw. *Chambers Pillar Historical Reserve:* Chambers Pillar, named by John McDouall Stuart in 1860, is a 40 m high solitary rock pillar left standing on a Simpson Desert plain after 340 million years of erosion. It served as a landmark for early pioneers and explorers and is best viewed at dawn or dusk; 149 km s. *Mereenie Loop:* links Alice Springs, Kings Canyon, Uluṟu and Kata Tjuṯa via the West MacDonnell Ranges and Glen Helen. A permit is required because a section of the route passes through Aboriginal land; map and permit from visitor centre. *Tours:* experience scenic attractions and Aboriginal culture by foot, bus or coach, train, limousine, 4WD safari, Harley-Davidson motorcycle, camel, horse, aeroplane, helicopter or hot-air balloon; brochures at visitor centre.

See also RED CENTRE, p. 382

Aileron
Map ref. 638 H5

ⓘ Aileron Roadhouse, Stuart Hwy; (08) 8956 9703.

The highlight of the year at this popular rest stop on the Stuart Highway is the annual cricket match between local grape farmers and government officials from the Department of Primary Industries. There are even attendant seagulls, which are made by sticking parts of packing-cases onto sticks and painting them white.

🏠 **Aileron Hotel Roadhouse** The roadhouse is a welcome oasis with a swimming pool, Aboriginal art, playground and picnic and barbecue facilities. A 17 m sculpture of Charlie Portpot, a local rainmaker, stands beside the roadhouse which offers meals, including a roast for Sunday lunch, and accommodation. There is also an adjoining campsite. Stuart Hwy.

🎪 *Cricket Match:* dates from visitor centre.

🛏 *Aileron Hotel and Roadhouse:* modern roadhouse rooms; Stuart Hwy; (08) 8956 9703.

⊗ **Ryans Well Historical Reserve** The reserve is named after Ned Ryan, a 19th-century stonemason and bushman who was an expert at sinking wells. He accompanied John McKinlay on his ill-fated exploration of Arnhem Land in 1866. When they became trapped on the East Alligator River during the wet season, Ryan and another bushman fashioned a raft out of the skins of 27 pack horses to negotiate their escape. Ryans Well was hand-dug in 1889 as part of an attempt to encourage settlement in the NT. Today there is a plaque beside the well explaining the process of raising water. 7 km SE.

Glen Maggie Homestead: ruins of 1914 homestead, once used as a telegraph office but abandoned in 1934; 7 km SE. *Native Gap Conservation Reservation:* sacred Aboriginal site with picnic area surrounded by cypress pines and magnificent views of the Hahn Range; 12 km SE.

See also RED CENTRE, p. 382

Arltunga Bush Hotel
Map ref. 639 K6 | 641 N1

ⓘ Arltunga Historical Reserve Visitor Centre, (08) 8956 9770; or Arltunga Bush Hotel, (08) 8956 9797.

Arltunga was named after a subgroup of the Arrernte people who had lived in the area for at least 22 000 years before Europeans arrived. When gold was discovered in 1887, prospectors travelled 600 kilometres from the Oodnadatta railhead, often on foot, to get there. When the gold ran out, the people left, and the only remaining signs of life today are the hotel (closed 1 December to 1 March) and adjoining campground. Ruins of the town have been well preserved by the dry climate.

⊗ **N'Dhala Gorge Nature Park** The shady gorge features extensive walking tracks that provide access to a large number of rock-art sites with carvings and paintings, including more than 6000 petroglyphs. The carvings are of 2 distinct types – finely pecked and heavily pounded – and are thought to represent 2 different periods. There are also rare plants in the park such as the peach-leafed poison bush and the undoolya wattle. Access by 4WD only. 53 km sw.

Arltunga Historical Reserve: ruins of Arltunga, some of which have been restored, including police station and gaol, mines and the Government Battery and Cyanide Works (1896). The visitor centre has displays on the history of the town; behind the hotel. **Ruby Gap Nature Park:** the site of Central Australia's first mining rush, in 1886, when rubies were thought to have been found. After the stones proved to be relatively valueless garnets the boom went bust and people left. The stunning gorges are now popular sites for bushwalking and camping. Track closures possible Nov–Apr due to wet conditions; 37 km E. **Trephina Gorge Nature Park:** known for its sheer quartzite cliffs, red river gums and sandy creek bed. Several waterholes attract native wildlife and provide a beautiful setting for bushwalking, swimming, camping and picnicking; 43 km w.

See also RED CENTRE, p. 382

Barrow Creek
Pop. 11
Map ref. 639 I2

 Barrow Creek Hotel; (08) 8956 9753.

 107.3 FM ABC Territory Radio

Although its appearance today is that of a small wayside stop on the highway, Barrow Creek was originally an important telegraph station. It was also the site of an 1874 punitive expedition against the Kaytej people by police after a telegraph station master and linesman were killed during an assault by 20 Kaytej men. This attack (thought to have been a reaction to the abuse of an Aboriginal woman) is the only known planned attack on staff of the Overland Telegraph.

Old Telegraph Station This restored stone building (1872) is set against the breathtaking backdrop of the Forster Ranges. It is 1 of 15 telegraph stations that formed the original network from Port Augusta to Port Darwin. A key is available from the hotel for those who wish to look inside. Stuart Hwy.

Barrow Creek Hotel: outback pub (1932), with original bar, cellar and tin ceilings, and memorabilia of the area on display; Stuart Hwy. **Cemetery:** graves of early settlers and local characters; information available at the hotel.

See also RED CENTRE, p. 382

Batchelor
Pop. 477
Map ref. 632 E7 | 634 D5

i Information booth, Tarkarri Rd; (08) 8976 0045.

93.7 8KIN FM, 98.9 FM ABC Territory Radio

Established as a large air force base during World War II, Batchelor became prominent with the discovery of uranium at nearby Rum Jungle in 1949. Today Batchelor thrives on tourism, in particular, because of its close proximity to the increasingly popular Litchfield National Park.

Karlstein Castle Czech immigrant Bernie Havlik worked at Rum Jungle and was a gardener there until his retirement in 1977. As a gardener he had been frustrated by a rocky outcrop that was too large to move and too difficult to keep tidy, so he decided to build over it. Havlik spent 5 years constructing a mini replica of the original Karlstein Castle that still stands in Bohemia. He added finishing touches, despite serious illness, and died just after completion. Rum Jungle Rd.

Coomalie Cultural Centre: bush tucker garden plus display of Aboriginal works and culture; Batchelor Institute, cnr Awilla Rd and Nurudina St.

Lingalonga Festival: cultural festival; Aug/Sept.

Batchelor Butterfly Cafe: good barra and buffalo; 8 Meneling Rd; (08) 8976 0199. **Monsoon Cafe:** tasty burgers and cheesecake; Litchfield Park Rd; (08) 8978 2077.

Historic Retreat: restored 1950s guesthouse; 19 Pinaroo Cres; (08) 8976 0554. **Lake Bennett Wilderness Resort:** stunning resort set in 125 ha of tropical bushland on the shore of an 81 ha freshwater lake; Chinner Rd, Winnellie; (08) 8976 0960 or 1800 999 089. **Rum Jungle Bungalows:** bush cabins; 10 Meneling Rd; (08) 8976 0555.

Litchfield National Park Sandstone formations and monsoon rainforest feature in this easily accessible park. There are fantastic swimming spots: plunge into the rainforest-fringed pool at Wangi Falls, swim beneath the cascading Florence Falls or relax in the waters of Buley Rockhole. Do not miss the Lost City (access by 4WD only), a series of windswept formations that eerily resemble the ruins of an ancient civilisation, and the magnetic termite mounds, so-called because they all align north–south. (08) 8976 0282; 20 km w.

Lake Bennett Wilderness Resort: this resort has a plethora of birdlife and native fauna that can be enjoyed in the many serene picnic areas. A range of activities are available including abseiling, swimming and barramundi fishing. Dining and accommodation also on-site; Chinner Rd; (08) 8976 0960; 18 km NE. **Batchelor Air Charter:** scenic flights, parachuting and gliding; Batchelor Aerodrome; 1 km w. **Rum Jungle Lake:** canoeing, kayaking, diving and swimming; 10 km w.

See also AROUND DARWIN, p. 380

Borroloola
Pop. 775
Map ref. 635 M11 | 637 M2

i Lot 384, Robinson Rd; (08) 8975 8799.

 102.9 8MAB FM, 106.1 FM ABC Territory Radio

Located beside the McArthur River, Borroloola is a small settlement with a chequered past. As a frontier town and port in the 19th century it was a base for rum smuggling from Thursday Island. It became known as the home of criminals, murderers and alcoholics, a reputation it lost only when it was virtually deserted in the 1930s. Today Borroloola's fortunes have vastly improved and it is popular with fishing and four-wheel-drive enthusiasts. Although it lies on Aboriginal land, no permit is required to enter.

Police Station Museum: built in 1886, the museum is the oldest surviving outpost in the NT and displays memorabilia and photographs that illustrate the town's history; Robinson Rd. **Cemetery:** pioneer graves; Searcy St and other scattered sites; map from visitor centre.

Barra Classic: Easter. **Rodeo:** Aug.

Heartbreak Hotel Cape Crawford: budget rooms with pub food; Cnr Carpentaria and Tablelands hwys, Cape Crawford; (08) 8975 9928. **King Ash Bay Lodge:** stopover between WA and Queensland; Batten Point Rd, King Ash Bay; (08) 8975 8998 or (08) 8975 9650.

Cape Crawford This charming town is an excellent base for exploring Bukalara rocks (60 km E) and the Lost City (20 km SE). Bukalara rocks are a mass of chasms winding through ancient sandstone structures (the area is very remote and a guide is

NORTHERN TERRITORY

recommended). The Lost City is a collection of sandstone turrets, domes and arches formed by water seeping through cracks and eroding the sandstone. It is an important Aboriginal ceremonial site and accessible only by air or 4WD. Flights can be arranged from Cape Crawford. 110 km sw.

King Ash Bay: popular fishing spot year-round; 40 km NE. *Caranbirini Conservation Reserve:* protects weathered rock escarpments and semi-permanent waterhole rimmed by riverine vegetation and open woodland, along with many native birds. Surrounding the waterhole are 25 m sandstone spires providing a vivid contrast in colour and shape to the surrounding countryside; 46 km sw. *Barranyi (North Island) National Park:* sun-drenched wilderness with long sandy beaches and excellent angling. No permit is required, but visitors are requested to register with the Borroloola Ranger Station. Offshore; (08) 8975 8792; 70 km NE. *Lorella Springs:* campground and caravan park at thermal springs. The road is unsealed and accessible only during the dry season; 170 km NW. *Limmen Bight River Fishing Camp:* ideal conditions for barramundi and mud crabs. Accommodation is available but check road access in wet season; 250 km NW. *Fishing charters:* river and offshore fishing trips; bookings at visitor centre. *Scenic flights:* over town and the islands of the Sir Edward Pellew Group; brochure at visitor centre.

See also GULF TO GULF, p. 381

Daly Waters

Pop. 20
Map ref. 634 H12 | 636 H3

 Daly Waters Pub, Stuart St; (08) 8975 9927.

106.1 FM ABC Territory Radio

The nearby springs, from which this tiny settlement takes its name, were named after the governor of South Australia by John McDouall Stuart during his south–north crossing of Australia in 1862. The town's size belies its historical importance as the first international refuelling stop for Qantas in 1935.

Daly Waters Pub Known as one of the great authentic Australian pubs with characters to match. The knickers donated by patrons and stapled to the beam above the bar have all been removed. Accommodation and meals are available with the menu including 'bumnuts on toast' and 'ambuggers'. Stuart St.

Campdraft: Sept.

Daly Waters Aviation Complex: display on local aviation in the oldest hangar in the NT (1930). Key available from Daly Waters Pub; off Stuart Hwy; 1 km NE. *Tree:* marked with an 'S', reputedly by explorer John McDouall Stuart; 1 km N. *Dunmarra:* roadhouse and accommodation; 44 km s. *Historic marker:* commemorates the joining of north and south sections of the Overland Telegraph Line; 79 km s. *Larrimah:* remains of historic WW II building at Gorrie Airfield and museum with relics of the local transport industry and WW II; 92 km N.

See also GULF TO GULF, p. 381

Elliott

Pop. 353
Map ref. 637 I5

Elliott Hotel, Stuart Hwy; (08) 8969 2069.

102.9 8KIN FM, 105.3 FM ABC Territory Radio

Elliott is a shady one-street town that is used as a cattle service stop. Stock being transported from the north are given a chemical tick bath here to prevent infection of herds in the south. The

town was named after Lieutenant Snow Elliott, the officer in charge of an army camp on this site during World War II.

 Nature Walk: interpretive signs introduce native flora and its traditional Aboriginal uses; details from visitor centre.

Mardi Gras: Apr.

Renner Springs This roadside stop on the Stuart Hwy is thought of as the place where the tropical Top End gives way to the dry Red Centre. It was named after Frederick Renner, doctor to workers on the Overland Telegraph Line. Dr Renner discovered the springs when he noticed flocks of birds gathering in the area. Fuel, supplies and meals are available and there are pleasant picnic and barbecue facilities. 91 km s.

Newcastle Waters: once-thriving old droving town featuring historic buildings and a bronze statue, The Drover; 19 km NW.

See also GULF TO GULF, p. 381

Glen Helen Resort

Map ref. 638 G7 | 640 C3

ⓘ Namatjira Dr; (08) 8956 7489; www.glenhelen.com.au

106.1 8ACR FM, 783 AM ABC Territory Radio

This small homestead-style resort is an excellent base for exploring the superb scenery of Glen Helen Gorge and other attractions in West MacDonnell National Park. Its facilities include accommodation, restaurant, bar, entertainment, tour information and an attractive natural swimming hole.

Glen Helen Gorge This breathtaking sandstone formation was created by the erosive action of the Finke River over thousands of years. There is a beautiful walk along the Finke River with towering cliffs providing a habitat for black-footed wallabies. Helicopter flights provide awe-inspiring views over Mt Sonder. 300 m E.

West MacDonnell National Park: majestic mountain range and wilderness surrounding Glen Helen Resort and featuring Ormiston Gorge (12 km NE), Ochre Pits (21 km E) and the Larapinta Trail; see *Alice Springs*. *Tnorala (Gosse Bluff) Conservation Reserve:* huge crater, 25 km in diameter, formed when a comet struck earth over 130 million years ago, with excellent views from Tylers Pass. Access permit, from visitor centre, is included with Mereenie Loop permit (Mereenie Loop links West MacDonnells with Kings Canyon Resort in the south-west); 50 km sw.

See also RED CENTRE, p. 382

Hermannsburg

Pop. 555
Map ref. 638 H7 | 640 D5

 Ntaria Supermarket; (08) 8956 7480; www.hermannsburg.com.au

106.1 8ACR FM, 783 AM ABC Territory Radio

This Aboriginal community lives on the site of a former mission station established by German Lutherans in 1877. During the first 14 years, they recorded the Arrernte language and culture, compiled an Arrernte dictionary and translated the New Testament into the local language. From 1894 to 1922 the mission was run by Pastor Carl Strehlow, who restored and constructed most of the extant buildings. His son, T. G. H. Strehlow, assembled a vast collection of anthropological items relating to the Arrernte way of life. Renowned artist Albert Namatjira,

JABIRU

Pop. 1140
Map ref. 633 O4 | 634 G5

ⓘ 6 Tasman Plaza; (08) 8979 2548.

📻 100.5 Flow FM, 747 AM ABC Territory Radio

Located deep within Kakadu National Park, Jabiru was first established because of the nearby uranium mine and, although this still operates, the town is now a major centre for the thousands who come to explore Kakadu each year.

🏠 **Gagudju Crocodile Holiday Inn** This NT icon is a 250 m crocodile-shaped building that really only resembles a crocodile from the air. The entrance (the mouth of the crocodile) leads to a cool marble reception area, designed to represent a billabong, and accommodation is in the belly of the beast. The design was approved by the Gagudju people, to whom the crocodile is a totem, and was a finalist at the prestigious Quaternario Architectural Awards in Venice. Flinders St.

Aurora Kakadu Lodge and Caravan Park: accommodation laid out in traditional Aboriginal circular motif; Jabiru Dr.

🌼 *Gubbalunya (Oenpelli) Open Day:* the Aboriginal community of Gunbalunya (Oenpelli) opens its doors to visitors, with sports, art and Aboriginal culture; Aug. *Mahbilil Festival:* music, dance and artistic expression celebrating Kakadu; Sept.

🍴 *Escarpment Restaurant:* stylish, modern Australian; Gagudju Crocodile Holiday Inn, Flinders St; (08) 8979 9000. *Jabiru Golf Club:* good, well-priced food; Jabiru Dr; (08) 8979 2575. *Jabiru Sports & Social Club:* steak, barra and Sunday roast; Lakeside Dr; (08) 8979 2326. *The Bark Hut Inn:* good pub fare; Arnhem Hwy, Annaburroo; (08) 8978 8988. *Mimi Restaurant:* relaxed, outdoor seating; Gagudju Lodge Cooinda, Kakadu Hwy, Jim Jim; (08) 8979 0145. *The Wetlands Restaurant:* buffet breakfast and dinner; Aurora Kakadu, Arnhem Hwy, South Alligator; (08) 8979 0166.

🛏 *Gagudju Crocodile Holiday Inn:* luxury rooms in a crocodile; Flinders St; (08) 8979 9000. *Aurora Kakadu:* comfortable mid-range accommodation; Arnhem Hwy, South Alligator; (08) 8979 0166 or 1800 818 845. *Cape Don Lighthouse:* historic lighthouse keeper's residence; Cobourg Peninsula; (08) 8979 0030. *Gagudju Lodge Cooinda:* comfort by the billabong; Kakadu Hwy, Jim Jim; (08) 8979 0145. *Mount Borradaile Safari Camp:* wilderness safari camp; Mt Borradaile, Arnhem Land; (08) 8927 5240. *Peppers Seven Spirit Bay Wilderness Lodge:* luxury coastal wilderness stay; Garig Gunak Barlu National Park, Cobourg Peninsula; (08) 8979 0281.

⊗ **Kakadu National Park** A World Heritage site listed for both its natural value and cultural significance, Kakadu is a place of rare beauty and grand landscapes, abundant flora and fauna, impressive rock art and ancient mythology. The largest national park in Australia, it encompasses the flood plain of the South Alligator River system and is bordered to the east by the massive escarpment of the Arnhem Land Plateau. The wide-ranging habitats, from arid sandstone hills, savannah woodlands and monsoon forests to freshwater flood plains and tidal mudflats, support an immense variety of wildlife, some rare, endangered or endemic. There are over 50 species of mammal, including kangaroos, wallabies, quolls, bandicoots, bats and dugong, as

[FLOOD PLAIN OF THE SOUTH ALLIGATOR RIVER, KAKADU NATIONAL PARK]

well as a plethora of reptiles and birdlife. With around 5000 rock-art sites, the park has the world's largest and possibly oldest collection of rock art, which reveals the complex culture of the Aboriginal people since the Creation Time, when their ancestors are believed to have created all landforms and living things. Nourlangie Rock shows a variety of styles including X-ray art, which illustrates the anatomy of humans and animals in rich detail. Other highlights of the park include Jim Jim Falls and Twin Falls, the Yellow Water wetland area, and sunset at Ubirr rock, with free ranger tours at 5pm each day from May–Nov. Also stop in at the Warradjan Aboriginal Cultural Centre in Cooinda, which features educational displays and exhibitions. *Travellers note: Kakadu is a special place. It is important to respect the land and its people and refrain from entering restricted areas such as sacred sites, ceremonial sites and burial grounds. For more information contact (08) 8938 1100.*

Tourist walk: 1.5 km stroll from town centre through bush to Bowali Visitor Centre, which features an audiovisual presentation and interpretive displays on Kakadu. *Scenic flights:* over Kakadu parklands to see inaccessible sandstone formations standing 300 m above vast flood plains, seasonal waterfalls, wetland wilderness, remote beaches and ancient Aboriginal rock-art sites; 6 km E. *Ranger Uranium Mine:* open-cut mine with educational tours available; bookings through tours office, 1800 089 113; 9 km E. *Aboriginal cultural tours:* day tours and cruises; contact visitor centre.

See also KAKADU & ARNHEM LAND, p. 379

KATHERINE

Pop. 5848

Map ref. 634 F8

[ENTRANCE TO KATHERINE GORGE SYSTEM]

ⓘ Cnr Lindsay St and Stuart Hwy; (08) 8972 2650 or 1800 653 142; www.visitkatherine.com.au

📻 101.3 Katherine FM, 106.1 FM ABC Territory Radio

Katherine, on the south side of the Katherine River, has always been a busy and important area for local Aboriginal groups, who used the river and gorge as meeting places. Explorer John McDouall Stuart named the river on his way through in 1862 after the second daughter of James Chambers, one of his expedition sponsors. The town grew up around an Overland Telegraph station and was named after the river. Today its economic mainstays are the Mount Todd goldmine, tourism and the Tindal RAAF airbase.

🏠 *Katherine Museum:* built as an air terminal in 1944–45, the museum houses artefacts, maps, photographs and farming displays. There is also memorabilia relating to Dr Clyde Fenton, who as a pioneer medical aviator and Katherine's Medical Officer between 1934 and 1937 serviced an area of 8 000 000 sq km in a second-hand Gypsy Moth he bought for £500. The plane is on display. Check opening times; Gorge Rd; (08) 8972 3945. *Railway Station Museum:* displays of the area's railway history with an old steam engine adjacent to the museum; closed weekends; Railway Tce. *School of the Air:* see displays about the history of the school and listen in on lessons; open Apr–Oct, closed on weekends; Giles St. *O'Keefe House:* built during WW II and used as the officers' mess, it became home to Sister Olive O'Keefe, whose work with the Flying Doctor and Katherine Hospital from the 1930s to 1950s made her a NT identity. The house is one of the oldest in town and is a classic example of bush ingenuity, using local cypress pine, corrugated iron and flywire; open 1–3pm Mon–Fri May–Sept; Riverbank Dr. *NT Rare Rocks:* unusual rock and gem displays; Zimmin Dr. *Self-guide walks:* including Pioneer Walk and Arts and Crafts Trail; brochures from visitor centre.

🎋 *Tick Markets:* Lindsay St; 1st Sat each month Apr–Sept. *Country Music Muster:* Apr/May. *Katherine Cup:* horseracing; May. *Canoe Marathon:* Aug. *Flying Fox Festival:* community festival, theatre and music; Aug.

🍴 *Katherine Country Club:* traditional Australian; Pearce St, off Victoria Hwy; (08) 8972 1276. *Katie's Bistro:* good cooking; Knotts Crossing Resort, cnr Giles and Cameron sts; (08) 8972 2511.

Kumbidgee Lodge Tea Rooms: barramundi a specialty; 4739 Gorge Rd; (08) 8971 0699. *The Carriage Stonegrill Restaurant & Bar:* hot-rock cooking; Paraway Motel, 35 First St; (08) 8972 2644. *The Katherine Club:* value-for-money; Cnr Second St and O'Shea Tce; (08) 8972 1250.

🛏 *Donkey Camp B&B:* rammed-earth homestead; Pandanus Farm, Lot 3233 Gorge Rd; (08) 8972 1986. *Hotel All Seasons Katherine:* modern tropical setting; Stuart Hwy; (08) 8972 1744. *Knotts Crossing Resort:* tropical landscape, rooms and cabins; Cnr Giles and Cameron sts; (08) 8972 2511. *Maude Creek Country Lodge:* private rustic retreat; Gorge Rd; (08) 8971 1814. *Top Springs Hotel:* pub oasis; Cnr Buchanan and Buntine hwys, Top Springs; (08) 8975 0767.

✴ **Nitmiluk National Park** This 292 800 ha wilderness is owned by the Jawoyn people and managed jointly with NT Parks & Wildlife Commission. The Katherine River flows through a broad valley that narrows dramatically between the high sandstone cliffs of the magnificent Nitmiluk Gorge. High above the floodline, on the overhangs of the ancient rock walls, are Aboriginal paintings thousands of years old. The best way to explore the gorge is by flat-bottomed boat (daily cruises; bookings at visitor centre), but canoe hire is available. Another highlight of the park is Edith Falls (Leliyn), which drops into a paperbark- and pandanus-fringed natural pool that is a popular swimming spot. There are signposted bushwalks, picnic areas and campsites. Fauna in Nitmiluk includes many reptile and amphibian species, kangaroos and wallabies in higher reaches and rare birds such as the hooded parrot and Gouldian finch. The countryside is at its best Nov–Mar although the weather is hot. (08) 8972 1886; 29 km NE.

Knotts Crossing: site of region's first Overland Telegraph station (1870s) around which the original township of Katherine developed. By 1888 there was a hotel, store and police station. The hotel lost its licence in 1916 and the store was given a Gallon Licence. The Gallon Licence Store (now a private residence) operated until 1942; Giles St; 2 km E. *Natural hot springs:* on the banks of the Katherine River with picnic facilities and pleasant walking trails; Victoria Hwy; 3 km S. *Low Level Nature Reserve:* weir built by US soldiers during WW II, now a popular waterhole for swimming and canoeing (bring own canoe). The river is teeming with barramundi, black bream and northern snapping turtles; 3 km S. *Springvale Homestead:* originally the home of Alfred Giles, this is the oldest remaining homestead in NT (1879). Accommodation, restaurant, swimming pool and camping; Shadforth Rd; 8 km W. *Cutta Cutta Caves Nature Park:* 1499 ha of the only accessible tropical limestone caves in the NT with fascinating formations 15 m underground; regular tours each day; 37 km SE. *Manyallaluk Aboriginal Community:* camping and Aboriginal cultural tours; bookings essential, (08) 8975 4727; 100 km NE. *Flora River Nature Park:* great campsites, interesting mineral formations, pools and cascades along the river; 110 km SW. *Tours:* magnificent scenery can be enjoyed from helicopter tours, scenic flights, 4WD safaris, barramundi fishing expeditions and horseback trail rides; brochures at visitor centre.

See also GULF TO GULF, p. 381

the first Aboriginal to paint landscapes in a European style, was born at the mission in 1902. In 1982 the mission and its land was returned to the Arrernte. Visitors are restricted to the shop, petrol station and historic precinct.

 Historic precinct The National Heritage–listed mission site comprises about 13 main buildings, mostly stone, the earliest dating from 1877 but generally from the period 1897–1910. They include Strehlow's House (1879), home of the pastor in charge of the mission and now Kata-Anga Tea Rooms with a reputation for delicious apple strudel; old manse (1888), currently a watercolour gallery housing work by Aboriginal artists of the Hermannsburg school (guided tours available); old schoolhouse (1896); tannery (1941); and Old Colonists House (1885), now a museum displaying historic items from the missionary era.

Finke Gorge National Park For millions of years the Finke River has carved its way through the weathered ranges, creating red-hued gorges and wide valleys. There are astonishing rock formations and dry creek beds that wind through sandstone ravines, where rare flora flourishes. The park's most famous feature, Palm Valley, is a refuge for about 3000 red cabbage palms (*Livistona mariae*), which are found nowhere else in the world. The 46 000 ha area is great for bushwalking: a 1.5 km climb leads to Kalarranga Lookout for views of the amazing Amphitheatre rock; the 5 km Mpaara Walk with informative signs explains the mythology of Western Arrernte culture; and the 2 km Arankaia Walk passes through the lush oasis of Palm Valley. Park access by 4WD only. (08) 8951 8290; 20 km s.

Monument to Albert Namatjira: a 6 m red sandstone memorial to the legendary artist; Larapinta Dr; 2 km E. *Wallace Rockhole Aboriginal community:* cultural tours and camping; 46 km SE.

See also RED CENTRE, p. 382

Jabiru

see inset box on previous page

Kings Canyon Resort

Map ref. 638 F8

ℹ️ Luritja Rd; (08) 8956 7442; www.kingscanyonresort.com.au

Kings Canyon Resort, in Watarrka National Park, is an excellent base from which to explore the region. It has various standards of accommodation, a petrol station, supermarket, laundry, tennis courts and swimming pools.

Watarrka National Park This park's many rock holes and gorges provide refuge from the harsh conditions for many species of plants and animals. The great attraction is Kings Canyon, an enormous amphitheatre with sheer sandstone walls rising to 270 m. The 870 m Carmichael Crag is known for its majestic colours, which are particularly vibrant at sunset. There are well-signed trails. The Rim Walk is a boardwalk through prehistoric cycads in the lush Garden of Eden and takes in unusual rock formations such as the Lost City. There are wonderful views across the canyon. The Kings Creek Walk is a 1 hr return walk along the canyon floor. The 6 km (3–4 hr) Kings Canyon Walk is rough going and recommended only for experienced walkers. Tours of the park include Aboriginal tours and scenic flights; brochures available from visitor centre. (08) 8951 8211.

Kings Creek Station: working cattle and camel station with campsites and accommodation. Quad (4-wheeled motorcycle),

helicopter and camel tours of the area; 36 km SE. *Mereenie Loop:* links Alice Springs, Kings Canyon, Uluṟu and Kata Tjuṯa via the West MacDonnell Ranges and Glen Helen. Permit required because a section of the route passes through Aboriginal land; map and permit from visitor centre.

See also RED CENTRE, p. 382

Mataranka

Pop. 249
Map ref. 634 H9

ℹ️ Stockyard Gallery, Stuart Hwy; (08) 8975 4530.

📻 106.1 FM ABC Territory Radio

Visitors are lured to Mataranka for its thermal springs and its sense of literary history. Jeannie Gunn, author of *We of the Never Never*, lived at nearby Elsey Station in the early 20th century. The town has adopted the term 'Never Never', using it to name a museum and a festival. Generally the phrase now refers to the vast remote area of inland northern Australia.

Stockyard Gallery: showcases NT artists' work, including leather sculpture; Devonshire teas available; Stuart Hwy. *Territory Manor:* restaurant and accommodation with daily feeding of barramundi at 9.30am and 1pm (open to the public); Stuart Hwy. *We of the Never Never Museum:* outdoor displays of pioneer life, railway and military history and the Overland Telegraph; open Mon–Fri; Stuart Hwy. *Giant termite mound:* sculpture with recorded information; Stuart Hwy.

Back to the Never Never Festival: celebration of the outback including a cattle muster; May. *Art show:* May. *Rodeo:* Aug.

Mataranka Homestead Tourist Resort: good food in bush setting; Homestead Rd; (08) 8975 4544. *Territory Manor Holiday Park:* barra and beef; Martin Rd, off Stuart Hwy; (08) 8975 4516.

Coodardie Station Stay: family station stay; Stuart Hwy; (08) 8975 4460. *Territory Manor Motel & Caravan Park:* surrounded by lush gardens; Martins Rd, off Stuart Hwy; (08) 8975 4516

Elsey National Park The park encircles the Roper River, with rainforest, paperbark woodlands, and tufa limestone formations at Mataranka Falls. The thermal pools at Mataranka Springs and nearby Bitter Springs are believed to have therapeutic powers. At Mataranka Thermal Pool water (34°C) rises from underground at the rate of 30.5 million litres per day to provide a beautiful swimming spot surrounded by palm trees. The Roper River offers excellent canoeing (hire available) and barramundi fishing. There are scenic walking tracks through pockets of rainforest with wildlife observation points and camping areas. The walk from Twelve Mile Yards leads to the small but beautiful Mataranka Falls. Mataranka Homestead Tourist Resort is a replica of Jeannie Gunn's home, Elsey Homestead, and offers accommodation and camping. The replica was used in the 1982 film *We of the Never Never*. (08) 8975 4560; 5 km E.

Elsey Cemetery: graves of outback pioneers immortalised by Jeannie Gunn, who lived on Elsey Station from 1902 to 1903; 20 km SE. *We of the Never Never:* a cairn marks the site of the original homestead near the cemetery; 20 km SE.

See also GULF TO GULF, p. 381

NORTHERN TERRITORY

Nhulunbuy

Pop. 4111
Map ref. 635 N4

 Chamber of Commerce, Endeavour Sq; (08) 8987 1985.

 106.9 Gove FM, 990 AM ABC Territory Radio

Located on the north-eastern tip of Arnhem Land on the Gove Peninsula, Nhulunbuy and its surrounds are held freehold by the Yolngu people. Originally a service town for the bauxite-mining industry, it is now the administrative centre for the Arnhem region and a pleasant and relaxed hideaway. Access is by a year-round daily air service from Darwin or Cairns or, with a permit, by four-wheel drive through Arnhem Land.

Gayngaru Wetlands Interpretive Walk The path surrounds an attractive lagoon that is home to around 200 bird species. There are 2 viewing platforms and a bird hide, as well as signs near local flora explaining their uses in Aboriginal food and bush medicine. Visitors can take the Winter walk or Tropical Summer walk, which is shorter as a result of higher water levels. Centre of Nhulunbuy.

Garma Festival: celebration of the arts and culture; Aug. *Beach Volleyball Day:* Sept. *Annual Ball:* Sept. *John Jones Memorial Billfish Classic:* Oct/Nov.

Katie's Kitchen: home-style cooking; Drimmie Head Rd; (08) 8987 3077. *Macassans Restaurant:* modern Australian; The Arnhem Club, 1 Franklyn St; (08) 8987 0600. *The Walkabout Lodge Restaurant:* modern Australian with good seafood; 12 Westal St; (08) 8987 1777. *Bistro Sea:* steak, seafood and Asian dishes; 35 Bougainvillea Dr, Alyangula; (08) 8987 7100. *Golf Shed Bistro:* Australian and Asian dishes; Alyangula Golf Club, 1 Alebewa Rd, Alyangula; (08) 8987 6060. *Seagrass Restaurant:* modern Australian with Asian influences; Dugong Beach Resort, 1 Bougainvillea Dr, Alyangula; (08) 8987 7077 or 1800 877 077.

Dugong Beach Resort: modern luxury cabins and rooms; 1 Bougainvillea Dr, Alyangula; (08) 8987 7077 or 1800 877 077. *Gove Peninsula Motel:* modern motel rooms; 1 Matthew Flinders Way; (08) 8987 0700. *Walkabout Lodge:* modern hotel; 12 Westal St; (08) 8987 1777.

Buku-Larrnggay Mulka This renowned community-based Aboriginal art museum was set up to educate visitors in the ways of local law and culture, and to share the art of the Yolngu people. 'Buku-Larrnggay' refers to the feeling on your face as it is struck by the first rays of the sun. 'Mulka' is a sacred but public ceremony and means to hold or protect. A permit is not required for a museum visit. Open Mon–Fri and Sat morning; (08) 8987 1701; 20 km SE.

Dhamitjinya (East Woody Island) and Galaru (East Woody Beach): island with long sandy beaches, tropical clear blue water and amazing sunset views; 3 km N. *Nambara Arts and Crafts:* traditional and contemporary Aboriginal art and craft; 15 km NW. *Tours:* include boat charters for outstanding game, reef and barramundi fishing, eco and cultural tours with Yolngu guides, 4WD tours, birdwatching and croc-spotting tours and bauxite-mine tours. Details from visitor centre.

Travellers note: Visitors intending to drive to Nhulunbuy must obtain a permit from the Northern Land Council beforehand, (08) 8987 8500; conditions apply. Allow 2 weeks for processing. A recreation permit is also required for travel outside the Nhulunbuy Town Lease, available from Dhimurru Land Management, (08) 8987 3992.

See also KAKADU & ARNHEM LAND, p. 379

Noonamah

Pop. 485
Map ref. 632 E4

 Noonamah Tavern, Stuart Hwy; (08) 8988 1054.

106.1 FM ABC Territory Radio

Noonamah is a tiny town outside Darwin at the centre of numerous parks and reserves. It is a great base to experience wildlife, native bushland and safe swimming spots (something of a rarity, considering the Northern Territory's crocodile population).

Bamurru Plains: luxury lodges; Swim Creek Station, Harold Knowles Rd; (02) 9571 6399 or 1300 790 561. *Eden at Fogg Dam:* tropical B&B; 530 Anzac Pde, Middle Point; (08) 8988 5599. *Mary River Houseboats:* explore the waterway by houseboat; Corroboree Billabong, off Arnhem Hwy; (08) 8978 8925. *Mary River Park:* bush cabins; Mary River Crossing, Arnhem Hwy; (08) 8978 8877. *Point Stuart Wilderness Lodge:* comfortable wilderness stay; Point Stuart Rd, Point Stuart; (08) 8978 8914.

Territory Wildlife Park This 400 ha bushland park provides an easy way to view native animals in their natural habitat. They can be seen from walking trails or a motorised open train. A tunnel leads through an extensive aquarium that represents a Top End river system, where visitors can come face to face with a 3.7 m crocodile. Other highlights include a bird walk, nocturnal house and daily show of birds of prey. 14 km SW.

Didgeridoo Hut: see Aboriginal craftspeople make didgeridoos and weave baskets and dilly bags. Works are for sale in the gallery and there is an emu farm on-site; 8 km N. *Lakes Resort:* great facilities for watersports including waterski and jetski hire; accommodation available; 10 km SW. *Berry Springs Nature Park:* safe swimming in spring-fed pools in a monsoon forest with pleasant walking trails and picnic areas; 13 km SW next to Territory Wildlife Park. *Jenny's Orchid Garden:* huge and colourful collection of tropical orchids, many on sale in the nursery; 22 km NW. *Howard Springs Nature Park:* Swim in the freshwater springs and see barramundi and turtles or relax with a picnic in the shade by the children's pool. 23 km NW. *Manton Dam:* safe swimming, fishing, watersports and shady picnic spots; 25 km S. *Tumbling Waters Holiday Park:* fauna enclosure and caravan park; 26 km SW. *Fogg Dam:* wetland with prolific wildlife that is best viewed at sunrise or sunset; 41 km NE. *Window on the Wetlands:* interpretive centre offering insight into the Top End's fascinating wetland environments plus superb views over the Adelaide River flood plains; 40 km NE (7 km beyond Fogg Dam turn-off). *Adelaide River Jumping Crocodile Cruises:* see crocodiles jump out of the water with the lure of food. Several tours each day; bookings on (08) 8988 8144; 41 km NE (next to wetlands centre). *Fishing:* excellent barramundi fishing at Mary River Crossing (45 km E of Fogg Dam turn-off); several 4WD tracks lead north from here to prime fishing spots in Mary River National Park such as Corroboree Billabong (houseboat hire available).

See also AROUND DARWIN, p. 380

Pine Creek

Pop. 256
Map ref. 633 I12 | 634 F7

 Diggers Rest Motel, 32 Main Tce, (08) 8976 1442; or Shire office, (08) 8976 1391.

96.7 Mix FM, 106.1 FM ABC Territory Radio

The town, officially called Playford until 1973, was named Pine Creek by Overland Telegraph workers because of the prolific pine trees growing along the banks of the tiny creek. Today the town benefits from the reopened goldmine, one of the largest open-cut goldmines in the Northern Territory.

 Railway Station Museum The station (1888) is at the terminus of the uncompleted 19th-century transcontinental railway system and now houses photographs and memorabilia. The historic Beyer Peacock steam train was built at Manchester in England in 1877 and used in the film *We of the Never Never* (1982). The adjacent Miners Park points to an important visible link between the railway and the mines, which depended on the railway for survival. There are interpretive signs and displays of old mining machinery that reflect life on the goldfields. Main Tce.

Water Gardens: ponds with walking trails, birdlife and picnic spots; Main Tce. *National Trust Museum:* once a doctor's residence, military hospital then post office, building now houses a historical collection, including a display on the Overland Telegraph; open 11am–5pm Mon–Fri and 11am–1pm Sat Apr–Oct, 1–5pm Mon–Fri Nov–Mar; Railway Tce. *Enterprise Pit Mine Lookout:* panoramic views of open-cut goldmine that was once Enterprise Hill, but is now a water-filled pit; Enterprise Pit. *Gun Alley Gold Mining:* features restored steam ore crusher and gold-panning tours; Gun Alley Rd. *Bird Park:* tropical birds in lush garden setting; Gun Alley Rd. *Old Timers Rock Hut:* rock and mineral display; Jenson St. *Town walk:* takes in historic buildings and mining sites; brochure from visitor centre.

Races: horseracing; May. *Gold Rush Festival and Gold-panning Championships:* June. *Rodeo:* June.

Mayse's Cafe: good Australian homemade food; 40 Moule St; (08) 8976 1241.

Grove Hill Heritage Hotel: rustic, comfortable hotel; Goldfields Rd, Grove Hill Siding, via Adelaide River; (08) 8978 2489.

Butterfly Gorge Nature Park This park is a wilderness of sheer cliff-faces, dense vegetation and scenic shady river walks. Butterfly Gorge was named for the butterflies that settle in its rock crevices and is a beautiful and safe swimming and picnic spot. Access is by 4WD only. Open only during the dry season (May–Sept); 113 km NW.

Copperfield Recreation Reserve: safe swimming in deep-water lake and picnicking on foreshore plus a Didgeridoo Jam held each May; 6 km SW. *Bonrook Lodge and Station:* wild horse sanctuary with trail rides and overnight camps; 6 km SW. *Umbrawarra Gorge Nature Park:* good swimming, rock-climbing and walking trails; 22 km SW. *Tjuwaliyn (Douglas) Hot Springs Park:* sacred place for Wagiman women with hot springs; camping available; off Stuart Hwy; 64 km NW. *The Rock Hole:* attractive secluded waterhole; 4WD access only (via Kakadu Hwy); 65 km NE. *Gold fossicking:* several locations; licence required (available along with maps from visitor centre). *Kakadu National Park:* best-known park in the Top End, this is a massive tropical savannah woodland and freshwater wetland. Highlights nearby include the spectacular views at Bukbukluk Lookout (87 km NE) and the beautiful falls and permanent waterhole at Waterfall Creek (113 km NE). See *Jabiru*.

See also **AROUND DARWIN, p. 380**

Tennant Creek

Pop. 2922
Map ref. 637 J9

 Peko Rd; 1800 500 879; www.barklytourism.com.au

102.1 8CCC FM, 106.1 FM ABC Territory Radio

According to legend, this settlement emerged when a beer wagon broke down here. Gold was found in the area in the early 1930s and the town grew rapidly in the wake of Australia's last great gold rush. Gold and copper deposits still account for its role as a centre for the Barkly Tableland, an area larger than Victoria.

Nyinkka Nyunyu Cultural Centre This centre was built near a Warumungu sacred site and its name means 'home of the spiky-tailed goanna'. Dioramas illustrate the history of the area, an Aboriginal art gallery showcases the Tennant Creek art movement, and bush tucker, dance performances and displays explain the Aboriginal people's relationship with the land. The centre is set in landscaped gardens, which have plants used for bush tucker and medicine and feature 2 dance rings: 1 for men and 1 for women. Paterson St.

Tennant Creek Museum: housed in historic Tuxworth Fullwood House, an old WW II army hospital (1942), this museum has a photographic collection and displays of early mine buildings and equipment, a 1930s police cell and a steam tractor engine; open 2–4pm May–Sept, other times by appt with the visitor centre; Schmidt St. *Purkiss Reserve:* pleasant picnic area with swimming pool nearby; Ambrose St. *Anyinginyi Arts:* authentic Aboriginal art and craft; Irvine St. *Self-guide tours:* scenic drives and heritage walk; brochure from visitor centre. *Historical building:* old Australian Inland Mission built in 1934 of prefabricated corrugated iron is the oldest building in town; Paterson St.

Drag Racing: Apr. *Show:* cooking, craft and camels; July. *Cup Day:* horseracing; Aug. *Desert Harmony Festival:* arts and culture; Aug/Sept.

Anna's Restaurant: steak, chicken and barra; Bluestone Motor Inn, 1 Paterson St; (08) 8962 2617. *Fernanda's Restaurant:* Mediterranean cuisine; 1 Noble St; (08) 8962 3999. *Jajjikari Cafe:* cafe food in terrific setting; Nyinkka Nyunyu, Paterson St; (08) 8962 2699. *Margo Myles Steakhouse:* scotch fillets and T-bones, as well as Indian and Thai dishes; Tennant Creek Hotel, Paterson St; (08) 8962 2227. *Memories Restaurant:* home-style cooking; Tennant Creek Memorial Club, 48 Schmidt St; (08) 8962 2474.

Barkly Homestead: comfortable cool rooms; Cnr Tablelands and Barkly hwys; (08) 8964 4549. *Bluestone Motor Inn:* modern comfortable rooms; 1 Paterson St; (08) 8962 2617. *Eldorado Motor Inn:* refreshing oasis near lake; 195 Paterson St; (08) 8962 2402. *Threeways Roadhouse:* comfortable outback cabins and rooms; Cnr Stuart and Barkly hwys; (08) 8962 2744.

Battery Hill This comprises an underground mine and operational gold-processing plant. Visitors can see a 10-head stamp battery, 1 of 3 in Australia still in working order. There are daily tours of a modern underground mine with working machinery that displays gold extraction and crushing techniques. Bill Allen Lookout, just past the battery, offers panoramic views, with plaques identifying significant sites. Off Peko Rd; 1.5 km E.

Tennant Creek Cemetery: pioneer graves with plaques telling stories of battles with the elements and joys and hardships of pioneer life; 2 km S. *Mary Ann Dam:* artificial dam ideal for swimming, canoeing, windsurfing and picnics; 5 km NE. *Juno*

YULARA

Pop. 983
Map ref. 638 E10 | 640 D9

 Ayers Rock Resort; (08) 8957 7888.

 99.7 FM ABC Territory Radio, 100.5 8HA FM

Yulara is a resort town that was built specifically to cater for visitors coming to see Uluṟu and Kata Tjuṯa. It offers excellent visitor facilities and food and accommodation for all budgets. Advance bookings for accommodation are essential.

Information Centre: displays of geology, history, flora and fauna; spectacular photographic collection.

Bough House Restaurant: buffet features bush tucker; Outback Pioneer Hotel and Lodge, Ayers Rock Resort, Yulara Dr; (08) 8957 7601. **Kuniya Restaurant:** modern Australian; Sails in the Desert Hotel, Ayers Rock Resort, 174 Yulara Dr; (08) 8957 7888. **Pioneer BBQ and Bar:** barbecue and native meats; Ayers Rock Resort, Yulara Dr; (08) 8957 7888. **Sounds of Silence:** alfresco modern Australian; Ayers Rock Resort, Yulara Dr; (08) 8957 7888 or 1300 134 044. **Winkiku:** seafood buffet; Sails in the Desert Hotel, Ayers Rock Resort, 174 Yulara Dr; (08) 8957 7888.

Desert Gardens Hotel: modern rooms with views; Ayers Rock Resort, Yulara Dr; (08) 8957 7888 or 1300 134 044. **Emu Walk Apartments:** self-contained apartments; Ayers Rock Resort, Yulara Dr; (08) 8956 2000 or 1300 134 044. **Longitude 131°:** luxury eco-camping; Yulara Dr; (08) 8957 7131 or 1300 134 044. **Outback Pioneer Hotel and Lodge:** reasonably priced rooms and cabins; Ayers Rock Resort, Yulara Dr; (08) 8957 7605 or 1300 134 044. **Sails in the Desert Hotel:** five-star accommodation; Ayers Rock Resort, 174 Yulara Dr; (08) 8956 2200 or 1300 134 044. **The Lost Camel Hotel:** modern studio-style apartments; Ayers Rock Resort, Yulara Dr; (08) 8957 7650 or 1300 134 044. **Curtin Springs Cattle Station & Wayside Inn:** rustic outback rooms; Curtin Springs, Lasseter Hwy; (08) 8956 2906. **Erldunda Station B&B:** cottage on working cattle station; Erldunda Station, off Stuart Hwy; (08) 8956 0997.

Uluṟu Australia's most recognisable natural landmark and the largest monolith in the world, Uluṟu features stunning Aboriginal rock-art sites that can be viewed on guided walks and tours around the base. These sites highlight the rock's significance

[ULUṞU]

for Aboriginal people. The traditional owners prefer visitors not to climb Uluṟu and there are countless tales of a curse befalling those who take a piece of the rock home as a souvenir. The spectacular changing colours of Uluṟu at sunrise and sunset are not to be missed. 20 km SE.

Uluṟu-Kata Tjuṯa Cultural Centre: designed in the shape of 2 snakes, with displays of Aboriginal culture and sales of artwork; on approach road to Uluṟu; 17 km s. **Kata Tjuṯa:** remarkable rock formations, with spectacular Valley of the Winds walk, fantastic views and a variety of flora and fauna; 50 km w. **Tours:** helicopter, coach and safari tours. The Uluṟu Experience Night Show offers viewing and narration of Aboriginal and European interpretations of the night sky; bookings at visitor centre or at reception in accommodation centres.

See also RED CENTRE, p. 382

Horse Centre: horseriding and cattle drives; bush camping facilities; 10 km E. **Telegraph Station:** restored stone buildings (1872), once the domain of telegraph workers, whose isolated lives are revealed by interpretive signs; key is available from Battery Hill Visitor Centre; 12 km N. **Nobles Nob:** once the richest open-cut goldmine in Australia, this was founded by William Weaber, who was totally blind, and Jack Noble, who had only one good eye; tours available; 16 km E. **The Pebbles:** spectacular in their quantity, these are miniature versions of the Devils Marbles (huge balancing boulders found north of Wauchope). The site is sacred to the Munga Munga women; 16 km NW. **Three Ways Roadhouse:** good roadhouse meals at the junction of Stuart and Barkly hwys, with memorial to John Flynn, founder of the Royal Australian Flying Doctor Service, nearby; 25 km N. **Memorial**

Attack Creek Historical Reserve: memorial marks the encounter between John McDouall Stuart and local Aboriginal people; 73 km N. **Goldmining tours:** includes tour of early goldmine and fossicking; brochure from visitor centre.

See also RED CENTRE, p. 382

Ti Tree

Map ref. 639 I3

 Ti Tree Roadhouse, Stuart Hwy; (08) 8956 9741.

105.9 8ACR FM, 107.7 FM ABC Territory Radio

This rest stop on the Stuart Highway took its name from nearby Ti Tree Wells, the source of plentiful sweet water in the 1800s.

Today the desert region supports remarkably successful fruit and vegetable industries.

 Red Sand Art Gallery: Pmara Jutunta art with exhibitions and sales; food available; Stuart Hwy. **Ti Tree Park:** picnic area and playground; Stuart Hwy.

Central Mt Stuart Historical Reserve: the sandstone peak was noted by John McDouall Stuart as the geographical centre of Australia; no facilities, but a monument at the base; 18 km N.

See also RED CENTRE, p. 382

Timber Creek

Pop. 227
Map ref. 634 D10 | 636 D2

Max's Victoria River Boat Tours, Victoria Hwy; (08) 8975 0850.

106.9 FM Territory Radio

In 1855 explorer A. C. Gregory was the first European to visit this area as he followed the Victoria River south from the Timor Sea. His boat was wrecked at the site of Timber Creek, where he found the timber he needed to make repairs. The town today is growing in importance as a stop on the journey from the Kimberley in Western Australia to the major centres of the Northern Territory and as a gateway to Gregory National Park.

Timber Creek Police Station Museum: displays of historic artefacts in restored police station (1908); open 10am–12pm Mon–Fri; off Victoria Hwy. **Office for Parks & Wildlife Commission of the Northern Territory:** information for travellers to Gregory and Keep River national parks; Victoria Hwy. **Tours:** boat and fishing tours, river cruises (with abundant crocodiles) and scenic flights; brochures from visitor centre.

Fishing competitions: Apr–May. **Rodeo:** May. **Campdraft and Gymkhana:** Sept.

Bullo River Station: great outback experience; Bullo River Station via Timber Creek; (08) 9168 7375.

Gregory National Park This is the NT's second largest national park with 2 sections covering 13 000 sq km of ranges, gorges, sandstone escarpments, remnant rainforest, eucalypts and boab trees. There are opportunities for boating, canoeing and bushwalking, scenic flights and cruises, as well as Aboriginal and European heritage sites. Gregory's Tree (in the Victoria River section to the east) stands at Gregory's campsite with historic inscriptions and audio presentation. The tree also has special significance for the Ngarinman people and is a registered sacred site. The spectacular dolomite blocks and huge cliffs of Limestone Gorge can be found in the Bullita section to the west. Bullita station has traditional timber stockyards, an old homestead, interpretive displays and shady camping spots in summer. Check with Parks & Wildlife Commission for current access details; (08) 8975 0888; 31 km W and 92 km E.

Jasper Gorge: scenic gorge with permanent waterhole and Aboriginal rock art; 48 km SE. **Victoria River Roadhouse:** rest stop where the Victoria Hwy crosses the Victoria River; cruises, fishing trips and accommodation; several scenic walks in the area including the Joe Creek Walk (10 km W); 92 km E. **Keep River National Park:** rugged scenery, Aboriginal rock art and wildlife. Most trails are 4WD only; check with Parks & Wildlife Commission for current access details; (08) 9167 8827; 180 km W.

See also GULF TO GULF, p. 381

Wauchope

Pop. 10
Map ref. 637 J11 | 639 J1

Wauchope Hotel, Stuart Hwy; (08) 8964 1963.

106.1 FM ABC Territory Radio

Wauchope (pronounced 'walk-up') was established to cater for the wolfram-mining and cattle-farming communities nearby. Today it is a service town and tourist destination thanks to its proximity to the popular Devils Marbles.

Wauchope Hotel Once catering to workers at the old Wolfram Mines, this desert oasis now offers fuel, meals (licensed restaurant and takeaway), various standards of accommodation and an adjacent campground. The walls of the pub are adorned with signed bank notes (a 'bush bank' where customers pin deposits to the wall to be retrieved on a later visit) and photographs of patrons. The landscaped beer garden features native birdlife including Bill the talking cockatoo. Stuart Hwy.

Wauchope Hotel and Roadhouse: rustic outback pub; Stuart Hwy; (08) 8964 1963. **Wycliffe Well Holiday Park:** variety of cabins and camping; Wycliffe Well, Stuart Hwy; (08) 8964 1966 or 1800 222 195.

Wycliffe Well This roadhouse was the first in the NT to be allowed to sell water (at a penny a gallon). Once a market garden supplying troops during WW II, it now features pleasant picnic lawns surrounding Wycliffe Lake. The area is said to be at a cross-section of energy lines and has had many alleged UFO sightings (ranked 5th in the world for the number of sightings). Wycliffe Well also claims to have Australia's largest range of beers, but any connection between that and the UFO sightings is yet to be proven. Accommodation available. 17 km S.

Devils Marbles: large, precariously balanced granite boulders; 8 km N. **Davenport Range National Park:** isolated area with important Aboriginal heritage and waterhole ecology sites; high clearance vehicles or 4WD access only; advise travel plans at the Wauchope Hotel; (08) 8962 4599; 118 km E.

See also RED CENTRE, p. 382

NORTHERN TERRITORY

QUEENSLAND is...

Snorkelling or scuba diving among fish and coral in the GREAT BARRIER REEF / A

daytrip to one – or more – of the GOLD COAST'S many theme parks / Four-wheel driving

on FRASER ISLAND'S BEACHES / Fossicking for gemstones around ANAKIE,

RUBYVALE, SAPPHIRE or WILLOWS GEMFIELDS / Discovering tropical rainforest in

[WHITEHAVEN BEACH, WHITSUNDAY ISLANDS NATIONAL PARK]

QUEENSLAND

DAINTREE NATIONAL PARK / Taking a ride on the KURANDA SCENIC RAILWAY, returning via the Skyrail Rainforest Cableway / Sailing in the WHITSUNDAYS / Walking through NOOSA NATIONAL PARK, followed by a coffee and shopping on HASTINGS STREET / Travelling on the GULFLANDER train between Normanton and the old goldmining town of Croydon

QUEENSLAND is Australia's second largest state and offers numerous idyllic holiday destinations. Myriad islands, cays and atolls are scattered along its 6973-kilometre coastline. The Great Barrier Reef offers the ultimate in diving, and there are 2000 species of fish, dugongs, turtles and extensive coral gardens, all protected by World Heritage–listing.

By contrast, the arid west gives visitors a chance to experience some of Australia's unique outback in towns such as Winton, established by those searching for the lost Burke and Wills expedition. Winton also has a special place in Australian folklore as the location of Dagworth woolshed where Banjo Paterson wrote the iconic *Waltzing Matilda* in 1895.

Two-thirds of Queensland lies above the Tropic of Capricorn. In the monsoonal Far North, visitors can venture into magnificent ancient rainforests, like those of the Daintree National Park, where cool respite lies in places such as the boulder-strewn Mossman Gorge.

South of Brisbane is the famous Gold Coast. With more waterways than Venice and 300 days of sunshine each year, it is the perfect place for swimming and surfing. The theme parks here will terrify and astound, while in the hinterland, an emerald-green paradise allows visitors to soak up magnificent views among waterfalls and rainforest trees.

[PANDANUS PALM, NOOSA NATIONAL PARK]

Captain James Cook and his crew were the first Europeans to unexpectedly enjoy the Queensland coast after they ran aground on a reef near Cape Tribulation in 1770. Dutch explorer Willem Jansz had sailed along the western side of Cape York 164 years earlier, but received a hostile reception from the local Aboriginal people.

European settlement of Queensland occurred quite late compared with the rest of Australia. In 1824 a convict station was built near Moreton Bay to cater for the most intractable prisoners from southern gaols, but after a year of active resistance by Aboriginal tribes it was abandoned and relocated to where Brisbane stands today.

In recent years Queensland has shaken off its reputation as a quiet backwater. This modern state is fast becoming the envy of the rest of the country with its stunning natural features, relaxed pace and languid lifestyle, all enhanced by a climate close to perfect.

[A PAIR OF RAINBOW LORIKEETS]

fact file

Population 4 450 400
Total land area 1 722 000 square kilometres
People per square kilometre 2.3
Sheep and cattle per square kilometre 12
Length of coastline 6973 kilometres
Number of islands 1955
Longest river Flinders River (840 kilometres)
Largest lake Lake Dalrymple (dam), 220 square kilometres
Highest mountain Mount Bartle Frere (1622 metres), Wooroonooran National Park
Highest waterfall Wallaman Falls (305 metres), Girringun (Lumholtz) National Park
Highest town Ravenshoe (930 metres)
Hottest place Cloncurry (average 37°C in summer)
Coldest place Stanthorpe (46 days per year begin at below 0°C)
Wettest place Tully gets 4300 millimetres per year, and has a giant gumboot to prove it
Sunniest town Townsville (average 300 days of sunshine per year)
Most remote town Birdsville
Major industries Sugar and mining
Most famous person Steve Irwin, the 'Crocodile Hunter'
Number of 'big things' 39
Best beach Whitehaven Beach, Whitsunday Island
Local beer XXXX

gift ideas

Arts and crafts (The Valley Markets, Brisbane) Quirky, unusual and interesting handmade arts, crafts and fashion. See Markets p. 408, 404 D1

Beer glasses (XXXX Brewery, Brisbane) A little something from Queensland's iconic XXXX brewery. See Milton p. 411, 402 D4

Pineapple souvenirs (Big Pineapple, Nambour) Take home your own slice of the Sunshine State, to eat or keep. See Nambour p. 467, 647 G4

Ginger products (Buderim Ginger Factory, Yandina) All Queensland grown and made, including everything from ginger chocolate to ginger perfume. See Yandina p. 482, 647 F3

'Crocodile Hunter' souvenirs (Australia Zoo, Beerwah) Choose from an incredible range of souvenirs from this internationally renowned zoo. See Landsborough p. 457, 647 F5

Macadamia nuts (Nutworks, Yandina) Delicious and unusual produce, as well as skin products from this working nut factory. See Yandina p. 482, 647 F3

Great Barrier Reef mementos (Reef HQ, Townsville) Beautiful photos, books and souvenirs of the Great Barrier Reef. See Townsville p. 480, 650 G10

Tropical fruit (Cairns & The Tropics region) Black sapote, soursop and carambola are just some of the Dr Seuss–sounding tropical fruits you can taste and purchase. Visit Cape Tribulation Exotic Fruit Farm at Lot 5, Nicole Dr, Cape Tribulation, and other producers around Far North Queensland. See Cairns & The Tropics p. 425, 657

Australian Arabica coffee (The Australian Coffee Centre, Mareeba) The Skybury Coffee company makes pure Arabica coffee from beans grown near the Great Dividing Range. See Mareeba p. 459, 650 D2

Vodka and liqueurs (Tamborine Mountain Distillery, North Tamborine) Award-winning vodka, schnapps and other liqueurs in hand-painted bottles from Australia's smallest pot still distillery. 87–91 Beacon Rd, North Tamborine. See North Tamborine p. 469, 645 E8

BRISBANE is...

A bike ride through the CITY BOTANIC GARDENS / Breakfast by the river at the

POWERHOUSE arts centre / People-watching on fashionable JAMES

STREET / City views from MOUNT COOT-THA / The latest blockbuster expo at

the GALLERY OF MODERN ART / Riverside dining at EAGLE STREET PIER / An

adventure climb on the STORY BRIDGE / Hugging a koala at LONE PINE KOALA

SANCTUARY / A stroll along the RAINFOREST WALK and a swim at STREETS

BEACH in South Bank / A CityCat ferry cruise on the BRISBANE RIVER

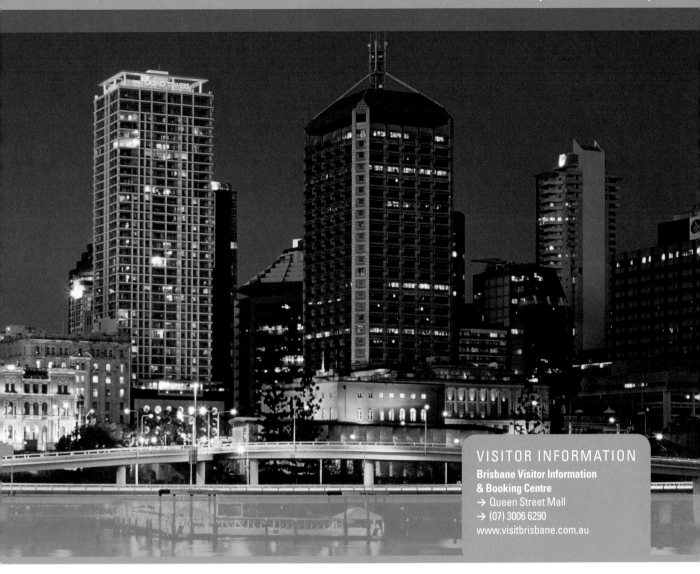

VISITOR INFORMATION
Brisbane Visitor Information & Booking Centre
→ Queen Street Mall
→ (07) 3006 6290
www.visitbrisbane.com.au

The subtropical climate may be warm, but Brisbane is decidedly cool. The population has doubled in the last two decades, and as a result, Brisbane has been busily reinventing itself. There is a lively young arts scene and the city has been ranked among the hottest places in the world for new music. Its young fashion designers are making a name for themselves, and the Gallery of Modern Art is bringing blockbuster exhibitions down under. But while the CBD skyline may be spiked by glittering high-rise buildings, and the river lined with big boats, thankfully, the city has lost little of its friendliness in the make-over. Life is as relaxed as ever, and firmly focused on the outdoors.

Brisbane's hilly terrain provides breathing space and a beautiful backdrop to the CBD. Step into the nearby suburbs and you will find stately Moreton Bay fig trees standing sentinel in the suburban streets and mango trees blooming in the backyards of those distinctive weatherboard houses on stilts known as 'Queenslanders'. With their shady verandahs and tin roofs just made for the patter of summer rain, you can still find them within walking distance of the CBD.

From the coast to the suburbs, the year-round warm climate means that Brisbane is tops for a holiday; whether you want city parks or national parks, markets or museums, nightlife or wildlife, you will find it all here.

City Centre

Despite the fact that it is the commercial and retail heart of Brisbane, the city centre retains the buoyant holiday spirit that pervades the entire Sunshine State. If you lose your way in the CBD grid, remember that the streets named after royal women all run north-east and parallel to each other, while the king-inspired streets run north-west.

Queen Street Mall 404 B4

With QueensPlaza, Myer Centre, Broadway on the Mall, the heritage-listed Brisbane Arcade and MacArthur Central (adjoining the GPO), Queen Street Mall offers something for everyone and is the hub of the CBD. Catering only to pedestrians (but with the central bus station conveniently located beneath), it is packed with people seven days a week. Along with a public stage, there are outdoor cafes and restaurants dotted down its centre. At the top (the George Street end) is the Conrad Treasury Casino *(see next entry)*, the Brisbane Square Library and surrounding eateries, and the bridge over to the South Bank parklands. At the other end, the mall leads onto ANZAC Square *(see below)* and Post Office Square. Cutting through the middle is Albert Street, leading to more shopping on Elizabeth Street, including the Elizabeth Arcade – a focus for edgy fashion – and Adelaide Street with the old Brisbane City Hall *(see below)* and the recently redeveloped King George Square. Get a literary insight into Brisbane by following the **Albert Street Literary Walk** – look for the 32 brass plaques in the pavement.

Conrad Treasury Brisbane 404 B4

One of Brisbane's spectacular buildings, the Treasury Building, built between 1885 and 1928, is now the Conrad Treasury casino. With restaurants, bars and live bands nightly, the casino is a top nightspot even if you don't want to play the tables. *George St; open 24 hours daily; admission free.*

ANZAC Square 404 C3

Popular with lunchtime office workers and foraging pigeons and herons alike, ANZAC Square, between Ann and Adelaide streets, is a peaceful retreat. The square's **Shrine of Remembrance**, built in 1930, honours the Australian soldiers who died in World War I with its eternal flame. In the pedestrian tunnel behind the square is the World War II **Shrine of Memories** (open Monday to Friday only) where you can see unit plaques, honour rolls and a mosaic made from hand-cut glass enamels and soils from official World War II cemeteries. From

ANZAC Square take the steps to the walkways over Adelaide Street to reach **Post Office Square**, another of Brisbane's grassy public squares. Opposite the square is the **General Post Office**, built in the 1870s; even with the busy post office crowds, you can still get an impression of its history.

Brisbane City Hall 404 B3

The newly revamped **King George Square** is a popular place for public gatherings, and it's here you will find the historic Brisbane City Hall. Built throughout the 1920s and opened in 1930, this impressive sandstone building is topped by a soaring 92-metre clock tower. Unfortunately there are no tours inside – City Hall is closed for repairs until late 2012. *Between Ann and Adelaide sts; (07) 3403 8888.*

Museum of Brisbane 404 B3

With City Hall closed for restoration, the Museum of Brisbane has moved to a temporary location just around the corner from King George Square. Also known as MoB, the museum has several exhibition spaces and celebrates the history, culture and people of Brisbane. Displays incorporate design, craft and visual arts. The MoB Store is a good spot to pick up something created by one of Brisbane's talented writers, artists or musicians. *157 Ann St; (07) 3403 4355; open daily; admission free.*

St John's Cathedral 404 C2

This striking example of Gothic-Revival architecture was designed in 1889 and construction began 17 years later. St John's has the distinction of being the last medieval construction project of its kind in the world.

climate

Queensland isn't called the 'Sunshine State' for nothing, and with an average of 300 days of sunshine each year, the south-east corner has (according to many) the most liveable climate in the state and possibly the country. Summers are hot and steamy; winters are mild and dry. Summer days in Brisbane average in the high 20s or low 30s. The hot days often build up to spectacular evening thunderstorms, and Brisbane's annual rainfall of approximately 1200 mm occurs mostly in summer. In winter the average temperature is 21°C – a very pleasant 'winter' for anyone from down south! Winter evenings can be a bit cool though, so make sure you pack at least one jumper.

J	F	M	A	M	J	J	A	S	O	N	D	
29	29	28	26	23	21	20	21	24	25	27	28	MAX °C
21	21	19	16	13	10	9	10	12	15	18	20	MIN °C
113	121	76	63	122	70	27	35	32	65	102	114	RAIN MM
8	8	7	7	7	5	3	3	4	5	9	9	RAIN DAYS

QUEENSLAND

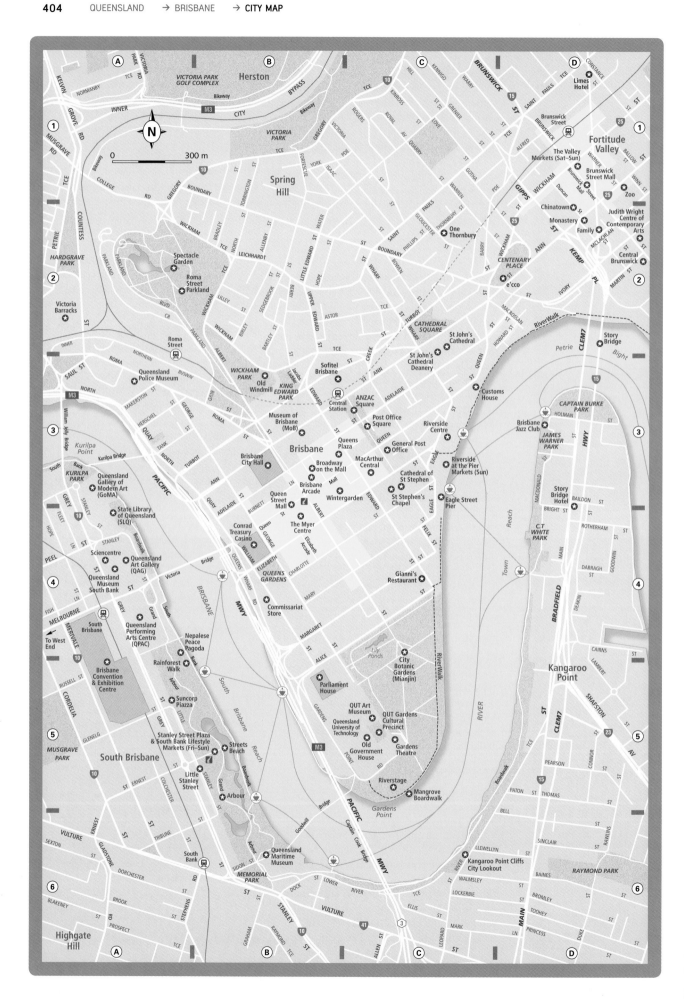

The original project ran out of funds and remained unfinished until, thanks to a recent injection of capital, was finally completed 120 years after it was originally conceived. It has the only fully stone-vaulted ceiling in Australia, as well as extensive woodcarvings by Queensland artists, 350-million-year-old fossiliferous marble and beautiful stained-glass windows. Next to the cathedral is the **Deanery**, built in 1850 and formerly the residence of Queensland's first governor, Sir George Bowen. Free tours are conducted daily. *373 Ann St; (07) 3835 2231.*

Cathedral of St Stephen 404 C3

This magnificent cathedral is a quiet place of worship amid the hustle and bustle of the city. The cathedral grounds include **St Stephen's Chapel**, the oldest surviving church in Queensland. Guided tours are available. *249 Elizabeth St; (07) 3336 9111.*

Commissariat Store 404 B4

Built by convicts in 1829 from Brisbane tuff – a local stone quarried at nearby Kangaroo Point – this is one of the oldest buildings in Brisbane (with newer additions). Today it is home to the offices, library and museum of the Royal Historical Society of Queensland. There is a convict display, and tours are available. *115 William St; (07) 3221 4198; open Tues–Fri.*

Foreshore

The serpentine Brisbane River curves its way through the whole city and seems to be everywhere at once. It is the place for award-winning restaurants, cafes and spectacular vistas. Ferries and CityCats stop at the Riverside Wharf and near the Botanic Gardens. The RiverWalk links many of the city's attractions. Hire a bike in the Botanic Gardens – it is a great way to see everything without having to mix it with the road traffic.

Customs House 404 C3

Built in 1889 and beautifully restored, this magnificent building on the Brisbane River served as the city's Customs House for almost a century until port activities shifted closer to the mouth of the river. Now a cultural and educational facility of the University of Queensland, it has function rooms and a brasserie with waterfront tables. On Sundays there are free guided tours. *399 Queen St; (07) 3365 8999; open daily; admission free.*

Riverside Centre & Eagle Street Pier 404 C3

These two neighbouring office precincts dominate the CBD reach of the river. By day they are the busy hub of corporate Brisbane, and their riverside cafes, bars and restaurants are packed with city professionals. At night the precincts turn on the glamour, and with the city lights twinkling on the water it's here you will find some of Brisbane's best-known and most-awarded restaurants. On Sundays they transform themselves once again, into the popular **Riverside at the Pier Markets** *(see Markets, p. 408)*. It's worth having a coffee on the boardwalk just to enjoy the views of the landmark **Story Bridge**, the largest steel cantilever bridge in Australia.

City Botanic Gardens 404 C5

These beautiful historic gardens, established in 1855 right in the heart of the city, are Queensland's oldest public gardens and recognised for both their natural and historic heritage. You can spend hours strolling along the avenues lined with majestic bunya pines and Moreton Bay figs, exploring the rainforest glade or taking the **Mangrove Boardwalk** along the bank of the river. Hidden gardens and shady nooks provide secluded picnic spots and, if you take the riverside path, you can enjoy stunning views of the river and Kangaroo Point Cliffs. Take a free guided tour, hire a bike or, if exercise isn't on the agenda, simply sit on the grassy foreshore and enjoy the views of the river and Kangaroo Point Cliffs. *Gardens Point, Alice St.*

QUEENSLAND

getting around

Brisbane has well-signed, well-maintained roads, but it's not an easy city for first-time visitors to negotiate. The region's growth has resulted in a crisscrossing network of major motorways and some significant new roadwork projects. In the centre itself, there are many one-way streets. To make matters more confusing, the Brisbane River twists its way through the city and suburbs. An up-to-date road map and some careful route planning at the beginning of each day is a good idea. As the city has grown more crowded, cycling has become a viable and healthy option for getting around and more locals are taking to their bikes. Brisbane boasts an ever-expanding network of generally picturesque bikeways and pedestrian paths. The Cycle2City facility under King George Square is a first for Australia and offers showers, lockers, laundry and bike security for local city workers and visitors alike.

Trains, buses and ferries cater for all needs and a couple of bus routes are designed specifically for visitors *(see below)*. A boat trip on the Brisbane River is a must. Plenty of tours are available to riverside tourist attractions *(see Walks & tours, p. 411)* and there is an excellent commuter ferry and catamaran (CityCat) service. The Cats travel at high speed and standing on the deck and feeling the cool wind in your hair is the best way to see Brisbane. The Go Card can be used on all transport – ferries, trains and buses – and offers discounts for frequent users. The Off Peak Daily offers cheaper travel between 9am and 3.30pm and on all weekends and gazetted public holidays.

Public transport Translink (bus, ferry, CityCat and rail) 13 1230.

Airtrain Train from the airport to the city and Gold Coast 1800 119 091.

Airport shuttle bus Coachtrans Airport Service (07) 3358 9700.

Motoring organisation RACQ 13 1905, roadside assistance 13 1111.

Car rental Avis 13 6333; Budget 1300 362 848; Europcar 1300 131 390; Hertz 1300 132 607; Thrifty 1300 367 227.

Taxis Black and White Cabs 13 1008; Yellow Cabs 13 1924.

Bus tours City Sights bus tours and The Loop (free bus circling the CBD) 13 1230.

Bicycle hire Bicycle Revolution (07) 3342 7829; Valet Cycle Hire Botanic Gardens 0408 003 198.

shopping

Queen Street Mall Brisbane's premier shopping precinct, with major department stores, malls and arcades including QueensPlaza, Myer Centre, Brisbane Arcade, MacArthur Central and Wintergarden. Also young labels in Elizabeth Street. Everything you'll ever need for retail therapy. 404 B4

Fortitude Valley For up-and-coming designer fashion and innovative chic, collectibles and books, art and trendy homewares, adventure gear and trinkets. 402 E3

Emporium More than 35 specialty retailers offering top-end fashion, jewellery, art, books, wine and food. 402 E3

Little Stanley Street, South Bank Edgy designer fashion, boutique homewares and gifts. 404 B5

Paddington For antiques, fashion and boutique homewares on Latrobe and Given terraces. 402 C3

Logan Rd, South Brisbane A quirky street of antiques, edgy fashion, accessories and homewares. 402 E5

Westfield Chermside Shopping Centre Huge mall on Brisbane's north side with 350 specialty stores, all the major department stores and a 16-cinema complex including a Gold Class theatre. 644 E6

Indooroopilly Shopping Centre A mall in Brisbane's western suburbs with over 250 specialty shops, major department stores, a gym and a 16-cinema complex. Fabulous shopping. 402 B5

Direct Factory Outlet (DFO) Brisbane Next to Brisbane Airport, this centre offers up to 120 discounted brands. 644 F6

Stones Corner Factory outlets and fashion seconds only 15 minutes south of the CBD. 402 E5

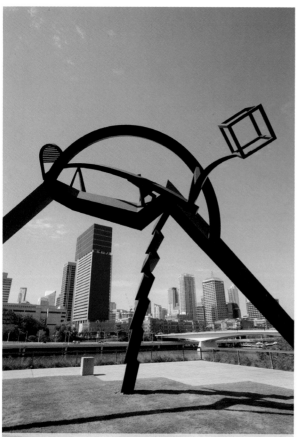

[SCULPTURE AT THE QUEENSLAND GALLERY OF MODERN ART]

QUT Gardens Cultural Precinct 404 C5

Launched in 2000, Queensland University of Technology's Gardens Cultural Precinct, at Gardens Point next to the City Botanic Gardens, encompasses **Old Government House**, the QUT Art Museum and the Gardens Theatre. Now run by QUT, the graceful sandstone Old Government House, built in 1860, was home to the Queensland governor for most of the state's first 50 years. *(07) 3138 8005; open 10am–5pm Sun–Fri; admission free.*

QUT Art Museum is housed in a 1930s neoclassical building and shows QUT's art collections, work by students and diverse contemporary exhibitions. *Open 10am–5pm Tues–Fri, 10am–8pm Wed, 12–4pm Sat–Sun; admission free.*

The cultural venue of the **Gardens Theatre** offers shows by QUT students and visiting international and Australian theatre companies.

Parliament House 404 B5

Overlooking the City Botanic Gardens, this grand old seat of government was built in 1868 (new buildings have since been added to the precinct). The two sandstone wings hold majestic staircases, stained-glass windows and ornate chandeliers. Fringed with palms, the parliamentary precinct is a showcase of Queensland's history. Watch the Queensland State Parliament in action from the visitors' gallery when the House is sitting, or when it's not in session take one of the 30-minute tours that are run on demand. *Cnr George and Alice sts; (07) 3406 7562; open daily; admission free.*

Roma Street Parkland & Surrounds

Formerly rail yards and engine sheds, this area has been transformed by the creation of the Roma Street Parkland. New pedestrian links give access from the city centre, so it is an easy stroll when you need a break from Queen Street shopping. If you are coming into town via train, hop off at Roma Street Station and head to the Queensland Police Museum nearby. The museum has displays on themes such as police heritage, the Dog Squad and police investigative techniques. Open 9am–4pm Mon–Fri, 10am–3pm last Sun of the month. The military museum at Victoria Barracks has a collection of weapons and medals from 1899 to 1980. Open 12–4pm Sun (or by appt).

Old Windmill 404 B3

Brisbane's oldest convict-built structure on Wickham Terrace is also Australia's oldest extant windmill. Built in 1828 to grind flour, it was also used as a treadmill for punishment. In 1861 it was converted into a signal station. Since then it has been used as both an observatory and a fire tower, and in 1934 the first successful experimental television transmittal was made from it. It no longer has its original sails and treadmill, but it remains as an evocative reminder of the convict past. An information board lists its fascinating history and it is a pleasant walk from the CBD up the Jacobs Ladder steps through the leafy King Edward Park.

Roma Street Parkland 404 A2

This huge subtropical garden is a wonderful haven in Brisbane's city centre and an easy walk from Queen Street through King George Square. The 16 hectares of parkland include landscaped gardens, Queensland's largest public art collection and hundreds of unique plants. Meander along the network of pathways or simply escape from the summer heat under the shade of one of the many mature trees. Kids can spend time in the playground or play on the Celebration Lawn. There is a lake precinct and a subtropical rainforest, and the **Spectacle Garden** is the parkland's horticultural heart. Enjoy a barbecue in one of the many picnic areas or have someone else do the cooking at the parkland's cafe. There are brochures for self-guide themed walks, or you can take a guided tour or hop on the trackless train that travels the paths.

South Bank

Set aside a day to spend at South Bank; with its large areas of parklands and some of Queensland's major cultural institutions, it's one of Brisbane's favourite places to play and celebrate. On the opposite side of the river to the CBD, it is an easy walk across Victoria Bridge from Queen Street, or the pedestrian-and-cycle-only Goodwill Bridge. Throughout the year thousands gather here for Christmas and New Year parties, and events such as the Brisbane Festival with its Riverfire pyrotechnic extravaganza. There are also regular concerts and multicultural events.

The Arbour

The beautiful kilometre-long Arbour – created by tendril-like metal columns covered in vibrant magenta bougainvillea – winds through the length of the South Bank precinct. Along the way, stop to watch some of the free entertainment – from buskers and street performers to international acts in the 2600-seat **Suncorp Piazza**. For something more peaceful, discover the ornate **Nepalese Peace Pagoda** set among tropical rainforest trees or take a detour and stroll along the shady **Rainforest Walk**, a raised boardwalk through the sort of subtropical vegetation for which Queensland is famed.

Kangaroo Point

You can walk east along the **Cliffs Boardwalk** to watch rock climbers and abseilers do their stuff on **Kangaroo Point Cliffs**, located on the bend of the river beyond the Captain Cook Bridge. If you're keen, you can learn to abseil on the spot. From the Kangaroo Point Cliffs City Lookout there are great views of the city.

Streets Beach 404 B5

A sandy beach right in the centre of Brisbane, Streets Beach has a crystal-clear lagoon with enough water to fill five Olympic swimming pools. Patrolled by lifesavers and with views across the Brisbane River to the CBD, the lagoon is tops with kids and sunbathers alike. Surrounded by tropical palms, there are plenty of barbecues and covered picnic areas.

South Bank Boardwalk

Walking or cycling along the riverside boardwalk is a great way to see the sights of South Bank. The precinct is also a popular eating spot, with more than 50 cafes, restaurants and bars, many overlooking the river. There are plenty of shady spots to sit back, relax and enjoy a good meal or a coffee among sculptures, tropical foliage and water features. For a great day out with the family there are exceptional barbecue areas ideal for private groups.

Queensland Performing Arts Centre 404 A4

This is the place for theatre, music and opera. The Cremorne Theatre is dedicated to experimental theatre; the Playhouse offers cutting-edge technology in stage design; the Lyric Theatre is the flagship of the centre, hosting everything from Opera Queensland performances to the latest blockbuster musical; and the Concert Hall is home to regular performances by the Queensland Orchestra as well as international classical, jazz and pop artists. At the ground-floor entrance of the Cremorne Theatre is the Tony Gould Gallery, the exhibition space for the **QPAC Museum**, which displays exhibitions related to the performing arts. There are cafes and a restaurant, perfect for post-theatre suppers. Guided tours of the centre must be booked in advance. *Cnr Grey and Melbourne sts; guided tours (07) 3840 7444; general admission free.*

Queensland Museum South Bank 404 A4

This excellent museum has an extensive natural history collection, including a fascinating endangered species exhibit, and displays on Queensland's Indigenous and European history. Interactive displays for kids sit alongside the skeleton of a humpback whale and dinosaur displays. Plan to spend a few hours here and take in **Sciencentre**, an interactive science experience. *Cnr Grey and Melbourne sts; open daily; general admission free.*

Queensland Art Gallery

Overlooking the Brisbane River, Brisbane's premier cultural attraction houses the state's permanent art collection as well as regular special exhibitions. Not to be missed is the Watermall, an internal feature that runs the entire length of the building and is flooded with natural light from a huge skylight. Free guided tours are available. The **Queensland Gallery of Modern Art (GoMA)**, which opened at the end of 2006, showcases cutting-edge contemporary art and is home to the highly successful Asia–Pacific Triennial of Contemporary Art. GoMA's architecture is equally impressive, encouraging a connection between the

top events

Paniyiri Greek Festival Enjoy Greek food, dance, music, cooking classes and live entertainment as Musgrave Park, South Brisbane, is transformed with markets, tavernas and all things Greek. May.

Queensland Winter Racing Carnival Excitement on and off the racecourse. May–June.

Brisbane International Film Festival Superb showcase of the latest in Australian and overseas film, with an international atmosphere. July–August.

Ekka (Royal Queensland Show) A Brisbane institution where the city meets the country for ten days, with fireworks and wild rides. August.

Brisbane Festival Queensland's largest celebration of the performing and visual arts, featuring fireworks, fantastic food and live music. September–October.

Brisbane Jazz Festival at the Powerhouse Some of the world's most acclaimed musicians perform innovative jazz. November.

Woodford Folk Festival Huge award-winning folk festival, just out of Brisbane, with local, national and international musicians and artists, and lots of stalls. December.

markets

Riverside at the Pier Markets Open-air markets on the city reach of the Brisbane River at Waterfront Place, with bric-a-brac, craft, fashion, food. Sun. 404 C3

South Bank Lifestyle Markets Street performances, art and craft, jewellery and live music. Fri night and Sat–Sun. 404 B5

The Valley Markets Brisbane's alternative markets, with vintage clothing, tarot readings, gifts, old books and an exciting atmosphere. Brunswick St Mall and Chinatown Mall; Sat–Sun. 404 D1

Farmers Markets at the Powerhouse Mix in with the locals combing the stalls for locally grown, farm-fresh produce, gourmet food, cut flowers and fresh seafood, all in the atmospheric surrounds of the Brisbane Powerhouse. New Farm, 2nd and 4th Sat each month. 403 F4

Davies Park Market West End Friendly, cosmopolitan markets on the river at Davies Park, West End, with fruit and veg, plenty of organics, bargains, art and craft, and free entertainment. Sat. 402 C4

Northey Street City Farm Organic Growers Markets Brisbane's only completely organic market, with organic produce and a nursery, set in a permaculture garden at Northey Street City Farm, Windsor. Sun. 402 E3

art and the public, and offering river views. *Stanley Pl; open 10am–5pm Mon–Fri, 9am–5pm Sat–Sun; general admission free.*

State Library of Queensland 404 A4

The State Library of Queensland must rank as one of the most beautiful repositories of books, archives, manuscripts, images, prints and maps you'll find anywhere. There are regular exhibitions and events (visit www.slq.qld.gov.au for details). *(07) 3840 7666; open 10am–8pm Mon–Thurs, 10am–5pm Fri–Sun.*

Queensland Maritime Museum 404 B6

No maritime enthusiast should miss this local institution, which is self-funded and run by volunteers. There are three galleries displaying relics, memorabilia and exhibits, such as a wall map of vessels lost in Queensland seas – more than 1500 since the

where to eat

Anise Bistro & Wine Bar Exciting small bar and equally exciting food at this tiny French treasure. 697 Brunswick St, New Farm; (07) 3358 1558; open Fri–Sat for lunch and Mon–Sat for dinner. 402 E4

Bretts Wharf Delicious seafood caught sustainably from local commercial fishers. 449 Kingsford Smith Dr, Hamilton; (07) 3868 1717; open daily for lunch and dinner. 403 F3

e'cco Fabulous modern Australian bistro; one of the very best in town. 100 Boundary St; (07) 3831 8344; open Tues–Fri for lunch and Tues–Sat for dinner. 404 D2

Gianni's Restaurant Mediterranean and Australian with an innovative and constantly changing menu using local seasonal produce. 12 Edward St; (07) 3221 7655; open Tue–Fri for lunch and Tue–Sat for dinner. 404 C4

Montrachet Local pinnacle of French cuisine; fun and relaxed with superb seafood. 224 Given Tce, Paddington; (07) 3367 0030; open Mon–Fri for lunch and Mon–Thurs for dinner. 402 D3

first recorded wreck in 1791. Look for displays on sailing, old diving equipment and the navigation instruments used by early explorers of Queensland's coastline; there's also an impressive collection of historic seagoing craft, ocean-liner replicas and nautical machinery. In the Dry Dock explore Australia's only remaining World War II frigate, HMAS *Diamantina*. You can also see a coal-fired, steam-powered 1925 tug, the SS *Forceful*. *Sidon St; open daily.*

Grey Street precinct 404 B5

The success of South Bank has spilled over into the adjoining area, especially Little Stanley and Grey streets, where you will find cafes and shops and people out and about enjoying the sunshine. **Little Stanley Street** is home to designer fashion stores, gourmet food shops and great cafes, bars and restaurants. Closed to traffic, **Stanley Street Plaza** also has eateries aplenty and buzzes day and night. **Grey Street**, a grand tree-lined boulevard, has shops, cafes, a hotel and a cinema complex as well as the nearby **Brisbane Convention and Exhibition Centre**, a 7.5-hectare complex used for regular trade and retail exhibitions.

Fortitude Valley

Known by the locals simply as 'the Valley', this cosmopolitan area of inner-city Brisbane is a fascinating mix of seedy history, stylish restaurants and alternative-lifestylers. These days it's more hip than hippie, and still dances to a rock 'n' roll beat as the seeding ground for young bands making their way onto the world stage. In 2007, Brisbane was named among the five hottest spots in the world by US magazine Billboard. *First settled in 1849 by 256 free settlers who arrived in Moreton Bay aboard the SS* Fortitude, *the Valley still retains much of its 19th-century heritage. Its old buildings are home to many private art galleries and artists' studios. The creative hub is the Judith Wright Centre of Contemporary Arts.*

Brunswick Street Mall 404 D1

Dominated for almost a century by the McWhirters building, formerly a department store and now stylish apartments with shops at street level, Brunswick Street is packed with shoppers at weekends cruising through the **Valley Markets** where the vibe is busy but always relaxed *(see Markets, this page)*. Free bands play in the mall on Saturdays and Sundays, and at night crowds flock to the restaurants and nightclubs. Enjoy the alfresco dining at any time of day. Further up Brunswick Street, you will find another foodies' delight at **Central Brunswick**. For cutting-edge fashion go to Ann Street which runs across Brunswick Street, or to the TCB – formerly the TC Beirne Building – which links Chinatown with Brunswick Street Mall. Further down Ann Street there are more pubs and bars, including the GPO, in the old Fortitude Valley Post Office.

Chinatown 404 D2

Brisbane's Chinatown is a sensory delight. Restaurants offer excellent value and even better yum cha, supermarkets have traditional Chinese treasures and the busy Valley Markets extend into Chinatown at weekends. Elements of feng shui were used in the design of this mall on Duncan Street and you can expect to see peaceful practitioners of tai chi there on weekends. If you are in Brisbane in late January/early February, head to Chinatown for Chinese New Year celebrations.

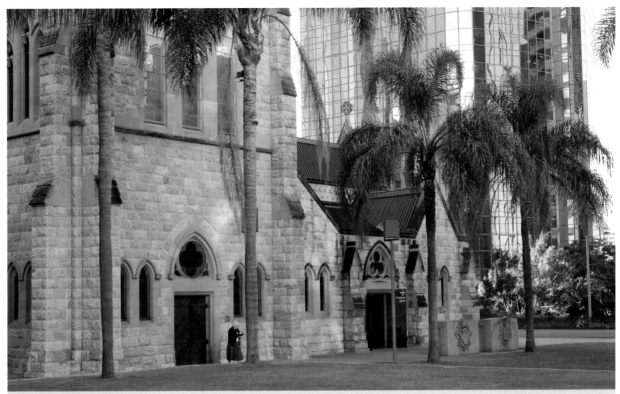

[CATHEDRAL OF ST STEPHEN]

James Street precinct 402 E3

Lined with shade trees, James Street is Brisbane's hottest new lifestyle precinct, where homewares and furniture stores cater to the cashed-up new inner-city residents, while outdoor cafes, restaurants and bars satisfy appetites for good coffee, fine dining and cocktails. The **James Street Market** is an excellent spot for picking up fresh food and produce along with flowers, nuts and juices. The **Centro** development includes a cinema complex. A short walk across Ann Street, **Emporium** has a big 'village square' of outdoor cafes, restaurants, high-end fashion shops, gifts and bookshops. A French-inspired hotel is here, along with the adjoining French restaurant and patisserie Belle Epoque.

New Farm & Newstead

Adjoining Fortitude Valley are other lively suburbs well worth a visit. New Farm is located on a peninsula created by the deep curves of the Brisbane River. Further along the river, Newstead and Teneriffe's historic wool stores and warehouses have been converted into stylish apartments, cafes and shops.

New Farm Park 403 F4

Originally an 1846 racecourse until it was bought by the Brisbane City Council in 1913, New Farm Park is a favourite spot for locals at any time, in any season. Stroll through the rose garden, picnic under the trees, listen to a band in the Rotunda, contemplate the river, and let the kids loose in the much-prized playground. First settled in the 1800s, the inner-city suburb of New Farm has a growing population and changing dynamic. The strongly Italian local community has now been joined by fashion-conscious

young inner-urbans. There is still a village feel, however, with outdoor cafes, fashion shops, art galleries and bookshops.

Newstead & Teneriffe Renewal Project 403 F3

Between New Farm and Breakfast Creek, these suburbs once encompassed one of Brisbane's major industrial precincts. Its deep-water frontage made it the perfect dock for ships and in the late 19th century a railway was built, bringing export wool from the booming inland sheep properties. In 1987 development zoning was changed from industrial to high-density residential, and these days the rugged industrial architecture of the old wool stores, warehouses, wharves and laneways provides the framework for stylish restaurants, cafes and bars, and antiques and homewares shops.

where to stay

Emporium Hotel Modern, luxury boutique hotel in a precinct of up-market shops and restaurants, just a short walk to Fortitude Valley. 1000 Ann St, Fortitude Valley; (07) 3253 6999 or 1300 883 611. 402 E3

Limes Hotel Australia's first Design Hotel; each of the 21 rooms has a balcony or courtyard with hammock, plus there's a rooftop bar. 142 Constance St, Fortitude Valley; (07) 3852 9000. 404 D1

One Thornbury Boutique B&B in a character building built in 1886, close to CBD and Fortitude Valley. 1 Thornbury St, Spring Hill; (07) 3839 5334. 404 C2

Sofitel Brisbane Luxury in an unbeatable location with proximity to the CBD and adjacent Central Railway. 249 Turbot St; (07) 3835 3535. 404 B3

QUEENSLAND

entertainment

Cinema Major cinemas can be found at the Myer Centre in the city (a Birch Carroll & Coyle complex) and at most of the big suburban malls. See the *Courier-Mail* for movie times. If you're in town in August you can catch the Brisbane International Film Festival (BIFF). Brisbane is a city devoted to film festivals. Look out for them throughout the year.

Live music The Valley is the centre of Brisbane's live music scene and has been the birthplace of the 'Valley Sound' – a collective name for some of Australia's best and most innovative bands. Crowded with partying people most evenings, Brunswick and Ann streets are lined with fantastic bars, pubs, nightclubs – including the award-winning multilevel Family, and the monastically imbued Monastery – and alternative music venues such as the Zoo, a Brisbane institution. Kangaroo Point has some good live-music venues, including the renowned Story Bridge Hotel and the Brisbane Jazz Club. For jazz you could also head to West End. Popular alternative acts play gigs at the Tivoli in the Valley; international acts play the Brisbane Entertainment Centre out at Boondall. Buy a copy of the *Courier-Mail* on Thursdays and Fridays for music listings, or pick up one of the free street papers such as *Time Off* for details of what's on.

Classical music and performing arts Brisbane has a pulsing creative life with theatres of all sizes spread throughout the city. For high-end performing arts and music, the premier venue is the Queensland Performing Arts Centre at South Bank, which includes the Concert Hall and the Lyric Theatre. The Powerhouse, on the river at New Farm, is the place to go for world-ranking contemporary music, dance and theatre. The Judith Wright Centre of Contemporary Arts in the Valley focuses on cutting-edge contemporary performance. West End is the address of the Queensland Ballet, in the Thomas Dixon Centre. The Valley has a number of smaller venues for experimental and alternative theatre, and there are often live street performances taking place in Brunswick Street Mall. The Roundhouse Theatre in the Kelvin Grove Urban Village is the venue for the La Boite Theatre Company and some brilliant productions. See the *Courier-Mail* for details of what's on.

Brisbane Powerhouse 403 F4

This live arts precinct, in the restored 100-year-old New Farm Powerhouse, is the place to go for contemporary music, theatre, dance and art. Go to www.brisbanepowerhouse.org for details of upcoming shows. The landmark building itself is worth a visit and it is a great spot for lunch, dinner or just a coffee by the river. Every second and fourth Saturday its forecourts are packed with locals foraging for the best in fresh food at the Farmers Markets. It's also popular with dog owners and the markets run a doggie cafe *(see Markets, p. 408). 119 Lamington St, New Farm; (07) 3358 8622; open 9am–5pm Mon–Fri, 12–4pm Sat.*

Newstead House 403 F3

Brisbane's oldest residence, Newstead House was built in 1846 by Patrick Leslie, the first white settler on the Darling Downs. Beautifully restored, with its spacious verandahs, formal gardens, and lawns running down to the river, it offers an image of the quintessential Australian homestead. *Newstead Park, Breakfast Creek Rd, Newstead; (07) 3216 1846; open 10am–4pm Mon–Thurs, 2–5pm Sun.*

Breakfast Creek 403 F3

Named by explorer John Oxley in 1826 when he stopped one morning to eat while charting the Brisbane River, Breakfast Creek sits on a wide, open stretch of water. Here you will find the historic **Breakfast Creek Hotel** – or the 'Brekkie Creek', as it is affectionately dubbed by the locals. Built in 1889, but given a stunning contemporary renewal in 2003, this Queensland institution is the ideal place for top-class steak and a cold beer. Nearby is **Breakfast Creek Wharf** with restaurants, cafes and river boat tours.

Inner North-east

Miegunyah 403 E3

Built in 1886 in traditional Queensland fashion with long verandahs and ornate ironwork, Miegunyah has been restored to its original style. It is now home to the Queensland Women's Historical Association and serves as a memorial to the state's pioneering women. Take a guided tour or enjoy morning or afternoon tea on the wide verandah overlooking the garden. *35 Jordan Tce, Bowen Hills; (07) 3252 2979; open 10.30am–3pm Wed, 10.30am–4pm Sat–Sun.*

Racecourse Road & Hamilton 403 F2

Drive through Hamilton and Ascot if you want to see some stunning examples of grand 19th-century Queensland homes. And if you feel like a flutter and a day out at the races, **Eagle Farm** is the state's premier track. Racecourse Road, which runs from the river to the racecourse, is the place to go for smart outdoor restaurants and cafes – and if you need to pick up a hat for the occasion, there are some excellent high-end fashion shops. On Kingsford-Smith Drive, **Brett's Wharf** has an acclaimed seafood restaurant and a ferry stop. Further along the river, the newer **Portside** development is Brisbane's international cruise-ship terminal and offers smart restaurants, quality shopping and cinemas.

Inner East

Bulimba & Woolloongabba 402 E5

The renewal and expansion of Brisbane has seen the proliferation of cafe and shopping strips right across the inner suburbs from north to south. It's in the suburbs that you will find some of the best coffee and most innovative little gift, homewares and fashion shops. On the southside, Oxford Street at **Bulimba** offers a leafy strip that is a short ferry ride from the CBD, and provides a pleasant break from the city bustle. **Logan Road** is one of Brisbane's main thoroughfares, but running south from the Story Bridge through Woolloongabba there is a little dog-leg behind the **Gabba** cricket ground that's a 19th-century hideaway of antique shops, tiny cafes, top restaurants, young designer fashion and quality homewares.

Inner South

West End 402 C4

Close to the CBD but a million miles away in mood, this is the suburb of choice for artists, students and those seeking a low-key lifestyle. If you want buildings with character, a multicultural mix of cafes and restaurants, organic provedores and alternative fashion, this is the place to find them. You can see19th-century houses throughout the suburb and the 1912 Gas Stripping Tower in Davies Park is a local landmark. The park is also home to organic markets on Saturdays *(see Markets, p. 408).*

Inner West

Milton 402 D4

Dominated by the iconic XXXX Brewery *(see next entry)* and the legendary sportsground the Suncorp Stadium, formerly Lang Park, Milton is also known for the bustling Park Road. Developed 20 years ago and endowed with a mock mini-Eiffel Tower, this is a lively street of restaurants and cafes, fashion, jewellery and bookshops. There are more restaurants, cafes and delis at nearby **Baroona Road** and **Rosalie.**

XXXX Brewery 402 D4

Brisbanites are familiar with the pungent smell of brewing beer occasionally wafting from the Castlemaine Perkins XXXX Brewery. For beer-loving visitors, the brewery's Ale House is a must. Bookings are recommended for tailored tours that finish with a beer sampling. *Cnr Black and Paten sts (just off Milton Rd), Milton; (07) 3361 7597; open 9am–5.30pm Mon–Tues and Thurs–Fri, 9am–8pm Wed, 10am–3.30pm Sat.*

Paddington 402 C3

Known for its distinctive style, the streets of this hilly inner-city suburb are lined with old timber cottages and on **Latrobe** and **Given terraces** many have been converted into small shops, cafes and businesses. Together, the two terraces make for a very long shopping strip that changes in character from one end to the other. At the Latrobe end there are some excellent antique shops and small art galleries along with quirky cafes and recycled fashion shops. Closer to the city, Given Terrace offers quality fashion, an organic provedore and some of Brisbane's best

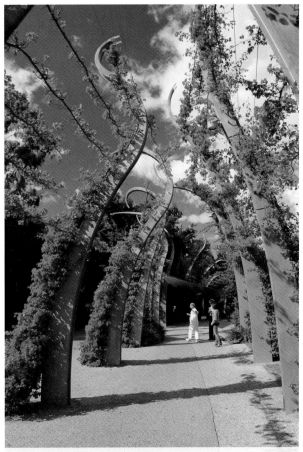

[COLOURFUL ARBOUR IN SOUTH BANK]

restaurants. Also here is the popular Paddington Tavern, better known to locals as the 'Paddo'. **Caxton Street**, at the Petrie Terrace end of Paddington, is close to the Suncorp Stadium and offers nightlife and a variety of bars and restaurants.

walks & tours

Balloons Over Brisbane See the sun rise over Brisbane city at dawn – take a hot-air balloon flight, followed by a gourmet champagne breakfast. Bookings on (07) 3844 6671.

Brisbane CityWalk Explore Brisbane's green heart on this leisurely, self-guide walking tour that takes in the CBD's highlights via its three main parkland areas: the City Botanic Gardens, South Bank and Roma Street Parkland. Brochure available from the visitor centre in the Queen Street Mall.

Brisbane's Living Heritage Network Grab a copy of the Network's *Experience Guide* and take a trip back in time on these excellent self-guide tours of historic districts in the city and surrounds. Brochures available from the visitor centre and Brisbane City Council. (07) 3403 8888.

City Sights Bus Tours See the cultural and historic attractions of Brisbane in comfort. Set your own pace – you can hop off and on the clearly signed buses at any time. Brochure and tickets available from the visitor centre or call 13 1230 or (07) 3404 8888 for more information.

Gonewalking Discover Brisbane on foot with the help of experienced Brisbane City Council volunteers, or buy a copy of *Great Brisbane*

Walks from Brisbane City Council or a good bookshop to plan your own. (07) 3403 8888.

Ghost Tours Scare yourself silly on one of a variety of serious ghost tours exploring Brisbane's haunted history. You can also pick up a copy of the Haunted Brisbane guidebook. Bookings on (07) 3344 7265.

Moreton Bay Cruises Explore beautiful Moreton Bay on one of the many cruises on offer. Details from the visitor information centre.

River tours Travel the river up to Lone Pine with Mirimar Cruises (1300 729 742) or enjoy a fine meal with stunning views on a Kookaburra River Queen cruise ((07) 3221 1300).

Story Bridge Adventure Climb Take in spectacular 360-degree views of the city on this 2.5-hour climb up Brisbane's iconic Story Bridge. Bookings on 1300 254 627.

Wynnum Manly Heritage Trail Once you've explored historic Brisbane, do the same in the bayside area. Brochures available from the Wynnum Manly visitor centre.

QUEENSLAND

West

Toowong 402 C4

Toowong Cemetery has more than 100 000 graves, some dating back to 1875. Its headstones tell the story of the trials, tribulations and triumphs of Queensland's early settlers. This is also the final resting place of one prime minister, two Queensland governors, 13 Queensland premiers, 11 Queensland Labor leaders, at least 15 Brisbane mayors and many other prominent political,

[HISTORIC GRAND VIEW HOTEL, CLEVELAND]

religious, sports, arts and business figures. Also built at the end of the 19th century, but very much a part of the living, the **Regatta Hotel** enjoys self-proclaimed 'oarsome' river views. A stunning revamp in 2001 has made it a dining and drinking spot that well deserves its popularity. The CityCat stops here.

Mount Coot-tha Forest 402 A4

To get a bearing on Brisbane's geography, drive up **Sir Samuel Griffith Drive** to the **Mount Coot-tha Lookout.** You will see the Brisbane River snaking through leafy suburbs, impressive views of the CBD and, unless it's very hazy, the islands in Moreton Bay. To the west are rugged bush-covered ranges. Look down at your feet and you will see that the lookout's paving reflects the layout of the city, the river and the ocean. There are beautiful walks and picnic areas in the park, including the local favourite, **J. C. Slaughter Falls.**

Brisbane Botanic Gardens – Mount Coot-tha 402 B4

At the foot of Mount Coot-tha, these botanic gardens are well worth a visit for the Bonsai House, Fern House, Japanese Garden, the Tropical Dome and the Australian Plant Communities section, which showcases native species. Free guided walks are available. Located in the gardens is the **Sir Thomas Brisbane Planetarium**, which holds a range of regular and special events, some involving planetarium astronomers. *Mt Coot-tha Rd, Toowong; (07) 3403 2535; open daily; admission free.*

Lone Pine Koala Sanctuary 645 D5

The world's largest and oldest koala sanctuary, Lone Pine has more than 130 koalas. Visitors can hold koalas, handfeed kangaroos and get up close to many other species in a natural environment. The sanctuary is set on 20 hectares next to the Brisbane River. You can get to Lone Pine by road (11 kilometres from the city) or catch Mirimar's Wildlife Cruise *(see Walks & tours, p. 411)*. There are informative talks daily. *Jesmond Rd, Fig Tree Pocket; (07) 3378 1366; open daily.*

sport

Brisbane's weather is perfect for sport, and Brisbane's stadiums are state of the art. If **AFL** (Australian Football League) is your passion, you can't miss the Brisbane Lions at their home ground, the Gabba, proving that Victoria no longer has a monopoly on AFL. The Gabba is also home to Queensland **cricket** – watch the Bulls defend the state's cricketing honour. You will find the Gabba (known formally as the Brisbane Cricket Ground) in the suburb of Woolloongabba, south of Kangaroo Point.

Rugby League is a way of life in Queensland, culminating in State of Origin. You can watch the Brisbane Broncos, the city's rugby league team, at the redeveloped Lang Park (also known as Suncorp Stadium), a Brisbane sporting institution in Milton. Ticket-holders enjoy free public transport on match days. Or show your true colours by supporting the Reds, Queensland's **Rugby Union** team, at their matches, which are also at Lang Park.

The Brisbane International **tennis** tournament attracts the world's leading players in the first week of January. Matches are held at the Queensland Tennis Centre in Tennyson, opened in 2009.

If you prefer the sport of thoroughbreds, head to Brisbane's **horseracing** venues at Doomben and Eagle Farm. Or for car racing at its loudest and most thrilling, head south for the **Gold Coast SuperGP** in October.

Outer North

The northern bayside suburbs of Scarborough, Redcliffe, Brighton, Margate, Sandgate and Shorncliffe were popular holiday places for Brisbanites prior to World War II, and the legacy lives on in the form of beautiful old boarding houses, mature gardens, the Redcliffe Jetty (although now rebuilt) and Shorncliffe Pier. Together they form a pleasant coastal drive (between 25 minutes and 45 minutes from Brisbane), with plenty of worthwhile places to stop.

Northern beaches 644 F3

Eating fish and chips at Morgans Seafood, a renowned local institution in **Scarborough**, while watching pelicans glide and seagulls wheel over the bobbing trawlers against a background of the Glass House Mountains, is a must-do. Travel south to **Redcliffe**, the site of Queensland's first European settlement in 1824, and follow one of the heritage trails (ask at the information centre for brochures). Redcliffe has good beaches and a landscaped foreshore lined with little cafes – great for coffee with a view over to the Moreton Island sandhills. Its jetty is a popular

day tours

Mount Glorious The sleepy settlement of Mount Glorious lies to the north-west of the city in Brisbane Forest Park, a 28 500-hectare reserve of subtropical forests and hills. Mount Glorious is the base for a number of enjoyable walking tracks. Nearby Wivenhoe Lookout offers panoramic views of the surrounding country. For more details see p. 415

Daisy Hill State Forest Close to Brisbane's south-eastern suburbs is Daisy Hill State Forest, best known for its large colony of koalas. The Daisy Hill Koala Centre has a variety of displays and, from a tower, you can see koalas in their favourite place – the treetops. 1300 130 372. For more details see p. 415

Bribie Island Connected to the mainland by a bridge near Caboolture, Bribie is the most accessible of the Moreton Bay islands. Fishing, boating and crabbing are popular activities. For a quiet picnic and walk, visit Buckleys Hole Conservation Park at the southern end. For more details see p. 416

Moreton Island This impossibly beautiful sand island is mostly national park, reached by passenger ferry from Eagle Farm or vehicular ferry from the Port of Brisbane. Vehicle access is four-wheel drive only, but guided tours are available. Walking, swimming, fishing and dolphin-watching are some of the activities on offer. The big sand hills are a must-visit attraction. For more details see p. 416

North Stradbroke Island A favourite getaway for Brisbanites, Straddie, as it's affectionately known, is the most developed of the Moreton Bay islands, with small townships at Point Lookout, Dunwich and Amity. Visit Blue Lake National Park, at the centre of the island, for swimming and walking (access by four-wheel drive or a 45-minute walk), or enjoy ocean views along the North Gorge Headlands Walk. The island is reached by vehicular ferry from Cleveland. For more details see p. 416

The Gold Coast An hour's drive from Brisbane, the Gold Coast is arguably Australia's most famous and busiest holiday region, with beautiful surf beaches and huge theme parks – perfect for kids of all ages. All activities on offer, from deep-sea fishing and golf to dining and shopping, are of international-resort standard. For more details see p. 417

Gold Coast Hinterland Dubbed the 'green behind the gold', the region offers a peaceful retreat from the bustle of the coast. Follow the winding scenic road up to Lamington National Park, part of a World Heritage area and Queensland's most visited park. It preserves a rainforest environment and a large wildlife population with many bird species, including bowerbirds and lyrebirds. For more details see p. 417

Toowoomba Travel to Toowoomba from Brisbane and you will find yourself climbing the Great Dividing Range. This grand old lady of the Darling Downs is perched on the edge of the escarpment at 800 metres above sea level. It's not dubbed the 'Garden City' for nothing – Toowoomba is famous for its parks, gardens and tree-lined streets, and each September it celebrates the Carnival of the Flowers. The city has also long been known for its antique shops and tea parlours, and these days also offers good coffee and innovative restaurants. For more details see p. 418

---

fishing spot and the little cafe here is decorated with historical photos. There's also a memorial to John Oxley, who landed in 1823, and a plaque dedicated to Mathew Flinders, who came ashore here in 1799. **Margate** beach has a string of shaded picnic spots with lovely bay views. At **Woody Point**, you will find the historic Belvedere Hotel, built in the 1890s.

Alma Park Zoo 644 E3

Set in award-winning rainforest gardens, the zoo is 30 minutes north of the city, inland from Redcliffe. It displays both Australian and exotic animals, and offers the chance to get up close to many species. You can touch koalas, and feed kangaroos and deer in the walk-through enclosures – all great for kids. *Alma Rd, Dakabin; open daily.*

Eastern Bayside

Wynnum & Manly 644 G7

Half an hour east of the city, Wynnum and Manly offer an easy-reach bayside experience. The **Wynnum North Mangrove Circuit** is worth a look, especially for wildlife – watch out for fish and migrating birds. If you're feeling active, hire a bike to ride the 1.5-kilometre **Esplanade** from Manly to Lota. The **Manly Boat Harbour** is a vista of yachts, and charters and boat hire for both fishing and sailing are available. Tours to the island of St Helena also depart from here. This island is two-thirds national park, and served as a penal settlement between 1867 and 1932. Prison life is recalled in the stark but strangely beautiful structures that remain. North of Wynnum, at the mouth of the Brisbane River,

is the 19th-century **Fort Lytton**. A museum at the fort (open only on Sundays and public holidays) interprets Queensland's military and social history from 1879. Further north is the **Port of Brisbane**, which offers public tours and a visitor centre. *Wynnum–Manly Visitor Information Centre: 43A Cambridge Pde, Manly; (07) 3348 3524.*

Outer Eastern Bayside

Cleveland 644 H8

About 40 minutes south-east of Brisbane, leafy Cleveland is the centre of the Redland Bay district. The area is rich in history, so follow the heritage trail from the Old Courthouse to explore it. Enjoy the colourful Cleveland Bayside Markets on Sundays or try one of the delicious counter meals at Brisbane's oldest pub, the 1851 **Grand View Hotel** – with Queensland's oldest banyan tree out front. Another historic building is **Ormiston House**, built in 1862 and now restored and open to visitors. *(07) 3286 1425; open Sun afternoons Mar–Nov.*

It is at Cleveland that you can catch a ferry or water taxi to North Stradbroke Island *(see Day tours, on this page)*. South of Cleveland, Victoria Point and Redland Bay offer good fishing. Boats can be hired along this section of the coast.

REGIONS
queensland

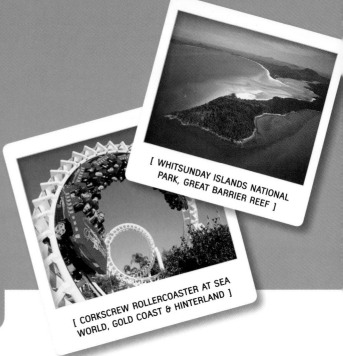

[WHITSUNDAY ISLANDS NATIONAL PARK, GREAT BARRIER REEF]

[CORKSCREW ROLLERCOASTER AT SEA WORLD, GOLD COAST & HINTERLAND]

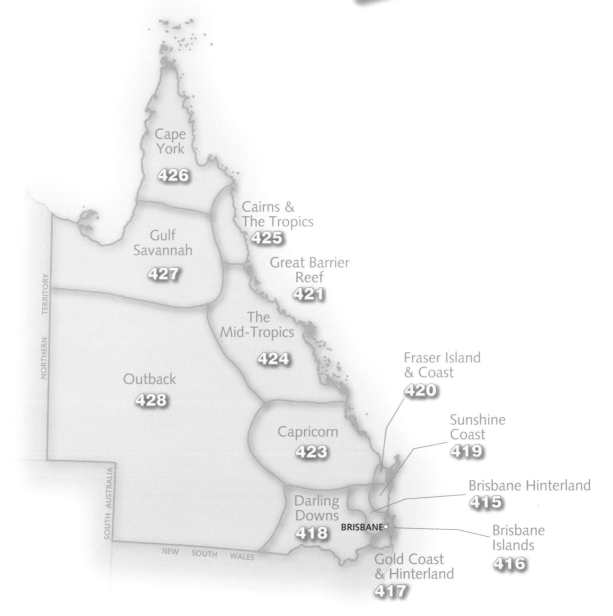

Cape York
426

Cairns &
The Tropics
425

Gulf
Savannah
427

Great Barrier
Reef
421

The
Mid-Tropics
424

Fraser Island
& Coast
420

Outback
428

Sunshine
Coast
419

Capricorn
423

Brisbane Hinterland
415

Darling
Downs
418

BRISBANE

Brisbane
Islands
416

Gold Coast
& Hinterland
417

NORTHERN TERRITORY

SOUTH AUSTRALIA

NEW SOUTH WALES

BRISBANE HINTERLAND

Heavily forested hills create a subtropical haven just a stone's throw away from Brisbane's hustle and bustle.

[LUSH GREENERY NEAR BRISBANE FOREST PARK]

Booubyjan Homestead Two Irish brothers, the Clements, took up this run near Goomeri in 1847, beginning with sheep and then moving to cattle in the 1880s. Many generations later, the property is still in the family. The homestead, open daily, provides a glimpse of pioneering life in Queensland's early years.

South Burnett This comfortable slice of rural Queensland invites you to the historic timber towns of Blackbutt and Yarraman, and to wineries along the scenic Barambah Wine Trail. Go to Nanango or Kilkivan to fossick for gold and bed down for the night in a B&B or farmstay.

Bunya Mountains This isolated spur of the Great Dividing Range is a cool, moist region of waterfalls, green and scarlet king parrots, and the remaining stands of bunya pine, a species much depleted by early timber-getters. Walk the easy 4-kilometre Scenic Circuit from the Dandabah camping area, which winds through rainforest to Pine Gorge Lookout.

Brisbane Forest Park Few cities have an attraction such as Brisbane Forest Park on their doorstep, with its pristine rainforest, towering trees, cascading waterfalls, deep pools, mountain streams and incredible wildlife. The small settlement of Mount Glorious is a base for forest walking tracks. Wivenhoe Lookout, 10 kilometres further on, has superb views west to Lake Wivenhoe.

TOP EVENTS

MAR	Wine and Food in the Park Festival (Kingaroy)
MAY	Pine Rivers Festival (Strathpine)
MAY	Pumpkin Festival (Goomeri)
AUG	Peanut Festival (Kingaroy)
OCT	Annual Fishing Competition (Bjelke-Petersen Dam, south-east of Murgon)
OCT	Funfest (Nanango)

CLIMATE

MOUNT GLORIOUS

	J	F	M	A	M	J	J	A	S	O	N	D	
	25	24	24	21	18	16	15	17	20	22	24	25	MAX °C
	18	17	17	15	12	10	9	9	11	14	15	17	MIN °C
	238	252	222	129	126	84	86	56	57	114	123	167	RAIN MM
	15	16	16	12	11	8	8	7	7	10	11	13	RAIN DAYS

ANIMAL ANTICS

Walkabout Creek Wildlife Centre, in Brisbane Forest Park, features a freshwater creek environment populated with water dragons, frogs, platypus, pythons and fish. The Australian Woolshed, just past Samford, re-creates life on a sheep station. Shearing demonstrations, ram shows and cattle-dog demonstrations are staged daily, while native animals roam freely around the property. Daisy Hill State Forest is a pocket of eucalypt forest and acacia scrub 25 kilometres south of Brisbane, where visitors can scan the canopy for koalas from a treetop tower. The Daisy Hill Koala Centre in the central picnic area has information about koalas and their habitats.

→ For more detail see maps 644, 645, 647 & 653. For descriptions of ⦿ towns see Towns from A–Z (p. 429).

QUEENSLAND

BRISBANE ISLANDS

The islands of Moreton, North Stradbroke and Bribie are holiday destinations with endless white beaches, lakes and pockets of forest, while St Helena draws visitors keen to discover remnants of its penal settlement.

[CYLINDER BEACH, NORTH STRADBROKE ISLAND]

St Helena Island   This low sandy island, 8 kilometres from the mouth of the Brisbane River, was used as a prison from 1867 to 1932. It was dubbed 'the hell-hole of the South Pacific'. Historic ruins remain and are protected in the island's national park. Tours of the island depart from the Brisbane suburbs of Manly and Breakfast Creek.

North Stradbroke Island   'Straddie' is a coastal and bushland paradise, with contained pockets of development. Blue Lake National Park is an ecologically significant wetland; access is by four-wheel drive or a 45-minute walk. Other island walking trails include the popular North Gorge Headland Walk. Travel to North Stradbroke by vehicular ferry from Cleveland. The ferry arrives at Dunwich, the site of a 19th-century quarantine and penal centre.

Bribie Island   About a third of Bribie is protected by national park. See the magnificent birdlife and spectacular wildflower displays on one of the Bicentennial bushwalks, or go fishing, boating or crabbing. Woorim, in the south-east, is an old-fashioned resort with great surfing beaches. Nearby, Buckleys Hole Conservation Park has good picnic spots for daytrippers and walking tracks to the beach. The island is connected to the mainland by a bridge east of Caboolture.

Moreton Island   Almost all of this large island is national park. It is also mainly sand, with 280-metre Mount Tempest possibly the world's highest stable sandhill. On the east coast is an unbroken 36-kilometre surf beach, with calmer beaches on the west coast. Get to the island by passenger or vehicular ferry from Scarborough or the Brisbane River. A four-wheel drive and a permit are required for self-drive touring.

TOP EVENTS

AUG	Bribie Island Greek Festival (Bribie Island)
SEPT	Festival in the Ruins (celebrates the history and ecology of St Helena Island)

CLIMATE

MORETON ISLAND

J	F	M	A	M	J	J	A	S	O	N	D	
33	32	32	32	31	30	30	31	32	34	35	34	MAX °C
23	23	23	21	19	18	17	16	18	20	21	23	MIN °C
326	331	287	115	22	10	8	4	5	17	65	198	RAIN MM
20	20	19	11	6	4	4	2	2	5	12		RAIN DAYS

MARINE LIFE

The marine population of Moreton Bay includes dolphins, whales, dugongs and turtles. Visitors to Moreton Island can see dolphins at the Tangalooma Wild Dolphin Resort, where a care program has been developed, or at several spots along the western shore. Migrating humpback whales can be seen between July and November from Cape Moreton and from North Gorge Headland on North Stradbroke Island. Pumicestone Channel, between Bribie and the mainland, is a haven for turtles, dolphins and dugongs. Diving and snorkelling facilities are available on all three islands, allowing visitors to explore the crystal waters and rich underwater life of this magnificent bay.

→ For more detail see maps 644, 645, 647 & 653. For descriptions of ⓣ towns see Towns from A–Z (p. 429).

GOLD COAST & HINTERLAND

With unbelievably good weather and no less than 35 beautiful beaches, the Gold Coast has become Australia's biggest holiday destination.

[BURLEIGH HEADS ARTS AND CRAFTS MARKET]

Warner Bros. Movie World This popular theme park south of Oxenford offers visitors the chance to 'meet' their favourite Hollywood characters and see the business of movie-making up close. Rides include the Wild West Falls Adventure and the Road Runner Rollercoaster (for toddlers).

See Brisbane Islands region on page 416

South Stradbroke Island
South Stradbroke, separated from North Stradbroke by the popular fishing channel Jumpinpin, is a peaceful alternative to the Gold Coast. Access is by launch from Runaway Bay. Cars are not permitted; once on the island visitors must walk or cycle.

Golf at Sanctuary Cove
With 40 courses, the Gold Coast is one of the Southern Hemisphere's great golfing destinations. Sanctuary Cove boasts two championship courses: the exclusive Pines and the immaculate Palms.

Surfers Paradise
Surfers Paradise is the Gold Coast's signature settlement – high-rise apartments fronting one of the state's most beautiful beaches. The first big hotel was built here in the 1930s, among little more than a clutch of shacks.

Lamington National Park Part of a World Heritage area, this popular park preserves a wonderland of rainforest and volcanic ridges, crisscrossed by 160 kilometres of walking tracks. The main picnic, camping and walking areas are at Binna Burra and Green Mountains, sites of the award-winning Binna Burra Mountain Lodge and O'Reilly's Rainforest Retreat. Don't miss the Tree Top Walk for an up-close look at the canopy's flora.

Currumbin Wildlife Sanctuary
Be captivated by the wild and roaming animals in this National Trust reserve. The crocodile wetlands let you get up close, and the daily feedings in the aviary make for a loud and exciting experience.

TOP EVENTS

JAN	Magic Millions Racing Carnival (Gold Coast Turf Club)
MAY–JUNE	Blues on Broadbeach Music Festival (Broadbeach)
JUNE	Country and Horse Festival (Beaudesert)
AUG–SEPT	Gold Coast Show (Southport)
OCT	Springtime on the Mountain (Tamborine Mountain)
OCT	Gold Coast SuperGP (Surfers Paradise)

GOLDEN BEACHES

The Gold Coast is a surfers' mecca and, mixed with the fabulous weather, also the perfect destination for a relaxing beach holiday. Best for surfers are the southern beaches, including Currumbin and Kirra Point (in Coolangatta), said to have one of the ten best breaks in the world. Greenmount Beach, in Coolangatta, is great for families, as is Tallebudgera, which offers both estuary and ocean swimming. Towards Surfers Paradise the crowds get larger, but the beaches are still spectacular. Surfers Paradise is renowned for its beachfront – try out your volleyball skills in the free competition near Cavill Avenue. There is an open-ocean beach on The Spit, near Main Beach, with the marine park Sea World close by. For a more remote option, try the 22 kilometres of beach on the east coast of South Stradbroke Island. Once you've soaked up enough magnificent Gold Coast sunshine, you could explore the island's wetlands and rainforest.

CLIMATE

COOLANGATTA

	J	F	M	A	M	J	J	A	S	O	N	D	
	28	28	27	25	23	21	20	21	22	24	26	26	MAX °C
	20	20	19	17	13	11	9	10	12	15	17	19	MIN °C
	184	181	213	114	124	122	96	103	49	108	137	166	RAIN MM
	14	15	16	14	10	9	7	9	9	11	11	13	RAIN DAYS

→ For more detail see maps 645, 646 & 653. For descriptions of ⓣ towns see Towns from A–Z (p. 429).

QUEENSLAND

DARLING DOWNS

This region's rich volcanic soil yields some of the country's most magnificent gardens. Winter, a popular time for touring, is known locally as 'Brass Monkey Season'.

[JIMBOUR HOUSE WINERY, NEAR DALBY]

Jondaryan Woolshed
This 1859 woolshed on historic Jondaryan Station is the centrepiece of a complex of old farm buildings. Sheepdog and shearing demonstrations are held daily, and for a taste of yesteryear, visitors can sit down for a yarn over the billy tea and damper.

Toowoomba Japanese garden A thousand visitors a week stroll the 3 kilometres of paths at Ju Raku En, a Japanese garden at the University of Southern Queensland. Opened in 1989, it showcases the harmony and beauty of ancient Japanese garden design with its lake, willowy beeches, islands, bridges, stream and pavilion.

Queen Mary Falls
Stretching for 55 kilometres along the Great Dividing Range, World Heritage–listed Main Range National Park boasts impressive peaks and escarpments, and the delightful Queen Mary Falls. At the falls, which are part of the Murray-Darling, one of Australia's longest river systems, there's a 400-metre cliff walk that takes you to the top, as well as a 2-kilometre circuit trail revealing distinct changes in the vegetation.

Allora This historic town lies just off the highway between Toowoomba and Warwick. Victorian verandahed shopfronts and three old timber hotels line the main street. St David's Anglican Church (1888) is one of Queensland's finest timber churches. Glengallan Homestead, south of town, was built in 1867, during the golden age of pastoralism.

Granite Belt wineries Queensland's only significant wine region is on an 800-metre plateau in the Great Dividing Range, around Ballandean and Stanthorpe. Over 40 boutique wineries, many with tastings and sales, grow major grape varieties on the well-drained granite soils, favouring soft reds made from shiraz and merlot grapes.

TOP EVENTS

FEB	Melon Festival (Chinchilla, odd-numbered years)
MAR	Cotton on to Energy Festival (Dalby)
MAY	Opera in the Vineyards (Ballandean Estate Winery)
AUG	Australian Heritage Festival (Jondaryan Woolshed)
SEPT	Carnival of Flowers (Toowoomba)
OCT	Campdraft and Rodeo (Warwick)

CLIMATE

TOOWOOMBA

J	F	M	A	M	J	J	A	S	O	N	D	
28	27	26	23	20	17	16	18	21	24	26	28	MAX °C
17	17	15	12	9	6	5	6	9	12	14	16	MIN °C
135	122	95	63	60	58	54	40	48	73	89	120	RAIN MM
12	11	11	8	8	8	7	6	7	8	10	11	RAIN DAYS

GARDENS OF THE DOWNS

The climate and soils of the Darling Downs have created one of Australia's great gardening districts. Toowoomba has 150 public parks and gardens, including the Scented Garden – for visually impaired people – and the 6-hectare mountainside Boyce Gardens, with 700 species of trees, shrubs and perennials. Warwick is known for its roses, particularly the red 'City of Warwick', best seen in the Jubilee Gardens. There are superb private gardens throughout the region – some open daily, some seasonally and some as part of the Open Garden Scheme; check with an information centre for details.

→ For more detail see maps 652–3. For descriptions of ⊤ towns see Towns from A–Z (p. 429).

SUNSHINE COAST

Bathed by the blue Coral Sea and fringed by native bush, the Sunshine Coast has near-perfect weather, with winter temperatures around 25°C.

[DRIVING NEAR THE GLASS HOUSE MOUNTAINS]

Mountain villages The 70-kilometre scenic drive here is one of Queensland's best. Starting on the Bruce Highway near Landsborough, it passes the antique shops, B&Bs, galleries and cafes of the pretty mountain villages of Maleny, Montville, Flaxton and Mapleton, offering beautiful coastal and mountain views along the way. The drive ends near Nambour.

Glass House Mountains These 20-million-year-old crags, the giant cores of extinct volcanoes, mark the southern entrance to the Sunshine Coast. Glass House Mountains Road leads to sealed and unsealed routes through the mountains, with some spectacular lookouts along the way. There are walking trails, picnic grounds, and challenges aplenty for rockclimbers.

The coloured sands of Teewah Located in the Cooloola section of Great Sandy National Park, these coloured sands rise in 40 000-year-old cliffs. It is thought that oxidisation or decaying vegetation has caused the colouring; Aboriginal legend attributes it to the slaying of a rainbow serpent.

Gondola ride on the Noosa River A very special way to appreciate Noosa's surrounds is on a gondola cruise with Gondolas of Noosa. It doesn't get much better than gliding through Noosa Sound's calm waters listening to the strains of Italian opera as the sun goes down. This is also a very romantic mode of transport when eating at Ricky's River Bar and Restaurant – catch the gondola at the Sheraton wharf, but be sure to book beforehand.

Coastal towns The southern towns of Caloundra, Mooloolaba and Maroochydore make pleasant daytrips from Brisbane or good spots for an extended family holiday, with patrolled surfing beaches and protected lakes and rivers for boating and fishing. Central Noosa Heads offers luxury hotels, top restaurants, hip bars and stylish boutiques, as well as the pandanus-fringed beaches of Noosa National Park.

TROPICAL PRODUCE

The Sunshine Coast hinterland, with its subtropical climate and volcanic soils, is renowned for its produce. Nambour's Big Pineapple symbolises the importance of food as an industry and a tourist attraction. Visitors can take a train, trolley and boat through a plantation growing pineapples and other fruit, macadamia nuts, spices and flowers. Yandina's Ginger Factory, the world's largest, sells ginger products including ginger ice-cream. For freshly picked local fruit and vegetables, visit the Wednesday- and Saturday-morning markets at Eumundi, north of Yandina.

TOP EVENTS

JAN	Ginger Flower Festival (Yandina)
JULY	Family Fishing Classic (Rainbow Beach)
SEPT	Scarecrow Festival (Maleny)
SEPT	Jazz Festival (Noosa Heads)
SEPT	Seafood Festival (Tin Can Bay)
OCT	Gold Rush Festival (Gympie)

CLIMATE

NAMBOUR

J	F	M	A	M	J	J	A	S	O	N	D	
30	29	28	26	24	22	21	22	25	27	28	29	MAX °C
19	20	18	15	12	9	8	8	10	14	16	18	MIN °C
242	262	236	149	143	91	92	53	48	105	141	176	RAIN MM
16	18	18	13	13	9	9	8	9	12	12	13	RAIN DAYS

→ For more detail see maps 647, 648 & 653. For descriptions of ⊕ towns see Towns from A–Z (p. 429).

QUEENSLAND

FRASER ISLAND & COAST

This region features all of Queensland's signature attractions: spectacular white beaches, coloured sand cliffs, wildflower heathland and rainforest, and whale-watching in Hervey Bay.

[FOUR-WHEEL DRIVING, FRASER ISLAND]

Fraser Island's dingoes   Roaming around on the world's largest sand island is what is thought to be the purest strain of dingoes in eastern Australia. By the time these native dogs arrived on the mainland – they came with Asian seafarers around 5000 years ago – Fraser Island was already disconnected from the continent, and the dingoes swam the few kilometres across Great Sandy Strait. Unlike most mainland dingoes, they have not been hybridised by contact with domestic dogs.

WARNING: Dingoes have been known to attack. Stay with small children and never feed or coax animals.

Hervey Bay   This once sleepy settlement is now a booming resort town. The bay itself is a large, calm body of water warmed by tropical currents. The area's protected beaches are perfect for family swimming. Other popular activities include sailing, diving, windsurfing, fishing, kayaking, whale-watching and skydiving.

Maryborough Heritage Walk and Drive   Established in 1847, Maryborough is one of Queensland's oldest and best-preserved provincial cities. A self-guide brochure leads visitors through tree-lined streets, past heritage sites and well-restored Queenslander houses, and along the historic streetscape of Wharf Street.

Fraser Island's east coast   Also Fraser Island's surf coast this takes in the beautiful Seventy Five Mile Beach; The Cathedrals, 15-metre sheer cliffs composed of different-coloured sands; the wreck of the *Maheno*, a trans-Tasman luxury liner; and Eli Creek, a freshwater creek filtered through the dunes, where visitors can float beneath the pandanus trees.

Lake McKenzie   World Heritage–listed Fraser Island is distinguished by its 40 perched dune lakes, formed by water collecting on an impermeable layer of decaying matter. Idyllic Lake McKenzie is definitely one of the most beautiful of these freshwater lakes – its shallow water is dazzling aquamarine and ringed by white sandy beaches backed by paperbark trees. To swim here, in some of the purest drinking water in the world, is a wonderful experience.

Great Sandy Strait   This narrow strait between the mainland and Fraser Island makes for good boating; there are houseboats and other vessels for hire. Drop into the Kingfisher Bay Resort and Village on Fraser Island, facing the strait. Look out for dugongs, the world's only plant-eating marine mammals, and fish at the mouth of the Mary River, around River Heads.

Map labels

CORAL SEA · Burrum Heads · BURRUM COAST NP · Hervey Bay · HERVEY BAY · GREAT SANDY NATIONAL PARK · The Cathedrals · Maheno wreck · FRASER ISLAND · Seventy Five Mile Beach · Eli Ck · Lake Lenthall · River Heads · Lake McKenzie (Boorangoora) · MARYBOROUGH · Mary River · POONA NP · MOUNT BAUPLE NP · Great Sandy Strait · N · 0   10 km

TOP EVENTS

EASTER	Amateur Fishing Classic (Burrum Heads)
APR–MAY	Bay to Bay Yacht Race (Tin Can Bay to Hervey Bay)
AUG	Whale Festival (Hervey Bay)

CLIMATE

MARYBOROUGH

J	F	M	A	M	J	J	A	S	O	N	D	
31	30	29	27	25	22	22	23	26	28	29	31	MAX °C
21	21	19	17	13	10	9	9	12	15	18	20	MIN °C
166	173	159	90	80	67	54	40	43	75	85	128	RAIN MM
13	14	14	12	11	8	7	6	6	8	9	11	RAIN DAYS

WHALE-WATCHING

At the start of winter humpback whales begin migrating to the warmer waters of Hervey Bay. Visitors are never far behind them, many making their way up the coast for the chance to see these amazing creatures offshore. Each year around 2000 humpback whales migrate from the Antarctic to Australia's eastern subtropical coast. Between July and November, up to 400 rest and regroup in Hervey Bay. For an up-close view of the majestic whales, various tours operate from the boat harbour in town.

→ For more detail see maps 648 & 653. For descriptions of ⊕ towns see Towns from A–Z (p. 429).

GREAT BARRIER REEF

Australia's most prized and visited natural destination extends over 2000 kilometres, taking in tropical islands, rare and brilliantly coloured corals, exotic fish, and sea-going mammals and birds.

Tropical North Islands

[SNORKELLING, GREAT BARRIER REEF]

Lizard Island   This northernmost island has tourist facilities, gamefishing, snorkelling, diving and bushwalking. The small, luxurious resort has bungalow-style lodgings (maximum 80 people) or camping (maximum 20 people); camping permits from Cairns parks office.

Fitzroy Island   A low-key destination with a national park, white coral beaches and magnificent flora and fauna for bushwalking, diving and snorkelling. Cabins and hostel-style accommodation (maximum 160 people) and camping (maximum 20 people) are available.

Bedarra Island   This island of untouched tropical beauty is off-limits to day visitors and children under 15. There's bushwalking, snorkelling, fishing, swimming, windsurfing, sailing and tennis, and an exclusive resort (maximum 30 people).

Orpheus Island   A small island surrounded by coral reefs and protected by national park, Orpheus offers birdwatching, watersports, glass-bottomed boat tours, island walks and fishing. There's a five-star resort (maximum 74 people) or bush camping (maximum 54 people); camping permits from Ingham parks office.

Green Island   A true coral cay covered with thick tropical vegetation, with glass-bottomed boats for reef viewing and an underwater observatory. This popular daytrip destination has a small resort (maximum 90 people).

Dunk Island   National park with walking tracks through rainforest, and prolific birdlife, butterflies and wild orchids. Go parasailing, waterskiing, sailing, clay-target shooting and horseriding. Resort accommodation (maximum 360 people) and camping (maximum 30 people).

Hinchinbrook Island   National park with a wonderland of mountains, tropical vegetation, waterfalls and sandy beaches for snorkelling, swimming, fishing and bushwalking. Small, low-key resort (maximum 45 people).

Magnetic Island   With a national park and beautiful beaches, activities include horseriding, bushwalking, snorkelling, parasailing, swimming, fishing, sea-kayaking and reef excursions. There's a permanent population and accommodation from budget to deluxe.

ISLAND ACCESS

Magnetic Island 8 kilometres NE of Townsville.
From Townsville, by vehicular ferry, catamaran or water taxi.
Orpheus Island 80 kilometres N of Townsville.
From Townsville or Cairns, by sea plane.
Hinchinbrook Island 5 kilometres E of Cardwell.
From Cardwell, by launch.
Bedarra Island 35 kilometres NE of Cardwell.
From Dunk Island, by launch.
Dunk Island 5 kilometres SE of Mission Beach.
From Cairns, by plane. From Clump Point near Mission Beach, by launch.
From Wongaling Beach and South Mission Beach, by water taxi.
Fitzroy Island 30 kilometres SE of Cairns.
From Cairns, by catamaran.
Green Island 27 kilometres NE of Cairns.
From Cairns, by catamaran, sea plane or helicopter.
Lizard Island 93 kilometres NE of Cooktown.
From Cairns or Cooktown, by plane or sea plane.

CLIMATE

FITZROY ISLAND

	J	F	M	A	M	J	J	A	S	O	N	D	
	31	30	29	28	26	24	24	25	27	29	30	31	MAX °C
	12	12	10	8	7	5	4	5	6	7	9	10	MIN °C
	27	25	31	60	89	100	106	103	86	68	40	35	RAIN MM
	6	5	7	11	5	18	17	18	15	13	9	7	RAIN DAYS

QUEENSLAND

→ For more detail see maps 649, 650, 651, 653, 655 & 657. For descriptions of ⓣ towns see Towns from A–Z (p. 429).

GREAT BARRIER REEF

Whitsunday Islands

Daydream Island A small island of volcanic rock, coral and dense tropical foliage. Daydream has a Kids Club, tennis, outdoor cinema, watersports centre, snorkelling, diving, and reef and island trips. Luxurious resort (maximum 900 people).

South Molle Island Numerous inlets and splendid views of Whitsunday Passage, plus great wildflowers in spring and early summer. There's golf, bushwalking, snorkelling, scuba diving, windsurfing and sailing. Medium-size resort (maximum 520 people).

Hayman Island Close to the outer reef, with fishing, sightseeing trips, scenic flights, diving, watersports, Kids Club and whale-watching excursions. Luxury resort (maximum 450 people).

Whitsunday Island Entirely uninhabited national park, with a beautiful 7-kilometre white silica beach and complex mangrove system. Camping only (maximum 40 people); details from Airlie Beach parks office.

Hamilton Island A large island with a wide range of facilities and activities, shops, marina and fauna park. There's windsurfing, sailing, fishing, scuba diving, parasailing, helicopter rides, tennis, squash, and reef and inter-island trips. Resort (maximum 1500 people).

Lindeman Island Secluded beaches, national park, and prolific birds and butterflies, a golf course, and full range of watersports and other island activities. Club Med resort (maximum 460 people).

Brampton Island National park and wildlife sanctuary with fine golden beaches, snorkelling trail, bushwalking, sea-plane trips and watersports. Resort-style accommodation (maximum 280 people).

Map labels (Whitsunday)

South Molle Island
West Molle Island (Daydream Island)
Hayman Island
Hook Island
Whitsunday Island
Airlie Beach
Shute Harbour
Proserpine
Hamilton Island
CONWAY NATIONAL PARK
Lindeman Island
Long Island
N
0   50 km
Brampton Island
MACKAY
CORAL SEA

ISLAND ACCESS

Whitsunday Islands

Brampton Island 32 kilometres NE of Mackay.
From Mackay, by light plane or launch. From Hamilton Island, by plane.

Lindeman Island 67 kilometres N of Mackay.
From Airlie Beach or Shute Harbour, by light plane or boat. From Mackay, by plane. From Hamilton Island, by boat or plane.

Hamilton Island 16 kilometres SE of Shute Harbour.
Direct flight from Sydney, Brisbane and Melbourne; connections from all major cities. From Shute Harbour, by launch.

South Molle Island 8 kilometres E of Shute Harbour.
From Shute Harbour or Hamilton Island, by launch.

Daydream Island 5 kilometres NE Shute Harbour.
From Shute Harbour or Hamilton Island, by launch or helicopter.

Whitsunday Island 25 kilometres E of Shute Harbour.
From Shute Harbour or Airlie Beach, by boat.

Hayman Island 25 kilometres NE of Shute Harbour.
Direct flight to Hamilton Island from Sydney and Brisbane (connections from all major cities), then by launch to Hayman Island. From Airlie Beach, by water taxi.

Southern Reef Islands

Lady Elliot Island 80 kilometres NE of Bundaberg.
From Bundaberg or Hervey Bay, by plane.

Heron Island 72 kilometres NE of Gladstone.
From Gladstone, by catamaran or charter helicopter.

Great Keppel Island 48 kilometres NE of Rockhampton.
From Rockhampton, by light plane. From Yeppoon, by launch.

Southern Reef Islands

Great Keppel Island With white sandy beaches and unspoiled tropical island scenery, there's tennis, waterskiing, diving, snorkelling, fishing, sea-kayaking, golf, parasailing, coral viewing and island cruises. Kids Club during holidays. Camping, cabins and lodge-style accommodation (maximum 650 people).

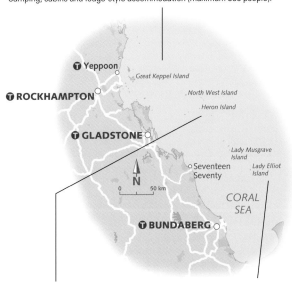

Map labels (Southern Reef)

Yeppoon
Great Keppel Island
ROCKHAMPTON
North West Island
Heron Island
GLADSTONE
Lady Musgrave Island
Seventeen Seventy
Lady Elliot Island
N
0   50 km
CORAL SEA
BUNDABERG

Heron Island A small coral cay, entirely national park, with turtle-nesting site, birdwatching and prolific flora, diving and snorkelling, and reef and ecology walks. Resort-style accommodation (maximum 250 people).

Lady Elliot Island A small coral cay with 19 major dive sites, bird rookeries, turtle-nesting site and whale-watching opportunities. Low-key resort (maximum 140 people), ranging from budget to island suites.

CLIMATE

HAMILTON ISLAND

	J	F	M	A	M	J	J	A	S	O	N	D	
	30	30	29	27	25	23	22	23	25	28	29	30	MAX °C
	25	25	24	23	21	19	18	18	20	22	23	24	MIN °C
	13	322	262	242	159	100	80	59	23	52	89	215	RAIN MM
	15	18	19	19	18	12	10	11	7	8	8	13	RAIN DAYS

CAPRICORN

Relatively untouched by commercial development, this region features remote beaches and unspoiled bushland.

[CARNARVON NATIONAL PARK]

Gemfields Some of the world's richest sapphire fields are found around the tiny, ramshackle settlements of Anakie, Sapphire, Rubyvale and Willows Gemfields, approximately 50 kilometres west of Emerald. Fossicking licences can be bought on the gemfields for a small fee.

Mount Morgan This goldmining town south of Rockhampton has hardly changed in a century. Take a tour to the Southern Hemisphere's largest excavation, or see the ancient dinosaur footprints in nearby caves.

Rockhampton The town has many heritage buildings – particularly grand are those in Quay Street. There is also an excellent discovery centre at the Customs House, and historic botanic gardens.

Capricorn Coast Thirteen beaches stretch out along Keppel Bay, taking in Yeppoon, Emu Park and Keppel Sands. Elsewhere, picturesque bays are framed by rocky headlands, pockets of rainforest, peaceful estuarine waters and wetlands.

Carnarvon National Park Carnarvon Gorge, the signature attraction of Carnarvon National Park, bends and twists its way around 30 kilometres of semi-arid terrain. Within its sandstone walls exists a cool, green world of delicate ferns and mosses fed by Carnarvon Creek. The 298 000-hectare park also contains some magnificent Aboriginal rock-art sites.

Rum town On the southern coast of the Capricorn region is the city of Bundaberg, renowned for its parks and gardens, in particular the Botanical Gardens, with the excellent Hinkler House Memorial Museum.

Mon Repos turtle rookery Mon Repos Conservation Park is one of Australia's most important turtle rookeries. From November to March there is an on-site interpretative centre and guided night tours.

Map labels
CORAL SEA
GOODEDULLA NP
Rubyvale · Sapphire ⊕
Anakie∘ ⊕ Emerald
Willows Gemfields∘
SNAKE RANGE NP · Lake Maraboon
⊕ Springsure
Blackwater ⊕
BLACKDOWN TABLELAND NP
ROCKHAMPTON
Fitzroy
Yeppoon ⊕
Emu Park
Keppel Sands
Keppel Bay
GREAT BARRIER REEF
River
Mount Morgan ⊕
CURTIS ISLAND NP
Curtis Island
GLADSTONE ⊕
EURIMBULA NP
Awoonga Reservoir
Bustard Bay
Seventeen Seventy
Agnes Water
DEEPWATER NATIONAL PARK
Biloela ⊕
Miriam Vale
CANIA GORGE NP
LITTABELLA NP
Lake Monduran
MON REPOS CP
CARNARVON NATIONAL PARK
Camarvon Gorge · Carnarvon Ck
NUGA NUGA NP
Lake Nuga Nuga
PALMGROVE NP
Theodore∘
ISLA GORGE NP
⊕ Monto
Gin Gin ⊕
BUNDABERG ⊕
BURRUM COAST NP
EXPEDITION NATIONAL PARK
PRECIPICE NP
GOOD NIGHT SCRUB NP
Childers ⊕
GREAT DIVIDING RANGE
⊕ Taroom∘
Mundubbera∘
Biggenden ⊕
⊕ Gayndah
MOUNT WALSH NP
0   50 km   N

TOP EVENTS

MAR	1770 Longboard Classic (surfing competion, Agnes Water)
MAR	Harbour Festival (Gladstone, includes finish of Brisbane–Gladstone Yacht Race)
JUNE	Orange Festival (Gayndah, odd-numbered years)
SEPT	Bundy in Bloom Festival (Bundaberg)
SEPT	Seafood Festival (Gladstone)
OCT	Rocky Barra Bounty (Rockhampton)

CLIMATE

ROCKHAMPTON

J	F	M	A	M	J	J	A	S	O	N	D	
32	31	30	29	26	23	23	25	27	30	31	32	MAX °C
22	22	21	18	14	11	9	11	14	17	19	21	MIN °C
136	141	103	47	52	35	31	29	24	48	68	105	RAIN MM
11	12	10	7	7	5	5	4	4	7	8	10	RAIN DAYS

DISCOVERY COAST

Seventeen Seventy, a small town on a narrow, hilly peninsula above an estuary, was named to mark Captain Cook's landing at Bustard Bay on 24 May 1770. Today's visitors come for the views from the headland north across the bay, and for fishing, mudcrabbing and boating. Agnes Water, a few kilometres south, has Queensland's northernmost surfing beach; rolling surf and a balmy climate attract visitors all year-round. Eurimbula National Park, just across Round Hill Inlet from Seventeen Seventy, has dunes, mangroves, salt marshes and eucalypt forests. From Agnes Water, an 8-kilometre track south to Deepwater National Park is suitable for four-wheel drives only. The long beaches of this park form a breeding ground for loggerhead turtles.

→ For more detail see maps 648, 653 & 654–5. For descriptions of ⊕ towns see Towns from A–Z (p. 429).

THE MID-TROPICS

An alternative to some of Queensland's busier coastal areas, The Mid-Tropics has stretches of sandy shoreline, warm tropical waters and rainforest.

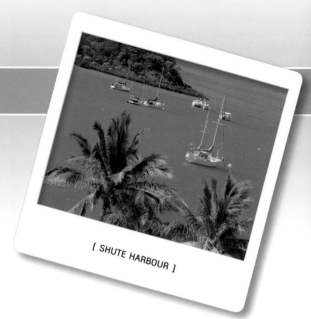

[SHUTE HARBOUR]

Marine attractions   At Reef HQ in Townsville, touch-tanks and underwater-viewing tunnels reveal some of the Great Barrier Reef's ecological mysteries. Next door, the Museum of Tropical Queensland features a full-scale reproduction of the bow of HMS *Pandora*, a British vessel wrecked on the reef in 1791.

Wreck diving   A must for divers is the SS *Yongala* wreck, which sank near Cape Bowling Green during a cyclone in 1911, and lay undiscovered for half a century. Despite being under water for almost 100 years, details such as the engine room, toilets, portholes and most of the ship's name are still evident. The marine life is excellent, with beautiful corals, giant groupers and trevally, barracuda, stingrays, turtles and hundreds of other sea creatures.

Hibiscus Coast   Steep rainforest-clad hills plunge to rocky headlands and white sandy beaches in this lovely and surprisingly peaceful district north of Mackay. Cape Hillsborough National Park offers the most pristine scenery, with kangaroos often seen hopping along the deserted beaches.

Charters Towers   Charters Towers was Queensland's second largest city during the 1870s gold rush; at that time it was known as 'The World' because of its cosmopolitan population. Today it is a showpiece, with many beautifully preserved buildings including the Bank of Commerce, now restored as the New World Theatre Complex. The 'Ghosts of Gold' Heritage Trail allows visitors to experience the town's glamorous history.

Map labels

GIRRINGUN NATIONAL PARK
Cardwell
Hinchinbrook Island
Ingham
PALUMA RANGE NP
GREAT
TOWNSVILLE
GREAT BASALT WALL NP
BOWLING GREEN BAY NP
Cape Bowling Green
Charters Towers
Ayr
BARRIER
WHITE MOUNTAINS NATIONAL PARK
Ravenswood
Bowen
Lake Dalrymple
Proserpine
Airlie Beach
GREAT BARRIER REEF MARINE PARK
Brampton Island
CAPE HILLSBOROUGH NP
Lake Buchanan
EUNGELLA NP
N
0   50 km
NAIRANA NATIONAL PARK
HOMEVALE NP
MACKAY
Sarina
Moranbah
DIPPERU NP
REEF
CORAL SEA
Clermont
JUNEE NP
BYFIELD NP

→ For more detail see maps 649, 650, 654–5 & 657. For descriptions of ⊤ towns see Towns from A–Z (p. 429).

TOP EVENTS

APR–MAY	Ten Days in the Towers (Charters Towers)
MAY	Australian Italian Festival (Ingham)
JULY	Festival of the Arts (Mackay)
JULY–AUG	Australian Festival of Chamber Music (Townsville)
SEPT	Burdekin Water Festival (Ayr)
OCT	Greek Fest (Townsville)

CLIMATE

MACKAY

J	F	M	A	M	J	J	A	S	O	N	D	
30	29	28	27	24	22	21	22	25	27	29	30	MAX °C
23	23	22	20	17	14	13	14	16	20	22	23	MIN °C
293	311	303	134	104	59	47	30	15	38	87	175	RAIN MM
16	17	17	15	13	7	7	6	5	7	9	12	RAIN DAYS

HERITAGE

This region preserves some interesting pockets of heritage. Ravenswood, east of Charters Towers, is now almost a ghost town. It flourished in the second half of the 19th century as a centre for the surrounding goldfields, and many of its buildings from this period are in a near-original state. West of Mackay is Greenmount Historic Homestead – now a museum – built in 1915 on the Cook family's grazing property. Bowen, established in 1861, is north Queensland's oldest town. The diverse history here is recorded in 25 street murals detailing the stories, personalities and events of the towns past.

CAIRNS & THE TROPICS

Tourists flock to this region to experience its ancient rainforest and coastline fronting part of the world's most spectacular reef. The national parks here offer camping, wildlife-watching and four-wheel driving.

[THE ELUSIVE SOUTHERN CASSOWARY, DAINTREE NATIONAL PARK]

Cooktown Captain Cook beached the *Endeavour* near the site of Cooktown in 1770. The town was built a century later when gold was discovered on the Palmer River to the south-west. Cooktown has excellent botanic gardens dating from the 1880s, and cruises travel along the river and out to the reef.

Atherton Tableland This 900-metre-high tableland south-west of Cairns is a productive farming district, thanks to the high rainfall and rich volcanic soil. Near Yungaburra is the remarkable Curtain Fig Tree, a strangler fig that has subsumed its host, sending down a curtain of roots. Volcanic lakes and spectacular waterfalls, including Millaa Millaa Falls and Zillie Falls, are among the other scenic attractions.

Whitewater rafting on the Tully River The Tully River, which descends from the Atherton Tableland through rainforest gorges, is one of Queensland's three main rafting rivers (the other two are the Barron and North Johnstone). It receives one of the highest annual rainfalls in Australia, explaining its rapids, which are pretty ferocious in parts, and has more than 45 individual rapids up to grade 4. In short, it's perfect for whitewater rafting.

Daintree National Park The Mossman Gorge section of this park takes visitors into the rainforest's green and shady heart via an easy 2.7-kilometre walk to the Mossman River. The Cape Tribulation section is a rich mix of coastal rainforest, mangroves, swamp and heath.

Tjapukai Aboriginal Cultural Park An Aboriginal group, originally a dance company, set up this park in Smithfield to make their unique Far North Queensland culture more accessible. In the theatres you can hear Aboriginal creation stories and watch Aboriginal dance, and in the Camp Village you can learn to throw a boomerang.

Map labels

CORAL SEA
ENDEAVOUR RIVER NP
Cooktown
CEDAR BAY NP
Palmer R.
GREAT
DAINTREE NATIONAL PARK
Cape Tribulation
Daintree
DAINTREE NP
Mossman
Port Douglas
DIVIDING
HANN TABLELAND NP
Kuranda
Palm Cove
Smithfield
BARRON GORGE NP
CAIRNS
Mareeba
Gordonvale
Lake Tinaroo
Atherton
Yungaburra
RUSSELL RIVER NP
Herberton
Babinda
WOOROONOORAN NP
Millaa Millaa
Innisfail
Ravenshoe
Mourilyan
RA
TULLY GORGE NP
KURRIMINE BEACH NP
Koombooloomba Dam
Tully
Mission Beach
HULL RIVER NP
EDMUND KENNEDY NP

0   40 km   N

QUEENSLAND

TOP EVENTS

MAY	Village Carnivale (Port Douglas)
JUNE	Discovery Festival (Cooktown)
AUG–SEPT	Festival Cairns (Cairns)
OCT	Walkamin Country Music Festival (Mareeba)
OCT	Yungaburra Folk Festival (Yungaburra)
OCT	Palm Cove Fiesta (Palm Cove)

CLIMATE

CAIRNS

	J	F	M	A	M	J	J	A	S	O	N	D	
	31	31	30	29	28	26	26	27	28	29	31	31	MAX °C
	24	24	23	22	20	18	17	18	19	21	22	23	MIN °C
	413	435	442	191	94	49	28	27	36	38	90	175	RAIN MM
	18	19	20	17	14	10	9	8	8	8	10	13	RAIN DAYS

TROPICAL RAINFORESTS

The World Heritage Wet Tropics Area covers 894 000 hectares along the eastern escarpment of the Great Dividing Range between Townsville and Cooktown, and features rainforest, mountains, gorges, fast-flowing rivers and countless waterfalls. The rainforest here is one of the oldest continually existing rainforests on earth, with an estimated age of more than 100 million years. It represents major stages in the earth's evolutionary history and has the world's greatest concentration of primitive flowering plants, or 'green dinosaurs', as they are known. Its biological diversity is astounding; while the Wet Tropics covers just 0.1 per cent of the continent, it contains 30 per cent of Australia's marsupial species, 60 per cent of its bats and 62 per cent of its butterflies.

→ For more detail see maps 650, 651 & 657. For descriptions of ⊤ towns see Towns from A–Z (p. 429).

CAPE YORK

One of Australia's last undeveloped frontiers, Cape York showcases some of the country's finest Aboriginal rock art, spectacular wildlife and amazing landscapes.

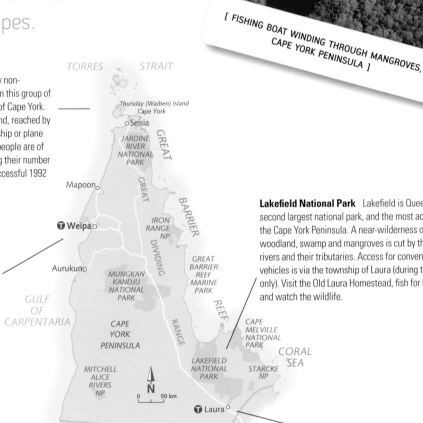

[FISHING BOAT WINDING THROUGH MANGROVES, CAPE YORK PENINSULA]

Torres Strait Islands   Australia's only non-Aboriginal indigenous people come from this group of around 100 islands off the northern tip of Cape York. The commercial centre is Thursday Island, reached by ferry from Seisia or Punsand Bay or by ship or plane from Cairns. The Torres Strait Islander people are of Melanesian descent and include among their number the late Eddie Mabo, famous for his successful 1992 land claim in Australia's High Court.

Weipa   The world's largest bauxite deposits are found around Weipa. In 1961 Comalco built a modern mining town, with all facilities, on the site of an Aboriginal mission station and reserve. Today the company offers tours of its mining operations. The fishing around Weipa (and indeed the whole of the cape) is excellent.

Lakefield National Park   Lakefield is Queensland's second largest national park, and the most accessible on the Cape York Peninsula. A near-wilderness of grassland, woodland, swamp and mangroves is cut by three major rivers and their tributaries. Access for conventional vehicles is via the township of Laura (during the Dry only). Visit the Old Laura Homestead, fish for barramundi and watch the wildlife.

Quinkan country   To the south-east of Laura are the spectacular Aboriginal rock-art sites of Split Rock and Gu Gu Yalangi. Encompassing the area between Laura and Cooktown, these form just a small part of one of the largest collections of prehistoric rock art in the world. The most distinctive works are the Quinkan figures, stick-like figures representing spirits that emerge suddenly from rock crevices.

TOP EVENTS

JUNE	Laura Aboriginal Dance and Cultural Festival (Laura, odd-numbered years)
JUNE	Mabo Day (Torres Strait Islands)
JULY	Coming of the Light Festival (Torres Strait Islands)
SEPT	Torres Strait Cultural Festival (Torres Strait Islands, even-numbered years)

CLIMATE

WEIPA

	J	F	M	A	M	J	J	A	S	O	N	D	
	32	31	32	32	32	31	30	32	33	35	35	33	MAX °C
	24	24	24	23	21	20	19	19	20	21	23	24	MIN °C
	421	401	338	82	6	2	1	1	1	14	98	256	RAIN MM
	22	21	20	10	3	2	1	1	1	3	8	16	RAIN DAYS

ABORIGINAL CAPE YORK

Before white people arrived, the Aboriginal people of Cape York were divided into two main groups – East Cape and West Cape – with many language and cultural groups within this broad division. The distinctive art of the East Cape people survives in the rock-art galleries around Laura, some of the most extensive and unusual in Australia. The Aboriginal groups of West Cape, an area that proved largely resistant to European expansion, maintained sizeable pockets of land around Mapoon and Aurukun. Native title legislation since the 1950s has handed much of the West Cape back to its Aboriginal owners.

Map labels: TORRES STRAIT; Thursday (Waiben) Island; Cape York; Seisia; JARDINE RIVER NATIONAL PARK; GREAT; GREAT; BARRIER; Mapoon; Weipa; IRON RANGE NP; DIVIDING; Aurukun; MUNGKAN KANDJU NATIONAL PARK; GREAT BARRIER REEF MARINE PARK; REEF; GULF OF CARPENTARIA; CAPE YORK PENINSULA; RANGE; CAPE MELVILLE NATIONAL PARK; CORAL SEA; MITCHELL ALICE RIVERS NP; LAKEFIELD NATIONAL PARK; STARCKE NP; N; 0   50 km; Laura

→ For more detail see maps 656–7 & 658. For descriptions of ⊤ towns see Towns from A–Z (p. 429).

GULF SAVANNAH

A remote and far-flung area of Queensland, this region is characterised by vast tracts of savannah grasslands, lagoons and mangrove-lined estuaries.

[CANOEING IN BOODJAMULLA (LAWN HILL) NATIONAL PARK]

Tourist train Every Wednesday the *Gulflander* leaves Normanton on a 153-kilometre journey to the historic goldmining town of Croydon. With stops at points of interest along the line, the trip takes four hours. Travellers can explore Croydon with a local guide and return to Normanton on Thursday.

Fossicking around Mount Surprise
The historic rail town of Mount Surprise has excellent gemfields in its vicinity that are perfect for fossicking, especially for topaz, quartz and aquamarine. Mount Surprise Gems in Garland Street (which doubles as the visitor centre) runs tours to nearby fossicking spots, so you don't need to worry about licences. If you're out of luck on the field, you can always purchase the stunning gemstones in town.

Boodjamulla (Lawn Hill) National Park
Lawn Hill Gorge, about 205 kilometres from Burketown, is this remote park's main attraction. The gorge has given life to an oasis of lush rainforest. Canoeing, swimming and walking are the main activities, and Aboriginal rock-art sites are accessible at two locations.

Riversleigh Fossil Site The fossils in this World Heritage–listed part of Boodjamulla (Lawn Hill) National Park record the evolution of mammals over 20 million years, as the vegetation changed from rainforest to semi-arid grassland. Guided tours provide an insight into the ancient world, and there is a self-guide interpretive trail.

Lava tubes Undara, an Aboriginal word for long, accurately describes the tubes in Undara Volcanic National Park east of Mount Surprise. At 160 kilometres, one of the lava tubes here is the longest on earth. The caves in nearby Chillagoe–Mungana Caves National Park are a feast for the senses, with bat colonies and richly decorative stalactites and stalagmites. Tours are necessary to visit both the tubes and the caves. The incredible geological history of the area is detailed at The Hub in Chillagoe.

TOP EVENTS

EASTER	World Barramundi Championships (Burketown)
EASTER	Barra Classic (Normanton)
APR	Fishing Competition (Karumba)
APR–MAY	Gregory River Canoe Marathon (Gregory)
MAY	Chillagoe Big Weekend (Chillagoe)
JUNE	Normanton Show and Rodeo (Normanton)

CLIMATE

NORMANTON

J	F	M	A	M	J	J	A	S	O	N	D	
35	34	34	34	32	29	29	31	34	36	37	36	MAX °C
25	25	24	22	19	16	15	17	20	23	25	25	MIN °C
260	249	158	31	8	9	3	2	3	10	44	143	RAIN MM
14	14	9	2	1	1	1	0	0	1	4	9	RAIN DAYS

FISHING THE GULF

The gulf is one of Australia's true fishing frontiers. Anglers can fish the rivers – the Nicholson, Albert, Flinders, Norman and Gilbert – as well as the coastal beaches and the offshore waters and reefs of the gulf, accessible via the island resorts. Karumba, on the Norman River estuary, is a popular base for both river and offshore anglers. Sweers Island, in the Wellesley group, has a fishing resort offering access to thousands of hectares of reef, where coral trout, parrotfish, sweetlip and sea perch (and in winter, pelagics such as mackerel and tuna) are plentiful. Mornington Island is home to the Birri Fishing Resort, offering crabbing and sport- and bottom-fishing, all with professional masters. You can also stay at Escott Barramundi Lodge on the Nicholson River, reached via Burketown. Fishing charters take you along the nearby lagoons and rivers, where you can catch barramundi, catfish and mangrove jack.

→ For more detail see maps 656–7 & 659. For descriptions of ⊤ towns see Towns from A–Z (p. 429).

QUEENSLAND

OUTBACK

Outback Queensland is remote, sparsely populated and — in parts — beautiful. Many legends of Australia's pioneering days evolved here, and are celebrated in the region's museums and monuments.

[OLD MAILBOX AT CRAVENS PEAK, BOULIA]

Mount Isa   This is Queensland's largest outback town. For a quintessential outback experience, visit Outback at Isa, complete with underground mining tunnels and mining machinery. Nearby is the Kalkadoon Tribal Centre and Cultural Keeping Place, with artefacts of the fierce and proud Kalkadoon people.

Channel Country   Monsoon rains in the tropical north flood the hundreds of inland river channels that meander through Queensland's south-west. Here cattle graze on huge semi-desert pastoral holdings. Spectacular red sandhills are found in the area, particularly in Simpson Desert National Park, beyond Birdsville. On certain nights under certain conditions, the town of Boulia, capital of the Channel Country, is handed over to the realm of the Min Min reputedly a strange ball of white light that hovers above the ground, disappearing, reappearing and moving around at will. The Min Min Encounter in town is an impressive centre where you can soak up the stories surrounding this outback legend.

Waltzing Matilda Centre   The area surrounding Winton is known as Matilda Country, because Australia's most famous song, *Waltzing Matilda*, was written by Banjo Paterson at nearby Dagworth Station in 1895. A tribute to the character and life of the Australian swagman, the Waltzing Matilda Centre provides an interesting look at the nation's history. Among other things, it incorporates the regional gallery, interactive exhibits and the Matilda Museum, harking back to Winton's pioneering days and the first days of Qantas (whose first office was registered here in 1920).

Barcaldine   This 'Garden City of the West' was the first Australian town to tap the waters of the Great Artesian Basin, an event commemorated by the town's giant windmill. The Australian Workers Heritage Centre, in town, recollects the 1891 Shearers' Strike that led to the formation of the Australian Workers Party, forerunner of the Australian Labor Party. It also features re-created work precincts in tribute to all the workers who helped shape early Australia.

Australian Stockman's Hall of Fame and Outback Heritage Centre   This impressive institution is a lasting tribute to the outback people – Indigenous, European settler and current-day inhabitants alike. The imaginative displays show the development of the outback. Don't miss the nearby Qantas Founders Outback Heritage Museum, which tells the story of the oldest airline in the English-speaking world.

TOP EVENTS

APR	Dirt and Dust Festival (Julia Creek)
APR	Surf Carnival (Kynuna)
AUG	Isa Rodeo (Mount Isa)
AUG	Drover's Camp Festival (Camooweal)
SEPT	Birdsville Cup Racing Carnival (Birdsville)
SEPT	Bilby Festival (Charleville)

CLIMATE

LONGREACH

	J	F	M	A	M	J	J	A	S	O	N	D	
	37	36	35	31	27	24	23	26	30	34	36	37	MAX °C
	23	23	20	16	12	8	7	8	12	17	20	22	MIN °C
	58	68	43	10	13	5	4	3	3	16	16	44	RAIN MM
	7	7	5	3	3	2	2	2	2	4	4	6	RAIN DAYS

ANCIENT ANIMALS

Queensland's outback is a veritable feast of fossils that document its changing ecological history. There is a fossil collection at Flinders Discovery Centre in Hughenden, its main exhibit being the replica skeleton of *Muttaburrasaurus langdoni* (the real thing was found in 1963 in a creek near Muttaburra). Kronosaurus Korner in Richmond is well known for its vertebrate fossils, and the Riversleigh Fossil Centre in Mount Isa showcases the tremendous findings of the Riversleigh Fossil Site. At Lark Quarry Conservation Park south-west of Winton, the preserved tracks of a dinosaur stampede lie protected under a shelter.

→ For more detail see maps 652, 654, 659, 660–1 & 662–3. For descriptions of ⦿ towns see Towns from A–Z (p. 429).

[RAINFOREST CANOPY, DAINTREE NATIONAL PARK]

LEGEND

ⓘ VISITOR INFORMATION

RADIO STATIONS

IN TOWN

WHAT'S ON

WHERE TO EAT

WHERE TO STAY

NEARBY

Airlie Beach

Pop. 2752
Map ref. 649 F5 | 655 J3

ⓘ 277 Shute Harbour Rd; (07) 9496 6665 or 1800 819 366; www.destinationwhitsundays.com.au

📻 89.9 FM ABC Local Tropical North, 94.7 Hot FM

Airlie Beach is at the centre of the thriving Whitsunday coast. This tropical holiday town offers a cosmopolitan blend of bars, restaurants and shops just metres from the beach. From Abel Point Marina, daytrips to the outer Great Barrier Reef and Whitsunday islands are on offer. Watersports available include sailing, snorkelling, diving and fishing. Nearby Shute Harbour is one of the largest marine passenger terminals in Australia and, along with Airlie Beach, services the majority of the Whitsunday islands.

Airlie Beach Lagoon: safe, year-round swimming in landscaped environment; foreshore. **Whale watching:** tours July–Sept depart Abel Point Marina; details from visitor centre. **Sailing:** be it traditional sailing, adventure or luxury crewed; details from visitor centre. **Skydiving:** tandem skydive and take in the stunning views from very high above; (07) 4946 9115.

Community market: Airlie Beach Esplanade; Sat mornings. **Meridien Marinas Race Week:** sailing; Aug. **Whitsunday Fun Race:** competitions for cruising yachts; Aug/Sept. **Festival of Sport:** includes triathlon; Sept.

Déjà Vu: modern Australian; Golden Orchid Dr; (07) 4948 4309. **Air Whitsunday Peppers Palm Bay daytrip:** seaplane tour with lunch; Air Whitsunday, Whitsunday Airport; (07) 4946 9111. **Daydream Island Day Tripper:** lunch cruise;

Fantasea Cruises, 11 Shute Harbour; (07) 4946 5111 or 1800 650 851.

Airlie Waterfront B&B: waterfront location; Cnr Broadwater Ave and Mazlin St; (07) 4946 7631. **Pinnacles Resort and Spa:** luxury resort; 16 Golden Orchid Dr; (07) 4948 4800. **Whitsunday Terraces:** great views from these self-contained apartments; 5 Golden Orchid Dr; (07) 4946 6788 or 1800 075 062.

Conway National Park Covering 35 km of coastline, this park is renowned for its natural beauty and as the habitat of the Proserpine rock wallaby (endangered species). Walks start in Airlie Beach and Shute Harbour. The Mt Rooper Lookout is a highlight, featuring a panoramic view over Hamilton, Dent, Long and Henning islands. Access the park off the road to Shute Harbour; (07) 4967 7355; 3 km SE.

Islands of Whitsunday Passage These islands offer an abundance of sights and activities, whether they be the sports and social activities at the resorts on Hamilton, Daydream and Hayman islands, or the more secluded island experience on Whitsunday, Hook and South Molle. Whitsunday Island is famous for the white sand and clear water of Whitehaven Beach. The waterfalls on Hook Island are impressive, as are the butterflies on the shores of the island's aptly named Butterfly Bay. Big-game enthusiasts strive to catch black marlin off Hayman Island Sept–Nov.

Crocodile safaris and fishing trips: to nearby coastal wetlands; details from visitor centre. **Scenic flights:** various tours over the 74 Whitsunday islands; details from visitor centre.

See also THE MID-TROPICS, p. 424

Allora

Pop. 920
Map ref. 653 L10

i 49 Albion St (New England Hwy), Warwick; (07) 4661 3122;
www.southerndownsholidays.com.au

89.3 Rainbow FM, 747 AM ABC Southern QLD

Allora is a charming town in the Darling Downs, central to its
rich agricultural surrounds. Explored and settled with stud farms
in the 1840s, Allora's main street is noted for its well-preserved
historic buildings and old-time country feel.

Allora Museum: noted for its replica of the Talgai Skull,
an Aboriginal cranium dating back 15 000 years; open 1.30–4pm
Sun; old courthouse, Drayton St. *St David's Anglican Church:*
built in 1888 and said to be one of the finest timber churches
in country Queensland; Church St. *The Gnomery:* over 100
different moveable handcrafted toys that feature in a theatre
performance; New England Hwy.

Glengallan Farmers Markets: 1st Sun of each season.
Heritage Weekend: Jan. *Allora Show:* Feb. *Allora Auction:* cars to
farm machinery; June.

Goomburra Forest Retreat: peaceful retreat; 268 Forestry
Reserve Rd; (07) 4666 6058.

Goomburra, Main Range National Park Located in the
western foothills of the Great Dividing Range, this park has short
walks around Dalrymple Creek and spectacular views from Mt
Castle and Sylvesters lookouts. Take the Inverramsay Rd 40 km
E to the forest. The last 6 km is unsealed and may be impassable
following heavy rain. (07) 4666 1133; 49 km E.

Glengallan Homestead and Heritage Centre: restored 1867
sandstone mansion. Documents and photos chronicle its history as
a pastoral station; open Thurs–Sun; New England Hwy; 11 km S.

See also DARLING DOWNS, p. 418

Aramac

Pop. 340
Map ref. 654 D9 | 661 P9

i Post office, 22 Gordon St; (07) 4651 3147;
www.aramac.qld.gov.au

540 AM ABC Western QLD

Aramac is a small service town west of the Great Dividing Range.
The town was named by explorer William Landsborough; the
name is an acronym for the name of Queensland premier Sir
Robert Ramsay Mackenzie (RRMac). The town's sole water
supply is from two bores that tap into the Great Artesian Basin.

Harry Redford Interpretive Centre: photographic
exhibition of cattle drives, also local arts and crafts; Gordon St.
White Bull replica: commemorating Captain Starlight's arrest for
cattle stealing; Gordon St. *Tramway Museum:* with old rail motor
and historical exhibits; McWhannell St.

Harry Redford Cattle Drive: May–June. *Ballyneety
Rodeo:* Sept.

Lake Dunn This freshwater lake and its surrounds have
greatest appeal to birdwatchers. It is also popular for swimming
and fishing. Follow signs to 'The Lake'; 68 km NE.

Forest Den National Park This remote park is an important
wildlife sanctuary due to its semi-permanent waterholes. Have a
picnic next to Torrens Creek and go birdwatching at dusk. 4WD
recommended. Torrens Creek Rd; (07) 4652 7333; 110 km N.

Gray Rock: large sandstone rock engraved with the names of
hundreds of Cobb & Co travellers. This was once the site of a

hotel – a nearby cave was used as the hotel's cellar. 35 km E. *Lake
Galilee:* 15 000 ha saltwater lake with large waterfowl population;
some of access road unsealed; 100 km NE.

See also OUTBACK, p. 428

Atherton

Pop. 6249
Map ref. 650 D3 | 651 D9 | 657 L7

i Cnr Silo and Main sts; (07) 4091 4222;
www.athertontableland.com

97.9 Hot FM, 720 AM ABC Far North QLD

Originally called Prior's Pocket and renamed in 1885, this
town is the commercial hub of the Atherton Tableland. It is
an area renowned for its volcanic crater lakes, waterfalls and
fertile farmlands. Surrounding the town is dense rainforest that
abounds in birdlife, and the nearby parks and forests offer a
variety of watersports, bushwalking and outdoor activities.

Chinese Interpretive Centre and Old Post Office Gallery
Atherton once had a large population of Chinese working for
local timber cutters. This centre exhibits photos of these days and
has artefacts and works by local artists and potters. Tours of the
nearby Hou Wang Temple, built in 1903 and recently restored,
depart from here. Open Wed–Sun; Herberton Rd.

Hallorans Hill Conservation Park: walk to the rim of this
extinct volcanic cone on the Atherton Tableland, where there is a
spectacular lookout and informative displays; off Kennedy Hwy.
Crystal Caves: explore underground tunnels and chambers lined
with crystals, fossils and fluorescent minerals. The above-ground
Fascinating Facets shop sells a range of jewellery and gemstones;
Main St. *Birds of Prey:* interactive bird show featuring some
amazing aerial predators; shows 11am and 2pm Wed–Sun (closed
Feb, Mar and Nov); Herberton Rd; (07) 4091 6945.

VP60 Celebrations: military parade; Aug. *Maize
Festival:* Aug.

Tolga Woodworks Cafe and Gallery: gourmet cafe food;
Kennedy Hwy, Tolga; (07) 4095 4488.

Atherton Rainforest Motor Inn: garden adjoins rainforest;
Cnr Simms Rd and Kennedy Hwy; (07) 4095 4141. *The Summit
Rainforest Retreat:* Land for Wildlife property; 22 Twelfth Ave;
(07) 4091 7300. *Barking Owl Retreat:* 2 secluded cottages;
409 Hough Rd, Kairi; (07) 4095 8455.

Lake Tinaroo With 200 km of shoreline, Lake Tinaroo is
ideal for fishing, waterskiing and sailing. Walking tracks circle
the lake, and dinghies and houseboats are available for hire. The
Danbulla Forest Drive is a scenic 28 km drive. 15 km NE via Kairi.

Hasties Swamp National Park: local and migratory birds visit
this swamp, including whistling ducks and magpie geese;
(07) 4091 1844; 3 km S. *Tolga:* this town has a railway
museum and craft outlets; 5 km N. *Wongabel State Forest:*
important wildlife refuge in Wet Tropics World Heritage Area.
An informative heritage trail gives an insight into Aboriginal
culture and history; Kennedy Hwy; 8 km S.

See also CAIRNS & THE TROPICS, p. 425

Ayr

Pop. 8094
Map ref. 649 B2 | 654 H2 | 657 O12

i Burdekin Visitor Information Centre, Bruce Hwy,
Plantation Creek Park; (07) 4783 5988;
www.burdekintourism.com.au

97.1 Sweet FM, 630 AM ABC North QLD

This busy town south-east of Townsville is surrounded by sugarcane fields – the most productive in Australia – and is the largest mango-growing area in the country. On the north side of the Burdekin River, it is linked to Home Hill to the south by the 1097-metre Silver Link Bridge, which ensures the towns are not cut off when the river floods.

Burdekin Cultural Complex: 530-seat theatre, library and activities centre. The forecourt has distinctive Living Lagoon water feature; Queen St. **Gubulla Munda:** 60 m carpet snake sculpture is the totem for the Juru Tribe, who were the original inhabitants of the area. Nearby Juru Walk passes through remnant dry tropical rainforest; Bruce Hwy, southern entrance to Ayr.

Market: Plantation Creek Park; Bruce Hwy; Sun (not 4th Sun of the month). **Barra Rush:** fishing competition; Feb. **Auto Fest:** car show; Apr. **Water Festival:** Sept.

Home Hill This small town is just south of Ayr over the Silver Link. The towering tea trees along the main street bear plaques commemorating the town's pioneering families. The Silver Link Interpretive Centre in Eighth Ave gives a photographic history of the Burdekin River Bridge. Ashworth's Tourist Centre houses Ashworth's Jewellers, the Rock Shop and the impressive Treasures of the Earth Display, while Zaro's Cultural Gallery has original islander artworks. The Canefield Ashes cricket competition is held in Apr, the Burdekin Grower Race Day in May and the Harvest Festival in Nov; 12 km s.

Hutchings Lagoon: watersports; 5 km NW. **Brandon Heritage Precinct:** includes district's oldest church, St Patrick's (1897), now a local history museum. Ye Olde Machinery Place has an antique farm machinery display; 6 km N. **Lynchs Beach:** beach walks, birdwatching, swimming and fishing. Departure point for dive trips to world-famous shipwreck, SS *Yongala*; 18 km N. **Mt Kelly:** Great views of surrounding farmlands; 18 km sw. **Charlies Hill:** WW II historic site; 24 km s. **Groper Creek:** great fishing spot with camping available; 24 km SE. **Horseshoe Lagoon:** birdwatching; 35 km N. **Mt Inkerman:** good views at top, plus picnic and barbecue facilities; 30 km s. **Burdekin Dam:** biggest dam in Queensland, holding the equivalent of 4 Sydney Harbours. Fishing and camping on offer; 180 km NW.

See also THE MID-TROPICS, p. 424

Babinda
Pop. 1168
Map ref. 650 E4 | 651 G10 | 657 M7

i Cnr Bruce Hwy and Munro St; (07) 4067 1008.

 94.9 Kool FM, 720 AM ABC Far North QLD

A small sugar town south of Cairns, Babinda boasts abundant wildlife, secluded swimming holes and untouched rainforest in its surrounds. In adjacent Wooroonooran National Park are the state's two highest mountains, Mount Bartle Frere (1622 metres) and Mount Bellenden Ker (1592 metres).

M&J Aboriginality: a family business specialising in traditional Aboriginal artefacts. Make your own didgeridoo or learn how to throw a boomerang; Howard Kennedy Dr; (07) 4067 1660.

Harvestfest: celebrate the start of the cane season; May.

Wooroonooran National Park Part of the Wet Tropics World Heritage Area, the park has endemic species of plants and animals and spectacular walks through tropical rainforest. Swim in the watering hole at Josephine Falls, located at the base of Mt Bartle Frere, or see the Boulders, a large group of rocks worn smooth by tropical rains. Also visit the Mamu Canopy Rainforest Walk, which has spectacular views of the North Johnstone Gorge. Access off Bruce Hwy, west of Babinda; (07) 4061 5900.

Deeral: departure point for cruises through rainforest and saltwater crocodile haunts of the Mulgrave and Russell rivers. Deeral Cooperative makes footwear and Aboriginal artefacts; Nelson Rd; 14 km N. **Bramston Beach:** small community behind long palm-lined beach; Bruce Hwy s to Miriwinni, then 12 km E. **Russell River National Park:** small park on the coast with good birdwatching, swimming and canoeing; no facilities, 4WD access; (07) 4046 6600; 6 km N of Brampton Beach.

See also CAIRNS & THE TROPICS, p. 425

Barcaldine
Pop. 1338
Map ref. 654 D10 | 661 P10

i Oak St; (07) 4651 1724; www.barcaldine.qld.gov.au

 100.9 West FM, 540 AM ABC Western QLD

After the 1891 Shearers' Strike, the Australian Labor Party was born in this pastoral and rail town located some 100 kilometres east of Longreach. Barcaldine's supply of artesian water ensures its status as 'Garden City of the West'; the streets are named after trees.

Australian Workers Heritage Centre This centre is a tribute to the working men and women of Australia – the shearers, teachers, policemen and other workers who helped build the nation. The interpretive displays also cover the events leading to the formation of the Labor Party. Open 9am–5pm Mon–Sat, 10am–4pm Sun and public holidays; Ash St; (07) 4651 2422.

Tree of Knowledge: was a large ghost gum, which stood outside the railway station. It was fatally poisoned in 2006, but is being preserved and will be placed inside an $8 million memorial; Oak St. **Folk Museum:** display of historical memorabilia from the area; Cnr Gidyea and Beech sts. **Roses 'n' Things:** sit among over 800 roses of various varieties while enjoying Devonshire tea; Coolibah St. **National Trust–classified buildings:** Masonic lodge, Beech St; Anglican church, Elm St; shire hall, Ash St. **Murals and musical instruments:** Barcaldine is home to several murals including one painted by the late D'Arcy Doyle. There are also 2 musical instruments in the parks, which visitors are free to play; Oak St. **Between the Bougainvilleas Heritage Trail:** this award-winning heritage trail showcases Barcaldine's varied and colourful history; details from visitor centre. **Artesian Country tours:** including some to Aboriginal carvings and caves; details from visitor centre. **Bike hire:** a gold coin donation will allow you to cycle around the town at your own leisure and take in all the sites.

Mini steam-train rides: depart Folk Museum; last Sun each month (Mar–Oct). **Easter in the Outback:** Easter. **Tree of Knowledge Festival:** festival includes the Revfest, goat races, May Day parade and markets; May.

Bicentennial Park: has botanical walk through bushland; Blackall Rd; 9 km s. **Lloyd Jones Weir:** great fishing and birdwatching venue; 15 km sw.

See also OUTBACK, p. 428

QUEENSLAND

Beaudesert

Pop. 5386
Map ref. 551 F1 | 557 N1 | 645 C9 | 653 N10

 Historical Museum, 54 Brisbane St; (07) 5541 3740; www.bsc.qld.gov.au

101.5 Beau FM, 747 AM ABC Southern QLD

Beaudesert lies in the valley of the Logan River, in the Gold Coast hinterland. The town was built up around the homestead of Edward Hawkins – his property was immense, comprising land from the coast to the Logan River. Those origins continue with the area noted for its dairying, beef cattle, and fruit and vegetable produce, making the country markets a great attraction.

Centre for Arts and Culture: the region's newest attraction and hub for musicians, artists, comedians and film buffs. State-of-the-art auditorium for large performances as well as intimate spaces; Brisbane St. **Historical Museum:** displays of old machinery and tools; Brisbane St. **Community Arts Centre:** art gallery, teahouse and craft shop; Enterprise Dr.

Market: Westerman Park; 1st Sat each month. **Bikes and Bands Charity Fesitval:** food and music; Feb. **Rodeo:** May. **Equine Expo:** June. **Country and Horse Festival:** June. **Beaudesert Show:** Sept.

Barney Creek Vineyard Cottages: 3 private cottages; 198 Seidenspinner Rd, Barney View; (07) 5544 3285. **Cedar Glen Farmstay:** homestead and private cottages; 3338 Kerry Rd, Lost World Valley; (07) 5544 8170. **Katandra Mountain Farm House:** pets welcome, including horses; 3213 Kerry Rd, Lost World Valley; 1800 503 475. **Worendo Cottages:** also has cooking school; 97 Cedar Glen Rd, Darlington; (07) 5544 8104.

Mt Barney National Park A remote park where the rugged peaks of Barney, Maroon, May and Lindesay mountains stand as remnants of the ancient Focal Peak Shield Volcano. The walks are not for the inexperienced, but picnicking at Yellow Pinch at the base of Mt Barney is an alternative. The challenging 10 hr ascent to Mt Barney's summit on the Logan's Ridge track rewards walkers with spectacular views; 55 km sw.

Darlington Park: recreation area with picnic/barbecue facilities; 12 km s. **Tamrookum:** has a fine example of a timber church; tours by appt; 24 km sw. **Bigriggen Park:** recreation area with picnic/barbecue facilities; 30 km sw. **Rathdowney:** great viewpoint from Captain Logan's Lookout in John St; 32 km s. **Lamington National Park:** 40 km sw; see Nerang.

See also GOLD COAST & HINTERLAND, p. 417

Biggenden

Pop. 644
Map ref. 648 B5 | 653 L4

 Rose's Gallery Cafe Shoppe, George St; (07) 4127 1901; www.biggenden.qld.gov.au

102.5 Breeze FM, 855 AM ABC Wide Bay

This agricultural town south-west of the city of Bundaberg, known as the 'Rose of the Burnett', is proud of its impressive range of roses in the main street. Situated in a valley, the majestic ranges of Mount Walsh National Park tower over the town.

Historical Museum: exhibits history of shire and life of the early pioneers; open Thurs and 2nd Sat each month, or by appt; Brisbane St; (07) 4127 5137. **Blacksmith Shop:** established in 1891, this recently restored shop contains displays and relics; open by appt; George St; (07) 4127 1298.

Market: Lions Park; 3rd Sat each month. **Biggenden Show:** May. **Dallarnil Sports Day:** June. **Auto Spectacular:** Aug. **Rodeo:** Nov.

Mt Walsh National Park Featuring the impressive Bluff Range, this wilderness park commands the skyline. Walks take in rugged granite outcrops and gullies and are for the experienced bushwalker only. From the picnic area the views are still commanding; Maryborough Rd; (07) 4121 1800; 8 km s.

Mt Woowoonga: bushwalking in a forestry reserve; picnic and barbecue facilities; 10 km NW. **Coalstoun Lakes National Park:** protects 2 volcanic crater lakes. Walk up the northern crater for a view over the rim; 20 km sw. **Coongara Rock:** a volcanic core surrounded by rainforest; 4WD access only; 20 km s. **Chowey Bridge:** 1905 concrete arch railway bridge, one of 2 surviving in the country; 20 km NW. **Brooweena:** small town with Pioneer Museum; Biggenden Rd; 30 km SE. **Paradise Dam:** this 30 000-megalitre dam took 4 years to build and has a tourist centre. Walking track and fishing areas nearby; barbecue facilities; 35 km NW.

See also CAPRICORN, p. 423

Biloela

Pop. 5369
Map ref. 653 J2

 Queensland Heritage Park, Exhibition Ave; (07) 4992 2400; www.biloela.com

96.5 Sea FM, 837 AM ABC Capricornia

This thriving town in the fertile Callide Valley is part of the Banana Shire, but do not expect to find any bananas grown here. The area was actually named after a bullock called 'Banana', whose job was to lure wild cattle into enclosures, a difficult feat that was much applauded by local stockmen.

Queensland Heritage Park Exhibition Originally an exhibition at the Expo '88 in Brisbane, the park is home to the famous silo, which stands 28 m tall. Inside are exhibitions on the history of the Callide and Dawson valleys as well as scenes of rural life. Also in the complex is Pioneer Place, home to Biloela's first church and railway station, where photographs and memorabilia document the area's past. Exhibition Ave.

Spirit of the Land Mural: amazing mural depicting the history of women in the shire; State Farm Rd. **Greycliffe Homestead:** original slab hut converted to a museum showcases the area's pioneering heritage; open by appt; Gladstone Rd; (07) 4992 1572.

Rotary Car, Ute and Bike Show: Mar. **Biloela Rockfest:** Mar. **Callide Fishing Competition:** Mar. **Callide Valley Show:** May. **Old Wheels in Motion (Callide):** festival celebrating farm machinery and vintage cars; July. **Arts Festival (Brigalow):** Oct. **Food and Comedy Festival:** Oct. **Coal and Country Festival (Moura):** Oct.

Mt Scoria Known locally as the 'Musical Mountain' because of the basalt columns at the top that ring when hit with another rock. Walks and trails around the mountain. 14 km s.

Thangool: renowned for its race days; 10 km SE. **Callide Dam:** excellent for boating, fishing and swimming; 12 km NE. **Callide Power Station:** near Callide Dam. **Callide Mine Lookout:** view over Biloela, the mine and the dam; 18 km NE, past dam. **Kroombit Tops National Park:** 25 km E; see Gladstone. **Baralaba:** historic village; watersports on the Dawson River; 100 km NW.

See also CAPRICORN, p. 423

Birdsville

i Wirrari Centre, Billabong Blvd; (07) 4656 3300.

540 AM ABC Western QLD

Birdsville is a tiny town at the northern end of the Birdsville Track, a major cattle route developed in the 1880s. In the 1870s the first European settlers arrived in the area. By 1900 the town was flourishing, boasting three hotels, several stores, a customs office and a cordial factory. When, after Federation in 1901, the toll on cattle crossing the border was abolished, the town's prosperity slowly declined. John Flynn, the famous 'Flynn of the Inland', opened an Australian Inland Mission at Birdsville in 1923. Cattle remains a major trade, as well as the tourism accompanying four-wheel-drive enthusiasts keen to take on the Birdsville Track and Simpson Desert National Park.

Working Museum: housed in 6 buildings, the museum showcases an array of old relics from tools to pottery and farming equipment. Join proprietor John Menzies for a tour and demonstration in harness making and coach building; tours daily at 9am, 11am and 3pm; Waddie Dr. *Blue Poles Gallery:* art by local painter Wolfgang John. Cafe on-site; Graham St. *Artesian bore:* water comes out at near boiling point from this 1219 m deep bore; behind the bore is a geothermal power plant; Graham St. *Adelaide Street:* ruins of Royal Hotel (1883), a reminder of Birdsville's boom days; Birdsville Hotel (1884), still an important overnight stop for travellers; cemetery, housing the grave sites of early pioneers.

Rodeo and Bronco Branding: May. *Birdsville Gift:* footrace; June. *Birdsville Cup Racing Carnival:* the 1st meeting of this annual event was held in 1882 and the tradition continues on the claypan track south-east of town. Held 1st Fri and Sat in Sept, when the population swells to over 6000.

Birdsville Caravan Park: centre of town; 1 Florence St; (07) 4656 3214. *Birdsville Hotel:* legendary pub; Adelaide St; (07) 4656 3244.

Simpson Desert National Park West of Birdsville, this arid national park is the largest in Queensland. The parallel windblown sand dunes are enormous – up to 90 m high, about 1 km apart, and can extend up to 200 km. A self-guide drive includes 10 sites, starting at the eastern park boundary and following the track to Poeppel's Corner. Walking any distance is not recommended and a 4WD is essential. Visit only between Apr and Oct, *see note below*; (07) 4656 3249; 65 km w.

Waddi Trees and Dingo Cave Lookout: 14 km N. *Big Red:* huge sand dune; 35 km w. *Bedourie:* Eyre Creek runs through town providing waterholes that are home to the endangered bilby and peregrine falcons; 191 km N.

Travellers note: Travel in this area can be hazardous, especially in the hotter months (approximately Oct–Mar). Motorists are advised to check the RACQ Road Conditions Report on 1300 130 595 (or www.racq.com.au) for information before departing down the Birdsville Track and to advise police if heading west to Simpson Desert National Park. There is no hotel or fuel at Betoota, 164 km E, but fuel is available at Windorah, 375 km E.

See also OUTBACK, p. 428

Blackall

i Shamrock St; (07) 4657 4637; www.blackall.qld.gov.au

95.1 West FM, 540 AM ABC Western QLD

Blackall is west of the Great Dividing Range in sheep and cattle country, and was home to the legendary sheep-shearer Jackie Howe. In 1892 he set the record of shearing 321 sheep with blade shears in less than eight hours at Alice Downs Station.

Fossilised tree stump: preserved tree stump estimated to be possisbly 225 million years old; Shamrock St. *Major Mitchell Memorial Clock:* commemorates the founding of Blackall in 1846; Shamrock St. *The Black Stump:* the reference point used when the area was surveyed in 1886. Beautiful mural painting of the stump at the site; Thistle St. *Jackie Howe Memorial:* statue of the legendary shearer who holds the record for shearing 321 sheep in 7 hrs 40 min; Shamrock St. *Historic Ram Park:* incorporates the living history of the Blackall district, with shearing occuring all year-round; Shamrock St. *Pioneer Bore:* first artesian bore sunk in Queensland, with display of replica drilling plant; Aqua St.

Blackall Show: May. *Campdraft:* May. *Heartland Festival:* May. *Christmas in July:* July. *Flower Show:* Sept. *Springtime Affair:* celebration of the season; Sept.

Idalia National Park Renowned habitat of the yellow-footed rock-wallaby, which can be spotted at Emmet Pocket Lookout (which also has amazing panoramic views) or along the Bullock Gorge walking track. A self-guide drive begins at the information centre, 12 km beyond the park entrance. (07) 4652 7333; 70 km sw on Yaraka Rd; at Benlidi siding turn south.

Blackall Wool Scour: restored steam-driven wool-processing plant with demonstrations of machinery (steam operating May–Sept only); Evora Rd; 4 km N.

See also OUTBACK, p. 428

Blackwater

i Central Highlands Regional Council, McKenzie St; (07) 4980 5555.

92.7 4BCB FM, 1548 AM ABC Capricornia

Blackwater is west of Rockhampton in the Capricorn region and is known as the coal capital of Queensland. The coal is transported directly from coalmines south of town to Gladstone by train. The name 'Blackwater' is not a reference to the effects of mining operations, however, but comes from the discolouration of local waterholes caused by tea trees.

Japanese Garden complex This ornate traditional Japanese garden was constructed over 8 months in 1998. It symbolises the relationship Blackwater shares with its sister town Fujisawa in Japan. The complex also houses the newly opened Blackwater International Coal Centre, which has interactive and interpretive touch-screen displays, a cinema screening films on coal mining and a cafe. There is also a craft shop and information centre that was once the town station. Capricorn Hwy.

Lions Park: displays the flags of 37 nations to commemorate the nationality of every worker on the coalmines. In terms of size and variety, the display is second only to that of the United Nations'

QUEENSLAND

building in New York; Capricorn Hwy to the west of town. *Helicopter flights over Blackwater Coal Mine:* see the mine in action; details from visitor centre.

 May Day Festival: May. *World Dingo Trap Throwing Competition:* July. *Rodeo:* Oct. *Craft Fair and Art Exhibition:* regional arts and crafts exhibit; Oct.

Blackdown Tableland National Park This national park offers spectacular scenery over mountains and lowlands, including some beautiful waterfalls. It is the traditional home of the Ghungalu people, whose stencil art can be seen on the 2.8 km Mimosa Culture Track. Walk through to Rainbow Falls Gorge and swim in rockpools. (07) 4986 1964; 30 km E to turnoff.

Bedford Weir: dam excellent for fishing; 20 km N. *Comet:* in town is the Leichhardt Dig Tree, where the explorer buried letters and marked the tree 'dig'; 30 km W.

See also CAPRICORN, p. 423

Boonah

Pop. 2282
Map ref. 551 D1 | 557 N1 | 645 A9 | 653 M10

i Boonah–Fassifern Rd; (07) 5463 2233; www.scenicrim.qld.gov.au

100.1 Rim FM, 747 AM ABC Southern QLD

Boonah is set in the picturesque Fassifern Valley, surrounded by hills. Once noted as a 'beautiful vale' by 19th-century explorers, a little expedition in the surrounding region will reveal the beauty and ruggedness of the area. West of town is Main Range National Park, part of the Scenic Rim.

Cultural Centre: incorporates regional art gallery; open Mon–Fri, gallery open Wed–Sun; High St. *Art and Soul:* local art and photography; Walter St. *Gliding and ultralight tours:* flights over the Scenic Rim; details from visitor centre.

Country market: Springleigh Park; 2nd and 4th Sat each month. *Rodeo:* Apr. *Country Show:* May. *SPAR Arts Festival:* Sept. *Orchid Show:* Oct.

Stark House B&B: 3 rooms with ensuites; 143 Kalbar Connection Rd, Kalbar; (07) 5463 9365. *Wiss House B&B:* heritage-listed luxury; 7 Ann St, Kalbar; (07) 5463 9030. *Zengarra Country House:* music pavilion enchants guests; 2225 Lake Moogerah Rd, Moogerah; (07) 5463 5600.

Main Range National Park A World Heritage–listed park of rugged mountains and landscapes with spectacular lookouts. There are walks starting at the Cunninghams Gap and Spicers Gap campsites. See the varied birdlife, including the satin bowerbird, on the 8.4 km return Box Forest track. Access park from Cunningham Hwy; (07) 4666 1133; 40 km W. In the south of the park is Queen Mary Falls; *see Killarney.*

Templin: has historical museum chronicling the history of the area; 5 km NW. *Kalbar:* historic German town with magnificent buildings including the heritage-listed Wiss Emporium; 10 km NW. *Moogerah Peaks National Park:* excellent for birdwatching, and with lookouts over the Fassifern Valley. The Frog Buttress at Mt French is one of the best rock-climbing sites in Queensland; contact EPA on 1300 130 372 for more information; 12 km W. *Lakes Maroon and Moogerah:* ideal for camping and watersports; 20 km S and SW.

See also GOLD COAST & HINTERLAND, p. 417

Boulia

Pop. 206
Map ref. 660 F8

i Min Min Encounter, Herbert St; (07) 4746 3386; www.outbackholidays.tq.com.au

102.5 Hot FM, 106.1 ABC FM North West QLD

Boulia is the capital of the Channel Country and is on the Burke River, named after the ill-fated explorer Robert O'Hara Burke. The town is famous for random appearances of the mysterious Min Min light, a ball of light that sometimes reveals itself to travellers at night. The isolated Diamantina National Park nearby is a haven for threatened species.

Stonehouse Museum: built in 1888, this National Trust–listed site was one of the first houses built in western Queensland. It is now a museum housing the history of the Jones family, as well as Aboriginal artefacts and photographs; Pituri St. *Min Min Encounter:* high-tech re-creation of the Min Min light, with outback characters as your guide; Herbert St. *Red Stump:* warns travellers of the dangers of the Simpson Desert; Herbert St. *Corroboree Tree:* last known of the Pitta Pitta community; near Boulia State School.

Rodeo Races and Campdraft: Easter. *Camel Race:* July. *Back to Boulia:* traditional games weekend; Sept.

Desert Sands Motel: 11 motel units, 1 self-contained unit and real Australian hospitality; Herbert St; (07) 4746 3000. *The Australian Hotel:* iconic outback pub; Herbert St; (07) 4746 3144.

Diamantina National Park This remote park south-east of Boulia is rich in colours and landscapes. Follow the 157 km Warracoota self-guide circuit drive to view the spectacular sand dunes, claypans and ranges and many rare and threatened species in their native habitat, including the greater bilby, kowari and peregrine falcon. Canoe or fish in the winding creeks and rivers. 4WD access only. Roads may become impassable after rain; check road conditions before travelling; (07) 4652 7333; 147 km SE.

Ruins of Police Barracks: 19 km NE. *Cawnpore Hills:* good views from summit; 108 km E. *Burke and Wills Tree:* on the west bank of the Burke River; 110 km NE. *Ruins of Min Min Hotel:* burned down in 1918, where the Min Min light was first sighted; 130 km E.

See also OUTBACK, p. 428

Bowen

Pop. 7483
Map ref. 649 E4 | 655 J3

i Bruce Hwy next to Big Mango, Mount Gordon; (07) 4786 4222; www.tourismbowen.com.au

88.0 Explore FM, 630 AM ABC North QLD

At the north of the Whitsundays, Bowen is positioned within 5 kilometres of eight pristine beaches and bays. Named after the state's first governor, Bowen was established in 1861 – the first settlement in north Queensland. The town and surrounding area is well known for its mangoes, the Big Mango being testimony to the fact. Bowen has more recently gained fame as the film set for Baz Luhrmann's epic movie, *Australia.*

Historical murals Around the buildings and streets of Bowen's town centre are 25 murals by local and national artists, each illustrating an aspect of the region's history. The mural by Australian artist Ken Done was displayed at Expo '88. A new mural is commissioned every 2 years.

Historical Museum: covers history of area; open 9.30am–3.30pm Mon–Fri, 10am–12pm Sun Sept–Apr, closed Feb and Mar; Gordon St. *Summergarden Theatre:* styled on the classic movie houses of Southern California. Used now to screen films and stage performances; Murroona Rd.

Bowen Show: June. *Polocrosse Carnivale:* June. *Bowen River Rodeo (Collinsville):* July. *Bowen Fest:* Aug. *Bowen Family Fishing Classic:* Sept. *Coral Coast Festival:* Oct. *Bowen Cup:* Oct.

Rose Bay Resort: apartments on the bay; 2 Pandanus St, Rose Bay; (07) 4786 9000.

Bays and beaches Choose from 8 excellent spots for swimming, snorkelling and fishing in spectacular surrounds. Rose and Horseshoe bays are connected by a walking track with panoramic views over the ocean; a sidetrack leads to Murray Bay. Impressive corals and fish can be found at Grays, Horseshoe, Murray and Rose bays. Diving enthusiasts should head to Horseshoe and Murray bays. For a more exclusive swim, visit secluded Coral Bay. Details and directions from visitor centre.

Big Mango: tribute to the local Kensington Mango, grown since the 1880s. A shop sells all things mango-related – the mango ice-cream is a highlight; Bruce Hwy, Mt Gordon; 7 km s. *Gloucester Island National Park:* group of secluded islands 23 km offshore, part of the Great Barrier Reef, boasting beaches and rainforest. Campers must be self-sufficient and obtain a permit. Access via private boat from Dingo Beach, Hideaway Bay, Bowen or Airlie Beach; (07) 4967 7355. *Cape Upstart National Park:* remote granite headland flanked with sandy beaches; self-sufficient visitors only; access by boat, ramps at Molongle Bay and Elliot River; (07) 4967 7355; 50 km NW. *Collinsville:* coalmine tours can be arranged at Bowen visitor centre; 82 km sw.

See also THE MID-TROPICS, p. 424

Buderim

Pop. 34 454
Map ref. 647 G4 | 648 F12 | 653 N7

ⓘ Old Post Office, Burnett St; (07) 5477 0944; www.buderim.com

 90.3 FM ABC Coast, 91.1 Hot 91 FM

Buderim is just inland from the Sunshine Coast, high on the fertile red soil of Buderim Mountain, a plateau overlooking the surrounding bushland and ocean. With its wide streets and abundance of small-scale art and craft galleries, it escapes the crush of nearby towns like Maroochydore and Mooloolaba.

Pioneer Cottage This restored 1876 National Trust timber cottage is one of Buderim's earliest houses and retains many of its original furnishings. Now home to the local historical society, it has exhibits on the history of the town and its surrounds. Open 11am–3pm daily; Ballinger Cres; (07) 5450 1966.

Buderim Forest Park: subtropical rainforest reserve and a great place for a picnic or barbecue. In the south, via Quorn Cl, is the Edna Walling Memorial Garden and Serenity Falls; in the north, via Lindsay Rd, is Harry's Restaurant and a boardwalk along Martins Creek. *Foote Sanctuary:* rainforest walks and more than 80 bird species; car entry via Foote St. *Arts and crafts galleries:* various shops selling locally made items; Main St. *Ginger Shoppe:* while the Buderim Ginger Factory may have relocated to Yandina, you can purchase products from the shop; Burnett St.

Australia Day celebrations: parade and fair; Jan.

Parle on Buderim B&B: guest privacy is paramount; 6 Parle Crt; (07) 5450 1413.

Mooloolah River National Park: 6 km SE; *see Mooloolaba.*

See also SUNSHINE COAST, p. 419

Bundaberg

see inset box on next page

Burketown

Pop. 176
Map ref. 656 A7 | 659 D4

ⓘ Old Post Office (Apr–Sept); or council offices (Oct–Mar), Musgrave St, (07) 4745 5100; www.burkeshirecouncil.com

 567 AM ABC North West QLD

Burketown is on the edge of the Gulf of Carpentaria, on the dividing line between the wetlands to the north and the Gulf Savannah plains to the south. It was named after the ill-fated explorer Robert Burke, who was the first European (with partner William John Wills) to arrive in the area. Regularly in spring, the natural phenomenon known as Morning Glory takes over the horizon at dawn between Burketown and Sweers Island, offshore. The clouds appear as rolling tube-like formations and can extend for more than 1000 kilometres.

Museum and Information Centre: in the original post office, with displays on the history of the area plus local arts and crafts. Open Apr–Oct; Musgrave St. *Artesian bore:* operating for over 100 years and quite a sight to see due to the build up of minerals; The Great Top Rd.

World Barramundi Championships: Easter. *May Day Weekend (Gregory):* May. *Arts and Crafts Festival:* Aug. *Campdraft:* Sept.

Burketown Caravan Park: pet friendly; Sloman St; (07) 4745 5118. *Burketown Pub:* ensuite units and hotel rooms; Cnr Beames and Musgrave sts; (07) 4745 5104. *Adels Grove:* range of accommodation, close to national park; Lawn Hill; (07) 4748 5502.

Boodjamulla (Lawn Hill) National Park Approximately 90 km w of the town of Gregory, this park is steeped in Aboriginal, pastoral and evolutionary history. Highlights include canoeing in lush Lawn Hill Gorge, home to the Waanyi rock-art sites of Wild Dog Dreaming and Rainbow Dreaming, and the early-morning climb to Island Stack. The park's Riversleigh section contains some of the world's most significant mammalian fossils; public access is restricted to D site. Access to the park by conventional vehicle is best from Cloncurry; 4WD access from Burketown, Mount Isa and Camooweal; 200 km sw.

Original Gulf Meatworks: machinery relics of this once-thriving industry; just north of town. *Colonial Flat:* site of the Landsborough Tree. Blazed by the explorer in 1862 on his search for Burke and Wills, it became the depot camp for search parties and the resting place of Landsborough's ship Firefly – the first ship to enter the Albert River; 5 km E. *Nicholson River wetlands:* breeding ground for crocodiles, fish and birds; 17 km w. *Bluebush Swamp:* large wetland area ideal for birdwatchers; 30 km sw. *Sweers Island:* excellent spot for lure and fly fishing, plus golden beaches and over 100 species of birds; access by aircraft or boat, details from visitor centre; 30 km N. *Leichhardt Falls:* picturesque flowing falls in rainy months; 71 km SE.

QUEENSLAND

BUNDABERG

Pop. 59 766

Map ref. 648 D2 | 653 M3

i 271 Bourbong St; (07) 4153 8888 or 1300 722 099; www.bundabergregion.info

93.9 Hitz FM, 855 AM ABC Wide Bay

Bundaberg, the southernmost access point to the Great Barrier Reef, is proud of its parks and gardens. Even more recognisable is its world-famous amber spirit, Bundaberg Rum, and the surrounding fields of sugarcane. In harvest season, from July to November, the cane fires give the area a smoky haze. As the sugar industry was being developed in the 1880s, and Australian labour costs were rising, South Sea Islanders were placed under 'contract' to work on the cane fields as a cheap alternative. In fact, the majority of these labourers had been lured from their island homes onto boats under the pretence of trading goods. In 1901, when Australia's Commonwealth government was established, the Kanakas (as the labourers were known) were allowed to return home. A Kanaka-built basalt stone wall can still be seen near Bargara, a short distance north-east of town. Bundaberg more proudly claims the aviator Bert Hinkler as one of its own. In 1928 Hinkler was the first to successfully fly from England to Australia in a flight of just over 15 days.

Bundaberg Botanical Gardens In this picturesque setting stand many buildings from Bundaberg's past. Hinkler House Memorial Museum, inside Bert Hinkler's relocated Southampton home, is a tribute to him and to aviation history. Fairymead House Sugar Museum, a restored plantation house, recalls years of sugar production, and the nearby Historical Museum chronicles the general history of the area. To see more of the grounds, take the restored steam train around the lakes, which runs every Sun (also Wed on school holidays); Mt Perry Rd.

Bundaberg Rum Distillery: discover the distillation process first-hand; tours daily; Avenue St. *Schmeider's Cooperage and Craft Centre:* demonstrations of barrel making and glass-blowing, and sales of local crafts and handmade crystal jewellery; Alexandra St. *Arts Centre:* 3 galleries devoted to local and visiting art exhibitions; cnr Barolin and Quay sts. *Baldwin Swamp Conservation Park:* boardwalks and pathways, waterlily lagoons, abundant birdlife and native fauna; Steindl St. *Tropical Wines:* taste unique wines made from local fruit; Mt Perry Rd. *Alexandra Park and Zoo:* historic band rotunda, cactus garden, zoo (free admission); riverbank, Quay St. *Whaling Wall:* a 7-storey-high whale mural; Bourbong St. *Heritage city walk:* self-guide walking tour of 28 significant sites and buildings; starts at historic post office, Barolin St. *Bundaberg Barrel:* giant barrel and home to Bundaberg Brewed Drinks. With interactive tours, holographic 3D adventure and free sampling; Bargara Rd.

Shalom College Markets: local crafts; Fitzgerald St; every Sun. *PCYC Markets:* Maryborough St; 2nd Sun each month. *Big House Piano:* music at Fairymead House; 1st Sun each month. *Aussie Country Muster:* music festival; May. *Bundaberg Show:* May. *International Air Show:* July. *Multicultural Food and Wine Festival:* Aug. *Bundy in Bloom Festival:* celebration of spring; Sept. *Arts Festival:* Oct. *Bundy Thunder:* power boat spectacular; Nov. *Port2Port Yacht Rally:* Nov.

[LOGGERHEAD TURTLE AT MON REPOS CONSERVATION PARK]

Reef Gateway Motor Inn: Best Western member; 11 Takalvan St; (07) 4132 6999. *Kacy's Bargara Beach Motel:* on the waterfront; Cnr Bauer St and Esplanade, Bargara; (07) 4130 1100. *Kelly's Beach Resort:* self-contained villas; 6 Trevors Rd, Bargara; (07) 4154 7200 or 1800 246 141.

Mon Repos Conservation Park This park contains the largest and most accessible mainland loggerhead turtle rookery in eastern Australia. Between Nov and Mar these giant sea turtles come ashore to lay their eggs. Hatchlings leave their nests for the sea from mid-Jan to late Mar. Access to the park is restricted during these times – guided night tours depart from the park information centre for viewing turtles up-close. When turtles are not hatching, snorkelling and exploring the rockpools are popular. (07) 4159 1652; 15 km NE.

Burrum Coast National Park Broken into 2 sections, this national park offers a variety of landscapes and activities. In the northern Kinkuna section it is relatively undeveloped. The vegetation along the beach is rugged and spectacular, and birdwatching in the wallum heath is a highlight. Access is via Palm Beach Road; 14 km SW; 4WD and sand-driving experience are necessary. The southern Woodgate section is more developed, with boardwalks and established tracks that allow the visitor to see abundant wildlife from every vantage. Access is via Woodgate, a small town with a magnificent ocean beach; (07) 4131 1600; 57 km S.

Hummock Lookout: panoramic view of Bundaberg, cane fields and coast; 7 km NE. *Meadowvale Nature Park:* rainforest and walkway to Splitters Creek; 10 km w. *Sharon Nature Park:* rainforest, native fauna and walkway to Burnett River; 12 km SW. *Bargara:* coastal town with a popular surf beach and year-round fishing on man-made reef. Turtles often nest at nearby Neilson Park, Kelly's and Rifle Range beaches; 13 km NE. *Fishing spots:* area renowned for its wide variety of fishing. Excellent spots at Burnett Heads (15 km NE), Elliott Heads (18 km SE) and Moore Park (21 km NW). *Mystery craters:* 35 small craters in sandstone slab, the origin of which causes much debate, but confirmed to be over 25 million years old; 25 km sw. *Littabella National Park:* lagoons and billabongs surrounded by tea tree forest. Many sand tracks for the 4WD enthusiast can be found at nearby Norval Park Beach; (07) 4131 1600; 38 km nw. *Lady Elliot and Lady Musgrave islands:* excellent spots for snorkelling and fishing.

Wilderness camping on Lady Musgrave; seabird nesting on Lady Elliot during summer; sea access from Bundaberg Port plus air access to Lady Elliot from Hinkler Airport.

See also Capricorn, p. 423

Gregory: small outback town that holds the Gregory River Canoe Marathon in May; 113 km s. *Fishing and boat tours:* to nearby estuaries and Wellesley Islands; details from visitor centre.

See also Gulf Savannah, p. 427

Burleigh Heads

Pop. 7606

Map ref. 551 G1 | 557 O1 | 645 G10 | 646 F8 | 653 N11

 Shop 14B, Coolangatta Pl, Cnr Griffith and Warner sts, Coolangatta; 1300 309 440; www.verygoldcoast.com.au

89.3 4CRB FM, 91.7 FM ABC Gold Cast

Burleigh Heads is a suburb of the Gold Coast and is situated between Coolangatta and the tourist mecca Surfers Paradise. It is known for its breathtaking scenery, highlighted by the stunning Burleigh Head National Park. The famed south-easterly swells and surrounding parklands make the beaches on Burleigh Heads some of the best in the world, attracting international surfing tournaments. The relaxed charm of Burleigh Heads can be enjoyed from under the beachside pines and pandanus palms or in a nearby restaurant overlooking the stunning Pacific Ocean.

Burleigh Head National Park: take the 2.8 km Ocean View circuit to experience the coastal vegetation, rainforest and mangroves or go to Tumgun Lookout to watch for dolphins and humpback whales (seasonal); access from Goodwin Tce; 1300 130 372. *David Fleay Wildlife Park:* displays Queensland's native animals in a natural setting with the only display of Lumholtz's tree kangaroo and mahogany gliders in the world. The park also has crocodile feeding in summer and Aboriginal heritage programs; West Burleigh Rd. *Paramount Adventure Centre:* enjoy a rush of adrenaline and adventure at the Gold Coast's largest adventure centre. Choose from indoor rock climbing, kayaking, mountain-biking or take part in a learn-to-surf program; Hutchinson St.

Burleigh Art and Craft Market: beachfront; last Sun each month. *Coolangatta Markets:* beachfront; 2nd Sun each month. *Burleigh Car Boot Sale:* Stocklands Shopping Centre Car Park; 2nd Sun each month. *Quiksilver Roxy Pro Surfing:* Feb/Mar. *Gold Coast Cup Outrigger Canoe Marathon:* Apr. *Wintersun Festival:* Coolangatta; May/June. *Coolangatta Gold:* famous ironman and ironwoman race; Oct.

Vecchia Roma: traditional Italian family restaurant; 1748 Gold Coast Hwy, cnr West Burleigh Rd; (07) 5535 5988. *Fish & Wine:* very fine fish dishes; Relections Tower 2, 110 Marine Pde, Coolangatta; (07) 5536 7775.

Hillhaven Holiday Apartments: great ocean-view apartments; 2 Goodwin Tce; (07) 5535 1055. *Sands*

Mediterranean Resort: good-value apartments; 220 The Esplanade, North Burleigh; (07) 5535 7188 or 1300 302 733. *Bella Mare Holiday Apartments:* near several beaches; 5 Hill St, Coolangatta; (07) 5599 2755. *Sanctuary Beach Resort:* good family resort; 47 Teemangum St, Currumbin; (07) 5598 2524. *Sanctuary Lake Apartments:* near wildlife sanctuary; 1/40 Teemangum St, Currumbin; (07) 5534 3344.

Currumbin Wildlife Sanctuary This 20 ha reserve is owned by the National Trust. There are free-ranging animals in open areas, the Crocodile Wetlands with raised walkways over pools of freshwater and saltwater crocodiles, a walk-through rainforest aviary and a miniature railway. A highlight is the twice-daily feeding of wild rainbow lorikeets. The 'Wildnight Tours' are interactive tours to see the nocturnal wildlife. 8 km se.

Springbrook National Park, Mt Cougal section This small section of the park contains a subtropical rainforest remnant and is part of the Gondwana Rainforests of Australia World Heritage Area. Mt Cougal's twin peaks and the Currumbin Valley are an interesting and diverse landscape. There is a scenic drive through the valley and a walking track through rainforest, past cascades, to the remains of an old bush sawmill. End of Currumbin Creek Rd; 27 km sw. Springbrook and Natural Bridge sections: *see Nerang*.

Palm Beach: popular golden-sands beach that has won Queensland's Cleanest Beach Award in previous years; 4 km se. *Superbee Honeyworld:* live displays, Walks with Bees tour, honey making and sales; opposite sanctuary; 8 km se. *Olson's Bird Gardens:* large landscaped aviaries in subtropical setting with a lilly pilly hedge maze; Currumbin Creek Rd; 16 km sw. *Greenmount and Coolangatta beaches:* sheltered white-sand beaches with beautiful views of the coast; 13 km se. *Rainbow Bay:* sheltered beach excellent for swimming. Walk along the coast to Snapper Rocks; 15 km se. *Snapper Rocks:* top surf area with the 'Superbank', one of the world's longest point breaks; 15 km se. *Point Danger:* named by Captain Cook as he sailed by. It offers excellent panoramic views over the ocean and coast. Catch a glimpse of dolphins from the Captain Cook Memorial Lighthouse; 15 km se. *Tom Beaston Outlook (Razorback Lookout):* excellent views; behind Tweed Heads; 16 km se.

See also Gold Coast & Hinterland, p. 417

Caboolture

Pop. 17 739

Map ref. 644 E1 | 645 D1 | 647 F7 | 653 N8

 Bruce Hwy, Burpengary; 1800 833 100; www.moretonbay.qld.gov.au

105.1 4OUR FM, 612 AM ABC Brisbane

QUEENSLAND

CAIRNS

Pop. 122 732

Map ref. 650 E2 | 651 F7 | 657 M6

ⓘ **Cairns & Tropical North Visitor Information Centre,**
51 The Esplanade; (07) 4051 3588; www.tropicalaustralia.com.au

📻 102.7 4CA FM, 801 AM ABC Far North QLD

This modern, colourful city is the capital of the Tropical North, but was once a service town for the sugar plantations to the south. Tourism boomed with the airport's upgrade in 1984 and the influx of visitors and commercial enterprises resulted in the unusual mix of modern architecture and original Queenslander homes that can be seen today. The Esplanade traces the bay foreshore and blends city life with the natural attractions of the Coral Sea. With Cairns' superb location – the Great Barrier Reef to the east, mountain rainforests of the Wet Tropics and plains of the Atherton Tableland to the west, and palm-fringed beaches to the north and south – it is a good base for many activities. For fishing enthusiasts, Cairns is famous for its black marlin.

🏠 **Flecker Botanic Gardens** Established in 1886 as a recreational reserve, they are now the only wet tropical botanic gardens in Australia. The gardens display tropical plants from around the world, including a number of endangered species and over 200 species of palm. Follow the boardwalks through remnant lowland swamp to adjacent Centenary Lakes to see turtles and mangrove birds. Access gardens via Collins Ave.

Mt Whitfield Conservation Park: 2 major walking tracks through forested mountain range to summit for views of Cairns and Coral Sea; behind botanic gardens. **Royal Flying Doctor Service Visitor Centre:** highlights the history and achievements of the service, with aircraft display; closed Sun; Junction St. **McLeod Street Pioneer Cemetery:** honours local pioneers. **Tanks Art Centre:** multipurpose centre in revamped WW II oil storage tanks,

including gallery with local art; Collins Ave. **Regional Gallery:** local artists exhibit in this National Trust–classified building; cnr Shields and Abbott sts. **Cairns Museum:** displays of Aboriginal, gold-rush, timber and sugarcane history; open 10am–4pm Mon–Sat; cnr Lake and Shields sts. **Undersea World Aquarium:** variety of tropical fish. See the sharks being fed by divers; ground floor, Pier Marketplace. **Bulk Sugar Terminal:** guided tours by arrangement during crushing season (June–Nov); (07) 4051 3533; Cook St. **Foreshore Promenade:** landscaped area with safe swimming lagoon; foreshore; closed Wed mornings. **Kuranda Scenic Railway:** trip through Barron Gorge to rainforest village of Kuranda; leaves Cairns Railway Station in Bunda St; *see also Kuranda*. **Game fishing:** boats moor at Marlin Marina, Marlin Jetty and Trinity Wharf and you can arrange fishing trips from here; end of Spence St. **Dive schools:** contact visitor centre for details.

🌴 **Rusty's Market:** Grafton and Sheridan sts; Fri, Sat and Sun. **Esplanade Market:** every Sat. **Cairns Show:** July. **Cairns Cup:** Aug. **Festival Cairns:** Aug–Sept.

🍴 **Bayleaf Balinese Restaurant:** Balinese food with flair; Bay Village Tropical Retreat, cnr Lake and Gatton sts; (07) 4051 4622. **Blue Sky Brewery:** hearty meals and beers; 34–42 Lake St; (07) 4057 0500. **Bushfire Flame Grill:** world menu with Brazilian flame grill and Japanese barbecue; Pacific International Hotel, cnr The Esplanade and Spence St; (07) 4044 1879. **Food Trail Tours:** tastes of tropical produce; pick-ups from Cairns and northern beaches accommodation; (07) 4032 0322. **Genkai:** fine Japanese dining; Sebel Cairns Hotel, Village La; (07) 4031 1300.

🛏 **Hides Hotel:** affordable heritage pub; 87 Lake St; (07) 4051 1266 or 1800 079 266. **Pacific International Hotel:**

[SWIMMING LAGOON, CAIRNS ESPLANADE]

spacious rooms and friendly staff; Cnr The Esplanade and Spence St; (07) 4051 7888 or 1800 079 001. *Pullman Reef Hotel Casino:* luxurious up-market hotel; 35–41 Wharf St; (07) 4030 8888.

Great Barrier Reef and islands Take a tour, charter a boat or fly to see some of the spectacular sights just offshore. Rainforest-covered Fitzroy Island to the east has impressive snorkelling sites at Welcome and Sharkfin bays. Follow the Secret Garden track to see wildlife up-close, including Ulysses butterflies and emerald doves. Green Island to the north-east is a true coral cay and the surrounding reef is home to magnificent tropical fish; they can be seen from a glass-bottom boat, in the underwater observatory or by snorkelling. Smaller Michaelmas and Upolo cays to the north-east are important sites for ground-nesting seabirds. The surrounding waters are excellent for reef swimming. For tours contact visitor centre.

Tjapukai Aboriginal Cultural Park The group began as an Aboriginal dance company in 1987, but the demand for more cultural information prompted the move to this large park.

Four theatres, both live and film, illustrate the history and culture of the rainforest people of Far North Queensland. The interactive camp village and 'Tjapukai By Night' live-theatre experience are highlights. Smithfield; (07) 4042 9900; 11 km NW.

Beaches: incredible 26 km of beaches extending from Machans Beach on north bank of Barron River, 9 km N, north to Ellis Beach. *Skyrail Rainforest Cableway:* spectacular gondola ride through rainforest to Kuranda; departs Caravonica Lakes, 11 km N. *Bungee tower:* bungee jump from platform through rainforest in Smithfield, 13 km N; contact visitor centre for details. *Crystal Cascades:* walks by cascades. Also an excellent spot for cooling off; end of Redlynch Valley; 18 km SW. *Lake Morris and Copperlode Dam:* walking tracks; 19 km SW. *Barron and Freshwater valleys:* bushwalking, hiking, whitewater rafting and camping to the west and north-west of Cairns; contact visitor centre for details. *Safaris:* 4WD to Cape York and the Gulf Country; contact visitor centre for details.

See also CAIRNS & THE TROPICS, p. 425

At the northern edge of Greater Brisbane and the southern opening to the Sunshine Coast, Caboolture is surrounded by subtropical fruit farms. The town was settled in 1842 after the restricted land around Moreton Bay penal colony was opened up. The historical village north of town exhibits much of this history. Bribie Island to the east has spectacular aquatic and wildlife attractions, which bring many visitors to the region.

Trail of Reflections: self-guide trail of open-air artwork and sculptures around town that illustrate the history of the area; starts in King St; details from visitor centre.

Market: showgrounds, Beerburrum Rd; Sun mornings. *Country Music Festival:* Apr/May. *Medieval Tournament:* July. *Caboolture Show:* Aug. *Rodeo:* Nov/Dec.

Caboolture Riverlakes Motel: overlooks riverside parklands; 14 Morayfield Rd; (07) 5499 1766. *Beachmere Palms Motel:* 6 quiet waterside units; 30 Biggs Ave, Beachmere; (07) 5496 8577.

Bribie Island This island park is separated from the mainland by Pumicestone Passage, where mangroves flourish and dugongs, dolphins, turtles and over 350 species of birds live. National park covers about a third of the island and offers secluded pristine white beaches. Follow the Bicentennial Bushwalks to discover the park on foot, boat along Pumicestone Passage or 4WD along the ocean beach (permit required). Fishing and surfing are popular at Woorim Beach, just north of which are old WW II bunkers. See migratory birds in summer at Buckleys Hole Conservation Park on the south-west tip of the island. Bridge access to island; 21 km E.

Ferryman cruises: cruise the waters of Pumicestone Passage; (07) 3408 7124. *Caboolture Historical Village:* over 50 restored buildings of historical importance house museums, with themes including maritime and transport; open 9.30am–3.30pm daily; Beerburrum Rd; 2 km N. *Airfield:* Warplane and Flight Heritage

Museum with displays of WW II memorabilia and restored fighter planes. Tiger Moth and Mustang flights and gliding on offer; McNaught Rd; 2 km E. *Sheep Station Creek Conservation Park:* walks through open forest. See remains of the old bridge on original road leading from Brisbane to Gympie; 6 km SW. *Abbey Museum:* traces growth of western civilisation with displays of art and antiques; open 10am–4pm Mon–Sat; just off road to Bribie Island; 9 km E. *Woodford:* the town has one of the largest narrow-gauge steam locomotive collections in Australia; Margaret St; 22 km NW. *Mt Mee State Forest:* boardwalks through subtropical rainforest and lookouts over Neurum Valley, Moreton Bay and surrounds; 23 km W. *Donnybrook, Toorbul and Beachmere:* coastal fishing towns to the east.

See also BRISBANE ISLANDS, p. 416

 Caloundra — Pop. 87 596 — Map ref. 647 H5 | 648 F12 | 653 N8

7 Caloundra Rd; (07) 5420 6240 or 1800 644 969; www.caloundratourism.com.au

90.3 FM ABC Coast

This popular holiday spot at the southern tip of the Sunshine Coast was once a retirement haven. It now boasts a diverse population of retirees and young Brisbane commuters keen on the seaside lifestyle. The nearby beaches offer a variety of watersports – the calm waters of Golden Beach are especially popular with windsurfers. The fishing between Bribie Island and the mainland in Pumicestone Passage is excellent.

Queensland Air Museum Founded by members of the Aviation Historical Society of Australia in 1973, this museum collects important relics of Queensland's aviation heritage. Memorabilia on display includes old fighter planes and bombers. Airport, Pathfinder Dr; (07) 5492 5930.

QUEENSLAND

Caloundra Regional Art Gallery: local and touring art exhibitions; open 10am–4pm Wed–Sun; Omrah Ave. *Ben Bennet Botanical Park:* easy walks through natural bushland; Queen St. *Suncoast Helicopter Flights:* over Glass House Mountains and Sunshine Coast; bookings on (07) 5499 6900. *Caloundra Cruises:* morning, lunchtime and afternoon cruises, as well as sunset charters. Scenic Pumicestone Passage cruises have spectacular views of Bribie Island and Moreton Bay; bookings on (07) 5492 8280. *Blue Water Kayak Tours:* paddle in the tranquil Moreton Bay Marine Park.

 Country Market: Bulcock St; Sun. *City Show:* May. *Cairns Cup:* June. *Open Cockpit Weekend:* July. *Taste of the Coast:* food and wine festival; July. *Bowls Carnival:* July–Aug. *Classic Boat Regatta:* Aug. *Art and Craft Festival:* Oct. *Caloundra Music Festival:* Oct.

Alfie's Mooo Char and Bar: steak from paddock to plate; Cnr Otranto Tce and The Esplanade, Bulcock Beach; (07) 5492 8155. *Between the Flags Restaurant:* Lifesaving Club bistro; Ormonde Tce; (07) 5491 8418. *Cafe by the Beach:* popular surf cafe; 12 Seaview Tce, Moffat Beach; (07) 5491 9505. *The Moorings Cafe:* masters of big breakfasts; 84 The Esplanade, Golden Beach; (07) 5492 2466.

Bluewater Point and Deepwater Point Resort: quiet spot on the river; 13 Nicklin Way, Minyama; (07) 5477 9900. *Currimundi Lakeside B&B:* gourmet breakfasts; 1 Rosea Crt; (07) 5493 9123. *Dicky Beach Family Holiday Park:* on a patrolled beach; Beerburrum St; (07) 5491 3342.

Currimundi Lake Conservation Park This unspoiled coastal park offers quiet walks beside the lake and through to the beach. Canoe and swim in the lake or see the finches and friarbirds in the remnant wallum heath. In spring the wildflowers are spectacular. Access from Coongara Espl; 4 km N.

Opals Down Under: opal-cutting demonstrations and 'scratch patch' where visitors fossick for their own gemstones; 14 km NW. *Aussie World:* family fun-park in native garden setting, with over 30 rides and games, Side Show Alley and one of the country's growing number of Ettamogah Pubs, based on Ken Maynard's cartoon; Palmview; 18 km NW. *Surrounding beaches:* include patrolled beaches of Bulcock, Kings, and Dicky with the wreck of SS *Dicky* (1893); excellent fishing at Moffat and Shelly beaches. *Scenic drives:* taking in the beaches to the north, the Blackall Range with art galleries and views of the Sunshine Coast, and the Glass House Mountains with magnificent walks and scenery; details from visitor centre.

See also BRISBANE ISLANDS, p. 416

Camooweal

Pop. 197
Map ref. 637 P10 | 659 A9 | 660 C1

ⓘ Drovers Camp, Camooweal; (07) 4748 2022.

📻 102.5 Hot FM, 567 AM ABC North West QLD

North-west of Mount Isa, Camooweal is the last Queensland town before the Northern Territory border. It was once the centre for enormous cattle drives travelling south. Some say that the town is a suburb of Mount Isa, which would make the 188 kilometres of Barkly Highway between Mount Isa and Camooweal one of the longest main streets in the world. To the south of town are the incredible Camooweal Caves, a series of sinkhole caves that have evolved over millions of years.

Barkly Tableland Heritage Centre: museum in National Trust–classified building exhibiting droving history; open 9am–4pm Mon–Fri, 9am–12pm Sat–Sun; Barkly Hwy. *Historic buildings:* the Drovers and Freckleton's stores; Barkly Hwy.

 Cricket tournament: Apr. *Campdraft:* June. *Horseracing:* Aug. *Drovers Camp Festival:* Aug.

Camooweal Caves National Park On the Barkly Tableland, this national park is still evolving as water continues to filter through the soluble dolomite to create and transform the extensive cave system. The underground caves are linked by vertical shafts and only the experienced caver should attempt them. The Great Nowranie Cave is excellent to explore with an 18 m drop at the opening (climbing gear is essential). Caves may flood during wet season. If exploring the caves, inform local police or ranger beforehand. 4WD access is recommended. (07) 4722 5224; 24 km S.

Cemetery: headstones tell local history; 1 km E. *Boodjamulla (Lawn Hill) National Park:* around 300 km N via Gregory; *see* Burketown.

See also OUTBACK, p. 428

Cardwell

Pop. 1251
Map ref. 650 E7 | 657 M9

ⓘ Rainforest and Reef Information Centre, 142 Victoria St; (07) 4066 8601; www.gspeak.com.au/cardwell

📻 91.9 Kool FM, 630 AM ABC North QLD

Cardwell is a coastal town overlooking Rockingham Bay and the nearby islands of the Great Barrier Reef. Ferries transport visitors to nearby Hinchinbrook Island, the largest island national park in Australia. Between the island and the mainland is Hinchinbrook Channel (Cardwell is at the northern edge), a popular spot for fishing and a sheltered area for houseboats.

Bush Telegraph Heritage Centre This complex comprises the old post office and telegraph station, in operation 1870–1982, and the original magistrates court and gaol cells. An informative history of communications and the region is provided through interpretive displays. Open 10am–1pm Mon–Fri, 9am–12pm Sat, other times by appt; Bruce Hwy; (07) 4066 2412.

Rainforest and Reef Information Centre: interpretive centre that acquaints visitors with landscape, flora and fauna of northern Queensland; Bruce Hwy, near jetty. *Coral Sea Battle Memorial Park:* large war memorial that commemorates the WW II battle off the coast between Australian/US forces and the Japanese; beachfront. *Boat hire and cruises:* explore the tropical waters and islands to the east at the helm of a yacht, houseboat or cruiser, or travel with an organised cruise; details from visitor centre. *Snorkelling and scuba-diving tours:* details from visitor centre.

 Market: Cardwell Espl; 1st Sun each month. *Coral Sea Battle Memorial Commemoration:* May. *Seafest:* Aug. *Fishing Classic (Port Hinchinbrook):* Sept.

Cardwell Beachfront Motel and Holiday Units: 6 units, close to beach; Cnr Bruce Hwy and Scott St; (07) 4066 8776. *Mudbrick Manor:* 5 rooms and suites; Lot 13 Stoney Creek Rd; (07) 4066 2299. *Port Hinchinbrook Resort:* cabins and apartments; 1 Front St; (07) 4066 2000 or 1800 220 077.

Hinchinbrook Island National Park An amazing variety of vegetation covers this island park, including rainforest, wetlands, forests and woodlands. The 32 km Thorsborne Trail on the east coast is renowned for its spectacular scenery as it winds past waterfalls and along pristine beaches. Many people allow 4 days or more for the walk, camping on a different beach each night.

Hikers must be self-sufficient and bookings are essential (limited number of walkers allowed). Shorter walks are from the camping areas at Macushla and The Haven. Access the island via ferry from Cardwell or Lucinda; (07) 4066 8601.

Scenic drive in Cardwell State Forest: this 26 km circuit from Cardwell takes in a lookout, waterfalls, swimming holes and picnic spots; begins on Braesnose St. *Edmund Kennedy National Park:* boardwalk through extensive mangrove forests and variety of other vegetation to beach, with spectacular view of islands. This park is a habitat of the endangered mahogany glider; (07) 4066 8601; 4 km N. *Five Mile Swimming Hole:* attractive picnic and swimming spot safe from crocodiles, sharks and stingers; 7 km S. *Dalrymple's Gap:* original service path and stone bridge through range; 15 km S. *Brook Islands:* nesting area for Torresian imperial pigeons (Sept–Feb). Excellent snorkelling on reef of northern 3 islands. Sea access only; 30 km NE. *Murray Falls:* climb the steep 1 km path to viewing platform over falls and surrounds; 42 km NW. *Girringun (Lumholtz) National Park:* travel through World Heritage rainforest on road (dry weather only) to the 3-tier 91 m Blencoe Falls; (07) 4066 8601; 71 km W; *see Ingham for southern parts of park.*

See also THE MID-TROPICS, p. 424

Charleville
Pop. 3275
Map ref. 652 B5 | 663 P5

 Matilda Hwy; (07) 4654 3057; www.murweh.qld.gov.au

 101.7 Triple C FM, 603 AM ABC Western QLD

Charleville is in the heart of mulga country on the banks of the Warrego River and at the centre of a rich sheep and cattle district. By the late 1890s the town had its own brewery, ten hotels and 500 registered bullock teams. Cobb & Co recognised the value of Charleville's location on a major stock route and opened a coach-building factory in 1893. There are also strong links with aviation: the first London–Sydney flight landed here in 1919, Qantas' first fare-paying service took off in 1922 and record-setting aviator Amy Johnson landed nearby in 1930. Charleville marks the terminus of the Westlander rail service from Brisbane.

 Cosmos Centre This centre explores the Australian night sky and its significance to Aboriginal culture. There are multimedia displays, nightly shows and interactive areas where the wonders of the sky are observed through powerful Meade Telescopes. The outback night sky has never looked so beautiful; Matilda Hwy; (07) 4654 7771.

Royal Flying Doctor Service Visitor Centre: museum displaying memorabilia from the past and present. View the documentary entitled A Day in the Life of the Flying Doctor; Old Cunnamulla Rd. *Historic House Museum:* a wonderful example of early Queensland architecture. Machinery displays including steam engine and a rail ambulance in restored Queensland National Bank building; open 9am–3pm Mon–Fri, 9am–12pm Sat, other times by appt; Alfred St. *Vortex Gun:* in 1902 this 5 m long gun was used in an unsuccessful rain-making experiment; Bicentennial Park, Matilda Hwy. *Heritage trail:* self-guide walk past heritage buildings; brochure from visitor centre. *Bilby Tours:* one of Australia's most rare and endangered animals, bilbies are captively bred in Charleville. Get up-close and personal with these marsupials on the night tour; details from visitor centre.

 Market: Historic House Museum; 1st Sat each month. *Charleville Show:* May. *Bilby Festival:* food, music and celebration of National Bilby Day; Sept.

 Evening Star Tourist Park: on a cattle station; Adavale Rd; (07) 4654 2430. *Hotel Corones:* famous Queensland outback hotel; 33 Wills St; (07) 4654 1022. *Mulga Country Motor Inn:* luxury in the outback; Cunnamulla Rd; (07) 4654 3255. *Waltzing Matilda Motor Inn:* comfort close to town; 125 Alfred St; (07) 4654 1720.

 Tregole National Park This semi-arid national park has a vulnerable and fragile ecosystem. It is largely made up of ooline forest – rainforest species dating back to the Ice Age. Follow the 2.1 km circuit track to see the diverse vegetation and spectacular birds of the park. (07) 4654 1255; 99 km E via Morven.

Monument: marks the spot where Ross and Keith Smith landed with engine trouble on the first London–Sydney flight; 19 km NW.

See also OUTBACK, p. 428

Charters Towers
Pop. 7978
Map ref. 654 F3

 74 Mosman St; (07) 4761 5533; www.charterstowers.qld.gov.au

 95.9 Hot FM, 630 AM ABC North QLD

Charters Towers is in the Burdekin Basin south-west of Townsville. The town's gold rush began on 25 December 1871 when Aboriginal horse-boy Jupiter discovered gold while looking for lost horses. He brought gold-laden quartz to his employer, Hugh Mosman, who rode to Ravenswood to register the claim, and the gold rush was on. Between 1872 and 1916 Charters Towers produced ore worth £25 million. At the height of the gold rush it was Queensland's second largest city and was commonly referred to as 'The World' because of its cosmopolitan population. This rich history can be seen in the preserved streetscapes of 19th- and 20th-century architecture. To the north-west of Charters Towers is the 120-kilometre Great Basalt Wall, a lava wall created from the Toomba basalt flow.

 Ghosts of Gold Heritage Trail This informative tour reveals the rich history of the town in the district known as 'One Square Mile'. Over 60 heritage-listed buildings are in the precinct. Of particular interest are the re-created workings of the Stock Exchange in Mosman St; the once heavily mined Towers Hill (1.5 km W) with interpretive walking trails and a film screening at night; and the Venus Gold Battery in Millchester Rd, an old gold-processing plant where the 'ghosts' come alive. Starts in the orientation centre behind the visitor centre.

Charters Towers Folk Museum: local historical memorabilia; Mosman St. *Civic Club:* once a gentlemen's club, this remarkable building (1900) still contains the original billiard tables; Ryan St. *Rotary Lookout:* panoramic views over region; Fraser St.

 National Trust Markets: Stock Exchange Arcade; 1st and 3rd Sun each month. *Showgrounds Markets:* Cnr Mary and Show sts; 2nd Sun each month. *Goldfield Ashes Cricket Carnival:* Jan. *Rodeo:* Easter. *Ten Days in the Towers:* festival including music and bush poets; Apr–May. *Country Music Festival:* May Day weekend. *Charters Towers Show:* July.

 Bluff Downs Historic Station: experience station life; 29 km off Lynd Hwy; (07) 4770 4084.

QUEENSLAND

Dalrymple National Park This small national park on the Burdekin River comprises mainly woodland and is an important area for native animals including rock wallabies and sugar gliders. A highlight is the 4 million-year-old solidified lava wall, the Great Basalt Wall, parts of which are accessible from this park. The site of the old Dalrymple township is also of interest. Contact the ranger before setting out on any walks. (07) 4722 5224; 46 km N.

Ravenswood: another gold-rush centre, but now 'not quite a ghost town'. Two hotels remain as magnificent examples of the prosperity of this town's wealthy beginnings. It's worth taking a stroll down Main St, which resembles a set from an old movie; 85 km E. *Greenvale:* near the Gregory Development Rd with a roadhouse, caravan park, golf course and the well-known Three Rivers Hotel, made famous by Slim Dusty's song of the same name; 209 km NW. *Burdekin Falls Dam:* recreation area with barramundi fishing; 165 km SE via Ravenswood. *Blackwood National Park:* a woodland park of undulating hills and stony ridges. See the Belyando blackwood trees that give the park its name, and walk on fire trails to discover the park's interesting birdlife including squatter pigeons and speckled warblers; (07) 4722 5224; 180 km S.

See also THE MID-TOPICS, p. 424

Childers
Pop. 1352
Map ref. 648 C4 | 653 M4

ℹ️ Palace Hotel (Childers Memorial), 72 Churchill St; (07) 4126 1994.

📻 102.5 Breeze FM, 855 AM ABC Wide Bay

Childers is a picturesque National Trust town south of Bundaberg, part of the state's sugarcane belt. With leafy streets and a lovely outlook over the surrounding valleys, the town's history has been blighted by fire. One ravaged the town in 1902 (though many of the heritage buildings survived) and another engulfed a backpacker's hostel in 2000, tragically killing 15 people and making international news. A memorial to those lost in this fire stands in Churchill Street. Thankfully life has returned to normal in Childers and the flow of backpackers on the fruit-picking trail is as strong as ever.

Pharmaceutical Museum: collection of memorabilia including leather-bound prescription books and Aboriginal wares; open 8.45am–4.30pm Mon–Fri, 8.30am–12pm Sat; Churchill St. *Historical complex:* area of historic buildings including school, cottage and locomotive; Taylor St. *Baker's Military and Memorabilia Museum:* 16 000 items on display covering all the major wars, including uniforms and communications equipment; closed Sun (open by appt); Ashby La. *Childers Art Gallery:* Churchill St. *Snakes Downunder:* informative exhibits on native snakes; open 9am–3pm, closed Wed; Lucketts Rd. *Historic Childers:* self-guide town walk past historic buildings; highlight is the Old Butcher's Shop (1896) in Churchill St.

Village Market: historical society; 3rd Sun each month. *Festival of Cultures:* a week of celebrations also includes workshops by visiting artists and performers; July.

🏨 *Gateway Motor Inn:* quiet and comfortable; Cnr Bruce Hwy and Butchers Rd; (07) 4126 1288 or 1800 100 603.

 Flying High Bird Habitat The native vegetation here is home to 600 bird species. Follow the boardwalk tracks to see the many Australian parrots and finches. Cnr Bruce Hwy and Old Creek Rd, Apple Creek; 5 km N.

Buxton and Walkers Point: unspoiled fishing villages to the east. *Woodgate:* coastal town to the north-east with 16 km beach. Access to Burrum Coast National Park is from here; *see Bundaberg.* *Goodnight Scrub National Park:* 27 km W; *see Gin Gin.*

See also CAPRICORN, p. 423

Chillagoe
Pop. 223
Map ref. 650 A3 | 657 J6

ℹ️ The Hub, 23 Queen St; (07) 4094 7111; www.chillagoehub.com.au

 720 AM ABC Far North QLD

Chillagoe is a small outback town west of Cairns and the Atherton Tableland. Once a thriving mining town after silver and copper deposits were found in 1887, the town was practically deserted after the smelter closed in 1940. Chillagoe's history and the well-preserved Aboriginal rock art and limestone caves in the area make it a popular spot with visitors.

🏛️ **The Hub** This major interpretive centre is constructed from local materials including marble and copper. Informative displays cover the geographical history of the local landscape (dating back 2 billion years), the town's mining and pioneering past and the region's Aboriginal heritage. Queen St; (07) 4094 7111.

Heritage Museum: displays on local history and relics of old mining days; Hill St. *Historic cemetery:* headstones from early settlement; Railway Line Rd. *Historical walks:* self-guide or guided walks taking in the old State Smelter and disused marble quarry just south of town; details from visitor centre.

Big Weekend and Rodeo: May. *Annual Wheelbarrow Race:* May. *Country Music Festival:* July.

Chillagoe–Mungana Caves National Park The impressive rugged limestone outcrops and magnificent caves of this park, south of town, are studied by scientists world-wide. The cave system was originally an ancient coral reef and is home to a wide variety of bats. Fossilised bones, including those of a giant kangaroo, have been discovered in the caves. Guided tours only; tickets from The Hub. Above ground are magnificent Aboriginal rock paintings at Balancing Rock. (07) 4046 6600; 7 km S.

Mungana: Aboriginal rock paintings at the Archways. Also a historic cemetery; 16 km W. *Almaden:* small town where cattle own the main street; 30 km SE. *4WD self-guide adventure trek:* mud maps and clues provided; details from visitor centre. *Tag-along tours:* full- and half-day tours visiting Aboriginal sites, marble quarries and other places; details from visitor centre.

See also GULF SAVANNAH, p. 427

Chinchilla
Pop. 3684
Map ref. 653 J7

ℹ️ Warrego Hwy; (07) 4668 9564; www.chinchilla.org.au

📻 97.1 Breeze FM, 747 AM ABC Southern QLD

Chinchilla is a prosperous town in the western Darling Downs. Explorer Ludwig Leichhardt named the area in 1844 after the local Aboriginal name for the native cypress pines, 'jinchilla' – there are still many in town. Today Chinchilla is known as the 'melon capital' of Australia as it produces around 25 per cent of the country's watermelons.

Historical Museum: a varied collection of memorabilia including steam engines, a replica 1910 sawmill and a slab cottage. Also an excellent display of local petrified wood known as 'Chinchilla Red'; open 9am–4pm Wed–Sun; Villiers St. **Pioneer Cemetery**: headstones tell early history. Also a monument to Ludwig Leichhardt; Warrego Hwy.

 Melon Festival: odd-numbered years, Feb. **Market:** Warrego Hwy; Easter Sat. **Rotary May Day Celebrations:** May. **Chinchilla Show:** May. **Polocrosse Carnival:** Sept. **Grand Father Clock Campdraft:** Oct. **Mardi Gras:** Nov. **Chinchilla Cup:** Dec.

 Cactoblastis Memorial Hall: dedicated to the insect introduced from South America to eradicate the prickly pear cactus; Boonarga, 8 km E. **Fossicking:** for petrified wood at nearby properties; licences and details from visitor centre. **Fishing:** good spots include Charleys Creek and the Condamine River; details from visitor centre. **Chinchilla Weir:** popular spot for boating and waterskiing, plus freshwater fishing for golden perch and jewfish; 10 km S.

See also DARLING DOWNS, p. 418

Clermont
Pop. 1851
Map ref. 649 B12 | 654 H9

i Cnr Herschel and Karmoo sts; (07) 4983 4755; www.isaac.qld.gov.au

102.1 4HI FM, 1548 AM ABC Capricornia

Clermont is in the central highlands south-west of Mackay. It was established over 130 years ago after the discovery of gold at Nelson's Gully. At first the settlement was at Hood's Lagoon, but was moved to higher ground after a major flood in 1916 in which 63 people died. To the east of Clermont are the prominent cone-shaped mountains of Peak Range National Park. The Wolfgang Peak between Clermont and Mackay is particularly spectacular.

Hood's Lagoon and Centenary Park Walk the boardwalks in this picturesque setting to see the colourful birdlife. The park has interesting memorials and monuments that include the Sister Mary MacKillop grotto, an Aboriginal monument and a war memorial. The tree marker at the flood memorial plaque demonstrates how high the water rose. Access via Lime St.

Railway Wagon Murals: paintings on 4 original wagons depict industries within the Belyando Shire; Hershel St. **The Stump:** memorial to the 1916 flood; Cnr Drummond and Capricorn sts.

Rodeo: Apr. **Clermont Show:** May. **Campdraft:** June. **Gold and Coal Festival:** Aug. **Country Music Festival:** Oct.

Cemetery: headstones dating back to 1860s and mass grave of 1916 flood victims; 2.5 km NE. **Clermont Museum and Heritage Park:** museum exhibits historic artefacts and machinery, including the steam engine used to shift the town after flood and historic buildings, such as the old Masonic lodge, with displays of local family histories; open daily, times vary; (07) 4983 3311; 4 km NW. **Remnants of Copperfield:** old coppermining town with museum in original Copperfield store, chimneystack, and cemetery containing 19th-century graves of coppermines; 5 km S. **Theresa Creek Dam:** popular spot for waterskiing, sailboarding and fishing (permit required). Bushwalks nearby; off Peakvale Rd; 17 km SW. **Blair Athol open-cut mine:** free half-day tour to see the largest seam of steaming coal in the world; departs from Clermont Visitor Centre; Blair Athol; 23 km NW. **Blackwood National Park:** 187 km NW; *see*

Charters Towers. **Fossicking for gold:** obtain licence and fossicking kit to start the search in nearby area; details from visitor centre.

See also THE MID-TROPICS, p. 424

Clifton
Pop. 1065
Map ref. 653 L10

i Council offices, 70 King St; (07) 4697 4222; www.clifton.qld.gov.au

91.9 CFM, 747 AM ABC Southern QLD

Clifton is south of Toowoomba in the fertile agricultural lands of the Darling Downs. The town's charming street facades have been a popular backdrop for many Australian movies, including the epic film adaptation of The *Thorn Birds*. The town is a vision of colour during the renowned annual Rose and Iris Show.

Historical Museum: in the old butter factory, with displays of early implements and farm life; open 1st and 3rd Sun each month; King St. **Alister Clark Rose Garden:** largest Queensland collection of these roses; Edward St.

Clifton Show: Apr. **Country Week:** includes the Rose and Iris Show and horseracing; Oct.

Nobby This small town provided inspiration to writer Arthur Hoey Davis (Steele Rudd), author of *On Our Selection* and creator of the famous Dad and Dave characters. Rudd's Pub (1893) has a museum of pioneering memorabilia. Nearby is the burial site of Sister Kenny along with a memorial and museum dedicated to her – she was renowned for her unorthodox method of treating poliomyelitis. 8 km N.

Darling Downs Zoo Queensland's newest zoo is situated in the serene countryside where you can view native and exotic animals from Africa, South America and Asia. The zoo has a shady picnic area as well as barbecue facilities and a small kiosk. Open weekends, public and school holidays, or by appt (for large groups); Gatton–Clifton Rd; (07) 4696 4107; 10 km E.

Leyburn: holds the Historic Race Car Sprints in Aug; 30 km W.

See also DARLING DOWNS, p. 418

Cloncurry
Pop. 2385
Map ref. 659 F11 | 660 H3

i Mary Kathleen Park, McIlwraith St; (07) 4742 1361; www.cloncurry.qld.gov.au

102.5 Hot FM, 567 AM ABC North West QLD

Cloncurry is an important mining town in the Gulf Savannah region. In 1861 John McKinlay, leading a search for Burke and Wills, reported traces of copper in the area. Six years later, pastoralist Ernest Henry discovered the first copper lodes. During World War I Cloncurry was the centre of a copper boom and the largest source of the mineral in Australia. Copper prices slumped postwar and a pastoral industry was developed. Today main industries include grazing, coppermining and goldmining. The town's interesting history extends to aviation as well. Qantas was conceived here – the original hangar can still be seen at the airport – and the town became the first base for the famous Royal Flying Doctor Service in 1928.

John Flynn Place This complex includes the RFDS Museum, with history on the service and memorabilia including

QUEENSLAND

the first RFDS aircraft and an original Traegar pedal wireless. There is also the Fred McKay Art Gallery, with changing exhibits of local art, the Alfred Traegar Cultural Centre and the Alan Vickers Outdoor Theatre. Open 8am–4.30pm Mon–Fri, 9am–3pm Sat–Sun (May–Sept); Cnr Daintree and King sts.

Mary Kathleen Memorial Park: with buildings from abandoned uranium mining town of Mary Kathleen including Old Police Station and Town Office – now a museum with historic items such as Robert O'Hara Burke's water bottle, local Aboriginal artefacts and a comprehensive rock, mineral and gem collection. Visitor information centre is also on-site; McIlwraith St. *Shire hall:* restored 1939 building; Scarr St. *Cemeteries:* varied cultural background of Cloncurry can be seen in the 3 cemeteries: Cloncurry Old Cemetery, including the grave of Dame Mary Gilmore (Sir Hudson Fyshe Dr); Afghan Cemetery (part of Cloncurry Old Cemetery); and Chinese Cemetery (Flinders Hwy). *Original Qantas hangar:* airport; Sir Hudson Fyshe Dr. *Historic buildings:* including the post office, Brodie Hardware Store and the Post Office Hotel; brochure from visitor centre.

 Markets: Florence Park, Scarr St; 1st Sat each month. Mary Kathleen Park, McIlwraith St; 4th Sun each month. *Cloncurry Show:* June. *Stockman's Challenge and Campdraft:* night rodeo; July. *Rockhana:* mineral and gem festival; July. *Merry Muster Rodeo:* July/Aug. *Art Show:* Sept. *Battle of the Mines:* rugby league carnival; Oct. *Cloncurry Cup:* Oct.

Gidgee Inn Motel: rammed-earth motel; Matilda Hwy; (07) 4742 1599.

Rotary Lookout: over Cloncurry and the river; Mt Isa Hwy; 2 km w. *Chinamen Creek Dam:* peaceful area with abundant birdlife; 3 km w. *Ernest Henry Copper and Gold Mine:* tours available. Departs from Mary Kathleen Park; 29 km NE. *Burke and Wills cairn:* near Corella River; 43 km w. *Kajabbi:* town holds Yabby Races in May; 77 km NW. *Kuridala:* this one-time mining town is now a ghost town. Explore the ruins including the old cemetery; 88 km s. *Fossicking:* for amethysts and other gemstones; details from visitor centre.

See also OUTBACK, p. 428

Cooktown

Pop. 1339
Map ref. 657 L3

ⓘ Nature's Powerhouse, Cooktown Botanic Gardens, Finch Bay Rd; (07) 4069 6004 or 1800 174 895; www.cook.qld.gov.au

📻 105.7 FM ABC Far North QLD

Cooktown is the last main town before the wilderness that is Cape York. In 1770, Captain Cook beached the *Endeavour* here for repairs after running aground on the Great Barrier Reef. Cooktown was founded more than 100 years later after gold was discovered on the Palmer River. It became the gold-rush port with 37 hotels and a transient population of some 18 000, including 6000 Chinese. Nearby are some of the most rugged and remote national parks in Australia. They form part of the Wet Tropics World Heritage Area and are a special experience for today's intrepid explorers.

🏛 **James Cook Museum** Housed in the old convent school (1888), this museum documents Aboriginal life prior to European settlement, Cook's voyages and the 1870s gold-rush past. Relics include the anchor from the *Endeavour*. Helen St.

Botanic Gardens: these are the oldest botanic gardens in Queensland, with native, European and exotic plants. The 'Cooktown Interpretive Centre: Nature's Powerhouse' has botanical and wildlife illustrations, and there are also walking trails to Cherry Tree and Finch bays; Walker St. *Historic cemetery:* documents the varied cultural heritage of Cooktown and includes the grave of tutor, early immigrant and heroine Mary Watson; Boundary Rd. *Chinese shrine:* to many who died on the goldfields; near cemetery. *Cooktown Wharf:* dates back to 1880s and is an excellent spot for fishing. *The Milibi Wall:* collage of traditional art by local Aboriginal people; near wharf. *Fishing:* spanish mackerel and barramundi at the wharf. *Walking trails:* plenty around the town and outlying areas, including the Scenic Rim and Wharf and Foreshore Walk; details from visitor centre.

🌴 *Market:* Lions Park; Sat. *Discovery Festival:* re-enactment of Cook's landing; June. *Cooktown Races:* July. *Art Festival:* Aug. *Agricultural Show:* Aug. *Wallaby Creek Festival (Rossville):* music festival; Sept.

🛏 *The Sovereign Resort Hotel:* quality hotel in colonial building; 128 Charlotte St; (07) 4043 0500. *Mungumby Lodge:* 10 ensuite bungalows; Mungumby Rd, Helenvale; (07) 4060 3158.

◉ **Lizard Island National Park** Comprises 6 islands to the north-east of Cooktown surrounded by the blue waters and coral reefs of the northern Great Barrier Reef. Four of the islands are important seabird nesting sites. Lizard Island is a resort island popular for sailing and fishing. Also on offer is snorkelling in the giant clam gardens of Watsons Bay. Walk to Cooks Look for a spectacular view. There are 11 species of lizard here, and green and loggerhead turtles nest in late spring. Regular flights depart from Cairns; charter flights depart from Cairns and Cooktown; charter or private boat hire is available at Cooktown. (07) 4069 5777 (use same contact number for all national parks below).

Endeavour River National Park: just north of town is this park of diverse landscapes, including coastal dunes, mangrove forests and catchment areas of the Endeavour River. Most of the park is accessible only by boat (ramps at Cooktown); southern vehicle access is via Starcke St, Marton. *Black Mountain National Park:* impressive mountain range of granite boulders and a refuge for varied and threatened wildlife; Cooktown Developmental Rd; (07) 4069 5777; 25 km s. *Helenvale:* small town with historic Lions Den Hotel (est. 1875) and rodeo in June; 30 km s. *Rossville:* town with markets every 2nd Sat and Wallaby Creek Folk Festival at Home Rule Rainforest Lodge in Sept; 38 km s. *Cedar Bay (Mangkal-Mangkalba) National Park:* this remote coastal park is an attractive mix of rainforest, beaches and fringing reefs, with a variety of wildlife including the rare Bennett's tree kangaroo. Walk on the old donkey track once used by tin miners (remains of tin workings can be seen). Access by boat or by the walking track, which starts at Home Rule Rainforest Lodge, Rossville, 38 km s. *Elim Beach and the Coloured Sands:* spectacular beach with white silica sandhills and surrounding heathlands. The Coloured Sands are found 400 m along the beach (Aboriginal land, permit required from Hope Vale Community Centre); 65 km N. *Cape Melville National Park:* this rugged park on the Cape York Peninsula has spectacular coastal scenery. Much of the plant life is rare, including the foxtail palm. Visitors must be self-sufficient; 4WD access only in dry weather; southern access via Starcke homestead, western access via Kalpower Crossing in Lakefield National Park; 140 km NW. *Flinders Group National Park:* comprising 7 continental islands in Princess Charlotte Bay. There are 2 self-guide trails taking in bushfoods and Aboriginal rock-art sites on Stanley Island. Access by charter or private boat or sea plane; 195 km NW. *Sportfishing safaris:* to nearby waterways; details from visitor centre. **Guurrbi Aboriginal Tours:** full- and half-day tours of Aboriginal rock-art sites and informative history of bush tucker and traditional medicine; details from visitor centre. **Bicentennial National Trail:** 5000 km trail that runs from Cooktown to Healesville in Victoria, for walkers, bike riders and horseriders. It is possible to do just a section of trail; details from visitor centre.

Travellers note: *Before driving to remote areas check road conditions and restrictions with Queensland Parks & Wildlife Service, 5 Webber Espl, Cooktown, (07) 4069 5777.*

See also CAIRNS & THE TROPICS, p. 425

Crows Nest

Pop. 1443
Map ref. 653 L8

 Hampton Visitor Information Centre, 8623 New England Hwy, Hampton (12 km S); (07) 4697 9066 or 1800 009 066; www.crowsnest.info

100.7 C FM, 747 AM ABC Southern QLD

On the western slopes of the Great Dividing Range north of Toowoomba is the small town of Crows Nest. It was named after Jimmy Crow, a Kabi-Kabi Aboriginal man who made his home in a hollow tree near the present police station. He was an invaluable source of directions for passing bullock teams staying overnight in the area. A memorial to Crow can be found in Centenary Park.

Carbethon Folk Museum and Pioneer Village: many interesting old buildings and over 20 000 items of memorabilia documenting the history of the shire; open 10am–3pm Thurs–Sun; Thallon St. **Bullocky's Rest and Applegum Walk:** a 1.5 km track follows the creeks to Hartmann Park and a lookout over Pump Hole. Visit in late winter to see the beautiful wildflowers; entry from New England Hwy.

Village Markets: arts, crafts and local produce; 1st Sun each month. **Crows Nest Day:** children's worm races, crow calling competitions and battle of the band concert; Oct.

Bunnyconnellen Olive Grove and Vineyard: self-contained studio; Swain Rd; (07) 4697 9555.

Crows Nest National Park This popular park features a variety of landscapes, including granite outcrops and eucalypt forest. The wildlife is spectacular: see the platypus in the creek and the brush-tailed rock wallabies on the rocky cliffs. A steep track from the creek leads to an excellent lookout over Crows Nest Falls; follow this further to Koonin Lookout for spectacular views over the gorge, known locally as the Valley of Diamonds. (07) 4699 4333; 6 km E (look for sign to Valley of Diamonds).

Holland Wines: offers a vast collection of exquisite wines: 5 km N. **Bunnyconnellen Olive Grove and Vineyard:** perfect getaway for couples with rooms available. Enjoy the magnificent wines and gourmet food; open weekends; Swain Rd, off New England Hwy, 10 km N. **Lake Cressbrook:** set among picturesque hills is this excellent spot for windsurfing and boating. Fish the lake for silver perch; 17 km E. **Ravensbourne National Park:** a small park comprising remnant rainforest and wet eucalypt forest with over 80 species of birds, including the black-breasted button-quail that can be seen feeding on the rainforest floor on the Cedar Block track. Many bushwalks start at Blackbean picnic area; Esk–Hampton Rd; (07) 4699 4333; 25 km SE. **Beutel's Lookout:** picnic area with scenic views across the Brisbane Valley; adjacent

to Ravensbourne National Park; 25 km SE. **Goombungee:** historic town with museum. Famous for running rural ironman and ironwoman competitions on Australia Day; 32 km W.

See also DARLING DOWNS, p. 418

Croydon

Pop. 255
Map ref. 656 F8

 Samwell St; (07) 4745 6125; www.croydon.qld.gov.au

105.9 FM ABC Far North QLD

Croydon is a small town on the grassland plains of the Gulf Savannah. It marks the eastern terminus for the Gulflander train service, which leaves each Thursday morning for Normanton. The train line was established in the late 1800s to service Croydon's booming gold industry. Many original buildings dating from 1887 to 1897, and classified by the National Trust and Australian Heritage Commission, have been restored to the splendour of the town's goldmining days.

Historical precinct: many restored buildings bring the rich history of Croydon to life. Highlights include the old courthouse with original furniture, and the old hospital featuring original hospital documents. **Outdoor Museum:** displays mining machinery from the age of steam; Samwell St. **Old Police Precinct and Gaol:** historic documents and access to gaol cells; Samwell St. **General Store and Museum:** restored store in the old ironmongers shop; Sircom St.

Poddy Dodger Festival: June.

Mining Museum: interesting display of early mining machinery including battery stamper; 1 km N. **Historic cemetery:** includes old Chinese gravestones; 2 km S. **Chinese temple site:** Heritage-listed archaeological site preserving 50 years of Chinese settlement that followed the gold discoveries of the 1880s. Take the Heritage Trail to see how the Chinese lived; on road to Lake Belmore. **Lake Belmore:** one of many sites for birdwatching, along with beautiful picnic areas and barbecue facilities. Also swimming, waterskiing and fishing (limits apply); 5 km N.

See also GULF SAVANNAH, p. 427

Cunnamulla

Pop. 1218
Map ref. 655 A9 | 663 N9

 Centenary Park, Jane St; (07) 4655 8470; www.paroo.info

96.5 Triple C FM, 603 AM ABC Western QLD

Cunnamulla is on the Warrego River, north of the New South Wales border. It is the biggest wool-loading station on the Queensland railway network, with two million sheep in the area. Explorers Sir Thomas Mitchell and Edmund Kennedy were the first European visitors, arriving in 1846 and 1847 respectively, and by 1879 the town was thriving with regular Cobb & Co services to the west. In 1880, Joseph Wells held up the local bank but could not find his escape horse. Locals bailed him up in a tree that is now known as the Robber's Tree and can be found in Stockyard Street. The wetland birdlife in the area, particularly the black swans, brolgas and pelicans, is spectacular.

Cunnamulla Fella Centre Art Gallery and Museum: gallery showcases different artist exhibitions throughout the year, while the musem displays the rich history and heritage of the town and wider Paroo shire; Jane St. **Yupunyah Tree:** planted by Princess Anne; Cnr Louise and Stockyard sts. **Outback Botanic**

QUEENSLAND

Gardens and Herbarium: Matilda Hwy. *Outback Dreaming Arts and Crafts:* exhibits and sales of local Aboriginal art; Stockyard St. *The Heritage Trail:* discover the days of the late 1880s on this self-guide trail; details from visitor centre.

Cunnamulla Outback Masters Games: odd-numbered years, Apr. *Horseracing:* Aug. *Cunnamulla Festival and Bullride Championships:* Nov.

Nardoo Station: ensuite rooms and camp sites; Matilda Hwy; (07) 4655 4833.

Wyandra: small town featuring Powerhouse Museum and Heritage Trail; 100 km N. *Noorama:* remote sheep station that holds picnic races each Apr; 110 km SE. *Culgoa Floodplain National Park:* 195 km SE; *see St George.*

See also OUTBACK, p. 428

Daintree
Pop. 78
Map ref. 651 D2 | 657 L4

ℹ 5 Stewart St; (07) 4098 6133; www.daintreevillage.asn.au

📻 639 AM ABC Far North QLD

The unspoiled township of Daintree lies in the tropical rainforest of Far North Queensland, at the heart of the Daintree River catchment basin surrounded by the McDowall Ranges. Daintree began as a logging town in the 1870s. Now tourism is the major industry with the Daintree River and World Heritage rainforest nearby. Saltwater crocodiles can be seen in the mangrove-lined creeks and tributaries of the Daintree River.

Daintree Timber Gallery: hand-crafted pieces from local woods exhibited and sold. Also displays showcasing local history, including logging past; Stewart St. *Eliza's Rainforest Gallery:* handmade pottery of pixies, elves and gnomes; Stewart St.

Julaymba: elegant, contemporary bush flavours; Daintree Eco Lodge & Spa, 20 Daintree Rd; (07) 4098 6100 or 1800 808 010. *Papaya Cafe:* try the crocodile dishes; 3–5 Stewart St; (07) 4098 6173.

Daintree Eco Lodge & Spa: *Daintree Valley Haven:* 3 self-catering cabins; Stewart Creek Rd; (07) 4098 6206. *Daintree Wild B&B:* 4 rooms in wildlife park; 2054 Daintree Rd; (07) 4098 7272.

 Daintree National Park Arguably Australia's most beautiful and famous rainforest. The lush tangle of green protected within it is an incredible remnant from the days of Gondwana, forming part of the Wet Tropics World Heritage Area. This park, which is split into 3 distinct sections – Mossman Gorge, Cape Tribulation and Snapper Island – will dazzle visitors with its diverse landscapes, which, apart from beautiful rainforest, include canopies of sprawling fan palms, deserted mangrove-lined beaches and boulder-strewn gorges.

Daintree Discovery Centre: informative displays for visitors. A boardwalk and aerial walkway passes through the rainforest canopy; 11 km SE. *Wonga Belle Orchid Gardens:* 3.5 ha of lush gardens; 17 km SE. *Cape Tribulation:* spectacular beaches and reefs. Reef tours and horseriding on beach can be arranged at visitor centre or Mason's Shop in Cape Tribulation; for details call (07) 4098 0070; access via Daintree River cable ferry (car ferry runs 6am to 12am). *River cruises:* to see the saltwater crocodiles and plentiful birdlife; details from visitor centre. Horseriding tours: in Cape Tribulation; (07) 4041 3244.

Travellers note: Beware of estuarine crocodiles that live in the sea and estuaries; never cross tidal creeks at high tide, swim in creeks,

prepare food at water's edge or camp close to deep waterholes. Beware of marine stingers between Oct and Mar.

See also CAIRNS & THE TROPICS, p. 425

Dalby
Pop. 9775
Map ref. 653 K8

ℹ Thomas Jack Park, Cnr Drayton and Condamine sts; (07) 4662 1066; www.dalby.info

📻 89.9 FM Dalby Community Radio, 747 AM ABC Southern QLD

Sitting at the crossroads of the Warrego, Moonie, Condamine and Bunya highways, Dalby is conveniently linked to all of Australia's capital cities. It was a small rural town until the soldier resettlement program after World War II in which the population influx allowed the surrounding agricultural industry to thrive. It is now a relaxed country town with uncluttered landscapes, charismatic local pubs and home-grown produce.

Thomas Jack Park: beautifully landscaped park with playground equipment and tranquil lagoon; Cnr Drayton and Condamine sts. *Cultural and Administration Centre:* regional art gallery and cinema; Drayton St. *Pioneer Park Museum:* comprises historic buildings, household and agricultural items and a craft shop; Black St. *The Crossing:* an obelisk marks the spot where explorer Henry Dennis camped in 1841; Edward St. *Historic cairn:* pays homage to the cactoblastis, the Argentinean caterpillar that controlled prickly pear in the 1920s; Myall Creek picnic area, Marble St. *Myall Creek Walk:* walk along banks of Myall Creek to see varied birdlife. *Heritage walk:* self-guide walk provides insight into town's history; brochure from visitor centre.

Cotton on to Energy Festival: 4-day festival; Mar. *Country Race Days:* Newmarket Races; Mar. Picnic Races: May. Saints Race Day: July. Plough Inn Cup: Aug. *Dalby Show:* Apr. *Spring Art Show:* Sept. *Spring Garden Week:* Sept.

Lake Birdwater Conservation Park The 350 ha lake is an important breeding ground for waterfowl. There are over 240 species of bird that can be seen from the short walks around the lake. Waterskiing and boating are popular on the main body of the lake when it is full (permit required); 29 km SW.

Historic Jimbour House: attractive French homestead, formal gardens and boutique winery; 29 km N. *Bell:* small town at the base of Bunya Mountains with traditional arts and crafts stores; 41 km NW. *Cecil Plains:* cotton town with historic murals and Cecil Plains Homestead. Also a popular spot for canoeing down Condamine River; 42 km S. *Rimfire Vineyards and Winery:* boutique winery offering tastings; 47 km NE. *Bunya Mountains National Park:* 63 km NE; *see Kingaroy.*

See also DARLING DOWNS, p. 418

Emerald
Pop. 10 999
Map ref. 655 I10

ℹ Clermont St; (07) 4982 4142; www.emerald.qld.gov.au

 96.3 4EEE FM, 1548 AM ABC Capricornia

Shady Moreton Bay fig trees line the main street in Emerald, an attractive town at the hub of the Central Highlands. Emerald was established in 1879 as a service town while the railway from Rockhampton to the west was being constructed. Several fires ravaged the town in the mid-1900s, destroying much of this early history. The largest sapphire fields in the Southern Hemisphere are nearby, where visitors can fossick for their own gems.

Pioneer Cottage Complex: historic cottage and lock-up gaol with padded cells. There is also a church and a communications museum; Morton Park, Clermont St. *Botanic Gardens:* walk around native display, herb garden and melaleuca maze. You can also visit a traditional bush chapel and ride the monorail; banks of Nogoa River. *Railway station:* restored 1900 National Trust–classified station with attractive lacework and pillared portico; Clermont St. *Fossilised tree:* 250 million years old; in front of town hall. *Mosaic pathway:* 21 pictures depict 100 years of Emerald history; next to visitor centre. *Van Gogh Sunflower Painting:* largest one (on an easel) in the world; Morton Park, Clermont St.

Sunflower Festival: Easter. *Gemfest:* Aug.

Sapphire gemfields To the west of Emerald is the largest sapphire-producing area in the Southern Hemisphere, incorporating Rubyvale, Sapphire, Anakie and Willows gemfields. The towns feature walk-in mines, fossicking parks, gem-faceting demonstrations, jewellers and museums. Obtain a licence and map of the mining areas from local stores or the Department of Natural Resources in Emerald to start fossicking. Rubyvale offers 4WD tours of gemfields including Tomahawk Creek; 43 km w.

Lake Maraboon/Fairbairn Dam: popular spot for watersports and fishing, especially for the red claw crayfish; 18 km s. *Capella:* first town settled in the area. See its history at the Capella Pioneer Village. The Crafts Fair and Vintage Machinery Rally is held in Sept; 51 km nw. *Local cattle stations and farm stays:* day tours in nearby area; details from visitor centre.

See also Capricorn, p. 423

Esk

Pop. 1163
Map ref. 647 A8 | 653 M8

2 Redbank St; (07) 5424 4000; www.somerset.qld.gov.a

95.9 Valley FM, 747 AM ABC Southern QLD

Esk is a heritage town in the Upper Brisbane Valley renowned for its beautiful lakes and dams where watersports are popular. Deer roam in the grazing country north of town, progeny of a small herd presented to the state by Queen Victoria in 1873.

Antiques and local crafts: numerous shops in town.

Market: Highland St; Sat. *Multicultural Festival:* July. *Picnic Races:* July. *Rail Trail Fun Run:* July. *Esk Show:* Aug.

Lakes and dams Known as the Valley of the Lakes, this region is popular for swimming, fishing and boating. Lake Wivenhoe (25 km e) is the source of Brisbane's main water supply. Walk to the Fig Tree Lookout for a panoramic view or ride a horse around the lake. Lake Somerset (25 km ne) is on the Stanley River and is a popular waterskiing spot. Atkinson Dam (30 km s) also attracts watersports enthusiasts.

Caboonbah Homestead: museum that houses the Brisbane Valley Historical Society, with superb views over Lake Wivenhoe; closed Thurs; 19 km ne. *Coominya:* small historic town; 22 km se. *Ravensbourne National Park:* 33 km w; *see Crows Nest. Skydiving:* take a tandem dive over the valley; contact visitor centre for details. *Brisbane Valley Rail Trail:* picturesque 148 km rural trail for biking enthusiasts. Trail runs between Fervale and Lowood, and Moore and Blackbutt. *Kilcoy:* small and unassuming farming town that claims to be the home of the

Yowie, Australia's equivalent of the Bigfoot or Yeti. There is a large wooden statue in town of the supposed creature; 60 km n.

See also Brisbane Hinterland, p. 415

Eulo

Pop. 108
Map ref. 663 M9

Centenary Park, Jane St, Cunnamulla; (07) 4655 2481; www.paroo.info

Eulo is on the banks of the Paroo River in south-west Queensland and was once a centre for opal mining. The town was originally much closer to the river but, after severe flooding, moved to where it currently stands. Eulo's population is variable as beekeepers travel from the south every winter so their bees can feed on the precious eucalypts in the area.

Eulo Queen Hotel: owes its name to Isobel Robinson who ran the hotel and reigned over the opal fields in the early 1900s; Leo St. *Eulo Date Farm:* taste the famous date wine; open Mar–Oct; western outskirts. *WW II air-raid shelter:* part of Paroo Pioneer Pathways; self-guide brochure available from visitor centre. *Destructo Cockroach Monument:* commemorates the death of a champion racing cockroach; near Paroo Track, where annual lizard races are held. *Eulo Queen Opal Centre:* opals, Aboriginal art and jewellery on display and for purchase; Leo St. *Lizard Lounge:* beautiful picnic area inspired by the frill-necked lizard; Cunnamulla Rd. *Fishing:* on the Paroo River; details from visitor centre.

Currawinya National Park The lakes and waterholes of Paroo River form an important refuge for the abundant birdlife of this park. The 85 km circuit track for vehicles starts at the Ranger Station and is the best way to view the park. See the black swans and grebes at Lake Wyara or go canoeing at Lake Numulla. For an excellent outlook over the park, climb the Granites. 4WD necessary to reach the lakes. (07) 4655 4143; 60 km sw.

Mud springs: natural pressure valve to artesian basin that is currently inactive; 9 km w. *Yowah:* small opal-mining town where visitors can fossick for opals or take a tour of the minefields. The 'Bluff' and 'Castles' provide excellent views over the minefields. Yowah holds a craft day in June and the Opal Festival in July, which includes an international opal jewellery competition; 87 km nw. *Lake Bindegolly National Park:* walk to the lakes to see pelicans and swans. The 9.2 km lake circuit track may flood after rain. No vehicles are allowed in the park; 100 km w. *Thargomindah:* pick up a mud map at visitor centre for Burke and Wills Dig Tree site; (07) 4655 3173; 130 km w. *Noccundra Waterhole:* good fishing spot on Wilson River; 260 km w.

See also Outback, p. 428

Gatton

Pop. 5296
Map ref. 653 L9

Lake Apex Dr; (07) 5462 3430; www.gatton.qld.gov.au

100.7 C FM, 747 AM ABC Southern QLD

In the Lockyer Valley west of Brisbane, Gatton was one of the first rural settlements in Queensland. The much recorded and debated 'Gatton Murders' that occurred in 1898 were the subject of Australian writer Rodney Hall's novel *Captivity Captive*. The graves of the three murdered siblings can still be seen in the cemetery. The Great Dividing Range provides a scenic

QUEENSLAND

backdrop to the surrounding fertile black soil, excellent for vegetable produce.

Gatton & District Historical Society Museum: complex of 11 buildings depicting the social history of the region; open 1–4pm or by appt; Freemans Rd. **Lake Apex:** park and complex include the historic village with preserved heritage buildings, memorabilia and Aboriginal carvings. Follow the walking tracks to see the diverse birdlife; Old Warrego Hwy.

Markets: Rotary Park, 1st Sat each month; Showgrounds, 2nd Sat each month. **Clydesdale and Heavy Horse field days:** Apr/May. **Gatton Show:** July. **Multicultural Festival:** Aug.

Agricultural College: opened in 1897. Drive through the grounds that are now part of the University of Queensland; 5 km E. **Helidon:** town noted for its sandstone – used in many Brisbane buildings – and spa water; 16 km w. **Glen Rock Regional Park:** at the head of East Haldon Valley, this park boasts rainforest gorges, creeks and excellent valley views; 40 km s. **Tourist drive:** 82 km circuit through surrounding countryside that includes farm visits; contact visitor centre for details.

See also Brisbane Hinterland, p. 415

Gayndah

Pop. 1747
Map ref. 653 L5

ⓘ Historical Museum, 3 Simon St; (07) 4161 2226; www.gayndah.qld.gov.au

📻 91.5 FM Burnett River Radio, 855 AM ABC Wide Bay

Gayndah, in the Capricorn region, is one of Queensland's oldest towns. Founded in 1849, it was once competing with Brisbane and Ipswich to be the state's capital. Main Street's heritage buildings and landscaped gardens illustrate the long history of the town, which is now central to a rich citrus-growing industry.

Historical Museum An award-winning museum with several historic buildings, displays, photographs and memorabilia that illustrate the town's changing history from small settlement to thriving agricultural centre – a highlight is a restored 1884 cottage. There is also an interesting display on the lungfish and its link between sea and land animals. Simon St.

Market: Jaycees Park; 1st Sun each month. **Gayndah Show:** Mar. **Orange Festival:** odd-numbered years, June. **Triathlon:** Oct.

Lookouts: several in area offering views over Burnett Valley; closest to town is Archers Lookout, atop the twin hills 'Duke and Duchess' overlooking town. **Claude Warton Weir:** excellent spot for fishing and picnics; 3 km w. **Ban Ban Springs:** natural springs and picnic area; 26 km s.

See also Capricorn, p. 423

Gin Gin

Pop. 888
Map ref. 648 B2 | 653 L3

ⓘ Mulgrave St; (07) 4157 3060.

📻 93.1 Sea FM, 855 AM ABC Wide Bay

Some of Queensland's oldest cattle properties surround this pastoral town south-west of Bundaberg. The district is known as 'Wild Scotchman Country' after James McPherson, Queensland's only authentic bushranger. His antics are re-enacted every March at the Wild Scotchman Festival.

Historical Society Museum: displays memorabilia of pioneering past in 'The Residence' – a former police sergeant's

house. The old sugarcane locomotive The Bunyip forms part of the historic railway display; open 8.30am–3.30pm Mon–Fri, 8.30am–12pm Sat, other times by appt; Mulgrave St. **Courthouse Gallery:** fine-arts gallery in refurbished old courthouse; Mulgrave St.

Market: Historical Museum; Sat. **Jazz and Shiraz:** Wonbah Winery; Aug. **Auto Machinery Show:** Aug. **Cane Burning and Whipcracking Festival:** Aug. **Didgeridoo Festival:** Aug/Sept. **Santa Fair:** Dec.

Goodnight Scrub National Park A dense remnant hoop pine rainforest in the Burnett Valley, this park is home to over 60 species of butterfly. Have a bush picnic at historic Kalliwa Hut, used during the logging days of the park. Drive up to One Tree Hill (4WD only) for a spectacular panoramic view over the area, on a clear day, all the way to Bundaberg. Turn-off is 10 km south of Gin Gin; (07) 4131 1600.

Lake Monduran: an excellent spot for watersports and fishing (permit from kiosk). Catch a barramundi or Australian bass, or walk the 6 km of tracks in the bush surrounds; 24 km NW. **Boolboonda Tunnel:** longest non-supported tunnel in the Southern Hemisphere. It forms part of a scenic tourist drive; brochure available from visitor centre; 27 km w. **Mount Perry:** small mining town, home to mountain-bike racing in June; 55 km sw.

See also Capricorn, p. 423

Gladstone

Pop. 42 902
Map ref. 653 L1 | 655 N12

ⓘ Marina Ferry Terminal, Bryan Jordan Dr; (07) 4972 4000; www.gladstoneregion.org.au

📻 95.1 Sea FM, 837 AM ABC Capricornia

Gladstone is a modern city on the central coast of Queensland. Matthew Flinders discovered Port Curtis, Gladstone's deep-water harbour, in 1802, but the town did not truly develop until the 1960s. Today it is an outlet for central Queensland's mineral and agricultural wealth – a prosperous seaboard city with one of Australia's busiest harbours. Set among hills with natural lookouts over the harbour and southern end of the Great Barrier Reef, Gladstone is popular for swimming, surfing and fishing – especially for mud crabs and prawns.

Tondoon Botanic Gardens: displays of all-native species of the Port Curtis region with free guided tours on weekends. Also offers a recreational lake and Mt Biondello bushwalk; Glenlyon Rd. **Gladstone Regional Art Gallery and Museum:** local and regional art with history exhibitions; closed Sun; Cnr Goondoon and Bramston sts. **Maritime Museum:** artefacts and memorabilia document 200 years of port history; open Thurs and Sun; Auckland Pt. **Potters Place:** fine-art gallery and craft shop; Dawson Hwy. **Gecko Valley Winery:** tastings and sales of award-winning wines; closed Mon; Bailiff Rd. **Barney Point Beach:** historic beach including Friend Park; Barney St. **Waterfall:** spectacular at night when floodlit; Flinders Pde.

Markets: Calliope River Historical Village; selected dates (6 times a year). **Sunfest:** youth sports and arts program; Jan. **Harbour Festival:** includes the finish of the Brisbane to Gladstone Yacht Race; Mar. **Woodworker's Art and Crafts Weekend (Calliope):** July. **Multicultural Festival:** Aug. **Seafood Festival:** Sept.

Auckland Hill B&B: heritage house in centre of town; 15 Yarroon St; (07) 4972 4907. **Rydges Gladstone Hotel:** spacious rooms; 100 Goondoon St; (07) 4970 0000 or 1300 857 922.

Xenia Central Studio Accommodation: self-catering rooms and suites; 166 Auckland St; (07) 4972 2022. *Glassford Creek Station Farmstay:* working cattle station; Boxvale, Builyan; (07) 4974 1185.

 Capricornia Cays National Park This park, 60–100 km offshore from Gladstone, protects the 9 coral islands and cays that form the southern end of the Great Barrier Reef. The islands are important nesting sites for seabirds and loggerhead turtles. North West Island has walking tracks through forests dominated by palms and she-oaks. The most popular activities are reef walking, diving and snorkelling in the spectacular reefs or visiting the renowned dive sites on Heron Island. Access is by private boat or charter from Gladstone; air access to Heron Island. There is seasonal closure to protect nesting wildlife. (07) 4971 6500 (same number for all national parks in the area).

Boyne Island: with beautiful foreshore parks and beaches. Home to the Boyne–Tannum Hookup Fishing Competition in June. The Boyne Aluminium Smelter is Australia's largest and has an information centre and tours every Fri. The island and its twin town of Tannum Sands are linked by bridge; 25 km SE. *Tannum Sands:* small community offering sandy beaches with year-round swimming, picturesque Millennium Way along the beach and 15 km of scenic walkways known as the Turtle Way. Wild Cattle Island, an uninhabited national park at the southern end of the beach, can be reached on foot at low tide; 25 km SE. *Calliope:* small rural community with excellent fishing in nearby Calliope River with abundant mud crabs, salmon and flathead. The Calliope River Historical Village documents Port Curtis history in restored buildings and holds regular art and craft markets; 26 km SW. *Lake Awoonga:* a popular spot for swimming, skiing (permit required) and fishing. It has walking tracks and recreational facilities, and holds the Lions Lake Awoonga Family Fishing Festival each Sept; 30 km S. *Mt Larcom:* spectacular views from the summit; 33 km W. *Castle Tower National Park:* a rugged park of granite cliffs and the outcrops of Castle Tower and Stanley mountains. Only experienced walkers should attempt the climb to Mt Castle Tower summit, where there are superb views over the Boyne Valley and Gladstone. Access by foot or boat from Lake Awoonga; access by car from Bruce Hwy; 40 km S. *Kroombit Tops National Park:* this mountain park is on a plateau with sandstone cliffs and gorges, waterfalls and creeks. Drive the 90 min return loop road to explore the landscapes and walk to the site of a WW II bomber crash; 4WD recommended; 75 km SW via Calliope. *Curtis Island National Park:* at the north-east end of the island is this small park with a variety of vegetation and excellent spots for birdwatching. There are no walking tracks, but the 3–4-day hike along the east coast is worthwhile; access by boat from Gladstone or the Narrows. *Great Barrier Reef tours:* cruises depart from the Gladstone Marina; Bryan Jordan Dr.

See also **Capricorn**, p. 423

Goondiwindi

Pop. 5031
Map ref. 556 H1 | 653 I11

ⓘ Cnr McLean and Bowen sts; (07) 4671 2653; www.goondiwindi.qld.gov.au

📻 101.9 Coast FM, 711 AM ABC Western QLD

Beside the picturesque MacIntyre River in the western Darling Downs is this border town. Explored by Allan Cunningham in 1827 and settled by pastoralists in the 1830s, the town derives its name from the Aboriginal word 'gonnawinna', meaning 'resting place of the birds'.

 Customs House Museum: explore local history in the restored 1850 customs house; closed Tues; McLean St. *Victoria Hotel:* renowned historic pub with tower; Marshall St. *Goondiwindi Cotton and Gin:* one of the largest cotton manufacturers in Australia; bus tours available, contact visitor information centre for details. *River Walk:* watch abundant birdlife and wildlife on 2 km walk along MacIntyre River; starts at Riddles Oval, Lagoon St. *'Goondiwindi Grey' Statue:* tribute to famous racehorse Gunsynd; Apex Park, MacIntyre St. *Fishing:* some of Queensland's best fishing in and around the town, Murray cod and yellow-belly in abundance.

Market: Town Park, Marshall St; 2nd Sun each month. *Hell of the West Triathlon:* Feb. *Gourmet in Gundy:* Sept. *Spring Festival:* coincides with flowering of jacarandas and silky oaks; Oct.

 Southwood National Park This brigalow-belah forest park was once known as 'Wild Horse Paradise'. Have a bush picnic and look for the black cockatoos in the belah trees, or visit at night and go spotlighting for feathertail gliders. 4WD is recommended. Access from Moonie Hwy; (07) 4699 4355; 125 km NW.

Botanic Gardens of Western Woodlands: 25 ha of native plants of the Darling Basin. Also here is a lake popular for swimming and canoeing; access from Brennans Rd; 1 km W. *Toobeah:* small town famous for its horse events; 48 km W.

See also **Darling Downs**, p. 418

Gordonvale

Pop. 4421
Map ref. 650 E3 | 651 F8 | 657 M6

ⓘ Cnr Bruce Hwy and Munro St, Babinda; (07) 4067 1008.

📻 103.5 Hot FM, 801 AM ABC Far North QLD

Gordonvale is a sugar-milling town just south of Cairns with well-preserved streetscapes, historic buildings and the 922-metre-high Walsh's Pyramid that forms the backdrop to the town. People flock to the mountain in August for a race to the top. The town's less glorious claim to fame is that cane toads were released here in 1935 in an attempt to eradicate sugarcane pests.

 Settlers Museum: with displays and dioramas depicting early pioneer life in the shire. Includes blacksmith's shop, old store and a Chinese display; open 10am–2pm Mon–Sat (closed Dec–Feb); Gordon St.

 Goldsborough Valley State Forest The lowland rainforest along the Goldsborough Valley is protected here. Walk to the falls along the 1.6 km Kearneys Falls track and learn about the local Aboriginal culture and customs from the informative displays. The 18 km historic Goldfields Trail travels through nearby Wooroonooran National Park to the Boulders near Babinda; 25 km SW via Gillies Hwy.

Mulgrave River: runs next to Gordonvale and is popular for swimming, canoeing, kayaking and bushwalking. *Wooroonooran National Park:* waterfalls, walking tracks and Walsh's Pyramid; 10 km S; *For the southern sections see Babinda and Millaa Millaa.* *Orchid Valley Nursery and Gardens:* tours of tropical gardens; 15 km SW. *Cairns Crocodile Farm:* crocodiles and other native wildlife with daily tours; around 5 min north on road to Yarrabah.

See also **Cairns & The Tropics**, p. 425

QUEENSLAND

Gympie

Pop. 10 933
Map ref. 648 D9 | 653 M6

i Mary Street Information Booth, (07) 5483 6656; or Cooloola Regional Information Centre, Matilda's Roadhouse Complex, Bruce Hwy, Kybong (15 km s), (07) 5483 5554 or 1800 444 222; www.cooloola.org.au

96.1 Zinc FM, 1566 AM ABC Wide Bay

On the banks of the Mary River on the Sunshine Coast is the major heritage town of Gympie. It was established when James Nash discovered gold in the area in 1867 and started Queensland's first gold rush to save the state from near bankruptcy. The field proved extremely rich – four million ounces had been found by the 1920s. The gold slowed to a trickle soon after, but the dairy and agricultural industries were already well established. See the attractive jacarandas, silky oaks, cassias, poincianas and flame trees that line the streets.

Mary Valley Heritage Railway Known locally as the 'Valley Rattler', this restored 1923 steam train takes the visitor on a 40 km journey through the picturesque Mary Valley. The train departs Gympie every Wed, Sat and Sun on its way to Imbil, where it stops before returning. Special tours run each Sat. Tickets and information from visitor centre; inquiries (07) 5482 2750.

Woodworks, Forestry and Timber Museum: exhibits memorabilia from old logging days including a steam-driven sawmill; closed Sat; Fraser Rd. *Deep Creek:* gold-fossicking area; permits from visitor centre; Counter St. *Public gallery:* local and visiting art exhibitions in heritage building; Nash St. *Heritage walk:* self-guide walk includes the Stock Exchange and Town Hall; details from visitor centre. *Trail rides:* horseriding through Kiah Park and Mary Valley; details from visitor centre.

Market: Gympie South State School; 2nd and 4th Sun each month. *Gympie Show:* May. *Race the Rattler:* a race against the historic steam train; June. *Fishing Classic:* Rainbow Beach; July. *Rodeo and Woodchop (Mary Valley):* Aug. *Country Music Muster:* Amamoor State Forest; Aug. *Art Festival (Mary Valley):* Sept. *Gold Rush Festival:* Oct.

Amamoor State Forest Over 120 native animal species find shelter in this protected forest, a remnant of the woodlands and vegetation that used to cover the Cooloola region. See the platypus in Amamoor Creek at dusk or take the Wonga walk or Cascade circuit track starting across the road from Amama. The renowned outdoor music festival, the Country Music Muster, is held in the forest on the last weekend in Aug. 30 km s.

Gold Mining Museum: delve into the area's goldmining history. It includes Andrew Fisher House (Fisher was the first Queenslander to become prime minister); 5 km s. *Mothar Mountain:* rockpools and forested area for bushwalking and excellent views; 20 km se. *Imbil:* picturesque town with excellent valley views. There is a market every Sun, and the nearby Lake Borumba offers great conditions for watersports and fishing – especially for golden perch and saratoga. Take the 14 km Imbil Forest Drive through scenic pine plantations just south of town; 36 km s. *Mary Valley Scenic Way:* enjoy this scenic route through towns of the valley, pineapple plantations and grazing farms; it runs south between Gympie and Maleny, via Kenilworth.

See also SUNSHINE COAST, p. 419

Herberton

Pop. 974
Map ref. 650 C4 | 651 C10 | 657 L7

i Herberton Mining Museum, 1 Jacks Rd; (07) 4096 3474; www.herbertonvisitorcentre.com.au

Known as the 'Village in the Hills', Herberton sits about 1000 metres above sea level on the south-west ranges of the Atherton Tableland. The first settlement on the tableland, it was established in 1880 when two prospectors discovered tin in the area. It was a thriving tin-mining town, the most important in the Herbert River field, until the mine's closure in 1978.

Mining Museum: explore local mining history in this richly informative museum, with displays of antique machinery, an array of minerals and rocks, and multimedia shows. A short walking track takes you past mining relics that made up the Great Northern Claim, now a heritage-listed site; 1 Jacks Rd. *Spy and Camera Museum:* houses some of the world's rarest, oldest and smallest cameras. See Russian spy cameras and cameras from Hitler's Germany; Grace St.

Ghost Walks: 3 times a year the ghosts of former miners and Herberton residents 'materialise' to retell their stories; dates vary, details from visitor centre.

Mt Hypipamee National Park Set on the Evelyn Tableland, this park boasts high-altitude rainforests and a climate that attracts birdlife and possums, including the green and lemuroid ringtail possums. The park is known locally as 'The Crater' because of its sheer-sided volcanic explosion crater 70 m wide. Walk to the viewing deck for the best vantage point, or see the Dinner Falls cascade down the narrow gorge. (07) 4091 1844; 25 km s.

Herberton Range State Forest: the temperate climate attracts a variety of wildlife in this rainforest park, including the attractive golden bowerbird. Walk to the summit of Mt Baldy for panoramic views over the tableland (the steep ascent should be attempted only by experienced walkers); Rifle Range Rd, between Atherton and Herberton. *Irvinebank:* many heritage-listed buildings including Mango House, Queensland National Bank Building and Loudoun House Museum; 26 km w on unsealed road. *Emuford:* small town featuring a historic stamper battery and museum; 51 km w.

See also CAIRNS & THE TROPICS, p. 425

Hughenden

Pop. 1154
Map ref. 654 B4 | 661 N4

i Flinders Discovery Centre, Gray St; (07) 4741 1021; www.hughenden.com

1485 AM ABC North West QLD

Hughenden is on the banks of the Flinders River, Queensland's longest river, west of the Great Dividing Range. The first recorded Europeans to pass here were members of Frederick Walker's 1861 expedition to search for explorers Burke and Wills. Two years later Ernest Henry selected a cattle station and Hughenden came into existence. The black volcanic soil in the region is rich with fossilised bones, particularly those of dinosaurs.

Flinders Discovery Centre Learn about the Flinders Shire history in this complex. The fossil exhibition's centrepiece is the 7 m replica skeleton of *Muttaburrasaurus langdoni*, a dinosaur found in Muttaburra (206 km s) – it was the first entire fossil skeleton found in Australia. The Historical Society also documents the shire history in their display. Gray St; (07) 4741 1021.

HERVEY BAY

Pop. 48 156
Map ref. 648 F4 | 653 N4

ⓘ Cnr Urraween and Maryborough–Hervey Bay rds;
(07) 4125 9855 or 1800 811 728; www.herveybay.qld.gov.au

107.5 FM Fraser Coast Community Radio, 855 AM ABC Wide Bay

Hervey (pronounced 'Harvey') Bay is the large area of water between Maryborough and Bundaberg, protected by Fraser Island. It is also the name of a thriving city spread out along the bay's southern shore. The climate is ideal and during winter there is an influx of visitors, not only for the weather, but also for the migrating humpback whales that frolic in the bay's warm waters between July and November. Hervey Bay is promoted as 'Australia's family aquatic playground' – there is no surf and swimming is safe, even for children. Fishing is another popular recreational activity, especially off the town's kilometre-long pier.

Botanic Gardens: interesting orchid conservatory; Elizabeth St. *Historical Museum:* recalls pioneer days in 19 historic buildings, including an 1898 slab cottage; open Fri–Sun; Zephyr St. *Sea Shell Museum:* shell creations and displays, including 100-million-year-old shell; Esplanade. *Neptune's Reefworld:* animals of the ocean, including performing seals; Pulgul St. *M & K Model Railways:* award-winning miniature gardens and model trains. Ride the replica diesel train; open Tues–Fri; Old Maryborough Rd. *Thrillseeker's Amusement Park:* rides include the Bungee Rocket; Hervey Bay Rd. *Dayman Park:* memorial commemorates landing of Matthew Flinders in 1799 and the Z-Force commandos who trained there on the Krait in WW II. *Regional Gallery:* includes regularly changing exhibitions of local artists plus touring exhibitions from state and national galleries; open Tues–Sat; Old Maryborough Rd. *Scenic walkway:* cycle or walk 15 km along the waterfront. *Whale-watching tours:* half- and full-day tours to see the migratory whales off the coast, departing from Boat Harbour; contact visitor centre for details.

Nikenbah Markets: Nikenbah Animal Refuge; 1st and 3rd Sun each month. *Koala Markets:* Elizabeth St; 2nd and 4th Sun each month. *Fraser Coast Multicultural Festival:* Mar. *Fraser Coast Show:* May. *World's Biggest Pub Crawl:* June. *Mary Poppins Festival:* July. *Whale Festival:* Aug. *Seafood Festival:* Aug. *Hervey Bay Jazz and Blues Festival:* Nov.

Bayswater: seafood the specialty; 26–34 Hibiscus St; (07) 4194 9700. *Enzo's on the Beach:* seaside cafe, meals can be served on the beach; 351A The Esplanade, Scarness; (07) 4124 6375. *Gatakers Landing Restaurant:* outdoor dining, delicious seafood; Cnr The Esplanade and Mant St, Point Vernon, Gatakers Bay; (07) 4124 2470. *Moonlight and Day Away Cruises:* leave the mainland for lunch; from Urangan Boat Harbour; 1800 072 555.

Breakfree Great Sandy Straits: on the water's edge; 17 Buccaneer Dr, Urangan; (07) 4128 9999 or 1300 553 800. *Emeraldene Inn & Eco-Lodge:* rooms and apartments; 166 Urraween Rd; (07) 4124 5500. *Peppers Pier Resort:* 129 units on 6 floors; 26–34 Hibiscus St; (07) 4194 9700.

Fraser Island World Heritage–listed Fraser Island is the largest sand island in the world. It is an ecological wonder with lakes and forests existing purely on sand. Protected within Great Sandy National Park, the island is an oasis of beaches, beautifully coloured sand cliffs, more than 40 freshwater lakes and the spectacular tall rainforests. The island is also home to a variety of wildlife, including migratory birds and rare animals such as the ground parrot and Illidge's ant-blue butterfly. Fraser Island's dingoes are one of the purest strains in the country. Offshore, see the turtles, dugong and dolphins soak up the warm waters and, between Aug and Nov, look out for migrating humpback whales. There are a variety of walks around the island, as well as swimming spots and scenic drives. Care should be taken around the island's dingo population. Stay with children, walk in groups, never feed or coax the dingoes and keep all food and rubbish in vehicles or campground lockers. Vehicle and camping permits from Queensland Parks & Wildlife Service, 13 1304.

Great Sandy Strait: the Mary and Susan rivers to the south of Hervey Bay run into this strait where the visitor can see spectacular migratory birds, including the comb-crested jacana. Hire a houseboat to travel down the strait; contact visitor centre for details. *Toogoom:* quiet seaside resort town. Feed the pelicans on the boardwalk; 15 km w. *Burrum Heads:* pleasant holiday resort at the mouth of the Burrum River with excellent beaches and fishing. Visit at Easter for the Amateur Fishing Classic; 20 km NW. *Burrum Coast National Park:* 34 km NW; *see Bundaberg. Brooklyn House:* historic old Queenslander pioneer house; Howard; 36 km w. *Lady Elliot Island:* fly to the island for a day to snorkel on the fabulous reef; contact visitor centre for details. *Scenic flights:* over Hervey Bay and Fraser Island in a Tiger Moth or other small plane; contact visitor centre for details.

See also Fraser Island & Coast, p. 420

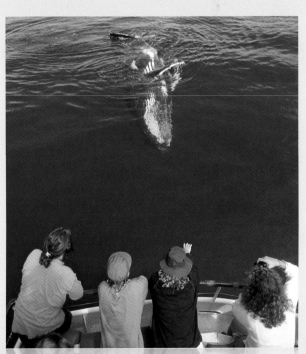

[VIEWING A HUMPBACK WHALE ON A WHALE-WATCHING TOUR]

QUEENSLAND

Historic Coolibah Tree: blazed by Walker in 1861 and again by William Landsborough in 1862 when he was also searching for Burke and Wills, and their 2 companions; east bank of Station Creek, Stansfield St East. *Flinders Poppy Art and Craft Cottage:* unique range of handmade art and craft items for sale; open 10am–2pm daily (hours can vary); Gray St.

Market: Lions Rotary Park; last Sun each month. *Country Music Festival:* Apr. *Horseracing:* Apr and Sept. *Hughenden Show:* June. *Porcupine Gorge Challenge:* fun run; June. *Arid Lands Festival:* camel endurance race; Aug. *Outback Scrap:* Aug. *Bullride:* Sept.

Porcupine Gorge National Park The coloured sandstone cliffs of this park are a delight and contrast with the greenery surrounding Porcupine Creek. The gorge, known locally as the 'mini Grand Canyon', has been formed over millions of years and can be seen from the lookout just off Kennedy Development Rd. Walk down into the gorge on the 1.2 km track, but be warned, the steep walk back up is strenuous. (07) 4722 5224; 61 km N.

Basalt Byways: discover the Flinders Shire landscapes on these 4WD tracks. Cross the Flinders River and see the Flinders poppy in the valleys. The longest track is 156 km; access on Hann Hwy; 7.3 km N. *Prairie:* small town with mini-museum and historic relics at Cobb & Co yards; 44 km E. *Mt Emu Goldfields:* fossicking and bushwalking; 85 km N. *Torrens Creek:* the town, a major explosives dump during WW II, was nearly wiped out by 12 explosions when firebreaks accidentally hit the dump. Visit the Exchange Hotel, home of the 'dinosaur steaks'; 88 km E. *Kooroorinya Falls:* the small falls cascade into a natural waterhole, excellent for swimming. Walk and go birdwatching in surrounding bushland; 109 km SE via Prairie. *White Mountains National Park:* rugged park with white sandstone outcrops and varied vegetation. Burra Range Lookout on Flinders Hwy has excellent views over the park. There are no walking tracks; (07) 4722 5224; 111 km E. *Chudleigh Park Gemfields:* gem-quality peridot found in fossicking area (licence required); 155 km N. *Moorrinya National Park:* important conservation park protecting 18 different land types of the Lake Eyre Basin. The park is home to iconic Australian animals, such as koalas, kangaroos and dingoes, and includes remains of the old sheep-grazing property Shirley Station. Walking is for experienced bushwalkers only; (07) 4722 5224; 178 km SE via Torrens Creek.

See also OUTBACK, p. 428

Ingham

Pop. 4603

Map ref. 650 E8 | 657 M10

Tyto Wetlands Information Centre, Bruce Hwy (Townsville Rd); (07) 4776 5211; www.hinchinbrooknq.com.au

 91.9 FM Kool, 630 AM ABC North QLD

Ingham is a major sugar town near the Hinchinbrook Channel. Originally, Kanaka labourers were employed in the surrounding sugarcane fields, but after their repatriation at the beginning of the 20th century, Italian immigrants took their place (the first Italians arrived in the 1890s). This strong Italian heritage is celebrated in the Australian Italian Festival each May. Ingham is at the centre of a splendid range of national parks. The Wallaman Falls in Girringun (Lumholtz) National Park is a highlight as the largest single-drop falls in Australia.

Hinchinbrook Heritage Walk and Drive: displays at each historic site in Ingham and the nearby township of Halifax illustrate the dynamic history of the shire. It starts at the Shire

Hall in Ingham; brochure available from visitor centre. *Memorial Gardens:* picturesque waterlily lakes and native tropical vegetation. They include Bicentennial Bush House with displays of orchids and tropical plants (open weekdays); Palm Tce.

Conroy Hall Markets: McIlwraith St; 2nd Sat each month. *Raintree Market:* Herbert St; 3rd Sat each month. *Ingham Arts Festival:* Apr. *Australian Italian Festival:* May. *Bullride:* June. *Ingham Show:* July. *Horseracing:* Aug. *Family Fishing Classic:* Sept. *Maraka Festival:* Oct.

Noorla Heritage Resort: tiffin, tapas, cakes and curry; 5–9 Warren St; (07) 4776 1100 or 1800 238 077.

Noorla Heritage Resort: Art Deco villa; 5–9 Warren St; (07) 4776 1100 or 1800 238 077.

Girringun (Lumholtz) National Park The Wallaman Falls section (50 km W) is in the Herbert River Valley and features waterfalls, gorges and tropical rainforest. See the crimson rosellas on the 4 km return walk from the Falls Lookout to the base of Wallaman Falls – look out for platypus and water dragons. Take a scenic drive around the Mt Fox section of the park (75 km SW) or walk the 4 km return ascent to the dormant volcano crater. There are no formal tracks and the ascent is for experienced walkers only. 4WD is recommended in both sections during the wet season; *see Cardwell for northern parts of park*; (07) 4066 8601 (same number for other national parks in area); 20 km NW.

Paluma Range National Park The Jourama Falls section of the park (24 km S) is at the foothills of the Seaview Range. Walk the 1.5 km track through rainforest and dry forest to the Jourama Falls Lookout (take care crossing the creek) to see the vibrant birdlife including azure kingfishers and kookaburras. The Mt Spec section of the park (40 km S) features casuarina-fringed creeks in the lowlands and rainforest in the cooler mountain areas. Drive to McClelland's Lookout for a spectacular view and take the 2 short walks from there to see the varied park landscapes; 49 km S.

Tyto Wetlands: 90 ha of wetlands with birdlife and wallabies. See the rare grass owl from the viewing platform; outskirts of town. *Cemetery:* interesting Italian tile mausoleums; 5 km E. *Forrest Beach:* sandy 16 km beach overlooking Palm Islands. Stinger-net swimming enclosures are installed in summer; 20 km SE. *Taylors Beach:* popular family seaside spot for sailing with excellent fishing and crabbing in nearby Victoria Creek; 24 km E. *Hinchinbrook Island National Park:* resort island to the north-east; sea access from Lucinda; 25 km NE; *see Cardwell*. *Lucinda:* coastal village on the banks of the Herbert River at the southern end of the Hinchinbrook Channel. Take a safari or fishing tour through the channel. Stinger-net swimming enclosures are installed in summer; 27 km NE. *Broadwater State Forest:* swimming holes, walking tracks and birdwatching; 45 km W. *Orpheus Island National Park:* this rainforest and woodland park is a continental resort island in the Palm Islands surrounded by a marine park and fringing reefs. Snorkel and dive off the beaches or take in the wildlife on the short track from Little Pioneer Bay to Old Shepherds Hut; access is by private or charter boat from Lucinda or Taylors Beach.

See also THE MID-TROPICS, p. 424

Innisfail

Pop. 8260
Map ref. 650 E4 | 651 H11 | 657 M7

i 24 Bruce Hwy, Mourilyan; (07) 4063 2655;
www.innisfailtourism.com.au

 98.3 Kool FM, 720 AM ABC Far North QLD

Innisfail has seen destruction by cyclone more than once – most recently cyclone Larry in 2006, which destroyed homes and much of the town's banana plantations. But today Innisfail seems to have mostly recovered and travellers come to work during fruit-picking season. The parks and walks on the riverside, as well as the classic Art Deco buildings in the town centre, add to the charm of this town. The area is also renowned for its sugar industry and the excellent fishing in nearby rivers, beaches and estuaries.

Innisfail and District Historical Society Museum: documents local history; Edith St. *Chinese Joss House:* reminder of Chinese presence during gold-rush days; Owen St. *Warrina Lakes and Botanical Gardens:* recreational facilities and walks; Charles St. *Historical town walk:* see classic Art Deco architecture of the town and historic Shire Hall on self-guide or guided town walk; details from visitor centre.

Market: ANZAC Memorial Park; 3rd Sat each month. *Innisfail Show:* July. *Game Fishing Tournament:* Sept. *Karnivale:* Oct. *Innisfail Cup:* Oct.

Eubenangee Swamp National Park This important park protects the last of the remnant coastal lowland rainforest around Alice River, which is part of the Wet Tropics Region. See the rainforest birds on the walk from Alice River to the swamp where jabirus and spoonbills feed. (07) 4067 6304; 13 km NW.

Flying Fish Point: popular spot for swimming, camping and fishing; 5 km NE. *Johnstone River Crocodile Farm:* daily feeding shows at 11am and 3pm; 8 km NE. *Ella Bay National Park:* small coastal park with beach and picnic spot; (07) 4067 6304; 8 km N. *North Johnstone River Gorge:* walking tracks to several picturesque waterfalls; 18 km W via Palmerston Hwy. *Wooroonooran National Park:* 33 km W; *see Millaa Millaa*. *Crawford Lookout:* for spectacular views of North Johnstone River; 38 km W off Palmerston Hwy.

See also CAIRNS & THE TROPICS, p. 425

Ipswich

Pop. 155 000
Map ref. 644 A9 | 645 B5 | 647 D12 | 653 M9

i 14 Queen Victoria Pde; (07) 3281 0555;
www.ipswichtourism.com.au

94.9 FM River, 747 AM ABC Southern QLD

Ipswich is Queensland's oldest provincial city with diverse heritage buildings throughout its streets. In 1827 a convict settlement was established alongside the Bremer River to quarry the nearby limestone deposits used in Brisbane's stone buildings. In 1842 the settlement, simply called 'Limestone', opened to free settlers and was in 1843 renamed Ipswich. The impressive Workshops Rail Museum honours Ipswich as the birthplace of Queensland Railways. Australia's largest RAAF base is in the suburb of Amberley.

Workshops Rail Museum In the North Ipswich railyards, this museum offers diverse historical displays, interactive exhibitions and an impressive variety of machinery. Watch workers restore old steam trains, or look into the future of rail by taking a simulated ride in the high-speed tilt train. North St.

Global Art Links Gallery This art gallery and social history museum merges heritage and the present day at the Old Town Hall. See the local and visiting exhibitions in the Gallery, partake in the interactive displays of Ipswich history in the Hall of Time, walk through the Indigenous installation in the Return to Kabool section, or try electronic finger-painting in the Children's Gallery. D'Arcy Doyle Pl.

Queens Park Nature Centre: native flora, animals and a bird aviary; Goleby Ave. *Ipswich Heritage Model Railway Club:* miniature trains; activity days on the 1st Sat and 3rd Sun of each month, visits at other times by appt; via Workshops Rail Museum. *Historical walk:* self-guide walk to see the renowned heritage buildings, churches and excellent domestic architecture of Ipswich, including the Uniting Church (1858) and Gooloowan (1864); outstanding colour brochure available from visitor centre.

Showground Market: Salisbury Rd; Sun. *Farmers Market:* Leichhardt Community Centre; 1st Sat each month (June–Nov). *Handmade Expo:* over 50 stalls of handmade arts and crafts; 3rd Sat each month (Aug–Dec). *Ipswich Cup:* horseracing; June. *Circus Train:* month-long event with circus performers and train rides; Sept–Oct. *Jacaranda Festival (Goodna):* Oct. *Rodeo:* Nov.

 Cotton's Restaurant: modern Australian steakhouse; Spicers Hidden Vale, 617 Mt Mort Rd, Grandchester; (07) 5465 5900. *Woodlands of Marburg:* modern Australian in heritage house; 174 Seminary Rd, Marburg; (07) 5464 4777.

Parkview Colonials B&B: colonial houses with ensuite rooms; 72 Chermside Rd; (07) 3812 3266. *Spicers Hidden Vale:* luxury resort; 617 Mt Mort Rd, Grandchester; 1300 881 435. *Woodlands of Marburg:* heritage mansion; 174 Seminary Rd, Marburg; (07) 5464 4777.

Queensland Raceway: home to the Queensland 500 and host of the V8 Supercar Series. Winternationals Drag-racing Championship runs every June; 15 km W. *Wolston House:* historic home at Wacol; open weekends and public holidays; 16 km E. *Rosewood:* heritage town with St Brigid's Church, the largest wooden church in the South Pacific. The Railway Museum, with restored carriages and wagons and displays of area's industrial heritage, runs scenic steam-train rides on the last Sun of each month; museum open every Sun; 20 km W. *Recreational reserves:* popular picnic and leisure spots to the north-east of Ipswich include College's Crossing (7 km), Mt Crosby (12 km) and Lake Manchester (22 km).

See also BRISBANE HINTERLAND, p. 415

Isisford

Pop. 262
Map ref. 654 B11 | 661 N11

i Council offices, St Mary St; (07) 4658 8900;
www.isisford.qld.gov.au

104.5 FM West, 603 AM ABC Western QLD

Isisford is a small outback community south of Longreach. In the mid-1800s large stations were established in the area. This brought hawkers, keen on trading their goods to the landowners. Two such hawkers were brothers William and James Whitman who, after their axle broke trying to cross the Alice River, decided

  QUEENSLAND

to stay and established Isisford in 1877. First called Wittown, after the brothers, it was renamed in 1880 to recall the nearby Barcoo River ford and Isis Downs Station. The town provided inspiration to iconic Australian poet Banjo Paterson, in particular his poems Bush Christening and Clancy of the Overflow.

 Outer Barcoo Interpretation Centre: features the world-class fossil exhibit of *Isisfordia duncani,* reported to be the ancestor of all modern crocodilians. Also local arts and crafts, town relics and theatrette; St Mary St. **Whitman's Museum:** photographic exhibition documents Isisford's history; St Mary St. **Barcoo Weir:** excellent spot for fishing and bush camping.

Sheep and Wool Show: May. **Fishing Competition and Festival:** July. **Horse and Motorbike Gymkhana:** June/July. **Isisford Ross Cup:** horseracing; Oct.

Oma Waterhole: popular for fishing and watersports, and home to a fishing competition and festival mid-year (subject to rains); 15 km sw. **Idalia National Park:** 62 km se; *see Blackall.*

See also OUTBACK, p. 428

Julia Creek

Pop. 368
Map ref. 659 H11 | 661 J3

i Cnr Burke and Quarrell sts; (07) 4746 7690; www.mckinlay.qld.gov.au

99.5 FM Rebel, 567 AM ABC North West QLD

Julia Creek became known as 'The Gateway to the Gulf' after the road to Normanton was sealed in 1964. Pioneer Donald MacIntyre was the first to settle when he established Dalgonally Station in 1862. Julia Creek is actually named after his niece. A monument to Donald and his brother Duncan (an explorer who led a search for Leichhardt) can be seen by the grave site on the station boundary. The district's main industries are cattle, sheep and mining. It is also home to a rare and endangered marsupial, the Julia Creek dunnart, a tiny nocturnal hunter found only within a 100-kilometre radius of town.

Duncan MacIntyre Museum: local pioneering and cattle history; Burke St. **Opera House:** photographic display of McKinlay Shire; closed weekends; Julia St. **Historical walk:** stroll the 38 signposted historical sites around the town; map from visitor centre.

Dirt and Dust Festival: Apr. **Horseracing:** Apr–Aug. **Campdraft and Rodeo:** May, June and Aug. **Cultural Capers:** Oct.

WW II bunkers: remains of concrete bunkers used to assist navigation of allied aircraft; western outskirts near airport. **Punchbowl waterhole:** popular area for swimming and fishing on the Flinders River; 45 km ne. **PROA Redclaw Farm:** 12 ponds with over 16 000 redclaw; 75 km se. **Sedan Dip:** popular swimming, fishing and picnicking spot; 100 km n.

See also OUTBACK, p. 428

Jundah

Pop. 93
Map ref. 663 J1

i Dickson St; (07) 4658 6930; www.outbackholidays.tq.com.au

101.7 FM Triple C, 540 AM ABC Western QLD

Jundah is at the centre of the Channel Country and its name comes from the Aboriginal word for women. Gazetted as a town in 1880, for 20 years the area was important for opal mining, but lack of water caused the mines to close. The waterholes and channels of the Thomson River are filled with yabbies and fish, including yellow-belly and bream. The spectacular rock holes, red sand dunes and beauty of Welford National Park are the natural attractions of this outback town.

Jundah Museum: documents area's early pioneer heritage; Perkins St. **Post Office:** beautiful shopfront mural; Dickson St.

Race Carnival: Oct. **Wooly Caulfield Cup:** sheep races; Oct.

Welford National Park This park protects mulga lands, Channel Country and Mitchell grass downs – 3 types of natural vegetation in Queensland. See the rare earth homestead (1882) that is now listed by the National Trust (not open to the public) or go wildlife-watching to see pelicans and whistling kites at the many waterholes of the Barcoo River. There are 2 self-guide drives that start at the campground: one through the mulga vegetation to the scenic Sawyers Creek; the other a desert drive past the impressive red sand dunes. 4WD is recommended. Roads are impassable in wet weather; call 000 or Jundah police station on (07) 4658 6120 in emergency. (07) 4652 7333; 20 km s.

Stonehenge: named not for the ancient English rock formation, but for the old stone hut built for visiting bullock teams. Nearby on the Thomson River are brolgas and wild budgerigars; 68 km ne. **Windorah:** holds the International Yabby Race in Sept; 95 km s.

See also OUTBACK, p. 428

Karumba

Pop. 522
Map ref. 656 C6 | 659 G4

i Karumba Library, Walker St, (07) 4745 9582; or call Normanton Visitor Information Centre, (07) 4745 1065; www.gulf-savannah.com.au

98.1 FM Rebel, 567 AM ABC North West QLD

Karumba is at the mouth of the Norman River in the Gulf Savannah. It is the easiest access point for the Gulf of Carpentaria, the key reason the town is the centre for the Gulf's booming prawn and barramundi industries. During the 1930s, the town was an important refuelling depot for the airships of the Empire Flying Boats, which travelled from Sydney to England. Fishing enthusiasts will enjoy the untouched waters of the gulf and nearby rivers that offer an abundance of fish.

Barramundi Discovery Centre: barramundi display and information; Riverside Dr. **Ferryman cruises:** tours include birdwatching, gulf sunset and night crocodile spotting; depart Karumba boat ramp; (07) 4745 9155. **Charters and dinghy hire:** discover the renowned fishing spots in the Gulf or on the Norman River on a charter or hire a dinghy; Karumba Port. **Heritage walk:** self-guide walk; brochure from Karumba library.

Market: Sunset Tavern; Sun. **Fishing Competition:** follows Easter event at Normanton; Apr. **Norman River Duck Race:** June.

End of the Road Motel: where the outback meets the ocean; Karumba Point; (07) 4745 9599.

 Wetland region: extending 30 km inland from Karumba are the wetlands, habitat of the saltwater crocodile and several species of birds, including brolgas and cranes. **Cemetery:** early-settlement cemetery when Karumba was known as Norman Mouth telegraph station; 2 km n on road to Karumba Pt. **Karumba Pt:** boat hire available; note presence of saltwater crocodiles; 3 km n. **Sweers Island:** island in the Gulf with beaches, abundant birdlife, excellent fishing and caves; access is by boat or air; details from visitor centre.

See also GULF SAVANNAH, p. 427

Kenilworth

Pop. 238
Map ref. 647 E3 | 648 D11 | 653 M7

 4 Elizabeth St; (07) 5446 0122; www.kenilworthguide.org.au

 91.1 Hot FM, 612 AM ABC Brisbane

West of the Blackall Range in the Sunshine Coast hinterland is Kenilworth. This charming town is known for its handcrafted cheeses and excellent bushwalking. The spectacular gorges, waterfalls, creeks and scenic lookouts make Kenilworth State Forest a popular spot for bushwalking, camping and picnics.

Kenilworth Cheese Factory: tastings and sales of local cheeses; Charles St. **Historical Museum:** machinery and dairy display and audiovisual show; open 10am–3pm Sun or by appt; Alexandra St; (07) 5446 0581. **Lasting Impressions Gallery:** fine-art gallery; Elizabeth St. **Artspace Gallery:** local art on display; Elizabeth St.

Kenilworth Cheese, Wine and Food Festival: Easter. **Kenilworth Celebrates:** arts festival; Sept–Oct.

Another Time Another Place: 2 cabins beside a billabong; 2576 Eumundi–Kenilworth Rd; (07) 5472 3134.

Kenilworth State Forest This diverse park is in the rugged Conondale Ranges. The rainforest, tall open forest and exotic pines are home to birds and wildlife, including the threatened yellow-bellied glider. There are walks signposted, but a highlight is the steep 4 km return hike from Booloumba Creek to the summit of Mt Allan, where the forest and gorge views are breathtaking. Visit Booloumba Falls from the Gorge picnic area (3 km return) or picnic in the riverine rainforest at Peters Creek. Turn-off to the park is 6 km sw.

Kenilworth wineries: tastings and sales at boutique wineries; 4 km N. **Kenilworth Bluff:** steep walking track to lookout point; 6 km N. **Conondale National Park:** this small forest reserve west of the Mary River is suitable only for experienced walkers. Take the 37 km scenic drive, starting in the adjacent Kenilworth Forest, to enjoy the rugged delights of the park; (07) 5446 0925. **Lake Borumba:** picnics and watersports, and home to a fishing competition each Mar; 32 km NW.

See also SUNSHINE COAST, p. 419

Killarney

Pop. 833
Map ref. 551 C2 | 557 L1 | 653 L11

 49 Albion St (New England Hwy), Warwick; (07) 4661 3122; www.southerndownsholidays.com.au

The attractive small town of Killarney is on the banks of the Condamine River close to the New South Wales border. It is appealingly situated at the foothills of the Great Dividing Range and is surrounded by beautiful mountain scenery.

Spring Creek Mountain Cafe & Cottages: local produce, great views; 1503 Spring Creek Rd; (07) 4664 7101.

Adjinbilly Rainforest Retreat Cabins: true eco-friendly accommodation; Lot 10 Adjinbilly Rd; (07) 4664 1599. **Spring Creek Mountain Cafe & Cottages:** cooking classes add interest; 1503 Spring Creek Rd; (07) 4664 7101.

Main Range National Park, Queen Mary Falls section The Queen Mary Falls section of this World Heritage–listed park is right on the NSW border. Most of the vegetation is open eucalypt, but in the gorge below the falls is subtropical rainforest.

Follow the 2 km Queen Mary Falls circuit to the lookout for a stunning view of the 40 m falls and continue down to the rockpools at the base. If you are lucky, the rare Albert's lyrebird might be seen on the walk or the endangered brush-tailed rock-wallaby on the cliffs. 11 km E. *See also Boonah.*

Dagg's and Brown's waterfalls: stand behind Brown's Falls and see the 38 m Dagg's Falls; 4 km S. **Cherrabah Homestead Resort:** offers horseriding and fabulous bushwalking; 7 km S.

See also DARLING DOWNS, p. 418

Kingaroy

Pop. 7619
Map ref. 648 A10 | 653 L7

 128 Haly St (opposite silos); (07) 4162 6272; www.kingaroy.qld.gov.au

 96.3 FM Kingaroy, 747 AM ABC Southern QLD

Kingaroy is a large and prosperous town in the South Burnett region. The town's name derives from the Aboriginal word 'Kingaroori', meaning red ant. Found in the area, this unique ant has gradually adapted its colour to resemble the red soil plains of Kingaroy. The town is the centre for Queensland's peanut and navy-bean industries, and its giant peanut silos are landmarks. The region's relatively new wine industry is thriving with excellent boutique wineries close by. Kingaroy was also the home of Sir Johannes (Joh) Bjelke-Petersen, former premier of Queensland.

Heritage Museum: formerly the Kingaroy Power House, the museum depicts the history of Kingaroy under the themes of people, power and peanuts. Historical displays include machinery, photos and videos on the peanut and navy-bean industries; Haly St. **Art Gallery:** local and regional artists; open 10am–3pm Mon–Fri; Civic Sq, Glendon St. **The Peanut Van:** sales of local 'jumbo' peanuts; Kingaroy St. **Apex Lookout:** panoramic views of town; Carroll Nature Reserve, Fisher St.

Wine and Food in the Park Festival: Mar. **Peanut Festival:** includes the Strong Man Games; Aug.

Belltower Restaurant: modern Australian, adjoins distillery; Cnr Schellbachs and Haydens rds; (07) 4162 7000.

Bethany Cottages: Bjelke-Petersen family farm; 218 Peterson Dr; (07) 4162 7046. **Deshon's Retreat:** pet-friendly bush cottage; 164 Haydens Rd; (07) 4163 6688. **Taabinga Homestead:** a National Estate homestead; 7 Old Taabinga Rd; (07) 4164 5531. **The Quilter's Rest:** accommodation and quilting classes; 562 Weens Rd; (07) 4162 3987.

Bunya Mountains National Park This important park is part of the Great Dividing Range and protects the world's largest natural Bunya-pine forest. It is a significant Aboriginal site as many feasts were held here with the bunya nuts as the main fare. There are many walking trails for beginners and the experienced alike, including the short Bunya Bunya Track or the 8.4 km return Cherry Plain Track. Have a bush picnic and see the many butterflies or go spotlighting to glimpse owls and mountain possums. (07) 4668 3127; 58 km SW.

Aboriginal Bora Ring: preserved site; Cnr Reagan and Coolabunia rds;17.5 km SW. **Mt Wooroolin Lookout:** excellent views over Kingaroy's farmlands; 3 km W. **Bethany:** tour the Bjelke-Petersen's property and taste the famous Bjelke-Petersen pumpkin scones; open Wed and Sat, bookings essential; (07) 4162 7046; off Goodger Rd; 9 km SE. **Wooroolin:** quaint town

QUEENSLAND

with many heritage buildings including the Grant Hotel (1916). The Gordonbrook Dam is an excellent spot for picnics and birdwatching from the hides; 18 km N. ***Scenic aeroplane flights:*** over the Burnett region daily; (07) 4162 2629. ***Scenic glider flights:*** over surrounding area; (07) 4162 2191.

See also BRISBANE HINTERLAND, **p. 415**

Kuranda

Pop. 1612
Map ref. 650 D2 | 657 L6

 Therwine St; (07) 4093 9311; www.kuranda.org

99.5 FM Sea, 801 AM ABC Far North QLD

This small village is set in tropical rainforest on the banks of the Barron River north-west of Cairns. Its beautiful setting attracted a strong hippie culture in the 1960s and 1970s and, while it still has a bohemian feel, tourism is now the order of the day. There are many nature parks and eco-tourism experiences on offer, along with plenty of art and craft workshops, cafes and a daily market. Even transport to and from the town has been developed into an attraction – the Scenic Railway and Skyrail, both with jaw-dropping views over World Heritage–listed rainforest.

Scenic Railway and Skyrail The Scenic Railway is an engineering feat over 100 years old with tunnels, bridges and incredible views of Barron Falls. It begins in Cairns and ends 34 km later in the lush garden setting of Kuranda Station. Travel by rail on the way up and take the Skyrail on the way back (or vice versa), a journey via gondola across the treetops (ends at Caravonica Lakes, 11 km N of Cairns). (07) 4038 1555.

Butterfly Sanctuary: large enclosure, home to over 1500 tropical butterflies, including the blue Ulysses and the Australian birdwing, the country's largest butterfly; Rod Veivers Dr. ***Birdworld:*** over 50 species of birds, including the flightless cassowary and some endangered species; close to the heritage markets. ***Koala Gardens:*** Australian animals in a natural setting; close to the heritage markets. ***The Aviary:*** birds, frogs, snakes and crocodiles; Thongon St. ***Arts and crafts shops:*** including Kuranda Arts Cooperative, next to Butterfly Sanctuary, and Doongal Aboriginal Arts and Crafts on Coondoo St. ***Emu Ridge Gallery and Museum:*** unique dinosaur skeleton, fossil and gemstone museum; Therwine St. ***Australian Venom Zoo:*** visit the most venomous snakes and spiders in the world; Coondoo St. ***World Famous Honey House:*** free tastings and live bee displays; open 9am–3pm; Therwine St. ***River cruises:*** depart daily from the riverside landing below the railway station.

Kuranda Heritage Markets: Rod Veivers Dr; daily. ***Kuranda Original Markets:*** behind the Kuranda Market Arcade; daily. ***New Kuranda Markets:*** 40 shops and stalls on Coondoo St; daily. ***Kuranda Spring Festival:*** Sept.

Cedar Park Rainforest Resort: very fine affordable food; 250 Cedar Park Rd; (07) 4093 7892.

Cedar Park Rainforest Resort: 6 individually decorated rooms; 250 Cedar Park Rd; (07) 4093 7892. ***Kuranda Rainforest Accommodation Park:*** several accommodation options; 88 Kuranda Heights Rd; (07) 4093 7316.

Barron Gorge National Park Most people experience this park via the Scenic Railway or Skyrail, but those who want to get away from the crowds could set out on one of the park's bushwalking tracks leading into pockets of World Heritage wilderness. Perhaps you'll spot a Ulysses butterfly, cassowary or tree kangaroo. If you haven't already seen Barron Falls from the train or Skyrail, make your way to Barron Falls lookout 3 km

from Kuranda. The falls are spectacular after rain. Access to the national park is via Cairns or Kuranda; (07) 4046 6600.

Kuranda Nature Park: wildlife, canoeing, swimming and rainforest tours aboard 4WD Hummers; 2 km W. ***Rainforestation Nature Park:*** rainforest tours, tropical fruit orchard, Pamagirri Aboriginal Dance troupe, Dreamtime walk, and a koala and wildlife park; 35 km E. ***Carrowong Wildlife Eco-tours:*** tours to see nocturnal, rare and endangered rainforest creatures; (07) 4093 7287.

See also CAIRNS & THE TROPICS, **p. 425**

Kynuna

Pop. 20
Map ref. 661 J5

 Roadhouse, Matilda Hwy; (07) 4746 8683.

95.9 FM West, 540 AM ABC Western QLD

Kynuna is a tiny outback town famous for inspiring Banjo Paterson to write his iconic tune, Waltzing Matilda. It is said that Samuel Hoffmeister, at the time of the Shearers' Strike, drank his last drink at the Blue Heeler Hotel and then killed himself at Combo waterhole (south of town). This story stirred Paterson to write the now famous ballad.

Blue Heeler Hotel: famous hotel with illuminated blue heeler statue on the roof. ***Kynuna Roadhouse:*** obtain a mudmap from the roadhouse to find the original Swagman's Billabong.

Surf Carnival: Apr.

Combo Waterhole Conservation Park The events described in *Waltzing Matilda* occurred in this park, which has waterholes lined with coolibahs. On the Diamantina River, the park is an important dry-weather wildlife refuge. See the Chinese-labour-constructed historic stone causeways from the 1880s or take the 40 min return waterhole walk. The turn-off to the park is 16 km E.

McKinlay Although the town is tiny, its famous Walkabout Creek Hotel was originally known as McKinlay Hotel and is the local watering hole in the film *Crocodile Dundee*, which starred famed Australian larrikin Paul Hogan. 74 km NW.

Swagman's Billabong: made famous in our national folk song; 2 km E.

See also OUTBACK, **p. 428**

Laidley

Pop. 2387
Map ref. 647 A12 | 653 M9

 Lockyer Valley Tourist Information Centre, Jumbo's Fruit Barn Complex, Warrego Hwy, Hatton Vale (8 km N); (07) 5465 7642; www.laidley.qld.gov.au

100.7 C FM, 747 AM ABC Southern QLD

Laidley is in the Lockyer Valley in the Brisbane hinterland. The surrounding agricultural farmland produces an abundance of fresh fruit and vegetables, which can be taste-tested at the country market. The quality of Laidley's produce comes from the region's fertile soil, which explains why the town is known as 'Queensland's country garden'.

Das Neumann Haus Restored and refurbished in 1930s style, this 1893 historic home is the oldest in the shire. It was built by a German immigrant, whose carpentry skills can be seen in the excellent details of the building. It houses a local history museum and exhibits local art and craft. Open Thurs–Sun; William St.

Historical walk: self-guide walk to heritage sites; contact visitor centre for details.

Village market: Main St; Fri. *Country market:* Ferrari Park; last Sat each month. *Rodeo:* Apr. *Heritage Day:* Apr. *Laidley Show:* July. *Spring Festival:* flower and art show, craft expo, street parade and markets; Sept. *Art Exhibition:* Oct. *Christmas Carnival:* Dec.

 Branell Homestead B&B: luxurious homestead accommodation; 12 Paroz Rd; (07) 5465 1788. *Frog Hollow Barnstay:* guests enjoy the orchard; 19 Hughes Rd, Plainland; (07) 5465 6616.

Laidley Pioneer Village: original buildings from old township including blacksmith shop and slab hut; 1 km s. *Narda Lagoon:* flora and fauna sanctuary with picturesque suspension footbridge over lagoon; adjacent to pioneer village. *Lake Dyer:* beautiful spot for fishing, picnics and camping; 1 km w. *Lake Clarendon:* birdwatching area; 17 km NW. *Laidley Valley Scenic Drive:* attractive drive to the south of Laidley through Thornton.

See also BRISBANE HINTERLAND, p. 415

Landsborough

Pop. 2807
Map ref. 647 F5 | 648 E12 | 653 N8

ⓘ Historical Museum, Maleny St; (07) 5494 1755; www.landsboroughtown.com.au

90.3 FM ABC Coast QLD, 91.1 Hot FM

Landsborough is just north of the magnificent Glass House Mountains in the Sunshine Coast hinterland. It was named after the explorer William Landsborough and was originally a logging town for the rich woodlands of the Blackall Ranges.

Historical Museum: this excellent local museum documents the history of the shire through memorabilia, photographs and artefacts; open 9am–3pm Thurs–Mon; Maleny St. *De Maine Pottery:* award-winning clay pottery by Joanna De Maine; open Thurs–Mon; Maleny St.

Market: School of Arts Memorial Hall; Sat.

Glass House Mountains National Park This park protects 8 rugged volcanic mountain peaks. The open eucalypt and mountain heath landscape is a haven for many threatened and endangered animals. Three tracks lead to mountain lookouts that provide panoramic views of the Sunshine Coast hinterland. Only experienced walkers should attempt climbing to any of the summits. (07) 5494 3983; 13 km SW.

Australia Zoo Once a small park, this zoo was made famous by 'The Crocodile Hunter', Steve Irwin, who was tragically killed by a stingray in 2006. Originally developed by Irwin's parents, the complex is now over 20 ha and home to a wide range of animals. See the otters catching fish, the birds of prey tackling the skies, the ever-popular crocodile demonstrations or feed the kangaroos by hand in the Kids Zoo. The complex also has important breeding programs for threatened and endangered species. 4 km s.

Dularcha National Park: scenic park with excellent walks. 'Dularcha' is an Aboriginal word describing blackbutt eucalyptus country; (07) 5494 3983; 1 km NE. *Big Kart Track:* largest outdoor go-kart track in Australia, open for day and night racing and includes the 'Bungee Bullet'; 5 km N. *Beerburrum State Forest:* short walks and scenic drives to lookouts; access from Beerburrum; 11 km s.

See also SUNSHINE COAST, p. 419

Laura

Pop. 225
Map ref. 657 J3

ⓘ Quinkan Centre, Peninsula Development Rd; (07) 4060 3457; www.quinkancc.com.au

92.5 FM 4CA, 106.1 FM ABC Far North QLD

Laura is a tiny town in Far North Queensland that boasts only a few buildings, including the quaint old Quinkan Pub nestled in the shade of mango trees. The area to the south-east of town is known as Quinkan country after the Aboriginal spirits depicted at the incredible Split Rock and Gu Gu Yalangi rock-art sites. Every two years Laura hosts possibly the biggest Indigenous event on Australia's calendar – the Laura Dance and Cultural Festival.

Quinkan Centre: photos and relics of Quinkan Country are on display here. Guided tours, which include rock-art sites, can also be booked from the centre; Peninsula Development Rd; (07) 4060 3457.

Laura Aboriginal Dance and Cultural Festival: around 25 Cape York and Gulf communities gather at a traditional meeting ground by the Laura River. Traditional dance, music, and art and craft feature at the 3-day event; odd-numbered years, June. *Laura Annual Race Meeting:* race meeting on river flat that has run since 1897, and includes dances and rodeo; June.

Split Rock and Gu Gu Yalangi rock-art sites These are Queensland's most important Aboriginal art sites. Hidden behind a tangle of trees in the chasms and crevices of the sandstone escarpment, a diorama of Aboriginal lore and culture unfolds. The Quinkan spirits – the reptile-like Imgin and stick-like Timara – can be found hiding in dark places. There are also dingoes, flying foxes, kangaroos, men, women and many hundreds of other things, both obvious and mysterious. More sites exist nearby, though only these 2 are accessible to the public. Bookings through the Quinkan Centre; 12 km s.

Lakefield National Park This park is Queensland's second largest and a highlight of any visit to the Cape. The large rivers and waterholes are excellent for fishing and boating in the dry season, but become inaccessible wetlands in the wet season. In the south is the Old Laura Homestead, once en route to the Palmer River Goldfields, and in the north are plains dotted with spectacular anthills. See the threatened gold-shouldered parrot and spectacled hare-wallaby in the rainforest fringes of the Normanby and Kennedy rivers. 4WD is recommended. Access only in the dry season (Apr–Nov); (07) 4069 5777; entrance is 27 km N.

Lakeland Downs: bananas and coffee are the main fare cultivated from the area's rich volcanic soil, which is also ideal for a variety of fruit and vegetables; 62 km s.

See also CAPE YORK, p. 426

Longreach

see inset box on next page

Mackay

see inset box on page 461

Maleny

Pop. 1299
Map ref. 647 E4 | 648 E12 | 653 N7

ⓘ 25 Maple St; (07) 5499 9033; www.brbta.com

91.1 Hot FM, 612 AM ABC Brisbane

  RADIO STATIONS   IN TOWN   WHAT'S ON   WHERE TO EAT   WHERE TO STAY   NEARBY

Pop. 2977

Map ref. 654 B10 | 661 N10

 Qantas Park, Eagle St; (07) 4658 3555;
www.longreach.qld.gov.au

104.5 FM West, 540 AM ABC Western QLD

On the Thomson River, Longreach is the largest town in central-west Queensland. It epitomises the outback and features the renowned Australian Stockman's Hall of Fame, devoted to the outback hero. In 1922, Longreach became the operational base for Qantas and remained so until 1934. The world's first Flying Surgeon Service started from Longreach in 1959.

Australian Stockman's Hall of Fame and Outback Heritage Centre This impressive centre was developed as a tribute to the men and women who opened up outback Australia for settlement, industry and agriculture. It deals with everything from Australia's Indigenous heritage and the challenges of outback education and communication to the life of the modern-day stockman. Highlights include a photo gallery, an old blacksmith's shop and a 1920s kitchen. Open 9am–5pm daily; Landsborough Hwy; (07) 4658 2166.

Qantas Founders Outback Heritage Museum This modern museum details the commercial flight history of the second-oldest airline in the world. Explore the restored original 1922 hangar with displays on early flights and a replica Avro 504K. Or visit the exhibition hall to see how flying has evolved over the last century. Longreach Airport, Landsborough Hwy; (07) 4658 3737.

Powerhouse Museum: displays of old agricultural machinery, power station and local history museum; open 2–5pm Apr–Oct; Swan St. *Botanical Gardens:* walking and cycling trails; Landsborough Hwy. *Banjo's Outback Theatre and Woolshed:* bush poetry, songs and shearing in shearing shed; near airport. *Qantas Park:* replica of original Qantas booking office, it now houses the information centre; Eagle St. *Heritage buildings:*

highlights include the courthouse (1892) in Galah St and the railway station (1916) in Sir Hudson Fysh Dr. *Kinnon and Co:* offers horse-drawn adventure tours; bookings through the Station Store; (07) 4658 2006.

Easter in the Outback: Easter. *Outback Muster and Drovers Reunion:* May. *Rodeo:* July. *Fishing Competition:* Aug. *Horseracing:* Nov.

Albert Park Motor Inn: 4-star rooms, garden setting; Cnr Stork and Ilfracombe rds; (07) 4658 2411.

Lochern National Park The Thomson River plays an important role in this national park as its many waterholes are a sanctuary for a variety of birds. Camp beside the billabong in true outback style at Broadwater Hole and watch the brolgas and pelicans. For visitors passing through, drive the 16 km Bluebush Lagoon circuit to see the natural attractions of this park and glimpse Australian favourites – the kangaroo and emu. Visitors must be self-sufficient. Check road conditions before departing – roads may be impassable in wet weather; (07) 4652 7333. Turn-off 100 km s onto Longreach–Jundah Rd, then further 40 km.

Thomson River: fishing, bushwalking and swimming; 4.6 km NW. *Ilfracombe:* once a transport nucleus for the large Wellshot Station to the south, now an interesting outdoor machinery museum runs the length of this town on the highway. Another feature of town is the historic Wellshot Hotel, with a wool press bar and local memorabilia; 27 km E. *Starlight's Lookout:* said to be a resting spot of Captain Starlight. Enjoy the scenic view; 56 km NW. *Sheep and cattle station tours:* visit local stations to try out mustering and shearing; contact visitor centre for details. *Thomson River cruises:* contact visitor centre for details.

See also OUTBACK, p. 428

[CATTLE MUSTERING NEAR LONGREACH]

A steep road climbs from the coast to Maleny, at the southern end of the Blackall Range. The surrounding area is lush dairy country, although farmland is increasingly being sold for residential development. The town's peaceful community lifestyle and picturesque position, with views to the coast and Glass House Mountains, make it popular with artists.

Arts and crafts galleries: excellent quality galleries throughout town.

Handcraft Markets: Community Centre, Maple St; Sun. *Chainsaw to Fine Furniture Expo:* May. *Spring Fair and Flower Show:* Sept. *Scarecrow Festival:* Sept. *Fine Art Show:* Sept. *Festival of Colour:* Oct. *Christmas Show:* Nov.

Terrace of Maleny: seafood with style; Cnr Mountain View and Landsborough Maleny rds; (07) 5494 3700. *Le Relais Bressan:* French Provincial; 344 Flaxton Dr, Flaxton; (07) 5445 7157. *Tree Houses Restaurant:* imaginative international food; 5 Kondalilla Falls Rd, Montville; (07) 5445 7650 or 1800 444 350.

Bendles Cottages: 5 cottages with rural views; 937 Montville Rd; (07) 5494 2400. *Eyrie Escape:* 3 suites and resort facilities; 316 Brandenburg Rd, Bald Knob; 0414 308 666. *The Frog House:* luxury ensuite rooms with views; 73 Mountain View Rd; (07) 5499 9055.

Kondalilla National Park This park has scenic walks, subtropical rainforest and the spectacular Kondalilla Falls. The 4.6 km return Falls Circuit track passes rockpools to the falls, which drop 90 m. (07) 5494 3983; 21 km N via Montville.

Mary Cairncross Park: this beautiful park was donated to the community in 1941 as protected rainforest after the fierce logging days of the early 1900s. Walk through the rainforest to see superb panoramic views; 7 km SE. *Baroon Pocket Dam:* popular spot for fishing and boating. Follow the boardwalks through rainforest; North Maleny Rd; 8 km N. *Montville:* main street lined with cafes, giftshops, potteries and art and craft galleries. The town also has a growing wine industry; 16 km NE. *Flaxton:* charming tiny village surrounded by avocado orchards. Visit the quality art and craft galleries, Flaxton Grove Winery and miniature English village; 19 km NE. *Flaxton Barn:* model Swiss and German railway with tearooms; 21 km N via Flaxton. *Maleny–Blackall Range Tourist Drive:* this 28 km scenic drive is one of the best in south-east Queensland. Drive north-east from Maleny through to Mapleton, stopping off at museums, antique shops, fruit stalls and tearooms along the way, as well as taking in spectacular views. The drive can be extended to Nambour.

See also SUNSHINE COAST, p. 419

 Mareeba

Pop. 6806
Map ref. 650 D2 | 651 D7 | 657 L6

i Heritage Museum, Centenary Park, 345 Byrnes St; (07) 4092 5674; www.mareebaheritagecentre.com.au

92.3 FM Rhema, 720 AM ABC Far North QLD

Mareeba was the first town settled on the Atherton Tableland by pastoralist John Atherton in 1877. Tobacco production began in the 1950s, but was deregulated only a few years ago. Today the area produces mangoes, coffee and sugarcane. The morning balloon flights over the tableland are spectacular.

Heritage Museum: local history exhibits and information centre; Centenary Park, Byrnes St. *Art Society Gallery:* Centenary

Park. *Barron River Walk:* walk along the banks to swimming hole. *Bicentennial Lakes:* park with plantings to encourage wildlife. Explore the park on the walking tracks and bridges; Rankine St. *The Coffee Works:* see the production of coffee and taste-test the results; 136 Mason St. *The Australian Coffee Centre:* this complex offers a 54-seat cinema, coffee labratory and restaurant. Daily tours take you through the coffee plantation and include tastings. Open 9am–5pm daily; 136 Ivicevic Rd.

Market: Centenary Park; 2nd and 5th Sat each month (if applicable). *Great Wheelbarrow Race:* Mareeba to Chillagoe; May. *Rodeo:* July. *Multicultural Festival:* Aug. *Walkamin Country Music Festival:* Oct.

Biboohra Bush Retreat B&B: homestead near wetland reserve; 326 Pickford Rd, Biboohra; (07) 4093 2787. *Jabiru Safari Lodge:* exceptional nature experience; Pickford Rd, Biboohra; (07) 4093 2514 or 1800 788 755.

Mareeba Tropical Savanna and Wetland Reserve This conservation reserve of over 2400 ha and 12 lagoons is home to birds, mammals, fish and freshwater crocodiles. Take a self-guide trail by hiring a timber canoe, a tour cruise or the guided 'Twilight Reserve Safari' (with cheese and wine afterwards). Open Apr–Dec (dry season); tour bookings on (07) 4093 2514; turn-off at Biboohra (7 km N).

Mako Trac International Racetrack: Australia's best track and fastest go karts. Also 18-hole minigolf course; Springs Rd, 2 km W. *de Brueys Boutique Wines:* taste world-class tropical fruit wines, liqueurs and ports; Fichera Rd, 4 km E. *The Beck Museum:* aviation and military collection; Kennedy Hwy; 5 km S. *Warbird Adventures Adventure flights:* experience the thrill of a flight in a real Warbird; museum open Wed–Sun; Kennedy Hwy, 5 km S. *Mango Winery:* produces white wine from 'Kensington Red' mangoes; Bilwon Rd, Biboohra; 7 km N. *Granite Gorge:* impressive boulder and rock formation; 12 km SW off Chewko Rd. *Emerald Creek Falls:* walk 1.9 km and see the water as it tumbles down the mountain between massive boulders; Cobra Rd; 12 km SE. *Davies Creek National Park:* walk the 1.1 km Davies Creek Falls circuit to see the falls crashing over boulders; (07) 4091 1844; 22 km E. *Dimbulah:* small town with museum in restored railway station; 47 km W. *Tyrconnell:* historic mining town with tours of goldmine; 68 km NW via Dimbulah. *Scenic balloon flights:* over Atherton Tableland; details available from visitor centre.

See also CAIRNS & THE TROPICS, p. 425

 Maroochydore

Pop. 17 500
Map ref. 647 G4 | 648 F11 | 653 N7

i Cnr Sixth Ave and Melrose Pde; (07) 5459 9050 or 1800 882 032; www.discovermaroochy.com.au

91.9 FM Sea, 612 AM ABC Brisbane

A popular beach resort, Maroochydore is also the business centre of the Sunshine Coast. The parklands and birdlife on the Maroochy River and the excellent surf beaches began to attract a growing tourist interest in the 1960s, which has only increased since. An incredible range of watersports is available.

Maroochy River: enjoy diverse birdlife and parklands on the southern bank with safe swimming. *Endeavour Replica:* replica of Captain Cook's ship; David Low Way. *The Esplanade:* atmospheric strip of cafes, restaurants and clothing stores.

 QUEENSLAND

Market: Cnr Fishermans Rd and Bradman Ave; Sun mornings. *Cotton Tree Street Markets:* King St; Sun mornings.

Ebb: riverside location, contemporary menu; 6 Wharf St; (07) 5452 7771. *Boat Shed:* laid-back eatery with day beds; The Esplanade at Cotton Tree; (07) 5443 3808. *The Wine Bar Restaurant:* 40 wines by the glass, modern Australian; 4–8 Duporth Ave; (07) 5479 0188.

Amytis Gardens Retreat & Spa: 4 luxury mountain cabins; 51 Malones Rd; (07) 5450 0115. *Novotel Twin Waters Resort:* many types of accommodation; Ocean Dr, Twin Waters; (07) 5448 8000 or 1800 072 277.

Mt Coolum National Park Located above the surrounding sugarcane fields, the mountain offers cascading waterfalls after rain. The park is generally undeveloped, but take the rough 800 m trail to the summit to be rewarded with panoramic views of the coast. (07) 5447 3243; 13 km N via Marcoola.

Nostalgia Town: emphasises humour in history on a train ride through fantasy settings. Markets every Fri and Sat; Pacific Paradise; 7 km NW. *Bli Bli:* attractions include medieval Bli Bli Castle, with dungeon, torture chamber and doll museum, the 'Ski 'n Surf' waterski park and the Aussie Fishing Park. Take a cruise through Maroochy River wetlands; 9 km NW. *Marcoola:* coastal town with quiet beach; 11 km N. *Coolum Beach:* coastal resort town with long sandy beach; 17 km N. *Eco-Cruise Maroochy:* cruises to Dunethin Rock through sugarcane fields; details from visitor centre.

See also SUNSHINE COAST, p. 419

Maryborough
Pop. 21 499
Map ref. 648 E6 | 653 N5

ⓘ City Hall, Kent St; (07) 4190 5742 or 1800 214 789; www.maryborough.qld.gov.au

📻 103.5 FM Mix, 855 AM ABC Wide Bay

Maryborough is an attractive city on the banks of the Mary River. Its fine heritage buildings and famous timber Queenslander architecture date back to the early years of settlement, when Maryborough was a village and port. Maryborough Port was an important destination in the mid-1800s as over 22 000 immigrants arrived from Europe. Today the Mary River is a popular spot for relaxed boating and some good fishing.

Bond Store Museum: located in the Portside Centre, this museum documents the history of the region from a river port to the present day; open 9am–4pm Mon–Fri, 10am–1pm Sat–Sun; Wharf St. *Customs House Museum:* also in the Portside Centre, this important cultural heritage museum depicts the area's industries and early immigration and Kanaka history; Wharf St. *Military and Colonial Museum:* fascinating look at local military and colonial history; open 9am–3pm daily; Wharf St. *Mary Poppins statue:* statue of the famed and magical nanny in honour of author Pamela Lyndon Travers, who was born in the town in 1899; Cnr Kent and Richmond sts. *Central Railway Station, Mary Ann:* replica of Queensland's first steam engine with rides in Queens Park every Thurs, market day, and last Sun each month; Lennox St. *Queens Park:* unusual domed fernery and waterfall; Cnr Lennox and Bazaar sts. *Elizabeth Park:* extensive rose gardens; Kent St. *ANZAC Park:* includes Ululah Lagoon, a scenic waterbird sanctuary where black swans, wild geese, ducks and waterhens may be handfed; Cnr Cheapside and Alice sts. *Heritage walk:* self-guide walk past 22 historic buildings,

including the impressive City Hall, St Paul's bell tower (with pealing bells) and National Trust–listed Brennan and Geraghty's Store. The walk starts at City Hall, Kent St; brochure available from visitor centre. *Heritage drive:* a highlight is the original site of Maryborough (until 1885), where a series of plaques document its history. Drive starts at City Hall; brochure available from visitor centre. *Ghost tours:* discover the town's ghostly past on tours that run once a month; details from visitor centre.

 Heritage markets: Cnr Adelaide and Ellena sts; Thurs. *World's Greatest Pub Crawl:* June. *Mary Poppins Festival:* July. *Technology Challenge:* Sept. *Maryborough Masters Games:* Sept/Oct.

Teddington Weir: popular for watersports; 15 km s. *Tiaro:* excellent fishing for Mary River cod in surrounding waterways. See the historic Dickabram Bridge over the river, and nearby Mt Bauple National Park; 24 km SW. *Tuan Forest:* bushwalking; 24 km SE. *Fraser Island:* World Heritage–listed sand island to the east of town; *see Hervey Bay.*

See also FRASER ISLAND & COAST, p. 420

Miles
Pop. 1164
Map ref. 653 I7

ⓘ Historical Village, Murilla St; (07) 4627 1492; www.murilla.qld.gov.au

📻 94.5 FM Rebel, 747 AM ABC Southern QLD

Miles is in the Western Downs. Ludwig Leichhardt passed through this district on three expeditions and named the place Dogwood Crossing. The town was later renamed Miles in honour of a local member of parliament. After spring rains, this pocket of the Darling Downs is ablaze with wildflowers.

Dogwood Crossing @ Miles This modern cultural centre combines history and art in an innovative space. The excellent Wall of Water displays imagery and stories of the local people – a novel way of discovering the personal history of Miles. The art gallery has changing exhibitions from local and regional artists. There is an IT centre and library also on-site. Murilla St.

Historical Village: a pioneer settlement with all types of early buildings, a war museum, shell display and lapidary exhibition; Murilla St. *Wildflower excursions:* some of the most beautiful wildflowers in Australia; details from visitor centre.

 St Luke's market: Dawson St; 2nd Sat each month. *Miles Show:* May. *Back to the Bush:* includes the Wildflower Festival; Sept. *Beef, Bells and Bottle Tree Festival:* massive month-long celebration including country music bash, bush poetry and fishing competition; even-numbered years, Sept.

Condamine: small town known for inventing the Condamine Bell, a bullfrog bell that, hung around bullocks, can be heard up to 4 km away. A replica and history display are in Bell Park. There is excellent fishing on the Condamine River, and the town holds a famous rodeo in Oct; 33 km s. *The Gums:* tiny settlement with historic church and nature reserve; 79 km s. *Glenmorgan:* the Myall Park Botanical Gardens; 134 km SW.

See also DARLING DOWNS, p. 418

Millaa Millaa
Pop. 289
Map ref. 650 D4 | 651 E11 | 657 L7

ⓘ Millaa Millaa Tourist Park, Millaa Millaa–Malanda Rd; (07) 4097 2290; www.tablelands.org/millaa-millaa.html

MACKAY

Pop. 72 848

Map ref. 649 G8 | 655 K5

ℹ️ **Mackay Tourism**, Old Town Hall, 320 Nebo Rd; (07) 4952 2677 or 1300 130 001; www.mackayregion.com

📻 101.9 FM 4MK, 630 AM ABC North QLD

The city of Mackay is an intriguing blend of 1800s and Art Deco heritage buildings mixed with modern-day architecture. Sugar was first grown here in 1865, and Mackay now produces around one-third of Australia's sugar crop and has the world's largest bulk-sugar loading terminal.

🏠 **Artspace Mackay** This modern art gallery forms part of the Queensland Heritage Trails Network. The museum documents Mackay's history with an interesting permanent exhibition entitled 'Spirit and Place: Mementoes of Mackay'. The gallery section has changing exhibits of both local and international artwork. Closed Mon; Gordon St.

Old Town Hall: houses the Heritage Interpretive Centre with displays on Mackay's history and visitor information; Sydney St. *Regional Botanic Gardens:* follow the picturesque boardwalk over a lagoon and explore specialised gardens of plants of the central coast; Lagoon St. *Queens Park:* includes the Orchid House that displays over 3000 orchids; Goldsmith St. *Heritage walk:* self-guide walk of 22 heritage buildings; brochure available from visitor centre. *City cemetery:* 1.5 km heritage walk; Greenmount Rd. *Horizons Mosaic:* locally constructed mosaics of the Mackay region's natural attractions; Victoria St. *Mackay Museum:* local artefacts with a research area and souvenirs for sale; open 10am–2pm every Thurs and 1st Sun each month; Casey Ave. *Great Barrier Reef tours:* snorkelling, diving, reef fishing and sailing tours; details at visitor centre.

🌴 **Market:** showgrounds, Milton St; Sat mornings. *City Centre Markets:* Victoria St; Sun mornings. *Walkers Markets:* Harbour Rd; weekends. *Seaforth Markets*: Palm Ave; Sun mornings. *Troppo Treasure Markets:* showgrounds; 2nd Sun each month. *Seaforth Fishing Classic:* Apr. *Festival of the Arts:* July. *River to Reef Festival:* Aug. *Sugartime Festival:* Sept.

🍴 **Church on Palmer:** international cuisine; 15 Palmer St; (07) 4944 1466. *George's Thai on the Marina:* top-notch Thai food; Mulherin Dr; (07) 4955 5778. *Sorbello's Italian Restaurant:* affordable Italian; 166 Victoria St; (07) 4957 8300.

🛏️ **Clarion Hotel Mackay Marina:** 79 suites with views; Mulherin Dr; (07) 4955 9400 or 1800 386 386. *Lantern Motor Inn and Restaurant:* 16 units in tropical gardens; 149–151 Nebo Rd; (07) 4951 2188. *Ocean International:* beachfront hotel; 1 Bridge Rd; (07) 4957 2044 or 1800 635 104. *Comfort Resort Blue Pacific:* waterfront location; 26 Bourke St, Blacks Beach; (07) 4954 9090 or 1800 808 386. *Broken River Mountain Resort:* a platypus haven; Eungella Dam Rd, Eungella National Park; (07) 4958 4000.

✖️ **Eungella National Park** This ecologically diverse park is home to some unusual plants and animals including the Eungella gastric brooding frog and the Mackay tulip oak. A highlight of the visit is seeing the platypus in Broken River from the viewing

[SUGARCANE HARVESTING NEAR MACKAY]

deck. Visit the Finch Hatton Gorge section of the park where the waterfalls, swimming holes and walking tracks are breathtaking. For the more adventurous, try sailing through the rainforest canopy on the eco-tour Forest Flying. Finch Hatton Gorge turn-off is just before Eungella. Broken River is 6 km s of Eungella; (07) 4944 7800 (same phone number for national parks below).

Northern beaches: visit fabulous beaches including Harbour (patrolled, fishing), Town, Blacks (area's longest beach), Bucasia, Illawong, Eimeo, Lamberts (excellent lookout) and Shoal Point. *Farleigh Sugar Mill:* tours during crushing season, July–Oct; 15 km N. *That Sapphire Place:* sapphire display and gem-cutting demonstrations; 20 km W. *Greenmount Homestead:* restored historic home with pioneering history museum; open 9.30am–12.30pm, closed Sun; Walkerston; 20 km W. *Homebush:* small town offers art and craft gallery, orchid farms and self-drive tour through historic area; 25 km S. *Melba House:* the home where Dame Nellie Melba spent the 1st year of her married life. It is now home to Pioneer Valley Visitor Centre; Marian; 28 km W. *Mirani:* small town in the Pioneer Valley with museum and Illawong Fauna and Flora Sanctuary; 33 km W. *Kinchant Dam:* popular spot for watersports and fishing; 40 km W. *Hibiscus Coast:* comprises the quaint coastal towns of Seaforth, Ball Bay and Cape Hillsborough; 43 km NW. *Cape Hillsborough National Park:* scenic coastal park with sandy beaches, tidal rockpools and walking trails; access from Hibiscus Coast, 44 km NW. *Smith Islands National Park:* the largest island of this group is Goldsmith, with long sandy beaches and snorkelling in surrounding reefs; access is by private boat or water taxi; 70 km NE via Seaforth. *Cumberland Island National Park:* this group of islands off Mackay coast is popular for boating and also an important rookery for flat back and green turtles; access is by private boat or water taxi. *Brampton Island:* resort island at southern end of Whitsunday Passage with pristine beaches and coral reef; sea and air access. *Nebo:* historic town of Mackay region, with local artefacts and pioneering history at the Nebo Shire Museum. Nebo holds a Campdraft in Sept; 93 km SW.

See also THE MID-TROPICS, p. 424

See also THE MID-TROPICS, p. 424

QUEENSLAND

 RADIO STATIONS   IN TOWN   WHAT'S ON   WHERE TO EAT   WHERE TO STAY   NEARBY

97.9 FM Hot, 720 AM ABC Far North QLD

Millaa Millaa is at the southern edge of the Atherton Tableland, and is central to a thriving dairy industry. The 17-kilometre Waterfall Circuit and rainforest-clad Wooroonooran National Park are just two of the natural attractions that bring visitors to the mild climate of this town.

Eacham Historical Society Museum: documents history of local area, with special interest in dairy and timber industries; opening times vary, contact museum for more information; Main St; (07) 4097 2147.

Wooroonooran National Park, Palmerston section More than 500 types of rainforest trees means the landscape in this park is both diverse and breathtaking. Walks include a 5 km return track leading to spectacular gorge views at Crawford's Lookout and a short 800 m track to glimpse the Tchupala Falls. A popular activity in the park is whitewater rafting on the North Johnstone River; companies include RnR Adventures; bookings on (07) 4041 9444. Access via Palmerston Hwy; (07) 4061 5900; 25 km sw.

Waterfall Circuit This 17 km circuit road includes the Zillie, Ellinjaa and Mungalli falls, as well as the popular Millaa Millaa Falls, a great spot for swimming, with walks leading to other waterfalls. The circuit road is mostly sealed and the route leaves and rejoins Palmerston Hwy east of town.

Millaa Millaa Lookout: panoramic views of tablelands and national parks; 6 km w. *Misty Mountains walking trails:* short- and long-distance tracks through World Heritage–listed Wet Tropics, many of which follow traditional Aboriginal paths of the Jirrbal and Mamu people; details from visitor centre. *Hillside Eden Garden:* award-winning garden featured on the television program *Better Homes and Gardens*, with stunning camellias and rhododendrons; Tarzali, 20 km N.

See also Cairns & The Tropics, p. 425

Miriam Vale
Pop. 362
Map ref. 653 L2

ⓘ Discovery Coast Information Centre, Roe St (Bruce Hwy); (07) 4974 5428; www.gladstonerc.qld.gov.au

 93.5 FM Hot, 855 AM ABC Wide Bay

Miriam Vale lies south-east of Gladstone, in the hinterland of the 'Discovery Coast'. The town is renowned for its charming hospitality, its historic fig trees in the main street and its mud-crab sandwiches. The hinterland and coastal national parks are ideal places for bushwalking, four-wheel driving and horseriding.

Edge on Beaches Resort: 4 pools, many beaches; Cnr Captain Cook Dr and Beaches Village Circuit, Agnes Water; (07) 4902 1200. *The Beach Shacks:* totally tropical and relaxed; 578 Captain Cook Dr, Seventeen Seventy; (07) 4974 9463.

Deepwater National Park A diverse vegetation covers this coastal park, including paperbark forests, swamp mahogany, Moreton Bay ash and subtropical rainforest. Walk along the sandy beaches or enjoy the birdlife of the freshwater stream, Deepwater Creek. Bush camp at Wreck Rock, and explore the rockpools. 4WD access only; (07) 4131 1600; 63 km NE via Agnes Water.

Eurimbula National Park: rugged coastal park with walks along the beach, canoeing on Eurimbula Creek, fishing, and scenic views from Ganoonga Noonga Lookout. 4WD recommended; (07) 4131 1600; access between Miriam Vale and Agnes Water; 50 km NE. *Agnes Water:* this coastal town has the most northerly surfing beach in Queensland. A local history museum includes

documents of Cook's voyage in 1770. The town holds the surfing competition 1770 Longboard Classic each Mar; 57 km NE. *Seventeen Seventy:* Captain Cook, while on his discovery voyage, made his second landing on Australian soil at the town site. Today the seaside village has the Joseph Banks Environmental Park and is the departure point for daytrips and fishing charters to the Great Barrier Reef and Lady Musgrave Island; 63 km NE.

See also Capricorn, p. 423

Mission Beach
Pop. 517
Map ref. 650 E5 | 657 M8

ⓘ Porter Promenade; (07) 4068 7099; www.missionbeachtourism.com

 88.5 FM 4KZ, 630 AM ABC North QLD

Mission Beach is named for the Aboriginal mission established in the area in 1914. The beach that features in the town's name is a 14-kilometre-long strip of golden sand fringed by coconut palms and World Heritage–listed wet tropical rainforest. Artists, potters, sculptors and jewellers have settled in the area, now reliant on the strong tourism industry of the coast.

Porter Promenade: woodcarving exhibition and rainforest arboretum; next to visitor centre. *Ulysses Link Walking Trail:* this 1.2 km pathway along the foreshore features local history, sculptures and mosaics. *Great Barrier Reef tours:* cruises and day tours to islands and reefs depart from Clump Point Jetty daily. *Boat, catamaran and jetski hire:* details from visitor centre.

Market: Porter Promenade; 1st Sat and 3rd Sun each month. *Monster Markets:* Recreation Centre, Cassowary Dr; last Sun each month (Easter–Nov). *Banana Festival:* Aug. *Aquatic Festival:* Oct.

Lillypads: 2 tropical garden chalets; 1375 Cassowary Dr; (07) 4088 6133. *Mission Beach Resort:* all rooms lead to a pool; Wongaling Beach Rd; (07) 4088 8288 or 1800 079 024. *Sejala on the Beach:* luxuriously rustic beach huts; Pacific Pde; (07) 4088 6699.

Family Islands The Family Islands National Park protects this 14 km stretch of islands. The most northerly of the group, Dunk Island, is a popular holiday destination with spectacular forest, rainforest and 14 km of walking tracks. The resort is private but camping is available. The less-developed islands of Wheeler and Coombe are perfect for bush camping (visitors must be self-sufficient). There is air service to Dunk Island from Cairns and Townsville or ferry from Clump Point. Islands are accessible by water taxi from Wongaling Beach.

Clump Mountain National Park: this scenic park boasts remnant lowland rainforest, an important habitat for the southern cassowary. A highlight is the 4 km Bicton Hill Track to the summit lookout over Mission Beach and coast; just north of Mission Beach on Bingil Bay Rd; (07) 4722 5224. *Historic cairn:* commemorates the ill-fated 1848 Cape York expedition of Edmund Kennedy; South Mission Beach Espl. *Aboriginal Midju:* display of Aboriginal culture; adjacent to cairn. *Wet Tropics walking trails:* the area around Mission Beach offers spectacular rainforest walks, including the Lacy Creek Forest circuit (1.2 km) in the major cassowary habitat of Tam O'Shanter National Park, the Kennedy Trail (7 km) past lookouts and along beaches, and the trails in Licuala State Forest; brochure available from visitor centre. *Adventure activities:* include tandem parachuting, kayak trips and whitewater rafting; details from visitor centre.

See also Cairns & The Tropics, p. 425

Mitchell

Pop. 942
Map ref. 652 E6

 ⓘ Great Artesian Spa Complex, 2 Cambridge St; (07) 4623 8171; www.visitmitchell.com.au

102.9 FM Outback Radio 4VL, 711 AM ABC Western QLD

Mitchell, a gateway to the outback, is on the banks of the Maranoa River at the western edge of the Darling Downs. But, located as it is on the Great Artesian Basin, it does not suffer the dry heat or exhibit the arid landscape typical of the region. The town was named after Sir Thomas Mitchell, explorer and Surveyor-General of New South Wales, who visited the region in 1846. Its long pastoral history is shown in the fine examples of heritage buildings on the main street.

Kenniff Courthouse This courthouse was in use from 1882 to 1965. It held the murder trials for the Kenniff Brothers, infamous bushrangers who killed a policeman and station manager in 1902. The courthouse is now a museum with a bushranger exhibition, visual display, and art and craft sales. The landscaped grounds incorporate a community mosaic, an operating artesian windmill and a small billabong. Cambridge St.

Great Artesian Spa Complex: with relaxing waters in a garden setting, this is Australia's largest open-air spa; Cambridge St. *Graffiti murals:* depict the past, present and future of the Booringa Shire; around town. *Art galleries:* including the Maranoa Art Gallery and Nalingu Contemporary Indigenous Gallery. *Horse-drawn wagon tours:* in season; details from visitor centre.

Mitchell Rodeo: Mar/Apr. *Maranoa Diggers Races:* Apr. *Campdraft:* Mar. *Agricultural Show:* May. *Mitchell Show:* May. *Fire & Water Festival:* Sept/Oct. *Bushstock Contemporary Musical Festival:* Oct. *Christmas in the Park:* Dec.

Berkeley Lodge Motor Inn: near Great Artesian Spa centre; 20–30 Cambridge St; (07) 4623 1666. *Bonus Downs Farmstay:* fully catered options available; Bollon Rd; (07) 4623 1573.

Carnarvon National Park, Mt Moffatt section This section of the park is mainly for driving, with short walks to scenic spots. See the sandstone sculptures of Cathedral Rock, Marlong Arch and Lot's Wife, or visit the Tombs for the ancient stencil art of the Nuri and Bidjara people. The high-country woodlands and forest are home to a variety of wildlife, and birdwatching for raptors and lorikeets is exceptional. 4WD recommended; (07) 4984 4505; 256 km N. Gorge section: *see Roma.* Ka Ka Mundi section: *see Springsure.* Salvator Rosa section: *see Tambo.*

Neil Turner Weir: birdwatching and picnics; 3.5 km NW. *Fisherman's Rest:* good fishing spot; 6 km W. *Maranoa River Nature Walk:* informative 1.8 km circuit walk starting at Fisherman's Rest. *Kenniff Statues:* depict the story of the brothers at their last stand; 7 km S. *Major Mitchell Cruises:* cruises down Maranoa River departing from Rotary Park, Neil Turner Weir; bookings at visitor centre. *Aboriginal tours:* guided tours run by Nalingu Aboriginal Corporation; details from visitor centre.

See also OUTBACK, p. 428

Monto

Pop. 1155
Map ref. 653 K3

 ⓘ Touch screen in Newton St; or council offices, 51A Newton St, (07) 4166 9999; www.monto.qld.gov.au

105.1 FM Rebel, 855 AM ABC Wide Bay

Monto, one of the most recent towns in the Capricorn region, was settled in 1924. It is the centre of a rich dairy and beef cattle district and is set picturesquely on a plateau surrounded by rolling hills.

Monto History Centre: local history displays and videos; closed Sat–Sun; Cnr Kelvin and Lister sts. *Historical and Cultural Complex:* variety of historic artefacts and a mineral display; Flinders St.

Country Craft Market: Mulgildie Hall; 1st Sun every month. *Campdraft:* Mar. *Fishing Classic:* Mar. *Horseracing:* Mar. *Monto Show:* Apr. *Monto Festival:* June. *Annual Cattle Drive and Trail Ride:* Aug. *Monto Garden Expo:* Oct.

Cania Gorge Caravan and Tourist Park: campsites, cabins and villas; Phil Marshall Dr; (07) 4167 8188.

Cania Gorge National Park Part of Queensland's sandstone belt, this park has cliffs, gorges and caves of spectacular colours. The freehand Aboriginal art around the park is a reminder of the area's ancient heritage. There are over 10 walks of varying length and difficulty. See the park's goldmining history on the 1.2 km return Shamrock Mine track or experience breathtaking park views from the Giant's Chair Lookout, reached on the longer Fern Tree Pool and Giant's Chair circuit. (07) 4167 8162; 25 km NW.

Mungungo: small town with boutique Waratah Winery; 13 km N. *Lake Cania:* excellent spot for watersports, fishing (permit required) and walking to lookout. Annual Lake Cania Fishing Classic is held here every Mar; 11 km N via Cania Gorge Picnic Area. *Kalpower State Forest:* hoop pine and rainforest vegetation. 4WD or walk rugged tracks to scenic lookouts; 40 km NE. *Wuruma Dam:* swimming, sailing and waterskiing; 50 km S.

See also CAPRICORN, p. 423

Mooloolaba

Pop. 7376
Map ref. 647 H4 | 648 F11 | 653 N7

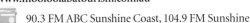 **ⓘ** Cnr First Ave and Brisbane Rd; (07) 5478 2233; www.mooloolabatourism.com.au

90.3 FM ABC Sunshine Coast, 104.9 FM Sunshine

Mooloolaba is a popular holiday destination on the Sunshine Coast. Its fabulous beaches, restaurants, nightlife and resort-style shopping contribute to the constant influx of families and young people eager for the sun. Mooloolaba Harbour is one of the safest anchorages on the east coast and the base for a major prawning and fishing fleet.

UnderWater World This award-winning complex has a fantastic 80 m walkway through seawater 'ocean', with displays of the Great Barrier Reef and underwater creatures. There are daily shows, including the seal show and crocodile feeding. Spend 15 min swimming with a seal or dive in with sharks (bookings essential). The Touch Tank is a less daunting alternative to get up-close to the animals of the sea; Wharf Complex, Parkyn Pde.

Mooloolaba Harbour: popular spot for parasailing, scuba diving and cruises; contact visitor centre for tour operators.

Triathlon: Mar. *Etchells Australian Winter Championship:* yacht race; June.

Aegean Apartments: 5-storey block with views; 14 River Espl; (07) 5444 1255 or 1800 644 155. *Breakfree Seamark:* 12-storey apartment block; 29 First Ave; (02) 8248 2350 or

 QUEENSLAND

1300 130 601. *Mantra Zanzibar:* family-friendly high-rise; 47–51 The Esplanade; (07) 5444 5633 or 1300 553 800.

 Alexandra Headland: popular coastal town with views to the Maroochy River and Mudjimba Island. Extensive beaches and parklands on the foreshore. Surf lessons and board hire are available from Mooloolaba Wharf; just north of Mooloolaba. *Mooloolah River National Park:* take a canoe down Mooloolah River, ride along the bike trail or walk on the fire trails in this remnant wallum heath park; straddles Sunshine Motorway; (07) 5494 3983; 6 km sw. *Yachting and game fishing:* trips to nearby offshore reefs; details from visitor centre.

See also SUNSHINE COAST, p. 419

Moranbah

Pop. 7131
Map ref. 649 C10 | 655 I7

i Library, town square; (07) 4941 4500; www.isaac.qld.gov.au

96.9 FM Rock, 104.9 FM ABC Tropical North QLD

Moranbah is a modern mining town south-west of Mackay. It was established in 1969 to support the huge open-cut coalmines of the expanding Bowen Coal Basin. Coking coal is railed to the Hay Point export terminal just south of Mackay.

Federation Walk: 1 km scenic walk starts at Grosvenor Park; Peak Downs Hwy. *Historical walk:* self-guide trail past interesting sites and heritage buildings of town; brochure from visitor centre.

Australia Day Street Party: Jan. *May Day Union Parade and Fireworks:* May.

Tours to Peak Downs Mine: leaves from town square the last Wed each month; bookings at visitor centre. *Isaacs River:* recreational area with historic monuments and a hiking trail in dry weather; 13 km s. *Lake Elphinstone:* camping, recreation activities, waterskiing, boating and fishing; 70 km N.

See also THE MID-TROPICS, p. 424

Mossman

Pop. 1740
Map ref. 650 D1 | 651 D3 | 657 L5

 Call council offices, (07) 4099 9444; or Cairns & Tropical North Visitor Information Centre, 51 The Esplanade, Cairns, (07) 4051 3588; www.cairnsgreatbarrierreef.org.au

92.5 FM 4CA, 639 AM ABC Far North QLD

The town of Mossman, in Far North Queensland, is set among green mountains and fields of sugarcane. Originally named after the explorer Hugh Mosman, the town changed the spelling of its name from Mosman to Mossman to avoid being confused with the Sydney suburb.

Market: Foxton Ave; Sat. *Christmas Party:* Dec.

 Papillon B&B: 2 rooms overlooking pool; 36 Coral Sea Dr; (07) 4098 2760. *Silky Oaks Lodge & Healing Waters Spa:* fantastic treehouse and rainforest rooms; Finlayvale Rd; (07) 4098 1666.

Cooya Beach and Newell: coastal towns with popular beaches to the north-east. *Daintree National Park:* including the magnificent Mossman Gorge; 5 km w; *see also Daintree. Karnak Rainforest Sanctuary:* amphitheatre and rainforest; 8 km N. *High Falls Farm:* tropical fruit orchard, market garden and open-air restaurant in rainforest setting; 9 km N. *Wonga:* small town with an excellent beach and orchid gardens; 18 km N.

See also CAIRNS & THE TROPICS, p. 425

Mount Isa

Pop. 18 856
Map ref. 659 D11 | 660 F3

 Outback at Isa, 19 Marian St; (07) 4749 1555 or 1300 659 660; www.mountisa.qld.gov.au

102.5 Hot FM, 567 AM ABC North West QLD

The city of Mount Isa is the most important industrial, commercial and administrative centre in north-west Queensland, an oasis of civilisation in outback spinifex and cattle country. But before John Campbell Miles first discovered a rich silver-lead deposit in 1923, the area was undeveloped. Today Mount Isa Mines operates one of the world's largest silver-lead mines. Mount Isa is also one of the world leaders in rodeos, holding the third largest, which attracts rough-riders from all over Queensland and almost doubles the town's population.

Outback at Isa This modern complex shows the splendours of Queensland's outback country. Don a hard hat and take a guided tour of the 1.2 km of underground tunnels in the Hard Times Mine. The Indigenous, pioneering and mining history of Mount Isa is explored in the Sir James Foots building, and the Outback Park offers a scenic lagoon and informative walking trail. Marian St; 1300 659 660.

Riversleigh Fossil Centre This award-winning centre explores the significant discoveries of the Riversleigh Fossil Site (267 km NW). Through colourful displays, the ancient animals and landscapes come alive. The theatrette shows an excellent film on the fossil story so far and a visit to the laboratory with a working palaeontologist brings fossil discovery up-close as precious material is extracted from rocks. Adjacent to Outback at Isa.

Kalkadoon Tribal Centre: preserves the heritage and culture of the Indigenous Kalkadoon people. There are displays of artefacts and guided tours by Kalkadoon descendants; open weekdays; Centenary Park, Marian St. *National Royal Flying Doctor Service Visitor Centre:* informative video, historic and modern memorabilia and photo display; open weekdays; Barkly Hwy. *Trust Tent House:* an example of the housing provided for miners in the 1930s and 1940s that was designed for good ventilation in extreme conditions; open by appt only; Fourth Ave; (07) 3229 1788. *School of the Air:* discover how distance education works in the outback; Abel Smith Pde. *City Lookout:* overview of city and mine area; Hilary St. *Underground Hospital:* tours of hospital built in WW II; Deighton St. *Rodeo Walk of Fame:* walk the road paved with the names of Mount Isa rodeo legends; Rodeo Dr. *Mount Isa Mine:* the mine's lead smelter stack is Australia's tallest free-standing structure (265 m); informative surface tours available; details from visitor centre. *Donaldson Memorial Lookout:* lookout and walking track; off Marian St.

Market: Library carpark, Sat. *Mining Expo:* Apr. *Mount Isa Cup:* horseracing; June. *Mount Isa Show:* June. *Isa Rodeo:* Aug. *Mardi Gras:* Aug. *Fishing Classic:* Sept.

Lake Moondarra: artificial lake for picnics and barbecues, swimming, watersports and birdwatching. Home of the Fishing Classic in Sept; 20 km N. *Mt Frosty:* old limestone mine and swimming hole (not recommended for children as hole is 9 m deep with no shallow areas); 53 km E. *Lake Julius:* canoe at the lake or see the Aboriginal cave paintings and old goldmine on the nature trails; 110 km NE. *Station visits:* feel the outback spirit at one of the stations in the area; details from visitor centre. *Safari tours:* to Boodjamulla (Lawn Hill) National Park and Riversleigh Fossil Fields; details from visitor centre. *Air-charter flights:* to barramundi fishing spots on Mornington and Sweers islands in the Gulf of Carpentaria; details from visitor centre.

See also OUTBACK, p. 428

Mount Morgan

Pop. 2444
Map ref. 655 M11

 Heritage Railway Station, 1 Railway Pde; (07) 4938 2312; www.mountmorgan.com

98.5 FM 4YOU, 837 AM ABC Capricornia

Located in the Capricorn region south-west of Rockhampton is the quaint historic mining town of Mount Morgan. Said to be the largest single mountain of gold in the world, Mount Morgan's gold supply was discovered and mined from the late 1800s. What was a big mountain is now a big crater – the largest excavation in the Southern Hemisphere. In the mine's heyday, around 1910, the town was home to about 14 000 people.

Railway Station: historic station with tearooms, rail museum and a restored 1904 Hunslett Steam Engine that operates regularly; Railway Pde. *Historical Museum:* varied collection of memorabilia traces history of this mining town; Morgan St. *Historic suspension bridge:* built in the 1890s and spans the Dee River. *Historic cemetery:* features the Chinese Heung Lew (prayer oven) and the Linda Memorial to men killed in underground mines (1894–1909); off Coronation Dr. *The Big Stack:* 76 m high 1905 brick chimney used to disperse mining fumes; at the mine site.

Lions Club Market: Apex Park Cemetery; 3rd Sat each month. *Golden Mount Festival:* May. *Mount Morgan Show:* Aug.

Leichhardt Hotel: 12 hotel rooms, shared bathrooms; 52 Morgan St; (07) 4938 1851.

The Big Dam: good boating and fishing; 2.7 km N via William St. *Wowan:* town featuring the Scrub Turkey Museum in old butter factory; 40 km sw. *Tours:* tour to the open-cut Mount Morgan Mine and ancient clay caves with dinosaur footprints; details available from visitor centre.

See also CAPRICORN, p. 423

Mount Surprise

Pop. 162
Map ref. 657 J8

 Bedrock Village Caravan Park, Garland St (Savannah Way), (07) 4062 3193; or Mount Surprise Gems, Garland St, (07) 4062 3055; www.gulf-savannah.com.au

97.9 FM Hot, 105.3 FM ABC Far North QLD

Mount Surprise is a historic rail town in the Gulf Savannah. Its name comes from the surprise the Aboriginal people felt when they were resting at the base of the mountain and the loud white people of Ezra Firth's pioneer party arrived in 1864. The region has excellent gemfields for fossicking, especially for topaz, quartz and aquamarine. The town is on the edge of the Undara lava field, formed from the craters of the McBride Plateau. The lava caves can be explored in Undara Volcanic National Park.

Savannahlander This unique train journey shows the rugged delights and beautiful landscapes between Mount Surprise and Cairns. Departing from Mount Surprise Station each Sat, the train stops at various towns in the Gulf Savannah region. There are also trips between Mount Surprise and Forsayth. Bookings on (07) 4053 6848.

Old Post Office Museum: documents the bush history of the region in a historic 1870 building; opposite railway station. *Mount Surprise Gems:* runs tours to nearby fossicking spots and provides licences; Garland St.

Campdraft: Aug.

Undara Experience: accommodation in railway carriages; Savannah Way; (07) 4097 1900 or 1800 990 992.

Undara Volcanic National Park The cooling molten lava of an erupted volcano formed the 90 km of hollow underground lava tubes, the longest in the world. You can only explore the tubes by guided tour; bookings on 1800 990 992; day tours also run from Bedrock Village. See the eggcup-shaped crater on the 2.5 km Kalkani Crater circuit or go birdwatching to see some of the park's 120 bird species. (07) 4046 6600; 42 km E.

O'Brien's Creek: renowned for quality topaz; obtain a licence before fossicking; 37 km NW. *Tallaroo Hot Springs:* 5 natural springs created over centuries; open Easter–Sept; 48 km NW. *Forty Mile Scrub National Park:* vine-thicket park on the McBride Plateau with informative short circuit track from day area; (07) 4046 6600; 56 km E. *Georgetown:* small town once one of many small goldmining settlements on the Etheridge Goldfields; noted for its gemstones, especially agate, and gold nuggets; 82 km W. *Forsayth:* old mining town; 132 km SW. *Cobbold Gorge:* guided boat tours through sandstone gorge; bookings essential (07) 4062 5470. A full-day tour to Forsayth and the gorge also runs from Bedrock Village; 167 km SW via Forsayth. *Agate Creek:* fossick for gemstones; 187 km SW via Forsayth.

See also GULF SAVANNAH, p. 427

Mourilyan

Pop. 423
Map ref. 650 E5 | 651 H12 | 657 M7

 Cnr Eslick St and Bruce Hwy, Innisfail; (07) 4061 7422.

98.3 FM Kool, 720 AM ABC Far North QLD

Mourilyan is a small town in Far North Queensland. It is the bulk-sugar outlet for the Innisfail area. The history of this thriving industry can be seen at the Australian Sugar Industry Museum.

Australian Sugar Industry Museum This large museum was opened in 1977. Its permanent displays include a museum collection of photographs, books, documents and an incredible display of machinery that includes a steam engine, reputedly one of the largest ever built. See the audiovisual display on the history of Australia's sugar industry and tour the art gallery. Cnr Bruce Hwy and Peregrine St; (07) 4063 2656.

Paronella Park This 5 ha park was the vision of immigrant sugarcane worker José Paronella. After making his fortune, he started building a mansion on the site (1930–1946). Floods and other natural disasters have ruined the grand buildings, despite rebuilding efforts. Now the visitor can walk through the ruins, admire the spectacular rainforest and birdlife, swim near the falls and have Devonshire tea at the cafe. 17 km SW.

Etty Bay: quiet tropical beach with caravan and camping facilities; 9 km E.

See also CAIRNS & THE TROPICS, p. 425

Mundubbera

Pop. 1055
Map ref. 653 K4

 Historical Museum, Dugong St; or call council offices, (07) 4165 4101 or (07) 4165 4549.

93.1 FM Sea, 855 AM ABC Wide Bay

Mundubbera is on the banks of the Burnett River and is the main citrus-growing area in Queensland. Fruit pickers flock to the town in the cooler months. The unusual company 'Bugs for Bugs' produces a group of predatory bugs that reduces the need for pesticides. The rare Neoceratodus, or lungfish, is found in the Burnett and Mary rivers.

Historical Museum: local history; Leichhardt St. **Heritage Centre:** several displays of early settlement history; Durong Rd. **Jones Weir:** popular spot for fishing; Bauer St. **'Meeting Place of the Waters':** 360-degree town mural; Cnr Strathdy and Stuart–Russell sts. **Bugs for Bugs:** company that breeds insects; tours by appt only; Bowen St; (07) 4165 4663. **Pioneer Place:** gorgeous park with picnic facilities right in the middle of town.

Morning Market: Uniting Church: 3rd Sat each month. **Mundubbera Show:** May.

Auburn River National Park In this small park the Auburn River flows through a sheer-sided gorge and over granite boulders in the riverbed. Dry rainforest grows on the upper part of the tough track that leads down the side of the gorge to the river. An easier walk is the 150 m trail to the lookout above the Auburn River. Opposite the campsite catch a glimpse of the nesting peregrine falcons. 4WD is recommended in wet weather. (07) 4165 3905; 40 km sw.

Enormous Ellendale: the big mandarin, another addition to the 'big' monuments of Queensland; outskirts of town at the Big Mandarin Caravan Park. **Golden Mile Orchard:** impressive orchard with tours; 5 km s. **Eidsvold:** town at the centre of beef cattle country featuring the Historical Museum Complex and Tolderodden Environmental Park; 37 km nw.

See also CAPRICORN, p. 423

Murgon

Pop. 2133
Map ref. 648 A9 | 653 L6

i Queen Elizabeth Park; (07) 4168 3864; www.murgon.qld.gov.au

90.7 FM Crow, 855 AM ABC Wide Bay

Murgon, known as 'the beef capital of the Burnett', is one of the most attractive towns in southern Queensland. Settlement dates from 1843, but the town did not really develop until after 1904, when the railway arrived and the large stations of the area were divided up. The town's name comes from a lily pond, found on Barambah Station, which was the site of the first pastoral property in the area.

 Queensland Dairy Museum: static and interactive displays illustrating the history of the dairy industry, with special interest in the development of butter; Gayndah Rd.

Murgon Show: Mar. **Barambah Blowout Bull Ride:** Mar/Apr. **Kids Kapers:** fun day for the kids including a treasure hunt; May. **Dairy Heritage Festival:** June. **Rotary Arts Festival:** Sept/Oct. **Barambah Shakin' Grape Festival:** Oct. **Christmas Carnival:** Dec.

Boat Mountain Conservation Park The flat-topped crest in this park looks like an upturned boat, hence the name. The views from the top are panoramic and take in the surrounding agricultural valley. There are 2 lookout walks and an excellent 1.8 km circuit track. Watch for the bandicoot digs along the way. 20 km ne via Boat Mountain Rd.

Jack Smith Conservation Park This park comprises valuable remnant dry rainforest that used to cover the region before clearing for agriculture began. Have a picnic overlooking the South Burnett Valley before taking the 20 min return track through scrub to see the abundant birdlife of the park; 13 km n.

Cherbourg: small Aboriginal community featuring the Ration Shed Precinct displaying a pictorial history of the area; 5 km se. **Wondai:** attractions include the Regional Art Gallery, Heritage Museum and South Burnett Timber Industry Museum. Town hosts Garden Expo in September; 13 km s. **Bjelke-Petersen Dam:** popular spot for watersports and fishing (boat hire available) with various accommodation styles at Yallakool Tourist Park. The dam is home to the Annual Fishing Competition in Oct; 15 km se. **Goomeri:** known as 'clock town' for its unique memorial clock in the town centre. It has numerous antique stores and holds the Pumpkin Festival in May; 19 km ne. **Booubyjan Homestead:** historic home (1847) open to public; 43 km n via Goomeri. **Kilkivan:** Queensland's first discovery of gold was here in 1852. Try fossicking for gold or visit the lavender farm and historical museum. The town holds the Great Horse Ride in Apr; 44 km ne. **Proston:** small community featuring Sidcup Castle and Crafts Museum (open Wed–Mon); 54 km w. **Lake Boondooma:** watersports, fishing and the Fishing Competition in Feb; 74 km nw via Proston. **Barambah Wine Trail:** within 15 km of Murgon, in the Moffatdale and Redgate areas, are 7 excellent wineries with tastings and sales; visit by car or bus tour. **Bicentennial National Trail:** a 5330 km trail for walkers, bike riders and horseriders – you can do just a part of the trail. It runs through Kilkivan. **Fossicking:** semi-precious stones in Cloyna and Windera region; details from visitor centre.

See also BRISBANE HINTERLAND, p. 415

Muttaburra

Pop. 106
Map ref. 654 C8 | 661 O8

i Post office, Sword St; (07) 4658 7147; www.muttaburra.com

104.5 FM West, 540 AM ABC Western QLD

Despite being a tiny outback community, Muttaburra has much to promote in its history. Famous cattle duffer Harry Redford (Captain Starlight) planned his daring robbery at nearby Bowen Downs Station in 1870. He stole 1000 head of cattle (thinking they wouldn't be missed) and drove them 2400 kilometres into South Australia. He was arrested and tried; the jury acquitted him, probably because his daring was so admired. These events were the basis for Rolf Boldrewood's novel *Robbery Under Arms*. More recently, a skeleton of an unknown dinosaur was found in 1963 in a creek close to the Thomson River. It was named Muttaburrasaurus. A replica can be seen in Bruford Street.

Dr Arratta Memorial Museum: this museum has medical and hospital displays with original operating theatres and wards; tours by appt; (07) 4658 7287. **Cassimatis General Store and Cottage:** restored store depicts the original family business in early 1900s. The adjacent cottage was home to the Cassimatis family; tours by appt; (07) 4658 7287.

Anzac Day Celebrations: Apr. **Landsborough Flock Ewe Show:** June. **Horseracing:** Aug. **Christmas Celebrations:** Dec.

Muttaburra Cemetery: outskirts of town; 1 km w. **Agate fossicking:** 5 km w. **Pump Hole:** swimming and fishing for golden perch and black bream; 5 km e. **Broadwater:** part of Landsborough River for fishing, birdwatching, bushwalking and camping; 6 km s.

See also OUTBACK, p. 428

Nambour

Pop. 13 532
Map ref. 647 F3 | 648 E11 | 653 N7

ⓘ 5 Coronation Ave; (07) 5476 1933;
www.nambourtown.com.au

 90.3 FM ABC Coast, 91.1 Hot FM

Nambour is a large, unpretentious service town in the Sunshine Coast hinterland. Development began in the 1860s and sugar has been the main crop since the 1890s. Small locomotives pull loads of sugarcane across the main street to Moreton Central Mill, a charming sight during the crushing season (July–October). The town's name is derived from the Aboriginal word for the local red-flowered tea tree.

Sunshine Coast Show: June. *Queensland Home Garden Expo:* July. *Australia's Greatest Rock Event:* Sept.

Chez Claude: tiny French treasure; 4 Pine Grove Rd, Woombye; (07) 5442 1511.

Mapleton Falls National Park Volcanic columns jut out of Pencil Creek just before the creek's water falls 120 m to the valley floor. Walk to the falls lookout or see panoramic views of the Obi Obi Valley from Peregrine Lookout. Birdwatchers will delight at the early morning and dusk flights of the park's numerous bird species. (07) 5494 3983; 3 km sw of Mapleton.

The Big Pineapple Complex and Macadamia Nut Factory The 16 m fibreglass pineapple makes this complex hard to miss. Inside are displays on the tropical fruit industry. The complex has a variety of interesting activities, including the Plantation Train, Harvest Boat Ride, Rainforest Walk and Nutmobile through macadamia orchards. Open from 9am daily; (07) 5442 1333. 7 km s.

Mapleton: attractive arts and crafts town in the Blackall Range; holds the Yarn Festival in Oct; 15 km w; *see also Maleny. Mapleton Forest Reserve:* with excellent drive through bunya pines and blackbutt forests starting just north of Mapleton. Along the drive, walk to the top of the waterfall from Poole's Dam and take the short Piccabeen Palm Groves Walk. The drive ends with spectacular views from Point Glorious.

See also SUNSHINE COAST, p. 419

Nanango

Pop. 3085
Map ref. 648 A11 | 653 L7

ⓘ Henry St; (07) 4171 6871; www.nanango.qld.gov.au

 89.1 C FM, 747 AM ABC Southern QLD

Nanango is one of the oldest towns in Queensland. Gold was mined here from 1850 to 1900 and fossickers still try their luck today. The industrial Tarong Power Station and Meandu Coal Mine are nearby, yet Nanango still retains a welcoming country atmosphere.

Historic Ringsfield House: excellent example of colonial architecture of the 1900s. It houses the historical society and period furnishings; open weekdays, Sat–Sun by appt; Cnr Alfred and Cairns sts; (07) 4163 3345. *Tarong Power Station Display:* models and displays; adjacent to visitor centre.

Market: showgrounds; 1st Sat each month. *Nanango Show:* Apr. *Nanart:* art show; Apr/May. *Country Music Muster:* Sept. *Funfest:* Oct.

The Palms National Park Located at the Brisbane headwaters is this vine forest and subtropical rainforest park.

Have a bush picnic and then take the 20 min Palm Circuit track through natural vegetation and along boardwalks. (07) 4699 4355; 42 km sw.

Tipperary Flat: tribute park to early pioneers with old goldmining camp, displays and walking track; 2 km E. *Seven-Mile Diggings:* gold- and gem-fossicking; permit from visitor centre; 11 km SE. *Yarraman:* historic timber town with heritage centre and 'mud maps' for region; 21 km S. *Maidenwell:* small town with Astronomical Observatory and Coomba Falls nearby; 28 km sw. *Blackbutt:* picturesque timber town with country markets 3rd Sun each month; 41 km SE.

See also BRISBANE HINTERLAND, p. 415

Nerang

Pop. 16 066
Map ref. 551 G1 | 645 F9 | 646 D6 | 653 N10

ⓘ Cavill Walk, Surfers Paradise; (07) 5538 4419.

 92.1 FM Breeze, 612 AM ABC Brisbane

Nerang is in the Gold Coast hinterland. Today the town is much more similar in character to that dense urban strip of coast than to the small rural centre it started out as in the mid-1800s.

Nerang Forest Reserve On the north-west fringe of Nerang is this hilly rainforest and open eucalypt reserve. An excellent way of exploring the landscape is on the 2.8 km return Casuarina Grove Track through rainforest and along the creek. Look out for the black cockatoos. The reserve is a popular spot for horseriders and cyclists (permit required).

Nerang River: this gorgeous river flows through town, providing a popular spot for picnics, boating, fishing and watersports.

Farmers market: Lavelle St; Sun.

Riviera B&B: French food and friendly hosts; 53 Evanita Dr; (07) 5533 2499. *Binna Burra Mountain Lodge:* cabins, tents and guesthouse accommodation; Binna Burra Rd, Beechmont; (07) 5533 3622 or 1300 246 622. *O'Reilly's:* great location and accommodation; Lamington National Park Rd, via Canungra; (07) 5502 4911 or 1800 688 722.

Springbrook National Park This rainforest park forms part of the Scenic Rim of mountains. The Springbrook section has an information centre, from which a short walk leads to a spectacular lookout over the Gold Coast. Access is via Springbrook (39 km sw). The Natural Bridge section features a unique rock arch over Cave Creek. Take the 1 km rainforest walk to see the natural bridge where Cave Creek plunges through an eroded hole to a cavern below. There are tours to see the glow worms or a 3 km night trail through rainforest; bookings on (07) 5533 5239. Park information (07) 5533 5147; 38 km sw. Mt Cougal section: *see Burleigh Heads.*

Lamington National Park This beautiful park to the south-west of Nerang protects the world's largest subtropical rainforest. It is a popular bushwalking and scenic park with spectacular waterfalls and mountain landscapes. Have a picnic with the rosellas and brush turkeys or go on a bushwalk – there are over 20. Access to the Green Mountains section is via Canungra; (07) 5544 0634. Binna Burra is accessed via Beechmont; (07) 5533 3584.

Carrara: nearby town offers scenic balloon flights over the Gold Coast, (07) 5578 2244, and holds weekend markets; 5 km SE. *Hinze Dam on Advancetown Lake:* sailing and bass-fishing;

 QUEENSLAND

NOOSA HEADS

Pop. 3658

Map ref. 647 H1 | 648 F10 | 653 N7

ℹ️ **Hastings St roundabout; or Noosa Marina (Tewantin);**
(07) 5430 5000; www.visitnoosa.com.au

📻 90.3 FM ABC Sunshine Coast, 101.3 FM Noosa
Community Radio

Noosa Heads, commonly known as Noosa, is a coastal resort
town on Laguna Bay on the Sunshine Coast. The relaxed lifestyle,
the weather and the safe year-round swimming make this a
popular holiday destination. Cosmopolitan Hastings Street offers
a relaxed cafe lifestyle, and within walking distance are the natural
attractions of superb coastal scenery and the protected coves,
surfing beaches and seascapes of Noosa National Park.

🏠 *Noosa Main Beach:* safe family swimming. *David Hart
Galleries:* featuring Australian investment artists including Pro
Hart; Hastings St. *Adventure sports:* on the spectacular coastal
waters of the Coral Sea and inland waterways. Activities include
kite surfing, high-speed boating, surfing lessons and kayaking.
Camel safaris: 2 hr beach and bushland safari on Noosa's North
Shore; (07) 5442 4402. *Scenic flights:* contact visitor centre
for details.

🎪 *Farmers market:* AFL ground, Weyba Rd; Sun mornings.
Festival of Surfing: Mar. *Noosa Mardi Gras Recovery Week:*
a week-long festival following the Sydney Gay and Lesbian
Mardi Gras; Mar. *Mayfiesta:* food and wine on the Noosa River;
May. *Celebration of Australian Food and Wine:* May. *Noosa
Longweekend:* arts festival; July. *Noosa Enduro:* Mountain-bike
race; July. *Half Marathon:* Aug. *Jazz Festival:* Sept. *Beach Car
Classic:* Sept. *Triathlon Multi-sport Festival:* Oct/Nov.

🍴 *Berardo's Bistro on the Beach:* inspired by French bistros;
Hastings St; (07) 5448 0888. *Berardo's Restaurant and Bar:*
the place for a special night out; Hastings St; (07) 5447 5666.
Sails: delicious food overlooking the beach; Cnr Park Rd and
Hastings St; (07) 5447 4235. *Harvest:* signature dish of grilled
lamb pizza; 1808 David Low Way, Coolum; (07) 5446 4314.

River House Restaurant: fresh, local, modern cuisine; 301
Weyba Rd, Noosaville; (07) 5449 7441. *Wasabi:* award-winning
Japanese; 2 Quamby Pl, Noosa Sound; (07) 5449 2443.

🛏️ *Eumarella Shores:* 2 lakeside cottages; 251 Eumarella Rd;
(07) 5449 1738. *Lake Weyba Cottages:* lakeside cottages and
pavilions; 79 Clarendon Rd; (07) 5448 2285. *Netanya Noosa:*
beachfront luxury boutique hotel; 75 Hastings St; (07) 5447 4722
or 1800 072 072. *Sheraton Noosa Resort & Spa:* sophisticated
and relaxed; 14–16 Hastings St; (07) 5449 4888. *Villa Alba:*
4 luxurious villas; 191 Duke Rd, Doonan; (07) 5449 1900.

🧭 **Noosa National Park** This largely untouched rocky
coastline national park covering 454 ha of seascape has walks
of varying length through rainforest and heathland. Escape the
summer crowds of Noosa with the 8.4 km return Tanglewood
Track in the Noosa headland to Hells Gate, a popular lookout
and whale-viewing spot. Return via the coastal track for scenic
ocean views. Access the park via Park Rd in Noosa Heads,
the coastal boardwalk from Hastings St, or Sunshine Beach;
(07) 5447 3243.

Great Sandy National Park, Cooloola section This park has
stunning coloured sands, beaches, lakes, forests and sand dunes,
all of which are protected. Many rare and threatened species call
it home. There are walks for all ranges of fitness and stamina
from short circuit walks to overnight hikes. For the serious
walker, there is the 2–4-day Cooloola Wilderness Trail with bush
camping. For less strenuous activity, picnic in the rainforest at
Bymien or see the Teewah Coloured Sands (multicoloured sand
cliffs). There is also camel-riding, horseriding and surfing, as well
as commercial tours from Brisbane, Noosa and Rainbow Beach,
and 4WD tours to Fraser Island. The park is separated from the
Sunshine Coast by Noosa River and is accessed via vehicle ferry
from Tewantin. Access from the north is via Rainbow Beach;
4WD recommended. (07) 5449 7792; 14 km N.

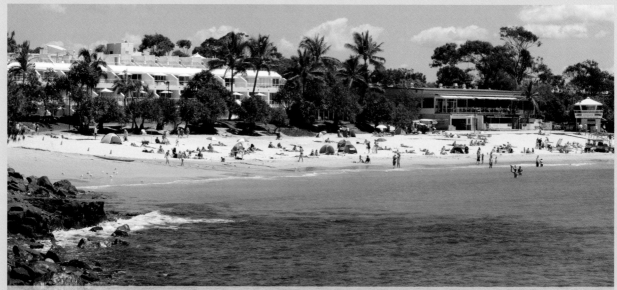

[NOOSA MAIN BEACH]

Laguna Lookout: views of Noosa River, lakes and hinterland; on Noosa Hill. *Sunshine Beach:* golden beach popular for surfing; 3 km SE. *Noosaville:* family-style area with Noosa River as focal point; departure point for river cruises; 5 km SW. *Lake Cooroibah:* ideal for boating, sailing and windsurfing; access by car or boat from Noosaville. *Tewantin:* Noosa Marina in Parkyn Court with restaurants, art gallery, boat hire and cruise tours. The Big Shell and the House of Bottles are nearby; 7 km W. *Tewantin State Forest:* hilly rainforest and eucalypt forest reserve with 10 min walk to Mt Tinbeerwah Lookout offering a panoramic view over Noosa River, lakes and hinterland; 10 km W via Tewantin. *Noosa River and the Everglades:* the river extends over 40 km north into Great Sandy National Park. Take a cruise into the Everglades – waters known for their reflections – and to Harry's Hut, a relic of timber-cutting days. Kayak and canoe hire on offer, as well as camping facilities; contact visitor centre for details. *Eumundi:* famed markets every Wed and Sat (also Thurs night Dec–Jan); *see Yandina;* 21 km SW.

See also SUNSHINE COAST, p. 419

10 km SW. *Historic River Mill:* 1910 arrowroot mill; 10 km W. *Mudgeeraba:* holds the Somerset Celebration of Literature in Mar. Nearby is the Gold Coast War Museum with militia memorabilia and skirmish paintball; 12 km S. *Paradise Country:* this 12 ha Aussie farm offers half-day tours with camel rides, whip cracking, boomerang throwing, sheep shearing demonstrations, and damper and billy tea by a campfire; Entertainment Rd, Oxenford; (07) 5573 8270; 15 km N. *Outback Spectacular:* night-time show that brings Australia's outback to life with stunt riders, stockmen and a barbecue dinner; show starts at 7.30pm Tues–Sun; Pacific Mwy, Oxenford; (07) 5573 3999; 15 km N.

See also GOLD COAST & HINTERLAND, p. 417

Normanton

Pop. 1098
Map ref. 656 D7 | 659 G4

ℹ️ Cnr Landsborough and Caroline sts; (07) 4745 1065; www.gulf-savannah.com.au

📻 101.7 Rebel FM, 567 AM ABC North West QLD

Normanton thrived as a port town in the late 1800s when the gold rush was on in Croydon. The Normanton-to-Croydon railway line, established at that time, today runs the award-winning *Gulflander* tourist train. More recently, Australia's largest saltwater crocodile, known as Krys the Savannah King, was shot at nearby Archer's Creek in 1957. A life-size replica of his body, over 8 metres long, can be seen in the council park.

🏠 *Normanton Railway Station:* National Trust–listed Victorian building; Matilda St. *Original well:* settlers used it for drawing water; Landsborough St. *Giant Barramundi:* big monument to the fish; Landsborough St. *Scenic walk and drive:* self-guide tours to historic buildings including the Old Gaol in Haig St and the restored Bank of NSW building in Little Brown St; brochure available from information centre in the Burns Philip Building. **Gulflander:** this historical 140 km railway journey from Normanton to Croydon reveals the remote beauty of the Gulf Savannah; departs 8.30am Wed and returns Thurs afternoons. *Gulflander* also runs regular sunset tours with billy tea and damper, and other short trips. *'Croc Spot' Cruise:* at sunset on the Norman River; departs Norman Boat Ramp 5pm Mon–Sat. *Norman River fishing tours:* fishing trips and boat hire for barramundi and estuary fish; details from visitor centre.

🌴 *Barra Classic:* Easter. *Normanton Show and Rodeo:* June.

🛏️ *Purple Pub & Brolga Palms Motel:* character-filled pub, comfortable motel; Landsborough St; (07) 4745 1324.

🧭 *Lakes:* attract jabirus, brolgas, herons and other birds; on the outskirts of Normanton. *Shady Lagoon:* bush camping, birdwatching and wildlife; 18 km SE. *Fishing:* catching barramundi is very popular in the area – try the spots at Norman River in Glenore (25 km SE), Walkers Creek (32 km NW) or off the bridges or banks in Normanton. *Burke and Wills cairn:* last and most northerly camp of Burke and Wills (Camp 119) before their fatal return journey; off the Savannah Hwy; 30 km SW. *Bang Bang Jump Up rock formation:* a solitary hill on the surrounding flat plains with excellent views; Matilda Hwy; 106 km SW. *Dorunda Station:* cattle station offering barramundi and saratoga fishing in lake and rivers; accommodation is available; 197 km NE. *Kowanyama Aboriginal community:* excellent barramundi fishing, guesthouse and camping; permit to visit required from Kowanyama Community Council; 359 km NE.

See also GULF SAVANNAH, p. 427

North Tamborine

Pop. 1272
Map ref. 645 E9 | 646 B4 | 653 N10

ℹ️ Doughty Park, Main Western Rd; (07) 5545 3200; www.tamborinemtncc.org.au

📻 88.9 Breeze FM, 612 AM ABC Brisbane

North Tamborine is one of the towns on the Tamborine Mountain ridge in the Gold Coast hinterland. Numerous galleries, arts and crafts shops and boutique wineries make it and the nearby towns of Tamborine Village, Eagle Heights and Mount Tamborine popular weekend getaways. Tamborine National Park covers most of the mountain – the Witches Falls section was Queensland's first national park, listed in 1908.

🏠 *Tamborine Mountain Distillery:* award-winning distillery with a range of liqueurs, schnapps, vodkas and spirits; Beacon Rd. *Mt Tamborine Winery and Cedar Creek Estate:* tastings and sales; Hartley Rd. *Hang-gliding:* off Tamborine Mountain; Main Western Rd; (07) 5543 5631 or contact visitor centre. *Tamborine Trolley Co:* provides tours of mountain, including weekend hop-on hop-off tour to major sights; (07) 5545 2782.

QUEENSLAND

Produce market: showgrounds (green shed); Sun mornings. *Tamborine Mountain Markets:* showgrounds, Main Western Rd; 2nd Sun each month. *Scarecrow Festival:* May. *Mountain Show:* Sept. *Springtime on the Mountain:* open gardens and mini-markets; Oct. *Craft Extravaganza:* Oct. *Tamborine Mountain Classic:* bike, run or walk; Nov.

Songbirds in the Forest: modern Australian, lovely setting; Songbirds Rainforest Retreat, Tamborine Mountain Rd; (07) 5545 2563. *The Polish Place:* hearty Polish food and drink; 333 Main Western Rd; (07) 5545 1603. *Cork 'n Fork Winery Tours:* local wineries and lunch; Tamborine Mountain Plateau; (07) 5543 6584.

Pethers Rainforest Retreat: adults-only luxury retreat; 28B Geissmann St; (07) 5545 4577. *Songbirds Rainforest Retreat:* villas in the forest; Tamborine Mountain Rd; (07) 5545 2563. *The Polish Place:* European-style chalets; 333 Main Western Rd; (07) 5545 1603.

Tamborine National Park This picturesque mountain park protects remnant subtropical rainforest. Waterfalls, cliffs and beautiful walks make it a popular spot for visitors. The scenic drive visits the major waterfalls and lookouts and there are 22 km of walks on offer. Walk highlights are the 5.4 km Jenyns Falls circuit track and the 3 km Witches Falls circuit track, both leading to spectacular waterfalls. Park access points are on Tamborine–Oxenford Rd; (07) 5576 0271.

Eagle Heights: pretty village to the north-east with the Gallery Walk on Long Rd featuring excellent local crafts; Botanical Gardens in Forsythia Dr are set on 9 ha of rainforest with a variety of plants; historic buildings are on show at the Heritage Centre, Wongawallen Rd. *Thunderbird Park:* wildlife sanctuary, horseriding, laser skirmish, ropes course and fossicking for 'thunder eggs'; Tamborine Mountain Rd. *Heritage and Mud Brick wineries:* tastings and sales; Mt Tamborine; 5 km s.

See also GOLD COAST & HINTERLAND, p. 417

Oakey

Pop. 3653
Map ref. 653 K9

ⓘ Library, 64 Campbell St; (07) 4692 0154.

📻 102.7 FM 4DDB, 747 AM ABC Southern QLD

Oakey is an agricultural town on the Darling Downs, surrounded by beautiful rolling hills and black-soil plains. It is also the base for the aviation division of the Australian army.

Bernborough: bronze statue of famous local racehorse; Campbell St. *Oakey Historical Museum:* local memorabilia; Warrego Hwy. *Australian Army Aviation Museum:* every aircraft flown by the Australian army since WW II is represented at the museum through originals and replicas. Other aircraft can also be viewed, from the early wood Box Kite to the hi-tech Blackhawk Helicopter; at army base on Corfe Rd.

 Jondaryan Woolshed Built in 1859 and still shearing under steam power, this woolshed is a memorial to pioneers of the wool industry. The complex includes the huge woolshed, historic buildings, and machinery and equipment collections. Visitors can see the shearing and sheepdog demonstrations or sit down to some billy tea and damper. Events are held throughout the year, including the Working Draft-horse Expo in June and the Australian Heritage Festival in Aug. Off Warego Hwy; 22 km NW.

See also DARLING DOWNS, p. 418

Palm Cove

Pop. 1215
Map ref. 650 D2 | 651 F6 | 657 L5

ⓘ Paradise Village Shopping Centre, Williams Espl; (07) 4055 3433; www.palmcove.net

📻 99.5 Sea FM, 639 AM ABC Far North QLD

Serene Palm Cove, north-west of Cairns, has white, sandy beaches and streets lined with palm trees. It is essentially a resort village, with locals and tourists alike soaking up the relaxed Far North atmosphere. The lifestyle is based around the water – fishing off the jetty, horseriding along the beach and swimming in the Coral Sea's crystal-clear blue water.

Reef tours: to Green Island and the Great Barrier Reef; depart Palm Cove jetty daily. *Day tours:* to Atherton Tableland and surrounds; details from visitor centre.

Palm Cove Fiesta: Oct.

Nu Nu Restaurant: award-winning Asian and Mediterranean fusion cuisine; 123 Williams Espl; (07) 4059 1880. *Reef House Restaurant:* modern Australian; The Sebel Reef House and Spa, 99 Williams Espl; (07) 4055 3633. *Vivo Bar and Grill:* colonial-style eatery, Italian influences; 45 Williams Espl; (07) 4059 0944.

Angsana Great Barrier Reef: world-renowned spa, absolute beach frontage; 1 Veivers Rd; (07) 4055 3000. *Peppers Beach Club & Spa:* luxury resort with rainforest lagoon pool; 123 Williams Espl; (07) 4059 9200 or 1300 987 600. *Sea Temple Resort & Spa:* contemporary Asian-style spa resort; 5 Triton St; (07) 4059 9600 or 1800 010 241. *The Sebel Reef House & Spa:* colonial-style architecture; 99 Williams Espl; (07) 4055 3633 or 1800 079 052.

Clifton Beach: resort village with park-lined beach and attractions such as Wild World, an interactive animal zoo, and Outback Opal Mine, with simulated mine and displays of Australia's most famous stone; 3 km s. *Hartley's Crocodile Adventures:* prides itself on the range of habitats that can be seen from extensive boardwalks and river cruises. Presentations include crocodile and snake shows and koala feeding; 15 km N. *Rex Lookout:* stunning coastal views; 17 km N.

See also CAIRNS & THE TROPICS, p. 425

Pomona

Pop. 1003
Map ref. 647 F1 | 648 E10 | 653 N7

ⓘ Railway Station Gallery, Station St; (07) 5485 2950.

📻 92.7 Mix FM, 612 AM ABC Brisbane

This small and relaxed farming centre is in the northern hinterland of the Sunshine Coast. Mount Cooroora rises 439 metres above the town. Each July mountain runners from around the world flock to attempt the base–summit and back again race, the winner being crowned King of the Mountain.

Majestic Theatre: authentic silent movie theatre with cinema museum and regular screenings; Factory St. *Noosa Shire Museum:* tribute to shire's past in old council chambers; Factory St. *Railway Station Gallery:* converted station featuring local art; open Tues–Sat; Station St.

Country market: Stan Topper Park; 2nd and 4th Sat each month. *King of the Mountain:* July. *Silent Movie Festival:* at the Majestic Theatre; Nov.

Noosa Avalon Cottages: peaceful rural retreat; 292 Pomona–Kin Kin Rd; (07) 5485 1959.

Boreen Point This sleepy town is on the shores of Lake Cootharba. The town features a 2.4 km walk from Teewah Land to Noosa's north shore beaches, and boardwalks into the surrounding wetlands. There are holiday cottages, and boat hire is available on Lake Cootharba. Try the many watersports on offer, including canoeing and kayaking. Windsurfing and yachting competitions are held here throughout the year. The lake is near where Mrs Eliza Fraser spent time with Aboriginal people after the wreck of Stirling Castle on Fraser Island in 1836; 19 km NE.

Cooroy: large residential area with excellent art gallery and cultural centre in the Old Butter Factory. The Noosa Botanical Gardens and Lake Macdonald are nearby; 10 km SE.

See also SUNSHINE COAST, p. 419

Port Douglas

Pop. 951
Map ref. 650 D1 | 651 D4 | 657 L5

ⓘ Call council offices, (07) 4099 9444; or Cairns & Tropical North Visitor Information Centre, 51 The Esplanade, Cairns, (07) 4051 3588; www.cairnsgreatbarrierreef.org.au

 106.3 Velvet Radio, 639 AM ABC Far North QLD

Port Douglas lies on the serene waters of a natural harbour in tropical North Queensland. Once a small village, it is now an international tourist destination. The town is surrounded by lush vegetation and pristine rainforests, and offers a village lifestyle with shops, galleries and restaurants. Its tropical mountain setting, the pristine Four Mile Beach and its proximity to the Great Barrier Reef make Port Douglas an ideal holiday destination. The drive from Cairns to Port Douglas is one of the most scenic coastal drives in Australia.

 Rainforest Habitat Wildlife Sanctuary This sanctuary covers an area of 2 ha and is home to over 1600 animals. Walk along the boardwalks through the 4 habitats of North Queensland – rainforest, wetlands, woodlands and grasslands. There are regular guided tours of the sanctuary, and the special daily events of Breakfast with the Birds and Habitat After Dark (runs July–Oct). Cnr Captain Cook Hwy and Port Douglas Rd.

Flagstaff Hill: commands excellent views of Four Mile Beach and Low Isles; end of Island Point Rd. *Dive schools:* details from visitor centre. *Great Barrier Reef tours:* over 100 operators offer reef tours to outer Great Barrier Reef and Low Isles; details from visitor centre. *Cane-toad racing:* nightly at 8.15pm; Ironbar pub, 5 Macrossan St.

 Market: Anzac Park; Sun. *Village Carnivale:* May.

 Balé: modern Italian with style; Peppers Balé Resort, 1 Balé Dr; (07) 4084 3000. *Nautilus Restaurant:* magical forest setting, whole coral trout is a highlight; 17 Murphy St; (07) 4099 5330. *Port O'Call Bar & Bistro:* affordable international fare; Port O'Call Eco Lodge, cnr Port St and Craven Cl; (07) 4099 5422. *Salsa Bar and Grill:* excellent food in a relaxed setting; 26 Wharf St; (07) 4099 4922.

 Macrossan House Boutique Holiday Apartments: comfortable apartments near good restaurants; 19 Macrossan St; (07) 4099 4366. *Peppers Balé Resort:* pavilion-style resort; 1 Balé Dr; (07) 4084 3000. *Port O'Call Eco Lodge:* high-standard budget accommodation; Cnr Port St and Craven Cl; (07) 4099 5422. *Sheraton Mirage Port Douglas Resort:* luxury on the beach; Davidson St; (07) 4099 5888 or 1800 073 535. *Thala*

Beach Lodge: secluded deluxe bungalows; Private Rd, Oak Beach; (07) 4098 5700.

 Tours: horseriding, sea-kayaking, rainforest tours, Lady Douglas paddlewheel cruises, 4WD safaris and coach tours to surrounding areas; details available from visitor centre.

See also CAIRNS & THE TROPICS, p. 425

Proserpine

Pop. 3314
Map ref. 649 E5 | 655 J4

ⓘ Whitsunday Information Centre, Bruce Hwy; (07) 4945 3711 or 1300 717 407; www.tourismwhitsundays.com.au

Proserpine is the inland sugar town and service centre of the Whitsunday Shire. It was named after the Roman goddess of fertility, Proserpina, for the rich and fertile surrounding lands.

 Historical Museum: local history dating back to settlement; closed weekends, open by appt; Bruce Hwy. *Cultural Centre:* displays local Aboriginal artefacts and has regular cinema screenings; Main St. *Pioneer Park and Mill Street Park:* beautiful spots with shady trees perfect for a picnic.

 Proserpine Show: June. *Harvest Festival:* includes the World Championship Cane Cutting event; Oct.

 Lake Proserpine at Peter Faust Dam: boat hire, waterskiing, fishing and swimming. The Cedar Creek Falls are nearby; 20 km NW on Crystalbrook Rd. *Conway National Park:* 28 km E; *see Airlie Beach. Midge Point:* coastal community and an ideal spot for bushwalking, fishing, crabbing and swimming; 41 km SE. *Crocodile safaris:* take a nature tour on an open-air tractor and cruise through mangrove river system on *Proserpine River;* bookings on (07) 4946 5111.

See also THE MID-TROPICS, p. 424

Quilpie

Pop. 563
Map ref. 663 L5

ⓘ Brolga St; (07) 4656 2166; www.quilpie.qld.gov.au

 104.5 FM Outback Radio 4VL, 603 AM ABC Western QLD

Quilpie is on the banks of the Bullo River in the outback's famous Channel Country. The town was established as a rail centre for the area's large sheep and cattle properties. Today it is better known as an opal town and, in particular, for the 'Boulder Opal'. The world's largest concentration of this opal is found in the area surrounding Quilpie. The town takes its name from the Aboriginal word 'quilpeta', meaning 'stone curlew'.

 Museum and gallery: historical and modern exhibitions; closed Sat–Sun from Oct–Mar; visitor centre, Brolga St. *St Finbarr's Catholic Church:* unique altar, font and lectern made from opal-bearing rock; Buln Buln St. *Opal sales:* various town outlets. *Lyn Barnes Gallery:* outback-inspired paintings; Brolga St.

 Kangaranga Doo: Aug/Sept. *Wool and Flower Show:* includes show and rodeo; Sept.

 Mariala National Park The park was formerly used to breed Cobb & Co horses in the early 1900s. It is remote with spectacular contrasts – the rich red earth mixed with green vegetation of mulga trees and shrubs. The threatened yellow-footed rock wallaby and pink cockatoo find refuge in this park. There are no formal walking trails. You can bush camp, but visitors must

QUEENSLAND

be self-sufficient. 4WD is recommended; roads may become impassable in the wet season. (07) 4654 1255; 130 km NE.

Lake Houdraman: popular watersports and recreation area; river road to Adavale; 6 km NE. *Baldy Top:* large geological formation with spectacular views; 6 km S. *Opal fields:* guided tours (no general access); details from visitor centre; 75 km W. *Toompine:* historic hotel, cemetery and designated opal-fossicking areas nearby; 76 km S. *Eromanga:* this place is reputedly Australia's furthest town from the sea. It features the Royal Hotel, once a Cobb & Co staging post, and holds a rodeo at Easter; 103 km W.

See also OUTBACK, p. 428

Ravenshoe
Pop. 914
Map ref. 650 D4 | 651 D12 | 657 L7

 24 Moore St; (07) 4097 7700; www.ravenshoevisitorcentre.com.au

97.9 Hot FM, 720 AM ABC Far North QLD

At 930 metres, Ravenshoe is the highest town in Queensland. Situated on the Atherton Tableland, it is surrounded by World Heritage rainforest, with 350 species of birds, 14 species of kangaroos and 12 species of possums. Once a town with a thriving logging industry, a new, alternative-lifestlye population has now developed.

Nganyaji Interpretive Centre: showcases the lifestyle of the local Jirrbal people, including hunting techniques and community life; Moore St. *Scenic train-ride:* heritage steam-train ride to nearby Tumoulin; details available from visitor centre.

Market: railway station; 4th Sun each month. *Torimba Garden Party:* Sept. *Torimba Festival:* includes Festival of the Forest and mardi gras; Oct.

Innot Hot Springs These natural thermal springs reputedly have healing powers. The spring water was originally bottled and sent to Europe as a healing remedy until the 1900s. 3 km E of the town is the Windy Hill Wind Farm. 32 km SW.

Millstream Falls National Park: enjoy the 1 km return walk past falls and rockpools to the Millstream Falls, the widest single-drop waterfall in Australia; (07) 4091 1844; 3 km SW. *Tully Falls:* walk 300 m to Tully Falls (in wet season) and the gorge; 25 km S. *Lake Koombooloomba:* popular spot for swimming, watersports, camping and fishing for barramundi; 34 km S. *Mount Garnet:* old tin-mining town with prospecting sites nearby; 47 km W.

See also CAIRNS & THE TROPICS, p. 425

Richmond
Pop. 554
Map ref. 661 L3

 Kronosaurus Korner, 91–93 Goldring St; (07) 4741 3429 or 1300 576 665; www.richmond.qld.gov.au

99.7 Rebel FM, 540 AM ABC Western QLD

This small town on the Flinders River in the Gulf Country serves the surrounding sheep and cattle properties. The town's main street is lined with beautiful bougainvilleas. In recent years Richmond has become the centre of attention as an area rich in marine fossils dating back around 100 million years, when outback Queensland was submerged under an inland sea.

Kronosaurus Korner This marine fossil museum has a renowned collection of vertebrate fossils, all found in the Richmond Shire. The museum and exhibition space holds more than 200 exhibits, including the 100-million-year-old armoured dinosaur Minmi, Australia's best-preserved dinosaur. There

is also an activity centre, children's discovery area and fossil preparation area where visitors can watch the palaeontologist at work. Guided museum tours, as well as tours to nearby fossicking sites with a palaeontologist, are available (groups of 10 or more, bookings essential). Goldring St; (07) 4741 3429.

Cobb & Co coach: beautifully restored coach with informative history display; Lions Park, Goldring St. *Gidgee Wheel Arts and Crafts:* local craft; Harris St. *Lake Fred Tritton:* recreational lake for waterskiing, picnics and walks. Enjoy the Richmond Community Bush Tucker Garden, which showcases beautiful native plants and was a finalist for the Banksia Environmental Awards; eastern outskirts. *Cambridge Store:* replica of the old Cambridge Downs Homestead from the late 1800s; contains memorablia and machinery from pioneer days; Goldring St. *Heritage walk:* follow the self-guide trail with informative history at each stop. It includes the historic flagstone and adobe building, Richmond Hotel, St John the Baptist Church and the Pioneer Cemetery; brochure available from visitor centre.

Fossil Festival: even-numbered years, Apr/May. *Richmond Great Outback Challenge:* sports carnival; odd-numbered years, Oct.

 Fossicking sites: guided tours to nearby areas; details from visitor centre.

See also OUTBACK, p. 428

Rockhampton
Pop. 68 832
Map ref. 655 M11

 Customs House, 208 Quay St; (07) 4922 5339; capricorntourism.com.au

98.5 4YOU FM, 837 AM ABC Capricornia

Rockhampton is a prosperous city that straddles the Tropic of Capricorn. It is known as the beef capital of Australia, with some 2.5 million cattle in the region. Quay Street is Australia's longest National Trust–classified streetscape, with over 20 heritage buildings set off by flowering bauhinia and brilliant bougainvilleas. Watch out for the bent-wing bat exodus in summer at Mount Etna, just north of the town, and the summer solstice light spectacular in early December to mid-January at the Capricorn Caves.

Mt Archer National Park On the north-east outskirts of Rockhampton in the Berserker Ranges, this park provides a backdrop to the city. Take a scenic drive up the mountain to Frazer Park for panoramic views. Explore the open forest and subtropical vegetation of the mountain on the 11 km walk from top to bottom. Be advised that the return trip is quite strenuous. Other shorter walks lead to scenic lookouts. Access to the summit is via Frenchville Rd; to the base via German St; (07) 4936 0511.

Botanic Gardens Set on the Athelstane Range, these heritage-listed gardens are over 130 years old. There are tropical displays, an orchid and fern house, a Japanese-style garden and the bird haven of Murray Lagoon. The city zoo has free entry and koala and lorikeet feedings at 3pm daily. Access via Spencer and Ann sts.

Customs House: this heritage building (1901) houses the visitor centre and 'Rockhampton Discovery Centre' exhibition, which introduces the visitor to the history, culture and lifestyle of Rockhampton; Quay St. *Archer Park Station and Steam Tram Museum:* interactive displays document the history of rail transport in Rockhampton. A fully restored Purrey Steam Tram operates 10am–1pm every Sun; closed Sat; Cnr Denison and Cambridge sts. *Kershaw Gardens:* follow the Australian native flora Braille Trail; Bruce Hwy. *Rockhampton City Art Gallery:* changing exhibitions featuring various well-known Australian artists such as Sidney Nolan; Victoria Pde. *Great Western Hotel:* operates weekly rodeos at an indoor arena; Stanley St. *Fitzroy River:* a great spot for watersports, rowing and fishing. A barrage in Savage St that separates tidal salt water from upstream fresh water provides opportunities for barramundi fishing. *Capricorn Spire:* marks the line of the Tropic of Capricorn; Curtis Park, Gladstone Rd. *Heritage walk:* self-guide trail around city centre; brochure available from visitor centre.

Garden Expo: Apr. *Beef Australia:* every 3 years, May. *Rocky Swap Meet:* Aug. *Big River Jazz:* Sept. *Rocky Barra Bounty:* Oct.

Coffee House Luxury Apartment Motel: right in the centre of town; Cnr William and Bolsover sts; (07) 4927 5722. *Henderson Park Farm Retreat:* 2 cabins beside a creek; 88 Barretts Rd, Barmoya; (07) 4934 2794.

Dreamtime Cultural Centre: displays on Aboriginal and Torres Strait Islander culture set on ancient tribal site. Guided tours available; open 10am–3.30pm Mon–Fri; 7 km N on Bruce Hwy. *Old Glenmore Historic Homestead:* National Trust–classified complex of historic buildings and displays; open by appt only; 8 km N. *Rockhampton Heritage Village:* heritage buildings with unusual Time after Time clock collection and Life before Electricity exhibition; Parkhurst; 9 km N. *St Christopher's Chapel:* open-air chapel built by American servicemen; Emu Park Rd; 20 km E. *Capricorn Caves:* guided tours and wild caving adventures through limestone cave system. Visit in Dec for Carols in the Caverns; 23 km N. *Mt Hay Gemstone Tourist Park:* thunder-egg fossicking and sales; 38 km W. *Capricorn Coast Scenic Loop tourist drive:* through coast and hinterland. *Great Keppel Island:* catch the cruise boat from Rosslyn Bay to visit the beautiful white sandy beaches and clear blue waters of the island; perfect spot for snorkelling and watersports.

See also CAPRICORN, p. 423

Roma

Pop. 5983
Map ref. 652 G6

Big Rig Visitor Information Centre, 2 Riggers Rd; (07) 4622 4355; www.romaregionalcouncil.qld.gov.au

101.7 4RRR FM, 711 AM ABC Western QLD

Roma is in the Western Downs region and was named after the wife of Queensland's first governor. Roma boasts a few historic 'firsts' for Queensland and Australia. In 1863 Samuel Symons Bassett brought vine cuttings to Roma and Queensland's first wine-making enterprise began – Romaville Winery is still running today. In the same year Captain Starlight faced trial in Roma for cattle stealing. Australia's first natural gas strike was at Hospital Hill in 1900. The excellent complex in town, The Big Rig, documents the oil and gas industry since this discovery.

The Big Rig This unique complex is set on an old oil derrick and features historic oil rigs and machinery displays. Photographs, memorabilia and multimedia displays provide a comprehensive history of oil and gas discovery and usage in Australia from 1900 to the present day. A highlight is the sound and light show on summer nights. Adjacent to the complex is a historic slab hut, recreational area and 1915 mini steam train that travels on a 1.4 km circuit. Riggers Rd.

Roma–Bungil Cultural Centre: a 3D mural by local artists depicting Roma's history; Cnr Bungil and Injune rds. *Heroes Avenue:* heritage-listed street of bottle trees commemorating local soldiers who died in WW I; Bungil St. *Romavilla Winery:* Queensland's oldest winery; Northern Rd.

RSL Market: RSL Hall; 1st Sun each month. *Easter in the Country:* Easter. *Picnic Races:* Apr. *Polocrosse Club Annual Carnival:* Aug. *Roma Cup:* Bassett Park; Nov. *Christmas Street Party:* Dec.

Carnarvon Gorge Wilderness Lodge: safari cabins near national park; via Rolleston; (07) 4984 4503.

Carnarvon National Park, Gorge section The Carnarvon Creek winds through the steep-sided Carnarvon Gorge, flanked by white sandstone cliffs. There are over 21 km of walks through rainforest to waterfalls and caves, and incredible Aboriginal rock art can be found throughout the park – see rock engravings, stencils and paintings at Cathedral Cave and the Art Gallery. The turn-off to the park is 199 km N on Carnarvon Developmental Rd; (07) 4984 4505. Mt Moffatt section: *see Mitchell.* Ka Ka Mundi section: *see Springsure.* Salvator Rosa section: *see Tambo.*

Roma Salesyard: largest inland cattle market in Australia with sales on Tues and Thurs; 4 km E. *Meadowbank Museum:* historic vehicle and machinery collection, and farm animals; 12 km W. *Surat:* large town featuring the Cobb & Co Changing Station Complex with museum, art gallery, aquarium and information centre. Visit the award-winning Villacoola Winery or go fishing for Murray cod on Balonne River; 78 km SE.

See also DARLING DOWNS, p. 418

St George

Pop. 2411
Map ref. 652 F9

Cnr The Terrace and Roe St; (07) 4620 8877; www.balonne.qld.gov.au

102.9 FM 4ROM, 711 AM ABC Western QLD

On the banks of the Balonne River is the Darling Downs town of St George. It is the last post in southern Queensland before the heavily populated east coast finally gives way to the sparseness of the outback. The river crossing was discovered by explorer Sir Thomas Mitchell on St George's Day, 1846, giving the town its name. St George is often referred to as the inland fishing capital of Queensland with lakes and rivers nearby, which also support the area's rich cotton, grape and grain industry.

Heritage Centre: historic buildings and a local history museum featuring Aboriginal display; Victoria St. *The Unique Egg:* carved, illuminated emu eggs; Balonne Sports Store; Victoria St. *Town murals:* around town, depicting scenes of St George's history. *Riversands Vineyard:* boutique winery on the banks of the Balonne River; Whytes Rd. *Jack Taylor Weir:* Sir Thomas Mitchell cairn commemorating the explorer's landmark crossing in 1846; western outskirts.

St George Show: with rodeo; May. *Boolba Wool and Craft Show:* May. *Horseracing:* July. *Nindigully Campdraft:* Sept. *Family Fishing Competition:* Sept. *Nindigully Country Music Spectacular:* includes pig races; Nov.

Beardmore Dam: popular spot for watersports and picnics in surrounding parklands. It offers excellent fishing for yellow-belly and Murray cod; 21 km N. *Moon Rocks Farm:* home to the

QUEENSLAND

famous melons, as well as other fresh produce grown on-site; 24 km SE. ***Ancient rock well:*** hand-hewn by Aboriginal people, possibly thousands of years ago; 37 km E. ***Nindigully:*** town where the film *Paperback Hero* was filmed. Historic 1864 hotel, as well as an annual bull ride and motorbike enduro; 44 km SE. ***Boolba:*** holds the impressive Boolba Wool and Craft Show each May; 50 km W. ***Rosehill Aviary:*** one of Australia's largest collections of native parrots; 64 km W. ***Begonia Historical Homesetad:*** grazing property with farmstay and museum; 73 km N. ***Thallon:*** small town with excellent swimming and fishing at Barney's Beach on the Moonie River. The nearby Bullamon homestead (1860), mentioned in Steele Rudd's *Memoirs of Corporal Keeley*, has original shingle roof and canvas ceilings; tours by appt (07) 4625 9217; 76 km SE. ***Bollon:*** large koala population in river red gums along Wallan Creek and a heritage and craft centre in George St; 112 km W. ***Thrushton National Park:*** undeveloped park of mulga scrub, sand plains and woodlands; access in dry weather only and 4WD recommended; (07) 4624 3535; 132 km NW. ***Culgoa Floodplain National Park:*** in the Murray–Darling basin, this park, with over 150 species of birds, is excellent for birdwatchers. There are no formal walking tracks and visitors must be self-sufficient. 4WD recommended; access via Brenda Rd, Goodooga; (07) 4654 1255; 200 km SW.

See also DARLING DOWNS, p. 418

Sarina
Pop. 3284
Map ref. 649 G8 | 655 K6

ⓘ Sarina Tourist Art and Craft Centre, Bruce Hwy; (07) 4956 2251; www.sarina.qld.gov.au

 93.5 Kids FM

Sarina is in the hinterland of what has been dubbed the Serenity Coast, at the base of the Connor Range. It is central to the Queensland sugar belt. To the east and south are fine beaches, many of which are renowned fishing spots.

 Sarina Sugar Shed: Australia's only fully operational miniature sugar mill and distillery. Take a tour and watch the complex process of turning sugar canes into granules. There are also multimedia presentations and a novelty shop on-site; closed Sun; Railway Sq. ***Sarina Tourist Art and Craft Centre:*** excellent variety of local art and craft as well as visitor centre; Bruce Hwy. ***'Field of Dreams' Historical Centre:*** local industry history and memorabilia; open 10am–2pm Tues, Wed and Fri; Railway Sq.

Market: showgrounds; last Sun each month. ***Mud Trials:*** buggy racing on a mud track; May. ***Scope Visual Arts Competition:*** May. ***Discover Sarina Festival:*** May.

 Cape Palmerston National Park This remote park features rugged coastal landscapes of headlands, swamps and sand dunes. Watch for the soaring sea eagles overhead or the birdlife around the swamp. There are spots for bush camping. The park has no official walking tracks, but the outlook from the cape is spectacular. 4WD recommended. (07) 4944 7800; 46 km SE via Ilbilbie.

Beaches: including Grasstree and Half Tide beaches to the north-east (Grasstree hosts annual bike race; date depends on tidal conditions); also Sarina Beach (east), popular for boating, fishing and swimming, with a lookout over the coast, and Armstrong Beach (south), great for swimming, prawning and fishing. ***Hay Point Lookout:*** viewing gallery at Hay Point and Dalrymple Bay coal terminal complex – informative video and excellent views; 12 km N. ***Salonika Beach:*** attractive beach with amazing wildlife, including loggerhead turtles and whales in season; adjacent to Hay Point Lookout. ***Lake Barfield:*** picnic area and bird sanctuary; 12 km N. ***Carmila:*** small town with beach just to the east. Visit the nearby Flaggy Rock Exotic Fruit Garden for delicious ice-cream; 65 km S. ***Clairview:*** popular spot for beach fishing and crabbing; 73 km S. ***St Lawrence:*** once a major port, this town is now a historical tribute to past days with many historic buildings and the remains of the wharf; 110 km S.

See also THE MID-TROPICS, p. 424

Springsure
Pop. 828
Map ref. 655 I12

ⓘ Information shed, Rolleston Rd; or call council offices, (07) 4984 1166.

 94.7 Hot FM, 1548 AM ABC Capricornia

Mount Zamia towers over Springsure, a small valley town in the Central Highlands, settled in the 1860s. Springsure's early history is dominated by conflicts between local Aboriginal groups and the intruding European settlers. The 1861 massacre of 19 Europeans at Cullin-la-ringo is commemorated at Old Rainworth Fort.

 Aboriginal Yumba-Burin (resting place): in Cemetery Reserve, containing 3 bark burials (around 600 years old). ***Rich Park Memorials:*** includes cattleyard displays and a Dakota engine from a plane that crashed during WW II. ***Historic Hospital:*** heritage-listed building (1868) includes museum.

 Horseracing: Mar. ***Springsure Show:*** May.

 Minerva Hills National Park The park includes the Boorambool and Zamia mountains and has unusual wildlife, such as the fawn-footed melomys, on a 2.2 km walking track to a spectacular lookout, or have a bush picnic at Fred's Gorge. (07) 4984 1716; 4 km W of Springsure, part of road unsealed.

Carnarvon National Park, Ka Ka Mundi section This remote section of the park is in Queensland's brigalow belt and features undulating plains and sandstone cliffs. See the king parrots and fig birds around the springs and creeks or the area's pastoral history at the old cattleyards near the springs. (07) 4984 1716; west on Springsure–Tambo Rd for 50 km, then south on Buckland Rd. Mt Moffatt section: *see Mitchell*. Gorge section: *see Roma*. Salvator Rosa section: *see Tambo*.

Old Rainworth Historical Complex: National Trust–listed buildings of old storehouse built after 1861 massacre; open 9am–2pm weekdays (closed Thurs), 9am–5pm Sat–Sun; 10 km S.

See also CAPRICORN, p. 423

Stanthorpe
Pop. 4268
Map ref. 551 A3 | 557 L2 | 653 K11

ⓘ 26 Leslie Pde; (07) 4681 2057 or 1800 060 877; www.granitebeltwinecountry.com.au

 90.1 Breeze FM, 747 AM ABC Southern QLD

Stanthorpe is the main town in the Granite Belt and mountain ranges along the border between Queensland and New South Wales. The town came into being after the discovery of tin at Quartpot Creek in 1872, but the mineral boom did not last. The climate is cool, said to be the coldest in Queensland, but the numerous wineries in the vicinity are welcoming. Visit in spring to see the fruit trees, wattles and wildflowers in bloom.

 Heritage Museum: displays the region's past in historic buildings, such as a schoolroom, gaol and shepherd's hut; closed Mon–Tues; High St. ***Regional Art Gallery:*** touring and local exhibitions; open Mon–Fri, Sat–Sun afternoons; Weeroona Park, Marsh St.

 Market in the Mountains: Cnr Marsh and Lock sts; 2nd and 4th Sun each month. *Apple and Grape Harvest Festival:* even-numbered years, 1st weekend in Mar. *Rodeo:* Mar. *Brass Monkey Season: winter festival;* June–Aug. *Primavera:* Sept–Nov. *Australian Small Winemakers Show:* Oct.

Vineyard Cafe: regional food and wine; New England Hwy, Ballandean; (07) 4684 1270.

Beverley Bush Cottages: 2 cottages and licensed restaurant; 25 Turner La, Severnlea; (07) 4683 5100. *Granite Gardens:* 3 cottages amid 2000 roses; 90 Nicholson Rd, Thorndale; (07) 4683 5161.

Granite Belt Wine Region Around Stanthorpe are over 40 boutique wineries open for tastings and sales. To the north, among others, are Old Caves Winery and Heritage Wines at Cottonvale; 12 km N. High-quality wineries are near Glen Aplin; 11 km SW. Ballandean, 21 km SW, features Golden Grove, Winewood, Bungawarra and Robinson's Family wineries. The Ballandean Estate holds Opera in the Vineyard in May and Jazz in the Vineyard in Aug/Sept. Brochure from visitor centre; bus tours available.

Girraween National Park The stunning granite and creek scenery is popular with bushwalkers. It is a remarkable Queensland park, not only for its cooler weather, but also because it is home to animals that are rarely seen in the tropical state, such as the common wombat. There is a variety of walks, from short to overnight hikes (taking in adjacent Bald Rock National Park). Of particular note is the 3 km return track to the Pyramid, which has panoramic views. Visit in spring to see the wildflower display. (07) 4684 5157 (same number for national parks below); turn-off 40 km S of Stanthorpe; further 8 km to park.

Mt Marlay: excellent views; 1 km E. *Storm King Dam:* popular spot for picnics, canoeing, waterskiing, and fishing for Murray cod and silver perch; 26 km SE. *Boonoo Boonoo National Park (NSW):* spectacular waterfall; 60 km SE. *Bald Rock National Park (NSW):* incredible granite rock formation (second biggest monolith in the world); 65 km SE. *Sundown National Park:* rugged national park of gorges and high peaks. Go birdwatching to see the herons and azure kingfishers along the river or take the short Red Rock Gorge Lookout Track for spectacular views; 80 km SW. *Heritage trail:* a historical drive tour of surrounding towns; brochure from visitor centre.

See also DARLING DOWNS, p. 418

 Strathpine
Pop. 9534
Map ref. 644 D5 | 645 D3 | 647 F10 | 653 N9

ℹ Pine Rivers Tourism Centre, Daisy Cottage, cnr Gympie and South Pine rds; (07) 3205 4793; www.brisbanehinterland.com

97.3 4B FM, 612 AM ABC Brisbane

Strathpine is north of Brisbane in the Pine Rivers region, a district that includes the forested areas and national parks closest to the capital. Taking advantage of this rural setting so close to the city are a number of art and craft industries.

Pine Rivers Festival: May.

Brisbane Forest Park This natural bushland forest park has a scenic drive from the south-east corner to lookouts, mountain

towns and attractive landscapes, ending at Lake Wivenhoe. There are many picnic spots – Jollys Lookout is a highlight, with views over Brisbane, the valley and north to the Glass House Mountains. A guide to the park's walks is available from the park headquarters at 60 Mt Nebo Rd, The Gap. Access via Ferny Hills.

Lake Samsonvale: fishing, watersports and bushwalking; 8 km NW. *Old Petrie Town:* heritage park that holds markets each Sun and the popular Twilight Markets 1st Fri each month (Jan–Oct) then every Fri (Nov–Dec). Catch the free bus from Petrie Railway Station; 9 km N. *Alma Park Zoo:* palm garden and subtropical rainforest zoo with native and exotic animals. Feed the koalas and explore the Friendship Farm for children; Alma Rd, Dakabin; 14 km N. *Australian Woolshed:* demonstrations of shearing, spinning and working sheepdogs; bush dances with bush band; Ferny Hills; 16 km SW. *Osprey House:* environmental centre; Dohles Rocks Rd; 18 km N. *Brisbane's Vineyard:* wine tastings and sales; Mt Nebo Rd, Mount Nebo; 46 km SW.

See also BRISBANE HINTERLAND, p. 415

Surfers Paradise
see inset box on next page

Tambo
Pop. 346
Map ref. 652 B2 | 663 P2

ℹ Council offices, Arthur St; (07) 4654 6133; www.tambo.qld.gov.au

100.3 Outback Radio 4LG FM, 603 AM ABC Western QLD

Tambo is the oldest town in central-western Queensland. It was established in the mid-1860s to service the surrounding pastoral properties, which it continues to do today. This long history can be seen in the heritage buildings on Arthur Street.

Old Post Office Museum: display of historic photographs; Arthur St. *Tambo Teddies Workshop:* produces popular all-wool teddies; Arthur St. *Coolibah Walk:* nature walk along banks of the Barcoo River.

Tambo Stock Show: Apr. *Day/Night Rodeo:* Oct. *Market Day:* Dec.

Carnarvon National Park, Salvator Rosa section One of the more remote sections of the park, Salvator Rosa is a perfect spot to escape the crowds. The attractive Nogoa River and Louisa Creek flow through the valley. See the spectacular rock formations, Belinda Springs and other natural attractions on the self-guide trail, which starts at the Nogoa River camping area. (07) 4984 4505; 130 km E. Mt Moffatt section: *see Mitchell.* Gorge section: *see Roma.* Ka Ka Mundi section: *see Springsure.*

Wilderness Way: a 420 km self-guide drive including Aboriginal rock art, historic European settlement sites and the Salvator Rosa section of the Carnarvon National Park. Check road conditions before departing; brochure available from council office.

See also OUTBACK, p. 428

Taroom
Pop. 626
Map ref. 653 I4

ℹ 17 Kelman St; (07) 4628 6113.

102.1 Rebel FM

Taroom is on the banks of the Dawson River in the Capricorn region. Since settlers took up land in 1845, cattle raising has been

QUEENSLAND

SURFERS PARADISE

Pop. 18 501

Map ref. 551 G1 | 557 O1 | 645 G10 | 646 F6 | 653 N10

i Gold Coast Tourism Bureau, Cavill Walk; (07) 5538 4419 or 1300 309 440; www.verygoldcoast.com.au

89.3 4CRB FM, 91.7 FM ABC Coast

Surfers Paradise is the Gold Coast's signature settlement – high-rise apartments fronting one of the state's most beautiful beaches. The first big hotel was built here in the 1930s, among little more than a clutch of shacks. Since then the area has become an international holiday metropolis, attracting every kind of visitor from backpacker to jetsetter.

Circle on Cavill: exciting new-generation shopping and leisure precinct with Circle Big Screen entertainment; access via Surfers Paradise Blvd, Cavill and Ferny Aves. *Orchid Avenue:* famous strip with the best live music in town. *Ripley's Believe It or Not:* the 12 galleries of amazing feats, facts and figures will surprise and amaze. There are interactive displays and movies that bring events to life; Raptis Plaza, Cavill Ave. *Haunted House:* from the creators of Dracula's world-famous cabaret, this walk-through attraction offers 5 levels of fright and a shop of horrors; Surfers Paradise Blvd. *Q1 Observation Deck:* the tallest residential building in the world, the Q1 Observation Deck gives breathtaking panoramic views from Brisbane to Byron Bay at 230m above sea level; Hamilton Ave. *Adventure activities and tours:* try surfing lessons or scenic flights to see Surfers Paradise in a new light or take a tour to the Gold Coast hinterland; contact visitor centre for details. *Minus 5 Ice Lounge:* Circle on Cavill. *Flycoaster and Bungee Rocket:* thrill rides; Cypress Ave. *Aquaduck Tours:* take an adventure on both land and water in this amphibious vehicle; departs Orchid Ave.

Surfers Paradise Markets: The Esplanade, between Hanlan St and Elkhorn Ave; every Wed and Fri evening. *Broadbeach Markets:* Kurrawa Park; 1st and 3rd Sun each month. *Lantern Market:* Broadbeach Mall; Fri nights May–Sept. *Farmers Market:* Marina Mirage Shopping Centre; 1st Sat each month. *Magic Millions Racing Carnival:* Jan. *Gold Coast Big Day Out:* Music festival; Jan. *Australian Beach Volleyball Championships:* Mar. *Blues on Broadbeach Music Festival:* May–June. *GC Bazaar:* month-long festival of fashion, food and fun; June. *Gold Coast Marathon:* July. *Tastes of the Gold Coast Festival:* Aug. *Tastes of Broadbeach Festival Food, Wine and Jazz Festival:* Aug. *Gold Coast Show:* Aug–Sept. *Gold Coast Eisteddfod:* Aug–Sept. *Go Xtreme Festival:* actions sports at the Mudgeeraba Showgrounds: Sept. *Gold Coast Indy 300:* Oct. *New Year's Eve fireworks:* Dec.

Absynthe: innovative French and Australian cuisine; Q1 Building, Surfers Paradise Blvd; (07) 5504 6466. *Chill on Tedder:* great seafood, delicious desserts; Shop 10/26 Tedder Ave, Main Beach; (07) 5528 0388. *Kurrawa Surf Club:* modern bistro; Old Burleigh Rd, Broadbeach; (07) 5538 0806. *Moo Moo The Wine Bar and Grill:* modern steakhouse; Broadbeach on the Park Resort, 2685 Gold Coast Hwy, Broadbeach; (07) 5539 9952. *Ristorante Fellini:* classic Italian fine dining; Marina Mirage, Sea World Dr, Main Beach; (07) 5531 0300.

Q1 Resort & Spa: world's tallest residential tower; Hamilton Ave; (07) 5630 4524 or 1300 792 008. *Surfers Paradise Marriott Resort & Spa:* excellent facilities throughout; 158 Ferny Ave; (07) 5592 9800. *Chevron Palms Resort:* good-value low-rise; 50 Stanhill Dr, Chevron Island; (07) 5538 7933. *Harbour Side Resort:* good value close to attractions; 132 Marine Pde, Southport; (07) 5591 6666. *Palazzo Versace:* world's first designer hotel; Sea World Dr, Main Beach; (07) 5509 8000 or 1800 098 000. *Sea World Resort:* park entry with accommodation packages; Sea World Dr, Main Beach; (07) 5591 0000.

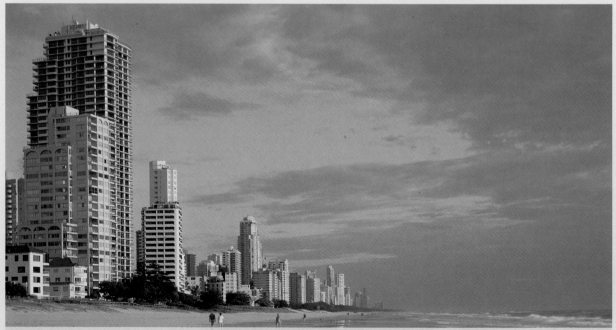

[HIGH-RISE BUILDINGS ALONG SURFERS PARADISE'S BEACHFRONT]

Sofitel Gold Coast: child-friendly and luxurious; 81 Surf Pde, Broadbeach; (07) 5592 2250 or 1800 074 465. ***Surfers Paradise YHA:*** dorms and doubles, no under 18s; 70 Sea World Dr, Main Beach; (07) 5571 1776. ***The Ritz Resort:*** desirable northern aspect; 8 Philip Ave, Broadbeach; (07) 5531 5185.

 Broadbeach The cosmopolitan heart of the Gold Coast has sophisticated wine bars, chic cafes, sun-drenched beaches and a vibrant nightlife. Visit Pacific Fair, Australia's largest shopping centre, hit the famous Conrad Jupiters Casino and try your luck at some blackjack, or stroll down to Kurrawa Beach, home of Australia's major surf lifesaving competition. 3 km s.

Main Beach This wealthy area just north of Surfers Paradise is awash with trendy boutiques and chic eateries. The Southport Spit Jetty, or The Spit as it's commonly known, is home to Sea World and the famous Palazzo Versace Hotel, as well as many specialty shops, restaurants, outdoor cafes and weekend entertainment at Marina Mirage and Mariner's Cove. It is also a hot spot for fishing while diving can be done at the nearby wreck of the *Scottish Prince*. 3 km N.

South Stradbroke Island This resort island boasts peaceful coves to the west and lively ocean beaches to the east, separated by wetland and remnant rainforest. See the abundant bird and butterfly species and discover the pleasures of windsurfing and sailing on either a daytrip or longer stay. Access by ferry or private boat from Runaway Bay Marina; 11 km N.

Theme parks The Gold Coast is the theme park capital of Australia, with 4 major theme parks in the Oxenford and Coomera areas. Warner Bros. Movie World is 'Hollywood on the Gold Coast' with thrilling rides, stunts and shows that will interest all ages. Just down the road is Wet 'n Wild Water World. Enjoy the thrill-seeking rides or relax on Calypso Beach. Further north is Dreamworld, which has a diverse range of attractions from The Giant Drop (the tallest free-fall in the world) to the famous *Big Brother* House. Next to Dreamworld is Whitewater World, which has the latest technology in water theme-park slides and is home to the 'world's best' water slide.

Gold Coast Arts Centre: art gallery incorporating contemporary and historical Australian art. Evandale sculpture walk nearby; Bundall Rd; 2 km w. ***Miami and Nobby beaches:*** both beaches are separated by a headland known as Magic Mountain. Miami is home to many diehard surfers; 6 km s. ***The Broadwater:*** sheltered waterways excellent for boating (hire available), watersports and shore walks; access from Labrador and Southport; 5 km N. ***Surfers Riverwalk:*** scenic 9 km walk from Sundale Bridge at Southport to Pacific Fair at Broadbeach. ***Sanctuary Cove:*** famous area for championship golf courses. Hire a houseboat or take a cruise; 23 km NW. ***High-speed racing:*** 3 professional circuit tracks to test the visitor's driving skills in V8 Supercars, Commodores and WRXs. Courses at Ormeau and Pimpama; Pacific Hwy towards Brisbane; 33 km NW.

See also GOLD COAST & HINTERLAND, p. 417

---

the main local industry. The coolibah tree in Taroom's main street was marked 'L. L.' by explorer Ludwig Leichhardt on his 1844 trip from Jimbour House near Dalby to Port Essington, north of Darwin.

 Museum: old telephone-exchange equipment, farm machinery and items of local history; open 9am–3pm Mon and Fri or by appt; Kelman St; (07) 4627 3231.

 Campdraft: Apr and Oct. ***Taroom Show:*** May. ***Rodeo:*** July.

 Expedition National Park This remote park features the 14 km Robinson Gorge. The 4 km return track leads to an excellent lookout. Only experienced walkers should attempt the rough track down into the gorge. The Cattle Dip Lookout overlooks a permanent waterhole reached via the 8 km return Shepherd's Peak Trail or from the carpark at the lookout. 4WD recommended; some of the road is gravel. (07) 4624 3535; 128 km NW.

Lake Palm Tree Creek: rare Livistona palms; 15 km N. ***Murphy Conservation Park:*** pristine lake with birdlife, and picnic and camping spots. It was the site of Leichhardt's campsite in 1844; 30 km N. ***Glebe Weir:*** waterskiing and fishing; 40 km NE. ***Wandoan:*** the local heritage trail in the town visits all the major sights, including the Waterloo Plain Environmental Park; brochure from visitor centre in Royd St; 59 km s. ***Scenic and historic drives:*** self-drive tours to nearby sights; brochure from visitor centre.

See also CAPRICORN, p. 423

Texas

Pop. 694

Map ref. 557 J3 | 653 J12

i Newsagency, 19 High St; (07) 4653 1384; texasqld4385.com.au

90.1 Breeze FM, 711 AM ABC Western QLD

Texas lies alongside the Dumaresq River (pronounced Du-meric) and the Queensland–New South Wales border. Its name comes from the similarity between an 1850s land dispute in the area to a dispute between the Republic of Texas and Mexico. The town was originally on the river flat, 2 kilometres from its current position. Severe floods forced the move. Remains of the original town can be seen on the river off Schwenke Street.

 Heritage Centre and Tobacco Museum: located in the old police building (1893), with memorabilia that shows 100 years of the tobacco industry, as well as horse-drawn vehicles, mini shearing shed and the gaol; open Sat or by appt; Fleming St; (07) 4653 1410. ***Art Gallery:*** local and touring art exhibitions; open Tues–Sat; High St. ***Riverside Freezing and Rabbit Works:*** interpretive display on the rabbit skins factory and Aboriginal artefacts; open by appt; Mingoola Rd; (07) 4653 1453.

 Heritage Centre Markets: Heritage Centre; 1st Sat in June and Dec. ***Texas Show:*** July. ***Country Music Roundup:*** Sept. ***Horseracing:*** Dec.

 Beacon Lookout: regional views; 3 km SE on Stanthorpe Rd. ***Cunningham Weir:*** site where Allan Cunningham crossed

QUEENSLAND

 RADIO STATIONS IN TOWN WHAT'S ON WHERE TO EAT WHERE TO STAY NEARBY

the Dumaresq River in 1827; 31 km w off Texas–Yelarbon Rd. *Glenlyon Dam:* excellent fishing spot; 45 km se. *Inglewood:* Texas's twin town at the centre of Australia's olive industry. Visit Inglewood Heritage Centre for local memorabilia (open 2nd and last Sat each month or by appt). Tour the local olive groves and follow the scenic drives in area; brochure available; 55 km n. *Coolmunda Reservoir:* picnics, boating and fishing; 75 km ne via Inglewood. *Dumaresq River:* winding river popular for canoeing and fishing, and hiking through wilderness areas along its banks.

See also Darling Downs, p. 418

Theodore

Pop. 442
Map ref. 653 I3

i The Boulevard; (07) 4993 1900.

 96.5 Sea FM, 855 AM ABC Wide Bay

Theodore, first called Castle Creek, was the site of Queensland's first irrigation project, opened in 1924. With its rich black soils, the town is surrounded by pastoral and grazing properties, with sheep, cattle, sorghum, wheat and cotton. Located on the Dawson River, irrigation has resulted in palm-lined streets and a tropical air. The town was named after Edward (Red Ted) Theodore, union leader then Queensland premier from 1919 to 1925.

Theodore Hotel: only cooperative hotel in Queensland; The Boulevard. *Dawson Folk Museum:* provides local history; open by appt; Second Ave; (07) 4993 1686.

Fishing Competition: Mar. *Theodore Show:* May.

Isla Gorge National Park This highland park has gorges and spectacular rock formations. The camping area overlooks the gorge and a 2 km return walk leads to the Isla Gorge Lookout. If staying overnight, watch the changing colours of the sandstone cliffs as the sun sets. (07) 4627 3358; turn-off 35 km s.

Theodore Weir: popular spot for fishing; southern outskirts of town. *Moura:* major cattle town that holds the annual Coal and Country Festival in Aug; 48 km nw. *Cracow:* where gold was produced from famous Golden Plateau mine 1932–76; 49 km se.

See also Capricorn, p. 423

Tin Can Bay

Pop. 1920
Map ref. 648 F8 | 653 N6

i Cooloola Regional Information Centre, Matilda's Roadhouse Complex, Bruce Hwy, Kybong (15 km s of Gympie); (07) 5483 5554 or 1800 444 222; www.tincanbaytourism.org.au

 96.1 Zinc FM, 855 AM ABC Wide Bay

Tin Can Bay is a well-known fishing and prawning region northeast of Gympie. It was originally known as Tuncanbar to the local Aboriginal people. The town is a relaxing hamlet offering watersports on the quiet waters of Tin Can Bay inlet.

Environmental Walkway: a 9.5 km trail for birdwatching on the Tin Can Bay foreshore. *Boat and yacht hire:* cruise the inlet and Sandy Strait; Tin Can Bay Marina. *Canoeing:* eco-tours down estuaries; (07) 5486 4417. *Norman Point boat ramp:* see the dolphins up-close before 10am; access point to waterways.

Yacht Race: May. *War Birds:* model planes and helicopters; May. *Seafood Festival:* Sept.

Rainbow Beach This relaxing coastal town to the east across the inlet offers a pristine sandy beach popular with surfers. The Family Fishing Classic is held here each July. For adventure, try paragliding from the Carlo Sand Blow; bookings on (07) 5486 3048. Tours include dolphin ferry cruises, safaris and 4WD tours. The road south (4WD) leads to the coloured sands and beaches of the Cooloola section of Great Sandy National Park; *see Noosa Heads.* Rainbow Beach is 41 km e by road.

Carlo Point: great for fishing and swimming. There is also boat access to the inlet, with houseboats and yachts available for hire; 43 km e via Rainbow Beach. *Inskip Point:* camp along the point or take the car ferry to Fraser Island; 53 km ne via Rainbow Beach.

See also Sunshine Coast, p. 419

Townsville

see inset box on next page

Tully

Pop. 2459
Map ref. 650 E6 | 657 M8

i Bruce Hwy; (07) 4068 2288.

 90.3 Kool FM, 630 AM ABC North QLD

At the foot of Mount Tyson, Tully receives one of the highest annual rainfalls in Australia – around 4200 millimetres. This abundance of rain supports swift rapids on the Tully River – an attraction for any whitewater-rafting enthusiast. The area was settled in the 1870s by a family keen on growing sugarcane, and the town grew when the government decided to build a sugar mill in 1925. Sugarcane remains a major industry.

Tully Sugar Mill: informative tours in the crushing season (approximately June–Nov); tickets from the visitor centre. *Golden Gumboot:* 7.9 m high gumboot erected to celebrate Tully as Australia's wettest town.

Tully Show: July. *Golden Gumboot Festival:* Sept.

Tully Gorge Alcock State Forest This state forest incorporates the Tully Gorge and the raging waters of the Tully River. Visit the Frank Roberts Lookout for gorge views, take the Rainforest Butterfly Walk and visit the Cardstone Weir boardwalk in the afternoons to watch rafters negotiate the rapids. Head to the top reaches of the river for superb scenery and swimming. Visit in dry season only (May–Dec); 40 km w.

Alligator's Nest: beautiful rainforest with swimming in stream; 10 km s. *Tully Heads:* estuary and beachside fishing; separated from Hull Heads by Googorra Beach; 22 km se. *Echo Creek Walking Trail:* take this guided trail through rainforest, walking a traditional Aboriginal trading route with Jirrba guides; turn-off after Euramo; 30 km sw. *Murray Upper State Forest:* rainforest walks to cascades, rockpools and Murray Falls; turn-off 38 km s. *Misty Mountains walking trails:* day walks or longer (up to 44 km) in Wet Tropics World Heritage Area; details from visitor centre. *Whitewater rafting:* operators run from Tully to the renowned rapids of the Tully River; details from visitor centre.

See also Cairns & The Tropics, p. 425

Warwick

Pop. 12 564
Map ref. 551 B1 | 557 L1 | 653 L10

i 49 Albion St (New England Hwy); (07) 4661 3122; www.southerndownsholidays.com.au

 89.3 Rainbow FM, 747 AM ABC Southern QLD

Warwick is an attractive city set alongside the willow-shaded Condamine River. It is known as the 'Rose and Rodeo City', as the Warwick Rodeo dates back to the 1850s, and the parks and

TOOWOOMBA

Pop. 114 479
Map ref. 653 L9

 86 James St; (07) 4639 3797 or 1800 331 155; www.toowoombaholidays.info

100.7 CFM, 747 AM ABC Southern QLD

Toowoomba is a city with a distinctive charm and graciousness in its wide, tree-lined streets, colonial architecture and over 240 parks and gardens. The city is perched 700 metres above sea level on the rim of the Great Dividing Range. It began in 1849 as a small village near an important staging post. It is now the commercial centre for the fertile Darling Downs where visitors are captivated by the mild summers, crisp leafy autumns and vibrant springs.

Cobb & Co Museum The museum traces the history of horse-drawn vehicles in the Darling Downs region. It has an excellent collection of carriages, from old wagons to Cobb & Co coaches. The museum has expanded to include exhibits depicting the settlement history of the Downs and Aboriginal history. There is also an interactive discovery centre for children. Lindsay St; (07) 4639 1971.

Parks and gardens No trip to the 'Garden City' would be complete without a visit to some of the superb parks and gardens. Lake Annand is a popular recreation spot with boardwalks, bridges and ducks; MacKenzie St. There are imposing European trees in Queen's Park, which also includes the Botanic Gardens; Lindsay and Margaret sts. Laurel Bank Park features the unique Scented Garden, designed for the visually impaired; cnr Herries and West sts. Birdwatchers should visit Waterbird Habitat where native birds can be watched from observation platforms and floating islands; MacKenzie and Alderley sts. The impressive Japanese Garden, at the University of Southern Queensland, is the largest in Australia; off West St.

Regional Art Gallery: changing exhibitions in Queensland's oldest gallery; open 10am–4pm Tues–Sat, 1–4pm Sun; Ruthven St. *Royal Bull's Head Inn:* National Trust–listed building (1859); open Wed–Sun or by appt; Brisbane St, Drayton. *Empire Theatre:* live theatre in this restored Art Deco building, opened in 1911; Neil St. *Picnic Point:* offers views of Lockyer Valley, mountains and waterfall. Enjoy the recreational facilities and walks through bushland. Perfect venue for Music in the Park concerts during summer; Tourist Dr, eastern outskirts. *City tour:* self-guide drive to major city attractions, starting at visitor centre; brochure available from visitor centre.

Markets: Wilsonton Shopping Centre and PCYC James St, Sun; Queen's Park, 3rd Sun each month. *Toowoomba Royal Show:* Mar. *Easterfest:* music festival; Easter. *Carnival of Flowers:* Sept.

Spotted Cow Hotel: European beers and food; 296 Ruthven St; (07) 4639 3264. *Veraison:* modern Australian, good wine list; 205 Margaret St; (07) 4638 5909. *Weis:* legendary smorgasbord; 2 Margaret St; (07) 4632 7666.

James Cottage B&B: 2 ensuite rooms in Federation-style home; 128 James St; (07) 4637 8377. *Quality Hotel Platinum International:* modern hotel; 326 James St; (07) 4634 0400 or

[COBB & CO MUSEUM]

1800 880 310. *Vacy Hall:* National Trust mansion; 135 Russell St; (07) 4639 2055.

Highfields: growing town featuring Orchid Park, Danish Flower Art Centre and Historical Village with vintage machinery and buildings; 12 km N. *Cabarlah:* small community that has the Black Forest Hill Cuckoo Clock Centre and holds excellent country markets on the last Sun each month; 19 km N. *Southbrook:* nearby Prestbury Farm offers accomodation and the experience of rural life; 34 km SW. *Lake Cooby:* fishing, walking and picnic facilities; 35 km N. *Pittsworth:* in town is the Pioneer Historical Village featuring a single-teacher school, early farming machinery and a display commemorating Arthur Postle, or the 'Crimson Flash', once the fastest man in the world; village open 10am–1pm Tues, Wed, Thurs and Sun or by appt; (07) 4693 1660; 46 km SW. *Yandilla:* here you'll find the quaint, steeped All Saints Anglican Church (1877), the oldest building in the shire; 77 km SW. *Millmerran:* colourful murals illustrate the history of this industrial town, including the dairy industry mural at the Old Butter Factory, and the mural on the water reservoir showing the development of transport. The town's historical museum is open Tues–Thurs; 87 km SW. *Scenic drives:* take in places such as Spring Bluff, with old railway station and superb gardens (16 km N), Murphys Creek, Heifer Creek and the Valley of the Sun; brochure available from visitor centre.

See also DARLING DOWNS, p. 418

 RADIO STATIONS   IN TOWN   WHAT'S ON   WHERE TO EAT   WHERE TO STAY   NEARBY

TOWNSVILLE

Pop. 143 329

Map ref. 649 A1 | 650 G10 | 654 G1 | 657 N11

i Bruce Hwy, (07) 4778 3555 or 1800 801 902; or
The Mall Information Centre, Flinders Mall, (07) 4721 3660;
www.townsvilleholidays.info

106.3 Mix FM, 630 AM ABC North QLD

Despite Townsville being Australia's largest tropical city, it
has retained the relaxed tropical atmosphere of its smaller
counterparts. In 1864 sea captain Robert Towns commissioned
James Black to establish a settlement on Cleveland Bay to service
the new inland cattle industry. The many historic buildings found
around Cleveland Bay are a reminder of this heritage. The city's
proximity to the Great Barrier Reef has allowed Townsville to be
increasingly recognised as a centre for research into marine life.
The foreshore also caters for more cosmopolitan tastes with The
Strand's blend of cafes and restaurants combined with tropical
parks and spectacular views to Magnetic Island.

Reef HQ Home to the headquarters for the Great Barrier
Reef Marine Park Authority, this underwater observatory is both
informative and visually breathtaking. Its living reef is the largest
'captive' reef in the world. Get up-close at the touch pools or
see marine feeding and dive shows. Open 9.30am–5pm daily;
Flinders St East.

Museum of Tropical Queensland: featuring artefacts from
wreck of HMAS *Pandora*; Flinders St East. *North Queensland
Military Museum:* displaying military artefacts; open 9am–12pm
Mon, Wed and Fri, 10am–2pm Sun; Kissing Point. *Maritime
Museum:* maritime items of historical significance; Palmer St.
Rock Pool Baths: year-round swimming; The Strand. *Perc Tucker
Regional Art Gallery:* local and touring exhibitions; Flinders
Mall. *Botanic Gardens:* Anderson Park, Kings Rd. *Imax Dome*

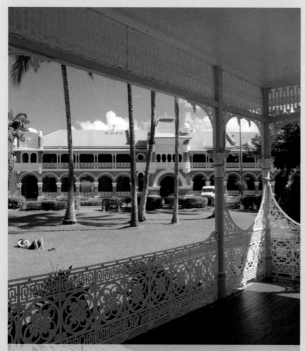

[TROPICAL GARDENS OUTSIDE THE OLD QUEENS HOTEL,
THE STRAND]

Theatre: excellent viewing experience in this theatre, the first
of its kind in the Southern Hemisphere; Flinders St East. *Town
Common Conservation Park:* a coastline park with prolific
birdlife, Aboriginal Plant Trail and forest walks; Pallarenda Rd.
Castle Hill Lookout: off Stanley St. *Jupiters Townsville Hotel and
Casino:* Sir Leslie Thiess Dr. *Ferry Terminal:* for Magnetic Island,
and daytrips and dive cruises to the Great Barrier Reef as well as
extended cruises to the Whitsundays; Flinders St. *Coral Princess:*
cruise to Cairns via resort islands and reef on a luxury catamaran;
contact visitor centre for details. *Adventure activities:* numerous
tour operators offer jetskiing, waterskiing, abseiling, whitewater
rafting and more; contact visitor centre for details. *Dive schools:*
contact visitor centre for details.

Showground Market: Sun. *Cotters Market:* Flinders Mall;
Sun. *Horseshoe Bay Market:* Beachside Park, Magnetic Island; last
Sun each month. *Opal Fashion Bash:* Apr. *Italian Festival:* May.
Townsville Show: June. *Australian Festival of Chamber Music:*
July/Aug. *Townsville Cup:* horseracing; July (weather permitting).
Palmer Street Jazz Festival: Aug. *Greek Festival:* Oct.

Michel's Restuarant: international fare; 7 Palmer St;
(07) 4724 1460. *Watermark:* seafood and steaks; 72–74 The
Strand; (07) 4724 4281.

Jupiters Townsville Hotel and Casino: 4.5-star hotel; Sir
Leslie Thiess Dr; (07) 4722 2333 or 1800 079 210. *Balgal Beach
Holiday Units:* simple beachside units; 284 Ocean Pde; Balgal
Beach; (07) 4770 7296. *Hidden Valley Cabins:* carbon-neutral
resort; Pine Creek Rd, Hidden Valley; (07) 4770 8088 or
1800 466 509.

Magnetic Island Over half of this beautiful island is covered
by the Magnetic Island National Park. The sandy beaches, granite
headlands and hoop pine rainforest make this an attractive
daytrip, or stay overnight in the private accommodation on offer.
See the natural attractions by taking some of the many walks
around the island or hire a bike for a different view. Snorkel and
swim at Sandy Bay and see spectacular views from the old
WW II forts. Access the island from Townsville by Fast Ferry,
vehicle barge or passenger ferry. 8 km NE.

Bowling Green Bay National Park This coastal park offers much
for the self-sufficient visitor. Granite mountains blend with a
variety of landscapes including saltpans and mangrove country.
Walk along Alligator Creek to see cascades and waterfalls. Stay
overnight at the Alligator Creek campsite and go spotlighting to
glimpse brush-tail possums and sugar gliders. (07) 4722 5224;
turn-off Bruce Hwy 28 km SE; park is further 6 km.

Billabong Sanctuary: covering 10 ha of rainforest, eucalypt forest
and wetlands. See koala feeding and crocodile shows. Bruce Hwy;
17 km SE. *Giru:* small community with waterfalls, bushwalks and
swimming nearby; 50 km SE.

See also THE MID-TROPICS, p. 424

gardens have an abundance of roses. There is even a red rose cultivated especially for Warwick – the City of Warwick Rose (or Arofuto Rose). The area was explored by Allan Cunningham in 1827, and in 1840 the Leslie brothers established a sheep station at Canning Downs. Warwick was eventually established in 1849 on the site that Patrick Leslie selected. The surrounding pastures support famous horse and cattle studs.

 Australian Rodeo Heritage Centre: follow the history and relive the glory of the Australian Professional Rodeo Association's greatest champions; open 10am–3pm Mon–Sat or by appt; Alice St. **Pringle Cottage:** historic home (1870) housing large historic photo collection, vehicles and machinery; closed Mon–Tues; Dragon St. **Warwick Regional Art Gallery:** local and touring exhibitions; closed Mon; Albion St. **Jubilee Gardens:** see the displays of roses that Warwick is famous for; Cnr Palmerin and Fitzroy sts. **Lookout:** viewing platform for regional views; Glen Rd. **Historic walk or drive:** self-guide tour of historic sandstone buildings dating from the 1880s and 1890s; brochure from visitor centre.

Rock Swap Festival: Easter. **Jumpers and Jazz:** July. **Campdraft and Rodeo:** Oct.

Spicers Peak Lodge Restaurant: up-market modern Australian; Wilkinsons Rd, Maryvale; (07) 4666 1083 or 1300 773 452.

Coachman's Inn Warwick: modern suites and apartments; 91 Wood St; (07) 4660 2100. **Spicers Peak Lodge:** small luxury resort; Wilkinsons Rd, Maryvale; (07) 4666 1083 or 1300 773 452.

 Leslie Dam: watersports, fishing and swimming; 15 km w. **Main Range National Park:** 61 km NE; *see Boonah and Killarney*. **Heritage drive:** 80 km cultural drive in region; brochure from visitor centre.

See also DARLING DOWNS, p. 418

Weipa

Pop. 2832
Map ref. 658 B7

ℹ️ Evans Landing; (07) 4069 7566.

📻 100.9 KIG FM, 1044 AM ABC Far North QLD

This coastal part of Cape York was reputedly the first area in Australia to be explored by Europeans (1605). The town of Weipa was built in 1961 on the site of a mission station and Aboriginal reserve, and is now home to the world's largest bauxite mine. Although the town is remote, it offers a full range of services for travellers.

 Western Cape Cultural Centre This centre was established to introduce the visitor to the culture of western Cape York. The range of artefacts and photos bring the area's Indigenous and European history alive. A highlight is the ceramic wall mural depicting sacred images of the local Aboriginal people. There is also information about the landscapes and ecosystems of the Cape, and sales of local arts and crafts. Open 10am–3pm daily; Evans Landing; (07) 4069 7566.

Tours of bauxite mine: guided tours provide insight into the mining process at Weipa; details from visitor centre. **Fishing tours:** Weipa's fishing spots can be explored on tours; details from visitor centre. **Boat and houseboat hire:** details from visitor centre.

Fishing Competition: June. **Bullride:** Aug.

Thursday Island and the Torres Strait The islands of the Torres Strait stretch from the tip of Cape York Peninsula to Papua New Guinea and comprise 17 inhabited islands. The first Europeans passed through the Islands in the 1600s, and by the late 1800s a pearling industry was established, which continues today along with crayfishing, prawning and trochus industries. Thursday Island is the administrative centre. Visit the Torres Strait Island Cultural Centre – it preserves the cultural heritage of the islands and documents their art, culture, geography and history in an excellent interpretive display. Other surrounding islands worth a visit are Friday Island where you can see pearls being cultivated at Kazu; Horn Island, which was an important posting for Australian Troops in WW II; and Badu Island, where you can enjoy traditional dances, arts and crafts and food. Getting to the Islands involves either a flight from Cairns, a trip on a cargo vessel from Cairns (through Seaswift, (07) 4035 1234), or a ferry ride from Cape York (through Peddells, (07) 4069 1551).

Jardine River National Park This remote park is on the north-east tip of Cape York Peninsula. It was known to early explorers as the 'wet desert' because of its abundant waterways, but lack of food. These waters attract varied birdlife including the rare palm cockatoo. See the Fruit Bat Falls from the boardwalk or fish in restricted areas. 4WD access only. Visit between May–Oct; off Peninsula Development Rd, south of Bamaga; (07) 4069 5777.

Fishing and camping: a number of areas developed for the well-equipped visitor. **Mungkan Kandju National Park:** wilderness park of open forests, swamps and dense rainforest. There is excellent birdlife around lagoons and bushwalking along Archer River. 4WD access only; visit between May–Nov; (07) 4060 1137; turn-off 29 km N of Coen. **Mapoon:** camping and scenery; permit required; 85 km N. **Iron Range National Park:** this important lowland tropical rainforest park is a haven for wildlife. There is good fishing at Chili Beach, and bush camping for self-sufficient visitors only. 4WD recommended; visit only between Apr–Sept; (07) 4060 7170; 216 km E.

Travellers note: *Roads to the Cape may become impassable during the wet season (Nov–Apr). Motorists are advised to check the RACQ Road Conditions Report on 1300 130 595 (or www.racq.com.au) before departing. Permits for travel over Aboriginal land can be sought in Weipa; details from visitor centre. Beware of crocodiles in rivers, estuaries and coastal areas. Also beware of marine stingers in coastal areas (Oct–Apr) and swim within enclosures where possible.*

See also CAPE YORK, p. 426

Winton

Pop. 983
Map ref. 661 L7

ℹ️ Waltzing Matilda Centre, 50 Elderslie St; (07) 4657 1466; www.matildacentre.com.au

📻 95.9 West FM, 540 AM ABC Western QLD

The area surrounding Winton is known as Matilda Country, as Australia's most famous song, *Waltzing Matilda*, was written by Banjo Paterson at nearby Dagworth Station in 1895. Combo Waterhole (near Kynuna) was the setting for the ballad and the tune had its first airing in Winton. A less auspicious event in Winton's history was the declaration of martial law in the 1890s following the Shearers' Strike. In 1920 the first office of Qantas was registered here. The town's water supply comes from

QUEENSLAND

deep artesian bores at a temperature of 83°C. The movie *The Proposition* was filmed in the town in 2004.

Waltzing Matilda Centre Created as a tribute to the life of the swagman. The centre incorporates the 'Billabong Courtyard' with its sound and light show, the regional art gallery, interactive exhibits showcasing the swagmans life in 'Home of the Legend' hall, and the Matilda Museum that harks back to Winton's pioneering days and the first days of Qantas. Elderslie St; (07) 4657 1466.

Royal Theatre: historic open-air movie theatre and museum, one of the oldest still operating in Australia; Elderslie St. *Corfield and Fitzmaurice Store:* charming National Trust–listed store with diorama of Lark Quarry dinosaur stampede; Elderslie St. *Gift and Gem Centre:* displays and sales; the 'Opal Walk' leads to the theatre museum; Elderslie St. *Arno's Wall:* ongoing concrete-wall creation proudly containing 'every item imaginable'; Vindex St. *North Gregory Hotel:* built in 1878, this historical structure has been ravaged by 3 separate fires. Artwork and opal collection on display; Elderslie St.

Winton Show: June. *Opal Expo:* July. *Camel Races:* July. *Rodeo:* Aug. *Outback Festival:* odd-numbered years, Sept.

North Gregory Hotel Motel: family friendly; 67 Elderslie St; (07) 4657 1375.

Lark Quarry Conservation Park This park features the preserved tracks of a dinosaur stampede from 93 million years ago – the only track of this type known in the world. The stampede occurred when a Therapod chased a group of smaller dinosaurs across the mud flats. The 'trackways' are sheltered and can be visited on a tour (details from visitor centre). The park also offers a short walk past ancient rock formations, known as the Winton Formation, to a lookout over the region. 110 km sw.

Bladensburg National Park The vast plains and ridges of this park provide an important sanctuary for a variety of wildlife, including kangaroos, dunnarts and emus. Skull Hole (40 km s) has Aboriginal paintings and bora ceremonial grounds and is believed to be the site of a late-1880s Aboriginal massacre. Walking should only be attempted by experienced bushwalkers. 'Route of the River Gums', a self-drive tour, shows the region's varied landscapes. (07) 4652 7333; drive starts 8 km s.

Carisbrooke Station: a working sheep station with Aboriginal cave paintings and scenic drives in the surrounds; day tours and accommodation available; 85 km sw. *Opalton:* see the remains of the historic town or try fossicking for opals in one of the oldest fields in Queensland; licence available from visitor centre; 115 km s. *Air charters and ground tours:* to major regional sights; details from visitor centre.

See also OUTBACK, p. 428

Yandina
Pop. 1078
Map ref. 647 F3 | 648 E11 | 653 N7

ℹ Yandina Historic House, 3 Pioneer Rd (at the roundabout); (07) 5472 7181.

📻 90.3 AM ABC Coast FM, 91.1 Hot FM

Yandina is in the Sunshine Coast hinterland north of Nambour. The first land claims in the area were made here in 1868. It is now home to The Ginger Factory, the largest of its kind anywhere, giving rise to Yandina's title of 'Ginger Capital of the World'.

The Ginger Factory This award-winning complex is devoted to everything ginger. Visitors can see Gingertown, watch ginger-cooking demonstrations, see ginger being processed and ride on the historic Queensland Cane Train through subtropical gardens with acres of tropical plants, water features and a plant nursery – a highlight are the stunning flowering gingers. Pioneer Rd.

Yandina Historic House: local history display, arts and crafts, art gallery and visitor centre; Pioneer Rd. *Nutworks Macadamia Processes:* see processing of macadamia nuts and taste-test the results; opposite The Ginger Factory. *Fairhill Native Plants and Botanic Gardens:* fabulous nursery and gardens – a must for any native-plant buff; also includes the excellent Elements Restaurant, with breakfast, lunch and afternoon tea in botanic garden setting; Fairhill Rd. *Heritage trail:* self-guide trail around town sights; brochure from visitor centre.

Market: town centre; Sat. *Ginger Flower Festival:* Jan.

Spirit House: superb Thai food; 20 Ninderry Rd, Yandina; (07) 5446 8994.

Ninderry House: 3 ensuite rooms; 8 Karnu Dr; (07) 5446 8556. *Ninderry Manor Luxury Retreat:* 3 guest rooms, hosts are qualified masseurs; 12 Karnu Dr; (07) 5472 7255.

Eumundi This historic town has a variety of excellent galleries to visit, including some with Indigenous Australian art. Also sample exquisite handcrafted chocolates at Cocoa Chocolate, all made on-site (Etheridge St); or browse through the maze of shelves at Berkelouw Books in the main street. The impressive country markets are renowned for their size with over 600 stalls. The quality of the fresh produce, art and craft and cut flowers, along with the wonderful atmosphere, brings visitors to the town each Wed and Sat, and on Thurs night Dec–Jan; 10 km N.

Wappa Dam: popular picnic area; west of Yandina. *Yandina Speedway:* offers a variety of motor races; call (07) 5446 7552 for details; just west on Wappa Falls Rd.

See also SUNSHINE COAST, p. 419

Yeppoon
Pop. 13 282
Map ref. 655 M10

ℹ Capricorn Coast Tourist Information Centre, Scenic Hwy; (07) 4939 4888 or 1800 675 785; www.capricorncoast.com.au

📻 91.3 FM Radio Nag

The popular coastal resort of Yeppoon lies on the shores of Keppel Bay. Yeppoon and the beaches to its south – Cooee Bay, Rosslyn Bay, Causeway Lake, Emu Park and Keppel Sands – are known as the Capricorn Coast. Great Keppel Island Resort lies 13 kilometres offshore and is a popular holiday destination offering great swimming, snorkelling and diving.

The Esplanade: attractive strip of shops, galleries and cafes overlooking parkland and crystal-clear water. *Doll and Antiquity Museum:* Hidden Valley Rd.

Market: showgrounds; Sat mornings. *Fig Tree Markets:* 1st Sun each month. *Australia Day Celebrations:* Jan. *Yeppoon Show:* June. *Ozfest:* World Cooeeing Competition; July. *Village Arts Festival:* Aug. *Rodeo:* Sept. *Yeppoon Tropical Pinefest:* Sept/Oct.

Capricorn Resort Yeppoon: family-friendly golf resort; Farnborough Rd; (07) 4939 5111 or 1300 857 922.

Great Keppel Island Popular island holiday destination with over 15 beaches to explore, swim and relax on. There is snorkelling and diving offshore and walks exploring the island's centre, including an interesting Aboriginal culture trail. Various styles of accommodation are offered. Access is by ferry from Keppel Bay Marina at Rosslyn Bay Harbour. 7 km s.

Byfield National Park This coastal park offers uninterrupted views of the ocean from its long beaches. Explore the open woodlands and forest or take in coastal views from the headlands at Five Rock and Stockyard Point. Fishing and boating are popular at Sandy Point at the south of the park. 4WD only; experience in sand driving is essential. (07) 4936 0511; 32 km N.

Boating: bareboat and fishing charters, sea access to Great Keppel Island and nearby underwater observatory, and water taxis to Keppel Bay islands; all from Keppel Bay Marina; 7 km s. *Wetland Tour:* Australian nature tour at Rydges Capricorn International Resort; 9 km N. *Cooberrie Park:* noted flora and fauna reserve; 15 km N. *Emu Park:* small village community with historical museum and interesting 'singing ship' memorial to Captain Cook – the sea breezes cause hidden organ pipes to make sounds. There is a Service of Remembrance to American troops each July, and Octoberfest is held each Oct; 19 km s. *Byfield State Forest:* the extremely rare Byfield fern is harvested here. Walks include the 4.3 km Stony Creek circuit track through rainforest and the boardwalk along Waterpark Creek; adjacent to Byfield National Park. *Keppel Sands:* this popular spot for fishing and crabbing is home to the excellent emerging Joskeleigh South Sea Island Museum, with the Koorana Crocodile Farm nearby; 38 km sw. *Keppel Bay Islands National Park:* this scenic group of islands is popular for walks, snorkelling, reef-walking and swimming; private boat or water taxi from Keppel Bay Marina; (07) 4933 6595. *Capricorn Coast Coffee:* Australia's largest coffee plantation; tours available; details from visitor centre. *Scenic flights:* over islands and surrounds from Hedlow Airport (between Yeppoon and Rockhampton); details from visitor centre.

See also CAPRICORN, p. 423

Yungaburra

Pop. 932
Map ref. 650 D3 | 651 E9 | 657 L7

ⓘ Allumbah Pocket Cottages, Gillies Hwy, (07) 4095 3023; or Nick's Swiss–Italian Restaurant, Gillies Hwy, (07) 4095 3330; www.athertontableland.com

 102.5 4KZ FM, 720 AM ABC Far North QLD

Yungaburra is a historic town on the edge of the Atherton Tableland. Originally a resting spot for miners, it was slow to develop. The tourism boom did not hit until the coastal road opened from Cairns in 1926. Today the town offers craft shops, galleries, cafes and restaurants.

Historical precinct walk: take this self-guide walk past heritage buildings, including the popular Lake Eacham Hotel in Cedar St; brochure available from visitor centre. *Platypus viewing platform:* see the elusive animal at sunrise and sunset; Peterson Creek, Gillies Hwy. *Galleries, craft and gem shops:* various outlets in town.

Market: renowned produce and craft market; Gillies Hwy; 4th Sat each month. *Tour de Tableland:* bike race; May. *Malanda Show:* July. *Folk Festival:* Oct.

Eden House: modern Australian; 20 Gillies Hwy; (07) 4089 7000. *Flynn's Licensed Restaurant:* European-influenced fare; 17 Eacham Rd; (07) 4095 2235. *Nick's Restaurant and Yodeller's Bar:* Swiss-Italian; 33 Gillies Hwy; (07) 4095 3330.

Eden House Retreat & Mountain Spa: cottages and villas; 20 Gillies Hwy; (07) 4089 7000. *Mt Quincan Crater Retreat:* romantic retreat; Peeramon Rd; (07) 4095 2255. *Williams Lodge:* luxury suites in historic family home; Cedar St; (07) 4095 3449.

Crater Lakes National Park The 2 volcanic lakes, Lake Eacham (8 km E) and Lake Barrine (12 km NE), are surrounded by rainforest and offer watersports, bushwalking and birdwatching. Look for the eastern water dragons along the 3 km track around Lake Barrine or take a wildlife cruise on the lake. There is a children's pool at Lake Eacham, a self-guide trail through the rainforest and a 3 km circuit shore track. Both lakes are popular recreation areas. (07) 4091 1844.

Malanda Malanda is a small town in the middle of rich dairy-farming country. It claims the longest milk run in the world (to Alice Springs) and boasts the still-operating 19th-century Majestic Theatre, and the Gourmet Food Factory specialising in local produce. On the southern outskirts of town is the Malanda Falls Conservation Park, with signposted rainforest walks, and the Malanda Environmental Centre, which has displays on local history, vulcanology, flora and fauna. The Malanda Falls actually flow into the local swimming pool. 20 km s.

Curtain Fig Tree: spectacular example of strangler fig with aerial roots in curtain-like formation; 2.5 km sw. *Tinaburra:* a great spot for swimming and watersports on Lake Tinaroo; boat ramp provides access. Nearby Seven Sisters are 7 volcanic cinder cones; 3 km N. *Lake Tinaroo:* watersports and fishing; travel around on a houseboat or dinghy – hire available; north of Yungaburra. *Heales Outlook:* spectacular views over Gillies Range; 16 km NE. *Tinaroo Falls Dam outlet:* views over lake; 23 km N.

See also CAIRNS & THE TROPICS, p. 425

 RADIO STATIONS   IN TOWN   WHAT'S ON   WHERE TO EAT   WHERE TO STAY   NEARBY

TASMANIA is...

Shopping for fresh produce and crafts at Hobart's SALAMANCA MARKET / Walking

through a forest canopy at the TAHUNE FOREST AIRWALK / A cruise down

the GORDON RIVER from Strahan / Bushwalking in CRADLE MOUNTAIN—

LAKE ST CLAIR NATIONAL PARK / Learning the chilling history behind PORT

[TROUSER BAY, FLINDERS ISLAND]

TASMANIA

ARTHUR HISTORIC SITE / Visiting cellar doors along the TAMAR VALLEY

WINE ROUTE / Taking the one-hour walk to the lookout over WINEGLASS BAY in

Freycinet National Park / A chairlift ride to the top of THE NUT, Stanley / Discovering

CATARACT GORGE and the nearby landscaped gardens in Launceston

TASMANIA

is bursting with wonderful surprises. A winding country road can suddenly reveal a colonial village, a boutique vineyard or a breathtaking ocean view like that of Wineglass Bay. From landscape and history to food and culture, Australia's island state is a feast for travellers.

Although it is Australia's smallest state – only 296 kilometres from south to north and 315 kilometres east to west – Tasmania's territory also includes the Bass Strait islands and subantarctic Macquarie Island. A population of just over 500 000 is eclipsed by over half a million visitors each year, and Tasmania is famous for its friendly, welcoming and relaxed pace of life.

Tasmania's Indigenous peoples have been here for around 35 000 years, and despite the terrible impact of white settlement, they are a large and increasingly influential community today. Middens are common around the coastline, showing where generations of Aboriginal people cooked shellfish meals.

Abel Tasman sighted and named Van Diemen's Land in 1642, closely followed by French and British explorers. The British – never keen to be outdone by the French – acted in 1803 to establish a presence on the River Derwent. With the arrival of the British, white settlement

[SLEEPY BAY, FREYCINET PENINSULA]

got off to a rollicking and violent start as a penal colony for the first 50 years.

In more recent history, Tasmania is the home of the world's first 'green' political party. Local environmental politics captured international attention in the 1980s when the No Dams campaign saved the Franklin River from being flooded for a hydro-electric scheme.

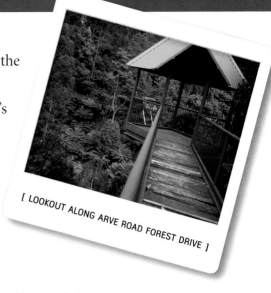

[LOOKOUT ALONG ARVE ROAD FOREST DRIVE]

The island's spirited cultural life includes the renowned Tasmanian Symphony Orchestra, award-winning author Richard Flanagan, and many arts and literary events.

Although two-thirds of the land is too harsh for farming, Tasmania has a growing reputation for boutique agriculture and aquaculture. A gastronomic circumnavigation of the island offers as much diversity as the landscape and a chance to discover Tasmania's cool-climate wines, fresh seafood, fruits and fine cheeses.

fact file

Population 504 400
Total land area 68 102 square kilometres
People per square kilometre 7.1
Sheep per square kilometre 49.6
Length of coastline 2833 kilometres
Number of islands 1000
Longest river South Esk River (252 kilometres)
Largest lake Lake Gordon (hydro-electric impoundment) (271 square kilometres)
Highest mountain Mount Ossa (1614 metres), Cradle Mountain–Lake St Clair National Park
Coldest place At Liawenee in August the average minimum temperature is – 1.8°C
Longest place name Teebelebberrer Mennapeboneyer (Aboriginal name for Little Swanport River)
Best beach Wineglass Bay, Freycinet National Park
Biggest surfable wave Shipstern Bluff near Port Arthur
Tallest tree At 99.6 m, the Arve Valley's giant swamp gum 'Centurion' is the world's tallest eucalypt
Most famous son Ricky Ponting, captain of the Australian cricket team
Most famous daughter Danish Crown Princess Mary Donaldson
Quirkiest festival National Penny Farthing Championships, Evandale
Most expensive gourmet produce Stigmas of *Crocus sativus*, grown on a saffron farm, which can attract a price of $30 000 per kilogram
Local beers Cascade in the south; Boags in the north

gift ideas

Arts and crafts (Salamanca Market, Hobart) A range of fantastic products on offer, including Jemma Clements' hand-blown perfume bottles and More Than Skin Deep handcrafted vegetable soaps. See Salamanca Place p. 492, 492 C3

Huon pine box (Handmark Gallery, Hobart) Buttery aromatic wood endemic to Tasmania and treasured by woodworkers. 77 Salamanca Pl, Hobart. 492 C3

Peter Dombrovskis poster (Wilderness Society Shop, Hobart) Haunting wilderness images by the man whose photographs influenced Tasmanian conservation history, including the protection of the Franklin River against flooding. Galleria building, 33 Salamanca Pl, Hobart. 492 C3

Leatherwood honey in decorative tin (Tasmanian Honey Company, Perth) Full-flavoured honey from the nectar of trees found in Tasmania's rainforest wilderness. See Longford p. 519, 675 H11

Tasmanian Devil soft toy (Tasmanian Devil Conservation Park, Taranna) You can't snuggle up with the real thing, so cuddle a stuffed version of this famous marsupial. See Eaglehawk Neck p. 513, 671 M8

Shell necklace (Queen Victoria Museum and Art Gallery, Launceston) Tasmania's Aboriginal women string traditional necklaces of iridescent blue-green maireener shells. See Launceston p. 520, 675 G10

Sweets (Richmond) Enter the town's old-fashioned lolly shop to find giant Tasmania-shaped freckles or uniquely Tasmanian Esmeraldas (coconut ice covered in toffee). See Richmond p. 524, 669 J3

Ghosts of Port Arthur book or DVD (Port Arthur) Scare your friends witless with tales of strange apparitions, available from the giftshop. See Port Arthur p. 525, 669 M9

Oysters (Barilla Bay, Cambridge) Tasmania's deep, cool and flowing waters are the key to large and juicy oysters. Barilla Bay will package them for air travel. 1388 Tasman Hwy, Cambridge. 669 J5

Cheese (King Island Dairy, King Island) King Island's world-famous, handcrafted cheeses can be bought directly from the Fromagerie Tasting Room next to the factory in Loorana. The company's range covers everything from soft white cheeses to aged cheddars, yoghurts and desserts. See Currie p. 510, 671 O11

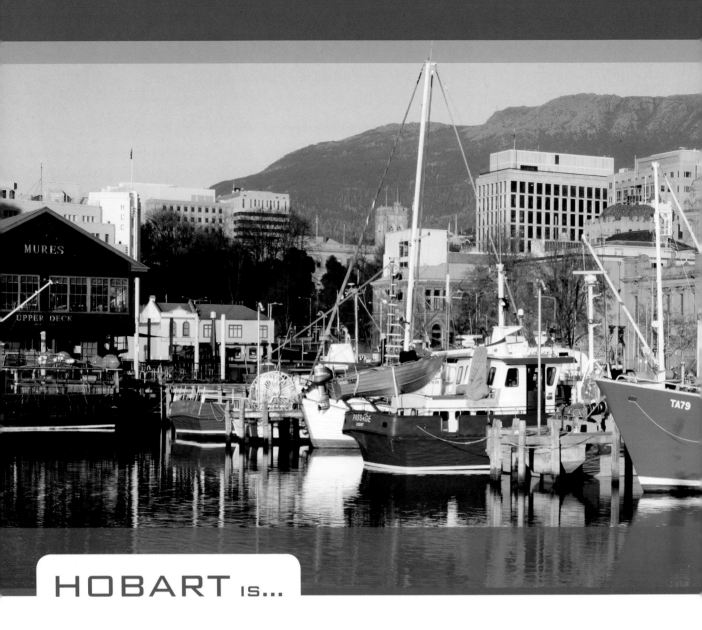

HOBART is...

Shopping for fresh produce and crafts at SALAMANCA MARKET / Fish and chips at

CONSTITUTION DOCK / A drive to the summit of MOUNT WELLINGTON / Exploring

Hobart's WATERFRONT / An afternoon at the ROYAL TASMANIAN BOTANICAL

GARDENS / Wandering around historic BATTERY POINT / A visit to the TASMANIAN

MUSEUM AND ART GALLERY / A counter meal in a warm, colonial-era pub / Having

breakfast and a browse around THE HENRY JONES ART HOTEL / Watching beer production

at CASCADE BREWERY / Coffee and a movie at North Hobart's independent STATE CINEMA

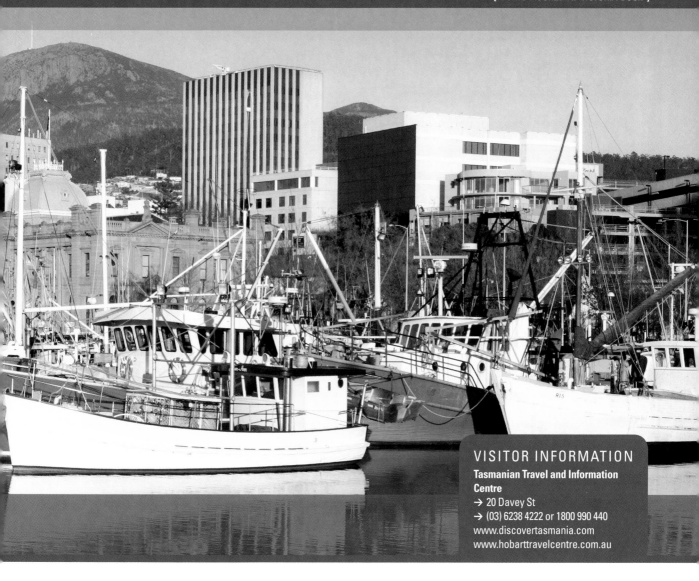

VISITOR INFORMATION

Tasmanian Travel and Information
Centre
→ 20 Davey St
→ (03) 6238 4222 or 1800 990 440
www.discovertasmania.com
www.hobarttravelcentre.com.au

At the southern tip of Australia, Hobart lies nestled between the slopes of Mount Wellington and the Derwent estuary. It was the second city after Sydney to be established, yet today it is the smallest of the capitals with just 210 000 people enjoying its glorious location and unhurried, easy-going lifestyle.

Impelled to set up colonies in the face of French exploration, the English established Hobart at Sullivans Cove in 1804 on land known to its Aboriginal inhabitants as Nibberloonne. Whaling and sealing brought wealth to the town, its dockside soon dotted with taverns doing a brisk trade among seafarers and traders. Hobart's fortunes still centre on its deep-water harbour, but these days fishing trawlers and freighters moor alongside tourist ferries, Antarctic research vessels and luxury ocean liners.

Boasting internationally recognised temperate wilderness on its doorstep, Hobart's abundance of natural beauty propelled it to the forefront of environmental politics in 1972, becoming home to the world's first 'green' political party. With a cosmopolitan literary and arts culture centred on a handful of hip galleries and cafes around the waterfront, but without the hustle and bustle of bigger cities, Hobart has turned small-city attributes to its advantage with its laid-back friendly vibe.

SEE PAGE 492

MAP LEGEND

⊕ Attraction

🄸 Tourist information

⊕ Where to eat & Where to stay

Shopping precinct

Downtown Hobart

Downtown Hobart is centred on the intersection of Elizabeth and Liverpool streets. There are fashion and department stores, specialty shops, banks, cafes and restaurants in the surrounding streets and arcades. Shops are open Monday to Saturday until 5pm, and on Sundays the larger stores open 10am to 4pm.

Elizabeth Mall 492 C2

Surrounded by shops and cafes, this busy meeting place is a favourite with shoppers, young people and buskers. A visitor information booth is open in the mall on weekdays until 4.30pm and from 10am until 2pm on Saturdays.

Cat and Fiddle Arcade 492 C2

There are several shopping arcades in the main retail area of Hobart, but the Cat and Fiddle Arcade's nursery rhyme musical clock lends it a certain charm. Much to the delight of children, it plays 'Hey Diddle Diddle' on the hour as moving parts provide accompanying action. The arcade runs between the Elizabeth Mall and Murray Street.

Liverpool Street 492 B3, C2

This is Hobart's main downtown shopping strip, with interesting arcades and side streets. **Bank Arcade** (between Argyle and Elizabeth streets) will tempt you with breads, spices and tiny cafes. **Mathers Lane** and **Criterion Street**, further along towards Murray Street, will interest those with a taste for good coffee and all things retro.

Elizabeth Street 492 B2

North of the mall, Elizabeth Street continues up a gentle slope towards North Hobart. In the first few blocks there is a cluster of shops selling polar fleece and outdoor equipment, followed by interesting cafes and antique shops.

Northern Waterfront

The northern waterfront of Sullivans Cove is the busiest, smelliest and most fascinating part of the working dock, both on and off the water. Along the Hunter Street waterfront contemporary apartments sit next to recycled 19th-century buildings, with Mount Wellington as the backdrop.

Constitution and Victoria docks 492 C2

Constitution Dock and neighbouring Victoria Dock are the heart of Sullivans Cove. There are several excellent seafood restaurants nearby

as well as dockside punts offering some of the best takeaway fish and chips in Australia. Every New Year, Constitution Dock comes alive when the annual Sydney and Melbourne to Hobart yachts cross the finish line of these gruelling ocean races. Every two years **Franklin Wharf** hosts the Australian Wooden Boat Festival, the largest gathering of historic craft in the Southern Hemisphere *(see Top events p. 494).*

Federation Concert Hall 492 C2

This concert hall is the home of the Tasmanian Symphony Orchestra and was designed to give priority to quality acoustics. Described as both intimate and grand, it seats over 1000 people. *1 Davey St; TSO Box Office 1800 001 190.*

The Henry Jones Art Hotel 492 D2

Facing Victoria Dock, this multi-award-winning hotel complex is established in what was once the IXL jam factory, owned by Hobart's first and most famous entrepreneur, Henry Jones. Alongside are galleries of fine Tasmanian furniture and Aboriginal art, cafes and restaurants. *25 Hunter St; (03) 6210 7700.*

Tasmanian Museum and Art Gallery 492 C2

This historic museum and gallery complex is home to Australia's finest collection of colonial art and Huon pine furniture. The zoology galleries will introduce you to Tasmania's unique wildlife including a glimpse of the extinct Tasmanian tiger or *thylacine*. There's also a gallery dedicated to Tasmanian Aboriginal culture. *40 Macquarie St; (03) 6211 4177; open 10am–5pm daily; tours 2.30pm Wed–Sun; admission free.*

Maritime Museum of Tasmania 492 C2

Located inside the impressive Neoclassical Carnegie Building, this museum brings to life Tasmania's rich maritime history. It displays

climate

Hobart's weather is changeable at any time of the year, so be prepared! Summer is mild with temperatures in the mid-20s, but sometimes the forecast highs are only reached for a short time as a cool sea breeze kicks in most afternoons. There are windless, sun-drenched days and chilly nights in autumn, but winter brings temperatures in the low teens and blustery cold conditions. Snow is rare in Hobart, but often settles on Mount Wellington's summit.

J	F	M	A	M	J	J	A	S	O	N	D	
23	22	20	17	13	11	10	12	14	17	19	21	MAX °C
11	11	10	8	6	4	3	4	6	7	9	10	MIN °C
44	39	42	47	42	49	48	46	47	55	54	51	RAIN MM
3	3	3	4	4	5	5	5	5	6	4	4	RAIN DAYS

TASMANIA

pictures and equipment from the whaling era, models of various ships and fascinating relics from shipwrecks. *Cnr Davey and Argyle sts; (03) 6234 1427; open 9am–5pm daily.*

Southern Waterfront

The docks on the southern side of Sullivans Cove are surrounded by remarkable historic buildings. The work of the docks continues amid cafes, restaurants and pubs, contributing to the area's lively atmosphere.

Salamanca Place 492 C3

The sandstone warehouses along Salamanca Place are undoubtedly Australia's finest row of Georgian dockside buildings, packed with interesting shops and galleries.

Hobart's famous **Salamanca Market** is held here every Saturday, offering an amazing variety of tempting produce, arts and crafts, and the chance to meet local artisans. *(03) 6238 2843; 8.30am–3pm Sat.*

For 150 years, merchants conducted their business from the Salamanca warehouses alongside some notoriously rowdy pubs and hotels. **Knopwoods Retreat** still does a brisk trade and is popular for Friday night drinks. Nearby, at the **Salamanca Arts Centre** a free street party featuring local musicians is held every Friday evening.

Parliament House 492 C3

Situated behind the trees in Parliament Square, Hobart's majestic Parliament House faces out to the waterfront. Designed by the colonial architect John Lee Archer and built by convicts as the first Customs House, it became the home of Tasmania's parliament in 1856. *Between Salamanca Pl and Murray St; bookings (03) 6233 2288; visitors gallery open on sitting days; tours 10am and 2pm Mon–Fri, except sitting days.*

Castray Esplanade and Princes Wharf 492 C3

Built in 1870 to provide a promenade for the people of Hobart, Castray Esplanade runs behind Princes Wharf. At the city end of the esplanade are restaurants specialising in Tasmanian seafood. The Taste of Tasmania festival takes place in **Princes Wharf No. 1 Shed** at the beginning of January.

For most of the year, Princes Wharf is a working dock, berthing Antarctic research and supply vessels. The CSIRO Marine Research Laboratories are situated at the Battery Point end. On the hill are the original **Signal Station** and **Mulgrave Battery**, which was built in 1818 during panic about a rumoured Russian invasion. They are now part of Princes Park.

The octagonal **Tide House**, next to the **Ordnance Stores**, is the point from which all distances are measured in Tasmania.

Battery Point

Battery Point, built to house the workers and merchants of the port, is on the hill behind Salamanca Place. Its compact size and village atmosphere make it a perfect place to explore on foot.

Kelly's Steps 492 C3

At the end of Kelly Street, historic Kelly's Steps connect Salamanca Place to Battery Point. They were built in 1839 by Captain James Kelly, an adventurer who made a comfortable living from sealing and whaling. Kelly's good fortune was short-lived, however, and by 1842 he was bankrupt and destitute following the death of his wife and seven of his children. After a run-in with the law over another man's wife, he died at age 67.

Arthurs Circus 492 C4

Exploring Arthurs Circus, just off Hampden Road at the top of Runnymede Street, is like walking into an intact Georgian streetscape – so be sure to bring your camera. The 16 cottages were built around a circular village green between 1847 and 1852, and they are still private residences today.

Hampden Road 492 C4

Hampden Road begins at a cluster of antique shops near Sandy Bay Road and heads downhill to Castray Esplanade, which winds through the heart of Battery Point.

One of the earliest grand houses in Battery Point is **Narryna Heritage Museum**, built in 1836 by one of Hobart's early sea captains and now set up as a heritage museum. Visitors can wander through the house and see how a comfortable life would have been lived in early Hobart. The kitchen is especially worth a look. *103 Hampden Rd; (03) 6234 2791; open 10.30am–5pm Mon–Fri, 12.30–5pm Sat–Sun in summer, 10.30am–5pm Tues–Fri, 2–5pm Sat–Sun in winter.*

Trumpeter Street 492 C4

A few streets away, at the top end of Trumpeter Street is the **Shipwright's Arms Hotel** which has traded under this name since 1846. The front bar has a distinctive nautical atmosphere with every inch of wall space covered with photographs of vessels that have sailed on the River Derwent. A few doors down the hill, across Napoleon Street, are **Mr Watson's Cottages**, a row of simple Georgian brick dwellings built in 1850. Behind are the boat building slip yards that date back to the 1830s.

getting around

Metro buses regularly service the city and suburbs at peak times and less frequently during weekends. Timetables are displayed at most bus stops and are available from the Metro shop in the Hobart Bus Terminal at the Macquarie Street end of Elizabeth Street. An all-day ticket allows you to catch any number of buses after 9am Monday to Friday, and anytime on weekends.

On the river you can order a water taxi from Watermans Dock to Bellerive, Lindisfarne, Wrest Point or the Botanical Gardens. There are also cruise boats operating from Franklin Wharf. Information is available harbourside and from the Tasmanian Travel and Information Centre, (03) 6238 4222.

The 15-kilometre Inter-City Cycleway runs alongside a rail track between Hobart's waterfront and the northern suburb of Claremont. With a paved surface and no hills, it's popular with commuters and recreational riders alike. Bikes of all types can be hired from the Hobart end of the cycleway.

Public transport Metro bus information line 13 2201.

Airport shuttle bus Airporter City Hotels Shuttle 1300 385 511; TenBuckBus Airporter 0419 382 240.

Motoring organisation RACT 13 2722, roadside assistance 13 1111.

Car rental Autorent Hertz (03) 6237 1111; Avis 13 6333 or (03) 6234 4222; Bargain Car Rentals (03) 6234 6959; Budget 13 2727 or (03) 6234 5222; Europcar 1800 030 118; Lo-cost Autorent (03) 6231 0550; Thrifty 1300 367 227.

Campervan and 4WD rental Britz 1800 038 171; Cruisin' Tasmania 1300 664 485; Tasmania Campers 1800 627 074; Tasmanian Campervan Hire 1800 807 119.

Taxis Australian Taxi Service 0411 286 780; Executive Taxi Service 0411 488 734; Taxi Combined Services 13 2227; United Taxis 13 1008; Yellow Cabs 13 1924.

Ferries Hobart Yellow Water Taxi 0407 036 268.

Bicycle hire Derwent Bike Hire (daily weather permitting); Cenotaph, Regatta Ground 0428 899 169.

Macquarie Street

Macquarie Street has always been Hobart's main thoroughfare, its classical buildings adding an air of sophistication. The area is now populated by government offices, lawyers' premises and consulting rooms.

Franklin Square 492 C2

Franklin Square is a peaceful city park and bus terminal. On sunny days it's a popular spot for city workers to eat lunch and a favourite meeting place for young people. Hobart's first Government House was built in Franklin Square but by 1858 the timber and thatch building was almost collapsing, so it was replaced by this park. At its centre a formal fountain supports a statue of Sir John Franklin, Arctic explorer and Governor of Tasmania (1837–43).

TASMANIA

top events

King of the Derwent Maxi yachts battle to capture the crown. January.

MONA FOMA Hobart grooves with two weeks of eclectic jazz, rock, hip-hop and indie music. January.

Royal Hobart Regatta A family regatta and fireworks display since 1838. February.

Australian Wooden Boat Festival Biennial dockside celebration of maritime history. February (odd-numbered years).

Ten Days on the Island International island culture comes to Tasmania. March–April (odd-numbered years).

Targa Tasmania State-wide classic car rally. April–May.

Antarctic Tasmania Midwinter Festival Celebrating all things cold at the winter solstice. June.

Festival of Voices For four days winter is warmed by singers and choirs from all over Australia gathering to sing their hearts out. July.

Royal Hobart Show Four days of competitions and displays bringing country life to town. October.

Sydney to Hobart and Melbourne to Hobart yacht races Gruelling races end with a dockside party, and a crowd of people to welcome the yachts no matter what time of the day or night. December.

The Taste Festival Hobart sparkles with fun activities and waterfront gourmet indulgence. December–January.

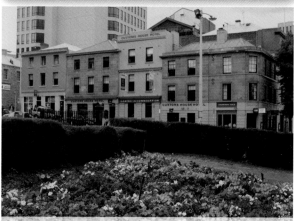

[STATE PARLIAMENT HOUSE GARDENS AND HERITAGE BUILDINGS]

shopping

Salamanca Place, City Fine craft and Tasmanian art. 492 C3

Elizabeth Street, City Gifts, outdoor clothing and antiques. 492 B2

Liverpool Street, City Fashion and jewellery. 492 C2

Cat and Fiddle Arcade, City Bargain fashion and sportswear. 492 C2

Bathurst Street, City Fine furniture and antiques. 492 C2

Sandy Bay Road, Battery Point Antique furniture, china and books. 492 C3

Sandy Bay Road, Sandy Bay Stylish fashion stores. 492 B4

Eastlands Shopping Centre, Rosny Park Hobart's largest undercover suburban mall. 490 E4

Corner of Macquarie & Murray streets 492 C3

A short walk up Macquarie Street from Franklin Square, this remarkable intersection has a historic sandstone building on every corner. It was once the administrative centre of Hobart and today offers panoramic views down Macquarie Street's elegant heritage streetscape past the Georgian **Ingle Hall**, built in 1814, and the Art Deco *Mercury* newspaper building, to the **Cenotaph** in the distance.

On one corner **St David's Cathedral**, rebuilt several times, stands where there have been churches since 1817. The present cathedral was substantially rebuilt in 1909 and its bell tower was completed in 1936. Across Murray Street, **Hadleys Hotel** stands on the site of a hotel dating back to the 1830s. Dating to the same era, the **Treasury Buildings** are still used as government offices today. The 1875 **Derwent and Tamar Building** used to have a set of punishment stocks outside the front door as the Hobart Gaol was once its neighbour.

St David's Park 492 C3

On Davey Street, at the city end of Salamanca Place, this formal English-style walled park still has old headstones displayed in the lower section – a reminder that this was the colony's first burial ground. It was made into a park in 1926, with a rotunda and sweeping lawns shaded by huge English trees. *Cnr Davey St and Sandy Bay Rd.*

Anglesea Barracks 492 B3

On the hill at the top of Davey Street is Australia's oldest military establishment still in use. There is a military museum to explore, some elegant Georgian buildings and a pair of 1770s bronze cannons. *Davey St; (03) 6237 7160; grounds open daily; museum open 9am–1pm Tues and Thurs; tours 11am Tues.*

Queens Domain

Queens Domain is a bush reserve on the hill overlooking the Derwent River, to the north-east of the city centre. It has soccer fields, a tennis centre, a cricket oval and an aquatic centre. In Glebe ('The Glebe' to locals), there are magnificent weatherboard Federation houses built on some of the steepest streets you will ever find.

Government House 490 D4

Next door to the Botanical Gardens, Tasmania's Neo-Gothic Government House is one of the finest viceregal residences in the Commonwealth. Built in 1857 from local timbers and sandstone excavated on-site, it dominates the riverside slopes between Hobart and the Tasman Bridge. *Lower Domain Rd; open to the public one Sunday each year; phone (03) 6234 2611 for the exact date; admission free.*

Royal Tasmanian Botanical Gardens 490 D4

These superb botanical gardens were established in 1818, and today they are one of the best in Australia. There is a restaurant, a beautiful old-world conservatory and greenhouses, an extensive Japanese garden and, of course, ABC gardener Peter Cundall's famous veggie patch. *Lower Domain Rd; (03) 6236 3076; open daily; admission free; entry to conservatory and discovery centre by gold coin donation.*

Inner North

Heading north out of Hobart city along Elizabeth Street is a strip of hip cafes, bars and eateries in North Hobart. Here you can linger over coffee and cake during the day or kick up your heels and take in the local music scene at night.

Elizabeth Street, North Hobart 492 B1

This cosmopolitan strip is busy day and night. At the Federal Street end, the independent **State Cinema** shows arthouse and foreign films in Hobart's only old cinema. Further down the street there is a wide choice of casual restaurants, bistros, cafes and takeaway outlets. *State Cinema, 375 Elizabeth St; (03) 6234 6318.*

On the Burnett Street corner, the **Republic Bar & Cafe** is a popular meeting place for an eclectic mix of musos, artists, writers, activists and students. There is live music every night of the week, complemented by excellent counter meals.

Cornelian Bay 490 D3

Cornelian Bay is tucked away north of the Botanical Gardens and easily accessible from the Inter-City Cycleway. A popular swimming beach for families in the 1950s and 1960s, it is now a tranquil waterside park reminiscent of a bygone era with barbecue facilities, an all-access playground and a row of historic Edwardian boatsheds. There is also a contemporary restaurant and a kiosk selling gourmet ice-cream and takeaway coffee.

Around both sides of the bay there are walking trails offering excellent views of the Tasman Bridge. Along these tracks, a careful eye will discover the charcoal and shell-midden evidence of past Aboriginal occupation.

Runnymede 490 C3

Built in 1836, this Georgian villa has had a number of distinguished owners including a bishop, a captain and the first lawyer to qualify in the colony. It's now in the hands of the National Trust and has been restored and refurbished to its former glory as an 1860s mansion. *61 Bay Rd, New Town; open 10am–4.30pm Mon–Fri, 12–4.30pm Sat–Sun.*

North

Between the Derwent River and Mount Wellington, Hobart's northern suburbs sweep over gently sloping hills and around the meandering foreshore. There are suburban shopping strips at Moonah and Glenorchy, catering to the retail needs of nearby suburban areas.

Tasmanian Transport Museum 490 B2

This museum contains a restored and working collection of steam engines, locomotives and carriages from Tasmania's unique and fascinating railway history. There are also some of the old trams and trolley buses that used to run on Hobart's streets. Visitors can browse through displays in the relocated New Town suburban train station, a relic from a bygone era. Occasional main-line trips are scheduled. *Anfield St, Glenorchy; (03) 6272 7721; open 1–4pm Sat–Sun and public holidays.*

markets

Glenorchy Showgrounds Market Trash and treasure, craft, produce and occasionally livestock. Royal Hobart Showgrounds, Glenorchy; 8am–2pm Sun. 490 B2

Island Markets Hobart's only undercover market selling produce Wed–Sun, and arts, crafts, plants and sweets Fri–Sun. 54–56 Gormanston Rd, Moonah. 490 C3

Sorell Market Produce, craft, and trash and treasure. Sorell Memorial Hall, Cole St; most Sun and public holidays. 669 K4

The Market Unique Tasmanian-designed and made jewellery, books, cards, craft and food. Masonic Temple, 3 Sandy Bay Rd; 10am–3pm 1st Sun each month. 492 C3

See also Salamanca Market, p. 492

where to stay

Islington Hotel Hobart's most glamorous boutique hotel in a fine Regency mansion. 321 Davey St; (03) 6220 2123. 492 A4

The Henry Jones Art Hotel Super-stylish luxury waterfront accommodation in Hobart's historic sandstone warehouses. 25 Hunter St; (03) 6210 7700. 492 D2

The Old Woolstore Apartment Hotel Multi-level apartment complex behind a heritage street facade, just a short stroll from Hobart's picturesque waterfront. 1 Macquarie St; (03) 6235 5355 or 1800 814 676. 492 C2

Wrest Point Fantastic views from Wrest Point's landmark tower and temptations in the casino below. 410 Sandy Bay Rd, Sandy Bay; 1800 703 006. 490 D5

Zero Davey Boutique Apartments Groovy waterfront apartment complex offering fabulous luxury, hip contemporary design and cool modern decor. 15 Hunter St; (03) 6270 1444 or 1300 733 422. 492 D2

where to eat

Jackman & McRoss Bakery Vibrant bakery cafe with very good coffee and heavenly sweet and savoury pastries. 57–59 Hampden Rd, Battery Point; (03) 6223 3186; open daily for breakfast, lunch and afternoon tea. 492 C4

Lebrina Restaurant Award-winning, sophisticated dining with French style and Italian flavour in an elegant historic cottage. 155 New Town Rd, New Town; (03) 6228 7775; open Tues–Sat for dinner. 490 C4

Mezethes Greek Taverna Lively crowded taverna for those with a passion for authentic Greek chargrilled seafood and meats. Salamanca Arts Centre; (03) 6224 4601; open daily for breakfast, lunch and dinner. 492 C3

Mures Upper Deck Perched above the dockside sights, sounds and smells, this is Hobart's best-loved seafood restaurant. Victoria Dock; (03) 6231 1999; open daily for lunch and dinner. 492 C2

Smolt Mediterranean-style dining and late-night 'small plates' with a piazza outlook and hip modern interior. 2 Salamanca Sq; (03) 6224 2554; open daily for breakfast, lunch and dinner. 492 C3

entertainment

Cinema   There are multiscreen cinemas at Glenorchy in the northern suburbs, in Bligh Street opposite Eastlands on the eastern shore and in Collins Street in the city. These are ideal for mainstream and latest-release movies. If your taste leans towards arthouse films, try the independent State Cinema in Elizabeth Street, North Hobart. See the *Mercury* for details of films being shown.

Live music   Hobart has a small but thriving live-music scene based around a handful of pub venues. For a night of great blues you can't beat the Republic Bar & Cafe in North Hobart, and for original rock and roots head to the Alley Cat Bar in North Hobart or the Brisbane Hotel in the city. There are plenty of late-night pubs and clubs around Sullivans Cove including Syrup, Isobar, Bar Celona, Irish Murphy's, Lark Distillery and the Telegraph Hotel. Check out Thursday's gig guide in the *Mercury*.

Classical music and performing arts   Hobart's unique Theatre Royal is the venue for visiting stage companies and occasional local productions, including the annual University Review. Classical music is usually performed at the Federation Concert Hall, and the Derwent Entertainment Centre hosts large events. A livelier theatre scene is supported by smaller venues such as the intimate Backspace Theatre behind the Theatre Royal. The Playhouse in Bathurst Street is home to an amateur theatrical society and the Peacock Theatre specialises in contemporary works in its small space at the Salamanca Arts Centre. See the *Mercury* for details of what's on.

Moorilla Estate 490 B2

Italian migrant and visionary Claudio Alcorso developed this vineyard in 1955 and put Tasmania's excellent cool-climate wines on the map. The estate is 12 kilometres upriver from Hobart's city centre by high-speed catamaran from Brooke Street Pier. Enjoy lunch or dinner, taste wines from the cellar door or sample pilsner, ale and wheat beer brewed at Moo Brew on-site. Moorilla Estate is also the home of the new **Museum of Old and New Art**, which opens in 2011 to show an outstanding

private collection of pieces celebrating the twin themes of sex and death. *655 Main Rd, Berriedale; (03) 6277 9900; restaurant open daily for lunch, dinner Fri–Sat.*

Cadbury Visitor Centre 490 B1

Among their many other chocolate delights, Cadbury's factory at Claremont makes the 90 million Freddo frogs eaten every year in Australia. Visitors can watch an informative DVD, see a demonstration of chocolate being moulded, taste the raw materials and indulge themselves in the factory shop and cafe (which makes excellent hot chocolate). *100 Cadbury Rd, Claremont; 1800 627 367; open 8am–4pm (last presentation at 3pm) Mon–Fri Sept–May, 9am–3pm (last presentation at 2pm) Mon–Fri June–Aug.*

Inner South

The prosperous southern suburbs of Hobart extend from Battery Point south along the river to Taroona and Kingston, and up into the foothills of Mount Wellington. Around the shopping area on Sandy Bay Road there are narrow streets of cottages, providing digs for students from the nearby University of Tasmania campus. Davey Street and Sandy Bay Road are lined with impressive mansions while the hills above are dotted with contemporary houses with spectacular outlooks.

Wrest Point Casino 490 D5

A Hobart landmark since it opened in 1973, the iconic Wrest Point tower houses Australia's first legal casino. From its rotating top-floor restaurant (open daily for dinner and lunch on Fridays) there are views of the Derwent River from the Tasman Bridge to Storm Bay, and to Mount Wellington behind the city. Be there at sunset for the most amazing views. *410 Sandy Bay Rd; 1800 703 006.*

Sandy Bay Beach 490 D6

Sandy Bay Beach has been a popular swimming beach for decades. Lawns beside the beach provide a relaxing place for a family barbecue, to kick a footy with the kids or take a leisurely

grand old buildings

Lenna of Hobart   When Alexander McGregor made a fortune from whaling he built this rich, Italianate mansion on a cliff overlooking the cove so he could keep an eye on shipping movements. Now it's a stylish boutique hotel. 20 Runnymede St, Battery Point.

Hebrew Synagogue   Australia's first synagogue and a rare example of Egyptian Revival architecture. Argyle St (between Liverpool and Bathurst sts), City.

Theatre Royal   Australia's oldest theatre, with a highly decorated interior and a resident ghost. Laurence Olivier called it 'the best little theatre in the world'. 29 Campbell St, City *(see Walks & tours, p. 497)*.

Town Hall   Classical Revival design by Henry Hunter, it stands where Hobart's founder, David Collins, pitched the first tent. Macquarie St (between Elizabeth and Argyle sts), City.

Penitentiary Chapel and Criminal Court   Underground passages, solitary cells and an execution yard. Cnr Brisbane and Campbell sts, City *(see Walks & tours, p. 497)*.

City Hall   Built from a competition-winning design in 1915, it is perhaps Hobart's most underrated public building. Macquarie St (between Market and Campbell sts), City.

T & G Building   Built for an insurance company, it has an Egyptian-inspired clock tower. Cnr Collins and Murray sts, City.

Hydro-Electric Commission Building   The design brief said that it should represent the new age of electricity, and its Art Deco facade suggests energy and modernity. Cnr Elizabeth and Davey sts, City.

Colonial Mutual Life Building   Inter-war building with Gothic gargoyles, Moorish balconies, Art Deco chevrons and multicoloured roofing tiles. Cnr Elizabeth and Macquarie sts, City.

St George's Anglican Church   Built by two noted colonial architects – the body in 1836–38 by John Lee Archer, and the spire in 1847 by James Blackburn – this is Australia's finest Classical Revival church. 28 Cromwell St, Battery Point.

stroll. There are a number of nearby eateries, including a fine-dining seafood restaurant in the old regatta pavilion, a tiny wood-fired pizza restaurant on the foreshore, a beachside contemporary wine bar and a Chinese restaurant on Sandy Bay Road.

Female Factory 490 C5

Serving at various times as a rum distillery, contagious diseases hospital, home for 'imperial lunatics' and, most recently, as a fudge factory, this historic site was also a female prison for 50 years. The nearby Remembrance Garden was created in 1995. Visitors can take a tour of the site and have an 1830s-style 'Morning Tea with the Matron' in her refurbished cottage. *16 Degraves St, South Hobart; open 9am–4pm Mon–Fri; Morning Tea with the Matron bookings (03) 6223 1559; Mon, Wed and Fri.*

Cascade Brewery 490 B5

Cascade beers have been brewed here since 1824, making it Australia's oldest brewery. Locally grown hops, Tasmanian barley and mountain water combine to produce one of Australia's top beers. There are several brewery tours daily with samples included. *140 Cascade Rd, South Hobart; bookings (03) 6224 1117; open daily.*

Mount Nelson Signal Station 490 D6

In 1811 on a visit to Van Diemen's Land, Governor Macquarie ordered that a signal station be erected on 350-metre 'Nelson Hill' to relay sightings of boats to Hobart. The site affords sweeping views of the Derwent Valley and Storm Bay, and there is a restaurant with a spectacular outlook – especially at night.

Taroona Shot Tower 667 E12

Towering above the winding Channel Highway south of Taroona, this 58-metre-tall sandstone tower was erected to make lead shot

[SALAMANCA MARKET]

walks & tours

Hobart Historic Tours Guided walks of Hobart or Battery Point with great stories of the early days, an informative tour discovering Hobart's polar links, or a pub crawl with colourful tales thrown in. Bookings on (03) 6278 3338 or 0429 843 150.

Art Deco in Hobart Self-guide tour brings Hobart's collection of Art Deco buildings to life. Brochure available from the Tasmanian Travel and Information Centre.

Hobart Rivulet Tour Follow a guide into this underground rivulet to discover Hobart's hidden history. Bookings on (03) 6238 4222 or 1800 990 440.

River cruises Combine a river cruise with delicious food and wine; step back into history aboard a square rigger; or cruise to Cadbury Schweppes Chocolate Factory, Moorilla Estate winery or Peppermint Bay. Catamarans and jet boats head out into Storm Bay for a thrilling ride. For information and timetables head to the Brooke Street Pier area in Sullivans Cove, or phone Captain Fells (03) 6223 5893, Navigators (03) 6223 1914, Peppermint Bay Cruises 1300 137 919, The Cruise Company 1800 990 200, Hobart Yellow Water Taxi 0407 036 268, Wild Thing Adventures 1300 137 919, Hobart Harbour Jet 0404 078 687 or Windeward Bound Sailing Adventures 0418 120 399.

Kayak tours Get a sea-level perspective on Hobart's waterfront with a daytime or evening paddle around the docks. Blackaby's Sea Kayaks 0418 124 072; Freycinet Adventures (03) 6257 0500; Roaring 40s Ocean Kayaking (03) 6267 5000.

Ghost Tours of Hobart and Battery Point Comfy shoes and nerves of steel are needed for this sunset tour of Hobart's spooky past. Bookings on 0439 335 696.

Old Rokeby Historic Trail A self-guide tour of the outer suburb of Rokeby, one of Hobart's earliest rural districts. Brochures available at the trailhead in Hawthorn Place, Rokeby. (03) 6247 6925.

Theatre Royal Tour A guided tour backstage. Bookings on (03) 6233 2299; 11am Mon, Wed and Fri.

Penitentiary Chapel Historic Site Grim history of gallows, cells and tunnels illustrated by lamplight if you dare. Bookings on 0417 361 392.

Sullivans Cove Walks Guided evening and day walks around the waterfront unveiling Hobart's past. Bookings on (03) 6245 1208 or 0409 252 318.

Louisa's Walk Follow the bleak life of convict Louisa Ryan to the Female Factory where she was imprisoned. Bookings on (03) 6229 8959 or 0437 276 417.

Mount Wellington Walks Guided walks delving into the history, botany and ancient past of this intriguing mountain. Bookings on 0439 551 197.

Mount Wellington Descent Plummet down from Mount Wellington's 1270-metre summit to sea level on a mountain bike. Gloves and ear warmers supplied. Bookings on (03) 6228 4255 or 1800 064 726.

TASMANIA

sport

The **Sydney to Hobart Yacht Race**, held in December, is Hobart's premier sporting event. Other twilight and weekend sailing events take place on the Derwent throughout the year.

A state-wide Australian Rules **football** league is up and running, with games played at the North Hobart Football Oval. In summer the action shifts to Bellerive Oval – Tasmania's premier **cricket** ground *(see entry on this page).*

Hobart has an international-standard **hockey** centre at New Town, and national and international games attract large crowds. In January the Domain Tennis Centre hosts the Moorilla Hobart International **tennis** tournament, and Hobart's **horseracing** calendar is dominated by the Hobart Cup, run at Tattersall's Park in February.

Tasmania lays claim to Australia's very first **golf** course at Bothwell. Around Hobart there is a nine-hole course on the eastern shore at Rosny Park, while 18-hole courses are at Kingston Beach in the southern suburbs and Claremont In the north.

in 1870. The tower summit and its remarkably good views of the Derwent are reached via hundreds of steps. There is a tearooms on-site to help you recover from the climb. *234 Channel Hwy, Taroona; (03) 6227 8885; open daily.*

Inner East

The 'eastern shore', as it is locally known, is a residential area spreading along the River Derwent south to the beachside suburbs of Howrah, Rokeby and Lauderdale. It is reached by travelling over the arching Tasman Bridge.

Bellerive 490 E4

Bellerive was settled in the 1820s. Today it's a quiet suburban village overlooking the river, bordered by a marina to the north and sandy beaches to the south. Back in 1885, in a nervous response to reported sightings of Russian ships in the Derwent, a military fort was built on **Kangaroo Bluff**. Its guns were never fired, but can still be seen today mounted over a network of tunnels and bunkers. *(03) 6248 4053; open daily; admission free.*

Bellerive's best-known landmark is the **Bellerive Oval**, home to the **Tasmanian Cricket Museum** and **Max Atwell Memorial Library**. This picturesque oval hosts Tests and one-day matches, and is the home ground of the state cricket team – the Tasmanian Tigers – and the site of their 2007 inaugural Pura Cup victory. *Derwent St, Bellerive; tour bookings (03) 6282 0433; museum open 10am–3pm Tues–Thurs, 10am–12pm Fri; oval tours 10am Tues, or by arrangement.*

East

Beyond the eastern shore's built-up areas, the peninsula between Storm Bay and Frederick Henry Bay is a favourite haunt for surfers, within an easy drive from the city. Few tourists head out this way so there are crowd-free surf breaks and plenty of long deserted dune-backed beaches.

Rokeby 667 H9

Rokeby is a 20-minute drive out of Hobart along the South Arm Highway. It was settled in 1809 and quickly became an important food-producing area for the growing colony, with Tasmania's first crops of wheat and apples harvested here.

St Matthew's Church houses a collection of notable items including its organ, which was the first keyboard brought to Australia. Tasmania's first chaplain, the notorious Reverend Robert Knopwood, spent his last days in the Rokeby area and was buried in a plain coffin, with no nameplate, in St Matthew's churchyard. *Cnr King St and North Pde.*

Storm Bay beaches 669 K7, L5

Surrounding Hobart's outer-eastern suburbs there are some lovely sheltered beaches that are well worth a visit. The beaches facing south into Storm Bay are excellent surfing spots and usually uncrowded. **Clifton Beach** is a popular surfing location reached via a turn-off from the South Arm Highway, while a further 8 kilometres south the **Goat Bluff** cliff-top lookout offers spectacular views of wild and deserted surf beaches on either side of the bluff.

For a swim in the waves at a safe, patrolled beach, head to **Carlton** (take the turn-off to Dodges Ferry from the Arthur Highway, after Sorell).

day tours

Richmond This small settlement just north of Hobart is probably Australia's best-preserved Georgian colonial village. Highlights include the convict-built Richmond Bridge, Australia's oldest bridge; the gaol, which predates Port Arthur; and galleries and cafes housed in historic shopfronts and cottages. For more details see p. 501

Tasman Peninsula The stunning setting of Port Arthur – lawns, gardens, cliffs – and the beauty of its sandstone buildings belie the site's tragic history. Other sites on the peninsula worth a look include the spectacular rock formations and blow holes around Eaglehawk Neck. For more details see p. 501

Derwent Valley The Derwent Valley, with its neat agricultural landscape and historic buildings, forms one of the loveliest rural areas of Australia, reminiscent of England. Visit the trout hatchery of Salmon Ponds, the National Trust–classified New Norfolk, and the hop museum at Oast House. For more details see p. 501

D'Entrecasteaux Channel The beauty and intricacy of Tasmania's south-eastern coastline can be experienced on a leisurely drive south from Hobart. There are stunning water views, particularly at Tinderbox (via Kingston), and Verona Sands at the Huon River entrance. At Kettering, a car ferry goes to remote Bruny Island. For more details see p. 501

Huon Valley The Huon Valley is the centre of a growing gourmet food industry. The signposted Huon Trail follows the valley between rows of apple trees, with a backdrop of forested mountains. In the far south, at Hastings, visitors can tour a dolomite cave and swim in a thermal pool. For more details see p. 501

REGIONS
tasmania

[TASMANIAN DEVIL]

[SCOPARIA IN BLOOM, WALLS OF
JERUSALEM NATIONAL PARK]

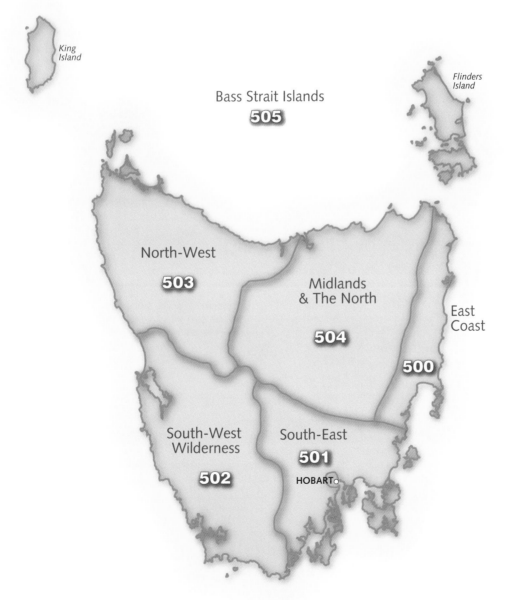

King
Island

Flinders
Island

Bass Strait Islands
505

North-West
503

Midlands
& The North
504

East
Coast

500

South-West
Wilderness

South-East
501

502

HOBART○

EAST COAST

Tasmania's premier seaside destination boasts exquisite coastal scenery, historic sites, gourmet produce, a lush hinterland and, offshore, a rich marine environment.

[WINEGLASS BAY, FREYCINET NATIONAL PARK]

Fishing The fishing is excellent along this coast, particularly around St Helens, which is the base for those planning to fish the East Australian Current for tuna, marlin and shark. For land-based and inshore anglers there is the long, narrow estuary of Georges Bay. And for those who prefer the eating to the catching, fish and chip shops like Captain's Catch in St Helens and restaurants like Kabuki by the Sea near Swansea specialise in only the freshest east-coast seafood.

Penguin tours in Bicheno Every night at dusk, Bicheno Penguin Tours allows people to get very close to these beautiful little creatures as they return from their day's fishing. At the peak of the season, close to 600 birds inhabit the rookery. It's a popular and magical wildlife experience, run in an environmentally sensitive way.

Mount William National Park This fairly remote park, created in 1973, protects Tasmania's forester kangaroo and many bird species. The view from Mount William takes in the sandy beaches and coastal heath of the state's north-east corner and extends north to the Furneaux Islands and south to St Marys.

Underwater wonders The underwater landscape of the east coast is an unsung wonder. Offshore from Bicheno is Governor Island Marine Reserve. Here, beneath clear waters, granite outcrops create cliffs, caves and deep fissures, which provide a home for diverse marine communities. Glass-bottomed boat and diving tours are available.

Freycinet Peninsula This long, narrow paradise features forests, cliffs, beaches and walking trails. The beautiful Peninsula Walking Track ends at Wineglass Bay, regarded by many as one of the world's best beaches. Coles Bay, which now has an up-market resort, is a peaceful base from which to explore the area.

TOP EVENTS

JAN	St Helens Regatta and Seafood Festival
MAR	Fingal Valley Festival (Fingal)
MAR	Tasmanian Game Fishing Classic (St Helens)
EASTER	Jazz Concert (Freycinet Vineyard, near Bicheno)
JUNE	Winter Solstice Festival (St Marys)

CLIMATE

BICHENO

J	F	M	A	M	J	J	A	S	O	N	D	
21	21	20	19	16	14	14	15	16	17	18	20	MAX °C
13	13	12	10	9	7	6	6	7	8	10	11	MIN °C
52	57	59	60	58	61	53	51	44	56	58	69	RAIN MM
8	8	8	9	9	9	9	10	9	10	10	10	RAIN DAYS

EAST COAST GOURMET TRAIL

Much of this region's appeal lies in its magnificent seafood. Visitors can taste and buy oysters at Freycinet Marine Farm near Coles Bay, and buy crays, oysters and scallops from Wardlaw's Cray Store at Chain of Lagoons. The area is also known for its dairy produce – try the cheddar at Pyengana Dairy Company in the tiny river town of Pyengana. Kate's Berry Farm near Swansea is a gourmet institution, specialising in fresh berries and berry products. At Swansea Wine and Wool Centre visitors can taste the pinots and chardonnays of the small local wine industry.

→ For more detail see maps 671 & 673. For descriptions of ⓣ towns see Towns from A–Z (p. 506).

SOUTH-EAST

Little development has ensured the preservation of many colonial sites in this region, including Port Arthur Historic Site.

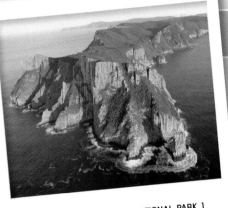

[CAPE PILLAR, TASMAN NATIONAL PARK]

Trout fishing The region's lakes and rivers boast some of Australia's best freshwater fishing. A favourite among trout anglers is the Ouse River, which joins the Derwent north of Hamilton. Other spots include the Clyde, Jordan and Coal rivers east of the Derwent, and the Tyenna, Styx and Plenty rivers west of the Derwent.

Tahune Forest AirWalk Tahune Forest Reserve's most famous attraction is its treetop walk, the award-winning AirWalk. The last section of the suspended steel path is cantilevered and hangs 48 metres above the Huon and Picton rivers that converge below – not for the faint of heart.

Hastings Caves This cave and thermal spring complex near Dover features the magnificent Newdegate Cave, with 245 steps leading to its vast chambers of formations created over more than 40 million years. Tours of its stalactites, stalagmites and helictites (distorted stalactites) run daily.

Southern Tasmanian Wine Route Tasmania's first vineyard was established at New Town (now a suburb of Hobart) in 1821. The modern industry began in 1958 when Claudio Alcorso set up the now acclaimed Moorilla Estate on the Derwent. Today a number of wineries fan out from Hobart, with most offering cellar-door tastings.

Tasmanian Devil Conservation Park The feature of this park is undeniably the Tasmanian devils, fierce-looking black creatures the size of small dogs. The park also has displays on the thylacine (Tasmanian tiger), regarded as extinct despite unconfirmed sightings.

Port Arthur Historic Site Port Arthur is one of Australia's most significant historic sites. Imposing sandstone prison buildings are set in 40 hectares of spectacular landscaping. Highlights are the ghost tours and summer boat trips to the Isle of the Dead, the final resting place for convicts and prison personnel alike.

TOP EVENTS

JAN	Cygnet Folk Festival (Cygnet)
FEB–MAR	International Highland Spin-In (wool-spinning competition, Bothwell, odd-numbered years)
MAR	Taste of the Huon (different town each year)
MAR	Village Colonial Fair (Richmond)
OCT	Olie Bollen Festival (Dutch community festival, Kingston)
NOV	Huon Agricultural Show (Huonville)

CLIMATE

NEW NORFOLK

	J	F	M	A	M	J	J	A	S	O	N	D	
	24	24	21	18	14	11	11	13	15	17	19	21	MAX °C
	11	11	10	7	5	3	2	3	5	6	8	10	MIN °C
	40	35	39	48	45	49	48	47	49	55	47	50	RAIN MM
	8	7	9	10	11	12	13	14	13	14	12	11	RAIN DAYS

THE CONVICT SYSTEM

Reminders of Australia's convict years are a feature of Tasmania's south-east. The island was colonised in 1803 as a penal settlement, and over the next 50 years 52 227 males and 12 595 females – 46 per cent of the entire Australian convict consignment – were transported to its remote shores. Many prisoners worked on public buildings and infrastructure until the early 1820s, after which most were assigned to free settlers. Reoffending convicts from other prison colonies were sent to Port Arthur from 1830, and in the following years, a penal settlement for re-convicted criminals was built there. Conditions were harsh and escape almost impossible. Some of the state's most emotive and colourful stories stem from its convict past and can be appreciated at the Coal Mines Historic Site (north of Port Arthur) and Eaglehawk Neck, while the fruits of convict labour can be seen in many early structures, such as those in the heritage town of Richmond.

TASMANIA

→ For more detail see maps 667, 668–9 & 670–1. For descriptions of ⓣ towns see Towns from A–Z (p. 506).

SOUTH-WEST WILDERNESS

This almost uninhabited landscape of mountains, rivers, waterfalls, gorges and 1000-year-old trees contains the famous Franklin River.

[WEST COAST WILDERNESS RAILWAY]

Zeehan   A walk around National Trust–classified Zeehan reveals something of its heyday in the late 19th century, when it was a booming silver-mining town known as Silver City. Back then it had 26 hotels; the few that remain include the Grand Hotel, which encompasses Gaiety Theatre (once the largest concert hall in Australia). Other buildings of historical interest include the post office, bank and St Luke's Church, and the West Coast Pioneers' Memorial Museum is great for learning about the mines.

Franklin–Gordon Wild Rivers National Park   One way to visit this grand wilderness is by boat from Strahan. Cruises run up the Gordon to Heritage Landing, where there is a short walk to a 2000-year-old Huon pine. For a little more adventure, guided whitewater rafting trips begin near the Lyell Highway east of Queenstown and run down the Franklin River.

Strathgordon   Strathgordon is the place to see Tasmania's massive hydro-electricity industry at work. Sights along Gordon River Road include the huge lakes Pedder and Gordon, the Gordon Dam and the underground Gordon Power Station. Bushwalkers can enter Southwest National Park via the Creepy Crawly Nature Trail.

West Coast Wilderness Railway   One of Tasmania's most recent tourist attractions is a restored 1896 rack-and-pinion railway that travels 34 kilometres across wild rivers and through pristine forests. The journey begins at Queenstown, a mining town huddled beneath some huge and ominous hills, and finishes at Strahan, a charming village on Macquarie Harbour.

South Coast Track   This six-to-nine-day walk along the entirely uninhabited south coast has become a mecca for experienced trekkers. The walk starts at Cockle Creek and finishes at Melaleuca, where you can either continue walking north or take a prearranged flight out. The track crosses an unforgettable landscape of mountain ranges, rivers, swampy plains and wild beaches.

TOP EVENTS

| JAN | Mount Lyell Picnic (Strahan) |

CLIMATE

STRATHGORDON

	J	F	M	A	M	J	J	A	S	O	N	D	
	19	20	17	14	12	9	9	10	12	13	16	17	MAX °C
	10	10	9	7	5	4	3	3	4	5	7	8	MIN °C
	150	111	150	208	235	218	270	283	270	253	187	199	RAIN MM
	17	14	18	20	22	22	25	25	24	23	20	20	RAIN DAYS

PRESERVING THE WILDERNESS

The 1972 flooding of Lake Pedder for the Gordon River Hydro-Electric Scheme sparked a campaign to preserve the south-west wilderness from further inroads. Despite the region's 1982 World Heritage listing, the Tasmanian government pressed on. Conservationists blockaded a proposed dam site from December 1982 until the election of a new federal Labor government in March 1983. Arrests and clashes with police made headlines and earned the movement support from mainstream Australia and abroad. Finally, federal legislation to stop the project survived a High Court challenge. The historical and ecological significance of the south-west wilderness is imaginatively presented at the Strahan Visitor Centre.

→ For more detail see maps 668, 670, 672 & 674. For descriptions of ⊤ towns see Towns from A–Z (p. 506).

NORTH-WEST

This region features unparalleled views of Bass Strait, farmland and the beauty of Cradle Mountain–Lake St Clair National Park.

[DOVE LAKE, CRADLE MOUNTAIN–LAKE ST CLAIR NATIONAL PARK]

Woolnorth The Van Diemen's Land Company, which was granted tracts of north-west Tasmania in the 1820s, still owns this sheep, cattle and plantation-timber property. Tours from Smithton include a visit to the wind farm and to spectacular Cape Grim, where the air is reputedly the world's cleanest.

The Nut Historic Stanley is dominated by the 152-metre-high volcanic Circular Head (known as The Nut), Tasmania's version of Uluṟu. A steep stairway and a chairlift go to the cliff-top, where a 40-minute circuit walk offers spectacular views.

Bass Highway The spectacular scenery on the Ulverstone to Stanley section of this highway recalls Victoria's Great Ocean Road. The route's highlights include the little penguins at the village of Penguin, the Lactos Cheese Tasting Centre in Burnie, the colourful fields of Table Cape Tulip Farm near Wynyard, and the picturesque town of Boat Harbour.

Pieman River cruise Corinna is a delightful spot with a goldmining heritage. Once a bustling town and river port, today it is a popular launching pad for cruises (or canoeing trips) down the Pieman River, compared by many to the mighty Gordon. Daily four-hour return trips aboard Pieman River Cruises' *Arcadia II* pass lush rainforest incorporating stands of majestic Huon pine on the way to rugged Pieman Head, where you can go ashore and explore untouched wilderness.

Cradle Mountain–Lake St Clair National Park This magnificent glaciated landscape is part of the Tasmanian Wilderness World Heritage Area. While the park has become synonymous with the Overland Track, it also includes some fantastic short walks. Take the three-hour circuit around Dove Lake in the north for views of the majestic Cradle Mountain from all angles.

Map labels

Three Hummock Island
Hunter Island
Robbins Island
Cape Grim
Woolnorth
Stanley 🅣
The Nut
BASS STRAIT
Smithton 🅣
Marrawah
ROCKY CAPE NATIONAL PARK
Boat Harbour
Wynyard 🅣
SOUTHERN OCEAN
N
0   20 km
BURNIE 🅣
Penguin 🅣
DEVONPORT 🅣
NARAWNTAPU NP
Ulverstone 🅣
Port Sorell 🅣
SAVAGE RIVER NATIONAL PARK
Latrobe 🅣
Sheffield 🅣
Lake Paloona
Lake Barrington
Waratah 🅣
Pieman Head
Pieman
Corinna
Lake Pieman
Lake Mackintosh
Lake Cethana
Dove Lake
Cradle Mountain
Rosebery 🅣
Lake Murchison
Mount Ossa
CRADLE MOUNTAIN–LAKE ST CLAIR NATIONAL PARK
Lake St Clair

TOP EVENTS

JAN	Henley-on-the-Mersey Regatta (Latrobe)
FEB	Festival in the Park (Ulverstone)
MAR	Taste the Harvest Festival (Devonport)
MAR	Rosebery Miners, Axemen, Bush and Blarney Festival (Rosebery)
MAR	Rip Curl West Coast Classic (near Marrawah)
OCT	Burnie Shines (month-long festival, Burnie)

CLIMATE

WARATAH

	J	F	M	A	M	J	J	A	S	O	N	D	
	18	18	16	12	10	8	7	8	10	12	14	16	MAX °C
	6	7	6	4	3	2	1	1	2	3	4	5	MIN °C
	110	95	123	174	213	229	251	251	226	204	168	142	RAIN MM
	16	14	18	21	23	23	25	25	24	23	20	18	RAIN DAYS

OVERLAND TRACK

The 85-kilometre Overland Track, one of Australia's most awe-inspiring treks, takes walkers into the heart of Tasmania's alpine wilderness, past lakes and tarns, buttongrass heath, wildflowers, woodland and rainforest. It runs the length of Cradle Mountain–Lake St Clair National Park and passes Mount Ossa, Tasmania's highest peak. Each year about 9000 people attempt the five-to-eight-day trek. While you can choose to do the walk with a group and a guide, staying in well-appointed private huts along the way, most people do the walk unguided. There are 12 basic, unattended huts for overnight stays, but these quickly fill up, so be prepared to camp. Summer is the best season for walking here, but even then walkers need to prepare for all conditions.

TASMANIA

→ For more detail see maps 670, 672–3, 674 & 675. For descriptions of 🅣 towns see Towns from A–Z (p. 506).

MIDLANDS & THE NORTH

This area, reminiscent of rural England, features elegant mansions and small cottages. It's also home to some excellent wineries and gourmet food spots.

[ROSS PIONEER HOME]

A stroll through Launceston   Begin at Princes Square, a serene park surrounded by Georgian churches. Walk north up John Street to one of Australia's oldest synagogues, and then to the town hall and some imposing Victorian bank buildings. Continue past a restored Georgian warehouse to the elegant customs house facing the river. Lastly, walk south along the river to Launceston's star attraction, Cataract Gorge, where you can hike, swim, take the chairlift and cross the suspension bridge; at night it's lit in spectacular fashion.

Ben Lomond National Park   Tasmania's best skiing is to be found on Ben Lomond Range, a plateau rising to over 1575 metres. The scenery is magnificent, especially the view from Legges Tor, Tasmania's second highest peak. The park also offers easy bushwalking and is ablaze with wildflowers in spring and early summer.

Trout fishing   Tasmania's Central Plateau Conservation Area is famous for the wild trout that inhabit literally thousands of lakes, tarns and connecting streams. Although bushwalking is the only option to reach many lakes in this wilderness, plenty of the most famous waters, such as Arthurs Lake and Great Lake, can be reached by road; these two lakes are the very best and most popular trout waters, producing consistent quality fish. Bronte Lagoon is also highly regarded, particularly for fly-fishing.

Woolmers Estate   Regarded as Australia's most significant colonial property, Woolmers (near Longford) has buildings, antique cars, photographs, art and furniture that reflect the life of six generations of one family, from 1817 to the present day. The Servants Kitchen Restaurant serves morning and afternoon teas.

Ross   This tiny village (founded in 1812) boasts the decoratively carved Ross Bridge, a fine example of convict construction. Female convicts were held at Ross Female Factory nearby, which visitors can tour today. The wool centre explains the other focus of this charming town.

Map labels

BASS STRAIT
NARAWNTAPU NATIONAL PARK
Bridport
George Town
Gladstone
Pipers Brook
Beauty Point
Scottsdale
Beaconsfield
Lilydale
Derby
Exeter
LAUNCESTON
Deloraine
MOLE CREEK KARST NATIONAL PARK
Hadspen
BEN LOMOND NATIONAL PARK
Mole Creek
Westbury
Longford
Evandale
Legges Tor
Lake Rowallan
CENTRAL PLATEAU CONSERVATION AREA
WALLS OF JERUSALEM NATIONAL PARK
Great Lake
Arthurs Lake
N   0   20 km
Campbell Town
Miena
Lake Sorell
Bronte Lagoon
Lake Echo
Ross
Lake Crescent
Oatlands

TOP EVENTS

JAN	Tamar Valley Folk Festival (George Town)
FEB	Launceston Cup (horseracing, Launceston)
FEB	Festivale (food and wine, Launceston)
FEB	Village Fair and National Penny Farthing Championships (Evandale)
FEB	Exeter Show (Exeter)
NOV	Tasmanian Craft Fair (Deloraine)

TASMANIAN WINE ROUTE

The wineries of northern Tasmania hug the banks of the River Tamar, extending east out to Pipers Brook and Lilydale. Pipers Brook Vineyard, established in 1974, is the largest and best-known producer in the region. Cool-climate varieties ripen well in northern Tasmania, and the superb quality of the wines has much to do with the dry, warm autumn. Local riesling, pinot noir and sparkling wines are gaining international recognition, while cabernet sauvignon, pinot gris, sauvignon blanc, chardonnay and gewurztraminer are also grown. Start a self-guide driving tour by picking up a Tasmanian Wine Route brochure at a visitor centre.

CLIMATE

LAUNCESTON

	J	F	M	A	M	J	J	A	S	O	N	D	
	23	23	21	17	14	11	11	12	14	16	19	21	MAX °C
	10	10	9	7	5	3	2	3	4	6	7	9	MIN °C
	44	39	38	55	62	62	78	78	64	62	51	51	RAIN MM
	8	7	8	10	12	13	15	16	13	13	11	10	RAIN DAYS

→ For more detail see maps 670–1, 672–3, 674 & 675. For descriptions of ⊤ towns see Towns from A–Z (p. 506).

BASS STRAIT ISLANDS

These islands are known for their gourmet produce, fauna and windswept beauty, and offer low-key holidays with a range of activities available.

[CATARAQUI POINT, KING ISLAND]

Killiecrankie diamond Flinders Island is home to the elusive Killiecrankie diamond, which is actually topaz, a semi-precious stone. You can try your luck fossicking around Killiecrankie Bay or nearby Mines Creek, designated as official fossicking areas. The stone you're looking for is usually colourless, but sometimes pale blue or amber gems can be found.

King Island produce King Island has, in recent years, developed a strong reputation for quality produce, for everything from cheese to beef. The island's name is synonymous with award-winning cheeses and creams made from unpasteurised milk. The peerless double brie and camembert can be sampled at King Island Dairy, north of Currie.

Wybalenna Wybalenna ('black man's home') was set up on Flinders Island in 1834 to house around 160 Aboriginal people, the few survivors of Tasmania's pre-European population of over 4000. Less than a third of the people held there survived the appalling living conditions. Located near Emita, it is one of the most important – albeit tragic – historic sites in Tasmania, and includes a National Trust–restored church and cemetery.

Strzelecki National Park The granite Strzelecki Range occupies the south-west corner of Flinders Island. On a clear day, the highlight of this largely undeveloped park is a five-hour-return walk to the summit of Strzelecki Peaks, offering spectacular views across Franklin Sound.

Wreck diving In the storm-lashed waters around King Island lie almost 60 shipwrecks. The best known is the *Cataraqui*, which sank in 1845 off the coast south of Currie with the loss of 399 immigrants and crew, making it Australia's worst peacetime disaster. A number of wrecks around the island are accessible to scubadivers; diving tours are available.

TOP EVENTS

MAR	King Island Imperial 20 (marathon from Naracoopa to Currie, King Island)
EASTER	Three Peaks Race (sailing and hiking event visiting Lady Barron, Flinders Island)
OCT	Flinders Island Show (Flinders Island)
NOV–DEC	King Island Horseracing Carnival (Currie)

CLIMATE

CURRIE

	J	F	M	A	M	J	J	A	S	O	N	D	
	20	21	20	17	15	14	13	13	14	16	17	19	MAX °C
	13	13	13	11	10	9	8	8	8	9	10	11	MIN °C
	36	39	48	68	99	102	124	115	84	75	60	52	RAIN MM
	11	10	14	17	21	22	24	24	21	19	15	13	RAIN DAYS

FISHING

The Bass Strait islands offer superb coastal fishing. On Flinders Island Australian salmon, flathead, gummy shark, silver trevally, pike and squid can be caught from the rocks and beaches. From Lady Barron, Emita and Killiecrankie several charter boats take anglers offshore for catches of all of the above as well as snapper, yellowtail kingfish, trumpeter and various species of tuna. On King Island there is excellent fishing for Australian salmon, flathead and whiting from the beaches along the east coast. South of Currie is British Admiral Reef, where boat-anglers can try for morwong, warehou, yellowtail kingfish and squid.

→ For more detail see maps 670 (inset), 671 (inset) & 673. For descriptions of ⊕ towns see Towns from A–Z (p. 506).

TASMANIA

[CRADLE MOUNTAIN–LAKE ST CLAIR NATIONAL PARK]

LEGEND

ⓘ VISITOR INFORMATION

📻 RADIO STATIONS

🏠 IN TOWN

🎏 WHAT'S ON

🍴 WHERE TO EAT

🛏 WHERE TO STAY

🧭 NEARBY

Adventure Bay

Pop. 620
Map ref. 669 I11 | 671 K10

ⓘ Bruny D'Entrecasteaux Visitor Centre, 81 Ferry Rd, Kettering; (03) 6267 4494; www.brunyisland.org.au

📻 95.3 Huon FM, 936 AM ABC Local Radio

Adventure Bay is the primary town on largely undeveloped Bruny Island, a peaceful retreat for many Tasmanians with its striking landscape untainted by excessive tourism. The island is more accurately two islands joined by a narrow isthmus. On one side the coast is pounded by the waves of the Pacific, and on the other it is gently lapped by the waters of the D'Entrecasteaux Channel. After a long Aboriginal occupation, Europeans discovered the islands. Captain Cook's interaction with the Aboriginal people was largely amicable, but the sealers who subsequently came to Bruny decimated the population. Of those who survived, Truganini is the most famous. Memorials dot the island, standing as stark reminders of the grim past amid the spectacular scenery.

🏠 **Eco-cruise** Arguably one of Tasmania's greatest attractions, this 3 hr cruise takes in the seal colonies, penguins, dolphins, humpback whales and abundant birdlife in the area. It focuses on the ecological and historical nature of the coastline. The tour leaves from Adventure Bay daily; bookings on (03) 6293 1465.

Morella Island Retreat: hothouse, cafe and gum tree maze. *Bligh Museum of Pacific Exploration:* constructed from handmade convict bricks and housing displays of island history.

🍴 *Bruny Island Cheese Co:* cafe with cheese tastings; 1807 Bruny Island Main Rd, Great Bay; (03) 6260 6353. *Get Shucked*

Oyster Farm: fresh Pacific oysters; 1650 Bruny Island Main Rd, Great Bay; 0428 606 250. *The Hothouse Cafe:* home-cooked fare in casual surrounds; 46 Adventure Bay Rd; (03) 6293 1131.

🛏 *Adventure Bay Eco Village:* old-fashioned beachside shacks; 1005 Main Rd, Cookville; (03) 6293 2096 or 1300 889 557. *Bruny Beach House:* modern beach house; Nebraska Rd, Dennes Point; 0419 315 626. *Poppies on the Beach:* secluded beachside A-frame cabin; Main Rd, Great Bay; (03) 6293 1131. *The Tree House:* luxurious waterfront pole-house; 66 Matthew Flinders Dr, Alonnah; 0405 192 892.

🧭 **Bushwalking** Bruny Island is a bushwalker's delight. At the southern tip is South Bruny National Park with stunning scenery and several tracks. Labillardiere State Reserve has a vast range of vegetation including eucalypt woodlands, shrublands, herblands and wildflowers. The rainforest at Mavista Falls is another breathtaking spot, as is Cape Queen Elizabeth. Check with visitor centre for details.

Truganini memorial: boardwalk and lookout; on isthmus between islands; 11 km N. *Birdlife:* little penguins and short-tailed shearwaters on Bruny's ocean beaches. *Cape Bruny Lighthouse:* second oldest lighthouse in Australia (1836); South Bruny National Park via Lunawanna; 29 km SW. *Beaches:* many good swimming beaches (details from visitor centre); Dennes Point Beach on North Bruny has picnic facilities and Cloudy Bay (turn left at Lunawanna) is a magnificent surf beach.

See also SOUTH-EAST, p. 501

Beaconsfield

Pop. 1055
Map ref. 673 J6 | 675 E7

ℹ️ **Tamar Visitor Centre, Main Rd, Exeter; (03) 6394 4454 or 1800 637 989; www.tamarvalley.com.au**

📻 91.7 FM ABC Local Radio, 103.7 FM City Park Radio

Now a modest apple-growing centre in Tasmania's north, Beaconsfield was once the wealthiest gold town in Tasmania. Gold rush–era relics include two massive Romanesque arches at the old pithead of the Tasmania Gold Mine. The Gold Festival is held each December and draws a large crowd. Tourism increased significantly in Beaconsfield following the dramatic rescue of two trapped miners in 2006.

🏛️ *Beaconsfield Mine and Heritage Centre* This mine constantly struggled with water problems, but still managed to produce 26 tonnes of gold before it was closed in 1914. There's now a museum complex along with a miner's cottage.

Beaconsfield Walk of Gold: self-guide historical walk that starts at the Heritage Centre; 1.8 km round trip with signage; West St. *Van Diemen's Land Gallery:* art and craft; Weld St. *Gem and Stone Creations:* gallery and giftshop; Weld St.

🍴 *Tamar Valley Wholefoods & Coffee Shop:* cafe and organic groceries; 110B Weld St; (03) 6383 1120.

🛏️ *Exchange Hotel:* friendly heritage pub; 141 Weld St; (03) 6383 1113. *Tamar River Retreat:* riverside cottages; 123 Kayena Rd, Kayena; (03) 6394 7030.

🧭 **Holwell Gorge** This is a fern-covered gorge with beautiful waterfalls in the Dazzler Range to the west of town. There are basic picnic facilities at the eastern entrance and a 3 hr return hiking track. Contact Parks & Wildlife Service on 1300 135 513; access is via Holwell or Greens Beach rds; 8 km w.

Auld Kirk: convict-built church (1843) at Sidmouth with views of Batman Bridge, which features a 100 m A-frame across the River Tamar; 13 km se. *Wineries:* cellar-door tastings and sales to the east of town around Rowella, Kayena and Sidmouth; Sidmouth is 13 km e. *Lavender House:* exhibition fields of 70 varieties of lavender, plus tearooms with specialty lavender scones and giftshop with 50 health and beauty products; 15 km e.

See also Midlands & The North, p. 504

Beauty Point

Pop. 1113
Map ref. 673 J6 | 675 E6

ℹ️ **Tamar Visitor Centre, Main Rd, Exeter; (03) 6394 4454 or 1800 637 989; www.tamarvalley.com.au**

📻 91.7 FM ABC Local Radio, 95.3 Tamar FM

Beauty Point is the base for the Australian Maritime College and is also a good spot for fishing and yachting. The town's main attractions are Seahorse World and Platypus House.

🏛️ **Seahorse World** The centre acts as a breeding farm for aquariums and the Chinese medicine market, but also studies endangered species to ensure their survival. Take a guided tour to see how seahorses are bred – newborns are the size of a child's fingernail. There's also a touch pool and expo centre for local wines and craft. Inspection Head Wharf, Flinders St; (03) 6383 4111.

Platypus House This centre has 3 live displays: one with platypus and native beaver rats, another with Tasmanian butterflies, and a third with many Tasmanian leeches, blood-sucking worms and spiders. Scientists here are currently conducting research into a disease attacking the Tasmanian platypus population. Inspection Head Wharf, Flinders St; (03) 6383 4884.

Sandy Beach: safe swimming spot.

🌴 *Three Peaks Race:* 3-day sailing and mountain-climbing event that begins in town each Easter, heading north to Flinders Island, then south down the east coast to Hobart.

🍴 *Carbones Cafe:* Italian cuisine with a view; 225 Flinders St; (03) 6383 4099. *Tamar Cove Restaurant:* casual, family-friendly restaurant; 4421 West Tamar Hwy; (03) 6383 4375.

🛏️ *Beauty Point Cottages:* riverbank cottages or homestead suites; 14 Flinders St; (03) 6383 4556. *Kateland Manor Estate B&B:* elegant luxury B&B; 170 West Arm Rd; 0418 128 742. *Pomona Spa Cottages:* 3 Federation-style cottages; 77 Flinders St; (03) 6383 4073. *Greens Beach Luxury Escape:* glass-fronted beach house; 19 Pars Rd, Greens Beach; 0408 376 211.

🧭 **Narawntapu National Park** This park is a popular spot for horseriding and waterskiing (conditions apply), and has excellent walks such as the 5 hr walk from Badger Head to Bakers Beach. Contact Parks & Wildlife Service on 1300 135 513; access via Greens Beach or via Badger Head or Bakers Beach rds.

York Town monument: site marks the first settlement in northern Tasmania (1804); 10 km w. *Kelso and Greens Beach:* popular holiday towns to the north-west.

See also Midlands & The North, p. 504

Bicheno

see inset box on next page

Bothwell

Pop. 377
Map ref. 671 J4

ℹ️ **Australasian Golf Museum, Market Pl; (03) 6259 4033; www.bothwell.com.au**

📻 95.7 Heart FM, 936 AM ABC Local Radio

Australia's first golf course was created in Bothwell in 1837, making golf a point of pride. There are many craft shops and art galleries in town, as well as over 50 National Trust–classified buildings.

🏛️ **Heritage Walk** Bothwell has 53 colonial cottages, churches, houses and official buildings around Queens Park. Notable are the Georgian brick Slate Cottage and St Luke's Church. The best way to appreciate the historic buildings is by a self-guide walking tour; pamphlet from visitor centre.

Australasian Golf Museum: displays of golfing memorabilia and history. The museum also sells award-winning Tasmanian Highland Cheese and local tartan; Market Pl. *Bothwell Grange:* guesthouse with tearooms and art gallery; Alexander St.

🌴 *International Highland Spin-In:* odd-numbered years, Feb–Mar.

🍴 *Bothwell Fat Doe Bakery & Coffee Shop:* excellent pies and pastries; 12 Patrick St; (03) 6259 5551. *Castle Hotel:* great counter meals; 14 Patrick St; (03) 6259 5502.

🛏️ *The Priory Country Lodge:* exclusive fishing lodge; 2 Wentworth St; (03) 6259 4012.

🧭 **Ratho** Home to the first game of golf in Australia, Ratho was the elegant 'gentleman's residence' of Alexander Reid in the early 1800s. It is a stone house with wooden Ionic columns. The famous golf course is still intact and in use. Lake Hwy; 3 km w.

BICHENO

Pop. 639
Map ref. 671 O1 | 673 O11

 Foster St; (03) 6375 1500; www.gsbc.tas.gov.au

 89.7 FM ABC Local Radio, 98.5 Star FM

Bicheno (pronounced 'bish-eno') was set up as a whaling and sealing centre in 1803, predating the official settlement of Van Diemen's Land by a few months. A local Aboriginal women, Waubedebar, became a heroine after saving two white men from drowning in a storm. Landmarks in town bear her name and her grave is in Lions Park. After a short stint as a coal port, during which time the population increased considerably, Bicheno relaxed back into what it does best – fishing – and is known for its abundant seafood. Situated on the east coast, the town has the mildest climate in Tasmania. It is blessed with sandy beaches and popular dive spots, and draws holiday-makers from far afield. Native rock orchids, unique to the east coast, bloom in October and November.

Bicheno Penguin Tours Join a tour at dusk to watch little penguins return home from the sea. On most nights they waddle right past you as they make their way through the coastal vegetation to their burrows. Tours depart from operator's office on Burgess St; bookings on (03) 6375 1333.

Scuba diving Bicheno has one of the best temperate dive locations in the world. The Bicheno Dive Centre runs tours to over 20 locations, including Governor Island Marine Reserve. In winter, divers have been known to swim among pods of dolphins or near migrating whales. Bookings on (03) 6375 1138.

Bicentennial Foreshore Walk: a 3 km track with great views, this walk starts at Redhill Beach and continues to the blowhole. *The Gulch:* natural harbour; foreshore. *Whalers Lookout:* off Foster St. *Sea Life Centre:* aquarium stocked with Tasmanian marine life; features include a touch tank, licensed restaurant, giftshop and the Enterprise, a trading ketch built in Hobart in 1902; 1 Tasman Hwy; (03) 6375 1121. *Scenic boat*

tours: glass-bottom boat tours in The Gulch; bookings on (03) 6375 1294. *Fishing tours:* rock lobster and premium gamefishing in particular; details from visitor centre.

Cyrano Restaurant: casual French cuisine; 77 Burgess St; (03) 6375 1137. *Facets Restaurant and Bar:* modern Australian; Diamond Island Resort, 69 Tasman Hwy; (03) 6375 0100. *Sip Cafe:* funky, colourful cafe; Seaview at Bicheno, 29 Banksia St; (03) 6375 1247.

Bicheno Gaol Cottages: historic self-contained cottages; Cnr Burgess and James sts; (03) 6375 1266. *Bicheno Hideaway:* oceanfront chalets; 179 Harvey's Farm Rd; (03) 6375 1312. *Diamond Island Resort:* award-winning beachfront apartments; 69 Tasman Hwy; (03) 6375 0100. *Aurora Beach Cottage:* timber and stone cottages; 207 Champ St, Seymour; (03) 6375 1774.

East Coast Natureworld This park offers encounters with the region's diverse fauna. The often-misunderstood Tasmanian devil is here, as are Forester kangaroos, Cape Barren geese and Bennett's wallabies. (03) 6375 1311; 8 km N.

Douglas–Apsley National Park This national park is Tasmania's last largely undisturbed area of dry eucalypt forest. It encompasses the catchments of the Denison, Douglas and Apsley rivers and has stunning gorges and waterfalls. There is a viewing platform at Apsley Gorge Lookout and Waterhole, and safe swimming spots. Contact Parks & Wildlife Service on 1300 135 513; 14 km NW.

Freycinet National Park: begins directly south of town; *see Coles Bay. Vineyards:* to the south-west of town, including Springbrook Vineyard and adjacent Freycinet Vineyard, which hosts a jazz concert each Easter; 18 km SW on Tasman Hwy. *Scenic flights:* offered by Freycinet Air over the region; bookings on (03) 6375 1694.

See also EAST COAST, p. 500

[ORANGE LICHEN–COVERED ROCKS ALONG BICHENO'S COASTLINE]

Trout fishing: in nearby lakes, rivers and streams; contact visitor centre for details.

See also SOUTH-EAST, p. 501

Bridport

Pop. 1325
Map ref. 673 L5

ⓘ Main Rd; (03) 6356 1881; www.northeasttasmania.com.au

📻 91.7 FM ABC Local Radio, 103.7 FM City Park Radio

Bridport is a popular seaside holiday retreat for Launceston and Scottsdale residents. It has many safe swimming beaches and fishing.

🏠 **Bridport Wildflower Reserve** Best during Sept and Oct, this wildflower reserve spans 50 ha of coastal heath and woodland. There is a 2.2 km walking track that covers the length of the reserve and takes in scenic Adams Beach. Access via Main St.

Tom's Turnery: functional and souvenir woodturning; 31 Edward St.

🌴 *Bridport Triathlon:* Jan.

✗ *Bridport Bay Inn Bistro & Woodfired Pizza:* seafood and tasty pizzas; 105 Main St; (03) 6356 1238. *Bridport Cafe:* environmentally aware gourmet Mediterranean cafe; 89 Main St; (03) 6356 0057. *Flying Teapot Cafe & Gallery:* garden cafe; 1800 Bridport Rd; (03) 6356 1918.

🛏 *Barnbougle Cottages:* golf course and cottages; 425 Waterhouse Rd, Barnbougle Dunes; (03) 6356 0094. *Bridaire:* old-fashioned B&B with ocean views; 32 Frances St; (03) 6356 1438. *Bridport Resort:* seaside spa villas; 35 Main St; (03) 6356 1789. *Platypus Park Country Retreat:* self-contained farmstay; 20 Ada St; (03) 6356 1873.

◎ *Waterhouse Protected Area:* offers 6700 ha of coastal bush camping, rockpools, sand dunes and beaches. Access via the old goldmining village, Waterhouse; 26 km E. *Wineries:* south-west of town around Pipers Brook and include Delamere, Dalrymple and Pipers Brook; cellar-door tastings and sales.

See also MIDLANDS & THE NORTH, p. 504

Bruny Island

see Adventure Bay

Burnie

Pop. 77 408
Map ref. 672 F5

ⓘ Tasmanian Travel and Information Centre, Civic Centre Plaza, off Little Alexander St; (03) 6434 6111; www.tasmaniantravelcentre.com.au

📻 102.5 FM ABC Local Radio, 106.1 Coast FM

The first European pioneers believed the Burnie area to be agriculturally rich, but high rainfall and dense forests covering the surrounding hills made farming virtually impossible. The deep waters in Emu Bay, however, rescued the community by providing an ideal port for the local industries of tin and timber. Today Burnie, Tasmania's fourth largest city, is a vibrant city with beautiful parklands and charming heritage buildings.

🏠 **Burnie Park** This park has lawns, shaded walkways, diverse native flora and animal enclosures with ducks, swans, wallabies, emus, peacocks and rabbits. Burnie Inn, the city's oldest building,

is in the park and has been restored as a teahouse. A brochure is available from the park information centre. Bass Hwy.

Pioneer Village Museum: re-creation of old Burnie town that houses almost 20 000 items from the late 1800s and early 1900s; Civic Centre Plaza. Little Penguin Observation Centre: free guided tours Oct–Feb; Parsonage Point; 0437 436 803. *Creative Paper:* recycled-paper art with demonstrations and activities; tours available daily; Old Surrey Rd. *Walking track:* 17 km track that skirts the city; start at boardwalk. *Australian Paper:* mill tours held 2pm Mon–Fri; Bass Hwy; bookings on (03) 6430 7882. *The Cheese Tasting Centre:* dairy samples and other specialty produce; Old Surrey Rd. *Hellyers Road Distillery:* makers of single malt whisky; tours, tastings, sales and licensed eatery; open 9.30am–5.30pm daily; Old Surrey Rd, adjacent to Cheese Tasting Centre. *Burnie Regional Art Gallery:* impressive collection of Australian contemporary prints; open 10am–4.30pm Mon–Fri, 1.30–4.30pm Sat, Sun and public holidays; Wilmot St.

🌴 *Burnie Farmers Market:* Wivenhoe Showgrounds; 1st and 3rd Sat morning each month. *Burnie Ten:* 10 km road race; Oct. *Burnie Shines:* month-long community festival; Oct.

✗ *Bayviews Restaurant and Lounge Bar:* smart seafront bistro; 1st floor, North Tce; (03) 6431 7999. *Cafe Europa:* Mediterranean fare; Cnr Cattley and Wilson sts; (03) 6431 1897. *Rialto Gallery Restaurant:* traditional Italian; 46 Wilmot St; (03) 6431 7718.

🛏 *Apartments Down Town:* opulent Art Deco apartments; 52 Alexander St; (03) 6432 3219. *Glen Osborne House:* glorious heritage mansion; 9 Aileen Cres; (03) 6431 9866. *Seabreeze Cottages:* cottages from bygone eras; 6 Mollison St and 82 Bass Hwy, Cooee; (03) 6435 3424.

◎ **Emu Valley Rhododendron Gardens** Considered the city's floral emblem, the rhododendron has pride of place in Burnie. These gardens have over 9000 wild and hybrid rhododendrons on display in a natural 12 ha amphitheatre, and host the floral festival in Oct. Open Aug–Feb; off Cascade Rd; 6 km S.

Fern Glade: tranquil reserve on Emu River with walking tracks and picnic areas; off Old Surrey Rd; 5 km W. *Annsleigh Garden and Tearooms:* voted one of the 10 best gardens in Australia and comprising 2 ha of beautiful gardens and novelty buildings, plus souvenirs and food; open Sept–May; Mount Rd; 9 km S. *Upper Natone Forest Reserve:* popular picnic spot; Upper Natone Rd; 30 km S. *Lake Kara:* good trout fishing; signposted from Hampshire; 30 km S. *Bushwalks and waterfalls:* many in area, but Guide Falls (near Ridgley, 17 km S) is most accessible.

See also NORTH-WEST, p. 503

Campbell Town

Pop. 776
Map ref. 671 L1 | 673 L11

ⓘ Heritage Highway Museum and Visitor Centre, 103 High St; (03) 6381 1353; www.campbelltowntasmania.com

📻 95.7 Heart FM, 1161 AM ABC Local Radio

This small town has been prominent in Tasmania's history: the first telephone call in the Southern Hemisphere was made from here to Launceston; the British Commonwealth's first agricultural show was held here in 1839, and the event is still held today; and it is the birthplace of Harold Gatty, the first person to fly around the world.

TASMANIA

Heritage buildings Of the 35 heritage buildings listed on the National Estate, The Grange, an old manor house built in the centre of town in 1840, is possibly the grandest. Others include the Fox Hunter's Return, Campbell Town Inn and Red Bridge, a 3-arched structure built over the Elizabeth River by convicts in the 1830s. There is a map in Grange Park at the northern end of High Street that lists the main historic buildings.

Heritage Highway Museum: displays on local history and the first round-the-world flight navigation; 103 High St.

Market: Town Hall; 4th Sun each month. *Great Painting Race:* Jan. *Agricultural show:* Australia's oldest; June.

Caledonia Bistro: hearty pub meals; 118 High St; (03) 6381 1158. *Zeps Cafe:* travellers cafe with city vibe; 92 High St; (03) 6381 1344. *St Andrews Inn:* international menu in historic surrounds; 12819 Midland Hwy, Cleveland; (03) 6391 5525.

The Broadwater on Macquarie: secluded fishing cabin; 'Barton', 2464 Macquarie Rd; (03) 6398 5114. *Foxhunters Return:* convict-built coaching inn; 132 High St; (03) 6381 1602. *The Gables:* Art Deco B&B and cottages; 35 High St; (03) 6381 1347. *St Andrews Inn:* restored coaching inn; 12819 Midland Hwy, Cleveland; (03) 6391 5525.

Fishing: Macquarie River, just west of town, and Lake Leake, 30 km E, are 2 good trout-fishing spots in the area.

See also MIDLANDS & THE NORTH, p. 504

Coles Bay

Pop. 473
Map ref. 671 O3

ℹ️ Freycinet National Park; (03) 6256 7000; www.freycinetcolesbay.com

📻 98.5 Star FM, 106.1 FM ABC Local Radio

Coles Bay is a tiny town with a few stores and facilities. It is a gateway to the spectacular scenery of The Hazards, Wineglass Bay and Freycinet Peninsula.

Fishing competition: Southern Game Fishing Club; Mar. *Three Peaks Race:* sailing and mountain-climbing event; Easter. *Freycinet Challenge:* running, sea-kayaking, and road and mountain-bike racing at Freycinet Lodge; Oct. *Mark Webber Challenge:* Nov.

Madge Malloys: super fresh seafood; 3 Garnet Ave; (03) 6257 0399. *The Bay Restaurant:* tranquil, intimate dining; Freycinet Lodge, Freycinet National Park; (03) 6225 7016 or 1800 420 155. *The Edge Restaurant:* fine seafood and gorgeous views; Edge of the Bay Resort, 2308 Main Rd; (03) 6257 0102. *The Oystercatcher:* rustic seafood cafe and takeaway; 6 Garnet Ave; (03) 6257 0033.

Cove Beach Apartments: colourful modern apartments; 97 The Esplanade; 0417 609 151. *Freycinet Beach Apartments:* architect-designed minimalist apartments; Meika Crt, Swanwick; 0428 245 336. *Freycinet Lodge:* beautiful bushland cabins; Freycinet National Park; 1800 084 620. *Iluka Holiday Centre:* family-friendly budget cabins; The Esplanade; (03) 6257 0115 or 1800 786 512.

Freycinet National Park This park is world renowned for its stunning coastal scenery, challenging rock climbs, abundant wildlife, and range of walking tracks. The park is covered in wildflowers, including 60 varieties of ground orchid. Visitors can take the 1 hr walk to the lookout over stunning Wineglass

Bay, or the 2.5 hr return walk to the beach. There are many safe swimming beaches and waterskiing, scuba diving, canoeing and sailing facilities. Check with visitor centre for details.

Freycinet Marine Farm: working oyster farm with guided tours and sampling; open 5–6pm Mon–Fri; tour bookings on (03) 6257 0140; 9 km NW. *Moulting Lagoon Game Reserve:* wetlands of international importance with many bird species; 12 km NW. *Fishing:* Great Oyster Bay is a renowned fishing spot – species include flathead and Australian salmon. Coles Bay is also a base for big-game fishing, particularly southern bluefin tuna in autumn; contact visitor centre for tour details.

See also EAST COAST, p. 500

Currie

Pop. 745
Map ref. 671 O11

ℹ️ The Trend, Edward St, Currie; (03) 6462 1355 or 1800 645 014; www.kingisland.org.au

📻 88.5 FM ABC Local Radio, 88.9 Coast FM

Located in Bass Strait, Currie is the main town on King Island. The island is well known for its gourmet produce, including superb soft cheeses and grass-fed beef. The Roaring Forties are responsible for many of the 57 shipwrecks scattered around the island. The island now has five lighthouses (to avoid any further disaster), including one at Cape Wickham, which at 48 metres is the tallest lighthouse in the Southern Hemisphere.

King Island Cultural Centre: local arts, community projects, resident artists and personal stories of King Island residents; Currie Harbour. *King Island Historical Society Museum:* memorabilia of the island; open 2–4pm daily in summer, closed in winter; Lighthouse St. *The Boathouse Gallery:* displays and sales of pottery, sculptures and paintings, plus barbecue facilities; Edward St. *Observatory:* tours when sky is clear; Rifle Range Rd. *King Island Maritime Trail:* track with interpretive signs takes in shipwreck sites; details from visitor centre. *Tours:* full- and half-day tours of the island run by King Island Coaches; bookings on (03) 6462 1138.

King Island Imperial 20: marathon from Naracoopa to Currie; Mar. *King Island Show:* Mar. *King Island Dramatic Society Play:* Mar. *Queenscliff to Grassy Yacht Race:* Mar. *King Island Horseracing Carnival:* Nov/Dec.

Boomerang by the Sea: perfect seafood, panoramic views; Golf Club Rd; (03) 6462 1288. *King Island Bakery:* gourmet pies and breads; 5 Main St; (03) 6462 1337. *Parers King Island Hotel Bistro:* hearty pub-style meals; Main St; (03) 6462 1633. *Kings Cuisine at the Bold Head Brasserie:* local-produce-driven menu; Grassy Club, 10 Main Rd, Grassy; (03) 6461 1003.

Boomerang by the Sea: comfy seaside motel with views; Golf Club Rd; (03) 6462 1288 or 1800 221 288. *Devil's Gap Retreat:* private coastal cottages; Charles St; (03) 6462 1180. *Naracoopa Holiday Units:* beachside cottages; Beach Rd, Naracoopa; (03) 6461 1326. *Portside Links:* modern units with harbour views; Grassy Harbour Rd, Grassy; (03) 6461 1134.

King Island Dairy Internationally recognised for its cheeses, King Island Dairy has a Fromagerie Tasting Room with an excellent range of brie, camembert, cheddar, washed rind, triple cream and many others. The cows graze year-round, which makes their milk better for cheese production. Loorana; 9 km N.

Fishing: excellent salmon, flathead and whiting fishing from east-coast beaches; morwong, warehou, yellowtail kingfish and squid fishing at British Admiral Reef; 3 km s of Currie. *Penguins:* see them return to shore at dusk at Grassy in the south-east; 25 km SE. *King Island Kelp Craft:* specialising in the rare form of bull kelp handcrafts, with displays and sales; 6 Currie Rd, Grassy; 25 km SE. *Naracoopa:* seaside town with growing tourist industry; 25 km E. *Seal Rocks State Reserve:* covers 800 ha, with calcified forest and stunning cliffs at Seal Rocks; 30 km s. *Lavinia Nature Reserve:* 6400 ha of ocean beaches, heath, dunes, wetland bird habitats, lagoons and a rare suspended lake formation. Lavinia Point has a popular surfing beach; 40 km NE. *Cape Wickham:* lighthouse on rugged cliffs; north of Egg Lagoon; 45 km NE. *Surfing:* King Island is an ideal location for surfing.

See also BASS STRAIT ISLANDS, p. 505

Cygnet

Pop. 840
Map ref. 668 G8 | 671 J9

 Huon River Jet Boats and Visitor Centre, Esplanade, Huonville; (03) 6264 1838; www.huonjet.com

98.5 Huon FM, 936 AM ABC Local Radio

Cygnet was originally named Port de Cygne Noir by French admiral Bruni D'Entrecasteaux – after the black swans in the bay. However, in 1915 two local troopers were assaulted in a pub brawl and, in an attempt to avoid eternal infamy, the town name was changed to Cygnet. Now it is a fruit-growing and alternative-lifestyle community. In spring, the surrounding area blooms with magnificent wattle, apple and pear blossom.

Living History Museum: memorabilia, historic photos; open Thurs–Sun; Mary St. *Trading Post:* antiques, second-hand treasures and collectibles; Mary St. *Town square:* Presbytery, Catholic church (with stained-glass windows dedicated to lost miners) and convent; popular photo spot. *Phoenix Creations:* turns recycled materials into one-off furniture and crafts; Mary St. *Near and Far:* handcrafts and gifts; Mary St.

Cygnet Folk Festival: music, dance and art festival; Jan.

Lotus Eaters Cafe: worldly cuisine and relaxed surrounds; 10 Mary St; (03) 6295 1996. *The School House Coffee Shop:* casual cafe in heritage building; 23A Mary St; (03) 6295 1206. *The Red Velvet Lounge:* popular, eclectic cafe/restaurant; 24 Mary St; (03) 6295 0466.

Cygnet Hotel: budget-priced heritage rooms; 77 Mary St; (03) 6295 1267. *Hartzview Vineyard:* private vineyard homestead; 70 Dillons Rd, Gardners Bay; (03) 6295 1623. *Riverside:* serene and stylish riverside house; 35 Graces Rd, Glaziers Bay; (03) 6295 1952.

Birdwatching: black swans and other species inhabit Port Cygnet; viewing areas off Channel Hwy. *Wineries:* many including Hartzview Wine Centre, known for pinot noir, ports and liqueurs. There are cellar-door tastings and sales; Gardners Bay; 10 km SE. *Beaches:* good boat-launching facilities and beaches at Randalls Bay (14 km s), Egg and Bacon Bay (15 km s) and Verona Sands (18 km s). *Nine Pin Point Marine Nature Reserve:* reef; near Verona Sands; 18 km s. *Fishing:* sea-run trout and brown trout from the Huon River; west and south of town. *Berry orchards:* orchards with pick-your-own sales.

See also SOUTH-EAST, p. 501

Deloraine

Pop. 2242
Map ref. 673 I8 | 675 C10

 Great Western Tiers Visitor Centre, 98–100 Emu Bay Rd; (03) 6362 3471; www.greatwesterntiers.net.au

91.7 FM ABC Local Radio, 103.7 FM City Park Radio

Deloraine has become the artistic hub of northern Tasmania. Artists are inspired by the magnificent scenery, working farms and hedgerows, and the Great Western Tiers nearby. Situated on the Meander River, Deloraine is Tasmania's largest inland town and a busy regional centre that has been classified by the National Trust as a town of historical significance.

Yarns Artwork in Silk Created by more than 300 people and taking 10 000 hours to complete, Yarns is a 200 m reflection of the Great Western Tiers of Tasmania in 4 large panels. Accompanied by an audio presentation and sound and light effects, the Yarns presentation operates every half-hour. 98 Emu Bay Rd.

Jahadi Tours and Art Gallery Jahadi Indigenous Experience runs half- and full-day tours in and around Deloraine that take in the natural landscape and focus on Aboriginal sites such as caves, middens and rock shelters. Tours are organised for a maximum of 8 people to ensure a personal experience; bookings on (03) 6363 6172. The Jahadi Art Gallery exhibits artwork from local Indigenous artists; 900 Mole Creek Rd.

Deloraine Folk Museum: showcases the life of a country publican with exhibition gallery, garden, dairy, blacksmith's shop and family history room; 98 Emu Bay Rd. *Galleries:* sales and exhibits of local artwork from paintings to furniture. Venues include Gallery B on Emu Bay Rd, Artifakt on Emu Bay Rd, Artist's Garret on West Church St and Bowerbank Mill on the Bass Hwy.

Market: showgrounds, Lake Hwy; 1st Sat each month plus 3rd Sat Feb–May. *Tasmanian Craft Fair:* largest working craft fair in Australia; Nov.

Christmas Hills Raspberry Farm Cafe: 'go straight to dessert'; Bass Hwy, Elizabeth Town; (03) 6362 2186. *etc (Elizabeth Town Bakery Cafe):* super roadside licensed cafe; 5783 Bass Hwy, Elizabeth Town; (03) 6368 1350.

Bonney's Inn: award-winning historic B&B; 19 West Pde; (03) 6362 2974. *Bowerbank Mill B&B:* 4-storey restored flour mill; 4455 Meander Valley Rd; (03) 6362 2628. *Peppers Calstock:* exclusive 19th-century boutique hotel; Highland Lakes Rd; (03) 6362 2642. *Three Willows Vineyard B&B:* organic vineyard homestead; 46 Montana Rd, Red Hills; 0438 507 069.

Liffey Falls State Reserve Liffey Falls is surrounded by cool–temperate rainforest species of sassafras, myrtle and leatherwood. There is a 45 min return nature walk from the picnic area through lush tree ferns, taking in smaller falls along the way. Contact Parks & Wildlife Service on 1300 135 513; 29 km s.

Exton: tiny township full of antique shops and charming old cottages; 5 km E. *41 Degrees South Aquaculture:* salmon farm, wetlands and ginseng nursery, with tastings and cafe; Montana Rd; 8 km w. *Ashgrove Farm Cheeses:* sales and tastings of English-style cheeses; Elizabeth Town; 10 km NW. *Lobster Falls:* 2 hr return walk from roadside through riverside forest with lookout and wide variety of local birdlife; 11 km w. *Quamby Bluff:* solitary mountain behind town, with 6 hr return walking track to summit starting near Lake Hwy; 20 km s. *Meander Falls:* stunning falls reached by 5–6 hr return trek for experienced

 TASMANIA

walkers that also takes in the Tiers. Shorter walks are outlined at information booth in forest reserve carpark; 28 km s. **Fishing:** excellent trout fishing in Meander River (north and south of town) and Mersey River (around 20 km ᴇ). **Scenic drive:** through Central Highlands area via Golden Valley to Great Lake, one of the largest high-water lakes in Australia. Check road conditions with Parks & Wildlife Service; (03) 6259 8348.

See also MIDLANDS & THE NORTH, p. 504

Derby
Pop. 302
Map ref. 673 N6

ⓘ Derby Tin Mine Centre, Main St; (03) 6354 1062; www.northeasttasmania.com.au

📻 91.7 FM ABC Local Radio, 94.5 Sea FM

This small north-eastern town was born when tin was discovered in 1874 and the 'Brothers Mine' opened two years later. The Cascade Dam was built and the mine prospered until 1929, when the dam flooded and swept through the town, killing 14 people. The mine closed and, although it eventually reopened, the town never fully recovered. Tourists stroll through the charming streets to view the old buildings and tin mine memorabilia.

🏠 **Derby Tin Mine Centre** The town's major attraction, the centre is a reconstruction of this old mining village. It includes a miner's cottage, general store, butcher's shop, huge sluice and the historic Derby gaol. The old Derby School houses a comprehensive museum with history displays, gemstones, minerals and tin-panning apparatus. Main St.

Red Door Gallerae: paintings, carvings and furniture; Main St. **Bankhouse Manor:** arts, crafts and collectibles; Main St.

🌴 **Derby River Derby:** raft race down Ringarooma River with markets, exhibitions and children's activities; Oct.

✕ **Berries Cafe:** cute country-style cafe; 72 Main St; (03) 6354 2520.

🛏 **Cobblers Accommodation:** rustic miner's cottage; 63 Main St; (03) 6354 2145. **Tin Dragon Trail Cottages:** peaceful rural cottages; 3 Coxs La, Branxholm; (03) 6354 6210. **Winnaleah Hotel:** comfortable pub rooms; 12 Main St, Winnaleah; (03) 6354 2331.

🧭 **Ralphs Falls** The longest single-drop waterfall in Australia. A 20 min return walk under a myrtle rainforest canopy arrives at Norms Lookout at the top of the falls. From here views of the Ringarooma Valley, Bass Strait and the Furneaux Islands. Picnic and barbecue facilities are available. 15 km ꜱᴇ of Ringarooma.

Gemstone fossicking: Weld River in Moorina, where the largest sapphire in Tasmania was discovered; Tasman Hwy; 8 km ɴᴇ. **Miners cemetery:** historic cemetery where early tin miners, including some Chinese, were buried; Moorina; 8 km ɴᴇ. **Fishing:** excellent trout fishing along Ringarooma River north of town.

See also MIDLANDS & THE NORTH, p. 504

Devonport
Pop. 22 317
Map ref. 672 H6 | 675 A6

ⓘ 92 Formby Rd; (03) 6424 4466; www.devonporttasmania.travel

📻 100.5 FM ABC Local Radio, 104.7 Coast FM

Devonport, on the banks of the Mersey River, is the home port of the *Spirit of Tasmania I* and *II*. This vibrant seaport city is framed by the dramatic headland of Mersey Bluff, beautiful coastal

reserves and parklands, and Bass Strait. The community is fuelled by farming, manufacturing and, of course, tourism.

🏠 **Home Hill** A National Trust property, this was home to prime minister Joseph Lyons and Dame Enid Lyons, along with their 12 children. The rich collection of personal material provides insight into Australian political life and international relations during the momentous events of the mid-20th century. Joseph Lyons was Tasmania's premier from 1923 to 1928 and became prime minister in 1932. He is the only Tasmanian to have achieved the 'top job'. Dame Enid became the first female member of the House of Representatives in 1943 and was sworn in as the first female federal minister of the Crown in 1949. The Home Hill property comprises a beautiful old building in well-maintained gardens of wisteria and imposing trees. 77 Middle Rd; (03) 6424 3028.

Tiagarra Aboriginal Culture Centre and Museum Meaning 'keep' or 'keeping place', Tiagarra is one of the few preserved Aboriginal rock carvings sites in Tasmania. A 1 km circuit walk takes in the carvings. An adjoining art centre exhibits over 2000 artefacts. Dioramas depict the lifestyle of the original inhabitants. Bluff Rd, Mersey Bluff; (03) 6424 8250.

Don River Railway Owned and operated by the Van Diemen Light Railway Society; the train offers short rides along Don River to Coles Beach. On-site is a museum housing the largest collection of old steam locomotives and passenger carriages in Tasmania. Train rides hourly. Forth Main Rd, Don; (03) 6424 6335.

Devonport Maritime Museum & Historical Society: features detailed models and displays from the days of sail, through the age of steam, to the present seagoing passenger ferries. 6 Gloucester Ave; (03) 6424 7100. **Imaginarium Science Centre:** learn and enjoy everyday science through hands-on, interactive exhibitions, displays, science shows and special events. Something for all age groups. Entrance off the Wenvoe St carpark; (03) 6423 1466. **Devonport Regional Gallery:** displays the work of established and emerging Tasmanian artists in a century-old building; 45–47 Stewart St; (03) 6424 8296. **Mersey River Cruises:** enjoy the scenery and history of this busy port; operates Nov–Apr; departs from pontoon opposite visitor centre, Formby Rd. **Australian Weaving Mills Factory Outlet:** factory seconds for Dickies and Dri-Glo products; 45 Tasman St. **Devonport Lighthouse:** striking icon completed in 1899 and part of the National Estate; Mersey Bluff. **Scenic flights:** through Tasair from Devonport airport; bookings on (03) 6427 9777.

🌴 **Devonport Cup:** Jan. **Apex Regatta:** Mar. **Taste the Harvest Festival:** Mar. **Devonport Jazz Weekend:** July. **Devonport Show:** Nov. **Athletic and Cycling Carnivals:** Dec.

✕ **Essence Food and Wine:** fine dining, licensed; 28 Forbes St; (03) 6424 6431. **Hawley's Gingerbread House:** hearty fare close to ferry terminal; 71 Wright St, East Devonport; (03) 6427 0477. **High Tide Waterfront Restaurant:** stylish riverside dining; 17 Devonport Rd; (03) 6424 6200. **Taco Villa:** popular Mexican restaurant; Shop 4, 1 Kempling St; (03) 6424 6762.

🛏 **Birchmore of Devonport:** central historic B&B; 8–10 Oldaker St; (03) 6423 1336. **Mersey Bank Apartments:** luxury apartments above various restaurants; 153–159 Rooke St; (03) 6423 5141. **Glencoe Rural Retreat:** French-style luxury B&B; 1468 Sheffield Rd, Barrington; (03) 6492 3267.

🧭 **Tasmanian Arboretum** 58 ha reserve of rare native and exotic plants and trees. Picnic areas, walking tracks and a lake where you can watch waterbirds and platypus. Eugenana; 10 km s.

House of Anvers Chocolate Factory: the total chocolate experience – manufacturing viewing room, chocolate museum and tasting centre. Bass Hwy; 10 km SW. *Braddon's Lookout:* panoramic view of coastline; near Forth; 16 km W. *Kelcey Tier Nature Walk:* 160 ha of native bushland and 3.6 km circuit walk with superb views of Devonport and Mersey River.

See also NORTH-WEST, p. 503

Dover

Pop. 461
Map ref. 668 F10 | 671 J10

 Forest and Heritage Centre, Church St, Geeveston; (03) 6297 1836; www.forestandheritagecentre.com

95.3 Huon FM, 936 AM ABC Local Radio

Dover lies beside the waters of Esperance Bay and the D'Entrecasteaux Channel, with the imposing figure of Adamson's Peak in the background. The three islands directly offshore, Faith, Hope and Charity, were named perhaps to inspire the convicts held at the original probation station. The town is a popular destination for yachting enthusiasts.

Commandant's Office: well-preserved remnant of Dover's penal history; Beach Rd.

Dover Hotel: local fare in homely pub; Main Rd; (03) 6298 1210. *Gingerbread House Bakery Cafe:* breakfasts and light lunches; Cnr Station St and Main Rd; (03) 6298 1502.

Driftwood Cottages: bayside cottages; Bayview Rd; (03) 6298 1441. *Riseley Cottage B&B:* spacious, elegant accommodation; 170 Narrows Rd, Strathblane; (03) 6298 1630.

Faith Island: several historic graves; access by boat. *Walking trails:* epic Tasmanian Trail to Devonport, as well as Dover Coast and Duckhole Lake tracks; details from visitor centre. *Beaches:* safe swimming beaches surround town.

See also SOUTH-EAST, p. 501

Dunalley

Pop. 310
Map ref. 669 M6 | 671 M7

 Dunalley Hotel, 210 Arthur Hwy; (03) 6253 5101.

97.7 Tasman FM, 936 AM ABC Local Radio

A quaint fishing village, Dunalley is on the isthmus separating the Forestier and Tasman peninsulas from the mainland. Nearby is the Denison Canal, which is Australia's only purpose-built, hand-dug sea canal. The swing bridge that spans the canal has become quite a spectacle for visitors.

Tasman Monument Erected in 1942, this monument commemorates the landing of Abel Tasman and his crew. The actual landing occurred to the north-east on the Forestier Peninsula, near the fairly inaccessible Cape Paul Lamanon. Imlay St.

Dunalley Fish Market: fishmonger and cafe; 11 Fulham Rd; (03) 6253 5428. *Dunalley Hotel:* pub tucker, especially seafood; 210 Arthur Hwy; (03) 6253 5101. *Dunalley Waterfront Cafe:* contemporary cafe and collectibles; 4 Imlay St; (03) 6253 5122. *Murdunna Store:* roadside tea room; 4050 Arthur Hwy, Murdunna; (03) 6253 5196.

Potters Croft: loft rooms and gallery; 1 Arthur Hwy; (03) 6253 5469. *Beachbreaks:* glass-fronted beach house; 357 Marion Bay Rd, Bream Creek; (03) 6253 5476.

Copping Colonial and Convict Exhibition Housing a vast array of antiques and memorabilia from the convict era, it has the added highlight of containing one of only 3 cars manufactured in Australia in the 19th century. Arthur Hwy; (03) 6253 5373; 11 km N.

Marian Bay: popular swimming beach; 14 km NE.

See also SOUTH-EAST, p. 501

Eaglehawk Neck

Pop. 267
Map ref. 669 N7 | 671 M8

 Port Arthur Historic Site, Arthur Hwy, Port Arthur; (03) 6251 2310 or 1800 659 101.

97.7 Tasman FM, 936 AM ABC Local Radio

Present-day Eaglehawk Neck is a pleasant fishing destination, speckled with small holiday retreats and striking scenery. Situated on the narrow isthmus between the Forestier and Tasman peninsulas, Eaglehawk Neck was the perfect natural prison gate for the convict settlement at Port Arthur. Few prisoners escaped by sea, so Eaglehawk Neck was essentially the only viable way out. The isthmus was guarded by soldiers and a line of ferocious tethered dogs. Most convicts knew not to bother, but William Hunt, convict and former strolling actor, tackled the isthmus in a kangaroo skin. As two guards took aim with their muskets, their efforts were cut short by a plaintive shout coming from the kangaroo, 'Don't shoot! It's only me – Billy Hunt!'

Bronze dog sculpture: marks the infamous dogline; access by short walking track off Arthur Hwy. *Scuba diving:* the area has a huge diversity of dive sites including the spectacular formations of Sisters Rocks, the 25 m high giant kelp forests, the seal colony at Hippolyte Rock, the SS *Nord* wreck and amazing sea-cave systems; Eaglehawk Dive Centre; bookings on (03) 6250 3566. *Surfing:* good surf beaches at Eaglehawk Neck and Pirates Bay.

Eaglehawk Cafe & Guesthouse: local seasonal menu; 5131 Arthur Hwy; (03) 6250 3331. *Lufra Hotel:* counter meals; 380 Pirates Bay Dr; (03) 6250 3262 or 1800 639 532. *The Mussel Boys:* oysters, mussels, seafood and meats to delight; 5927 Arthur Hwy, Taranna; (03) 6250 3088.

Eaglehawk Cafe & Guesthouse: 2-storey weatherboard guesthouse; 5131 Arthur Hwy; (03) 6250 3331. *Lufra Hotel:* iconic Art Deco hotel; 380 Pirates Bay Dr; (03) 6250 3262 or 1800 639 532. *Four Seasons Holiday Cottages:* modern A-frame cabins; 5732 Arthur Hwy, Taranna; 0407 044 483. *Norfolk Bay Convict Station:* historic waterfront homestead; 5862 Arthur Hwy, Taranna; (03) 6250 3487.

Tasman National Park Tasman Blowhole, Tasmans Arch and Devils Kitchen are the key attractions here, occurring in rocks that are Permian in age (about 250 million years old). There are numerous walks, the full track reaching from Eaglehawk Neck to Fortescue Bay, and there are shorter walks to Tasmans Arch, Waterfall Bay and Patersons Arch. Check with visitor centre for details or contact Parks & Wildlife Service on 1300 135 513; 4 km SE.

Tasmanian Devil Conservation Park This animal-rescue centre features Tasmanian devils, quolls, eagles, wallabies, owls and wombats. There is a 1.5 km bird trail and free flight bird show, Kings of the Wind (11.15am and 3.30pm). The Tasmanian devil feeding time is worth waiting for (10am, 11am, 1.30pm and 5pm; 4.30pm in winter). Arthur Hwy, Taranna; (03) 6250 3230; 12 km S.

 RADIO STATIONS   IN TOWN   WHAT'S ON   WHERE TO EAT   WHERE TO STAY   NEARBY

TASMANIA

Tessellated Pavement: these rocks appear to have been neatly tiled, but their formation is entirely natural. Earth movements have fractured the pavement over the years. 1 km N. *Pirates Bay Lookout:* views across the bay, past the eastern side of Eaglehawk Neck to the massive coastal cliffs of the Tasman Peninsula; 1.5 km N. *Doo Town:* holiday town in which most of the houses bear names with variations of 'doo'; 3 km s. *Federation Chocolate:* chocolate factory with free tastings and historical museum; South St, Taranna; 10 km SW.

See also SOUTH-EAST, p. 501

Evandale
Pop. 1055
Map ref. 673 K9 | 675 H11

ⓘ Tourism and History Centre, 18 High St; (03) 6391 8128; www.evandaletasmania.com

📻 91.7 FM ABC Local Radio, 103.7 FM City Park Radio

Just south of Launceston is this classified town, with beautiful buildings of historical and architectural importance. Cyclists come from as far as the Czech Republic for the annual Penny Farthing Championships, a race along the triangular circuit in the centre of the town.

🏛 **Heritage walk** Evandale is best appreciated with a copy of the brochure *Let's Talk About Evandale*, which lists over 35 historic buildings and sites in the town and many more in the district. Among them are Blenheim (1832), which was once a hotel, St Andrews Uniting Church (1840) with its classic bell-tower and Doric columns, and the former Presbyterian Manse (1840). Brochure available from visitor centre.

Miniature railway: steam railway; open Sun; adjacent to market, Logan Rd.

🌺 *Market:* over 100 stalls; Falls Park, Russell St; Sun. *Village Fair and National Penny Farthing Championships:* largest annual event in the world devoted to racing antique bicycles; Feb. *Railex:* model railway exhibition; Mar. *Glover Prize:* Australia's second-richest art prize; Mar.

🍴 *Clarendon Arms Hotel:* hearty pub food; 11 Russell St; (03) 6391 8181. *Ingleside Bakery:* cafe and bakery; 4 Russell St; (03) 6391 8682. *Josef Chromy Cellar Door Cafe:* modern Australian vineyard restaurant; 370 Relbia Rd, Relbia, (03) 6335 8700.

🛏 *Grandma's House:* cute cottage in heritage garden; 10 Rogers La; (03) 6391 8444. *Greg and Gill's Place:* 2 self-contained apartments; 35 Collins St; (03) 6391 8248. *Solomon Cottage:* B&B in old bakery; 1 High St; (03) 6391 8331. *Wesleyan Chapel:* antique church to yourself; 28 Russell St; (03) 6331 9337.

🧭 **Clarendon House** Just north of Nile is the stunning National Trust residence, Clarendon House. It was built in 1836 by James Cox, a wealthy grazier and merchant, and has been restored by the National Trust. Clarendon's high-ceilinged rooms, extensive formal gardens and range of connected buildings (dairy, bakehouse, gardener's cottage and stable) make it one of the most impressive Georgian houses in Australia. (03) 6398 6220; 8 km s.

Ben Lomond National Park Site of Tasmania's largest alpine area and premier ski resort, this park has both downhill and cross-country skiing, with ski tows and ski hire. The park also offers walking tracks and picnic areas in summer. Legges Tor, the second highest point in Tasmania, has spectacular views. The area blooms with alpine wildflowers in summer. Contact Parks & Wildlife Service on 1300 135 513; 47 km E.

Symmons Plains International Raceway: venue for national V8 Supercars meeting in Nov. A track is open for conditional public use; bookings on (03) 6398 2952; 10 km s. *John Glover's grave:* burial site of prominent Tasmanian artist beside church designed by Glover; Deddington; 24 km SE. *Trout fishing:* in North Esk and South Esk rivers.

See also MIDLANDS & THE NORTH, p. 504

Exeter
Pop. 339
Map ref. 673 J7 | 675 F8

ⓘ Tamar Visitor Centre, Main Rd, Exeter; (03) 6394 4454 or 1800 637 989; www.tamarvalley.com.au

📻 91.7 FM ABC Local Radio, 95.3 Tamar FM

Exeter is a small community in Tasmania's north-east, best known for its scenic surroundings. It lies just north of Launceston, in the centre of Tamar Valley wine country, which, along with cold-climate wines, has a variety of orchards.

 John Temple Gallery: beautiful, framed Tasmanian photographs.

🌴 *Show:* Feb.

🍴 *Exeter Bakery:* great selection of pastries, slices and gourmet rolls including their famous scallop pies; 104 Main Rd: (03) 6394 4069. *Koukla's:* home-style Greek; 285 Gravelly Beach Rd; (03) 6394 4013. *Daniel Alps at Strathlynn:* award-winning regional fine dining; 95 Rosevears Dr, Rosevears; (03) 6330 2388. *Estelle Restaurant at Rosevears Estate:* hip winery restaurant; Rosevears Vineyard, 1A Waldhorn Dr, Rosevears; (03) 6330 1800.

🛏 *Viewenmore Villa for Two:* elevated octagonal house; 312 Rosevears Dr, Rosevears; 0421 422 779. *Conmel Cottage:* old-world 1-bedroom cottage; 125 Rosevears Dr, Rosevears; (03) 6330 1466. *Rosevears Vineyard Retreat:* modern chalets with vineyard views; 1A Waldhorn Dr, Rosevears; (03) 6330 1800. *Aspect Tamar Valley Resort:* quirky Swiss-village chalets; 7 Waldhorn Dr, Grindelwald; (03) 6330 0400 or 18000 TAMAR.

🧭 **Brady's Lookout** This scenic lookout was once the hideout of bushranger Matthew Brady, who used the high vantage point to find prospective victims on the road below. Today the site is more reputable, but retains its magnificent view of the Tamar Valley and is an ideal picnic spot. 5 km SE.

Glengarry Bush Maze: excellent family venue with maze and cafe; closed in winter, except Wed; Jay Dee Rd, Glengarry; 8 km SW. *Paper Beach:* 5 km return walking track to Supply River, where there are ruins of the first water-driven flour mill in Tasmania; 9 km E. *Artisan Gallery and Wine Centre:* displays and sales of Tasmanian arts, crafts and wines from smaller, independent vineyards in the area; Robigana; 10 km N. *Tamar Valley Resort at Grindelwald:* resort in Swiss architectural style with Swiss bakery, chocolatier, crafts, souvenirs and a world-class minigolf course; 10 km SE. *Notley Fern Gorge:* 11 ha wildlife and rainforest sanctuary with giant man-ferns and moss-covered forest. A 2 hr return walk leads to Gowans Creek; Notley Hills; 11 km SW. *Tasmanian Wine Route:* a string of wineries with cellar-door tastings and sales runs on either side of the Tamar, north and south of town. Closest to Exeter are wineries around Rosevears, 10 km s; brochure available from visitor centre.

See also MIDLANDS & THE NORTH, p. 504

Fingal

 Old Tasmanian Hotel Community Centre, Main Rd; (03) 6374 2344.

100.3 Star FM, 1161 AM ABC Local Radio

Poet James McAuley wrote of Fingal's 'blonding summer grasses', 'mauve thistledown' and the river that 'winds in silence through wide blue hours, days'. Indeed, the crags of Ben Lomond National Park and the lush valley make Fingal a quiet inspiration for many writers. The town was established in 1827 as a convict station and distinguished itself by becoming the headquarters of the state's coal industry. Just north of Fingal, at Mangana, Tasmania's first payable gold was discovered in 1852.

Historic buildings There are many heritage buildings throughout the township, particularly in Talbot St, including the Holder Brothers General Store (1859), St Peter's Church (1867) and Fingal Hotel (1840s), which claims to stock the largest collection of Scotch whiskies in the Southern Hemisphere.

Fingal Valley Festival: incorporates the World Coal Shovelling Championships and Roof Bolting Championships; Mar.

Glenesk Holiday Cottage: country cottage with brass beds; 9 Talbot St; (03) 6374 2195. *Mayfield Manor:* 100-year-old country manor; 18 Talbot St; (03) 6374 2285. *The Fingal Hotel:* pub-style accommodation; 4 Talbot St; (03) 6374 2121. *St Pauls River Cabins:* modern cabins with access to trout fishing; 1207 Royal George Rd, Avoca; (03) 6384 2211.

Evercreech Forest Reserve This reserve is home to the impressive White Knights, the tallest white gums in the world, including a specimen 89 m high. A 20 min circuit walk passes through a man-fern grove and blackwoods, then up a hill for a superb view. There is also a 45 min return walk to Evercreech Falls, and many picnic and barbecue spots. Contact Forestry Tasmania on 1800 367 378; on the road to Mathinna; 30 km N.

Avoca: small township with many historical buildings; 27 km sw. *Mathinna Falls:* magnificent 4-tier waterfall over a drop of 80 m, with an easy 30 min return walk to falls base; 36 km N. *Ben Lomond National Park:* see Evandale; 72 km NW.

See also EAST COAST, p. 500

Flinders Island

see Whitemark

Geeveston

 Forest and Heritage Centre, Church St; (03) 6297 1836; www.forestandheritagecentre.com

95.3 Huon FM, 936 AM ABC Local Radio

Geeveston, on the cusp of enormous Southwest National Park, is driven by thriving timber and forestry industries, and slow-moving timber trucks frequent the roads. Swamp Gum, the trunk of a logged eucalypt 15.8 metres in length and weighing 57 tonnes, stands on the highway as the town's mascot. The other principal industry, apple farming, is responsible for the magnificent apple blossom in late September.

Forest and Heritage Centre Comprising 4 different sections, including the Forest Room and Hartz Gallery, the centre offers a comprehensive look at forest practices with computer games, timber species exhibits and a woodturning viewing area. Church St; (03) 6297 1836.

Southern Design Centre Tasmanian timber furniture is lovingly crafted on-site here. Watch resident artisans demonstrate skills in various mediums and browse the showrooms for art and craft, exquisite giftware and home furnishings. 11 School Rd.

Geeveston Highlands Salmon and Trout Fishery: world's first catch-and-release Atlantic salmon fishery with a 1.6 ha salmon lake and 0.4 ha trout lake. Fly-fishing tuition available; bookings on (03) 6297 0030; 172 Kermandie Rd. *Bears Went Over the Mountain:* sales of teddy bears and assorted antiques; 2 Church St.

Tasmanian Forest Festival: biennial event in Mar.

Apple Core Cafe: friendly eatery; 13 George St; (03) 6297 1100.

Bears over the Mountain: teddy-bear-themed B&B; 2 Church St; (03) 6297 0110. *Cambridge House:* grand Edwardian B&B; 2 School Rd; (03) 6297 1561.

Hartz Mountains National Park The Huon Valley used to be wholly glaciated and this national park displays some remarkable glacial features and morainal deposits. Lake Hartz is the largest of the glacial lakes that surround the 1255 m high Hartz Mountain. There are walking tracks through forests of Tasmanian waratah, snow gums, yellow gum and alpine heath, and Waratah Lookout affords fantastic views. Self-guide brochure and park pass are available from the visitor centre. Off Arve Rd; 23 km sw.

Tahune Forest AirWalk Opened in 2001, this is the longest and highest forest canopy walk in the world. It stretches 597 m through the treetops of the Tahune Forest Reserve and, at its highest point, is 48 m above the forest floor. It provides a bird's-eye view of wet eucalypt forest and the Huon and Picton rivers. Within the forest, visitors can go fishing, rafting and camping. Tickets from visitor centre; 28 km w.

Arve Forest Drive: scenic drive following the Arve River Valley that takes in the Look-In Lookout (an information booth and lookout perch), the Big Tree Lookout (remarkable, large swamp gum), picnic areas and the Keoghs Creek Walk (a great short streamside walk); 10 km w. *Southwest National Park:* Tasmania's largest national park offers walking tracks of varying difficulty, beautiful scenic drives and plentiful fishing. Contact Parks & Wildlife Service in Huonville for up-to-date information on track and weather conditions; (03) 6264 8460; 60 km s.

See also SOUTH-EAST, p. 501

George Town

 Cnr Victoria St and Main Rd; (03) 6382 1700; www.georgetown.tas.gov.au

91.7 FM ABC Local Radio, 95.3 Tamar FM

George Town is Australia's third oldest settlement, after Sydney and Hobart, and Tasmania's oldest town. European settlement can be traced back to 1804 when William Paterson camped here after running his ship, HMS *Buffalo*, aground at York Cove. Ignoring the disaster, he ran up the flag, fired three shots in the air and played the national anthem. A memorial stands at Windmill Point to honour this optimism.

TASMANIA

The Grove: this classic Georgian stone house (c. 1838) was the home of Mathew Friend, the port officer and magistrate of the settlement; 25 Cimitiere St. *York Cove:* scenic cove where George Town's centre was built, with mooring and pontoon facilities, and restaurants. *Self-guide Discovery Trail:* walking route through town; brochure from visitor centre. *George Town Watch House:* community history room and female factory display; Macquarie St.

Tamar Valley Folk Festival: Jan.

Cove Restaurant: Mediterranean-influenced modern Tasmanian; York Cove, 2 Ferry Blvd; (03) 6382 9990. *The Pier Hotel Bistro:* bistro with pizzas; 5 Elizabeth St; (03) 6382 1300.

Ben Hyrons Cottage: historic cottage B&B; 40 Anne St; (03) 6382 1399. *Charles Robbins:* stylish modern foreshore apartments; 3 Charles Robbins Pl; (03) 6382 4448. *Tam O'Shanter Views:* isolated glass-fronted beach house; 29 Seascape Dr, Tam O'Shanter; 0412 146 166

Low Head This popular holiday retreat has safe swimming and surf beaches. The Maritime Museum is housed in Australia's oldest continuously used pilot station and has fascinating displays of memorabilia discovered in nearby shipwrecks. At the Tamar River's entrance stands a 12 m high lighthouse, built in 1888, behind which lies a little penguin colony. Penguin-watching tours start around sunset; bookings on 0418 361 860; 5 km N.

Mt George Lookout: scenic views of George Town, the north coast, and south to the Western Tiers. The lookout has a replica of a Tamar Valley semaphore mast used to relay messages in the 1800s; 1 km E. *Fishing:* excellent fishing at Lake Lauriston and Curries River Dam; 13 km E. *Lefroy:* old goldmining settlement, now a ghost town, with ruins of old buildings; 16 km E. *Hillwood Strawberry Farm:* sales and pick-your-own patch, along with sampling of local fruit wines and cheeses; 24 km SE. *Seal tours:* cruises to Tenth Island fur seal colony, a short distance offshore in Bass Strait; bookings on (03) 6382 3452. *Tasmanian Wine Route:* many wineries to the east of town with cellar-door sales and tastings; brochure from visitor centre. *Beaches:* the area has many beautiful beaches including East Beach (facing Bass Strait and ideal for walking, swimming and surfing) and Lagoon Beach on the Tamar River (for family swimming).

See also MIDLANDS & THE NORTH, p. 504

Gladstone

Pop. 42
Map ref. 673 05

ℹ Gladstone Hotel, 37 Chaffey St; (03) 6357 2143.

📻 91.7 FM ABC Local Radio, 93.7 Star FM

The north-eastern district surrounding Gladstone was once a thriving mining area, yielding both tin and gold. Today many of the once-substantial townships nearby are ghost towns. Gladstone has survived, but its successful mining days have long since given way to tourism. It acts as a tiny service centre for surrounding dairy, sheep and cattle farms, as well as for visitors to Mount William National Park, and has the distinction of being Tasmania's most north-easterly town.

Gladstone cemetery: A historic reminder of the miners, including many Chinese, who were drawn to the area; Carr St.

 Bay of Fires Lodge: walk-in luxury lodge; Mt William National Park; (03) 6392 2211. *Gladstone Hotel:* basic pub accommodation; Chaffey St; (03) 6357 2143.

Mt William National Park With rolling hills, rugged headlands and pristine beaches this park offers swimming, fishing, diving and bushwalking. Georges Rocks and Eddystone Pt are favoured diving spots, while Ansons Bay is well known for bream and Australian bass fishing. Walks vary in difficulty and are signposted. At Eddystone Pt, at the southern end of the park, stands a historic, pink-granite lighthouse. Contact Parks & Wildlife Service on 1300 135 513; 25 km E.

Bay of Fires Walk This 4-day guided walk takes in the best of Mt William National Park while offering first-class accommodation and catering. The highlight (along with the scenery) is kayaking in Ansons Bay and, of course, bedding down for the night in the architecturally superb Bay of Fires Lodge, surrounded by bush. (03) 6391 9339.

Blue Lake: disused tin mine filled with brilliant blue water (coloured by pyrites) and safe for swimming and waterskiing; South Mt Cameron; 8 km S. *Cube Rock:* large granite monolith on an outcrop, reached by 3 hr return climb; South Mt Cameron; 8 km S. *Beaches:* magnificent beaches to the north, including Petal Pt; 25 km N. *Geological formations:* impressive granite formations between Gladstone and South Mt Cameron. *Gem fossicking:* smoky quartz, topaz and amethyst can be found in the district; contact visitor centre for details.

See also MIDLANDS & THE NORTH, p. 504

Hadspen

Pop. 1929
Map ref. 673 K8 | 675 G10

ℹ Launceston Travel and Information Centre, Cornwall Square Transit Centre, 12–16 St John St, Launceston; (03) 6336 3133 or 1800 651 827; www.ltvtasmania.com.au

📻 93.7 FM ABC Local Radio, 103.7 FM City Park Radio

Hadspen's best-known resident, Thomas Reibey III, became premier of Tasmania after being fired as archdeacon of Launceston's Church of England. Reibey was prepared to fund construction of Hadspen's Church of the Good Shepherd, but withdrew his offer after a dispute with the bishop, who allegedly discovered Reibey's unorthodox sexual preferences and refused the 'tainted' money. As a result, the church only reached completion in 1961, more than 100 years later.

Historic buildings: Hadspen's Main Rd is lined with heritage buildings, including the Red Feather Inn (c. 1844) and Hadspen Gaol (c. 1840).

Carrick Inn: traditional pub fare; 46 Meander Valley Hwy, Carrick; (03) 6393 6143. *Rutherglen Bistro:* family dining; Rutherglen Holiday Village, Bass Hwy; (03) 6393 6307.

Red Feather Inn: coaching inn turned French Provincial hotel; 42 Main St; (03) 6393 6506. *The Stables at Hawthorn Villa:* self-contained units in historic gardens; Cnr Bass Hwy and Bishopsbourne Rd, Carrick; (03) 6393 6150.

Entally House Thomas Reibey's original abode, built in 1819, is one of the most impressive heritage homes in the state. Entally has sprawling gardens (maintained by Parks & Wildlife Service), Regency furniture and other antiques, as well as a stunning riverside location on the South Esk River. 1 km W.

Carrick: neighbouring town with historical buildings. It hosts Agfest, one of Australia's biggest agricultural field days, in May; 10 km SW. *Tasmanian Copper Gallery:* sales and exhibitions of original copper artworks; 1 Church St, Carrick; 10 km SW.

See also MIDLANDS & THE NORTH, p. 504

Hamilton

Pop. 300
Map ref. 668 F1 | 671 I5

 Council offices, Tarleton St; (03) 6286 3202.

 97.1 Mid FM, 936 AM ABC Local Radio

Hamilton, an unspoilt National Trust–classified town, has avoided the commercialisation found in some parts of the state. Its buildings and tranquil lifestyle just outside Hobart conjure up an image of 1830s Tasmania.

 Hamilton Sheep Centre Demonstrates sheepshearing methods and the use of working farm dogs. Farm tours can be arranged, with meals provided. Bookings on (03) 6286 3332.

Glen Clyde House: convict-built c. 1840, this place now houses an award-winning craft gallery and tearooms; Grace St. *Hamilton Heritage Museum:* small museum with artefacts and memorabilia of the area; Old Warder's Cottage, Cumberland St. *Jackson's Emporium:* sells local products and wines; Lyell Hwy. *Heritage buildings:* many buildings of historical importance include the Old Schoolhouse (1856) and St Peter's Church (1837), which is notable for having just 1 door to prevent the once largely convict congregation from escaping.

 The Highlander Arms: hearty pub-style meals; Tarraleah Estate, 5 Oldina Dr; (03) 6289 0111. *Wildside Restaurant:* gourmet dining; Tarraleah Estate, 5 Oldina Dr, Tarraleah; (03) 6289 0111.

 Hamilton's Cottage Collection: convict-built cottages; 'Uralla', Main Rd; (03) 6286 3270. *McCauley's Cottage:* 1846 garden cottage; 21 Franklin Pl; (03) 6286 3232. *The Old Schoolhouse:* 2-bedroom cottages; Lyell Hwy; (03) 6286 3292. *Tarraleah:* award-winning Art Deco mountain luxury; 5 Oldina Dr, Tarraleah; (03) 6289 0111.

 Lake Meadowbank: popular venue for picnics, boating, waterskiing and trout fishing; 10 km NW.

See also SOUTH-EAST, p. 501

Hastings

Pop. 35
Map ref. 668 F11 | 671 I10

 Hastings Caves and Thermal Springs Centre, Hastings Cave Rd; (03) 6298 3209.

 95.3 Huon FM, 936 AM ABC Local Radio

Hastings lies in Tasmania's far south and is known for the stunning dolomite caves to the west of town. The caves were discovered in 1917 by a group of timber workers who, among others, flocked to the small town in more prosperous days.

 Southport Hotel Bar & Restaurant: Australia's southernmost counter meals; 8777 Huon Hwy, Southport; (03) 6298 3144.

 The Jetty House: eco-friendly bayside homestead: 8848 Huon Hwy, Southport; (03) 6298 3139. *Lune River Cottage:* 3 affordable rooms; Lot 2, Lune River Rd, Lune River; (03) 6298 3302. *Southern Forest B&B:* 3 modern rooms; 30 Jager Rd, Southport; (03) 6298 3306.

 Hastings Caves and Thermal Springs This is the only cave system in Tasmania occurring in dolomite rather than limestone. Newdegate Cave, which began forming more than 40 million years ago, has stalactites, stalagmites, columns, shawls, flowstone and the more unusual helictites, making it – and especially

Titania's Palace within it – one of Australia's most beautiful caves. Tours run throughout the day. Near Newdegate Cave is a thermal pool surrounded by native bushland. It remains at 28°C year-round and is an extremely popular swimming and picnic spot. The Sensory Trail, an easy walk through magnificent forest, starts near the pool. 8 km NW.

Ida Bay Railway: originally built to carry dolomite, the train now carries passengers to Deep Hole Bay along a scenic section of track. Train times change, so ring for details (03) 6298 3110; Lune River Rd; 5 km S. *Lunaris:* gemstone display and shop; Lune River Rd; 5 km S. *Southport:* seaside resort town and one of the oldest settlements in the area; good fishing, swimming, surfing and bushwalking; 6 km SE. *Cockle Creek:* the southernmost point of Australia that can be reached by car, the town is surrounded by beautiful beaches and mountainous terrain and is the start of the 10-day South Coast walking track; 25 km S. *Hastings Forest Tour:* this self-drive tour begins off Hastings Rd west of town, leads north to the Esperance River, then heads to Dover. Short walks and picnic spots en route; map available from visitor centre.

See also SOUTH-EAST, p. 501

Huonville

Pop. 1814
Map ref. 668 G7 | 671 J8

 Huon River Jet Boats and Visitor Centre; Esplanade; (03) 6264 1838; www.huonjet.com

 98.5 Huon FM, 936 AM ABC Local Radio

Huonville produces more than half of Tasmania's apples and is surrounded by blossoming fields of apples, cherries, plums, pears, berries and hops. Although relatively small, it is a prosperous community and the largest town in the Huon Valley.

 Apple and Heritage Centre This centre houses 3 attractions: the museum, providing a comprehensive insight into the lives of Huon Valley's early settlers; Apple Blossom's Gifts, with a selection of gifts, souvenirs and samples of local products; and The Starving Artist, an art gallery and heritage apple orchard. 2064 Huon Hwy; (03) 6266 4345.

Huon River Jet Boats: exciting 35 min jet-boat rides along Huon River rapids; river cruises also on offer, and aqua-bikes and pedal boats for hire; bookings on (03) 6264 1838; Esplanade.

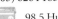 *Market:* Websters Car Park, Cool Store Rd; 10am–2pm, 2nd and 4th Sun each month. *A Taste of the Huon:* festival venue changes towns yearly; check visitor centre for details; Mar. *Huon Agricultural Show:* biggest 1-day agricultural show in state; Nov.

 Huon Manor: classy seafood dishes; 1 Short St; (03) 6264 1311. *Home Hill Winery Restaurant:* dramatic award-winning vineyard restaurant; 38 Nairn St, Ranelagh; (03) 6264 1200. *Petty Sessions:* exciting Tasmanian fare; 3445 Huon Hwy, Franklin; (03) 6266 3488.

 Huon Bush Retreats: eco-friendly forest cabins; 300 Browns Rd, Ranelagh; (03) 6264 2233. *Kay Creek Cottage:* storybook garden cottage hideaway; 17 Kay St, Franklin; (03) 6266 3524. *Matilda's of Ranelagh:* elegant Victorian guesthouse; 2 Louisa St, Ranelagh; (03) 6264 3493.

 Ranelagh Almost an outer suburb of Huonville, Ranelagh has the atmosphere of a charming English village, complete with an old oast house to process the hops. 5 km NW.

TASMANIA

Wooden Boat Centre – Tasmania: workshop and interpretive centre; Main St, Franklin; 8 km sw. *Glen Huon Model Village:* features doll and rock display including the 'crooked man'; open Sept–May; Glen Huon; 8 km w. *Studio Karma:* studio, gallery and home of Terry Choi-Lundberg; original paintings, quality cards and prints of the artist's work; open 10am–4pm Thurs–Sun, by appt May–Sept; Glen Huon; 8 km w. *Pelverata Falls:* stunning waterfall with medium-to-difficult walk over scree slope; 14 km SE. *Huon Bushventures:* 4WD tours of the region; bookings on (03) 6264 1838. *Fishing:* good trout fishing in Huon River and tributaries.

See also SOUTH-EAST, p. 501

Kettering

Pop. 389
Map ref. 668 H8 | 671 K8

ⓘ Bruny D'Entrecasteaux Visitor Centre, 81 Ferry Rd; (03) 6267 4494; www.tasmaniaholiday.com

📻 95.3 Huon FM, 936 AM ABC Local Radio

The area around Kettering, in the state's south-east, was first explored in 1792 by Bruni D'Entrecasteaux, after whom the surrounding channel is named. The town was settled in the 1800s by timber cutters, sealers and whalers, and the community was a transient one. Kettering is now principally the launching point to Bruny Island, but is charming in its own right with a sheltered harbour full of yachts and fishing vessels.

🏠 *Oyster Cove Marina:* well-known marina with boats for hire, skippered cruises and fishing charters; Ferry Rd. *Ocean-kayaking:* guided day tours with Roaring 40s Ocean Kayaking company; bookings on (03) 6267 5000. *Herons Rise Vineyard:* picturesque vineyard specialising in cool-climate white and pinot noir wines; sales; 120 Saddle Rd.

🍴 *Farm Gate Cafe:* gourmet provedore and cafe; Cnr Channel Hwy and Saddle Rd; (03) 6267 4497. *Fleurtys Cafe:* uniquely Tasmanian gourmet meals; 3866 Channel Hwy, Birchs Bay; (03) 6267 4078. *Peppermint Bay Dining Room:* top Tasmanian gourmet food; 3435 Channel Hwy, Woodbridge; (03) 6267 4088.

🏨 *Anstey Barton:* ultra-luxurious modern mansion; 82 Ferry Rd; (03) 6267 4199. *Herons Rise Vineyard Cottages:* rustic vineyard cottages; 100 Saddle Rd; (03) 6267 4339. *Tulendena:* peaceful garden cottage; 29 Bloomsbury La; (03) 6267 4348.

🧭 **Peppermint Bay** This is one of Tasmania's top gastronomic experiences, with a first-class restaurant and a store full of local products. There is also an arts and crafts gallery and fine views across the waterfront. The Peppermint Bay Cruise, departing from Hobart and touring the D'Entrecasteaux Channel along the way, is another way to visit this spectacular location; bookings on 1800 751 229. 3435 Channel Hwy, Woodbridge; 5 km s.

Woodbridge Hill Handweaving Studio: weaving tuition and sales of products woven from silk, cotton, linen, wool, alpaca, mohair and collie-dog hair; Woodbridge Hill Rd; 4 km s. *Channel Historical and Folk Museum:* displays of historical memorabilia of the D'Entrecasteaux Channel region; closed Wed; 2361 Channel Hwy, Lower Snug; 5 km N. *Conningham:* good swimming and boating beaches; 6 km N. *Snug Falls:* pleasant 1.5 hr return walk to falls; 8 km N. *Grandvewe Sheep Cheesery:* 15 different types of cheese at Tasmania's only sheep cheesery; Birchs Bay; 9 km s. *Bruny Island ferry:* trips throughout the day from Ferry Rd Terminal; for information on the island, *see Adventure Bay.*

See also SOUTH-EAST, p. 501

King Island

see Currie

Kingston

Pop. 17 286
Map ref. 669 I6 | 671 K8

ⓘ Council offices, Civic Centre, 15 Channel Hwy; (03) 6211 8200; www.kingborough.tas.gov.au

📻 92.1 Hobart FM, 936 AM ABC Local Radio

Almost an outer suburb of Hobart, this pleasant seaside town sits just beyond the city limits. Its literary claim to fame is that Nobel Laureate Patrick White holidayed at Kingston Beach as a child.

🏠 **Australian Antarctic Headquarters** This centre houses displays on the dramatic events of Antarctic exploration, including historic photographs and items such as Sir Douglas Mawson's sledge. Open Mon–Fri; Channel Hwy; (03) 6232 3209.

🌴 *Rotary Market:* library carpark; Sun. *Olie Bollen Festival:* Dutch festival; Oct.

🍴 *Citrus Moon Cafe:* wholefoods cafe; 23 Beach Rd; (03) 6229 2388. *Doms Asian Teahouse:* South-East Asian; Shop 9A Opal Drive Shopping Centre, Blackmans Bay; (03) 6229 7633. *The Beach:* popular beachside bistro; 14 Ocean Espl, Blackmans Bay; (03) 6229 7600. *Pear Ridge:* French-style food from a potager garden; 1683 Channel Hwy, Margate; (03) 6267 1811.

🏨 *Anubha Mountain Health Retreat:* pampering resort with magnificent views; 680 Summerleas Rd; (03) 6239 1573. *D'Entrecasteaux:* charming provincial boutique hotel; 77 Howden Rd, Howden; (03) 6267 1161. *Kingston Beach Motel:* budget rooms in great location; Cnr Beach Rd and Osbourne Espl, Kingston Beach; (03) 6229 8969. *Tranquilla:* sunny seaside B&B; 30 Osbourne Espl, Kingston Beach; (03) 6229 6282.

🧭 **Shot Tower** This tower, one of the state's most historic industrial buildings (with a National Trust 'A' classification), was completed in 1870. There are wonderful views of the Derwent Estuary from the top of the 66 m structure and at the base there is a museum and a craft shop. Channel Hwy, Taroona; 4 km NE.

Kingston Beach: safe swimming beach at the mouth of the River Derwent; 3 km SE. *Kingston Beach Golf Course:* well-regarded course with specific holes picked by international players as their favourites; Channel Hwy. *Boronia Hill Flora Trail:* 2 km track follows ridge line between Kingston and Blackmans Bay through remnant bush; begins at end of Jindabyne Rd and finishes at Peter Murrell Reserve, well known for its many native orchids; Kingston. *Blackmans Bay blowhole:* small blowhole at the northern end of the beach that is spectacular in stormy weather; Blowhole Rd; 7 km s. *Alum Cliff walk:* great walk from Browns River area along the coastal cliffs to Taroona. *Train:* 1950s passenger train (non-operational) with tearooms in the buffet car, adjacent antique sales and Sun market; Margate; 9 km s. *Tinderbox Marine Reserve:* follow the underwater snorkel trail; Tinderbox; 11 km s. *Scenic drives:* south through Blackmans Bay, Tinderbox and Howden, with magnificent views of Droughty Pt, South Arm Peninsula, Storm Bay and Bruny Island from Piersons Pt. *Fishing:* good fishing at Browns River. Red Tag Trout runs tours from Kingston; bookings on (03) 6229 5896. *Horseriding:* trail rides at Cheval Equitation; bookings on (03) 6229 4303.

See also SOUTH-EAST, p. 501

Latrobe

Pop. 2846
Map ref. 672 H6 | 674 H2 | 675 B7

 48 Gilbert St; (03) 6421 4699; www.latrobetasmania.com.au

100.5 FM ABC Local Radio, 104.7 Coast FM

Latrobe was once Tasmania's third largest settlement with inns, hotels, a hospital and no less than three newspapers in circulation. As it was the best place to cross the Mersey River, it became the highest-profile town on the north coast. Since the early 19th century, however, Latrobe has ceded its importance as a port town and relaxed into a gentler pace.

Australian Axeman's Hall of Fame This attraction honours the region's renowned axemen and details the role of the town in the creation of woodchop competition. Also featured at the facility is the Platypus and Trout Experience, including an interactive display of Tasmanian wildlife heritage. There is also a cafe and giftshop selling local crafts and souvenirs. 1 Bells Pde.

Platypus tours: with a LandCare guide; check at visitor centre for departure times and cost; bookings on (03) 6426 1774. *Court House Museum:* located in a heritage building under the National Trust register with over 600 prints and photographs; open 1–4pm Tues–Fri, other times by appt; Gilbert St; (03) 6426 2777. *Sherwood Hall Museum:* original home of pioneering couple Thomas Johnson and Dolly Dalrymple; open 10am–4pm daily Oct–Mar, Tues and Thurs or by appt in other months; Bells Parade. *Anvers Confectionery:* factory of well-known Belgian chocolatier, this outlet has tastings and sales of premium chocolates, fudges and pralines; 9025 Bass Hwy. *Sheean Memorial Walk:* 3 km return walk commemorating local soldiers and WW II hero; Gilbert St. *Bells Parade Reserve:* beautiful picnic ground along riverbank where town's docks were once located; River Rd. *Historical walk:* starts at western end of Gilbert St and turns into Hamilton St.

Markets: Gilbert St; 7am–2pm Sun. *Henley-on-the-Mersey regatta:* Jan. *Chocolate Winterfest:* July. *Latrobe Wheel Race:* prestige cycling event; Dec. *Latrobe Gift footrace:* Dec.

House of Anvers: European cafe; 9025 Bass Hwy; (03) 6426 2703. *Lucas Hotel:* excellent bistro meals; 46 Gilbert St; (03) 6426 1101.

Lucas Hotel: quiet ensuite rooms; 46 Gilbert St; (03) 6426 1101. *Lucinda B&B:* Victorian mansion in parkland gardens; 17 Forth St; (03) 6426 2285. *Sherwood View:* rural B&B; 298 Coal Hill Rd; (03) 6426 2797.

Warrawee Forest Reserve An excellent place for platypus viewing, swimming, bushwalking and barbecues. A 5 km walking track winds through sclerophyll forest and a boardwalk has been installed around the lake to allow disabled access to trout fishing. Tours are run by LandCare; bookings on (03) 6426 2877; 3 km s.

Henry Somerset Orchid Reserve: over 40 native orchids and other rare flora; Railton Rd; 7 km s.

See also NORTH-WEST, p. 503

Launceston

see inset box on next page

Lilydale

Pop. 292
Map ref. 673 K7 | 675 H8

 Launceston Travel and Information Centre, Cornwall Square Transit Centre, 12–16 St John St, Launceston; (03) 6336 3133 or 1800 651 827; www.ltvtasmania.com.au

91.7 FM ABC Local Radio, 95.3 Tamar FM

Originally called Germantown, this small north-eastern township is better known for the 'Englishness' of its gardens and the almost French quality of its countryside. Yet the bushwalks through surrounding reserves and waterfalls are distinctly Australian, with native temperate rainforests lining the trails.

Painted Poles: scattered throughout the village centre are 15 hydro poles painted by professional and community artists to show the local history.

Lilydale Tavern: good pub staples; 1983 Main Rd; (03) 6395 1230. *Pipers Brook Winery Cafe:* acclaimed vineyard cafe; 1216 Pipers Brook Rd, Pipers Brook; (03) 6382 7527.

Eagle Park and Cherry Top: passive-solar mudbrick house; 81 Lalla Rd, Bottom Downie; (03) 6395 1167.

Lilydale Falls Situated within the temperate rainforest of Lilydale Park, the waterfall is at the end of a pleasant 5 min walk through ferns and eucalypts. A picnic area and playground are on-site, as well as 2 oak trees planted in 1937 from acorns picked near Windsor Castle in England to commemorate the coronation of King George VI. 3 km N.

Tamar Valley Wine Route: numerous vineyards between Lilydale and Pipers Brook include Providence (4 km N), Clover Hill (12 km N) and Brook Eden (15 km N); *see also Launceston*; brochure from visitor centre. *Walker Rhododendron Reserve:* 12 ha park reputed to have the best rhododendron display in Australia. Other species are also on display; Lalla; 4 km W. *Appleshed:* teahouse with local art and craft; Lalla; 4 km W. *Hollybank Forest Reserve:* 140 ha forest reserve with Australia's first continuous cable treetop tour, arboretum, picnic facilities and information centre with details on walking tracks; marked turn-off near Underwood; 5 km s. *Mt Arthur:* 3 hr return scenic walk to summit (1187 m); 20 km SE. *Bridestowe Estate Lavender Farm:* this is one of the world's largest single commercial lavender farms; 296 Gillespies Rd, Nabowla; 26 km N.

See also MIDLANDS & THE NORTH, p. 504

Longford

Pop. 3030
Map ref. 673 K9 | 675 G12

 JJ's Bakery at the Old Mill Cafe, 52 Wellington St; (03) 6391 2364

91.7 FM ABC Local Radio, 103.7 FM City Park Radio

Longford was established when numerous settlers from Norfolk Island were given land grants in the area in 1813. Fittingly, the district became known as Norfolk Plains, while the settlement itself was called Latour. Today Longford is classified as a historic town and serves the rich agricultural district just south of Launceston.

Historic buildings These include the Queen's Arms (1835) in Wellington St, Longford House (1839) in Catherine St and the Racecourse Hotel (1840s) in Wellington St, which was originally built as a railway station then used as a hospital and later a pub, and in which a patron was murdered after stealing

TASMANIA

LAUNCESTON

Pop. 99 676

Map ref. 673 K8 | 675 G10

ⓘ Cornwall Square Transit Centre, 12–16 St John St;
(03) 6336 3133 or 1800 651 827; www.ltvtasmania.com.au

📻 91.7 FM ABC Local Radio, 103.7 FM City Park Radio

Tasmania's second largest city and a busy tourist centre,
Launceston lies nestled in northern hilly country where the
Tamar, North Esk and South Esk rivers meet. An elegantly laid-
back place, Launceston has the highest concentration of 19th-
century buildings in Australia. Yet it is also a city of contrasts,
where modern marinas meet graceful Georgian and Victorian
streetscapes and parks – and you're seldom without a view of the
Tamar River or surrounding valley.

Cataract Gorge This is one of Launceston's outstanding
natural attractions. Historic Kings Bridge spans the Tamar River
at the gorge entrance. Above the cliffs on the north side is an
elegant Victorian park with lawns, European trees, peacocks
and a restaurant. The world's longest single-span chairlift and
a suspension bridge link this area to First Basin's lawns on the
south side, which has a swimming pool and a kiosk. Walks and
self-guide nature trails run on both sides of the gorge.

Queen Victoria Museum and Art Gallery This is considered one
of the best regional museums in Australia, with permanent
exhibits on Aboriginal and convict history, Tasmanian flora
and fauna, colonial art, a Chinese joss house, a blacksmith
shop and many temporary exhibitions. Other features include
Phenomena Factory – an interactive science centre for kids of
all ages – as well as the Launceston Planetarium and a railway
museum. Renovations are currently being done on the museum's
original Royal Park building, which should reopen in 2011. In
the meantime, all exhibits are housed in the Inveresk building;
2 Invermay Rd, Inveresk; (03) 6323 3777.

Boags Brewery J Boag and Son Brewery was where James Boag
commenced his brewing tradition on the banks of the Esk River
in 1852. Full tours of the brewery start and finish at the Boags
Centre for Beer Lovers. The centre houses a museum and a retail
store. Open Mon–Fri; William St; (03) 6332 6300.

City Park: magnificent 5 ha park with European deciduous
trees, it features a Japanese Macaque monkey enclosure, the
John Hart conservatory, annual display beds, senses garden,
and monuments; Cnr Tamar and Brisbane sts. *Seaport:* new
riverside complex with restaurants, shops, marina and hotel at
the head of the Tamar River. *Design Centre of Tasmania:* houses
Australia's only museum collection of contemporary wood
design. Runs exhibitions and tours of crafts, design and art, both
nationally and internationally; City Park. *National Automobile
Museum of Tasmania:* displays over 40 fully restored classic
vehicles spanning 100 years of style and technical achievement;
Cimitiere St. *Ritchies Mill & Stillwater River Cafe & Restaurant:*
a 4-storey grain mill from the 1800s, now home to one of
Launceston's most renowned restaurants. The award-winning
Stillwater restaurant opened on the ground floor of the Mill in
2000, while The Mill Providore & Gallery is located on the 1st
and 2nd floor of the mill, showcasing local Tasmanian produce,
art and design; Paterson St. *Aurora Stadium:* the home of AFL

[BOAGS CENTRE FOR BEER LOVERS]

football in Tasmania, the stadium hosts 5 rostered matches per
year and a variety of other events. *Walking tour:* self-guide tour
takes in 25 places of historical importance including Morton
House, Milton Hall and Princes Sq, where the fountain was
changed from a half-naked nymph to a pineapple after locals
objected; brochure from visitor centre. *Waverley Woollen Mills:*
Australia's oldest woollen mill, with tours and showroom; open
Mon–Fri; Waverley Rd. *Old Umbrella Shop:* unique 1860s
shop preserved by the National Trust and housing a giftshop
and information centre; George St. *Aquarius Roman Baths:*
relaxation centre with Tepidarium (warm bath), Caldarium
(hot bath), Spa Alveus (therapeutic spa) and hot rooms; open
9am–9pm; George St. *Scenic flights:* Tasmanian Aero Club at
Launceston Airport; bookings on (03) 6391 8330.

Launceston Cup: state's biggest race day; Feb. *Festivale:*
food and wine; Feb. *MS Fest:* major youth music festival; Feb.
Launceston Regatta & Henley on Tamar: annual boat race;
Mar. *National Trust Tasmanian Heritage Festival:* Apr. *Agfest:*
Tasmania's largest agricultural show; May. *Royal Launceston
Show:* Oct. *Tamar Valley Classic:* yacht race; Nov.

Black Cow Bistro: beef connoisseur's heaven; Cnr George
and Paterson sts; (03) 6331 9333. *Calabrisella:* traditional Italian;
56 Wellington St; (03) 6331 1958. *Flip:* creative burgers; 23
George St; (03) 6334 6844. *Smokey Joe's Creole Cafe:* Caribbean
and Cajun Creole; 20 Lawrence St; (03) 6331 0530. *Stillwater
River Cafe & Restaurant:* fine Asian-inspired dining: Ritchies
Mill, 2 Bridge Rd; (03) 6331 4153.

Fiona's of Launceston: old-style central B&B;
141A George St; (03) 6334 5965. *Peppers Seaport:* swish riverside
hotel; 28 Seaport Blvd; (03) 6345 3333. *The Lido Apartments:*
1930s Art Deco apartments; 47–49 Elphin Rd; (03) 6337 3000.
TWOFOURTWO: hip, contemporary luxury apartments;
242 Charles St; (03) 6331 9242. *Werona Heritage
Accommodation:* opulent Federation hillside mansion;
33 Trevallyn Rd, Trevallyn; (03) 6334 2272.

Tamar Valley Wine Route With around 24 vineyards in the area, Pipers Brook Vineyard is one of the state's biggest names, and makes beautiful gewurztztraminer and pinot noir. Its cellar also offers tastings of its Ninth Island Label and Kreglinger sparkling wines. Other wineries worth visiting include Bay of Fires and Tamar Ridge. For masterpieces in sparkling, visit Clover Hill, whose picturesque cellar door is perfect for a picnic lunch, and Jansz, with its modern, architectural wine room featuring an interpretive centre. Brochures are available from the visitor centre.

Franklin House A National Trust–listed Georgian building, Franklin House was built by convicts in 1838 for a Launceston brewer. It is furnished elaborately with period pieces and is a popular historical attraction. 6 km s.

Punchbowl Reserve: spectacular park with rhododendron plantation, a small gorge and native and European fauna in natural surroundings; 5 km sw. *Trevallyn State Reserve:*

neighbour to the Cataract Gorge, good picnic spot with trail rides, kayaking, walking tracks and water activities at Trevallyn Dam; 6 km w. *Cable hang-gliding:* Australia's only cable hang-gliding simulator; closed weekdays May–Nov; Reatta Rd; 6 km w. *Tamar Island Wetlands:* urban wetlands reserve; a haven for birdlife, with a 3 km boardwalk to Tamar Island, pleasing views from the middle of the river and an outstanding Interpretation Centre that offers visitors the opportunity to learn about the great value of the wetlands; 9 km NW. *Launceston Lakes and Wildlife Park:* Tasmanian devils, emus, wallabies and other native fauna. Good fly-fishing in the lakes with tuition available; 17 km w. *Grindelwald:* Swiss village designed for relaxation, which has the chalet-themed Tamar Valley Resort and Swiss-style shopping square with specialty shops including Swiss chocolates and bakery, crafts and souvenirs; 19 km NW.

See also **MIDLANDS & THE NORTH, p. 504**

and swallowing 2 gold sovereigns from local farmhands. The Racecourse Hotel is now a guesthouse and restaurant. Also on Wellington St is Christ Church, an 1839 sandstone building with outstanding stained-glass windows, pioneer gravestones and a clock and bell presented by George VI. Path of History is the self-guide walk; brochure available from visitor centre.

Walk: track along the South Esk River. *The Village Green:* originally the site of the town market, now a picnic and barbecue spot; Cnr Wellington and Archer sts.

Longford Picnic Day Races: held at the oldest operating racecourse in Australia; Jan. *Blessing of the Harvest Festival:* celebration of the rural tradition with parade and Sheaf Tossing Championships; Mar.

JJs Bakery and Old Mill Cafe: historic bakery cafe; 52 Wellington St; (03) 6391 2364. *The Racecourse Inn Restaurant:* elegant modern Australian; 114 Marlborough St; (03) 6391 2352. *The River's Edge Cafe:* Italian-inspired garden cafe; The River's Edge Venue, 38 Tannery Rd; (03) 6391 2559.

Longford Boutique Accommodation: luxury heritage B&B; 6 Marlborough St; (03) 6391 2126. *The Racecourse Inn:* rose-covered convict-brick B&B; 114 Marlborough St; (03) 6391 2352. *Woolmers Estate:* timeless colonial cottages; Woolmers La; (03) 6391 2230.

Woolmers Estate Woolmers was built c. 1817 by the Archer family, who lived there for 6 generations. Tours of the house, the outbuildings, the gardens and the National Rose Garden are conducted daily and the Servants Kitchen restaurant serves morning and afternoon teas. Lyell Hwy; (03) 6286 3332; 5 km s.

Brickendon: historic Georgian homestead built in 1824, now a working farm and historic farm village; open Wed–Sun June–July, Tues–Sun Sept–May; 2 km s. *Perth:* small town with historic buildings, including Eskleigh and Jolly Farmer Inn, and market on Sun mornings; 5 km NE. *Tasmanian Honey Company:* tastings and sales of excellent range of honeys including

leatherwood and flavoured varieties; 25A Main Rd, Perth; 5 km NE. *Woodstock Lagoon Wildlife Sanctuary:* 150 ha sanctuary for nesting waterfowl; 9 km w. *Cressy:* good fly-fishing at Brumby's Creek, especially in Nov when mayflies hatch; 10 km s.

See also **MIDLANDS & THE NORTH, p. 504**

Miena

Pop. 104
Map ref. 671 I1 | 673 I11

ℹ️ Great Lake Hotel, Great Lake Hwy; (03) 6259 8163.

📻 91.7 FM ABC Local Radio, 95.7 Heart FM

Miena is on the shores of Great Lake on Tasmania's Central Plateau and has been popular with anglers since brown trout were released into the lake in 1870. The Aboriginal name (pronounced 'my-enna') translates to 'lagoon-like'. The surrounding region, known as the Lake Country, can become very cold, with snow and road closures, even in summer.

Great Lake Hotel: fireside counter meals; 3096 Marlborough Hwy; (03) 6259 8163.

Central Highlands Lodge: lodge for fly-fishing devotees; Haddens Bay; (03) 6259 8179. *Great Lake Hotel:* lakeside rooms and apartments; 3096 Marlborough Hwy; (03) 6259 8163. *Shannon Rise Lodge:* self-contained lodge; 52 Lake Hwy, Haddens Bay; (03) 5334 3851 *Skittleball Plain Homestead:* isolated rustic cabin; Little Pine Lagoon; (03) 6424 1288.

Fishing The 22 km Great Lake is the second largest freshwater lake in Australia and has excellent trout fishing. But Arthurs Lake, 23 km E, is said to be even better. The Highland Dun mayflies that hatch in summer generate an abundance of speckled brown trout, drawing fly-fishing enthusiasts. West of Liawenee (about 7 km N) are more locations for fly-fishing in isolated lakes and tarns of the Central Plateau Conservation Area (4WD recommended for several lakes, while some are accessible only to experienced bushwalkers). Lakes are closed over winter.

Bushwalking: along the shores of Great Lake. *Circle of Life:* bronze sculptures by Steven Walker, each representing an aspect of the region's history; Steppes; 27 km SE. *Waddamana Power Museum:* housed in the first station built by the Hydro-Electric Corporation, it includes history of hydro-electricity in Tasmania; 33 km S. *Lake St Clair:* a boat service from Cynthia Bay provides access to the north of the lake and to the renowned 85 km Overland Track, which passes through Cradle Mountain–Lake St Clair National Park; *see Sheffield;* 63 km W.

See also MIDLANDS & THE NORTH, p. 504

Mole Creek

Pop. 223
Map ref. 672 H8 | 674 H5 | 675 A11

 46 Pioneer Dr; (03) 6363 1487; www.greatwesterntiers.org.au

91.7 FM ABC Local Radio

Mole Creek is named after the nearby creek that 'burrows' underground. Most visitors come to explore the limestone caves in Mole Creek Karst National Park. The unique honey from the leatherwood tree, which grows only in the west-coast rainforests of Tasmania, is also a drawcard. Each summer, apiarists transport hives to the nearby leatherwood forests.

Stephens Leatherwood Honey Factory At the home of Tasmania's unique aromatic honey, visitors can see clover and leatherwood honey being extracted and bottled. Tastings and sales are available. Open Mon–Fri; 25 Pioneer Dr; (03) 6363 1170.

Mole Creek Tiger Bar: local hotel with information and memorabilia on the Tasmanian tiger; Pioneer Dr.

Laurel Berry Restaurant: local produce and flavours; Mole Creek Guest House, 100 Pioneer Dr; (03) 6363 1399.

Blackwood Park Cottages: delightfully romantic garden cottages; 445 Mersey Hill Rd; (03) 6363 1208. *Old Wesley Dale Heritage Accommodation:* cosy stone cottage; 1970 Mole Creek Rd; (03) 6363 1212.

Mole Creek Karst National Park Set in the forests of the Western Tiers, this national park protects the Marakoopa and King Solomons caves, spectacular caverns of calcite formations created by underground streams. Marakoopa Cave has a magnificent glow-worm display, while King Solomons Cave offers coloured stalagmites and stalactites and sparkling calcite crystals. Guided tours daily; details (03) 6363 5182; 13 km W.

Alum Cliffs Gorge: spectacular 30 min return walk; 3 km NE. *Trowunna Wildlife Park:* see Tasmanian devils and other native fauna; 4 km E. *The Honey Farm:* over 50 flavours of honey and an interactive bee display; open Sun–Fri; Chudleigh; 8 km E. *Devils Gullet State Reserve:* World Heritage area with natural lookout on a 600 m high cliff, reached by 30 min return walking track; 40 km SE. *Wild Cave Tours:* adventure tours to caves that are closed to the general public; bookings on (03) 6367 8142. *Cradle Wilderness Tours:* guided 4WD tours; bookings on (03) 6363 1173. *Walls of Jerusalem National Park:* the park is accessible on foot only, from the end of the road that turns off around 15 km W of Mole Creek and heads down to Lake Rowallan. With glacial lakes, pencil pines and dolerite peaks, it is a wonderland for self-sufficient and experienced bushwalkers.

See also MIDLANDS & THE NORTH, p. 504

New Norfolk

Pop;. 5232
Map ref. 668 G4 | 671 J6

 Derwent Valley Visitor Information Centre, Circle St; (03) 6261 3700; www.newnorfolk.org

96.1 Hobart FM, 936 AM ABC Local Radio

This National Trust–classified town has a look similar to that of Kent in England. Located on the River Derwent in Tasmania's south-east, the town was named for the European settlers from the abandoned Norfolk Island penal settlement who were granted land here. The district is also renowned for its hops industry, and has more recently become a mecca for those seeking antiques and collectibles.

Oast House A working oast house from 1867 to 1969, the building has since been converted into a museum that showcases the growing and processing of hops. A cafe and craft market are on-site. Tynwald Park Reserve, Lyell Hwy.

Tynwald House: charming rural residence next to the Oast House, with restaurant; Tynwald Park Reserve. *Old Colony Inn:* heritage house (1835) with folk museum, restaurant and craft shop, and Australia's largest antique doll's house; Montagu St. *Church of St Matthew:* reputedly the oldest church in Tasmania (1823), with striking stained-glass windows; Bathurst St. *Rosedown:* beautiful rose and daffodil gardens along riverbank. Bookings preferred, (03) 6261 2030; closed May–Sept; 134 Hamilton Rd. *Antique and collectibles outlets:* over 15 in the town; details from visitor centre. *Bush Inn Hotel:* longest continually licensed hotel in Tasmania. *Jet-boat rides:* on River Derwent rapids; bookings on (03) 6261 3460. *River walk:* from Esplanade to Tynwald Park Wetlands Conservation Area. *Scenic lookout:* Peppermint Hill, off Blair St. *Self-guide historical walks:* brochure from visitor centre; Circle St.

Drill Hall Market: collectibles and antiques; Stephen St; daily.

Possum Shed Cafe: riverside cafe; 1654 Gordon River Rd, Westerway; (03) 6288 1364. *The Bush Inn:* generous pub meals; 49–51 Montagu St; (03) 6261 2256. *Tynwald:* fine Provençal food; 1 Tynwald Rd; (03) 6261 2667.

Explorers Lodge: elegant 1940s guesthouse; 105 Derwent Tce; (03) 6261 1255. *Rosie's Inn Private Hotel:* lacy, floral B&B in pretty gardens; 5 Oast St; (03) 6261 1171. *Tynwald:* fairytale mansion in riverside gardens; 1 Tynwald Rd; (03) 6261 2667. *Woodbridge on the Derwent:* exclusive and world-class luxury hotel; 6 Bridge St; (03) 6261 5566.

Mt Field National Park Tasmania's first national park, Mt Field is best known for the impressive Russell and Lady Barron falls. Most walks pass through lush ferns and rainforests, while the Pandani Grove walk traverses the glaciated landscapes of the mountain country to Lake Dobson. A visitor centre on-site offers interpretive displays. Contact Parks & Wildlife Service on 1300 135 513; 40 km NW.

Norske Scog Boyer Mill: the first in the world to manufacture newsprint from hardwoods; tours available Tues and Thurs; Boyer; 5 km E. *Salmon Ponds:* first rainbow and brown trout farm in Australia, in operation since 1864. There is also a Museum of Trout Fishing and a restaurant; Plenty; 11 km NW. *Possum Shed:* locally made crafts and collectibles, and cafe with delectable coffee; Gordon River Rd, Westerway; 31 km NW. *Styx Tall Tree Reserve:* small reserve with the tallest hardwood trees in the world, the giant swamp gums, which grow to 92 m; 73 km W via Maydena.

See also SOUTH-EAST, p. 501

Oatlands

Pop. 540
Map ref. 671 K3

 Heritage Highway Tourism Centre, 85 High St; (03) 6254 1212; www.heritagehighwaytasmania.com.au

97.1 Mid FM, 936 AM ABC Local Radio

Approaching Oatlands from the north, look out for the topiary and striking metal sculptures by the roadside. The topiaries are a local tradition from the 1960s, while the recently created metal sculptures depict earlier times in the district. The town is on the shores of Lake Dulverton and has the largest collection of Georgian sandstone buildings in a village environment – with much of the stone from local quarries.

Callington Mill Built in 1836, the old mill is a feature of Oatlands that was fully operational until 1892. After being battered by the elements and gutted by fire in the early 1900s, it was finally restored as part of Australia's bicentenary. The view from the top floor takes in Lake Dulverton. Old Mill La.

Lake Dulverton: the lake is stocked with trout and onshore is a wildlife sanctuary protecting many bird species. Popular picnic spot; Esplanade. *Fielding's Ghost Tours:* tours run by local historian Peter Fielding; bookings on (03) 6254 1135. *Historical walk:* takes in the many Georgian buildings, including the convict-built Court House (1829); *'Welcome to Historic Oatlands'* brochure from visitor centre. *Scottish, Irish and Welsh Shop:* stocks over 500 tartans, clan crests, badges, pins, and arts and crafts; open Sun–Mon and Thurs–Fri; 64 High St. *Skulduggery:* mystery tour game following true crime clues around town; available from visitor centre.

Oatlands Open Day: Oct.

Casaveen: country-style lunches; 44 High St; (03) 6254 0044.

Lakeview Cottage: shared cottage accommodation; 3 Lake St; (03) 6245 1212. *Oatlands Lodge:* convict-built Georgian manor; 92 High St; (03) 6254 1444. *Waverley Cottage Collection:* heritage cottages; Bow Hill Rd; (03) 6254 1264.

Convict-built mud walls: 13 km s on Jericho Rd. *Fishing:* excellent trout fishing in Lake Sorell and Lake Crescent; 29 km NW.

See also MIDLANDS & THE NORTH, p. 504

Penguin

Pop. 2949
Map ref. 672 G5

 78 Main Rd; (03) 6437 1421; www.coasttocanyon.com.au

91.7 FM ABC Local Radio, 106.1 Coast FM

This northern seaside town was named after the little penguins that shuffle up the beaches, and images of the iconic bird are peppered around town. The largest example is the much-photographed Big Penguin, which stands 3 metres tall on the beachfront and is the town's premier attraction.

Dutch Windmill The windmill was presented to the town during Australia's bicentenary to commemorate the Dutch explorers and settlers. There is also a colourful tulip display in spring and play equipment on-site. Hiscutt Park, off Crescent St.

Penguins: each evening penguins come ashore; check with visitor centre for tour details; Sept–Mar. *Johnsons Beach Reef:* popular walking spot at low tide when reef is exposed. *Penguin Roadside*

Gardens: originally a labour of love for 2 town residents, now a flourishing garden beside the road; Old Coast Rd to Ulverstone. *Chocolate Lovers:* quality European and Australian chocolates of all varieties; 100 Main Rd.

Market: over 300 stalls undercover; Arnold St; Sun.

Neptune Grand Bistro: beachside pub; 84 Main Rd; (03) 6437 2406. *The Groovy Penguin Cafe:* arty retro cafe; 74 Main Rd; (03) 6437 2101. *Wild:* Asian-inspired fine Tasmanian fare; 87 Main Rd; (03) 6437 2000.

The Madsen: classic seaside boutique hotel; 64 Main Rd; (03) 6437 2588.

 Dial Range Walks Excellent tracks include the walk up Mt Montgomery (5 km s) with magnificent views from the summit, and Ferndene Gorge (6 km s). The Ferndene Bush Walk takes in an old silver-mine shaft, Thorsby's Tunnel. Brochures on walks from visitor centre highlight more trails.

Penguin Cradle Trail This 80 km trail heads inland from the coast to the world-famous Cradle Mountain. Sections of the walk vary in difficulty. It takes 6 days to complete, but access roads mean that sections can be done as day or overnight trips.

Pioneer Park: beautiful gardens with picnic facilities and walks; Riana; 10 km sw. *Scenic drive:* along coast to Ulverstone.

See also NORTH-WEST, p. 503

Pontville

Pop. 2170
Map ref. 669 I3 | 671 K6

 Council offices, Tivoli Rd, Gagebrook; (03) 6268 7000.

96.1 Hobart FM, 936 AM ABC Local Radio

The area around Pontville (declared a town in 1830) was first explored by Europeans when Hobart experienced severe food shortages in the early 1800s. Soldiers were sent north to kill emus and kangaroos. One of them, Private Hugh Germain, is allegedly responsible for the unusual names found in the region, such as Bagdad, Jericho, Lake Tiberius and Jordan River. Legend has it that Germain carried copies of *Arabian Nights* and *The Bible* and found his inspiration within.

Historic buildings Many buildings remain from Pontville's early days, including the Romanesque St Mark's Church (1841), The Sheiling (1819) and The Row, thought to have been built in 1824 as soldiers quarters. On or adjacent to Midland Hwy.

The Crown Inn Bistro: friendly country pub; 256 Midland Hwy; (03) 6268 1235.

Lythgo's Row Cottages: whitewashed Georgian terrace; 253 Midland Hwy; (03) 6268 1665. *Armytage House:* 1830s barn meets stylish luxury; 1702 Midland Hwy, Bagdad; (03) 6268 6354.

Bonorong Wildlife Park: popular attraction showing Tasmanian devils, quolls, echidnas, koalas, wombats and Forester kangaroos; Briggs Rd, Brighton; 5 km s. *Historic towns:* Brighton (3 km s), Tea Tree (7 km E), Bagdad (8 km N), Broadmarsh (10 km w) and Kempton (19 km N).

See also SOUTH-EAST, p. 501

Port Arthur

see inset box on next page

 RADIO STATIONS   IN TOWN   WHAT'S ON   WHERE TO EAT   WHERE TO STAY   NEARBY

 TASMANIA

Port Sorell

Pop. 2209
Map 673 I6 | Map 675 C6

i Latrobe Visitor Centre, River Rd, Bells Pde, Latrobe; (03) 6421 4699; www.latrobetasmania.com.au

📻 100.5 FM ABC Local Radio, 104.7 Coast FM

This holiday town on the Rubicon River enjoys a mild and sunny climate nearly all year-round. It was established in the early 1820s, but sadly, many of its oldest buildings were destroyed by bushfires. The port is now a fast-developing coastal retreat for retirees and beach lovers.

🏠 *The jetty:* good fishing for cocky salmon, mullet, flathead, cod and bream. There are views to Bakers Beach and Narawntapu National Park. Behind caravan park on Meredith St. *Port Sorell Conservation Area:* 70 ha of coastal reserve with much flora and fauna. Guided tours available; bookings on (03) 6428 6072; Park Espl. *Estuary:* boating and safe swimming areas.

🎪 *Market:* Memorial Hall; 1st and 3rd Sat each month Sept–May. *Port Sorell Regatta:* Jan.

✕ *Hawley House:* elegant candlelit dinners; Hawley Beach; (03) 6428 6221.

🛏 *Hawley House:* peacocks, pets and a rooftop bath; Hawley Beach; (03) 6428 6221. *Sails on Port Sorell:* modern apartments on an unspoilt beach; 54 Rice St; (03) 6428 7580. *Tranquilles:* romantic luxury B&B; 9 Gumbowie Dr; (03) 6428 7555. *Shearwater Country Club:* self-contained resort accommodation; The Boulevard, Shearwater; (03) 6428 6205.

🕐 *Shearwater:* holiday town with shopping centre and good beach access; 5 km N. *Hawley Beach:* safe swimming, good fishing and historic Hawley House (1878) offering meals; 6 km N. *Walk:* 6 km return track from Port Sorell to Hawley Beach, offering excellent views of Narawntapu National Park and coastline. Starts at beach end of Rice St.

See also NORTH-WEST, p. 503

Queenstown

Pop. 2120
Map ref. 670 D1 | 672 D11 | 674 A10

i Queenstown Galley Museum, Cnr Sticht and Driffield sts; (03) 6471 1483.

📻 90.5 FM ABC Local Radio, 92.1 FM West Coast 7XS

The discovery of gold and other mineral resources in the Mount Lyell field in the 1880s led to the rapid emergence of Queenstown. Continuous mining here from 1893 to 1994 produced over 670 000 tonnes of copper, 510 000 kilograms of silver and 20 000 kilograms of gold. Operations began again in 1995, and are now owned by the Indian company Sterlite Industries. The town has modern facilities, but its wide streets and remaining historic buildings give it an old-mining-town flavour. In certain lights, multicoloured boulders on the hillsides, denuded through a combination of felling, wildfire, erosion and poisonous fumes from the smelter, reflect the sun's rays and turn to amazing shades of pink and gold. However, many Tasmanians view the place as a haunting reminder of the devastating impact humans can have on their environment.

🏠 **Galley Museum** The museum is housed in the Imperial (1898), Queenstown's first brick hotel, and displays over 800 photographs and general memorabilia of the history of the west coast. Cnr Sticht and Driffield sts.

West Coast Wilderness Railway This restored 1896 rack-and-pinion railway travels over 34 km of river and forest track to Strahan. It crosses 40 bridges and passes through pristine wilderness areas. Bookings on 1800 628 288.

Spion Kop Lookout: views of Queenstown and surrounding mountains; off Bowes St. *Paragon Theatre:* cinema; McNamara St. *Historical walk:* takes in 25 locations of historical importance; '*The Walkabout Queenstown*' brochure from visitor centre.

✕ *Penghana B&B:* à la carte traditional dining; 32 The Esplanade; (03) 6471 2560; dinner for non-guests by arrangement.

🛏 *Empire Hotel:* beautifully ornate, regal hotel; 2 Orr St; (03) 6471 1699. *Mount Lyell Anchorage:* Edwardian bungalow; 17 Cutten St; (03) 6471 1900. *Penghana B&B:* magnificent stately mansion; 32 The Esplanade; (03) 6471 2560. *Derwent Bridge Chalets:* cosy forest chalets; 15478 Lyell Hwy, Derwent Bridge; (03) 6289 1000.

🕐 *Mt Lyell Mines:* guided tours of the mines north of town, either surface (1 hr) or underground (3.5 hrs); bookings on (03) 6471 1472. *Iron Blow:* original open-cut mine where gold was discovered in 1883; Gormanston; 6 km E. *Linda:* ghost town; 7 km E. *Mt Jukes Lookout:* superb panoramic views; 7 km S. *Lake Burbury:* excellent brown and rainbow trout fishing; picnic areas; 8 km E. *Nelson Falls:* short walk through temperate rainforest leads to falls; 23 km E. *Valley views:* spectacular views from Lyell Hwy as it climbs steeply out of town.

See also SOUTH-WEST WILDERNESS, p. 502

Richmond

Pop. 879
Map ref. 669 J3 | 671 K6

i Old Hobart Town model village, 21A Bridge St, opposite Henry St; (03) 6260 2502; www.richmondvillage.com.au

📻 97.7 Tasman FM, 936 AM ABC Local Radio

Richmond, just north of Hobart, is one of the most important historic towns in Tasmania. Richmond Bridge is the oldest surviving freestone bridge in Australia, built by convicts under appalling conditions in 1823. The situation was so bad that one convict committed suicide by throwing himself off the bridge. Other convicts beat and killed an overseer who was known for his cruelty; legend has it that his ghost still haunts the bridge.

🏠 **Old Hobart Town** Taking 3 years to build, this is an intricate model of Hobart in the 1820s. A remarkable feat, it is also historically accurate. Bridge St.

Richmond Gaol One of Australia's best preserved convict prisons, built in 1825 and once the abode of convict Ikey Solomon, said to be the inspiration for Dickens' Fagin. Self-guide tours. Bathurst St; (03) 6260 2127.

Richmond Maze and Tearooms: 2-stage maze with surprise ending, puzzle corner, gardens and Devonshire tea; Bridge St. *Historical walk:* many heritage buildings throughout town include Ivy Cottage, Village Store and Richmond Arms; '*Let's Talk About Richmond*' brochure from visitor centre. *Art Galleries:* local arts and crafts in heritage buildings include Saddlers Court (c. 1848); Bridge St. *Olde Time Portraits:* photographs of people in period costume; Bridge St. *Prospect House:* historic Georgian mansion built in 1830s, supposedly haunted by the ghost of its past owner; restaurant; Richmond Rd.

🎪 *Richmond Village Colonial Fair:* Mar.

PORT ARTHUR

Pop. 499
Map ref. 669 M9 | 671 M9

ⓘ Port Arthur Historic Site, Arthur Hwy; (03) 6251 2300 or 1800 659 101; www.portarthur.org.au

📻 97.7 Tasman FM, 936 AM ABC Local Radio

This historic settlement on the scenic Tasman Peninsula was one of Australia's most infamous penal settlements from the 1830s to the 1870s. Over 12 000 convicts from Britain, some of whom did nothing more than steal some food to survive, were shipped to Port Arthur, dubbed 'Hell on Earth'. They lived under threat of the lash and experimental punitive measures that often drove them to madness. This grim past is offset by the stark beauty of the sandstone buildings overlooking the tranquil, often misty, waters of the bay. Port Arthur is Tasmania's number one tourist attraction.

Port Arthur Historic Site Over 30 buildings and restored ruins sit on 40 ha of land, illuminating the life of the convicts and their guards. Day entry tickets include a guided historical walking tour, access to the visitor centre, interpretation gallery and museum, and a harbour cruise in summer. Lantern-lit ghost tours depart at dusk and tours of the Isle of the Dead, the cemetery for the colony, unravel emotive stories of the convicts. The site's heritage gardens have been restored and replanted to reflect the style of the original plantings; guided and self-guide walks are available. Cruises and guided tours operate daily to the site of incarceration of juvenile male convicts at nearby Point Puer. Details from visitor centre; Arthur Hwy.

Port Arthur Memorial Garden: dedicated to the victims of the 1996 tragedy at the site in which 35 people were killed by a gunman. *Convict Trail drive:* scenic drive; brochure from visitor centre.

Eucalypt: modern Australian cafe; 6962 Arthur Hwy; (03) 6250 2555. *Felons Bistro:* quality regional menu; Port Arthur Historic Site Visitor Centre; (03) 6251 2310 or 1800 659 101. *Lemo's Seafood and Roast Restaurant:* casual Asian-inspired eatery with glorious views; 6555 Arthur Hwy; (03) 6250 3403. *The Commandant's Table:* friendly country pub; 256 Midland

[PORT ARTHUR HISTORIC SITE]

Hwy; (03) 6268 1235. *The Fox & Hounds Inn:* traditional fireside pub fare; 6789 Arthur Hwy; (03) 6250 2217.

Port Arthur Villas: villas at the historic site; 52 Safety Cove Rd; (03) 6250 2239 or 1800 815 775. *Sea Change Safety Cove:* 2-storey guesthouse with views; 425 Safety Cove Rd; (03) 6250 2719. *Stewarts Bay Lodge:* bayside timber cottages; 6955 Arthur Hwy; (03) 6250 2888. *Brick Point Cottage:* waterside retro shack; 241 Safety Cove Rd, Safety Cove; 0438 070 498.

Remarkable Cave Created by wave erosion, Remarkable Cave affords spectacular views along the coastline to Cape Raoul. It is in Tasman National Park and is the starting point of a 4–5 hr return walk to Crescent Bay. 6 km s.

Palmers Lookout: views of harbour and coastline; 3 km s. *Coal Mines Historic Site:* Tasmania's first operational mine, with self-guide tours; 30 km NW. *Tasman Island Wilderness Cruise:* 2 hr cruise exploring the beautiful coastal scenery of Tasman National Park; bookings on (03) 6223 1914. *Historical nature walk:* to nearby Stewarts Bay; brochure from visitor centre.

See also SOUTH-EAST, p. 501

Abby's Restaurant: classical dining by candlelight; Prospect House, 1384 Richmond Rd; (03) 6260 2207. *Ashmore on Bridge Street:* light meals, excellent coffee; 34 Bridge St; (03) 6260 2238. *Richmond Wine Centre:* licensed modern Australian cafe; 27 Bridge St; (03) 6260 2619. *Meadowbank Estate:* fine modern European dishes; 699 Richmond Rd, Cambridge; (03) 6248 4484.

Hatcher's Manor: themed farmstay accommodation complex; 73 Prossers Rd; (03) 6260 2622. *Mrs Currie's House:* 2-storey Georgian B&B; 4 Franklin St; (03) 6260 2766. *Mulberry Cottage B&B:* B&B with heritage show included in the tariff; 23A Franklin St; (03) 6260 2664.

ZooDoo This Wildlife Park is on a 330 ha farm with native fauna such as Tasmanian devils, galahs, emus and the rare albino pademelon wallaby. Middle Tea Tree Rd; (03) 6260 2444; 7 km w.

Southern Tasmanian Wine Route: vineyards north of town include Stoney (6 km N) and Crosswinds (10 km NW); brochure from visitor centre. *Scenic drive:* north through Campania (8 km) and Colebrook (19 km).

See also SOUTH-EAST, p. 501

Rosebery

Pop. 1032
Map ref. 672 D9 | 674 A7

ⓘ Hay's Bus Services, 10–12 Esplanade; (03) 6473 1247.

📻 92.1 FM West Coast 7XS, 106.3 FM ABC Local Radio

Like the nearby towns of Queenstown, Strahan and Zeehan, Rosebery found its economic niche in mining. The region is also known for its ancient rainforests, home to unique fauna and Huon pine, one of the oldest living things on earth.

Mine tours: surface tours of the Pasminco mine; bookings on (03) 6473 1247.

Rosebery Miners, Axemen, Bush and Blarney Festival: Irish music festival; Mar.

Tullah Lakeside Chalet Restaurant: pub fare beside scenic lake; Tullah Lakeside Resort, Farrell St, Tullah; (03) 6473 4121.

Mount Black Lodge: wilderness lodge amid stunning scenery; Hospital Rd; (03) 6473 1039.

Montezuma Falls The highest in Tasmania, the falls plummet 113 m and are accessed from Williamsford in a 3 hr return walk. The track winds through beautiful rainforest and there is a viewing platform at the falls. 11 km sw.

Wee Georgie Wood Steam Train: a 2 km ride along a scenic track on the fully restored steam train runs 1st Sun afternoon each month Sept–Apr; Tullah; 12 km NE. **Mt Murchison:** difficult but worthwhile 4 hr return walk rising 1275 m through ancient alpine forests; 14 km SE. **Lake Johnson Reserve Tour:** alpine nature tour offering a close-up look at a stand of 10 000-year-old Huon pines; bookings on (03) 6473 1247. **Hays Trout Tours:** fishing tours of west-coast lakes and rivers, Aug–Apr; bookings on (03) 6473 1247. **Fishing:** good trout fishing in nearby lakes Rosebery, Mackintosh and Murchison; north and east of town.

See also NORTH-WEST, p. 503

Ross

Pop. 270
Map ref. 671 L2 | 673 L12

ⓘ Tasmanian Wool Centre, Church St; (03) 6381 5466; www.taswoolcentre.com.au

📻 97.1 Mid FM, 936 AM ABC Local Radio

One of the oldest and most beautiful bridges in Australia spans the Macquarie River in Ross. Completed in 1836, the bridge was designed by colonial architect John Lee Archer and constructed by convicts, one of whom, Daniel Herbert, was given a pardon for his efforts. Herbert was responsible for 186 beautiful stone carvings along the side of the bridge, comprising images of animals, plants, Celtic gods and goddesses, and even the governor of the time, George Arthur. Ross Bridge is a point of pride in this Midlands town and it complements the many old sandstone buildings that adorn the main street. The town's central junction reveals the different aspects of Ross's history and, perhaps, its potential. The four corners are known as Temptation (hotel), Recreation (town hall), Salvation (church) and Damnation (gaol).

Tasmanian Wool Centre Regional attraction housing a museum, wool exhibition and retail area – all illustrating the national importance of the wool industry. Church St.

Ross Female Factory Site Archaeologically the most intact female convict site in Australia, this operated as a probation station for female convicts and their babies in the 19th century. The women were trained as domestic help and hired out to landowners in the area. The Overseer's Cottage has a historical display and model. Off Bond St; (03) 6223 1559.

Heritage walk: takes in 40 historic buildings in town, including Uniting Church (1885); booklet from visitor centre. **Old Ross General Store and Tearoom:** Devonshire tea and bakery, home of the famous Tassie scallop pie; Church St. **Skulduggery:** mystery tour game, following true crime clues around town; available from visitor centre. **T-Spot:** has an array of tea and coffee produce, homewares, gifts and alpaca products; Bridge St.

Old Ross Bakery and Tearooms: stone-walled tearooms; 31 Church St; (03) 6381 5422. **Ross Village Bakery:** treats from the wood-fired oven; 15 Church St; (03) 6381 5246.

Colonial Cottages and Ross B&B: central heritage accommodation; 12 Church St; (03) 6381 5354. **Man O'Ross Hotel:** sandstone country hotel; 35 Church St; (03) 6381 5445. **Ross Village Bakery Inn:** wake to freshly baked bread; 15 Church St; (03) 6381 5246. **Somercotes:** colonial property immersed in history; Mona Vale Rd; (03) 6381 5231.

Fishing There is world-class fly-fishing for brown trout in Macquarie River and some of the state's best trout-fishing lakes (Sorell, Crescent, Tooms and Leake) are within an hour's drive.

See also MIDLANDS & THE NORTH, p. 504

St Helens

Pop. 2051
Map ref. 673 O8

ⓘ St Helens History Room, 61 Cecilia St; (03) 6376 1744.

📻 93.7 Star FM, 1584 AM ABC Local Radio

This popular resort on the shores of Georges Bay is renowned for its crayfish and scalefish, which help maintain a thriving restaurant industry. The nearby beaches have pristine white sand dunes and a mild climate year-round.

St Helens History Room: thematic display of local history, with wooden interactive models; Cecilia St. **Beaches:** bay beaches ideal for swimming and coastal beaches for surfing. **Fishing:** Scamander River has excellent bream and trout fishing. Charter boats and tours are available for deep-sea fishing and dinghy hire is available for bay fishing. Check with visitor centre for details.

St Helens Regatta and Seafood Festival: Jan. **Athletic Carnival:** Jan. **Tasmanian Game Fishing Classic:** Mar. **Seafood and Symphony:** Mar.

Latris Restaurant: seafood straight from the boat; Marine Pde; (03) 6376 1170. **Margot:** French-style bistro; 15 Pendrigh Pl; (03) 6376 2594. **Ocean View Restaurant:** Asian-flavoured seafood dishes; Tidal Waters Resort, 1 Quail St; (03) 6376 1999. **Angasi:** acclaimed modern restaurant in top spot; 64A Main Rd, Binalong Bay; (03) 6376 8222. **Holy Cow Cafe:** cheesemaker's licensed cafe; Pyengana Dairy Company, St Columba Falls Rd, Pyengana; (03) 6373 6157. **Pub in the Paddock:** good-value counter meals, home to 2 pigs that guzzle beer; 250 St Columba Falls Rd, Pyengana; (03) 6373 6121.

The Old Headmasters House: grand antique-furnished B&B; 74 Cecilia St; (03) 6376 1125. **Tidal Waters Resort:** stylish foreshore resort; 1 Quail St; (03) 6376 1999. **Bay of Fires Character Cottages:** beachside cottages with postcard views; 64–74 Main Rd, Binalong Bay; (03) 6376 8262. **Bed in the Treetops:** treetop pole-house B&B; 701 Binalong Bay Rd, Binalong Bay; (03) 6376 1318.

Binalong Bay: this small holiday town with gorgeous beaches is renowned for its excellent surf and rock-fishing. 11 km NE. **St Helens Point:** walks with stunning coastal scenery along Maurouard Beach; brochure from visitor centre; 9 km S. **Bay of Fires Conservation Area:** named by Captain Furneaux for the Aboriginal campfires burning along the shore as he sailed past in 1773, this area features magnificent coastal scenery, good beach fishing and camping. Aboriginal middens are found in the area. A guided walk takes in the scenery to the north (*see Gladstone for details*); begins 9 km N. **Beaumaris:** good beaches and lagoons;

12 km s. **Blue Tier Forest Reserve:** walks with wheelchair access and interpretive sites; 27 km NW. **St Columba Falls:** dropping nearly 90 m, the falls flow down a granite cliff-face to the South George River. Walks through sassafras and myrtle lead to a viewing platform; 38 km W.

See also EAST COAST, p. 500

St Marys

Pop. 524
Map ref. 673 O9

 St Marys Coach House Restaurant, 34 Main St; (03) 6372 2529.

100.3 Star FM, 102.7 FM ABC Local Radio

Despite being the chief centre of the Break O'Day Plains, St Marys is a small town overshadowed by the magnificent St Patricks Head in the eastern highlands. The roads to and from St Marys venture through picturesque forests or down through the valley.

Rivulet Park: platypus, Tasmanian native hens and picnic and barbecue facilities; Main St. **St Marys Railway Station:** restored with cafe, Woodcraft Guild and Men's Shed giftshop; Esk Main Rd. **St Marys Hotel:** iconic building; Main St.

New Year's Day Races: Jan. **Winter Solstice Festival:** June. **Car Show:** June. **St Marys to Fingal Bicycle Race:** Oct.

eScApe Cafe: licensed cafe and gallery; 21 Main St; (03) 6372 2444. **Mt Elephant Pancake Barn:** well-known creperie set in rainforest overlooking Chain of Lagoons; Tasman Hwy, Elephant Pass; (03) 6372 2263. **White Sands Resort Restaurant:** French-accented fine dining; 21554 Tasman Hwy, Ironhouse Point; (03) 6372 2228.

Rainbow Retreat: carbon-neutral eco-cabins; 1 Gillies Rd; (03) 6372 2168. **Ivory Fields Spa Retreat and Herb Farm:** revitalising country retreat; 56 Davis Gully Rd, Four Mile Creek; (03) 6372 2759. **White Sands Resort:** sun-soaked coastal resort; 21554 Tasman Hwy, Ironhouse Point; (03) 6372 2228.

St Patricks Head: challenging 1 hr 40 min return walk to top of rocky outcrop for great 360-degree views of coast and valley; 1.5 km E. **South Sister:** an easier lookout alternative to St Patricks Head, a 10–15 min walk leads through stringybarks and silver wattles to spectacular views of Fingal Valley; 3 km NW. **Cornwall:** miners wall and Cornwall Collectables shop; 6.5 km W. **Falmouth:** small coastal township with several convict-built structures, fine beaches and good fishing; 14 km NE. **Scamander:** holiday town with sea- and river-fishing, good swimming, and walks and drives through forest plantations; 17 km N. **Douglas–Apsley National Park:** see Bicheno; 25 km SE.

See also EAST COAST, p. 500

Scottsdale

Pop. 1967
Map ref. 673 M6

 Forest EcoCentre, 96 King St; (03) 6352 6520; www.northeasttasmania.com.au

91.7 FM ABC Local Radio, 103.7 FM City Park Radio

Scottsdale, the major town in Tasmania's north-east, serves some of the richest agricultural and forestry country in the state. Indeed, as Government Surveyor James Scott observed in 1852, it has 'the best soil in the island'. A visitor to the town in 1868 noted with some surprise that the town had 'neither police station nor public house, but the people appear to get on harmoniously enough without them'. Present-day Scottsdale (now with both of those establishments) still retains a sense of harmony.

Forest EcoCentre A state-of-the-art centre built to principles of ecological sustainability, this place showcases the story of the forests through greenhouse-style interpretive displays and interactive features. King St.

Anabel's of Scottsdale: National Trust building now used as a restaurant and quality motel, set in exquisite gardens; King St. **Trail of the Tin Dragon:** discover the history of Chinese miners who came to the region more than 100 years ago; brochure from visitor centre.

The Steak Out: surf 'n turf meals; 13–15 King St; (03) 6352 2248.

Anabel's of Scottsdale: motel-style garden units; 46 King St; (03) 6352 3277. **Beulah Heritage B&B:** antique-furnished Victorian house; 9 King St; (03) 6352 3723. **Willow Lodge:** grand country home; 119 King St; (03) 6352 2552.

 Bridestowe Estate Lavender Farm One of the word's largest lavender-oil producers, Bridestowe is renowned for growing lavender that is not contaminated by cross-pollination. Tours are available in the flowering season (Dec–Jan) and there are lavender products for sale. Nabowla; (03) 6352 8182; 13 km W.

Mt Stronach: very popular 45 min climb to views of the north-east; 4 km S. **Cuckoo Falls:** uphill 2–3 hr return walk to falls; Tonganah; 8 km SE. **Springfield Forest Reserve:** popular picnic spot and 20 min loop walk through Californian redwoods, English poplars, pines and native flora; 12 km SW. **Sidling Range Lookout:** views of town and surrounding countryside; 16 km W. **Mt Maurice Forest Reserve:** walks incorporating Ralph Falls; 30 km S.

See also MIDLANDS & THE NORTH, p. 504

Sheffield

Pop. 1035
Map ref. 672 H7 | 674 H3 | 675 A8

 5 Pioneer Cres; (03) 6491 1036; www.sheffieldcradleinfo.com.au

91.7 FM ABC Local Radio, 104.7 Coast FM

Inspired by the Canadian town Chemainus, the people of Sheffield devised an attraction to encourage tourism, commissioning an artist to cover the town in murals depicting local history and scenery. Since then, murals have popped up all over town. As a result, there are many arts and crafts places in town, including marble-making and an open art space.

Story of the Sheffield Murals: audio tour that explains how the town went from rural decline to thriving outdoor art gallery; available from visitor centre. **Kentish Museum:** exhibits on local history and hydro-electricity; open 10am–3pm daily; Main St. **Blue Gum Gallery:** arts and crafts; at visitor centre. **Steam train:** Red Water Creek Steam and Heritage Society runs a train 1st weekend each month; Cnr Spring and Main sts. **Badgers Range Kimberley's Lookout:** 90 min return, with short, steep sections. Views along the walk; access from High St, Sheffield North.

Market: Claude Road Hall; 3rd Sun every 3rd month. **Steam Fest:** Mar. **Mural Fest:** Apr. **Daffodil Show:** Sept.

Highlander Restaurant & Scottish Scone Shop: daytime tea rooms, evening restaurant; 60 Main St; (03) 6491 1077.

 RADIO STATIONS   IN TOWN   WHAT'S ON   WHERE TO EAT   WHERE TO STAY   NEARBY

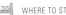 TASMANIA

Yvette's: excellent coffee, gourmet meals; 43 Main St; (03) 6491 1893. **Highland Restaurant:** fine Tasmanian cuisine; Cradle Mountain Lodge, 4038 Cradle Mountain Rd, Cradle Mountain; (03) 6492 2100. **Weindorfers:** country-style cafe; 1447 Claude Rd, Gowrie Park via Sheffield; (03) 6491 1385.

Cradle Mountain Highlanders Cottages: 12 rustic timber cabins; 3876 Cradle Mountain Rd, Cradle Mountain; (03) 6492 1116. **Cradle Mountain Lodge:** award-winning wilderness lodge; 4038 Cradle Mountain Rd, Cradle Mountain; (03) 6492 2100. **Cradle Mountain Wilderness Village:** secluded modern chalets; Cradle Mountain Rd, Cradle Mountain; (03) 6492 1500. **Discovery Holiday Park:** cottages, cabins and camping; 3832 Cradle Mountain Rd, Cradle Mountain; (03) 6492 1395. **Eagles Nest Retreat:** ultra-luxury amid spectacular scenery; 3 Browns Rd, West Kentish; (03) 6491 1511. **Waldheim Cabins:** rustic cabins in national park; Parks and Wildlife Service, Cradle Mountain–Lake St Clair National Park; (03) 6492 1110.

Cradle Mountain–Lake St Clair National Park Covering 124 942 ha, this national park has over 25 major peaks, including the state's highest, Mt Ossa, and possibly its most spectacular, Cradle Mountain. The terrain is marked by pristine waterfalls, U-shaped valleys, dolerite formations, forests of deciduous beech, Tasmanian myrtle, pandani and King Billy pine, and swathes of wildflowers. At the southern end of the park lies Lake St Clair. Cruises operate daily. There are many tracks for all levels of experience; check with the rangers for up-to-date information on conditions. The 3 major tracks are the Overland Track, covering 85 km and one of Australia's best-known walks for experienced, well-equipped walkers; Dove Lake Loop Track, suitable for everyone; and Summit Walk, an 8 hr return walk to the top of Cradle Mountain. The Overland Track can also be done in style, staying in well-appointed huts and with all meals provided. Contact (03) 6391 9339 for more information. For other general information, contact one of the visitor centres: Cradle Mountain (03) 6492 1110; Lake St Clair (03) 6289 1172; 61 km sw.

Tasmazia Claiming to be the world's largest maze complex, Tasmazia has a variety of mazes, model village, honey boutique, pancake parlour and lavender farm. Lake Barrington Nature Reserve; (03) 6491 1934; 14 km sw.

Stoodley Forest Reserve: experimental tree-farm forest, with a 40 min loop walk through European beech, Douglas fir, radiata pine and Tasmanian blue gum. Picnic areas; 7 km NE. **Lake Barrington Estate Vineyard:** tastings and sales; open Wed–Sun Nov–Apr; West Kentish; 10 km w. **Railton:** known as the 'Town of Topiary', Railton has over 100 living sculptures; 11 km NE. **Mt Roland:** well-marked bushwalks to the summit, which rises to 1234 m, with access from Claude Rd or Gowrie Park; 11 km sw. **Lake Barrington:** internationally recognised rowing course created by Devils Gate Dam. Picnic and barbecue facilities along the shore; 14 km sw. **Wilmot:** this 'Valley of Views' has magnificent views of the mountains of Cradle country and Bass Strait, novelty letterbox trail, and the original Coles store and family homestead; 38 km w.

See also NORTH-WEST, p. 503

| Smithton | Pop. 3363 |
| | Map ref. 672 C4 |

ⓘ Stanley Information Centre, 45 Main Rd, Stanley; (03) 6458 1330 or 1300 138 229.

 88.9 Coast FM, 91.3 FM ABC Local Radio

This substantial town is renowned for its unique blackwood-swamp forests. Smithton services the most productive dairying and vegetable-growing area in the state and, with several large sawmills, is also the centre of significant forestry reserves and the gateway to The Tarkine.

Circular Head Heritage Centre: artefacts and memorabilia detailing the area's pioneering history; 8 King St. **Lookout tower:** excellent views from Tier Hill; Massey St. **Western Esplanade Community Park:** popular picnic spot overlooking the mouth of the Duck River, with fishing and walks; Western Espl. **Britton Brothers Timber Mill:** tours of the mill by appt (03) 6452 2522; Brittons Rd, southern outskirts of town.

Bridge Bistro: pub grub in modernised surrounds; Bridge Hotel/Motel, 2A Montagu St; (03) 6452 1389. **Kauri Bistro:** bistro fare in vast log cabin; Tall Timbers Hotel, Scotchtown Rd; (03) 6452 2755 or 1800 628 476. **Marrawah Tavern:** counter meals; Comeback Rd, Marrawah; (03) 6457 1102. **Tarkine Forest Adventure:** licensed cafe; Bass Hwy; (03) 6456 7199.

Rosebank Cottages Collection: country-style cottages; 46 Brooks Rd and 40 Goldie St; (03) 6452 2660. **Tall Timbers Hotel:** hotel complex showcasing Tasmania's timber; Scotchtown Rd; (03) 6452 2755 or 1800 628 476.

Allendale Gardens These gardens are linked to a rainforest area by 3 easy loop walks that take in the Fairy Glades, a section constructed for children, and towering 500-year-old trees. Peacocks roam the gardens, where Devonshire tea is available. Open Oct–Apr; Edith Creek; (03) 6456 4216; 13 km s.

River and Duck Bay: good fishing and boating; 2 km N. **Sumac Lookout:** amazing views over Arthur River and surrounding eucalypt forest; 4 km s on Sumac Rd. **Milkshake Hills Forest Reserve:** exquisite picnic spot among eucalypts and rainforest; 10 min loop walk or 1 hr return walk to hill-top; 40 km s. **Surfing:** excellent, but turbulent surf beaches near Marrawah where Rip Curl West Coast Classic is held in Mar; 51 km sw. **Arthur River cruises:** trips into pristine wilderness of Arthur Pieman Protected Area; run Sept–June; 70 km sw. **Gardiner Point:** 'Edge of the World' plaque; 70 km sw. **Woolnorth tours:** coach tours visit spectacular Cape Grim cliffs, wind farm, and Woolnorth sheep, cattle and timber property; bookings on (03) 6452 1493.

See also NORTH-WEST, p. 503

| Sorell | Pop. 4179 |
| | Map ref. 669 K4 | 671 L6 |

ⓘ Gordon St; (03) 6269 2924.

 97.7 Tasman FM, 936 AM ABC Local Radio

The south-eastern town of Sorell was founded in 1821, and was important in early colonial times for providing most of the state's grain. It was named after Governor Sorell who attempted to curb bushranging in Tasmania, but ironically the town was later targeted by bushranger Matthew Brady, who released the prisoners from gaol and left the soldiers imprisoned in their place.

Historic buildings There are 3 churches listed in the National Estate, most notably St George's Anglican Church (1826). There are also many heritage buildings including the Old Rectory (c. 1826), Old Post Office (c. 1850) and Bluebell Inn (c. 1864).

Orielton Lagoon: important habitat for migratory wading birds on western shore of town. **Pioneer Park:** popular picnic spot with barbecue facilities; Parsonage Pl.

STANLEY

Pop. 459
Map ref. 672 D3

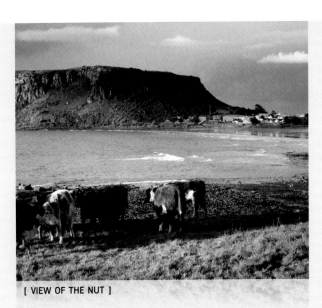

[VIEW OF THE NUT]

i 45 Main Rd; 1300 138 229; www.stanley.com.au

📻 88.9 Coast FM, 91.3 FM ABC Local Radio

This quaint village nestles at the base of an ancient outcrop called The Nut, which rises 152 metres with sheer cliffs on three sides. Matthew Flinders, upon seeing The Nut in 1798, commented that it looked like a 'cliffy round lump resembling a Christmas cake'. Today visitors come to see this 'lump' and the historic township.

The Nut The remains of volcanic rock, The Nut looms above the surrounding sea and provides spectacular coastal views. Visitors can either walk to the summit along a steep and challenging track or take the chairlift from Browns Rd. There is a 40 min circuit walk along cliffs at the summit.

Historic buildings: many in the wharf area, including the bluestone former Van Diemen's Land (VDL) Company store in Marine Park. *Lyons Cottage:* birthplace of former prime minister J. A. Lyons, with interesting memorabilia; Alexander Tce. *Hearts and Craft:* fine Tasmanian craft; shop closes during quieter months; 12 Church St. *Discovery Centre Folk Museum:* displays of local history; Church St. *Touchwood:* quality craft and woodwork; 31 Church St. *Cemetery:* graves of colonial architect John Lee Archer and explorer Henry Hellyer; Browns Rd. Stanley Seaquarium: Tasmanian marine species including huge rock lobsters and giant crabs; Fishermans Dock; (03) 6458 2052. *Penguins & Platypus Tours:* evening tours to see little penguins and platypus in their natural environment Sept–Apr; bookings on (03) 6458 1455. *Seal cruises:* daily trips to see offshore seal colonies; bookings on 0419 550 134.

Melbourne to Stanley Yacht Race: Nov.

Hursey Seafoods: freshest seafood ever; 2 Alexander Tce; (03) 6458 1103. *Old Cable Station Restaurant:* intimate fine dining; 435 Greenhills Rd, West Beach; (03) 6458 1312. *Stanley's on the Bay:* nautical-themed seafood fine dining; 15 Wharf Rd; (03) 6458 1404.

🛏 *@ VDL Stanley:* luxury modernised bluestone warehouse; 16 Wharf Rd; (03) 6458 2032. *Abbey's Cottages:* 7 heritage cottages; various locations in Stanley; (03) 6458 1430 or 1800 222 397. *Beachside Retreat West Inlet:* secluded futuristic eco-cabins; 253 Stanley Hwy; (03) 6458 1350. *Horizon Deluxe Apartments:* contemporary glass-fronted style; 88 Dovecote Rd; 0448 521 115.

Highfield Historic Site The headquarters of VDL Co, Highfield contains a homestead with 12 rooms, a chapel, convict barracks, a schoolhouse, stables, a barn, workers' cottages and large gardens. Green Hills Rd; 2 km N.

Dip Falls: double waterfall in dense rainforest and eucalypts. There is a picnic area nearby; 40 km SE off hwy, via Mawbanna.

See also NORTH-WEST, p. 503

Market: Cole St; Sun (weekly in summer, fortnightly in winter; check with visitor centre for current schedule).

Barilla Bay: oysters, seafood and ... oysters; 1388 Tasman Hwy, Cambridge; (03) 6248 5454.

Cherry Park Estate: fruit farm B&B; 114 Pawleena Rd; (03) 6265 2271. *Flimby:* convict-built country B&B; 68 Rosendale Rd; (03) 6265 2979. *Sorell Barracks:* Sorell's oldest buildings; 31 Walker St; (03) 6265 1572. *Steeles Island Beach Cottages:* rustic homestead and cabins; Steeles Island via River St, Carlton Beach; (03) 6265 8077.

Sorell Fruit Farm Offers pick-your-own patches as well as ready-picked. Fruits available in season include berries, apricots, cherries, pears, nashi, nectarines and peaches. Devonshire tea at the cafe. Open Oct–May; Pawleena Rd; (03) 6265 2744; 2 km E.

Southern Tasmanian Wine Route: many vineyards east of town include Orani (3 km E) and Bream Creek (22 km E); brochure

from visitor centre. *Beaches:* around Dodges Ferry and Carlton; 18 km S.

See also SOUTH-EAST, p. 501

Strahan

see inset box on next page

Swansea

Pop. 558
Map ref. 671 N3 | 673 N12

i Swansea Bark Mill and East Coast Museum, 96 Tasman Hwy; (03) 6257 8094.

📻 98.5 Star FM, 106.1 FM ABC Local Radio

Perched on Great Oyster Bay, Swansea looks out to the Freycinet Peninsula. It is part of the Glamorgan/Spring Bay shire, the oldest rural municipality in the country, and many fine old buildings testify to its age. Today it is a popular holiday destination.

TASMANIA

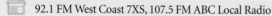

STRAHAN

Pop. 635
Map ref. 670 C2 | 672 C12

 The Esplanade; (03) 6472 6800.

92.1 FM West Coast 7XS, 107.5 FM ABC Local Radio

This pretty little port on Macquarie Harbour, on Tasmania's west coast, is the last stop before a long stretch of ocean to Patagonia. Sometimes considered the loneliest place on earth, it was dubbed 'The Best Little Town in the World' by the *Chicago Tribune* and continues to attract visitors. Strahan (pronounced 'strawn') came into being as a penal colony operating from the isolated station of Sarah Island. Known as a particularly cruel environment, the station was shut down in 1833, but not before convict Alexander Pearce had managed to escape. Pearce and seven others set off for Hobart but found the terrain too tough to overcome. Pearce, alone when discovered, was suspected of cannibalism. The following year he again escaped and again killed and ate his cohort. Pearce finally made it to Hobart, where he was executed.

Visitor centre The centre has an impressive historical display on Tasmania's south-west, including Aboriginal history, European settlement, and events such as the fight to save the Franklin River from being dammed in the early 1980s. In the amphitheatre there is an audiovisual slideshow and a nightly performance of 'The Ship That Never Was', about convict escapes. The Esplanade.

Morrison's Mill: one of 4 remaining Huon pine sawmills in Tasmania; tours available; The Esplanade. *Strahan Woodworks:* woodturning, arts and crafts; The Esplanade. *Tuts Whittle Wonders:* carvings from forest wood; Reid St. *Ormiston House:* built in 1899 and a fine example of Federation architecture surrounded by magnolia trees and expansive gardens. Morning and afternoon teas are served; Bay St. *Water Tower Hill Lookout:* views of township and harbour; Esk St. *West Coast Wilderness Railway: see Queenstown.*

Mount Lyell Picnic: Jan.

Franklin Manor: distinguished fine dining; The Esplanade; (03) 6471 7311. *Hamers Hotel:* bistro meals; The Esplanade; (03) 6471 7191. *Risby Cove:* contemporary à la carte dining; The Esplanade; (03) 6471 7572. *Schwochs Seafoods:* excellent little seafood cafe; The Esplanade; (03) 6471 7500.

Aloft Boutique Accommodation: central contemporary apartments; 15 Reid St; (03) 6471 8095. *Ormiston House:* grand Federation mansion; The Esplanade; (03) 6471 7077. *Risby Cove:* waterline views and sublime reflections; The Esplanade;

[CRUISE BOAT ON THE GORDON RIVER]

(03) 6471 7572. *Wheelhouse Luxury Apartments:* glass-fronted cliff-top luxury; 4 Frazer St; (03) 6471 7777.

Franklin–Gordon Wild Rivers National Park This park now has World Heritage listing after an earlier state government tried to dam the Franklin River. Protests were so heated and widespread that the federal government and High Court stepped in and vetoed the proposal, saving the dense temperate rainforest and wild rivers that make up the park. Visitors can go canoeing and whitewater rafting, and there are many bush trails for experienced walkers. A 4-day walk to Frenchmans Cap takes in magnificent alpine scenery. The 40 min return walk to Donaghys Hill is easier and overlooks the Franklin and Collingwood rivers. Contact Parks & Wildlife Service on 1300 135 513. Gordon River cruises depart from Strahan; bookings on 1800 420 500. 36 km SE.

Peoples Park: popular picnic spot in botanical gardens setting with a 1 hr return walk to Hogarth Falls through marked rainforest; 2 km E. *Ocean Beach:* Tasmania's longest beach (36 km) offers horseriding, beach fishing and the opportunity to see short-tailed shearwaters in their burrows Oct–Mar; 6 km W. *Henty Sand Dunes:* vast sand dunes with sandboards and toboggans for hire; 12 km N. *Cape Sorell Lighthouse:* 40 m high lighthouse built in 1899; 23 km SW. *Sarah Island:* ruins of convict station with tours available; check with visitor centre; 29 km SE. *Scenic flights:* bird's-eye views of Gordon River, Sir John Falls and Franklin River valley; bookings on (03) 6461 7718.

See also SOUTH-WEST WILDERNESS, p. 502

Swansea Bark Mill and East Coast Museum The only restored black-wattle bark mill in Australia has machinery that still processes the bark for tanning leather. The museum has comprehensive displays on life in the 1820s, and the adjoining Wine and Wool Centre has wines from over 50 Tasmanian vineyards and textiles from around the state. A cafe and tavern complete the complex. Tasman Hwy; (03) 6257 8094.

Historical walk: self-guide tour takes in charming heritage buildings including Morris' General Store (1838), run by the Morris family for over 100 years, and Community Centre (c. 1860),

featuring the unusually large slate billiard table made for the 1880 World Exhibition; brochure from visitor centre. *Waterloo Point:* 1 km walking track leads to viewpoint to see short-tailed shearwaters at dusk and Aboriginal middens; Esplanade Rd.

Kate's Berry Farm: sinfully lavish berry desserts; Addison St; (03) 6257 8428. *The Banc:* modern Australian fine dining; Cnr Franklin and Maria sts; (03) 6257 8896. *The Ugly Duck Out:* international fare; 2 Franklin St; (03) 6257 8850. *Kabuki by the Sea:* cliff-top Japanese restaurant; 12164 Tasman Hwy, Rocky Hills; (03) 6257 8588.

Amos House and Swansea Ocean Villas: motel rooms and self-catering villas; 3 Maria St; (03) 6257 8656. *Meredith House:* colonial B&B; 15 Noyes St; (03) 6257 8119. *Swansea Cottages and Sherbourne Lodge:* country-style cottages and lodge suites; 43 Franklin St; (03) 6257 8328. *Avalon Coastal Retreat:* ultra-chic cliff-top villa; 11922 Tasman Hwy, Rocky Hills; 1300 361 136.

 Spiky Bridge Built by convicts in 1843, the bridge was pieced together without the aid of mortar or cement. The spikes – vertical fieldstones – prevented cattle from falling over the sides. The beach nearby has a picnic area and good rock-fishing. 7.5 km s.

Coswell Beach: good spot for viewing little penguins at dusk; 1 km s along coast from Waterloo Pt. *Duncombes Lookout:* splendid views; 3 km s. *Mayfield Beach:* safe swimming beach with walking track from camping area to Three Arch Bridge. There is also great rock- and beach-fishing; 14 km s. *Vineyards:* Springvale, Coombend, Freycinet and Craigie Knowe vineyards all have cellar-door sales on weekends and holidays; 15 km N. *Lost and Meetus Falls:* bushwalks past beautiful waterfalls in dry eucalypt forest. Sheltered picnic area is nearby; 50 km NW.

See also EAST COAST, p. 500

Triabunna

Pop. 798
Map ref. 669 N1 | 671 M5

 Cnr Charles St and Esplanade West; (03) 6257 4772.

 90.5 FM ABC Local Radio, 97.7 Tasman FM

When Maria (pronounced 'mar-eye-ah') Island was a penal settlement, Triabunna (pronounced 'try-a-bunnah') was a garrison town and whaling base. After an initial boom, this small, south-east coast town settled into relative obscurity, content with its role as a centre for the scallop and abalone industries.

 Tasmanian Seafarers' Memorial: commemorates those who lost their lives at sea; Esplanade. *Girraween Gardens and Tearooms:* with large lily pond, day lilies, roses and agapanthus; Henry St.

 Spring Bay Seafest: Easter.

 Girraween Gardens and Tearooms: light meals and snacks; 4 Henry St; (03) 6257 3458. *Scorchers by the River:* casual gourmet cafe; 1 Esplanade, Orford; (03) 6257 1033. *Gateway Cafe:* great lunches and pancakes; 1 Charles St, Orford; (03) 6257 1539.

 Barton Retreat: modern luxury with 'wow' factor; 53 Barton Ave, Double Creek; 1300 763 132. *Sanda House Colonial B&B:* historic stone cottage; 33 Walpole St, Orford; (03) 6257 1527.

 Maria Island National Park After the convicts were moved to Port Arthur, the island was leased to Italian merchant Diego Bernacchi, who envisaged first a Mediterranean idyll and then a cement works. Both projects were short-lived. Today, bushwalks are popular. The extensive fossil deposits of the Painted Cliffs are magnificent and the historic penal settlement of Darlington is also of interest. Daily ferry to the island from town. Contact Parks & Wildlife Service on 1300 135 513; 7 km s.

Orford: pleasant walk along Old Convict Rd following Prosser River; 7 km sw. *Thumbs Lookout:* stunning views of Maria Island; 9 km sw. *Church of St John the Baptist:* heritage church (1846) with a stained-glass window (taken from England's Battle Abbey) depicting John the Baptist's life; Buckland; 25 km sw.

Beaches: safe swimming beaches around area; contact visitor centre for details.

See also SOUTH-EAST, p. 501

Ulverstone

Pop. 9761
Map ref. 672 G6 | 674 G1

 13–15 Alexandra Rd; (03) 6425 2839; www.coasttocanyon.com.au

 91.74 FM ABC Local Radio, 106.1 Coast FM

At the mouth of the Leven River on the north central coast, Ulverstone has some of Tasmania's finest tourist beaches. Relax along these sweeping beaches, cycle through waterfront parklands, take coastal and forest walks, or explore spectacular Leven Canyon and the nearby caves.

 Discover the Leven Cruise A fun 1.5 hr guided tour of the upper Leven River in Ulverstone. Tours leave daily, in the cutest little passenger vessel in Tasmania. Tasma Pde; (03) 6425 2839.

Riverside Anzac Park: amazing children's playground, great picnic facilities and an interesting fountain. The park is named after a pine tree grown from a seed taken from Gallipoli; Beach Rd. *Fairway Park:* has a giant waterslide; Beach Rd. *Shropshire Park:* has a footpath inscribed with details from 75-year history of the Royal Australian Navy; Dial St. *Legion Park:* magnificent coastal setting; Esplanade. *Tobruk Park:* includes Boer War Memorial; Hobbs Pde. *Ulverstone Local History Museum:* interesting display of old business facades and other memorabilia; Main St. *Shrine of Remembrance:* clock-tower memorial designed and built by European immigrants in 1953; Reibey St. *Ulverstone Lookout:* views over town; Upper Maud St. *Woodcraft Gallery and Workshop:* demonstrations, private tutoring and sales; open Tues, Thurs and Sat; Reibey St.

 Market: The Quadrant Carpark; every 2nd Sat. *Hobbies and craft expo:* Jan. *Festival in the Park:* Feb. *Twilight Rodeo:* Jan/Feb. *Carnival of the Grasshopper:* Mar. *Forth Valley Blues Festival:* Mar. *Doll, Bear and Miniature Extravaganza:* July. *NW Woodcraft Exhibition:* Nov. *Cradle Coast Rotary Art Exhibition:* Nov. *Ulverstone Agricultural Show:* Nov. *Christmas Mardi Gras:* Dec.

 The Atrium: family-oriented restaurant; The Lighthouse Hotel, 33 Victoria St; (03) 6425 1197. *Furners Hotel:* good pub meals; 42 Reibey St; (03) 6425 1488. *Pedro's the Restaurant:* casual waterside seafood; Ulverstone Wharf; (03) 6425 6663.

 Boscobel of Ulverstone: restored French Provincial–style mansion; 27 South Rd, West Ulverstone; (03) 6425 1727. *Moonlight Bay Guesthouse:* homely seaside B&B; 141 Penguin Rd, West Ulverstone; (03) 6425 1074. *Westella:* ornate Gothic guesthouse; 68 Westella Dr; (03) 6425 6222. *Winterbrook:* elegant B&B; 28 Eastland Dr; (03) 6425 6324.

 Leven Canyon There are walking tracks to a viewing platform with spectacular views down this 250 m ravine. Picnic and barbecue facilities are nearby. 41 km s.

Gunns Plains Caves: these limestone caves are well-lit for visitors. Daily tours take in an underground river and glow worms. Check visitor centre for tour departure times. 24 km sw. *Wing's Wildlife Park:* wildlife exhibits, trout and reptile display and animal nursery are all to be found here – including Tasmanian devils.

Gunns Plains; (03) 6429 1151; 24 km SW. *Miniature railway:* 3rd Sun each month; 2 km E. *Goat Island Sanctuary:* cave and good fishing, but walking access to island at low tide only; 5 km W. *Penguins:* view little penguins at dusk; Leith; 12 km E. *Preston Falls:* scenic views; 19 km S. *Winterbrook Falls:* 5 hr return walk to the falls for fit bushwalkers; 46 km S. *Fishing:* good fishing on beach (especially Turners Beach), river and estuary; contact visitor centre for details. *Beaches:* safe swimming beaches to east and west of town; contact visitor centre for details.

See also NORTH-WEST, p. 503

Waratah

Pop. 223
Map ref. 672 E7 | 674 A3

ⓘ Wynyard Visitor Centre, 8 Exhibition Link, Wynyard; (03) 6443 8330; www.wowtas.com.au

103.3 FM ABC Local Radio, 106.1 Coast FM

Waratah was the site of the first mining boom in Tasmania. Tin deposits were discovered in 1871 by James 'Philosopher' Smith, and by the late 1800s the Mount Bischoff operation was the richest tin mine in the world. The mine closed in 1947.

Waratah Museum and Giftshop: displays early photographs and artefacts of the area and provides brochure for self-drive tour of town; Smith St. *Waratah Waterfall:* in the centre of town; Smith St. *Philosopher Smith's Hut:* replica of late-19th-century miner's hut; Smith St. *St James Anglican Church:* first church in Tasmania to be lit by hydro-power; Smith St. *Lake Waratah:* pleasant picnic and barbecue area with rhododendron garden and walks to Waratah Falls; English St.

Bischoff Hotel: Queen Anne–style hotel; 20 Main St; (03) 6439 1188. *Waratah's O'Connor Hall Guest House and B&B:* ornate Victorian heritage homestead; 2 Smith St; (03) 6439 1472.

Savage River National Park The rainforest here is the largest contiguous area of cool–temperate rainforest surviving in Australia. Excellent for self-sufficient bushwalking as well as fishing, 4WD and kayaking in the adjacent regional reserve. Contact Parks & Wildlife Service on 1300 135 513; access tracks lead off the main road out of Waratah; around 20 km W.

Fishing: excellent trout fishing in rivers and lakes in the area, including Talbots Lagoon; 20 km E. *Old mines:* walks and drives to old mining sites; brochure from visitor centre.

See also NORTH-WEST, p. 503

Westbury

Pop. 1357
Map ref. 673 J8 | 675 E11

ⓘ Great Western Tiers Visitor Centre, 98–100 Emu Bay Rd, Deloraine; (03) 6362 3471; www.greatwesterntiers.org.au

91.7 FM ABC Local Radio, 103.7 FM City Park Radio

Westbury's village green gives the town an English air. Just west of Launceston, the town was surveyed in 1823 and laid out in 1828, the assumption being that it would be the main stop between Hobart and the north-west coast. Originally planned as a city, it never grew beyond the charming country town it is today.

The village green Used for parades and fairs in the 1830s, the village green is still the focal point and fairground of Westbury – with one small difference: prisoners are no longer put in the stocks for all to see. King St.

White House This collection of buildings, enclosing a courtyard, was built in 1841. Later additions include a coach depot, a bakery and a flour mill. The house has an excellent collection of 17th- and 18th-century furniture and memorabilia, and a magnificent doll's house. The outbuildings house a toy museum as well as early bicycles, vintage cars and horse-drawn vehicles. The restored bakery serves refreshments. Open Sept–June; King St.

Pearn's Steam World: said to be the largest collection of working steam traction engines in Australia; Bass Hwy. *Westbury Maze and Tearoom:* hedge maze composed of 3000 privet bushes; open Oct–June; Bass Hwy. *Culzean:* historic home with beautifully maintained temperate-climate gardens; open Sept–May; William St. *Westbury Mineral and Tractor Shed:* museum of vintage tractors and farm machinery featuring a scale-model tractor exhibition; Veterans Row.

Maypole Festival: Mar. *St Patrick's Day Festival:* Mar.

Andy's Bakery Cafe: pastries and gelato; 45 Meander Valley Rd; (03) 6393 1846. *Fitzpatricks Inn:* fine European-style dishes; 56 Meander Valley Hwy; (03) 6393 1153. *Hobnobs Restaurant:* sophisticated provincial-style food; 47 William St; (03) 6393 2007.

Elm Wood: gabled cottages in English gardens; 10 Lonsdale Prom; (03) 6393 2169. *Fitzpatricks Inn:* stylish renovated coaching inn; 56 Meander Valley Hwy; (03) 6393 1153. *Westbury Gingerbread Cottages:* central period cottages; 52 William St; (03) 6393 1140.

Fishing: good trout fishing at Four Springs Creek (15 km NE) and Brushy Lagoon (15 km NW).

See also MIDLANDS & THE NORTH, p. 504

Whitemark

Pop. 598
Map ref. 670 B10

ⓘ 4 Davies St, (03) 6359 2380 or 1800 994 477; www.flindersislandonline.com.au

91.7 FM ABC Local Radio

Flinders Island in Bass Strait is the largest of the 52 islands in the Furneaux Group, once part of a land bridge that joined Tasmania to the mainland. It's a beautiful place, but with a tragic history. In 1831 Tasmania's Aboriginal people, depleted to fewer than 160, were isolated on Flinders Island. A lack of good food and water meant that by 1847, when the settlement was finally abandoned, only 46 Aboriginal people remained. The Wybalenna Historic Site at Settlement Point stands as a reminder of the doomed community. Whitemark is the island's largest town.

Bowman History Room: displays of memorabilia show Whitemark since the 1920s; rear of E. M. Bowman & Co, 2 Patrick St. *Diving and snorkelling:* tours to shipwreck sites, limestone reefs and granite-boulder formations including Chalky Island Caves and Port Davies Reef; bookings on (03) 6359 8429. *Fishing tours:* from Port Davies to Prime Seal Island for pike and salmon, and Wybalenna Island for couta; bookings on (03) 6359 8429.

Three Peaks Race: annual sailing and hiking race from Beauty Pt to Flinders Island, then down the coast to Hobart. It coincides with local produce markets and children's activities at Lady Barron; Easter. *Bass Strait Golf Classic:* June. *Flinders Island Show:* local and off-shore exhibitors; showgrounds; Oct.

Sweet Surprises: coffee and light meals; 5 Lagoon Rd; (03) 6359 2138. *Furneaux Tavern and Shearwater Restaurant:* seafood with a view; 11 Franklin Pde, Lady Barron; (03) 6359 3521.

Interstate Hotel: budget heritage rooms; Patrick St; (03) 6359 2114. *Partridge Farm:* luxurious bush hideaways; Badger Corner; (03) 6359 3554. *Echo Hills:* farm cottage; Madeleys Rd, Lackrana; (03) 6359 6509. *Palana Beach House:* secluded timber beach house; 4758 Palana Rd, Palana; griggsys@gmail.com.

Strzelecki National Park The only national park in the Furneaux Group, featuring the Peaks of Flinders and Mt Strzelecki, and wetlands, heathland and lagoons. A 5 hr return walk to the summit of Mt Strzelecki is steep, but affords excellent views of Franklin Sound and its islands. Trousers Pt, featuring magnificent rust-red boulders and clear waters, is located just outside the park. Contact Parks & Wildlife Service on 1300 135 513; 15 km s.

Emita Museum This museum, run by the Historical Society, has a wide range of memorabilia and houses displays on the short-tailed shearwater industry, the War Service Land Settlement and the nautical and natural histories of Flinders Island. Open 1–4pm Sat–Sun; Settlement Point Rd, Emita; 18 km NW.

Patriarchs Wildlife Sanctuary: privately owned sanctuary with a vast range of birdlife and wallabies, which can be handfed; access via Lees Rd, Memana; 30 km NE. *Logan Lagoon Wildlife Sanctuary:* houses a great diversity of birdlife in winter including the red-necked stint, common greenshank and eastern curlew; east of Lady Barron; 30 km SE. *Mt Tanner:* lookout with stunning views of the northern end of the island and Marshall Bay; off West End Rd; Killiecrankie; 40 km N. *Port Davies:* from the viewing platform see short-tailed shearwaters fly into their burrows at dusk. An enormous colony of these birds breed here between Sept and Apr and then set out on an annual migration to the Northern Hemisphere. West of Emita; 20 km NW. *Fossicking:* Killiecrankie diamonds, a form of topaz released from decomposing granite, are found along the beach at Killiecrankie Bay; brochure at visitor centre; 43 km NW. *Beachcombing:* rare paper-nautilus shells wash up along the island's western beaches.

See also BASS STRAIT ISLANDS, p. 505

Wynyard

Pop. 4810
Map ref. 672 E5

i 8 Exhibition Link; (03) 6443 8330; www.wowtas.com.au

102.5 FM ABC Local Radio, 106.1 Coast FM

This small centre at the mouth of the Inglis River has charming timber buildings and is located on a stunning stretch of coastline in an extremely fertile pocket of the state.

Gutteridge Gardens: riverside gardens in the heart of town; Goldie St. *Nature walks:* include boardwalk along Inglis River; brochure at visitor centre. *Wonders of Wynyard:* an exhibition of veteran vehicles that includes one of the oldest Ford models in the world; Exhibition Link.

Wynyard Farmers' Market: 2nd and 4th Sat each month. *Bloomin' Tulips Festival:* Oct.

Buckaneers: popular seafood eatery; 4 Inglis St; (03) 6442 4101. *The Riverview:* international fare; The Waterfront, 1 Goldie St; (03) 6442 2531. *Jolly Rogers on the Beach:* modern beachside bistro; 1 Port Rd, Boat Harbour Beach; (03) 6445 1710.

Alexandria: classical, stylish Federation B&B; 1 Table Cape Rd; (03) 6442 4411. *Cape Cottage:* quaint bush cottage; 8A Elfrida Ave, Sisters Beach; (02) 4784 1248. *The Harbour House:* funky beachfront pads; Port Rd, Boat Harbour Beach;

(03) 6442 2135. *The Winged House:* cantilevered masterpiece perched cliff-side; 400 Tollymore Rd, Table Cape; (02) 9906 3224.

Boat Harbour This is a picturesque village ideal for diving and spearfishing. Boat Harbour Beach (4 km NW of town) has safe swimming, marine life in pools at low tide, fishing and waterskiing. 10 km NW.

Rocky Cape National Park With some of the best-preserved Aboriginal rock shelters and middens in Tasmania, the park incorporates the pristine Sisters Beach. Contact Parks & Wildlife Service on 1300 135 513. 29 km NW.

Fossil Bluff: scenic views from an unusual geological structure where the oldest marsupial fossil in Australia was found; 3 km N. *Table Cape Lookout:* brilliant views of the coast from 190 m above sea level. En route to lookout is Table Cape Tulip Farm, with tulips, daffodils and Dutch irises blooming Sept–Oct. From lookout a short walk leads to an old lighthouse; 5 km N. *Flowerdale Freshwater Lobster Haven:* restaurant and artificial lakes stocked with lobster; 6.5 km NW. *Fishing:* Inglis and Flowerdale rivers provide excellent trout fishing; also good sea-fishing around Table Cape. *Scenic flights:* the best way to appreciate the patchwork colours of the fields in the area; bookings at Wynyard Airport (03) 6442 1111. *Scenic walks and drives:* brochure from visitor centre.

See also NORTH-WEST, p. 503

Zeehan

Pop. 846
Map ref. 672 D10

i West Coast Pioneers Memorial Museum, Main St; (03) 6471 6225.

90.5 FM ABC Local Radio, 92.1 FM West Coast 7XS

After silver-lead deposits were discovered here in 1882, Zeehan boomed and between 1893 and 1908 the mine yielded ore worth $8 million, which led to its nickname, the 'Silver City of the West'. However, from 1910 the mine started to slow and Zeehan declined, threatening to become a ghost town. Fortunately, the nearby Renison Bell tin mine has drawn workers back to the area.

West Coast Pioneers Memorial Museum The old Zeehan School of Mines building (1894) has been converted into a comprehensive museum outlining the local history with extensive mineral, geological and locomotive collections. Main St.

Historic buildings: boom-era buildings on Main St include Gaiety Theatre, once Australia's largest theatre. *Scenic drives:* self-guide drives in town and nearby; brochure from visitor centre.

Maud's Restaurant: pub-style dishes; Hotel Cecil; 99–101 Main St; (03) 6471 6221.

Hotel Cecil and Old Miners Cottages: grand old hotel; 99–101 Main St; (03) 6471 6221. *Corinna Wilderness Experience:* patch of civilisation amid rainforest wilderness; Pieman River, Corinna; (03) 6446 1170.

Fishing: Trial Harbour (20 km W) and Granville Harbour (35 km NW) are popular fishing spots. *Lake Pieman:* boating and good trout fishing; 42 km NW. *Cruises:* tour the Pieman River, leaving from fascinating former goldmining town, Corinna; bookings on (03) 6446 1170; 48 km NW.

See also SOUTH-WEST WILDERNESS, p. 502

 RADIO STATIONS IN TOWN WHAT'S ON WHERE TO EAT WHERE TO STAY NEARBY

TASMANIA

ROAD ATLAS

Inter-City Route Maps

The inter-city route maps and distance charts will help you plan your route between major cities. As well, you can use the maps during your journey, since they provide information on distances between towns along the route, roadside rest areas and road conditions. The table below provides an overview of the routes mapped. The inter-city route maps can be found on pages 536–8.

INTER CITY ROUTES	DISTANCE	TIME
Sydney–Melbourne via Hume Hwy/Fwy 31 M31	879 km	12 hrs
Sydney–Melbourne via Princes Hwy/Fwy 1 A1 M1	1039 km	15 hrs
Sydney–Brisbane via New England Hwy 1 15	995 km	14 hrs
Melbourne–Adelaide via Western & Dukes hwys M8 A8 M1	729 km	8 hrs
Melbourne–Adelaide via Princes Hwy M1 A1 B1 M1	911 km	11 hrs
Melbourne–Brisbane via Newell Hwy M31 A39 39 A39 A2	1676 km	20 hrs
Darwin–Adelaide via Stuart Hwy 1 87 A87 A1	3026 km	31 hrs
Adelaide–Perth via Eyre & Great Eastern hwys A1 1 94	2700 km	32 hrs
Adelaide–Sydney via Sturt & Hume hwys A20 20 31	1415 km	19 hrs
Perth–Darwin via Great Northern Hwy 95 1	4032 km	46 hrs
Sydney–Brisbane via Pacific Hwy 1 1 M1	936 km	14 hrs
Brisbane–Darwin via Warrego Hwy A2 85 87 1	3406 km	39 hrs
Brisbane–Cairns via Bruce Hwy M1 A1	1703 km	20 hrs
Hobart–Launceston via Midland Hwy 1	197 km	3 hrs
Hobart–Devonport via Midland & Bass hwys 1 B52 1	279 km	4 hrs

Legend

═══▯═══	Freeway, with toll
▬ M31 ▬ 31 ▬	Highway, sealed, with National Highway Route Marker
▬ A1 ▬ 1 ▬	Highway, sealed, with National Route Marker
▬ 5 ▬	Highway, sealed, with Metroad Route Marker
───────	Highway, unsealed
▬ C141 ▬ 26 ▬	Main road, sealed, with State Route Marker
───────	Main road, unsealed
───────	Connector road, on central city maps only
──→──	Other road, with traffic direction, on central city maps only
───────	Other road, sealed
───────	Other road, unsealed
───────	Vehicle track
··········	Walking track
=========	Mall, on central city maps only
──●──	Railway, with station
──●──	Underground railway, with station
▼ 114 ▼	Total kilometres between two points
▼ 45 ▼	Intermediate kilometres
───────	State border
▬ ▬ ▬ ▬	Fruit fly exclusion zone boundary
∿∿∿	River, with waterfall
⬭	Lake, reservoir
⬭	Intermittent lake
～～	Coastline, with reefs and rocks

SYDNEY ◎	State capital city
GEELONG ◎	Major city / town
Deniliquin ◎	Town
Caldwell ○	Other population centres / localities
Rorruwuy ○	Aboriginal community
Karoonda Roadhouse ▣	Roadhouse
Nullagong ▫	Pastoral station homestead
ESSENDON	Suburb, on suburbs maps only
Unley	Suburb, on central city maps only
THE TWELVE APOSTLES ◉	Place of interest
✈	Airport
✛	Landing ground
★	Lighthouse
+	Hill, mountain, peak
●	Gorge, gap, pass, cave or saddle
●	Waterhole
⚒	Mine site
▨	National park
▨	Other reserve
▨	Aboriginal / Torres Strait Islander land
▨	Other named area
▨	Prohibited area
❶	Text entry in A to Z listing

Maps are in a Lamberts Conformal Conic Projection
Geocentric Datum Australia, 1994 (GDA94)

SYDNEY–MELBOURNE
via HUME HIGHWAY/ FREEWAY 31 M31

SYDNEY–MELBOURNE
via PRINCES HIGHWAY/ FREEWAY 1 A1 M1

SYDNEY–BRISBANE
via NEW ENGLAND HIGHWAY 1 15

MELBOURNE–ADELAIDE
via WESTERN & DUKES HIGHWAYS M8 A8 M1

MELBOURNE–ADELAIDE
via PRINCES HIGHWAY M1 A1 B1 M1

MELBOURNE –BRISBANE
via HUME, NEWELL, GORE & WARREGO HIGHWAYS M31 A39 39 A38 A2

DARWIN– ADELAIDE
via STUART HIGHWAY 1 87 A87 A1

ADELAIDE– PERTH
via PRINCES, EYRE & GREAT EASTERN HIGHWAYS A1 1 94

ADELAIDE– SYDNEY
via STURT & HUME HIGHWAYS A98 20 31

PERTH– DARWIN
via GREAT NORTHERN, VICTORIA & STUART HIGHWAYS 95 1

MAPS

NEW SOUTH WALES and AUSTRALIAN CAPITAL TERRITORY

INTER-CITY ROUTES		DISTANCE
Sydney–Melbourne via Hume Hwy/Fwy	31 M31	879 km
Sydney–Melbourne via Princes Hwy/Fwy	1 A1 M1	1039 km
Sydney–Brisbane via New England Hwy	1 15	995 km
Sydney–Brisbane via Pacific Hwy	1 1 M1	936 km
Sydney–Adelaide via Hume & Sturt hwys	31 20 A20	1415 km

0   0.25   0.5   0.75   1 km

Accommodation ■
Establishment Hotel 1 D5
Four Points by Sheraton 2 C7
Four Seasons Hotel Sydney 3 D4
InterContinental Sydney 4 E5
Novotel Sydney on Darling Harbour 5 A8
The Observatory Hotel 6 C4
Park Hyatt Sydney 7 D2
Sebel Pier One Sydney 8 D2
Shangri-La Hotel Sydney 9 D4
Sydney Central YHA Hostel 10 D11
Sydney Harbour Marriott Hotel 11 E5
The Westin Sydney 12 D7
The York Suites & Residences 13 C5
Note: Only a sample range of accommodation
is listed; inclusion is not necessarily a
recommendation.

General Information ■
Cadmans Cottage (NPWS Info. Centre) 14 D3
Central Railway Station 15 D12
City Central Police Station 16 C9
Coach Tour Departures 17 E3
General Post Office 18 D6
Interstate & Country Coach Terminal 19 D12
Motoring Organisation (NRMA) 20 D7
Qantas Travel Centre 21 D5
Sydney Ferries 22 E4
Sydney Visitor Centre 23 D3

Places of Interest ■
The Art Gallery of NSW 24 G7
Australian Museum 25 F9
Australian National Maritime Museum 26 B7
Campbell's Storehouse 27 D3
Chinatown 28 C10
Chinese Garden of Friendship 29 C10
Government House 30 F4
Hyde Park Barracks Museum 31 F7
IMAX Theatre 32 C9
Justice & Police Museum 33 E4
Museum of Contemporary Art 34 D4
Museum of Sydney 35 E5
Parliament of NSW 36 F6
Powerhouse Museum 37 B10
Queen Victoria Building 38 D8
Royal Botanic Gardens 39 G6
St Mary's Cathedral 40 F8
Star City (casino, hotel & theatres) 41 A7
State Library of NSW 42 F6
Susannah Place Museum 43 D4
Sydney Aquarium 44 C7
Sydney Harbour Bridge 45 E1
Sydney Harbour Bridge Visitor Centre 46 D3
Sydney Observatory Museum 47 C4
Sydney Opera House 48 F3
Sydney Tower 49 E7
Sydney Town Hall 50 D8
Victoria Barracks 51 H12

0   0.25   0.5   0.75   1 km

A   B   C   D   Joins map 542   E   F   G   H

TO LANE COVE

WARRINGAH   RD   TO LANE COVE

Cammeray

St Leonards   **Crows Nest**

North Cremorne

St Leonards

Wollstonecraft

St Leonards Park

FALCON   ST   FALCON   ST

North Sydney ANZAC Memorial Club

ANZAC Park

Cammeray Golf Club

Cammeray Park

Cammeray Tennis Club

MILITARY   RD   TO BALMORAL

Neutral Bay Village Shopping Centre

Big Bear Shopping Centre

North Sydney Boys High School

North Sydney Girls High School

Mater Misericordiae Hospital

TAFE NSW Northern Sydney Institute

Brennan Park

North Sydney Police Station

Marist College North Shore

St Marys North Sydney

North Sydney Oval

Nth Sydney Leagues Bowling Club

Forsyth Park

Neutral Bay Public School

Neutral Bay

Neutral Bay Club Ten. & Bowls

Waverton

Waverton Park Bowling Club

Waverton Park

Australian Catholic Uni

Tennis Centre

St Thomas Anglican Church

North Sydney Council

McGrath's Art Gallery

Rydges North Sydney

North Sydney Demonstration School

Monte Sant' Angelo College

Wenona Girls School

Stanton Library

Willow Tree Park

North Sydney

Sydney Church of England Grammar School

Greenwood Plaza

Graythwaite Nursing Home

St Peters Pres.

St Francis Xavier Christ Church

North Sydney

Watt Park

Quibaree Park

Clark Park

Kirribilli Tennis Centre

Anderson Park

Aust. Customs

Marina

Neutral Bay Wharf

'Nutcote' (May Gibbs)

Kurraba Point Wharf

Kurraba Point Reserve

Hodgson Lookout

Spains Lookout

Kurraba Point

McMahons Point

Berrys Bay

Marina

Sawmillers Reserve

Lavender Bay

Vibe Hotel North Sydney

Milsons Point

Milson Park

Sydney Flying Squadron

Ensemble Theatre

North Sydney Wharf

Careening Cove

Balls Head Reserve

Balls Head

Luna Park

Milsons Point Wharf

North Sydney Olympic Pool

Loreto (school)

Kirribilli

St Aloysius Catholic College

Royal Sydney Yacht Squadron

Wudyong Point

McMahons Point Wharf

McMahons Point

Blues Point Reserve

Blues Point

Kirribilli Lookout

Kirribilli Wharf

Dr. Mary Booth Res

Kirribilli House

Admiralty House

Beulah Street Wharf

Kirribilli Point

Priv. Hospital

Mosman Bay

Taronga Zoo

Ferries to Parramatta

Ferries to Birkenhead Darling Harbour

Walsh Bay

Ferry to Manly

Dawes Point

Sebel Pier One Sydney

Dawes Point Park

Pylon Lookout & Harbour Bridge Exhibition

Harbour Bridge

Sydney Harbour Tunnel

SYDNEY HARBOUR

Capt. Henry Waterhouse Res

Bennelong Point

Sydney Opera House

PORT JACKSON

Millers Point

Wharf Theatre

Sydney Ports Marine Base

Campbell's Storehouse

Campbells Cove

Ferry to Watsons Bay

TO SYDNEY   Joins map 540

Accommodation ■
Harbourside Apartments 1 C9
North Sydney Harbourview Hotel 2 D7
Rydges North Sydney 3 D5
Sovereign Inn Crows Nest 4 B3
Vibe Hotel North Sydney 5 E8
Note: Only a sample range of
accommodation is listed; inclusion is
not necessarily a recommendation.

General Information ■
Motoring Organisation (NRMA) 6 D6
North Sydney Police Station 7 C4
North Sydney Post Office 8 D6
Stanton Library 9 D4

Places of Interest ■
Campbell's Storehouse 10 D12
Don Bank Museum 11 C6
Mary MacKillop Museum 12 C6
North Sydney Olympic Pool 13 E10
'Nutcote' (May Gibbs) 14 H7
Sydney Harbour Bridge 15 E10
Sydney Opera House 16 F12

N

1   2   3   4   5   6   7   8   9   10   11   12

0   2   4   6   8   10 km

Joins map 545

Joins map 544

For more detail on Central Sydney & North Sydney see pages 540 & 541

Joins map 553

Joins map 555
Joins map 549
Joins map 555
Joins map 549

For more detail on Newcastle see page 548

For more detail on Sydney & Surrounds see pages 544–5

Joins map 555
Joins map 554
Joins map 553

For more detail on the Blue Mountains see pages 546–7

TO MUDGEE

TO BATHURST

TO MITTAGONG

0 5 10 15 20 km

Joins map 555
Joins map 543
Joins map 553

For more detail on Sydney
Suburbs see page 542

TO NEWCASTLE

TO SHELLHARBOUR

NEWCASTLE

Accommodation ■
Aloha Motor Inn 1 A9
Backpackers Newcastle 2 A5
Hotel Novocastrian 3 H5
Quality Hotel Noah's on the Beach 4 H5
The Clarendon Hotel 5 E5
Travelodge Newcastle Hotel 6 C6
Note: Only a sample range of
accommodation is listed; inclusion is
not necessarily a recommendation.

General Information ■
City Hall 7 E5
Ferry Terminal 8 F5
Newcastle Railway Station 9 G5
Police 10 G6
Post Office 11 F5
Visitor Information 12 E5

Places of Interest ■
Band Rotunda 13 F6
Bogey Hole (swimming pool) 14 G6
Christ Church Cathedral 15 F6
Civic Theatre 16 D5
Convict Stockade 17 G5
Cooks Hill Galleries 18 D6
Customs House 19 G5
Fort Scratchley 20 H4
Harbour Square 21 D5
Historical Navigation Tower 22 E6
Hunter Street Mall 23 F5
King Edward Park 24 F7
Lee Wharf 25 D5
Maritime & Military Museums 26 H4
Merewether Baths 27 B11
Newcastle Region Art Gallery 28 E6
Obelisk 29 F6
Queens Wharf 30 F5
Soldiers Baths (swimming pool) 31 H5
Sydney Seaplanes 32 D5
War Memorial Cultural Centre 33 E6

0 5 10 15 20 km

A B C D Joins map 550 E F G H

Joins map 550
Joins map 555
Joins map 543

TO GLOUCESTER

BARRINGTON TOPS NP
Cockcrow Mountain
Mount Malumla
Mount Royal
Mount Cabre Bald
MOUNT ROYAL NP
Mount Carrow

BARRINGTON TOPS NATIONAL PARK
Gloucester Gap
The Pinnacle
The Mountaineer
Mount Nelson

RUNNING CREEK NR
Stratford
Craven
THE GLEN NR
KYLE RANGE

LAWLERS RANGE
BUCKETTS WAY
Wards River
Weismantels
GHIN-DOO-EE NP
Cabbage Tree Mountain
Upper Myall

Salisbury
Salisbury Gap
Chichester Gap
Chichester Reservoir
Mount Toonumbue
Prickly Peak
Karuah
BLACK BULGA SCA

Eccleston
Spring Mountain
Belgrave Mountain
Bandon Grove
KILLARNEY NR
MONKERAI NR
Peach Tree Mountain
Poppers Mountain
Conical Mountain
Markwell

Lake Saint Clair
Big Black Jack Mountain
Little Black Jack Mountain
Lostock
Halton
Bendolba
Mount Butterwicki
Monkerai Mountain
Stroud Road
Winns Mountain
Rosenthal

Glennies Creek Dam
St Clair
Lostock Dam
Mount Razorback
STROUD RD
Dungog
Mount Ebsworth
Stroud
Bulahdelah

Mirannie
Gresford
East Gresford
RANGE
Mount Richardson
Pilchers Mountain
Mount Ararat
Alison
Marshdale
BUCKETTS WAY
Booral
MYALL LAKES NATIONAL PARK
Burdekins Gap
TO TAREE

Mirannie Mountain
GRESFORD RD
Tangory Pass
Mount Brackin
Trevallyn
Hilldale
Wallarobba
Brookfield
Flat Tops
Mount Douglas
Glen William
KARUAH NR
Skertchleys Island
Mount George
Bombah Broadwater

Glendon Brook
Tangory Mountain
Mount Durham
Lambs Mountain
DUNGOG RD
Vacy
Martins Creek
Mount Johnstone
Glen Martin
Ironstone Mountain
The Branch

BELFORD NP
NEW ENGLAND
Branxton
North Rothbury
Lochinvar
Allandale
Rothbury
Paterson
Glen Oak
TOWN
Clarence Town
WALLAROO NR
Limeburners Creek
Rooke Island

Rosebrook
Woodville
Mount Torrance
Seaham
CLARENCE
KARUAH NR
Karuah
Carrington
North Arm Cove
Tea Gardens
Hawks Nest
MYALL LAKES NP
Cabbage Tree Island
Yacaaba Head
Tomaree Head

MAITLAND
St Peters
Bolwarra
Hinton
Morpeth
Duckenfield
Nelsons Plains
PACIFIC HWY
Grahamstown Lake
MEDOWIE SCA
WORIMI NR
Big Swan Bay
Little Swan Bay
Corrie
Point Stephens

WERAKATA NP
HUNTER VALLEY WINERIES
HUNTER VALLEY ZOO
Nulkaba
CESSNOCK
Abermain
Weston
Kurri Kurri
Heddon Greta
Thornton
RAYMOND TERRACE
Beresfield
Medowie
TILLIGERRY HABITAT
Lemon Tree Passage
Corlette
Nelson Bay
Shoal Bay
Fingal Bay
TOMAREE NP
Point Stephens

Bellbird
Neath
Pelaw Main
RICHMOND VALE RAILWAY MUSEUM
Kitchener
Tomago
Hexham
HUNTER REGION BOTANIC GARDENS
PROHIBITED AREA
FIGHTER WORLD
Williamtown
Salt Ash
OAKVALE FARM & FAUNA WORLD
Anna Bay
Boat Harbour
Morna Point
Fingal Point

Quorrobolong
Mulbring
Minmi
Seahampton
KOORAGANG NR Fullerton Cove
STOCKTON SAND DUNES
Stockton Bight

Brunkerville
West Wallsend
Wallsend
Elermore Vale
Islington
Hamilton
Stockton
NEWCASTLE
Wickham
New Lambton
Cardiff
Boolaroo
Warners Bay
Cooks Hill
Merewether
Charlestown

WATAGANS NATIONAL PARK
Martinsville
Killingworth
Awaba
Toronto
Rathmines
Balmoral
Belmont
Redhead
Little Redhead Point
Redhead Point

Avondale
Cooranbong
Eraring
Dora Creek
Wangi Wangi
Blacksmiths
Swansea
Nine Mile Beach

Mandalong
Morisset
Beauty Point
Bonnells Bay
Yarrawonga Park
Silverwater
Brightwaters
Windermere Park
Nords Wharf
Stinky Point
JILLIBY SCA

Wyee Point
Gwandalan
Mannering Park
Catherine Hill Bay
The Basin

Wyee
Doyalson
Lake Munmorah
Chain Valley Bay
Flat Rocks Point
Bongon Head

Jillibi
Wyong
Tuggerawong
Gorokan
Toukley
Budgewoi
Bird Island
Birdie Beach
Lakes Beach
Norah Head
Norahville

TO SINGLETON
TO SYDNEY

TASMAN SEA

For more detail on Newcastle see page 548

N

Joins map 543
TO SYDNEY

0   20   40   60 km

A   B   C   D   E   F   G   H

Yarrowyck
Brushgrove
Rocky River
Uralla
Dangarsleigh
Hillgrove
Jeogla
Wollomombi
ARMIDALE
TO GLEN INNES
HISTORIC TOWN
Mount Butler
Mount John
The Brothers
Mount Davidson
Black Mountain
Bora Mountain
CATHEDRAL ROCK NP
Round Mountain
Ebor
Darkwood
POINT LOOKOUT
BICENTENNIAL NATIONAL TRAIL
Dorrigo
DORRIGO NP
Thora
BELLINGER RIVER NP
COFFS HARBOUR
Boambee
Bindarri NP
Bonville
SAWTELL
BONGIL BONGIL

Kentucky
Wollun
Winterbourne Gorge
Blue Nobby Mountain
Lower Creek
CUNNAWARRA NP
COMARA RANGE
NEW ENGLAND NP
Killiekrankie Mountain
JUUGAWAARRI NR
Missabotti
JAANINGGA NR
Bellingen
Raleigh
Mylestom
Valla Beach
Hyland Park
Nambucca Heads

Woolbrook
Walcha Road
Walcha
Moona Plains
Yarrowitch
Mount Lofthole
Mount Enmore
Blue Mountain
Apsley River
Mount Hannah
Table Top Mountain
OXLEY
WILD
RIVERS
Comara
O'Sullivans Gap
Bellbrook
CARRAI NP
Bitter Vine Mountain
Jobs Mountain
Mount Comara
Mount Woorong Woorong
Broads Mountain
Taylors Arm
The Brothers
Warrell Creek
Eungai Creek
Stockyard Mountain
Bowraville
Macksville
Scotts Head
YARRAHAPPINI NP
Stuarts Point

Niangala
Black Mountain
Ohio Peak
High Mountain
Dobrabad Mountain
Mount Sugarloaf
Brackendale
Tia
NEW ENGLAND
DIVIDING
RANGE
MUMMEL
Fifes Knob NR
THE CASTLES NR
NATIONAL
WILLI
WILLI
NP
Double Head Mountain
Mount Mystery
Mount Parabel
Willawarrin
Mount + Banda Banda
KUMBATINE NP
Green Hill
Euroka
Collombatti Rail
Clybucca
Smithtown
Gladstone
Kinchela
Frederickton
Kempsey
TRIAL BAY GAOL
South West Rocks
Jerseyville
Smoky Cape
Korogoro Point
Hat Head
Kemps Corner
HAT HEAD NP

Halton
Lostock
Eccleston
Niangala
NGULIN NR
Mount Carrington
GULF
NP
Rowleys
COTTAN-BIMBANG NP
Mount Seaview
KOOREBANG NP
Jaspers + Peak
Birdwood
Pappinbarra
JASPER
NR
Mount Cairncross
Rollands Plains
Telegraph Point
MARIA NP
PACIFIC
LIMEBURNERS CREEK NR
Big Hill Point
Point Plomer
Kundabung
Crescent Head
Racecourse Head
North Shore Beach

TOMALLA NR
TUGGOLO CREEK NR
MERNOT NR
NOWENDOC NP
Nowendoc
Cooplacurripa
BARAKEE NP
BUGAN NR
MONKEYCOT NR
ELLENBOROUGH FALLS
Elands
BIRIWAL BULGA NP
Comboyne
Byabarra
BAGO BLUFF NP
OLD BOTTLEBUTT
Wauchope
Timbertown HISTORIC TOWN
PORT MACQUARIE
SEA ACRES RAINFOREST CENTRE
Tacking Point
LAKE INNES NR
Lighthouse Beach
Lake Cathie
Long Flat
Beechwood
Pembroke
Ellenborough
Bagnoo

WOKO NP
Mount Myra
BRETTI NR
Bretti
TAPIN TOPS NP
KILLABAKH NR
COORABAKH NP
Killabakh
Marlee
Lorne
Kendall
Kew
Herons Creek
QUEENS LAKE NR
Grants Beach
Bonny Hills
North Haven
Laurieton
Dunbogan
Dunbogan Beach
Diamond Head
Watson Taylors Lake
CROWDY BAY NP
Bobin
Wyoming
Lansdowne
Johns River
Moorland
Kylies Beach
Crowdy Head

GREAT
Front Mountain
Boranei Mountain
Mount McKenzie
BARRINGTON TOPS
BICENTENNIAL NATIONAL TRAIL
Upper Bowman
Rookhurst
Bundook
Mount George
Wingham
TAREE
Tinonee
Cundletown
Oxley Island
Harrington
Manning Point
Coopernook
Rawdon Vale
Copeland
Barrington
BUCKETTS WAY
Belbora
Burrell Creek
Purfleet
Old Bar
Wallabi Point
Gloucester

Salisbury
Gloster NP
Salisbury
RUNNING CREEK NR
Stratford
Craven
THE GLEN NR
Krambach
Nabiac
Diamond Beach
Halladays Point
KHAPPINGHAT NR
DARAWANK NR
Nine Mile Beach
Cape Hawke
FORSTER-TUNCURRY
Bennetts Head

Gresford
East Gresford
Trevallyn
Hilldale
Vacy
Bandon Grove
Bendolba
Wards River
Weismantels
GHIN-DOO-EE NP
Upper Myall
Wang Wauk
Willina
Coolongolook
Bunyah
Wallis Island
Green Point
Seven Mile Beach
TASMAN

Lostock
Dungog
Alison
Marshdale
Flat Tops
Booral
Stroud Road
Markwell
Rosenthal
WALLINGAT NP
Coomba
Wallis Lake
Tiona
Elizabeth Beach
Blueys Beach
Bald Head

Trevallyn
Brookfield
Glen William
Glen Martin
Clarence Town
Stroud
Bulahdelah
Pacific Palms
Bungwahl
Smiths Lake
Seal Rocks
Sugarloaf Point
Myall Lake
SEA

Rosebrook
Woodville
Martins Creek
Paterson
Glen Oak
Limeburners Creek
WALLAROO NR
KARUAH NR
The Branch
Mount George
Bombah Broadwater
MYALL LAKES NP
Mungo Brush
Tamboy
Broughton Island
Little Broughton Island
Fiona Beach

Bolwarra
Morpeth
MAITLAND
Heddon Greta
Beresfield
Thornton
RAYMOND TERRACE
Seaham
Nelsons Plains
Karuah
North Arm Cove
Carrington
TILLIGERRY HABITAT
KOALA RES
Lemon Tree Passage
Hawks Nest
Tea Gardens
Port Stephens
PACIFIC

Maitland
Woodville
Glen
Williamtown
KOORAGANG NR
Salt Ash
Nelson Bay
Anna Bay
Boat Harbour
Shoal Bay
TOMAREE NP
Fingal Bay

Mimmi
Wallsend
Stockton
Nobbys Head
NEWCASTLE
TO SYDNEY
Stockton Bight

For more detail on Newcastle & Surrounds see page 549

TO TOOWOOMBA

QUEENSLAND

WARWICK

NEW SOUTH WALES

NEW ENGLAND

Joins map 557

TO GLEN INNES

Boonah

Beaudesert

NERANG

GOLD COAST

WARNER BROS.
MOVIE WORLD,
DREAMWORLD,
WET 'N' WILD
WATER WORLD,
SEA WORLD,
SURFING

Mudgeeraba

For more detail on
Brisbane & Surrounds,
South see page 645

Murwillumbah

Banora Point
Chinderah
Kingscliff

Bogangar

Hastings Point
Pottsville

BORDER RANGES NP

LAMINGTON NP

MOUNT BARNEY NP

Ocean Shores

Brunswick Heads

CAPE BYRON
LIGHTHOUSE,
WATEGO BEACH,
WHALES

Mullumbimby

Byron Bay

Cape Byron

Suffolk
Park

Jews Point

Kyogle

Lennox Head

Casino LISMORE

Wollongbar Alstonville

BALLINA

Coraki

Evans Head

CORAL

SEA

BUNDJALUNG
NATIONAL
PARK

Woodburn

New
Italy

PROHIBITED AREA

Iluka

Yamba

Maclean

Angourie

YURAYGIR
NATIONAL
PARK

Junction
Hill

GRAFTON

South
Grafton

Brooms Head

WASHPOOL

NATIONAL

PARK

GIBRALTAR
RANGE
NP

Wooli

SOLITARY ISLANDS MP

North Solitary
Island

North Rock

Red Rock

Corindi Beach

Arrawarra

Woolgoolga

Sandy Beach

Emerald Beach

South Solitary Island

Korora

COFFS HARBOUR

Boambee

SAWTELL

Dorrigo

BONGIL BONGIL NP

TASMAN SEA

Bellingen

Urunga

TO PORT MACQUARIE

0   0.5   1   1.5   2 km

A   B   C   D   Joins map 553   E   F   G   H

Tarrawanna

TO SYDNEY

Corrimal Pk
RAILWAY

Corrimal

Corrimal Beach
Tourist Park

Corrimal
SLSC

ILLAWARRA ESCARPMENT
STATE CONSERVATION AREA

Mt Pleasant
Colliery

Towradgi Creek

Fernhill

Balgownie

Towradgi Park

Rocks

Towradgi
Point

Towradgi

Guest Park

Towradgi
SLSC
Northern Beach

**Mount
Pleasant**

**Mount
Ousley**

**Fairy
Meadow**

Fairy
Meadow

Fairy
Meadow
SLSC

ILLAWARRA
ESCARPMENT
STATE
CONSERVATION
AREA

Wollongong
Science
Centre &
Planetarium

University of
Wollongong
Innovation
Campus

Thomas
Dalton
Park

Brandon
Park

TASMAN

N

University of
Wollongong

TAFE NSW
Illawarra
Institute

18
Wollongong
Botanic
Gardens

School

Stuart
Park

SEA

**North
Wollongong**

North Wollongong
SLSC

North
Wollongong
Beach

**Mount
Keira**

Keiraville

Keira
Village Park

Gwynneville

Wiseman
Park

Beaton
Park

Swimming
Pool

Wollongong Harbour

Rocks

Flagstaff Hill
Park

Flagstaff
Point

City Beach
SLSC

Gilmore
Park

2

1

5

9

4

8

10

WOLLONGONG

14
7
11
16
19
12
17

Roy
Johanson
Park

**West
Wollongong**

Wollongong
Hospital

13

Figtree

Harry
Graham
Park

Mangerton

Mangerton
Park

McCabe Park

Stewart
Park

WIN
Stadium

Showground

Wollongong
Golf
Club

Fig Tree
Park

Westfield
Figtree S.C.

Coniston

JJ Kelly
Park

Sid Parrish
Park

**Mount
St Thomas**

Coniston

Wollongong
Greenhouse
Park

TO KIAMA

**Port Kembla
Steel Works**

Joins map 553

N of document — legend:

Accommodation ■
Belmore All Suite Hotel 1 F9
Boat Harbour Motel 2 F8
The City Beach Motel 3 F9
Downtown Motel 4 F9
Hotel Ibis Wollongong 5 E9
Novotel Wollongong Northbeach 6 F7
Park Street Serviced Apartments 7 F7
Note: Only a sample range of
accommodation is listed; inclusion is
not necessarily a recommendation.

General Information ■
Coach Terminal 8 E8
Motoring Organisation (NRMA) 9 E9
Police Headquarters 10 E9
Post Office 11 F9
WIN Sports & Entertainment Centres 12 F9
Wollongong Railway Station 13 D9
Wollongong Visitor Centre 14 F9

Places of Interest ■
Illawarra Historical Society Museum 15 F9
Illawarra Performing Arts Centre 16 F9
International Centre 17 F9
Wollongong Botanic Garden 18 C6
Wollongong City Gallery 19 F9

Joins map 544
Joins map 542
Joins map 565
Joins map 567

0   5   10   15   20 km

TO SYDNEY

For more detail
on Wollongong
see page 552

TO GOULBURN

TO ULLADULLA

**JERVIS BAY
TERRITORY**
BOODEREE NATIONAL PARK
Cape St George

TASMAN

SEA

Joins map 556

Joins map 559

For more detail
on the ACT
see page 564

For more detail on
the Mid North Coast
see page 550

For more detail on
Newcastle & Surrounds
see page 549

For more detail on
the Central Coast
see page 543

For more detail on Sydney &
Surrounds see pages 544–5

For more detail on the
Southern Highlands
see page 553

For more detail on the
Snowy Mountains &
The South Coast
see pages 566–7

TASMAN SEA

Joins map 652
Joins map 653
Joins map 561
Joins map 554
Joins map 555

0   20   40   60   80   100 km

Joins map 554

QUEENSLAND
NEW SOUTH WALES

WARNINGS: In outback Australia, long distances separate some towns. Travellers should familiarise themselves with prevailing conditions before departure and take care to ensure their vehicle is roadworthy. Adequate supplies of petrol, water and food should be carried at all times.

In central Australia, rainfall can make some roads impassable, even with a 4WD vehicle. Full information on road conditions should be obtained from local authorities before departure.

SOUTH AUSTRALIA
NEW SOUTH WALES

STRZELECKI DESERT

STURT NATIONAL PARK

STURT NP

MUTAWINTJI NATIONAL PARK

MUTAWINTJI NATURE RESERVE

PAROO-DARLING NP

PAROO-DARLING SCA

PAROO-DARLING NP

KINCHEGA NP

BROKEN HILL

Joins map 556

0   0.25   0.50   0.75   1 km

Joins map 563

Accommodation ■
Best Western Motel Monaro 1 F12
The Brassey of Canberra 2 E11
Crowne Plaza Hotel Canberra 3 D4
The Griffin Hotel & Spa 4 E11
Hyatt Hotel Canberra 5 C8
Hotel Kurrajong 6 D10
Medina Executive James Court 7 D2
Olims Hotel Canberra 8 F3
Rydges Capital Hill Hotel 9 D11
Rydges Lakeside Canberra Hotel 10 C4
Note: Only a sample range of
accommodation is listed; inclusion is
not necessarily a recommendation.

General Information ■
Bus Interchange 11 D3
Canberra Railway Station 12 G12
General Post Office 13 C3
Jolimont Centre 14 C3
Motoring Organisation (NRMA) 15 D2
Police Station 16 C4
Qantas Travel Centre 17 C3

Places of Interest ■
Australian National University 18 B4

Australian War Memorial 19 G4
Blundell's Cottage 20 F6
Canberra Glassworks 21 F11
Canberra Museum and Gallery 22 D3
Canberra Theatre Centre 23 D4
Captain Cook Memorial Water Jet 24 C6
High Court of Australia 25 E8
Legislative Assembly of the ACT 26 D4
The Lodge 27 A10
Manuka Oval 28 D12
Museum of Australian
   Democracy 29 C8
National Capital Exhibition 30 D6
National Carillon 31 F8
National Film & Sound Archive 32 B4
National Gallery of Australia 33 E8
National Library of Australia 34 D7
National Museum of Australia 35 B6
National Portrait Gallery 36 D8
Parliament House 37 B10
Questacon – The National Science &
   Technology Centre 38 D8
St John the Baptist Church 39 E5

TO GOULBURN

Braddon

Northbourne
Oval

Ainslie Public
School

Mt Ainslie
Lookout

Canberra
Nature
Park

Ainslie
Hostel

CSIRO Head Office

Campbell
High School

Remembrance
Nature Park

CANBERRA

City
Hill

Casino
Canberra

Reid

Reid
Park

Australian
War Memorial

FAIRBAIRN AV

TO AIRPORT

St John's
Schoolhouse
Museum

St John the
Baptist Church

Campbell

Campbell
Public School

St Thomas
More Convent

Swimming
Pool

West Basin

Acton Ferry Terminal
& Boat Hire

LAKE

National Museum
of Australia

Acton
Peninsula

Nerang Pool

National Capital
Exhibition

Regatta Point

Captain Cook
Memorial Water Jet

Gallipoli Reach

Central
Basin

BURLEY

Russell

Australian–
American
Memorial

Canberra
Nature Park

Attunga Point

Southern Cross
Yacht Club

Lotus
Bay

Lennox
Gardens

Flynn
Place

National Library of
Australia

National
Carillon

Aspen
Island

NORTHCOTT

Stirling

Rose
Gardens

Questacon – The National
Science & Technology
Centre

High Court
of Australia

National Gallery
of Australia

Grevillea
Park

Yarralumla

Rose
Gardens

Parkes

National
Portrait
Gallery

Kings Avenue
Bridge

Bowen
Place

GRIFFIN

East
Basin

Molonglo River

National Archives
of Australia

Capital
Hill

Parliament
House

Barton

Bowen Park

Jerrabomberra
Wetlands

TO WODEN

ADELAIDE AV

The Lodge

Forrest
Public School

National Jewish
Memorial Centre

Serbian
Orthodox
Church

York
Park

Telopea Park
High School

Canberra
Glassworks

Old Bus Depot
Markets (Sun)

Kingston

Boat Harbour

Jerrabomberra
Creek

Deakin

Manuka
Oval

Collins Park

TO QUEANBEYAN

Canberra
Railway
Museum

Joins map 563

Joins map 565

Joins map 566

Joins map 566

Joins map 567

For more detail on Canberra
Suburbs see page 563

Joins map 554

Joins map 555

Joins map 585

Joins map 583

0   20   40   60   80   100 km

Key places

A1 Grogan, Milvale, Stockinbingal, Bethungra, Frampton, Cootamundra, Harden, Murrumburrah, Gundagai, Nangus, Coolac, Tumblong, Mount Adrah, Adelong, Batlow, Laurel Hill, Tumbarumba, Tooma, Greg Greg, Towong, Khancoban, Biggara, Tom Groggin, Geehi, Charlotte Pass, Wairewa, Bete Bolong, Tostaree, Newmerella, Orbost, Marlo, Buchan, Murrindal, W Tree

B Bribbaree, Crowther, Thuddungra, Wirrimah, Monteagle, Young, Maimuru, Wombat, Boorowa, Kingsvale, Nubba, Wallendbeen, Cunningar, Galong, Binalong, Jugiong, Bookham, Adjungbilly, Burrinjuck, Brungle, Tumorrama, Gocup, Tumut, Gilmore, Bondo, Windowie, Wereboldera, Goobarragandra, Talbingo, Pilot Hill, Yarrangobilly, Kiandra, Cabramurra, Old Adaminaby, Anglers Reach, Sue City, Khancoban, Gungahlin, Guthega, Perisher, Smiggin Holes, Thredbo, Moonbah, Dalgety, Paupong, Matong, Bungarby, Numbla Vale, Tombong, Bombala, Wulgulmerang, Suggan Buggan, Deddick, Amboyne Crossing, Tubbut, Karoonda Roadhouse, Gelantipy, Butchers Ridge, Seldom Seen Roadhouse, Deliicknora, Bendoc, Bonang, Goongerah, Errinundra, Combienbar, Club Terrace, Tonghi Creek, Noorinbee, Murrungowar, Tabbara, Cann River, Bellbird Creek, Cabbage Tree Creek, Tamboon

C Breakfast Creek, Godfreys Creek, Bendick Murrell, Murringo, Frogmore, Rye Park, Kangiara, Tangmangaroo, Wee Jasper, Burrinjuck, Yass, Bowning, Goondah, Jerrawa, Dalton, Murrumbateman, Gundaroo, Sutton, Belconnen, Canberra, Tharwa, Royalla, Williamsdale, Michelago, Bredbo, Adaminaby, Eucumbene, Anglers Reach, Shannons Flat, Colinton, Jerangle, Numeralla, Cooma, Cooma West, Bunyan, Rock Flat, Kybeyan, Berridale, Jindabyne, Coonerang, Kydra, Nimmitabel, Bukalong, Cathcart, Rocky Hall, Wyndham, Craigie, Mila, Haydens Bog, Delegate River, Delegate, Bendoc, Bonang, Chandlers Creek, Weeragua, Noorinbee North, Gipsy Point

D Reids Flat, Bigga, Tuena, Taylors Flat, Blanket Flat, Peelwood, Rugby, Binda, Kennys Creek, Bevendale, Biala, Grabben Gullen, Kialla, Crookwell, Roslyn, Breadalbane, Gunning, Collector, Bellmount Forest, Currawang, Gundaroo, Bungendore, Hoskinstown, Rossi, Braidwood, Captains Flat, Ballalaba, Reidsdale, Majors Creek, Krawarree, Kain, Araluen, Numeralla, Countegany, Yowrie, Wandella, Cobargo, Brogo, Bemboka, Morans Crossing, Kameruka, Candelo, Bibbenluke, Wolumla, Pambula, Greigs Flat, Nethercote, Towamba, Buldah, Wroxham, Timbillica, Wangarabell, Noorinbee, Genoa, Gipsy Point, Mallacoota

E Isabella, Porters Retreat, Fullerton, Golspie, Richlands, Roslyn, Woodhouselee, Chatsbury, Tarlo, Gurrundah, Kingsdale, Komungla, Bungonia, Windellama, Nerriga, Sassafras, Lake Bathurst, Tarago, Boro, Lower Boro, Corang, Gundillion, Anembo, Colinton, Peak View, Jerangle, Numeralla, Chakola, Bunyan, Bega, Numbugga, Tanja, Kalaru, Tathra, Wolumla, Tura Beach, Merimbula, Pambula Beach, Eden, Boydtown, Kiah, Wonboyn

F Mount Werong, Wombeyan Caves, High Range, Bannaby, Penrose, Tallong, Wingello, Marulan, Tallong, Windellama, Nerriga, Sassafras, Tarago, Durras, Mongarlowe, Long Flat, Currowan Creek, Nelligen, Araluen, Oranmeir, Mogo, Bimbimbie, Mogendoura, Bergalia, Turlinjah, Nerrigundah, Belowra, Eurobodalla, Bodalla, Central Tilba, Tilba Tilba, Cobargo, Quaama, Brogo, Wapengo, Bega, Merimbula

G Warragamba, Silverdale, Werombi, Nattai, Colo Vale, Berrima, Sutton Forest, Exeter, Penrose, Moss Vale, Robertson, Bundanoon, Kangaroo Valley, Cambewarra, Bomaderry, Nowra, Nowra Hill, Yalwal, Falls Creek, Milton, Kings Point, Ulladulla, Burrill Lake, Tabourie Lake, Bawley Point, Kioloa, Pebbly Beach, Durras, Long Beach, Batemans Bay, Malua Bay, Rosedale, Broulee, Moruya, Moruya Heads, Congo, Meringo, Tuross Head, Potato Point, Dalmeny, Narooma, Bermagui, Bermagui South, Mimosa Rocks NP

H Liverpool, Campbelltown, Heathcote, Appin, Helensburgh, Stanwell Park, Wollongong, Port Kembla, Windang, Shellharbour, Bass Point, Kiama, Jamberoo, Gerringong, Shoalhaven Heads, Greenwell Point, Culburra, Callala Bay, Vincentia, Huskisson, St Georges Basin, Jervis Bay, Sussex Inlet

Inset notes

For more detail on the Southern Highlands see page 553

For more detail on the ACT see page 564

For more detail on the Snowy Mountains & The South Coast see pages 566–7

TASMAN SEA

Joins map 565

| A | B | C | D | E | F | G | H |

TO YASS

Gundagai
South Gundagai
DOG ON THE TUCKER BOX
Kangaroo Mountain
Adjungbilly
BLACK ANDREW NR
Black Andrew Mountain
OAK CREEK NR
Mount Boambolo
Keswick
Ruthfield
Gundaroo

Tumblong
Mount Adrah
HWY
Mount Brae
Mount Narrangullen
WEE JASPER NR
Wee Jasper
Mount Spring

TO WAGGA WAGGA
STURT HWY
Mount Adrah
Mount Horeb
MUDJARN NR
Tumorrama
Mount Wee Jasper
WADDYS PLAIN
BARTON HWY
Sutton

HUME HWY
Mount Yaven
ELLERSLIE NR
SNOWY
Gocup
Mount Hartwood
BRINDABELLA NATIONAL PARK
Hall
Gungahlin
Ginninderra
Mitchell

TO ALBURY
Tarcutta
Adelong
Tumut
Bondo
BOBBYS PLAINS
Snow Gum Mountain
NEW SOUTH WALES
AUSTRALIAN CAPITAL TERRITORY
Belconnen
CANBERRA

Oberne
Windowie
Gilmore
Argalong
Mount Lickhole
Brindabella Mountain
MOUNT STROMLO OBSERVATORY
Coppins Crossing
Canberra Airport
Fyshwick

Humula
Mount Oberne
Spyglass Mountain
Wereboldera
Wondalga
Goobarragandra
Mount Hovell
Mount Bramina
CANBERRA DEEP SPACE COMMUNICATION COMPLEX
QUEANBEYAN
Burt

DOWNFALL NR
BLOWERING DAM LOOKOUT
Blowering Reservoir
Ugly Mountain
Black Bottle Mountain
BIMBERI
TIDBINBILLA
Tidbinbilla Peak
RED ROCKS GORGE NR
Tuggeranong
BULLEN RANGE
Jerrabomberra

Carabost
Batlow
Kunama
Talbingo
Bogong Mountain
KOSCIUSZKO
FIERY RANGE
Aggie Gap
NATURE RESERVE
Mount Ginini
Corin Dam
BILLY RA
Williamsdale
Royalla
LONDON BRIDGE LIMESTONE FORMATION

Rosewood
Laurel Hill
Pilot Hill
TUMUT 3 POWER STATION
Talbingo Dam
Big Talbingo Mountain
NATIONAL
Mount Jackson
Blackfellows Gap
NAMADGI
Cotter
FORMER SPACE TRACKING STATION
Mount Tennent
Mount McKeahnie
For more detail on the ACT see page 564

Glenroy
HUME & HOVELL WALKING TRACK
Cumberland Gap
Yarrangobilly
Yarrangobilly Mountain
PARK
Leura Gap
Corin Peak
Mount Murray
NATIONAL
Michelago

Tumbarumba
COURABYRA NR
Granite Mountain
Yarrangobilly Caves
CAVES
Rules Point
Dairymans Gap
Skains Mountain
Howells Peak
Tantangara Reservoir
Mount Scabby
SCABBY RANGE NR
Mount Gudgenby
PARK
Mount Kelly
Mount Burra
Mount Bullongong
TINDERRY NATURE RESERVE

Pilot Reef Mountain
Round Top Mountain
BLANKET PLAIN
GULF PLAIN
Mount Nungar
Mount Morgan
Sentry Box Mountain
Shanahans Mountain
Mount Holland
BURNT SCHOOL NR

Ikes Mountain
CLARKES HILL NR
Sue City
Gooandra
NUNGAR PLAIN
YAOUK NATURE RESERVE
Yaouk
BICENTENNIAL NATIONAL TRAIL
ACT
STRIKE-A-LIGHT NR

JINGELLIC NATURE RESERVE
Walwa
Ournie
BOGANDYERA NATURE RESERVE
Tooma
TUMUT 2 POWER STATION
Kiandra
Tantangara Mountain
Gang Gang Mountain
WORLD'S LARGEST TROUT
NSW
Colinton
Mount Clear
Gungoandra Gap
Jerangle
Mount Wangrah

BURROWA-PINE MOUNTAIN NP
Cudgewa North
Welaregang
Mount Welaregang
The Sisters
Cabramurra
Tumut Pond Reservoir
Tabletop Mountain
Mount Denison
SNOWY
Adaminaby
JONES PLAIN
RESERVE
Shannons Flat
Riversdale
Bredbo
Connollys Gap
Mount Dowling

Tintaldra
Greg Greg
Lighthouse Mountain
Far Bald Mountain
Round Mountain
Anglers Reach
Wyandra
Montillo
Caddigat
Oakvale
Wathonga
Rothlyn
Overda

Cudgewa
Colac Colac
Thowgla
Corryong
Towong Upper
Khancoban
Bradneys Gap
Toorna Res
The Dargals
Spencers Peak
KOSCIUSZKO
Barneys Gap
Mount Hudson
Cosey Corner
Lake Eucumbene
Five Springs
Bernina
Morees
Crookshanks Peak
Murrumbucca
Dromore
Chakola
Peak View

TO WODONGA
Thowgla Upper
Nariel Gap
Mount Sugarloaf
Biggara
Khancoban Pondage
MURRAY 1 POWER STATION
NATIONAL
RANGE
NIMMO PLAIN
Nimmo
Eucumbene
Montana
Bellevue
Buckenderra
Peak Valley
Yalcowinna
Cooma Llama Farm
Rosebrook
COORNARTHA NR
Bunyan
Numeralla

Nariel
Mount Barlow
SCAMMELL'S LOOKOUT
The Twins
The Pinnacle
Geehi Res
WAY
Schlink Pass
Island Bend Pondage
PARK
NIMMO NR
Rocky Plain
Rosemont
Murlingbung
Middlingbank
Lake Plain
COOMA GLADSTONE LOOKOUT
Woodend
NUMERALLA NR

Mount Bunroy
Mount Unicorn
OLSENS LOOKOUT
Mount Tate
Island Bend
Wilsons Valley
SNOWY VALLEY LOOKOUT
Kalkite Gap
Glengyle
MOUNT GLADSTONE LOOKOUT
Cooma West
Cooma
AUSTRALIAN ALPS
Guthega
Mount Anton
Mount Blue Cow
Perisher
Carruthers Peak
Smiggin Holes
Bullocks Flat
Kalkite
Kiah Lodge
Kiah Lake
EUCUMBENE TROUT FARM
Gunyah
Snowy Mountains Airport
Brookfield Park
Woodstock
Carlaminda

Nariel
Mount Morgan
Granuaille Mountain
Geehi
Mount Townsend
SKI AREA
Sawpit Creek
East Jindabyne
Lake Jindabyne
Yerenbah
Berridale
Hazeldean
Arable
Cherrytree
Manaroo
Sunny Corner

AUSTRALIA'S HIGHEST MOUNTAIN
Mount Kosciuszko
Charlotte Pass
Crackenback Peak
GADEN TROUT HATCHERY
SNOWY REGION VISITOR CENTRE
Jindabyne
Coolamatong
Dutton Plain
Cottage Creek
Ravensworth
Myalla
Milton Park
Rock Flat
Dangelong
Kybeyan

Thredbo
Tom Groggin
Penderlea
Moonbah
Moonbah Mountain
Lynwood
Waterford
Glen Miln
NGADANG NR
Snowy Station
Allawah
Severn Park
The Twins
BOBUNDARA NR
Coonerang
Caringa
DANGELONG NR

ALPINE WAY DRIVE
Mount Terrible
Round Mountain
Mount Stony
GROSSES PLAIN
Dimboola
Dalgety
Manara
Jinny Brother Peak
Bobingha
Gourock
Nimmitabel

ALPINE NATIONAL PARK
KOSCIUSZKO NATIONAL PARK
VICTORIA
NEW SOUTH WALES
JACK WALLS RA
PAUPONG NR
Beloka
Gallaroi
IRONMUNGY NR
Conhoonbula
Maffra
Old Curry Flat
Kookabunna
Yandra
Highland Grange
Hurlstone
Kydra
Clermont

Buenba Gap
Mount Murphy
GREAT
DIVIDING
RANGE
BARRY
The Big Rocks
Bald Peak
Milligans Creek
Murranumbla
Paupong
Ironmungy
Numbla Vale
Finister
Boco
SNOWY RIVER
Avonlake
Bungee Peak
Brooklyn
Shirley
Le Tompe
Bellevue
Bull Mountain

Mount Misery
Round Mountains
Mount Cobberas Number 2
The Pilot
The Beehive
The Red Hill
Pinch Mountain
Black Jack River
Boundary Creek
Jimenbuen
Johns Peak
Matong
Bungarby
Jimenbuen
Yarrandod
MERRIANGAAH NATURE RESERVE
SHERWINS RANGE
Pleasant View
Grannys Hill
MONARO HWY
TO BOMBALA

Joins map 565

| A | B | C | D | E | F | G | H |

0   10   20   30   40 km

For more detail on the
Southern Highlands
see page 553

MAPS

VICTORIA

588–9

Mildura
Robinvale
Ouyen

590–1

Swan Hill
Kerang

Nhill
Warracknabeal
Charlton
Dimboola
Horsham
St Arnaud

584–5

Cobram
Echuca
Rutherglen
Wodonga
Corryong
Shepparton
Wangaratta
Rochester

581

592–3

Maryborough
Stawell
Castlemaine
Ararat
Ballarat

579
Bendigo

Euroa
Benalla
Bright
Seymour
Mansfield

Casterton
Coleraine
Hamilton

Alexandra

586–7

Heywood
Portland
Port Fairy
Warrnambool
Colac
Terang
Lorne

580

570
Geelong
Ocean Grove
Torquay

MELBOURNE
Healesville
Cranbourne
Mornington
Wonthaggi
Warragul
Morwell
Foster
Yarram

Bairnsdale
Lakes Entrance
Orbost

571

582–3

574–5

572–3

INTER-CITY ROUTES		DISTANCE
Melbourne–Sydney via Hume Hwy/Fwy	M31 31	879 km
Melbourne–Sydney via Princes Hwy/Fwy	B1 A1 1	1039 km
Melbourne–Adelaide via Western & Dukes hwys	M8 A8 M1	729 km
Melbourne–Adelaide via Princes Hwy	M1 A1 B1 M1	911 km
Melbourne–Brisbane via Newell Hwy	M31 A39 39 A39 A2	1676 km

0   0.25   0.5   0.75   1 km

Accommodation ■
Adelphi Hotel 1 E7
Crown Towers 2 C9
Jasper Hotel 3 C4
Langham Hotel 4 D8
Lygon Lodge 5 D3
Melbourne Marriott Hotel 6 E5
Novotel Melbourne on Collins 7 D7
Park Hyatt Melbourne 8 G5
Radisson on Flagstaff Gardens 9 B5
The Rialto 10 B8
Sofitel Melbourne on Collins 11 F6
Somerset Gordon Place 12 E5
The Westin Melbourne 13 D7
Note: Only a sample range of
accommodation is listed; inclusion is
not necessarily a recommendation.

General Information ■
Bus Day Tour Departure Point 14 D6
City Police Station 15 A9
Flinders Street Station 16 E8
General Post Office 17 C6
Melbourne River Cruises 18 E8
The Melbourne Transit Centre 19 C4
Melbourne Visitor Centre 20 E7
Motoring Organisation (RACV) 21 C7
Qantas Travel Centre 22 D7
Regional & Interstate Coach Terminal 23 A7
Southern Cross Station 24 A8

Places of Interest ■
Aust. Centre for Contemporary Art 25 D10
The Block Arcade 26 D7
Chinatown 27 E6

Chinese Museum 28 E5
Cooks' Cottage 29 G6
Crown Entertainment Complex 30 B9
Eureka Tower & Eureka Skydeck 88 31 D9
Federation Square 32 E8
Fire Services Museum 33 G5
The Ian Potter Centre: NGV Australia 34 E7
IMAX Theatre 35 E3
La Trobe's Cottage 36 G12
Melbourne Aquarium 37 B9
Melbourne Central 38 D5
Melbourne Convention Centre 39 B9
Melbourne Cricket Ground (MCG) 40 H8
Melbourne Museum 41 E3
Melbourne Park 42 G8
Melbourne Town Hall 43 D7
National Sports Museum 44 H8
Old Melbourne Gaol 45 D4
Parliament of Victoria 46 F5
Performing Arts Museum 47 E8
Polly Woodside 48 A10
Queen Victoria Market 49 B4
Queensbridge Square 50 C9
Royal Arcade 51 D7
Royal Botanic Gardens 52 H11
Royal Exhibition Building 53 F3
St Patrick's Cathedral 54 G5
St Paul's Anglican Cathedral 55 E7
Shrine of Remembrance 56 F11
Sidney Myer Music Bowl 57 F9
Southgate 58 D8
State Library of Victoria 59 D5
Victorian Arts Centre 60 E9

0 5 10 15 20 km

TO SEYMOUR

Joins map 573

TO MANSFIELD

N

TO WOODS POINT

Joins map 570

Joins map 573

TO PHILLIP ISLAND

Joins map 573

TO WARRAGUL

For more detail on Mornington & Bellarine Peninsulas see pages 574–5

Major places:
Tyaak, Strath Creek, Reedy Creek, Flowerdale, Hazeldene, Break O Day, Yea, Limestone, Murrindindi, Alexandra, Eildon, Thornton, Acheron, Taggerty, Buxton, Marysville, Narbethong, St Fillans, Kinglake West, Kinglake Central, Kinglake, Kinglake East, Castella, Toolangi, Strathewen, St Andrews, Hurstbridge, Yarra Glen, Healesville, Coldstream, Lilydale, Gruyere, Seville, Woori Yallock, Launching Place, Yarra Junction, Millgrove, Warburton, Wesburn, Gladysdale, Powelltown, Noojee, Nunawading, Mitcham, Ringwood, Croydon, Mooroolbark, Wandin North, Silvan, Kalorama, Olinda, Monbulk, Macclesfield, Emerald, Cockatoo, Gembrook, Belgrave, Tecoma, Upwey, Ferntree Gully, Rowville, Lysterfield, Dandenong, Noble Park, Hallam, Narre Warren, Berwick, Beaconsfield, Upper Beaconsfield, Officer, Pakenham, Cranbourne, Clyde, Cardinia, Nar Nar Goon, Tynong, Garfield, Bunyip, Longwarry, Drouin West, Rokeby, Buln Buln, Neerim, Neerim South, Neerim Junction, Nayook, Labertouche, Jindivick, Tarago, Crossover

A B C D E F G H

Joins map 572

TO WERRIBEE

1

Rothwell
SERENDIP SANCTUARY
AVALON RACEWAY
Lara
Lara Lake
Werribee South
Lake Borrie
Western Treatment Plant
Beacon Point

2

Hovell Park
Rosewall
Lovely Banks
Moorabool
Norlane
Corio
North Shore
Avalon
Avalon Airport
LIMEBURNERS LAGOON NATURE RESERVE
Point Lillias
Point Wilson
WILDLIFE RESERVE
Port Phillip
Batesford
TO BALLARAT
MIDLAND

Joins map 572

3

Hamlyn Heights
Geelong North
Rippleside
Drumcondra
GEELONG
Geelong East
Fyansford
Point Henry
Corio Bay
Outer Harbour
Point Richards
Port Richards Channel
Port Bellarine
Port Bellarine
Portarlington
Point George
Indented Head
Indented Head

For more detail on Geelong see page 576

4

Buckley Falls
Highton
Wandana Heights
Belmont
Geelong South
Thomson
Breakwater
Moolap
Marshall
St Albans Park
Grovedale
Leopold
Curlewis
Clifton Springs
Drysdale
Murradoc
CLIFTON SPRINGS GOLF COURSE
DRYSDALE REC RES
BELLARINE PENINSULA RAILWAY
PORTARLINGTON GOLF COURSE
Bellarine
St Leonards

5

Mount Dunned
Connewarre
WILDLIFE RESERVE
Lake Connewarre
Wallington
ADVENTURE PARK
A MAZE 'N GAMES
Fenwick
Marcus
Marcus Hill
Mannerim
BELLARINE PENINSULA
Edwards Point
Duck Island
PORT PHILLIP HEADS MARINE NP
Swan Bay
Swan Island
Swan Point
LOWER BLUFF WILDLIFE RESERVE
PORT PHILLP HEADS MARINE NP
Mud Islands

6

JIRRAHLINGA KOALA & WILDLIFE RESERVE
Barwon Heads
Ocean Grove
Collendina
Lake Victoria
BARWON HEADS GOLF CLUB
Barwon Head
Point Lonsdale
Point Impossible
Breamlea
Point Lonsdale
Lonsdale Bay
MARITIME CENTRE, BELLARINE PENINSULA RAILWAY, HISTORIC TOWN
Queenscliff
BLACK LIGHTHOUSE, FORT QUEENSCLIFF, WHITE LIGHTHOUSE
FERRIES
PORT PHILLIP HEADS MARINE NP

7

SURFWORLD AUSTRALIA
Torquay
Jan Juc
Half Moon Bay
SURFING
POINT DANGER MARINE SANCTUARY
FORT NEPEAN
PORT PHILLIP HEADS MARINE NP
PROHIBITED AREA
LONDON BRIDGE
MORNINGTON
Point Nepean
Observatory Point
Monash Lighthouse
Portsea
Point King
Sorrento
COLLINS SETTLEMENT HISTORIC SITE
Capel Sound
South Channel Island

8

PENINSULA
NATIONAL
PARK
Jubilee Point
Blairgowrie
Rye
Tootgarook
Rosebud West
Rosebud
McCrae
ROSEBUD COUNTRY CLUB

9

MORNINGTON
PENINSULA
Rye Ocean Beach
Saint Andrews Beach
Boneo
Fingal
MORNINGTON PENINSULA NATIONAL PARK

10

Gunnamatta Beach
NATIONAL
PARK
CAPE SCHANCK LIGHTHOUSE
Cape Schanck

11

12

BASS STRAIT

A B C D E F G H

Scale: 0 0.25 0.5 0.75 1 km

Joins map 574

TO BALLARAT
TO MELBOURNE
TO HAMILTON
TO COLAC
TO TORQUAY
TO QUEENSCLIFF

Geelong North
Hamlyn Heights
Drumcondra
Herne Hill
Geelong West
Newtown
GEELONG
Geelong East
Thomson
Geelong South
Highton
Belmont
Breakwater
CORIO BAY

Accommodation ■
Aberdeen Motor Inn 1 D6
Best Western Geelong Motor Inn 2 D4
Colonial Lodge Motel 3 D8
Comfort Inn Bay City Geelong 4 F6
Mercure Hotel Geelong 5 D6
Riverglen Holiday Park 6 B9
Shannon Motor Inn 7 B5
Note: Only a sample range of
accommodation is listed; inclusion is
not necessarily a recommendation.

General Information ■
Geelong Hospital 8 F6
Geelong Railway Station 9 D5
Geelong Transport
Interchange 10 E5
Motoring Organisation (RACV) 11 E5
Police 12 D5
Post Office 13 E5
Town Hall 14 E5

Visitor Information 15 E5

Places of Interest ■
Balyang Sanctuary 16 A8
Barwon Grange 17 C8
Barwon Valley Park 18 B9
Botanic Gardens 19 G6
Christ Church 20 E6
Customs House 21 E5
Eastern Beach 22 F5
Ford Discovery Centre 23 E5
Geelong Gallery 24 E5
Geelong Racecourse 25 G10
The Heights 26 A6
National Wool Museum 27 E5
Old Geelong Gaol 28 F7
Osborne House 29 D1
Geelong Performing
Arts Centre 30 D5
Pottage Jewellery & Crafts 31 E6
Wintergarden 32 E6

Joins map 574

Joins map 574

0   0.5   1   1.5   2 km

Joins map 579
Joins map 579
Joins map 579

Invermay

Wendouree

Invermay Park

Ballarat North

Black Hill

Nerrina

Soldiers Hill

Brown Hill

BALLARAT

Ballarat Central

Mount Pleasant

Canadian

Redan

Delacombe

Sebastopol

TO ARARAT

TO HAMILTON

TO MELBOURNE

TO GEELONG

Lake Wendouree

Victoria Park

Accommodation ■
Ballarat Mid City Accommodation & Conference Centre 1 D6
Best Western Bakery Hill Motel 2 F6
Best Western Ballarat 3 F8
Central City Motor Inn 4 F6
Comfort Inn Main Lead 5 F7
Craig's Royal Hotel 6 E6
Eureka Lodge Motel 7 H6
George Hotel 8 E6
The Lake View 9 C5
Mercure Ballarat Hotel & Convention Centre 10 F8
Miners Retreat Motel 11 H6
Peppinella Motel 12 A10
Ravenswood Cottage 13 E5
Reid's Guest House 14 E6
Sovereign Hill Lodge 15 F8
Sovereign Park Motor Inn 16 F7
Sovereign Views Apartments 17 F8
Victoriana Motor Inn 18 H5
Note: Only a sample range of accommodation is listed; inclusion is not necessarily a recommendation.

General Information ■
Ballarat Base Hospital 19 D6
Ballarat Railway Station 20 E6
Motoring Organisation (RACV) 21 E6
Police Station 22 E6
Post Office 23 E6
Visitor Information 24 E6, E7

Places of Interest ■
Adam Lindsay Gordon Craft Cottage 25 A5
Aquatic & Hockey Centre 26 A5
Art Gallery of Ballarat 27 E6
Ballarat Tramway Museum 28 A6
Ballarat Wildlife Park 29 H7
The Eureka Centre 30 H6
Gold Museum 31 F8
Her Majesty's Theatre 32 E6
The Mining Exchange Gold Shop 33 E6
Montrose Cottage and Museum 34 F7
The Robert Clark Conservatory 35 A5
Sovereign Hill Historical Park 36 F8
Town Hall 37 E6

0   200   400   600 m

North
Bendigo

N

Accommodation ■
Abode Bendigo 1 F3
Alexandra Place 2 F6
Barclay 'on View' Motor Inn 3 C7
Bendigo Haymarket Motor Inn 4 G8
Bendigo McIvor Motor Inn 5 H8
Best Western Cathedral Motor Inn 6 B9
Comfort Inn Julie-Anna 7 H4
Comfort Inn Central Deborah 8 A11
Hotel Shamrock 9 D8
Hunter House 10 D10
Oval Motel 11 C7
Note: Only a sample range of
accommodation is listed; inclusion is
not necessarily a recommendation.

General Information ■
All Saints Old Cathedral 12 C8
Base Hospital 13 E4
Bendigo Railway Station 14 E11
Motoring Organisation (RACV) 15 E10
Municipal Offices 16 E8
Police 17 E8
Post Office 18 E9
Sacred Heart Cathedral 19 B9
Town Hall 20 E8
Visitor Information 21 D8

Places of Interest ■
Alexandra Fountain 22 D9
Bendigo Art Gallery 23 C8
Bendigo Woollen Mills 24 H6
Capital Theatre 25 C8
Central Deborah Gold Mine 26 A11
Chinese Joss House 27 H1
Conservatory Gardens 28 E8
Discovery Science &
  Technology Centre 29 E11
Dudley House 30 C8
Golden Dragon Museum 31 E7
Tram Depot Museum 32 G6
Vintage Tram 33 A11

Joins map 579

Joins map 579

Joins map 579

Joins map 579

BENDIGO

TO ECHUCA
TO INGLEWOOD
TO CASTLEMAINE
TO HEATHCOTE

0 10 20 30 40 50 km

A B C D E F G H

Joins map 565

Joins map 585

Joins map 565

Joins map 583

For more detail
on the ACT
see page 564

For more detail on the
Snowy Mountains &
The South Coast
see pages 566–7

ACT

NAMADGI
NP

Tooma
Welaregang
Greg Greg
Towong
The Sisters
BOGANDYERA
NR
CLARKES
HILL NR
Maragle
Mountain

Towong
Upper
Biggara
Khancoban
Khancoban
Pondage

KOSCIUSZKO
NATIONAL
PARK

Kiandra
Cabramurra
Mount
Black Jack

SNOWY

Adaminaby
Anglers
Reach
Old
Adaminaby
Lake
Eucumbene
Eucumbene

BICENTENNIAL
NATIONAL
TRAIL

SCABBY
RANGE
NR

YAOUK
NR

Shannons
Flat

Colinton
Jerangle

Bredbo

Kain
Gundillion

BURNT SCHOOL NR
STRIKE-A-LIGHT
NR
Anembo

Geehi
Guthega
Mount
Blue Cow
Perisher
Smiggin
Holes
Charlotte
Pass
Bullocks
Flat
SKI AREA
Island
Bend
Sawpit
Creek
Wilsons
Valley
Kalkite
East Jindabyne
Lake
Jindabyne

Buckenderra
Middlingbank

Bunyan

Cooma

Cooma
West

Numeralla
Countegany
Belowra

Berridale
Jindabyne
Penderlea
Thredbo
Tom Groggin
Moonbah

Rock
Flat
Coonerang

Kybeyan
Yowrie
Wandella

MYALLA NR
WULLWYE
NR
NGADANG
NR

Dalgety
Beloka
IRONMUNGY
NR
Paupong

Nimmitabel
Kydra

Numbla
Vale

Bungarby

Matong
Horseshoe
Gap
MERRIANGAAH
NATURE RESERVE

Ando
Bukalong

Bemboka
Numbugga

Bega
Brogo

SOUTH EAST
FOREST NP

SOUTH
EAST
FOREST

Morans
Crossing
Bimbaya
Kameruka
Candelo
Wolumla

Tombong
Bibbenluke

Cathcart

Bombala

Merimbula
Pambula
Pambula
Beach
Lochiel
Greigs Flat

GREAT
NEW

ALPINE NATIONAL PARK

KOSCIUSZKO
NATIONAL
PARK

Suggan
Buggan
Hanging
Rock
Amboyne
Crossing
Tubbut
Deddick
Delegate
River

Wulgulmerang
Seldom Seen
Roadhouse
Dellicknora
Delegate
Mila
Craigie

Rocky
Hall
Wyndham
Burragate
Nethercote

Eden
Boydtown
East
Boyd
Kiah

Karoonda
Roadhouse
Gelantipy
Glenmore

Haydens
Bog
Bendoc
Bonang

SOUTH

VICTORIA

BONDI
GULF
NR

Butchers Ridge
W Tree
Murrindal

SNOWY
RIVER

NATIONAL

PARK

ERRINUNDRA NATIONAL PARK
Goongerah

Ellery Saddle
Errinunda
Combienbar

Buldah

COOPRACAMBRA
NATIONAL
PARK
Wroxham
Wangarabell

SOUTH
EAST
FOREST NP
Towamba

Pericoe

MOUNT
IMLAY
NP

BEN
BOYD
NP

WALES

Wonboyn
Lake

Buchan
Chandlers
Creek
Weeragua
Noorinbee
North

Timbillica

NADGEE
NATURE
RESERVE

Wairewa
Bete Bolong
Jarrahmond
Waygara
Orbost
Brodribb
River
Tabbara
Club
Terrace
Tonghi
Creek
Noorinbee
Cann River

LIND
NP

Genoa
Gipsy
Point

Tostaree
PRINCES
Newmerella
Marlo
Murrungowar
RAINFOREST RESERVE
Bellbird
Creek
Cabbage Tree
Creek
ALFRED NP

GIPPSLAND

Mallacoota
Bastion
Point
Gabo
Island

Sandy
Point
Point
Ricardo
Cape Conran
CAPE CONRAN
COASTAL PARK
Bemm
River
Tamboon
Sydenham
Inlet

Point Hicks
Cape Everard
Rame
Head

CROAJINGOLONG NATIONAL PARK
Little Rame Head
Sandpatch Point
The Skerries
Wingan
Inlet
Mount
Victoria
Cape Howe

BASS STRAIT

TASMAN SEA

A B C D E F G H

Joins map 584

A B C D E F G H

Joins map 593

1 Malmsbury · Drummond · Kyneton · Denver · Spring Hill · Tylden · Little Hampton · Fern Hill · Carlsruhe · Cobaw · Newham · High Camp · Broadford · Tyaak · Reedy Creek · Strath Creek · Kerrisdale · SWITZERLAND FLORA RESERVE · Ghin Ghin · Homewood · Yea · Cathkin · Korella · Mount Prospect · Fawcett · Molesworth · Alexandra · LAKE EILDON · LAKE EILDON NP · Piries · Goughs Bay · Macs Cove · Delatite · Howqua · The Pinnacle

2 Trentham · Newbury · Barrys Reef · Blackwood · Bullengarook East · Woodend · Macedon · Mount Macedon · Barringo · New Gisborne · Bolinda · Lancefield · Willowmavin · Kilmore · Waterford Park · Wandong · Heathcote Junction · Upper Plenty · Clonbinane · Flowerdale · Hazeldene · Break O Day · Murrindindi · Mount Dorothy · Taggerty · Rubicon · Buxton · Acheron · Thornton · Snobs Creek · Eildon · LAKE EILDON NP · Mount Torbreck · Kevington · Ten Mile · Jamieson

3 Greendale · Korobeit · Myrniong · The Highlands · Colmadai · Darley · BACCHUS MARSH · BRISBANE RANGES NP · Rossyline Res · Gisborne · Couangalt · The Gap · Toolern Vale · Bulla · Diggers Rest · Jurunjung · SUNBURY · Mickleham · Kalkallo · Donnybrook · Woodstock · Craigieburn · Wollert · Mernda · Yan Yean · Nutfield · Arthurs Creek · St Andrews · WHITTLESEA · Humevale · Kinglake West · Kinglake Central · Kinglake · KINGLAKE NATIONAL PARK · Pheasant Creek · Castella · Toolangi · Glenburn · Dixons Creek · St Fillans · Narbethong · BICENTENNIAL NATIONAL TRAIL · Cambarville · SKI AREA · Marysville · Mount Arnold · Stockmans Reward · A1 Mine Settlement · Woods Point · Mount Matlock · Matlock · Jericho · Red Jacket

4 Glenmore · Rowsley · Parwan · Melton South · Exford · MELTON · Rockbank · Sydenham · Keilor · Melton Res · Deer Park · Mount Cottrell · Truganina · St Albans · Essendon · Preston · Fawkner · Brunswick · Footscray · MELBOURNE · Richmond · Doncaster · Templestowe · Eltham · Greensborough · Hurstbridge · Warrandyte · YARRA VALLEY WINERIES · Yering · Yarra Glen · Coldstream · Healesville · HEALESVILLE SANCTUARY · YARRA RANGES NATIONAL PARK · McMahons Creek · Upper Yarra Reservoir · Warburton · Violet Town · Aberfel · Matlock

5 Balliang · Balliang East · Little River · Lara · Werribee · Hoppers Crossing · Tarneit · Williamstown · Altona · Laverton · Point Cook · RAAF BASE WILLIAMS · Brighton · Sandringham · Elsternwick · Caulfield · Moorabbin · Oakleigh · Cheltenham · Mentone · Mordialloc · Glen Waverley · Box Hill · Ringwood · Croydon · Lilydale · Seville · Wandin North · Woori Yallock · Millgrove · DANDENONG RANGES NP · Boronia · Ferntree Gully · Belgrave · Monbulk · Macclesfield · Nangana · Gladysdale · Three Bridges · Powelltown · Noojee · Toorongo · Icy Creek · Fumina · Myrrhee · Tanjil Bren · SKI AREA · Mt Baw Baw · BAW BAW NATIONAL PARK

6 Corio · Lara · Point Wilson · HISTORIC TOWN · GEELONG · Belmont · Leopold · Clifton Springs · Portarlington · Indented Head · Bellarine · Drysdale · Marshall · Wallington · St Leonards · BELLARINE PENINSULA · Marcus Hill · Emerald · Cockatoo · Gembrook · BUNYIP STATE PARK · Upper Beaconsfield · Beaconsfield · Berwick · Officer · Pakenham · Maryknoll · Garfield North · Labertouche · Tonimbuk · Jindivick · Tarago · Rokeby · Drouin West · Neerim · Neerim South · Crossover · Neerim East · Hill End · Willow Grove · BULL BEEF CREEK FLORA & FAUNA RESERVE · MOONDARRA STATE PARK · Tanjil South · C466

7 Breamlea · Barwon Heads · Ocean Grove · Point Lonsdale · Portsea · Queenscliff · HISTORIC TOWN · Sorrento · Rosebud · Dromana · Rye · Safety Beach · MORNINGTON · Mount Martha · Moorooduc · Tyabb · Hastings · Baxter · Pearcedale · Somerville · Frankston · Seaford · Carrum · Carrum Downs · Cranbourne South · Clyde · CRANBOURNE · Cardinia · Tooradin · Koo-wee-rup · Modella · Ripplebrook · Longwarry · Drouin · Drouin South · Brandy Creek · Buln Buln · Buln Buln East · Warragul · Nilma · Darnum · Shady Creek · Westbury · Yarragon · Trafalgar · MOE · Newborough · Yallourn North

8 MORNINGTON PENINSULA NATIONAL PARK · Cape Schanck · Flinders · West Head · The Nobbies · Seal Rocks · PENGUIN PARADE · Phillip Island · Cowes · Ventnor · Rhyll · Newhaven · San Remo · Anderson · Kilcunda · Dalyston · FRENCH ISLAND NP · Tortoise Head · Tankerton · Corinella · Coronet Bay · Bass · Woolamai · Kongwak · Glen Forbes · Grantville · The Gurdies · Woodleigh · Bena · Kernot · Krowera · Jumbunna · Outtrim · Korumburra · Ruby · Arawata · Woorarra · Hallston · Mirboo North · Budgeree · Boolarra · Allambee · Darlimurla · Delburn · Churchill · MORWELL · Mirboo · Budgeree East · Rytor

9 BASS STRAIT · Wonthaggi · Coal Point · Cape Paterson · BUNURONG MARINE PARK · Archies Creek · Powlett River · Dudley · Inverloch · Pound Creek · Tarwin Lower · Venus Bay · Buffalo · Koonwarra · Tarwin · Meeniyan · Dumbalk · Leongatha · Leongatha South · Turtons Creek · Fish Creek · Hoddle · Foster · Toora · Welsh · Port Franklin · Barry Point · Welshpool · Binginwa · Woo · Mount Best · Hazel Park

10 CAPE LIPTRAP COASTAL PARK · Arch Rock · Waratah North · Waratah Bay · Walkerville · Sandy Point · Duck Point · Yanakie · CORNER INLET MARINE AND COASTAL PARK · Corner Inlet · Mount Roundback · Mount Norgate

11 Walkerville South · Bell Point · SHALLOW INLET MARINE AND COASTAL PARK · Grinder Point · Cape Liptrap · WILSONS PROMONTORY NATIONAL PARK · Shellback Island · Tongue Point · Norman Island · Mount Leonard · WILSONS PROMONTORY COASTAL WALKS · Mount Vereker

12 TASMAN SEA · Dannevig Island · Great Glennie Island · Kanowna Island · South West Point · Anser Island · Tidal River · Norman Bay · Oberon Bay · Oberon Point · Mount Oberon · South Peak · Mount Norgate · South East Point · Waterloo Bay · WILSONS PROMONTORY MARINE PARK

For more detail on Melbourne & Surrounds see pages 572–3

−38° 30′   −39° 00′

Spirit of Tasmania ferries Melbourne to Devonport

A B C D E F G H

0 10 20 30 40 50 km

I J K L M N O P

awmill
element *Mount No 3+
The
Pinnacle *Mount
Cobbler AUSTRALIAN
ALPS *Mount
Selwyn Hotham
Heights SKI AREA Cobungra Anglers Rest Lake
Omeo Benambra Mount
Bung Bung ALPINE Mount
Stradvote Suggan Buggan

Mirimbah The
Monument ALPINE *Mount Despair Mount
Freezeout Dinner Plain GREAT RANGE Cobungra Hinnomunjie C543 21 Mount
Tambo NATIONAL Mount
Wombargo Hanging
Rock 1

Mount
Stirling The
Horn *Mount Speculation Mount
Tabletop ALPINE 112 Mount George B500 Omeo Mount
Cook Mount
Simson PARK Black
Mountain Wulgulmerang

Mount
Buller SKI
AREA *Mount
Thom Mount Lowlos *Dargo
High Plains NATIONAL ALPINE Mount Parslow Omeo Mount
Shaw Bindi Mount
Deception Seldom
Seen
Roadhouse 2

NATIONAL The Bluff *Mount
Darling Mount
Darling Wonnangatta BICENTENNIAL
NATIONAL
TRAIL Mount
Mungobala Cassilis Mount Stawell The Sugarloaf *Mount Bindi Mount
Statham Karoonda
Roadhouse Gelantipy

Mount
McKinty Mount Short Mount
Lamit Tongio West Tongio Mount
Hopeless Glenmore Mount
Stewart W Tree SNOWY
RIVER

PARK (WONNANGATTA MOROKA UNIT) Crooked
River Swifts Creek Mount Nurjong Timbarra NATIONAL
PARK 3

Primrose
Gap Dargo Waterford Stirling Battle Point 121 Tambo
Crossing Buchan 4

Licola ALPINE NATIONAL PARK Castleburn Cobbannah The Basin Deptford B500 Buchan
South FLORA RESERVE
MOTTLE RANGE Sandy
Point

GIPPSLAND Culloden Glenaladale Woodglen Wuk Wuk Lindenow Calulu Wy Yung Clifton
Creek Wiseleigh Bruthen Nowa
Nowa Wairewa Bete Bolong 5

Valencia
Creek Stockdale Briagolong Coongulmerang Lindenow
South BAIRNSDALE Lucknow Nicholson Sarsfield Mossiface Tambo
Upper Colquhoun 95 Tostaree Waygara Jarrahmond
Newmerella A1 HWY

Glenmaggie Coongulla Bushy Park Munro PROVIDENCE PONDS
FLORA & FAUNA RESERVE Harrow Forge
Creek Eagle
Point Lake King Nungurner Kalimna
West Lake Tyers 6

Heyfield Maffra Stratford Perry
Bridge Clydebank Goon Nure Paynesville GIPPSLAND
LAKES Lakes
Entrance

SALE Longford The Heart Seacombe Lake Wellington GIPPSLAND
LAKES
COASTAL
PARK 7

TRARALGON Rosedale Dutson Paradise Beach
Golden Beach TASMAN 8

Stradbroke GIFFARD
FLORA
RESERVE Seaspray SEA

Yarram Woodside Woodside Beach 9

Port Albert NOORAMUNGA MARINE
AND COASTAL PARK N 10

BASS STRAIT 12

I J K L M N O P

Joins map 559

A B C D E F G H

1
2
3
4
5
6
7
8
9
10
11
12

Joins map 591
Joins map 593
Joins map 582

NEW SOUTH WALES

VICTORIA

Jimaringle, Burraboi, Wakool, Yallakool, Barham, Koondrook, McMillans, Cohuna, Leitchville, Gunbower, Patho, Torrumbarry, Bald Rock, Terrick Terrick, Sylvaterre, Mologa, Roslynmead, Mitiamo, Kotta, Prairie, Tennyson, Lockington, Milloo, Diggora, Dingee, Tandarra, Drummartin, Hunter, Kamarooka, Summerfield, Neilborough East, Raywood, Neilborough, Woodvale, Goornong, Eaglehawk, Huntly, Bagshot, Epsom, Fosterville, Barnadown, Myola, Muskery East, BENDIGO, Junortoun, Longlea, Axedale, Kangaroo Flat, Strathfieldsaye, Axe Creek, Knowsley, Mandurang, Eppalock, Lake Eppalock, Emu Creek, Sedgwick, Pilchers Bridge, Derrinal, Ravenswood South, Harcourt North, Sutton Grange, Myrtle Creek, Mia Mia, Barkers Creek, Harcourt, Faraday, Golden Point, Redesdale, Chewton, Elphinstone, Barfold, Metcalfe, Sidonia, Fryerstown, Taradale, Malmsbury, Drummond, Langley, Baynton, Lauriston, Kyneton, Spring Hill, Denver, Tylden, Carlsruhe, Little Hampton, Fern Hill, Trentham, Newbury, Woodend, Macedon, Mount Macedon

Dahwilly, Deniliquin, Caldwell, Bunnaloo, Allandale, Mathoura, Picnic Point, Womboota, Moira, Manorbar, Barnes, Barmah, Moama, ECHUCA, Echuca Village, Kanyapella, Yambuna, Bamawm Extension, Bamawm, Strathallan, Simmie, Kyvalley, Nanneella, Fairy Dell, Ballendella, Rochester, Timmering, Strathmerton, Corop, Stanhope, Rushworth, Whroo, Colbinabbin, Wanalta, Elmore, Colbinabbin West, Toolleen, Angustown, Goulburn Weir, Bailieston, Redcastle, Graytown, Costerfield, Heathcote, Argyle, Tooborac, Pyalong, Glenaroua, High Camp, Broadford, Lancefield, Willowmavin, Kilmore, Romsey, Bylands, Darraweit Guim, Wandong, Heathcote Junction, Monegeetta, Barringo

Conargo, Redbank, Forest Creek, Mayrung, Lara, Tadji, Logie Brae, Naringal, RIVERINA, Blighty, Maial, Finley, Berrigan, Tocumwal, Picola North, Picola, Barwo, BARMAH STATE PARK, Bearii, Mywee, Koonoomoo, Strathmerton, Cobram, Ulupna, Yarroweyah, Nathalia, Waala, Katunga, Numurkah, Mulwala, Yarrawonga, Burramine South, Boosey, Katamatite, Bathumi, Barooga, Telford, Kotupna, Kaarimba, Mundoona, Invergordon, Youanmite, Youarang, Tungamah, Wilby, Almonds, Undera North, Bunbartha, Marungi, Katandra West, Katandra, Yabba North, Yundool, Lake Rowan, Yeerip, Lancaster, Zerust, Congupna, Dookie, Boxwood, Devenish, Bungeet, Gillieston, Merrigum, Lemnos, Pine Lodge, Cosgrove, Thoona, Ardmona, SHEPPARTON, Major Plains, Nooramunga, Cooma, Byrneside, MOOROOPNA, Tatura, MIDLAND, Nalinga, Goorambat, Harston, Kialla West, Kialla, Tamleugh North, Gowangardie, Koonda, Chesney Vale, Tamick, Toolamba, Tamleugh, Earlston, Winton North, Glenrowan West, Arcadia, Miepoll, Murchison East, Moglonemby, Tarnook, Goomalibee, Winton, Murchison, Moorilim, Riggs Creek, Baddaginnie, Benalla, Glenrowan West, Boundary, Wahring, Violet Town, Balmattum, Boho, Warrenbayne, Yin Barun, Lurg, Nagambie, Creighton, Longwood, Euroa, Harrys Creek, Marraweeny, Lima, Mallum, Tatong, Tabilk, Locksley, Monea, Longwood East, Sheans Creek, Kelvin View, Boho South, Molyullah, Moorngag, Samaria, Avenel, Mangalore, Gooram, Strathbogie, Kithbrook, Boho Creek Junction, Lima East, Wrightley, Seymour, Whiteheads Creek, Dropmore, Ruffy, Terip Terip, MOUNT SAMARIA STATE PARK, Puckapunyal, Highlands, Caveat, Gobur, Merton, Dry Creek, Barjarg, Nilahcootie, Tallarook, Trawool, Kanumbra, Woodfield, Bonnie Doon, Maindample, Bridge Creek, Mansfield, Glenaroua, Kerrisdale, Ghin Ghin, Yarck, Fawcett, Piries, Broadford, Tyaak, Yea, Homewood, Molesworth, Koriella, Cathkin, LAKE EILDON NATIONAL PARK, Sunday Creek, Reedy Creek, Strath Creek, Flowerdale, Limestone, Alexandra, Delatite, Goughs Bay, Macs Cove, Waterford Park, Clonbinane, Hazeldene, Forderdale, Acheron, Thornton, Eildon, Howqua, Break O Day, Murrindindi, Snobs Creek, Rubicon, Taggerty, Jamieson

For more detail on the Goldfields see page 579

Joins map 581

For more detail on the
High Country see pages 586-7

Joins map 558
Joins map 603
Joins map 601
Joins map 590

Joins map 588

Joins map 601

Joins map 592

A B C D E F G H

1 2 3 4 5 6 7 8 9 10 11 12

MALLEE RD

Parilla

Pinnaroo

Panitya

Murrayville

Danyo

Cowangie

Tutye

HWY

Boinka

Underbool

Timberoo South

Bronzewing

Woornack

A79

SUNRAYSIA

B220

Gypsum

Tempy

Speed

Turriff West

Turriff

Gama

SCORPION SPRINGS CONSERVATION PARK

B57

BORDERTOWN

NGARKAT CONSERVATION PARK

133

Mount Shaugh

MOUNT SHAUGH CP

BIG DESERT WILDERNESS PARK

WYPERFELD

Mount Observatory

Mount Jenkins

BIG DESERT

NATIONAL

PARK

Mount Mattingley

Dering

Baring

Patchewollock

Willa

Yarto

Dattuck

Nypo

Hopetoun West

Burroin

Lascelles

HWY

B200

Hopetoun

Lake Albacutya

Yaapeet

Albacutya

Pella

Goyura

Hopevale

Rosebery

FLORA & FAUNA RESERVE

Rainbow

Kenmare

Beulah West

Galaquil

Beulah

Beulah East

Galaquil East

PINNAROO

Lowan Vale

Wirrega

Mount Edgerley

Telopea Downs

Werrap

Pullut

Brentwood

Dalmalee

Brim

Lah

Perenna

Baker

Netherby

Lorquon West

Lake Hindmarsh

Ellam

Willenabrina

Angip

Yellangip

Crymelon

Batchica

Bangera

DUKES

Cannawigara

Broughton

Yanac

Lorquon

Woorak West

Jeparit

Peppers Plains

Tarranyurk

Aubrey

Warracknabeal

Homecroft

Mundulla

Bordertown

Yanac South

Propodollah

Boyeo

Balrootan North

Woorak

GLENLEE FLORA RES.

Glenlee

Antwerp

Cannum

Mellis

HWY

WESTERN

Dinyarrak

Yearinga

Yarrock

Sandsmere

Bleak House

Diapur

Tarranginnie

Nhill

Salisbury

Kiata

Gerang Gerung

Arkona

Katyil

Wallup

Ailsa

Sheep Hills

Nullan

Wolseley

Serviceton

Lillimur

Kaniva

Miram

Yanipy

A8

Lawloit

Winiam

Winiam East

BORUNG

Dart Dart

Murra Warra

Blackheath

Kellalac

Custon

Leeor

Lillimur South

Miram South

Kinimakatka

C234

Minyip

B57

Western Flat

Bangham

LITTLE

DESERT

WIMMERA

NATIONAL

PARK

Wail

Dimboola

WEST WAIL FLORA RES

A8

Byrneville

Kalkee

B200

Kewell

Rupanyup North

Coromby

NARACOORTE

The Gap

Wallabrook

Frances

Minimay

Morea

Peronne

Goroke

Nurcoung

Grass Flat

Quantong

Vectis

Pimpinio

Jung

Murtoa

Rupanyup

RIDDOCH

A66

Binnum

Neuarpurr

Mortat

Booroopki

Dopewora

Gymbowen

Duffholme

NURCUONG FLORA RES

Mitre

Arapiles

Natimuk

Dahlen

Dooen

Longerenong

Drung Drung

BARRABOOL FLORA RES

Ashens

Rupanyup South

Lubeck

Tallageira

Bringalbert

Ozenkadnook

Kangawall

Karnak

MT ARAPILES-TOOAN STATE PARK

Mount Arapiles

Tooan

WIMMERA

Haven

HORSHAM

McKenzie Creek

Drung Drung South

Marma

Kybybolite

Benayeo

Patyah

Ullswater

HWY

99

Miga Lake

JILPANGER FLORA & FAUNA RESERVE

Clear Lake

Lower Norton

Wonwondah North

Wonwondah East

Wal Wal

Naracoorte

Apsley

Awonga

Charam

Noradjuha

Jallumba

Nurrabiel

Connangorach

Mockinya

Laharum

Golton Gorge

Dadswells Bridge

Glenorch

A8

BOOL LAGOON GAME RESERVE

NARACOORTE CAVES

Struan

Joanna

Langkoop

Edenhope

Wombelano

Toolondo

Brimpaen

Wartook

THE GRAMPIANS

Mount Difficult

Lake Lonsdale

Glenroy

A66

Wrattonbully

GLEN ROY CP

Poolaijelo

Powers Creek

Kadnook

Harrow

BLACK RANGE STATE PARK

C222

Mount Zero

Mount Stapylton

Mount Dryden

Comaum

Coonawarra

DERGHOLM STATE

Moree

Chetwynd

Pigeon Ponds

Balmoral

Glenisla

A200

HENTY

GRAMPIANS NATIONAL PARK

Halls Gap

WONDERLAND WALKS

Mount Victory

Victoria Gap

Mount Rosea

Moker

Pomo

Dorodong

PARK

Tarrayoukyan

Englefield

Rocklands Reservoir

Mount Thackeray

Triplet Peak

Mount William

SOUTH AUSTRALIA

VICTORIA

0 10 20 30 40 50 km

1
2
3
4
5
6
7
8
9
10
11
12

I J K L M N O P

VICTORIA

NEW SOUTH WALES

Mittyack
Wood Wood
Miralie
Yarraby
Daytrap EXCLUSION
Chinkapook
Ryanby
Chillingollah
Nowie North
Nyah
Nyah West
Vinifera
Beverford
Speewa
Beverford
Woorinen North
Tyntynder Central
Tyntynder South
Woorinen
Swan Hill
Murray Downs

Mallan
Moulamein
Cunninyeuk
Dhuragoon
Inverness
Niemur
Noorong
Jimaringle
Werai
Burraboi

Pier Millan
Nandaly
Nyarrin
Ninda
Sea Lake
Boigbeat
Banyan
Woomelang
Watchupga
Curyo
Kinnabulla
Reedy Dam
Birchip
Narraport
Morton Plains
Watchem
Massey
Corack East
Corack
Teddywaddy
Wooroonook
Jeffcott North
Jeffcott
Litchfield
Lake Buloke
Carron
Lawler
Laen North
Donald
Dooboobetic
Laen
Rich Avon
Swanwater West
Burrereo
Banyena
Burrum
Traynors Lagoon
Avon Plains
Marnoo
Lallat
Wallaloo
Wallaloo East
Callawadda
Kanya
Morri Morri
Campbells Bridge
Navarre
Greens Creek
Tulkara
Joel Joel
Landsborough
Shays Flat
Warrenmang
Bridge Inn
Stawell
Joel South
Great Western
Glenlofty
Dunneworthy
Norval
Armstrong
Warra Yadin
Ben Nevis
Eversley
Rhymney Reef
Ararat

Waitchie
Gowanford
Ultima
Lalbert Road
Meatian
Culgoa
Tittybong
Warne
Kalpienung
Nullawil
Whirily
Dumosa
Ninyeunook
Wycheproof
Fairview
Glenloth
Narrewillock
Lake Marmal
Glenalbyn
Teddywaddy
Barakee
Charlton
Woosang
Buckrabanyule
Wychitella
Fernihurst
Korong Vale
Fiery Flat
Nine Mile
Wedderburn
Wedderburn Junction
Yeungroon
Coonooer Bridge
Gooroc
Berrimal
Slaty Creek
Cope Cope
Kurraca West
Gowar East
Kurraca
Fentons Creek
St Arnaud
Logan
Kooreh
Carapooee
Burkes Flat
Wehla
Inglewood
Kingower
Rheola
Arnold West
Arnold
Beazleys Bridge
Rostron
Emu
Cochranes Creek
McIntyre
Llanelly
Stuart Mill
Winjallok
Moliagul
Murphys Creek
Tarnagulla
Newbridge
Leichardt
Barkly
Moyreisk
Bealiba
Painswick
Laanecoorie
Marong
Redbank
Archdale
Goldsborough
Dunolly
Bromley
Shelbourne
Moonambel
Natte Yallock
Dunluce
Betley
Eddington
Eastville
Redbank
Rathscar
Timor West
Timor
Havelock
Baringhup
Landsborough
Moores Flat
Bowenvale
Alma
Maryborough
Carisbrook
Moolort
Percydale
Avoca
Homebush
Adelaide Lead
Golden Point
Craigie
Glenpatrick
Amphitheatre
Bung Bong
Daisy Hill
Majorca
Strathlea
Newstead
Crowlands
Elmhurst
Green Hill Creek
Lamplough
Amherst
Talbot
Clydesdale
Warrak
Mount Lonarch
Caralulup
Dunach
Glengower
Campbelltown
Yandoit
Glenluce

Long Plains
Tyrrell Downs
Lake Tyrrell
Lake Timboram
Lake Lalbert
Boundary
The Marsh
Tresco West
Kunat
Tresco
Lake Tutchewop
Beauchamp
Lake Charm
Sandhill Lake
Lake Bael Bael
Normanville
Fairley
Budgerum
Cannie
Quambatook
Towaninny
Oakvale
Gredgwin
Leaghur State Park
Appin
Appin South
Leaghur
Canary Island
Mimmindie
Yando
Canary Island South
Gladfield
Catumnal
Boort
Durham Ox
Mysia
Jarklin
Borung
Calivil
Pompapiel
Bears Lagoon
Fruit Fly Exclusion Zone
Serpentine
Tandarra
Salisbury West
Kurting
Bridgewater On Loddon
Sebastian
Raywood
Derby
Campbells Forest
Woodvale
Huntly
Epsom
Goornong
Bagshot
Eaglehawk
Maiden Gully
Marong
BENDIGO
Kangaroo Flat
Strathfieldsaye
Lockwood
Lockwood South
Mandurang
Axe Creek
Emu Creek
Sedgwick
Eppalock
Ravenswood
Nuggetty
Walmer
Ravenswood South
Pilchers Bridge
Lake Eppalock
Derrinal
Bet Bet
Betley
Welshmans Reef
Gowar
Harcourt
Barkers Creek
Sutton Grange
Myrtle Creek
Heathcote
Argyle
Perkins Reef
Maldon
Harcourt North
Mia Mia
Joyces Creek
Castlemaine
Chewton
Faraday
Redesdale
Guildford
Yapeen
Fryerstown
Metcalfe
Sidonia
Vaughan
Elphinstone
Barfold
Sandon
Tarradale
Baynton
Langley
Malmsbury

Moulamein
Noorong
Ballbank
Gonn Crossing
Murrabit
Myall
Capels Crossing
Koondrook
Barham
Westby
Koroop
Kerang East
Kerang South
Tragowel
McMillans
Langville
Mincha
Bald Rock
Macorna
Gunbower
Leitchville
Womboota
Caldwell
Yallakool
Wakool
Bunnaloo
Kow Swamp
Patho
Torrumbarry
Wharparilla North
Wharparilla
Kotta
Bamawm Extension
Bamawm
Lockington
Ballendella
Diggora
Milloo
Tennyson
Dingee
Prairie
Drummartin
Hunter
Kamarooka
Summerfield
Neilborough East
Neilborough
Greater Bendigo NP
Fosterville
Barnadown
Myola
Muskerry East
Toolleen
Knowsley
Axedale
Longlea
Junortoun
Strathfieldsaye

Kerang
Cohuna
Pyramid Hill
Sylaterre
Yarrawalla South
Mologa
Mitiamo
Terrick Terrick
Terrick Terrick NP
Roslynmead

Donald
Maryborough
Maldon

For more detail on the Goldfields see page 579

B400
B260
B220
B79
C234
C239
A79
B240
B400
A300
A790
B280
B75
B180
M79
A8
B180

SUNRAYSIA HWY
CALDER HWY
LODDON VALLEY HWY
MURRAY VALLEY HWY
WIMMERA HWY
MIDLAND HWY
PYRENEES HWY
GREAT DIVIDING RANGE
ST ARNAUD RANGE NP
KOOYOORA STATE PARK
RICHMOND PLAINS
PYRENEES WINERIES

HISTORIC TOWN
HISTORIC TOWN

Joins map 589
Joins map 584

Joins map 590

Joins map 601

0   10   20   30   40   50 km

I   J   K   L   M   N   O   P

Stawell

Ararat

Beaufort

BALLARAT

Maryborough

Castlemaine

Maldon

Kyneton

Daylesford

Woodend

Macedon

Gisborne

SUNBURY

MELTON

Riddells
Creek

Lancefield

Romsey

Mount Helen
Buninyong

BACCHUS
MARSH

Ballan

Diggers
Rest

Creswick

Camperdown

Terang

Cobden

Colac

Elliminyt

Winchelsea

GEELONG

Clifton
Springs

Leopold

Drysdale

Portarlington

St
Leonards

Ocean
Grove

Queenscliff

Point Lonsdale

Sorrento

Rye

Barwon
Heads

Torquay

Anglesea

Lorne

Apollo Bay

Princetown

BASS   STRAIT

TASMAN SEA

N

For more detail on the
Goldfields see page 579

For more detail on Melbourne
& Surrounds see pages 572–3

For more detail on the
Great Ocean Road
see page 580

1

2

3

4

5

6

7

8

9

10

11

12

MAPS

SOUTH AUSTRALIA

INTER-CITY ROUTES		DISTANCE
Adelaide–Darwin via Stuart Hwy	A1 A87 B7 1	3026 km
Adelaide–Perth via Eyre & Great Eastern hwys	A1 1 94	2700 km
Adelaide–Sydney via Sturt & Hume hwys	A20 20 31	1415 km
Adelaide–Melbourne via Dukes & Western hwys	M1 A8 M8	729 km
Adelaide–Melbourne via Princes Hwy	M1 B1 A1 M1	911 km

Accommodation ■
Adelaide Central YHA 1 C8
Adelaide Paringa Motel 2 D8
Austral Hotel 3 F8
BreakFree Directors Studios 4 B9
Chifley on South Terrace 5 E10
Country Comfort Adelaide 6 E10
Hilton Adelaide 7 D9
InterContinental Adelaide 8 D7
Majestic Old Lion Apartments 9 F4
Quality Hotel Old Adelaide 10 D3
Rockford Adelaide 11 C8
The Sebel Playford Adelaide 12 D7
Stamford Plaza Adelaide Hotel 13 D7
Note: Only a sample range of
accommodation is listed; inclusion is
not necessarily a recommendation.

General Information ■
Adelaide Police Station 14 E9
Adelaide Railway Station 15 D7
Central Bus Station 16 C9
Country & Interstate Rail Terminal 17 A10
Explorer Tram Depot 18 D7
General Post Office 19 D8
Glenelg Tram Terminus 20 C7
Motoring Organisation (RAA) 21 E8
Popeye Cruises 22 D7
Qantas Travel Centre 23 D7
SA Visitor & Travel Centre 24 D7
Visitor Information 25 D8

Places of Interest ■
Adelaide Aquatic Centre 26 C3
Adelaide Central Market 27 D9
Adelaide Convention Centre 28 D7
Adelaide Entertainment Centre 29 A4
Adelaide Festival Centre 30 D7
Adelaide Oval 31 D6
Adelaide Town Hall 32 D8
Adelaide Zoo 33 F6
Art Gallery of SA 34 E7
Ayers House 35 F7
Botanic Gardens of Adelaide 36 F7
Chinatown 37 D9
Edmund Wright House 38 D8
Elder Hall 39 E7
Elder Park 40 D7
Government House 41 D7
Historic Adelaide Gaol 42 B6
JamFactory 43 C7
Light's Vision 44 C5
Lion Arts Centre 45 C7
Migration Museum 46 E7
Museum of Classical Archaeology 47 E7
National Wine Centre of Australia 48 G7
Parliament House 49 D7
South Australian Museum 50 E7
State Library of South Australia 51 E7
Tandanya 52 F8
University of Adelaide 53 E7

0   5   10   15 km

Joins map 597

TO PORT WAKEFIELD
TO BURRA
TO NURIOOTPA
TO NURIOOTPA

A1
A32
A20
STURT HWY
GAWLER RD
BAROSSA
VALLEY WAY
B19

Kangaroo Flat
Rosedale
Two Wells
Lewiston
North Para River
Rowland Flat
GAWLER
Sandy Creek
Lyndoch
B31

Middle Beach
Port Gawler
Angle Vale
SANDY CREEK CP
Pewsey Vale Peak

PORT WAKEFIELD RD
OLD PORT WAKEFIELD RD
ANGLE VALE RD
Virginia
SMITHFIELD
A20
Para River
Williamstown
WARREN CP
B34

PORT GAWLER CONSERVATION PARK
Bolivar
NORTH RD
Direk
Edinburgh Aerodrome
ELIZABETH
BLACK TOP RD
PARA WIRRA RECREATION PARK
Mount Gawler
South Para Dam
HALE CP
CRICKS MILL RD

St Kilda
Point Grey
Pelican Point
TORRENS ISLAND CP
Torrens Island
WATERLOO CORNER RD
SALISBURY
Little Para Reservoir
Little Para Dam
South Para Reservoir
WARREN RESERVOIR
WARREN RD
CROMER CP
RANGE
B34

N

OUTER HARBOR
NORTH HAVEN
OSBORNE
TAPEROO
LEFEVRE PENINSULA
LARGS NORTH
A16
A13
SALISBURY HWY
PARAFIELD
Parafield Airport
GREEN FIELDS
A20
PARA HILLS
A18
TEA TREE GULLY
COBBLER CREEK RP
Kersbrook
Mount Gould
Forreston
Birdwood
GOULD RANGE
B31
B34

SEMAPHORE
Point Malcolm
PORT ADELAIDE
DRY CREEK
NORTHFIELD
GRAND JUNCTION RD
ANSTEY HILL RP
Houghton
Millbrook Reservoir
Gumeracha
Mount Torrens
MOUNT LOFTY RANGE
B10

GULF
ALBERTON
KILBURN
DUDLEY PARK
NORTH RD
EAST RD
GORGE RD
O-BAHN
HOPE VALLEY RESERVOIR
A11
BLACK HILL CP
Kangaroo Creek Reservoir
Kangaroo Creek Dam
MONTACUTE CP
CUDLEE CREEK CP
Mount Torrens
B31
B34

ALBERT PARK
GRANGE
BOWDEN
NORTH ADELAIDE
A7
ROSTREVOR
MAGILL
PORTRUSH RD
MORIALTA CP
KENNETH STIRLING CP
Lobethal
FOREST RANGE

For more detail on Central Adelaide see page 595

ST VINCENT
Adelaide Airport
A6
ADELAIDE
A17
KESWICK
HORSNELL GULLY CP
GREENHILL RD
Uraidla
Summertown
Charleston
CHARLESTON CP

TAPLEYS HILL RD
GOODWOOD
UNLEY PARK
WATERFALL GULLY
Woodside
B34

ANZAC HWY
CROSS RD
GLENELG
Holdfast Bay
ASCOT PARK
MITCHAM
A13
BELAIR
BROWNHILL CREEK RP
CLELAND CP
MOUNT GEORGE CP
Stirling
Mount Lofty
Aldgate
Oakbank
Balhannah
Brukunga
SOUTH RD

HOVE
MARION
GLENALTA
BELAIR NP
EDEN HILLS
BLACKWOOD
Upper Sturt
Heathfield
Bridgewater
Hahndorf
Summit Reservoir
Nairne

BRIGHTON
SEACLIFF
A15
MARINO CP
Marino Rocks Lighthouse
EXP RD
MARK OLIPHANT CP
STURT GORGE RP
MAIN RD
Mylor
TOTNESS RP
Mount Barker
PRINCES HWY
M1

HALLETT COVE CONSERVATION PARK
REYNELLA
Happy Valley Reservoir
Littlehampton
MOUNT BARKER
EASTERN RD
OLD PRINCES HWY
FWY
TO MURRAY BRIDGE

LONSDALE
A13
MORPHETT VALE
M2
Clarendon
SCOTT CREEK CONSERVATION PARK
Mount Bold Reservoir
Echunga
Wistow
CHRISTIES BEACH
PORT NOARLUNGA
A15
NOARLUNGA CENTRE
MAIN RD
Mount Bold Dam
Kangarilla
B34
SOUTH RD

ONKAPARINGA RIVER NATIONAL PARK
Blewitt Springs
DASHWOOD GULLY RD
Meadows
Macclesfield
B37
LONG VALLEY RD

MOANA SANDS CP
SEAFORD
OLD NOARLUNGA
Ochre Point
Moana
Maslin Beach
TATACHILLA RD
McLaren Flat
KANGARILLA
McLaren Vale
Mount Wilson
BROOKMAN RD
BATTUNGA RD
Woodchester
Hartley
Bletchley
B23
A13
B33
B34

TO VICTOR HARBOR
Joins map 598

0   5   10   15   20 km

A   B   C   D   E   F   G   H

LEFEVRE PENINSULA
Taperoo
Largs North
Peterhead
Semaphore
Point Malcolm
Port Adelaide
Hendon
Albert Park
Grange

TO TWO WELLS   TO GAWLER
Tea Tree Gully
Millbrook Reservoir
Forreston
Dry Creek
Pooraka
Northfield
Houghton
Gumeracha
B10
B30
THE TOY FACTORY
ANSTEY HILL REC PARK
B31
Kangaroo Creek Reservoir
Cheltenham
Kilburn
Hope Valley Res
Woodville
Croydon
Ovingham
North Adelaide
Rostrevor
BLACK HILL CP
MORIALTA CP
MONTACUTE
Lobethal
Charleston
Bowden

ADELAIDE HILLS, CLELAND WILDLIFE PARK, INDIAN PACIFIC TRAIN, THE GHAN, JUNCTION MARKETS, R.M. WILLIAMS OUTBACK HERITAGE MUSEUM
ADELAIDE
Keswick
Goodwood
Unley Park
Waterfall Gully
Summertown
PENFOLDS MAGILL ESTATE
HORSNELL GULLY CP
Uraidla
KENNETH STIRLING
Oakbank
B34
Woodside
Adelaide Airport
Mitcham
Torrens Park
Belair
CLELAND CP
Stirling
PETALUMA'S BRIDGEWATER MILL WINERY
Balhannah
Bridgewater
Holdfast Bay
Glenelg
Edwardstown
Marion
Clovelly Park
BELAIR NP
Mount Lofty
Aldgate
EASTERN
Hahndorf
Nairne

Warradale
Hove
Brighton
Seacliff
Eden Hills
Glenalta
Heathfield
Mylor
Littlehampton
MARINO CP
Blackwood
HISTORIC TOWN
M1
FWY
Marino Rocks Lighthouse
STURT GORGE RECREATION PARK
MARK OLIPHANT CONSERVATION PARK
Mount Barker
HALLETT COVE CONSERVATION PARK
Happy Valley Reservoir
SCOTT CREEK CP
B33
Echunga
Wistow
Reynella
Onkaparinga
Mount Bold
Lonsdale
M2
Morphett Vale
Clarendon
Mount Bold Reservoir
Christie Downs
Christies Beach
Noarlunga Centre
River
Kangarilla
B33
Port Noarlunga
ONKAPARINGA RIVER NP
Meadows
Macclesfield
ONKAPARINGA RIVER RECREATION PARK
Blewitt Springs
B33
Seaford
McLaren Flat
Old Noarlunga
MOANA SANDS CP
McLaren Vale
Mount Wilson
SOLDIERS MEMORIAL GARDENS
Ochre Point
Maslin Beach
McLaren Vale Wineries
Strathalbyn
Port Willunga
A15
VICTOR HILL
KYEEMA CONSERVATION PARK
Aldinga
Willunga
Ashbourne
Aldinga Beach
MOUNT MAGNIFICENT CP
FINNISS CP
B37
ALDINGA SCRUB CONSERVATION PARK
Silver Sands
COX SCRUB CP
Sandergrove
Aldinga Bay
B23
Mount Compass
Yundi
THE STEAM RANGER TOURIST RAILWAY
Sellicks Beach
LOOKOUT
Nangkita
Myponga Beach
Mount Compass
LOOKOUT
Tooperang
Finniss
Haycock Point
Myponga Reservoir
Myponga
SCOTT CP
Gilberts
CURRENCY CREEK WINERY
Carrickalinga
B23
MYPONGA CP
YULTE CP
Currency Creek
CANOE TREE
Normanville
SPRING MOUNT
HINDMARSH FALLS
MIDDLETON WINERY
Clayton
Yankalilla Bay
Yankalilla
GLACIER ROCK
MOUNT BILLY CP
CROWS NEST LOOKOUT
MALLEEBAA WOOLSHED
Goolwa
Rapid Head
Second Valley
FLEURIEU
Hindmarsh Valley
Goolwa Aerodrome
Hindmarsh Island
Rapid Bay
URIMBIRRA WILDLIFE PARK, GREENHILLS ADVENTURE PARK
Middleton
COCKLE TRAIN
Mount Rapid
SOUTH
Port Elliot
Mundoo Island
Delamere
RANGE
Victor Harbor
Pullen Island
SIR RICHARD PENINSULA
LOOKOUT
HEYSEN TRAIL, CAPE JERVIS LIGHTHOUSE
B37
PENINSULA
Granite Island
FAIRY PENGUINS
HORSE-DRAWN TRAM, S.A. WHALE CENTRE
Cape Jervis Lands End
B23
Waitpinga
Wright Island
Rosetta Head (The Bluff)
Encounter Bay
COORONG NATIONAL PARK
Cape Jervis
TALISKER CP
King Head
West Island
Fishery Beach
DEEP CREEK CONSERVATION PARK
Parsons Beach
NEWLAND HEAD CONSERVATION PARK
Porpoise Head
Tunkalilla Beach
Tunk Head
Waitpinga Beach
Newland Head

GULF
ST VINCENT

BACKSTAIRS PASSAGE
Ferry to Kangaroo Island
Cuttlefish Bay
Snapper Point
Cape Coutts
LASHMAR CP
Antechamber Bay
Red House Bay
Cape St Albans
THE PAGES CONSERVATION PARK
North Page
South Page
The Pages
SOUTHERN
OCEAN
KANGAROO ISLAND
Cape Saint Alban Lighthouse
Moncrieff Bay
Cape Willoughby Lighthouse
LESUEUR CONSERVATION PARK
Cape Willoughby
Windmill Bay
SIMPSON CR
MACDONNELL (DUDLEY) PENINSULA
Cape Hart

Joins map 597
Joins map 597
TO MURRAY BRIDGE
Joins map 601
Joins map 599

For more detail on Adelaide Suburbs see page 596

0 10 20 30 40 km

Joins map 605

A B C D E F G H

Joins map 604
Joins map 605

TO MARREE
D83
TO INNAMINCKA
D96

Minagoona Lake
Leigh Creek
OCHRE CLIFFS
Avondale
Mount Lyndhurst
STRZELECKI TRACK
Mount Lyndhurst
Lyndhurst
21
Mount Playfair
Mount Parry
Myrtle Springs Gorge
Myrtle Springs
Mount Hutton
COALFIELD
B83
Mount Telford
Jacob Gap
Burr Well
WEEDNA PLAINS
Mount Rose
Ilyteena Gap
Yerelina
Mount Harris
Mount Crocker
Mount Neil
Pepegoona Gorge
Mount Adams
North Mulga

Leigh Creek
Leigh Creek Aerodrome
Copley
COPLEY
Leigh Creek
The Cutaway
Mountain of Light
Mount Aroona
RED RANGE
Depot Springs
Camel Gap
Silver Gap
Mount Serle
Frome Gap
Angepena
Mount Rowe
Owieandana
The Plateau
Changeweather
Streak Gorge
Cleft Peak
Bunyip Chasm
GAMMON RANGES
YANKANINNA RANGE
VULKATHUNHA-GAMMON RANGES NATIONAL PARK
Compass Pass
Yankaninna
NORTH
Needles
The Pinnacles
Idninha
Arkaroola
ARKAROOLA WILDERNESS SANCTUARY
Mount Oliphant
Mount McDonnell
Mount Ward
Mount Painter
East Painter Gorge
American Gap
Mount Warren Hastings
BARARRANA GORGE
Yudnamutana Gorge
Paralana Outstation
ARKAROOLA RD
Mount Jacob
Tilite Gorge
Wooltana
Nepouie Peak
Mount McKinlay
Balcanoona Gorge
Italowie Gap
WEETOOTLA GORGE
Balcanoona
The Bluff
PARK HEADQUARTERS
VULKATHUNHA-GAMMON RANGES NATIONAL PARK

Red Gorge
Mudlapena Gap
Manners Well
Mount Jeffery
Mount Coffin
Mount Morris
Mount Wallace
Evans Outstation
Mulka Gap
Nepabunna
Oocaboolina Outstation
COPLEY
135
ITALOWIE GORGE
Italowie Gap
McKinlay Ck
Wertaloona
Mount Dormer

Puttapa Gap
Mount Bayley (Puttapa)
Mount Deception
Mount Greig
Warraweena
Mount Hack
Mount Goddard
FLINDERS RANGES
BALD HILL RANGE
CAMPBELL RANGES
NANTAWARRINNA
Mount Uro
Waukawoodna
Mount Corner
BIG MORO GORGE
Arrowie Gorge
Mount Robert
LAKE FROME RECREATION RESERVE

Trebilcock Gap
Beltana
Puttapa
Beltana Roadhouse
RED RA
Moorillah
Mount Stuart
Mount Gill
Mount Tilley
Warraween Gap
Main Gap
Waukawoodna Gap
Nantawarrinna
Pinda Springs
Mount Roebuck
STIRRUP IRON RA
Deep Bore Gap
Mulga View
WEARING GORGE
Wearing
Teatree Outstation
MOUNT CHAMBERS GORGE
Lake Frome

Nilpena
Hannigan Gap
Mooloolao
Patawarta Gap
Point Well
Narrina
Mount Brooke
Mount John
Mount Chambers

GLASS GORGE
Breakneck Gorge
Oratunga
Mount Samuel Proper
Mount Falkland
Mount Mary
Mount Elkington
Angorigina
Nildottie Gap
EREGUNDA VALLEY
Mount Lucius
Mount Lyall
Mount Frome
Wyamba Outstation
Frome Downs

Motpena
Parachilna
HEYSEN TRAIL PARACHILNA GORGE
Mount Falkland
Blinman
Alpana
ANGORICHINA TOURIST VILLAGE
GREAT WALL OF CHINA
Mount Emily
SECOND PLAIN
GRINDSTONE RA
Wirrealpa
Wirrealpa
Balcoracana

Commodore
Kanyaka Peak
ABC RA
SOUTH
Mount Barloo
Mount Barbara
Mount Hayward
BRACHINA GORGE
AROONA VALLEY (RUINS)
Walkandi Peak
Gum Creek
Bulls Gap
FLINDERS RANGES NATIONAL PARK
The Bunkers
LOVES MINE RA
Wyamba Outstation

Lake Station
Brachina Gap
Mount Rupert
BUNYEROO GORGE
Edeowie
FLINDERS RANGES
Oraparinna
Mount Bell
Mount Sunderland
BUNKERS CONSERVATION RESERVE
Mount Caernarvon
Mount Mantell
Martins Well
Erudina

Mount Burns
Edeowie Gorge
Mount Abrupt
St Mary Peak
Bunyeroo Valley
Upalinna Outstation
Willow Springs
STOKES HILL LOOKOUT
WESTERN PLAIN
MORALANA PLAIN
Mount Boorong
Wilpena
Upalinna
Buffalo

Moralana
Merna Mora
Mount Palmerston
Greg Peak
Wilpena
POUND GAP
WILPENA POUND
Mount Kanyanna
Oliphant Bagge
Binye Peak
SCARED CANYON
Curnamona

Hells Gate
Mernmerna
WANGARRA LOOKOUT
Moonarie
RAWNSLEY PARK STATION
555
ARKAROO ROCK
Prelinna
Mount Aleck
Woolyana
MORALANA SCENIC DRIVE
Ulowdna
Mount Neville
Mount Josephine

THREE SISTERS RANGE
Three Sisters
Worro Downs
WONOKA HISTORIC SITE (RUINS)
Arkaroola
Little
Memmerna
ELDER RANGE
FLINDERS
CHACE RA
Mount Desire
White Gap
Red Gap
Warcowie
Shaggy Ridge
BLACK RA
Willipa
Mount Davidson

HODKINA (RUINS)
Wild Dog Glen
Yappala
Pine Flat
Fairleigh
JARVIS HILL LOOKOUT
Hawker
Glen Lyle
Glen Oak
SOUTH
WILLOW PLAINS
Black Gap
Mount Craig
Mount Ernest
Holowilena
The Bluff
Bibliando
Killawarra Outstation

Mount Elm
Gum Vale
Yourumbulla Peak
The Oaks
YOURAMBULLA CAVES
B80
B83
Niggly Gap
Worumba
Mount Sims
Holowilena South
Mount Plantagenet
Glenorchy

TO PORT AUGUSTA
TO PETERBOROUGH
Joins map 605

N

Joins map 604

Joins map 611

A B C D E F G H

GREAT AUSTRALIAN BIGHT

SOUTHERN OCEAN

PORT AUGUSTA

Streaky Bay

PORT LINCOLN

Whyalla

Tumby Bay

Coffin Bay

Cummins

Wallaroo

Moonta

Yorketown

Kingscote

KANGAROO ISLAND

EYRE PENINSULA

YORKE PENINSULA

SPENCER GULF

INVESTIGATOR STRAIT

GAWLER RANGES NATIONAL PARK

LAKE GAIRDNER NATIONAL PARK

COFFIN BAY NATIONAL PARK

LINCOLN NP

FLINDERS CHASE NATIONAL PARK

INNES NP

SIR JOSEPH BANKS GROUP CONSERVATION PARK

NEPTUNE ISLANDS CONSERVATION PARK

For more detail on the Peninsulas & Kangaroo Island see page 599

N

Joins map 606

Joins map 611

Joins map 602

WARNING: While visitors are permitted in the township of Woomera, entry to the Woomera Prohibited Area is by permit only, except in the immediate corridors of the Stuart Highway and the road from Coober Pedy to William Creek. Camping is not permitted in the area.

Joins map 639

Joins map 609

Joins map 604

WARNING: Visitors planning to enter the Desert Parks are required to contact National Parks and Wildlife SA. A Desert Parks Pass is necessary.

WARNING: While visitors are permitted in the township of Woomera, entry to the Woomera Prohibited Area is by permit only, except in the immediate corridors of the Stuart Highway and the road from Coober Pedy to William Creek. Camping is not permitted in the area.

0   20   40   60   80   100 km

I   J   K   L   M   N   O   P

SIMPSON DESERT NATIONAL PARK

EYRE DEV. RD

Mount Collins

1

Diamantina River

BIRDSVILLE 114

Durrie

DEVELOPMENTAL

Betoota

Mount Leonard

Mount Hal

51

RD 51

Cuddapan

Lake Cuddapan

STURT STONY DESERT

Mount Lewis

Roseberth

Shallow Lake

Moonda Lake

Planet Downs Outstation

Birdsville

CORDILLO

Mount Oakes

Haddon Corner

2

QUEENSLAND

SOUTH AUSTRALIA

The West Lake

Alton Downs

Pandie Pandie

Lake Coninnie

Lake Short

STURT STONY DESERT

KACHUMBA PLAIN

Curalle Tin Shed

26° 00'

SIMPSON DESERT CONSERVATION PARK

D83

The Sisters

Nulla Outstation

Gilpeppee Outstation

3

SIMPSON DESERT

Diamantina

Lake Etamunbanie

Mount Howie

Lake Yamma Yamma (MacKillop)

Cooper

SIMPSON DESERT RECREATION RESERVE

New Alton Downs

Clifton Hills Outstation

Lake Uloowaranie

RAINBOW PLAIN

Mount Gow

My Mountain

PLANET

4

STURT STONY DESERT

TRACK (OUTSIDE)

Mount Mckinlay

STRZELECKI DESERT

RD

Cordillo Downs

Arrabury

The Gibbers

STRZELECKI DESERT

Lake Marroopootanie

Clifton Hills

BIRDSVILLE

Lake Apanburra

Lake Goyder (Coolangirie)

Lake Toontoowaranie

RD

Lake Pure

Lake Pure

Joes Outstation

5

27° 00'

516

133

STURT STONY DESERT

Mount Gason

Coori Coori Tillie Lakes

COONGIE LAKES NATIONAL PARK

Coongie Lake

Mitkacaldratillie Lakes

INNAMINCKA RECREATION RESERVE

Old Karmona Cottage

Mona Downs Outstation

Lake Koodnanie

MONTEPIRIE

St Anne's Cottage

WAY

6

D83

Mount Sullivan

Lake Howitt

CORDILLO

Nappa Merrie

SOUTH AUSTRALIA

QUEENSLAND

Cooper

TRACK

WARNINGS: In outback Australia, long distances separate some towns. Travellers should familiarise themselves with prevailing conditions before departure and take care to ensure their vehicle is roadworthy. Adequate supplies of petrol, water and food should be carried at all times.

In central Australia, rainfall can make some roads impassable, even with a 4WD vehicle. Full information on road conditions should be obtained from local authorities before departure.

If visitors intend diverting off public roads within Aboriginal Land areas, a permit is required from the relevant Aboriginal authority.

Fly Lake

Gidgealpa

TRACK

Mount McLeod

Innamincka

44

ADVENTURE

NAPPA

MERRIE

7

Mount Hogarth

Cooper

Innamincka

Mungeranie Gap

Mungerannie Roadhouse

STURT STONY DESERT

DILLONS HWY

47

SANTOS 166

28° 00'

8

TRACK

Lake Warrakalanna

TRACK

60

TRACK

50

Orientos

Tennappera

Theare Hill

Mulka

Lake Hope (Pando)

Cooper

INNAMINCKA RECREATION RESERVE

RD

Epsilon

9

D96

STRZELECKI

Santos

STRZELECKI DESERT

Etadunna

BYPASS

FLOOD

TRACK

Lake Killamperpunna

Therua Hill

Mount Wells

Lake Hope

OLD

Merty Merty

Naryilco

Pigeon Lake

10

204

Mount Kauto

Lake Gregory

STRZELECKI RECREATION RESERVE

120

Omicron

Old Naryilco

34

Dulkaninna

Mount Flint

STRZELECKI

Corner Store

Bollards Lagoon

Fortville House

Toona House

Warri House

11

D83

Mount Jervois

Mount Way

Lake Blanche

127

Cameron Corner

Fortville Bore

Fort Grey

Binerah Downs

Olive Downs

Binerah Well

STURT NP

layton

Coongarra

NEW SOUTH WALES

Whitecatch House

Lake Stewart

Waka

133

Mount King

Mount Playford

The Bluff

Murnpeowie

D96

Mount Hopeless

Lake Callabonna

STRZELECKI DESERT

Stone Hut

Hewart Downs

Gum Vale

Gum Vale Gorge

12

Tilcha

Tilcha

Mount Sturt

Mount Sturt

40

I   J   K   L   M   N   O   P

A   B   C   D   Joins map 638   E   F   G   H

Joins map 623

Joins map 621

KATITI ABORIGINAL LAND TRUST

NGAANYATJARRA CENTRAL RESERVE

MURRAY RANGE

Warlpapuka

Pirntirri Mulari

MORGAN RANGE

Mount Fanny

Arnold Creek

Mount Aloysius

Mount Maria

Anumarrapirti

TOMKINSON RA

Mount Daisy Bates

Mount Gosse

Surveyor Generals Corner

GUNBARREL

Mount Hinckley

Kalka

Pipalyatjara

Mount Davies

Mount West

Boundary Peak

Mount Samuel

Mount Cockburn

Mount Le Hunte

Mount Jenkins

Mount Mann

MANN

HWY

Aparawatatja

Mount Edwin

Mount Berry

Kanypi

RANGES

Mount Whinham

GUNBARREL

213

PETERMANN

ABORIGINAL

LAND TRUST

NORTHERN TERRITORY
SOUTH AUSTRALIA

Mount Robert

Alpara

Britten Jones (Ulaiyanya)

HWY

63

Mulgai Park

Mogat Fraser

Mount Woodward

Amata

Mount Davenport

THE

MUSGRAVE

Mount Woodroffe (Ngarutjaranya)

128

Mount Hardy

The Deering Hills

Mount Cooparinna

Mount Caroline (Ulkiyanya)

ANANGU

Mount Kintore

Mount Harriet

PITJANTJATJARA

Pirrilyungka

BUSINESS

ABORIGINAL

RD

Mount Moulden

Mount Agnes

Mount Harcus

Mount Tietkens

Mount Crombie (Ulpara)

YANKUNYTJATJARA

LANDS

NGAANYATJARRA

CENTRAL

RESERVE

Mount Copley

Mount Wooltarlinna

Mount Hoare

Mount Holder

Mount Sir Thomas

BIRKSGATE RA

Mount Lindsay

408

N

GREAT

LIZZIE LIGHTFOOT RANGE

COMET RANGE

ANANGU

PITJANTJATJARA

YANKUNYTJATJARA

Mount Poondinna

VICTORIA

LANDS

DESERT

GREAT

VICTORIA

DESERT

SOUTH AUSTRALIA
WESTERN AUSTRALIA

WARNINGS: In outback Australia, long distances separate some towns. Travellers should familiarise themselves with prevailing conditions before departure and take care to ensure their vehicle is roadworthy. Adequate supplies of petrol, water and food should be carried at all times.

In central Australia, rainfall can make some roads impassable, even with a 4WD vehicle. Full information on road conditions should be obtained from local authorities before departure.

If visitors intend diverting off public roads within Aboriginal Land areas, a permit is required from the relevant Aboriginal authority.

UNNAMED

CONSERVATION

PARK

ANNE

BEADELL

HWY

271

ANNE

BEADELL

HWY

MARALINGA

Wanna Lakes

Serpentine Lakes

GREAT

VICTORIA

TJARUTJA

LANDS

DESERT

Joins map 621

GREAT VICTORIA DESERT

Forrest Lakes

NATURE RESERVE

Nurrari Lakes

Wyola Lake

Halinor Lake

LAKE

RD

DEY-DEY

Lake Dey-Dey

Lake Maurice (Carle-Thulka)

BUSINESS

ABORIGINAL

HWY

A   B   C   D   Joins map 610   E   F   G   H

Joins map 608

Joins map 621

0 20 40 60 80 100 km

Joins map 609

I J K L M N O P

WARNING: While visitors are permitted in the township of Woomera, entry to the Woomera Prohibited Area is by permit only, except in the immediate corridors of the Stuart Highway and the road from Coober Pedy to William Creek. Camping is not permitted in the area. Note the overlap with Aboriginal Land where you need additional seperate permits.

Wirrida

Lake Wirrida

Ingomar

Phar Lap
Outstation

Mount
Sandy

Wilkinson
Lakes

STUART HWY

A87

Minikata

Mc Douall Peak

Comet

Mount
Soward

MARALINGA
DEFENCE
LAND
(PROHIBITED
AREA)

MARALINGA
TJARUTJA
LANDS

Lake Anthony

Jumbuck

Commonwealth
Hill

Gina
Outstation

367

1

2

Indooroopilly
Outstation

Half Moon
Lake

WOOMERA
PROHIBITED
AREA

Goode
Outstation

Bulgunnia.

98

Irria
Outstation

Muckanippie
Outstation

Bradman
Outstation

Carne
Outstation

Ooraminna Outstation

Lake Bring

Mulgathing

Mount
Christie

Durkin
Outstation

Johns
Outstation

Whymlet

Lake
Labyrinth

Ambrosia
Outstation

Gibraltar
Outstation

Ealbara
Outstation

Mentor
Outstation

Mount
Eba

3

Ooldea

Bates

TRANS

AUSTRALIAN

Wynbring

Warrior
Outstation

Carnding Road
Outstation

Tarcoola

Lake
Moolkra

Big Tank
Outstation

North
Well

Lake
Harris

4

NULLARBOR
CREATION
RESERVE

Lyons
Camp

Malbooma
Outstation

RAILWAY

Wilgena

80

Kingoonya

Lake Ifould

Mount
Finke

Yerda

5

Lake Tallacootra

143

YELLABINNA RECREATION RESERVE

LAKE GAIRDNER
NATIONAL PARK

Kokatha

YALATA
ABORIGINAL
RESERVE

85

Lake
Everard

6

Yalata

Yalata
Roadhouse

Glyde Hill
Outstation

Lake
Everard

WAHGUNYAH
CONSERVATION
PARK

55

EYRE

YUMBARRA
CR

YUMBARRA CONSERVATION PARK

Lake
Acraman

7

GREAT
AUSTRALIAN
BIGHT
MARINE NP

Nundroo
Roadhouse

39

202

Bookabie

Cundilippy

YUMBARRA CR

PUREBA
CR

PUREBA CONSERVATION PARK

Mount John

Kondoolka

96

Nundroo

Pintumba

Coorabie

91

35

Koonibba

Northedge

Mount
Wallaby

Mount
Pollard

Yarna

Wookata

FOWLERS
BAY CR

Fowlers Bay

Penong

A1

73

Marbra

Corrong

Watchbrae

NUNNYAH
CR

Winlippee Peak

Mount Hiltaba

Mount
St Mungo

8

Cape Adieu
Cheetima Beach

Cape
Nuyts

Point Fowler

CHADINGA
CR

CHADINGA CR

Lake MacDonnell

Black Peak

NULLARBOR
PLAIN DRIVE

EYRE

Mudamuckla

92

Oak Valley

Mount
Pyramid

NUYTS REEF CP

SURFING
Cactus Beach
Point Sinclair

Thevenard

Ceduna

Denial
Bay

40

Chinbingina

KOOLGERA CR

Waroona
Peak

POINT BELL CR

Point
Bell

Point Peter

Kara-Pine

Nunjikompita

Mount Centre

Purdie Islands

St Peter Island

Goat Island

Cape D'Estrees

Smoky Bay

Carawa

222

Wirrulla

A1

Wirrambie

GAWLER
RANGES
NP

9

Lacy Island

Evans
Island

Eyre Island

Smoky
Bay

30

Flagstaff

109

Petina

Yantanabie

Gawler
View

Mount
Granite

Scrubby
Peak

NUYTS ARCHIPELAGO CP

Franklin
Islands

ACRAMAN
CREEK CP

Haslam

27

Cungena

GAWLER
RANGES
CR

Kaibree

Scrubby
Peak

74

ISLES OF
ST. FRANCIS CP

St Francis Island

Point Dillon

St Mary Bay
Point Brown

Point
Collinson

Gascoigne Bay

Streaky
Bay

B100

Chilpanunda

Capietha

Poochera

Mount
Granite

10

Corvisart Bay

Cape Bauer

Eba Island

Chandada

62

Coolgrana

The Bald Hills

Mount Jane

28

FLINDERS HWY

33

Wyoming

Minnipa

16

Streaky Bay

Point Westall

Maryvale

Mount
Cooper

Tootla

Yandra

Conglima

Moonlight
Flat

Carina

Yaninee

Yanerbie Beach

SCEALE BAY CR

Sceale Bay

Calca

CALPATANNA
WATERHOLE
CP

Mount Hall

Colley

Yandra

Lake
Yaninee

11

Slade Point

Searcy Bay

Mount Msery

KULLIPARU
CP

Mount Damper

Mount
Damper

OCEAN

Point Labatt

Baird
Bay

Cape Radstock

Port
Kenny

Venus Bay

124

VENUS BAY CP

COCATA
CP

Anxious Bay

Talia

B100

Talia Beach

Kooringal

Mount
Wedge

Mount
Wedge

12

LAKE
NEWLAND
CP

Lake Newland

FLINDERS
HWY

86

Colton

B91

WALDEGRAVE
ISLANDS
CP

Mount Fairy

Bramfield

I J K L M N O P

Joins map 602

Joins map 604

MAPS

WESTERN AUSTRALIA

INTER-CITY ROUTES		DISTANCE
Perth–Adelaide via Great Eastern & Eyre hwys	94 1 A1	2700 km
Perth–Darwin via Great Northern Hwy	1 95	4032 km

0   0.25   0.5   0.75   1 km

A   B   C   D   E   F   G   H

Accommodation ■
Duxton Hotel Perth 1 E6
Holiday Inn City Centre Perth 2 C5
Hyatt Regency Perth 3 G7
Ibis Perth 4 C5
Miss Maud Swedish Hotel 5 D5
Novotel Perth Langley 6 E7
Parmelia Hilton Perth 7 B5
Royal Hotel 8 C5
Rydges Perth 9 C5
Seasons of Perth 10 D5
Sheraton Perth Hotel 11 F7
Note: Only a sample range
of accommodation is listed;
inclusion is not necessarily
a recommendation.

General Information ■
Barrack Street Jetty 12 C7
Esplanade Railway Station 13 C6
General Post Office 14 D5
Motoring Organisation (RAC) 15 B4
Perth Railway Station 16 D5
Qantas Travel Centre 17 C5
Transperth City Busport 18 C6
Wellington St Bus Station 19 C4
West Australian
Tourist Centre 20 D5
William Street Underground
Platforms 21 D5

Places of Interest ■
Art Gallery of WA 22 D5
Barracks Archway 23 B5
Botanic Gardens 24 A7
Central Government
Building 25 D6
Deanery 26 D6
Forrest Place 27 D5
Gov Stirling Statue 28 D6
Government House 29 D6
Hay Street Mall 30 D5
Kings Park 31 A6
London Court 32 D6
Murray Street Mall 33 D5
Old Court House 34 D6
Old Mill 35 A8
Parliament House 36 A5
Perth Concert Hall 37 E6
Perth Cultural Centre 38 D4
Perth Institute of
Contemporary Arts 39 D4
Perth Mint 40 F6
Perth Town Hall 41 D6
Perth Zoo 42 C11
Scitech Discovery Centre 43 A3
Swan Bells 44 D7
WA Museum 45 D4
WACA Oval 46 H7

Joins map 614

TO FREMANTLE   Joins map 614   TO FREMANTLE

Joins map 615

Joins map 618

Joins map 617

Joins map 624

Joins map 622

Joins map 620

WITTENOOM: Due to the presence of blue asbestos in and around Wittenoom, townsite status has officially been removed. Electricity, water and postal services have ceased and there are no longer any licensed accommodation providers in the area. Any found to be offering accommodation are doing so without health permits.

For more detail on the Pilbara see pages 626–7

Joins map 619

Joins map 622

Joins map 619

TOOLONGA NR

KALBARRI NP

WANDANA NR

INDIAN

OCEAN

GERALDTON

Dongara-Denison
Port Denison

Northampton

Mullewa

Mount Magnet

Yalgoo

Morawa

Three Springs

Carnamah

Coorow

Mingenew

Eneabba

Leeman

Green Head

Jurien Bay

Cervantes

NAMBUNG NP
THE PINNACLES

Cataby Roadhouse

Lancelin

Two Rocks

Yanchep

Guilderton

Gingin

Bindoon

Moora

Dandaragan

Badgingarra

Coomberdale

Miling

Bindi Bindi

New Norcia

Calingiri

Wongan Hills

Dalwallinu

Wubin

Pithara

Watheroo

Ballidu

Cadoux

Koorda

Bencubbin

Mukinbudin

Beacon

Wialki

Bonnie Rock

Merredin

Nungarin

Bruce Rock

Bodallin

Marvel Loch

Westonia

Southern Cross

Yellowdine

GREAT EASTERN HWY

BOORABBIN NATIONAL PARK

KALGOORLIE-BOULDER

Coolgardie

Kambalda

Ora Banda

Broad Arrow

Menzies

Leonora

Leinster

Agnew

Sandstone

NORTHERN HWY

Cue

Mount Magnet

Yalgoo

PERTH

Fremantle

ROCKINGHAM

MANDURAH

Singleton

Pinjarra

Waroona

Harvey

Australind

BUNBURY

Collie

Capel

Donnybrook

BUSSELTON

Dunsborough

Cape Naturaliste

Margaret River

Augusta

Cape Leeuwin

Manjimup

Pemberton

Northcliffe

Walpole

Denmark

ALBANY

Little Grove

Mount Barker

Kojonup

Katanning

Cranbrook

Wagin

Narrogin

Boddington

York

Northam

Mundaring

Beverley

Brookton

Pingelly

Cuballing

Wickepin

Kulin

Wave Rock

Hyden

Lake King

Newdegate

Lake Grace

SOUTH COAST HWY

Ravensthorpe

Hopetoun

Bremer Bay

FITZGERALD RIVER NP

STIRLING RANGE NP

Kalgan

Cheyne Beach

SOUTHERN OCEAN

For more detail on South Western
Western Australia see page 618

LEEUWIN-NATURALISTE NP

WALPOLE-NORNALUP NATIONAL PARK

VALLEY OF THE GIANTS,
TREE TOP WALK

0   50   100   150   200 km

Joins map 623
Joins map 608
Joins map 610

WARNINGS: In outback Australia, long distances separate some towns. Travellers should familiarise themselves with prevailing conditions before departure and take care to ensure their vehicle is roadworthy. Adequate supplies of petrol, water and food should be carried at all times.

In central Australia, rainfall can make some roads impassable, even with a 4WD vehicle. Full information on road conditions should be obtained from local authorities before departure.

If visitors intend diverting off public roads within Aboriginal Land areas, a permit is required from the relevant Aboriginal authority.

Joins map 624

WITTENOOM: Due to the presence of blue asbestos in and around Wittenoom, townsite status has officially been removed. Electricity, water and postal services have ceased and there are no longer any licensed accommodation providers in the area. Any found to be offering accommodation are doing so without health permits.

For more detail on the Pilbara see pages 626–7

Joins map 619

Joins map 620

0   50   100   150   200 km

I   J   K   L   M   N   O   P

GREAT   SANDY   DESERT

KEARNEY

Mount
Fothringham

Thomas
Peak   Lake Dennis

Mount
Ford   Lake White   YININGARRA
ABORIGINAL
LAND TRUST

ROUTE   —21° 00'

WAPET   ROBERTS   Lake
RANGE   Wills   1

Farewell
Lakes

610   STANSMORE   Warri   Lake Hazlett   Mount   LAKE
RANGE   Peak   Russell

Percival   MACKAY
Lakes
Bremner +
Peak   **GREAT**   Mount   2
Tobin   **SANDY**   Bilbarrd   Lindsay
Lake   Outstation
632   STOCK   **DESERT**   NGAANYATJARRA   —22° 00'

RD   Mount
Shoesmith   CENTRAL
CANNING   AUSTRALIA

WAPET   NGAANYATJARRA   LAND

Lake   RD   MARUWA   3
Auld   ROUTE   Lake   Mount
Gary   Mackay   Morris
Lake   Junction   TRUST
Dora   KIWIRRKURRA   —23° 00'

Lake   STOCK   487   Mount
Blanche   TERRY   Kiwirrkurra   Webb   Mount
Lake   RANGE   NGAANYATJARRA   Lindsay   4
Mount Eva   George   KIWIRRKURRA   RD   Inini   Kintore   Tinki
Lake
Winifred   Mount   Mount
Greene   Mount
TALAWANA   NGAANYATJARRA   Main   Yuwalki

CANNING   HWY   TROPIC   OF   CAPRICORN   Mount   HAASTS BLUFF
TRACK   ABORIGINAL   5
RUNTON   BARON   SIR   LAND TRUST
RANGES   Windy   RA   FREDERICK   —24° 00'
Corner   NGAANYATJARRA   RANGE
Lake   KURLKUTA   Lake Anec
Disappointment

Skeleton
Pass   Dabbalya
Gorge

Joins map 622

WARNINGS: In outback Australia, long distances separate some towns. Travellers should familiarise themselves with prevailing conditions before departure and take care to ensure their vehicle is roadworthy. Adequate supplies of petrol, water and food should be carried at all times.

In central Australia, rainfall can make some roads impassable, even with a 4WD vehicle. Full information on road conditions should be obtained from local authorities before departure.

If visitors intend diverting off public roads within Aboriginal Land areas, a permit is required from the relevant Aboriginal authority.

Beware of crocodiles in rivers, estuaries and coastal areas.

Beware of marine stingers in coastal areas (October to April). Swim within enclosures where possible.

INDIAN   OCEAN

For more detail on the Pilbara see pages 626–7

Joins map 634
Joins map 636
Joins map 638

TIMOR SEA

INDIAN OCEAN

JOSEPH BONAPARTE GULF

KIMBERLEY

GREAT SANDY DESERT

WESTERN AUSTRALIA

NORTHERN TERRITORY

For more detail on the Kimberley
see pages 628–9

INDIAN   OCEAN

N

PORT HEDLAND
South Hedland

WITTENOOM: Due to the presence of blue asbestos in and around Wittenoom, townsite status has officially been removed. Electricity, water and postal services have ceased and there are no longer any licensed accommodation providers in the area. Any found to be offering accommodation are doing so without health permits.

Joins map 619

Joins map 619

0 20 40 60 80 100 km

TIMOR SEA

JOSEPH BONAPARTE GULF

KIMBERLEY

KALUMBURU

Kalumburu

BARTON PLAIN

ANJO PENINSULA

Cape Londonderry
Cape Talbot
Glycosmis Bay
Koolama Bay
Lesueur Island
Cape Rulhieres
Cape Bernier
Cape Hay
Old Mission
Cape Keats
Port Keats (Wadeye)
Peppimenarti
Merrepen
Un-Marr
Moyle
Yeder
MOYLE PLAIN
Emu Point

DALY RIVER / PORT KEATS ABORIGINAL LAND TRUST

MACADAM RANGE

Wudapuli
Kubuyirr
Kuy
Tree Point
Injin Beach
Ditchi
Nangu
Treachery
Ngarinthi
Fossil Head
New Moon Inlet
Swamp Point
Kultchill

TABLE PLAIN

QUEENS CHANNEL
Quoin Island
Keyling Inlet
Fitzmaurice

BRADSHAW FIELD TRAINING AREA

Bradshaw
The Tombs

OOMBULGURRI

Cape St Lambert
Reveley Island
Buckle Head
Thurburn Bluff
Sharp Peak
Cape Dussejour
Lacrosse Island
Rocky Island
Pelican Island
Turtle Point
Cape Dornett
Knobi Peak

CAMBRIDGE GULF

NINGBING RANGE

DRYSDALE RIVER NATIONAL PARK

ASHTON RANGE

COUCHMAN RANGE

FORREST RIVER

NOOGOORA BURR QUARANTINE AREA

Wyndham
PRISON TREE
PARRYS LAGOONS NR
PALM SPRINGS NR
Buttons Gap
Cave Spring Gap

KEEP RIVER NATIONAL PARK EXTENSION (PROPOSED)

KEEP RIVER NP

Kununurra

Bucket Springs (Doojum)
Policemans Hole
Bubble Bubble

VICTORIA HWY

Bulla
East Baines Gorge

TO TIMBER CREEK

ZEBRA ROCK GALLERY
CARR BOYD RANGES
PINKERTON RANGE

GREGORY NATIONAL PARK

Home Valley
EMMA GORGE
El Questro
VOYAGES EL QUESTRO WILDERNESS PARK
Palmer Pass
Grimwood Gap
Salmond Gorge

Durack River
Ellenbrae
Pentecost Downs (Karunjie)
Scotty Salmond Gorge
Gibb River (Ngallagunda)
GIBB RIVER RD

MINERS POOL
Drysdale River

DOON DOON

Carlton Gorge
Argyle Historic Homestead
ORD RIVER DAM, LAKE ARGYLE TOURIST VILLAGE
Lake Argyle
The Twins

Rosewood
Argyle Downs
Waterloo

NAGURUNGURU ABORIGINAL LAND TRUST

Amanbidji

GLEN HILL
ARGYLE DIAMOND MINE

Bow River
Gordons Gorge
Patterson Gorge

Spring Creek
Bamboo Springs
Mistake Creek

MALNGIN 2 ABORIGINAL LAND TRUST

Limbunya

Warmun-Turkey Creek Roadhouse
Warmun
Texas Downs
Mabel Downs

Nelson Springs

MALNGIN ABORIGINAL LAND TRUST

DAGURAGU ABORIGINAL LAND TRUST

VIOLET VALLEY

CONSERVATION RESERVE

BUNGLE BUNGLES
PURNULULU NATIONAL PARK

DUNCAN RD

NORTHERN TERRITORY
WESTERN AUSTRALIA

TABLELANDS
Yulumbu (Tableland)
Crocodile Gorge
SIR JOHN GORGE
NARRIE RANGE
Lansdowne
Bedford Downs
Mount Wells

Kirkimbie
BUNTINE HWY
Nicholson
Inverway (Mamadi)
Riveren
Bunda

HOOKER CREEK ABORIGINAL LAND TRUST

KIMBERLEY

LEOPOLD RANGES

KING LEOPOLD RANGES

O'Donnell River Gorge
One Palm Tree Gorge
Neville Gorge
Halls Creek
CHINA WALL
OLD HALLS CREEK
Sophie Downs
Alice Downs
Crocodile Gorge
Marella Downs
Flora Valley
Old Flora Valley

Birrindudu

BIRRINDUDU RANGE

Moola Bulla
Koongie Park
Rockhole
DUNCAN RD
Saw Tooth Gorge
Lamboo
Eagle Hawk Crossing Gorge
Old Lamboo
Ruby Plains

DENISON PLAINS

YINGUALYALYA ABORIGINAL LAND TRUST

CENTRAL DESERT ABORIGINAL LAND TRUST

MUELLER RANGE
NORTHERN HWY
TANAMI RD
GREAT NORTHERN HWY

GORDON DOWNS (RINGERS SOAK)
TANAMI DESERT

GREAT NORTHERN HWY

WARNINGS: In outback Australia, long distances separate some towns. Travellers should familiarise themselves with prevailing conditions before departure and take care to ensure their vehicle is roadworthy. Adequate supplies of petrol, water and food should be carried at all times.

In central Australia, rainfall can make some roads impassable, even with a 4WD vehicle. Full information on road conditions should be obtained from local authorities before departure.

If visitors intend diverting off public roads within Aboriginal Land areas, a permit is required from the relevant Aboriginal authority.

Beware of crocodiles in rivers, estuaries and coastal areas.

Beware of marine stingers in coastal areas (October to April). Swim within enclosures where possible.

Joins map 634
Joins map 636
Joins map 625

MAPS

NORTHERN TERRITORY

INTER-CITY ROUTES	DISTANCE
Darwin–Adelaide via Stuart Hwy	3026 km
Darwin–Perth via Great Northern Hwy	4032 km
Darwin–Brisbane via Warrego Hwy	3406 km

0   10   20   30   40 km

Joins map 634

Joins map 634

I   J   K   L   M   N   O   P

1
2
3
4
5
6
7
8
9
10
11
12

WARNINGS: In outback Australia, long distances separate some towns. Travellers should familiarise themselves with prevailing conditions before departure and take care to ensure their vehicle is roadworthy. Adequate supplies of petrol, water and food should be carried at all times.

In central Australia, rainfall can make some roads impassable, even with a 4WD vehicle. Full information on road conditions should be obtained from local authorities before departure.

If visitors intend diverting off public roads within Aboriginal Land areas, a permit is required from the relevant Aboriginal authority.

Beware of crocodiles in rivers, estuaries and coastal areas.

Beware of marine stingers in coastal areas (October to April). Swim within enclosures where possible.

MARY RIVER
NATIONAL PARK
(PROPOSED)

Point
Stuart

Finke
Bay

SWIM
CREEK
PLAIN

CARMOR
PLAIN

KAKADU
NATIONAL
PARK

KAKADU
NATIONAL
PARK

PART OF
JABILUKA
SPECIAL
MINERAL
LEASE

Oenpelli
Oenpelli
Aerodrome
Cannon
Hill
Kungarrewarl

UBIRR
ART SITE
Ubirr
Woelk (Red
Lily Lagoon)
Border Store
Cahills Crossing

EAST ALLIGATOR
RANGER STATION

Mudginberri
Mudginberri

EXCISION
FOR
MINING
PURPOSES

JABILUKA
ABORIGINAL
LAND
TRUST

Hunters
Camp
Jabiru
GAGUDJU
CROCODILE
HOLIDAY INN

Mount
Brockman

ARNHEM

LAND

KOONGARRA

ABORIGINAL

LAND

TRUST

FOUR MILE HOLE

TWO MILE HOLE

Aurora
Kakadu
Resort

GUNGARRE
MONSOON
RAINFOREST
WALK

MAMUKALA
WETLANDS WALK
Chirracarwoo
Lagoon

Mumakala

BOWALI VISITOR CENTRE
& PARK HEADQUARTERS

HWY

HWY

Nourlangie
(Anlarrh)

ILAGADJARR
WETLANDS WALK

Baroalba

BABOALBA SPRINGS
(GUBARA)

Muirella
Park

NANGALUWAR
ART SITE

NOURLANGIE
ROCK
Koongarra

KAKADU

NATIONAL

PARK

Gurdurunguranjdju
(Alligator Billabong)

YELLOW WATER
(NGURRUNGURRUDJBA)
BILLABONG

COOINDA

Giinda

WARRADJAN
ABORIGINAL
CULTURAL CENTRE

MARDUGAL
BILLABONG WALK
Jim Jim Billabong

Mirrai
Lookout

Paradise Farm

Urgdurr
(Spring
Peak)

Patonga Airstrip
Patonga

Golondjorr
(Deaf Adder
Outstation)

Deaf
Adder
Gorge

MOUNT
BUNDEY
TRAINING
AREA

Mount
Partridge

KAKADU
ABORIGINAL
LAND
TRUST

JIM JIM FALLS
PLUNGE POOL
WALK

BARRKMALAM
(JIM JIM FALLS)

GUNGKURDUL
(TWIN FALLS)

MARY RIVER
NATIONAL PARK
(PROPOSED)

Coirwong Gorge

GUNGURAL
RECREATION
AREA

Maguk
(Barramundie Gorge)

MAGUK PLUNGE
POOL WALK

Goodparla

HWY

GUNLOM WATERFALL
CREEK FALLS

GUNLOM
LOOKOUT WALK

Koolpin
Gorge

BUKBUKLUK
LOOKOUT

YIRMIKMIK
WALKING
TRACKS

Mary River
Station

Mount
Callanan

Mount
Daniels

Gimbat

GIMBAT
RECREATION
AREA

Mary River
Roadhouse

KAKADU
NATIONAL
PARK

GUNLOM
ABORIGINAL
LAND
TRUST

ARNHEM

LAND

ABORIGINAL

LAND

TRUST

Pine Creek

TO KATHERINE

NITMILUK
(KATHERINE GORGE)
NATIONAL
PARK

MANYALLALUK
ABORIGINAL
LAND
TRUST

0   50   100   150 km

I   J   K   L   M   N   O   P

ARAFURA   SEA

N

WARNINGS: In outback Australia, long distances separate some towns. Travellers should familiarise themselves with prevailing conditions before departure and take care to ensure their vehicle is roadworthy. Adequate supplies of petrol, water and food should be carried at all times.

In central Australia, rainfall can make some roads impassable, even with a 4WD vehicle. Full information on road conditions should be obtained from local authorities before departure.

If visitors intend diverting off public roads within Aboriginal Land areas, a permit is required from the relevant Aboriginal authority.

Beware of crocodiles in rivers, estuaries and coastal areas.

Beware of marine stingers in coastal areas (October to April). Swim within enclosures where possible.

Cape Wessel
Mort Point
Jensen Bay
Sphinx Head
Red Point
Marchinbar Island
Hopeful Bay
Guluwuru Island
Raragala Island
Wigram Island
Truant Island
Cotton Island
Cape Wilberforce
Bremer Island
Nhulunbuy
Yirrkala
Gunyangara
Cape Arnhem
GOVE PENINSULA
Mount Harold
Port Bradshaw

North Crocodile Reef
Stevens Island
Burgunngura Island
Drysdale Island
North West Crocodile Island
Graham Island
Jirrgari Island
Alger Island
Inglis Island
Refuge Bay
Elcho Island
Warnga Point
Point Napier
Buckingham Bay
Mooroongga Island
Yabooma Island
Cape Stewart
Galiwinku
Howard Island
Garniyak
Burrum
Rorruwuy
Arnhem Bay

ARNHEM LAND
Maningrida
Maningrida Aerodrome
Ji-Marda
Milingimbi
Castlereagh Bay
Marlwon
Gurrgurr
Nangak
Nanak
Ankabadbirri
Ji-Balbal
Gatji
Ngangalala
Ramingining
Gilirri
Old Arafura
Gapuwiyak
Mirrngadja Village
Dhamiyaka
Gurrumuru
Wanyanmera Point
Garrthalala
Birany Birany
Point Alexander
Dudly Island
Cape Grey

Yikarrakkal
Manmoyi
Gamarrawan
Malnjangarnak
ABORIGINAL
LAND TRUST
Malgawa
Dhunganda
Donydji
Koolatong
Barrapunta
Mount Parsons
Mount Fawcett
Baniyala
Grindall Point
Cape Shield
Isle Woodah
Blue Mud Bay
Wardlaea Bay
Point Arrowsmith

CENTRAL
RANGE
PARSONS
RANGE
BATH
RANGE
Mount Ramsay
Mount Rankine
Bennet Bay
Bickerton Island (Amakalyuwakba)
Port Langdon
Mount Jean
Mount Weir
Mount Marumba
Bulman
Mount Catt
Marraya
Milyakburra
Umbakumba
Mamalimandja Point
Alyangula
Ilyungmadja Point
Mountain Valley
Mainoru
Mount Leane
Phelp
Angurugu
Miwul
GROOTE EYLANDT
Yedikba
Ungwariba Point
Mainoru
YARRAWIRRIE PLAINS
Wumajbarr
Rantyirrity Point
Tasman Point
Yanbakwa
Marangula Bay
ARNHEM LAND ABORIGINAL LAND TRUST

Mount Throsby
Sowden Peak
Numbulwar
South Point
Cape Beatrice
GULF
Mount Karman
Mount Furner
Boomerang Lagoon
Wanmatri
Mumpumampu
Nyinpinti Point
Edward Island
Warrakunta Point

URAPUNGA ABORIGINAL LAND TRUST
Moroak
Mount Chapman
Nummerloori
Mount Moore
Limmen Bight
Maria Island
OF

HWY
Roper Bar Store
Ngukurr
Nulawan
Roper Valley
Larrpayanji
Mount Fisher
Mount Bokall
Mount Roper
MARRA ABORIGINAL LAND TRUST
CARPENTARIA

MANGARRAYI ABORIGINAL LAND TRUST
ALAWA 1 ABORIGINAL LAND TRUST
LIMMEN NATIONAL PARK (PROPOSED)
Mount Young
Yarnarndu Inlet
Minyerri
Mount Colton
ALAWA ABORIGINAL LAND TRUST
YYINTYI RANGE
BARRANYI (NORTH ISLAND) NATIONAL PARK

Hodgson River Station
Nathan River
Rawali Inlet
West Island
North Island
Investigator Bay
Vanderlin Island
Nutwood Downs
Lorella Spring
Bing Bong
Centre Island
Stokes Bay
Webinger Point
WURRALIBI ABORIGINAL LAND TRUST
Minamia
Limmen Gate
NARWINBI ABORIGINAL LAND TRUST
Manangoora
LIMMEN NATIONAL PARK (PROPOSED)
Wandangula
Mara
Warby Outstation
Bauhinia Downs
Jangurrie
Billengarrah
Borroloola
Tawallah
CARANBIRINI CONSERVATION RESERVE
Seven Emu
CARPENTARIA
Broadmere
MAMBALIYA RRUMBURRIYA WUYALIYA ABORIGINAL LAND TRUST
BUKALARA RANGE
GARAWA ABORIGINAL LAND TRUST
Cooee Hill
Tanumbirini
McArthur River Mine Aerodrome
Mount Mirmbulligan
Mount Ine
BULLWADDY CONSERVATION RESERVE
O T Downs
HWY
McArthur River
Heartbreak Hotel
Spring Creek
NT
QLD
Tully Inlet

Joins map 637

WARNINGS: In outback Australia, long distances separate some towns. Travellers should familiarise themselves with prevailing conditions before departure and take care to ensure their vehicle is roadworthy. Adequate supplies of petrol, water and food should be carried at all times.

In central Australia, rainfall can make some roads impassable, even with a 4WD vehicle. Full information on road conditions should be obtained from local authorities before departure.

If visitors intend diverting off public roads within Aboriginal Land areas, a permit is required from the relevant Aboriginal authority.

Beware of crocodiles in rivers, estuaries and coastal areas.

Beware of marine stingers in coastal areas (October to April). Swim within enclosures where possible.

0   50   100   150 km

Joins map 635

ARAFURA SEA

I   J   K   L   M   N   O   P

MANGARRAYI
ABORIGINAL
LAND TRUST

Minyerri

ALAWA 1
ABORIGINAL
LAND
TRUST

LIMMEN
NATIONAL
PARK
(PROPOSED)

YIYINYI
RANGE

BARRANYI (NORTH ISLAND)
NATIONAL PARK

1

Hodgson River
Station

West
Island

North Island

ALAWA
ABORIGINAL
LAND
TRUST

Nutwood
Downs

18

Rawali Inlet

Bing
Bong

Batten
Point

Centre
Island

Stokes Bay

WURRALIBI
ABORIGINAL
LAND TRUST

GULF
OF
CARPENTARIA

2

Minamia

88

Mount
Marmbulligan

Limmen
Gate

LIMMEN
NATIONAL
PARK
(PROPOSED)

Lorella
Spring

NARWINBI
ABORIGINAL
LAND
TRUST

Wandangula

Manangoora

Vanderlin
Island

Seven
Emu

-16° 00'

Mount
Joe

Bauhinia
Downs

Billengarrah

35

Borroloola

Jangurrie

Mara 28

Warby
Outstation

26

CARPENTARIA

139

Broadmere

McArthur River Mine
Aerodrome

Tawallah

CARANBIRINI
CONSERVATION
RESERVE

42

65

3

Cooee Hill

270

Tanumbirini

BULLWADDY
CONSERVATION
RESERVE

30

21

O T
Downs

37

44

110

84

HWY

BUKALARA
RANGE

Spring
Creek

Robinson
River

GARAWA
ABORIGINAL
LAND
TRUST

104

Tully Inlet

Hayfields

43

McArthur
River

58

Heartbreak
Hotel

McArthur
River

HWY

37

1

Mallapunyah

4

MAMBALIYA
RRUMBURRIYA
WUYALIYA
ABORIGINAL
LAND
TRUST

Kiana

Gold

58

Echo
Gorge

495

-17° 00'

Newcastle

Beetaloo

43

BARKLY
TABLELAND

HWY

115

Kiana

Calvert
Hills

59

Westmoreland

5

Elliott

19

19

200

STUART

Ucharonidge

Mungabroom

STOCK

Eva
Downs

Walhallow

ROUTE
Anthony
Lagoon

CALVERT

16

Cresswell
Downs

223

Benmara

Bamadjina
Claypan

80

WAANYI /
GARAWA
ABORIGINAL
LAND
TRUST

-18° 00'

6

BARKLY

16

229

377

20

Cresswell

Caulfield
Clay Flats

BOODJAMULLA
(LAWN HILL)
NATIONAL
PARK

Renner
Springs

JUNCTION
RESERVE

72

11

Tarrabool
Lake

75

Fish   Hole

Murun
Murula

7

Helen Springs

39

Mount
Willieray

Mount
Hawker

Muckaty

87

Corella Lake

Ngunarra

100

Lake Sylvester

RANKEN

CONNELLS
LAGOON
CONSERVATION
RESERVE

100

Mount
Morgan

Mittiebah

Mount
Drummond

Carrara

BARKLY
TABLELAND

New Herbert
Vale

Old Herbert Vale

-19° 00'

8

Banka Banka
Outstation

50

136

45

Brunchilly

70

Rockhampton
Downs

Wogyala

46

Lake De Burgh

WARUMUNGU ABORIGINAL
LAND TRUST

WARUMUNGU
ABORIGINAL
LAND TRUST

Playford

TABLELANDS

76

MITTIEBAH
RANGE

Mount
Lamb

Alexandria

21

65

Gallipoli

Kalumpurlpa

Phillip
Creek

29

Mungalawurru

Three Ways
Roadhouse

18

Likkaparta

BARKLY

98

187

66

89

54

Alroy
Downs

BURUDU
ABORIGINAL
LAND TRUST

98

Norfolk

No 3
Outstation

Morstone

9

Warrego

24

31

25

Tennant Creek

Kunayungku
Outstation

HWY

87

KURNTURLPARA
ABORIGINAL
LAND TRUST

Barkly
Homestead

Dalmore
Downs

Mount
Lamb

Kerringnew
Swamp

Oolgoolgarri
Swamp

GULANGULU
ABORIGINAL
LAND TRUST

80

76

10

MUNGKARTA
ABORIGINAL
LAND TRUST

139

Mount
Figg

Ngurrutji

WAKAYA ABORIGINAL
LAND TRUST

122

141

263

HWY

UDOONGUL
ABORIGINAL
LAND TRUST

Soudan

21

31

Avon
Downs

27

30

13

Camooweal

A2

-20° 00'

CAMOOWEAL
CAVES
NP

Mungkarta

Kalinjarri

52

69

Wutunugurra

Kurundi

Kuninelli
Outstation

21

Canteen
Creek

ANURRETE
ABORIGINAL
LAND
TRUST

56

URANDANGI   RD

101

Don

Old
Wooroona

Wooroona

11

DEVIL'S MARBLES

Wauchope

DEVILS
MARBLES

Mount
Cairns

Singleton

DAVENPORT

DAVENPORT
RANGE
NATIONAL
PARK

49

Hatches
Creek

95

Austral
Downs

Mount
Michael

Arcadia

55

Bullecourt

Wycliffe Well
Roadhouse

Numagalong

Wycliffe
Well

21

Ali-Curung

61

Imangara

76

RANGE

100

Elkedra

Mount
Alone

Elkedra
River

Annitowa

SANDOVER

14

147

HWY

Alpurrurulam

Lake
Nash

21

Georgina

53

59

12

Mount
Strzelecki

OSBORNE

110

RA

Mount
Morphett

WARRABRI
ABORIGINAL
LAND
TRUST

Joins map 639

Joins map 659

Joins map 660

NORTHERN TERRITORY

QUEENSLAND

Joins map 636

WARNING: Visitors planning to travel along the Larapinta Drive through Aboriginal Land require a permit. Check road conditions before departing; 4WD vehicle may be required.

For more detail on Uluru–Kata Tjuta National Park see page 640

WARNING: Visitors planning to travel along Tjukaruru Road through Aboriginal Land require a permit. A second permit is required for those venturing over the WA border.

Joins map 623

Joins map 608

Joins map 609

0   50   100   150 km

I   J   K   L   Joins map 637   M   N   O   P

1

KARLANTIJPA SOUTH ABORIGINAL LAND TRUST
Numagalong
Wauchope
Singleton
DAVENPORT
DAVENPORT RANGE NP
Canteen Creek
ANURRETE ABORIGINAL LAND TRUST
Mount Michael
Arcadia
Bullecourt 59
55

Wycliffe Well Roadhouse
Ali-Curung
Imangara
RANGE
Hatches Creek
Alpurrurulam
Lake Nash
Georgina
53
RD

2

WARRABRI ABORIGINAL LAND TRUST
OSBORNE RA
110
Mount Strzelecki
Mount Morphett
Mount Nelson
Tara
Elkedra
Elkedra
Annitowa
14
HWY
Georgina
Headingly

STUART HWY
87
RAILWAY
Barrow Creek
SPRING RANGE
Mount Stirling
90
Wilora
Ampilatwatja
Indaringinya
Ammaroo
579
Sandover
157
River
Ermanne
Argadargada
IRRMARNE ABORIGINAL LAND TRUST
Mount Hogarth
Urandangi
URANDANGI RD
TOBERMOREY

3

AHAKEYE ABORIGINAL LAND TRUST
Mount Tops
Mount Octy
Arawerr
Irrwelty
Derry Downs
Perety
Ooratippra
ANATYE ABORIGINAL LAND TRUST
Manners Creek

Ti-Tree
Pmara Jutunta
DAWSON SPRINGS
Atneltyey
SANGARAPA ABORIGINAL LAND TRUST
Mount Skinner
Utopia
Arapunya
Lucy Creek
Warlpeyangrere
DONOHUE HWY
12
101
Tobermorey
116

4

Chianina
Woolla Downs
Atartinga
Delmore Downs
Waite River
Delny
Dneiper
Mount Swan
DULCIE RANGE NATIONAL PARK
DULCIE RA
Mount Sainthill
Arthur
Mount Pozieres
Mount Guide
Marqua
TOOMBA RANGE
Mount Harriet

Mount Ewart
Bushy Park
Engawala
Mount Swan
Plenty
Huckitta
Jinka
Orrtipa-Thurra
PLENTY
River
Marqua
Mount Remecke
Mount Alfred

5

PLENTY
Gemtree
12
Atitjere
Mount Riddock
Mount Palmer
Mount Brassey
HARTS RA
486
Jervois
HWY
Akarnenehe
Mount Cornish
ADAM RANGE
Mount Woods
TOKO RANGE

Yambah
MACDONNELL RANGES
RANGES
ARLTUNGA HISTORICAL RESERVE
Claraville
Mount Ruby
Indiana
Mount Lloyd
Atula
TROPIC OF CAPRICORN
ATNETYE ABORIGINAL LAND TRUST
Mount Knuckey
Mount Gardiner
Mount Beck

6

TREPHINA GORGE NATURE PARK
HISTORIC TOWN, LARAPINTA TRAIL, THE GHAN
ALICE SPRINGS
ROSS HWY
Ross River
N'DHALA GORGE NATURE PARK
Arltunga Bush Hotel
RUBY GAP GORGE
RUBY GAP NATURE PARK
Illogwa
Hale
Lake Caroline
Ethabuka

STANDLEY CHASM
Iwupataka
6
Owen Springs
87
Amoonguna
SANTA TERESA ABORIGINAL LAND TRUST
OLD GHAN RAILWAY
Ringwood
Limbla
URETYINGKE ABORIGINAL LAND TRUST
Mount Isabel
Numery

7

OWEN SPRINGS RESERVE
201
Mount Oolarinna
Santa Teresa (Ltyente Purte)
Todd River
Little Well (Alutalkwa)
Todd River Downs

RAINBOW VALLEY
Stuarts Well
Orange Creek
Deep Well
Allambi
RODINGA RA
PMERE NYENTE ABORIGINAL LAND TRUST

8

Mount Gloaming
Titjikala
Mount Rodinga
217
The Twins
SIMPSON DESERT
SIMPSON DESERT NATIONAL PARK

YEWERRE ABORIGINAL LAND TRUST
CHAMBER'S PILLAR HISTORICAL RES
Idracowra
Horseshoe Bend

9

Mount Duff
Mount Casuarina
Mount Musgrave
Mount Rumbalara
MAC CLARK (ACACIA PEUCE) CONSERVATION RESERVE

10

Lilla Creek
Finke
New Crown
Mount Peebles
Andado
APATULA ABORIGINAL LAND TRUST
Mount Kingston
Mount Watt

Umbeara
Mount Gordon
147
Mount Grundy
PMER ULPERRE INGWEMIRNE ARLETHERRE ABORIGINAL LAND TRUST

11

Kulgera
Mount Cecil
Mount Etingimbra
Mount Wilyunpa
Mirranponga Pongunna Lake
Poeppel Corner

NORTHERN TERRITORY
SOUTH AUSTRALIA

Mount Darling
Mount Parloo
Mount Mead
Mount Dare
Mount Apperda
SIMPSON DESERT
SIMPSON DESERT
Lake Thomas
SIMPSON DESERT CONSERVATION PARK

Tieyon
WITJIRA NATIONAL PARK
Mount Hammersley
SIMPSON DESERT RECREATION

12

Mount Howe
Mount Irwin
Mount Tieyon
Mount Barr
Mount Ross
Mount Emeroo
Mount Attacherikanna
RESERVE
Poolowanna Lake
Lake Griselda
Peera Peera Poolanna Lake

ANANGU PITJANTJATJARA YANKUNYTJATJARA LANDS
BAGOT RA
Hamilton
Mount Deane

I   J   K   L   Joins map 606   M   N   O   P

For more detail on Alice Springs & the MacDonnell Ranges see page 640–1

WARNINGS: In outback Australia, long distances separate some towns. Travellers should familiarise themselves with prevailing conditions before departure and take care to ensure their vehicle is roadworthy. Adequate supplies of petrol, water and food should be carried at all times.

In central Australia, rainfall can make some roads impassable, even with a 4WD vehicle. Full information on road conditions should be obtained from local authorities before departure.

If visitors intend diverting off public roads within Aboriginal Land areas, a permit is required from the relevant Aboriginal authority.

NORTHERN TERRITORY
QUEENSLAND

Joins map 660
Joins map 662

Joins map 638

TO YUENDUMU

TANAMI

WEST MACDONNELL NATIONAL PARK

WARNING: Visitors planning to travel along the Larapinta Drive through Aboriginal Land require a permit. Check road conditions before departing; 4WD vehicle may be required.

WARNING: Visitors planning to travel along Tjukaruru Road through Aboriginal Land require a permit. A second permit is required for those venturing over the WA border.

WARNINGS: In outback Australia, long distances separate some towns. Travellers should familiarise themselves with prevailing conditions before departure and take care to ensure their vehicle is roadworthy. Adequate supplies of petrol, water and food should be carried at all times.

In central Australia, rainfall can make some roads impassable, even with a 4WD vehicle. Full information on road conditions should be obtained from local authorities before departure.

If visitors intend diverting off public roads within Aboriginal Land areas, a permit is required from the relevant Aboriginal authority.

MAPS

QUEENSLAND

INTER-CITY ROUTES	DISTANCE
Brisbane–Sydney via New England Hwy	995 km
Brisbane–Sydney via Pacific Hwy	936 km
Brisbane–Melbourne via Newell Hwy	1676 km
Brisbane–Darwin via Warrego Hwy	3406 km
Brisbane–Cairns via Bruce Hwy	1703 km

0   0.25   0.5   0.75   1 km

Joins map 644
Joins map 644

A   B   C   D   E   F   G   H

1
2
3
4
5
6
7
8
9
10
11
12

TO CHERMSIDE

Gona Barracks
Victoria Park Golf Course
Centenary Aquatic Centre
Tennis Courts
Brisbane Grammar School Lower Oval
Brisbane Girls Grammar School
Brisbane Boys Grammar School
Victoria Park
St Josephs College
Spring Hill
Primary School
Fortitude Valley
Brunswick Street
McWhirters Apartments
ChinaTown
Duncan St
Petrie Terrace
Spectacle Garden
Amphitheatre
Roma Street Parkland
St Andrews War Memorial Hospital
All Hallows School
Philip Bacon Galleries
Victoria Barracks
Holy Spirit Hospital
Old Windmill
MiM Plaza
St John's Cathedral
Deanery
Admiralty Towers
Petrie Bight
Kangaroo Point
Captain Burke Park
Customs House
RIVER
Brisbane Transit Centre
Police HQ
Brisbane Dental Hospital
ANZAC Square
Post Office Square
Riverside Centre
Holman Street Wharf
James Warner Park
Roma St
King Edward Park
Central
GPO
RACQ
Riverside @ the Pier Markets (Sun)
Riverside Wharf
Uniting Church
King George Square
Myer Centre
Cathedral of St Stephen
BRISBANE
Eagle St Pier
Old St Stephen's Chapel
Waterfront
Eagle Street Wharf
CT White Park
Qld Gallery of Modern Art
State Library of Qld
Queen Street Bus Stn
Elizabeth Arcade
Thornton Street Wharf
Pedestrian Underpass
Kangaroo Point
Queensland Qld Art Gallery
Qld Museum
Queens Gardens
Edward Street Wharf
Mt Olivet Hospital
North Quay Wharf
Cultural Centre
Queensland Performing Arts Centre
South Bank
South Brisbane
Brisbane Convention & Exhibition Centre
Queensland Conservatorium, Griffith Univ.
Heliport
Parliament House
City Botanic Gardens (Mianjin)
St Marys Anglican Church
South Bank Institute of Technology Kangaroo Point campus
Brisbane Southbank Institute of Technology campus
South Brisbane
Suncorp Piazza
QUT Gardens Point Wharf
South Bank 1 & 2 Wharf
Queensland University of Technology
Gardens Point Campus
Old Government House
Kiosk
Mangrove Boardwalk
Musgrave Park
Stanley St Plaza
Streets Beach
River Stage & Amphitheatre
Gardens Point
Kangaroo Point Cliffs City Lookout
Brisbane State High School
South Bank 3 Wharf
Raymond Park
TAFE College
Dry Dock
River Plaza Wharf
Queensland Maritime Museum
Highgate Hill
Sommerville House (Girls school)
St Laurences College
Mater Medical Centre
Mater Private Hospital
Woolloongabba
Brisbane Cricket Ground (The Gabba)
Mater Mothers Hospital
Mater Childrens Hospital
TO BEENLEIGH

Accommodation
BASE Backpacker Central 1 D5
Brisbane Marriott Hotel 2 F4
Chifley at Lennons 3 D6
Hilton Brisbane 4 E6
Holiday Inn Brisbane 5 C5
Hotel Conrad 6 D7
Hotel Grand Chancellor Brisbane 7 C3
Mantra on Queen 8 F3
Mercure Hotel Brisbane 9 C6
Novotel Brisbane 10 E4
Park Regis North Quay 11 B5
Rydges South Bank Hotel 12 C9
The Sebel Suites Brisbane 13 E7
Sofitel Brisbane 14 E4
Stamford Plaza Brisbane Hotel 15 F7
Urban Brisbane 16 C4
Note: Only a sample range of accommodation is listed; inclusion is not necessarily a recommendation.

General Information
Brisbane Transit Centre 17 B5
Central Railway Station 18 D5
City Police Station 19 E7
General Post Office 20 E5
RACQ 21 E5
Qantas Travel Centre 22 E5

Roma Street Station 23 B4
Visitor Information 24 D9,D6

Places of Interest
Arbour 25 D9
Brisbane City Hall 26 D6
Brisbane Cricket Ground (The Gabba) 27 H12
Brunswick Street Mall 28 G2
Cathedral of St Stephen 29 E6
Chinatown 30 G2
City Botanic Gardens 31 F8
Commissariat Store 32 D8
Conrad Treasury Casino 33 D7
Customs House 34 F4
Eagle Street Pier 35 F6
Museum of Brisbane 36 D6
Old Government House 37 E8
Old Windmill 38 D5
Parliament House 39 E8
Queen Street Mall 40 D6
Queensland Art Gallery 41 B7
Queensland Maritime Museum 42 D11
Queensland Museum 43 B7
Queensland Performing Arts Centre 44 C8
St John's Cathedral 45 F4
State Library of Qld 46 B7
Streets Beach 47 D9

Joins map 644

0 5 10 15 20 km

A B C D Joins map 647 E F G H

Joins map 647

TO WOODFORD
Wamuran Basin
Wamuran
TO BEERWAH
TO NAMBOUR
BULLOCK CREEK CP
PUMICESTONE
Mermaid Lagoon
BRIBIE ISLAND
NORTH WEST CHANNEL
27° 00'

D'AGUILAR
Mount Mee
WARARBA CREEK CP
Campbells Pocket
48
Moodlu
D'AGUILAR HWY
85
TOORBUL CP
Meldale
Toorbul
Ningi
BRIBIE ISLAND NATIONAL PARK
Banksia Beach

1

Mount Byron
BYRON CREEK CP
BRISBANE RANGE
Rocksberg
CABOOLTURE
Morayfield
11
BRIBIE ISLAND RD
85
21
Ningi
Godwin Beach
Bellara
FIRST AVE
Woorim
BONGAREE
Skirmish Point

2

NATIONAL
Mount Pleasant
58
DAYBORO RD
SHEEP STATION CREEK CP
Burpengary
60
M1
Beachmere
South Point
Red Beach
Bald Point

Upper Laceys Creek
Dayboro
MOUNT
Narangba
58
27
Kurwongbah
FRESHWATER NP
DECEPTION BAY
North Reef
Deception Bay
Castlereagh Point
Combie Trader Ferry to Moreton Island

3

PARK
The Bulls Knob
Mount Sim Jue
D'AGUILAR NATIONAL PARK
Kobble
22
WINN RD
Lake Samsonvale
73
North Pine Dam
Sideling Creek Dam
Dakabin
KALLANGUR
26
ROTHWELL
ANZAC AVE
BRUCE
25
Redcliffe Airport
SCARBOROUGH
Osbourne Point
Queens Beach
KIPPA-RING
REDCLIFFE
Redcliffe Point
Moreton Bay (Quandamook)
MAIN CHANNEL

4

TO ESK
31
MOUNT GLORIOUS RD
Mount Kobble
Mount Samson
Clear Mountain
18
PETRIE
LAWNTON
M1
MANGO HILL
HAYS INLET CP
Clontarf Point
Suttons Beach
WOODY POINT
Juno Point

5

Mount Glorious
Upper Cedar Creek
Closeburn
Yugar
Highvale
HOUSE MOUNTAIN RA
Mount O'Reilly
GLORIOUS RD
Samford
74
WARNER
STRATHPINE
BRAY PARK
BALD HILLS
BRACKEN RIDGE
CARSELDINE
BRIGHTON
Bramble Bay
SANDGATE
SHORNCLIFFE
Cabbage Tree Head
For more detail on Central Brisbane see page 643
Mud Island (Bungumba)

MOUNT NEBO
Mount Nebo
Camp Mountain
46
22
FERNY GROVE
UPPER KEDRON
ALBANY CREEK
28
ZILLMERE
ASPLEY
GEEBUNG
NUDGEE
BOONDALL
Brisbane Airport
MUD ISLAND CONSERVATION PARK

6

Joins map 645
D'AGUILAR NATIONAL PARK
NEBO RD
19
31
40
Enoggera Reservoir
Gold Creek Reservoir
ARANA HILLS
KEPERRA
STAFFORD
CHERMSIDE
KEDRON
VIRGINIA
TOOMBUL
NUNDAH
HENDRA
MEEANDAH
Fisherman Islands
South Point
St Helena Island (Noogoon)
ST HELENA ISLAND NP
Green Island (Milwarpa)

Horse Mountain
Lake Manchester
Mermaid Mountain
GALLIPOLI BARRACKS MILITARY AREA
THE GAP
ASHGROVE
NEWMARKET
ENOGGERA
PADDINGTON
MILTON
BRISBANE
LINDUM
WYNNUM
HEMMANT
MANLY
Oyster Point
Darling Point
23

7

DANDYS RANGE
Brookfield
KENMORE HILLS
Mount Coot-tha
TOOWONG
WEST END
INDOOROOPILLY
COORPAROO
MURARRIE
MANLY
LOTA
THORNESIDE
King Island (Erobin)
Waterloo Bay
Wellington Point

Borallon
Pine Mountain
Mount Crosby
MOUNT CROSBY RD
37
Pullenvale
KENMORE
CHAPEL HILL
FIG TREE POCKET
CORINDA
FAIRFIELD
ANNERLEY
CAMP HILL
MOUNT GRAVATT
CARINDALE
BIRKDALE
WELLINGTON POINT
ORMISTON
Raby Bay
Cleveland Point
27° 30'

8

TO TOOWOOMBA
WARREGO
Chuwar
Karalee
Karana Downs
BELLBOWRIE
MOUNT OMMANEY
OXLEY
ROCKLEA
ARCHERFIELD
Mount Petrie
Leslie Harrison Dam
Tingalpa Reservoir
CAPALABA
CLEVELAND
Oyster Point
Sandy Island

A2
38
Barellan Point
Moggill
DARRA
RIVERVIEW
WACOL
INALA
Archerfield Airport
SUNNYBANK
RUNCORN
MOUNT COTTON RD
44
THORNLANDS
Point Halloran

9

EAST IPSWICH
LEICHHARDT
NEW CHUM
REDBANK
GOODNA
CAMIRA
ELLEN GROVE
FOREST LAKE
M2
KURABY
SPRINGWOOD
DAISY HILL
45
Mount Cotton
Victoria Point
Redland Bay

YAMANTO
IPSWICH
CHURCHILL
15
Swanbank Lagoon
REDBANK PLAINS
SPRINGFIELD
CALAMVALE
WOODRIDGE
KINGSTON
SLACKS CREEK
VENMAN BUSHLAND NP
BEENLEIGH
REDLAND BAY
33

10

TO WARWICK
CUNNINGHAM
CENTENARY
93
98
Purga
Ripley
WHITE ROCK CONSERVATION PARK
GREENBANK MILITARY TRAINING AREA
Greenbank
BORONIA HEIGHTS
BROWNS PLAINS
CRESTMEAD
LOGANLEA
BETHANIA
WATERFORD
HOLMVIEW
CARBROOK WETLANDS CP
Bayview Island
Pannikin Island

Peak Crossing
MOUNT PERRY CONSERVATION PARK
Mount Goolman
Mount Blaine
Bundamba (Dalys) Lagoon
Round Mountain
LINDSAY
19
North Maclean
TAMBORINE RD
BEENLEIGH
Woongoolba
SOUTHERN MORETON BAY ISLANDS NP
Lagoon Island
Long Island

11

Limestone Ridge
FLINDERS PEAK CONSERVATION PARK
Flinders Peak
Mount Welcome
Mount Wilbraham
Kagaru
13
Jimboomba
MOUNT LINDSAY
WATERFORD RD
Logan Village
Buccan
BUCCAN CP
PLUNKETT CONSERVATION PARK
92
Ormeau
M1
Jacobs Well

12

IPSWICH
TO BEAUDESERT
Joins map 645
TO TAMBORINE
TO NERANG
Pimpama

A B C D E F G H

0   10   20   30 km

TO GYMPIE   TO GYMPIE

A B C D E F G H

1 2 3 4 5 6 7 8 9 10 11 12

GREAT SANDY
NATIONAL PARK

Gallangowan

AMAMOOR   RANGE

KANDANGA   RANGE

KILCOY

Kandanga

Mount Cooroora

BRUCE

Big Shell
Beach

Laguna
Bay

Noosa
Head

Tewantin

Noosa Heads
Sunshine
Beach

Cooroy

Noosaville

MOUNT
COOROY

BEACHES

NOOSA

Marcus Beach

Imbil

Brooloo

Eumundi

VILLAGE
MARKETS

Peregian Beach

NATIONAL

Mount Gibberagee

Mount Kandanga

KENILWORTH

HERITAGE
RAILWAY

Borumba Dam

North Arm

Yandina

THE GINGER
FACTORY,
NUTWORKS

Coolum Beach

PARK

Diaper Mountain

Burumba Mountain

EUMUNDI

Kenilworth

BLACKALL RANGE

Mapleton

FERNTREE
CREEK NP

Yaroomba
Point Arkwright

MOUNT COOLUM
NATIONAL PARK

Marcoola

Jimna

MAPLETON
FALLS
NP

SUNSHINE
CASTLE

Bli Bli

Maroochydore Aerodrome

Mount Monsildale

Summer
Mountain

Mount Walli

KONDALILLA
NP

NAMBOUR

THE MINIATURE
ENGLISH VILLAGE

TRIUNIA
NP

Woombye

MACADAMIA
NUT FACTORY

Mudjimba

MAROOCHY RIVER CP

MALENY

Flaxton

CONONDALE NATIONAL
PARK

Mount
Langley

Montville

Palmwoods

MAROOCHYDORE

Yednia

Conondale

KENILWORTH

Baroon
Pocket Dam
Lake
Baroon

EUDLO
CREEK

Forest
Glen

BUDERIM

SUPERBEE
HONEY
FACTORY

MOOLOOLABA

Point Cartwright

UNDERWATER WORLD

Linville

RD

Maleny

Eudlo

AUSSIE WORLD
ETTAMOGAH PUB,
HOUSE OF HERBS,
OPALS DOWN
UNDER

Buddina

Mount
Pascoe

CONONDALE
RANGE

Mooloolah

MOOLOOLAH
RIVER
NP

Warana

CORAL

PALMVIEW CP

Mount
Spencer

MCCARTHYS
LOOKOUT

DULARCHA
NP

CURRIMUNDI LAKE CP

Moore

D'AGUILAR

Moffat
Head

CALOUNDRA

Caloundra Head

The Round
Mountain

Mount Miva

BEERWAH

Landsborough

WAY

BIG KART
TRACK

Nurinda

Gregors
Creek

Harlin

BRISBANE

Mount
Lional

Peachester

Mount
Marysmokes

AUSTRALIA
ZOO

QUEENSLAND
AIR MUSEUM

Deep
Water
Point

Beerwah

KILCOY

Coochin Creek

BRIBIE
ISLAND

Brait
Mountain

Yimbun

Kilcoy

GLASS HOUSE
MOUNTAINS

Mount
Beerwah

Glass House Mountains

SEA

Ivory Creek

CRESSBROOK
CONSERVATION
PARK

Woodford

GLASS HOUSE
MOUNTAINS
NATIONAL
PARK

BRIBIE
ISLAND

Biarra

Mount
Archer

Beerburrum

BRIBIE
ISLAND
NATIONAL
PARK

Toogoolawah

D'AGUILAR
NP

Delaneys
Creek

Wamuran
Basin

Wamuran

CABOOLTURE
HISTORICAL
VILLAGE

Donnybrook

BULLOCK CREEK CP

Meldale

Toorbul

Banksia
Beach

Mount Beppo

Somerset
Dam

BYRON CREEK
CP

Mount Mee

WARARBA
CREEK
CP

Campbells
Pocket

Modlu

Ningi

Caboonbah

Lake
Somerset

Rocksberg

Elimbah

CABOOLTURE

BRIBIE

ISLAND

Bellara

Woorim

The Gap

Coal
Creek

Crossdale

Morayfield

Godwin
Beach

BONGAREE

Murrumba

Mount Pleasant

Upper Laceys
Creek

SHEEP STATION
CREEK CP

Burpengary

South Point

BUCKLEYS HOLE CP

Bald Point
Beach

Gallanani

Esk

The Bull
Knob

Dayboro

Narangba

FRESHWATER
NP

Beachmere

Deception
Bay

Combie Trader
Ferry to Moreton Island

Mount Hallen

WIVENHOE

Bryden

Dundas

Kobble

DAYBORO

ALMA PARK
ZOO

Deception Bay

North Reef

For more detail on Brisbane
Suburbs see page 644

Mount
Mugowie

Moombra

WIVENHOE
LOOKOUT

D'AGUILAR
NP

Lake
Kobble

Mount
Samson

Dakabin

Kallangur

Castlereagh Point
Scarborough
Osbourne Point

Buaraba

ESK

Lake
Wivenhoe

Mount
Glorious

MOUNT
GLORIOUS

Upper
Cedar
Creek

Petrie

Lawnton

Mango
Hill

HAYS
INLET

Redcliffe
Redcliffe Point

Kippa-Ring

Suttons Beach

Moreton Bay
(Quandamook)

Coominya

Patrick
Estate

BRISBANE

Clarendon

Ardmory

D'AGUILAR
NP

Closeburn

Yugar

Warner

Bray
Park

Brighton

Strathpine

Bramble
Bay

Tangalooma Flyer
Ferry to Moreton Island

Mount
Tarampa

Wivenhoe
Pocket

MOUNT
NEBO

Highvale

Samford

Albany Creek

Bald
Hills

Carseldine

Sandgate

Cabbage Tree Head

Mud Island
(Bungumba)

Tarampa

Lowood

Fairneyview

Mount
Nebo

Camp Mountain

Ferry
Hills

Arana
Hills

Aspley

Zillmere

Boondall

Shorncliffe

MUD ISLAND CP

Juno
Point

Fisherman
Islands

Glenore Grove

Fernvale

JOLLY'S
LOOKOUT

AUSTRALIAN
WOOLSHED

Ferry
Grove

Keperra

Virginia

Brisbane
Airport

St Helena Island
(Noogoon)

ST HELENA
ISLAND NP

Plainland

WARREGO

Prenzlau

Coolana

Minden

Borallon

Wahora

MCAFEES
LOOKOUT

Mount
Crosby

Enoggera

The Gap

Newmarket

Doomben

Eagle Farm

Oyster Point

Green Island
(Milwarpa)

Thorneside

Laidley

Hatton Vale

Marburg

Haigslea

Karana Downs

Chuwar

Karalee

Moggill

Pullenvale

Kenmore Hills

Brookfield

Kenmore

Indooroopilly

Paddington

Toowong

BRISBANE

STREETS BEACH

Morningside

Wynnum
Darling Point

Manly

Wellington
Point

Peel Island
(Turkroar)

Birkdale

Rosewood

Walloon

East Ipswich

Booval

New
Chum

Riverview

Wacol

Ommaney

Oxley

Rocklea

Archerfield

Sunnybank

Camp
Hill

Mount
Gravatt

Cleveland
Point

Capalaba

Ormiston

ORMISTON
HOUSE

OLD COURT
HOUSE

Grandchester

Calvert

IPSWICH

Leichhardt

Yamanto

Goodna

Camira

Redbank Plains

Redbank

Ellen
Grove

Pallara

Richlands

Archerfield
Airport

Darra

Runcorn

Burbank

Alexandra
Hills

Cleveland

Tingalpa

Thornlands

Victoria
Point

Coochiemudlo
Island

MacLeay
Island

0   10   20   30   40   50 km

TO GLADSTONE

Mount Bonito
Mount Whaggo
Lake Monduran
Mount Gaeta
Black Mountain
Red Mountain
KALPOWAR RD
BRUCE HWY

Yandaran
Avondale
Moore Park
MOUTH OF KOLAN RIVER CP
Flagstone Creek
Fred Haigh Dam
Bucca
Bingera
BUCCA RD
Kolan River

South Head
Burnett Heads ☉ TURTLES
Bargara
BARUBBRA ISLAND CP

BUNDABERG ⊕

GIN GIN
Gin Gin ⊕
MOUNT PERRY RD
Clayton
Elliott Heads
Coonarr

Mount Perry
North Double Peak
Mount Gongiberoo
Mount Prazier

A1
Wallaville
Walla Weir
ISIS HWY
Cordalba
Apple Tree Creek
Childers
GOODWOOD RD
Goodwood
ISS Balancing Storage Dam

Sandy Cape
Sandy Cape Lighthouse ★
Manann Beach
Rooney Point
North Ngkala Rocks
South Ngkala Rocks
Platypus Bay
Orchid Beach
Marloo Bay
Orchid Beach
Waddy Point
Indian Head
GREAT
FRASER ISLAND
SANDY
Corroboree Beach
FRASER ISLAND
NATIONAL
THE CATHEDRALS
The Pinnacles
MAHENO WRECK
Maheno Beach
PARK

BURRUM COAST NATIONAL PARK
Hervey Bay
Woodgate
Walkers Point
Buxton
Burrum Heads
North Shore Point
Port of Maryborough
Toogoom

GOOD NIGHT SCRUB NP
Booyal
BRUCE HWY
Mount Blande
Mount Stradman
Dallarnil
HWY
Junction Mountain
Howard
Lenthalls Dam
Lake Lenthall
Torbanlea
Point Vernon
Pialba
HERVEY BAY ⊕
WHALES ☉
Blackfellow Point
Woody Island
Mangrove Point
South Point
Rainbow Gorge
Happy Valley
River Heads
North Head
Shoulder Point
KINGFISHER BAY RESORT & VILLAGE
Turkey Island
Eurong
Seventy Five Mile Beach

BICENTENNIAL NATIONAL TRAIL
Byrnestown
Biggenden
MOUNT WALSH NP
ISIS
Mount Havilah
Scrubby Mountain
Coalstoun Lakes
Mount Walla
Mount Brian
BAN BAN SPRINGS
BURNETT HWY
Brooweena
MARYBOROUGH
Aramara
BIGGENDEN RD
Mungar
HISTORIC TOWN
MARYBOROUGH ⊕
Boonlye Point
Moonboom Islands
POONA NP
Maaroom
GREAT SANDY STRAIT
Mount Marcella
Ettiewyn
Dovedale
BROOWEENA
Sunny Glen
Owanyilla
WOOLOOGA RD
Tiaro
MOUNT BAUPLE NP
Bauple
Tuan
Snout Point
Cowra Point
Elbow Point
WIDE BAY TRAINING AREA
Hook Point
Inskip Point
Rainbow Beach
Double Island Point

Mount Kola
Miva
Gundiah
Grassy Mountain
Mount Neerdie
Mount Eaton
Tansey
Cloyna
Wooloога
Gunaldah
Neerdie
TIN CAN BAY RD
Tin Can Bay ⊕
GREAT
Kilkivan
WIDE BAY HWY
Goomeri
BRUCE HWY
GYMPIE FOREST RESERVE
A1
SANDY
CORAL
Murgon ⊕
Cherbourg
CHERBOURG
Wondai
SOUTH BURNETT WINERIES
A3
Tingoora
Wooroolin
Memerambi
Crawford
Kingaroy ⊕
Haabinga
BRISBANE RANGE
KILCOY RD
Manumbar
Gallangowan
Nanango ⊕
Yarraman
A3
Upper Yarraman
D'AGUILAR
Blackbutt
17
Benarkin
Moore
Nurinda
Googa Googa

BURNETT HWY
GYMPIE ⊕
Mount Boulder
Boreen Point
Teewah
Lake Cootharaba
NATIONAL
SEA
Amamoor
Kandanga
Imbil
Brooloo
Cooran
Pomona
Cooroy
Tewantin
Noosaville
Noosa Head
Noosa Heads ⊕ BEACHES
Sunshine Beach
NOOSA NATIONAL PARK
Marcus Beach
Peregian Beach
Kenilworth
North Arm
Eumundi
VILLAGE MARKETS
Yandina
THE GINGER FACTORY
Coolum Beach
Yaroomba
Marcoola
Mapleton
BIG PINEAPPLE
Woombye
Palmwoods
Montville
NAMBOUR ⊕
KONDALILLA NP
Mudjimba
MAROOCHYDORE ⊕
MOOLOOLABA ⊕
UNDERWATER WORLD
Point Cartwright
Buderim
Forest Glen
Buddina
Warana
MOOLOOLAH RIVER NP
CONONDALE NATIONAL PARK
Condale
Maleny
Eudlo
Mooloolah
QUEENSLAND AIR MUSEUM
MCCARTHYS LOOKOUT
Bli Bli
Peachester
Landsborough
CALOUNDRA ⊕
Caloundra Head
Coochin Creek
Beerwah
AUSTRALIA ZOO
BRIBIE ISLAND
TO CABOOLTURE

For more detail on Brisbane & Surrounds, North see page 647

Joins map 653

TO GAYNDAH

0 20 40 60 80 100 km

Joins map 657

For more detail on Cairns & Surrounds see page 651

TOWNSVILLE

0 500 m

CLEVELAND BAY

South Townsville

Accommodation
Aquarius on the Beach 1 F1
Holiday Inn Townsville 2 G3
Leisure Inn Plaza Hotel 3 G3
Reef Lodge Backpackers 4 H2
Rydges Southbank Townsville Hotel 5 G3
Note: Only a sample range of accommodation is listed; inclusion is not necessarily a recommendation.

General Information
Police Station 6 G3
Post Office 7 G2
Qantas Travel Centre 8 G2
Town Hall 9 G2
Townsville Transit Centre 10 H3

Vehicle Ferry Terminal 11 H2
Visitor Information 12 G2

Places of Interest
Perc Tucker Regional Gallery 13 G2
Flinders Mall 14 G3
Jupiters Townsville Hotel & Casino 15 H1
Maritime Museum of Townsville 16 H2
Museum of Tropical Queensland 17 H2
Reef HQ Aquarium & Imax Dome Theatre 18 H2
St James Cathedral 19 G2
Townsville Entertainment & Convention Centre 20 H1

Joins map 654

Joins map 663

0   25   50   75   100 km

I   J   K   L   M   N   O   P

CORAL SEA

GLADSTONE
Boyne Island
Tannum Sands

Calliope

Biloela

Moura

Monto

Mundubbera

Gayndah

Miles
Chinchilla

Dalby

TOOWOOMBA
IPSWICH
BRISBANE

Pittsworth

WARWICK

Goondiwindi

Stanthorpe

Smithfield

NEW SOUTH
WALES

BUNDABERG
Bargara
Burnett Heads

Childers

HERVEY
BAY

MARYBOROUGH

Tin Can Bay

GYMPIE

Noosa Heads
Sunshine Beach
Peregian Beach
Coolum Beach
NAMBOUR
BUDERIM
MAROOCHYDORE
MOOLOOLABA
CALOUNDRA

Kingaroy
Nanango

Murgon
Cherbourg
Wondai

CABOOLTURE
BONGAREE
Beachmere

Landsborough
Beerwah
Woodford
Elimbah

Kilcoy

Crows Nest
Highfields

Gatton
Laidley
Rosewood

NERANG
Mudgeeraba
Beaudesert

Boonah
Jimboomba

Murwillumbah
Chinderah
Banora Point
Kingscliff
Bogangar
Pottsville
Ocean Shores
Brunswick Heads
Byron Bay

Kyogle
Mullumbimby

LISMORE
Casino
Wollongbar
Alstonville
BALLINA
Suffolk Park
Lennox Head

CORAL SEA

GOLD COAST

WARNER BROS.
MOVIE WORLD,
DREAMWORLD,
WET 'N' WILD
WATER WORLD,
SEA WORLD,
SURFING

For more detail on
Fraser Coast
see page 648

For more detail on Brisbane &
Surrounds see pages 645 & 647

I   J   K   L   M   N   O   P

1
2
3
4
5
6
7
8
9
10
11
12

Joins map 657
Joins map 661
Joins map 663
Joins map 652

0 25 50 75 100 km

For more detail on The Whitsunday Coast see page 649

WARNINGS: In outback Australia, long distances separate some towns. Travellers should familiarise themselves with prevailing conditions before departure and take care to ensure their vehicle is roadworthy. Adequate supplies of petrol, water and food should be carried at all times.

In central Australia, rainfall can make some roads impassable, even with a 4WD vehicle. Full information on road conditions should be obtained from local authorities before departure.

If visitors intend diverting off public roads within Aboriginal Land areas, a permit is required from the relevant Aboriginal authority.

Beware of crocodiles in rivers, estuaries and coastal areas.

Beware of marine stingers in coastal areas (October to April). Swim within enclosures where possible.

CORAL SEA

GREAT BARRIER REEF

SOUTH PACIFIC OCEAN

CORAL SEA

I J K L M N O P

1 2 3 4 5 6 7 8 9 10 11 12

CAPE UPSTART NP
Cape Upstart
Gumlu
Guthalungra
Bowen
Merinda
Delta
MOUNT ABERDEEN NP
Binbee
Collinsville
Scottville
Proserpine
Cannonvale Airlie Beach
GLOUCESTER ISLAND NP
WHITSUNDAY GROUP
WHITSUNDAY ISLANDS NP
WHITSUNDAY ISLANDS, WHITEHAVEN BEACH
CONWAY NP
Conway Beach
Midge Point
Bloomsbury
SMITH ISLANDS NP
SOUTH CUMBERLAND ISLANDS NP
Elaroo Yalboroo
Calen
Seaforth Ball Bay
Mount Ossa
EUNGELLA NP
Mount Charlton
Eungella
Finch Hatton
Gargett
Kuttabul
Mirani Marian
Bucasia Eimeo
Shoal Point
Farleigh
MACKAY
Slade Point
Walkerston
Eton
Homebush
Bakers Creek
Half Tide
Hector
HOMEVALE NP
Homevale
Glenden
Grasstree
Sarina
Campwin Beach
Sarina Beach
Armstrong Beach
NORTHUMBERLAND ISLANDS NP
Exvale
Nebo
Braeside
Koumala
CAPE PALMERSTON
Ilbilbie
Moranbah
Coppabella
DIPPERU NP
West Hill
WEST HILL NP
Carmila
Flaggy Rock
Collaroy
BROAD SOUND ISLANDS NP
PERCY ISLES NP
Morpeth
Killarney
Clairview
Broad Sound
Port of St Lawrence
St Lawrence
SHOALWATER BAY
Dysart
Barmount
Ogmore
MOUNT O'CONNELL NP
SHOALWATER BAY TRAINING AREA
Middlemount
Rocky Crossing
Marlborough
Kunwarara
Tieri
Capella
Gregory
Merimal
Glen Geddes
Canoona
BYFIELD NP
GOODEDULLA NATIONAL PARK
Yaamba
Milman
The Caves
Farnborough
Yeppoon
Emerald
Blackwater
Comet
Bluff
Leichhardt
Dingo
Goowarra
Wallaroo
Duaringa
Gogango
Westwood
Warren
Kabra
ROCKHAMPTON
Gracemere
Midgee
Mulambin
Kinka
KEPPEL BAY ISLANDS NP
Emu Park
Keppel Sands
Joskeleigh
South Yaamba
Ridgelands
Parkhurst
Tungamull
BLACKDOWN TABLELAND NP
Mount Morgan
Bouldercombe
Bajool
Port Alma
CURTIS ISLAND NP
Dululu
Wowan
Mount Larcom
Yarwun
Ambrose
Raglan
Marmor
GLADSTONE
Springsure
Rannes
Goovigen
Jambin
Baralaba
Calliope
Boyne Island
Tannum Sands
EURIMBULA NP
Lady Musgrave Island
Turkey Beach
CAPRICORNIA CAYS NATIONAL PARK

A B C D E F G H

Joins map 658

1

WARNINGS: In outback Australia, long distances separate some towns. Travellers should familiarise themselves with prevailing conditions before departure and take care to ensure their vehicle is roadworthy. Adequate supplies of petrol, water and food should be carried at all times.

In central Australia, rainfall can make some roads impassable, even with a 4WD vehicle. Full information on road conditions should be obtained from local authorities before departure.

If visitors intend diverting off public roads within Aboriginal Land areas, a permit is required from the relevant Aboriginal authority.

Beware of crocodiles in rivers, estuaries and coastal areas.

Beware of marine stingers in coastal areas (October to April). Swim within enclosures where possible.

-15° 00'

-16° 00'

-17° 00'

18° 00'

19° 00'

-20° 00'

ARAFURA SEA

GULF OF CARPENTARIA

CAPE YORK PENINSULA

GULF COUNTRY

STAATEN RIVER NATIONAL PARK

CURLEW RANGE

Pormpuraaw

Kowanyama

MITCHELL ALICE RIVERS NP

Strathgordon

WELLESLEY ISLANDS
White Cliffs
Mornington Island
Lingnoonganee (Wallaby) Island
Cape Van Diemen
Weediah Bay
Sydney Island
Bountiful Islands
Bentinck Island
Sweers Island
SOUTH WELLESLEY ISLANDS
Tarrant Point
Pasco Inlet

Karumba
FINUCANE ISLAND NP
Kangaroo Point
Disaster Inlet
Morning Inlet

Escott
Burketown
Yarrum
NARDOO
JOHNNIES PLAIN
Armraynald

Maggieville
Mutton Hole
Normanton
Magowra
Shady Lagoon
Glenore Crossing
Timora

BURKE
Glencoe
Stirling
Vanrook
Myra Vale
Lotus Vale
Delta Downs
Double Lagoon
Point Austin
Accident Inlet

Miranda Downs
Old Miranda Homestead
TWELVE MILE PLAIN

Blackbull
GULF DEVELOPMENTAL
Croydon
Belmore
Guildford
Ellavale
Gum Creek
Wallabadah Outstation
Tabletop
Strathmore

Gilbert River
Lake Calo
Inorunie
Alehvale
Huonfels
Georgetown
Paramount

GREGORY
Mittagong
Idalia
Langlo Vale
Malacura
Paddys
Mount Clark

Claraville
Vena Park

GULF COUNTRY

Iffley
Wondoola
Bang Bang
Donors Hill
SIMPSON PLAIN

BURKETOWN
NORMANTON RD
Invetleigh
Wernadinga
ARMSTRONG PLAIN
Milgarra
McAllister
Mount Victoria
Neumayer Valley
Warren Vale
Yappar Station
Belmore
Florence Holding

Floraville
Alexandra
Talawanta
Augustus Downs
Fiery Downs Outstation
Nardoo
Lorraine
WILLS DEVELOPMENTAL

Burke & Wills Roadhouse
Kamileroi
Ten Mile Waterhole
Canobie
Cowan Downs

White Gorge
American Gorge
Gleeson
Mount Fox
Byron House Mountain
The Knob
MADCAP PLAIN
Alcala
WALLA PLAIN
Violet Vale

Mount Stanley
Mount Mckeon
Gereta
Lake Julius
Kajabbi
Granada
Coolullah
The Nobbies
Clonagh
Bendigo Park
Dalgonally

Etta Plains
Balootha
Millungera
Mount Brown
Numil Downs
Taldora
Myola
Lyrian Waterhole
Earles Camp Waterhole

Momba
Prospect
Esmeralda
North Head
South Head
Glenora
Nara
Perpendicular Peak
Robinhood
Agate Creek
Iona
Bald Mountain
Mount Spinifex
Lawnvale
Forsayth
Mount Tabletop

Pioneer
Victoria Vale
Bellfield
Perryvale
Waitan
Strathpark
Mount Norman
Saxby Downs
Bunda Bunda

RANGE

0 25 50 75 100 km

I J K L M N O P

WAKOOKA

Bizant

Breeza Plains
Outstation

CAPE
MELVILLE
NP

TURTLE
GROUP
NP

LIZARD ISLAND NP

Eyrie
Reef

Lizard Is
Palfrey Is

1

LAKEFIELD

Koolburra
Mountain

Koolburra

MUNBURRA
RESOURCES
RES

Turtle Group

Martin Reef

310

Hann River
Roadhouse

PARK

NATIONAL

Mount Stuckey (Numbaumbar)

STARCKE
NP

Lookout Point

Flattery
Harbour

Cape Flattery

CORAL

2

Moreheads

GREAT

Mount
Jack

BRIDGE
CREEK
NP

MOUNT WEBB NP

Mount
Baird

THREE ISLANDS NP

GREAT

SEA

KIMBA

PALMERVILLE

CAMP
83

HOPE
VALE

Cape
Bedford

Forrester Reef

BARRIER

15° 00'

Pinnacles

Laura

BICENTENNIAL
NATIONAL
TRAIL

Marton

Hope
Vale

South Cape
Bedford

ENDEAVOUR RIVER NP

Cooktown

Walker Bay

REEF

3

CAPE
YORK
PENINSULA

Fairlight

QUINKAN

McCormack

BLACK MOUNTAIN NP

Archer Point

Helenvale

GREAT

DIVIDING

WEST
QUINKAN

Mount Lukin

Lakeland

Rossville

CEDAR BAY
NP

Cedar Bay

Rattlesnake Point
(North Head)

Ayton

MARINE

4

Mount
Emma

PALMER GOLDFIELD
RESOURCES RES

Palmer River
Roadhouse

Mount
Eykin

Racecourse
Mountain

Wujal Wujal

DAINTREE
NATIONAL PARK

Cape Tribulation

St Crispin Reef

16° 00'

RANGE

DAINTREE
(WORLD
HERITAGE)

Daintree

Cow Bay
Cape Kimberley

HOPE ISLANDS NP

5

Bellevue

DAINTREE
NP

Wonga

Mossman

Trinity Bay

LOW ISLES
LIGHTHOUSE

Tongue Reef

PARK

Mount Carbine

Port Douglas
Craiglie

Cooya Beach

FOUR MILE
BEACH

Michaelmas Reef

Maryfarms

Julatten

Oak Beach

CAPTAIN COOK
HIGHWAY DRIVE
Trinity Bay

Arlington
Reef

Mount Molloy

Ellis Beach

Palm Cove

6

Mount
Mulligan

HANN
TABLELAND
NP

Koah

Clifton Beach
Smithfield

Kuranda

Green Is

KURANDA SCENIC
RAILWAY,
AUSTRALIAN
BUTTERFLY
SANCTUARY

Kingsborough

Biboohra

Heights

Mareeba

BARRON
GORGE
NP

CAIRNS

Fitzroy Is

GREAT
BARRIER
REEF

Mungana

Chillagoe

Dimbulah

Tabacum

Edmonton

Gordonvale

Sudbury Reef

17° 00'

CHILLAGOE
MUNGANA
CAVES NP

Almaden

Mutchilba

Walkamin

Aloomba

Fishery Falls

Petford

Tinaroo Falls

Tolga

Kairi

Tinaburra

Atherton

Yungaburra

Deeral

Russell Is

RUSSELL RIVER NP

Gibson Reef

7

BULLERINGA
NATIONAL
PARK

Ootann

Herberton

Malanda

Babinda

Miriwinni

Bramston Beach

ELLA BAY NP

Irvinebank

Watsonville

Kalunga

WOOROONOORAN
NP

Millaa Millaa

Flying Fish Point

Innisfail

Tumoulin
Ravenshoe

Mourilyan

South Johnstone

8

Bullock
Creek

Munderra

Innot Hot
Springs

Mena Creek

Cowley Beach

COWLEY BEACH TRAINING AREA

KURRIMINE BEACH NP

Kurrimine Beach

Cardstone

El Arish

Bingil Bay

Silkwood

Mission Beach

Wongaling Beach

Springfield

BICENTENNIAL
NATIONAL
TRAIL

FORTY MILE
SCRUB NP

KOOMBOOLOOMBA
FOREST RESERVE

Koombooloomba
Dam

Tully

South Mission Beach

Dunk Is

Bedarra Is

REEF

Cabana

Mount
Eliza

TULLY FALLS
FOREST RESERVE

Euramo

Tully Heads

9

GULF
DEV

Mount
Surprise

UNDARA
VOLCANIC
NATIONAL
PARK

Glen
Ruth

Bilyana

EDMUND KENNEDY NP

Kennedy

Rockingham Bay

South Is

Cape Sandwich

Einasleigh

MOUNT-ROSEY
RESOURCES RESERVE

KINRARA
NP

Abergowrie

Cardwell

GIRRINGUN

HINCHINBROOK ISLAND
NP

Kinrara

Lannercost

NATIONAL

Hillcock
Point

PALM
ISLANDS

Trunk
Reef

10

Kidston

Oasis
Roadhouse

Greenvale

Trebonne

Lucinda

Halifax

Pelorus Is (North Palm Island) (Yanooa)

ORPHEUS ISLAND NP

Ingham

Toobanna

Taylors
Beach

Great Palm Island

White Rock (Albino Rock)

Greenvale

Christmas
Creek

Forrest
Beach

Michael
Creek

Bambaroo

HALIFAX BAY WETLANDS NP

11

BLACKBRAES
RESOURCES
RESERVE

PALUMA
RANGE NP

Mutarnee

Balgal Beach

MAGNETIC ISLAND NP

Paluma

Rollingstone

Rattlesnake Is

Halifax Bay

Horseshoe Bay

Nelly Bay

Bluewater

Jalloonda

Pallarenda

Picnic Bay

Cape Cleveland

BLACKBRAES
NATIONAL
PARK

Blue Water
Springs
Roadhouse

TOWNSVILLE
FIELD
TRAINING
AREA

Thuringowa

TOWNSVILLE

HISTORIC
TOWN

Bowling

Cape Bowling
Green

12

Cape Upstart

BOWLING
GREEN
BAY NP

Alligator Creek

Cungulla

BOWLING GREEN
BAY NP

Alva

GREAT BASALT WALL NP

DALRYMPLE
NP

Reid River

Woodstock

Giru

Brandon

Ayr

Home Hill

I J K L M N O P

For more detail on Townsville to Cairns Region see page 650

For more detail on The Whitsunday Coast see page 649

0   25   50   75   100 km

WARNINGS: In outback Australia, long distances separate some towns. Travellers should familiarise themselves with prevailing conditions before departure and take care to ensure their vehicle is roadworthy. Adequate supplies of petrol, water and food should be carried at all times.

In central Australia, rainfall can make some roads impassable, even with a 4WD vehicle. Full information on road conditions should be obtained from local authorities before departure.

If visitors intend diverting off public roads within Aboriginal Land areas, a permit is required from the relevant Aboriginal authority.

Beware of crocodiles in rivers, estuaries and coastal areas.

Beware of marine stingers in coastal areas (October to April). Swim within enclosures where possible.

N

ARAFURA   SEA

WELLESLEY ISLANDS
Rocky Is
White Cliffs
Bidgagun Bay
Mornington Island
Gubungura
Gee Wee
Denham Is
Lingnoonganee (Wallaby) Is
Cape Van Diemen
Sydney Is
Gerrigroo Point
Bountiful Islands
Forsyth Is
Bayley Is

GULF

GULF COUNTRY

OLD DOOMADGEE

Allen Island
Oaktree Point
Bentinck Island
Sweers Island
Tarrant Point

OF

CARPENTARIA

Point Austin
Accident Inlet
Delta Downs
Lotus Vale
Double Lagoon
Glencoe

Pasco Inlet
Kangaroo Point
FINUCANE ISLAND NP
Gore Point
Morning Inlet

Karumba
Bynoe Inlet
Maggieville
BURKE DEV.
Mutton Hole

DOOMADGEE

Escott
Burketown
Normanton
Shady Lagoon
Glenore Crossing
GULF DEV. RD
Timora

WAANYI

Corinda
Tirranna Roadhouse
Doomadgee
Armraynald
NARDOO RD
Magowra
NORMANTON RD
Gum Creek

GARAWA ABORIGINAL LAND TRUST

Bowthorn
Brinawa
Wernadinga
Inverleigh
McAllister
Milgarra

Mount Oscar
Almora
Floraville
BURKETOWN
BURKETOWN RD
Warren Vale
Yappar Station

BARKLY TABLELAND

BOODJAMULLA (LAWN HILL) NATIONAL PARK

Lawn Hill
Kunkulla
Augustus Downs
Neumayer Valley
Mount Victoria
Bang Bang
Wondoola
Vena Park
Claraville

Highland Plains
Gregory Downs
Yeldham
Talawanta
Donors Hill
Iffley
GULF COUNTRY

New Herbert Vale
Lawn Hill Gorge
Adels Grove
Kamarga
Nardoo
WILLS RD
Wombool
Cowan Downs
Myola

Old Herbert Vale
RIVERSLEIGH FOSSIL SITE
Riversleigh
Mount Merlin
Lorraine
Coolibah Outstation
Earles Camp Waterhole

Gallipoli
Saxby Roundup

NORTHERN TERRITORY   QUEENSLAND

Norfolk
CAMOOWEAL
Burke & Wills Roadhouse
Ten Mile Waterhole
Lynian Waterhole

Morstone
Thorntonia
Mount Oxide
Kamileroi
Gleeson
Boomarra
Canobie
Arizona

GREGORY DOWNS
Undilla
BARKLY TABLELAND
Gunpowder
Mount Fox
Dobbyn
Coolullah
Alkala
Violet Vale
Kalmeta
Numil Downs
Millungera

BARKLY
Camooweal
CAMOOWEAL CAVES NP
Mount Mckeon
The Nobbies
Bellman
Brinard
Etta Plains
Mount Little
Balootha

URANDANGI
Yelvertoft
Gereta
Kajabbi
Granada
Clonagh
Dalgonally
Manfred Downs

Old Wooroona
Barkly Downs
Calton Hills
Mount Remarkable
Mount Roseby
Quamby
Ernestina Plains
Alva Downs

Wooroona
Glenroy
Mount Maggie
SEDAN DIP
Corella Park
Oorindi
FLINDERS HWY
Julia Creek

Mingera
New May Downs
Lake Moondarra
MOUNT ISA
BARKLY HWY
Cloncurry
Gilliat
Kamerooka

Mount Michael
Bullecourt
Lake Mary Kathleen
The Three Sisters
Mount Philip
Roxmere
Mount Connor
Mount Noma
Rutchillo
Coolreagh

Lake Nash
DIAMANTINA DEV. RD
Malbon Vale
Black Mountain
Malbon
Kays Peak
LANDSBOROUGH HWY

Headingly
Sheila Outstation
Mount Woodhouse
Bushy Park
Duchess
Devoncourt
Kuridala
McKinlay
Eulolo

Ashover
Mount Collis
Mount Tracey

URANDANGI NORTH RD

Joins map 660
Joins map 639
Joins map 606
Joins map 605

WARNING: Visitors planning to enter the Desert Parks are required to contact National Parks and Wildlife SA. A Desert Parks Pass is necessary.

WARNINGS: In outback Australia, long distances separate some towns. Travellers should familiarise themselves with prevailing conditions before departure and take care to ensure their vehicle is roadworthy. Adequate supplies of petrol, water and food should be carried at all times.

In central Australia, rainfall can make some roads impassable, even with a 4WD vehicle. Full information on road conditions should be obtained from local authorities before departure.

If visitors intend diverting off public roads within Aboriginal Land areas, a permit is required from the relevant Aboriginal authority.

I J K L M N O P

Blackall

Landsborough

Welford National Park

Idalia National Park

Hell Hole Gorge NP

Mariala National Park

Tambo

Augathella

Charleville Sommariva

Diamantina Dev.

Windorah

Diamantina

Eromanga Quilpie Cheepie Cooladdi Fox Trap Roadhouse

Mitchell Hwy

Toompine Roadhouse

Wyandra

Coleman Range

Mcgregor Range

Grey Range

Norley Range

Moriarty Range

Strzelecki Desert

Bulloo Range

Noccundra

Thargomindah

Lake Bindegolly NP

Yowah

Eulo **Cunnamulla**

Balonne Hwy

Currawinya National Park

Culgoa Floodplain NP

QUEENSLAND
NEW SOUTH WALES

Hungerford Barringun

Ledknapper NR

Culgoa NP

Enngonia

Mitchell Hwy

Wanaaring Yantabulla

Nocoleche NR

MAPS

TASMANIA

671

620

672–3

Tasmania

667

INTER-CITY ROUTES	DISTANCE
Hobart–Launceston via Midland Hwy	197 km
Hobart–Devonport via Midland & Bass hwys	279 km

Approximate Distances TASMANIA	Burnie	Campbell Town	Deloraine	Devonport	Geeveston	George Town	Hobart	Launceston	New Norfolk	Oatlands	Port Arthur	Queenstown	Richmond	Rosebery	St Helens	St Marys	Scottsdale	Smithton	Sorell	Strahan	Swansea	Ulverstone
Burnie		200	101	50	391	204	333	152	328	247	432	163	304	110	300	263	222	88	318	185	267	28
Campbell Town	200		99	150	191	119	133	67	128	47	232	304	104	357	122	85	137	288	118	344	67	172
Deloraine	101	99		51	290	103	232	51	227	146	331	207	203	211	199	162	121	189	217	247	166	73
Devonport	50	150	51		341	154	283	102	278	197	382	213	254	160	250	213	172	138	268	235	217	22
Geeveston	391	191	290	341		310	58	258	95	144	157	308	85	361	313	276	328	479	84	348	197	363
George Town	204	119	103	154	310		252	52	247	166	351	310	223	314	182	182	83	292	237	350	186	176
Hobart	333	133	232	283	58	252		200	37	86	99	250	27	303	265	228	270	421	26	290	139	305
Launceston	152	67	51	102	258	52	200		195	114	299	258	171	262	167	130	70	240	185	298	134	124
New Norfolk	328	128	227	278	95	247	37	195		81	136	213	64	266	250	213	265	416	63	253	176	300
Oatlands	247	47	146	197	144	166	86	114	81		175	257	57	310	169	132	184	335	71	297	125	219
Port Arthur	432	232	331	382	157	351	99	299	136	175		349	87	402	312	275	369	520	73	389	186	404
Queenstown	163	304	207	213	308	310	250	258	213	257	349		277	53	426	389	328	253	276	40	389	191
Richmond	304	104	203	254	85	223	27	171	64	57	87	277		330	226	189	241	392	14	317	123	276
Rosebery	110	357	211	160	361	314	303	262	266	310	402	53	330		410	373	332	222	329	75	442	138
St Helens	300	122	199	250	313	182	265	167	250	169	312	426	226	410		37	99	388	240	466	126	272
St Marys	263	85	162	213	276	182	228	130	213	132	275	389	189	373	37		136	351	203	429	89	235
Scottsdale	222	137	121	172	328	83	270	70	265	184	369	328	241	332	99	136		310	255	368	204	194
Smithton	88	288	189	138	479	292	421	240	416	335	520	253	392	222	388	351	310		406	275	355	116
Sorell	318	118	217	268	84	237	26	185	63	71	73	276	14	329	240	203	255	406		316	113	290
Strahan	185	344	247	235	348	350	290	298	253	297	389	40	317	75	466	429	368	275	316		429	213
Swansea	267	67	166	217	197	186	139	134	176	125	186	389	123	442	126	89	204	355	113	429		239
Ulverstone	28	172	73	22	363	176	305	124	300	219	404	191	276	138	272	235	194	116	290	213	239	

Distances on this chart have been calculated over main roads and do not necessarily reflect the shortest route between towns.

0   0.25   0.5   0.75   1 km

Accommodation ■
Barton Cottage 1 F9
Colville Cottage 2 G9
Grand Mercure Hobart Hadleys Hotel
   & Apartments 3 E7
The Henry Jones Art Hotel 4 G6
Leisure Inn Hobart Macquarie 5 E8
Lenna of Hobart 6 G8
The Old Woolstore Apartment Hotel 7 G6
Salamanca Inn 8 F8
Somerset on the Pier 9 G7
Note: Only a sample range of
accommodation is listed; inclusion is
not necessarily a recommendation.

General Information ■
Brooke Street Pier 10 F7
General Post Office 11 F7
Hobart Transit Centre 12 D8
Metro Tasmania Bus Terminal 13 F7
Motoring Organisation (RACT) 14 D6
Police Headquarters 15 F6
Qantas Travel Centre 16 E7
Tasmanian Travel &
   Information Centre 17 F7
Tigerline Coach Terminal 18 E6

Places of Interest ■
Arthur's Circus 19 G9
Cat and Fiddle Arcade 20 E7
Cenotaph 21 G5
Constitution Dock 22 F7
Elizabeth Street Mall 23 E7
Federation Concert Hall 24 G6
Franklin Square 25 F7
Gasworks Shopping Village 26 G6
Government House 27 G3
Ingle Hall 28 F7
Kelly's Steps 29 G8
Maritime Museum of Tasmania 30 F7
Narryna Heritage Museum 31 F9
Parliament House 32 F8
Penitentiary Chapel & Criminal Court
   (National Trust HQ) 33 E5
Queens Domain 34 E3
Salamanca Arts Centre 35 G8
Salamanca Place 36 F8
Signal Station 37 G8
State Library/Allport Library
   & Museum of Fine Arts 38 E7
Tasmanian Museum &
   Art Gallery 39 F7
Theatre Royal 40 F6
Town Hall 41 F7
Victoria Dock 42 G7
Wrest Point Tasmania 43 G12

INDEX OF PLACE NAMES

This index includes all towns, localities, roadhouses and national parks shown on the maps and mentioned in the text. In addition, it includes major places of interest, landforms and water features.

Place names are followed by a map page number and grid reference, and/or the text page number on which that place is mentioned. A page number set in **bold** type indicates the main text entry for that place. For example:

Barcaldine Qld 654 D10, 661 P10, 428, **431**

Barcaldine	– Place Name
Qld	– State
654 D10, 661 P10	– Barcaldine appears on these map pages
428, **431**	– Barcaldine is mentioned on these pages
431	– Main entry for Barcaldine

The alphabetical order followed in the index is that of 'word-by-word' – a space is considered to come before 'A' in the alphabet, and the index has been ordered accordingly. For example:

White Hills
White Mountains
White Rock
Whitefoord
Whiteheads Creek
Whiteman

Names beginning with Mc are indexed as Mac and those beginning with St as Saint.

The following abbreviations and contractions are used in the index:

ACT	–	Australian Capital Territory
JBT	–	Jervis Bay Territory
NSW	–	New South Wales
NP	–	National Park
NT	–	Northern Territory
Qld	–	Queensland
SA	–	South Australia
Tas.	–	Tasmania
Vic.	–	Victoria
WA	–	Western Australia

Bagshot Vic. 579 G2, 584 A8, 591 O9

Bailieston Vic. 584 D9, 204

Baird Bay SA 602 A4, 611 N11, 279

Bairnsdale Vic. 583 M5, 159, **163–4**, 200, 210

Bajool Qld 655 M11

Bakara SA 601 E2, 603 M8

Baker Vic. 590 E6

Bakers Creek Qld 649 G8, 655 K6

Bakers Hill WA 615 F3, 618 D4

Bakers Swamp NSW 554 F3

Baking Board Qld 653 J7

Balaklava SA 599 H4, 603 J7, **247**

Balcatta WA 614 D5

Balcombe Vic. 575 J6

Bald Hills Qld 644 E5, 645 D3, 647 F10

Bald Rock Vic. 559 I12, 584 A5, 591 O6

Bald Rock NP NSW 551 A4, 557 L3, 653 L12, **98**, 475

Bald Rock NP Qld 551 A4

Baldivis WA 614 D11, 615 C7

Baldry NSW 554 E3

Balfes Creek Qld 654 E3

Balfour Tas. 672 B6

Balgal Beach Qld 650 F9, 657 M11

Balgo Hills WA 625 N10

Balgowan SA 599 D4, 602 H7, 264

Balgowlah NSW 542 G6, 543 C12, 545 M8

Balgownie NSW 552 C3, 553 F4

Balhannah SA 596 F8, 597 D9, 598 H3

Balingup WA 616 G6, 618 C9, 620 C10, **318**

Balintore Vic. 572 B8, 580 B1, 593 L8

Ball Bay Qld 649 G7, 655 K5, 461

Balladonia WA 621 K7, 310, **318**, 322

Balladoran NSW 556 C11

Ballajura WA 614 D5, 615 C4

Ballalaba NSW 554 G11, 565 E5, 567 J5

Ballan Vic. 572 F3, 579 F11, 593 N4, 163

Ballan North Vic. 572 F3, 579 F10, 593 N4

Ballandean Qld 551 A4, 557 K3, 653 K12, 418, 475

Ballangeich Vic. 580 D7, 592 H7

Ballarat Vic. 572 D3, 577, 579 C10, 593 M4, 154, 162, **166–7**

Ballark Vic. 572 E4, 579 E12, 593 N5

Ballaying WA 618 F8

Ballbank NSW 558 H10, 591 N3

Balldale NSW 559 N11, 585 J4

Ballendella Vic. 584 B6, 591 P8

Balliang Vic. 572 F5, 582 A4, 593 O5

Ballidu WA 618 D1, 620 C5

Ballimore NSW 554 F1, 556 D12

Ballina NSW 551 G5, 557 O3, 653 N12, **40**

Balls Pyramid NSW 37

Ballyrogan Vic. 593 J3

Balmattum Vic. 584 F9, 586 B6

Balmoral NSW 543 F4, 549 B10

Balmoral Vic. 590 E12, 592 E2, 172

Balnarring Vic. 570 E12, 573 J10, 575 K8, 582 C7, 180

Balnarring Beach Vic. 575 K9

Balook Vic. 583 I8

Balranald NSW 558 H7, 589 M9, **40–1**

Balrootan North Vic. 558 C12, 590 E7

Balumbah SA 602 E4, 604 D11

Bamaga Qld 658 C3

Bamawm Vic. 559 I12, 584 B6, 591 P7

Bamawm Extension Vic. 584 B6, 591 P7

Bambaroo Qld 650 E9, 657 M10

Bambill Vic. 558 C6, 588 E7, 603 P8

Bamboo Creek WA 622 F2, 624 F12, 627 L4

Bambra Vic. 572 D9, 580 E2, 593 M8

Bamganie Vic. 572 D6, 593 M6

Banana Qld 653 I2

Bancroft Qld 653 K3

Bandiana Vic. 554 A12, 585 K6, 587 I2, 214

Bandon Grove NSW 549 D3, 550 B9, 555 M2

Banealla SA 601 F6, 603 N12

Bangadilly NP NSW 553 A4, 555 I8, 565 F2

Bangalow NSW 551 G4, 557 O3, 653 N12, 53

Bangerang Vic. 590 H6

Bangham SA 590 B8, 601 G8

Bangor Tas. 673 K7, 675 H7

Baniyala NT 635 M6

Banksia NSW 545 L10

Banksia Beach Qld 644 G1, 647 G7

Banksia Grove WA 614 C3

Bankstown NSW 542 C8, 545 K9

Bannaby NSW 554 H8, 565 F2

Bannerton Vic. 558 F7, 589 J9

Bannister NSW 554 G8, 565 E2

Bannister WA 615 G9, 618 D6

Bannockburn Vic. 572 E7, 593 N7

Banora Point NSW 551 H2, 557 O2, 645 G12, 646 H11, 653 N11

Banyan Vic. 591 I3

Banyena Vic. 591 I9

Bar Beach NSW 548 C9

Barabba SA 597 B2, 599 H4

Baradine NSW 556 D8

Barakee NP NSW 550 B6, 557 J11

Barakula Qld 653 J6

Baralaba Qld 653 I1, 655 L12, 432

Baranduda Vic. 585 K6, 587 I3

Barcaldine Qld 654 D10, 661 P10, 428, **431**

Barellan NSW 554 A7, 559 N7

Barellan Point Qld 644 B8

Barfold Vic. 579 H6, 584 A11, 591 P12, 593 P1

Bargara Qld 648 D2, 653 M3, 436

Bargo NSW 553 D3, 555 J8, 565 G2

Barham NSW 559 I10, 584 A2, 591 O4, 35, **41**

Baring Vic. 558 D9, 588 G12, 590 G2

Baringhup Vic. 579 D5, 591 N11, 593 N1

Barjarg Vic. 584 G10, 586 D8

Bark Hut Inn NT 632 H6

Barkers Creek Vic. 579 F6, 584 A10, 591 O11, 593 O1

Barkly Vic. 591 K11

Barkly Homestead NT 637 L9

Barkly Tableland NT & Qld 393, 440

Barkstead Vic. 572 E2, 579 E9, 593 N3

Barmah Vic. 559 J12, 584 D5

Barmah State Park Vic. 157, **178**

Barmedman NSW 554 C6, 559 P6

Barmera SA 558 A6, 601 G1, 603 N7, 241, **247–8**

Barmundu Qld 653 K1

Barnadown Vic. 579 H2, 584 B8, 591 P9

Barnard Island Group NP Qld 650 F5, 651 H12, 657 M8

Barnawartha Vic. 554 A12, 559 N12, 585 J6, 586 H2, 170

Barnes NSW 559 J12, 584 C5

Barnes Bay Tas. 669 I8, 671 K8

Barongarook Vic. 572 B10, 580 B3, 593 L9, 172

Barongarook West Vic. 572 B9, 580 B2, 593 K8

Barooga NSW 559 L11, 584 G4, 35, 157, 170

Barool NP NSW 551 B8, 557 L5

Baroota SA 603 I3, 604 G11

Barossa Valley SA 221, 233, **238**, 246, 263, **270**, **279**

Barpinba Vic. 572 B7, 593 L7

Barraba NSW 556 H7, **41**, **43**

Barrakee Vic. 591 L7

Barramunga Vic. 572 B11, 580 C4, 593 L9

Barranyi (North Island) NP NT 635 N10, 637 N1, 381, 388

Barraport Vic. 558 H11, 591 M6

Barringo Vic. 570 B1, 579 H9, 582 B2, 584 B12

Barrington NSW 550 C8, 555 M1, 557 J12

Barrington Tas. 672 H7, 674 G3

Barrington Tops NP NSW 549 A1, 550 A8, 555 L1, 557 I12, 26, **65**

Barringun NSW 561 M2, 652 A11, 663 N11

Barron Gorge NP Qld 650 D2, 651 E6, 657 L6, **456**

Barrow Creek NT 639 I2, **387**

Barry NSW 554 G5, 557 I11

Barrys Reef Vic. 572 F2, 579 F9, 582 A2, 593 O3

Barton ACT 562 D10

Barton Vic. 593 I2

Barunga NT 634 G8

Barunga Gap SA 599 G2, 603 I6

Barwidgee Creek Vic. 585 K8, 586 H5

Barwo Vic. 584 D5

Barwon Downs Vic. 572 C10, 580 C3, 593 L9

Barwon Heads Vic. 572 G9, 574 C6, 580 H2, 582 A7, 593 O8, **198**

Baryulgil NSW 551 C6, 557 M4

Basin View NSW 553 C11, 567 O2

Basket Swamp NP NSW 551 B5, 557 L3, 653 L12

Bass Vic. 573 L11, 575 O11, 582 E8

Bass Landing Vic. 575 N11

Bass Strait Islands Tas. 505

Batchelor NT 632 E7, 634 D5, **387**

Batchica Vic. 558 E12, 590 H6

Bateau Bay NSW 543 E8, 545 P2

Batehaven NSW 554 H12, 567 L6

Batemans Bay NSW 554 H12, 565 F6, 567 L6, **42**

Bates SA 611 J3

Batesford Vic. 572 F7, 574 A2, 593 N7

Bathumi Vic. 584 H5, 586 E1

Bathurst NSW 554 H5, 30, **43**

Bathurst Island NT 634 D, 367, 377, 380

Batlow NSW 554 D11, 565 A5, 566 C4, 585 P3, 34, **43–4**

Battery Hill NT 393

Battery Point Tas. 667 E8, 666 F8, 492, 494, 496, 497

Bauhinia Qld 652 H2

Bauhinia Downs NT 635 L11, 637 L2

Baulkham Hills NSW 542 C5, 545 J7

Bauple Qld 648 D7, 653 M5

Baw Baw NP Vic. 573 P6, 582 H5, 583 I5, 150, **194**, 210

Bawley Point NSW 555 I11, 565 F5, 567 N5

Baxter Vic. 570 E10, 573 J9, 575 K5, 582 D6

Bay of Fires Tas. 516, 526

Bayles Vic. 573 M9, 582 E6

Baynton Vic. 584 B11, 591 P12, 593 P2

Bayswater Vic. 570 G6, 571 A8

Bayswater WA 614 E5

Bayview NSW 542 H4, 543 C10, 545 N6

Beachmere Qld 644 F2, 645 E1, 647 F8, 653 N8, 439

Beachport SA 601 E10, **248**

Beacon WA 618 F1, 620 D5

Beaconsfield Tas. 673 J6, 675 E7, **507**

Beaconsfield Vic. 570 G8, 571 B11, 573 K7, 575 N3, 582 E6

Beagle Bay WA 624 H6, 628 B9, 321

Bealiba Vic. 579 A3, 591 L10, 176

Beardmore Vic. 583 I5

Beargamil NSW 554 E3

Bearii Vic. 559 K11, 584 E4

Bears Lagoon Vic. 558 H12, 591 N7

Beauchamp Vic. 591 L3

Beaudesert Qld 551 F1, 557 N1, 645 C9, 653 M10, 417, **432**

Beaufort SA 599 G3, 603 I6

Beaufort Vic. 572 A2, 593 K3, 166–7

Beaumaris Tas. 673 O8, 526

Beaumaris Vic. 575 J1

Beauty Point NSW 543 E5, 549 A11, 565 E8, 567 K11

Beauty Point Tas. 673 J6, 675 E6, **507**

Beazleys Bridge Vic. 591 J9

Beckom NSW 554 B7, 559 O7

Bedarra Island Qld 421

Bedgerebong NSW 554 D4

Buckland Vic. 585 K10, 586 H8
Buckleboo SA 602 E3, 604 D10
Buckley Vic. 572 E8, 580 F1, 593 N8
Buckrabanyule Vic. 558 G12, 591 L7
Budawang NP NSW 554 H11, 565 E5, 567 L4
Buddabaddah NSW 561 O11
Budderoo NP NSW 553 D7, 555 J9, 565 G3, 24, **72**, 92, 94
Buddigower NSW 554 B6, 559 O6
Buddina Qld 647 H4, 648 F12
Buderim Qld 647 G4, 648 F12, 653 N7, **435**
Budgeree Vic. 573 P11, 582 H8
Budgeree East Vic. 582 H8
Budgerum Vic. 591 L4
Budgewoi NSW 543 F6, 549 B12
Buffalo Vic. 573 O12, 582 G9
Buffalo Creek Vic. 585 J9, 586 H6
Buffalo River Vic. 585 J9, 586 H6
Bugaldie NSW 556 D9
Bugilbone NSW 556 D5
Bugong NP NSW 553 C8, 555 I9, 565 G3
Builyan Qld 653 L2
Bukalong NSW 565 C9, 581 E6
Bukkulla NSW 557 I5
Bulahdelah NSW 549 H4, 550 C10, 555 N3, **49**, **51**
Bulart Vic. 592 F3
Buldah Vic. 565 C10, 581 E9
Bulga NSW 555 K3
Bulgandramine NSW 554 E2
Bulgobac Tas. 672 E8, 674 B5
Bulla NT 625 P4, 629 P5, 634 C11, 636 C2
Bulla Vic. 570 C4, 573 I4, 582 B3
Bullaburra NSW 544 E6, 546 H9
Bullarah NSW 556 E4
Bullaring WA 618 F6, 620 E8
Bullarook Vic. 572 D3, 579 D10, 593 M4
Bullarto Vic. 572 F2, 579 F9, 593 N3, 177
Bullarto South Vic. 572 F2, 579 F9
Bullengarook Vic. 572 G3, 579 H10, 582 A2, 593 O4
Bullengarook East Vic. 572 G3, 579 H10, 582 A2
Bulleringa NP Qld 657 I7
Bullfinch WA 618 H2, 620 F6
Bullhead Creek Vic. 585 M8, 587 K4
Bulli NSW 553 G4
Bullioh Vic. 585 M7, 587 L3
Bullita NT 395
Bullock Creek Qld 650 A5, 657 J7
Bullocks Flat NSW 566 D10, 581 B4, 33, 72, 73
Bullsbrook WA 614 E2, 615 C3, 618 C4, 620 C7
Bullumwaal Vic. 583 M4
Bulman NT 635 J6
Buln Buln Vic. 571 H12, 573 N8, 582 G6
Buln Buln East Vic. 571 H12, 573 O8, 582 G6
Bulwer Qld 645 G1, 653 N8
Bulyee WA 618 F5, 620 D8
Bumbaldry NSW 554 E6

Bumberry NSW 554 E4
Bumbunga SA 599 G2, 603 I6
Bunbartha Vic. 559 K12, 584 E6
Bunburra Qld 551 D1, 645 A9
Bunbury WA 616 D4, 618 C8, 620 C9, **323**
Bundaberg Qld 648 D2, 653 M3, **436–7**
Bundaburrah NSW 554 D5
Bundalaguah Vic. 583 K6
Bundaleer Forest Reserve SA 259
Bundalong Vic. 559 M12, 584 H5, 586 E1
Bundalong South Vic. 584 H6, 586 E2
Bundanoon NSW 553 A7, 555 I9, 565 G3, 24, **51**
Bundarra NSW 557 I7
Bundeena NSW 542 E11, 545 L12, 555 K7
Bundella NSW 556 F10
Bunding Vic. 572 E3, 579 E10, 593 N4
Bundjalung NP NSW 551 F7, 557 O5, 62, 71
Bundook NSW 550 C8, 555 N1, 557 K12
Bundure NSW 559 M9
Bung Bong Vic. 579 A6, 591 L12, 593 L1
Bunga NSW 565 E8, 567 K12
Bungador Vic. 580 A2, 593 K8
Bungal Vic. 572 E4, 579 E11, 593 N5
Bungarby NSW 565 C9, 566 F12, 581 E5
Bungaree Vic. 572 D3, 579 D10, 593 M4
Bungawalbin NP NSW 551 F6, 557 N4
Bungeet Vic. 584 H7, 586 D3
Bungendore NSW 554 G10, 564 H5, 565 D4, 567 I3, 31, **91**, 125
Bungil Vic. 554 B12, 585 M6, 587 L2
Bungle Bungle NP *see* **Purnululu NP**
Bungonia NSW 554 H9, 565 F3, **66**
Bungowannah NSW 554 A12, 585 K5, 587 I1
Bungulla NSW 551 A5, 557 L4, 653 L12
Bungulla WA 618 F4
Bunguluke Vic. 558 G12, 591 L6
Bungunya Qld 556 F1, 652 H10
Bungwahl NSW 550 D10, 555 N3
Buninyong Vic. 572 D4, 579 C11, 593 M4, **166**
Bunjil's Shelter Vic. 208
Bunnaloo NSW 559 J11, 584 B3, 591 P5
Bunnan NSW 555 J1, 556 G12
Buntine WA 620 C5
Bunya Mountains NP Qld 653 K7, 415, 446, **455**
Bunyah NSW 550 D9, 555 N2
Bunyan NSW 565 C7, 566 G9, 581 F3
Bunyip Vic. 571 E12, 573 M8, 582 F6
Buraja NSW 559 M11, 585 I4

Burbank Qld 645 E5, 647 G12
Burbong NSW 563 H7, 564 G5, 566 H3
Burcher NSW 554 C5, 559 P5
Burekup WA 616 E3, 618 C8
Burgooney NSW 554 A4, 559 N4
Burke & Wills Dig Tree SA 258, 434
Burke & Wills Roadhouse Qld 656 B10, 659 F8
Burkes Flat Vic. 579 A2, 591 L9
Burketown Qld 656 A7, 659 D4, 427, **435**, **437**
Burleigh Head NP Qld 645 G10, 646 F8, 437
Burleigh Heads Qld 551 G1, 557 O1, 645 G10, 646 F8, 653 N11, **437**
Burleigh Waters Qld 646 F8
Burnbank Vic. 579 A7, 591 L12, 593 L2
Burnett Heads Qld 648 D1, 653 M3
Burnie Tas. 672 F5, 503, **509**
Burns WA 614 B3, 615 B4
Burns Creek Tas. 673 L8
Burnt Yards NSW 554 F5
Buronga NSW 588 G6
Burpengary Qld 644 E2, 645 D1, 647 F8, 653 N8
Burra SA 603 K5, 233, 239, **250–1**
Burraboi NSW 559 I10, 584 A1, 591 O2
Burracoppin WA 618 G3, 620 E6
Burradoo NSW 553 B5
Burraga NSW 554 G6
Burragate NSW 581 G8
Burramine South Vic. 584 G5, 586 C1
Burrandana NSW 554 B10, 559 P10, 585 M2
Burrawang NSW 553 C6, 555 I9, 565 G3, 24, 92
Burrell Creek NSW 550 D8, 555 N1, 557 K12
Burren Junction NSW 556 D6
Burrereo Vic. 591 I8
Burrier NSW 553 B9, 567 N1
Burrill Lake NSW 555 I11, 565 G5, 567 N4
Burringbar NSW 551 G3, 557 O2, 653 N11
Burringurrah WA 619 F6, 622 C7
Burrinjuck NSW 554 E9, 565 B3
Burroin Vic. 558 E10, 590 H3
Burrowa–Pine Mountain NP Vic. 554 C12, 559 P12, 566 A7, 585 O6, 587 N2, **173**
Burroway NSW 556 B11
Burrowye Vic. 554 C12, 559 P12, 585 N6, 587 M2
Burrum Vic. 591 I9
Burrum Coast NP Qld 648 D3, 653 M4, **436**, 442, 451
Burrum Heads Qld 648 E4, 653 N4, 420, 451
Burrumbeet Vic. 572 C2, 579 B9, 593 L3
Burrumbuttock NSW 554 A11, 559 N11, 585 K4
Burswood WA 614 E6, 615 C5
Burwood NSW 542 D7
Burwood Vic. 573 J6

Bushfield Vic. 580 C7, 592 G8
Bushy Park Tas. 668 F3, 671 I6
Bushy Park Vic. 583 K5
Busselton WA 616 C6, 618 B9, 620 B10, 307, **321–2**
Butchers Ridge NSW 565 A10
Butchers Ridge Vic. 581 A8, 583 P2, 587 P12
Bute SA 599 F2, 603 I6
Butler Tanks SA 602 E6
Butlers Gorge Tas. 670 G3
Butmaroo NSW 554 G10, 565 D4, 567 I2
Butterfly Gorge Nature Park NT 393
Butterleaf NP NSW 551 A7, 557 K5
Buxton NSW 553 D3, 555 I8, 565 G2
Buxton Qld 648 D4, 653 M4, 442
Buxton Vic. 571 F4, 573 N3, 582 F2, 586 B12, 193
Byabarra NSW 550 E6, 557 L11
Byaduk Vic. 592 E5, 155, 181
Byaduk North Vic. 592 E5
Byawatha Vic. 585 J7, 586 G3
Byfield NP Qld 655 N10, **483**
Byford WA 614 F9, 615 D7, 618 C5
Bylands Vic. 570 D1, 573 J2, 582 C2, 584 C12
Bylong NSW 555 I2
Bymount Qld 652 F5
Byrne Vic. 585 I8, 586 F5
Byrneside Vic. 584 D7
Byrnestown Qld 648 A5, 653 L4
Byrneville Vic. 590 G8
Byrock NSW 561 N7
Byron Bay NSW 551 H4, 557 O3, 653 N12, 2, 3, 28, **53**

C

Cabarita Vic. 558 D6, 588 G6
Cabarlah Qld 653 L9, 479
Cabawin Qld 653 I8
Cabbage Tree Creek Vic. 565 B12, 581 C11, 200
Cable Beach WA 289, 314, **321**
Caboolture Qld 644 E1, 645 D1, 647 F7, 653 N8, **437**
Caboonbah Qld 647 B7, 653 M8
Cabramatta NSW 542 B7, 545 J9, 555 J7, 565 H1
Cabramurra NSW 554 D12, 565 B6, 566 D7, 581 B1, 3
Cactus Beach SA 221, 244, 251
Cadbury Visitor Centre Tas. 496
Cadell SA 603 M6, 269
Cadney Homestead SA 609 N7
Cadoux WA 618 E2, 620 D6
Cahills Crossing NT 633 P2, 634 H4
Caiguna WA 621 M7, 310, 318, **322**, 325
Cairns Qld 650 E2, 651 F7, 657 L6, 399, 425, 426, **438–9**, 481
Cairns Bay Tas. 668 F9, 671 I9
Calala NSW 557 I9
Calamvale Qld 644 E9, 645 D6
Calca SA 602 A3, 611 N11
Calder Tas. 672 E5

D

S

Sackville North NSW 545 J3
Saddleworth SA 603 K6
Safety Bay WA 614 C11, 615 B8
Safety Beach NSW 551 E11, 557 N7
Safety Beach Vic. 570 D11, 573 I9, 575 I7, 582 C7
St Albans NSW 543 A6, 555 K5
St Albans Vic. 570 C5, 573 I5, 582 B4, 593 P5
St Albans Park Vic. 574 B4
St Andrews Vic. 570 G3, 571 B5, 573 K4, 582 D3
St Andrews Beach Vic. 574 G9
St Arnaud Vic. 591 K9, 154, 162, **205**
St Arnaud Range NP Vic. 591 K10, **205**
St Aubyn Qld 653 L8
St Clair NSW 549 A3, 555 L2
St Fillans Vic. 571 F5, 573 M4, 582 F3
St George Qld 652 F9, **473–4**
St Georges Basin NSW 553 C11, 555 I10, 565 G4, 567 O2
St Helena Island Qld 416
St Helena Island NP Qld 644 G6, 645 F4, 647 H11, 653 N9
St Helens Tas. 673 O8, 500, **526–7**
St Helens Vic. 580 A7, 592 F7
St Ives NSW 542 F5, 543 B11, 545 L7
St James Vic. 584 G7, 586 C3
St Kilda SA 596 B4, 597 B7, 599 H6, 601 B2, 603 J8
St Kilda Vic. 570 D6, 573 I6, 582 C5
St Kitts SA 597 F3
St Lawrence Qld 649 H11, 655 K8, 474
St Leonards NSW 541 A2, 542 F7, 545 L8
St Leonards Tas. 673 K8, 675 H10
St Leonards Vic. 570 B9, 572 H8, 574 F4, 582 B6, 593 P7, 176
St Marys NSW 544 H7, 547 O11
St Marys Tas. 673 O9, 500, **527**
St Patricks River Tas. 673 L7
St Pauls Qld 658 C1
St Peter Island SA 611 M9
St Peters NSW 543 F1, 549 B7
Sale Vic. 583 K7, 159, 163, **205**
Salisbury NSW 549 C2, 550 A9, 555 L2
Salisbury SA 596 D4, 597 C7, 599 H6, 601 B2, 603 J8
Salisbury Vic. 558 C12, 590 E7
Salisbury West Vic. 579 D1, 591 N8
Sallys Flat NSW 554 H4
Salmon Gums WA 621 I8
Salmon Ponds Tas. 668 G3, 498
Salt Ash NSW 549 E8, 550 B12
Salt Creek SA 601 E6
Salter Springs SA 597 C1, 599 H4, 601 B1, 603 J7
Saltwater River Tas. 669 L7, 671 L8
Samaria Vic. 584 H9, 586 D7
Samford Qld 644 C5, 645 C3, 647 E10

San Remo Vic. 573 K11, 575 N11, 582 D8, 174
Sanctuary Cove Qld 645 F8, 646 E3, 653 N10
Sanctuary Point NSW 553 D11
Sandalwood SA 601 F3, 603 M9
Sandbanks NP Qld 658 F9
Sandergrove SA 598 H6, 601 C4
Sanderston SA 597 H7, 601 D2, 603 K8
Sandfire Roadhouse WA 624 F10, 627 N1
Sandfly Tas. 668 H6, 671 J8
Sandford Tas. 669 K6, 671 L7
Sandford Vic. 592 D3, 601 H11
Sandgate Qld 644 F5, 645 E3, 647 F10
Sandhill Tas. 675 G3
Sandhill Lake Vic. 558 H11, 591 M4
Sandigo NSW 554 A9, 559 N9
Sandilands SA 599 E5, 602 H8
Sandon Vic. 579 E7, 591 N12, 593 N2
Sandringham Vic. 570 D7, 573 J6, 575 J1, 582 C5
Sandsmere Vic. 558 B12, 590 C7, 601 H7
Sandstone WA 620 F1, 622 F12
Sandy Bay Tas. 666 D10, 667 D9, 669 I6, 671 K7
Sandy Bay Beach Tas. 496
Sandy Beach NSW 551 E11, 557 N7
Sandy Creek SA 596 F2, 597 D5
Sandy Creek Vic. 585 L7, 587 J4
Sandy Creek Upper Vic. 585 L7, 587 J4
Sandy Flat NSW 551 A6, 557 L4
Sandy Hill NSW 551 B5, 557 L3, 653 L12
Sandy Hollow NSW 555 J2, 84
Sandy Point NSW 542 C9, 545 J10, 554 H10, 565 E4, 567 K2
Sandy Point Vic. 581 A10, 582 G10, 583 P4, 180
Sangar NSW 559 M11, 584 H3
Santa Barbara Qld 645 F8, 646 E3
Santa Teresa (Ltyente Purte) NT 639 J7, 641 L6
Sapphire NSW 557 J5
Sapphire Qld 654 H10, 447
Sapphiretown SA 599 E11, 602 H11
Sarabah NP Qld 551 F1, 557 N1, 645 D10, 653 N10
Sarah Island Tas. 530
Saratoga NSW 543 D8, 545 O3
Sarina Qld 649 G8, 655 K6, **474**
Sarina Beach Qld 649 G8, 655 K6
Sarsfield Vic. 583 N5
Sassafras NSW 553 A11, 555 I10, 565 F4, 567 M2
Sassafras Tas. 672 H7, 675 B7
Sassafras Vic. 571 B9, 198
Sassafras East Tas. 673 I7, 675 C7
Saunders Islands NP Qld 658 E5
Savage River Tas. 672 C8
Savage River NP Tas. 672 D6, 674 A1, **532**
Savannahlander Qld 465
Savenake NSW 559 M11, 584 H4

Sawmill Settlement Vic. 583 I1, 585 I11, 586 F10
Sawpit Creek NSW 566 D9, 581 C3, 73
Sawtell NSW 550 H1, 551 E12, 557 N8
Sawyers Valley WA 614 H5, 615 E4
Sayers Lake NSW 558 G1, 560 F12
Scaddan WA 621 I9
Scamander Tas. 673 O8, 527
Scarborough NSW 553 G3, 555 J8, 565 H2
Scarborough Qld 644 F3, 645 E2, 647 G9
Scarborough WA 614 C5, 615 B5, 618 B5, 620 B7, 299
Scarsdale Vic. 572 B4, 579 B11, 593 L4
Sceale Bay SA 602 A3, 611 N11
Scenic Railway and Skyrail Kuranda Qld 456
Scheyville NSW 542 B2, 545 J5
Scheyville NP NSW 542 B2, 545 J4, 555 J6
Schofields NSW 542 A4, 545 I6, 547 P10
School Hill Vic. 575 I9
Scone NSW 555 K1, 556 H12, **94**
Scotsburn Vic. 572 D4, 579 C11, 593 M4
Scott NP WA 616 C10, 618 B10, 620 B11
Scotts Creek Vic. 580 G9, 593 J9
Scotts Head NSW 550 G3, 557 M9, 78
Scottsdale Tas. 673 M6, **527**
Scottville Qld 649 C5, 655 I4
Sea Elephant Tas. 671 P11
Sea Lake Vic. 558 F10, 591 J3
Seabird WA 618 B3
Seacliff SA 596 B9, 597 B10, 598 E3, 601 B3
Seacombe Vic. 583 L7
Seaford SA 596 A11, 597 A11, 598 E5
Seaford Vic. 570 E9, 573 J8, 575 K3, 582 D6
Seaforth Qld 649 F7, 655 K5, 461
Seaforth WA 614 F8
Seaham NSW 543 H1, 549 D6, 550 A11, 555 M3
Seahampton NSW 543 F3, 549 C9
Seal Bay Conservation Park SA 236, **260**
Seal Rocks NSW 550 E10, 555 N3, 51
Seal Rocks Vic. 150, **174**
Seaspray Vic. 583 K8, 205
Seaton Vic. 583 J6
Seaview Vic. 573 N10, 582 G7
Seawinds Vic. 574 H8
Sebastian Vic. 579 F2, 591 O9
Sebastopol NSW 554 C8, 559 P8
Sebastopol Vic. 572 C3, 577 C12, 579 C10
Second Valley SA 598 B8, 599 G10, 601 A4, 603 I11, 285
Sedan SA 597 H5, 601 D2, 603 L8
Sedgwick Vic. 579 G4, 584 A9, 591 O11
Seelands NSW 551 D8, 557 M5
Seisia Qld 658 C3

Selbourne Tas. 673 J8, 675 E10
Selby Vic. 571 B9
Seldom Seen Roadhouse Vic. 565 A10, 581 A8, 583 P2, 585 P12, 587 P11
Sellheim Qld 650 F12, 654 F2
Sellicks Beach SA 598 D6, 599 H9, 601 B4, 603 J10, 245
Semaphore SA 596 B5, 597 A8, 598 E1
Separation Creek Vic. 572 C11, 580 D5, 593 M10
Seppeltsfield SA 597 E4, 603 K8
Serpentine Vic. 591 N8
Serpentine WA 614 F11, 615 D8, 618 C6
Serpentine NP WA 614 G11, 615 D8, 618 C6, 620 C8
Serviceton Vic. 558 B12, 590 B7, 601 H7
Seven Mile Beach Tas. 669 K5, 671 L7
Seven Mile Beach NP NSW 553 E9, 555 J9, 565 G3, 567 P1, 74
Sevenhill SA 599 H2, 603 J6, 239
Seventeen Seventy Qld 653 M1, 462
Severnlea Qld 551 A3, 557 K2, 653 K11
Seville Vic. 570 H6, 571 C8, 573 L5, 582 E4
Sexton Hill NSW 646 H11
Seymour Tas. 673 O10
Seymour Vic. 584 D10, 157, **206**
Shackleton WA 618 F4, 348
Shadforth NSW 554 G5
Shady Creek Vic. 573 O8, 582 G6
Shannon Tas. 671 I2, 673 I11
Shannon WA 617 D3, 618 D11, 620 D11
Shannon NP WA 617 D3, 618 D11, 620 C11, 347
Shannons Flat NSW 554 F12, 564 B12, 565 C6, 566 F7, 581 E1
Shark Bay WA 312, 328
Shay Gap WA 622 E1, 624 E11, 627 L3
Shays Flat Vic. 591 J11, 593 J1
Sheans Creek Vic. 584 F9, 586 B7
Shearwater Tas. 675 C6, 524
Sheep Hills Vic. 558 E12, 590 H7
Sheffield Tas. 672 H7, 674 H3, 675 A8, **527–8**
Shelbourne Vic. 579 E4, 591 N10
Shelford Vic. 572 D7, 593 M6
Shelley Vic. 585 N7, 587 M3
Shellharbour NSW 553 F6, 555 J9, 565 H3, 24, **94–5**
Shelly Beach NSW 40
Shelly Beach Tas. 669 N2, 671 M5
Shenton Park WA 614 D6
Sheoaks Vic. 572 E6, 593 N6
Shepherds Flat Vic. 572 E1, 579 E8, 593 N2, 151
Shepparton Vic. 584 E7, **206**
Sherbrooke Vic. 571 B9
Sheringa SA 602 C6, 254
Sherlock SA 601 E4, 603 M10
Sherwood WA 614 F8
Shipley NSW 544 C5, 546 E7
Shirley Vic. 593 J3

Publications manager
Astrid Browne

Project manager
Melissa Krafchek

Editors
Janet Austin, Juliette Elfick, Elizabeth Watson, Emma Adams, Melissa Krafchek, Tracy O'Shaughnessy, Stephanie Pearson

Researchers
Anthony Roberts, Emily Hewitt, Eddie Pavuna

Design
Erika Budiman

Layout
Megan Ellis, Mike Kuszla

Cartographers
Paul de Leur, Claire Johnston, Bruce McGurty, Emily Maffei, Jason Sankovic

Indexer
Fay Donlevy, Sarah Fraser

Photo selection
Melissa Krafchek

Pre-press
PageSet Digital Print & Pre-press

Writers
NEW SOUTH WALES Introduction by Carolyn Tate; Sydney by Ruth Ward, Jill Varley, Nick Dent; Towns by Carolyn Tate; Where to Eat and Where to Stay by Frances Bruce; AUSTRALIAN CAPITAL TERRITORY Canberra by Alexandra Payne, Natasha Rudra, Margaret Wade; Where to Eat and Where to Stay by Kirsten Lawson, Natasha Rudra; VICTORIA Introduction by Rachel Pitts, Melissa Krafchek; Melbourne by Rachel Pitts, Melissa Krafchek, Michelle Bennett, Heidi Marfurt; Towns by Karina Biggs, Antonia Semler; Where to Eat and Where to Stay by Tricia Welsh; SOUTH AUSTRALIA Introduction by Sue Medlock; Adelaide by Terry Plane, Rachel Pitts, Ingrid Ohlsson, Peter Dyson, Janice Finlayson, Jenny Turner; Towns by Karina Biggs, Rachel Pitts; Where to Eat and Where to Stay by Quentin Chester; WESTERN AUSTRALIA Introduction by Heather Pearson; Perth and Towns by Heather Pearson; Where to Eat and Where to Stay by Carmen Jenner; NORTHERN TERRITORY Introduction and Darwin by David Hancock, Gillian Hutchison; Towns by Carolyn Tate, Helen Duffy, David Hancock, Gillian Hutchison; Where to Eat and Where to Stay by David Hancock; QUEENSLAND Introduction by Sue Medlock; Brisbane by Alexandra Payne, Pamela Robson, Rowan Roebig; Towns by Karina Biggs; Where to Eat and Where to Stay by Liz Johnston; TASMANIA Introduction and Hobart by Sue Medlock; Towns by Emma Schwarcz; Where to Eat and Where to Stay by Sue Medlock

Explore Australia Publishing Pty Ltd
85 High Street, Prahran, Victoria 3181

Explore Australia Publishing Pty Ltd is a division of Hardie Grant Publishing Pty Ltd

hardie grant publishing

This twenty-ninth edition published by Explore Australia Publishing Pty Ltd, 2010

First published by George Phillip & O'Neil Pty Ltd, 1980
Second edition 1981
Third edition 1983
Reprinted 1984
Fourth edition 1985
Fifth edition 1986
Sixth edition published by Penguin Books Australia Ltd, 1987
Seventh edition 1988
Eighth edition 1989
Ninth edition 1990
Tenth edition 1991
Eleventh edition 1992
Twelfth edition 1993
Thirteenth edition 1994
Fourteenth edition 1995
Fifteenth edition 1996
Sixteenth edition 1997
Seventeenth edition 1998
Eighteenth edition 1999
Nineteenth edition 2000
Twentieth edition 2001

Twenty-first edition 2002
Twenty-second edition published by Explore Australia Publishing Pty Ltd, 2003
Twenty-third edition 2004
Twenty-fourth edition 2005
Twenty-fifth edition 2006
Twenty-sixth edition 2007
Twenty-seventh edition 2008
Twenty-eighth edition 2009

Copyright © Explore Australia Publishing Pty Ltd, 2010

The maps in this publication incorporate data copyright © Commonwealth of Australia (Geoscience Australia), 2006. Geoscience Australia has not evaluated the data as altered and incorporated within this publication, and therefore gives no warranty regarding accuracy, completeness, currency or suitability for any particular purpose.

Copyright Imprint and currency – VAR Product and PSMA Data

"Copyright. Based on data provided under licence from PSMA Australia Limited (www.psma.com.au)".

Hydrography Data (May 2006)
Parks & Reserves Data (May 2006)
Transport Data (November 2009)

Disclaimer
While every care is taken to ensure the accuracy of the data within this product, the owners of the data (including the State, Territory and Commonwealth governments of Australia) do not make any representations or warranties about its accuracy, reliability, completeness or suitability for any particular purpose and, to the extent permitted by law, the owners of the data disclaim all responsibility and all liability (including without limitation, liability in negligence) for all expenses, losses, damages, (including indirect or consequential damages) and costs which might be incurred as a result of the data being inaccurate or incomplete in any way and for any reason.

Maps contain Aboriginal Land data (2005), which is owned and copyright of the relevant Queensland, Northern Territory, South Australia and Western Australia state government authorities. The authorities give no warranty in relation to the data (including accuracy, reliability, completeness or suitability) and accept no liability (including without limitation, liability in negligence) for any loss, damage or costs (including consequential damage) relating to any use of the data.

ISBN 13 978 1 74117 338 3

10 9 8 7 6 5 4 3 2 1

All rights reserved. Without limiting the rights under copyright reserved above, no part of this publication may be reproduced, stored in or introduced into a retrieval system, or transmitted in any form or by any means (electronic, mechanical, photocopying, recording or otherwise) without the prior written permission of both the copyright owner and the above publisher of this book.

Printed and bound in China by C & C Offset Printing Co. Ltd

Publisher's Note: Every effort has been made to ensure that the information in this book is accurate at the time of going to press. The publisher welcomes information and suggestions for correction or improvement. Write to the Publications Manager, Explore Australia Publishing, 85 High Street, Prahran, Victoria 3181, Australia, or email info@exploreaustralia.net.au

Disclaimers: The publisher cannot accept responsibility for any errors or omissions. The representation on the maps of any road or track is not necessarily evidence of public right of way or safe travelling conditions.

Assistance with research

The publisher would like to thank the following organisations for assistance with information:

Australian Bureau of Statistics
Bureau of Meteorology
National Road Transport Commission
St John Ambulance
Tristate Fruit Fly Committee

New South Wales
Roads and Traffic Authority
New South Wales National Parks & Wildlife Service
Tourism New South Wales

Australian Capital Territory
Australian Capital Territory Land Information Centre
Australian Capital Tourism Corporation

Victoria
VicRoads
Parks Victoria
Tourism Victoria

South Australia
Transport SA
Primary Industries and Resources South Australia
National Parks & Wildlife South Australia, Department of Environment & Heritage
South Australian Tourism Commission

Western Australia
Main Roads Western Australia
Department of Indigenous Affairs Western Australia
Aboriginal Lands Trust
Department of Conservation & Land Management Western Australia
Western Australia Tourism Commission

Northern Territory
Department of Transport and Infrastructure
Northern and Central land councils
Northern Territory Department of Infrastructure, Planning and the Environment
Parks Australia
Northern Territory Tourist Commission

Queensland
Department of Main Roads
Queensland Department of Natural Resources & Mines
Queensland Parks & Wildlife Service
Tourism Queensland

Tasmania
Department of Infrastructure, Energy & Resources
Parks and Wildlife Service
Tourism Tasmania

USEFUL INFORMATION

STATE TOURIST BUREAUS

New South Wales
Sydney Visitor Centres
Level 1, cnr Argyle and Playfair sts
The Rocks
(02) 9240 8788; 1800 067 676

33 Wheat Rd, Darling Harbour
(02) 9240 8788; 1800 067 676
www.visitnsw.com

Canberra
Canberra and Region Visitors Centre
330 Northbourne Ave, Dickson
1300 554 114
www.visitcanberra.com.au

Victoria
Melbourne Visitor Centre
Federation Square
Cnr Flinders and Swanston sts
Melbourne
(03) 9658 9658
www.visitvictoria.com

Victorian Tourism Information
Service
13 2842

South Australia
South Australian Visitor and Travel
Centre
18 King William St, Adelaide
(08) 8463 4547; 1300 764 227
www.southaustralia.com

Western Australia
Western Australian Visitor Centre
Cnr Forrest Pl and Wellington St
Perth
(08) 9483 1111; 1800 812 808
www.westernaustralia.com

Northern Territory
Tourism Top End
6 Bennett St
Darwin
(08) 8980 6000; 1300 138 886
www.tourismtopend.com.au

Visitor Information Centre Alice
Springs
60 Gregory Tce, Alice Springs
(08) 8952 5800; 1800 645 199
www.centralaustraliantourism.com

Queensland
Brisbane Visitor Information Centre
Queen Street Mall
Between Albert and Edward sts,
Brisbane
(07) 3006 6290
www.queenslandholidays.com.au

Tasmania
Tasmanian Travel and Information
Centre
20 Davey St, Hobart
(03) 6238 4222
www.discovertasmania.com.au

MOTORING ORGANISATIONS

Roadside assistance is one of the
most valued services of Australia's
state-based motoring organisations.
The country-wide network of these
organisations gives members access
to virtually the same services in
every state and territory.

Roadside assistance (country-wide)
13 1111

New South Wales
National Roads and Motorists'
Association (NRMA)
74–76 King St, Sydney
13 1122
www.mynrma.com.au

Australian Capital Territory
National Roads and Motorists'
Association (NRMA)
Shop CG5/6 City Walk, Civic
13 1122
www.mynrma.com.au

Victoria
Royal Automobile Club of Victoria
(RACV)
485 Bourke St, Melbourne
13 7228
www.racv.com.au

South Australia
Royal Automobile Association (RAA)
55 Hindmarsh Sq, Adelaide
(08) 8202 4600
www.raa.net

Western Australia
Royal Automobile Club of Western
Australia (RAC)
832 Wellington St, West Perth
13 1703
www.rac.com.au

Northern Territory
Automobile Association of Northern
Territory (AANT)
79–81 Smith St, Darwin
(08) 8925 5901
www.aant.com.au

Queensland
Royal Automobile Club of
Queensland (RACQ)
261 Queen St, Brisbane
13 1905
www.racq.com.au

Tasmania
Royal Automobile Club of Tasmania
(RACT)
Cnr Patrick and Murray sts, Hobart
13 2722
www.ract.com.au

For Motorcyclists
Motorcycle Riders Association
Australia
www.mraa.org.au

ROADS AND TRAFFIC AUTHORITIES

For licensing and registration,
information on vehicle standards,
and road condition reports.

New South Wales
Roads and Traffic Authority
19 York St, Sydney
13 2213
www.rta.nsw.gov.au

Australian Capital Territory
Road Transport Authority
Dickson Motor Registry
13–15 Challis St, Dickson
13 2281
www.rego.act.gov.au

Victoria
VicRoads Customer Service Centre
459 Lygon St, Carlton
13 1171
www.vicroads.vic.gov.au

South Australia
Transport SA
EDS Centre
108 North Tce, Adelaide
13 1084
www.transport.sa.gov.au

Western Australia
Main Roads Western Australia
Don Aitken Centre
Waterloo Cres, East Perth
13 8138
www.mainroads.wa.gov.au

Northern Territory
Northern Territory Transport Group
Motor Vehicle Registry Darwin
18 Goyder Rd, Parap
1300 654 628
www.transport.nt.gov.au

Queensland
Queensland Transport
229 Elizabeth St, Brisbane
13 2380
www.transport.qld.gov.au

Tasmania
Transport Division
Department of Infrastructure,
Energy and Resources
10 Murray St, Hobart
1300 135 513
www.transport.tas.gov.au

ACCOMMODATION

General
State-based motoring organisations
are a good point of contact for
information on accommodation in
motels, apartments and caravan
parks. All share a comprehensive
accommodation database that can
be accessed from their websites (see
listings on this page).

Caravan Parks
Top Tourist Parks
(08) 8363 1901
www.toptouristparks.com.au

BIG4 Holiday Parks
1800 738 044
www.big4.com.au

Family Parks of Australia
1300 855 707
www.familyparks.com.au

Bed and Breakfasts
Bed and Breakfast Australia
www.bedandbreakfast.com.au

Backpackers
VIP Backpackers Resorts of Australia
(07) 3395 6111
www.vipbackpackers.com

YHA Australia
(02) 9261 1111
www.yha.com.au

EMERGENCY

**DIAL 000 FOR POLICE,
AMBULANCE & FIRE BRIGADE**

AUSTRALIA-WIDE DISTANCE CHART

Approximate Distances AUSTRALIA

	Adelaide	Albany	Albury	Alice Springs	Ayers Rock/Yulara	Bairnsdale	Ballarat	Bathurst	Bega	Bendigo	Bordertown	Bourke	Brisbane	Broken Hill	Broome	Bunbury	Cairns	Canberra	Carnarvon	Ceduna	Charleville	Coober Pedy	Darwin	Dubbo	Esperance	Eucla	Geelong	Geraldton
Adelaide		2662	965	1537	1578	1010	625	1198	1338	640	274	1129	2048	514	4268	2887	3207	1197	3568	772	1582	847	3026	1194	2183	1267	711	3086
Albany	2662		3487	3585	3626	3672	3287	3720	4000	3302	2936	3388	4310	2773	2626	335	5466	3719	1300	1890	3841	2895	4428	3526	479	1395	3373	818
Albury	965	3487		2362	2403	336	412	466	427	313	679	779	1407	865	5093	3712	2764	348	4393	1597	1232	1672	3851	553	3008	2092	382	3911
Alice Springs	1537	3585	2362		443	2547	2162	2595	2875	2177	1811	2263	2979	1648	2731	3810	2376	2594	4114	1695	2320	690	1489	2401	3106	2190	2248	4009
Ayers Rock/Yulara	1578	3626	2403	443		2588	2203	2636	2916	2218	1852	2304	3226	1689	3174	3851	2819	2635	4532	1736	2763	731	1932	2442	3147	2231	2289	4050
Bairnsdale	1010	3672	336	2547	2588		388	802	328	423	736	1115	1743	1119	5278	3897	3100	455	4578	1782	1568	1857	4036	863	3193	2277	349	4096
Ballarat	625	3287	412	2162	2203	388		878	716	124	351	996	1747	754	4893	3512	3104	760	4193	1397	1449	1472	3651	893	2808	1892	86	3711
Bathurst	1198	3720	466	2595	2636	802	878		531	779	1180	569	1000	958	5011	3945	2416	309	4626	1830	1022	1905	3769	205	3241	2325	848	4144
Bega	1338	4000	427	2875	2916	328	716	531		751	1064	994	1399	1447	5436	4225	2910	222	4906	2110	1447	2185	4364	630	3521	2605	677	4424
Bendigo	640	3302	313	2177	2218	423	124	779	751		366	872	1623	696	4908	3527	2980	661	4208	1412	1325	1487	3666	769	2823	1907	210	3726
Bordertown	274	2936	679	1811	1852	736	351	1180	1064	366		1138	1922	788	4542	3161	3257	1071	3842	1046	1591	1121	3300	1068	2457	1541	437	3360
Bourke	1129	3388	779	2263	2304	1115	996	569	994	872	1138		922	615	4442	3613	2078	772	4294	1498	453	1573	3200	364	2909	1993	1082	3812
Brisbane	2048	4310	1407	2979	3226	1743	1747	1000	1399	1623	1922	922		1537	4648	4535	1703	1241	5216	2420	742	2495	3406	854	3831	2915	1745	4734
Broken Hill	514	2773	865	1648	1689	1119	754	958	1447	696	788	615	1537		4379	2998	2693	1097	3679	883	1068	958	3137	753	2294	1378	840	3197
Broome	4268	2626	5093	2731	3174	5278	4893	5011	5436	4908	4542	4442	4648	4379		2417	4045	5214	1451	3750	3989	3421	1870	4806	2745	3255	4979	1921
Bunbury	2887	335	3712	3810	3851	3897	3512	3945	4225	3527	3161	3613	4535	2998	2417		5691	3944	1091	2115	4066	3120	4219	3751	664	1620	3598	609
Cairns	3207	5466	2764	2376	2819	3100	3104	2416	2910	2980	3257	2078	1703	2693	4045	5691		2619	5428	3576	1625	3066	2803	2211	4987	4071	3102	5890
Canberra	1197	3719	348	2594	2635	455	760	309	222	661	1071	772	1241	1097	5214	3944	2619		4625	1829	1225	1904	3972	408	3240	2324	730	4143
Carnarvon	3568	1300	4393	4114	4532	4578	4193	4626	4906	4208	3842	4294	5216	3679	1451	1091	5428	4625		2796	4747	3801	3253	4432	1628	2301	4279	482
Ceduna	772	1890	1597	1695	1736	1782	1397	1830	2110	1412	1046	1498	2420	883	3750	2115	3576	1829	2796		1951	1005	3184	1636	1411	495	1483	2314
Charleville	1582	3841	1232	2320	2763	1568	1449	1022	1447	1325	1591	453	742	1068	3989	4066	1625	1225	4747	1951		2026	2747	817	3362	2446	1500	4265
Coober Pedy	847	2895	1672	690	731	1857	1472	1905	2185	1487	1121	1573	2495	958	3421	3120	3066	1904	3801	1005	2026		2179	1711	2416	1500	1558	3319
Darwin	3026	4428	3851	1489	1932	4036	3651	3769	4364	3666	3300	3200	3406	3137	1870	4219	2803	3972	3253	3184	2747	2179		3564	4547	3679	3737	3723
Dubbo	1194	3526	553	2401	2442	863	893	205	630	769	1068	364	854	753	4806	3751	2211	408	4432	1636	817	1711	3564		3047	2131	891	3950
Esperance	2183	479	3008	3106	3147	3193	2808	3241	3521	2823	2457	2909	3831	2294	2745	664	4987	3240	1628	1411	3362	2416	4547	3047		916	2894	1160
Eucla	1267	1395	2092	2190	2231	2277	1892	2325	2605	1907	1541	1993	2915	1378	3255	1620	4071	2324	2301	495	2446	1500	3679	2131	916		1978	1819
Geelong	711	3373	382	2248	2289	349	86	848	677	210	437	1082	1745	840	4979	3598	3102	730	4279	1483	1500	1558	3737	891	2894	1978		3797
Geraldton	3086	818	3911	4009	4050	4096	3711	4144	4424	3726	3360	3812	4734	3197	1921	609	5890	4143	482	2314	4265	3319	3723	3950	1160	1819	3797	
Grafton	1845	4177	1184	3052	3093	1397	1544	825	1069	1420	1719	808	330	1404	4975	4402	2033	911	5083	2287	1069	2362	3733	651	3698	2782	1542	4601
Horsham	433	3095	531	1970	2011	577	192	997	905	218	159	1067	1841	599	4701	3320	3145	879	4001	1205	1520	1280	3459	987	2616	1700	278	3519
Kalgoorlie–Boulder	2184	886	3009	3107	3148	3194	2809	3242	3522	2824	2458	2910	3832	2295	2338	779	4988	3241	1460	1412	3363	2417	4140	3048	407	917	2895	978
Katherine	2712	4114	3537	1175	1618	3722	3337	3455	3880	3352	2986	2886	3092	2823	1556	3905	2489	3658	2939	2870	2433	1865	314	3250	4233	3365	3423	3409
Kununurra	3224	3602	4049	1687	2130	4234	3849	3967	4392	3864	3498	3398	3604	3335	1044	3393	3001	4170	2427	3382	2945	2377	826	3762	3721	3877	3935	2897
Longreach	2098	4357	1748	1804	2247	2084	1965	1538	1963	1841	2107	969	1175	1584	3473	4582	1109	1741	4856	2467	516	2494	2231	1333	3878	2962	2016	4781
Mackay	2670	4932	2029	2451	2894	2365	2369	1681	2106	2245	2544	1544	968	2159	4120	5157	735	1884	5503	3042	1091	3141	2878	1476	4453	3537	2367	5356
Meekatharra	3055	1159	3880	3978	4019	4065	3680	4113	4393	3695	3329	3781	4703	3166	1467	950	5444	4112	627	2283	4234	3288	3269	3919	1278	1788	3766	541
Melbourne	733	3395	313	2270	2311	277	111	779	605	146	459	978	1676	842	5001	3620	3033	661	4301	1505	1431	1580	3759	822	2916	2000	72	3819
Mildura	394	2916	571	1791	1832	825	460	804	956	402	417	870	1654	294	4522	3141	2948	803	3822	1026	1323	1101	3280	800	2437	1521	546	3340
Moree	1567	3829	926	2704	2745	1262	1294	578	1003	1141	1482	441	481	1056	4608	4054	1838	781	4735	1939	702	2014	3366	373	3350	2434	1264	4253
Mount Gambier	452	3114	721	1989	2030	697	309	1187	1025	433	186	1324	2098	856	4720	3339	3402	1069	4020	1224	1777	1299	3478	1244	2635	1719	365	3538
Mount Isa	2706	4754	2383	1169	1612	2719	2600	2173	2598	2476	2742	1604	1810	2219	2838	4979	1207	2736	4221	2864	1151	1859	1596	1968	4275	3359	2651	4691
Newcastle	1553	3930	704	2805	2846	917	1116	338	589	1017	1427	768	821	1157	5111	4155	2341	431	4836	2040	1205	2115	3869	404	3451	2535	1086	4354
Perth	2700	410	3525	3623	3664	3710	3325	3758	4038	3340	2974	3426	4348	2811	2230	187	5504	3757	904	1928	3879	2933	4032	3564	738	1433	3411	422
Port Augusta	307	2355	1132	1230	1271	1317	932	1365	1645	947	581	1033	1955	418	3961	2580	3111	1364	3261	465	1486	540	2719	1171	1876	960	1018	2779
Port Hedland	3921	2025	4746	3264	3707	5100	4546	4979	5259	4561	4195	4647	5181	4032	601	1816	4578	4978	850	3149	4522	3954	2403	4785	2144	2654	4632	1320
Port Lincoln	647	2289	1472	1570	1611	1657	1272	1705	1985	1287	921	1373	2295	758	4149	2514	3451	1704	3195	399	1826	880	3059	1511	1751	894	1358	2713
Port Macquarie	1804	4136	942	3011	3052	1155	1354	565	827	1255	1665	859	584	1363	5150	4361	2287	669	5042	2246	1244	2321	3908	610	3657	2741	1324	4560
Renmark	250	2772	715	1647	1688	969	604	948	1100	546	269	1014	1798	438	4378	2997	3092	947	3678	882	1467	957	3136	944	2293	1377	690	3196
Rockhampton	2336	4598	1695	2486	2929	2031	2035	1347	1772	1911	2210	1210	634	1825	4155	4823	1069	1550	5504	2708	831	3176	2913	1142	4119	3203	2033	5022
Sydney	1414	3936	565	2811	2852	759	977	211	431	780	1169	780	966	1169	5222	4161	2479	292	4772	1965	974	2121	3638	340	3387	2471	1231	4360
Tamworth	1534	3866	893	2741	2782	1186	1233	457	858	1109	1408	589	573	1093	4880	4091	2110	700	4772	2051	974	2051	3638	340	3387	2471	1231	4290
Tennant Creek	2043	4091	2868	531	949	3053	2668	2836	3261	2683	2317	2267	2473	2154	2225	4316	1870	3039	3608	2201	1814	1196	983	2631	3612	2696	2754	4078
Toowoomba	1921	4183	1280	2852	3099	1616	1620	956	1357	1496	1795	795	127	1410	4521	4408	1705	1199	5089	2293	615	2368	3279	727	3704	2788	1618	4607
Townsville	2862	5121	2419	2061	2504	2755	2759	2071	2496	2635	2871	1733	1358	2348	3730	5346	345	2274	5113	3231	1280	2751	2488	1866	4642	3726	2757	5545
Wagga Wagga	948	3470	145	2345	2386	481	550	321	402	426	822	711	1262	848	5076	3695	2619	249	4376	1580	1164	1655	3834	408	2991	2075	527	3894
Warrnambool	649	3311	567	2186	2227	534	174	1052	862	298	383	1170	1933	829	4917	3536	3278	987	4217	1421	1623	1496	3675	1067	2832	1916	185	3735

Distances on this chart have been calculated over main roads and do not necessarily reflect the shortest route between towns.

Refer to page 665 for distance chart of Tasmania.